Comments About
'Bed & Breakfasts and Country Inns'

"Our office went crazy over this book. The quality of the inns and the quality of the book is phenomenal! Send us 52 books." – M. B., Westport, Conn.

"Outstanding! We were offering a variety of inn guide books, but yours was the only one guests bought." – J.A., White Oak Inn, Ohio.

"My husband and I have really enjoyed our Bed & Breakfast free night for the past two summers. Such a good offer. Thanks!" – B.C., Houston, Texas.

"The 300 women who attended my 'Better Cents' seminar went wild for the Free Night book. I brought my copy and showed them the value of the free night program. They all wanted to get involved. Thank you so much for offering such a great value." – R.R., Making Cents Seminars, Texas.

"We loved our stay thanks to your offer!" – P. N., Lake Lure, NC

"Thank you for offering this special! It allowed us to get away even on a tight budget." – D. L. Pittsburgh, Pa.

"Have just finished reading a friend's copy. Fantastic! Thank you!" – B.A., Pensacola, Fl.

"This made our vacation a lot more reasonable. We got the best room in a beautiful top-drawer inn for half the price." – L.A., Irvine, Calif.

"I used your book and free night offer and took my 17-year-old daughter. It was our first B&B visit ever and we loved it. (We acted like friends instead of parent vs. teenager for the first time in a long time.) It was wonderful!" – B. F., Clinton, N.J.

"Thanks! Do we love your B&B offer! You betcha! The luxury of getting a two-day vacation for the cost of one is Christmas in July for sure. Keep up the good work." – R.R., Grapevine, Texas.

"What a great idea for gifts. I'm ordering five to use as birthday, housewarming and thank-you gifts." – J.R., Laguna Niguel, Calif.

"The best thing since ice cream – and I love ice cream!" – M. C., Cape May, N.J.

"Out of 25 products we presented to our fund raising committee your book was number one and it generated the most excitement." – H. U., Detroit, Michigan.

Comments From Innkeepers

"The guests we receive from the Buy-One-Night-Get-One-Night-Free program are some of the most wonderful people. Most are first time inngoers and after their first taste of the inn experience they vow that this is the only way to travel." – Innkeeper, Mass.

"Guests that were staying here last night swear by your guide. They use it all the time. Please send us information about being in your guide." – Innkeeper, Port Angeles, Wash.

"The people are so nice! Please keep up the great program!"
– K. C, Avon Manor Inn, Avon-By-the-Sea, N.J.

"We would like to express our appreciation for the Free Night programs. We had an excellent response to the certificates. It has helped us fill our vacancies during the weekdays and in the slower time of the season. Keep up the good work!" – Hacienda Vargas, Sante Fe, N. M.

"Your book is so widely distributed that we booked up a room all the way from Japan!"
– Rose Inn, Ithaca, N.Y.

"We've just received the new edition. Congratulations on this magnificent book. You've done it again!" – Gilbert House, Charleston, W. V..

"We want to tell you how much we love your book. We have it out for guests to use. They love it! Each featured inn stands out so well. Thank you for the privilege of being in your book."
– Fairhaven Inn, Bath, Me.

"American Historic Inns is wonderful! We are proud and delighted to be included. Thank you for creating such a special guidebook." – The Heirloom, Ione, Calif.

"Your new edition has maintained the fine quality of previous editions and we are very pleased to be included." – The Victoriana 1898, Traverse City, Mich.

"Thanks so much for all your hard work. We receive the largest number of guidebook referrals from your book." – Saddle Rock Ranch, Sedona, Ariz.

"We are thrilled with your book. We appreciate your incredible traveling spirit captured in these pages!"
– Thorwood, Hastings, Minn.

"We tell all our guests about the Free Night promotion and how to participate. However, we also remind them to visit with us again. Almost 100% said they will–and do so! We must be doing something right. Thanks again for this unique opportunity." – House on the Hill, Lake George, N. Y.

"What a great deal for everyone involved. Thanks for the opportunity!"
– Victoria & Albert Inn, Abingdon, Va.

"We've had guests return two or three times after discovering us through your book. They have turned into wonderful guests and friends." – Port Townsend, Wash.

"The response to your book has been terrific and the guests equally terrific! Many are already returning. Thanks for all your hard work." – Rockport, Mass.

"We love your book and we also use it. Just went to New Orleans and had a great trip."
– Gettysburg, Penn.

"This has been one of the best B&B programs we have done and the guests have been delightful. Thanks!" – Eastern Shore, Md.

"We are grateful that so many of our old friends and new guests have found us through your book. We always recommend your publications to guests who wish to explore other fine country inns of New England." – Georgette & Albert Levis, Vermont innkeepers.

Media Comments

"...lighthouses , schoolhouses, stage coach stops, llama ranches, ...There's lots to choose from and it should keep B&B fans happy for years." – Cathy Stapells, Toronto Sun.

"...helps you find the very best hideaways (many of the book's listings appear in the National Register of Historic Places.)" – Country Living.

"I love your book!" – Lydia Moss, Travel Editor, McCall's.

"Delightful, succinct, detailed and well-organized. Easy to follow style..." – Don Wudke, Los Angeles Times.

"Pay for one night at a nearby country inn and get the second night free...Among them is the very fine L'Auberge Provencale...The goal of the program, sponsored by the Association of American Historic Inns, is to introduce first-timers to inn stays but frequent inn guests also are eligible for the bargain." – James Yenckel, Washington Post.

"This is one of the best guidebooks of its kind. It's easy to use, accurate and the thumbnail sketches give the readers enough description to choose among the more than 1,000 properties detailed and thousands others listed." – Dallas Morning News.

"One of the better promotions we've seen." – Baton Rouge Advocate.

"...thoughtfully organized and look-ups are hassle-free...well-researched and accurate...put together by people who know the field. There is no other publication available that covers this particular segment of the bed & breakfast industry – a segment that has been gaining popularity among travelers by leaps and bounds. The information included is valuable and well thought out." – Morgan Directory Reviews.

"Readers will find this book easy to use and handy to have. The Sakachs have conveyed their love of historic inns and have shared that feeling and information in an attractive and inviting guide. An excellent, well-organized and comprehensive reference for inngoers and innkeepers alike." – Inn Review, Kankakee, Illinois.

"This guide has become the favorite choice of travelers and specializes only in professionally operated inns and B&Bs rather than homestays (lodging in spare bedrooms)." – Laguna Magazine.

"This is the best bed and breakfast book out. It outshines them all!" – Maggie Balitas, Rodale Book Clubs.

"Most of us military families have lived all over the world, so it takes an unusual book, service or trip to excite us! As I began to look through the book by Tim and Deborah Sakach, my heart beat faster as I envisioned what a good time our readers could have visiting some of these very special historic bed and breakfast properties." – Ann Crawford, Military Living.

"Absolutely beautiful!" – KQIL talk show radio.

"This is a great book. It makes you want to card everything." – KBRT Los Angeles radio talk show.

"All our lines were tied up! We received calls from every one of our 40 stations (while discussing your book.)" – Business Radio Network.

"For a delightful change of scenery, visit one of these historical inns. (Excerpts from Bed & Breakfasts and Country Inns follow.) A certificate for one free consecutive night (minimum two nights stay) can be found in the book" – Shirley Howard, Good Housekeeping.

Comments about the Inns in
'Bed & Breakfast and Country Inns'

"Your wonderful stories brought us all together. You have created a special place that nurtures and brings happiness and love. This has been a dream!" – Captain Josiah Mitchell House, Freeport, Me.

"Closet feeling to heaven on Earth." – Fensalden, Albion, Calif.

"Absolutely the most charming, friendly and delightful place we have ever stayed at."
– Gingerbread Mansion, Ferndale, Calif.

"We spend many nights in hotels that look and feel exactly alike whether they are in Houston or Boston. Your inn was delightful. It was wonderful to bask in your warm and gracious hospitality."
– Madison Street Inn, Santa Clara, Calif.

"Thank you for sharing your ranch with us. It has been the highlight of our trip."
– B&B at Saddle Rock Ranch, Sedona, Ariz.

"You've spoiled us completely. Keep the joy going." – Shaw's Fancy B&B, Annapolis, Md.

"What hotel room could ever compare to a large room in a 115-year-old house with 12-foot ceilings and a marble fireplace with hosts that could become dear longtime friends?"
– Betsy's B&B, Baltimore, Md.

"Business travel has never been so good." – Clements House, Grants Pass, Ore.

"Next time I'll bring company. It's much too romantic to be here alone!"
– Rockwell House, Bristol, R. I.

"What a romantic place and such outrageous food!!" – Arlington Inn, Arlington, Vt.

"We couldn't believe such a place existed. Now we can't wait to come again."
– Manchester Highlands Inn, Manchester Center, Vt.

"Without a doubt the loveliest country inn it has ever been my pleasure to stay in."
– Birch Hill Inn, Manchester Village, Vt.

"A weekend in a good country inn, such as the Londonderry, is on a par with a weekend on the ocean in Southern Maine, which is to say that it's as good as a full week nearly anyplace else."
– Londonderry Inn, South Londonderry, Vt.

"Best breakfast on the island, the perfect B&B." – Breakfast at Tiasquam, Chilmark, Mass.

"Best weekend we've ever had." – La Vista Plantation, Fredericksburg, Va.

"Your hospitality far exceeds any we've experienced and truly made our stay one we'll treasure."
– Inn at Levelfields, Lancaster, Va.

"We have stayed at inns for 15 years, and yours is at the top of the list as best ever!"
– Gilbert House, Charles Town, W.Va.

"This is the creme de la creme. The most wonderful place I have stayed at bar none including ski country in the U.S. and Europe." – Old Miners' Lodge, Park City , Utah.

"Dorothy can have Kansas, Scarlett can take Tara, Rick can keep Paris – I've stayed at Cedar Hill Farm." – Cedar Hill Farm, Lancaster, Pa.

"Full of charm. As beautiful as a fairy world." – Summer House, Mass.

"I prefer this atmosphere to a modern motel. It's more relaxed and love is everywhere!"
– Spray Cliff on the Ocean, Marblehead, Mass."

"Thank you for the wonderful time we had at your place. We give you a 5-star rating!"
– George Fuller House, Essex, Mass.

"We've been traveling all our lives and never have we felt more at home." – Brook Farm Inn, Lenox, Mass.

American Historic Inns™

Bed & Breakfasts
and
Country Inns

ᛒ ᛒ ᛒ ᛡ ᛡ ᛡ

by Tim & Deborah Sakach

Published by

AMERICAN
HISTORIC
INNS
INCORPORATED

PO Box 669
Dana Point
California
92629-0336

Bed & Breakfasts and Country Inns

ISBN 0-9615481-6-9

Front Cover:
The Scofield House Bed & Breakfast, Sturgeon Bay, Wisconsin
Innkeepers: William and Fran Cecil

Cover and book design:
David Sakach

Cover photos:
Tim Sakach

Senior Editor:
Stephen Sakach

Contributors:
Tiffany Crosswy, Alex Murashko
Lucy Pochek, Carol Zeihm

Database manager:
Sandy Imre

Database assistants:
Joyce Roll, Lisa Weddle

Digital scanning:
Jessie Collier, Josh Prizer
Suzanne Sakach

Although no lodging establishment paid to be included
in this book, they were solicited to participate in the promotion and
the guide. The descriptions contained herein were based on information
supplied by the establishments.

This book is printed on recycled paper. American Historic Inns, Inc. supports refor-
estation projects and volunteer tree planting and maintenance programs as a contribu-
tor to the National Tree Trust in Washington, D.C. and its America's Treeways
Program. More than 300 trees have been planted by American Historic Inns.

Printed in the United States of America.

10 9 8 7 6 5 4 3 2 1

Table Of Contents

How To Make A Reservation

1. **You must make ADVANCE reservations.** This offer is only valid by making reservations in advance directly with the participating lodging establishment AND when you identify yourself as having a Certificate from this promotion.

2. **You must identify yourself FIRST as holding a Certificate from this promotion, or the innkeeper is not obligated to honor the certificate.**

3. All FREE nights are subject to availability. In some cases this may mean that the lodging establishment has rooms but is projecting that those rooms will be filled with full-fare customers. Most hotels consider they are at full occupancy when they are about 80% filled, and then cut off all reduced-fare programs at that time. Smaller properties such as Bed & Breakfast homes and inns may use different formulas. Some set aside a specific number of rooms for Certificate holders and then will not accept any more reservations for the promotion after those rooms are filled. Some will accept Certificate holders at the last minute when they project that they will have rooms available.

4. Try to obtain a confirmation number, confirmation letter or the name of the person taking your reservation.

5. If you have children or pets coming with you, or if you smoke, be sure to tell the innkeeper in advance. Most Bed & Breakfasts and Country Inns are non-smoking. Accommodations for children or pets may be limited or non-existent at some of the smaller inns.

6. Understand the cancellation policy. A number of Bed & Breakfasts and Country Inns require a two-week or more notice of cancellation in order to refund your deposit. You should find out what the policy is at the same time you make your reservations.

7. All holidays are excluded. There may be other local events that are excluded as well.

8. This is a two-night minimum program and the two nights MUST BE CONSECUTIVE, i.e. "Monday and Tuesday," or "Sunday and Monday." You can stay longer, of course.

9. Always find out what meals, if any, are included in the rates and whether you will have to pay for meals on the second day. Not every establishment participating in this program provides a free breakfast.

10. Some locales require that bed tax be collected, even on FREE nights. If you have a question, check with the innkeeper or Chamber of Commerce or City Hall serving the area in which you wish to stay.

11. Request a brochure from participating inns before you make your reservation.

12. Don't forget to take this booklet with the certificate along with you.

The free night is given to you directly from the innkeeper in the hope that you or your friends will return and share your discovery with others. **The inns are not reimbursed by American Historic Inns, Inc.**

inn poorly kept or poorly managed. This type of business usually does not survive because an inn's success depends upon repeat guests and enthusiastic word-of-mouth referrals from satisfied guests. We do not promote these types of establishments.

Traveler or tourist

Travel is an adventure into the unknown, full of surprises and rewards. A seasoned "traveler" learns that even after elaborate preparations and careful planning, travel provides the new and unexpected. The traveler learns to live with uncertainty and considers it part of the adventure.

To the "tourist," whether "accidental" or otherwise, new experiences are disconcerting. Tourists want no surprises. They expect things to be exactly as they had envisioned them. To tourists we recommend staying in a hotel or motel chain where the same formula is followed from one locale to another.

We have found that inngoers are travelers at heart. They relish the differences in America's intimate historic bed & breakfasts and country inns. This is the magic that makes traveling from inn to inn the delightful experience it is.

Minimum stays

Many inns require a two-night minimum stay on weekends. A three-night stay is often required during holiday periods.

Cancellations

Cancellation policies are individual for each bed and breakfast. It is not unusual to see 7- to 14-day cancellation periods. Please verify the inn's policy if this is a concern.

What if the inn is full?

Ask the innkeeper for recommendations. They may know of an inn that has recently opened or one nearby but off the beaten path. Call the local Chamber of Commerce in the town you hope to visit. They may also know of inns that have recently opened. Please let us know of any new discoveries you make.

We want to hear from you!

We've always enjoyed hearing from our readers and have carefully cataloged all letters and recommendations. If you wish to participate in evaluating your inn experiences, use the **Inn Evaluation Form** in the back of this book. You might want to make copies of this form prior to departing on your journey. The authors read each evaluation form.

We hope you will enjoy this book so much that you will want to keep an extra copy or two on hand to offer to friends. Many readers have called to purchase our Free Night Certificate book for hostess gifts, birthday presents, or for seasonal celebrations. It's a great way to introduce your friends to America's enchanting country inns and bed & breakfasts.

floor of the main house has four dining rooms, a piano lounge and a glass-enclosed veranda. The guest rooms and suites here are furnished with antiques, while those in the new Victorian annex feature reproduction pieces. Covered walkways, verandas and gazebos flow among the massive hard-woods, gardens, courtyard and pool.

Innkeeper(s): Jean Ann Oglesby & Fain Casey.

Rates:$69-145. MC VISA AX DC DS CB. ContPlus Bkfst. EP. 48 rooms. Beds:KQT. Conference Rm. TV, Phone, AC in room. Golf. Tennis. Handicap access. Swimming. Fishing.

Seen in: *Southern Living, Anniston Star, Birmingham Post Herald, Birmingham News.*

Contact: Jean Ann Oglesby. Certificate may be used: As available.

Eutaw

Kirkwood Plantation

11. Kirkwood Dr
Eutaw 462
(205) 009

1860. Located on more than eight acres of green lawns, pecan trees and azaleas, this is a stately ante-bellum Greek Revival plantation house. There are eight Ionic columns on the front and side of the house and italian Carrara marble mantles adorn the first floor. Massive mirrors and a Waterford crystal chandelier add to the elegance of the inn's furnishings, most of which are original to the house. The owner gives tours of the planta-tion along with a history lesson on the Civil War and its influence on Kirkwood Plantation.

Innkeeper(s): Mary Swayze.

Rates:$75. Full Bkfst. 4 rooms with shared baths. Beds:QT. AC in room.

Contact: Mary Swayze. Certificate may be used: Any day, anytime.

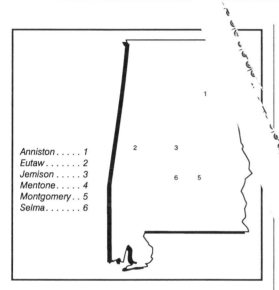

Anniston

The Victoria, a Country Inn & Restaurant

1604 Quintard Ave, PO Box 2213
Anniston 36201
(205)236-0503 Fax:(205)236-1138

1888. This Victorian estate, an Alabama landmark, occupies almost an entire square block on Quintard Avenue, Anniston's major thoroughfare. The first

Jemison

The Jemison Inn
212 Hwy 191
Jemison 35085
(205)688-2055 (800)438-3042

1930. Heirloom quality antiques fill this gabled brick house. A Victorian decor predominates. Casseroles, sausage, cheese grits and muffins comprise the inn's hearty breakfast.
Innkeeper(s): Nancy & Joe Ruzicka.
Rates:$55-60. MC VISA AX DC DS CB. Full Bkfst. AP available. Picnic lunches. Teas. Evening snacks. 3 rooms. 2 with shared baths. Beds:DT. AC in room. Bicycling. Handicap access. Fishing.
Seen in: *The Clanton Advertiser.*
Contact: Nancy Ruzicka. Certificate may be used: January-March, June-December.

"I've never had a better breakfast anywhere!"

Mentone

Mentone Inn
Highway 117, PO Box 284
Mentone 35984
(205)634-4836

1927. Mentone is a refreshing stop for those in search of the cool breezes and natural air conditioning of the mountains. Here antique treasures mingle with modern-day conveniences. A sun deck and spa complete the experience. Sequoyah Caverns, Little River Canyon and DeSoto Falls are moments away. The inn has its own hiking trails.
Innkeeper(s): Amelia Kirk.
Rates:$60-65. Full Bkfst. 12 rooms. Beds:Q. Conference Rm. AC in room. Fishing.
Seen in: *Birmingham News.*
Contact: Amelia Kirk. Certificate may be used: Sunday-Thursday.

Montgomery

Red Bluff Cottage B&B
551 Clay St, PO Box 1026
Montgomery 36101
(205)264-0056 Fax:(205)262-1872

1987. This raised cottage sits high above the Alabama River in Montgomery's historic Cottage Hill District. Guest rooms are on the first floor, while the kitchen, dining room, living room, sitting room and music room with piano and harpsichord are on the second floor. An upstairs porch has a panoramic view of the river plain, downtown Montgomery and the State Capitol building. Each of the guest rooms is furnished with family antiques, and the Granny's Room contains a three-quarter sleigh bed that belonged to the innkeeper's great-great-grandmother.
Innkeeper(s): Anne & Mark Waldo.
Rates:$55. MC VISA. Full Bkfst. 4 rooms. Beds:QT. AC in room.
Contact: Mark Waldo. Certificate may be used: All year.

Selma

Grace Hall B&B Inn
506 Lauderdale St
Selma 36701
(205)875-5744 Fax:(205)875-9967

1857. The first-floor rooms of this antebellum mansion open up to a New Orleans-style garden with ferns, fountains, and stone walls. Larger, more opu-

lent rooms can be found upstairs. A wood-burning fireplace in each room adds a romantic touch to an inn that has all the ambiance of 1860, but all the modern-day conveniences. The inn is located in one of three historic districts, and walking and driving tours are available to museums, cemeteries, and quaint shopping and antiquing.
Innkeeper(s): Joey & Coy Dillon.
Rates:$79-99. MC VISA AX. Full Bkfst. AP available. Teas. 6 rooms. Fireplaces. Beds:QDT. Conference Rm. TV, Phone, AC in room. Handicap access. Fishing.
Contact: Coy Dillon. Certificate may be used: Jan. 2-Feb. 13; Feb. 15-28; June 1-30; July 6-Aug. 30; Nov. 1 through Nov. 23; Nov. 28 through Dec. 22. All subject to availability.

Alaska

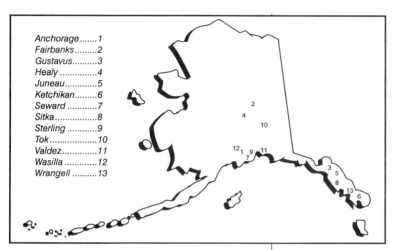

Anchorage

Aurora Winds B&B Resort

7501 Upper O'Malley
Anchorage 99516
(907)346-2533 Fax:(907)346-3192

1968. Situated on a hillside above Anchorage, this inn offers many amenities and features that the seasoned traveler has come to expect at the most luxurious accommodations. Guests can relax in an eight-person Jacuzzi after a workout in the exercise room. Other areas of enjoyment include a sauna, billiard room, two family rooms and three fireplaces. The inn is close to downtown, the airport, cross-country and downhill skiing. A full complement of culinary delights or an expanded continental breakfast is available in the dining room or at your door.

Innkeeper(s): James Montgomery.

Rates:$95-125. MC VISA AX. Gourmet Brkfst. Evening snacks. 5 rooms. Beds:Q. TV, Phone in room. Bicycling. Skiing. Spa. Sauna. Exercise room. Fishing.

Contact: James Montgomery. Certificate may be used: Sept. 15-May 15 only, two-night minimum stay.

Green Bough B&B

3832 Young St
Anchorage 99508
(907)562-4636

1960. Slip into freshly ironed sheets at night and awaken to aromas of cinnamon and coffee at Anchorage's oldest running B&B. The interior decor is reminiscent of German/country styles and enhanced by various Alaskana and a collection of award-winning, counted cross-stitch art done by the innkeeper's mother. An informal atmosphere lends itself to breakfasts at your own pace, and coming and going as you please. Days can be spent touring Anchorage or taking the train to Mt. McKinley's Denali Park.

Innkeeper(s): Jerry and Phyllis Jost.

Rates:$45-75. ContPlus Bkfst. 5 rooms. 3 with shared baths. Beds:KDT. Phone in room. Bicycling. Skiing. Swimming. Fishing.

Contact: Phyllis Jost. Certificate may be used: Sept. 15, 1994-May 15, 1995; Sept. 15, 1995-Dec. 31, 1995.

"Your charming company and home made this a highlight of our trip."

Fairbanks

A Pioneer B&B

1119 Second Ave
Fairbanks 99701
(907)452-5393

1906. Stay in an authentic pioneer cabin four blocks from the downtown area. Window boxes and gardens hold delphiniums, marigolds and snapdragons in summer. The cabin, a private accommodation behind the main house, has a well-stocked kitchen so you may create your own breakfast. Decorated in a simple style, there is an antique corner cabinet and a framed copy of a newspaper from 1906 that was found under the floor boards during the cabin's remodeling. The Chene River is two blocks away. The innkeepers own a Greek restaurant, Souvlaki's, six blocks from the B&B.

Innkeeper(s): Jack & Nancy Williams.

Rates:$65. MC VISA. Full Bkfst. 1 room. Beds:QD. Phone, Refrig. in room. Handicap access. Fishing.

Contact: Nancy Williams. Certificate may be used: Anytime we are open.

Gustavus

Glacier Bay Country Inn
PO Box 5, Mile 1 Tong Rd
Gustavus 99826
(907)697-2288 Fax:(907)697-2289

1986. The innkeepers assure guests that although a trip to their remote lodge is a bit of a challenge (reached by bush plane or Alaska Airlines shuttle),

it is definitely worthwhile. Set in a clearing, and surrounded by a lush, green forest and a mountain backdrop, the inn's design was derived from fairytale cottages that the innkeeper, Al Unrein, imagined in childhood. Its unique architecture includes multi-angled roofs, dormer windows, log-beamed ceilings and large porches. Take glacier tours, or go whale wathing or kayaking. The inn has a charter boat available for day and overnight fishing cruises for some of the best halibut and salmon around. All meals are included in the rate.

Innkeeper(s): Al & Annie Unrein.

Rates:$228. MC VISA AX. ContPlus Bkfst. AP available. Gourmet Brkfst, Dinner. Picnic lunches. Teas. 9 rooms. 1 with shared bath. Beds:QT. Farm. Bicycling. Fishing.

Contact: Annette & Al Unrein. Certificate may be used: May 10-20, Sept. 10-20.

Healy

Dome Home B&B
PO Box 262
Healy 99743
(907)683-1239

1982. As the name implies, this B&B is a geodesic dome having four levels and two living rooms. Ten living room windows look out to the Alaskan Range and surrounding foothills. The Dome Home is located on almost three acres and is 12 miles from the Denali National Park entrance. It is one-half mile from the George Parks Highway, and is within walking distance of a convenience store and restaurants. The innkeepers would be happy to suggest and arrange tours and sight seeing excursions of the area.

Innkeeper(s): Ann & Terry Miller.

Rates:$45-85. MC VISA. Full Bkfst. 6 rooms. 2 with shared baths. Fireplaces. Beds:QT. TV, Phone in room. Handicap access. Sauna.

Contact: Ann Miller. Certificate may be used: Sept. 15-May 20.

Juneau

Pearson's Pond Luxury Inn
4541 Sawa Cir
Juneau 99801
(907)789-3772 Fax:(907)789-6722

1986. View glaciers, visit museums and chance your luck at gold-panning streams, or simply soak in a hot tub surrounded by a lush forest and nestled next to a picturesque duck pond. Blueberries hang over the private decks of the guest rooms. A full, self-serve breakfast is provided each morning. Nearby trails offer excellent hiking, and the Medenhall Glacier is within walking distance. The sportsminded will enjoy river rafting or angling for world-class halibut and salmon.

Innkeeper(s): Steve & Diane Pearson.

Rates:$79-139. MC VISA DC CB. Full Bkfst. Evening snacks. 3 rooms. 1 with shared bath. Fireplaces. Beds:Q. TV, Phone, Refrig. in room. Tennis. Bicycling. Skiing. Handicap access. Spa. Swimming. Fishing.

Contact: Diane Pearson. Certificate may be used: October - April 30.

"A definite 10!"

Ketchikan

D & W B&B
412 D-1 Loop Rd N
Ketchikan 99901
(907)225-3273 (800)551-8654
Fax:(907)247-5337

1980. These rural B&B accommodations, located a few minutes' drive north of Ketchikan, provide guests with a completely outfitted two-bedroom apartment that sleeps six. A special welcome is extended to fishing parties. Ketchikan is known for its excellent salmon and halibut fishing and offers several fishing derbies each summer. A gas barbecue grill on the deck outside your room comes in handy for the catch of the day.

Innkeeper(s): Darrell & Wanda Vandergriff

Rates:$70. MC VISA. Full Bkfst. 3 rooms. 2 with shared baths. Beds:DT. TV, Phone, Refrig. in room. Swimming. Fishing.

Contact: Wanda Vandergriff. Certificate may be used: Oct. 1, 1994 through June 30, 1995; Oct. 1 through Dec. 31,1995.

Seward

"The Farm" B&B
PO Box 305, Salmon Creek Rd
Seward 99664
(907)224-5691 Fax:(907)224-2300

Known to Seward locals as "The Farm" (in name only), this peaceful inn sits on 20 acres of grass fields. It's not uncommon to see moose running through the property or eagles overhead. Innkeeper John Hoogland keeps guests entertained during breakfast with his sense of humor and although the fare is usually cold (20 brands of cereal are stocked) he claims the occasion can't be missed. There are plenty of wildlife tours in the area and Exit Glacier is six miles away.

Innkeeper(s): John W. Hoogland

Rates:$35-85. MC VISA. ContPlus Bkfst. EP. 11 rooms. 4 with shared baths. Beds:KQT. TV, Phone in room. Skiing. Handicap access. Swimming. Fishing.

Contact: Joanne Hoogland. Certificate may be used: September-May.

Sitka

Alaska Ocean View B&B
1101 Edgecumbe Dr
Sitka 99835
(907)747-8310 Fax:(907)747-8310

1987. This Alaska-style all-cedar home is located in a quiet neighborhood just one block from the seashore and the Tongass National Forest. Witness the spectacular Alaska sunsets over Sitka Sound and surrounding islands. On clear days, view Mt. Edgecumbe, which is an extinct volcano located on Kruzoff Island and looks like Mt. Fuji. Binoculars are kept handy for guests who take a special treat in viewing whales and eagles.

Innkeeper(s): Bill & Carole Denkinger.

Rates:$69-115. MC VISA. Full Bkfst. Gourmet Brkfst. 3 rooms. Beds:KQT. TV, Phone in room. Spa. Swimming. Fishing.

Contact: Carole Denkinger. Certificate may be used: October-May.

Sterling

Angler's Lodge & Fish Camp
PO Box 508, 36020 Stephen Dr
Sterling 99672
(907)262-1747 Fax:(907)262-6747

1987. Some of the finest sportfishing in Alaska is available 100 feet out the back door of this cedar flat log cabin lodge. Situated on the banks of the world famous Kenai River, guests have walking access to more than two miles of riverbank fishing. When the day is over, sit out back and watch the river go by, join other guests in telling your fish stories around the open fire, or relax in the outdoor hot tub. Bed & breakfast is offered to those staying a full week, with or without fishing.

Innkeeper(s): Roger & Marlene Byerly.

Rates:$50-100. MC VISA. Cont. Bkfst. AP available. Picnic lunches. 7 rooms. 3 with shared baths. Beds:DT. Bicycling. Skiing. Spa. Fishing.

Contact: Roger Byerly. Certificate may be used: May 1 to June 30 and Sept. 1 to Oct. 1.

Tok

Cleft of the Rock B&B
Sundog Trail Box 122
Tok 99780
(907)883-4219 (800)478-5646
Fax:(907)883-4219

1990. Guests can choose between spacious guest

rooms at this split-level inn or cabins. There is satellite TV and videos of Alaska for viewing pleasure. The innkeepers strive to make your stay a memorable experience. The inn is three miles west of Tok.

Innkeeper(s): John & Jill Rusyniak.

Rates:$45-85. MC VISA. Full Bkfst. Evening snacks. 3 rooms. Beds:KQT. Refrig. in room. Bicycling. Skiing. Sauna.

Contact: John Rusyniak. Certificate may be used: September, October - April.

Valdez

France Inn B&B
PO Box 1295
Valdez 99686
(907)835-4295

1978. Outstanding Alaskan scenery surrounds this B&B, which is a short walk from downtown Valdez and the Ferry Terminal. Prince William Sound serves as the focal point of the fishing community. Guests can tour the Alyeska Pipeline Terminal, take a Columbia Glacier tour, and visit the museum. Besides fishing, which is the main activity, there's live theater, festivals and special events to attend.

Innkeeper(s): Nancy & Miles France.

Rates:$50-75. ContPlus Bkfst. 4 rooms. 2 with shared baths. Beds:QDT. Bicycling. Skiing. Fishing.

Contact: Nancy France. Certificate may be used: August-May.

Wasilla

Yukon Don's B&B Inn
1830 E Parks Hwy #386
Wasilla 99654
(907)376-7472 Fax:(907)376-6515

1971. This inn, noted for its frontier memorabilia, was originally a sprawling dairy barn on a home-

stead farm in the Matanuska Valley. The inn's McComb Suite (named for the original homestead-

ers) is decorated with antique farm tools. A 100-foot-long, former feed bunk serves as a hallway to four other Alaskan-theme guest rooms. The hunting room features bear rugs, antlers, gun racks and duck print bedspreads. Innkeeper Don Tanner is known as the valley's Ambassador of Goodwill.

Innkeeper(s): Don & Kristan Tanner.

Rates:$65-105. VISA. ContPlus Bkfst. MAP available. 6 rooms. 4 with shared baths. Beds:QT. Conference Rm. TV, Phone, Refrig. in room. Farm. Skiing. Sauna. Exercise room. Swimming. Fishing.

Contact: Don Tanner. Certificate may be used: Sept. 15 to June 15, year-round if available.

Wrangell

Harding's Old Sourdough Lodge
1104 Peninsula, PO Box 1062
Wrangell 99929
(907)874-3613 (800)874-3613
Fax:(907)874-3455

1994. Located in Alaska's third oldest city, this inn has plenty of nearby activities. There's jet boat trips on the Stikene River, which is the fastest navigable river in North America. The area also boasts the largest springtime concentration of bald eagles. Nearby attractions include the Anan Black Bear Observatory, petroglyphs, museums that include exhibits on four ruling nations and three gold rushes, and Chief Shakes Tribal House & Totem Park.

Innkeeper(s): Bruce Harding.

Rates:$71. MC VISA AX DC. Full Bkfst. Picnic lunches. 18 rooms. 5 with shared baths. Beds:KT. Phone in room. Bicycling. Handicap access. Spa. Sauna. Swimming. Fishing.

Contact: Bruce Harding. Certificate may be used: October, November, December, January, February, March.

Arizona

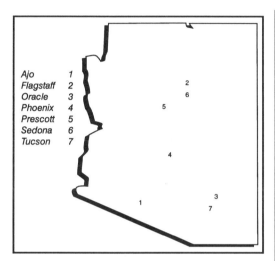

Ajo	1
Flagstaff	2
Oracle	3
Phoenix	4
Prescott	5
Sedona	6
Tucson	7

Ajo

The Mine Manager's House
One Greenway Dr
Ajo 85321
(602)387-6505 Fax:(602)387-6508

1919. Overlooking the Southwestern Arizona desert and a mile-wide copper mine pit, the Mine Manager's is a large Craftsman home situated on three acres. Built by the local copper mining industry, it has 10-inch thick walls. A library, coin laundry and gift shop are on the premises. The Greenway Suite features a marble tub and shower and two other suites boast two queen-size beds each. A full breakfast is served in the formal dining room.

Innkeeper(s): Jean & Micheline Fournier

Rates:$65-99. MC VISA. Full Bkfst. 5 rooms. Beds:Q. Phone in room. Handicap access. Spa.

Seen in: *Arizona Daily Star, Tucson Citizen, The Catalina-Oracle, Arizona Sun.*

Contact: Micheline Fournier. Certificate may be used: May & June, 1994 and 1995; September through December, 1994 and 1995, except holidays.

"The hospitality is what makes this place so inviting!"

Flagstaff

Comfi Cottages
1612 N Aztec
Flagstaff 86001
(602)774-0731

1920. Located in the heart of historic downtown Flagstaff, these cottages are freshly decorated and simply furnished with antiques and southwestern

pieces. Each two- or three-bedroom unit features polished wood floors, a wood stove and a washer and dryer. The kitchens are stocked with cooking utensils and breakfast foods. Fenced yards afford the convenience of picnic tables, lawn chairs and a barbeque grill. Guests may borrow bicycles to explore historic Flagstaff.

Innkeeper(s): Pat & Ed Wiebe.

Rates:$65-100. MC VISA. Full Bkfst. 4 rooms. Fireplaces. Beds:KQT. TV, Phone, Refrig. in room. Golf. Tennis. Skiing. Swimming. Horseback riding. Fishing.

Contact: Patricia Wiebe. Certificate may be used: January - April, Sunday-Thursday, September - December, Sunday-Thursday. None during May - August or holidays.

"Beautiful and relaxing. A port in the storm."

Inn at Four Ten

410 N Leroux
Flagstaff 86001
(602)774-0088

1907. Built by a wealthy banker, businessman and cattle rancher, this inn was first a stately family residence. Now fully renovated and elegantly decorated with antiques, stained glass and lace, the inn is a great home base for your Northern Arizona getaway. It's an easy jaunt to the Grand Canyon, volcanic and meteor craters, ancient Pueblo ruins, Hopi and Navajo villages, the Painted Desert, the red rocks of Sedona and Oak Creek Canyon.

Rates:$75-125. MC VISA AX. Full Bkfst. Picnic lunches. 9 rooms. 2 with shared baths. Fireplaces. Beds:KQT. Refrig. in room. Skiing. Handicap access.

Contact: Howard Krueger. Certificate may be used: Nov. 1-Dec. 20, 1994; Jan. 3-April 30, 1995; Nov. 1-Dec. 20, 1995.

Oracle

Triangle L Ranch B&B Retreat

PO Box 900
Oracle 85623
(602)896-2804 Fax:(602)896-9070

1890. This homestead ranch is situated in the high desert and oak woodland north of Tucson. Four housekeeping cottages are furnished in antiques. Rise to the din and clatter of geese, ducks and chickens. Winter guests are treated to a delectable breakfast in the large kitchen of the main ranch house, which boasts a wood-burning stove. In the warmer months, the meal is served on the airy front porch overlooking an iris garden. Innkeepers Margot and Tom Beeston possess a variety of unusual talents. Tom repairs and restores stringed instruments. His workshops are on the property and may be toured. Margot is licensed to rehabilitate injured or orphaned wildlife. She can provide guests with extensive knowledge of the local flora and fauna.

Innkeeper(s): Tom & Margot Beeston.

Rates:$80-95. MC VISA DS. Full Bkfst. 4 rooms. Fireplaces. Beds:QT. AC, Refrig. in room. Bicycling. Horseback riding.

Seen in: *Town & Country, Tucson Guide Quarterly.*

Contact: Margot Beeston. Certificate may be used: Anytime except holidays and February, March and April.

"An idyllic escape from the urban scene - we loved it."

Phoenix

Maricopa Manor

15 W Pasadena Ave, PO Box 7186
Phoenix 85011
(602)274-6302 Fax:(602)266-3904

1928. The secluded Maricopa Manor stands amid palm trees on an acre of land. The Spanish-styled house features four graceful columns in the entry hall, an elegant living room with a marble mantel and a music room with a grand piano and an Irish harp. The spacious suites are decorated with satins, lace, antiques and leather-bound books. Guests may relax on the deck, on the patio or in the gazebo spa.

Innkeeper(s): Mary Ellen & Paul Kelley.

Rates:$79-129. MC VISA AX. ContPlus Bkfst. 5 rooms. Fireplaces. Beds:KQ. TV, Phone, AC, Refrig. in room. Golf. Tennis. Spa. Swimming. Horseback riding.

Seen in: *Arizona Business Journal.*

Contact: Paul Kelley. Certificate may be used: June through August.

"I've stayed 200+ nights at B&Bs around the world, yet have never before experienced the warmth and sincere friendliness of Maricopa Manor."

Westways "Private" Resort Inn

PO Box 41624
Phoenix 85080
(602)582-3868 Fax:(602)561-2300

1939. The contemporary tone of this Spanish Mediterranean house refects the Southwest. The inn is on an acre landscaped with plants from the various regions of Arizona. There are palm, grapefruit and orange trees, mountain pines and desert cacti. The focal point of the courtyard is a tranquil Mexican fountain. A gratuity is charged.

Innkeeper(s): Darrell Trapp & Brian Kennedy.

Rates:$49-199. MC VISA AX. Full Bkfst. Gourmet Brkfst. Picnic lunches. Teas. Evening snacks. 8 rooms. Beds:Q. Conference Rm. TV, Phone, AC, Refrig. in room. Golf. Tennis. Bicycling. Spa. Exercise room. Swimming. Horseback riding.

Seen in: *Los Angeles Times, Travel Age West, Arizona Republic.*

Contact: Darrell Trapp. Certificate may be used: Year-round subject to advance reservations. Holiday periods only excluded.

"Personalized service made our stay memorable."

Prescott

Juniper Well Ranch
PO Box 10623
Prescott 86304
(602)442-3415

1992. A working horse ranch sits on the front 15 acres of this 50-acre, wooded property, which is surrounded by the Prescott National Forest. Guests are welcome to feed the horses, and children have been known to take a ride on a tractor with innkeeper David Bonham. Two log cabins sit farther back on the land where families can enjoy nature, "unlimited" hiking and seclusion. A summer house, which can be reserved by guests staying at the inn, has no walls, a sloping roof with skylight, and an eight-foot hot tub.

Innkeeper(s): David Bonham.

Rates:$105. MC VISA. Full Bkfst. 2 rooms. Beds:QT. Refrig. in room. Skiing. Handicap access. Spa. Fishing.

Contact: David Bonham. Certificate may be used: Monday through Thursday.

Marks House
203 E Union St
Prescott 86303
(602)778-4632

1894. In the 1890s four prominent residences dominated Nob Hill. One of them was the Marks House. Built by Jake Marks, cattle rancher and mine owner, it's now in the National Register. This Victorian mansion provides a special setting in which to enjoy rare antiques, gracious breakfasts and majestic sunsets. Fireplaces are in the living and dining rooms.

Rates:$75-120. MC VISA. Full Bkfst. 4 rooms. Beds:KQD. Conference Rm. Swimming. Fishing.

Contact: Dottie R. Viehweg. Certificate may be used: September through March, Sunday through Thursday only.

"Exceptional!"

Mt. Vernon Inn
204 N Mt Vernon
Prescott 86301
(602)778-0886 (800)574-7284

1900. Built by one of Prescott's prominent bootleggers, the inn is nestled among towering shade trees in the center of the Mt. Vernon Historical District, Arizona's largest Victorian neighborhood. The architecture of this grand house with its turret, gables, pediments and Greek Revival porch can best be described as whimsical. Cottages that once served as the carriage and tack houses also are

available.

Innkeeper(s): Sybil & John Nelson.

Rates:$60-110. MC VISA AX DS. Full Bkfst. Picnic lunches. Teas. Evening snacks. 4 rooms. Beds:QT. Phone in room. Bicycling. Handicap access. Swimming.

Contact: Sybil Nelson. Certificate may be used: Midweek, June through September; anytime October through May 25.

Prescott Pines Inn
901 White Spar Rd
Prescott 86303
(602)445-7270 (800)541-5374
Fax:(602)778-3665

1902. A white picket fence beckons guests to the veranda of this comfortably elegant country Victorian inn, originally the Haymore Dairy. There

are masses of fragrant pink roses, lavenders and delphiniums, and stately ponderosa pines tower above the inn's four renovated cottages, which were once shelter for farmhands. The acre of grounds includes a garden fountain and romantic tree swing.

Innkeeper(s): Jean Wu and Michael Acton.

Rates:$49-95. MC VISA. Full Bkfst. EP. 13 rooms. Fireplaces. Beds:KQ. Conference Rm. TV, Phone, AC, Refrig. in room. Golf. Tennis. Fishing.

Seen in: *Sunset Magazine, Arizona Republic News.*

Contact: Jean Wu. Certificate may be used: November through April, Sunday-Thursday only; exclude all major holiday periods.

"The ONLY place to stay in Prescott! Tremendous attention to detail."

Victorian Inn of Prescott B&B
246 S Cortez St
Prescott 86303
(602)778-2642

1893. The blue- and white-trimmed Victorian home with its tower and bay windows is a popular landmark of Prescott and is located one block from the historic town square. When it was constructed in the late 19th century, all the materials had to be brought in by train from the East Coast. Mauve and raspberry colors dominate the interior, which has been lovingly restored with many original fixtures. A favorite among the second-floor guest quarters is the spacious Victoriana Suite. Breakfast is a gourmet sit-down affair served on elegant china and linens.

Innkeeper(s): Tamia Thunstedt.

Rates:$90-135. MC VISA AX DS. Full Bkfst. Gourmet Brkfst. 4 rooms. 3 with shared baths. Beds:Q. Golf. Horseback riding. Fishing.

Seen in: *Arizona Republic*.

Contact: Tamia Thunstedt. Certificate may be used: Monday through Thursday.

Sedona

A Casa Lea Country Inn
PO Box 552
Sedona 86339
(602)282-2833 (800)385-7883

1994. This new inn was designed to showcase Arizona's history and native beauty. Hundreds of museum-quality artifacts surround guests as they feel the spirits of thousands of years of Native

Americans, pioneers, cowboys, Asians and Mexican caballeros. You can adventure in the rustic past while enjoying the luxuries of present. The inn's hosts, Lea and Vincent, have a variety of backgrounds. They can tell stories about the experiences of a clayworker, an educator, fisherman, writer, gardener, historian, outdoor enthusiast and more.

Innkeeper(s): Lea Pace.

Rates:$119-229. MC VISA. Full Bkfst. Gourmet Brkfst. Picnic lunches. Teas. Evening snacks. 11 rooms. Fireplaces. Beds:KQT. Conference Rm. TV, Phone, AC, Refrig. in room. Handicap access. Spa. Sauna. Fishing.

Contact: Lea Pace. Certificate may be used: January & December except for local and national events. Sunday - Thursday.

B&B at Saddle Rock Ranch
255 Rock Ridge Dr
Sedona 86336
(602)282-7640

1926. History, romance and elegance will highlight your stay at the Saddle Rock Ranch. The house has often been featured in motion pictures depicting the Old West. Nipper, the RCA Victor dog, greets visitors at the front door. The house is constructed of native red rock, beamed ceilings and wood and flagstone floors. Guest suites feature fieldstone fire-

places and panoramic vistas of the surrounding red rocks.

Innkeeper(s): Fran & Dan Bruno.

Rates:$100-130. Full Bkfst. Gourmet Brkfst. Teas. 3 rooms. Fireplaces. Beds:KQT. Conference Rm. TV, AC in room. Golf. Tennis. Bicycling. Skiing. Spa. Swimming. Horseback riding. Fishing.

Seen in: *Arizona Republic, Longevity Magazine, Sedona Red Rock News, Esquire Magazine*.

Contact: Fran Bruno. Certificate may be used: Monday through Thursday, Nov. 14, 1994-Feb. 28, 1995. Weekends and holiday periods not included.

"Thank you for sharing your ranch with us. It has been the highlight of our trip."

Greyfire Farm B&B
1240 Jacks Canyon Rd
Sedona 86351
(602)284-2340

1980. Pine trees frame this homestay located in the valley between Sedona and Wild Horse Mesa, a Western movie location. The Canyon Suite, decorated with antiques and contemporary furniture, offers views into Jacks Canyon and Red Rock Buttes. There's a patio where breakfast is served in good weather. Two guest horses may be accommodated on the farm's two acres. Three golf courses are nearby.

Innkeeper(s): David J. Payne & Elaine Ross.

Rates:$80-90. MC VISA. Full Bkfst. 2 rooms. Beds:Q. AC in room. Farm. Golf. Tennis. Horseback riding. Stables. Fishing.

Contact: Elaine Ross. Certificate may be used: July, August, December, January, February (1994 & 1995). Sunday through Thursday, holidays excluded.

Territorial House, An Old West B&B
65 Piki Dr
Sedona 86336
(602)204-2737 (800)801-2737
Fax:(602)204-2230

1974. This red rock and cedar two-story ranch home, nestled in the serene setting of Juniper and Cottonwood, is a nature lover's delight. Guests can see families of quail march through the landscape of cacti, plants and red rock or hear the call of coyotes as they drift off to sleep. The territorial decor includes Charles Russell prints collected from taverns throughout the Southwest. More than 40 western movies were filmed in Sedona.

Innkeeper(s): John & Linda Steele.

Rates:$90-130. MC VISA. Full Bkfst. Teas. 4 rooms. Fireplaces. Beds:KQT. TV, Phone, AC in room. Bicycling. Skiing. Swimming. Fishing.

Contact: John Steele. Certificate may be used: December, January, February, July, August, excluding weekends and holidays.

Tucson

Casa Alegre B&B Inn
316 E Speedway
Tucson 85705
(602)628-1800 Fax:(602)792-1880

1915. Innkeeper Phyllis Florek decorated the interi-
or of this bed and breakfast with artifacts that
reflect the history of Tuscon, such as Native

American pieces and antique mining tools. Wake
up to the aroma of fresh coffee and join other
guests as you enjoy fresh muffins, fruit and other
breakfast treats, such as cheese pancakes with raspberry preserves. The Arizona sitting room opens to
a large patio and pool area. In the afternoon,
refreshments are served on the patio or enjoy them
in front of the rock fireplace. Abundant shopping
and sightseeing are found nearby.

Innkeeper(s): Phyllis Florek.

Rates:$55-95. MC VISA DS. Full Bkfst. Gourmet Brkfst. Teas. 4 rooms.
Fireplaces. Beds:KQT. Conference Rm. AC in room. Golf. Tennis. Skiing.
Spa. Fishing.

Seen in: *Arizona Times.*

Contact: Phyllis Florek. Certificate may be used: Anytime except
January, February and March.

"Enjoyed your excellent care."

Catalina Park Inn
309 E 1st St
Tucson 85705
(602)792-4541 Fax:(602)792-4541

1927. Relax in the expansive living room of this
finely crafted country inn while listening to classical music and warming to the fireplace. Located in
Tucson's historic West University District, this inn
is only blocks from the University of Arizona and
Fourth Avenue's eclectic shops and restaurants.
Cozy rooms include down pillows and comforters, a
montage of colorfully patterned linens and a sitting
area.

Innkeeper(s): Mark Hall & Paul Richard.

Rates:$90-130. MC VISA. ContPlus Bkfst. 3 rooms. Beds:QD. TV,
Phone, AC in room. Bicycling.

Contact: Mark Hall. Certificate may be used: April through December,
1995. Based upon availability.

The Gable House
2324 N Madelyn Circle
Tucson 85712-2621
(602)326-4846 (800)756-4846

1930. Clark Gable lived in this adobe home during
the early 1940s. After his wife Carole Lombard
died, it was his favorite retreat for peace and quiet.
Situated on one acre in a residential area of central
Tucson, the Gable House features a blend of Santa
Fe Pueblo Indian and Mexican motifs. Therapeutic
massage is available on the premises.

Innkeeper(s): Albert Cummings & Phyllis Fredona.

Rates:$50-75. ContPlus Bkfst. 4 rooms. 2 with shared baths.
Fireplaces. Beds:K. Phone, AC in room. Golf. Tennis. Skiing. Spa.
Swimming. Horseback riding. Fishing.

Contact: Albert Cummings. Certificate may be used: Anytime.

La Posada Del Valle
1640 N Campbell Ave
Tucson 85719
(602)795-3840 (800)495-3840
Fax:(602)795-3840

1929. This Southwest adobe has 18-inch thick
walls, which wrap around to form a courtyard.
Ornamental orange trees surround the property,
which is across the street from the University
Medical Center. All the rooms have outside
entrances and open to the patio or overlook the
courtyard and fountain. Furnishings include
antiques and period pieces from the '20s and '30s.
Afternoon tea is served.

Innkeeper(s): Tom & Karin Dennen.

Rates:$65-115. MC VISA. ContPlus Bkfst. Teas. 5 rooms. Beds:KQT.
Phone, AC in room. Tennis. Bicycling. Skiing. Sauna. Swimming.

Seen in: *Gourmet, Los Angeles Times, USA Today, Travel & Leisure.*

Contact: Karin Dennen. Certificate may be used: June 1 - Oct. 1, 1994;
June 1 - Oct. 1, 1995.

*"Thank you so much for such a beautiful home, roman-
tic room and warm hospitality."*

Paz Entera Ranch
PO Box 85400, 7501 N Wade Rd
Tucson 85743
(602)744-2481 (800)726-7554
Fax:(602)744-2691

1925. Nestled at the base of Fire Mountain, this
massive adobe and rock ranch house with traditional clusters of adobe casitas offers an ideal setting for
nature enthusiasts. Dove, quail and other desert
birds serve as wake-up calls. Huge jack rabbits,
roadrunners and cottontails run by to visit on this
30-acre property. Guests can indulge in a mountain
spring-fed swimming pool and Jacuzzi, shaded ham-

mocks, library, hiking and walking trails. The ranch house contains a baby grand piano and fireplace.

Innkeeper(s): Glenn & Molli Nickell.

Rates:$75-120. MC VISA AX DS. ContPlus Bkfst. Picnic lunches. 12 rooms. Beds:KQT. Conference Rm. AC in room. Handicap access. Spa. Swimming.

Contact: Molli Nickell. Certificate may be used: Off season, June 1 to Sept. 15.

The Peppertrees B&B

724 E University Blvd
Tucson 85719
(602)622-7167 Fax:(602)622-5959

1905. Two ancient peppertrees shade the front of this red brick territorial house, near the University of Arizona. Inside you will find English antiques inherited from the innkeeper's family. There is a patio filled with flowers and a fountain. Each of two newly built Southwest-style guest houses features two bedrooms and two bathrooms, a kitchen, laundry and a private patio. Blue-corn pecan pancakes and Scottish shortbread are house specialties. Peppertrees is within walking distance to the university, shops, theaters, museums and restaurants.

Innkeeper(s): Marjorie G. Martin.

Rates:$68-150. MC VISA DS. Full Bkfst. Teas. 5 rooms. Beds:KQT. Phone in room. Skiing. Swimming.

Seen in: *Tucson Guide, Travel Age West, Country, Tucson Homes & Gardens.*

Contact: Marjorie G. Martin. Certificate may be used: June 1-Sept. 15.

"We have not yet stopped telling our friends what a wonderful experience we shared at your lovely home."

Arkansas

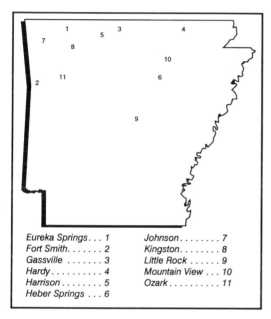

Eureka Springs

Arsenic & Old Lace B&B Inn
60 Hillside Ave
Eureka Springs 72632
(501)253-5454 (800)243-5223

1992. A new structure, but designed in the grand old Queen Anne Victorian style, this inn offers five guest rooms decorated with Victorian furnishings. Popular with honeymooners, the three upper-level guest rooms offer whirlpool tubs, as does one on the ground floor. The inn's gardens complement its attractive exterior, which includes a wraparound veranda and stone wall. Its location in the historic district makes it an excellent starting point for a sightseeing stroll.

Innkeeper(s): Gary & Phyllis Jones.

Rates:$77-150. MC VISA. Gourmet Brkfst. Teas. 5 rooms. Fireplaces. Beds:KQ. TV, AC in room. Fishing.

Contact: Phyllis Jones. Certificate may be used: November through April or anytime mid week (Sunday-Thursday).

Beaver Lake B&B
RR 2 Box 318, County Rd #998
Eureka Springs 72632
(501)253-9210

1990. This modern, woodplank farmhouse rests on the shoreline of Beaver Lake, providing easy access for fishing and swimming. Lake views are featured in the four guest rooms, which offer ceiling fans, country antique furnishings and queen beds. The rooms are named for the four seasons. Guests enjoy chatting around a wood stove in cool weather, and relaxing on the inn's wraparound porch when the weather is warmer. A pool table and writing desk are found in the recreation room. Hummingbirds are frequent visitors in summer.

Innkeeper(s): David & Elaine Reppel.

Rates:$50-70. Full Bkfst. 4 rooms. Beds:Q. AC in room. Swimming. Fishing.

Contact: Elaine Reppel. Certificate may be used: March 1 to May 31, Sunday through Thursday; Nov. 1 to Dec. 15, Sunday through Thursday.

Bridgeford House
263 Spring St
Eureka Springs 72632
(501)253-7853

1884. This peach-colored Victorian delight is nestled in the heart of the Eureka Springs historic district. Rooms feature antiques and are decorated in a wonderfully charming Victorian style with their own private entrance. Guests will enjoy the fresh, hot coffee and selection of teas in their suites, and the large gourmet breakfast is the perfect way to start the day. Enjoy the horse-drawn carriage rides down Eureka Springs' famed boulevard with its stately homes.

Innkeeper(s): Denise & Michael McDonald.

Rates:$75-95. MC VISA. Full Bkfst. Gourmet Brkfst. Evening snacks. 4 rooms. Beds:QT. TV, AC, Refrig. in room. Golf. Tennis. Swimming. Horseback riding. Fishing.

Seen in: *Times Echo Flashlight.*

Contact: Denise McDonald. Certificate may be used: Nov. 1 to Oct. 1, Sunday - Thursday, 1994 & 1995. No holidays.

"You have created an enchanting respite for weary people."

Cliff Cottage, A B&B Inn

42 Armstrong St
Eureka Springs 72632
(501)253-7409 (800)799-7409

1892. A turn-of-the-century "Painted Lady" Shingle Victorian and the newly constructed Place Next Door comprise this inn's guest accommoda-

tions. Listed in the National Register of Historic Places and in the midst of the historic district, this romantic inn is a huge favorite with honeymooners. Cliff Cottage features the Sarah Bernhardt and Lord Tennyson suites, each offering double whirlpool spas, king beds and mini-refrigerators.
Innkeeper(s): Sandra Smith.
Rates:$75-125. MC VISA. Full Bkfst. Gourmet Brkfst, Lunch, Dinner. Picnic lunches. Teas. Evening snacks. 4 rooms. Beds:KQ. TV, AC, Refrig. in room. Tennis. Swimming. Fishing.
Contact: Sandra Smith. Certificate may be used: Midweek (Monday - Thursday), off-season (January to April), holidays excluded.

Crescent Cottage Inn

211 Spring St
Eureka Springs 72632
(501)253-6022 Fax:(501)253-6234

1881. This classic Victorian inn was home to the first Governor of Arkansas after the Civil War. Two long verandas, where meals are served, overlook a breathtaking valley and two mountain ranges. The inn is situated on the quiet, residential end of the historic loop. A five-minute walk into town takes you past limestone cliffs, tall maple trees, beautiful gardens and refreshing springs. Try a ride on the steam engine train that departs nearby.
Innkeeper(s): Ralph & Phyllis Becker.
Rates:$68-115. MC VISA DS. Full Bkfst. Gourmet Brkfst. 5 rooms.

Beds:Q. TV, Phone, AC, Refrig. in room. Swimming. Fishing.
Contact: Ralph Becker. Certificate may be used: Nov. 1-20; Dec. 1-15; January-February (except 13-14); March; April 1-15 from Sunday-Thursday for all the months shown (preceding).

Crescent Hotel

Prospect St
Eureka Springs 72632
(501)253-9766 (800)342-9766
Fax:(501)253-5296

1886. This Eureka Springs landmark Victorian inn offers fine lodging and dining to its guests. Guest rooms vary in decor, ranging from modern to historic to Victorian. Some rooms boast king beds, refrigerators and other amenities. The inn is equipped to handle meetings, receptions and weddings, and guests will find many areas for relaxing and socializing, including a swimming pool.
Innkeeper(s): Dennis Hustead.
Rates:$24-145. MC VISA AX DC DS CB. Full Bkfst. AP available. Gourmet Brkfst, Lunch, Dinner. Picnic lunches. Teas. Evening snacks. 73 rooms. Beds:KQT. Conference Rm. TV, Phone, AC, Refrig. in room. Swimming. Fishing.
Contact: Dennis Hustead. Certificate may be used: Not October, no major holidays, on availability only.

Dairy Hollow House

515 Spring St
Eureka Springs 72632
(501)253-7444 (800)562-8650

1888. Dairy Hollow House, the first of Eureka Springs' bed and breakfast inns, consists of a restored Ozark vernacular farmhouse and a 1940s bungalow-style cottage, both in a national historic district. Stenciled walls set off a collection of Eastlake Victorian furnishings. Outstanding "*Nouveau 'zarks*" cuisine is available by reservation. Innkeeper Crescent Dragonwagon is the author of several books, including the award-winning *Dairy Hollow House Cookbook* and the new *Soup and*

Bread Cookbook, and was called upon to cater President Clinton's inaugural brunch in Washington, D.C.

Innkeeper(s): Ned Shank & Crescent Dragonwagon.

Rates:$125-165. MC VISA AX DC DS CB. Full Bkfst. EP. Evening snacks. 6 rooms. Fireplaces. Beds:Q. Conference Rm. Phone, AC, Refrig. in room. Spa. Swimming. Fishing.

Seen in: *Innsider, Christian Science Monitor, Los Angeles Times.*

Contact: Ned Shank. Certificate may be used: Midweek (Sunday-Thursday) nights, September, November, December, February, March for 1994 and 1995.

"The height of unpretentious luxury."

Ellis House at Trail's End
One Wheeler
Eureka Springs 72632
(501)253-8218 (800)243-8218

1933. This two-story Tudor home boasts views of Eureka Springs from each of its five suites. The hearty full breakfasts are eaten in a formal dining room, and an antique Palladin window offers a stunning view of the Ozarks below. Honeymooners enjoy the suites' amenities, including some with double whirlpool baths and king beds. The inn can accommodate family reunions, meetings and weddings. Guests often enjoy relaxing on the porch or strolling among its lush gardens and grounds.

Innkeeper(s): Jan Watson.

Rates:$89-129. MC VISA AX. Full Bkfst. Gourmet Brkfst. 5 rooms. Beds:KQT. Conference Rm. TV, Phone, AC in room. Swimming. Fishing.

Contact: Jan Watson. Certificate may be used: Weekdays Sunday - Thursday, excluding October, holidays and special events.

Heart of the Hills Inn
5 Summit
Eureka Springs 72632
(501)253-7468

1883. Three suites and a Victorian cottage comprise this antique-furnished homestead located just four blocks from downtown. The Victorian Room is furnished with a white iron bed, dresser, antique lamp and antique pedestal sink. Evening dessert is served. The honeymoon suite has a double Jacuzzi.

The village trolley stops at the inn.

Innkeeper(s): Jan Jacobs Weber.

Rates:$71-109. MC VISA. Gourmet Brkfst. Evening snacks. 4 rooms. Beds:KQT. TV, AC, Refrig. in room. Handicap access. Swimming. Fishing.

Seen in: *Carroll County Tribune's Peddler.*

Contact: Jan Weber. Certificate may be used: Anytime November through March, Sunday-Thursday, April-September, excluding holidays and special events.

"It was delightful - the bed so comfortable, room gorgeous, food delicious and ohhh those chocolates."

The Heartstone Inn & Cottages
35 King's Hwy
Eureka Springs 72632
(501)253-8916

1902. Described as a "pink and white confection," this handsome restored Victorian with its wraparound verandas is located in the historic district. The award-winning inn is filled with antiques and artwork from the innkeeper's native England. Live

music is featured; in May a fine arts festival and in September, a jazz festival. Afternoon refreshments are available on the sunny deck overlooking a wooded ravine. Pink roses line the picket fence surrounding the inviting garden.

Innkeeper(s): Iris & Bill Simantel.

Rates:$53-118. MC VISA AX DS. Gourmet Brkfst. 16 rooms. Fireplaces. Beds:KQ. Conference Rm. TV, AC, Refrig. in room. Golf. Spa. Swimming. Fishing.

Seen in: *Innsider Magazine, Arkansas Times, New York Times, Arkansas Gazette, Southern Living, Country Home.*

Contact: Iris Simantel. Certificate may be used: Sunday through Wednesday arrival. November through March-not good on holidays or special events. Other times last-minute only (call same day).

"Extraordinary! Best breakfasts anywhere!"

The Piedmont House B&B

165 Spring St
Eureka Springs 72632
(501)253-9258 (800)253-9258

1880. An original guest book from the inn's days as a tourist home is a cherished item here. The Piedmont offers the best views in town and is in the National Register.

Innkeeper(s): Sheri & Ron Morrill.

Rates:$59-89. MC VISA AX DC DS CB. Full Bkfst. Evening snacks. 8 rooms. Beds:QT. AC in room. Swimming. Fishing.

Seen in: *Arkansas Times*.

Contact: Sheri Morrill. Certificate may be used: Sunday through Thursday on space available.

"Wonderful atmosphere and your personalities are exactly in sync with the surroundings."

Sunnyside Inn

5 Ridgeway
Eureka Springs 72632
(501)253-6638 (800)554-9499

1883. Beautifully renovated, this National Register Queen Anne Victorian is located three blocks from town. Traditional Victorian decor is especially out-standing in the Rose Room with a carved, high oak bed and original rose stained-glass windows. The Honeymoon Suite features an Abe Lincoln era carved walnut bed with matching bureau. Country quiches, hot homemade cinnamon rolls and peach and blueberry cobblers are frequently served, some-times on the deck overlooking the wilderness area. Gladys seems to love innkeeping; she owned an inn in Alaska before coming to Eureka Springs.

Innkeeper(s): Gladys R. Foris

Rates:$60-95. MC VISA AX DC DS CB. Full Bkfst. 7 rooms. Beds:QT. Conference Rm. AC in room. Swimming. Fishing.

Contact: Gladys R. Foris. Certificate may be used: Tuesday through Thursday.

Taylor-Page Inn

33 Benton St
Eureka Springs 72632
(501)253-7315

1900. Within easy walking distance of downtown restaurants, shopping and trolley, this turn-of-the-century Square salt-box inn features Victorian and country decor in its three suites and rooms. Guests often enjoy relaxing in the inn's two sitting rooms. The suites offer ceiling fans, full kitchens, and sun-decks. The inn offers convenient access to antiquing, fishing, museums and parks.

Innkeeper(s): Jeanne Taylor.

Rates:$55-75. MC VISA. Cont. Bkfst. 5 rooms. 2 with shared baths. TV, Phone, AC, Refrig. in room. Handicap access. Fishing.

Contact: Jeanne Taylor. Certificate may be used: November, December, January, February, March, anytime. April through October Monday through Thursday.

Fort Smith

Beland Manor Inn B&B

1320 S Albert Pike
Fort Smith 72903
(501)782-3300 (800)334-5052

1950. Magnolia trees and pink and white azaleas surround this Colonial Revival mansion. Expansive lawns, hundreds of impatiens, a rose garden and patio adjoining a back garden gazebo, make the inn a popular setting for romantic weddings. Furnishings incorporate traditional pieces and antiques. A king-size four-poster rice bed makes the Bridal Suite the option of choice. Best of all is the three-course Sunday breakfast, often featuring Eggs Benedict with strawberry crepes for dessert.

Innkeeper(s): Mike & Suzy Smith.

Rates:$65-95. MC VISA AX. Gourmet Brkfst, Dinner. 6 rooms. Beds:KQT. Conference Rm. TV, Phone, AC in room. Bicycling. Handicap access. Swimming. Fishing.

Contact: Suzy Smith. Certificate may be used: January, March, September, November and December.

Thomas Quinn Guest House

815 North B St
Fort Smith 72901
(501)782-0499

1863. Nine suites with kitchenettes are available at this inn, which in 1916 added a second story and stately columns to its original structure. Located on the perimeter of Fort Smith's historic district, it is close to the art center, historic sites, museums and restaurants. Several state parks are within easy driving distance. Early morning coffee and tea are served.

Innkeeper(s): Virginia Whitfield.

Rates:$79. MC VISA AX DC DS CB. 9 rooms. Beds:D. TV, Phone, AC, Refrig. in room. Spa. Swimming. Fishing.

Contact: Gary Hammer. Certificate may be used: Anytime.

Gassville

Lithia Springs B&B

Rt 1 Box 77A Hwy 126
Gassville 72635
(501)435-6100

1890. Set on 39 acres of meadows and woods, this inn with its country decor is located between two fishing and boating lakes. Blanchard Springs Caverns, Silver Dollar City, Eureka Springs and the White and Buffalo Rivers are also nearby. Even though the springs are no longer active, the inn gained fame in the late 1800s because of the supposed cures of the medicinal springs. Breakfast can be enjoyed in the dining room or on the large screened front porch.

Innkeeper(s): Paul & Reita Johnson.

Rates:$45-50. Full Bkfst. 5 rooms. 2 with shared baths. Beds:QT. AC in room. Farm. Swimming. Fishing.

Contact: Paul Johnson. Certificate may be used: Any date except national holiday weekends.

Hardy

The Olde Stonehouse B&B Inn
511 Main St
Hardy 72542
(501)856-2983 (800)514-2983

1928. The stone fireplace which graces the comfortable living room of this former banker's home is set with fossils and unusual stones, including an Arkansas diamond. Lace tablecloths, china and silver make breakfast a special occasion. Each room is decorated to keep the authentic feel of the roaring '20s. The bedrooms have antiques and ceiling fans. Aunt Jenny's room boasts a clawfoot tub and a white iron bed, while Uncle Buster's room is filled with Depression-era furniture. Spring River is only one block away and offers canoeing, boating and fishing. Old Hardy Town caters to antique and craft lovers.

Innkeeper(s): Peggy & David Johnson.

Rates:$55-85. MC VISA AX DS. Full Bkfst. Gourmet Brkfst. Picnic lunches. Teas. Evening snacks. 9 rooms. Beds:QT. Conference Rm. Phone, AC in room. Golf. Tennis. Bicycling. Skiing. Swimming. Horseback riding. Fishing.

Seen in: Memphis Commercial Appeal, Jonesboro Sun.

Contact: Peggy Johnson. Certificate may be used: November-April, anytime, holidays excluded, special events excluded. May-October, Sunday through Thursday, holidays excluded, special events excluded.

Harrison

Queen Anne House
610 W Central
Harrison 72601-5006
(501)741-1304

1894. This Victorian is found in the Ozarks, within easy driving distance of Branson, Mo. The inn's lodging options include both guest rooms and a private cottage. A big-screen TV is available in the parlor, and another favorite lounging spot is on the

wraparound front porch. Guests enjoy a hearty breakfast in the glass-enclosed dining room before continuing their travels or heading out to explore the area's recreational and sightseeing opportunities. Dogpatch USA and Mystic Caverns are nearby.

Innkeeper(s): Anna Rose & Joe Avila.

Rates:$55-85. Full Bkfst. 4 rooms. 2 with shared baths. Beds:QD. AC, Refrig. in room. Bicycling. Fishing.

Contact: Anna Rose & Joe Avila. Certificate may be used: Anytime at regular rate (except for the month of October).

Heber Springs

Oak Tree Inn
1802 W Main
Heber Springs 72543
(501)362-7731 (800)959-3857

1983. Fishing and boating enthusiasts will appreciate this inn's proximity to Greers Ferry Lake and the Little Red River. The inn, a modern Colonial Revival home, offers six guest rooms. Cabins and a cottage also are available. Each of the inn's rooms is named for a prominent citizen who contributed to the growth of Cleburne County. Rooms feature ceiling fans, fireplaces, and wooden floors. Heber Springs is an easy getaway from Little Rock, and Wooly Hollow State Park is nearby.

Innkeeper(s): Freddie Lou Lodge.

Rates:$75-85. MC VISA DS. Full Bkfst. 6 rooms. Fireplaces. Beds:Q. AC in room. Golf. Tennis. Swimming. Fishing.

Seen in: USA Today, Brides Magazine, Vacation Magazine.

Contact: Freddie Lou Lodge. Certificate may be used: Sunday - Friday.

Johnson

Johnson House B&B
5371 S 48th St, PO Box 431
Johnson 72741
(501)756-1095

1882. Nestled in the rolling hillside between Fayetteville and Springdale, this handmade brick structure offers authentic Ozark hospitality. Guests can stroll the gardens and visit the inn's Smokehouse Antique Shop or play a game of horseshoes or croquet. At the end of the day, take in a spectacular Arkansas sunset, as seen from the upstairs veranda. Your hostess, will happily answer your questions on area attractions and history, and with advance notice she may pack a gourmet picnic lunch for your trip home.

Innkeeper(s): Mary K. Carothers

Rates:$75. Full Bkfst. Gourmet Brkfst. Picnic lunches. 3 rooms.

Beds:DT. AC in room. Farm. Handicap access. Swimming. Fishing.

Contact: Mary Carothers. Certificate may be used: November through February.

Kingston

Fool's Cove Ranch B&B
PO Box 10
Kingston 72742
(501)665-2986 Fax:(501)665-2986

1979. Situated in the Ozarks' Boston Mountain range, this 6,000-square-foot farmhouse, part of a family farm, offers 160 acres of field, meadow, and

forest. Guests who have had their horses test negative on a Coggins test may bring them along and utilize the farm's corrals. Guests may angle for bass or catfish in the pond. Favorite gathering spots are the roomy parlor and the outdoor hot tub. Area attractions include the Buffalo River, Dogpatch USA and several fine fishing spots.

Innkeeper(s): Mary Jo Sullivan.

Rates:$55-75. MC VISA AX DC DS CB. Full Bkfst. Picnic lunches. Evening snacks. 4 rooms. 3 with shared baths. Beds:Q. AC in room. Farm. Spa. Swimming. Fishing.

Contact: Mary Sullivan. Certificate may be used: Anytime, subject to availability.

Little Rock

The Carriage House B&B
1700 Louisiana
Little Rock 72206
(501)374-7032

1892. This turn-of-the-century Queen Anne Victorian is listed on the national, state and local historic registers. Guests stay in a restored carriage house adjacent to the innkeepers' home. Around the corner is the Governor's Mansion in the Quapaw Quarter. Guest rooms are tastefully furnished with informal antiques. A gourmet breakfast is served on the sunporch of the main house, and guests also are treated to afternoon tea.

Innkeeper(s): Dr. Dan & Sandra Cook.

Rates:$89. Gourmet Brkfst. Teas. 2 rooms. Beds:QD. AC in room.

Contact: Sandra Cook. Certificate may be used: Anytime, based on availability.

The Empress of Little Rock
2120 Louisiana St
Little Rock 72206
(501)374-7966

1850. Day lilies, peonies and iris accent the old-fashioned garden of this elaborate, three-story Queen Anne Victorian. A grand center hall opens to a double staircase, lit by a stained-glass skylight. The 7,500 square feet include a sitting room at the top of the tower. The original owner kept a private poker game going here and the stained-glass windows allowed him to keep an eye out for local authorities, who might close down his gambling activities. The Hornibrook Room features a magnificent Renaissance Revival bedroom set with a high canopy. The Tower bedroom has an Austrian walnut bed. Gourmet breakfasts are served in the dining room.

Innkeeper(s): Robert & Sharon Blair.

Rates:$85-125. MC VISA AX. Cont. Bkfst. Gourmet Brkfst. Teas. 5 rooms. Beds:QT. TV, Phone, AC, Refrig. in room. Bicycling.

Contact: Sharon Welch-Blair. Certificate may be used: Opening December, 1994. December, 1994 - December, 1995.

Quapaw Inn
1868 S Gaines
Little Rock 72206
(501)376-6873 (800)732-5591

1905. Innkeeper Dottie Woodwind swears Bill Clinton faithfully jogged past her Colonial Revival inn at 7 a.m. each day for 14 years before leaving for Washington, D.C. The roomy pink house offers a Honeymoon Suite. Three guests may be accommodated in Aunt Mary's Room, a country charmer with a unique handmade Dutch doll quilt and Gilbert bed. Be sure to inquire about dinner and theater packages.

Innkeeper(s): Dottie Woodwind.

Rates:$60-80. Full Bkfst. 3 rooms. Beds:KQT. TV, AC in room. Swimming. Fishing.

Contact: Dottie Woodwind. Certificate may be used: August.

Mountain View

Owl Hollow Country Inn

PO Box 1201, 219 S Peabody St
Mountain View 72560
(501)269-8699

1906. This historic two-story Federal-style inn is located within a block of Courthouse Square and downtown eateries and shops. A full breakfast is served at 8 a.m. before guests head out to explore the many attractions offered in the surrounding area, including Blanchard Springs Caverns and the Ozark Folk Center.

Innkeeper(s): George & Marilyn Ivy.

Rates:$55. Full Bkfst. 6 rooms. Beds:QT. AC in room. Swimming. Fishing.

Contact: George Ivy. Certificate may be used: Monday through Thursday, March 1 through Dec. 1, 1994 and 1995.

Wildflower B&B

100 Washington St, PO Box 72
Mountain View 72560
(501)269-4383 (800)591-4879

1918. The inn's wraparound porches are a gathering place for local musicians who often play old-time music. If you rock long enough you're likely to see an impromptu hootenanny in the Courthouse Square across the street. Since there are no priceless antiques, children are welcome. However, you may have to watch them (and yourself) because there's a tempting first-floor bakery that's always "fixin' up" divinity cookies, macaroons and hot breads.

Innkeeper(s): Todd & Andrea Budy.

Rates:$41-70. MC VISA DS. ContPlus Bkfst. 8 rooms. 2 with shared baths. Beds:DT. AC in room. Tennis. Swimming. Horseback riding. Fishing.

Seen in: *New York Times, Dan Rather & CBS, Midwest Living.*

Contact: Andrea Budy. Certificate may be used: Sunday-Thursday nights only in conjunction with one consecutive night's stay at regular rate.

"It's the kind of place you'll look forward to returning to."

Ozark

1887 Inn B&B

100 E Commercial
Ozark 72949
(501)667-1121

1885. At the foot of the Ozarks, this Queen Anne Victorian inn has been lovingly restored to its nat-ural beauty. The inn's accommodations include a Honeymoon/Anniversary Suite, an intimate spot for a romantic candlelight dinner arranged by the innkeeper. Desks, fireplaces and queen beds can be found in the rooms. The decor features antique Victorian and country furnishings. Receptions, special events and weddings are popular here. Less than two blocks away is the Arkansas River.

Innkeeper(s): Karen Britting.

Rates:$50-60. MC VISA AX DS. Full Bkfst. Gourmet Brkfst, Lunch, Dinner. Picnic lunches. Teas. Evening snacks. 5 rooms. 1 with shared bath. Fireplaces. Beds:Q. AC in room. Swimming. Fishing.

Contact: Karen Britting. Certificate may be used: Anytime rooms available.

California

Ahwahnee

Apple Blossom Inn B&B
44606 Silver Spur Tr
Ahwahnee 93601
(209)642-2001

1990. A bountiful organic apple orchard surrounds this inn, an attractive country cottage a short distance from Yosemite National Park. Visitors choose either the Red Delicious Room, with its two double beds and private entrance, or the Granny Smith Room, with queen bed and private balcony. Both rooms feature ceiling fans, private bath and sitting areas. Guests enjoy the inn's woodburning stove and the spa overlooking the woods.

Innkeeper(s): Edith, Lynn & Jenny Hays.

Rates:$60-85. MC VISA. ContPlus Bkfst. Teas. Evening snacks. 2 rooms. Beds:QD. AC in room. Skiing. Spa. Swimming. Fishing.

Contact: Lynn Hays. Certificate may be used: Sept. 1, 1994 through March 31, 1995; Sept. 1 through Dec. 31, 1995.

Alameda

Webster House Bed & Breakfast Inn
1238 Versailles Ave
Alameda 94501
(510)523-9697

1854. This fanciful Gothic Revival house bears the distinction of being the oldest house on the island as well as a city historical monument. Afternoon

tea is served upon check-in and dinner may be had by advance reservation. Rooms are decorated with antiques and there is a private cottage. Guests often enjoy breakfast next to the Victorian fountain and waterfall or on the large deck shaded by two coastal redwoods.

Innkeeper(s): Andrew & Susan McCormack.

Rates:$75-125. AX. Full Bkfst. Gourmet Brkfst, Lunch, Dinner. Teas. Evening snacks. 4 rooms. 1 with shared bath. Beds:Q. Golf. Bicycling. Swimming. Horseback riding. Fishing.

Seen in: *Bay Area Backroads, San Francisco Magazine, Innsider.*

Contact: Susan McCormack. Certificate may be used: Not to be used during holiday stays.

Albion

Fensalden Inn
PO Box 99
Albion 95410
(707)937-4042 (800)959-3850

1860. Originally a stagecoach station, Fensalden looks out over the Pacific Ocean as it has for more than 100 years. The Tavern Room has witnessed many a rowdy scene and if you look closely you can see bullet holes in the original redwood ceiling. The inn provides 20 acres for walks, whale-watching, viewing deer and bicycling. Relax with wine and hors d'oeuvres in the evening.

Innkeeper(s): Scott & Frances Brazil.

Rates:$85-130. MC VISA. Full Bkfst. AP available. Teas. 8 rooms. Fireplaces. Beds:KQT. Conference Rm. Refrig. in room. Golf. Tennis.

Bicycling. Handicap access. Swimming. Horseback riding. Fishing.

Seen in: *Sunset Magazine, Focus, Peninsula Magazine.*

Contact: R.S. Brazil. Certificate may be used: January to December: Sunday through Thursday only (except holidays). Subject to availability.

"Closest feeling to heaven on Earth."

Amador City

Mine House Inn
PO Box 245, S Hwy 49
Amador City 95601
(209)267-5900 (800)646-3473

1870. Housing the offices of one of the most profitable gold mines in the mother lode of 1853, known as the Keystone Mine, each room in this inn is named for its original function. All furnished with authentic 19th-century antiques, the rooms' names include the Vault, Bookkeeping, Directors, Mill Grinding and Assay rooms. The acre of land surrounding the Inn is shaded by 200-year-old oaks and pines. Just steps away is the historic downtown of Amador City with its charming shops and fine restaurants. Within easy driving distance are the towns of Volcano and Columbia.

Innkeeper(s): Allen & Rosario Mendy.

Rates:$65-90. MC VISA. ContPlus Bkfst. 8 rooms. Beds:DT. AC in room. Skiing. Swimming. Fishing.

Contact: Rosario Mendy. Certificate may be used: Sunday - Thursday excluding all holidays and June 1 - Sept. 15 through 1995.

Aptos

Apple Lane Inn
6265 Soquel Dr
Aptos 95003
(408)475-6868 (800)649-8988

1870. Ancient apple trees border the lane that leads to this Victorian farmhouse set on two acres of gardens and fields. Built by the Porter brothers, founding fathers of Aptos, the inn is decorated with Victorian wallpapers and hardwood floors. The original wine cellar still exists, as well as the

old barn and apple-drying shed used for storage after harvesting the orchard. Miles of beaches are within walking distance. The innkeepers were married at the inn and later purchased it.

Innkeeper(s): Doug & Diana Groom.

Rates:$80-150. MC VISA DS. Full Bkfst. Picnic lunches. 5 rooms. Beds:QT. Conference Rm. TV, Phone, Refrig. in room. Farm. Golf. Tennis. Bicycling. Swimming. Horseback riding. Fishing.

Seen in: *Santa Barbara Times, 1001 Decorating Ideas, New York Times.*

Contact: Diana Groom. Certificate may be used: Sunday-Thursday, November-April.

"Our room was spotless and beautifully decorated."

Mangels House

570 Aptos Creek Rd, PO Box 302
Aptos 95001
(408)688-7982

1886. Like the Spreckels family, Claus Mangels made his fortune in sugar beets, and built this house in the style of a Southern mansion. The inn, with its encircling veranda, stands on four acres of lawns and orchards. It is bounded by the Forest of Nisene Marks, 10,000 acres of redwood trees, creeks, and trails. Monterey Bay is three-quarters of a mile away.

Innkeeper(s): Jacqueline & Ron Fisher.

Rates:$98-145. MC VISA AX. Gourmet Brkfst. Evening snacks. 6 rooms. Fireplaces. Beds:KQT. Conference Rm. Golf. Tennis. Swimming. Horseback riding. Fishing.

Seen in: *Inn Serv, Innviews.*

Contact: Jacqueline Fisher. Certificate may be used: Sunday through Thursday (holiday weekends excepted).

"Compliments on the lovely atmosphere. We look forward to sharing our discovery with friends and returning with them."

Arroyo Grande

Arroyo Village Inn B&B

407 El Camino Real
Arroyo Grande 93420
(805)489-5926

1984. The travel section of the Los Angeles Times has featured many rare reviews of this country Victorian. Rooms feature extras such as balconies

and window seats. Laura Ashley prints complement the antiques. Day trips from the inn include Hearst Castle, wineries and mineral springs. Guests can test the water of local beaches on foot or ride up the coast on horseback. Breakfast features specialties such as homemade granola and breads, fresh fruit, omelets and French toast with caramel sauce and apple slices. A late afternoon tea provides wine and cheese or cookies and tea.

Innkeeper(s): John & Gina Glass.

Rates:$75-195. MC VISA AX DC DS. Full Bkfst. Gourmet Brkfst. Teas. 7 rooms. Beds:Q. Conference Rm. Phone, AC in room. Skiing. Swimming. Horseback riding. Fishing.

Seen in: *Los Angeles Times.*

Contact: Gina Glass. Certificate may be used: Sunday-Friday on $145 & up suites. Between September-June, Saturday and Sunday as available. All holidays and special event weekends excluded.

"Absolutely all the essentials of a great inn."

Auburn

Lincoln House B&B

191 Lincoln Way
Auburn 95603
(916)885-8880

1933. In the heart of California's gold country travelers will find the Lincoln House, a captivating Bungalow home. The romantic Shenandoah Room offers a queen-size bed and a view of the inn's koi fish pond. A petrified wood fireplace beautifully complements the southwest theme of the sitting room, and the dining room boasts a view of the

Sierra Nevada mountains. When they are not exploring historic Old Town Auburn, guests may take a dip in the inn's swimming pool or relax on its covered porch.

Innkeeper(s): Leslie & Stan Fronczak.

Rates:$69-89. MC VISA AX. Full Bkfst. Gourmet Brkfst. Teas. Evening snacks. 3 rooms. Beds:KQT. AC in room. Skiing. Fishing.

Contact: Leslie Fronczak. Certificate may be used: Sunday through Thursday, June, July, August. Anytime September through May. Holidays excluded.

Avalon

Catalina Island Seacrest Inn

201 Claressa Ave, PO Box 128
Avalon 90704
(310)510-0196 Fax:(310)510-1122

1907. The unique and romantic setting of Catalina Island is home to this inn, just a block from the ocean. The inn enjoys tremendous popularity with honeymooners, who love the in-room whirlpools and tubs for two offered in many of the guest rooms. The inn often hosts weddings and offers special packages, including round-trip transportation to the island and many other extras. Many guests enjoy exploring Avalon's shops and sights.

Innkeeper(s): Richard Duve.

Rates:$95-185. MC VISA AX DS. Cont. Bkfst. 7 rooms. Beds:KQ. TV, AC, Refrig. in room. Swimming. Fishing.

Contact: Norma Milne. Certificate may be used: Monday through Thursday, year-round, excluding August and holidays.

Ballard

Ballard Inn

2436 Baseline
Ballard 93463
(805)688-7770 (800)638-2466
Fax:(805)688-9560

1984. In the heart of Santa Barbara Wine Country, the Ballard Inn is in a quiet community of 81 families. The Figueroa Mountains serve as a backdrop to this inn filled with antiques, quilts and down comforters. Nearby adventures include visiting more than 15 wineries or hiking in the local mountains. The town of Los Olivos, which is minutes away, is home to 14 art galleries. A favorite pastime for guests is to relax while sitting on a wraparound porch that overlooks the town of Ballard and the mountain range.

Innkeeper(s): Kelly Robinson.

Rates:$160-195. MC VISA AX. Full Bkfst. 15 rooms. Fireplaces. Beds:KQT. Conference Rm. TV, Phone, AC in room. Bicycling. Handicap

access. Swimming. Fishing.

Contact: Kelly Robinson Certificate may be used: Sunday through Thursday, excludes holidays, upon availability.

Benicia

The Painted Lady

141 East F St
Benicia 94510
(707)746-1646

1896. This folk Victorian, located two blocks from the water, is close to the town's historic landmarks, and you can walk to cafes and shops, or take the paths to the Carquinex Straits and the harbor. The Rosario Room has antique furniture with a soft yellow background and climbing roses. A whirlpool tub is in the Daisy Room. It's 15 minutes to the ferry to San Francisco's waterfront and Napa Valley is a half-hour drive.

Innkeeper(s): Sally Watson.

Rates:$70-85. MC VISA. Full Bkfst. 2 rooms. Beds:Q. Swimming. Fishing.

Contact: Sally Watson. Certificate may be used: Sunday-Thursday, one room only (Rosario's Room), November-March.

Big Bear

Gold Mountain Manor Historic B&B

1117 Anita, PO Box 2027
Big Bear 92314
(909)585-6997

1931. This spectacular log mansion was once a hideaway for the rich and famous. Eight fireplaces provide a roaring fire in each room in fall and winter. The Lucky Baldwin Room offers a hearth made from stones of gold gathered in the famous Lucky Baldwin mine nearby. In the Clark Gable room is the fireplace Gable and Carole Lombard enjoyed on their honeymoon. Gourmet country breakfasts and afternoon hors d'oeuvres are served.

Innkeeper(s): John & Conny Ridgway.

Rates:$75-180. MC VISA. Full Bkfst. Gourmet Brkfst. Picnic lunches. Teas. 9 rooms. 6 with shared baths. Fireplaces. Beds:Q. Conference Rm. Bicycling. Skiing. Spa. Swimming. Fishing.

Contact: Conny Ridgway. Certificate may be used: Sunday through Thursday, excluding holidays and Christmas season.

"A majestic experience! In this magnificent house, history comes alive!"

Big Bear Lake

Eagle's Nest B&B
41675 Big Bear Blvd, Box 1003
Big Bear Lake 92315
(909)866-6465

1983. Named for the more than 50 American bald eagles that nest in and around Big Bear, this lodge-pole pine inn features a river rock fireplace in the parlor. Antiques, bronzed eagles and baskets of flowers provide a warm mountain setting. Surrounded by tall pine trees, the property also includes several cottage suites.
Innkeeper(s): James Joyce & Jack Draper.
Rates:$75-165. MC VISA. ContPlus Bkfst. Evening snacks. 15 rooms. Fireplaces. Beds:Q. TV, Phone, Refrig. in room. Golf. Bicycling. Skiing. Spa. Swimming. Horseback riding. Fishing.
Seen in: Los Angeles Times, Sun Living, AM Los Angeles.
Contact: Jack Draper. Certificate may be used: Sunday through Thursday, April, May, June, July, August and September.

"You are two superb hosts!"

Wainwright Inn B&B
43113 Moonridge Rd, PO Box 130406
Big Bear Lake 92315
(909)585-6914

1981. This Tudor-style B&B is located in a quiet, tree-filled residential area adjacent to Bear Mountain ski resort and golf course. The most popular accommodation is the Honeymoon Hideaway, with whirlpool for two, sleigh bed, fireplace, wet bar and private entrance. Canopy beds and English country antiques are found throughout the inn. Afternoon tea is served in the solarium and there's a massive brick fireplace in the Great Room.
Innkeeper(s): Shirin Berton & Jack Culler.
Rates:$85-155. MC VISA AX DC DS CB. Full Bkfst. Picnic lunches. Teas. 5 rooms. 2 with shared baths. Fireplaces. Beds:Q. Conference Rm. Refrig. in room. Golf. Bicycling. Skiing. Spa. Swimming. Horseback riding. Fishing.
Seen in: Los Angeles Times, Gourmet Getaway.
Contact: Shirin Berton. Certificate may be used: Midweek: January-November (excluding holidays and special events). Anytime: April, May, June (excluding holidays and special events).

Bishop

The Matlick House
1313 Rowan Ln
Bishop 93514
(619)873-3133 (800)898-3133

1906. Built by pioneers of the Owens Valley, this ranch house offers views of both the Sierra Nevadas

and White Mountains from most rooms. A full breakfast and evening wine and appetizers are served in the parlor or on the wraparound porch. Fly-fishing is within 15 minutes.
Innkeeper(s): Ray & Barbara Showalter.
Rates:$79-89. VISA AX DC DS. Full Bkfst. Picnic lunches. 5 rooms. Beds:QT. Phone, AC in room. Skiing. Swimming. Fishing.
Contact: Ray Showalter. Certificate may be used: Any except Memorial Day weekend.

Bolinas

Brighton Beach Haus
59 Brighton Ave, PO Box 57
Bolinas 94924
(415)868-9778

1900. The charming coastal town of Bolinas is home to this inn, which offers a comfortable European touch. Visitors select from four guest rooms, including the Marcello Room, which has a secluded deck perfect for moonlit conversations. The double canopy bed in the lavender Therese Room is another guest favorite, and the Angela Room sports a cozy down comforter on its queen bed. The intimate Rosa Room is found in the inn's upstairs loft. The Pacific Ocean is only a half-block from the inn, and Mt. Tamalpas State Park and the Point Reyes National Seashore are nearby.
Innkeeper(s): Charles Wols.
Rates:$95-120. MC VISA. Full Bkfst. MAP available. Gourmet Brkfst. 4 rooms. 4 with shared baths. Beds:QD.
Contact: Charles Wols. Certificate may be used: Midweek during season May 15-Sept. 15. Anytime during off season except holidays.

Bridgeport

The Cain House
340 Main St, PO Box 454
Bridgeport 93517
(619)932-7040 (800)433-2246
Fax:(619)932-7419

1920. The grandeur of the Eastern Sierra Mountains is the perfect setting for evening refreshments as the sun sets, turning the sky into a fiery, purple canvas. The innkeeper's experiences while traveling around the world have influenced The Cain House's decor to give the inn a European elegance with a casual western atmosphere. Travelers can take a short drive to the ghost town of Bodie where 10,000 people once lived in this gold-mining community. Outdoor enthusiasts can find an abundance of activity at Lake Tahoe, which is an hour-and-a-half away.

Innkeeper(s): Chris & Marachal Gohlich.

Rates:$80-135. MC VISA AX DC DS CB. Full Bkfst. EP. Evening snacks. 7 rooms. Tennis. Fishing.

Contact: Marachal Gohlich. Certificate may be used: Sunday-Thursday, April 15-Nov. 15.

Calistoga

Foothill House

3037 Foothill Blvd
Calistoga 94515
(707)942-6933 (800)942-6933
Fax:(707)942-5692

1892. This country farmhouse overlooks the western foothills of Mount St. Helena. Graceful old California oaks and pockets of flowers greet guests. Each room features country antiques, a four-poster bed, a fireplace and a small refrigerator. Breakfast is served in the sun room or is delivered personally to your room in a basket. Two rooms offer private Jacuzzi tubs.

Innkeeper(s): Gus & Doris Beckert.

Rates:$115-220. MC VISA AX. Gourmet Brkfst. Evening snacks. 3 rooms. Bicycling.

Seen in: *Herald Examiner.*

Contact: Doris Beckert. Certificate may be used: Nov. 1-March 31; Sunday through Thursday; holidays excluded.

"Gourmet treats served in front of an open fire. Hospitality never for a moment flagged."

Scarlett's Country Inn

3918 Silverado Trail N
Calistoga 94515
(707)942-6669 (800)870-6069

1900. Formerly a winter campground of the Wappo Indians, the property now includes a restored farmhouse. There are green lawns and country vistas of

woodland and vineyards. Each room has a private entrance and is air-conditioned. Breakfast is often served beneath the apple trees or poolside.

Innkeeper(s): Scarlett & Derek Dwyer.

Rates:$95-150. Full Bkfst. Teas. 3 rooms. Bicycling. Skiing. Swimming. Fishing.

Contact: Scarlett Dwyer. Certificate may be used: November through March on a Sunday through Thursday night.

"Wonderful, peaceful, serene."

Cambria

Olallieberry Inn

2476 Main St
Cambria 93428
(805)927-3222 Fax:(805)927-0202

1873. This Greek Revival house originally was built by a German pharmacist, but has been influenced by other owners, including dairy farmers and a Morro Bay fisherman. Restored and recently refurbished, the guest rooms feature handsome antique beds and sunken or claw-foot tubs. Afternoon wine and breakfast are served in a cheery gathering room overlooking Santa Rosa Creek. Guests can walk to shops and restaurants, and Hearst Castle is seven miles up the coast.

Innkeeper(s): Peter or Carol Ann Irsfeld.

Rates:$85-115. MC VISA. Full Bkfst. Teas. 6 rooms. Golf. Fishing.

Seen in: *Los Angeles Times, Elmer Dills Radio Show.*

Contact: Peter Irsfeld. Certificate may be used: Sunday-Thursday, except May 1 through Oct. 31 and holidays.

"Our retreat turned into relaxation, romance and pure Victorian delight."

The Squibb House

4063 Burton Drive
Cambria 93428
(805)927-9600 Fax:(805)927-9606

1877. For years visitors strolling through Cambria have stopped at the picket fence surrounding the Squibb House to admire its Italinate and Gothic Revival archicteture and to enjoy glimpses of the large garden. Some of the inn's custom furnishings were hand-made in the shop next door. Across the street are galleries, fine restaurants and interesting shops.

Innkeeper(s): Bruce Black.

Rates:$95-125. MC VISA. Cont. Bkfst. Teas. 5 rooms. Fireplaces. Beds:Q. Swimming. Fishing.

Contact: Bruce Black. Certificate may be used: Weeknights, Sunday-Thursday from October to May.

Camino

Camino Hotel B&B
4103 Carson Rd, PO Box 1197
Camino 95709
(916)644-7740 (800)200-7740

1888. Once a barracks for the area's loggers, this inn now caters to visitors in the state's famed gold country. Just east of Placerville, historic Camino is on the Old Carson Wagon Trail. Nine guest rooms are available, including the E.J. Barrett Room, a favorite with honeymooners. Other rooms feature names such as Pony Express, Stage Stop and Wagon Train. The family-oriented inn welcomes children, and a local park offers a handy site for their recreational needs. Popular area activities include antiquing, hot air ballooning and wine tasting.

Innkeeper(s): Paula Nobert & John Eddy.

Rates:$55-85. MC VISA AX DS CB. Full Bkfst. Picnic lunches. Evening snacks. 9 rooms. 6 with shared baths. Conference Rm. Golf. Tennis. Skiing. Swimming. Fishing.

Contact: Paula Nobert. Certificate may be used: Exclude weekends July through January.

Carmel

The Cobblestone Inn
PO Box 3185
Carmel 93921
(408)625-5222 Fax:(408)625-0478

1950. An exterior of wood and cobblestone gathered from the Carmel River provide a friendly facade for visitors to this bed and breakfast located two blocks from the heart of Carmel. Each guest room has its own cobblestone fireplace. The inn's country decor is enhanced with quilts, a colorful antique carousel horse and other early American antiques.

Innkeeper(s): Raymond Farnsworth.

Rates:$95-175. MC VISA AX. Full Bkfst. Picnic lunches. Teas. 5 rooms. Golf. Tennis. Fishing.

Seen in: *Country Inns, Honeymoons.*

Contact: Kim Post Watson. Certificate may be used: December - January, Sunday - Thursday.

Chico

Music Express Inn
1091 El Monte Ave
Chico 95928
(916)345-8376 Fax:(916)893-8521

1977. Music lovers will delight in this inn's warmth and charm. Seven air-conditioned guest rooms, all with private bath and cable TV, provide country-style comfort to those visiting the college town of Chico. Guests will awake to the smell of home-made bread or rolls. Visitors are welcome to tickle the ivories of the inn's Steinway grand piano. The innkeeper, a music teacher, is adept at many instruments and plays mandolin in a local band. The inn's library also lures many guests, and those who explore the surrounding area will find plenty of opportunities for antiquing and fishing.

Innkeeper(s): Irene Cobeen.

Rates:$72-75. MC VISA AX DS. Full Bkfst. 8 rooms. Conference Rm.

Contact: Irene Cobeen. Certificate may be used: Sunday through Thursday.

Dana Point

Blue Lantern Inn
34343 Street of the Blue Lantern
Dana Point 92629
(714)661-1304 (800)234-1425

1990. The inn is situated high on a blufftop overlooking a stunning coastline and the blue waters of Dana Point harbor with its pleasure craft, fishing boats and the tall ship Pilgrim. Each guest room features both a fireplace and a spa and there are private sundecks and mini-stereos. Afternoon tea, evening turn-down service and bicycles are just a few of the amenities available.

Innkeeper(s): Tom Taylor.

Rates:$135-350. MC VISA AX. Full Bkfst. Picnic lunches. Teas. 29 rooms. Conference Rm. Golf. Tennis. Swimming. Fishing.

Seen in: *LA Magazine, Oregonian, Orange County Register.*

Contact: Kim Post Watson. Certificate may be used: Sunday - Thursday.

Davis

University Inn B&B
340 "A" St
Davis 95616
(916)756-8648 (800)756-8648

1925. This Spanish-style inn features southwestern and country flavorings in its four guest rooms. The inn's name reflects its proximity to the UC Davis campus, and many guests incorporate college activities into their stays. The air-conditioned rooms feature cable TV, VCRs, phones, ceiling fans, desks and fireplaces. The inn offers many additional services, including child care, guest use of bicycles and limited pet boarding. Be sure to inquire about the inn's picnic lunches and afternoon teas. Sacramento is only 15 miles away.

Innkeeper(s): Ross Yancher/David Hiett

Rates:$55-65. MC VISA AX DC DS CB. ContPlus Bkfst. Picnic lunches. Teas. 4 rooms.

Contact: Ross Yancher. Certificate may be used: Anytime with the exception of special university events.

Dunsmuir

Dunsmuir Inn
5423 Dunsmuir Ave
Dunsmuir 96025
(916)235-4543

1925. Set in the Sacramento River Valley, this country-style inn may serve as a base for an assortment of outdoor activities. At the end of the day, guests can stop in at the inn's own Rosie's Ice Cream Parlor for an old-fashioned soda or delicious ice cream cone. Fishing in the crystal clear waters of the Upper Sacramento River is within walking distance. The innkeepers can suggest hiking trails and driving tours to mountain lakes, waterfalls, the Castle Crags State Park and Mt. Shasta.

Innkeeper(s): Jerry & Julie Iskra.

Rates:$55-65. MC VISA AX DC DS CB. ContPlus Bkfst. Picnic lunches. Evening snacks. 4 rooms.

Contact: Julie Iskra. Certificate may be used: October - December, 1994; January - April; October - December, 1995.

Eureka

"An Elegant Victorian Mansion"
1406 'C' St
Eureka 95501
(707)444-3144 (800)386-1888

1888. One of Eureka's leading lumber barons built this picturesque home made from 1,000-year-old virgin redwood. The inn is a state and national historic landmark. Original wallpapers, wool carpets

and beautiful light fixtures create a wonderfully authentic Victorian ambiance. A tuxedoed butler and your hosts, decked in period attire, will greet you upon arrival. Croquet fields and Victorian gardens surround the inn. The Vieyras can arrange horse-drawn carriage rides or boat cruises. Old-fashioned ice cream sodas are served and, to top it all off, each morning guests partake in a multi-course gourmet breakfast feast.

Innkeeper(s): Doug & Lily Vieyra.

Rates:$90-135. MC VISA. Full Bkfst. MAP available. Gourmet Brkfst. Picnic lunches. Teas. 4 rooms. 2 with shared baths. Conference Rm. Spa. Sauna. Exercise room.

Seen in: *Sunset, Westcoast Victorians, Washington Post, New York Times, Los Angeles Times, Portland Oregonian.*

Contact: Douglas Vieyra. Certificate may be used: Nov. 31 through March 1, except holidays and local special events. Valid only during midweek. Offer not good on weekends (Friday, Saturday, Sunday). Subject to availability.

"A magnificent masterpiece, both in architecture and service."

A Weaver's Inn
1440 B St
Eureka 95501
(707)443-8119

1883. This Queen Anne Colonial Revival is just as its name suggests—the home of a weaver. Innkeeper Dorothy Swendeman has her own fiber studio on the premises, which guests are invited to use. She will provide basic weaving and spinning instructions at special rates to her guests. Weavers and non-weavers alike will appreciate the romantic touches to each room of the inn. The Pamela Suite has a sitting room and a fireplace, while the Marcia Room includes a window seat. The full breakfast often features home-grown treats from the garden. Honeymooners can enjoy breakfast in bed.

Innkeeper(s): Bob & Dorothy Swendeman.

Rates:$60-85. MC VISA AX DS. Full Bkfst. Teas. 4 rooms. 2 with shared baths. Golf. Tennis.

Contact: Robert Swendeman. Certificate may be used: Sept. 15 to May 15.

"It's a charming inn, warm ambiance and very gracious hosts!"

Carter House
1033 Third St
Eureka 95501
(707)445-1390 (800)404-1390
Fax:(707)444-8062

1982. The Carters found a pattern book in an antique shop and built this inn according to the architectural plans for an 1890 San Francisco Victorian. (The architect, Joseph Newsom, also designed the Carson House across the street.) Three open parlors with bay windows and marble fireplaces provide an elegant backdrop for relaxing. Guests are free to visit the kitchen in quest of coffee and views of the bay. The inn is famous for its three-course breakfast, including an Apple Almond Tart featured in *Gourmet* magazine.

Innkeeper(s): Mark & Christi Carter.

Rates:$89-225. MC VISA AX DC DS CB. Full Bkfst. Gourmet Brkfst, Dinner. Teas. Evening snacks. 40 rooms. Fireplaces. Beds:KQ. Conference Rm. TV, Phone, Refrig. in room. Bicycling. Skiing. Handicap access. Spa. Sauna. Swimming. Fishing.

Seen in: *Sunset Magazine, U.S. News & World Report.*

Contact: Mark Carter. Certificate may be used: Off season, January - April.

"We've traveled extensively throughout the U.S. and stayed in the finest hotels. You've got them all beat!!"

The Daly Inn
1125 H St
Eureka 95501
(707)445-3638 (800)321-9656
Fax:(707)444-3636

1905. This 6,000-square-foot Colonial Revival mansion is located in the historic section of Eureka. Enjoy the Belgian antique bedstead, fireplace and view of

fish pond and garden from Annie Murphy's Room, or try the former nursery, Miss Martha's Room, with bleached pine antiques from Holland. Breakfast is served fireside in the inn's formal dining room or in the breakfast parlor or garden patio.

Innkeeper(s): Sue & Gene Clinesmith.

Rates:$65-130. MC VISA AX DS. Gourmet Brkfst. Evening snacks. 5 rooms. 2 with shared baths. Conference Rm. Golf.

Contact: Sue Clinesmith. Certificate may be used: Oct. 15 through April 15, holidays and special event weekends excluded.

"A genuine delight."

Hotel Carter
301 L St
Eureka 95501
(707)444-8062 (800)404-1390
Fax:(707)444-8062

1986. A new structure that manages to radiate old-time elegance and charm, this sophisticated inn offers a taste of the Victorian era as it also incorporates the modern. Contemporary artwork shares space with marble fireplaces and high ceilings in the inn's lobby. Its 23 guest rooms feature a variety of luxurious touches, including fireplaces, skylights, whirlpool tubs, VCRs, CD stereo systems and mini-refrigerators. Gourmet breakfasts add another element to the Hotel Carter's already impressive display of hospitality. Visitors to redwood country will enjoy exploring Eureka, home to more than 1,500 Victorian homes.

Innkeeper(s): Mark & Christi Carter.

Rates:$89-225. MC VISA AX DC DS CB. Full Bkfst. Gourmet Brkfst, Dinner. Teas. Evening snacks. 40 rooms. Conference Rm.

Contact: Mark Carter. Certificate may be used: Off season.

Ferndale

Gingerbread Mansion
400 Berding St
Ferndale 95536
(707)786-4000 (800)952-4136

1899. Built for Dr. H. J. Ring, the Gingerbread Mansion is now the most photographed of Northern California's inns. Near Eureka, it is in the fairy-tale Victorian village of Ferndale (a California Historical Landmark). Outside the inn are formal English gardens. Gingerbread Mansion is a unique combination of Queen Anne and Eastlake styles with elaborate gingerbread trim. Inside are spacious and elegant rooms including two suites with "his" and "her" bathtubs. There are four parlors. Bicycles are available for riding through town and the surrounding countryside.

Innkeeper(s): Ken Torbert.

Rates:$90-185. MC VISA AX. Full Bkfst. Teas. 9 rooms. Golf. Bicycling. Fishing.

Seen in: *Stockton Record, Country Inns, San Francisco Focus, Los Angeles Times.*

Contact: Kenneth Torbert. Certificate may be used: Nov. 1-April 30, 1994-1995, Sunday-Thursday, except during holiday periods or special event periods. (Offer valid through Dec. 1995.)

"Absolutely the most charming, friendly and delightful place we have ever stayed at."

Fort Bragg

Grey Whale Inn

615 N Main St
Fort Bragg 95437
(707)964-0640 (800)382-7244
Fax:(707)964-4408

1915. Built with old-growth redwood, this stately four-story inn has been skillfully renovated. Fourteen airy and spacious guest rooms include some with ocean views and cozy spaces from which to spot whales during the annual December-to-March migration. Other rooms feature amenities such as a fireplace, whirlpool tub for two, or private deck. Ask the innkeeper to help you arrange horseback riding on the beach, three blocks away. The inn is near the heart of downtown Fort Bragg.

Innkeeper(s): Colette & John Bailey.

Rates:$60-180. MC VISA AX DS. Full Bkfst. 14 rooms. Conference Rm. Golf. Tennis. Spa. Swimming. Horseback riding. Fishing.

Seen in: *Inn Times, San Francisco Examiner, Travel.*

Contact: Colette Bailey. Certificate may be used: Nov. 1 through Dec. 15, 1994; Jan. 2 to April 1, 1995; Nov. 1 - December, 1995. Friday, Saturday, holidays and special event periods always excluded.

"We are going to return each year until we have tried

each room. Sunrise room is excellent in the morning or evening."*

Pudding Creek Inn

700 N Main St
Fort Bragg 95437
(707)964-9529 (800)227-9529
Fax:(707)961-0282

1884. Originally constructed by a Russian count, the inn comprises two picturesque Victorian homes connected by an enclosed garden. There are

mounds of begonias, fuchsias and ferns. The Count's Room, in royal cranberry velvets, features inlaid redwood paneling, a stone fireplace and a brass bed. There is an enclosed hot tub with its own pond. A full breakfast is provided and you can reserve ahead for a picnic lunch. (Guests on a long coastal tour will appreciate the laundry service made available.)

Innkeeper(s): Garry & Carole Anloff & Jacque Woltman.

Rates:$55-125. MC VISA AX DS. Full Bkfst. Picnic lunches. Teas. Evening snacks. 10 rooms. Golf. Tennis. Bicycling. Swimming. Horseback riding. Fishing.

Seen in: *Evening Outlook.*

Contact: Jacque Woltman. Certificate may be used: Sunday-Thursday, holidays excluded, October-May.

"Best stop on our trip!"

The Rendevous Inn & Restaurant
647 N Main St
Fort Bragg 95437
(707)964-8142 (800)491-8142

1904. This turn-of-the-century inn offers visitors the convenience of lodging and dining. Six large guest rooms, all with private bath and queen beds, are designed with relaxation in mind, meaning television and phones are found elsewhere in the inn. Guests are encouraged to join others in the comfortable parlor for a glass or wine or beer, to watch TV, relax or socialize. Within walking distance are the Guest House Museum, Skunk Train and Glass and Pudding Creek beaches.

Innkeeper(s): Lionel & Rose Jacobs.

Rates:$55-95. MC VISA DS. Full Bkfst. EP. Gourmet Dinner. 6 rooms.

Contact: Lionel Jacobs. Certificate may be used: Sunday through Thursday year-round exception being holiday weekends.

Geyserville

Campbell Ranch Inn
1475 Canyon Rd
Geyserville 95441
(707)857-3476 (800)959-3878

1968. This ranch-style house on a hillside affords views of the picturesque local vineyards. There are copious decks, a tennis court, hot tub and swimming pool. Mary Jane, author of *"The Campbell Ranch Inn Cookbook,"* serves homemade pie and coffee each evening.

Innkeeper(s): Mary Jane & Jerry Campbell.

Rates:$100-165. MC VISA. Full Bkfst. Evening snacks. 5 rooms. Spa. Swimming.

Seen in: *Sunset, Country, The Healdsburg Tribune, San Francisco Examiner.*

Contact: George Campbell. Certificate may be used: November through March, Sunday through Thursday.

"The best of all possible worlds."

The Hope-Bosworth & Hope-Merrill House
PO Box 42, 21253 Geyserville Ave
Geyserville 95441
(707)857-3356 (800)825-4233
Fax:(707)857-4673

1875. The Hope-Merrill House is a classic example of the Eastlake Stick style that was so popular during Victorian times. Built entirely from redwood, the house features original wainscotting and silk-screened wallcoverings. A swimming pool, vineyard and gazebo are favorite spots for guests to relax.

The Hope-Bosworth House, on the same street, was built in the Queen Anne style by an early Geyserville pioneer who lived in the home until the 1960s. The front picket fence is covered with roses. Period details include oak woodwork, sliding doors, polished fir floors, and antique light fixtures. Guests will enjoy innkeeper Rosalie Hope's prize-winning breads with their full breakfasts.

Innkeeper(s): Bob & Rosalie Hope.

Rates:$95-140. MC VISA AX. Full Bkfst. Picnic lunches. 12 rooms. Conference Rm. Bicycling.

Seen in: *San Diego Union, Country Homes Magazine, Sunset Magazine, Sacramento Union.*

Contact: Kim Taylor. Certificate may be used: All year, Sunday through Thursday.

"Innkeepers extraordinaire." Leisure and Outdoor Guide.

Gilroy

Country Rose Inn - A Bed & Breakfast
PO Box 1804
Gilroy 95021-1804
(408)842-6646

1940. Amidst five wooded acres, a half-hour's drive south of San Jose, sits the aptly named Country Rose Inn. A roomy Dutch Colonial manor, this inn was once a farmhouse on the Lucky Hereford Ranch. Every room features a rose theme, including wallpaper and quilted bedspreads. Each window offers a relaxing view of horses grazing, fertile fields, or the tranquil grounds, which boast magnificent 100-year-old oak trees.

Innkeeper(s): Rose Hernandez.

Rates:$79-169. MC VISA. Full Bkfst. Gourmet Brkfst. Picnic lunches. Teas. 6 rooms. Conference Rm. Bicycling.

Seen in: *San Jose Mercury News, Houston Chronicle, San Jose Magazine, Contra Costa Times, Peninsula Times Tribune, Dispatch, Country News.*

Contact: Rose Hernandez. Certificate may be used: All times except Garlic Festival.

"The quiet, serene country setting made our anniversary very special. Rose is a delightful, gracious hostess and cook."

Grass Valley

Annie Horan's

415 W Main St
Grass Valley 95945
(916)272-2418 (800)273-7390

1874. Mine owner James Horan built this splendid Victorian house for his wife Mary. Today the exterior, parlor and guest quarters are as they were at the height of Gold Country opulence. Follow in the footsteps of Mark Twain, Bret Harte and Presidents Grant, Harrison and Cleveland, who visited the shops, pubs, restaurants and other spots located just beyond the inn.

Innkeeper(s): Tom & Pat Kiddy.

Rates:$79-97. Full Bkfst. Teas. 4 rooms. Conference Rm.

Contact: Patsy Kiddy. Certificate may be used: January - April 1 all seven nights. April 2 - Dec. 31, Sunday through Thursday, excluding holidays.

Golden Ore House B&B

448 S Auburn
Grass Valley 95945
(916)272-6872

1904. This striking country Victorian inn in the Sierra foothills has six guest rooms, all decorated with classy antiques gathered from local estates. The Parlour Room features elegant antique furniture, queen bed, shower and clawfoot tub. The Cedar Room's charms include a four-poster queen bed, and the Chestnut Room offers a romantic skylight and queen bed. Those two rooms share a bath and both feature pedestal sinks in the rooms.

Innkeeper(s): Allen & Joy Albonico.

Rates:$68-100. MC VISA. Full Bkfst. Gourmet Brkfst. Teas. 6 rooms. 3 with shared baths. Beds:QD. Golf. Tennis. Skiing. Swimming. Horseback riding. Fishing.

Contact: Joy Albonico. Certificate may be used: Sunday through Thursday only. No holidays, not good for November or December.

Groveland

The Groveland Hotel

18767 Main St, PO Box 481
Groveland 95321
(209)962-4000 (800)273-3314
Fax:(209)962-6674

1849. Located 25 miles from Yosemite National Park, the newly restored hotel features both an adobe building with 18-inch-thick walls constructed during the Gold Rush and a 1914 building erected to house workers for the Hetch Hetchy Dam. Both

feature two-story balconies. There is a Victorian parlor, a gourmet restaurant and a Western saloon. Guest rooms feature European antiques and down

comforters. The feeling is one of casual elegance.

Innkeeper(s): Peggy & Grover Mosley.

Rates:$85-175. MC VISA AX DC DS CB. ContPlus Bkfst. Gourmet Lunch, Dinner. Picnic lunches. Teas. Evening snacks. 17 rooms. Fireplaces. Beds:QT. Conference Rm. Phone, AC in room. Golf. Tennis. Skiing. Handicap access. Swimming. Horseback riding. Stables. Fishing.

Seen in: *Sonora Union Democrat, Peninsula Magazine.*

Contact: Peggy Mosley. Certificate may be used: Sunday - Thursday. Oct. 15-April 15, excluding holidays.

"Hospitality is outstanding."

Guerneville

Ridenhour Ranch

12850 River Rd
Guerneville 95446
(707)887-1033 Fax:(707)869-2967

1906. Located on a hill overlooking the Russian River, this ranch house is shaded by redwoods, oaks and laurels. There are seven guest rooms and a cottage overlooking the rose garden. The innkeepers are former restauranteurs from Southern California and provide a changing dinner menu for their guests. The Korbel Champagne cellars are nearby and it's a five-minute walk to the river.

Innkeeper(s): Fritz & Diane Rechberger.

Rates:$95-130. MC VISA AX. Full Bkfst. Gourmet Brkfst. Picnic lunches. 8 rooms. Fireplaces. Beds:Q. Conference Rm. TV in room. Golf. Bicycling. Handicap access. Spa. Horseback riding. Fishing.

Seen in: *Los Angeles Times, Orange County Register, Los Altos Town Crier, California Visitors Review.*

Contact: Diane Rechberger. Certificate may be used: Sunday through Thursday excluding holidays and weekends.

"Your hospitality and food will ensure our return!"

Santa Nella House

12130 Hwy 116
Guerneville 95466
(707)869-9488

1870. This Victorian farmhouse was the residence of the builder of the Santa Nella Winery. It was also the site of one of the first sawmills in the redwood lumber area and served as a stagecoach stop. An enchanting trail winds down to the Russian

River, and there is a sun deck and old pool table on the property. High ceilings, red carpets and antiques set the stage for a relaxing stay.

Innkeeper(s): Alan & Joyce Ferrington.

Rates:$90-100. MC VISA AX. Full Bkfst. Gourmet Brkfst. Teas. 4 rooms. Fireplaces. Beds:QT. Conference Rm. Spa. Swimming. Fishing.

Contact: Alan Ferrington. Certificate may be used: Middle of week - non-holiday.

"It is rare to find a home as warm and gracious as its owners."

Guernewood Park

Fern Grove Inn
16650 River Rd
Guernewood Park 95446
(707)869-9083 (800)347-9083
Fax:(707)869-2948

1926. Clustered in a village-like atmosphere, craftsman cottages have romantic fireplaces, private entrances and are decorated with freshly cut flowers. Your day starts with freshly brewed coffee and a leisurely buffet breakfast featuring renowned homemade muffins and pastries served in the relaxed atmosphere of the Common Room. The morning newspapers, soft classical music, warming fire and good conversation will stimulate your spirits. Innkeepers will provide you with concierge service throughout your stay.

Innkeeper(s): Robert Chok & Dennis Ekstrom

Rates:$59-159. MC VISA AX DC DS CB. ContPlus Bkfst. EP. Picnic lunches. Teas. Evening snacks. 20 rooms.

Contact: Dennis Ekstrom. Certificate may be used: Sunday - Thursday excluding July, August, September.

Half Moon Bay

Old Thyme Inn
779 Main St
Half Moon Bay 94019
(415)726-1616

1899. Redwood, harvested from nearby forests and dragged by oxen, was used to construct this Queen Anne Victorian on historic Main Street. Decorated in a distinctly English style, the inn boasts fireplaces and four-poster and

canopy beds. The skylight in the Garden Suite, above a double whirlpool tub, treats bathers to a view of the night sky. Innkeeper George has cultivated 80 varieties of herbs in his garden, and serious herbalists are provided with a cutting kit to take samples back home.

Rates:$75-220. MC VISA. Full Bkfst. 8 rooms. Fireplaces. Beds:Q. Conference Rm. TV, Refrig. in room. Golf. Tennis. Spa. Sauna. Swimming. Horseback riding. Fishing.

Seen in: *California Weekends, Los Angeles Magazine, San Mateo Times.*

Contact: George S. Dempsey. Certificate may be used: Monday - Thursday nights, Oct. 1 thru May 31.

"Furnishings, rooms and garden were absolutely wonderful."

Healdsburg

Camellia Inn
211 North St
Healdsburg 95448
(707)433-8182 (800)727-8182
Fax:(707)433-8130

1869. An elegant Italianate Victorian townhouse, the Camellia Inn has twin marble parlor fireplaces and an ornate mahogany dining room fireplace. Antiques fill the guest rooms, complementing Palladian windows and classic interior moldings. The award-winning grounds feature 30 varieties of camellias and are accentuated with a pool.

Innkeeper(s): Ray & Del Lewand.

Rates:$70-135. MC VISA AX. Full Bkfst. 9 rooms. Golf. Tennis. Swimming. Horseback riding. Fishing.

Seen in: *Sunset, Travel & Leisure, New York Times, San Fernando Valley Daily News, San Diego Union, Sacramento Bee, Healdsburg Tribune.*

Contact: Lucy Lewand. Certificate may be used: Sunday through Thursday, November through April, no weekends or holiday periods.

"A bit of paradise for city folks."

Madrona Manor, A Country Inn
1001 Westside Rd
Healdsburg 95448
(707)433-4231 (800)258-4003
Fax:(707)433-0703

1991. The inn is composed of four historic structures in a National Historic District. Surrounded by eight acres of manicured lawns and terraced flower and vegetable gardens, the stately mansion was built for John Paxton, a San Francisco businessman. Embellished with turrets, bay windows, porches, and a mansard roof, it provides a breathtaking view of surrounding vineyards. Elegant antique furnishings and a noteworthy restaurant add to the genuine country inn atmosphere. The Gothic-style Carriage House offers more casual lodging.

Innkeeper(s): John & Carol Muir.

Rates:$135-225. MC VISA AX DC DS. Full Bkfst. Gourmet Brkfst, Dinner. Picnic lunches. 21 rooms. Conference Rm. Golf. Tennis. Swimming. Horseback riding.

Seen in: *Gourmet, Woman's Day Home Decorating Ideas, Travel Leisure, US News, Diversions, Money, Goodhousekeeping, Sonoma Business.*

Contact: Carol Muir. Certificate may be used: Sunday through Thursday all year. Subject to availability. No holidays.

"Our fourth visit and better every time."

Raford House
10630 Wohler Rd
Healdsburg 95448
(707)887-9573 Fax:(707)887-9597

1880. Situated on more than four acres of rose gardens and fruit trees, this classic Victorian country estate was originally built as a summer home and ranch house in the 1880s. Just 70 miles north of San Francisco, The Raford House is nestled in the heart of the Sonoma County wine country, minutes away from award-winning wineries and many fine restaurants. Located close to the Russian River, between Healdsburg and the beautiful Northern California coast, the area has scenic country roads and a rugged coastline.

Innkeeper(s): Carole & Jack Vore.

Rates:$85-130. MC VISA. Full Bkfst. Evening snacks. 7 rooms. 2 with shared baths.

Contact: Jack Vore. Certificate may be used: Sunday through Thursday, November through March.

Idyllwild

Wilkum Inn B&B
26770 Hwy 243 at Toll Gate Rd
Idyllwild 92549
(909)659-4087

1938. The mountain village of Idyllwild is home to this charming inn, which offers European-style hospitality and a down-home atmosphere. Tall oaks and pines provide the perfect setting for a variety of birds and the ever-present squirrels. The inn offers four guest rooms, including the Eaves, a two-room suite with queen bed, open-beam ceiling and a lovely view of the surrounding pines. Another lodging option is a loft, which has its own kitchen and entrance and does not include breakfast or in-house amenities.

Innkeeper(s): Annamae Chambers & Barbara Jones.

Rates:$75-95. ContPlus Bkfst. Gourmet Brkfst. Evening snacks. 5 rooms. 2 with shared baths.

Seen in: *Los Angeles Times, Westways.*

Contact: Annamae Chambers/Barbara Jones Certificate may be used: Sunday/Monday or Thursday/Friday.

"Your inn really defines the concept of country coziness and hospitality."

Independence

Winnedumah Inn
PO Box 147, 211 N Edwards
Independence 93526
(619)878-2040 Fax:(619)878-2250

1927. This old hotel was built in a Spanish Colonial style with arches, stucco and a front portico. Its location is at the foot of the Eastern Sierra in Owens Valley. Independence offers a trout-filled steam, majestic scenery and nearby hiking and fishing. The inn's restaurant will provide box lunches for these excursions.

Innkeeper(s): Alan Bergman & Marvey Chapman.

Rates:$42-55. MC VISA AX. ContPlus Bkfst. MAP available. Picnic lunches. Teas. 20 rooms. 16 with shared baths. Beds:QT. AC in room. Skiing. Handicap access. Swimming. Fishing.

Contact: Marvey Chapman. Certificate may be used: Anytime Sept. 10 - May 20; weekdays May 21 - Sept. 9.

Inverness

Hotel Inverness
25 Park Ave, Box 780
Inverness 94937
(415)669-7393

1906. Guests rave about the outdoor breakfasts served in the garden or on the deck. Situated on the edge of a coastal village, Hotel Inverness overlooks Tomales Bay and is a short distance from Point Reyes National Seashore. The garden lawn accommodates picnics, lounging or croquet. Boasting one of the best bird-watching areas in the west, the inn has a park-like setting where one can relax and admire the surrounding wooded area. This great natural area reminds many of Yosemite National Park.

Innkeeper(s): Susie & Tom Simms.

Rates:$100-160. MC VISA. ContPlus Bkfst. 5 rooms.

Contact: Susie & Tom Simms. Certificate may be used: Non-holidays, Sunday through Thursday from Nov. 1, 1994 to April 30, 1995.

Ione

The Heirloom
214 Shakeley Ln, PO Box 322
Ione 95640
(209)274-4468

1863. A two-story Colonial with columns, balconies, and a private English garden, the antebellum Heirloom is true to its name. It has many family heirlooms and a square grand piano once owned by Lola Montez. The building was dedicated by the Native Sons of the Golden West as a historic site.

Innkeeper(s): Melisande Hubbs & Patricia Cross.

Rates:$60-95. MC VISA AX. Full Bkfst. Gourmet Brkfst. Teas. 6 rooms. 2 with shared baths. Fireplaces. Beds:KQT. AC in room. Golf. Tennis. Bicycling. Skiing. Handicap access. Swimming. Horseback riding. Fishing.

Seen in: *San Francisco Chronicle, Country Living.*

Contact: Melisande A. Hubbs. Certificate may be used: Sunday - Thursday.

"Hospitality was amazing. Truly we've never had such a great time."

Isleton

Delta Daze Inn
PO Box 607, 20 Main St
Isleton 95641
(916)777-7777

1926. Once a bawdy house and gambling den, the Delta Daze Inn still retains its old Wild West flavor. A soda fountain area in the parlor relives the era when it was used as a front for more notorious prohibition activities. The Deltanental Room, used for breakfast and conferences, features an 18th-century, stained-glass archway that overlooks the Sacramento River Delta.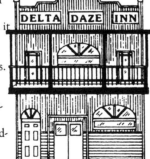

Innkeeper(s): Shirley & Frank Russell.

Rates:$70-125. MC VISA AX. Full Bkfst. Teas. 12 rooms. Conference Rm. Golf. Bicycling. Skiing. Swimming. Fishing.

Seen in: *Sunset Magazine.*

Contact: Shirley Russell. Certificate may be used: October through April, weekends only.

"Fun, great inn, squeaky clean, quiet."

Jackson

Court Street Inn
215 Court St
Jackson 95642
(209)223-0416 (800)200-0416

1872. This cheery yellow and white Victorian era house is accentuated with green shutters and a porch stretching across the entire front. Behind the house, a two-story brick structure that once served as a Wells Fargo office and a museum for Indian artifacts now houses guests. Hors d'oeuvres and wine are served in the dining room under a pressed, carved tin ceiling. Guests relax in front of a marble fireplace in the parlor topped by a gilded mirror. Guest rooms are decorated in antiques. Downtown is only two blocks away.

Innkeeper(s): Janet & Lee Hammond.

Rates:$75-130. MC VISA AX. Full Bkfst. Picnic lunches. Evening snacks. 6 rooms. Golf. Skiing. Spa. Fishing.

Seen in: *Amador Dispatch, Sunset.*

Contact: Janet Hammond. Certificate may be used: Sunday - Thursday, holidays excluded.

"Warm hospitality, great breakfasts, and genuine family atmosphere. All our friends will only hear wonderful thoughts about the Court Street Inn."

Gate House Inn
1330 Jackson Gate Rd
Jackson 95642
(209)223-3500 (800)841-1072
Fax:(209)223-3500

1903. This striking Victorian inn is listed on the National Register of Historic Places. Set on a hillside amid lovely gardens, the inn is within walking distance of a state historic park and several notable eateries. The inn's country setting, comfortable porches and swimming pool offer many opportunities for relaxation. Accommodations include three rooms, a suite and a romantic cottage with wood stove and whirlpool tub. All of the guest rooms feature queen beds and elegant furnishings. Nearby are several lakes, wineries and golf courses.

Innkeeper(s): Keith & Gail Sweet

Rates:$68-120. MC VISA DS. Full Bkfst. 6 rooms. Fireplaces. Beds:Q. AC in room. Bicycling. Skiing. Exercise room. Swimming. Fishing.

Contact: Keith Sweet. Certificate may be used: Anytime Monday through Thursday, weekends Jan. 5 - March 15 except for Valentine's and President's weekends.

Jamestown

Historic National Hotel B&B

77 Main St, PO Box 502
Jamestown 95327
(209)984-3446 (800)894-3446
Fax:(209)984-5620

1859. One of the 10 oldest continuously operating hotels in California, the inn maintains its original redwood bar where thousands of dollars in gold dust were spent. Electricity and plumbing were added for the first time when the inn was restored a few years ago. It is decorated with gold rush period antiques, brass beds and handmade quilts. The restaurant is considered to be one of the finest in the Mother Lode.

Innkeeper(s): Stephen & Pamela Willey.

Rates:$65-80. MC VISA AX DC DS CB. ContPlus Bkfst. EP. Gourmet Dinner. Picnic lunches. 11 rooms. 6 with shared baths. Beds:QT. Conference Rm. AC in room. Golf. Tennis. Skiing. Swimming. Horseback riding. Fishing.

Seen in: *Bon Appetit, California Magazine, Focus, San Francisco Magazine, Gourmet Magazine.*

Contact: Julie Adams. Certificate may be used: November - March.

"Excellent, wonderful place!"

Joshua Tree

Joshua Tree Inn

PO Box 340, 61259 29 Palms Hwy
Joshua Tree 92252
(619)366-1188 (800)366-1444

1953. The hacienda-style inn was once a '50s motel. It now offers Victorian-style rooms with king-size beds. Antiques and Old West memorabilia

add to the decor. The inn is one mile from the gateway to the 467,000-acre Joshua Tree National Monument.

Innkeeper(s): Evelyn & Dan Shirbroun.

Rates:$45-150. MC VISA AX DC. ContPlus Bkfst. AP available. Gourmet

Brkfst, Lunch, Dinner. Picnic lunches. Teas. Evening snacks. 10 rooms. Conference Rm. Swimming.

Seen in: *Los Angeles Times.*

Contact: Evelyn Shirbroun. Certificate may be used: Sunday through Friday.

"Quiet, clean and charming."

Julian

Julian Gold Rush Hotel

2032 Main St, PO Box 1856
Julian 92036
(619)765-0201 (800)734-5854

1897. The dream of a former slave and his wife lives today in this sole surviving hotel in Southern California's "Mother Lode of Gold Mining." This

Victorian charmer is listed in the National Register of Historic Places and is a designated State of California Point of Historic Interest (#SDI-09). Guests enjoy the feeling of a visit to Grandma's and a tradition of genteel hospitality.

Innkeeper(s): Steve & Gig Ballinger.

Rates:$64-145. MC VISA AX. Full Bkfst. Teas. 17 rooms. 12 with shared baths. Conference Rm. Tennis. Horseback riding. Fishing.

Seen in: *San Diego Union, PSA.*

Contact: Steve Ballinger. Certificate may be used: Valid Sunday-Thursday, excluding weekends and holidays. Rooms in historic part with shared baths.

"Any thoughts you have about the 20th century will leave you when you walk into the lobby of this grand hotel..." Westways Magazine.

Julian White House

3014 Blue Jay Dr, PO Box 824
Julian 92036
(619)765-1764 (800)948-4687

1978. Towering white pillars greet this inn's guests, who may feel they have traveled back in time to a Southern plantation. The attractive Colonial-style inn offers four luxurious guest rooms, including the Honeymoon Suite. The French Quarter Room features a New Orleans theme and Mardi Gras memorabilia, and the popular East Room boasts a goose down mattress and Laura Ashley linens on a queen-size Victorian-style brass bed. Guests often enjoy an evening at the Pine Hills Dinner Theatre, an easy walk from the inn.

Innkeeper(s): Mary & Alan Marvin.

Rates:$95-125. MC VISA. Full Bkfst. Gourmet Brkfst. Evening snacks. 4 rooms. Beds:QD. Skiing. Swimming. Horseback riding. Fishing.

Seen in: *San Diego Home/Garden, San Diego Union Tribune.*

Contact: Mary Sullivan-Marvin. Certificate may be used: Valid Monday-Thursday, not valid Easter week, Dec. 26-31, holidays excluded.

Random Oaks Ranch
3742 Pine Hills Rd, PO Box 454
Julian 92036
(619)765-1094 (800)262-3565

1987. Guests at this inn, which doubles as a thoroughbred horse ranch, choose from two elegant cottages. The English Squire Cottage features a marble fireplace, Queen Anne furniture and a half-canopy queen bed. The Victorian Garden Cottage offers a custom mantled fireplace, Queen Victorian cherry bed and sliding French doors. Both cottages sport private decks with spas, wet bars, microwave ovens and small refrigerators. Breakfast is served in the privacy of the cottages. The charming town of Julian is just two miles from the inn.

Rates:$120-145. MC VISA. Full Bkfst. Gourmet Brkfst. 4 rooms. Fireplaces. Beds:Q. Refrig. in room. Stables. Fishing.

Contact: Shari Foust-Helsel. Certificate may be used: Monday - Wednesday - holidays excluded through Dec. 1, 1995.

Rockin' A B&B
1531 Orchard Ln
Julian 92036
(619)765-2820

1981. This contemporary woodsided ranch inn found in the countryside outside Julian offers a relaxing getaway for city folk. The inn boasts a private bass fishing facility and guests also enjoy the farm animals found on the grounds. Three of the five guest rooms have private baths, and amenities include ceiling fans, a fireplace, spa and turndown service. The inn is a very popular anniversary and honeymoon destination. Visitors enjoy a full breakfast and evening snack and will find Julian a fun place to explore in their spare time.

Innkeeper(s): Gil & Dottie Archambeau

Rates:$86-102. MC VISA. Full Bkfst. AP available. Evening snacks. 5 rooms. 2 with shared baths. Fireplaces. Beds:KQ. Farm. Skiing. Spa. Fishing.

Contact: Gil Archambeau. Certificate may be used: Sunday through Thursday (excluding holidays).

Kernville

Kern River Inn B&B
119 Kern River Dr, PO Box 1725
Kernville 93238
(619)376-6750

1991. Located across from Riverside Park and the Kern River, this country-style inn boasts a wraparound porch featuring views and sounds of the river. Many of the guest rooms have stone fire-

places. The Whiskey Flats Room offers a whirlpool bath, full-river view and a red decor. Breakfast may include giant homebaked cinnamon rolls or sweetheart waffles. It's a short drive to the Sequoia National Forest.

Innkeeper(s): Jack & Carita Prestwich.

Rates:$69-89. MC VISA. Full Bkfst. Evening snacks. 6 rooms. Golf. Bicycling. Skiing. Fishing.

Seen in: *Bakersfield newspaper, Kern Valley Sun, Los Angeles Times, Valley Daily News.*

Contact: Jack Prestwich. Certificate may be used: Sunday through Thursday only. Nov. 1 through March 31, excluding holidays and special event days.

"Our fourth visit and we haven't been disappointed yet."

Laguna Beach

Carriage House
1322 Catalina St
Laguna Beach 92651
(714)494-8945

1925. A Laguna Beach historical landmark, this inn has a Cape Cod clapboard exterior. It housed an art gallery and a bakery before it was converted into apartments with large rooms and kitchens. Now as a cozy inn, each room has a private parlor. Outside, the courtyard fountain is shaded by a large carrotwood tree with hanging moss.

Innkeeper(s): Thom & Dee Taylor.

Rates:$95-150. ContPlus Bkfst. Evening snacks. 6 rooms. Golf. Tennis. Swimming.

Seen in: *Glamour Magazine, Los Angeles Times, Orange County Register.*

Contact: Dee Taylor. Certificate may be used: No weekends-holidays. Sunday through Thursday only. Not July or August.

"A true home away from home with all the extra touches added in."

Casa Laguna Inn
2510 S Coast Hwy
Laguna Beach 92651
(714)494-2996 (800)233-0449
Fax:(714)494-5009

1931. A romantic combination of California Mission and Spanish Revival architecture, the Mission House and cottages were built in the early '30s. The casitas were added in the '40s. The hillside setting of secluded gardens, winding paths and flower-splashed patios invites guests to linger and enjoy ocean views. Be sure to arrive in time to watch the sunset from the Bell Tower high above the inn. Ask for a quiet room at the back of the property.

Innkeeper(s): Ted & Louise Gould and Lee & Joan Kerr.

Rates:$105-205. MC VISA AX DC DS CB. ContPlus Bkfst. Teas. Evening snacks. 21 rooms. Conference Rm. Swimming.

Seen in: *Los Angeles Magazine, Houston Post.*

Contact: Louise Gould. Certificate may be used: After Labor Day to before July 1.

"What a fantastic place. Who needs a casa in Spain?"

Eiler's Inn
741 S Coast Hwy
Laguna Beach 92651
(714)494-3004 Fax:(714)497-2215

1935. This New Orleans-style inn surrounds a lush courtyard and fountain. The rooms are decorated with antiques and wallpapers. Wine and cheese is served during the evening in front of the fireplace. Named after Eiler Larsen, famous town greeter of Laguna, the inn is just a stone's throw from the beach on the ocean side of Pacific Coast Highway.

Innkeeper(s): Henk & Annette Wirtz.

Rates:$100-175. MC VISA AX. Gourmet Brkfst. 12 rooms. Beds:KQ. Golf. Tennis. Swimming. Fishing.

Seen in: *New York Times, Los Angeles Times, California Magazine, Home & Garden.*

Contact: Henk Wirtz. Certificate may be used: Sunday - Thursday.

"Who could find a paradise more relaxing than an old-fashioned bed and breakfast with Mozart and Vivaldi, a charming fountain, wonderful fresh-baked bread, ocean air, and Henk's conversational wit?"

Lake Arrowhead

Bracken Fern Manor
815 Arrowhead Villas Rd, PO 1006
Lake Arrowhead 92352
(909)337-8557 Fax:(909)337-3323

1929. Opened during the height of the '20s as Lake Arrowhead's first membership resort, this country inn provided refuge to Silver Screen heroines, the wealthy and the prominent. Old letters from the Gibson Girls found in the attic bespoke of elegant parties, dapper gentlemen, the Depression, Prohibition and homesick hearts. Each room is furnished with antiques collected from a lifetime of international travel. The Crestline Historical Society has its own museum, curator and a map of historical sites you can visit.

Innkeeper(s): Cheryl Weaver.

Rates:$80-175. MC VISA AX. Full Bkfst. Teas. Evening snacks. 10 rooms. 2 with shared baths. Beds:KQDT. Refrig. in room. Skiing. Spa. Sauna. Swimming. Fishing.

Contact: Cheryl Weaver. Certificate may be used: Sunday-Thursday, except holidays.

Lakeport

Forbestown Inn
825 Forbes St
Lakeport 95453
(707)263-7858 Fax:(707)263-7878

1863. Located in the downtown area, this early California farmhouse is two blocks from the lake. Wisteria drapes the front porch, overlooking the

inn's yard. The dining room, where Jack's gourmet breakfasts are served, has a wall of French windows looking out to the back garden with a tall redwood tree and handsome flagstone swimming pool. The innkeepers live in the carriage house next door. Clear Lake is fed by rain and underground sulfur and soda springs. The area has been acknowledged as having the cleanest air in California for the last three years.

Innkeeper(s): Jack & Nancy Dunne.

Rates:$85-110. MC VISA AX. Full Bkfst. Gourmet Brkfst. Teas. Evening snacks. 4 rooms. 3 with shared baths. Beds:KQ. TV in room. Bicycling. Spa. Swimming. Fishing.

Contact: Nancy Dunne. Certificate may be used: Sunday through Thursday excludes holidays. Oct. 1 to April 30.

Little River

Little River Inn
7750 Hwy 1
Little River 95456
(707)937-5942 Fax:(707)937-3944

1853. The 225 acres surrounding this handsomely gabled Victorian include a nine-hole golf course with panoramic ocean views, a driving range and putting green. Many of the guest rooms offer everyone's favorite ocean views and fireplaces. There is a garden dining room. Beachcombing is popular as is roaming, dining and shopping in Mendocino village, two miles to the north.

Innkeeper(s): Printah Platt.

Rates:$50-255. MC VISA AX. EP. 55 rooms. Fireplaces. Beds:KQT. Conference Rm. TV, Phone, Refrig. in room. Tennis. Fishing.

Contact: Susan McKinney. Certificate may be used: Monday-Thursday, November-May, excluding all holiday periods.

Lodi

Wine & Roses Country Inn
2505 W Turner Rd
Lodi 95242
(209)334-6988 Fax:(209)334-6570

1902. A 75-foot-long hedge of old-fashioned, pink Princess roses border the entrance to this cottage-style inn. The romantically landscaped six acres include white latticed arches, manicured lawns and wide borders of impatiens. Rooms are furnished with antiques, and the restaurant offers excellent dining in a garden setting. Although the inn enjoys popularity with honeymooners and business people, its location five miles off I-5 makes it an ideal midway stop between Los Angeles and San Francisco.

Innkeeper(s): Kris Cromwell, Del & Sherri Smith.

Rates:$99-145. MC VISA AX. Full Bkfst. Gourmet Brkfst, Dinner. Picnic lunches. Evening snacks. 10 rooms. Beds:QT. Conference Rm. Phone, AC in room. Golf. Tennis. Handicap access. Swimming. Horseback riding. Fishing.

Seen in: *Los Angeles Magazine, Business Tribune.*

Contact: Kris Cromwell. Certificate may be used: Sunday through Wednesday.

Los Angeles

Salisbury House
2273 W 20th St
Los Angeles 90018
(213)737-7817 (800)373-1778

1909. Located in Arlington Heights, the inn is part of the old West Adams area of Los Angeles. It features original stained and leaded-glass windows, wood-beamed ceilings, and an abundance of wood paneling. Used as a location for movies and commercials, Salisbury House is known for its gourmet breakfasts and old-fashioned graciousness.

Innkeeper(s): Sue & Jay German.

Rates:$75-100. MC VISA AX DS. Full Bkfst. Gourmet Brkfst. Teas. 5 rooms. 2 with shared baths. Beds:KQDT. Conference Rm. Phone, AC, Refrig. in room. Swimming. Fishing.

Seen in: *Sunset Magazine, Southern California Magazine, Los Angeles Magazine, Victorian Homes Magazine.*

Contact: Susan German. Certificate may be used: Anytime.

"The finest bed and breakfast we've seen. Not only is the house exquisite but the hospitality is unmatched!"

Mammoth Lakes

White Horse Inn
2180 Old Mammoth Rd, PO Box 2326
Mammoth Lakes 93546
(619)924-3656 (800)982-5657

1963. The innkeeper invites you to share your experiences of the day with other guests who socialize over cheese and wine in the knotty pine billiard room. Separate from the main house, the billiard room is complete with stone fireplace, bar and pool table. The honeymoon suite has a wood burning stove in an open sitting area and a canopy bed. The Emperor's room features an antique Chinese bed, an heirloom that is presented to the first-born son of each generation on his wedding day in anticipation of the birth of many more sons.

Innkeeper(s): Lynn Criss.

Rates:$65-150. MC VISA AX. Full Bkfst. Evening snacks. 5 rooms. 2 with shared baths. Fireplaces. Beds:KQT. TV in room. Skiing. Fishing.

Contact: Lynn Criss. Certificate may be used: Sunday through Thursday nights for a two-day minimum stay.

Mammoth/Crowley Lake

Rainbow Tarns

PO Box 1097, Rt 1

Mammoth/Crowley Lake 93546

(619)935-4556

1920. Just south of Mammoth Lakes, at an altitude of 7,000 feet, you'll find this secluded retreat amid three acres of hot springs, ponds, open meadows

and the High Sierra Mountains. Country-style here includes luxury touches, such as a double Jacuzzi tub, queen-size bed, down pillows and a skylight for star-gazing. In the '40s, ponds on the property served as a "U-Catch-Em;" folks rented fishing poles and paid 10 cents an inch for the fish they caught. Nearby Crowley Lake is still one of the best trout-fishing areas in California. Corrals are provided should you bring your horses for unlimited riding. Romantic country weddings are popular here.

Innkeeper(s): Lois Miles.

Rates:$95-125. Full Bkfst. 3 rooms. Golf. Bicycling. Skiing. Spa. Horseback riding. Fishing.

Seen in: *Mammoth-Sierra Magazine, Mammoth Winter, Eastern Sierra Fishing Guide, Mammoth-June Ski Preview.*

Contact: Lois Miles. Certificate may be used: Weeknights only.

"I love it! I'd rather stay here than go on to Tahoe!"

Mendocino

John Dougherty House

571 Ukiah St, PO Box 817

Mendocino 95460

(707)937-5266

1867. Early American furnishings and country-style stenciling provide the decor for this newly opened inn. Four rooms have outstanding water views, including the Captain's Room. The water tower room has an 18-foot ceiling and wood-burning stove.

Innkeeper(s): Dave & Marion Wells.

Rates:$95-175. MC VISA. Gourmet Brkfst. 8 rooms. Fireplaces. Beds:Q. TV, Refrig. in room. Golf. Tennis. Swimming. Fishing.

Seen in: *Mendocino Beacon.*

Contact: David Wells. Certificate may be used: Monday to Thursday, November to February. Holiday weeks excluded.

"The inn is beautiful and very comfortable."

Whitegate Inn

PO Box 150, 499 Howard St

Mendocino 95460

(707)937-4892 (800)531-7287

Fax:(707)937-1131

1883. When it was first built, the local newspaper called Whitegate Inn "one of the most elegant and

best appointed residences in town." It is resplendent with bay windows, a steep gabled roof, redwood siding and fishscale shingles. The house's original wallpaper and candelabras adorn the double parlors. There, an antique 1827 piano, at one time part of Alexander Graham Bell's collection, and inlaid pocket doors take you back to a simpler time. French and Victorian antique furnishings and a collection of early American cut glass add a crowning touch to the inn's elegant hospitality.

Innkeeper(s): Carol & George Bechtloff.

Rates:$79-175. MC VISA. EP. Gourmet Brkfst. 7 rooms. Fireplaces. Beds:KQT. Conference Rm. TV, Refrig. in room. Farm. Swimming.

Fishing.

Seen in: *Innsider, Country Inns.*

Contact: Carol Bechtloff. Certificate may be used: Sunday through Thursday nights, January-April, no holidays, no weekends.

"Made our honeymoon a dream come true."

Montara

The Goose & Turrets B&B
835 George St, PO Box 937
Montara 94037-0937
(415)728-5451 Fax:(415)728-0141

1908. This Northern Italian villa-style house has served as an art gallery, veteran's country club,

nursing home, church and nudist colony. It is now an antique-filled bed and breakfast. The Hummingbird Room includes a wood-burning stove and sitting area. All rooms have English towel warmers, goose-down comforters and desks. Southwest corn-pepper pancakes with salsa and sour cream are often served at breakfast along with Emily's entertaining stories about the old house. A water fountain, rose garden and herb garden are surrounded by a 20-foot-tall cypress hedge. The inn's white China geese are favorites of guests.
Innkeeper(s): Raymond & Emily Hoche-Mong.

Rates:$85-110. MC VISA AX DS. Full Bkfst. Teas. 5 rooms. Beds:KQDT. Golf. Swimming. Horseback riding. Fishing.

Seen in: *San Jose Mercury News, Half Moon Bay Review, Peninsula Times Tribune, San Mateo Times, Los Angeles Times, Tri-Valley Herald.*

Contact: Emily Hoche-Mong. Certificate may be used: Monday - Thursday, all year (holidays excluded).

"Lots of special touches. Great Southern hospitality — we'll be back."

Monte Rio

Highland Dell Inn
21050 River Blvd, PO Box 370
Monte Rio 95462-0370
(707)865-1759 (800)767-1759

1906. This chalet-style inn boasts Russian River views from many of the guest rooms. Recently renovated, its interiors are painted cheerfully to provide an airy background for antiques, Oriental rugs, and stained glass. For something unusual, you may wish to book the Bohemian Suite on the third floor to enjoy a red sunken tub, king bed and two wood stoves. Dinner is available on selected nights.
Innkeeper(s): Glenn Dixon & Anthony Patchett.

Rates:$60-225. MC VISA AX DS. Full Bkfst. Gourmet Brkfst, Dinner. 10 rooms. 2 with shared baths. Fireplaces. Beds:KQ. Conference Rm. TV in room. Golf. Tennis. Bicycling. Exercise room. Swimming. Horseback riding. Fishing.

Seen in: *Sunset Magazine, Press Democrat.*

Contact: Glenn Dixon. Certificate may be used: Anytime, subject to availability. Holidays excluded.

Monterey

The Jabberwock
598 Laine St
Monterey 93940
(408)372-4777

1911. Set in a half-acre of gardens, this Victorian inn provides a fabulous view of Monterey Bay and its famous barking seals. When you're ready to settle in for the evening, you'll find huge Victorian beds complete with lace-edged sheets and goose-down comforters. Early evening hors d'oeuvres and aperitifs are served in an enclosed veranda. After dinner, guests are tucked into bed with cookies and milk.
Innkeeper(s): Jim & Barbara Allen.

Rates:$100-180. MC VISA. Full Bkfst. Gourmet Brkfst. Evening snacks. 7 rooms. 4 with shared baths. Beds:KQ. Conference Rm. Golf. Tennis. Swimming. Horseback riding. Fishing.

Seen in: *Sunset Magazine, Travel & Leisure, Sacramento Bee, San Francisco Examiner, Los Angeles Times.*

Contact: Barbara Allen. Certificate may be used: Sunday - Thursday, November through April, except holiday periods.

"Not only were the accommodations delightful but the people were equally so."

Mount Shasta

Mount Shasta Ranch
1008 W.A. Barr Rd
Mount Shasta 96067
(916)926-3870 Fax:(916)926-6882

1923. This large two-story ranch house offers a full view of Mt. Shasta from its 60-foot-long redwood porch. Spaciousness abounds from the 1,500-square-foot living room with a massive rock fireplace to the large suites with private bathrooms that include large tubs and roomy showers. A full country breakfast may offer cream cheese-stuffed French toast or fresh, wild blackberry crepes. Just minutes away, Lake Siskiyou boasts superb fishing, sailing and swimming.

Innkeeper(s): Bill & Mary Larsen.

Rates:$45-95. MC VISA AX. Full Bkfst. Teas. 9 rooms. 5 with shared baths. Beds:QT. TV, AC in room. Skiing. Spa. Swimming. Fishing.

Contact: William Larsen. Certificate may be used: Anytime upon availability. Some restrictions apply for all holidays and summer weekends.

Murphys

Dunbar House, 1880
271 Jones St, PO Box 1375
Murphys 95247
(209)728-2897 (800)225-3764
Fax:(209)728-1451

1880. A picket fence frames this Italianate home, built by Willis Dunbar for his bride. Later, distinguished sons who served in the state assembly and ran the Dunbar Lumber Company lived here. On the porch, rocking chairs overlook century-old gardens. Inside are antiques, lace, quilts and clawfoot tubs. Breakfast is delivered to your room in a picnic basket, or you may join others by the fireplace in the dining room or in the garden.

Innkeeper(s): Bob & Barbara Costa.

Rates:$105-145. MC VISA AX. Full Bkfst. Evening snacks. 4 rooms. Fireplaces. Beds:Q. TV, Phone, AC, Refrig. in room. Golf. Tennis. Skiing. Spa. Swimming. Horseback riding. Fishing.

Seen in: *Los Angeles Times, Gourmet Magazine, Victorian Homes.*

Contact: Barbara Costa. Certificate may be used: Sunday - Thursday, excluding holidays.

"Your beautiful gardens and gracious hospitality combine for a super bed and breakfast."

Napa

The Blue Violet Mansion
443 Brown St
Napa 94559
(707)253-2583 Fax:(707)257-8205

1886. English lampposts, a Victorian gazebo, and a rose garden welcome guests to this blue and white Queen Anne Victorian. Listed in the National

Register, the house was originally built for a tannery executive. There are three-story bays, and from the balconies guests often view hot air balloons in the early morning. Three rooms feature two-person spas, and five have fireplaces. A full breakfast is served in the dining room. The innkeepers offer room service by request. Nearby is the wine train and restaurants.

Innkeeper(s): Bob & Kathy Morris.

Rates:$115-195. MC VISA AX. Full Bkfst. Gourmet Dinner. Picnic lunches. Evening snacks. 7 rooms. Fireplaces. Beds:KQ. Conference Rm. Bicycling. Swimming. Fishing.

Seen in: *American Painted Ladies Book.*

Contact: Kathleen Morris. Certificate may be used: Sunday through Thursday, holidays and Napa special events excluded.

The Hennessey House B&B
1727 Main St
Napa 94559
(707)226-3774 Fax:(707)226-2975

1889. This gracious Queen Anne Eastlake Victorian was once home to Dr. Edwin Hennessey, a Napa County physician. Pristinely renovated, the inn features stained-glass windows and a curving wraparound porch. A handsome hand-painted, stamped-tin ceiling graces the dining room. All rooms are furnished in antiques. The four guest rooms in the carriage house boast whirlpool baths, fireplaces or patios.

Innkeeper(s): Andrea Weinstein & Lauriann Nelay.

Rates:$80-155. MC VISA AX. Full Bkfst. 10 rooms. Fireplaces. Beds:KQT. TV, AC in room. Spa. Sauna.

Seen in: *AM-PM Magazine.*

Contact: Andrea Weinstein. Certificate may be used: November through June. Carriage House rooms only.

La Belle Epoque

1386 Calistoga Ave
Napa 94559
(707)257-2161 (800)238-8070
Fax:(707)226-6314

1893. This Queen Anne Victorian has a wine cellar and tasting room where guests can casually sip Napa Valley wines. The inn, which is one of the most unique architectural structures found in the wine country, is located in the heart of Napa's Calistoga Historic District. Beautiful original stained-glass windows include a window from an old church. A selection of fine restaurants and shops are within easy walking distance, as well as the riverfront, city parks and the Wine Train Depot. The train, which serves all meals, takes you just beyond St. Helena and back.

Innkeeper(s): Claudia and Merlin Wedepohl

Rates:$110-145. MC VISA AX DS. Full Bkfst. Gourmet Brkfst. 6 rooms. Fireplaces. Beds:KQ. AC in room. Fishing.

Contact: Merlin Wedepohl. Certificate may be used: Dec. 1, 1994-March 31, 1995, Monday-Thursday, holidays excluded.

La Residence Country Inn

4066 St Helena Hwy
Napa 94558
(707)253-0337 Fax:(707)253-0382

1870. This inn offers luxurious accommodations for those exploring the enchanting Napa Valley wine country. The uniquely decorated rooms in the French-style farmhouse or Gothic Revival Mansion are spacious and well-appointed, with fine antiques and designer fabrics. Many rooms also feature fireplaces, patios or spas. Guests will be impressed with the lovely gardens and pool area at the inn, not to mention the discreet but attentive service. Be sure to inquire about the picnic lunches, ideal for taking

along on excursions into the winery-rich valley.

Innkeeper(s): David Jackson, Craig Claussen.

Rates:$90-235. MC VISA. Full Bkfst. Picnic lunches. 20 rooms. 2 with shared baths. Fireplaces. Beds:Q. Conference Rm. Phone, AC in room. Handicap access. Spa. Sauna. Fishing.

Contact: David Jackson. Certificate may be used: Sunday-Thursday night, October to May.

Sybron House

7400 St Helena Hwy
Napa 94559
(707)944-2785 (800)944-2785

1978. The three-story tower of this new Victorian rises from a hillside overlooking Napa Valley. In the winter, breakfast is served with elegant china and silver in the formal dining room, and in summer, it's often provided on the redwood deck affording panoramic views of a dozen wineries including Inglenook, Silver Oak and Robert Mondavi.

Innkeeper(s): Cheryl and Denis Maddox.

Rates:$120-160. MC VISA AX. Full Bkfst. 4 rooms. Fireplaces. Beds:Q. Tennis. Spa.

Contact: Cheryl Maddox. Certificate may be used: February through May, excluding weekends and holidays. Weekdays include Sunday through Thursday.

"Your hospitality and warm personalities will never be forgotten."

Nevada City

Emma Nevada House

528 E Broad St
Nevada City 95959
(916)265-4415 (800)916-3662
Fax:(916)265-4415

1856. What is considered the childhood home of 19th-century opera star Emma Nevada now serves as an attractive Queen Anne Victorian inn. English roses line the white picket fence in front, and the forest-like back garden has a small stream with benches. The Empress' Chamber is the most romantic room with ivory Italian linens atop a French antique bed, a bay window and a massive French armoire. Some rooms have whirlpool baths. Guests enjoy relaxing in the hexagonal sunroom and on the inn's wraparound porches. Empire Mine State Historic Park is nearby.

Innkeeper(s): Ruth Ann Riese.

Rates:$100-150. MC VISA AX DS. Full Bkfst. Gourmet Brkfst. Teas. 6 rooms. Fireplaces. Beds:Q. TV, Phone, AC in room. Skiing. Handicap access. Swimming. Fishing.

Contact: Ruth Ann Riese. Certificate may be used: July 1-Nov. 23, 1994; May 1-Nov. 22, 1995 Sunday through Thursday, except holidays. Jan. 3-May 1, 1995 any day except holidays.

Flume's End B&B Inn

317 S Pine St
Nevada City 95959
(916)265-9665

1861. The peaceful sound of water accompanies your breakfast as you sit on the terrace overlooking Gold Run Creek. Flume's End is a Victorian inn named for the historic elevated flume on the property. (Flumes were used to conduct fresh water to the town.) Ask for the Garden Room and you'll enjoy a private Jacuzzi and deck set amid trees and waterfalls. A separate cottage is available as well. Interesting shopping and dining is just a stroll away.

Innkeeper(s): Terrianne Straw & Steve Wilson.

Rates:$75-135. MC VISA. Full Bkfst. Gourmet Brkfst. Evening snacks. 6 rooms. Fireplaces. Beds:Q. AC in room. Skiing. Swimming. Fishing.

Contact: Terrianne Straw. Certificate may be used: January through May, Sunday through Thursday excluding holidays.

Piety Hill Inn

523 Sacramento St
Nevada City 95959
(916)265-2245 (800)443-2245

1930. Nestled in the foothills of historic Nevada City, Piety Hill is composed of Victorian-style cottages clustered around a tree-shaded courtyard. The cottages are reminiscent of the gold rush era and furnished in early American, Victorian, and 1920s decor. Refreshments are found in the kitchenette of each cottage. A full breakfast is brought to the door every morning. Among the cedars in the one-acre garden is a gazebo spa.

Innkeeper(s): Linda Williams.

Rates:$75-135. MC VISA AX. Full Bkfst. MAP available. Gourmet Brkfst. 9 rooms. Fireplaces. Beds:KQD. Conference Rm. TV, Phone, AC, Refrig. in room. Skiing. Handicap access. Spa. Exercise room. Swimming. Fishing.

Contact: Linda Williams. Certificate may be used: Sunday to Thursday, no holiday or event day in town all year.

The Red Castle Inn

109 Prospect St
Nevada City 95959
(916)265-5135

1860. The Smithsonian has lauded the restoration of this four-story brick Gothic Revival known as "The Castle" by townsfolk. Its roof is laced with wooden icicles and the balconies are adorned with gingerbread. Within, there are intricate moldings, antiques, Victorian wallpapers, canopy beds and woodstoves. Verandas provide views of the historic city through cedar, chestnut and walnut trees, and

of terraced gardens with a fountain pond.

Innkeeper(s): Conley & Mary Louise Weaver.

Rates:$70-140. MC VISA. Full Bkfst. Gourmet Brkfst. Teas. 7 rooms. Beds:QD. Phone, AC in room. Golf. Tennis. Skiing. Swimming. Fishing.

Seen in: *Sunset, Gourmet, Northern California Home and Garden, Sacramento Bee, Los Angeles Times, Travel Holiday, Victorian Homes, Innsider, San Francisco Focus 1992 Grand Hotel Award.*

Contact: Mary Louise Weaver. Certificate may be used: Jan. 1 through Aug. 31 excepting holidays, Sunday through Friday.

"The Red Castle Inn would top my list of places to stay. Nothing else quite compares with it." Gourmet.

Nipomo

The Kaleidoscope Inn

Box 1297, 130 E Dana St
Nipomo 93444
(805)929-5444

1887. The sunlight that streams through the stained-glass windows of this charming Victorian creates a kaleidoscope effect and thus the name.

The inn is surrounded by gardens. Each romantic guest room is decorated with antiques and the library offers a fireplace. Fresh flowers add a special touch. Breakfast is either served in the dining room or in the gardens.

Innkeeper(s): Patty & Bill Linane.

Rates:$80. MC VISA AX. Full Bkfst. Gourmet Brkfst. 3 rooms. Beds:KQ. Conference Rm. Golf. Tennis. Swimming. Horseback riding. Fishing.

Seen in: *Santa Maria Times, Los Angeles Times, Country Magazine.*

Contact: Patricia Linane. Certificate may be used: November, 1994 to April, 1995. No three-day holidays.

"Beautiful room, chocolates, fresh flowers, peaceful night's rest, great breakfast."

Nipton

Hotel Nipton
HCI, Box 357
Nipton 92364
(619)856-2335 Fax:(702)896-6846

1904. This Southwestern-style adobe hotel with its wide verandas once housed gold miners and Clara Bow, wife of movie star Rex Bell. It is decorated in period furnishings and historic photos of the area. A 1920s rock and cactus garden blooms and an outdoor spa provides the perfect setting for watching a flaming sunset over Ivanpah Valley, the New York Mountains, and Castle Peaks. Later, a magnificent star-studded sky appears undimmed by city lights.

Innkeeper(s): Gerald & Roxanne Freeman.

Rates:$45. MC VISA DC CB. Cont. Bkfst. 4 rooms. 4 with shared baths. Beds:DT. Spa. Fishing.

Contact: Roxanne Freeman. Certificate may be used: Not on weekends or holidays.

Orland

The Inn at Shallow Creek Farm
4712 County Rd. DD
Orland 95963
(916)865-4093

1900. This vine-covered farmhouse was once the center of a well-known orchard and sheep ranch. The old barn, adjacent to the farmhouse, was a livery stop. The citrus orchard, now restored, blooms with 165 trees. Apples, pears, peaches, apricots, persimmons, walnuts, figs, and pomegranates are also grown here. Guests can meander to examine the Polish crested chickens, silver guinea fowl, Muscovy ducks, and African geese. The old caretaker's house is now a four-room guest cottage. Hundreds of narcissus grow along the creek that flows through the property.

Innkeeper(s): Mary & Kurt Glaeseman.

Rates:$55-75. ContPlus Bkfst. 4 rooms. 2 with shared baths. Beds:QT.

Phone, AC in room. Farm. Golf. Swimming. Fishing.

Seen in: *Adventure Road, Orland Press Register.*

Contact: Mary Glaeseman. Certificate may be used: Monday-Thursday all year.

"Now that we've discovered your country oasis, we hope to return as soon as possible."

Orosi

Mama Bear's Orchard B&B
42723 Road 128
Orosi 93647
(209)528-3614 (800)530-2327
Fax:(209)591-8439

1990. This country ranch home is situated on more than four acres of orange, Asian pear, pecan, walnut, cherry, persimmon, plum and banana trees, and the ranch is surrounded by grapevines. The Garden Room overlooks an enclosed Oriental garden complete with waterfall and koi fish pond. Mornings at Mama Bear's Orchard are serene and quiet except for the rooster's wake-up call heard in the distance. Your hostess is a fisherwoman, farmer, physician, photographer, lecturer and in the evenings she serves her homemade fruit-flavored Kitchen Cordial liqueur with freshly baked cookies.

Innkeeper(s): Manuela Fernandez.

Rates:$45-65. ContPlus Bkfst. 4 rooms. 2 with shared baths. Beds:KQ. AC in room. Farm. Bicycling. Skiing. Handicap access. Exercise room. Swimming. Fishing.

Contact: Manuela Fernandez. Certificate may be used: Nov. 1, 1994 to March 1, 1995; Nov. 1, 1995 to March 1, 1996.

Oroville/Berry Creek

Lake Oroville Bed and Breakfast
240 Sunday Drive
Oroville/Berry Creek 95916
(916)589-0700 (800)455-5253

1991. Situated in the quiet foothills above Lake Oroville, this country inn features panoramic views from the private porches that extend from each guest room. Two favorite rooms are the Rose Petal Room and the Victorian Room, both with lake views and whirlpool tubs. The inn's 40 acres are studded with oak and pine trees. Deer and songbirds abound.

Innkeeper(s): Ronald & Cheryl Damberger.

Rates:$65-110. MC VISA AX DS. Full Bkfst. Gourmet Brkfst. Evening snacks. 6 rooms. Beds:KQ. Conference Rm. Phone, AC in room. Golf. Tennis. Skiing. Handicap access. Swimming. Horseback riding. Fishing.

Seen in: *Oroville Mercury-Register.*

Contact: Cheryl Damberger. Certificate may be used: Sunday-Thursday (no holiday periods).

Pacific Grove

Gatehouse Inn

225 Central Ave
Pacific Grove 93950
(408)649-8436 (800)753-1881
Fax:(408)648-8044

1884. This Italianate Victorian seaside inn is just a block from the ocean and Monterey Bay. The inn

is decorated with Victorian and 20th-century antiques and touches of Art Deco. Guest rooms feature fireplaces, clawfoot tubs and down comforters. Some rooms have ocean views. The dining room boasts opulent Bradbury & Bradbury Victorian wallpapers as do some of the guest rooms. Afternoon hors d'oeuvres, wine and tea are served. The refrigerator is stocked for snacking.
Innkeeper(s): Lois DeFord.

Rates:$110-150. MC VISA AX. Full Bkfst. Picnic lunches. 8 rooms. Golf. Bicycling. Swimming. Horseback riding. Fishing.

Seen in: *San Francisco Chronicle, Monterey Herald, Time, Newsweek, Inland Empire Magazine, Bon Appetite.*

Contact: Lois DeFord. Certificate may be used: Sept. 15-Dec. 15; Jan. 5-May 20; Sunday-Thursday.

"Thank you for spoiling us."

Gosby House Inn

643 Lighthouse Ave
Pacific Grove 93950
(408)375-1287 (800)527-8828
Fax:(408)655-9621

1888. Built as an upscale Victorian inn for those visiting the old Methodist retreat, this sunny yellow mansion features an abundance of gables, turrets and bays. During renovation the innkeeper slept in all the rooms to determine just what antiques were needed and how the beds should be situated. Gosby

House is in the National Register.
Innkeeper(s): Shirley Butts.

Rates:$85-150. MC VISA AX. Full Bkfst. Picnic lunches. Teas. 22 rooms. 2 with shared baths. Beds:Q. Phone in room. Golf. Bicycling. Swimming. Fishing.

Seen in: *San Francisco Chronicle, Oregonian, Los Angeles Times, Travel & Leisure.*

Contact: Kim Post Watson. Certificate may be used: Oct. 1 - May 15, Sunday - Thursday.

Green Gables Inn

104 5th St
Pacific Grove 93950
(408)375-2095 Fax:(408)375-5437

1888. This half-timbered Queen Anne Victorian appears as a fantasy of gables overlooking spectacular Monterey Bay. The parlor has stained-glass panels framing the fireplace and bay windows looking

out to the sea. A favorite focal point is an antique carousel horse. Most of the guest rooms have panoramic views of the ocean, fireplaces, gleaming woodwork, soft quilts, and flowers. Across the street is the Monterey Bay paved oceanfront cycling path. (Mountain bikes may be borrowed from the inn.)

Innkeeper(s): Suzie Russo.

Rates:$100-160. MC VISA AX. Full Bkfst. Picnic lunches. Teas. 11 rooms. 4 with shared baths. Fireplaces. Beds:KQ. Conference Rm. Golf. Bicycling. Swimming. Fishing.

Seen in: *Travel & Leisure, Country Living.*

Contact: Kim Post Watson. Certificate may be used: December - January, Sunday - Thursday.

Palm Springs

Casa Cody Country Inn
175 S Cahuilla Rd
Palm Springs 92262
(619)320-9346 (800)231-2639
Fax:(619)325-8610

1920. Casa Cody, built by a relative of Wild Bill Cody and situated in the heart of Palm Springs, is the town's second-oldest operating inn. The San Jacinto Mountains provide a scenic background for

the tree-shaded spa, the pink bouganvillaea and the blue waters of the inn's two swimming pools. Each suite has a small kitchenette and features a soft-pink and turquoise Southwestern decor. Several have wood-burning fireplaces. There are Mexican pavers, French doors and private patios.

Innkeeper(s): Therese Hayes & Frank Tysen.

Rates:$45-175. MC VISA AX. Cont. Bkfst. 17 rooms. Fireplaces. Beds:KQT. Conference Rm. TV, Phone, AC, Refrig. in room. Golf. Tennis. Bicycling. Skiing. Spa. Swimming. Horseback riding. Fishing.

Seen in: *Seattle Times, San Diego Union-Tribune, Pacific Northwest, Palm Springs Life, Desert Sun, KCET Magazine, New York Times, San Diego Magazine, Alaska Airlines Magazine.*

Contact: Frank Tysen. Certificate may be used: All year except February and March, Sunday through Thursday, holidays excepted.

"Outstanding ambiance, friendly relaxed atmosphere."

Sakura, Japanese B&B
1677 N Via Miraleste at Vista Chino
Palm Springs 92262
(619)327-0705 (800)200-0705

Fax:(619)327-6847

1945. An authenthic Japanese experience awaits guests of this private home, distinctively decorated with Japanese artwork and antique kimonos. Guests are encouraged to leave their shoes at the door, grab kimonos and slippers and discover what real relaxation is all about. Guests may choose either American or Japanese breakfasts, and Japanese or vegetarian dinners also are available. The Palm Springs area is home to more than 70 golf courses and many fine shops. During the summer months, the innkeepers conduct tours in Japan.

Innkeeper(s): George & Fumiko Cebra.

Rates:$55-75. Full Bkfst. Teas. 3 rooms. 1 with shared bath. Beds:QT. TV, AC in room. Skiing. Spa. Swimming. Fishing.

Contact: George Cebra. Certificate may be used: Sunday through Thursday.

Palo Alto

Adella Villa
PO Box 4528
Palo Alto 94309
(415)321-5195 Fax:(415)325-5121

1920. This Tyrolean style house is located in an area of one-acre estates five minutes from Stanford University. Guest rooms feature whirlpool tubs and

a Japanese soaking tub. The music room boasts a 1920 mahogany Steinway grand piano. There is a solar-heated swimming pool set amidst manicured gardens.

Innkeeper(s): Tricia Young.

Rates:$105. MC VISA AX DC CB. Full Bkfst. EP. Teas. Evening snacks. 5 rooms. Beds:KQT. Conference Rm. TV, Phone, AC in room. Bicycling. Spa. Exercise room. Swimming. Fishing.

Contact: Tricia Young. Certificate may be used: All year. Anytime.

"This place is as wonderful, gracious and beautiful as the people who own it!"

Platina

Living Spring Farm & Guest Ranch

HCR 1, Box 611, Hwy 36
Platina 96076
(916)352-4338

1960. Anyone who has ever longed to visit a farm will enjoy this inn, which is dedicated to preserving the "old-fashioned" methods of farming. Visitors stay in an air-conditioned, farmstyle guest house, furnished in country decor and featuring private baths. Guests are encouraged to gain hands-on experience with as many farm tasks as they can manage, including cow milking, fruit picking, calf roping, crop harvesting and the processing of butter and cheese. Children enjoy arts and crafts and nature lessons. All meals, horseback riding and wagon rides are included in the rate.

Innkeeper(s): Will & Mary Gibbs, Fred & Sherry Morgan.

Rates:$150-200. Full Bkfst. AP available. Picnic lunches. 8 rooms. Beds:DT. AC in room. Farm. Handicap access. Stables. Fishing.

Contact: Mary Gibbs. Certificate may be used: March 1 - May 31, Sept. 15 - Dec. 31. All meals and horseback riding included.

Point Reyes Station

Carriage House

325 Mesa Rd, PO Box 1239
Point Reyes Station 94956
(415)663-8627 Fax:(415)663-8431

1920. This recently remodeled home boasts a view of Inverness Ridge. Each guest room is a suite furnished in antiques and folk art, and features a private parlor, television, and a fireplace. Children are welcome and cribs and daybeds are available. Point Reyes National Seashore has 100 miles of trails for cycling, hiking or horseback riding. If you bring your horse, the innkeeper will help you with overnight horse accommodations. Breakfast is brought to your room.

Innkeeper(s): Felicity & Bill Kirsch.

Rates:$100-120. Full Bkfst. 2 rooms. Fireplaces. Beds:QT. TV, Refrig. in room. Golf. Tennis. Bicycling. Swimming. Horseback riding. Fishing.

Contact: Felicity Kirsch. Certificate may be used: Sunday-Thursday.

"What a rejuvenating getaway. We loved it. The smells, sounds and scenery were wonderful."

Thirty-nine Cypress

39 Cypress St, Box 176
Point Reyes Station 94956
(415)663-1709

1980. The lures of the country and seashore are combined at this charming redwood home. Three guest rooms, all filled with country touches, feature patios with views of the bay and the peninsula. Julia, who was in charge of the natural history program at the Point Reyes National Seashore, will be happy to aid guests in planning their excursions. And Flora, the inn's well-behaved Australian cattle dog, will greet all comers, maybe even showing them the spa, cozily situated down the bluff with a view of the marsh below. Guests often enjoy eating breakfast at an outdoor table, overlooking the valley and its varied wildlife.

Innkeeper(s): Julia Bartlett.

Rates:$110-125. MC VISA AX. Full Bkfst. 3 rooms. Beds:Q. Spa. Swimming. Fishing.

Contact: Julia Bartlett. Certificate may be used: Midweek, non-holiday, November - March 15.

Tradewinds Bed & Breakfast

12088 Hwy One, PO Box 1117
Point Reyes Station 94956
(415)663-9326

1987. Offering its guests a panoramic view of the surrounding countryside is this comfortable ranch home, designed and built by the innkeeper. The inn offers many hand-crafted touches, which add to a feeling of warmth and luxury. One room boasts a double-wide whirlpool tub and French doors that open onto a deck. Corrals are available for guests who bring horses, and the surrounding area abounds with outdoor and nature activities.

Innkeeper(s): John Walker.

Rates:$90-110. ContPlus Bkfst. 2 rooms. Beds:Q. TV in room. Golf. Tennis. Handicap access. Spa. Swimming. Horseback riding. Fishing.

Contact: John Walker. Certificate may be used: Sunday, Monday, Tuesday, Wednesday, Thursday only.

The Tree House

PO Box 1075
Point Reyes Station 94956
(415)663-8720

1975. This homestay offers an outstanding view of Point Reyes Station from the deck and some of the guest rooms. The King's Room features a king-size waterbed while Queen Quarter boasts its own fireplace. A hot tub is tucked away in a cozy spot of the garden.

Innkeeper(s): Lisa Patsel.

Rates:$95-115. Full Bkfst. 4 rooms. Fireplaces. Beds:KQ. Phone in room. Spa. Stables.

Contact: Lisa Patsel. Certificate may be used: Sunday through Thursday only, no weekends or major holidays.

Quincy

The Feather Bed
542 Jackson St, PO Box 3200
Quincy 95971
(916)283-0102

1893. Englishman Edward Huskinson built this charming Queen Anne house shortly after he began his mining and real estate ventures. Ask for the secluded cottage with its own deck and clawfoot tub. Other rooms in the main house overlook downtown Quincy or the mountains. Check out a bicycle to explore the countryside.

Innkeeper(s): Bob & Jan Janowski.

Rates:$70-100. MC VISA AX DC DS. Full Bkfst. Gourmet Brkfst. Evening snacks. 7 rooms. Fireplaces. Beds:QT. Conference Rm. Phone, AC in room. Bicycling. Skiing. Handicap access. Swimming. Fishing.

Seen in: *Focus, Reno Gazette, SF Chronicle.*

Contact: Janet Janowski. Certificate may be used: September, 1994 through May, 1995; September, 1995 through December, 1995.

"After living and traveling in Europe where innkeepers are famous, we have found The Feather Bed to be one of the most charming in the U.S. and Europe!"

Rancho Cucamonga

Christmas House B&B Inn
9240 Archibald Ave
Rancho Cucamonga 91730
(909)980-6450

1904. This Queen Anne Victorian has been renovated in period elegance, emphasizing its intricate wood carvings and red and green stained-glass windows. Once surrounded by 80 acres of citrus groves and vineyards, the home, with its wide, sweeping veranda, is still a favorite place for taking in beautiful lawns and palm trees. The elegant atmosphere attracts the business traveler, romance-seeker and vacationer.

Innkeeper(s): Jay & Janice Ilsley.

Rates:$70-170. MC VISA AX DS. Full Bkfst. 6 rooms. 2 with shared baths. Fireplaces. Beds:QD. Conference Rm. Phone, AC in room. Golf. Tennis. Skiing. Spa. Swimming. Fishing.

Seen in: *Country Inns Magazine, Los Angeles Times, Elan Magazine.*

Contact: James Ilsley. Certificate may be used: Any night except Saturday night year-round except December.

"Coming to Christmas House is like stepping through a magic door into an enchanted land. Many words come to mind — warmth, serenity, peacefulness."

Red Bluff

The Jarvis Mansion
1313 Jackson St
Red Bluff 96080
(916)527-6901

1870. This Italianate mansion is located within Red Bluff's Victorian home tour area. Guest rooms are furnished in Victorian-era antiques. The city's historic downtown is within easy walking distance, and parts of it offer visitors modern shops behind 19th-century facades. The Sacramento River, with its boating, fishing and water skiing, is a quarter-mile from the inn. On the grounds, guests will find an enchanting gazebo. A cottage with kitchenette provides another lodging option.

Innkeeper(s): Dave & Tina Ebert.

Rates:$65-90. MC VISA. ContPlus Bkfst. 4 rooms. Beds:Q. TV, Phone, AC in room. Skiing. Swimming. Fishing.

Contact: David Ebert. Certificate may be used: Anytime - major holidays excluded.

Reedley

The Fairweather Inn B&B
259 S Reed Ave
Reedley 93654
(209)638-1918

1914. This Craftsman-style inn is situated on the bluffs of the Kings River, a half-hour's drive from Sequoia and Kings Canyon national parks. After a restful night in one of the inn's four guest rooms, all with queen beds, visitors will enjoy their gourmet breakfast in the dining room. The antique-filled inn is within walking distance of downtown restaurants and shops, and Reedley also offers a beautiful golf course near the river. Fresno and Visalia are 20 minutes away.

Innkeeper(s): Vi Demyan.

Rates:$75. MC VISA AX. Gourmet Brkfst. 4 rooms. 2 with shared baths. Beds:Q. AC in room. Skiing. Swimming. Fishing.

Contact: Violet Demyan. Certificate may be used: Sunday through Thursday.

Sacramento

Aunt Abigail's
2120 G St
Sacramento 95816
(916)441-5007 (800)858-1568

Fax:(916)441-0621

1912. This Colonial Revival inn, on an elm-lined street just minutes from the capitol building and convention center, offers gracious surroundings to both business and weekend getaway travelers. The inn's five guest rooms include The Margaret Room, with its four-poster, canopy queen bed, and the maroon and gray "country gentleman" Uncle Albert Room, with marble-floor bathroom and a queen bed. The inn's secluded garden spa is a favorite spot to relax after a busy day exploring California's capitol city and its surrounding area.

Innkeeper(s): Susanne & Ken Ventura.

Rates:$95-150. MC VISA AX DC DS CB. Full Bkfst. Evening snacks. 5 rooms. Beds:KQ. Phone, AC in room. Skiing. Spa. Swimming. Fishing.

Contact: Susanne Ventura. Certificate may be used: June through December excluding holidays and special event weekends.

Saint Helena

Deer Run Inn

3995 Spring Mtn Rd
Saint Helena 94574
(707)963-3794 (800)843-3408
Fax:(707)963-4567

1929. This secluded mountain home is located on four forested acres just up the road from the house used for the television show "Falcon Crest." A pine-tree-shaded deck provides a quiet spot for breakfast while watching birds and deer pass by. Your host, Tom, was born on Spring Mountain and knows the winery area well.

Innkeeper(s): Tom & Carol Wilson.

Rates:$95-125. AX. Full Bkfst. Gourmet Brkfst. 3 rooms. Fireplaces. Beds:KQ. TV, AC in room. Golf. Tennis. Swimming. Horseback riding.

Seen in: *Forbes, Chicago Tribune, Napa Record.*

Contact: Carol M. Wilson. Certificate may be used: November - March, Sunday through Thursday, holidays excluded.

"Very beautiful rooms, serene and comfortable."

Spanish Villa Inn

474 Glass Mountain Rd
Saint Helena 94574
(707)963-7483

1981. This contemporary Mission-style Spanish villa is nestled in a wooded valley in the Napa wine country, three miles from town. Guests will be charmed by the Tiffany lamp replicas found throughout the inn, including the guest rooms. A large sitting room and fireplace are favorite gathering spots. The quiet, country roads found in the area are popular for biking, jogging or walking. Don't miss the chance to visit nearby Calistoga, with its hang gliding and famous mud baths.

Innkeeper(s): Barbara.

Rates:$95-105. ContPlus Bkfst. 3 rooms. Beds:K. Farm. Swimming. Fishing.

Contact: Roy Bissember. Certificate may be used: Winter.

San Clemente

Casa de Flores B&B

184 Ave La Cuesta
San Clemente 92672
(714)498-1344

1974. Located a mile from the Pacific, you can enjoy a 180-degree view of the ocean, harbor and hills from this home. In a residential area, it was designed by your hostess. The Private Patio room offers skylights, a private spa and an ocean view. More than over 1,000 orchid plants are grown on the grounds. Grab a sand chair and towel and head for your own stretch of the five miles of San Clemente beaches. Whale watching and fishing charters are available at the Dana Point Harbor, 10 minutes away.

Innkeeper(s): Marilee Arsenault.

Rates:$75-100. Full Bkfst. Gourmet Brkfst. 2 rooms. Fireplaces. Beds:K. TV in room. Golf. Tennis. Spa. Swimming. Fishing.

Contact: Marilee Arsenault. Certificate may be used: Year-round except holidays.

San Francisco

Art Center/Wamsley Gallery/B&B

1902 Filbert St Corner - Laguna
San Francisco 94123
(415)567-1526

1857. The Art Center Bed & Breakfast was built during the Louisiana movement to San Francisco during the Gold Rush. It was  the only permanent structure on the path between the Presidio and Yerba Buena village. There are five guest suites here, convenient to much of San Francisco. The building is next to what is reputedly Washer Woman's Cove, a freshwater lagoon at the foot of Laguna Street that served as the village laundry.

Innkeeper(s): George & Helvi Wamsley.

Rates:$85-95. MC VISA AX DC DS CB. Full Bkfst. 5 rooms. Fireplaces. Beds:Q. TV, Refrig. in room. Spa. Fishing.

Seen in: *Richmond News, American Artist Magazine.*

Contact: Helvi Wamsley. Certificate may be used: January, February, March.

Country Cottage B&B

5 Dolores Terrace
San Francisco 94110
(415)479-1913 (800)452-8249
Fax:(415)921-2273

1906. Although just a mile from the city's center, this inn, at the end of a quiet street, provides the perfect escape from the non-stop excitement of San Francisco. The four country-style guest rooms feature American country antiques and queen-size brass beds. Complimentary wine is always available. Adding to the relaxing setting is a small, tree-lined patio area, a favorite spot for birdwatching. Before heading out for a day of sightseeing, guests enjoy a full breakfast in the inn's sunny kitchen. A streetcar stop is one block away.

Innkeeper(s): Susan or Richard Krelbich.

Rates:$65. MC VISA AX. Full Bkfst. 4 rooms. 4 with shared baths. Beds:Q. Tennis.

Contact: Susan Krelbich. Certificate may be used: November through April-anytime unless three-day weekends. May through October-Sundays through Thursdays only. If weekend is needed, last-minute calls and reservations accepted if we have room.

Dolores Park Inn

3641 17th St
San Francisco 94114
(415)621-0482 Fax:(415)621-0482

1874. The handsome Italianate Victorian entrance of this B&B welcomes guests to a sunny side of San Francisco, the Dolores Park area. There's a subtropical garden behind the wrought iron fence and inside, a balustrade with finials, ornate colonettes and other splendid architectural features. Within walking distance is Mission Dolores and many ethnic restaurants.

Innkeeper(s): Bernie, Leslie & Marissa Vielwerth.

Rates:$79-159. MC VISA. Full Bkfst. EP. AP available. Teas. 5 rooms. 4 with shared baths. Fireplaces. Beds:KQT. TV, Refrig. in room. Tennis.

Contact: Bernie Vielwerth. Certificate may be used: Monday-Thursday.

Golden Gate Hotel

775 Bush St
San Francisco 94108
(415)392-3702 (800)835-1118
Fax:(415)392-6202

1913. News travels far when there's a bargain. Half of the guests visiting this four-story Edwardian hotel at the foot of Nob Hill are from abroad. Great bay windows on each floor provide many of the rooms with gracious spaces at humble prices. An original bird cage elevator kept in working order floats between floors. Antiques, fresh flowers, and afternoon tea further add to the atmosphere. Union

Square is two-and-a-half blocks from the hotel.

Innkeeper(s): John & Renate Kenaston.

Rates:$59-99. MC VISA AX DC CB. Cont. Bkfst. Teas. 23 rooms. 9 with shared baths. Beds:QT. TV in room. Swimming. Fishing.

Seen in: *Los Angeles Times.*

Contact: John Kenaston. Certificate may be used: Available Sunday through Thursday from November through April, holidays excepted.

"Stayed here by chance, will return by choice!"

The Inn San Francisco

943 S Van Ness
San Francisco 94110
(415)641-0188 (800)359-0913
Fax:(415)641-1701

1872. Built on one of San Francisco's earliest "Mansion Rows" this 27-room Italianate Victorian is located near the civic and convention centers, close to Mission Dolores. Antiques, marble fireplaces and Oriental rugs decorate the opulent grand double parlors. Most rooms have featherbeds, Victorian wallcoverings and desks, while deluxe rooms offer private spas, fireplaces or bay windows.

Innkeeper(s): Marty Neely & Connie Wu.

Rates:$75-175. MC VISA AX DC DS CB. ContPlus Bkfst. Teas. 22 rooms. 5 with shared baths. Fireplaces. Beds:QT. Conference Rm. TV, Phone, Refrig. in room. Spa. Swimming. Fishing.

Seen in: *Innsider.*

Contact: Marty Neely. Certificate may be used: Anytime except weekends (Friday-Sunday) in August.

"...in no time at all you begin to feel a kinship with the gentle folk who adorn the walls in their golden frames."

No Name Victorian B&B

847 Fillmore St
San Francisco 94117
(415)479-1913 (800)452-8249
Fax:(415)921-2273

1895. Located in the historic district of Alamo Square, this Second Empire Victorian sits close to the Civic Center, Opera House, Davies Symphony Hall and Union Square. An 1830s wedding bed from mainland China adorns the honeymoon room. The massive hand-carved bed is believed to bring good spirits and luck to the couple who spend their wedding night there. Chinese antiques, a wood-burning fireplace, a city view and Chinese robes also are included. There's a family accommodation with a private entrance, full kitchen and a crib.

Innkeeper(s): Richard Kreibich.

Rates:$75-125. MC VISA AX. Full Bkfst. Teas. 6 rooms. 2 with shared baths. Fireplaces. Beds:QT. Tennis. Spa.

Contact: Susan Kreibich. Certificate may be used: November through April (anytime except three day weekends). May through October, Sunday-Thursday only. If a weekend is requested, last minute reservations accepted if we have room.

Petite Auberge

863 Bush St
San Francisco 94108
(415)928-6000 Fax:(415)775-5717

1919. This five-story hotel features an ornate baroque design with curved bay windows. Now transformed to a French country inn, there are antiques, fresh flowers and country accessories. Most rooms also have working fireplaces. It's a short walk to the Powell Street cable car.
Innkeeper(s): Richard Revaz.

Rates:$110-220. MC VISA AX. Full Bkfst. Picnic lunches. Teas. 26 rooms. Fireplaces. Beds:Q. TV, Phone in room. Golf. Tennis. Fishing.

Seen in: *Travel and Leisure, Oregonian, Los Angeles Times, Brides.*

Contact: Kim Post Watson. Certificate may be used: Nov. 1 - May 15, Sunday - Thursday.

"Breakfast was great, and even better in bed!"

Victorian Inn On The Park

301 Lyon St
San Francisco 94117
(415)931-1830 (800)435-1967
Fax:(415)931-1830
CA883076.TIF

1897. This grand three-story Queen Anne inn, built by William Curlett, has an open belvedere turret with a teahouse roof and Victorian railings. Silk-screened wallpapers, created especially for the inn, are accentuated by intricate mahogany and redwood paneling. The opulent Belvedere Suite features French doors opening to a Roman tub for two. Overlooking Golden Gate Park, the inn is 10 minutes from downtown.
Innkeeper(s): Lisa Benau.

Rates:$99-159. MC VISA AX DC DS CB. ContPlus Bkfst. Teas. 12 rooms. Fireplaces. Beds:QT. Phone in room. Golf. Tennis. Horseback riding.

Seen in: *Innsider Magazine, Country Inns, Good Housekeeping, New York Times, Good Morning America.*

Contact: Lisa Benau. Certificate may be used: Good Sundays thru Thursdays, Nov. 1 thru April 30.

"The excitement you have about your building comes from the care you have taken in restoring and maintaining your historic structure."

White Swan Inn

845 Bush St
San Francisco 94108
(415)775-1755 Fax:(415)775-5717

1908. This four-story inn is near Union Square and the Powell Street cable car. Beveled-glass doors open to a reception area with granite floors, an antique carousel horse and English artworks. Bay windows and a rear deck contribute to the feeling of an English garden inn. The guest rooms are decorated with softly colored English wallpapers and prints. All rooms have fireplaces. Turndown service is provided.
Innkeeper(s): Rich Revaz.

Rates:$145-250. MC VISA AX. Full Bkfst. Picnic lunches. Teas. 26 rooms. Fireplaces. Conference Rm. TV, Phone, Refrig. in room. Golf. Tennis. Swimming. Fishing.

Seen in: *Travel and Leisure, Victoria Magazine.*

Contact: Kim Post Watson. Certificate may be used: Nov. 1 - May 15, Sunday - Thursday.

"Wonderfully accommodating. Absolutely perfect."

San Gregorio

Rancho San Gregorio

5086 San Gregorio Rd, Box 54
San Gregorio 94074
(415)747-0810 Fax:(415)747-0184

1971. Built in the Mission style, this home appropriately rests on 15 acres that were part of an old Spanish land grant. Beamed redwood ceilings, terra cotta floors and Spanish furnishings reflect the old Spanish era. Fruits trees and gardens are sprinkled along the ranch's paths. Guests often find their way to the creek just below the inn where there is a picnic table. A barn on the property is more than 100 years old and is said to have been the site for many local dances when the Raynor family originally settled here in the late 1800s. San Francisco is 40 miles to the north.
Innkeeper(s): Bud & Lee Raynor.

Rates:$80-145. MC VISA AX DS. Full Bkfst. Evening snacks. 4 rooms. Fireplaces. Beds:KQT. Conference Rm. Refrig. in room. Farm. Golf. Bicycling. Spa. Swimming. Fishing.

Seen in: *Innsider Magazine, Country Magazine, Los Angeles Times, San Francisco Examiner.*

Contact: Lorraine Raynor. Certificate may be used: Suite (San Gregorio and Corte Madera) only, Sunday through Thursday, October through April only.

"A little bit of paradise."

San Luis Obispo

Heritage Inn
978 Olive St
San Luis Obispo 93405
(805)544-7440

1900. Once known as the Bachelor's Club, this graceful late Victorian housed bank executives from the Bank of Italy and other businessmen from the University. The rooms offer antiques, cheerful decor and some have fireplaces, bay windows and balconies. Wine and hors d'oeuvres are served in the evening, and on winter mornings breakfast is served fireside in the dining room.

Innkeeper(s): Lisa Davis & Nancy Pearson.

Rates:$85-95. MC VISA AX. Full Bkfst. Evening snacks. 9 rooms. 6 with shared baths. Fireplaces. Beds:QT. Swimming. Fishing.

Contact: Georgia Adrian. Certificate may be used: November-March, Monday-Thursday.

San Martin

Country Rose Inn B&B
455 Fitzgerald Ave #E
San Martin 95046
(408)842-0441 Fax:(408)842-6646

1940. This 1920s Dutch Colonial manor is surrounded by a grove of trees and Santa Clara Valley farmland. Guests can visit Henry Coe Wilderness State Park and Mission San Juan Bautista. Also nearby are the renowned wineries of Santa Clara Valley, the Santa Cruz Mountains and Monterey County. Catered events can be arranged for a variety of special occasions, from a breakfast meeting to a private or group retreat to a romantic country wedding sumptuously embellished. Up to 40 people can be accommodated for indoor events. The spectacular Pacific coast and Monterey Peninsula are a scenic road trip away.

Innkeeper(s): Rose Hernandez.

Rates:$72-169. MC VISA. Full Bkfst. Picnic lunches. Teas. 5 rooms. Fireplaces. Beds:KQT. Conference Rm. AC in room. Farm. Golf. Swimming. Fishing.

Seen in: *San Jose Magazine, Contra Costa Times, Houston Chronicle, Times Tribune, San Francisco Chronicle, Dispatch, Morgan Hill Times.*

Contact: Rose Hernandez. Certificate may be used: All times except Garlic festival or special events.

Santa Barbara

Glenborough Inn
1327 Bath St
Santa Barbara 93101
(805)966-0589 (800)962-0589
Fax:(805)564-2369

1865. This Craftsman-style inn recreates a turn-of-the-century atmosphere in the main house. There is also an 1880s cottage reminiscent of the Victorian era. Inside are antiques, rich wood trim and elegant fireplace suites with canopy beds. There's always plenty of firewood and an open invitation to the secluded garden hot tub. Breakfast is homemade and has been written up in *Bon Appetit* and *Chocolatier.*

Innkeeper(s): Michael Diaz.

Rates:$75-175. MC VISA AX DC DS CB. Full Bkfst. Gourmet Brkfst. 11 rooms. 6 with shared baths. Fireplaces. Beds:Q. Phone, Refrig. in room. Spa. Swimming. Fishing.

Seen in: *Houston Post, Los Angeles Times.*

Contact: Michael Diaz. Certificate may be used: Sunday - Thursday except holiday periods; October - December, 1994 & 1995; January - May, 1995. Reservations accepted seven days prior to arrival only.

"Both Tom & I are terminal romantics and as it is obvious that you must be also, suffice it to say that for grace & style you are hereby awarded the Blue Ribbon."

The Old Yacht Club Inn
431 Corona Del Mar
Santa Barbara 93103
(805)962-1277 (800)676-1676
Fax:(805)962-3989

1912. This California Craftsman house was the home of the Santa Barbara Yacht Club during the Roaring '20s. It was opened as Santa Barbara's first B&B and has become renowned for its gourmet food and superb hospitality. Innkeeper Nancy Donaldson is the author of *The Old Yacht Club Inn Cookbook.*

Innkeeper(s): Nancy Donaldson & Sandy Hunt.

Rates:$140-150. MC VISA AX DC DS. Full Bkfst. Gourmet Brkfst, Dinner. 9 rooms. Beds:KQ. Conference Rm. TV, Phone in room. Golf. Tennis. Bicycling. Spa. Swimming. Horseback riding. Fishing.

Seen in: *Los Angeles Magazine, Valley Magazine.*

Contact: Nancy Donaldson. Certificate may be used: Dec.1-16, 1994; Jan. 3-Feb. 28, 1995; Monday - Thursday evenings only. Excludes weekends and holidays.

"Donaldson is one of Santa Barbara's better-kept culinary secrets."

Olive House

1604 Olive St
Santa Barbara 93101
(805)962-4902 (800)786-6422
Fax:(805)899-2754

1904. This turn-of-the-century Craftsman-style inn offers elegant accommodations in its six guest rooms, which vary in amenities but share fine furnishings and stylings. Fireplaces and spas are available, and all rooms feature king or queen beds. Guests will enjoy the chance to partake of coffee or tea before their full breakfasts. And after a busy day of sailing, shopping or sightseeing, the afternoon tea is an absolute delight. The innkeeper also is more than happy to offer advice about the area's many fine dining establishments.

Innkeeper(s): Lois Gregg.

Rates:$105-175. MC VISA AX. Full Bkfst. EP. Teas. 6 rooms. Fireplaces. Beds:KQ. Conference Rm. TV, Phone in room. Spa.

Contact: Lois Gregg. Certificate may be used: Monday-Thursday, holiday periods excluded. December and January.

"Thank you for providing not only a lovely place to stay but a very warm and inviting atmosphere."

Santa Clara

Madison Street Inn

1390 Madison St
Santa Clara 95050
(408)249-5541 (800)491-5541
Fax:(408)249-6676

1890. This Queen Anne Victorian inn still boasts its original doors and locks, and "No Peddlers or Agents" is engraved in the cement of the original

carriageway. Guests, however, always receive a warm and gracious welcome to high-ceilinged rooms furnished in antiques, Oriental rugs and Victorian wallpaper.

Innkeeper(s): Theresa Wigginton.

Rates:$60-85. Full Bkfst. 6 rooms. 4 with shared baths. Golf. Tennis. Spa. Swimming.

Seen in: *Discovery Magazine.*

Contact: Theresa Wigginton. Certificate may be used: Anytime.

"We spend many nights in hotels that look and feel exactly alike whether they are in Houston or Boston. Your inn was delightful. It was wonderful to bask in your warm and gracious hospitality."

Santa Cruz

Babbling Brook B&B Inn

1025 Laurel St
Santa Cruz 95060
(408)427-2437 (800)866-1131
Fax:(408)427-2457

1796. This inn was built on the foundations of an 1870 tannery and a 1790 grist mill. Secluded, yet

within the city, the inn features a cascading waterfall, historic waterwheel and meandering creek on one acre of gardens and redwoods. Country French decor, cozy fireplaces, and deep-soaking whirlpool tubs are luxurious amenities of the Babbling Brook.

Innkeeper(s): Helen King.

Rates:$85-150. MC VISA AX DS CB. Full Bkfst. Teas. 12 rooms. Fireplaces. Beds:KQ. TV, Phone in room. Golf. Tennis. Handicap access. Spa. Swimming. Horseback riding. Fishing.

Seen in: *Country Inns, Yellow Brick Road, Times-Press-Recorder.*

Contact: Helen King. Certificate may be used: Space available basis only, October through April, no weekends or holidays.

"We were impressed with the genuine warmth of the inn. The best breakfast we've had outside our own home!"

The Darling House - A B&B Inn by the Sea

314 W Cliff Dr
Santa Cruz 95060
(408)458-1958

1910. It's difficult to pick a room at this oceanside

mansion. The Pacific Ocean Room features a fireplace and a wonderful ocean view. The Chinese Room might suit you as well with its silk-draped, hand-carved rosewood canopy wedding bed. Elegant oak, ebony, and walnut woodwork is enhanced by the antique decor of Tiffanys and Chippendales. Roses, beveled glass and libraries add to the atmosphere. Beyond the ocean-view veranda are landscaped gardens. Guests often walk to the wharf for dinner.

Rates:$125-145. ContPlus Bkfst. 5 rooms. 5 with shared baths. Beds:QDT. Conference Rm. Spa. Swimming. Fishing.

Seen in: *Modern Maturity, Pacific.*

Contact: Karen Darling. Certificate may be used: Sunday - Thursday, excluding holidays, November - April, 1994-1995.

"So pretty, so sorry to leave."

Pleasure Point Inn
2-3665 E Cliff Dr
Santa Cruz 95062
(408)475-4657

1940. This restored cliffside home is on three levels overlooking Monterey Bay. A new set of stairs goes down to picturesque Live Oak beach. All the rooms have a seaside or nautical decor. Best of all is the Pleasure Point Suite, with its own fireplace, private deck, clawfoot tub and Eastlake bed. Evening refreshments and a continental breakfast are served. Your hosts also offer a cruise or fishing trip along the Santa Cruz coastline on their 40-foot yacht.

Innkeeper(s): Sal & Margaret Margo.

Rates:$100-135. MC VISA. ContPlus Bkfst. AP available. 4 rooms. Fireplaces. Beds:Q. Refrig. in room. Swimming. Fishing.

Contact: Margaret Margo. Certificate may be used: Midweek Monday-Thursday.

Santa Monica

Channel Road Inn
219 W Channel Rd
Santa Monica 90402
(310)459-1920 Fax:(310)454-9920

1912. This shingle-clad building is a variation of the Colonial Revival Period, one of the few remaining in Los Angeles. The abandoned home was saved from the city's wrecking crew by Susan Zolla, with the encouragement of the local historical society. The rooms feature canopy beds, fine linens, custom mattresses and private porches. Chile Cheese Puff served with salsa is a popular breakfast speciality. The Pacific Ocean is one block away, and guests often enjoy borrowing the inn's bicycles to pedal along the 30-mile coastal bike path. In the evening, the inn's spectacular cliffside spa is popular.

Innkeeper(s): Susan Zolla & Kathy Jensen.

Rates:$85-200. MC VISA AX. Full Bkfst. Teas. 14 rooms. Beds:KQT. Conference Rm. TV, Phone in room. Bicycling. Handicap access. Spa. Swimming. Fishing.

Seen in: *Los Angeles Magazine, Brides Magazine.*

Contact: Susan Zolla. Certificate may be used: Sunday, Monday, Tuesday evenings Sept. 10 - Nov. 20, 1994; Jan. 3 - May 1, 1995.

"One of the most romantic hotels in Los Angeles."

Santa Rosa

Melitta Station Inn
5850 Melita Rd
Santa Rosa 95409
(707)538-7712

1880. Originally built as a stagecoach stop, this rambling structure became a freight depot for the little town of Melitta. Basalt stone quarried from

nearby hills was sent by rail to San Francisco where it was used to pave the cobblestone streets. Still located down a country lane, the station has been charmingly renovated. Oiled-wood floors, a rough-beam cathedral ceiling and French doors opening to a balcony are features of the sitting room. Wineries and vineyards stretch from the station to the town of Sonoma.

Innkeeper(s): Diane Crandon & Vic Amstadter.

Rates:$65-90. MC VISA. Full Bkfst. Gourmet Brkfst. 6 rooms. 2 with shared baths. Beds:Q. Conference Rm. Golf. Tennis. Swimming. Horseback riding. Fishing.

Seen in: *Los Angeles Times, New York Times, Press Democrat.*

Contact: Diane Crandon. Certificate may be used: Sunday - Thursday except holidays.

"Warm welcome and great food."

Sonoma

Starwae Inn
21490 Broadway
Sonoma 95476
(707)938-1374 (800)793-4792
Fax:(707)935-1159

1930. Behind clumps of morning glories and wild-flowers peeks this country home on three acres. Your innkeepers are both artists and their painting studios, dome-home and former pottery works comprise the inn. Each of the unpretentious cottages is decorated in an artsy style and includes figures, pencil drawings, pottery, art books and magazines. Up the road is a dairy farm with peacocks that show off along the fence.

Innkeeper(s): John Curry & Janice Crow.

Rates:$80-130. MC VISA. ContPlus Bkfst. 4 rooms. Fireplaces. Beds:Q. Conference Rm. AC, Refrig. in room. Bicycling. Fishing.

Contact: Janice Crow. Certificate may be used: Sunday through Thursday, except holiday weeks.

Trojan Horse Inn
19455 Sonoma Hwy
Sonoma 95476
(707)996-2430 (800)899-1925

1887. This blue Victorian farmhouse rests on the banks of Sonoma Creek. Recently restored, the pristine interiors offer antiques and a romantic country decor. The Bridal Veil Room has a canopied bed, woodburning stove and windows overlooking a magnolia tree, while a private Jacuzzi tub is a popular feature in the Grape Arbor Room. Bicycles, an additional outdoor Jacuzzi, flower gardens and grand old oak and pine trees add to the experience.

Innkeeper(s): Susan and Brian Scott.

Rates:$90-130. MC VISA AX DS. MAP available. Gourmet Brkfst. Teas. 6 rooms. Fireplaces. Beds:Q. Conference Rm. AC in room. Golf. Tennis. Bicycling. Handicap access. Spa.

Seen in: *Contra Costa Times, Mobil Travel Guide, Sonoma Index Tribune.*

Contact: Susan Scott. Certificate may be used: Sunday through Thursday excluding holiday weeks.

"We came for one night and stayed for four."

Sonora

Lavender Hill B&B
683 S Barretta St
Sonora 95370
(209)532-9024

1890. In the historic Gold Rush town of Sonora is this Queen Anne Victorian inn. Its four guest rooms include the Lavender Room, a mini-suite with desk, sitting area and clawfoot tub. After a busy day fishing, biking, river rafting or exploring nearby Yosemite National Park, guests may relax in the antique-filled parlor or watch cable TV in the sitting room. Admiring the inn's gardens from the wraparound porch is also a favorite activity. Be sure to ask about dinner theater packages.

Innkeeper(s): Jean & Charlie Marinelli.

Rates:$70-80. MC VISA. Full Bkfst. 4 rooms. 2 with shared baths. Beds:KQ. AC in room. Skiing. Swimming. Fishing.

Contact: Charles Marinelli, Sr. Certificate may be used: Sunday through Thursday only, dependent on availability.

Soquel

Blue Spruce Inn
2815 S Main St
Soquel 95073-2412
(408)464-1137 (800)559-1137
Fax:(408)475-0608

1875. Near the north coast of Monterey Bay, this old farmhouse has been freshly renovated and refitted with luxurious touches. The Seascape is a

favorite room with its private entrance, wicker furnishings and bow-shaped Jacuzzi for two. The Carriage House offers skylights above the bed, while a heart decor dominates Two Hearts. Local art, Amish quilts and featherbeds are featured throughout. Brunch enchiladas are the inn's speciality. Santa Cruz is two miles away.

Innkeeper(s): Pat & Tom O'Brien.

Rates:$80-125. MC VISA AX. Gourmet Brkfst. Picnic lunches. Evening snacks. 5 rooms. Fireplaces. Beds:QT. Conference Rm. TV, Phone, Refrig. in room. Golf. Tennis. Bicycling. Spa. Swimming. Horseback riding. Fishing.

Seen in: *Village View.*

Contact: Patricia O'Brien. Certificate may be used: Sunday-Thursday nights only all year.

"You offer such graciousness to your guests and a true sense of welcome."

Springville

Annie's B&B
33024 Globe Dr
Springville 93265
(209)539-3827 Fax:(209)539-2179

1900. A breathtaking view of the lovely Sierra Mountains greets guests at this inn, a farmhouse surrounded by green pastures and oak-covered hills. The inn's three guest rooms sport feather mattresses and quilts made by Annie's mother. All rooms offer private entrances and baths. Favorite spots for relaxing include the decks that overlook the pool-spa, and the living room, with its antique parlor stove. Guests will enjoy feeding Blossom, Annie's pet sow who weighs half a ton. A pot-bellied pig, Boo, also loves to eat treats. John operates a custom saddle shop on the grounds and guests are welcome to check it out.

Innkeeper(s): John & Ann Bozanich.

Rates:$75-85. MC VISA AX DC. Full Bkfst. Teas. Evening snacks. 3 rooms. Fireplaces. Beds:DT. TV, Phone, Refrig. in room. Farm. Skiing. Swimming. Stables. Fishing.

Contact: Ann Bozanich. Certificate may be used: Anytime except holidays, Apple Festival, Pow-Wow, Rodeo & Frontier Days.

Stinson Beach

Casa Del Mar
PO Box 238
Stinson Beach 94970
(415)868-2124 Fax:(415)868-2305

1989. Enjoy a quick getaway 35 minutes from the Golden Gate Bridge at this quiet coastal village. Casa Del Mar is a Mediterranean house on a hillside two blocks from the ocean, and guest rooms offer views of both the Pacific and Mount Tamalpais. The inn's garden was a teaching garden for the University of California. There are displays of model plots of vegetables, flowers, succulents and roses, passion flowers and fruit trees. Breakfast is

deliciously unique with such specialties as huevos rancheros, black bean and scallion pancakes and lemon walnut bread.

Innkeeper(s): Nancy Sullivan & Barbara Lee.

Rates:$100-200. MC VISA AX. Full Bkfst. Evening snacks. 6 rooms. Fireplaces. Beds:Q. Phone, Refrig. in room. Swimming. Fishing.

Contact: Rick Klein. Certificate may be used: Monday-Thursday, November-March excluding holiday seasons including Dec. 20-Jan. 2.

Templeton

Country House Inn
91 Main St
Templeton 93465
(805)434-1598 (800)362-6032

1886. This Victorian home, built by the founder of Templeton, is set off by rose-bordered gardens. It was designated as a historic site in San Luis Obispo County. All of the rooms are decorated with antiques and fresh flowers. Hearst Castle and six wineries are nearby.

Innkeeper(s): Dianne Garth.

Rates:$75-95. MC VISA DS. Gourmet Brkfst. 6 rooms. 2 with shared baths. Fireplaces. Beds:KQT. Swimming. Fishing.

Contact: Dianne Garth. Certificate may be used: Anytime except holidays, special events.

"A feast for all the senses, an esthetic delight."

Ukiah

Vichy Hot Springs Resort & Inn
2605 Vichy Springs Rd
Ukiah 95482
(707)462-9515 Fax:(707)462-9516

1854. This famous spa once attracted guests such as Jack London, Mark Twain and Teddy Roosevelt. Twelve rooms and two redwood cottages have been renovated for bed and breakfast, while the concrete 1860s baths remain unchanged. A new 12-foot spa and Olympic-size pool await your arrival. A magical waterfall is a 30-minute walk along a year-round stream.

Innkeeper(s): Gilbert & Marjorie Ashoff.

Rates:$125-160. MC VISA AX DC DS CB. Full Bkfst. EP. 14 rooms. Fireplaces. Beds:QT. Conference Rm. Phone, AC, Refrig. in room. Farm. Golf. Tennis. Bicycling. Spa. Swimming. Fishing.

Seen in: *Sunset, Mendocino Grapevine, Sacramento Bee, San Jose Mercury News, Gulliver (Japan), Oregonian, Contra Costa Times, Santa Rosa Press Democrat.*

Contact: Gilbert Ashoff. Certificate may be used: Sunday-Friday, September-December, 1994 no holidays; Sunday-Friday, January-May, 1995; Sunday-Thursday, June-September, 1995; Sunday-Friday, October-December, 1995 no holidays.

"Very beautiful grounds and comfortable accommodations."

Valley Center

Lake Wohlford B&B
27911 N Lake Wohlford Rd
Valley Center 92082
(619)749-1911 (800)831-8239

1993. This modern country log house, a short drive from Lake Wohlford in Northern San Diego County, offers a bounty for nature lovers. An adjacent wilderness preserve nicely complements the inn's own 48 acres, where guests may hike, jog and explore to their hearts' content. Guests will delight in the mountain views, the creekside hammock under sycamore trees and the inn's unique furnishings. San Diego Wild Animal Park and Lawrence Welk Village are nearby, as are several wineries and golf courses.
Innkeeper(s): Tatiana Ovanessoff & Nicholas Rottunda.
Rates:$88-128. MC VISA. Gourmet Brkfst. Picnic lunches. Teas. 5 rooms. 2 with shared baths. Beds:KQT. AC in room. Bicycling. Handicap access. Fishing.
Contact: Tatiana Ovanessoff. Certificate may be used: September through December.

Ventura

La Mer European B&B
411 Poli St
Ventura 93001
(805)643-3600

1890. This three-story Cape Cod Victorian overlooks the heart of historic San Buenaventura and the spectacular California coastline. Each room is decorated to capture the feeling of a specific European country. French, German, Austrian, Norwegian and English-style accommodations are available. Gisela, your hostess, is a native of

Siegerland, Germany. Midweek specials include romantic candlelight dinners, therapeutic massages and a mineral spa in the country.
Innkeeper(s): Gisela & Mike Baida.
Rates:$85-155. MC VISA. Full Bkfst. Picnic lunches. 5 rooms.

Fireplaces. Beds:KQT. Golf. Tennis. Bicycling. Swimming. Fishing.
Seen in: *Los Angeles Times, California Bride, Los Angeles Magazine.*
Contact: Gisela Baida. Certificate may be used: October through May.

"Where to begin? The exquisite surroundings, the scrumptious meals, the warm feeling from your generous hospitality! What an unforgettable weekend in your heavenly home."

Volcano

St. George Hotel
16104 Pine Grove-Volcano Rd
Volcano 95689
(209)296-4458

1862. This handsome old three-story hotel in the National Register features a double-tiered wraparound porch. There is a dining room, full bar and lounge area with fireplace. It is situated on one acre of lawns. An annex built in 1961 provides rooms with private baths. Volcano is a Mother Lode town that has been untouched by supermarkets and modern motels and remains much as it was during the Gold Rush.
Innkeeper(s): Marlene & Chuck Inman.
Rates:$110-130. MC VISA AX DC. Full Bkfst. MAP available. Gourmet Dinner. 20 rooms. 14 with shared baths. Beds:QDT. Conference Rm. Golf. Tennis. Skiing. Swimming. Horseback riding. Fishing.
Contact: Marlene Inman. Certificate may be used: Wednesday, Thursday, Friday, Sunday

"What is so precious about the hotel is its combination of graciousness and simplicity."

Westport

Howard Creek Ranch
40501 N Hwy One, PO Box 121
Westport 95488
(707)964-6725 Fax:(707)964-6725

1871. First settled as a land grant of thousands of acres, Howard Creek Ranch is now a 40-acre farm with sweeping views of the Pacific Ocean, sandy beaches and rolling mountains. A 75-foot bridge spans a creek that flows past barns and outbuildings to the beach 200 yards away. The farmhouse is surrounded by green lawns, an award-winning flower garden, and grazing cows and horses. This rustic rural location offers antiques, a hot tub and sauna.
Innkeeper(s): Charles & Sally Grigg.
Rates:$55-125. MC VISA AX. Full Bkfst. Gourmet Brkfst. Teas. 10 rooms. 2 with shared baths. Fireplaces. Beds:KQ. Refrig. in room. Farm. Spa. Sauna. Swimming. Stables.
Seen in: *California Magazine, Country Magazine.*

Contact: Sally Grigg. Certificate may be used: October through May, Sunday through Thursday.

"Of the dozen or so inns on the West Coast we have visited, this is easily the most enchanting one."

Yosemite/Coulterville

Hotel Jeffery
PO Box 440
Yosemite/Coulterville 95311
(209)878-3471 (800)464-3471
Fax:(209)878-3473

1851. This Gold Rush hotel was once a stagecoach inn for miners and passengers on their way to Yosemite. The historic Magnolia Saloon with its bat-wing entrance doors still provides an Old West flavor. Dancing and live weekend music may be heard in the guest rooms upstairs so it may be noisy for early sleepers but great fun for others.

Innkeeper(s): Louis Bickford & Karin Fielding.

Rates:$59-74. MC VISA. ContPlus Bkfst. 21 rooms. 16 with shared baths. Beds:T. Conference Rm. AC in room. Skiing. Swimming. Fishing.

Seen in: *Los Angeles Times, Motorland.*

Contact: Louis Bickford. Certificate may be used: Oct. 1 - March 31.

"Extremely friendly, excellent food."

Yosemite/Mariposa

Rockwood Gardens
5155 Tip Top Rd
Yosemite/Mariposa 95338
(209)742-6817 (800)859-8862
Fax:(209)742-7400

1989. Nestled among the pines in the Sierra foothills, this contemporary Prairie-style inn was designed and built to complement the natural beauty found nearby. A creek, oaks, pond and wildflower meadow all are part of the inn's setting. Guests often use the inn as headquarters when exploring the many wonders of Yosemite National Park. Visitors select from the Rose, Duck and Manzanita rooms. Stroll the grounds and relish the fine view of evening stars.

Innkeeper(s): Gerald & Mary Ann Fuller.

Rates:$65-90. DS. ContPlus Bkfst. 3 rooms. 2 with shared baths. Fireplaces. Beds:KQD. TV, AC in room. Skiing. Handicap access. Swimming. Fishing.

Contact: Mary Ann Fuller. Certificate may be used: Oct. 1 - Dec. 2, 1994; Jan. 2 - April 15, 1995; Oct. 1 - Dec. 2, 1995.

Yountville

Maison Fleurie
6529 Yount St
Yountville 94599
(707)944-2056

1880. Vines cover the two-foot thick brick walls of the Bakery, the Carriage House and the Main House of this French country inn. One of the Four Sisters Inns, it is reminiscent of a bucolic setting in Provence. Rooms are decorated in a pristine, romantic style, some with vineyard and garden views. Rooms in the Old Bakery have fireplaces. A pool and outdoor spa are available and you may borrow bicycles for wandering along the countryside.

Innkeeper(s): Roger Asbill.

Rates:$110-190. MC VISA AX. Full Bkfst. Picnic lunches. Teas. 13 rooms. Fireplaces. Beds:KQ. Phone, AC in room. Bicycling. Handicap access. Spa.

Contact: Roger Asbill. Certificate may be used: November - March, Sunday - Thursday.

Yuba City

Harkey House B&B
212 C St
Yuba City 95991
(916)674-1942

1874. An essence of romance fills this Victorian Gothic set in a lovely historic neighborhood. Every inch of the home has been given a special touch, from the knickknacks and photos in the sitting room to the quilts and furnishings in the guest quarters. The Harkey Suite features a brass bed with a down comforter and extras such as an adjoining library room and a pellet-burning stove. Breakfasts of muffins, fresh fruit, juice and freshly ground coffee are served in a glass-paned dining room or on the patio.

Innkeeper(s): Bob & Lee Jones.

Rates:$75-100. MC VISA AX DS. Gourmet Brkfst. 5 rooms. Fireplaces. Beds:Q. Conference Rm. TV, Phone, AC in room. Golf. Tennis. Bicycling. Skiing. Spa. Exercise room. Swimming. Horseback riding. Fishing.

Seen in: *Country Magazine.*

Contact: Robert Jones. Certificate may be used: Anytime.

"This place is simply marvelous...the most comfortable bed in travel."

Colorado

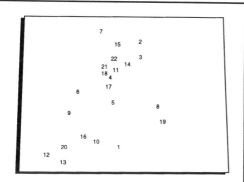

Alamosa

Cottonwood Inn
123 San Juan Ave
Alamosa 81101
(719)589-3882 (800)955-2623

1908. This refurbished Colorado bungalow is filled with antiques and paintings by local artists. The dining room set once belonged to Billy Adams, a Colorado governor in the 1920s. Blue-corn blueberry pancakes or flaming Grand Marnier omelets are the inn's specialties. A favorite day trip is riding the Cumbres-Toltec Scenic Railroad over the La Magna Pass, site of an Indiana Jones movie.
Innkeeper(s): Julie Mordecai.
Rates:$58-79. MC VISA AX DC DS CB. Full Bkfst. Gourmet Bkfst. Teas.

7 rooms. 2 with shared baths. Beds:KQ. Phone in room. Golf. Skiing. Swimming. Fishing.

Seen in: *Rocky Mountain News, Pueblo Chieftain.*

Contact: Julie Mordecai. Certificate may be used: November, 1994-February, 1995 and November, 1995-February, 1996.

"My husband wants to come over every morning for blueberry pancakes and strawberry rhubarb sauce."

Berthoud

Berthoud B&B
444 First St
Berthoud 80513
(303)532-4566 Fax:(303)532-4566

1895. With the Colorado Rocky Mountains as a backdrop and complete with a two-story turret and sweeping veranda, this inn reminds guests of a picture-perfect Victorian dollhouse. Tucked away in the turret is the Madame Pompadour Suite where Louis XV furniture graces the sitting area. The room is given a French country garden feel with its sleeping alcove with lavender walls; violet floral wallpaper, curtains and bed cover; and orchid carpet. A chandelier hangs from the turret ceiling above a huge, circular bed, and 11 windows give a view of the yard and its tall evergreens.
Innkeeper(s): Janet Foster & Gary Irwin.
Rates:$95-125. MC VISA AX DC DS. Full Bkfst. Gourmet Brkfst, Dinner. Picnic lunches. Teas. 7 rooms. Fireplaces. Beds:KQT. Conference Rm. TV, Phone, Refrig. in room. Farm. Tennis. Bicycling. Skiing. Spa. Sauna. Swimming. Fishing.

Contact: Janet Foster. Certificate may be used: Sunday - Thursday.

Boulder

The Magpie Inn
1001 Spruce St
Boulder 80302
(303)449-6528

1898. The Magpie Inn employed nine local interior designers to refurbish the mansion. Each room was given special and unique attention, with the focus being romance with a Victorian theme. The result is a collection of antiques, custom furniture and softly hued fabrics to elicit memories of an elegant home. Visual delights abound from marble fireplaces and fine paintings to old photographs and prints of Boulder.

Innkeeper(s): Nancy Raddatz.

Rates:$72-118. MC VISA DS. ContPlus Bkfst. 8 rooms. 2 with shared baths. Fireplaces. Beds:QT. Skiing. Fishing.

Contact: Teresa Koby. Certificate may be used: Sept. 15 - May 15, 1994 and 1995.

Breckenridge

The Walker House
103 S French St, PO Box 509
Breckenridge 80424
(303)453-2426

1875. Located in the beautiful ski town of Breckenridge with its historic past as a mining community, The Walker House is a three-story log home with Victorian accents. The innkeepers are happy to fulfill special diet requests and after-ski refreshments, including coffee, tea and cookies, are available anytime. Breakfast is served in a rustic dining room furnished with antiques and mining artifacts, or in the favorite gathering spot, the country kitchen. Lunch or dinner can be delivered by local restaurants.

Innkeeper(s): Sue Ellen Strong.

Rates:$89-112. Full Bkfst. Teas. Evening snacks. 2 rooms. 1 with shared bath. Beds:KQT. Skiing.

Contact: Sue Ellen Strong. Certificate may be used: Nov. 10-15, 1994; April 10 to May 15, 1995.

Buena Vista

Trout City Inn
Box 431
Buena Vista 81211
(719)495-0348

1987. Guests at this unique inn can sleep in an ele-

gant Victorian Pullman car or in the Drover's caboose. Located on 40 acres of the San Isabel National Forest, the inn's site is on the path of two famous mountain railroads. Although the historic narrow gauge train is stationary, the locomotive has been used for parades. The depot rooms are furnished in authentic Victorian style, but the berth mattresses are custom made—longer and a bit firmer than those of a hundred years ago.

Innkeeper(s): Juel & Irene Kjeldsen.

Rates:$38. MC VISA. Full Bkfst. MAP available. 4 rooms. Beds:DT. Conference Rm. Bicycling. Skiing. Swimming. Stables. Fishing.

Contact: Juel Kjeldsen. Certificate may be used: Weekdays, June 15 - Sept. 8.

Carbondale

Ambiance Inn
66 N 2nd St
Carbondale 81612
(303)963-3597 (800)350-1515

1975. This contemporary chalet-style home is located in the beautiful Crystal Valley between Aspen and Glenwood Springs. Year-round activities are numerous in the area, but ski buffs will be excited to know that Aspen and Snowmass are only a 30-minute drive away. Glenwood Springs and the world's largest hot springs are just 15 minutes away. Custom picnic baskets for outings are available with two days' advance notice. The New Orleans Library is adjacent to all three guest rooms on the second floor.

Innkeeper(s): Norma & Robert Morris.

Rates:$60-100. MC VISA. Full Bkfst. Gourmet Lunch. Picnic lunches. 4 rooms. Beds:Q. Refrig. in room. Golf. Tennis. Skiing. Swimming. Horseback riding. Fishing.

Seen in: Rocky Mountain News.

Contact: Norma Morris. Certificate may be used: Monday through Thursday, excluding July, August, September. No holidays.

Coalmont

Shamrock Ranch
4363 Rd 11
Coalmont 80430
(303)723-8413

1936. At an elevation of 8,800 feet and below the crest of the Continental Divide, the ranch is adjacent to thousands of acres of wilderness in the Routt National Forest. Overlooking the secluded cattle country of North Park, Colo., the lodge is built of native spruce logs and provides comfortable accommodations for 14 guests. The innkeepers like to provide a personalized touch and secluded atmosphere for your family or small group. Guests may enjoy horseback riding on fine saddle horses, with trail rides varying in pace to match experience or mood.

Innkeeper(s): Bruce & Cindy Wilson.

Rates:$70-85. VISA. Full Bkfst. MAP available. Gourmet Dinner. Picnic lunches. 4 rooms. 2 with shared baths. Beds:QT. Refrig. in room. Spa. Fishing.

Contact: Cindy Wilson. Certificate may be used: June 3, 1994 - Oct. 2, 1994 and June 1, 1995 - Oct. 1, 1995.

Colorado Springs

Black Forest B&B

11170 Black Forest Rd
Colorado Springs 80908
(719)495-4208 (800)809-9901
Fax:(719)495-0688

1984. Ponderosa pines, golden aspens and fragrant meadows surround this massive log home built on the highest point east of the Rocky Mountains. This rustic mountain setting is complete with 20 acres of beautiful country to explore. If you want to fully experience mountain living, the innkeepers will be more than happy to share their chores with you, which range from cutting firewood to planting Christmas trees on their tree farm. A greenhouse holds a indoor lap pool, sauna, fitness center and honeymoon suite.

Innkeeper(s): Robert & Susan Putnam.

Rates:$65-85. MC VISA AX. 4 rooms. Conference Rm. Exercise room.

Contact: Susan Putnam. Certificate may be used: November through April.

The Painted Lady

1318 W Colorado Ave
Colorado Springs 80904
(719)473-3165

1894. Once a popular restaurant in Old Colorado City, the Painted Lady has been remodeled into a bed and breakfast by its new owners. The three-

story Victorian is decorated in a warm, romantic

manner with lace and floral fabrics. Antique iron and four-poster beds, clawfoot tubs, and brass fixtures fill the guest rooms. Hearty breakfasts, served on the veranda in summer, might include seafood quiche or souffles and homemade breads.

Afternoon refreshments can be enjoyed in the parlor or on one of the porches.

Innkeeper(s): Valerie Maslowski.

Rates:$55-95. MC VISA DS. Full Bkfst. 4 rooms. 2 with shared baths. Beds:QD. Bicycling. Skiing. Swimming. Fishing.

Contact: Valerie Maslowski. Certificate may be used: Nov. 1 to April 30.

"Calm, peaceful. Our first B&B, very memorable."

Crawford

Sleeping Indian Mountain Lodge B&B

80082 Hwy 92, PO Box 21
Crawford 81415
(303)921-7378

1884. Offering the Western outdoor lifestyle of Colorado, this B&B is close to the Black Canyon National Monument, the West Elk Wilderness and the Crawford Reservoir. The area has many things to offer nature lovers, and the sporting activities change with the seasons. You may want to simply relax on the porches. The innkeeper is a language teacher and sculptor. Language and art workshops are held throughout the summer.

Innkeeper(s): Joanna Rodden.

Rates:$65. Full Bkfst. Gourmet Brkfst, Lunch. Picnic lunches. 9 rooms. 6 with shared baths. Beds:QT. Skiing. Swimming. Stables. Fishing.

Contact: Joanna Rodden. Certificate may be used: Hunting season (October-November) must be excluded. Any other dates according to occupancy.

Creede

Creede Hotel

1892 Main St
Creede 81130
(719)658-2608

1892. Built when Creede was a wild and booming mining town, the four restored rooms have provided a night's rest for some of the West's most colorful characters—Bat Masterson, Bob Ford and Calamity Jane, to name a few. The two rooms on the west side of this folk Victorian inn have access to a balcony overlooking Creede's historic Main Street. After dinner in the hotel dining room, guests can take in a performance at the highly acclaimed Creede Repertory Theatre next door.

Innkeeper(s): Catherine & Richard Ormsby.

Rates:$35-79. MC VISA DS. Full Bkfst. Gourmet Brkfst, Lunch, Dinner. Picnic lunches. Evening snacks. 6 rooms. Beds:QDT. Refrig. in room. Skiing. Swimming. Fishing.

Contact: Catherine Ormsby. Certificate may be used: Before Memorial weekend and between Memorial Day - June 15 and after Labor Day (September, Sunday - Thursday only).

Dillon

Swan Mountain Inn

PO Box 2900
Dillon 80435
(303)453-7903 (800)578-3687

1984. Less than seven miles from the outstanding ski areas of Keystone, Breckenridge and Copper Mountain, this cozy, country log home makes a perfect base for an array of Colorado activities. Rooms are individually decorated in down comforters and antiques. There's plenty to do when it's not ski season, including touring on the Summit County bike path and getting acquainted with the towns of Dillon and Breckenridge.

Innkeeper(s): Steve Gessner.

Rates:$50-100. MC VISA DS. AP available. MAP available. Gourmet Brkfst, Dinner. 4 rooms. 1 with shared bath. Beds:KQT. Skiing. Handicap access. Spa. Swimming. Fishing.

Contact: Robin Robson. Certificate may be used: Midweek, Sunday - Thursday. Except Thanksgiving & Christmas & March.

Dolores

Mountain View B&B

28050 County Rd P
Dolores 81323
(303)882-7861 (800)228-4592

1984. This sprawling ranch-type home has a magnificent view of the Mesa Verde National Park which is 12 miles away to its entrance. Besides spending a day or two touring the museum and cliff dwellings in Mesa Verde, guests can step outside this inn to enjoy its 22 acres of trails, woods and a small canyon with creek. In each direction, a short drive will take you to mountains, desert, canyon lands, mesa, forest lakes and world famous archaeological settings.

Innkeeper(s): Brenda & Cecil Dunn.

Rates:$49-59. MC VISA. Full Bkfst. 8 rooms. Beds:QT. Farm. Skiing. Spa. Swimming. Fishing.

Contact: Cecil Dunn Certificate may be used: Nov. 1, 1994-March 31, 1995.

Rio Grande Southern Hotel

101 S 5th St, PO Box 516
Dolores 81323
(303)882-7527 (800)258-0434

1893. Located in the town square, the inn has been in continuous use as a hostelry for more than 100 years. Having also served as a railroad hotel, it has a gift shop that offers the traveler a wide selection of gifts with a local and historical significance. The town is located at 7,000 feet elevation at the base of the San Juan Mountains, and close to the arid desert. This results in an exceptionally diverse environment. Both arid and alpine vegetation, wildlife and landscape are found in the regions surrounding the Dolores River Valley.

Innkeeper(s): Fred & Cathy Green.

Rates:$49-60. MC VISA. Full Bkfst. Picnic lunches. 3 rooms. Beds:QT. Conference Rm. Bicycling. Skiing. Fishing.

Contact: Cathy Green. Certificate may be used: Sept. 1-March 31.

Durango

The Leland House B&B Suites

721 E Second Ave
Durango 81301
(303)385-1920 (800)664-1920
Fax:(303)385-1967

1927. Each room of this two-story brick building is named after a historic figure associated with the Leland House, which has ties to a well-known builder, lumber company magnate, wool merchant and railroad executive. Gourmet breakfasts include the inn specialties of home-cooked granola and cranberry scones. Also, daily entrees include Southwestern burritos, filled French toast, pancakes or waffles topped with fresh fruit. Guests can tour the historic districts of Durango and browse through many fine shops, galleries and outlet stores.

Innkeeper(s): Kirk & Diane Komick.

Rates:$70-135. MC VISA. Full Bkfst. Gourmet Brkfst. Picnic lunches. 10 rooms. Beds:QD. TV, Phone, Refrig. in room. Skiing. Spa. Swimming. Fishing.

Contact: Diane Komick. Certificate may be used: Oct. 31 through May 15, excluding Dec. 15 through Jan. 2.

The Rochester Hotel

726 E Second Ave
Durango 81301
(303)385-1920 (800)664-1920
Fax:(303)385-1967

1892. This Federal-style inn's decor is inspired by many Western movies filmed in and around the town. The inn is located one block from the Historic Main Avenue District and two blocks from the Durango-Silverton Narrow Gauge Railroad. Conveniently located in a beautifully landscaped downtown setting, the building is an authentically restored late-Victorian hotel, fully furnished with antiques from the period.

Innkeeper(s): Kirk & Diane Komick.

Rates:$125-185. MC VISA. Cont. Bkfst. Gourmet Brkfst, Lunch. Teas. Evening snacks. 15 rooms. Beds:KQT. Conference Rm. TV, Phone in room. Skiing. Handicap access. Swimming. Fishing.

Contact: Diane Komick. Certificate may be used: April, May, June 1-15, Oct. 15-Dec. 15.

Scrubby Oaks B&B

PO Box 1047, 1901 Florida Rd
Durango 83102
(303)247-2176

1959. This Monterey-style inn sits on a hill at the south end of the Animas River Valley. Take a walk in winter along the ridge in ever-deepening snow where you will see elk grazing in the valleys and resident deer eating the last of the fruit left on the trees from the fall harvest. In the summer, listen to the quiet and enjoy a walk around the colorful gardens. Explore the house and take in the family antiques and photos, artworks and books found in all the rooms.

Innkeeper(s): Mary Ann Craig.

Rates:$65-75. Full Bkfst. Gourmet Brkfst. Evening snacks. 7 rooms. 4 with shared baths. Beds:KQT. Skiing. Sauna. Exercise room. Swimming. Fishing.

Contact: Mary Ann Craig. Certificate may be used: January, February, March.

The Verheyden Inn/Logwood B&B

35060 US Hwy 550 N
Durango 81301
(303)259-4396 (800)369-4082

1988. Large windows of this Western red cedar log structure make for great viewing of the upper Animas Valley. Deer often pass through this 15-

acre property with a stream, varieties of mountain trees and animal life. The perfect place to nap is a

hammock for two under oaks 50 feet away from the inn. All of the guest rooms are furnished with colorful home-stitched quilts to match the inn's Western decor. Breakfast menus range from hearty country fare to gourmet specialty dishes like quiches, casseroles and coffee cakes.

Innkeeper(s): Debby & Greg Verheyden.

Rates:$65-90. MC VISA. Full Bkfst. Gourmet Brkfst. Teas. Evening snacks. 6 rooms. Beds:Q. Skiing. Swimming. Stables. Fishing.

Contact: Debbie Verheyden. Certificate may be used: Oct. 1, 1994 through May 1, 1995. No holiday seasons.

Durango (Hesperus)

Blue Lake Ranch

16919 Hwy 140
Durango (Hesperus) 81326
(303)385-4537 Fax:(303)385-4088

1900. Built by Swedish immigrants, this renovated Victorian farmhouse is surrounded by spectacular flower gardens. The inn is filled with comforts such as down quilts, vases of fresh flowers and family antiques. The property is designated as a wildlife refuge and there is a cabin overlooking trout-filled Blue Lake. In the evening, guests enjoy soaking in the spa under star-studded skies, and in the morning dining on gourmet breakfasts.

Innkeeper(s): David & Shirley Alford.

Rates:$130-225. Gourmet Brkfst. Teas. 8 rooms. Fireplaces. Beds:KQT. Conference Rm. Phone, Refrig. in room. Farm. Golf. Tennis. Skiing. Spa. Swimming. Horseback riding. Fishing.

Seen in: *Colorado Home & Lifestyles, Durango Herald.*

Contact: Shirley Alford. Certificate may be used: Monday to Thursday, Nov. 1-May 1. Holiday weeks and weekends exlcuded.

"What a paradise you have created - we would love to return!!"

Empire

Mad Creek B&B

PO Box 404
Empire 80438
(303)569-2003

1881. This mountain town cottage has just the right combination of Victorian decor with its gingerbread trim on the facade, lace, flowers and antiques. Unique touches include door frames of old mineshaft wood, kerosene lamps, Eastlake antiques and complimentary cross-country ski gear and mountain bikes. Relax in front of the rock fireplace while watching a movie, peruse the library filled with local lore, or plan your next adventure with Colorado guides and maps. Empire, which was once a mining town, is conveniently located within 15 to 45 minutes of at least six major ski areas.

Innkeeper(s): Heather & Mike Lopez.

Rates:$49-69. MC VISA. Full Bkfst. Gourmet Brkfst. Teas. Evening snacks. 3 rooms. 2 with shared baths. Beds:Q. Bicycling. Skiing. Spa. Swimming. Fishing.

Contact: Heather Lopez. Certificate may be used: Weekday (Monday-Thursday), holidays excluded, December and March excluded, July and August excluded.

Georgetown

The Hardy House
605 Brownell St, Box 0156
Georgetown 80444
(303)569-3388

1880. With its late 19th-century charm, this red and white Victorian is nestled in a quaint mining town and is close to many major ski areas. In the summer you can tour historic Georgetown on the inn's bicycles, hike to the summits of nearby 14,000-foot-high peaks and picnic in alpine meadows or by mountain streams. Guests can relax by the pot-bellied stove or outdoors in the hot tub and when its time to bed down, sleep under feather comforters.

Rates:$73-77. MC VISA. Gourmet Brkfst. 4 rooms. Fireplaces. Beds:KQT. TV in room. Bicycling. Skiing. Spa. Fishing.

Contact: Michael Wagner Certificate may be used: 1994 and 1995 November - All dates except Thanksgiving Eve through Saturday of that week. Ruby room only. Also 1995 February except weekend preceeding Valentine's Day.

Grand Lake

Hummingbird B&B
132 Lakeview Dr
Grand Lake 80447
(303)627-3417

1992. This contemporary inn sits in a quaint mountain setting, close to Grand Lake, which is Colorado's largest natural lake. Wildlife is abundant in the area and you may view elk, deer and bighorn sheep most anytime of year. Shadow Mountain Lake and Lake Granby are nearby and all offer excellent water-sport activities. There are mountain bike and moped rentals in Grand Lake Village. The town is well known for its live theater performances.

Innkeeper(s): Dorothy & Leon Schnittker.

Rates:$60-65. MC VISA. Full Bkfst. Teas. Evening snacks. 3 rooms. Beds:KQDT. Golf. Tennis. Skiing. Swimming. Horseback riding. Fishing.

Contact: Dorothy Schnittker. Certificate may be used: May-October.

Green Mountain Falls

Outlook Lodge B&B
6975 Howard St, PO Box 5
Green Mountain Falls 80819
(719)684-2303

1889. Outlook Lodge was originally the parsonage for the historic Little Church in the Wildwood. Hand-carved balustrades surround a veranda that frames the alpine village view, and inside are many original parsonage furnishings. Iron bedsteads topped with patchwork quilts add warmth to the homey environment. This secluded mountain village is nestled at the foot of Pikes Peak.

Innkeeper(s): Patrick & Hayley Moran.

Rates:$45-70. MC VISA. Full Bkfst. 8 rooms. 2 with shared baths. Beds:Q. Conference Rm. Skiing. Swimming. Fishing.

Seen in: *Colorado Springs Gazette.*

Contact: Hayley Moran. Certificate may be used: Nov. 1 through March 31.

"Found by chance, will return with purpose."

Idaho Springs

St. Mary's Glacier B&B
336 Crest Drive
Idaho Springs 80452
(303)567-4084 Fax:(303)567-4084

1993. At an elevation of 10,500 feet, this inn claims to be the highest B&B in North America. Surrounded by snow-capped Continental Divide peaks, St. Mary's Glacier B&B is close to a cascading waterfall and crystalline mountain lakes. Each of the five distinctive suites is decorated in comfortable country charm with hand-sewn quilts and paintings by Colorado artist Pierre DeBernay. Two spacious suites feature king brass beds, whirlpool tubs and private decks with mountain views.

Innkeeper(s): Steve & Jackie Jacquin.

Rates:$75-125. MC VISA. Gourmet Brkfst, Lunch, Dinner. Evening snacks. 6 rooms. Beds:KQ. Conference Rm. Skiing. Spa. Fishing.

Contact: Stephen Jacquin. Certificate may be used: May 1-15, Dec. 1-15.

Lake City

The Cinnamon Inn B&B
426 Gunnison Ave, PO Box 533
Lake City 81235
(303)944-2641 (800)337-2335

1878. The kitchen of this country Victorian is a cozy gathering place full of antiques and curios. The bay window overlooks the backyard and affords a view of the San Juan Mountains. Guests can test their talent on a piano/harpsichord available in the Gathering Room. Many of the antiques found throughout the inn belonged to both innkeepers' grandparents or parents. Lake City is Colorado's largest Historical District and is filled with Victorian homes and 19th-century charm. A historical museum will take you back to the town's earlier days.

Rates:$59-95. MC VISA DS. Full Bkfst. Picnic lunches. Teas. 4 rooms. 2 with shared baths. Fireplaces. Beds:QD. TV in room. Skiing. Swimming. Fishing.

Contact: Gwendolyn Faber. Certificate may be used: October - December, 1994. January - May, 1995 and October - December, 1995.

Old Carson Inn
8401 County Rd 30, PO Box 144
Lake City 81235
(303)944-2511 (800)294-0608

1991. Located at an elevation of 9,400 feet, this massive log house provides a secluded mountain setting in a forest of aspens and spruce. The

Bonanza King Mine Room features a cathedral ceiling and soaring windows overlooking an aspen grove. American Indian artifacts and antiques are sprinkled throughout.

Innkeeper(s): Don & Judy Berry.

Rates:$60-95. MC VISA DS. Full Bkfst. AP available. Evening snacks. 7 rooms. Beds:KQ. Skiing. Spa. Fishing.

Seen in: *Rocky Mountain News, Country Inns.*

Contact: Judy Berry. Certificate may be used: October-May excluding holidays.

"Words are inadequate to express how very much we delighted in our stay at your beautiful home."

Leadville

The Apple Blossom Inn Victorian B&B
120 W 4th St
Leadville 80461
(719)486-2141 (800)982-9279

1879. Originally the home of Leadville banker Absalom Hunter, who lived here with his wife Estelle until 1918, the inn offers a glimpse into the good life of the late 19th century. Brass lights, beautiful crystal, fireplaces with Florentine tile, beveled mirrors, maple and mahogany inlaid floors, and stained-glass windows including one in a front window that gives The Apple Blossom Inn its name, are evidence to Hunter's prosperity. Innkeeper Maggie Senn invites guests to raid her cookie jar, which can include fresh brownies and chocolate chip cookies.

Innkeeper(s): Maggie Senn.

Rates:$59-79. MC VISA. Full Bkfst. MAP available. Picnic lunches. Evening snacks. 8 rooms. 5 with shared baths. Fireplaces. Beds:KQT. Refrig. in room. Skiing. Handicap access. Swimming. Fishing.

Contact: Margaret Senn. Certificate may be used: Sept. 20 - Nov. 20; April 1 - May 25.

The Leadville Country Inn
127 E Eighth St
Leadville 80461
(719)486-2354 (800)748-2354
Fax:(719)486-3886

1892. Built by a mining executive, this large Queen Anne Victorian boasts a shingled turret and a rounded porch. Upholstered walls, pull-chain toilets, an intricately carved fireplace mantel and a copper-lined wooded bathtub are some of the unique items found in the inn. The innkeepers can arrange a carriage or sleigh ride for guests.

Innkeeper(s): Sid & Judy Clemmer.

Rates:$52-127. MC VISA AX DC DS CB. Full Bkfst. Gourmet Brkfst, Lunch, Dinner. Picnic lunches. Teas. Evening snacks. 9 rooms. Beds:KQT. TV. Phone in room. Bicycling. Skiing. Handicap access. Spa. Swimming. Fishing.

Seen in: *Rocky Mountain News, The Herald Democrat.*

Contact: Sid Clemmer. Certificate may be used: Sunday through Friday, April and May. Sunday through Friday, October and November. Sunday through Thursday, December through March, holidays excluded.

"Everything was wonderful; the room, the romantic sleigh ride, dinner and most of all, the people."

Peri and Ed's Mountain Hideaway

201 W 8th St
Leadville 80461
(719)486-0716 (800)933-3715

1879. Families can picnic on the large lawn sprinkled with wildflowers under the soaring pines of
this former boarding house built during the boom
days of Leadville. Shoppers and history buffs can
enjoy exploring historic Main Street, one block
away. The surrounding mountains are a natural
playground offering a wide variety of activities, and
the innkeepers will be happy to let you know their
favorite spots and help with directions. The sunny
Augusta Tabor room features a sprawling king-size
bed with a warm view of the rugged peaks.

Innkeeper(s): Peri & Ed Solder.

Rates:$40-60. MC VISA AX DS. Full Bkfst. EP. 6 rooms. 3 with shared
baths. Beds:KQT. Skiing. Spa. Fishing.

Contact: Peri Solder. Certificate may be used: April 10 - June 15, Sept.
15 - Nov. 30.

Manitou Springs

Two Sisters Inn

10 Otoe Pl
Manitou Springs 80829
(719)685-9684

1919. Originally built by two sisters as the Sunburst
boarding house, the inn includes a honeymoon cottage in the back garden. The Victorian bed &
breakfast, nestled at the base of Pikes Peak, is one
block from the center of town and close to mineral
springs, art galleries, shops, restaurants, and the
beginning of the historic Manitou Springs Walking
Tour. The tour includes visiting 13 active springs,
which all have local lore. Guests come back to the
inn for the comradery with the innkeepers, who are
very active in their community and are willing to
share their part of the world.

Rates:$59-100. MC VISA DS. Gourmet Brkfst. 6 rooms. 2 with shared
baths. Fireplaces. Beds:D. Refrig. in room. Golf. Tennis. Skiing.
Swimming. Horseback riding. Fishing.

Seen in: *Rocky Mountain News, Gazette Telegraph, The Orlando
Sentinel.*

Contact: Sharon Smith. Certificate may be used: Nov. 15, 1994 through
April 15, 1995, Sunday through Thursday, excluding holidays and special events.

Minturn

Eagle River Inn

PO Box 100, 145 N Main St
Minturn 81645
(303)827-5761 (800)344-1750

1894. Earth red adobe walls, rambling riverside
decks, mature willow trees and brilliant flowers
enhance the secluded backyard of this
Southwestern-style inn. Inside, the lobby features
comfortable Santa Fe furniture, an authentic beehive fireplace and a ceiling of traditional latilas and
vegas. Baskets, rugs and weavings add warmth.
Guest rooms found on two floors have views of the
river or mountains. Minturn, which had its begin-
nings as a stop on the Rio Grande Railroad, is the
home of increasingly popular restaurants, shops and
galleries.

Innkeeper(s): Jane Leavitt.

Rates:$89-190. MC VISA AX. Full Bkfst. Evening snacks. 12 rooms.
Beds:KT. TV in room. Golf. Tennis. Bicycling. Skiing. Spa. Fishing.

Seen in: *Rocky Mountain News, Country Accents, Travel Holiday,
Resorts Magazine, Vail Valley Magazine.*

Contact: Jane Leavitt. Certificate may be used: Sunday-Thursday.

*"We love this place and have decided to make it a year-
ly tradition!"*

Pueblo

Abriendo Inn

300 W Abriendo Ave
Pueblo 81004
(719)544-2703 Fax:(719)542-6595

1906. This three-story, 7,000-square-foot
foursquare-style mansion is embellished with dentil
designs and wide porches supported by Ionic

columns. Elegantly paneled and carved oak walls
and woodwork provide a gracious setting for king-
size brass beds, antique armoires and Oriental rugs.
Breakfast specialties include raspberry muffins,
Italian strada and nut breads. Ask for the music
room with its own fireplace and bay window.

Innkeeper(s): Kerrelyn & Chuck Trent.

Rates:$54-89. MC VISA AX DC. Full Bkfst. Gourmet Brkfst. Evening snacks. 10 rooms. Beds:KQ. TV, Phone, AC in room. Swimming. Fishing.

Seen in: *Pueblo Chieftain, Rocky Mountain News.*

Contact: Kerrelyn M. Trent. Certificate may be used: Nov. 1 through March 31, all nights except Saturday.

"Thank you for warm hospitality, cozy environments and fine cuisine!"

Silverthorne

Mountain Vista B&B

PO Box 1398, 358 Lagoon Lane
Silverthorne 80498
(303)468-7700 (800)333-5165

1976. This modern mountain home makes a perfect base for the outdoor enthusiast. After a day of recreation, guests can relax by the fireplace or unwind in their rooms after slipping into robes provided for everyone. Located near the Dillon Reservoir, skiers will note that Keystone is nine miles, Arapahoe Basin 15 miles, Copper Mountain 11 miles, Breckenridge 13 miles and Vail 30 miles from the inn. During the summer, all that the magnificent Rocky Mountains have to offer is nearly at your doorstep. For bargain hunters, there are many factory outlet stores offering brand names within walking distance.

Innkeeper(s): Sandra Ruggaber.

Rates:$50-80. Full Bkfst. 3 rooms. 2 with shared baths. Beds:KQT. Skiing. Fishing.

Contact: Sandra Ruggaber. Certificate may be used: May through October.

Silverton

Grand Imperial Hotel

1219 Greene St
Silverton 81433
(303)387-5527 Fax:(303)387-5527

1882. This Victorian hotel, with its ornamental iron, three sets of wood-turned spiral staircases and dormer windows, is the oldest major structure in town. A large sun room on the third floor serves as a sitting room. Downstairs in the lounge, a full-service restaurant (meals extra) with antique back bar and stained-glass windows makes for a great gathering place. The Durango-Silverton narrow gauge train stops a short distance away and is the only train of its kind in existence. Downstairs are gift shops and art galleries.

Innkeeper(s): George & Nina Foster.

Rates:$30-150. MC VISA DS. AP available. Gourmet Dinner. Picnic lunches. Evening snacks. 40 rooms. Beds:KQT. Conference Rm. Skiing. Fishing.

Contact: George Foster II. Certificate may be used: Anytime other than July and August.

Smedleys B&B

1314 Greene St, PO Box 2
Silverton 81433
(303)387-5423 (800)342-4338
Fax:(303)387-5423

1979. Located above Smedleys Ice Cream Parlor and next door to The Pickle Barrel restaurant, this Victorian inn is ideal for families because of its three spacious one-bedroom suites, complete with living room, kitchen, private bath and color TV. Each suite has one queen and one sofa bed. Guests can really get the feel of this gold mining and railroad town by staying at the inn, which is within walking distance of many historic sites. Breakfast is served at The French Bakery restaurant.

Innkeeper(s): Fritz Klinke & Loren Lew.

Rates:$31-55. MC VISA AX DC DS CB. Full Bkfst. MAP available. 7 rooms. Beds:Q. TV, Refrig. in room. Skiing. Fishing.

Contact: Fritz Klinke. Certificate may be used: Anytime except July 15-Aug. 15.

Vail

Columbine Chalet B&B of Vail

PO Box 1407
Vail 81658
(303)476-1122 Fax:(303)476-8515

1980. The rooms at this Austrian-style chalet, located in the heart of famed Vail, are appropriately named the Sierra, Telluride and Matterhorn. An outdoor hot tub is a perfect place to soothe tired muscles after a day on bike trails or the ski slopes. It is located conveniently on Vail's free bus route. Afternoon snacks are served each day. Breakfast includes delicious treats such as waffles with strawberries and cream or breakfast burritos. Fruit, cereals and homemade breads or muffins also are served.

Innkeeper(s): Pat Funk.

Rates:$45-175. MC VISA. Full Bkfst. Picnic lunches. Teas. 3 rooms. Fireplaces. Beds:KQT. TV, Phone in room. Golf. Skiing. Spa. Swimming. Fishing.

Contact: Pat Funk. Certificate may be used: Spring-May-June 15-Sunday-Thursday nights. Fall-Oct. 1-Nov. 15-Sunday-Thursday nights. All other times: 24-hour advance reservations.

Winter Park

Alpen Rose B&B

244 Forest Trail, PO Box 769
Winter Park 80482
(303)726-5039 (800)531-1373

1960. The innkeepers of this European-style mountain B&B like to share their love of the mountains with guests. There is a superb view of the James and Perry Peaks from the large southern deck where you can witness spectacular sunrises and evening alpen glows. The view is enhanced by lofty pines, wildflowers and quaking aspens. Each of the bedrooms is decorated with treasures brought over from Austria, including traditional featherbeds for the queen-size beds. The town of Winter Park is a small, friendly community located 68 miles west of Denver.

Innkeeper(s): Robin & Rupert Sommerauer.

Rates:$65-95. MC VISA AX DS. Gourmet Brkfst. Teas. 5 rooms. Fireplaces. Beds:KQT. Skiing. Spa. Swimming. Fishing.

Contact: Robin Sommerauer. Certificate may be used: Weekdays, no holidays.

Woodland Park

Pikes Peak Paradise

PO Box 5760, 236 Pinecrest Rd
Woodland Park 80866
(719)687-6656 (800)728-8282
Fax:(719)687-9008

1988. This three-story Georgian Colonial with stately white columns rises unexpectedly from the wooded hills west of Colorado Springs. The entire south wall of the inn is made of glass to enhance its splendid views of Pikes Peak. A sliding glass door opens from each room onto a patio. Eggs Benedict and Belgian waffles are favorite breakfast dishes.

Innkeeper(s): Tim Stoddard, Martin Meier & Priscilla Arthur.

Rates:$85-150. MC VISA. Gourmet Brkfst. 5 rooms. Fireplaces. Beds:Q. Conference Rm. Refrig. in room. Skiing. Handicap access. Spa. Swimming. Fishing.

Seen in: *Rocky Mountain News*.

Contact: Tim Stoddard. Certificate may be used: Oct. 15 through May 15, Sunday-Thursday only.

Connecticut

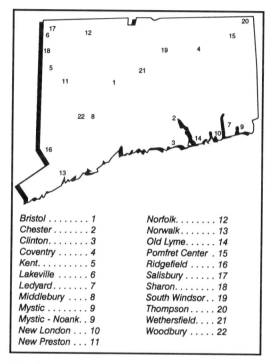

Bristol 1	Norfolk. 12
Chester 2	Norwalk. 13
Clinton. 3	Old Lyme. 14
Coventry 4	Pomfret Center . 15
Kent. 5	Ridgefield 16
Lakeville 6	Salisbury 17
Ledyard. 7	Sharon. 18
Middlebury 8	South Windsor. . 19
Mystic 9	Thompson 20
Mystic - Noank. . 9	Wethersfield. . . . 21
New London . . . 10	Woodbury 22
New Preston . . . 11	

Bristol

Chimney Crest Manor
5 Founders Dr
Bristol 06010
(203)582-4219

1930. This 32-room Tudor mansion possesses an unusual castle-like arcade and a 45-foot living room with a stone fireplace at each end. Many of the rooms are embellished with oak paneling and ornate plaster ceilings. The inn is located in the Federal Hill District, an area of large colonial homes.
Innkeeper(s): Dante & Cynthia Cimadamore.
Rates:$75-145. MC VISA AX. Full Bkfst. Teas. Evening snacks. 4 rooms. Beds:Q. Conference Rm. TV, Phone, AC, Refrig. in room. Skiing. Swimming. Fishing.

Seen in: *Record-Journal.*
Contact: Dante Cimadamore. Certificate may be used: November through March excluding holidays and murder mystery weekends.
"Great getaway - unbelievable structure. They are just not made like this mansion anymore."

Chester

The Inn at Chester
318 W Main St
Chester 06412
(203)526-4387 (800)949-7829
Fax:(203)526-4387

1776. More than 200 years ago, Jeremiah Parmelee built a clapboard farmhouse along a winding road named the Killingworth Turnpike. The Parmelee Homestead stands as a reflection of the past and is an inspiration for the Inn at Chester. Each of the rooms is individually appointed with Eldred Wheeler Reproductions. The Lincoln Suite has a sitting room with a fireplace. Enjoy lively conversation or live music while imbibing your favorite drink at the inn's tavern, Duck's Landing. Outside Duck's Landing a 30-foot fireplace soars into the rafters.
Innkeeper(s): Deborah Moore.
Rates:$85-205. MC VISA AX. ContPlus Bkfst. EP. Gourmet Dinner. Picnic lunches. 43 rooms. Beds:KQT. Conference Rm. Phone, AC in room. Tennis. Bicycling. Skiing. Sauna. Exercise room. Fishing.
Contact: Deborah Moore. Certificate may be used: Sunday - Friday, except holidays.

Clinton

Captain Dibbell House
21 Commerce St
Clinton 06413
(203)669-1646

1866. Built by a sea captain, this graceful Victorian house is only two blocks from the harbor where innkeeper Ellis Adams used to sail his own vessel.

A ledger of household accounts dating from the 1800s is on display, and there are fresh flowers in each guest room.

Innkeeper(s): Helen & Ellis Adams.

Rates:$60-85. MC VISA AX DS. Full Bkfst. Evening snacks. 4 rooms. Beds:KQT. AC in room. Tennis. Bicycling. Skiing. Swimming. Fishing.

Seen in: *Clinton Recorder, New Haven Register.*

Contact: Helen Adams. Certificate may be used: Sunday-Thursday, holidays excluded.

"This was our first experience with B&Bs and frankly, we didn't know what to expect. It was GREAT!"

Coventry

Maple Hill Farm B&B
365 Goose Ln
Coventry 06238
(203)742-0635 (800)742-0635

1731. This historic farmhouse still possesses its original kitchen cupboards and a flour bin used for generations. Family heirlooms and the history of the former home owners are shared with guests. There is a three-seat outhouse behind the inn. Visitors, of course, are provided with modern plumbing, as well as a screened porch and greenhouse in which to relax.

Innkeeper(s): Tony Felice/Mary Beth Gorke-Felice.

Rates:$60-75. MC VISA. Full Bkfst. 4 rooms. 3 with shared baths. Beds:DT. Farm. Golf. Bicycling. Spa. Exercise room. Swimming. Horseback riding. Stables. Fishing.

Seen in: *Journal Inquirer, Coventry Journal.*

Contact: Anthony Felice. Certificate may be used: Sunday through Thursday nights year around. Weekends in January, February, March, April, December except holidays and Valentine's Day.

"Comfortable rooms and delightful country ambiance."

Kent

Mavis' B&B
230 Kent Cornwall Rd
Kent 06757
(203)927-4334

1860. The living room of this Greek Revival home affords seasonal views of pastureland with sheep. Guests are pampered with luxurious towels (plenty of them), fresh flowers, late sleeping if desired, flexible check-in and check-out times and fancy tote with cookies and fruit for daily adventures. Walking is a pleasure on the two-acre property with a babbling brook. An antique shop is on premises and nearby, one can visit the Audubon Center, attend a music festival, galleries and wineries. Breakfasts are served with fine china, early pressed glassware and fine linens.

Innkeeper(s): Mavis & Don Scholl.

Rates:$85-95. MC VISA. ContPlus Bkfst. Teas. Evening snacks. 3 rooms. Beds:KQT. TV, Phone, Refrig. in room. Skiing. Fishing.

Contact: Donald and Mavis Scholl. Certificate may be used: Year round.

Lakeville

Wake Robin Inn
Rt 41 Sharon Rd
Lakeville 06039
(203)435-2515

1898. Once the Taconic School for Girls, this inn is located on 15 acres of landscaped grounds in the Connecticut Berkshires. A library has been added as well as antique furnishings. The recently renovated property also includes a few private cottages. An award-winning restaurant is on premises.

Innkeeper(s): H.J.P. Manassero.

Rates:$95-145. MC VISA AX DS. ContPlus Bkfst. Gourmet Dinner. Picnic lunches. Teas. 42 rooms. 2 with shared baths. Fireplaces. Beds:KQT. Conference Rm. TV, Phone, AC, Refrig. in room. Golf. Tennis. Bicycling. Skiing. Swimming. Horseback riding. Stables. Fishing.

Seen in: *Town & Country Magazine, Connecticut Magazine.*

Contact: Henri Manassero. Certificate may be used: Sunday through Thursday.

"A new sophistication has arrived in Lakeville, Conn. with the restoration of the Wake Robin Inn."

Ledyard

Applewood Farms Inn

528 Col Ledyard Hwy
Ledyard 06339
(203)536-2022 Fax:(203)536-4019

1826. Five generations of the Gallup family worked this farm near Mystic. The classic center-chimney Colonial, furnished with antiques and early-American pieces, is situated on 33 acres of fields and meadows. Stone fences meander through the property and many of the original outbuildings remain. It is in the National Register, cited as one of the best surviving examples of a 19th-century farm in Connecticut.

Innkeeper(s): Frankie & Tom Betz.

Rates:$115-125. MC VISA. Full Bkfst. 6 rooms. Fireplaces. Beds:KD. AC in room. Farm. Golf. Tennis. Skiing. Swimming. Fishing.

Seen in: *Country, New Woman.*

Contact: Frances Betz. Certificate may be used: Anytime upon availability, excluding holidays and holiday weekends, also excluding the months of August through Oct. 31.

"This bed & breakfast is a real discovery."

Middlebury

Tucker Hill Inn

96 Tucker Hill Rd
Middlebury 06762
(203)758-8334 Fax:(203)598-0652

1923. There's a cut-out heart in the gate that opens to this handsome three-story estate framed by an old stone wall. The spacious Colonial-style house is shaded by tall trees. Guests enjoy a parlor with fireplace and an inviting formal dining room. Guest rooms are furnished with a flourish of English country or romantic Victorian decor.

Innkeeper(s): Susan & Richard Cebelenski.

Rates:$60-100. MC VISA AX. Full Bkfst. Teas. 4 rooms. 2 with shared baths. Beds:KQT. Golf. Tennis. Skiing. Swimming. Horseback riding. Fishing.

Seen in: *Star, Waterbury American Republican.*

Contact: Susan Cebelenski. Certificate may be used: November-April.

"Thanks for a special visit. Your kindness never went unnoticed."

Mystic

The Whaler's Inn

20 E Main St
Mystic 06355
(203)536-1506 (800)243-2588
Fax:(203)572-1250

1901. This classical revival-style inn is built on the historical site of the Hoxie House, the Clinton House and the U.S. Hotel. Just as these famous 19th-century inns offered, the Whaler's Inn has the same charm and convenience for today's visitor to Mystic. Once a booming ship-building center, the town's connection to the sea is ongoing and the sailing schooners still pass beneath the Bascule Drawbridge in the center of town. The inn has indoor and outdoor dining available and more than 75 shops and restaurants are within walking distance.

Innkeeper(s): Dick Prisby.

Rates:$65-95. MC VISA AX. Cont. Bkfst. EP. 41 rooms. Beds:KQ. Conference Rm. TV, Phone, AC in room. Golf. Tennis. Swimming. Fishing.

Contact: Richard Prisby. Certificate may be used: Nov. 1, 1994 through April 1, 1995.

Mystic - Noank

Palmer Inn

25 Church St
Mystic - Noank 06340
(203)572-9000

1907. This gracious seaside mansion was built for shipbuilder Robert Palmer Jr. by shipyard craftsmen. It features a two-story grand columned

entrance, mahogany beams, mahogany staircase, quarter-sawn oak floors, and 14-foot ceilings. The

Lincrusta wallcovering, original light fixtures, and nine stained-glass windows remain.

Innkeeper(s): Patricia White.

Rates:$115-195. MC VISA AX. ContPlus Bkfst. EP. Teas. 6 rooms. Fireplaces. Beds:KQDT. Conference Rm. Tennis. Swimming. Fishing.

Seen in: *Boston Globe, Yankee, Norwalk Hour.*

Contact: Patricia Ann White. Certificate may be used: Sunday through Thursday, November through June excluding holidays.

"Tops for luxury." Water Escapes, by Whittemann & Webster.

New London

Queen Anne Inn & Antique Gallery
265 Williams St
New London 06320
(203)447-2600 (800)347-8818

1903. Several photographers for historic house books have been attracted to the classic good looks of the recently renovated and freshly painted Queen Anne Inn. The traditional tower, wrap-

around verandas, and elaborate frieze invite the traveler to explore the interior with its richly polished oak walls and intricately carved alcoves. Double stained-glass windows curve around the circular staircase landing. Period furnishings include brass beds and many rooms have their own fireplace. Afternoon tea is served.

Innkeeper(s): Tracey & Jim Cook.

Rates:$70-155. MC VISA AX DC DS. Full Bkfst. Teas. 10 rooms. 2 with shared baths. Fireplaces. Beds:KQT. Conference Rm. TV, Phone, AC, Refrig. in room. Spa. Fishing.

Seen in: *New London Day Features, New York Times.*

Contact: Tracey Rose Cook. Certificate may be used: November through May 1 excluding New Year's and Valentine's weekend as well as the first two weeks of January.

"Absolutely terrific - relaxing, warm, gracious - beautiful rooms and delectable food."

New Preston

Boulders Inn
East Shore Rd, Rt 45
New Preston 06777
(203)868-0541 Fax:(203)868-1925

1895. Outstanding views of Lake Waramaug and its wooded shores can be seen from the living room and many of the guest rooms and cottages of this country inn. The terrace is open in the summer for cocktails, dinner and sunsets over the lake. Antique furnishings, a basement game room, a beach house with a hanging wicker swing and a tennis court are all part of Boulders Inn.

Innkeeper(s): Kees & Ulla Adema.

Rates:$125-285. MC VISA AX. Full Bkfst. EP. MAP available. Gourmet Dinner. Teas. 17 rooms. Fireplaces. Beds:KQT. Conference Rm. Phone, AC, Refrig. in room. Tennis. Bicycling. Skiing. Handicap access. Swimming. Fishing.

Seen in: *The New York Times, Travel & Leisure, Country Inns.*

Contact: Stacy McBreairty. Certificate may be used: Midweek Nov. 1-May 1.

"Thank you for a welcome respite from the daily hurly-burly."

The Inn on Lake Waramaug
107 North Shore Rd
New Preston 06777
(203)868-0563 Fax:(203)868-9173

1795. Set on a hill overlooking Lake Waramaug, with acres of spacious lawns and towering sugar maples, this Colonial inn is well known for its guest rooms and cuisine. An indoor pool and sauna provide respite in winter while a private beach awaits in summer. Host John Koiter has been a white-water rafting guide and a member of the ski patrol.

Innkeeper(s): Nancy Conant.

Rates:$154-229. MC VISA AX. Full Bkfst. 23 rooms. Fireplaces. Beds:QT. Conference Rm. TV, Phone, AC in room. Tennis. Bicycling. Skiing. Sauna. Swimming. Fishing.

Seen in: *Washington Journal, Business Weekly, Record Journal.*

Contact: Nancy Conant. Certificate may be used: Sunday through Thursday, November through May.

"Guests, innkeepers and a pony all give the Inn on Lake Waramaug the kind of country inn character that most inns can only hope for." New England Get Aways.

Norfolk

Manor House
69 Maple Ave, PO Box 447
Norfolk 06058
(203)542-5690 Fax:(203)542-5690

1898. Charles Spofford, designer of London's subway, built this home with many gables, exquisite cherry paneling, and grand staircase. There are Moorish arches and Tiffany windows. Guests can enjoy hot-mulled cider after a sleigh ride, hay ride, or horse and carriage drive along the country lanes nearby. The inn was named by *Discerning Traveler* as Connecticut's most romantic hideaway.

Innkeeper(s): Hank & Diane Tremblay.

Rates:$95-160. MC VISA AX. Full Bkfst. Gourmet Brkfst. Evening snacks. 8 rooms. Fireplaces. Beds:KQT. Conference Rm. Golf. Tennis. Bicycling. Skiing. Swimming. Horseback riding. Fishing.

Seen in: *Boston Globe, Philadelphia Inquirer, Innsider Magazine, Rhode Island Monthly.*

Contact: Diane Tremblay. Certificate may be used: Sunday through Thursday excluding holidays.

"Queen Victoria, eat your heart out."

Weaver's House
58 Greenwoods Rd W
Norfolk 06058
(203)542-5108

1898. Easily found on the main street of the village, this inn overlooks the Yale-in-Norfolk estate and is a short walk from a library from the

Victorian period, the historical society, an antique store and a pub/restaurant. A fire in the wood-and-coal stove makes the sitting room cheerful in cool weather. The Yale Music Shed and Art Barn make summer evenings memorable.

Innkeeper(s): Arnold Tsukroff.

Rates:$45-58. MC VISA AX. Full Bkfst. 4 rooms. 4 with shared baths. Fireplaces. Beds:QT. Conference Rm. Skiing. Fishing.

Contact: Arnold Tsukroff. Certificate may be used: Nov. 1, 1994 through May 15, 1995.

Norwalk

Silvermine Tavern
194 Perry Ave
Norwalk 06850
(203)847-4558 Fax:(203)847-9171

1770. The Silvermine consists of the Old Mill, the Country Store, the Coach House, and the Tavern itself. Primitive paintings and furnishings, as well as family heirlooms, decorate the inn. Guest rooms and dining rooms overlook the Old Mill, the waterfall, and swans gliding across the millpond.

Innkeeper(s): Frank & Marsha Whitman, Jr.

Rates:$80-99. MC VISA AX DC. ContPlus Bkfst. Gourmet Lunch, Dinner. 10 rooms. Beds:DT. Conference Rm. Swimming. Fishing.

Seen in: *Advocate, Greenwich Time.*

Contact: Frank Whitman, Sr. Certificate may be used: No Friday arrival, no October usage.

Old Lyme

Bee and Thistle Inn
100 Lyme St
Old Lyme 06371
(203)434-1667 (800)622-4946
Fax:(203)434-3402

1756. This stately inn is situated along the banks of the Lieutenant River. There are five and one half acres of trees, lawns and a sunken English garden. The inn is furnished with Chippendale antiques and reproductions. A harpist plays in the parlor on Friday and Saturday evenings. Bee and Thistle was recently voted the most romantic inn in the state, as well as the most romantic dinner spot by readers of *Connecticut Magazine.*

Innkeeper(s): Bob & Penny Nelson.

Rates:$79-195. MC VISA AX DC. Full Bkfst. EP. Gourmet Brkfst, Lunch, Dinner. Teas. 12 rooms. 2 with shared baths. Beds:KQT. Phone, AC in room.

Seen in: *Countryside, Country Living, Money Magazine, New York.*

Contact: Robert Nelson. Certificate may be used: Sunday through Thursday excluding holidays.

Pomfret Center

Clark Cottage at Wintergreen
354 Pomfret St, Rt 44 & 169
Pomfret Center 06259
(203)928-5741 Fax:(203)928-1591

1890. Built for a landscape designer with seven children, this Victorian estate includes more than seven acres of flower and vegetable gardens and 100-year-old towering trees. Innkeeper Doris Geary can help you with your itinerary, which should include a visit to Sturbridge Village. The Williamsburg-like town, a 30-minute drive away, is steeped in Colonial lifestyle with authentic homes and traditional cooking. Doris will prepare breakfast to order if given the request the night before.
Innkeeper(s): Doris & Stanton Geary.

Rates:$60-75. MC VISA. Gourmet Brkfst. 5 rooms. 1 with shared bath. Fireplaces. Beds:QT. TV, Phone, AC in room. Bicycling. Skiing. Fishing.

Contact: Doris & Stanton Geary. Certificate may be used: Winter-January through April.

Ridgefield

West Lane Inn
22 West Ln
Ridgefield 06877
(203)438-7323 Fax:(203)438-7325

1849. This National Register Victorian mansion on two acres features an enormous front veranda filled with white bamboo chairs and tables overlooking a manicured lawn. A polished oak staircase rises to a third-floor landing and lounge. Chandeliers, wall sconces and floral wallpapers help to establish an intimate atmosphere. Although the rooms do not have antiques, they feature amenities such as heated towel racks, extra-thick towels, air conditioning and desks. The inn holds a AAA four-diamond award.
Innkeeper(s): Maureen Mayer.

Rates:$100-145. MC VISA AX DC CB. Cont. Bkfst. Evening snacks. 20 rooms. Fireplaces. Beds:Q. Phone, AC, Refrig. in room. Golf. Tennis. Bicycling. Swimming. Fishing.

Seen in: *Stanford-Advocate, Greenwich Times, Home & Away Connecticut.*

Contact: Maureen Mayer. Certificate may be used: Nov. 30 through April 30, Sunday through Thursday, excluding holidays.

"Thank you for the hospitality you showed us. The rooms are comfortable and quiet. I haven't slept this soundly in weeks."

Salisbury

Under Mountain Inn
482 Undermountain Rd
Salisbury 06068
(203)435-0242 Fax:(203)435-2379

1732. Situated on three acres, this was originally the home of iron magnate Jonathan Scoville. A thorned locust tree, believed to be the oldest in Connecticut, shades the inn. Paneling that now adorns the pub was discovered hidden between the ceiling and attic floorboards. The boards were probably placed there in violation of a Colonial law requiring all wide lumber to be given to the king of England. British-born Peter Higginson was happy to reclaim it in the name of the Crown.
Innkeeper(s): Peter & Marged Higginson.

Rates:$150-190. Full Bkfst. MAP available. Gourmet Dinner. Teas. 7 rooms. Beds:KQT. Skiing. Swimming. Fishing.

Seen in: *Travel & Leisure, Country Inns Magazine, Yankee, New England GetAways.*

Contact: Marged K. Higginson Certificate may be used: November thorugh April, Sunday through Thursday except during holidays.

"You're terrific!"

Sharon

1890 Colonial B&B
Rt 41, PO Box 25
Sharon 06069
(203)364-0436

1891. Summertime guests can find a cool place to sit on the screened porch of this center-hall Colonial home situated on five park-like acres. Guests visiting in the winter can warm up to any of the main floor fireplaces in the living room, dining room and den. Guest rooms are spacious and have high ceilings. A furnished apartment also is available with private entrance and kitchenette at special weekly rates.
Innkeeper(s): Carole "Kelly" Tangen.

Rates:$95-107. Full Bkfst. 5 rooms. Beds:QT. TV, Refrig. in room. Skiing. Swimming. Fishing.

Contact: Carole Tangen. Certificate may be used: Midweek, May 1 - Nov. 1, no holidays. Nov. 1 to May 1 anytime, no holidays.

South Windsor

Cumon Inn
130 Buckland Rd
South Windsor 06074
(203)644-8486 (800)286-6646
Fax:(203)644-0753

1970. This salt-box Colonial sits on 20 acres of a working farm and has a 100-mile view stretching from Mt. Tom to Connecticut River Valley. The inn features a sun room with hot tub, seedless grape arbor, gazebo, orchard, berry patch, pine grove and 1,000 white birch trees. There are sleigh rides and hay rides. Innkeeper Bill Krawski is more than happy to share farm chores with willing guests. If you weed the garden, you can raid the garden. Three cabins are surrounded by pine trees and next to a swimming hole.

Innkeeper(s): Bill Krawski.

Rates:$50-100. MC VISA. ContPlus Bkfst. Picnic lunches. Evening snacks. 8 rooms. 8 with shared baths. Beds:D. Farm. Bicycling. Skiing. Swimming.

Contact: Bill Krawski. Certificate may be used: Weekdays.

Thompson

Hickory Ridge Lakefront B&B
1084 Quaddick Town Farm Rd
Thompson 06277-2929
(203)928-9530

1990. Enjoy three wooded acres in the private rural setting of this spacious post-and-beam home. The

inn's property includes a chunk of the Quaddick Lake shoreline and canoes are available for guests. There's plenty of hiking to do with 17 private acres and access to miles of state lands. Quaddick State Park is within walking or bicycling distance. Breakfasts of baked goods and entrees are served at your convenience.

Innkeeper(s): Kenneth & Birdie Olson.

Rates:$65-75. Gourmet Brkfst. Picnic lunches. 3 rooms. 2 with shared baths. Beds:QT. Bicycling. Skiing. Handicap access. Swimming. Fishing.

Contact: Birdie Olson. Certificate may be used: Nov. - March including weekends. Other dates due to availability. Sunday - Thursday.

Wethersfield

Chester Bulkley House B&B
184 Main St
Wethersfield 06109
(203)563-4236

1830. Wide pine floors, hand-carved woodwork, working fireplaces and period pieces enhance the ambiance of this Greek Revival structure. Nestled in the historic village of Old Wethersfield and minutes from downtown Hartford, the inn offers a uniquely comfortable haven for business and holiday travelers. While visiting Hartford, guests may want to take in a performance of the opera, the symphony, the ballet or a Broadway show. Wethersfield is perfect for browsing the variety of quaint shops and touring historic homes and museums.

Innkeeper(s): Frank & Sophia Bottaro.

Rates:$55-85. MC VISA AX. Full Bkfst. 5 rooms. 2 with shared baths. Fireplaces. Beds:KQT. TV, Phone, AC in room. Bicycling.

Contact: Frank Bottaro. Certificate may be used: Jan. 2 - April 30; May 1 - Aug. 31; Monday - Thursday.

Woodbury

Merryvale B&B
1204 Main St South
Woodbury 06798
(203)266-0800

1789. Found in a town that has a reputation as the Antiques Capital of Connecticut, this B&B is a simple yet rambling Colonial. Guests can enjoy complimentary tea, coffee and biscuits throughout the day. A grand living room invites travelers to relax by the fireplace and enjoy a book from the extensive collection of classics and mysteries. Woodbury's charm, pride and determination to hold on to its way of life has been well publicized and many believe that this is where New England truly began.

Innkeeper(s): Gary & Pat Ubaldi Nurnberger.

Rates:$65-125. MC VISA AX. Full Bkfst. Gourmet Brkfst. Evening snacks. 4 rooms. Beds:KQT. AC in room. Skiing. Fishing.

Contact: Pat Ubaldi Nurnberger. Certificate may be used: Jan. 10 to March 31.

Delaware

Lewes

New Devon Inn

142 Second St
Lewes 19958
(302)645-6466
(800)824-8754
Fax:(302)645-7196

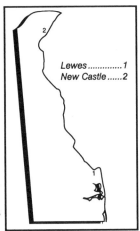

Lewes.............1
New Castle......2

1928. In the heart of
the historic district,
this inn boasts 24 indi-
vidually decorated
guest rooms. All rooms
feature antique beds
and turndown service.
The inn, which prefers guests over the age of 16,
also offers conference facilities, catering and convenient access to antiquing, beaches, dining and
sightseeing. Two suites also are available. The
shore is just a half-mile from the inn. Prime Hook
National Wildlife Refuge and Cape Henlopen State
Park are nearby.

Innkeeper(s): Barbara Lloyd, D. Dale Jenkins & Bernie Wash.

Rates:$60-105. MC VISA AX DC DS. Full Bkfst. Teas. Evening snacks.
26 rooms. Beds:QT. Conference Rm. Phone, AC in room. Golf. Tennis.
Handicap access. Swimming. Fishing.

Seen in: New York Times, Mid-Atlantic Country, National Geographic,
Entertainment Magazine.

Contact: Barbara A. Lloyd. Certificate may be used: Sept. 6, 1994 -
May 25, 1995.

Wild Swan Inn

525 Kings Hwy
Lewes 19958
(302)645-8550 Fax:(302)645-8550

1910. Lewes is a jewel among Delaware's coastal
towns. Home of the river pilots, who each year
shepherd hundreds of cargo ships up the Delaware
Bay, the town has a long and vital association with
the seas. Wild Swan is within walking distance of
downtown where several fine restaurants await you.
Museums, old churches, homes and plenty of history will satisfy your appetite to learn
more about the unique heritage of
Lewes. The surrounding
seascape and countryside are
ideal for cycling, running
and walking.

Innkeeper(s): Hope & Michael Tyler

Rates:$75-105. Full Bkfst. Gourmet
Brkfst. Evening snacks. 3 rooms.

Beds:Q. AC, Refrig. in room. Bicycling. Swimming. Fishing.

Contact: Michael Tyler. Certificate may be used: Sunday through
Thursday evenings from Oct. 1 to May 1, excluding holidays.

New Castle

The Jefferson House B&B

5 The Strand at the Wharf
New Castle 19720
(302)325-1025

1826. Overlooking the Strand and the Delaware
River, The Jefferson House served as a hotel, a
rooming house and a shipping-company office during Colonial times. On the side lawn is a "William
Penn landed here" sign. The inn features heavy
paneled doors, black marble mantels over the fireplaces and a fanlight on the third floor. There is
private access to the river, and a spa beckons guests
after a long day of sightseeing. Cobblestone streets
add to the quaintness of the first capital city of the
colonies.

Innkeeper(s): Martha Rispoli.

Rates:$54-85. MC VISA. Cont. Bkfst. 4 rooms. Fireplaces. Beds:D. TV,
AC, Refrig. in room. Golf. Tennis. Bicycling. Spa. Fishing.

Seen in: Roll Call.

Contact: Melvin Rosenthal. Certificate may be used: Monday through
Thursday nights excluding holidays or special events.

*"I loved sleeping on an old brass bed, in a room filled
with antiques and charm, just feet from where William
Penn landed in New Castle."*

Florida

Amelia Island

Elizabeth Point Lodge
98 S Fletcher Ave
Amelia Island 32034
(904)277-4851 (800)772-3359
Fax:(904)277-6500

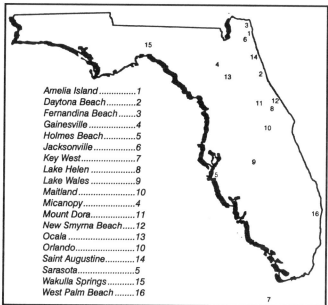

1992. Situated directly on the ocean, this newly constructed inn is in an 1890s Nantucket shingle-style design. Guest rooms feature king-size beds and oversized tubs. Two rooms have private whirlpools. Lemonade is served on the porch, which is filled with rockers for viewing the sea and its treasures of pelicans, dolphins and sea birds. Touring bikes, beach equipment and airport pickup are available.

Innkeeper(s): David & Susan Caples.

Rates:$95-150. MC VISA AX. Full Bkfst. EP. Gourmet Lunch. 25 rooms. Beds:KQT. Conference Rm. TV, Phone, AC in room. Golf. Tennis. Handicap access. Swimming. Horseback riding. Fishing.

Seen in: *Fernandina Beach News Leader.*

Contact: David Caples. Certificate may be used: January/February, 1995.

"The innkeeper's labor of love is evident in every detail."

The Fairbanks House
227 S Seventh St
Amelia Island 32034
(904)277-0500 (800)261-4838
Fax:(904)277-3103

1885. The living and dining room fireplace tiles of this Italianate-style mansion bring to life scenes from Shakespeare's works and "Aesop's Fables." Other features include polished hardwood floors, intricately carved moldings and eight other fireplaces that grace spacious rooms. Each of the guest rooms is furnished with a four-poster or canopied king, queen or twin beds, Jacuzzi and clawfoot tubs or showers. Guests can step outside to enjoy an inviting courtyard, swimming pool and gardens bursting with roses, palms and magnolias.

Innkeeper(s): Nelson & Mary Smelker.

Rates:$85-150. MC VISA AX DS. ContPlus Bkfst. Picnic lunches. 14 rooms. Beds:KQT. Conference Rm. TV, Phone, AC in room. Handicap access. Swimming. Fishing.

Contact: Nelson Smelker. Certificate may be used: Weekdays (Sunday - Thursday) Oct. 1, 1994 - March 15, 1995 and Oct. 1 to Dec. 31, 1995 excluding holidays. Reservations required.

Florida House Inn
22 S 3rd St, PO Box 688
Amelia Island 32034
(904)261-3300 (800)258-3301
Fax:(904)277-3831

1857. Located in the heart of a 50-block historic National Register area, the Florida House Inn is thought to be the oldest continuously operating tourist hotel in Florida. Recently renovated, the inn features a small pub, a guest parlor, a library and a New Orleans-style courtyard in which guests may enjoy the shade of 200-year-old oaks. Rooms are decorated with country pine and oak antiques, cheerful handmade rugs and quilts. The Carnegies and Rockefellers have been guests.

Innkeeper(s): Bob & Karen Warner.

Rates:$65-125. MC VISA AX DC CB. Full Bkfst. Picnic lunches. Teas. 10 rooms. Fireplaces. Beds:KQT. Conference Rm. TV, Phone, AC in room. Tennis. Handicap access. Spa. Swimming. Fishing.

Seen in: *Amelia Now, Tampa Tribune, Miami Herald, Toronto Star, Country Living, Ft. Lauderdale Sun Sentinel.*

Contact: Bob Warner. Certificate may be used: Sunday - Thursday.

Daytona Beach

Coquina Inn B&B
544 S Palmetto Ave
Daytona Beach 32114
(904)254-4969 (800)727-0678

1912. Located in the Daytona Beach Historic District, this handsome house boasts an exterior of coquina rock, blended from shells, arched windows,

and a picket porch on the second floor. The Jasmine Room is accentuated with a seven-foot canopy bed draped in floral fabric. French leather chairs, a fireplace and a Victorian tub are featured. A champagne package includes breakfast in bed, a fruit basket and fresh flowers. Lavish picnic lunches are available as well.

Innkeeper(s): Jerry & Susan Jerzykowski.

Rates:$75-150. MC VISA. Gourmet Brkfst, Dinner. Picnic lunches. 4 rooms. Fireplaces. Beds:QD. AC in room. Golf. Tennis. Bicycling. Skiing. Spa. Swimming. Fishing.

Seen in: *Florida Sports.*

Contact: Susan Jerzykowski. Certificate may be used: Sunday - Thursday or last minute for weekends excluding special events and holidays.

Fernandina Beach

The Taber House
PO Box 734, 15 N 4th St
Fernandina Beach 32035
(904)261-6391

1957. This inn offers three cottages, all authentic replicas of Victorian architecture, complete with gingerbread woodwork. Fernandina Beach, in Florida's very Northeast corner, boasts a charming historic district, of which the inn's cottages are at the geographic center. The innkeepers, veteran world travelers, have furnished each cottage with just the right touches, and each features one king or two queen beds, 27-inch cable TV with remote, phones, private entry and porch. Other thoughtful amenities are available, making this an ideal stop for those seeking a bit more privacy and pampering as they explore the historic area.

Innkeeper(s): Frances & Bo Taber.

Rates:$75-130. ContPlus Bkfst. 3 rooms. Beds:Q. TV, Phone, AC in room. Swimming. Fishing.

Contact: Frances Taber. Certificate may be used: Anytime.

Gainesville

Magnolia Plantation
309 SE Seventh St
Gainesville 32601
(904)375-6653

1885. This restored French Second Empire Victorian is in the National Register. Magnolia trees surround the house. Six guest rooms are filled with family heirlooms. All bathrooms feature clawfoot tubs and candles. Guests may enjoy the gardens, reflecting pool with waterfalls, and gazebo. Bicycles are also available. Evening wine and snacks are included. The inn is two miles from the University of Florida.

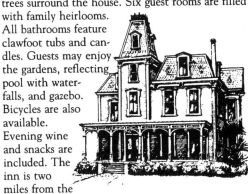

Innkeeper(s): Joe & Cindy Montalto.

Rates:$60-90. MC VISA AX. Full Bkfst. AP available. Evening snacks. 6 rooms. 2 with shared baths. Fireplaces. Beds:Q. AC in room. Bicycling. Swimming. Fishing.

Contact: Cindy Montalto. Certificate may be used: Sunday-Thursday, June, July, August.

"This has been a charming, once-in-a-lifetime experience."

Holmes Beach

Harrington House B&B
5626 Gulf Dr
Holmes Beach 34217
(813)778-5444

1925. A mere 40 feet from the water, this gracious home is set among pine trees and palms. Constructed in 1925 of 14-inch-thick coquina blocks, the house features a living room with a 20-

foot-high beamed ceiling, fireplace, '20s wallpaper and French doors. Many of the guest rooms have four-poster beds, antique wicker furnishings and French doors opening onto a deck overlooking the swimming pool and Gulf of Mexico. Kayaks are available for dolphin watching.

Innkeeper(s): Jo Adele & Frank Davis.

Rates:$79-159. MC VISA AX. Full Bkfst. Gourmet Brkfst. 13 rooms. Beds:KQT. TV, Phone, AC, Refrig. in room. Tennis. Bicycling. Handicap access. Spa. Swimming. Fishing.

Seen in: *Sarasota Herald Tribune, Island Sun, Islander Press, Westcoast Woman, Palm Beach Post, Tampa Tribune, Glamour Magazine, Atlantic Monthly Magazine.*

Contact: Frank Davis. Certificate may be used: May 1-Dec. 15, Sunday-Thursday, holidays excluded.

"Elegant house and hospitality."

Jacksonville

House on Cherry St
1844 Cherry St
Jacksonville 32205
(904)384-1999 Fax:(904)981-2998

1909. Seasonal blooms fill the pots that line the circular entry stairs to this Federal-style house on tree-lined Cherry Street. It was moved in two pieces to its present site on St. Johns River in the historic Riverside area. Traditionally decorated rooms include antiques, collections of hand-carved decoy ducks and old clocks that chime and tick. Most rooms overlook the river. Your hosts are a social worker and family doctor.

Innkeeper(s): Carol Anderson.

Rates:$75-90. MC VISA. Full Bkfst. Gourmet Brkfst. Evening snacks. 4 rooms. Beds:QT. Phone, AC in room. Golf. Tennis. Bicycling. Fishing.

Seen in: *Florida Wayfarer, Tampa Tribune, New York Times.*

Contact: Carol Anderson. Certificate may be used: June - September.

Key West

Eden House
1015 Fleming St
Key West 33040
(305)296-6868 (800)533-5397
Fax:(305)294-1221

1924. This charming art deco hotel was once a hot spot for writers, intellectuals and European travelers. Innkeeper Mike Eden improved the home,

adding a 10-person Jacuzzi, decks and gazebos. Ceiling fans and wicker furniture complete the tropical atmosphere found in each room. The home was the site for the Goldie Hawn movie, "Criss Cross." Next door Rich's Cafe boasts delicious cuisine by chef and owner Martin Busam. Breakfast is not included in the room price, but the restaurant offers gourmet entrees such as Shrimp Eggs Benedict and cinnamon coffee. For lunch and dinner, enjoy the German-style cuisine.

Innkeeper(s): Stephen & Joann Clement.

Rates:$55-275. MC VISA. EP. 40 rooms. 18 with shared baths. Beds:QT. Conference Rm. Phone, AC in room. Golf. Tennis. Bicycling. Spa. Swimming. Fishing.

Seen in: *Chicago Tribune, Woman's Day, Southern Living, Miami Herald.*

Contact: Stephane Clement. Certificate may be used: All year except holidays and special events.

"We feel lucky to have found such a relaxing place, and we look forward to returning."

Simonton Court

320 Simonton St
Key West 33040
(305)294-6386 (800)944-2687
Fax:(305)293-8446

1886. A variety of deluxe lodgings await this resort's visitors, including an inn, cottages and an elegant mansion. The inn, once a cigar factory, is now home to nine charming, individually decorated rooms. The six cottages are ideal for couples traveling together. The romantic mansion rooms all offer queen beds, VCRs and refrigerators. Fort Zachary Taylor State Historic Site and Beach, Truman's Little White House and the Key West Aquarium are nearby.

Innkeeper(s): Richard & Sue Clay Moloney.

Rates:$100-320. MC VISA AX DS. ContPlus Bkfst. 18 rooms. Beds:KQ. TV, Phone, AC, Refrig. in room. Spa. Swimming. Fishing.

Contact: Bill Wascher. Certificate may be used: June - September.

Lake Helen

Clauser's B&B

201 E Kicklighter Rd
Lake Helen 32744
(904)228-0310 (800)220-0310
Fax:(904)228-2337

1895. This three-story, turn-of-the-century vernacular Victorian inn is surrounded by a lovely variety of trees in a quiet, country setting. The inn is listed in the national, state and local historic registers, and offers eight guest rooms, all with private bath. Each room sports a different type of country decor, such as Americana, English and prairie. Guests enjoy hot tubbing in the Victorian gazebo or relaxing on the inn's porches, which feature rockers, a swing and cozy wicker furniture. Borrow a bike to take a closer look at the historic district. Stetson University, fine dining and several state parks are nearby.

Innkeeper(s): Tom & Marge Clauser.

Rates:$70-120. MC VISA AX DS. Full Bkfst. Picnic lunches. Evening snacks. 8 rooms. Beds:KQ. AC in room. Bicycling. Handicap access.

Spa. Swimming. Fishing.

Contact: Marge Clauser. Certificate may be used: Sunday-Thursday.

Lake Wales

Chalet Suzanne Country Inn & Restaurant

3800 Chalet Suzanne Dr
Lake Wales 33853-7060
(813)676-6011 (800)433-6011
Fax:(813)676-1814

1924. Carl & Vita Hinshaw are carrying on the traditions begun by Carl's mother, Bertha, who was known as a world-traveler, gourmet cook and antique-collector. Following the stock market crash and her husband's death, she turned her home into an inn and dining room. The whimsical architecture includes gabled roofs, balconies, spires and steeples. The restaurant received the Craig Claiborne award as one of the 121 best restaurants in the world.

Innkeeper(s): Carl & Vita Hinshaw.

Rates:$125-185. MC VISA AX DC DS CB. Full Bkfst. EP. MAP available. Gourmet Dinner. 30 rooms. Beds:KT. Conference Rm. TV, Phone, AC in room. Golf. Tennis. Handicap access. Swimming. Fishing.

Seen in: *Southern Living, Country Inns, National Geographic Traveler. Uncle Ben's 1992 award.*

Contact: Vita Hinshaw. Certificate may be used: Sunday - Thursday, based on availability.

"I now know why everyone always says, `Wow!' when they come up from dinner. Please don't change a thing."

Maitland

Thurston House

851 Lake Ave
Maitland 32751
(407)539-1911

1885. Just minutes from busy Orlando and the many attractions found nearby, this classic Queen Anne Victorian inn boasts a lakefront, countryside setting. Two of the inn's three screened porches provide views of Lake Eulalia. Two parlors provide additional relaxing spots, and many guests like to stroll the grounds, which feature fruit trees and several bountiful gardens.

Innkeeper(s): Carole & Joe Ballard.

Rates:$80-90. MC VISA AX. ContPlus Bkfst. 4 rooms. Fireplaces. Beds:QD. Phone, AC in room. Swimming. Fishing.

Contact: Carole Ballard. Certificate may be used: June & July; Sept. 1 through Dec. 20 (excluding Thanksgiving weekend).

Micanopy

Herlong Mansion
402 NE Cholokka Blvd, PO Box 667
Micanopy 32667
(904)466-3322

1845. This mid-Victorian mansion features four two-story carved-wood Roman Corinthian columns on its veranda. The mansion is surrounded by a garden with statuesque old oak and pecan trees. Herlong Mansion features leaded-glass windows, mahogany inlaid oak floors, 12-foot ceilings and floor-to-ceiling windows in the dining room. Guest rooms have fireplaces and are furnished with antiques.
Innkeeper(s): H.C. (Sonny) Howard, Jr.
Rates:$50-135. MC VISA. Full Bkfst. 11 rooms. Beds:KQT. AC in room. Bicycling. Swimming. Fishing.
Seen in: *Florida Trend.*
Contact: H. C. (Sonny) Howard, Jr. Certificate may be used: Sunday - Thursday other than holidays.

Mount Dora

Anapala Manor
347 E Third Ave
Mount Dora 32757
(904)735-3800

1926. This Mediterrean-style inn in Central Florida offers elegant accommodations to its guests, who will experience the Florida Boom furnishings of the 1920s. Guests will enjoy the convenience of early coffee or tea before sitting down to the inn's full breakfasts. Be sure to borrow a bicycle for a relaxing ride or take a soak in the inn's spa. Lake Griffin State Recreational Area and Wekiwa Springs State Park are within easy driving distance.
Innkeeper(s): Dolores & Bob Bersell.
Rates:$115-140. MC VISA AX DC DS CB. Full Bkfst. 3 rooms. Beds:Q. TV, Phone, AC in room. Bicycling.
Contact: Dolores Bersell. Certificate may be used: November - May.

New Smyrna Beach

Riverview Hotel
103 Flagler Ave
New Smyrna Beach 32169
(904)428-5858 (800)945-7416
Fax:(904)423-8927
1885. Conveniently located on Florida's

Intracoastal Waterway, this 18-room Florida Victorian once was home to a bridgetender. Four blocks away is the Atlantic Ocean. Guests also enjoy using the hotel's pool and bicycles. Several rooms offer views of the river or pool. Green Mound and Turtle Mound state archaeological sites are within easy driving distance, as is the Canaveral National Seashore. A popular area restaurant is found on the hotel grounds.
Innkeeper(s): Jim & Christa Kelsey.
Rates:$65-150. MC VISA AX DC DS CB. ContPlus Bkfst. 18 rooms. Beds:QT. Conference Rm. TV, Phone, AC in room. Bicycling. Swimming. Fishing.
Seen in: *Florida Living, Sun Sentinel.*
Contact: Christa Kelsey. Certificate may be used: Year-round not including Saturday night.

Ocala

Seven Sisters Inn
820 SE Fort King St
Ocala 34471
(904)867-1170 Fax:(904)732-7764

1888. This Queen Anne-style Victorian house is located in the heart of the historic district. Guests may relax on the large covered porches or visit with other guests in the Club Room. One of the innkeepers, Norma Johnson, is the eldest of seven sisters. Each room, named for one of the sisters, has a childhood picture of its namesake and is decorated in her favorite colors. The rooms feature king-size beds, sitting rooms, fireplaces and luxury linens. A gourmet breakfast includes caviar, homemade muffins and fresh fruits.
Innkeeper(s): Michele Mousin, Mgr.
Rates:$105-135. MC VISA AX DC DS. Gourmet Brkfst, Dinner. Picnic lunches. Teas. 7 rooms. Fireplaces. Beds:KQT. TV, Phone, AC in room. Handicap access. Swimming. Fishing.
Contact: Bonnie Morehardt. Certificate may be used: Sunday-Thursday only.

Orlando

The Courtyard at Lake Lucerne
211 N Lucerne Circle E
Orlando 32801
(407)648-5188 (800)444-5289
Fax:(407)246-1368

1883. The Courtyard at Lake Lucerne consists of three buildings: the Wellborn, an Art Deco building furnished in period style; the I.W. Phillips house, an antebellum-style manor with authentic Belle Epoque fittings and wraparound porches; and the Norment-Parry Inn, a Victorian-style house with English and American antiques. The Norment-Parry Inn is the oldest documented house still standing in Orlando and overlooks Lake Lucerne. The complex includes an elaborate turn-of-the-century fountain and lush gardens.

Innkeeper(s): Charles E., Sam & Paula Meiner.

Rates:$65-150. MC VISA AX. ContPlus Bkfst. 22 rooms. Beds:KQT. Conference Rm. TV, Phone, AC, Refrig. in room. Spa. Sauna. Swimming. Fishing.

Seen in: *Florida Historic Homes, Country Inns.*

Contact: Charles Meiner. Certificate may be used: All year, subject to availability.

"Best-kept secret in Orlando."

Saint Augustine

Carriage Way B&B
70 Cuna St
Saint Augustine 32084
(904)829-2467

1883. A two-story veranda dominates the facade of this square Victorian. Painted creamy white with blue trim, the house is located in the heart of the historic district. It's within a four-block walk to restaurants and shops and the Intracoastal Waterway. Guest rooms reflect the charm of a light Victorian touch, with brass, canopy and four-poster beds. Many furnishings have been in the house for 60 years. On Saturday evenings the dining-room table is laden with scrumptious desserts and coffee. A buffet breakfast is provided in the morning.

Innkeeper(s): Bill & Diane Johnson.

Rates:$80-105. MC VISA DS. Gourmet Brkfst. 9 rooms. Beds:Q. Phone, AC in room. Golf. Tennis. Bicycling. Swimming. Fishing.

Seen in: *Miami Herald, Florida Times Union, Palm Beach Post.*

Contact: Bill Johnson. Certificate may be used: Monday-Thursday, Sept. 10-Feb. 10, excluding holiday periods.

"Charming in every detail."

Castle Garden B&B
15 Shenandoah St
Saint Augustine 32084
(904)829-3839

1890. This newly-restored Moorish Revival-style inn features a castle-like facade of coquina stone. Among the six guest rooms are two honeymoon suites with sunken bedrooms, Jacuzzi tubs, and cathedral ceilings. Special touches include pillow chocolates and complimentary wine. An indoor chapel serves as the occasional wedding site.

Innkeeper(s): Bruce Kloeckner.

Rates:$55-150. MC VISA AX DS. Full Bkfst. Picnic lunches. Teas. 6 rooms. Beds:KQT. TV, AC in room. Golf. Tennis. Bicycling. Fishing.

Contact: Bruce Kloeckner. Certificate may be used: Monday through Thursday.

Old City House Inn & Restaurant
115 Cordova St
Saint Augustine 32084
(904)826-0113 Fax:(904)829-3798

1873. St. Augustine is a treasure bed of history and this inn is strategically located in the center. A red-tile roof covers this former stable, and a veranda

and courtyard add to the Spanish atmosphere. Gourmet breakfasts are prepared by innkeepers Bob and Alice Compton's son, John, whose recipes have been printed in Food Arts magazine. Inn guests are privy to the expansive breakfasts, but can join others for lunch and dinner in the restaurant. Appetizers include baked brie and Alligator Fritters. For lunch, unique salads, fresh fish and chicken create the menu, while dinner choices include gourmet standards such as Filet Mignon or a more unusual Seafood Strudel.

Innkeeper(s): Robert & Alice Compton.

Rates:$65-105. MC VISA AX DC. Full Bkfst. Gourmet Lunch, Dinner. Picnic lunches. 5 rooms. Beds:Q. TV, AC in room. Golf. Tennis. Bicycling. Skiing. Swimming. Horseback riding. Fishing.

Seen in: *Florida Times Union, Florida Trend, Ft. Lauderdale Sun Sentinal.*

Contact: Robert Compton. Certificate may be used: Will honor Sunday evening - Thursday.

Segul Inn B&B
47 San Marco Ave
Saint Augustine 32084
(904)825-2811 Fax:(904)824-3967

1914. This inn is located on the edge of St. Augustine's historic district. Marcie's Room features a king bed with handmade wedding-ring quilt, clawfoot tub, Victorian couch and private balcony. Martha Lee's Room boasts a queen bed and daybed in a separate sitting area. The full breakfasts feature homemade bread and jams, and may include George's pancakes or waffles. Be sure to inquire about discounts for senior citizens, members of the military and parents of Flagler College students.

Innkeeper(s): George & Nikki Lent.

Rates:$65-110. MC VISA. Full Bkfst. Teas. 3 rooms. Beds:KQT. AC in room. Bicycling.

Contact: Nikki Lent. Certificate may be used: Sunday through Thursday, excluding all holidays.

St. Francis Inn
279 St George St
Saint Augustine 32084
(904)824-6068

1791. Long noted for its hospitality, the St. Francis Inn is nearly the oldest house in town. A classic

example of Old World architecture, it was built by Gaspar Garcia who received a Spanish grant to the plot of land. Coquina was the main building material (Saint Augustine was founded in 1565.)

Innkeeper(s): Joe & Margaret Finnegan.

Rates:$49-140. MC VISA. ContPlus Bkfst. 14 rooms. Fireplaces. Beds:KQT. TV, AC, Refrig. in room. Golf. Tennis. Bicycling. Handicap access. Swimming. Fishing.

Seen in: *Orlando Sentinel.*

Contact: Joseph Finnegan, Jr. Certificate may be used: Sunday through Thursday nights from September to June (excluding holiday periods).

"We have stayed at many nice hotels but nothing like this. We are really enjoying it."

Wakulla Springs

Wakulla Springs Lodge & Conference Ctr
1 Spring Dr
Wakulla Springs 32305
(904)224-5950 Fax:(904)561-7251

1937. Financier Ed Ball built this Spanish-Moorish style lodge with its multitude of arches and fan windows. Now situated on 2,900 acres, the lodge's marbled terrace overlooks grounds lush with azaleas, camellias, dogwood and magnolias. The dining room overlooks Wakulla Springs, one of the world's largest natural springs, forming a four-and-a-half-acre lagoon. Glass-bottomed boats glide along the river inhabited with alligators, turtles, deer, nine species of herons and egrets, osprey and bald eagles. Films made here include early *Tarzan* movies with Johnny Weissmuller, and *Creature from the Black*

Lagoon. Rooms are furnished in the '30s style.

Innkeeper(s): Bill Roberts.

Rates:$70-100. MC VISA. Full Bkfst. Gourmet Dinner. Picnic lunches. 27 rooms. Beds:KQT. Conference Rm. Phone, AC in room. Handicap access. Fishing.

Seen in: *Southern Living Magazine, Family Circle.*

Contact: William Roberts. Certificate may be used: Sunday to Thursday nights only. No Fridays or Saturdays.

"...the lodge and surroundings cannot be matched anywhere!"

West Palm Beach

Hibiscus House
501 30th St
West Palm Beach 33407
(407)863-5633

1922. Built for John Dunkle, once the mayor of West Palm Beach, the Hibiscus House has period furniture, hand-loomed rugs, glossy pine floors, arched doorways and a marble hearth. Guests may relax in a gazebo draped with bougainvillea, on a second-floor terrace or in a quaint courtyard beside a small swimming pool. Airy guest rooms feature brass fans, armoires and potted palms. Fresh-picked fruit is served at the inn.

Innkeeper(s): Raleigh Hill & Colin Rayner.

Rates:$55-150. MC VISA. Full Bkfst. 7 rooms. Beds:Q. TV, Phone, AC in room. Bicycling. Swimming. Fishing.

Seen in: *Ft. Lauderdale-Sun Sentinel.*

Contact: Raleigh Hill. Certificate may be used: Subject to availability.

"You have such a warm and beautiful home. We have told everyone of our stay there."

Georgia

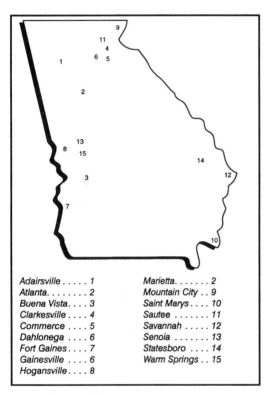

Adairsville

Old Home Place
764 Union Grove Church Rd SE
Adairsville 30103
(706)625-3649

1855. This country-style Greek Revival home in Northwest Georgia has three guest rooms, one with private bath. The rooms offer fireplaces and country decor, and guests will enjoy their country breakfasts, featuring homemade muffins and jams. The inn's convenient location midway between Atlanta and Chattanooga make it an ideal stop for busy city folk needing a getaway or travelers exploring the history-rich area. Allatoona Lake and Red Top

84

Mountain State Park are nearby.
Innkeeper(s): Vincent & Joan Mayer.
Rates:$42. ContPlus Bkfst. Evening snacks. 3 rooms. 2 with shared baths. Fireplaces. Beds:DT. Golf. Tennis. Fishing.
Contact: Joan Mayer. Certificate may be used: June, July, August, September, 1994/1995.

Atlanta

Ansley Inn
253 Fifteenth St NE
Atlanta 30309
(404)872-9000 (800)446-5416
Fax:(404)892-2318

1907. This Tudor inn, filled with handsome furnishings, is located in the historic Ansley Park district of midtown Atlanta. The inn once served as a chaperoned boarding house for young women, and modern-day guests sometimes return to revisit bygone courting days spent in the parlor. The inn's 15 well-appointed guest rooms feature cable TVs, wet bars and Jacuzzi baths. Some fireplaces and four-poster beds are available. Business travelers will find the staff more than willing to accommodate their needs. Nearby are the Atlanta Botanical Gardens, the theater district and access to MARTA, the city's award-winning subway system.
Innkeeper(s): Timothy Thomas.
Rates:$115-250. MC VISA AX DC DS CB. ContPlus Bkfst. EP. Teas. Evening snacks. 15 rooms. Fireplaces. Beds:QT. Conference Rm. TV. Phone, AC, Refrig. in room. Handicap access. Fishing.
Seen in: New York Times, Conde Nast Traveler, CNN, National Geographic Traveler.
Contact: Timothy Thomas. Certificate may be used: Sunday through Thursday.

Atlanta's Woodruff B&B
223 Ponce de Leon Ave
Atlanta 30308
(404)875-9449 (800)473-9449
Fax:(404)875-2882

1906. A gigantic oak shades the porches of this

beautifully renovated white brick mansion. Polished heart-of-pine floors are found throughout, and there's a staircase with heart shapes cut out of the banisters. Bright and airy rooms feature high ceilings, beveled mirrors and antique bedsteads. Favored Southern breakfasts are served in the dining room or by prior arrangement in your room. In the evening, fireside chats often include entertaining stories of Miss Bessie, a former owner of the house. Some of Atlanta's best restaurants are within a block of the inn.

Innkeeper(s): Douglas & Joan Jones.

Rates:$85-135. MC VISA AX DS. Full Bkfst. 10 rooms. 2 with shared baths. Fireplaces. Beds:DT. Conference Rm. Phone, AC in room. Spa.

Seen in: *CNN, Athens Magazine, Atlanta Business Chronicle, Atlanta Journal Constitution.*

Contact: Douglas Jones. Certificate may be used: Weekends and conventions subject to availability.

"They really show you what is meant by Southern hospitality."

Beverly Hills Inn

65 Sheridan Dr NE
Atlanta 30305
(404)233-8520 (800)331-8520
Fax:(404)233-8520

1929. Period furniture and polished-wood floors decorate this inn located in the Buckhead neighborhood. There are private balconies, kitchens and

a library with a collection of newspapers and books. The governor's mansion, Neiman-Marcus, Saks and Lord & Taylor are five minutes away.

Innkeeper(s): Mit Amin.

Rates:$90-160. MC VISA AX DC DS CB. ContPlus Bkfst. 18 rooms. Beds:Q. Conference Rm. Phone, AC, Refrig. in room. Golf. Tennis. Swimming.

Seen in: *Country Inns, Southern Living, Time.*

Contact: Mit Amin. Certificate may be used: All year subject to availability.

"Our only regret is that we had so little time. Next stay we will plan to be here longer."

Oakwood House B&B

951 Edgewood Ave NE
Atlanta 30307
(404)521-9320 (800)388-4403

1911. This post-Victorian house has seen duty as a boarding house, warehouse, travel agency, and psychologists' offices. The interior is very homey, with original moldings, stained glass, exposed brick, and traditional furnishings. Guests have the run of the house, as the owners live next door. It is situated in a suburb two miles from downtown Atlanta.

Innkeeper(s): Judy & Robert Hotchkiss.

Rates:$65-175. MC VISA. ContPlus Bkfst. 5 rooms. Beds:KQT. Conference Rm. Phone, AC in room. Exercise room.

Seen in: *Georgia B&B Council Christmas tour.*

Contact: Judy Hotchkiss. Certificate may be used: Sunday-Thursday, all special-event periods are exempt.

"Our family had a wonderful weekend."

Buena Vista

Morgan Towne House B&B

PO Box 522, No. 2 Church St
Buena Vista 31803
(912)649-3663

1880. A complimentary glass of lemonade upon guests' arrival is just the beginning of the charm offered at this Neoclassical inn, which prides itself on Southern hospitality. The inn is also home to a popular area restaurant. Guest rooms are furnished with period antiques and visitors may enjoy breakfast in bed if they wish. Be sure to inform the innkeepers if you are celebrating a birthday or anniversary. Andersonville, the historic Civil War prison camp, is an easy drive away.

Innkeeper(s): Claudine & Richard Morgan.

Rates:$50-60. MC VISA. Full Bkfst. Gourmet Brkfst, Lunch, Dinner. Picnic lunches. Teas. Evening snacks. 4 rooms. Beds:KQT. Conference Rm. Phone, AC in room. Fishing.

Contact: Claudine Morgan. Certificate may be used: Anytime.

Clarkesville

Burns-Sutton House

124 S Washington St, Box 992
Clarkesville 30523
(706)754-5565

1901. Located in Clarkesville's historic district, this three-story Queen Anne Victorian inn is listed in the National Register of Historic Places. Furnished with antiques and period pieces, the inn also boasts a beautiful exterior. Four magnificent magnolia trees are found in the front yard, adding to its elegant setting. Stained-glass windows, wraparound porches and four-poster canopy beds add to guests' enjoyment. A full country breakfast is served.

Innkeeper(s): JoAnn & John Smith.

Rates:$55-75. MC VISA AX. Full Bkfst. 7 rooms. 2 with shared baths. Fireplaces. Beds:QT. Conference Rm. TV, Phone, AC in room. Golf. Tennis. Skiing. Swimming. Horseback riding. Fishing.

Seen in: *Southern Living.*

Contact: JoAnn Smith. Certificate may be used: Weekdays, April through December, excluding October. Anytime January through March.

Commerce

The Pittman House B&B
81 Homer Rd
Commerce 30529
(706)335-3823

1890. An hour's drive from Atlanta is this four-square Colonial inn, found in the rolling hills of Northeast Georgia. The inn has four guest rooms, furnished in country decor. The surrounding area offers many activities, including Lake Lanier, Lake Hartwell, Hurricane Shoals, Crawford W. Long Museum, an outlet mall, a winery and a championship golf course. Innkeeper Tom Tomberlin, a woodcarver, has items for sale in an antique shop next to the inn.

Innkeeper(s): Tom & Dot Tomberlin.

Rates:$55-65. MC VISA. Full Bkfst. 4 rooms. 2 with shared baths. AC in room. Swimming. Fishing.

Contact: Tom Tomberlin. Certificate may be used: Sunday - Thursday. Friday & Saturday upon availability.

Dahlonega

Cavender Castle Winery
Hwy19/60 at Crisson Gold Mine
Dahlonega 30533
(706)864-4759

1989. This gothic-inspired castle is also home to a winery, and offers easy access to the many attractions of North Georgia's mountain country, including the Dahlonega Gold Museum. The inn sits atop Gold Hill, overlooking nine vine-covered acres. The Chardonnay Room boasts a mountain view and queen bed. Guests are welcome to play croquet or horseshoes, relax in the library, sample a taste of the Cavender's wines or explore the vineyards and gardens. The gourmet breakfast is served by candlelight.

Innkeeper(s): Wesley & Linda Phillips.

Rates:$65-85. Full Bkfst. Picnic lunches. Teas. 4 rooms. Beds:KQ. AC in room. Swimming. Fishing.

Contact: Linda Phillips. Certificate may be used: November, 1994 through April, 1995 (except holidays). November & December, 1995 (except holidays).

Worley Homestead Inn
410 W Main
Dahlonega 30533
(706)864-7002

1845. Four blocks from the historic town square is this beautiful old Colonial Revival inn. Several guest rooms are equipped with fireplaces, adding to the romantic atmosphere and Victorian ambiance. All the rooms feature antique beds. A popular spot for honeymooners and couples celebrating anniversaries, many guests take advantage of Dahlonega's proximity to the lures of the Chattahoochee National Forest.

Innkeeper(s): Bill & Mary Scott.

Rates:$55-75. MC VISA. Full Bkfst. 7 rooms. Fireplaces. Beds:D. TV, AC in room. Handicap access. Fishing.

Contact: Mary Scott. Certificate may be used: Winter season January - April.

Fort Gaines

John Dill House
PO Box 8, 102 S Washington St
Fort Gaines 31751
(912)768-2338 Fax:(912)768-2338

1820. This stately homestead, once a stagecoach stop, is just a mile from the Chattahoochee River in the state's Southwest region. The inn, listed with the national, state and local historic registers, boasts a fireplace in each of its nine guest rooms, all tastefully furnished in country decor and antiques. Features include oak floors, a 600-square-foot kitchen and more than $300,000 worth of antiques. Proceeds of the Elizabeth Dill Gift Shop, also on the grounds, go toward the costs of restoring the inn.

Rates:$50-70. Full Bkfst. MAP available. Gourmet Brkfst. Teas. 18 rooms. 9 with shared baths. Fireplaces. Beds:Q. Conference Rm. TV, AC in room. Handicap access. Swimming. Fishing.

Contact: Philip S. Kurland. Certificate may be used: November, December and January.

Gainesville

Dunlap House
635 Green St
Gainesville 30501
(404)536-0200 (800)264-6992
Fax:(404)503-7857

1910. Located on Gainesville's historic Green Street, this inn offers 10 uniquely decorated guest rooms, all featuring period furnishings. Custom-built king or queen beds and remote-controlled cable TV are found in all of the rooms, several of which have romantic fireplaces. Guests may help themselves to coffee, tea and light refreshments in the inn's common area. Breakfast may be enjoyed in guests' rooms or on the picturesque veranda, with its comfortable wicker furniture. The Quinlan Art Center and Lake Sidney Lanier are nearby.
Innkeeper(s): Ann & Ben Ventress.

Rates:$85-115. MC VISA AX. ContPlus Bkfst. 10 rooms. Fireplaces. Beds:KQT. TV, Phone, AC in room. Golf. Swimming. Fishing.

Seen in: *Southern Living, Atlanta Journal Constitution.*

Contact: Ben Ventress. Certificate may be used: Not available October & November.

Hogansville

Fair Oaks Inn
703 E Main St
Hogansville 30230
(706)637-8828

1901. This turn-of-the-century Victorian home is on the site of an original 1835 plantation. Each bedroom has a fireplace with authentic period mantels. There are a series of formal gardens with a swimming pool, and gazebo, lattice-covered swings and eight converted New Orleans street lights. The master suite has two fireplaces, a sitting room, bedroom with private bath, steam room and Jacuzzi. Breakfast is served in the formal dining room or on the sun porch.
Innkeeper(s): Ken Hammock & Wayne Jones.

Rates:$50-100. MC VISA. Gourmet Brkfst. 6 rooms. 3 with shared baths. Fireplaces. Beds:KQ. Phone, AC in room. Golf. Spa. Swimming. Fishing.

Contact: Kenneth Hammock. Certificate may be used: Sunday through Thursday.

Marietta

Whitlock Inn
57 Whitlock Ave
Marietta 30064
(404)428-1495 Fax:(404)427-5704

1900. This cherished Victorian has been recently restored and is in a National Register Historic District, located one block from the Marietta Square. To enjoy the best of Georgia's past, including family recipes and preserved Southern accents, be sure to arrive for afternoon tea and snacks served in the antique-filled parlor. Amenities even the Ritz doesn't provide (like fireplaces) are in every room and you can rock on the front verandas. There is a ballroom grandly suitable for weddings and business meetings.
Innkeeper(s): Sandy & Nancy Edwards.

Rates:$85. MC VISA AX DS. ContPlus Bkfst. Teas. 5 rooms. Fireplaces. Beds:QT. TV, Phone, AC in room. Handicap access.

Contact: Nancy Edwards. Certificate may be used: Weekdays, Monday - Thursday. (We have many weekend weddings.)

Mountain City

The York House
PO Box 126
Mountain City 30562
(706)746-2068 (800)231-9675

1896. Bill and Mollie York opened The York House as an inn in 1896, and it has operated con-

tinuously ever since. Two stories of shaded verandas overlook tall hemlocks, Norwegian spruce, lawns and mountains. Adjacent to the Old Spring House is a stand of pines that provides a romantic setting for weddings. Breakfast is carried to the room each morning on a silver tray, and each room is plumbed with natural spring water.
Innkeeper(s): Phyllis & Jimmy Smith.

Rates:$58-69. MC VISA AX DC DS CB. Cont. Bkfst. Teas. 13 rooms. Fireplaces. Beds:D. Conference Rm. TV, AC in room. Golf. Bicycling. Skiing. Handicap access. Swimming. Horseback riding. Fishing.

Seen in: *Blue Ridge Country, Mountain Review.*

Contact: James Smith. Certificate may be used: All times except month of October, Memorial weekend, 4th of July weekend and Labor Day weekend.

Saint Marys

Goodbread House

209 Osborne St
Saint Marys 31558
(912)882-7490

1870. In the heart of Saint Marys National Register Historic District, this Victorian Shingle inn offers four antique-filled guest rooms, all with fireplaces. Visitors will enjoy the original wood trim, high ceilings, pine floors and upstairs and downstairs verandas. Don't miss cocktail hour, where wine and cheese are served on the upstairs porch. The historic fishing village has many points of interest to explore, and the Cumberland Island Sea Shore, Kings Bay Naval Submarine Base and Crooked River State Park are close by.

Innkeeper(s): Betty & George Krauss.
Rates:$60. Full Bkfst. 4 rooms. Fireplaces. Beds:QDT. Phone, AC in room. Bicycling.
Contact: Betty Krauss. Certificate may be used: Summers - December & January.

The Historic Spencer House Inn

101 E Bryant St
Saint Marys 31558
(912)882-1872

1872. This large Folk Victorian once served as the village's finest hotel, and often hosted visitors who came to attend court sessions in what was once the county seat of Camden County. The inn and its 15 guest rooms are filled with fine antiques and reproductions. Three verandas are popular gathering spots for guests, who also may borrow a bicycle for a closer view of the village's charms. For the convenience of guests who arrive by boat, the inn is within two blocks of Lang's Marina, and one block from the Cumberland Island ferry mooring.

Innkeeper(s): Dale & Donna Potruski.
Rates:$65-100. MC VISA DS. ContPlus Bkfst. 15 rooms. Beds:KQT. Conference Rm. TV, Phone, AC in room. Swimming. Fishing.
Contact: Marci Price. Certificate may be used: Year-round except holidays/holiday weekends (Christmas, New Year's, Memorial Day, 4th of July, Labor Day, Thanksgiving).

Sautee

The Stovall House

Rt 1 Box 1476, Hwy 255 N
Sautee 30571
(706)878-3355

1837. This house, built by Moses Harshaw and restored in 1983 by Ham Schwartz, has received two state awards for its restoration. The handsome farmhouse has an extensive wraparound porch providing vistas of 28 acres of cow pasture, meadows and creeks. High ceilings, polished walnut woodwork and decorative stenciling provide a pleasant backdrop for the inn's collection of antiques. Victorian bathroom fixtures include pull-chain toilets and pedestal sinks. The inn has its own restaurant.

Innkeeper(s): Ham Schwartz.
Rates:$56-70. MC VISA. Cont. Bkfst. Gourmet Dinner. 5 rooms. Beds:KT. Farm. Golf. Tennis. Handicap access. Swimming. Horseback riding. Fishing.
Seen in: *The Atlanta Journal.*
Contact: P. Hamilton Schwartz. Certificate may be used: Sunday through Thursday (except October).

"Great to be home again."

Savannah

The Forsyth Park Inn

102 W Hall St
Savannah 31401
(912)233-6800

1893. This graceful yellow and white three-story Victorian features bay windows and a large veranda overlooking Forsyth Park. Sixteen-foot ceilings, polished parquet floors of oak and maple, and a hand-

some oak stairway provide an elegant background for the guest rooms. There are several whirlpool tubs, marble baths, four-poster beds and fireplaces.

Innkeeper(s): Hal & Virginia Sullivan.
Rates:$85-165. MC VISA AX DS. ContPlus Bkfst. 11 rooms. Fireplaces. Beds:KQT. AC in room. Golf. Tennis. Swimming. Fishing.
Seen in: *Savannah Morning News, Land's End Catalog, United Airlines Vis-A-Vis.*
Contact: Virginia Sullivan. Certificate may be used: Months of January and February, 1995, July and August, 1994 and 1995, Sunday through Wednesday, excluding holidays, special events and weekends. Not honored when booked through travel agents and reservation services. Must reserve directly with innkeeper.

"Breathtaking, exceeded my wildest dreams."

Senoia

Culpepper House
35 Broad St, PO Box 462
Senoia 30276
(404)599-8182 Fax:(404)599-8182

1871. This Queen Anne Victorian was built by a Confederate veteran and later occupied for 50 years by Dr. Culpepper. With original moldings, stained-glass windows and mantelpieces, the house is decorated in cozy Victorian clutter and comfortable whimsy. The inn offers guests Southern hospitality at its finest.

Innkeeper(s): Maggie Armstrong/Barb Storm.

Rates:$75. MC VISA. Full Bkfst. Gourmet Brkfst. 3 rooms. 2 with shared baths. Fireplaces. Beds:KQT. AC in room. Bicycling. Swimming. Fishing.

Seen in: *The Newman Times-Herald*.

Contact: Maggie Armstrong. Certificate may be used: Anytime.

"Thank you for your generous hospitality."

The Veranda
252 Seavy St, Box 177
Senoia 30276-0177
(404)599-3905 Fax:(404)599-0806

1906. Doric columns adorn the verandas of this 9,000-square-foot Neoclassical hotel. William Jennings Bryan stayed here, and it is said that Margaret Mitchell (*Gone With the Wind*) came here to interview Georgia veterans of the Civil War who held their annual reunion at the hotel. Furnishings include walnut bookcases owned by President William McKinley and a rare Wurlitzer player piano-pipe organ. There are Victorian collections of hair combs, walking canes, books and one of the largest assortments of kaleidoscopes in the Southeast.

Innkeeper(s): Jan Boal.

Rates:$85-105. MC VISA AX DS. Gourmet Brkfst, Lunch, Dinner. Teas. Evening snacks. 9 rooms. Fireplaces. Beds:QT. Conference Rm. AC in room. Tennis. Handicap access. Fishing.

Seen in: *Newnan Times Herald, Georgia Trend, Atlanta, Glamour, Southern Homes*.

Contact: Jan Boal. Certificate may be used: Sunday through Wednesday, October-November, 1995; Sunday through Wednesday, January-February, 1995.

"The mystique and reality of The Veranda are that you're being elaborately entertained by friends in their private home."

Statesboro

Statesboro Inn and Restaurant
106 S Main St
Statesboro 30458
(912)489-8628 (800)846-9466
Fax:(912)489-4785

1904. Visitors to the Georgia Southern University area often seek out this inn, a turn-of-the-century Neoclassical/Victorian home with 15 guest rooms, all beautifully furnished and featuring special amenities such as fireplaces, whirlpool baths or screened porches. The unique architecture includes bay windows, multiple gables and Tuscan columns. It is believed Blind Willie wrote the song "Statesboro Blues" in the Hattie Holloway Cabin on the grounds. Special dinner parties, receptions and conferences may be accommodated.

Innkeeper(s): Tony, Michele & Melissa Garges.

Rates:$65-75. MC VISA AX DC DS. Full Bkfst. Gourmet Brkfst, Dinner. 15 rooms. Fireplaces. Beds:KQ. Conference Rm. TV, Phone, AC, Refrig. in room. Handicap access.

Contact: Michele Garges. Certificate may be used: June 1 - Aug. 30; Nov. 15 - Dec. 31.

Warm Springs

Hotel Warm Springs B&B Inn
PO Box 351
Warm Springs 31830
(706)655-2114 (800)366-7616

1907. This three-story brick hotel once housed former President Franklin D. Roosevelt, who was drawn to the area by the warm spring waters. Seventeen guest rooms are available, including three suites. The Presidential Suite honors FDR and Eleanor Roosevelt, and is furnished with antiques and collectibles. Breakfasts are served in the Mezzanine, with its Queen Anne furniture and crystal teardrop chandelier. The surrounding area offers many picnicking, hiking and sightseeing opportunities.

Innkeeper(s): Lee & Gerrie Thompson.

Rates:$41-100. MC VISA AX DS. Full Bkfst. Picnic lunches. Teas. 17 rooms. Beds:KQDT. TV, AC in room. Fishing.

Contact: Lee Thompson. Certificate may be used: Sunday through Thursday, 1994/1995.

Hawaii

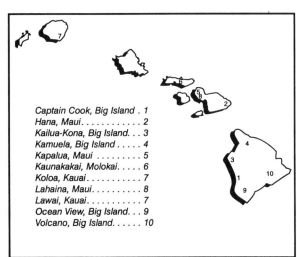

Captain Cook

Adrienne's B&B
RR 1, Box 8E
Captain Cook/Big Island 96740
(808)328-9726 (800)328-9726
Fax:(808)328-9787

1983. Nestled on the slopes of Mauna Loa and overlooking Honaunau Bay, this bed & breakfast is custom-built from cedar in the Kona style, with

open-beamed ceilings. Guest rooms are decorated in contemporary furnishings with private entrances and baths; two have private, ocean-view lanais. A continental breakfast is served on the lanai, where guests enjoy an unobstructed ocean view. A hot

tub, boogie boards and snorkeling equipment also are available to guests.

Innkeeper(s): Adrienne & Reg Batty.

Rates:$50-70. MC VISA. Cont. Bkfst. Teas. 4 rooms. Conference Rm. Spa. Exercise room.

Seen in: *This Week, Skin Diver, Modern Bride, Country Inns, Hawaii Magazine, Discover Hawaii.*

Contact: Adrienne Batty. Certificate may be used: Year-round except Dec. 17 to Jan. 17.

"A great retreat you have here."

Hana

Kaia Ranch & Co
PO Box 404, Ulaino Rd
Hana, Maui 96713
(808)248-7725

1992. This Hawaiian country farm consists of 27 acres that include park-like grounds offering fruit trees and flower gardens. If you stay in the Flower Studio you will enjoy your own kitchen and lanai. There are dogs, cats and horses on the property. The innkeeper trains horses and participates in local rodeos. A cedar chalet near Volcano National Park on the Big Island is also offered.

Innkeeper(s): John and Jo Loyce Kaia.

Rates:$75. Cont. Bkfst. 2 rooms. Beds:QT. Refrig. in room. Farm. Golf.

Contact: JoLoyce Kaia. Certificate may be used: No holidays.

Kailua-Kona

Adrienne's at Casa Del Sol B&B Inn
77-6335 Alii Dr
Kailua-Kona 96740
(808)326-2272 (800)328-9726
Fax:(808)326-2272

1982. This Mediterranean-style inn is in the heart of the famed Kona coast and between the quaint and historic village of Kailua (three miles to the north) and the modern Keahou Resort with its acclaimed Kona country club (three miles to the south). Breakfast is served at ocean or pool side and includes an array of tropical fruits, Kona coffee, homemade breads, muffins, local jellies and jams. Enjoy the famous Kona sunsets with the scent of fragrant citrus and exotic blossoms in the balmy air.

Innkeeper(s): Adrienne & Reg Batty.

Rates:$80-150. MC VISA. ContPlus Bkfst. Teas. 7 rooms. 2 with shared baths. Beds:KQT. Conference Rm. TV, Phone in room. Bicycling. Skiing. Spa. Swimming. Fishing.

Contact: Adrienne Batty. Certificate may be used: March through Nov. 15.

Hale Maluhia B&B

76-770 Hualalai Rd
Kailua-Kona 96740
(808)329-5773 (800)559-6627
Fax:(808)326-5487

1972. This one-acre estate was lovingly designed as a Hawaiian plantation-style home for many families to enjoy. The estate (House of Peace) has a Victorian and wicker interior with overstuffed sofas, antiques and Oriental rugs. Banana, mango, papaya, breadfruit and banyan trees edge and shade the compound. The hillsides are terraced with flower and vegetable gardens. Beach and snorkeling equipment are available at no charge, and the beaches are within a 15-minute drive. Holualoa is a sleepy, old coffee town on a mountain side above Kailua-Kona.

Innkeeper(s): Ken & Ann Smith.

Rates:$55-110. MC VISA AX DS. ContPlus Bkfst. 5 rooms. 2 with shared baths. Beds:KQT. Conference Rm. TV, Phone, Refrig. in room. Farm. Skiing. Handicap access. Spa. Exercise room. Swimming. Fishing.

Contact: N. K. Smith. Certificate may be used: July 15-Dec. 1, 1994 and 1995.

Kamuela

Kamuela Inn

PO Box 1994
Kamuela, Big Island 96743
(808)885-4243 Fax:(808)885-8857

1962. First-time visitors to the Big Island who drive

to the town of Kamuela might not believe their eyes when they see pine trees, cattle and horse

ranches, and mountain meadows instead of palm trees and tropical vegetation. This inn sits on horse country and is close to the famous Parker Ranch, which is the second-largest ranch in the United States. This 31-room country inn can be a cool break on your way from one side of the island to the other. The Hawaiian Style Cafe in town is a must stop for local islanders passing through and a good taste of traditional cuisine for visitors.

Innkeeper(s): Earnest Russell.

Rates:$54-165. MC VISA AX DC DS. Cont. Bkfst. 31 rooms. Beds:KQT. TV in room. Skiing. Handicap access. Swimming. Fishing.

Contact: Earnest Russell. Certificate may be used: All year.

Kapalua

The Kahili Maui

5500 Honoapiilani Rd
Kapalua, Maui 96761
(808)669-5635 (800)786-7387
Fax:(808)669-2561

1990. Enjoy the view from your private lanai at this modern inn located near several of the world's best beaches, including Kapalua Bay and Napili Beach. All studio and one-bedroom accommodations come with a complete kitchen and are decorated with fresh tropical flowers. After a day of playing on the championship Kapalua Golf Course next door or enjoying the waters of Maui, guests can relax by the pool or soak in the Jacuzzi. Casual or elegant dining are minutes away from the inn.

Innkeeper(s): Steve Weston.

Rates:$79-149. MC VISA AX DC. EP. 30 rooms. Beds:QT. TV, Phone, AC, Refrig. in room. Handicap access. Swimming. Fishing.

Contact: Steve Weston. Certificate may be used: Through 1995 subject to availability.

Kaunakakai

Kamalo Plantation

HC01, Box 300
Kaunakakai, Molokai 96748
(808)558-8236 Fax:(808)558-8236

1963. Ancient Hawaiian temple ruins built in the 13th and 14th century are found on the tropical, five-acre property of this Hawaiian Plantation-style home. A guest cottage is available away from the main house and surrounded by an acre of tropical garden. The ocean is only a five-minute walk away. The island of Molokai is known for its unique beauty and peaceful lifestyle. The innkeepers, who have lived and sailed in the islands for several years, can help you with information on shopping for local crafts, visiting museums and when festivals and special events take place.

Innkeeper(s): Glenn & Akiko Foster.

Rates:$65-75. ContPlus Bkfst. 3 rooms. 2 with shared baths. Beds:KT. Phone, Refrig. in room. Bicycling. Swimming. Horseback riding. Fishing.

Contact: Akiko Foster. Certificate may be used: April 1 to Oct. 31.

Koloa

Poipu B&B Inn
2720 Hoonani Rd, Poipu Beach
Koloa, Kauai 96756
(808)742-1146 (800)227-6478
Fax:(808)742-6843

1933. This restored plantation house preserves the character of old Kauai, while providing for every modern convenience. The handcrafted wood interiors and old-fashioned lanais provide the perfect backdrop for the ornate white Victorian wicker, carousel horses, pine antiques and tropical color

accents. Local art and handcrafts abound as one of the innkeepers is an avid collector and artist. The beach is one block away and the innkeepers can help you arrange every detail of your stay including helicopter tours, short-term health spa membership and dinner reservations.

Innkeeper(s): Dotti Cichon.

Rates:$110-225. MC VISA AX DC DS CB. ContPlus Bkfst. Teas. 8 rooms. Beds:KT. TV, AC, Refrig. in room. Handicap access. Spa. Swimming. Fishing.

Seen in: *Travel & Leisure, Travel-Holiday.*

Contact: Dotti Cichon. Certificate may be used: Oct. 1-Dec. 20 not including Thanksgiving week (in 1994 Nov. 18-28 excluded). Anytime on a space availability basis within 24 hours of arrival or at other times with advance reservations at our discretion. Please check.

"Thank you for sharing your home as well as yourself with us. I'll never forget this place, it's the best B&B we've stayed at."

Poipu Plantation
1792 Pee Rd
Koloa, Kauai 96756
(808)742-6757 (800)733-1632

Fax:(808)822-2723

1936. After the hurricane, which damaged much of Kauai, the island has had a chance to rebuild, renovate, and in many cases upgrade resort properties. The innkeepers at Poipu Plantation took the opportunity to install new amenities such as a hot tub in the barbecue area. Located on Kauai's sunny south shore, the family-owned and operated inn features a pleasant tropical decor. Within walking distance are many beautiful beaches and coves where tropical fish are plentiful.

Innkeeper(s): Evie Warner, Al Davis.

Rates:$70-80. MC VISA AX. Cont. Bkfst. 3 rooms. Beds:KQ. Conference Rm. TV in room. Golf. Tennis. Swimming. Horseback riding. Fishing.

Contact: Evelyn Warner. Certificate may be used: May and June and September, October, Nov. 15.

Lahaina

Old Lahaina House B&B
PO Box 10355
Lahaina, Maui 96761
(808)667-4663 (800)847-0761
Fax:(808)667-5615

1978. From the courtyard's private entrance, you are mere steps from a serene beach, perfect for swimming, snorkeling and whale watching. This inn is a leisurely walk to dining and unique shopping in Lahaina, a historic and culturally rich, old whaling town. The accommodations are comfortably appointed and feature the vibrant colors and decor of the Hawaiian Isles. The gracious innkeepers can offer guests special dining and shopping discounts as well as the best activity prices on Maui.

Innkeeper(s): John & Sherry Barbier.

Rates:$79-95. MC VISA AX. ContPlus Bkfst. 5 rooms. 3 with shared baths. Beds:KT. TV, Phone, AC, Refrig. in room. Bicycling. Swimming. Fishing.

Contact: John Barbier. Certificate may be used: Anytime depending on availability.

Lawai

Victoria Place B&B
PO Box 930
Lawai, Kauai 96765
(808)332-9300

1978. Three guest rooms open out to a pool area surrounded by hibiscus, gardenia and bougainvillea. The light and cheerful rooms are tiny but filled with native plants and flowers such as ginger and bird of paradise. For more spacious accommodations request the apartment. Innkeeper Edee Seymour loves to share her island secrets with guests and can direct you to hidden beaches off the tourist track. (She has received an award for being the friendliest person on the island.)

Innkeeper(s): Edee Seymour.

Rates:$75-105. ContPlus Bkfst. 5 rooms. Beds:KQT. Handicap access. Swimming.

Contact: Edee Seymour. Certificate may be used: April, September, November.

Ocean View

Bougainvillea B&B
PO Box 6045
Ocean View, Big Island 96704
(808)929-7089 (800)688-1763
Fax:(808)929-7089

Visitors to this Hawaiian Plantation-style home will be treated to the expertise of an innkeeper who has an extensive background in travel as the owner of an agency and as a teacher. All ground arrangements can be made through her. While using the inn as your base, you can enjoy the Hawaii of old as well as all the diversity the Big Island has to offer. The inn is located in a historic area near Volcano National Park.

Innkeeper(s): Martie Jean & Don Nitsche.

Rates:$57. MC VISA AX DC DS. ContPlus Bkfst. 5 rooms. Beds:QT. Phone in room. Farm. Bicycling. Spa. Fishing.

Contact: Martie Jean Nitsche. Certificate may be used: All year except Dec. 15-31 of 1994 and 1995 are blackout.

Volcano

Chalet Kilauea - The Inn at Volcano
PO Box 998
Volcano, Big Island 96785
(808)967-7786 (800)937-7786
Fax:(808)967-8660

1945. The Main House rooms of this chalet-style inn are uniquely decorated in different themes from around the world. Guests can have a safari experience in the Out of Africa room, a romantic interlude in the Continental Lace room, or a Far Eastern odyssey in the Oriental Jade room. Vacation homes, located in the Volcano Village, also are available with full kitchen, coffee and teas supplied. Some homes have wood-burning stoves and sunken bathtubs. Whether you stay at the Chalet or one of the vacation homes, you are invited to high tea in the afternoon between 4 and 5 p.m.

Innkeeper(s): Lisha & Brian Crawford.

Rates:$75-225. MC VISA DS. Gourmet Brkfst. Teas. 10 rooms. Fireplaces. Beds:KQT. TV, Phone, Refrig. in room. Fishing.

Contact: Lisha Crawford. Certificate may be used: Monday - Thursday excluding holidays and special events.

Hale Ohia Cottages
PO Box 758
Volcano, Big Island 96785
(808)967-7986 (800)455-3803
Fax:(808)967-8610

1931. These country cottages, nestled in the quaint Volcano Village area, are surrounded by Hawaiian gardens and lush forest. You can stroll the serene property on paths made of lava rock and enjoy the many orchids and native plants. Besides visiting the Volcano National Park, guests can tour the historic town of Hilo, which is only 23 miles away.

Innkeeper(s): Michael Tuttle.

Rates:$60-95. MC VISA DC. ContPlus Bkfst. Gourmet Lunch, Dinner. 6 rooms. Fireplaces. Beds:QDT. Conference Rm. Refrig. in room. Bicycling. Handicap access. Spa. Fishing.

Contact: Michael Tuttle. Certificate may be used: Sept. 10 through Oct. 31, 1994; Jan. 8-31, 1995.

Volcano Heart Chalet
11th St
Volcano, Big Island 96785
(808)248-7725

1987. This comfortable cedar home can be your base for visiting one of Hawaii's most fascinating landscapes. The entrance to Volcano National Park is just two miles away from this inn, which is nestled in a natural setting of tree ferns and ohia trees. The park features hiking trails around Kilauea volcano crater and through landscape that changes from forest to arid to tropical. The Volcano Art Center, volcano exhibit and observatory are a must for everyone and provide great insight into the Hawaiian culture.

Innkeeper(s): John & Jo Loyce Kaia.

Rates:$50. 3 rooms. Beds:QT. Exercise room. Swimming.

Contact: Jo Loyce Kaia. Certificate may be used: No holidays.

Idaho

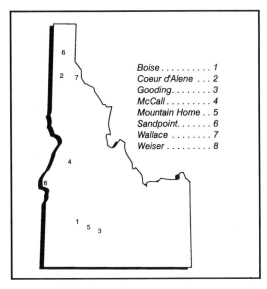

Boise

B&B at Victoria's White House
10325 W Victory Rd
Boise 83709
(208)362-0507 Fax:(208)445-7882

1980. Although the inn is not historic, it's
Colonial Revival-like architecture has incorporated

many vintage components saved from local historic
buildings, such as its banister, oak floors and fireplace mantels (gleaned from an old courthouse).
Bogus Basin may be seen from the suite, which fea-

tures a fireplace, large mirrored tub and parlor. In
spring, more than a thousand tulips welcome the
new season.

Innkeeper(s): Jeannette & Pablo Baldazo.

Rates:$75-95. Full Bkfst. Evening snacks. 3 rooms. Fireplaces. Beds:Q.
AC, Refrig. in room. Tennis. Swimming. Fishing.

Contact: Jeannette Baldazo. Certificate may be used: Year-round, based
on availability.

Coeur d'Alene

Greenbriar B&B Inn
315 Wallace
Coeur d'Alene 83814
(208)667-9660 (800)369-0026
Fax:(208)667-2231

1908. Winding mahogany staircases, woodwork and
window seats are features of Greenbriar, now in the
National Register. Antiques, imported Irish down
comforters with linen covers, sheer curtains, and
gabled ceilings decorate the guest rooms. The inn is
four blocks from Lake Coeur d'Alene, one of the
most beautiful lakes in the country.

Innkeeper(s): Kris & Bob McIlvenna.

Rates:$60-95. MC VISA AX DS. Full Bkfst. Gourmet Brkfst, Lunch,
Dinner. Teas. Evening snacks. 10 rooms. 2 with shared baths.
Beds:KQT. AC in room. Bicycling. Skiing. Spa. Swimming. Fishing.

Seen in: *Spokesman Review Chronicle, Downwind.*

Contact: Kristine McIlvenna. Certificate may be used: Only Oct. 1
through June 1.

*"It made our wedding celebration so special. You're a
real professional."*

Gooding

Gooding Hotel B&B
112 Main
Gooding 83330
(208)934-4374

1906. Travelers will appreciate the handy location
of this Colonial Revival inn, between Boise and

Twin Falls, just off Interstate 84. The historic hotel is listed with the National Register. Guests may avail themselves of the inn's two sitting rooms. Many attractions are found within a one-hour drive of the inn, including Malad Gorge State Park, Shoshone Falls, Shoshone Ice Caves, Snake River Canyon and Sun Valley.

Innkeeper(s): Lauren & Elsa Freeman.

Rates:$38-42. MC VISA. Full Bkfst. Gourmet Brkfst. 8 rooms. 8 with shared baths. Beds:QT. Phone, AC, Refrig. in room. Skiing. Swimming. Fishing.

Contact: Elsa Freeman. Certificate may be used: Anytime July 1, 1994 through Dec. 31, 1995 as long as room is reserved in advance and certificate is mentioned.

McCall

1920 House B&B

143 E Lake St, PO Box 1716
McCall 83638
(208)634-4661

1920. This restored home offers easy access to nearby recreation areas. The inn's three guest rooms have been lovingly decorated by the innkeepers with family heirlooms, antiques and unique touches. The sitting room boasts striking views of Payette Lake and Brundage Mountain, and guests also are welcome to enjoy the living room fireplace and library. Ponderosa State Park and the Brundage Mountain Ski Area are close by. Winter visitors should inquire about ski packages. Special arrangements may be made for weddings, showers, special dinners and picnic lunches.

Innkeeper(s): Bill & Bonni Shikrallah.

Rates:$65-70. Gourmet Brkfst, Lunch, Dinner. Picnic lunches. Teas. Evening snacks. 3 rooms. 3 with shared baths. Beds:Q. Skiing. Swimming. Fishing.

Contact: Bonni Shikrallah. Certificate may be used: March-June, October-December.

Northwest Passage B&B Lodge

201 Rio Vista, PO Box 4208
McCall 83638
(208)634-5349 (800)597-6658
Fax:(208)634-4977

1938. This mountain country inn rests on five acres and offers four guest rooms, two of them suites. Guests enjoy the inn's two sitting rooms, fireplace and full breakfasts. There are horse corrals on the premises, and most pets can be accommodated when arrangements can be made in advance. The inn is furnished in country decor and provides easy access to a myriad of recreational opportunites found in the area. Payette Lake is just a short dis-

tance from the inn, and the Brundage Mountain Ski Area and Ponderosa State Park are nearby.

Innkeeper(s): Steve & Barbara Schott.

Rates:$60-80. MC VISA DS. Full Bkfst. 6 rooms. Beds:QT. Conference Rm. Golf. Tennis. Skiing. Swimming. Horseback riding. Fishing.

Contact: Steve Schott. Certificate may be used: All year with advance reservations, except holiday weekends and winter carnival.

Mountain Home

The Rose Stone Inn

495 North 3rd East
Mountain Home 83647
(208)587-8866 (800)717-7673

1907. An easy getaway from Boise is this distinctive Queen Anne Victorian inn, which once served as a boardinghouse for the area's Basque immigrants. The inn's five rooms, all with queen beds, feature the influence of the Basques, many of whom came West to work as shepherds. The Olde World Room offers antiques, shower and clawfoot tub, while the Celebration Room sports a brass bed and floral canopy. Guests may eat breakfast in the dining area, turret, their rooms or on the outside veranda. A gift shop is on the premises. The surrounding area has many attractions, including skiing, golf, and a winery.

Innkeeper(s): Dorothy Halstead.

Rates:$35-65. MC VISA DC DS. Full Bkfst. Teas. 5 rooms. Beds:Q. Conference Rm. TV, Phone, AC, Refrig. in room.

Contact: Laurice Bentz. Certificate may be used: Monday through Thursday.

Sandpoint

Angel of the Lake B&B

410 Railroad Ave
Sandpoint 83864-1557
(208)263-0816

1895. Originally the home of Sandpoint's first mayor, this Queen Anne Victorian inn offers the feel of a bygone era and the picturesque setting of Lake Pend Oreille. The guest rooms, with their classic movie themes, will delight visitors, who select from the African Queen, Blazing Saddles, Casablanca and Gone with the Wind rooms, each

offering its own special ambiance and amenities. Views of the lake and the Cabinet Mountains are enjoyed at the inn, and another special treat is an outdoor hot tub. The Schweitzer Mountain ski area is just minutes from the inn.

Innkeeper(s): Tracy & Grace Bowser.

Rates:$65-75. MC VISA. Full Bkfst. 4 rooms. 2 with shared baths. Beds:KQ. Skiing. Spa. Swimming. Fishing.

Contact: Tracy Bowser. Certificate may be used: Sept. 1, 1994 through May 1, 1995. Not valid three-day holiday weekends or Dec. 17 through Jan. 1.

Wallace

The Beale House
107 Cedar St
Wallace 83873
(208)752-7151

1904. This attractive, three-story Colonial Revival home is listed in the National Register, as is the town of Wallace. Original parquet wood floor, antiques and memorabilia combine to lend an authentic aura of the past. Each of the five guest rooms offers a unique feature, such as a fireplace, balcony or wall of windows. The innkeepers are well versed in their home's history and guests are welcome to look over a photographic record of the house and its former owners. A backyard hot tub provides a lovely view of the mountains and creek. Recreational activities abound in the vicinity, famous for its silver mines.

Innkeeper(s): Jim & Linda See.

Rates:$75-100. MC VISA. Full Bkfst. Evening snacks. 5 rooms. 4 with shared baths. Fireplaces. Beds:DT. Skiing. Spa. Swimming. Fishing.

Contact: Linda See. Certificate may be used: May 1-June 30, Oct. 1-Nov. 30, Jan. 1-Feb. 15, only on Wednesday through Sunday. Would have to charge a minimum of $85 for the two nights.

Jameson B&B
304 Sixth St
Wallace 83873
(208)556-1554 Fax:(208)753-0981

1889. Wallace features many impressive turn-of-the-century homes, including this roomy Queen Anne Victorian. Arrangements may be made for family reunions, meetings and weddings. Area attractions include an arts center, mining museum, railroad museum and a silver mine tour. Be sure to take advantage of the town's walking tour.

Innkeeper(s): Rick Shaffer.

Rates:$57. MC VISA AX DS. Cont. Bkfst. Gourmet Dinner. Picnic lunches. 6 rooms. 6 with shared baths. Beds:QT. Conference Rm. Skiing. Exercise room. Swimming. Fishing.

Contact: Richard Shaffer. Certificate may be used: June 1 - Sept. 15 anyday.

Weiser

Galloway Inn B&B
1120 E Second St
Weiser 83672
(208)549-2659

1898. This three-story brick Victorian house boasts a turret and an octogonal tower with beveled-glass windows. Guest rooms feature antique furnishings and one has its own sun porch. A hearty country breakfast is served in the formal dining room. There is an acre of grounds with a hot tub under a gazebo and across the street is a park with a new swimming pool and tennis courts. The Weisler area is well known for big game hunting, pheasant hunting and trout fishing. The famous Old Time National Fiddler's Contest is held here each June. It's 60 miles to Hells Canyon, the deepest canyon in the United States.

Innkeeper(s): Eunia Gile.

Rates:$69. Full Bkfst. 5 rooms. 2 with shared baths. Beds:QT. AC in room. Golf. Spa.

Seen in: *Country*.

Contact: Eunia Gile. Certificate may be used: All year.

Illinois

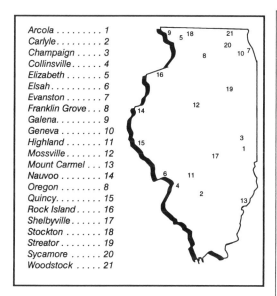

Arcola

Curly's Corner B&B
RR 2, Box 85B
Arcola 61910
(217)268-3352

1977. Less than a mile from Rockhome Gardens and in the middle of Amish Country, visitors will find Curly's Corner B&B, a one-story, air-conditioned brick ranch home. A lush expanse of lawn surrounds the attractive home. The other room boasts a king-size bed. The innkeepers, avid card players, also are available to drive guests on a tour of the area for a fee. Within easy driving distance are three state parks, the Shelbyville Wildlife Management Area and Lake Shelbyville.

Innkeeper(s): Warren & Maxine Arthur.

Rates:$50-60. Full Bkfst. 4 rooms. 2 with shared baths. Beds:KQT. TV, Phone, AC in room. Farm. Bicycling. Handicap access. Fishing.

Contact: Maxine Arthur. Certificate may be used: November through April.

Carlyle

Country Haus
1191 Franklin
Carlyle 62231
(618)594-8313 (800)279-4486
Fax:(618)594-8415

1898. This turn-of-the-century home features hardwood floors, an original tile mantel and a stained-glass window. Each guest room offers something special. The Wild Flower Room has a canopy bed

and is filled with wild flowers each summer. The Harvest Room offers owl-shaped lamps, a large selection of books and a clawfoot tub. Breakfasts are served in a family-style buffet with homebaked delicacies such as pineapple muffins, Swedish egg casserole and peaches and cream French toast. Unwind in the library or relax in the spa, located on the outside deck.

Innkeeper(s): Ron & Vickie Cook.

Rates:$45-55. MC VISA AX DC. Full Bkfst. 5 rooms. Beds:KQ. Phone, AC in room. Golf. Tennis. Skiing. Spa. Swimming. Fishing.

Seen in: *Great Lakes Sailor, Carlyle Laker, Union Banner, News-Democrat.*

Contact: Vickie Cook. Certificate may be used: Anytime except holiday weekends, i.e. Memorial Day, July 4, Labor Day, Easter, Christmas, Thanksgiving (Friday-Sunday, May 25-Sept. 15 excluded).

"Lovely, happy place to stay."

Champaign

The Golds B&B
2065 County Rd 525 E
Champaign 61821
(217)586-4345

1874. Visitors to the University of Illinois area may enjoy a restful experience at this inn, west of town in a peaceful farmhouse setting. Antique country furniture collected by the innkeepers over the past 25 years is showcased in the inn and is beautifully offset by early American stenciling on its walls. An apple tree and garden are on the grounds, and seasonal items are sometimes used as breakfast fare. Guests enjoy jogging on the inn's six acres, and often come across pheasants, rabbits and other wildlife. The inn's satellite TV and CD collection offer other opportunities for guests' enjoyment.
Innkeeper(s): Rita Gold.
Rates:$48. ContPlus Bkfst. 3 rooms. 2 with shared baths. Beds:T. AC, Refrig. in room. Farm. Golf. Skiing. Swimming. Fishing.
Seen in: *News Gazette*.
Contact: Rita Gold. Certificate may be used: Any time except special-event weekends.

Collinsville

Maggie's B&B
2102 N Keebler Rd
Collinsville 62234
(618)344-8283

1900. A rustic two-acre wooded area surrounds this friendly Victorian inn, once a boarding house. Rooms with 14-foot ceilings are furnished with exquisite antiques and art objects collected on

worldwide travels. Downtown St. Louis, the Gateway Arch and the Mississippi riverfront are just 10 minutes away.
Innkeeper(s): Margaret Leyda.

Rates:$35-70. MC VISA. Full Bkfst. Gourmet Brkfst. 5 rooms. 1 with shared bath. Fireplaces. Beds:QT. Conference Rm. TV, AC in room. Spa. Exercise room.
Seen in: *Collinsville Herald Journal, Innsider, Belleville News*.
Contact: Margaret Leyda. Certificate may be used: All year, Monday - Thursday nights.

"We enjoyed a delightful stay. You've thought of everything. What fun!"

Elizabeth

Ridgeview B&B
8833 S Massbach Rd
Elizabeth 61028
(815)598-3150

1919. The unique combination of a country schoolhouse and former artist's home greets guests of the Ridgeview B&B, which overlooks the scenic Rush Creek Valley in the state's Northwest corner. Once the residence of artist Thomas Locker, the Swiss-influenced inn now houses three guest rooms and a suite in its loft area, furnished in country-Southwest decor. The School Room sports an authentic, old-fashioned effect, with blackboard, small school desks and a library with an 1882 math book. The Art Room was once Thomas Locker's bedroom. Chestnut Mountain Ski Resort is nearby.
Innkeeper(s): Elizabeth (Betty) A. Valy.
Rates:$59-99. MC VISA AX. Full Bkfst. 4 rooms. Beds:KQ. Phone, Refrig. in room. Skiing. Fishing.
Contact: Elizabeth A. Valy. Certificate may be used: Sunday through Friday-no Saturdays, no holidays during September - October only. Two nights cannot be Friday-Saturday or Saturday-Sunday combination.

Elsah

Green Tree Inn
15 Mill St, PO Box 96
Elsah 62028
(618)374-2821

1850. Located in a New England-style village, this red clapboard inn is just a short walk from the Mississippi River. Opening onto a large front

porch, the first floor provides an 1850s country store with Victorian linens, lace, hand-blown glass, dried flowers, herbs and teas for sale. Each room is decorated in a period style and features a private porch. Monthly seminars offer insight into 19th-century perennial and herb gardening. Bicycles are provided so guests may enjoy the 16-mile Vadalabene bike trail that winds along the river and offers views of sailboats and the Delta Queen, and in winter, an occasional bald eagle.

Innkeeper(s): Mary Ann Pitchford.

Rates:$69-105. MC VISA. Full Bkfst. AP available. Gourmet Brkfst, Lunch, Dinner. Picnic lunches. Teas. Evening snacks. 10 rooms. Beds:KQ. Conference Rm. Phone, AC in room. Bicycling. Skiing. Handicap access. Swimming. Stables. Fishing.

Seen in: *Midwest Living, Chicago Tribune, Good Morning America.*

Contact: Mary Ann Pitchford. Certificate may be used: Tuesday, Wednesday, Thursday excluding holidays. July, August, November, December, January, February and March for Governor's Room.

"Thank you for the wonderful stay at your inn."

Evanston

Margarita European Inn
1566 Oak Ave
Evanston 60201
(708)869-2273 Fax:(708)869-2353

1927. This stately inn, once the proper home to young area working women, has a proud tradition in the city's history. The Georgian architecture is complemented by an impressive interior, featuring arched French doors, vintage period molding and a large parlor with floor-to-ceiling windows. Near the lakefront and Northwestern University, it also boasts a gourmet Italian restaurant, a library and large-screen TV room. Guests often enjoy renting a bike and exploring the area's many attractions, including 24 nearby art galleries.

Innkeeper(s): Judith Baker.

Rates:$55-90. MC VISA AX. Cont. Bkfst. Teas. 40 rooms. 27 with shared baths. Beds:KQT. Conference Rm. Phone in room.

Contact: Barbara Gorham. Certificate may be used: November through February.

Franklin Grove

Whitney B&B
1620 Whitney Rd
Franklin Grove 61031
(815)456-2526

1856. This historic Italianate inn, located in a tranquil, countryside farm setting, provides an ideal getaway for busy Chicago or Milwaukee residents or a convenient stop for those traveling the upper Midwest. Recognized by historical registers at the national, state and local levels, the Whitney B&B offers six guest rooms, many antique furnishings, feather beds and old-fashioned tubs. The inn's 161 acres are home to the Whitney #20 Crab Apple. Nearby are five state parks, the John Deere Home and Lincoln Monument State Memorial. Be sure to check out the non-alcoholic wine cellar and collectibles shop.

Innkeeper(s): Sheryl Lyons.

Rates:$50-75. Cont. Bkfst. 6 rooms. 3 with shared baths. Beds:KD. Farm. Golf. Tennis. Fishing.

Contact: Sheryl Lyons. Certificate may be used: Anytime available.

Galena

Felt Manor
125 S Prospect St
Galena 61036
(815)777-9093 (800)383-2830

1848. Overlooking the historic river town and its surrounding countryside is Felt Manor, a Second Empire Victorian inn. The inn's many unique fea-

tures include an underground ice house, original marble sinks and a double stairway that leads down to the street and is known as Felt's Folly, because it cost $40,000 to build back in 1850. The stairway is listed with the Library of Congress as a National Landmark. Marble fireplaces highlight the interior, where guests are encouraged to make use of the library and parlor.

Innkeeper(s): Laura & Dan Balocca.

Rates:$70-115. MC VISA AX. Full Bkfst. AP available. Gourmet Brkfst. Teas. 5 rooms. 2 with shared baths. Beds:QDT. Conference Rm. AC in room. Skiing. Swimming. Fishing.

Contact: Daniel Balocca. Certificate may be used: Any Sunday - Thursday night or any night December - April.

Mother's Country Inn

349 Spring St
Galena 61036
(815)777-3153

1838. Visitors have their choice of guest rooms or suites at Mother's Country Inn. The suites are located at Mother's II, a two-story home overlooking the levee on the Galena River. Each suite features antiques, wicker and wallpaper of the period. Guests will enjoy the added luxuries of fireplaces and whirlpool tubs after a

busy day exploring the history-rich area. The other building is a short walk from the city center. Breakfast is served in front of the sitting room fireplace and many guests relish a cup of coffee on the screened porch.

Innkeeper(s): Pat Laury.

Rates:$75-125. MC VISA. Cont. Bkfst. 11 rooms. Fireplaces. Beds:QT. Conference Rm. TV, Phone, AC, Refrig. in room. Farm. Skiing. Handicap access. Swimming. Fishing.

Contact: Patricia Laury. Certificate may be used: Sunday through Thursday year-round, no holiday weekends.

Park Avenue Guest House

208 Park Ave
Galena 61036
(815)777-1075

1893. A short walk from Grant Park sits this attractive Queen Anne Victorian with turret and wraparound porch. Gardens and gazebo add to this peaceful neighborhood charm, as does the original woodwork throughout. The Helen Room features a gas fireplace, TV, tub and shower, while the

Miriam Room's brass bed highlights a cheerful floral decor. The Anna Suite boasts a comfortable sitting room in the inn's turret area and the Lucille

Room is tastefully furnished in mauve, gray and white tones. The holiday decorations, including eight Christmas trees, are not to be missed.

Innkeeper(s): Sharon & John Fallbacher.

Rates:$80-100. MC VISA DS. ContPlus Bkfst. 4 rooms. Beds:QT. Skiing. Fishing.

Contact: Sharon Fallbacher. Certificate may be used: Midweek only, Sunday through Thursday, except holidays January, February, March & April.

Geneva

The Oscar Swan Country Inn

1800 W State St
Geneva 60134
(708)232-0173

1902. This turn-of-the-century Colonial Revival house rests on seven acres of trees and lawns. Its 6,000 square feet are filled with homey touches. There is a historic barn on the property and a gazebo on the front lawn. A pillared breezeway connects the round garage to the house. The stone

pool is round, as well. Nina is a home economics teacher and Hans speaks German and is a professor of business administration at Indiana University.

Innkeeper(s): Nina & Hans Heymann.

Rates:$75-139. MC VISA AX. Full Bkfst. 8 rooms. 3 with shared baths. Fireplaces. Beds:KQT. Conference Rm. Phone, AC, Refrig. in room. Golf. Skiing. Sauna. Swimming. Fishing.

Seen in: *Chicago Tribune, Windmill News.*

Contact: Nina Heymann. Certificate may be used: July, November, January, February, March and April. Sunday through Thursday.

"Thank you for making our wedding such a beautiful memory. The accommodations were wonderful, the food excellent."

Highland

Phyllis' B&B

801 Ninth St
Highland 62249
(618)654-4619

1910. Visitors to Highland, one of the country's largest Swiss settlements, have a home away from home at Phyllis' B&B, which prides itself on the ability to provide guests a quiet and restful stay. Fireplaces, ceiling fans and air conditioning help add to the comfort level at this Shingle Victorian inn. The five guest rooms include the Quilt and Wicker rooms, and the aqua and pink Angel Room is host to a lovely view. An outside deck is the perfect vantage point for birdwatching in the tree-lined neighborhood. The town square, with its festivals and summer music concerts, is nearby.

Innkeeper(s): Bob & Phyllis Bible.

Rates:$55. MC VISA. ContPlus Bkfst. 5 rooms. 2 with shared baths. Fireplaces. Beds:QDT. TV, Phone, AC, Refrig. in room. Golf. Tennis. Spa. Sauna. Exercise room. Swimming. Fishing.

Contact: Phyllis Bible. Certificate may be used: Anytime December through March.

Mossville

Old Church House Inn B&B

1416 E Mossville Rd
Mossville 61552
(309)579-2300

1869. This inn is a converted church. There are 18-foot ceilings, arched windows, Victorian-era antiques and an elevated library. Afternoon tea is presented between 4-6 p.m. in the dining room or in warmer weather, outdoors next to the rose and herb gardens. Guest rooms feature queen featherbeds and antique bedsteads. A gourmet continental breakfast buffet or sweetheart breakfast tray is available.

Innkeeper(s): Dean & Holly Ramseyer.

Rates:$69-99. MC VISA. ContPlus Bkfst. Picnic lunches. Teas. 3 rooms. 2 with shared baths. Beds:Q. AC in room. Bicycling. Skiing. Swimming. Fishing.

Seen in: *Chillicothe Bulletin, Journal Star.*

Contact: Dean Ramseyer. Certificate may be used: Monday through Thursday all year; weekends January and March. Private bath rate only.

"Your hospitality, thoughtfulness, the cleanliness, beauty, I should just say everything was the best."

Mount Carmel

Living Legacy Homestead

Box 146A, RR #2
Mount Carmel 62863
(618)298-2476

1870. This turn-of-the-century German homestead features both farmhouse and log house settings. Antiques and period furniture abound, and visitors experience the unique sight of the log house's exposed interior walls and loft. The 10-acre grounds are home to flower, herb and vegetable gardens, and guests also are free to roam the meadows, barnyard and wildlife areas. Nearby are the Beall Woods State Natural Area and the Wabash River. A gift shop featuring antiques, crafts and collectibles is on the premises.

Innkeeper(s): Edna Anderson.

Rates:$65-75. Full Bkfst. Evening snacks. 4 rooms. 2 with shared baths. Beds:DT. Conference Rm. Phone, AC in room. Farm.

Contact: Edna Anderson. Certificate may be used: Monday through Thursday nights; March through December.

The Poor Farm B&B

Poor Farm Rd
Mount Carmel 62863-9803
(618)262-4663 (800)646-3276

1915. This uniquely named inn served as a home for the homeless for more than a century. Today, the stately brick Federal-style structure hosts travelers and visitors to this lovely area of Southeast Illinois. Fireplaces and VCRs in the rooms add to guests' comfort and the inn also has bicycles available for those wishing to explore the grounds. The Poor Farm B&B sits adjacent to a recreational park with a well-stocked lake and is within walking distance of an 18-hole golf course and driving range.

Innkeeper(s): Liz & John Stelzer.

Rates:$45-85. MC VISA AX DS. Full Bkfst. MAP available. 4 rooms. Fireplaces. Beds:D. Conference Rm. Phone, AC in room. Farm. Bicycling. Handicap access. Swimming. Fishing.

Contact: Liz Stelzer. Certificate may be used: Monday - Thursday January - Nov. 15 except holidays.

Nauvoo

Mississippi Memories

Riverview Hgts, Box 291
Nauvoo 62354
(217)453-2771

1981. Spectacular sunsets and river views from this inn's two large decks greet guests at the Mississippi

Memories B&B, a modern farmhouse in a wooded riverfront setting. Guests may choose to breakfast on one of the decks, in the dining room or in the kitchen with Marge, who always serves up a hearty meal. Wintertime visitors often are able to spot bald eagles on the premises. The innkeepers, who own and run a large grain and livestock farm, often treat guests to an impromptu tour. Nauvoo State Park is nearby and in town are many historical sites, craft and antique shops and turn-of-the-century homes.

Innkeeper(s): Marge & Dean Starr.

Rates:$58-72. MC VISA. Full Bkfst. Teas. Evening snacks. 5 rooms. 3 with shared baths. Fireplaces. Beds:QD. Conference Rm. AC in room. Swimming. Fishing.

Seen in: *Country, Newslife.*

Contact: Marge Starr. Certificate may be used: Nov. 15 - Feb. 28.

"Our stay was delightful, and the name of your B&B certainly describes it perfectly."

Oregon

Historic Pinehill B&B
400 Mix St
Oregon 61061
(815)732-2061

1874. This classic Italianate country villa is listed in the National Register and features details such as marble fireplaces, French silk-screened mural wallpaper and down comforters. Guest rooms include the Somerset Maugham Room, with king bed, sitting area, fireplace and spa. The Emma Lytle Room, named for a former owner of the home who was an accomplished artist, features one of her original watercolors, a queen poster bed and antique Jenny Lind dressing table. Lowden and Castle Rock state parks are short drives from the inn. Be sure to try some of Pinehill's famous decorated fudge.

Innkeeper(s): Sharon A. Burdick.

Rates:$75-165. MC VISA. Gourmet Brkfst. Picnic lunches. Teas. Evening snacks. 5 rooms. Fireplaces. Beds:KQD. Conference Rm. AC, Refrig. in room. Golf. Tennis. Swimming. Horseback riding. Fishing.

Seen in: *Fox Valley Living Magazine, Victorian Sampler Magazine, Oregon Republican Reporter, Freeport Journal, The Winnetka Paper.*

Contact: Sharon A. Burdick. Certificate may be used: January through Aug. 31, Sunday - Thursday.

Quincy

Bueltmann Gasthaus
1680 Maine St
Quincy 62301
(217)224-8428

1889. This unique inn, with its massive stone porches, combines Queen Anne and Tudor stylings. Quincy, a Mississippi River town, was settled by German immigrant craftsmen. That influence is apparent at the Bueltmann Gasthaus, where Victorian lace curtains, purchased in Germany, and family heirloom rocking chairs add to the home's charm. The inn is located in the city's historic district, and on the grounds sits a two-story carriage house. Breakfast, which features homemade pastries and jams, is served in the formal dining room.

Innkeeper(s): Charlotte & David Bueltmann.

Rates:$50-60. ContPlus Bkfst. 4 rooms. 2 with shared baths. Beds:QT. Conference Rm. TV, Phone, AC in room. Fishing.

Contact: David Bueltmann. Certificate may be used: Weekdays only.

Rock Island

Potter House B&B
1906 7th Ave
Rock Island 61201
(309)788-1906 (800)747-0339

1907. This Colonial Revival mansion is in the National Register. Embossed leather wall coverings, mahogany woodwork and stained- and leaded-glass windows are special features. There is a solarium with a tile and marble floor and there are six fireplaces. A white Chinese carpet, antique beds and a round-tiled shower are features of the Palladian Room. Nearby are the Riverboat Casinos and a number of excellent restaurants.

Innkeeper(s): Nancy & Gary Pheiffer

Rates:$60-100. MC VISA AX DC DS CB. Gourmet Brkfst. 6 rooms. Fireplaces. Beds:QDT. Conference Rm. TV, Phone, AC in room. Golf. Tennis. Bicycling. Skiing. Swimming. Fishing.

Seen in: *Chicago Sun Times, Quad City Times.*

Contact: Nancy Pheiffer. Certificate may be used: Weeknights (Sunday - Thursday) Nov. 1 until June 1, 1995.

Shelbyville

The Shelby Historic House and Inn
816 W Main St
Shelbyville 62565
(217)774-3991 (800)342-9978

1903. This Queen Anne Victorian inn is listed in the National Register of Historic Places. The inn is well known for its conference facilities, and is less than a mile from Lake Shelbyville, one of the state's most popular boating and fishing spots. Guaranteed tee times are available at a neighboring championship golf course. Three state parks are nearby, and the Amish settlement near Arthur is within easy driving distance.

Innkeeper(s): Ken & Freddie Fry

Rates:$48-76. MC VISA AX DC DS CB. Cont. Bkfst. MAP available. 12 rooms. Beds:KT. Conference Rm. TV, Phone, AC in room. Swimming. Fishing.

Contact: Ken Fry. Certificate may be used: No weekends from May 25 through Sept. 16, 1994.

Stockton

Maple Lane Country Inn & Resort
3114 Rush Creek Rd
Stockton 61085
(815)947-3773 Fax:(815)847-3773

1954. The expansive grounds of this large Colonial Revival mansion, feature a guest house, gazebo, and several farm buildings. The full gourmet breakfast will delight guests. Historic Galena is within easy driving distance, as are several state parks.

Innkeeper(s): Rose & Bill Stout.

Rates:$77-300. Full Bkfst. Gourmet Brkfst. Picnic lunches. 12 rooms. Beds:QT. Conference Rm. AC, Refrig. in room. Farm. Skiing. Spa. Sauna. Swimming. Stables. Fishing.

Contact: Rose Stout. Certificate may be used: Sunday through Thursday, no holidays, not during October or hunting seasons.

Streator

Dicus House B&B
609 E Broadway St
Streator 61364
(815)672-6700 (800)262-1890

1890. A fine example of Stick/Eastlake Victorian architecture, this inn is recognized as a National Historic Place. The antique-filled inn regularly hosts Mystery Party weekends. Original woodwork, six marble fireplaces and the many antiques will impress guests, who are just a short drive from the Illinois River and its many recreational settings, including Rock and Matheison state parks. The surrounding area offers an abundance of community festivals and antique/collectible auctions.

Innkeeper(s): Felicia & Art Bucholtz.

Rates:$45-55. MC VISA. Full Bkfst. Evening snacks. 4 rooms. 2 with shared baths. Beds:KQ. AC in room. Skiing. Swimming. Fishing.

Contact: Felicia Bucholtz. Certificate may be used: Anytime January through April. Sunday - Thursday May to December, excluding holidays and special events.

Sycamore

Country Charm B&B
15165 Quigley Rd
Sycamore 60178
(815)895-5386 Fax:(815)895-5386

1911. Just outside DeKalb and the Northern Illinois University area lies this three-story stucco farmhouse. Despite its country setting, this inn offers many contemporary touches, including a sunken fireplace in the living room, several sitting rooms and a large-screen TV with surround sound. A wedding chapel adds to the inn's uniqueness. Guests and their children are encouraged to pet the farm animals, including Champ, the trick horse, who is known to correspond with some of the inn's younger customers. A city park is less than a half-mile stroll away.

Innkeeper(s): Howard & Donna Petersen.

Rates:$50-75. Full Bkfst. 3 rooms. Beds:KQ. AC in room. Farm. Fishing.

Seen in: *Dekalb Daily Chronicle.*

Contact: Donna Petersen. Certificate may be used: Nov. 1 through April 31.

"We had a very positive weekend because of your kindness."

Woodstock

The Bundling Board Inn
220 E South St
Woodstock 60098
(815)338-7054

1910. This inn provides the perfect getaway for Chicagoans, who are an easy car or train ride away. The Bundling Board, a Queen Anne Victorian home, is just two blocks from Woodstock's lovely town square. Antiques, quilts and crocheted bedspreads are found in the six guest rooms. The historic town boasts an opera house that is listed on the National Register of Historic Places, and is home to many festivals, fine dining and shopping establishments, including antiques. The Illinois Railroad Museum and Moraine Hills State Park are nearby.

Innkeeper(s): Karen Krajic.

Rates:$45-65. MC VISA DS. ContPlus Bkfst. 6 rooms. 3 with shared baths. Beds:Q. TV, AC in room. Skiing. Swimming. Fishing.

Contact: Karen Krajic. Certificate may be used: April through December.

Indiana

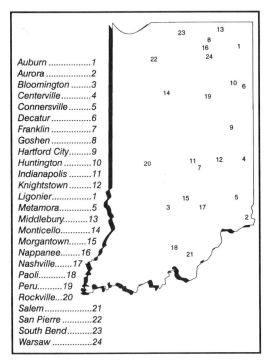

Auburn

Hill Top Country Inn
1733 CR 28
Auburn 46706
(219)281-2298

1920. Originally a pioneer log house, the Hill Top was also once a farmhouse before it was fashioned into the California Craftsman-style bungalow in the 1920s. Guests have their choice of the Front Parlour, Lavender & Lace or Country Slumber guest rooms, all with custom touches. A special feature of this inn is its Benny Bear Haven Room, where a single child will feel right at home and very grown up, while the child's parents enjoy the privacy of their own room. The Hill Top's antique-dominated kitchen is a favorite with many visitors.

Innkeeper(s): Chuck & Becky Derrow.
Rates:$45-70. Full Bkfst. 4 rooms. 3 with shared baths. Beds:KQT. Conference Rm. Phone, AC, Refrig. in room. Farm. Skiing. Swimming. Fishing.
Contact: Rebecca Derrow. Certificate may be used: From Sept. 10 through April.

Aurora

The Aurora Inn
220 4th Street
Aurora 47001
(812)926-4412

1895. One block from the water is the Aurora Inn, a Queen Anne Victorian just across the Ohio River from Kentucky and within easy driving distance of Cincinnati. This inn offers ceiling fans, bicycles and a library for its guests' convenience. Visitors may choose from four guest rooms, which feature mainly country decor. A scenic highway leads right out of Aurora, and the Perfect North Slopes Ski Area and Versailles State Park are close by.
Innkeeper(s): Steve & Beverly Reynolds.
Rates:$49-59. MC VISA. Full Bkfst. Picnic lunches. 4 rooms. 4 with shared baths. Beds:DT. AC in room. Bicycling. Skiing. Fishing.
Contact: Beverly A. Reynolds. Certificate may be used: November-December, 1994; March-May, 1995.

Bloomington

The Bauer House B&B
4595 N Maple Grove Rd
Bloomington 47404
(812)336-4383
IN882341.TIF

1864. This red brick farmhouse B&B boasts a double-tiered, columned porch welcoming guests to a peaceful stay. It is located three miles from downtown. A hearty Hoosier breakfast is served. Ask about the Hilly Hundred Bicycle Ride, Drum & Bugle competition and the Civil War reenactment days, all held nearby.

104

Innkeeper(s): Frank & Beverly Bauer.

Rates:$45. ContPlus Bkfst. 2 rooms. Beds:T. AC in room. Swimming. Fishing.

Seen in: *Herald Times.*

Contact: Beverly Bauer. Certificate may be used: Anytime based on availability March through November with prior reservation.

"Your place is peaceful and quiet, a place to enjoy."

Centerville

Historic Lantz House Inn
214 National Rd W
Centerville 47330
(317)855-2936 Fax:(317)935-0440

1823. This Federal-style inn with four guest rooms is listed with the National Register. The inn's age gives it significant historical value, and this rich tradition is reflected in The Lantz House's antique furnishings. Visitors select from four well-appointed guest rooms, all with fireplaces and desks. Guests may borrow bicycles from the inn to explore historic Centerville, and the inn also has an agreement with a large, neighboring farm so guests may hike, picnic or get a close-up view of farm operation. The surrounding area is rich with antiquing opportunities and several state campgrounds are nearby.

Innkeeper(s): Marcia Hoyt.

Rates:$65-85. VISA. Gourmet Brkfst. Picnic lunches. Evening snacks. 4 rooms. Fireplaces. Beds:Q. Conference Rm. Phone, AC in room. Bicycling. Fishing.

Contact: Marcia Hoyt. Certificate may be used: Oct. 15, 1994 to March 31, 1995.

Connersville

Maple Leaf Inn B&B
831 N Grand Ave
Connersville 47331
(317)825-7099 Fax:(317)825-4261
IN918751.TIF

1863. Large maple trees surround this Victorian home. Guest rooms are decorated with period furnishings, family quilts, and paintings by local artists. The house is close to town and antique shops.

Innkeeper(s): Angel & Cynthia Perez.

Rates:$55-65. MC VISA. ContPlus Bkfst. Gourmet Brkfst. Picnic lunches. 4 rooms. Fireplaces. Beds:QD. TV, Phone, AC in room. Golf. Bicycling. Swimming. Horseback riding. Fishing.

Seen in: *Water Valley Explorer.*

Contact: Cynthia Dorrel Perez. Certificate may be used: November-April.

"I'm going to tell all my friends about this place."

Decatur

Cragwood Inn B&B
303 N Second St
Decatur 46733
(219)728-2000

1900. This Queen Anne Victorian with four porches, gingerbread frosting, a turret and a graceful bay facade was built by a Decatur banker. Finely carved oak is magnificently displayed in the paneled ceilings, staircase and pillars of the parlor. An ornate tin ceiling, leaded-glass windows and a crystal chandelier are among other highlights. The four-poster bed in the Garden Room looks out through a Palladian window. The Turret Suite and the Blue Room have their own fireplace.

Innkeeper(s): George & Nancy Craig.

Rates:$60. MC VISA. Full Bkfst. Evening snacks. 5 rooms. 2 with shared baths. Fireplaces. Beds:QDT. Conference Rm. AC in room. Bicycling. Fishing.

Seen in: *Inside Chicago, Nipsco Folks, Great Lakes Getaway, Christmas Victorian Craft Magazine.*

Contact: Nancy Craig. Certificate may be used: November to April. Weekdays only May to October.

"Your wonderful hospitality, beautiful home and company made my trip that much more enjoyable."

Franklin

Oak Haven B&B
Route #2, Box 57
Franklin 46131-9519
(317)535-9491

1913. Nestled under the shade of several large trees lies the Oak Haven B&B, a modified American four-square home. The tranquil country setting

offers a peaceful change of pace from busy Indianapolis, less than a half-hour away. Handsome oak touches are featured, including a built-in coat rack and the furnishings in the Royal Oak Suite. Visitors are intrigued by the inn's "dumb waiter." A full country breakfast is served on fine china in the formal dining room.

Innkeeper(s): Alan & Brenda Smith.

Rates:$45-70. MC VISA. Full Bkfst. MAP available. Evening snacks. 3 rooms. 2 with shared baths. Beds:QT. AC in room. Farm. Skiing. Swimming. Fishing.

Contact: Brenda Smith. Certificate may be used: Sunday through Thursday only. Any month from now through Dec. 31, 1995.

Goshen

Waterford B&B
3004 S Main St
Goshen 46526
(219)533-6044

1856. This Italianate inn, listed with the National Register, features all Midwest antiques in its furnishing schemes. The innkeeper, an avid antiquer, can provide tips on where to buy in the surrounding area. A full breakfast is served at the Waterford, and guests also may relax in the sitting room or in front of the fireplace. The inn is a short distance from the state's chain of lakes, Amish country or famous South Bend, home of the University of Notre Dame.

Innkeeper(s): Judith Forbes.

Rates:$55. Full Bkfst. 2 rooms. Beds:DT. AC in room.

Contact: Judith Forbes. Certificate may be used: Jan. 1 through April 30.

Hartford City

De Coy's B&B
1546 W 100 N
Hartford City 47348
(317)348-2164

1920. Visitors will enjoy the relaxed atmosphere and "Hoosier" hospitality at this restored farmhouse, located midway between Ft. Wayne and Indianapolis. Tiann, an interior designer, has lovingly seen to the comfort and character of each guest room. The Pintail Room has an antique Murphy bed, and the Loon Room offers a double sleigh bed. Breakfasts feature homemade specialties prepared in the inn's thrasher kitchen. Nearby are Ball State, Indiana Wesleyan and Taylor universities.

Innkeeper(s): Tiann Coy.

Rates:$42-48. Full Bkfst. 5 rooms. 4 with shared baths. Beds:KQT. AC in room. Farm.

Contact: Tiann Coy. Certificate may be used: Anytime except local college events and local business bookings. Certificate must be presented when making reservation.

Huntington

Purviance House
326 S Jefferson
Huntington 46750
(219)356-4218

1859. This Italianate-Greek Revival house is listed in the National Register of Historic Places. The inn features a winding cherry staircase, parquet floors, original interior shutters, tile fireplaces, antique faucets, ornate ceiling designs, antiques and period reproductions. The gold parlor offers well-stocked bookshelves.

Innkeeper(s): Bob & Jean Gernand.

Rates:$40-55. MC VISA DS. Full Bkfst. 4 rooms. 4 with shared baths. Fireplaces. Beds:DT. Conference Rm. AC in room. Golf. Tennis. Skiing. Swimming. Fishing.

Seen in: *Huntington County TAB, Purdue Alumnus Magazine, Richmond Palladium-Item.*

Contact: Jean Gernand. Certificate may be used: Sunday - Friday, March 1 - Nov. 30.

"A completely delightful experience!"

Indianapolis

Renaissance Tower Historic Inn
230 E 9th St
Indianapolis 46204
(317)261-1652 (800)676-7786
Fax:(317)262-8648

1922. Nestled in the heart of one of Indianapolis' most historic areas, this hotel is listed in the National Register of Historic Places. The hotel features flamboyant construction details. Guest rooms

have cherry four-poster beds, Queen Anne furniture, elegant sitting rooms and scenic bay windows. Each suite has a European-style fully equipped kitchen.

Innkeeper(s): Judith Bennett Robbins.

Rates:$50. MC VISA AX. 81 rooms. Beds:D. Conference Rm. TV, Phone, AC, Refrig. in room. Swimming.

Seen in: *Indianapolis Business Journal, New York Times, Indianapolis Star, Muncie Star.*

Contact: Eva Bogar. Certificate may be used: Anytime that is not month of May, first weekend in October, nor first weekend in August. Guest must mention certificate prior to check-in.

"We were so pleased with your lovely decor in the rooms."

The Tranquil Cherub

2164 N Capitol Ave
Indianapolis 46202
(317)923-9036

1900. Visitors to the bustling Indianapolis area will appreciate the quiet elegance of the Tranquil Cherub, a Greek Revival home. The morning rou-

tine begins with freshly brewed coffee and juice served prior to breakfast, which is eaten in the oak-paneled dining room or on a back deck overlooking a pond. Guests may choose from the blue and white Victorian Room, with its antique wicker furniture and lace curtains, or the Gatsby Room, highlighted by its Art Deco-era four-poster cannonball bed. The jade green and navy Rogers Room features stained glass and an oak bedroom set that originated in an old Chicago hotel.

Innkeeper(s): Thom & Barb Feit.

Rates:$60-75. MC VISA. Full Bkfst. Gourmet Brkfst. Evening snacks. 4 rooms. 2 with shared baths. Beds:K. AC in room.

Contact: Barbara Feit. Certificate may be used: Monday-Thursday excluding special events.

Knightstown

Old Hoosier House

7601 S Greensboro Pike
Knightstown 46148
(317)345-2969 (800)775-5315

1836. The Old Hoosier House was owned by the Elisha Scovell family, who were friends of President Martin Van Buren, and the president stayed

overnight in the home. Features of the Victorian house include tall, arched windows and a gabled entrance. Rooms are decorated with antiques and lace curtains. Hearty Hoosier breakfasts include such specialties as a breakfast pizza of egg, sausage and cheese, and Melt-Away Puff Pancakes. The inn's eight acres are wooded, and the deck overlooks a pond on the fourth hole of the adjacent golf course.

Innkeeper(s): Jean & Tom Lewis.

Rates:$57-67. Full Bkfst. Gourmet Brkfst. Teas. Evening snacks. 4 rooms. Fireplaces. Beds:KQT. TV, Phone, AC, Refrig. in room. Golf. Tennis. Bicycling. Handicap access. Fishing.

Seen in: *Indianapolis Star News, New Castle Courier-Times, Indianapolis Monthly.*

Contact: Tom Lewis. Certificate may be used: Anytime.

"We had such a wonderful time at your house. Very many thanks."

Ligonier

Minuette

210 S Main St
Ligonier 46767
(219)894-4494

1898. This striking inn, with its Colonial Revival architecture and handcrafted interior, is listed in the National Register of Historic Places. Its four guest rooms offer visitors a peaceful respite after a day spent exploring Indiana's famous Amish country. Originally known as the Jacob Straus House, the inn was built by one of Ligonier's early Jewish

immigrant settlers. The Minuette features many elegant Victorian touches, such as handlaid mosaic tile, stained glass, handcarved woodwork, crystal chandeliers and beamed ceiling. Guests also enjoy innkeeper Jan Yinger's miniaturia work, which include doll houses.

Innkeeper(s): Ron & Jan Yinger.

Rates:$55. MC VISA. ContPlus Bkfst. Evening snacks. 4 rooms. Beds:QT. AC in room. Bicycling. Fishing.

Contact: Jan Yinger. Certificate may be used: All year.

Metamora

The Thorpe House Country Inn
Clayborne St, PO Box 36
Metamora 47030
(317)647-5425

1840. The steam engine still brings passenger cars and the gristmill still grinds cornmeal in historic Metamora. The Thorpe House is located one block from the canal. Rooms feature original pine and

poplar floors, antiques, stenciling and country accessories. Enjoy a hearty breakfast selected from

the inn's restaurant menu. (Popular items include homemade biscuits, egg dishes and sourdough pecan rolls.) Walk to the village to explore more than 100 shops.

Innkeeper(s): Mike & Jean Owens.

Rates:$70-125. MC VISA DS. Full Bkfst. Picnic lunches. Evening snacks. 5 rooms. Beds:DT. AC in room. Golf. Bicycling. Handicap access. Swimming. Fishing.

Seen in: *Cincinnati Enquirer, Electric Consumer, Indiana Business, Countryside Connection, Chicago Sun-Times.*

Contact: Jean Owens. Certificate may be used: Sunday-Thursday, April-August.

"Thanks to all of you for your kindness and hospitality during our stay."

Middlebury

Bee Hive B&B
PO Box 1191
Middlebury 46540
(219)825-5023

1984. This comfortable home was built with native, hand-sawn timber. Red oak beams and a special loft add country feel. Rooms include country decor and snuggly quilts, which are hand-made locally. Guests can spend the day relaxing or visit the nearby Amish communities. Visit local craft shops or other attractions, which include flea markets and the Shipshewana auction. The bed and breakfast is only four miles from the oldest operating mill in Indiana.

Innkeeper(s): Herb & Treva Swarm.

Rates:$52. MC VISA. Full Bkfst. 3 rooms. 3 with shared baths. Beds:Q. Phone, AC, Refrig. in room. Farm. Skiing. Fishing.

Contact: Herb & Treva Swarm. Certificate may be used: Anytime, rooms with shared bath only.

"What a great place to rest the mind, body and soul."

Patchwork Quilt Country Inn
11748 Cr 2
Middlebury 46540
(219)825-2417 Fax:(219)825-5172

Located in the heart of Indiana's Amish country, this inn offers comfortable lodging and fine food. Some of the recipes are regionally famous, such as the award-winning Buttermilk Pecan Chicken. All guest rooms feature handsome quilts and country decor, and The Loft treats visitors to a whirlpool tub and kitchenette. Ask about the four-hour guided tour of the surrounding Amish area. The alcohol- and smoke-free inn also is host to a gift shop.

Innkeeper(s): Susan Thomas & Maxine Zook.

Rates:$51-95. MC VISA. Full Bkfst. 11 rooms. 3 with shared baths. Beds:Q. AC in room. Skiing. Fishing.

Contact: Maxine Zook. Certificate may be used: Only in November & December, 1994; January, February & March, 1995.

Varns Guest House
PO Box 125, 205 S Main St
Middlebury 46540
(219)825-9666 (800)398-5424

1898. Built by the innkeepers' great-grandparents, this home has been in the family for more than 90 years. Recently restored, it is located on the town's tree-shaded main street. Guests enjoy gliding on the front porch swing while they watch Amish horses and buggies clip-clop past the inn. The Kinder Room features a whirlpool tub.

Innkeeper(s): Carl & Diane Eash.

Rates:$69. MC VISA. ContPlus Bkfst. 5 rooms. Beds:QT. AC in room. Fishing.

Seen in: *Heritage Country Magazine*.

Contact: Diane Eash. Certificate may be used: Nov. 15, 1994-March 30, 1995.

"In terms of style, decor, cleanliness and hospitality, there is none finer!"

Monticello

Zimmer Frei Haus
409 N Main St
Monticello 47960
(219)583-4061 Fax:(219)583-4061

1890. Many a business traveler has found a warm welcome at this Italianate inn, which among many other amenities features an office, with typewriter, fax machine and copier service also available. Handsome carved oak columns greet visitors who are welcome to eat breakfast inside if they wish, or on an outside patio under the shade of the inn's rare gymnaspermous tree. Two hours from Chicago and Indianapolis, Monticello is the gateway to both Lake Freeman and Lake Shafer, with its popular Indiana Beach. Call ahead for information about fishing charters.

Innkeeper(s): Kae & John Fuller.

Rates:$59. MC VISA. Full Bkfst. 2 rooms. Beds:Q. Conference Rm. AC in room. Golf. Tennis. Swimming. Fishing.

Contact: John Fuller. Certificate may be used: March 16 through Oct. 16, Monday through Thursday. Oct. 15 through March 15, all week.

Morgantown

The Rock House
380 W Washington St
Morgantown 46160
(812)597-5100

1894. James Smith Knight built this stone house with tower rooms, a three-room basement and an attic and delivery room. Knight made concrete blocks years before they were popular and embedded stones and rocks in them before they were dry. He also used seashells, jewelry, china dolls and even an animal skull to decorate the blocks. There is still a dumbwaiter used to lower food to the basement for cooling during the summer.

Innkeeper(s): Patricia & Lee Nabors.

Rates:$75-90. MC VISA. Full Bkfst. AP available. Gourmet Dinner. Teas. Evening snacks. 6 rooms. Beds:Q. AC in room. Skiing. Fishing.

Seen in: *Bloomington Herald-Times, Outdoor Indiana Magazine*.

Contact: Linda Landis. Certificate may be used: Anytime except October.

"I was so impressed with your hospitality and the little extra touches that added so much. I've already started spreading the word, and I'll be back myself."

Nappanee

The Victorian Guest House
302 E Market St
Nappanee 46550
(219)773-4383

1887. Listed with the National Register, this three-story Queen Anne Victorian inn was built by Frank Coppes, one of America's first noted kitchen cabi-

net makers. Nappanee's location makes it an ideal stopping point for those exploring the heart of Amish country, or visiting the South Bend or chain of lakes areas. Visitors may choose from six guest rooms, including the Coppes Suite, with its original golden oak woodwork, antique tub and stained glass. Full breakfast is served at the antique 11-foot dining room table. Amish Acres is just one mile from the inn.

Innkeeper(s): Bruce & Vickie Hunsberger.

Rates:$39-75. MC VISA. Full Bkfst. Teas. Evening snacks. 6 rooms. 2 with shared baths. Beds:QT. TV, Phone, AC in room. Swimming.

Contact: Vickie Hunsberger. Certificate may be used: Monday through Thursday, Nov. 1 to April 30.

Nashville

Story Inn
6404 S State Rd 135
Nashville 47448
(812)988-2273 Fax:(812)988-6516

1915. Marking the center of Story, Indiana, population 7, this rustic "Dodge City" style general store, with its weathered tin facade, is flanked by two illu-

minated Red and Gold Crown gas pumps set on the front porch. There's a first-floor restaurant that draws guests from hours away for its fancy desserts and delicious farm-fresh meals. Upstairs, where Studebaker buggies were previously assembled, attractive guest rooms now feature antique four-poster beds, quilts and down pillows.

Innkeeper(s): Gretchen & Bob Haddix.

Rates:$71-104. MC VISA DC DS. Full Bkfst. AP available. Gourmet Dinner. Picnic lunches. Teas. 13 rooms. Beds:QD. Conference Rm. AC, Refrig. in room. Tennis. Skiing. Horseback riding. Fishing.

Seen in: *New York Times, Chicago Tribune, Los Angeles Times, Midwest Living.*

Contact: Gretchen Haddix. Certificate may be used: Sunday, Monday, Tuesday, Wednesday and Thursday only-months of January, February, March, April, May only. No Sunday Monday on or after holiday.

"I never wanted to leave."

Paoli

Braxtan House Inn B&B
210 N Gospel St (SR 37)
Paoli 47454
(812)723-4677

1830. Thomas Braxtan, son of original Quaker settlers, was a business owner and stock trader who built this Victorian house. With 21 rooms, the inn

became a hotel when nearby mineral springs lured guests to Paoli. Oak, cherry, chestnut and maple woodwork are featured. The inn is furnished in antiques and highlighted with stained and leaded glass.

Innkeeper(s): Kate & Duane Wilhelmi.

Rates:$55-65. MC VISA AX DS. Full Bkfst. Evening snacks. 6 rooms. Beds:Q. Conference Rm. AC in room. Golf. Tennis. Skiing. Fishing.

Seen in: *Paoli News-Republican, Bloomington Herald Times, Courier-Journal.*

Contact: Kathrine Daschel. Certificate may be used: Exclude mid-December through end of February (weekends). All other times okay.

"Wonderful. Lovely hospitality."

Peru

Rosewood Mansion
54 N Hood St
Peru 46970
(317)472-7151 Fax:(317)472-5575

1872. Once a major stopover on the Erie-Wabash Canal route, Peru later became a railroad town where the Wabash Cannon Ball made its run. This elegant three-story Victorian manor is located on an acre of lawns and gardens. The inn's 10,000 square feet and 19 rooms include an oak-paneled library, a Victorian parlor, and a three-story staircase lighted with stained-glass windows. Furnishings are antiques and traditional pieces. Nearby attractions in the area are the Cole Porter Festival, the International Circus Hall of Fame, and the Mississinewa Reservoir.

Innkeeper(s): David & Lynn Hausner.

Rates:$65-85. MC VISA AX DS. Full Bkfst. 8 rooms. Beds:QT. Conference Rm. TV, Phone, AC in room. Swimming. Fishing.

Contact: David Hausner. Certificate may be used: Sunday/Monday nights.

Rockville

Suit's Us B&B
514 N College
Rockville 47872
(317)569-5660

1883. Sixty miles west of Indianapolis is this stately Colonial Revival inn. The inn offers a fireplace and library for visitors' comfort and relaxation, and guests also are welcome to use the inn's bicycles or its exercise room. Billie Creek Village is nearby and the Ernie Pyle State Historic Site and Raccoon State Recreation Area are within easy driving distance.

Innkeeper(s): Bob & Ann McCullough.

Rates:$50-125. Full Bkfst. 4 rooms. Beds:KQ. TV, AC in room. Bicycling. Exercise room. Swimming.

Contact: Ann McCullough. Certificate may be used: Sunday-Thursday, May 1-Nov. 1; Anytime Nov. 1-May 1.

Salem

Lanning House B&B
206 E Poplar St
Salem 47167
(812)883-3484

1873. Two structures comprise this inn, the original Lanning House, with three guest rooms, and The 1920s Annex, offering four additional rooms. The 1920s Annex also makes an ideal locale for meetings, reunions or small weddings. Salem is well known for its fine genealogical library, located in the Stevens Museum, just across the street. Both authentic and unique furnishings abound at the Lanning House, and a favorite of guests is the East Meets West Room, highlighted by Japanese artifacts from the owner's travels and a spindle trundle bed. French Lick and Louisville, Ky., are less than an hour away.

Innkeeper(s): Jeanette Hart.

Rates:$50-60. Full Bkfst. 8 rooms. 4 with shared baths. Beds:T. Phone, AC in room.

Contact: Jeanette Hart. Certificate may be used: Winter and early spring up to June.

San Pierre

Lomax Station
3153 S 900 W, RR 1 Box 128
San Pierre 46374
(219)896-2600 (800)535-6629
Fax:(219)896-2600

This country resort offers lodging for up to four people in each of its cabins and is an easy getaway from the hectic Chicago-Gary area. The cabins also feature kitchens, fireplaces, ceiling fans and sleeping lofts. The inn is adjacent to several wildlife sanctuaries and the Kankakee River. Lomax Station hosts many activities and special events, so be sure to call ahead for details. Guests enjoy hiking, picnicking and exploring the inn's 34 acres. A full breakfast is served and a restaurant is on the premises.

Innkeeper(s): Kim Parlin.

Rates:$45-85. Full Bkfst. 5 rooms. Fireplaces. Beds:DT. AC, Refrig. in room. Skiing. Handicap access. Fishing.

Contact: Kim Parlin. Certificate may be used: Anytime.

South Bend

Oliver Inn
630 W Washington St
South Bend 46601
(219)232-4545 Fax:(219)288-9788

1886. This stately Queen Anne Victorian sits amid 30 towering maples and was once home to Josephine Oliver Ford, daughter of James Oliver, of

chilled plow fame. Located in South Bend's historic district, this inn offers a comfortable library and eight inviting guest rooms, some with built-in fireplaces. The inn is within walking distance of downtown, and public transportation is available.

Innkeeper(s): Jacqui Thallemer.

Rates:$85-175. MC VISA AX. ContPlus Bkfst. Picnic lunches. 8 rooms. Fireplaces. Beds:KQT. Conference Rm. TV, Phone, AC in room. Skiing. Handicap access. Swimming. Fishing.

Contact: Lisa Maguire. Certificate may be used: November through March 31, not allowed on premium weekends such as Notre Dame football, parents' weekends.

Warsaw

Candlelight Inn
503 E Fort Wayne St
Warsaw 46580
(219)267-2906 (800)352-0640
Fax:(219)269-4646

1864. Canopy beds, pedestal sinks, clawfoot tubs and period antiques carry out the inn's "Gone With the Wind" theme. Scarlet's Chamber boasts rose wallpaper, a queen bed and mauve carpeting, while Rhett Butler's Chamber boasts navy walls, hardwood floors, walnut canopy bed, burgundy velvet sofa and a Jacuzzi tub.

Innkeeper(s): Ron & Lori McSorley.

Rates:$69-89. MC VISA AX. Full Bkfst. 6 rooms. Beds:KQ. TV, Phone, AC in room. Fishing.

Contact: Deborah Hambright. Certificate may be used: Anytime.

Iowa

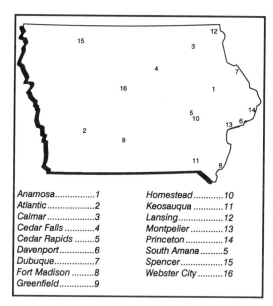

Anamosa

The Shaw House
509 S Oak
Anamosa 52205
(319)462-4485

1890. Framed by enormous old oak trees, this three-story Italianate mansion was built in the style of a Maine sea captain's house. Bordered by sweeping lawns and situated on a hillside on 45 acres, the inn provides views of graceful pastureland from the front porch swing and the tower. Polished oak, walnut and pine floors highlight the carved woodwork and antique furnishings. Guests can enjoy a short

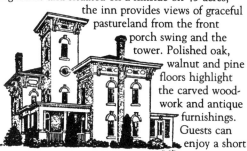

walk to downtown.

Innkeeper(s): Connie & Andy McKean.

Rates:$65-85. Full Bkfst. Evening snacks. 4 rooms. 1 with shared bath. Fireplaces. Beds:QT. Conference Rm. Phone, AC in room. Golf. Tennis. Bicycling. Skiing. Swimming. Horseback riding. Fishing.

Seen in: *Cedar Rapids Gazette, Anamosa Journal-Eureka.*

Contact: Constance McKean. Certificate may be used: As available.

"The views were fantastic as was the hospitality."

Atlantic

Chestnut Charm B&B
1409 Chestnut St
Atlantic 50022
(712)243-5652

1898. This Victorian manor features a sunroom, a fountained patio, natural hardwood floors and ornate woodwork. Most of the original artwork was done by Depression-era artists. The inn is decorated in the style of the '20s and '30s. A stained-glass window on the stairway overlooks the courtyard, which features a wading pool and bird bath. Each bed has a comforter that is handmade by one of the innkeepers, Barbara Stensvad.

Innkeeper(s): Barbara Stensvad.

Rates:$55-85. MC VISA. Full Bkfst. Gourmet Brkfst, Lunch, Dinner. 5 rooms. 2 with shared baths. Beds:KQD. AC in room. Golf. Tennis. Swimming. Fishing.

Seen in: *Atlantic News Telegraph.*

Contact: Barbara Stensvad. Certificate may be used: Anytime, no restrictions but advanced reservations are suggested.

"We truly had a wonderful weekend. Your hospitality was unsurpassed!"

Calmar

Calmar Guesthouse
RR 1, Box 206, 103 N St
Calmar 52132
(319)562-3851

1984. This beautifully restored Victorian was built

by John B. Kay, a lawyer and poet. Stained-glass windows, carved moldings, an oak-and-walnut staircase and gleaming woodwork highlight the gracious interior. A grandfather clock ticks in the living room. In the foyer, a friendship yellow rose is incorporated into the stained-glass window pane. Breakfast is served in the formal dining room. The Laura Ingalls Wilder Museum is nearby in Burr Oak. Smoking is not permitted.

Innkeeper(s): Art & Lucille Kruse.

Rates:$40-45. MC VISA AX. Full Bkfst. 5 rooms. 4 with shared baths. Beds:Q. TV, Phone, AC in room. Golf. Tennis. Skiing. Swimming. Fishing.

Seen in: *Iowa Farmer Today, Calmar Courier, Minneapolis Star-Tribune, Home and Away Magazine.*

Contact: Lucille Kruse. Certificate may be used: Sunday to Thursday, May to October.

"What a delight it was to stay here. No one could have made our stay more welcome or enjoyable."

Cedar Falls

The House by the Side of the Road
6804 Ranchero Rd
Cedar Falls 50613
(319)988-3691

1901. Located on 80 acres, this inn is a country-style farmhouse. Perfect for those seeking a retreat in the countryside, the rooms in the House by the Side of the Road feature ceiling fans and fireplaces. Corn and soybeans are raised on the property, located near Highway 20, a main link to Dubuque and to the Cedar Rapids area. A dinner boat ride on Shell Rock River can be arranged, and an Amish community is nearby for quilt shopping and crafts.

Innkeeper(s): Harlan & Marlys Hughes.

Rates:$40-45. Full Bkfst. AP available. 2 rooms. 2 with shared baths. Fireplaces. Beds:KQ. Phone, AC in room. Farm. Swimming. Fishing.

Contact: Marlys Hughes. Certificate may be used: Anytime available.

Cedar Rapids

Gwendolyn's B&B
1809 2nd Ave SE
Cedar Rapids 52403
(319)363-9731

1917. This recently remodeled Georgian inn features air-conditioned rooms with the added convenience of ceiling fans. Guests will enjoy the eclectic decor, courtesy of innkeeper Gwen Hall, who also prepares their gourmet breakfasts. Gwendolyn's, a family-oriented inn, also features a

conference room for its guests' use. Cross-country skiing, museums and parks are found nearby. Guests also may borrow a bicycle for a close-up view of Cedar Rapids.

Innkeeper(s): Gwen Hall.

Rates:$65-85. MC VISA. Gourmet Brkfst. Evening snacks. 3 rooms. 2 with shared baths. Beds:Q. Conference Rm. TV, Phone, AC in room. Bicycling. Skiing. Spa. Fishing.

Contact: Gwen Hall. Certificate may be used: January-April.

Davenport

River Oaks Inn
1234 E River Dr
Davenport 52803
(319)326-2629 (800)352-6016
Fax:(319)324-6920

1858. A charming Victorian gazebo greets guests of the River Oaks Inn, an Italianate beauty overlooking the Mississippi River. The inn, its gazebo and carriage house are listed with the National Register. Guests may choose from five bedrooms, including the River View Suite, with its king bed and sun porch. The Abner Davison room, named for the home's builder, features twin beds and a lovely bay window area. The three-bedroom Carriage House also boasts a hot tub room.

Innkeeper(s): Mary Jo & Ron Pohl.

Rates:$55-95. MC VISA. Full Bkfst. 5 rooms. Fireplaces. Beds:KQT. TV, Phone, AC, Refrig. in room. Skiing. Swimming. Fishing.

Contact: Mary Jo Pohl. Certificate may be used: Based on availability.

Dubuque

The Hancock House
1105 Grove Terrace
Dubuque 52001
(319)557-8989 Fax:(319)583-0813

1893. Victorian splendor can be found at The Hancock House, one of Dubuque's most striking

examples of Queen Anne architecture. Rooms feature period furnishings and offer views of the Mississippi River states of Iowa, Illinois and Wisconsin. The Hancock House, listed in the National Register, boasts several unique features, including a fireplace judged blue-ribbon best at the 1893 World's Fair in Chicago. Visitors also will enjoy the inn's authentic bathrooms, featuring clawfoot tubs and pull-chain water closets.

Innkeeper(s): Jim & Julie Gross.

Rates:$75-175. MC VISA AX DS. Gourmet Brkfst. 9 rooms. Fireplaces. Beds:Q. TV, Phone, AC in room. Skiing. Fishing.

Contact: Julie Gross. Certificate may be used: Sunday-Thursday nights, no holidays.

The Mandolin Inn
199 Loras Blvd
Dubuque 52001
(319)556-0069 (800)524-7996

1908. This three-story brick Edwardian with Queen Anne wraparound veranda boasts a mosaic-tiled porch floor. Inside are in-laid mahogany and rose-

wood floors, bay windows and a turret that starts in the parlor and ascends to the second-floor Holly Marie Room, decorated in a wedding motif. This room features a seven-piece French Walnut bedroom suite and a crystal chandelier. A three-course gourmet breakfast is served in the dining room with Italian tile depicting women's work at the turn-of-the-century. There is an herb garden outside the kitchen. A church is across the street and riverboat gambling is 12 blocks away.

Innkeeper(s): Jan Oswald.

Rates:$65-115. MC VISA AX DS. Gourmet Brkfst. Teas. 8 rooms. 4 with shared baths. Beds:KQ. AC in room. Golf. Tennis. Bicycling. Skiing. Swimming. Fishing.

Contact: Jan Oswald. Certificate may be used: Sunday through Thursday nights year round, July 1, 1994-Dec. 31, 1995.

"From the moment we entered the Mandolin, we felt at home. I know we'll be back."

Redstone Inn
504 Bluff St
Dubuque 52001
(319)582-1894

1892. This 23-room duplex, was built by pioneer industrialist A. A. Cooper as a wedding gift for his daughter Nell. The side occupied by Nell's family is of grand Victorian decor, generously embellished with turrets and porches. Maple and oak woodwork, beveled, leaded and stained-glass windows and marble and tile fireplaces are elegant features. Dubuque conservationists and business people converted the mansion into a luxurious antique-filled inn.

Innkeeper(s): Chris Weckerly, General Manager.

Rates:$60-175. MC VISA AX. ContPlus Bkfst. AP available. Teas. Evening snacks. 18 rooms. Fireplaces. Beds:QT. Conference Rm. TV, Phone, AC, Refrig. in room. Skiing. Spa. Fishing.

Seen in: *Country Inns, Journal Star, Midwest Living.*

Contact: Chris Weckerly. Certificate may be used: Sunday - Thursday only.

"Very nice!"

The Richards House
1492 Locust St
Dubuque 52001
(319)557-1492

1883. Innkeeper David Stuart estimates that it will take several years to remove the concrete-based

brown paint applied by a bridge painter in the '60s to cover the 7,000-square-foot, Stick-Style Victorian house. The interior, however, only needed a tad of polish. The varnished cherry and bird's-eye maple woodwork is set aglow under electrified gaslights. Ninety stained-glass windows, eight pocket doors with stained glass and a magnificent entryway reward those who pass through.

Innkeeper(s): Michelle Delaney, Manager.

Rates:$40-85. MC VISA AX DC DS CB. Full Bkfst. 6 rooms. 2 with shared baths. Fireplaces. Beds:Q. Conference Rm. TV, Phone, AC in room. Golf. Tennis. Skiing. Swimming. Fishing.

Seen in: *Collectors Journal, Telegraph Herald.*

Contact: David C. Stuart. Certificate may be used: Sunday through Thursday. Ask about Friday and Saturday (very limited availability, only November-April).

"Although the guide at the door had warned us that the interior was incredible, we were still flabbergasted when we stepped into the foyer of this house."

Stout House

1105 Locust
Dubuque 52001
(319)582-1890

1890. This Richardsonian-Romanesque mansion was built by Frank D. Stout for $300,000. The intricate wood carvings were a showcase for the finest skilled craftsmen of the day, working in rosewood, maple, oak and sycamore. One of the 10 wealthiest men in Chicago, Stout entertained Dubuque's upper crust elegantly in his rough-hewn sandstone house.

Innkeeper(s): Jim and Debbie Horvath.

Rates:$59-135. MC VISA AX. Full Bkfst. AP available. Evening snacks. 8 rooms. 4 with shared baths. Fireplaces. Beds:Q. Conference Rm. AC in room. Skiing. Spa.

Seen in: *Telegraph Herald, Country Inns, Innkeeping.*

Contact: Chris Wickerly. Certificate may be used: Good Sunday - Thursday only.

"The surroundings were exquisite."

Fort Madison

Kingsley Inn

707 Avenue H (Hwy. 61)
Fort Madison 52627
(319)372-7074 (800)441-2327
Fax:(319)372-7096

1858. Overlooking the Mississippi River, this century-old inn is located in downtown Fort Madison. Though furnished with antiques, all 14 rooms offer

modern amenities and private baths (some with whirlpools) as well as river views. Horsedrawn carriage and stagecoach rides are only steps away. Eleven miles away is historic Nauvoo, Illinois, the "Williamsburg of the Midwest."

Innkeeper(s): Myrna Reinhard.

Rates:$55-105. MC VISA AX DC DS. ContPlus Bkfst. 14 rooms. Beds:KQ. Conference Rm. TV, Phone, AC in room. Golf. Tennis. Swimming. Fishing.

Seen in: *The Hawkeye.*

Contact: Myrna Reinhard. Certificate may be used: Sunday - Thursday, November, 1994 - March, 1995 & November - December, 1995; Sunday - Thursday.

Mississippi Rose & Thistle Inn

532 Avenue F
Fort Madison 52627
(319)372-7044

1881. Gourmet suppers and picnics are available to guests with advance reservations at this beautiful, red brick Victorian inn. Breakfast specialties cooked by the innkeeper, a gourmet chef, include creamy scrambled eggs with sausage and vegetables in a butter crostade and B.J.'s Sticky Buns. There are three parlors including a game room. The first fort built west of the Mississippi is two blocks away. Also, two blocks away is the Catfish Bend Casino River Boat and not too much farther is the longest swing-span bridge in the world.

Innkeeper(s): Bill & Bonnie Saunders.

Rates:$70-105. MC VISA AX. Full Bkfst. Gourmet Brkfst, Lunch, Dinner. Picnic lunches. 4 rooms. Beds:KQ. Conference Rm. Phone, AC in room. Swimming. Fishing.

Contact: Bill Saunders. Certificate may be used: Sunday through Saturday, Sept. 20, 1994-May 24, 1995; May 30-Sept. 1, 1995; Sept. 20-Dec. 31, 1995.

Greenfield

The Wilson Home

RR 2, Box 132-1
Greenfield 50849
(515)743-2031

1918. Located on 20 acres, this B&B is highlighted by an indoor pool complex with a curving 40-foot pool. Guest rooms are above this building and feature Southwestern, country and traditional themes. The innkeepers are happy to guide hunters to private hunting lands known for excellent pheasant and quail hunting. Madison Country and its famous bridges are within a 20-minute drive.

Innkeeper(s): Wendy & Henry Wilson.

Rates:$75. Full Bkfst. Evening snacks. 3 rooms. 1 with shared bath. Beds:Q. Phone, AC in room. Farm. Golf. Tennis. Bicycling. Swimming. Horseback riding. Stables. Fishing.

Contact: Wendy Wilson. Certificate may be used: Sunday-Thursday night stays only September-April.

Homestead

Die Heimat Country Inn
1 Main St, Amana Colonies
Homestead 52236
(319)622-3937

1857. The Amana Colonies is a German settlement listed in the National Register. This two-story clapboard inn houses a collection of hand-crafted Amana furnishings of walnut and cherry. Country-style quilts and curtains add personality to each guest room. Nearby, you'll find museums, wineries and a woolen mill that imports wool from around the world.

Innkeeper(s): Jacki & Danner Lock.

Rates:$35-63. MC VISA DS. Full Bkfst. 19 rooms. Beds:Q. AC, Refrig. in room. Golf. Tennis. Bicycling. Skiing. Swimming. Fishing.

Contact: Jacklyn Lock. Certificate may be used: January - February only.

"Staying at Die Heimat has been one of our life's highlights. We loved the clean rooms, comfortable beds and history."

Keosauqua

Hotel Manning
100 Van Buren St
Keosauqua 52565
(319)293-3232 (800)728-2718

1899. This historic riverfront inn offers a peek at bygone days. Its steamboat gothic exterior is joined by an interior that strives for historic authenticity. The Shimek State Forest and Lacey-Keosauqua State Park are within easy driving distance, and a picnic lunch prepared at the inn would be ideal to take along. Full dining services are also available.

Innkeeper(s): Ron & Connie Davenport.

Rates:$35-65. MC VISA DS. Full Bkfst. Picnic lunches. 18 rooms. 8 with shared baths. Beds:Q. AC in room. Skiing. Handicap access. Swimming. Fishing.

Contact: Connie Davenport. Certificate may be used: Subject to availability.

Mason House Inn of Bentonsport
RR 2, Box 237
Keosauqua 52565
(319)592-3133

1846. A Murphy-style copper bathtub folds down out of the wall at this unusual inn built by Mormon craftsmen, who stayed in Bentonsport for one year on their trek to Utah. More than half of the furni-ture is original to the home, including a nine-foot walnut headboard and a nine-foot mirror. This is the only operating pre-Civil War steamboat inn in

Iowa. Guests can imagine the days when steamboats made their way up and down the Des Moines River, while taking in the scenery. A full breakfast is served, but if guests crave a mid-morning snack, each room is equipped with its own stocked cookie jar.

Innkeeper(s): Sheral & William McDermet.

Rates:$39-74. MC VISA. Full Bkfst. Picnic lunches. 9 rooms. 4 with shared baths. Beds:KQT. Conference Rm. AC in room. Golf. Bicycling. Skiing. Handicap access. Swimming. Fishing.

Seen in: *Des Moines Register, Fairfield Ledger, Friends.*

Contact: William McDermet. Certificate may be used: Sunday-Thursday.

"The attention to detail was fantastic, food was wonderful and the setting was fascinating."

Lansing

FitzGerald's Inn B&B
160 N 3rd St
Lansing 52151
(319)538-4872

1863. This newly remodeled Victorian inn with Queen Anne exterior and English-country interior features a breathtaking view of the Mississippi

River. FitzGerald's offers an ideal stopping point for visitors to this popular area of the upper Mississippi, known as the "mountains of the Midwest," 35 miles south of La Crosse, Wis. Tin

ceilings, patterned wood floors and many antiques provide guests with a comfortable setting for brief or extended stays.

Innkeeper(s): Marie & Jeff FitzGerald.

Rates:$60-75. DS. Full Bkfst. Teas. 5 rooms. 2 with shared baths. Beds:QD. AC in room. Skiing. Swimming. Fishing.

Contact: Marie FitzGerald. Certificate may be used: Valid November - April all week, upon availability.

Montpelier

Varners' Caboose

204 E 2nd, Box 10
Montpelier 52759
(319)381-3652

1958. Located halfway between Davenport and Muscatine, this original Rock Island Lines caboose rests on its own track behind the Verners' home, the former Montpelier Depot. Llamas and lambs are available for petting.

Innkeeper(s): Bob & Nancy Varner.

Rates:$55. Full Bkfst. 1 room. Beds:QT. AC, Refrig. in room. Fishing.

Contact: Nancy Varner. Certificate may be used: Anytime except special events and holidays.

Princeton

The Woodlands

27144 Levi Ln, PO Box 127
Princeton 52768
(319)289-3177 (800)257-3177
Fax:(800)666-0036

1975. A short drive from the bustling Quad Cities area, The Woodlands is a secluded treat for visitors who treasure the beauties of nature. Trees abound on the 26 acres that surround the picturesque two-story house. Gov. Terry Branstad, like many guests, found the inn's private wildlife refuge particularly compelling. The Woodlands offers privacy for those who seek it and pampering for guests who need more attention. The innkeeper, a world traveler, has furnished the Scandinavian-style home with many fascinating items, and guests will be impressed with the wonderful vistas provided by the viewing room.

Innkeeper(s): The Wallace Family.

Rates:$60-115. Gourmet Brkfst. Dinner. Picnic lunches. Teas. Evening snacks. 3 rooms. 1 with shared bath. Beds:KQT. Conference Rm. Phone, AC in room. Golf. Tennis. Bicycling. Skiing. Handicap access. Swimming. Fishing.

Seen in: *Iowa Lady, The Leader, The Quad City Times, AAA Home & Away Magazine.*

Contact: Elizabeth Anne Wallace. Certificate may be used: Anytime.

South Amana

Babi's B&B

Rt 1 B66, 2788 Hwy 6 Tr
South Amana 52334
(319)662-4381

1913. Babi, an Old World term for Grandma, provides an indication of the homestyle feeling featured at this inn, an ideal location for those visiting the nearby Amana Colonies. Babi's mini-retreat offers a variety of accommodations, including a hayloft, suite or separate rooms. The picturesque two-story farmhouse, with its comfortable country decor, is located on 10 tree-lined acres, and guests are free to explore the inn's grounds year-round.

Innkeeper(s): Tom & Marilyn Kessler.

Rates:$49-79. MC VISA. ContPlus Bkfst. Teas. Evening snacks. 8 rooms. 2 with shared baths. Beds:QT. AC in room. Farm. Golf. Tennis. Skiing. Swimming. Fishing.

Seen in: *Minneapolis Star Tribune, Cedar Rapids Gazette.*

Contact: Thomas Kessler. Certificate may be used: Dec. 15 through April.

Spencer

The Hannah Marie Country Inn

Rt 1, Hwy 71 S
Spencer 51301
(712)262-1286

1910. This beautifully restored farmhouse graces the green lawns and golden fields of corn that surround it. Guest rooms are decorated with down

comforters, Iowa-made quilts, antiques and lace curtains. The Sweetheart Room has an in-room clawfoot tub. Lunches and Mary's famous afternoon teas include Queen Victoria's Chocolate Tea or Tea with the Mad Hatter, all served in costume to the public in the Carl Gustav Dining Rooms. Guests are given walking sticks and parasols for strolling along the old creek. Picnic baskets are available for sale.

Innkeeper(s): Mary Nichols.

Rates:$50-85. MC VISA AX DS. Teas. 4 rooms. Beds:QD. AC in room. Farm. Golf. Swimming. Fishing.

Seen in: *Innsider, Midwest Living, Country Woman, Brides Magazine.*

Contact: Mary Nichols. Certificate may be used: Sunday-Thursday, April, May, October, November to mid-December. Excluding major holidays and Clay City Fair week in September.

"Just like coming home to an old friend."

Webster City

Centennial Farm B&B
1091 220th St
Webster City 50595
(515)832-3050

1900. Parts of the original homestead and barns have been incorporated into this farmhouse situated among fields of corn and soybeans. Tom and Shirley Yungclas are fourth-generation farmers here, and Tom was born in the downstairs bedroom. Guests can gather eggs for breakfast, poke about to view the 1929 Model A Ford and see the farm operation.

Innkeeper(s): Tom & Shirley Yungclas.

Rates:$35. Full Bkfst. Evening snacks. 2 rooms. 2 with shared baths. Beds:T. AC in room. Farm. Golf. Handicap access. Swimming. Fishing.

Seen in: *Fort Dodge Messenger, Freeman Journal.*

Contact: Shirley Yungclas. Certificate may be used: Any time space is available.

"The accommodations were excellent along with the great breakfasts."

Kansas

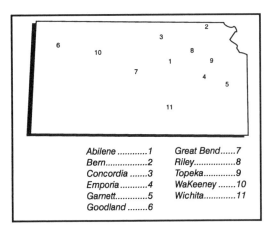

Abilene

Victorian Reflections B&B Inn
820 NW Third
Abilene 67410
(913)263-7774 (800)279-7774
Fax:(913)263-7701

1900. The son of the original owner of this inn was the childhood best friend of former President Dwight D. Eisenhower. Visitors to this Queen

Anne showpiece will marvel at the hand-carved staircase and luxurious formal living room. Beautifully preserved and reminiscent of a relaxed, bygone age, the inn offers a restful setting for its guests. The mauve and teal Hurd Room features a lovely view of Eisenhower Park, adjacent to the inn. Tennis and swimming facilities are available at the park.

Innkeeper(s): Don & Diana McBride.
Rates:$45-75. MC VISA DS. Full Bkfst. 4 rooms. Beds:D. TV, AC in

room. Tennis. Bicycling. Exercise room.
Contact: Diana McBride. Certificate may be used: Anytime.

Bern

Lear Acres B&B
Rt 1, Box 31
Bern 66408-9715
(913)336-3903

1918. A working farm just south of the Nebraska border, Lear Acres is exactly the downhome setting it appears to be. The two-story farmhouse features three spacious guest rooms, all with views of the surrounding countryside. Many of the inn's furnishings are period pieces from the early 1900s. Byron farms a variety of crops and manages a large livestock enterprise. Guests will be greeted by a menagerie of farm pets and animals, adding to the distinctly country atmosphere. The full breakfast features food from the innkeepers' farm and garden. Fall or winter guests may ask for Grandma's cozy feather bed.

Innkeeper(s): Byron & Toby Lear.
Rates:$35. Full Bkfst. 3 rooms. 3 with shared baths. Fireplaces.
Beds:DT. Phone, AC, Refrig. in room. Farm. Bicycling. Swimming. Fishing.
Contact: Toby Lear. Certificate may be used: Weekends with holiday exceptions.

Concordia

Crystle's B&B
508 W 7th St
Concordia 66901
(913)243-2192

1880. This Queen Anne Victorian inn has been recognized by its city's historical society. The home has been in the owner's family for four generations. Three of the inn's five guest rooms showcase Crystle's impressive plate collection. The inn is filled with charming Victorian touches, and a favorite feature is the 1916 Steinway grand piano

120

in the parlor. Guests may enjoy breakfast in their room, the inn's dining room or, weather permitting, on the sun-drenched front porch. Located in a

famous grain-production area of the state, Concordia offers much of interest. Be sure to take in the impressive Brown Grand Theatre.

Innkeeper(s): Jone Rhys.

Rates:$35-45. MC VISA. Gourmet Brkfst. 5 rooms. 4 with shared baths. Beds:Q. Conference Rm. AC in room. Swimming. Fishing.

Seen in: *Blade Empire, Innsider.*

Contact: Jone Rhys. Certificate may be used: Weekdays and September - April. Seven days a week.

Emporia

Plumb House B&B
628 Exchange
Emporia 66801
(316)342-6881

1910. Named for former owners of this restored Victorian Shingle home, the Plumb House offers elegant touches of that period's finery throughout its attractive interior. Try the Rosalie Room, with its pink roses and white lace, old-fashioned tub and rocking chair; or the Loft, a suite with not only a

view, but all the amenities of home, including TV, refrigerator and microwave. Be sure to inquire about the inn's two-hour Tea Party, available for

that extra-special occasion.

Innkeeper(s): Barbara Stoecklein.

Rates:$55-75. MC VISA. Full Bkfst. Gourmet Brkfst. Dinner. Picnic lunches. Teas. Evening snacks. 5 rooms. 1 with shared bath. Fireplaces. Beds:KQT. Conference Rm. TV, Phone, AC, Refrig. in room. Golf. Tennis. Swimming. Fishing.

Contact: Barbara Stoecklein. Certificate may be used: Anytime.

The White Rose Inn
901 Merchant St
Emporia 66801
(316)343-6336

1902. Emporia is a Midwest college town, and the White Rose Inn is a mere three blocks from Emporia State University. This Queen Anne Victorian home offers three private suites for its guests, all with a sitting room and queen beds. Each morning, guests will be treated to a different and delicious menu, and every afternoon tea or espresso is served. Guests who so desire may have breakfast in bed, and the innkeepers will happily arrange for a massage, manicure or pedicure. The inn also hosts weddings and family reunions.

Innkeeper(s): Samuel & Lisa Tosti.

Rates:$50-75. MC VISA AX. Gourmet Brkfst. Lunch. Picnic lunches. Teas. 3 rooms. Beds:Q. AC in room.

Contact: Samuel Tosti. Certificate may be used: Available for our first-time guests.

Garnett

Kirk House
145 W 4th Ave
Garnett 66032
(913)448-5813 Fax:(913)448-6478

1913. Those interested in the arts will love Kirk House. The innkeepers have backgrounds as art dealers, and count weaving and classical music among their other interests. Guests receive plenty of pampering at this inn, located in eastern Kansas, south of Ottawa. Food preparation and presentation are stressed here, with visitors enjoying a gourmet breakfast, afternoon tea and evening snacks. The inn also offers turndown service and a sitting room and library for further relaxation.

Innkeeper(s): Robert Logan, Robert Cugno & Angie Williams.

Rates:$60-90. Gourmet Brkfst. Teas. Evening snacks. 5 rooms. 4 with shared baths. Beds:QDT. Golf. Tennis. Swimming. Fishing.

Seen in: *Topeka Capital-Journal, The Anderson Countian.*

Contact: Robert Logan & Robert Cugno. Certificate may be used: Anytime.

Goodland

Heart Haven Inn
2145 Rd 64
Goodland 67735
(913)899-5171

1911. This farmhouse inn in rural Goodland, just off busy Interstate 70 in western Kansas, is the perfect getaway for weary travelers or those needing the refreshment of a country setting. An antique pump organ and Victrola phonograph player add to the authentic old-time aura. Guests choose from Baroque, Victorian or Western themes for their lodgings. The High Plains Museum is nearby.

Innkeeper(s): Cecil & Carol Bowen.
Rates:$335-65. Full Bkfst. Teas. 4 rooms. 2 with shared baths. Beds:QT. AC in room. Farm.
Contact: Carol Bowen. Certificate may be used: All year.

Great Bend

Peaceful Acres B&B
Rt 5, Box 153
Great Bend 67530
(316)793-7527

1900. A casual country setting greets guests at Peaceful Acres, a comfortable farmhouse with plenty of sheep, chicken, dogs and cats to entertain all visitors, especially children, who are more than welcome here. Activities abound for the youngsters and they also will enjoy the zoo in Great Bend, five miles away. Cheyenne Bottoms and Pawnee Rock are within easy driving distance.

Innkeeper(s): Dale & Doris Nitzel.
Rates:$30. Full Bkfst. 2 rooms. 2 with shared baths. Beds:QDT. AC in room. Farm. Fishing.
Contact: Doris Nitzel. Certificate may be used: Anytime.

Walnut Brook B&B
RR 3, Box 304
Great Bend 67530-9803
(316)792-5900 (800)300-5901
Fax:(316)792-5848

1924. Despite its country setting, this inn is a far cry from "roughing it." The innkeepers delight in treating guests to a stay they will never forget. The Walnut Brook is filled with beautiful oak woodwork and leaded glass. Visitors may enjoy their breakfast in the friendship garden or the cottage's breakfast nook. Guests may pet a lamb in a meadow, or stroll the grounds, breathing in the smells of fresh tar-

ragon and hollyhock. Others may opt for a dip in the pool or a soak in the sauna.

Innkeeper(s): Mike & Janet Hammeke.
Rates:$65. MC VISA DS. Full Bkfst. Gourmet Brkfst. Picnic lunches. Teas. Evening snacks. 2 rooms. 1 with shared bath. Beds:Q. TV, AC in room. Farm. Sauna. Exercise room. Stables. Fishing.
Contact: Janet Hammeke. Certificate may be used: Weeknights - year-round.

Riley

Trix's Riley Roomer
104 N Hartner
Riley 66531
(913)485-2654

1905. Visitors to nearby Kansas State University or Ft. Riley seeking a relaxed country setting may try Trix's Riley Roomer, a Folk Victorian farmhouse inn run by an antique collector. The rooms feature antique double beds and ceiling fans. There are those who say this area of Northeastern Kansas is one of the state's most beautiful, and guests can see for themselves as they explore three campgrounds and two lakes just a short drive from the inn.

Innkeeper(s): Trix Fasse.
Rates:$60-65. Full Bkfst. 3 rooms. 1 with shared bath. Beds:D. Phone, AC in room. Swimming. Fishing.
Contact: Trixie Fasse. Certificate may be used: Anytime.

Topeka

The Elderberry B&B
1035 SW Fillmore St
Topeka 66604
(913)235-6309

1887. Within walking distance of the state capitol building is this Queen Anne Victorian inn that once was home to a millinery parlor. The present owners have an impressive collection of hats and other accessories and have furnished the inn with an array of family antiques. Beveled glass and beautiful oak woodwork highlight the interior, and the guest rooms are filled with authentic touches of the 1880s. The paisley Holliday Room is named for the first president of the Atchison, Topeka and Santa Fe Railroad and the floral Gage Room for a famous local sculptor whose work is featured on the capitol grounds.

Innkeeper(s): Carol & Jerry Grant.
Rates:$45. Full Bkfst. Evening snacks. 2 rooms. Beds:QD. AC in room.
Seen in: *Topeka Metro News.*
Contact: Carol Grant. Certificate may be used: Availability only - no preferred times.

WaKeeney

Thistle Hill B&B

Rt 1, Box 93
WaKeeney 67672
(913)743-2644

1953. This modern cedar farmhouse sports a unique, "older" feel, aided mainly by its porch, which is reminiscent of the Old West. The interior features an oak-floored dining room and luscious views of the inn's gardens, farm and prairie. The second-story guest rooms include the Prairie Room, with a king-size round bed; the Sunflower Room, which boasts a handmade Kansas sunflower quilt and a view of the farm's working windmill; and the Oak Room, which offers a hide-a-bed for extra family members. Guests may explore a 60-acre prairie-wildflower restoration project, which attracts many species of birds.

Innkeeper(s): Mary & Dave Hendricks.
Rates:$55-65. Full Bkfst. Gourmet Brkfst. Evening snacks. 4 rooms. 2 with shared baths. Beds:QD. AC in room. Farm. Golf. Skiing. Swimming. Stables. Fishing.
Seen in: *Kansas Weekend Guide, Kansas City Star & Country Magazine.*
Contact: Mary Ruth Hendricks. Certificate may be used: October through March except second weekend in November.

Wichita

The Inn at the Park

3751 E Douglas
Wichita 67218
(316)652-0500 (800)258-1951
Fax:(316)652-0610

1909. This popular three-story brick mansion offers many special touches, including unique furnishings in each of its 11 guest rooms, three of which are

suites. Some of the rooms feature fireplaces, refrigerators or hot tubs, and all offer cable TV and VCRs. The inn's convenient location makes it ideal for business travelers or those interested in exploring Wichita at length. The inn's parkside setting provides additional opportunities for relaxation or recreation. Ask for information about shops and restaurants in Wichita's Old Town.

Innkeeper(s): Kevin Daves & Greg Johnson.
Rates:$89-139. MC VISA AX DS. ContPlus Bkfst. 11 rooms. Fireplaces. Beds:KQ. Conference Rm. TV, Phone, AC, Refrig. in room. Spa.
Seen in: *Wichita Business Journal.*
Contact: Lynda Weixelman. Certificate may be used: Anytime.

"This is truly a distinctive hotel. Your attention to detail is surpassed only by your devotion to excellent service."

Kentucky

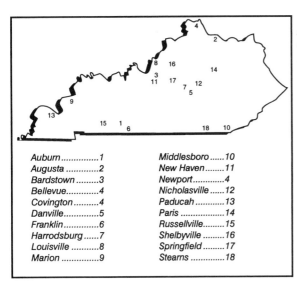

Auburn

David N. Williams Guest House
421 W Main St
Auburn 42206
(502)542-6019
KY907596.TIF

1938. This Southern Colonial mansion features mannequins dressed in vintage clothing. Guests may relax in the lounge, on the side porch or on the deck in the back of the house. The inn is furnished with antiques. The dressing room has an antique fainting couch. Guest rooms include the Primitive Room with chestnut pieces, the Maple Room, the Walnut Room, the Oak Room and the Cherry Room.

Innkeeper(s): David & Joy Williams.

Rates:$30-50. Full Bkfst. 4 rooms. 2 with shared baths. TV, AC in room.

Seen in: *Logan County News.*

Contact: Joy Williams. Certificate may be used: Anytime from April until October. Closed winter.

"I loved every second I spent in your beautiful home."

124

Augusta

Lamplighter Inn
103 W Second St
Augusta 41002
(606)756-2603

1800. This country inn is an hour's drive southeast of Cincinnati, not far from the shores of the Ohio River, in a county that once led the nation in wine production. The area's German influence is apparent at this inn and adjoining restaurant. The Pullman Room, with its railroad mementoes, and Actor's Room, decorated with playbills, posters and a theater seat, are popular with visitors. Be sure to inquire about Lamplighter Mystery parties, which also include dinner and music.

Innkeeper(s): Caroline & Kevin Froehlich.

Rates:$53-58. MC VISA. Full Bkfst. Gourmet Dinner. 9 rooms. Beds:QT. Conference Rm. TV, Phone, AC in room. Tennis. Handicap access. Exercise room.

Contact: Caroline Froehlich. Certificate may be used: Anytime.

Bardstown

The Mansion Bed & Breakfast
1003 N Third St
Bardstown 40004
(502)348-2586 Fax:(502)349-6098

1851. The Confederate flag was raised for the first time in Kentucky on this property. The beautifully crafted Greek Revival mansion is in the National Register of Historic Places. Period antiques and hand-crocheted bedspreads, dust ruffles and shams are featured in the guest rooms. There are more than three acres of tall trees and gardens. The Courthouse in historic Bardstown is nine blocks away.

Innkeeper(s): Joseph D. & Charmaine H. Downs.

Rates:$75-85. MC VISA DS. ContPlus Bkfst. 8 rooms. Beds:KDT. Conference Rm. AC in room.

Contact: Joseph Downs. Certificate may be used: Sunday -

Wednesday, May, June, July, August, October, 1994/1995. Sunday - Saturday, November, December, 1994; January, February, March, April, November, December, 1995.

Bellevue

Weller Haus B&B

319 Poplar St
Bellevue 41073
(606)431-6829

1880. Set in historic Taylor Daughter's District, five minutes across the Ohio River from downtown Cincinnati, this Victorian folk-style homestead is listed in the National Register. Special features include original millwork and a newly added, sky-lit great room with cathedral ceilings. A secluded garden adjoins the great room.

Innkeeper(s): Mary & Vernon Weller.

Rates:$60-110. MC VISA. ContPlus Bkfst. 5 rooms. Beds:QT. Conference Rm. TV, AC in room. Skiing. Swimming. Fishing.

Seen in: *The Downtowner, The Bellevue Community News.*

Contact: Mary Weller. Certificate may be used: Sunday through Thursday nights, holidays excluded.

"You made B&B believers out of us."

Covington

Sandford House

1026 Russell St
Covington 41011-3065
(606)291-9133

1820. Originally a fine example of Federal architecture, the inn underwent reconstruction after a fire in the 1880s and changed to a more Victorian style. The inn once served as a finishing school for young ladies and now offers two full apartments, a suite and one guest room. Guests enjoy a gourmet breakfast. The inn is in the heart of the Old Seminary Historic District, listed in the National Register. Just two blocks away is the Basilica.

Innkeeper(s): Dan & Linda Carter.

Rates:$55-85. MC VISA. Gourmet Brkfst. 4 rooms. Beds:QT. TV, Phone, AC, Refrig. in room. Swimming.

Contact: Linda Carter. Certificate may be used: Weeknights.

Danville

Twin Hollies Retreat B&B

406 Maple Ave
Danville 40422
(606)236-8954

1835. This Greek Revival-style house boasts elegant antiques and large rooms. In the National Register, the house is known as the Bridges-Fox House. A Jacuzzi overlooks the formal gardens. The innkeeper prepares tasty breakfasts featuring health conscious recipes. Guests often enjoy the historic walking tour of Danville.

Innkeeper(s): Mary Joe & John Bowling.

Rates:$75. Full Bkfst. Teas. 3 rooms. 2 with shared baths. Fireplaces. Beds:QT. Phone, AC in room. Farm. Bicycling. Handicap access. Spa. Swimming. Fishing.

Contact: Mary Joe Bowling. Certificate may be used: Anytime of the year.

"Such a beautiful spot, and warm hospitality. Like staying in Southern Living."

Franklin

College Street Inn

223 S College
Franklin 42134
(502)586-9352

1890. Visitors to Kentucky's scenic Cave Area will enjoy this Queen Anne Victorian inn midway between Bowling Green and Nashville. The inn's Southern gourmet breakfasts may include Eggs Rachel or pecan waffles, and guests may request Breakfast-in-a-Basket if they wish to dine in their rooms. An ornately carved fireplace mantel and built-in china cabinet highlight the inn's dining room. The guest rooms feature antique furnishings, ceiling fans and feather mattresses. Franklin's historic downtown is just two blocks away.

Innkeeper(s): Michael & Donna Houston.

Rates:$40-60. MC VISA. Full Bkfst. 4 rooms. 2 with shared baths. Beds:Q. TV, AC in room.

Contact: Donna Houston. Certificate may be used: October through April.

Harrodsburg

Canaan Land Farm B&B

4355 Lexington Rd
Harrodsburg 40330
(606)734-3984

1795. This National Register farmhouse, one of the oldest brick houses in Kentucky, is appointed with antiques, quilts and featherbeds. Your host is a shepherd and attorney while your hostess enjoys

raising Polypay and natural-colored sheep. Nubian and Angora goats, cows, donkeys, and a llama named Maxwell graze on the pastureland with the inn's sheep on the 189-acre farm. A clapboard addition houses two of the guest rooms and the Wool Room where the innkeeper spins and weaves.
Innkeeper(s): Fred & Theo Bee.

Rates:$55-85. Full Bkfst. 4 rooms. 1 with shared bath. Beds:D. AC in room. Farm. Golf. Spa. Swimming. Horseback riding. Fishing.

Seen in: *Danville Advocate.*

Contact: Theo Bee. Certificate may be used: Sunday-Thursday.

"You truly have a gift for genuine hospitality."

Louisville

Old Louisville Inn

1359 S Third St
Louisville 40208
(502)635-1574 Fax:(502)637-5892

1901. This 10,000-square-foot, three-story Beaux Arts inn boasts massive ornately carved mahogany

columns in the lobby. Rooms are filled with antiques gathered from local auctions and shops. The third-floor Celebration Suite, with its whirlpool bath, fireplace and king-size canopy bed, offers perfect honeymoon accommodations. The morning meal, including the inn's famous popovers, is served in the breakfast room, courtyard or in the guest rooms. The inn's location, in the heart of Louisville's Victorian district, makes sightseeing inviting. A romantic horse-and-carriage ride may be arranged.
Innkeeper(s): Marianne Lesher

Rates:$60-195. MC VISA. ContPlus Bkfst. AP available. Teas. 10 rooms. 3 with shared baths. Beds:KQT. Conference Rm. AC in room. Tennis. Handicap access.

Contact: Marianne Lesher. Certificate may be used: Sunday through Thursday. Excludes the Kentucky Derby weekend.

Rose Blossom

1353 S 4th St
Louisville 40203
(502)636-0295

1884. This spacious Second Empire Victorian is listed with the National Register. Among its 18 rooms are seven guest rooms, three with private bath. An oak stairwell and leaded glass in the entry hall and stairwell add to the home's authentic old-time aura. Ten fireplaces are found, some with carved mantels and decorative tile. The first-floor bath boasts a whirlpool tub, and Mary has amassed an impressive collection of fine plates and china. The University of Louisville is within easy walking distance.
Innkeeper(s): Mary Ohlmann.

Rates:$85. Full Bkfst. Gourmet Brkfst. 7 rooms. 4 with shared baths. Beds:KQT. AC in room.

Contact: Mary Ohlmann. Certificate may be used: Fall or Winter.

The Inn at the Park

1332 S 4th St
Louisville 40208
(502)637-6930 (800)700-7275

1886. An impressive sweeping staircase is one of many highlights at this handsome Richardsonian Romanesque inn, in the historic district of Old Louisville. Guests also will appreciate the hardwood floors, 14-foot ceilings and stone balconies on the second and third floors. The six guest rooms offer a variety of amenities, including cable TV, VCR, ceiling fans and a view of Central Park. Guests may enjoy breakfast in their rooms or in the well-appointed central dining area.
Innkeeper(s): Bob & Theresa Carskie.

Rates:$50-95. MC VISA AX. Full Bkfst. Gourmet Brkfst. Picnic lunches. Teas. Evening snacks. 6 rooms. 2 with shared baths. Fireplaces. Beds:KQ. Conference Rm. TV, Phone, AC in room. Swimming.

Contact: Theresa Carskie. Certificate may be used: Sunday - Thursday, Oct. 1 - March 31.

The Victorian Secret B&B

1132 S First St
Louisville 40203
(502)581-1914

1883. This three-story Queen Anne Victorian sports 11 fireplaces. Antiques and period furnishings are featured throughout the brick inn, located in Historic Old Louisville. Guest amenities include sundecks, washer-dryer facilities and a workout room with bench press, rowing machine and stationary bicycle.

Innkeeper(s): Nan & Steve Roosa.

Rates:$48-78. Cont. Bkfst. EP. 3 rooms. 2 with shared baths. Fireplaces. Beds:KQT. TV, AC in room. Skiing. Swimming.

Contact: Steven Roosa. Certificate may be used: Jan. 1 - Feb. 28.

Marion

LaFayette Club House

173 LaFayette Heights
Marion 42064
(502)965-3889

1921. This comfortable country farmhouse also serves as a popular dining spot on weekend evenings and for Sunday brunch. Its guest rooms feature family quilts and homemade bed coverings. Country-style furnishings are found throughout the inn, and two of the rooms offer a spa and refrigerator. Guests who relish good food will enjoy their stay here. Joyce, a well-known area caterer, has earned a fine reputation. Favorite relaxing spots include the front porch and gazebo. Nearby attractions include Crittenden County's Amish settlement, Land Between the Lakes and an outlet mall in Eddyville.

Innkeeper(s): Harley & Joyce Haegelin.

Rates:$38-56. MC VISA. Full Bkfst. Gourmet Brkfst, Lunch, Dinner. Picnic lunches. Teas. Evening snacks. 8 rooms. 5 with shared baths. Beds:QDT. Conference Rm. Phone, AC, Refrig. in room. Farm. Handicap access. Swimming. Fishing.

Contact: Harley Haegelin. Certificate may be used: January, February, March.

Middlesboro

The Ridge Runner B&B

208 Arthur Heights
Middlesboro 40965
(606)248-4299

1890. Bachelor buttons, lilacs and wildflowers line the white picket fence framing this 20-room brick Victorian mansion. Guests enjoy relaxing in its turn-of-the-century library and parlor filled with Victorian antiques. Ask for the President's Room and you'll enjoy the best view of the Cumberland Mountains. (The innkeeper's great, great-grandfather hosted Abe Lincoln the night before his Gettysburg address, and the inn boasts some heirlooms from that home.) A family-style breakfast is provided and special diets can be accommodated if notified in advance. Cumberland Gap National Park is five miles away.

Innkeeper(s): Sue Richards/Irma Gall.

Rates:$55-65. Full Bkfst. Evening snacks. 4 rooms. 2 with shared baths. Beds:QDT. Refrig. in room. Golf. Tennis.

Seen in: *Lexington Herald Leader.*

Contact: Susan Richards. Certificate may be used: November through September, no holiday weekends, i.e. Memorial Day, July 4th, Labor Day, Thanksgiving, Christmas.

New Haven

The Sherwood Inn

138 S Main St
New Haven 40051
(502)549-3386

1914. Since 1875 the Johnson family has owned the Sherwood Inn. A week after the original building burned in 1913, construction for the current

building began. In the National Register, the inn catered to passengers of the nearby L & N (Louisville and Nashville) Railroad. Antiques and reproductions complement some of the inn's original furnishings. The restaurant is open for dinner Wednesday through Saturday. The inn's slogan, first advertised in 1875 remains, "first class table and good accommodations."

Innkeeper(s): Errol & Cecilia Johnson.

Rates:$45-55. MC VISA. Full Bkfst. 5 rooms. 2 with shared baths. Beds:D. AC in room.

Seen in: *Kentucky Standard.*

Contact: Cecilia Johnson. Certificate may be used: Anytime.

"A memorable stop."

Newport

Gateway B&B
326 East 6th St
Newport 41071
(606)581-6447

1876. This charming Italianate won a National
Trust for Historic Preservation award in 1992 after
current owners/innkeepers Ken and Sandra Clift
turned a labor of love into a successful bed &
breakfast. The inn is located in East Newport's historic district, Kentucky's second-largest. An antique
organ and phonograph sit on either side of the fireplace in the music room. A view of the Tri-City
area is enjoyed from the rooftop deck. Guests may
opt to eat their full breakfast in the dining room or
kitchen. Downtown Cincinnati is just a five-minute
drive from the inn.

Innkeeper(s): Ken & Sandra Clift.

Rates:$60-70. MC VISA AX. Full Bkfst. 3 rooms. 2 with shared baths.
Beds:KT. Phone, AC in room. Swimming.

Contact: Ken Clift. Certificate may be used: Any night November
through January.

Nicholasville

Cedar Haven Farm
2380 Bethel Rd
Nicholasville 40356
(606)858-3849

1986. Enjoy the pastoral scene of Angus calves
from your post on the front porch of this 30-acre
working farm in the rolling Bluegrass area of
Jessamine County. A country farm breakfast
includes freshly baked bread and fruits from the
hosts' orchard. Nearby is Asbury College,
Shakertown and the Kentucky River Palisades.

Innkeeper(s): Jim & Irene Smith.

Rates:$40-50. Full Bkfst. 3 rooms. 2 with shared baths. Beds:QD.
Phone, AC in room. Farm. Swimming. Fishing.

Contact: Irene Smith. Certificate may be used: November-December,
1994; January-February, 1995; June-July, 1995; November-December,
1995.

The Sandusky House B&B
1626 Delaney Ferry Rd
Nicholasville 40356
(606)223-4730

1860. This Greek Revival inn rests in the tree-
lined countryside, surrounded by horse farms and
other small farms. Its tranquil setting offers a perfect getaway from busy nearby Lexington. The inn,

which is listed on Kentucky's state register, boasts
six porches, seven fireplaces and impressive brick
columns. The three guest rooms feature air condi-

tioning, desks, private baths and turndown service.
Area attractions include Asbury College,
Keeneland Race Course, the Mary Todd Lincoln
House and the University of Kentucky.

Innkeeper(s): Jim & Linda Humphrey.

Rates:$69. MC VISA. Full Bkfst. 3 rooms. Beds:D. TV, AC in room.
Farm. Fishing.

Contact: James Humphrey. Certificate may be used: Sunday-Thursday
anytime; weekends by availability. April and October and special events
excluded.

Paducah

The 1857's B&B
PO Box 7771, 127 Market House Sq
Paducah 42002
(502)444-3960 (800)264-5607

1857. Paducah's thriving, history-rich commercial
district is home to this Folk Victorian inn, located
in Market House Square. Guests choose from the
Master Bedroom, a suite featuring an antique queen
four-poster bed, and a guest room highlighted by a
Victorian highback bed. The popular third-floor
game room boasts a hot tub and impressive
mahogany billiard table. The Ohio River is an easy
walk from the inn, and guests also will enjoy an
evening stroll along the gas-lit brick sidewalks. The
inn occupies the second and third floors of a former
clothing store, with an Italian restaurant at street
level.

Innkeeper(s): Steve & Deborah Bohnert.

Rates:$65-75. MC VISA. ContPlus Bkfst. Evening snacks. 2 rooms. 1
with shared bath. Beds:Q. TV, Phone, AC in room. Spa. Swimming.

Contact: Deborah Bohnert. Certificate may be used: Anytime but April.

Paducah Harbor Plaza B&B
201 Broadway
Paducah 42001
(502)442-2698 (800)719-7799

1900. This striking, five-story brick structure was known as the Hotel Belvedere at the turn of the century. Guests now choose from four guest rooms on the second floor, where they also will find the arch-windowed Broadway Room, with its views of the Market House District and the Ohio River, just a block away. Breakfast is served in this room, which sports a 1911 player piano, cable TV and VCR. The guest rooms all feature different color schemes and each is furnished with antique furniture and handmade quilts.

Innkeeper(s): Beverly & David Harris.

Rates:$55-65. MC VISA AX. ContPlus Bkfst. EP. 4 rooms. 4 with shared baths. Beds:KQT. TV, Phone, AC in room. Bicycling. Swimming.

Contact: Beverly Harris. Certificate may be used: Anytime but April. May through December.

Paris

Rosedale B&B
1917 Cypress St
Paris 40361
(606)987-1845

1862. Once the home of Civil War General John Croxton, this low-roofed Italianate inn was voted prettiest B&B in the Bluegrass area by the Lexington Herald-Leader in 1992. The four lovingly decorated guest rooms feature Colonial touches and are filled with antiques and paintings. Fresh flowers, down comforters and ceiling fans add to the rooms' comfort and charm. The Henry Clay Room, with its twin four-poster beds, is one option for visitors. Guests may relax with a game of croquet or on one of the benches found on the inn's lovely three-acre lawn. Duncan Tavern Historic Shrine is nearby.

Innkeeper(s): Katie & Jim Haag.

Rates:$65. MC VISA. Full Bkfst. Gourmet Brkfst. Evening snacks. 4 rooms. 4 with shared baths. Beds:T. AC in room.

Contact: Katherine Haag. Certificate may be used: All but April and October weekends and first week of May.

Russellville

The Log House
2139 Franklin Rd
Russellville 42276
(502)726-8483 Fax:(502)726-2270

1976. This ideal log cabin retreat was built from hand-hewn logs from old cabins and barns in the area. Rooms are full of quilts, early American furnishings and folk art from around the world. The log walls and hardwood floors create an unparalleled atmosphere of country warmth. An impressive kitchen is decorated with an old-fashioned stove and crammed with knickknacks. Innkeeper Allison Dennis creates hand-woven garments and accessories in an adjacent studio. Nashville and Opryland are about an hour's drive, and the local area boasts a number of antique shops.

Innkeeper(s): Allison & Richard Dennis.

Rates:$75-85. MC VISA AX DS. Full Bkfst. 4 rooms. Fireplaces. Beds:QDT. Phone, AC in room. Spa. Swimming. Fishing.

Contact: Allison Dennis. Certificate may be used: Anytime.

Shelbyville

The Wallace House
613 Washington St
Shelbyville 40065
(502)633-4272

1804. This Federal-style inn, midway between Louisville and Frankfort, is listed in the National Register of Historic Places. Its five well-appointed guest suites all feature kitchenettes. The talented innkeepers (Donald is a physician, his wife a gifted pianist) enjoy golfing and gardening.

Innkeeper(s): Dr. & Mrs. Chatham.

Rates:$65-95. MC VISA. Cont. Bkfst. 5 rooms. Beds:KT. AC, Refrig. in room. Golf. Fishing.

Contact: Donald Chatham. Certificate may be used: Weekdays, winter.

Springfield

Maple Hill Manor
2941 Perryville Rd
Springfield 40069
(606)336-3075

1851. This brick Revival home with Italianate detail is a Kentucky Landmark home and is listed in the National Register of Historic Places. It features 13-1/2-foot ceilings, 10-foot doors, nine-foot

windows, a cherry spiral staircase, stenciling in the foyer, a large parlor with a fireplace, hardwood floors and period furnishings. The library has floor-to-ceiling mahogany bookcases. The large patio area is set among old maple trees.

Innkeeper(s): Bob & Kay Carroll.

Rates:$60-70. MC VISA. Full Bkfst. Evening snacks. 7 rooms. Fireplaces. Beds:QT. Conference Rm. Golf. Tennis. Horseback riding. Fishing.

Seen in: *Danville's Advocate-Messenger, Springfield Sun, Eastside Weekend, Courier Journal.*

Contact: Kathleen Carroll. Certificate may be used: Sunday through Thursday.

"Thank you again for your friendly and comfortable hospitality."

Stearns

Marcum-Porter House
PO Box 369, 35 Hume Dr
Stearns 42647
(606)376-2242 Fax:(502)875-3421

1902. This two-story frame home once housed employees of the Stearns Coal & Lumber Company. Many guests like to wander the grounds of the historic inn, which boast lovely gardens and shrubs. Golfers will enjoy a nearby nine-hole course, believed to be the second-oldest course in the state. Be sure to take a ride on the Big South Fork Scenic Railway during your stay. Area attractions include Big South Fork National Recreation Area, Cumberland Falls State Park and Yahoo Falls.

Innkeeper(s): Charles & Sandra Porter, Patricia Porter Newton.

Rates:$55-65. MC VISA. Full Bkfst. Gourmet Brkfst. 4 rooms. 3 with shared baths. Beds:D. Handicap access. Swimming. Fishing.

Contact: Patricia Porter Newton. Certificate may be used: Weekdays April through October.

Louisiana

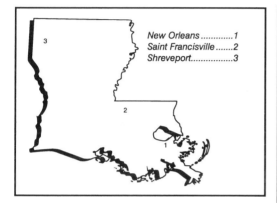

New Orleans 1
Saint Francisville 2
Shreveport.................3

New Orleans

Fairchild House

1518 Prytania
New Orleans 70130
(504)524-0154 (800)256-8096
Fax:(504)568-0063

1841. Set in the oak-lined Lower Garden District of New Orleans, this Greek Revival home was built by architect L.H. Pilie. The most prominent owner was cotton broker Louis Fairchild. Having undergone a recent renovation, the home has retained its elegant 19th-century setting. Afternoon wine, cheese and tea are included. The innkeepers feature a special honeymoon package and can arrange a four-day tour package of New Orleans.

Innkeeper(s): Rita Olmo & Beatriz Aprigliano.

Rates:$65-100. MC VISA AX. ContPlus Bkfst. Teas. 8 rooms. Beds:KQT. Phone, AC, Refrig. in room.

Contact: Beatriz Aprigliano. Certificate may be used: Sunday - Thursday.

"We felt very comfortable and welcome."

Glimmer Inn

1631 Seventh St
New Orleans 70115
(504)897-1895

1891. This is a simple Victorian house embellished with a two-story bay, a front porch and balcony. Eclectically appointed, there are antiques and modern furnishings and art. Rooms are spacious with 12-foot-high coved ceilings. St. Charles Avenue and the street car are one block away.

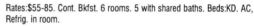

Innkeeper(s): Sharon Agiewich & Cathy Andros

Rates:$55-85. Cont. Bkfst. 6 rooms. 5 with shared baths. Beds:KD. AC, Refrig. in room.

Seen in: *The Times-Picayune.*

Contact: Sharon Agiewich. Certificate may be used: Nov. 28 - Dec. 22, 1994; Nov. 27 - Dec. 21, 1995; Jan. 3 - Feb. 15, 1994-1995.

"Your house is beautiful, breakfast yummy and hospitality superb!"

Lamothe House

621 Esplanade Ave
New Orleans 70116
(504)947-1161 (800)367-5858
Fax:(504)943-6536

1836. A carriageway that formerly cut through the center of many French Quarter buildings was enclosed at the Lamothe House in 1866, and is now the foyer. Splendid Victorian furnishings enhance moldings, high ceilings, and hand-turned mahogany stairway railings. Gilded opulence goes unchecked in the Mallard and Layfayette suites. Registration takes place in the second-story salon above the courtyard.

Innkeeper(s): Carol Chauppette.

Rates:$72-97. MC VISA AX. Cont. Bkfst. 20 rooms. Beds:DT. Conference Rm. TV, Phone, AC in room. Swimming. Fishing.

Seen in: *Houston Post, Travel & Leisure.*

Contact: Carol Chauppette. Certificate may be used: June, July, August, September.

The Prytania Park Hotel
1525 Prytania St
New Orleans 70130
(504)524-0427 (800)862-1984
Fax:(504)522-2977

1854. This hotel consists of a Victorian building and a new building. Request the older rooms to enjoy the English Victorian reproduction furnishings, garden chintz fabrics and 14-foot ceilings. Some of these rooms have fireplaces. Rooms in the new section feature refrigerators, microwaves and contemporary furnishings. It is one-half block from the historic St. Charles Avenue streetcar.

Innkeeper(s): Edward Halpern.

Rates:$89-189. MC VISA AX DC CB. Cont. Bkfst. EP. 62 rooms. Beds:KQT. TV, Phone, AC, Refrig. in room. Fishing.

Seen in: *New York Times.*

Contact: Edward Halpern. Certificate may be used: All year except special events.

"A little jewel." Baton Rouge Advocate.

The Victorian Guesthouse
1021 Moss St, Box 52257
New Orleans 70152-2257
(504)488-4640 (800)729-4640
Fax:(504)488-4639

1876. This Stick Victorian inn offers three guest rooms and two suites. Most of this family-oriented inn's rooms offer queen beds, with twins and a trundle also available. Tulane and Loyola universities are nearby, as are the Superdome, a golf course, shopping mall, Bayou Segnette State Park and the city zoo. The innkeepers have pet cats, but guests are asked to leave theirs at home.

Innkeeper(s): Jill & Charles Abbyad.

Rates:$80-125. ContPlus Bkfst. 5 rooms. Beds:QT. TV, Phone, AC in room. Fishing.

Seen in: *New York Times, National Geographic Traveler, Fodors, Frommers.*

Contact: Hazell Boyce. Certificate may be used: Sunday through Thursday, June through September excluding special events.

Saint Francisville

Green Springs Plantation
7463 Tunica Trace
Saint Francisville 70775
(504)635-4232 (800)457-4978

Fax:(504)635-3355

1990. Although this bluffland cottage, in the Feliciana style, was constructed just several years ago, its historic roots run deep. The inn rests on 150 acres that were owned by the innkeeper's family for 200 years, and on the grounds is a 2,000-year-old Indian mound. The inn's name comes from a

natural spring found in a glen on the property, and Big Bayou Sara Creek also is within the inn's borders. Visitors choose from three guest rooms, decorated in an attractive blend of antique and contemporary furnishings. A full plantation breakfast is served.

Innkeeper(s): Ivan & Madeline Nevill.

Rates:$85. MC VISA. Full Bkfst. MAP available. 3 rooms. Beds:QT. TV, AC in room. Farm. Fishing.

Contact: Madeline Nevill. Certificate may be used: June 1, 1994-February 1, 1995.

Shreveport

2439 Fairfield, A Bed & Breakfast
2439 Fairfield Ave
Shreveport 71104
(318)424-2424 Fax:(318)424-3658

1905. This turn-of-the-century Victorian mansion is located in the Highland historical district. The home is surrounded by English gardens, and guests can take in this view on their own private balcony, complete with rocking chairs and porch swings. English antiques and Amish quilts fill the guest rooms, which feature special extras such as Waverly linens, feather beds and down pillows and comforters. Each bath includes a whirlpool tub. The morning room is a cheerful place for a full English breakfast.

Innkeeper(s): Jimmy & Vicki Harris.

Rates:$85-125. MC VISA AX DC DS CB. Full Bkfst. Teas. 4 rooms. Fireplaces. Beds:KQ. TV, Phone, AC, Refrig. in room. Swimming.

Contact: Jimmy Harris. Certificate may be used: Sunday-Monday only.

Maine

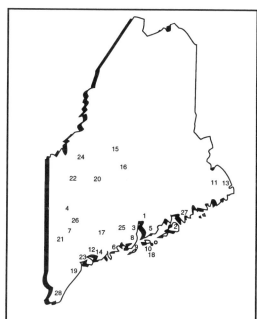

Bangor

Phenix Inn
20 Broad St
Bangor 04401
(207)947-3850 Fax:(207)947-3550

1873. Renovated in 1983, this four-story brick Victorian hotel offers a comfortable stay at an economical price in the downtown area. There are leather sofas in the lobby and solid mahogany beds in the rooms, some with canopies. There is a coffee shop and conference room, and both smoking and non-smoking rooms are available.

Innkeeper(s): Kim Haven.

Rates:$40-50. MC VISA AX DC DS. Cont. Bkfst. 35 rooms. Beds:QT. Conference Rm. TV, Phone, AC in room. Skiing. Handicap access. Fishing.

Contact: Kim Haven. Certificate may be used: Oct. 15-Jan. 1 and Jan. 1-June 1.

Bar Harbor

Balance Rock Inn on the Ocean
24 Albert Meadow
Bar Harbor 04609
(207)288-2610

1904. Built for a Scottish railroad tycoon, the Shingle-style structure was designed by a prestigious Boston architectural firm often used by wealthy summer residents of Bar Harbor. The inn is set on a secluded tree-covered property with views of the islands and Frenchman's Bay. Bar Harbor is two short blocks away. Off the back veranda, overlooking the pool, and past nearly an acre of sweeping lawns is the Historic Shore Path that winds its way around the waterfront.

Innkeeper(s): Nancy Cloud.

Rates:$145-395. MC VISA AX DS. Full Bkfst. EP. Evening snacks. 21 rooms. Fireplaces. Beds:KQ. Conference Rm. TV, Phone, AC, Refrig. in room. Sauna. Exercise room. Swimming. Fishing.

Contact: Nancy Cloud. Certificate may be used: May 8 to July 20, excluding 4th of July holiday; Sept. 1 - 30.

Manor House Inn

106 West St
Bar Harbor 04609
(207)288-3759 (800)437-0088

1887. Colonel James Foster built this 22-room Victorian mansion, now in the National Register. It is an example of the tradition of gracious summer living for which Bar Harbor was and is famous. In addition to the main house, there are several charming cottages situated in the extensive gardens on the property.
Innkeeper(s): Mac Noyes.

Rates:$50-155. MC VISA. Full Bkfst. Picnic lunches. Teas. 14 rooms. Fireplaces. Beds:KQT. Golf. Tennis. Bicycling. Swimming. Fishing.

Seen in: *Discerning Traveler.*

Contact: Mac Noyes. Certificate may be used: Sunday through Thursday, Oct. 15, 1994 through Nov. 15, 1994, April 15, 1995 through June 15, 1995, and Oct. 15, 1995 through Nov. 15, 1995.

"Wonderful honeymoon spot!"

The Maples Inn

16 Roberts Ave
Bar Harbor 04609
(207)288-3443

1903. This 15-room Victorian "summer cottage" once served wealthy summer visitors to Mt. Desert Island. Located on a quiet residential street, away

from Bar Harbor traffic, it has been tastefully restored and filled with Colonial and Victorian furnishings. The inn is within walking distance of shops, boutiques, and restaurants. Acadia National Park is five minutes away.
Innkeeper(s): Susan Sinclair.

Rates:$60-135. MC VISA DS. Full Bkfst. Gourmet Brkfst. Picnic lunches. Teas. 6 rooms. Fireplaces. Beds:Q. Golf. Tennis. Bicycling. Skiing. Swimming. Fishing.

Seen in: *San Diego Tribune, New York Times.*

Contact: Susan Sinclair. Certificate may be used: November-April, excluding holiday weekends.

Belfast

Adaline Palmer House

7 Franklin St
Belfast 04915
(207)338-5790

1845. Detailed woodwork and unusual terra-cotta fireplaces accent the beauty of this Greek Revival Cape. Afternoon wine is served in the formal living

room, which boasts an ornate tiled fireplace. The bedrooms feature pine floors and extras such as Oriental rugs or mahogany furniture. Breakfasts are served in a glassed-in porch decorated with wicker. Guests enjoy fresh fruit, homemade breads and a special main dish while they gaze at the gardens.
Innkeeper(s): Bob & Carol Lentilhon.

Rates:$45-50. Full Bkfst. 3 rooms. Beds:QT. Golf. Tennis. Swimming. Fishing.

Seen in: *Yankee Magazine Travel Guide, Maine Times.*

Contact: Robert Lentilhon. Certificate may be used: Anytime during season.

"We have yet to find the quaintness, personal attention and enjoyable conversation that we had during our stay."

Belfast Bay Meadows

90 Northport Ave, Rt 1
Belfast 04915
(207)338-5715 (800)335-2377
Fax:(207)338-5715

1910. This Victorian cottage is situated on five acres of meadow and bordered by large trees, while being fronted by the Penobscot Bay. Common areas include a sunny enclosed porch, a large living room and comfortable dining room. The inn is located a mile from the center of town and the municipal dock. There are numerous historic homes, antique shops and good restaurants nearby. Breakfast is served in the large, bright country kitchen, on the deck overlooking the meadow and bay or in the dining room.
Innkeeper(s): John & Patty Lebowitz.

Rates:$50-125. MC VISA AX DS. Full Bkfst. Gourmet Brkfst. 10 rooms. Beds:KQT. Handicap access. Swimming. Fishing.

Seen in: *Maine Times, Bangor Daily News.*

Contact: John Lebowitz. Certificate may be used: January-May, November, December.

Frost House B&B
6 Northport Ave
Belfast 04915
(207)338-4159

1908. Breakfast at this Victorian Shingle inn often is served on its picturesque turret porch. The inn is recognized as one of Maine's finest examples of

Victorian architecture. Hand-crafted woodwork is found throughout, and the three guest rooms have been furnished with period antiques to preserve the home's turn-of-the-century aura. Many of the inn's windows offer ocean views. Guests are welcome to borrow the tandem bicycle to tour downtown.

Innkeeper(s): John & Joan Lightfoot

Rates:$64-86. Full Bkfst. 3 rooms. Beds:KQ. Bicycling. Fishing.

Contact: Joan Lightfoot. Certificate may be used: May, June, September.

The Jeweled Turret Inn
16 Pearl St
Belfast 04915
(207)338-2304 (800)696-2304

1898. This grand Victorian is named for the staircase that winds up the turret, lighted by stained-and leaded-glass panels and jewel-like embellishments. It was built

for attorney James Harriman. Dark pine beams adorn the ceiling of the den, and the fireplace is constructed of bark and rocks from every state in the Union. Elegant antiques furnish the guest rooms of this National Register home.

Innkeeper(s): Carl & Cathy Heffentrager.

Rates:$65-85. Gourmet Brkfst. Teas. 7 rooms. Fireplaces. Beds:QDT. Golf. Tennis. Skiing. Swimming. Horseback riding. Fishing.

Seen in: *Republican Journal, Waterville Sentinel, Los Angeles Times.*

Contact: Cathy Heffentrager. Certificate may be used: April 1 to June 15, Oct. 21 to Nov. 30, no holidays.

"The ambiance was so romantic that we felt like we were on our honeymoon."

Bethel

Chapman Inn
PO Box 206 On the Common
Bethel 04217
(207)824-2657

1865. As one of the town's oldest buildings, this Federal Style inn has been a store, a tavern and a boarding house known as "The Howard." It was the home of William Rogers Chapman, composer, conductor and founder of the Rubenstein Club and the Metropolitan Musical Society in addition to the Maine Music Festival. The inn is a convenient place to begin a walking tour of Bethel's historic district. A private beach, located on Songo Pond, is just five miles away and is available in the summer and fall complete with canoe, picnic table and beach chairs.

Innkeeper(s): Sandra & "Bub" Wight.

Rates:$45-95. MC VISA AX. Full Bkfst. Gourmet Brkfst. Picnic lunches. Teas. Evening snacks. 4 rooms. Beds:DT. Refrig. in room. Bicycling. Skiing. Sauna. Swimming. Fishing.

Contact: Robin Zinchuk. Certificate may be used: Midweek winter (Dec. 26-March 15). Anytime fall, summer, spring, based on availability.

L'Auberge Country Inn
Mill Hill Rd, PO Box 21
Bethel 04217
(207)824-2774 (800)760-2774
Fax:(207)824-2774

1890. In the foothills of the White Mountains, surrounded by five acres of gardens and woods, this former carriage house was converted to a guest house in the 1920s. Among its seven guest rooms are two spacious suites. The Theater Suite offers a four-poster queen bed and dressing room. The Family Suite can accommodate up to six guests. Mount Abrahms and Sunday River ski areas are just minutes away.

Innkeeper(s): Werner Kohlmeyer.

Rates:$75-125. MC VISA AX DS. Cont. Bkfst. Gourmet Dinner. 7 rooms. Beds:QT. Conference Rm. Skiing. Handicap access. Swimming. Fishing.

Contact: Werner Kohlmeyer. Certificate may be used: Non-holiday week, Winter; Non-weekend, Winter; Summer, no restriction. Reservations required.

Blue Hill

Arcady Down East
HC 64, Box 370
Blue Hill 04614
(207)374-5576

This attractive Victorian Shingle inn, listed with the National Register, offers many authentic touches, including period antiques and tin ceilings. The inn's seven guest rooms include the Celebration Suite, perfect for honeymooners with its cozy fireplace and sitting area. Another favorite with visitors is the Captain's Quarters, featuring a skylight to help highlight its unique furnishings. The impressive coastal beauty of Acadia National Park is a short drive from the inn.

Innkeeper(s): Gene & Bertha Wiseman.

Rates:$95-110. MC VISA AX. Full Bkfst. 7 rooms. 2 with shared baths. Fireplaces. Refrig. in room. Bicycling. Skiing.

Contact: Bertha Wiseman. Certificate may be used: Anytime except month of August and holidays.

Boothbay

Kenniston Hill Inn
Rt 27, PO Box 125
Boothbay 04537
(207)633-2159 (800)992-2915

1786. The elegant clapboard home is the oldest inn at Boothbay Harbor and was occupied by the Kenniston family for more than a century. Four of

the antique-filled bedrooms have fireplaces. After a walk through the beautiful gardens or woods, warm up in the parlor next to the elegant, open-hearthed fireplace. Candlelit dinners are available November

through April and served in the parlor in front of a roaring fire. Boothbay Harbor offers something for everybody, including whale-watching excursions and dinner theaters.

Innkeeper(s): David & Susan Straight.

Rates:$50-110. MC VISA. Full Bkfst. MAP available. Gourmet Dinner. Teas. 10 rooms. Fireplaces. Beds:KQT. Bicycling. Skiing. Swimming. Horseback riding. Fishing.

Contact: Susan Straight. Certificate may be used: November and December, 1994 except holiday weekends or special packages. January through June, 1995 except holiday weekends or special packages.

"England may be the home of the original bed and breakfast, but Kenniston Hill Inn is where it has been perfected!"

Boothbay Harbor

Harbour Towne Inn
71 Townsend Ave, PO Box 266
Boothbay Harbor 04538
(207)633-4300 (800)722-4240
Fax:(207)633-7584

1895. This waterfront Victorian inn boasts 13 guest rooms and one suite. The Penthouse offers a private deck and an astonishing view of the harbor. Breakfast is served in the inn's Sunroom, and guests also may relax in the parlor, which has a fireplace. The inn's meticulous grounds include flower gardens and well-kept shrubs and trees. It's an easy walk to the village and its art galleries, restaurants and shops. The Ft. William Henry Memorial is nearby.

Innkeeper(s): George Thomas.

Rates:$49-195. MC VISA AX DS. ContPlus Bkfst. 13 rooms. Fireplaces. Beds:KQD. Conference Rm. TV, Refrig. in room. Skiing. Swimming.

Contact: George Thomas. Certificate may be used: Off season, excludes holidays and special events (Saturday nights November-December, April). Must identify certificate when making reservations.

Bridgton

The Hyland Coach House
60 S High St
Bridgton 04009
(207)647-8811

1859. Built on the site of an old tavern, this Federal house features Italianate arched windows with shutters and a large side porch. Hot chocolate is often served in the evening by the fireplace and in summer, iced tea is available on the porch. Quiches and freshly baked muffins are made for breakfast, and your hosts are happy to accommodate special requests. The garden is filled with tiger lilies and lilacs in summer and 500 yards away is Highland Lake for canoeing or swimming.

Innkeeper(s): Patricia W. Hill.

Rates:$50-60. Full Bkfst. Gourmet Brkfst. Teas. 5 rooms. 5 with shared baths. Beds:QT. Bicycling. Skiing. Swimming. Fishing.

Seen in: *The Bridgton News, Down East Magazine.*

Contact: Patricia Hill. Certificate may be used: Oct. 16 - May 16.

"The accommodations and our hosts were wonderful and very hospitable. The friendly atmosphere is charming and reminds us of the villages of England."

Tarry-a-While Resort

Box A, Highland Ridge Rd
Bridgton 04009
(207)647-2522

1800. The Tarry-a-While Resort brings the charm of Switzerland to the western hills of Maine with the help of innkeeper Hans, who was born in

Switzerland. The dining room features weathered barnboard paneling, pine tables, Swiss cowbells, a giant alpenhorn and a picture window looking down Highland Lake and across the White Mountains. Guests dine on gourmet Swiss cooking. The resort consists of a Victorian mansion, cottages and a social hall. Rooms have quaint old-world furnishings, including furniture handmade by Hans and painted with colorful flowers by Barbara.

Innkeeper(s): Hans & Barbara Jenni.

Rates:$8010-45. ContPlus Bkfst. 36 rooms. 10 with shared baths. Beds:KT. AC in room. Golf. Tennis. Bicycling. Swimming. Fishing.

Seen in: *Down East, Yankee Magazine.*

Contact: Barbara Jenni. Certificate may be used: Mid-June to mid-July (if available).

"The views, space, personal attention and laid-back ambiance is just what we needed on our precious vacation time."

Camden

Blue Harbor House, A Village Inn

67 Elm St, Rt 1
Camden 04843
(207)236-3196 (800)248-3196
Fax:(207)236-6523

1810. James Richards, Camden's first settler, built this Cape house on a 1768 homesite. (The King granted him the land as the first person to fulfill all

the conditions of a settler.) An 1810 carriage house has been refurbished to offer private suites, some with whirlpool tubs. Breakfast is served on the sun porch overlooking the Camden Hills. Dinner, available by reservation, can be a gourmet affair or an authentic Maine lobster bake on the lawn. The bustling harbor is a five-minute walk away.

Innkeeper(s): Jody Schmoll & Dennis Hayden.

Rates:$85-125. MC VISA AX DS. Full Bkfst. MAP available. Gourmet Brkfst, Dinner. Teas. 10 rooms. Beds:KQT. Conference Rm. TV, AC, Refrig. in room. Golf. Tennis. Bicycling. Skiing. Swimming. Horseback riding. Fishing.

Seen in: *Dallas Morning News, Discerning Traveler, Country Living.*

Contact: Jody Schmoll. Certificate may be used: Nov. 1 to July 1, excluding holidays. Subject to availability.

"I don't know when I've enjoyed my stay in a country inn more."

Castleview By The Sea

59 High St
Camden 04843
(207)236-2344 (800)272-8439

1856. Located on an acre of lawns and gardens, within a five-minute walk to the harbor, this classic American cape house overlooks the sea. Guest rooms feature wide pine floors, beamed ceilings, stained glass, and some have private porches. Take in the sun and sea from the favorite place at the inn, the ocean view decks.

Innkeeper(s): William Butler.

Rates:$75-130. MC VISA. Full Bkfst. Evening snacks. 3 rooms. Beds:KT. TV, Phone, AC, Refrig. in room. Tennis. Skiing. Swimming. Fishing.

Contact: William Butler. Certificate may be used: May or September or October or November.

Lord Camden Inn

24 Main St
Camden 04843
(207)236-4325 (800)336-4325
Fax:(207)236-7141

1983. Located in a restored brick building on the town's Main Street, the inn is decorated in American country antiques. A friendly staff will be happy to suggest some of the many activities in the area. Day sails and island picnics can be arranged and bicycle rentals are available for inland rides or to tour islands after a short ferry ride. Most guest rooms offer balconies with spectacular views of Camden Harbor, the village or the hills.

Innkeeper(s): Stuart & Mariane Smith.

Rates:$88-175. MC VISA AX. Cont. Bkfst. 31 rooms. Beds:KQT. Conference Rm. TV, Phone, AC, Refrig. in room. Skiing. Swimming. Fishing.

Contact: Stuart Smith. Certificate may be used: October, 1994 - May, 1995 excluding holidays.

Whitehall Inn

52 High St
Camden 04843
(207)236-3391 (800)789-6565
Fax:(207)236-4427

1834. It's easy to see why Edna St. Vincent Millay was so taken with this picturesque portion of the Maine coast. A recital of her poem, "Renascence," took place at this country inn, which has retained much of its original charm. Fifty rooms, including four suites, are available, each decorated in a unique and appealing way. Period antiques are found throughout the inn, and guests enjoy utilizing its many parlors, patios and porches. Across the street is the Maine House and the Wicker House, just a sample of many local sightseeing opportunities.

Innkeeper(s): Dewing Family.

Rates:$75-135. MC VISA AX. Full Bkfst. MAP available. Gourmet Brkfst, Dinner. Teas. 50 rooms. 4 with shared baths. Beds:KQT. Conference Rm. Phone in room. Tennis. Bicycling. Handicap access. Swimming. Fishing.

Contact: J.C. Dewing. Certificate may be used: June until mid-July and September, midweek.

Clark Island

Craignair Inn

533 Clark Island Rd
Clark Island 04859
(207)594-7644 Fax:(207)596-7124

1928. Craignair originally was built to house stonecutters working in nearby granite quarries.

Overlooking the docks of the Clark Island Quarry, where granite schooners once were loaded, this roomy, three-story inn is tastefully decorated with local antiques.

Innkeeper(s): Norman & Terry Smith.

Rates:$62-91. MC VISA AX. Full Bkfst. 22 rooms. 14 with shared baths. Beds:KT. Conference Rm. Phone in room. Tennis. Skiing. Spa. Swimming. Horseback riding. Fishing.

Seen in: *Boston Globe, Free Press.*

Contact: Theresa Smith. Certificate may be used: May 15 through June 30, excluding Memorial Day weekend, Labor Day through October 20.

"We thoroughly enjoyed our stay with you. Your location is lovely and private. Your dining room and service and food were all 5 star!"

Damariscotta

Brannon-Bunker Inn

PO Box 045, HCR 64 Rt 129
Damariscotta 04543
(207)563-5941

1820. This Cape-style house has been a home to many generations of Maine residents, one of whom was captain of a ship that sailed to the Arctic. During the '20s, the barn served as a dance hall. Later, it was converted into comfortable guest rooms. Victorian and American antiques are featured and there are collections of military and political memorabilia.

Innkeeper(s): Joe & Jeanne Hovance.

Rates:$55-65. MC VISA. Cont. Bkfst. 8 rooms. 2 with shared baths. Beds:QT. Skiing. Handicap access. Swimming. Fishing.

Seen in: *The Times-Beacon Newspaper.*

Contact: Joseph Hovance. Certificate may be used: April, May, June, Sunday through Thursday, no holiday weekends. September, October, November, Sunday through Thursday, no holiday weekends.

"Wonderful beds, your gracious hospitality and the very best muffins anywhere made our stay a memorable one."

Deer Isle

The Inn at Ferry Landing
RR1 Box 163, Old Ferry Rd
Deer Isle 04627
(207)348-7760

1850. Spectacular ocean views greet guests at this inn, which once served as a general store and livery stable, transporting goods, livestock and passengers on its ferry and steamboat. Now the inn serves as an ocean-lovers' delight, providing 180-degree views of sparkling blue waters and sailing. Visitors are served a full breakfast before they head out for a day of sightseeing, sunbathing or swimming. Guests also are treated to a refreshing afternoon tea and turndown service. The innkeepers enjoy antiquing.
Innkeeper(s): John & Maureen Deis.

Rates:$47-95. MC VISA. Full Bkfst. Picnic lunches. Teas. 7 rooms. 2 with shared baths. Fireplaces. Beds:QDT. Skiing. Swimming. Fishing.

Contact: Maureen Deis. Certificate may be used: Nov. 1, 1994-May 15, 1995 and Nov. 1, 1995-Dec. 15, 1995.

Dennysville

Lincoln House Country Inn
Rts 1 & 86
Dennysville 04628
(207)726-3953

1787. Theodore Lincoln, son of General Benjamin Lincoln, who accepted the sword of surrender from Cornwallis after the American Revolution, built

this house. The four-square Colonial looks out to the Dennys River and its salmon pools. John James Audubon stayed here on his way to Labrador. He loved the house and family so much that he named the Lincoln Sparrow in their honor.
Innkeeper(s): Mary & Jerry Haggerty.

Rates:$135-150. MC VISA AX. 11 rooms. 7 with shared baths. Conference Rm. Golf. Tennis. Skiing. Swimming. Fishing.

Seen in: *Good Housekeeping, Washington Post, New York Times.*

Contact: Mary Haggerty. Certificate may be used: June; third and fourth week of July; September.

"The food was delicious, the ambiance special."

Durham

The Bagley House
1290 Royalsborough Rd
Durham 04222
(207)865-6566 (800)765-1772
Fax:(207)353-5878

1772. Six acres of fields and woods surround the Bagley House. Once an inn, a store, and a schoolhouse, it is the oldest house in town. Guest rooms

are decorated with colonial furnishings and hand-sewn Maine quilts. For breakfast, guests gather in the country kitchen in front of a huge brick fireplace and beehive oven.
Innkeeper(s): Susan Backhouse & Suzanne O'Connor.

Rates:$65-100. MC VISA AX DS. Full Bkfst. Picnic lunches. Evening snacks. 5 rooms. Fireplaces. Beds:QDT. Conference Rm. Phone, Refrig. in room. Skiing.

Seen in: *Los Angeles Times, New England Getaways, Lewiston Sun.*

Contact: Suzanne O'Connor. Certificate may be used: Nov. 1 to June 30, stay one at full price, one night free.

"I had the good fortune to stumble on the Bagley House. The rooms are well-appointed and the innkeeper is as charming a host as you'll find."

Eastport

The Inn at Eastport
13 Washington St
Eastport 04631
(207)853-4307

1840. Skin-divers consider the waters near this Federal-style inn among the best in the United States. The innkeepers are more than happy to assist guests with their sightseeing efforts in America's most northeasterly city. The inn's antique furnishings, hardwood floors and black marble hearths will please visitors. Enjoy a soak in the inn's outdoor hot tub. The gourmet breakfasts may include wild blueberry pancakes. New Brunswick is just a 15-minute ferry ride away.
Innkeeper(s): Robert & Brenda Booker.

Rates:$55-65. MC VISA DS. Full Bkfst. 4 rooms. Beds:QD. Fishing.
Contact: Brenda Booker. Certificate may be used: Weekdays.

Weston House

26 Boynton St
Eastport 04631
(207)853-2907

1810. Jonathan Weston, an 1802 Harvard graduate, built this Federal-style house on a hill overlooking Passamaquoddy Bay. John Audubon stayed here as a guest of the Westons while awaiting passage to Labrador in 1833.

Innkeeper(s): Jett & John Peterson.

Rates:$50-70. Full Bkfst. Gourmet Brkfst. Dinner. Picnic lunches. Teas. 6 rooms. 5 with shared baths. Fireplaces. Beds:KQT. Conference Rm. TV in room. Golf. Bicycling. Fishing.

Seen in: *Downeast Magazine, Los Angeles Times, Boston Globe.*

Contact: Jett Peterson. Certificate may be used: September - June depending on availability.

"The most memorable bed and breakfast experience we have ever had."

Freeport

Captain Josiah Mitchell House

188 Main St
Freeport 04032
(207)865-3289

1789. Captain Josiah Mitchell was commander of the clipper ship *Hornet*. In 1865, en route from New York to San Francisco it caught fire, burned and was lost. The passengers and crew survived in three longboats, drifting for 45 days. When the boats finally drifted into one of the South Pacific Islands, Mark Twain was there and he befriended the Captain. The diary of Captain Mitchell parallels episodes of *Mutiny on the Bounty*. Flower gardens and a porch swing on the veranda now welcome guests to Freeport and Captain Mitchell's House.

Innkeeper(s): Alan & Loretta Bradley.

Rates:$52-82. MC VISA. Full Bkfst. 7 rooms. Beds:DT. Golf. Skiing. Spa. Fishing.

Seen in: *Famous Boats and Harbors.*

Contact: Alan Bradley. Certificate may be used: Nov. 15, 1994 to April 30, 1995, but excluding holidays and weekends.

"Your wonderful stories brought us all together. You

have created a special place that nurtures and brings happiness and love. This has been a dream!"

The Isaac Randall House

5 Independence Dr
Freeport 04032
(207)865-9295 (800)865-9295

1823. Isaac Randall's Federal-style farmhouse was once a dairy farm and a stop on the Underground Railway for slaves escaping into Canada. Randall was a descendant of John Alden and Priscilla

Mullins of the *Mayflower*. Longfellow immortalized their romance in *The Courtship of Miles Standish*. The inn is located on six wooded acres with a pond. Guest rooms are air-conditioned.

Innkeeper(s): Jim & Glynrose Friedlander.

Rates:$75-105. MC VISA. Full Bkfst. 8 rooms. Fireplaces. Beds:KQD. Conference Rm. TV, Phone, AC in room. Golf. Skiing. Spa. Swimming.

Contact: James Friedlander. Certificate may be used: Weekdays after Oct. 15, non-holiday weekends and weekdays between Jan. 1 and May 25. Weekdays in June.

"Enchanted to find ourselves surrounded by all your charming antiques and beautiful furnishings."

Greenville

The Lodge at Moosehead Lake

Upon Lily Bay Rd, Box 1175
Greenville 04441
(207)695-4400 Fax:(207)695-2281

1916. Westerly views of the lake can be enjoyed from four of the five guest rooms, living and dining rooms of this inn with its comfortable rustic decor. Each of the rooms has hand-carved, four-poster beds with dual control blankets and fireplaces. At the end of the day, relax in a Jacuzzi tub for two found in each private bath. The innkeepers enjoy pampering guests with gourmet meals, hors d'oeuvres and other fine amenities. Explore culinary delights in the lodge's own Lakeview Restaurant, a 25-seat bistro with French doors and the best view in the house. The shores of the lake are a stroll down a wooded trail.

Innkeeper(s): Roger & Jennifer Cauchi.

Rates:$85-185. MC VISA DS. Full Bkfst. 5 rooms. Fireplaces. Beds:Q. TV in room. Skiing. Swimming. Fishing.

Contact: Roger Cauchi. Certificate may be used: Nov. 1-April 30 excluding holidays and winter weekends.

Guilford

Trebor Inn
Golda Ct
Guilford 04443
(207)876-4070 (800)223-5509

1830. Seven guest rooms are available at this stately, turreted Victorian inn, which overlooks Guilford from high on a hill along the Moosehead Trail. Those who enjoy hunting bear, deer, partridge and pheasant should inquire about the inn's special rates for hunters. Meals are served family-style, and dinners are available on request. The family-oriented inn also accommodates business meetings, family reunions and weddings. Within five minutes of the inn, visitors will find basketball courts, a nine-hole golf course and tennis courts. Peaks-Kenny State Park and Sebec Lake are nearby.

Innkeeper(s): Robert & Larraine Vernal.

Rates:$35-60. MC VISA. Full Bkfst. Teas. 7 rooms. 5 with shared baths. Beds:DT. Skiing. Swimming. Fishing.

Contact: Larraine Vernal. Certificate may be used: Anytime but month of November.

Hallowell

Maple Hill Farm B&B Inn
RR 1, Box 1145, Outlet Rd
Hallowell 04347
(207)622-2708 (800)622-2708
Fax:(207)622-0655

1890. Visitors to Maine's capital city have the option of staying at this nearby inn, a peaceful farm setting adjacent to a 550-acre state wildlife management area that is available for canoeing, fishing and hunting. This Victorian Shingle inn was once a stagecoach stop and dairy farm. Guests may borrow a bicycle for a relaxing ride, or hop into a whirlpool tub after a busy day of sightseeing or other activities. The inn, with its 62-acre grounds, easily accommodates conferences, parties and receptions. Cobbossee Lake is a five-minute drive from

the inn.

Innkeeper(s): Scott Cowger.

Rates:$53-83. MC VISA AX DC DS CB. Full Bkfst. Picnic lunches. Teas. Evening snacks. 7 rooms. 3 with shared baths. Beds:QD. Conference Rm. Phone in room. Farm. Golf. Bicycling. Skiing. Handicap access. Swimming. Fishing.

Seen in: *Family Fun Magazine, An Explorer's Guide to Maine.*

Contact: Scott Cowger. Certificate may be used: May - October, Sunday - Wednesday. November - April, anytime but cannot select both Friday & Saturday.

Isle Au Haut

The Keeper's House
PO Box 26, Lighthouse Point
Isle Au Haut 04645
(207)367-2261

1907. Designed and built by the U.S. Lighthouse Service, the handsome 48-foot-high Robinson Point Light guided vessels into this once-bustling island

fishing village. Guests arrive on the mailboat. Innkeeper Judi Burke, whose father was a keeper at the Highland Lighthouse on Cape Cod, provides picnic lunches so guests may explore the scenic island trails. Dinner is served in the keeper's dining room. The lighthouse is adjacent to the most remote section of Acadia National Park. It's not uncommon to hear the cry of an osprey, see deer approach the inn, or watch seals and porpoises cavorting off the point. Guest rooms are comfortable and serene, with stunning views of the island's ragged shore line, forests and Duck Harbor.

Innkeeper(s): Jeff & Judi Burke.

Rates:$250. Full Bkfst. AP available. Gourmet Lunch, Dinner. Picnic lunches. 6 rooms. 6 with shared baths. Beds:D. Bicycling. Swimming. Fishing.

Seen in: *New York Times, USA Today, Los Angeles Times, Ladies Home Journal.*

Contact: Jeffrey Burke. Certificate may be used: May 1 through June 15; Oct. 16 through Oct. 31.

"Simply one of the unique places on Earth."

Kennebunkport

The Captain Fairfield House
PO Box 1308, 8 Pleasant St
Kennebunkport 04046
(207)967-4454 (800)322-1928

1813. Located in the historic district and only steps to the Village Green and Harbor, this sea captain's mansion features period furnishings in the guest

rooms. There are fireplaces, four-poster and canopy beds, down comforters and fresh garden flowers. Breakfast is served next to an open-hearth fireplace in the dining room.

Innkeeper(s): Dennis & Bonnie Tallagnon.

Rates:$99-160. MC VISA AX. Full Bkfst. Gourmet Brkfst. Teas. Evening snacks. 9 rooms. Fireplaces. Beds:QT. Conference Rm. AC in room. Golf. Tennis. Bicycling. Skiing. Swimming. Horseback riding. Stables. Fishing.

Contact: Bonnie Tallagnon. Certificate may be used: Midweek January through April; November and December (excluding holidays).

"A beautiful find, to be well recommended."

Cove House
S Maine St, PO Box 1615
Kennebunkport 04046
(207)967-3704

1793. This roomy Colonial Revival farmhouse overlooks Chick's Cove on the Kennebunk River. The inn's peaceful setting offers easy access to beaches, shops and town. Three guest rooms serve visitors of this antique-filled home. Guests enjoy full breakfasts, which often include the inn's famous blueberry muffins, in the Flow Blue dining room. A popular gathering spot for guests is the book-lined living room/library. Bicycles may be borrowed for a leisurely ride around the town. A cozy, secluded cottage with a screened front porch is another lodging option.

Innkeeper(s): Kathy, Bob & Barry Jones.

Rates:$70. MC VISA. Full Bkfst. Teas. 3 rooms. Beds:QT. Bicycling. Skiing. Swimming. Fishing.

Contact: Katherine Jones. Certificate may be used: Oct. 15, 1994 - May 15, 1995 excluding holidays and Prelude.

English Meadows Inn
141 Port Rd
Kennebunkport 04043
(207)967-5766

1860. Bordered by century-old lilac bushes, this Queen Anne Victorian inn and attached carriage house offer 11 guest rooms. The inn's well-tended

grounds, which include apple trees, gardens and lush lawns, invite bird-lovers or those who desire a relaxing stroll. Four-poster beds, afghans and hand-sewn quilts are found in many of the guest rooms, and visitors also will enjoy the talents of local artists, whose works are featured throughout the inn. Guests may eat breakfast in bed before heading out to explore Kennebunkport.

Innkeeper(s): Charles Doane.

Rates:$65-95. MC VISA. Full Bkfst. EP. Teas. 13 rooms. 4 with shared baths. Beds:QDT. Skiing. Swimming. Fishing.

Contact: Charles Doane. Certificate may be used: November-June (Sunday through Thursday).

Kennebunkport Inn
Box 111, One Dock Sq
Kennebunkport 04046
(207)967-2621 (800)248-2621
Fax:(207)967-3705

1899. The Kennebunkport Inn offers relaxation with its main lounge furnished with velvet loveseats and chintz sofas. Bedrooms are furnished with mahogany queen-sized beds, wing chairs and Queen Anne writing desks.

Innkeeper(s): Rick Griffin.

Rates:$63-179. MC VISA AX. Full Bkfst. EP. MAP available. 35 rooms. Beds:KQDT. TV in room. Swimming. Fishing.

Seen in: *Getaways for Gourmets, Coast Guide.*

Contact: Rick Griffin. Certificate may be used: Midweek, April 11 through June 23 or midweek Oct. 17 through Dec. 31. Cannot be combined with any other discounts or promotions.

"From check-in, to check-out, from breakfast through dinner, we were treated like royalty."

Kylemere House 1818
6 South St, PO Box 1333
Kennebunkport 04046-1333
(207)967-2780

1818. Located in Maine's largest historic district, this Federal-style house was built by Daniel Walker, a descendant of an original Kennebunkport family.

Later, Maine artist and architect Abbot Graves purchased the property and named it "Crosstrees" for its maple trees. The inn features New England antiques and brilliant flower gardens in view of the formal dining room in spring and summer. A full breakfast is provided. Art galleries, beaches, antiquing and golf are nearby.
Innkeeper(s): Ruth & Helen Toohey.
Rates:$80-135. MC VISA AX DS. Gourmet Brkfst. Teas. 4 rooms. Fireplaces. Beds:KQT. Bicycling. Swimming. Fishing.
Seen in: *Boston Globe, Glamour Magazine, Regis and Kathie Lee Show.*
Contact: Ruth Toohey. Certificate may be used: Mid-May to mid-June and November.

"Beautiful inn. Outstanding hospitality. Thanks for drying our sneakers, fixing our bikes. You are all a lot of fun!"

Maine Stay Inn & Cottages
34 Maine St, PO Box 500A
Kennebunkport 04046
(207)967-2117 (800)950-2117
Fax:(207)967-8757

1860. In the National Register, this is a square-block Italianate contoured in a low hip-roof design. Later additions reflecting the Queen Anne period include a suspended spiral staircase, crystal windows, ornately carved mantels and moldings, bay windows and porches. A sea captain built the handsome

cupola that became a favorite spot for making taffy. In the '20s, the cupola was a place from which to spot offshore rumrunners. Guests enjoy afternoon tea with stories of the Maine Stay's heritage.
Innkeeper(s): Lindsay & Carol Copeland.
Rates:$75-145. MC VISA AX DS. Full Bkfst. Teas. 17 rooms. Fireplaces. Beds:QT. TV, Refrig. in room. Golf. Tennis. Bicycling. Skiing. Swimming. Horseback riding. Fishing.
Seen in: *Boston Globe, Discerning Traveler, Montreal Gazette, Innsider, Tourist News, Down East.*
Contact: Lindsay Copeland. Certificate may be used: Midweek (Monday-Thursday), Oct. 24, 1994-June 15, 1995 and Oct. 23, 1995-Dec. 28, 1995.

"We have travelled the East Coast from Martha's Vineyard to Bar Harbor, and this is the only place we know we must return to."

Kingfield

The Inn on Winter's Hill
RR 1 Box 1272, Winter Hill Rd
Kingfield 04947
(207)265-5421 (800)233-9687
Fax:(207)265-5424

1895. The twin Stanley brothers (Stanley Steamer) designed this house on a lazy summer afternoon. Their creative genius resulted in an exciting example of Georgian Revival architecture, now restored to its original beauty. Today, it houses Julia's Restaurant which specializes in New England cuisine. There is a lighted skating rink and shuttle service to and from Sugarloaf USA.
Innkeeper(s): Diane Winnick.
Rates:$75-150. MC VISA AX DC DS CB. Full Bkfst. 20 rooms. Beds:KQ. Conference Rm. TV, Phone in room. Golf. Tennis. Skiing. Handicap access. Spa. Swimming. Fishing.
Seen in: *Skiing, The Franklin Journal.*
Contact: Carolyn Rainald. Certificate may be used: Anytime except holidays and holiday weeks July 1 - Dec. 24, 1994; midweek Jan. 1 - April 15, 1995; anytime except holidays and holiday weeks April 16 - Dec. 24, 1995. Not available Dec. 25-31, 1994 & 1995.

Naples

The Augustus Bove House
Corner Rts 302 & 114, RR1 Box 501
Naples 04055
(207)693-6365 Fax:(207)693-3833

1820. A long front lawn nestles up against the stone foundation and veranda of this house, once known as the Hotel Naples, one of the area's summer hotels in the 1800s. The guest rooms are decorated in a Colonial style and modestly furnished with antiques. Many rooms provide a view of Long Lake. A fancy country breakfast is provided.

Innkeeper(s): David & Arlene Stetson.

Rates:$55-85. MC VISA DS. Full Bkfst. 11 rooms. 4 with shared baths. Beds:KQT. TV, Phone, AC in room. Golf. Tennis. Bicycling. Skiing. Swimming. Horseback riding. Fishing.

Seen in: *Brighton Times.*

Contact: Arlene Stetson. Certificate may be used: Oct. 15 to June 15. Void June 16 through Oct. 14. Through December, 1995, void holidays.

"Beautiful place, rooms, and people."

The Inn at Long Lake
Lake House Rd, PO Box 806
Naples 04055
(207)693-6226 (800)437-0328

1906. Reopened in 1988, the inn housed the overflow guests from the Lake House resort 80 years ago. Guests traveled to the resort via the Oxford-

Cumberland Canal, and each room is named for a historic canal boat. The cozy rooms offer fluffy comforters and a warm, country decor in a romantic atmosphere. Warm up in front of a crackling fire in the great room, or enjoy a cool Long Lake breeze on the veranda while watching horses in nearby pastures. Murder-mystery weekends offer a spooky alternative to your getaway plans.

Innkeeper(s): Maynard & Irene Hincks.

Rates:$55-115. MC VISA AX DS. ContPlus Bkfst. 16 rooms. Beds:QDT. Conference Rm. TV, AC in room. Golf. Bicycling. Skiing. Swimming. Horseback riding. Fishing.

Seen in: *Bridgton News, Portland Press Herald.*

Contact: Maynard Hincks. Certificate may be used: Oct. 30, 1994 through May 21, 1995 and then Oct. 29, 1995 - Dec. 20, 1995.

"Convenient location, tastefully done and the prettiest inn I've ever stayed in."

New Harbor

Bradley Inn
HC 61, Box 361
New Harbor 04554
(207)677-2105 Fax:(207)677-3367

1900. The history-rich region of Pemaquid is home to this large Victorian Shingle inn, which offers 16

guest rooms. Many rooms sport views of St. John's Bay. Guests may enjoy bicycling, canoeing, exploring the tidal pools of the Rachel Carson Salt Pond, lawn games and swimming, and they also are free to play the inn's baby grand piano. There is a restaurant-pub on the premises. Be sure to inquire about arrangements for boating excursions, clambakes, picnic lunches and fishing charters.

Innkeeper(s): Chuck & Merry Robinson.

Rates:$85-140. MC VISA AX. Cont. Bkfst. Gourmet Dinner. 16 rooms. Beds:QT. Conference Rm. Phone in room. Golf. Tennis. Bicycling. Skiing. Swimming. Fishing.

Contact: C. W. Robinson. Certificate may be used: April 1-June 16; Oct. 11-Jan. 2.

Oquossoc

Oquossoc's Own B&B
Rangeley Ave, PO Box 27
Oquossoc 04964
(207)864-5584

1903. The recreation-rich mountains of Western Maine are home to this Victorian inn, which offers five guest rooms and easy access to local outdoor attractions. Basketball and tennis courts are nearby, and a grocery store and post office are within easy walking distance of the inn. Innkeeper Joanne Conner Koob is well known in the area for her catering skills. The Saddleback Mountain Ski Area, elevation 4,116 feet, is nearby.

Innkeeper(s): Joanne Conner Koob.

Rates:$55. MC VISA DS. Full Bkfst. AP available. MAP available. Gourmet Brkfst. Picnic lunches. 5 rooms. 5 with shared baths. Beds:DT. Tennis. Skiing. Swimming.

Contact: Joanne Conner Koob. Certificate may be used: Midweek, any month.

Portland

West End Inn
146 Pine St
Portland 04102
(207)772-1377 (800)338-1377

1871. Located in Portland's Western Promenade Historic District, this Georgian-style inn is one of many lovely Victorian-era homes found there. A full breakfast is offered, but guests may opt for lighter fare if they desire. An afternoon tea also is served, and provides a perfect opportunity to relax after an activity-filled day. The inn also offers facilities for meetings, reunions and wedding receptions. The Museum of Art and the University of South Maine are nearby.

Innkeeper(s): Teri Dizon & Beverly Williams.

Rates:$65-139. MC VISA AX. Full Bkfst. 5 rooms. Beds:KQT. TV, Phone in room. Skiing. Swimming. Fishing.

Contact: John Leonard. Certificate may be used: Nov. 1 - May 1, annually.

Rangeley

Northwoods
PO Box 79, Main St
Rangeley 04970
(207)864-2440

1912. This immaculate Colonial Revival home, which has all the original woodwork intact, has a magnificent view of Rangeley Lake. Inside, guests can find a doll house museum filled with porcelain dolls and antiques. Still largely unspoiled, the surrounding mountain and lake region offers a variety of activities and moose can be seen grazing and walking through the area. The inn's formal and prominent character is part of the unique residential architecture of the town. Although centrally located in Rangeley Village, Northwoods has a peaceful and lofty quality.

Innkeeper(s): Carol & Robert Scofield.

Rates:$60-75. Full Bkfst. Gourmet Brkfst. 4 rooms. 1 with shared bath. Beds:QT. Skiing. Swimming. Fishing.

Contact: Carol Scofield. Certificate may be used: Anytime except weekends or holidays July 1, 1994 through July 1, 1995.

Raymond

North Pines Health Resort
Raymond 04071
(207)655-7624 Fax:(207)655-3321

1928. This lakeside resort sits on 70 acres of pine forests, rolling hills and a mile-long waterfront. Owner Marlee Turner established the inn in 1980 as a place for people to go and work on inner health. Weight-loss programs are a big part of the experience and include special diets, instruction and spa treatments such as massages and facials. Accommodations include deluxe cabins and original cedar cabins by the lake, which have private or adjacent central modern facilities.

Innkeeper(s): Marlee Turner.

Rates:$70. MC VISA DS. Full Bkfst. EP. AP available. MAP available. Gourmet Brkfst, Lunch, Dinner. Picnic lunches. 38 rooms. 19 with shared baths. Conference Rm. Exercise room.

Contact: Marlee Turner. Certificate may be used: Spring and fall.

Round Pond

The Briar Rose B&B
Rt 32, Box 27
Round Pond 04564
(207)529-5478

1850. At the turn of the century, this house served the village of Round Pond as the Harbor View Hotel and hosted vacationers and those working with the busy shipping trade that once filled the tiny harbor. Guest rooms are large and airy with views of the harbor. Parlors are filled with books, magazines, games and other rainy-day entertainment. The winter parlor also offers a wood stove for chilly evenings. Within walking distance are country stores, antique shops, galleries and the working studios of local craftspeople. Sample fresh lobster picnic-style at the dock or in a waterfront restaurant.

Innkeeper(s): Anita & Fred Palsgrove.

Rates:$50-70. Full Bkfst. Picnic lunches. Evening snacks. 3 rooms. 2 with shared baths. Beds:QT. Phone in room. Skiing. Swimming. Fishing.

Contact: Anita Palsgrove. Certificate may be used: Anytime except July, August and holidays.

Saco

Crown 'N' Anchor Inn
121 North St, PO Box 228
Saco 04072-0228
(207)282-3829

1827. This Greek Revival house features both Victorian baroque and colonial antiques. A collection of British coronation memorabilia displayed throughout the inn includes 200 items. Guests gather in the Victorian parlor or the formal library. The innkeepers, two college librarians and an academic bookseller, lined the shelves with several thousand volumes, including extensive Civil War and British royal family collections and travel, theater and nautical books. The floor-to-ceiling windows of the Eliza Hitchcock Room overlook the Damariscotta River. Royal Dalton china, crystal and fresh flowers create a festive breakfast setting.

Innkeeper(s): John Barclay & Martha Forester.

Rates:$60-95. MC VISA. Full Bkfst. EP. Gourmet Brkfst. Teas. 6 rooms. Fireplaces. Beds:KQT. Conference Rm. TV in room. Skiing. Swimming. Fishing.

Seen in: *Lincoln County News, Yankee Magazine.*

Contact: John Barclay. Certificate may be used: Year-round, Monday through Thursday but not on national holidays.

"Absolute hospitality and helpfulness."

Searsport

Brass Lantern Inn
PO Box 407, Rt 1
Searsport 04974
(207)548-0150 (800)691-0150

1850. This Victorian inn is nestled at the edge of the woods on a rise overlooking Penobscot Bay. Showcased throughout the inn are many collectibles, antiques and family heirlooms, including an extensive doll collection. Enjoy breakfast in the dining room with its ornate tin ceiling, where you'll feast on Maine blueberry pancakes and other sumptuous treats. Centrally located between Camden and Bar Harbor, Searsport is known as the antique capital of Maine. There are many local attractions, including the Penobscot Marine Museum, fine shops and restaurants, as well as a public boat facility.

Innkeeper(s): Pat Gatto, Dan & Lee Anne Lee.

Rates:$50-75. MC VISA. Full Bkfst. 4 rooms. Beds:T. Swimming. Fishing.

Contact: Lee Anne Lee. Certificate may be used: Anytime except holiday weekends and August.

Homeport Inn
Rt 1 E Main St, PO Box 647
Searsport 04974
(207)548-2259 (800)742-5814

1861. Captain John Nickels built this home on Penobscot Bay. On top of the two-story historic landmark is a widow's walk. A scalloped picket

fence frames the property. Fine antiques, black marble fireplaces, a collection of grandfather clocks and elaborate ceiling medallions add to the atmosphere. Beautifully landscaped grounds sweep out to the ocean's edge. Some rooms have an ocean view.

Innkeeper(s): Dr. & Mrs. F. George Johnson.

Rates:$60-75. MC VISA AX DS. Full Bkfst. 10 rooms. 4 with shared baths. Beds:QT. Golf. Bicycling. Skiing. Handicap access. Fishing.

Seen in: *Yankee Magazine.*

Contact: F. George Johnson. Certificate may be used: Mondays through Thursdays inclusive all year except August, no holidays.

"Your breakfast is something we will never forget."

House Of Three Chimneys
Black Rd, Box 397
Searsport 04974
(207)548-6117

1850. Formerly a sea captain's home, the inn was built after the war of 1812 in Greek Revival style. The B&B features spacious parlors, dining room, family room with TV and fireplace and guest rooms. A wide variety of restaurants in the area include elegant fine dining, casual family dining, a tavern, bakery restaurant and lobster shack. Seaport is Maine's second-largest deep-water port. The town dock with boat ramp is open to the public.

Innkeeper(s): Patricia Collins-Stockton

Rates:$50-70. MC VISA. Full Bkfst. 4 rooms. Beds:KQT. AC in room. Skiing. Swimming. Fishing.

Contact: Patricia Collins-Stockton. Certificate may be used: Oct. 16-Dec. 30; April 1-May 15.

Thurston House B&B
8 Elm St, PO Box 686
Searsport 04974
(207)548-2213 (800)240-2213
Fax:(207)548-0161

1831. The innkeepers of this Colonial home proudly serve their "Forget About Lunch" breakfast, which consists of three courses, fresh prepared fruit, freshly baked hot breads and then a sumptuous entree course. Special diets are happily accommodated as well. Stephen Thurston was the pastor of the first Congregational Church in Searsport for the heart of the 19th century. He was one of the town's most prominent citizens as well. In 1853, the 242-ton brig named after Thurston was launched.

Innkeeper(s): Carl & Beverly Eppig.

Rates:$40-60. MC VISA. Full Bkfst. Gourmet Brkfst. Teas. 4 rooms. 2 with shared baths. Beds:DT. Golf. Tennis. Skiing. Handicap access. Swimming. Fishing.

Seen in: *Yankee Magazine, The Evening Times-Globe, The Great Hallowell-Searsport Antiques Rivalry.*

Contact: Carl Eppig. Certificate may be used: Nov. 1-May 31, 1994 and 1995.

South Thomaston

The Weskeag Inn
PO Box 213, Rt 73
South Thomaston 04858
(207)596-6676

1803. The backyard of this three-story house stretches to the edge of Weskeag River and Ballyhac Cove. Fifty yards from the house, there's a reversing white-water rapids, created by the 10-foot tide that narrows into the estuary. Guests often sit by the water's edge to watch the birds and the lobster fishermen. Sea kayakers can launch at the inn and explore the nearby coves and then paddle on to the ocean. The inn's furnishings include a mixture of comfortable antiques. Featherbed eggs are a house specialty.

Innkeeper(s): Gray & Lynne Smith.

Rates:$50-85. MC VISA. Full Bkfst. 9 rooms. 6 with shared baths. Beds:QDT. Golf. Tennis. Skiing. Swimming. Horseback riding. Fishing.

Contact: Lynne Smith. Certificate may be used: Jan. 1-May 31 and Oct. 16-Dec. 31, 1994; Jan. 1-May 31 and Oct. 16-Dec. 31, 1995.

Southwest Harbor

Lindenwood Inn
PO Box 1328
Southwest Harbor 04679
(207)244-5335

1906. Sea Captain Mills named his home "The Lindens" after stately linden trees in the front lawn. Elegantly refurbished, this historic house features many items collected from the new innkeeper's world travels. The rooms have sun-drenched balconies overlooking the harbor and its sailboats and lobster boats. A hearty full breakfast is served in the dining room with a roaring fireplace in the winter. From the inn you may take a tree-lined path down to the wharf.

Innkeeper(s): James King.

Rates:$55-155. MC VISA AX DS. Full Bkfst. 16 rooms. Beds:QT. TV in room. Bicycling. Skiing. Swimming. Fishing.

Seen in: *McCalls.*

Contact: James King. Certificate may be used: Oct. 30 to June 1.

"We had a lovely stay at your inn. Breakfast, room and hospitality were all first-rate. You made us feel like a special friend instead of a paying guest."

Stockton Springs

Whistlestop B&B
RFD 1 Box 639, Maple St
Stockton Springs 04981
(207)567-3726

1958. This traditional Cape Cod-style home, located on the edge of the village of Stockton Springs, overlooks quiet Stockton Harbor. Guests can relax on the patio or in the living room with grand piano, classical music and perhaps a fire in the hearth on cool evenings. Stockton Springs is located on Penobscot Bay, midway between Camden and Mount Desert Island. Guests taking a stroll

down to one of the rocky beaches can find an abundance of wildlife and flowers along the shore.

Innkeeper(s): David & Katherine Christie Wilson.

Rates:$45-65. Full Bkfst. EP. 2 rooms. 2 with shared baths. Beds:QT. Golf. Skiing. Swimming. Fishing.

Contact: Katherine Christie Wilson. Certificate may be used: Anytime except July, August and holiday weekends.

Stratton

Widow's Walk
171 Main St, PO Box 150
Stratton 04982
(207)246-6901

1892. Meals at this inn with its rambling Victorian architecture are served family-style in a paneled dining room overlooking Stratton Brook. After a long day of outdoor activity, guests can join others in front of the fire for a "gabfest," watch a special program on cable TV, or challenge a friend to ping pong or darts in the game room. The inn is 10 minutes away from Sugarloaf/USA and 15 minutes from Carrabassett Valley Ski Touring Center. There are lots of cross-country trails right in the neighborhood.

Innkeeper(s): Mary & Jerry Hopson.

Rates:$30-46. MC VISA. Full Bkfst. AP available. 6 rooms. 6 with shared baths. Beds:DT. Skiing. Fishing.

Contact: Mary Hopson. Certificate may be used: All times except Dec. 25-Jan. 1.

Tenants Harbor

East Wind Inn & Meeting House
PO Box 149
Tenants Harbor 04680
(207)372-6366 (800)241-8439
Fax:(207)372-6320

1974. Because of its proximity to the ocean, each of the inn's guest rooms has a view of the harbor. The inn was once a sail loft and the Meeting House was a captain's house. Spacious porches also afford a view, where guests can read and smell the salt air while rocking. Enjoy the beaches, tidal pools, berry picking and wildflowers. The nearby Farnsworth Art Museum has a permanent Wyeth collection, and another attraction is the Shore Village Lighthouse Museum.

Innkeeper(s): Tim Watts.

Rates:$60-110. MC VISA AX. Full Bkfst. EP. Gourmet Dinner. 25 rooms. 14 with shared baths. Beds:KQ. Phone in room. Skiing. Swimming. Fishing.

Contact: Maura Curley. Certificate may be used: November - April only.

Vinalhaven

Fox Island Inn
PO Box 451, Carver St
Vinalhaven 04863
(904)863-2122

1880. Discover island life during your stay at this country farmhouse-style inn where you are warmly welcomed to flea markets, church suppers and art shows featuring local artists. You can prepare a picnic in the guest kitchen before your day of exploring the coastal island of Vinalhaven, a fishing village nestled around picturesque Carver's Harbor. During the unstressed days you'll have time to jog (innkeepers are marathoners), pick berries, write, read, or just sit on a rock and contemplate the sea. You'll need to take a ferry from Rockland across scenic Penobscot Bay through islands surrounding Vinalhaven.
Innkeeper(s): Gail Reinertsen
Rates:$45-60. ContPlus Bkfst. 6 rooms. 6 with shared baths. Beds:DT. Bicycling.
Contact: Gail Reinertsen. Certificate may be used: May, June, September, October.

Waldoboro

Broad Bay Inn & Gallery
1014 Main St, PO Box 607
Waldoboro 04572
(207)832-6668

1830. This Colonial inn lies in the heart of an unspoiled coastal village. You'll find Victorian furnishings throughout and some guest rooms have canopy beds. Afternoon tea is served on the deck. An established art gallery displays works by renowned artists, as well as limited edition prints. Television, games and an art library are available in the common room.
Innkeeper(s): E. Libby Hopkins.
Rates:$35-70. MC VISA. Full Bkfst. Gourmet Brkfst. 3 rooms. 2 with shared baths. Beds:T. Tennis. Skiing. Swimming.
Seen in: *Boston Globe, Ford Times, Courier Gazette, Princeton Packet.*
Contact: E. Libby Hopkins. Certificate may be used: Monday through Thursday, anytime.

"Breakfast was so special - I ran to get my camera. Why, there were even flowers on my plate."

Tide Watch Inn
PO Box 94, 55 Pine St
Waldoboro 04572
(207)832-4987

1850. Located on the waterfront, the Tide Watch is a twin or mirror Colonial erected by brothers who wished to live side by side. The first five-masted schooners were built in front of the house, and for a time the inn was a boarding house for the shipbuilders.
Innkeeper(s): Mel & Cathy Hanson.
Rates:$50-60. Full Bkfst. 3 rooms. 2 with shared baths. Beds:T. Skiing. Swimming. Fishing.
Contact: Catherine Hanson. Certificate may be used: Nov. 1994 through June, 1995.

"Sumptuous breakfasts. We can't wait to come back."

Waterford

Kedarburn Inn
Rt 35 Box 61
Waterford 04088
(207)583-6182

1858. The innkeepers of this Victorian establishment invite guests to try a taste of olde English hospitality and cuisine at their inn, nestled in the foothills of the White Mountains in Western Maine. Located in a historic village, the inn sits besides the flowing Kedar Brook which runs to the shores of Lake Keoka. Each of the spacious rooms is decorated with handmade crocheted pillows, embroidered curtains, handsewn linens and arrangements of dried flowers. A variety of tea sandwiches, beverages, pastries, English biscuits and other tasty items are served for afternoon tea.
Innkeeper(s): Margaret & Derek Gibson.
Rates:$80-88. MC VISA AX. Full Bkfst. 6 rooms. 4 with shared baths. Beds:KT. AC in room. Golf. Skiing. Handicap access. Swimming. Fishing.
Seen in: *Maine Times.*
Contact: Margaret Gibson. Certificate may be used: April, May, June, August, September.

Lake House
Rts 35 & 37
Waterford 04088
(207)583-4182 (800)223-4182
Fax:(207)583-6618

1780. Situated on the common, the Lake House was first a hotel and stagecoach stop. In 1817, granite baths were constructed below the first floor. The inn opened as "Dr. Shattuck's Maine Hygienic

Institute for Ladies." It continued as a popular health spa until the 1890s. Now noted for excellent country cuisine, there are two dining rooms for non-smokers. Four guest rooms are upstairs. The spacious Grand Ballroom Suite features curved ceilings, a sitting room and a canopy bed. Views of Lake Keoka are enjoyed from the inn's veranda. A cozy guest bungalow with private porch sits behind the inn.

Innkeeper(s): Suzanne & Michael Uhl-Myers

Rates:$52-130. MC VISA AX. Full Bkfst. MAP available. Gourmet Dinner. 5 rooms. Beds:QT. AC in room. Golf. Tennis. Bicycling. Skiing. Swimming. Fishing.

Seen in: *Country Inns, Yankee Travel Magazine.*

Contact: Suzanne Uhl-Myers. Certificate may be used: Dec. 1 through March 31 (excluding Dec. 25-Jan. 2).

"Your hospitality was matched only by the quality of dinner that we were served."

West Boothbay Harbor

Lawnmeer Inn
PO Box 505
West Boothbay Harbor 04575
(207)633-2544 (800)633-7645

1899. This pleasant inn sits by the shoreline, providing a picturesque oceanfront setting. Located on a small, wooded island, it is accessed by a lift bridge. Family-oriented rooms are clean and homey, and there is a private honeymoon cottage in the Smoke House. The dining room is waterside and serves a Continental cuisine with an emphasis on seafood. Boothbay Harbor is two miles away.

Innkeeper(s): Lee & Jim Metzger.

Rates:$40-110. MC VISA. Full Bkfst. EP. 32 rooms. Beds:KQT. Conference Rm. Golf. Tennis. Swimming. Fishing.

Seen in: *Los Angeles Times, Getaways for Gourmets.*

Contact: Lee Metzger. Certificate may be used: Sunday through Thursday.

"Your hospitality was warm and gracious and the food delectable."

West Gouldsboro

Sunset House
Rt 186, HCR 60, Box 62
West Gouldsboro 04607
(207)963-7156 (800)233-7156

1898. This coastal country farm inn is situated near Acadia National Park. Naturalists can observe rare birds and other wildlife in an unspoiled setting. Seven spacious bedrooms are spread over three

floors. Four of the bedrooms have ocean views; a fifth overlooks a freshwater pond behind the house. During winter, guests can ice skate on the pond, while in summer it is used for swimming. The innkeepers have resident cats and poodles, and they also raise goats. Guests enjoy a full country breakfast cooked by Carl, who was an executive chef for 20 years.

Innkeeper(s): Kathy & Carl Johnson.

Rates:$59-79. MC VISA DS CB. Full Bkfst. EP. 6 rooms. 3 with shared baths. Beds:KT. Farm. Golf. Tennis. Bicycling. Skiing. Swimming. Fishing.

Contact: Kathy Johnson. Certificate may be used: Excluding August.

York

Dockside Guest Quarters
PO Box 205, Harris Island
York 03909
(207)363-2868

1900. This inn is located on Harris Island, a private peninsula in York Harbor. The "Maine House" is typical of large, cottage-style New England summer homes. Splendid water views encompass the ocean and harbor. Museum-quality antiques may be found. Guest rooms in the inn and cottages are cheerfully but simply appointed with painted furnishings and small print wallpapers or paneling. Waterfront dining is available at the inn's restaurant.

Innkeeper(s): The David Lusty Family.

Rates:$73-104. MC VISA. ContPlus Bkfst. Teas. 28 rooms. 2 with shared baths. Fireplaces. Beds:KQT. Conference Rm. Refrig. in room. Golf. Tennis. Bicycling. Skiing. Swimming. Fishing.

Seen in: *Boston Globe.*

Contact: Eric Lusty. Certificate may be used: Sunday-Thursday, 10/10/94-10/20/94; 10/21/94-5/1/95; 5/2/95-6/20/95; 10/21/95-12/31/95.

"We've been back many years. It's a paradise for us, the scenery, location, maintenance, living quarters."

York Beach

Homestead Inn B&B
8 S Main St (Rt 1A), PO Box 15
York Beach 03910
(207)363-8952

1905. This turn-of-the-century boarding house is next to Short Sands Beach. The original hard pine has been retained throughout. Bedrooms have a panoramic view of the ocean and hills. The house is kept cozy and warm by the heat of a woodstove and fireplace. Guests enjoy the sound of the surf and seagulls. Continental breakfast is offered on the sun deck or in the family dining room.

Innkeeper(s): Dan & Danielle Duffy.

Rates:$49-59. ContPlus Bkfst. Teas. Evening snacks. 4 rooms. 4 with shared baths. Beds:DT. Golf. Tennis. Bicycling. Swimming. Fishing.

Contact: Daniel Duffy. Certificate may be used: Anytime but restricted use in July and August, i.e. will accept in these months only 2-3 days prior to reservation dates.

York Harbor

Bell Buoy B&B
570 York St
York Harbor 03911
(207)363-7264

1884. Just a short walk to Long Sands Beach, this Victorian inn is located in prestigious York Harbor. You may want to stroll the Marginal Way along the ocean shore or catch the scenic trolley that stops across the street and takes you to points of interest while giving you a narrative about the town. After your day of enjoying the area, stop back for an afternoon tea, served at 5 p.m. to set your mood for one of the many outstanding restaurants in the area—some just a walking distance away. Breakfasts can be relished in the family dining room or on the porch.

Innkeeper(s): Wes & Kathie Cook

Rates:$60-75. Full Bkfst. Teas. Evening snacks. 5 rooms. 3 with shared baths. Beds:KQT. Swimming. Fishing.

Contact: Wesley Cook. Certificate may be used: November through May.

Maryland

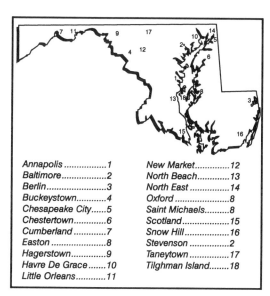

Annapolis

The Barn on Howard's Cove
500 Wilson Rd
Annapolis 21401
(410)266-6840

1850. This handsomely situated restored horsebarn features a deck with waterfront views. Step down from the deck to a deepwater dock for boating and fishing in the area. The inn's six wooded acres are on a cove of the Severn River just outside Annapolis, where your host is a professor at the Naval Academy. Antiques, old quilts, Oriental rugs and original paintings fill the rooms. A solarium overflowing with geraniums, impatiens and begonias frames pristine views of the water and woods.
Innkeeper(s): Graham & Libbie Gutsche.

Rates:$70. Full Bkfst. 2 rooms. 2 with shared baths. Beds:KDT. TV, AC, Refrig. in room. Fishing.

Contact: Mary Gutsche. Certificate may be used: Monday through Thursday year round.

Baltimore

Betsy's B&B
1428 Park Ave
Baltimore 21217
(410)383-1274 (800)899-7533
Fax:(410)728-8957

1870. This four-story townhouse features many elegant architectural touches. The hallway floor is laid in alternating strips of oak and walnut, and there are six carved-marble fireplaces. The most elaborate, carved in fruit designs, is in the dining room. The inn is decorated with handsome brass rubbings made by the owner during a stay in England.
Innkeeper(s): Betsy Grater.

Rates:$75. MC VISA AX DS. Full Bkfst. 3 rooms. Beds:KQT. Phone, AC in room. Spa. Swimming.

Seen in: Peabody Reflector, Baltimore/Washington Business Journal, Nation's Business, Times Herald, Baltimore Sun.

Contact: Betsy Grater. Certificate may be used: Sunday through Thursday.

"What hotel room could ever compare to a large room in a 115-year-old house with 12-foot ceilings and a marble fireplace with hosts that could become dear long-time friends?"

Union Square House B&B
23 S Stricker St
Baltimore 21223
(410)233-9064 Fax:(410)233-4046

1870. This restored Victorian Italianate townhouse is situated in "Millionaires' Row" of the Union Square Historic District. It faces Union Square Park with its gardens, trees, gracious domed gazebo and fountain, often the location for summertime concerts provided by local musicians. Rooms feature original plaster moldings, handsome woodwork and period furnishings. The University of Maryland, B&O Railroad Museum, Convention Center and the Inner Harbor are just a few blocks away.
Innkeeper(s): Joseph & Patrice Debes.

Rates:$80-115. MC VISA AX DS. Full Bkfst. MAP available. Gourmet Brkfst. Teas. Evening snacks. 3 rooms. Fireplaces. Beds:D. AC, Refrig. in room. Handicap access.

Contact: Joseph Debes. Certificate may be used: Sept. 15, 1994-Nov. 30, 1994; Jan. 15, 1995-April 30, 1995; Sept. 15, 1995-Nov. 30, 1995.

Berlin

Merry Sherwood Plantation

8909 Worcester Hwy
Berlin 21811
(410)641-2112 (800)660-0358
Fax:(410)641-3605

1859. This magnificent pre-Civil War mansion is a tribute to Southern plantation architecture. Antique period furniture, hand-woven, Victorian-

era rugs and a square grand piano are features. The ballroom, now a parlor for guests, boasts twin fireplaces and pier mirrors. (Ask to see the hidden cupboards behind the fireside bookcases in the library.) Nineteen acres of grounds are beautifully landscaped and feature azaleas, boxwoods and 125 varieties of trees.

Innkeeper(s): Kirk & Ginny Burbage.

Rates:$95-150. MC VISA. Gourmet Brkfst. 8 rooms. 2 with shared baths. Fireplaces. Beds:Q. AC in room. Golf. Swimming. Fishing.

Seen in: *Washinton Post, Baltimore Sun, Southern Living.*

Contact: Kirk Burbage. Certificate may be used: Monday to Friday, October through April. May through September, weekdays Sunday through Thursday. Promotion is available on weekends only if availability permits.

"Pure elegance and privacy at its finest."

Buckeystown

The Inn at Buckeystown

3521 Buckeystown Pike Gen Del
Buckeystown 21717
(301)874-5755 (800)272-1190

1897. Gables, bay windows and a wraparound porch are features of this grand Victorian mansion

located on two-and-a-half acres of lawns and gardens (and an ancient cemetery). Nearby St. John's Reformed Church, built in 1884, has been refur-

bished as a cottage. The inn features a polished staircase, antiques and elegantly decorated guest rooms. Ask for the Fireplace Room, which boasts a lavish canopy bed with draperies. At dinner, cream of lemon soup, German duck and West Virginia black walnut apple cake are house specialties. The village of Buckeystown is in the National Register.

Rates:$167-272. MC VISA AX. Full Bkfst. MAP available. Gourmet Brkfst, Dinner. 4 rooms. Fireplaces. Beds:QDT. Conference Rm. TV, Phone, AC, Refrig. in room. Skiing. Spa. Swimming. Fishing.

Seen in: *Mid-Atlantic, Innsider, The Washingtonian.*

Contact: Daniel R. Pelz. Certificate may be used: Year-round - Monday - Thursday. Not available weekends in October and holidays.

"The courtesy of you and your staff were the glue that bound the whole experience together."

Catoctin Inn and Antiques

3613 Buckeystown Pike
Buckeystown 21717
(301)874-5555 (800)730-5550

1780. The inn's four acres of dogwood, magnolias, maples and sweeping lawns overlook the village and the Catoctin Mountain range. Some special features of the inn include a library with marble fireplaces and a handsome wraparound veranda. A gazebo marks the site for weddings, showers and receptions for up to 150 guests. An antique shop on the property is housed in a two-story Victorian carriage house. Nearby villages to visit include Harper's Ferry, Antietam and New Market. Buckeystown's Monocacy River provides canoeing and fishing.

Innkeeper(s): Terry & Sarah MacGillivray.

Rates:$85. MC VISA AX DC DS CB. Gourmet Brkfst. 5 rooms. Fireplaces. Beds:Q. Conference Rm. TV, Phone, AC, Refrig. in room. Bicycling. Skiing. Fishing.

Contact: Terry MacGillivray. Certificate may be used: November-August, excluding September and October.

Chesapeake City

Bohemia House
1236 Town Point Rd
Chesapeake City 21915
(410)885-3024 Fax:(410)885-3040

1850. A long veranda stretches out across the front of this Victorian Italianate house, while a screened porch at the back overlooks the Bohemia River and the inn's 28 acres. The house was built by descendents of Kitty Knight, who saved Georgetown from the British. This Upper Eastern Shore area is referred to as Horse Country and there is an equine theme carried out in the inn's decor such as the Stewards Bench from the Coney Island Race Track. A conference room on the property makes it a suitable spot for corporate retreats, weddings, reunions and company picnics.

Innkeeper(s): Sally & Herbert Worsley.
Rates:$65-99. MC VISA AX DC. EP. Gourmet Brkfst, Lunch, Dinner. Teas. Evening snacks. 8 rooms. 1 with shared bath. Beds:KQT. Conference Rm. TV, Phone, AC in room. Bicycling. Exercise room. Swimming. Stables. Fishing.
Contact: Sally & Herbert Worsley. Certificate may be used: Through the week - no weekends or holidays.

Chestertown

The Chesapeake Club
PO Box 609
Chestertown 21620
(410)758-4793 (800)787-4667
Fax:(410)482-7189

1989. This three-story Colonial Revival manor house boasts a two-tiered veranda accentuated by six columns. The inn's 700 acres feature two ponds, a creek, woodlands, crops and a nature trail from which to enjoy the abundant wildlife on the property (wild turkey, quail, geese, duck and deer). There is a gun room, wine cellar, steam room, communications room and sauna among the inn's many amenities. Hunting is offered here on the estate, home to the Fairfield Shooting School. There are Sporting Clay ranges on the property as well.

Innkeeper(s): Erlene Schauber.
Rates:$75-95. MC VISA AX. Full Bkfst. 10 rooms. Beds:KT. Conference Rm. AC in room. Spa. Sauna. Swimming. Fishing.
Contact: Erleen Schauber. Certificate may be used: Weekdays, non-holiday or special event.

Hill's Inn
114 Washington Ave
Chestertown 21620
(410)778-4667 (800)787-4667
Fax:(410)778-1926

1877. This beautifully restored three-story yellow and green Queen Anne Victorian features porches and bay windows overlooking the inn's lawns. A dining room and double parlors are extra features. It's a short walk to the shops of charming High Street and Washington College.

Innkeeper(s): Janet Thompson.
Rates:$50-110. MC VISA AX DC DS. ContPlus Bkfst. Teas. 7 rooms. Beds:KT. AC in room. Swimming. Fishing.
Contact: Janet Thompson. Certificate may be used: Must be weekday, non-holiday or special-event weekends.

Lauretum Inn B&B
954 High St
Chestertown 21620
(410)778-3236 (800)742-3236

1870. At the end of a long winding driveway this massive Queen Anne Victorian commands a hilltop setting on six acres just outside of town. Inviting parlors and a porch are available to guests. Spacious guest rooms overlook the inn's lawns, often visited by deer in the early morning. Peg, the mother of 16 children, once plied the intracoastal waters on her 40-foot boat and can help you plan your stay in the area.

Innkeeper(s): Peg & Bill Sites.
Rates:$65-105. MC VISA DS. ContPlus Bkfst. 5 rooms. 2 with shared baths. Beds:QT. AC in room. Swimming. Fishing.
Contact: William Sites. Certificate may be used: Jan. 2-March 31.

The Inn at Mitchell House
8796 Maryland Parkway
Chestertown 21620
(410)778-6500

1743. This pristine 18th-century manor house sits as a jewel on 12 acres overlooking Stoneybrook

Pond. The guest rooms and the inn's several parlors are preserved and appointed in an authentic Colonial mood, heightened by handsome polished wide-board floors. Eastern Neck Island National Wildlife Refuge, Remington Farms, St. Michaels, Annapolis and nearby Chestertown are all delightful to explore. The Inn at Mitchell House is a popular setting for romantic weddings and small corporate meetings.

Innkeeper(s): Tracy & Jim Stone.

Rates:$68-100. MC VISA DS. Full Bkfst. Gourmet Lunch, Dinner. Teas. 6 rooms. 1 with shared bath. Fireplaces. Beds:KQT. AC, Refrig. in room. Farm. Golf. Tennis. Swimming. Horseback riding. Fishing.

Seen in: *Washingtonian, New York Magazine, Glamour, Philadelphia Enquirer, Baltimore Sun, Kent County News.*

Contact: James Stone. Certificate may be used: Valid Sunday through Thursday.

Cumberland

The Inn at Walnut Bottom
120 Greene St
Cumberland 21502
(301)777-0003 (800)286-9718
Fax:(301)777-1629

1815. Two historic houses comprise the Inn at Walnut Bottom: the 1815 Cowden House and the 1890 Dent house. There are two guest parlors.

Country antiques and reproduction furnishings decorate the old-fashioned rooms. Arthur's Restaurant provides homemade traditional cookery.

Innkeeper(s): Sharon Ennis Kazary.

Rates:$65-85. MC VISA AX DS. Full Bkfst. EP. Gourmet Lunch, Dinner. Picnic lunches. 12 rooms. 4 with shared baths. Beds:QT. Conference Rm. TV, Phone, AC in room. Bicycling. Skiing. Swimming. Horseback riding. Fishing.

Seen in: *Washington Post, Mid-Atlantic Country.*

Contact: Sharon Kazary. Certificate may be used: Sunday-Thursday nights, November through March, not including holidays and special events. Friday and Saturday nights, December and January, not including holidays and special events.

Easton

The Bishop's House B&B
214 Goldsborough St, PO Box 2217
Easton 21601
(410)820-7290 (800)223-7290
Fax:(410)820-7290

1880. This three-and-a-half-story clapboard and gabled roof home includes three spacious first-floor rooms with 14-foot-high ceilings and generously sized second-floor guest rooms with 12-foot ceilings.

Furnished with 19th-century oak, walnut and mahogany furniture, the inn offers its guests the ambiance of the Victorian era. Three guest rooms have working fireplaces. Located in Easton's Historic District, it is within three blocks of the Talbot County Court House, boutiques, antique shops, restaurants and historic sites.

Innkeeper(s): Diane & John Ippolito.

Rates:$75-110. Full Bkfst. 6 rooms. 2 with shared baths.

Contact: Diane Ippolito. Certificate may be used: December through September; not available for a Thursday-night stay.

The McDaniel House
14 N Aurora St
Easton 21601
(410)822-3704 (800)787-4667

1860. A wide veranda wraps around this three-story white Queen Anne Victorian, complete with octagonal tower, dormers and a wraparound porch. Located in the historic district, considered to be the "Colonial Capital of the Eastern Shore," it's within walking distance to the Classic Avalon Theater, Academy of Art, many good restaurants and unique shops. A large barn on the property often is used by cyclists for storing their bicycles while visiting the inn.

Innkeeper(s): Rosemary & SD Garrett.

Rates:$60-80. MC VISA AX. ContPlus Bkfst. 6 rooms. 1 with shared bath. Beds:KQD. AC in room. Fishing.

Contact: Rosemary Garrett. Certificate may be used: November-March.

Hagerstown

Beaver Creek House B&B
20432 Beaver Creek Rd
Hagerstown 21740
(301)797-4764

1905. History buffs enjoy this turn-of-the-century inn located minutes away from Antietam and Harpers Ferry National Historical Parks. The sur-

rounding villages house antique shops and some hold weekend auctions. The inn features a courtyard with a fountain and a country garden. Innkeepers Don and Shirley Day furnished the home with family antiques and memorabilia. Guests can sip afternoon tea or complimentary sherry in the elegant parlor or just relax on the porch and take in the view of South Mountain.

Innkeeper(s): Donald & Shirley Day.

Rates:$75-85. MC VISA AX DC DS. Gourmet Brkfst. 5 rooms. 2 with shared baths. Beds:DT. Conference Rm. AC in room. Golf. Tennis. Bicycling. Skiing. Swimming. Horseback riding. Fishing.

Seen in: *Baltimore Sun, Hagerstown Journal.*

Contact: Donald Day. Certificate may be used: Sunday through Thursday all year, holidays excluded.

Sunday's B&B
39 Broadway
Hagerstown 21740
(301)797-4331 (800)221-4828

1890. This Queen Anne Victorian is appropriately appointed with period antiques. Fresh flowers and fruit baskets are provided and guests are pampered with a full breakfast, afternoon tea, evening wine and cheese and for late evening, bedside cordials and truffles. Antietam, Harpers Ferry and the C&O

Canal are nearby.

Innkeeper(s): Bob Ferrino.

Rates:$85-95. Full Bkfst. Gourmet Dinner. Picnic lunches. Teas. 3 rooms. 2 with shared baths. Beds:QD. TV, AC in room. Golf. Tennis. Skiing. Swimming. Horseback riding. Fishing.

Contact: Bob Ferrino. Certificate may be used: Anytime.

"You made a wedding night in heaven."

Havre De Grace

The Spencer Silver Mansion
200 S Union Ave
Havre De Grace 21078
(410)939-1097 (800)780-1485

1896. This elegant granite Victorian mansion is graced with bays, gables, balconies, a turret and a gazebo veranda. The Victorian decor, with antiques and Oriental rugs, complements the house's carved-oak woodwork, fireplace mantels and parquet floors. The Concord Point Lighthouse (oldest continuously operated lighthouse in America) is only a walk away.

Innkeeper(s): Carol & Jim Nemeth.

Rates:$65-85. Full Bkfst. EP. Teas. 5 rooms. 3 with shared baths. Beds:QT. Conference Rm. Phone, AC in room. Tennis. Swimming. Fishing.

Seen in: *Mid-Atlantic Country.*

Contact: Jim Nemeth. Certificate may be used: Anytime except Saturday night may not be part of the two-night stay.

"A fabulous find."

Little Orleans

Town Hill Hotel
Beauty Spot of Maryland
Little Orleans 21766
(301)478-2794

1922. Said to be Maryland's first tourist hotel, this inn located on 10 acres is much as it was back in the '20s with the same metal furniture and faux wood metal dressers. The hotel is surrounded by thousands of acres of Green Ridge State Forest at the top of a 1,600-foot mountain. The front yard overlooks three states and seven counties. Rocky Gap State Park and White Tail ski area are a few minutes away. The inn's large dining room is available for dinner and is popular for wedding receptions and banquets. Ask if Florence's pineapple egg dish will be served at breakfast.

Innkeeper(s): Dick & Flo Essers.

Rates:$39-79. Full Bkfst. AP available. MAP available. Gourmet Dinner. Picnic lunches. 7 rooms. 3 with shared baths. Beds:D. Conference Rm. Skiing. Fishing.

Contact: Florence Essers. Certificate may be used: Not available month of October, weekends; first weekend in August, good any midweek time. Holiday weekends not available.

New Market

National Pike Inn
9 W Main St, PO Box 299
New Market 21774
(301)865-5055

1796. This red shuttered brick Federal house is one of the few inns remaining on the National Pike, the old East-West route between Baltimore and points west. The inn's Colonial decor includes wingback chairs, Oriental rugs and four-poster beds. There's a private courtyard and fountain bordered by azalea gardens.

Innkeeper(s): Tom & Terry Rimel.

Rates:$75-125. MC VISA. Full Bkfst. 5 rooms. 2 with shared baths. Beds:QD. Conference Rm. AC in room. Golf. Tennis.

Seen in: *Mid-Atlantic Country, Country Magazine.*

Contact: Terry Rimel. Certificate may be used: Monday, Tuesday, Wednesday, Thursday, year-round except New Year's Eve, special events or holidays.

"A total joy! A relaxed, charming and romantic setting."

North Beach

Angels in the Attic's Westlawn Inn
9200 Chesapeake Ave, PO Box 70
North Beach 20714
(410)257-1069

1903. Located just a block from Chesapeake Bay, this was one of the county's original guest houses. The inn's restoration has brought back to life a hand-painted mural of Winchester, Virginia, encircling the living and dining room. The Yankee Harbour room is furnished with antiques, quilts and a collection of sailor dolls. The inn is named after Angel, an African Gray parrot, but don't neglect to talk to Cupid, the Double Yellow Headed Amazon or visit the Chinese pugs in their own back garden playground.

Innkeeper(s): Denise England Devoe & Linda Travers.

Rates:$55-65. MC VISA. ContPlus Bkfst. Teas. 8 rooms. 6 with shared baths. Conference Rm. AC in room. Swimming. Fishing.

Contact: Denise England Devoe. Certificate may be used: Sunday through Thursday, no holidays.

North East

The Mill House B&B
102 Mill Ln
North East 21901
(410)287-3532

1710. The Mill House is a combination of two houses: one the mill owners' house and the other the former kitchen and maid's quarters. In the

Maryland Register of Historic Sites, the inn is filled with antiques such as an 18th-century tall case clock, four-poster beds and Victorian slipper chairs. Wildflowers now grow on the property's five acres in the marsh between the mill ruins and the North East River. The village features antique and craft shops and the Upper Bay Museum. Ten minutes away is a factory outlet mall.

Innkeeper(s): Lucia & Nick Demond.

Rates:$65-75. MC VISA. Full Bkfst. 2 rooms. 2 with shared baths. AC in room. Bicycling. Swimming. Fishing.

Contact: Lucia Demond. Certificate may be used: Sunday through Thursday.

Oxford

Oxford Inn/Pope's Tavern
510 S Morris St, PO Box 627
Oxford 21654
(410)226-5220 (800)292-5220

1900. Situated at the head of Town Creek and its docks, this inn has two dining rooms with authentic scale models of Chesapeake Bay sailing vessels featured as part of the nautical decor. The inn's sitting room overlooks Town Creek as does Tavern Hall, a third-floor room with four window-seat views of the quaint harbor. The inn is a part of "Biking Inn to Inn on the Eastern Shore" and can help you plan your cycling itinerary.

Innkeeper(s): Rick & Sue Schmitt.

Rates:$60-135. MC VISA DS. ContPlus Bkfst. Picnic lunches. Evening snacks. 11 rooms. 4 with shared baths. Beds:QDT. Conference Rm. AC in room. Swimming. Fishing.

Contact: Susan Schmitt. Certificate may be used: Sunday through

Thursday, April through November exclude February. Anytime December, January and March.

Saint Michaels

Kemp House Inn

412 Talbot St, PO Box 638

Saint Michaels 21663

(410)745-2243

1807. This two-story Georgian house was built by Colonel Joseph Kemp, a shipwright and one of the town forefathers. The inn is appointed in period furnishings accentuated by candlelight. Guest rooms include patchwork quilts, a collection of four-poster rope beds and old-fashioned nightshirts. There are several working fireplaces. Robert E. Lee is said to have been a guest.

Innkeeper(s): Steve & Diane Cooper.

Rates:$65-105. MC VISA DS. ContPlus Bkfst. 8 rooms. 2 with shared baths. Fireplaces. Beds:QT. AC in room. Golf. Swimming. Fishing.

Seen in: *Gourmet magazine.*

Contact: Diane Cooper. Certificate may be used: Sunday through Thursday nights excluding holidays.

Parsonage Inn

210 N Talbot St

Saint Michaels 21663

(410)745-5519 (800)394-5519

1883. A striking Victorian steeple rises next to the wide bay of this brick residence, once the home of Henry Clay Dodson, state senator, pharmacist and

brickyard owner. The house features brick detail in a variety of patterns and inlays, perhaps a design statement for brick customers. Porches are decorated with filigree and spindled columns. Laura Ashley linens, late Victorian-era furnishings, fireplaces and decks add to the creature comforts. Four 12-speed bikes await guests who wish to ride to Tilghman Island or to the ferry that goes to Oxford. Gourmet breakfast is served in the dining room.

Innkeeper(s): Willard Workman.

Rates:$80-130. MC VISA. Gourmet Brkfst. 8 rooms. Fireplaces.

Beds:KQ. Golf. Tennis. Bicycling. Handicap access. Swimming. Fishing.

Seen in: *Wilmington, Delaware News Journal, Philadelphia Inquirer.*

Contact: Willard Workman. Certificate may be used: Midweek, November through June.

"Striking, extensively renovated."

Scotland

St. Michael's Manor B&B

Box 17-A, Rt 5

Scotland 20687

(301)872-4025

1805. Twice featured on the Maryland House and Garden Tour, St. Michael's Manor is located on Long Neck Creek, a half mile from Chesapeake Bay. The original hand-crafted woodwork provides a handsome backdrop for the inn's antique collection. A three-acre vineyard and swimming pool are on the property.

Innkeeper(s): Joe & Nancy Dick.

Rates:$65. Full Bkfst. 4 rooms. 4 with shared baths. Beds:KQT. AC in room. Farm. Bicycling. Swimming. Fishing.

Contact: Nancy Dick. Certificate may be used: November 1 through March 31.

"Your B&B was so warm, cozy and comfortable."

Snow Hill

The River House Inn

201 E Market St

Snow Hill 21863

(410)632-2722 Fax:(410)632-2866

1860. This picturesque Gothic Revival house rests on the banks of the Pocomoke River and boasts its own dock. Its two acres roll down to the river over

long tree-studded lawns. Lawn furniture and a hammock add to the invitation to relax as do the inn's porches. Guest rooms are air-conditioned and some feature marble fireplaces. The 17th-century village of Snow Hill boasts old brick sidewalks and historic homes. Canoes and pontoon boats can be rented a block from the inn or you may wish to take Tillie the Tug's cruise.

Innkeeper(s): Larry & Susanne Knudsen.

Rates:$75-125. MC VISA AX. Full Bkfst. Picnic lunches. 9 rooms. Fireplaces. Beds:KQT. AC in room. Bicycling. Handicap access. Swimming. Fishing.

Contact: Larry Knudsen. Certificate may be used: Weekdays (Sunday - Thursday) all year; weekends (Friday - Saturday) November - April.

Stevenson

Gramercy B&B
1400 Greenspring Valley Rd, Box 119
Stevenson 21153-0119
(410)486-2405

1902. This beautiful English Tudor mansion was built as a wedding present for the daughter of Alexander Cassatt. There is a music room, library and parlors, all decorated with antiques and

Oriental rugs. Most of the guest rooms have fire-places and a few have Jacuzzi baths. Cookie, the inn's collie, loves taking guests on nature walks along the woodland trails to flush deer and fox out for viewing. There are commercial herb gardens, an orchard, a stream and flower gardens. The house was featured as the Decorator Showhouse to benefit the Baltimore Symphony. The inn is known for its delectable breakfasts.

Innkeeper(s): Dr. Ronald & Anne Pomykala.

Rates:$90-175. MC VISA DS. Gourmet Brkfst. 5 rooms. Fireplaces. Beds:K. Conference Rm. AC in room. Tennis. Spa. Exercise room. Swimming.

Contact: Anne Pomykala. Certificate may be used: Sunday-Thursday.

"The hospitality, atmosphere, food, etc. were top-notch."

Taneytown

Glenburn
3515 Runnymede Rd
Taneytown 21787
(410)751-1187

1840. Glenburn sits at the end of a winding drive that crosses Bear Branch Creek through park-like grounds. Once a boys' school, the inn features both a Georgian and Victorian section. Heirlooms gar-nered from three centuries are featured in the inn. A wraparound porch provides views and water sounds from Bear Branch. The inn's 200 acres boast pastures, a creek and woodland. There is a separate guest house. Nearby are vineyards, golf courses, museums, bike trails and the Catoctin Mountains.

Innkeeper(s): Robert & Elizabeth Neal.

Rates:$65-100. Full Bkfst. 5 rooms. 2 with shared baths. Beds:QDT. AC in room. Farm. Golf. Tennis. Skiing. Swimming. Horseback riding. Fishing.

Contact: Elizabeth Neal. Certificate may be used: Limited by available space.

Tilghman Island

Black Walnut Point Inn
Black Walnut Rd, PO Box 308
Tilghman Island 21671
(410)886-2452 Fax:(410)886-2053

1843. Located on 57 beautiful acres set aside as a wildlife sanctuary, this handsome Colonial Revival manor commands views from its private peninsula location. Charter fishing and island and river cruis-es can be arranged by the innkeepers. From its bay-side hammock to its nature walk, swimming pool and lighted tennis court, the inn provides an amaz-ingly private getaway. Accommodations are in the main house as well as the Riverside Cottage. The Cove Cottage has its own kitchen and screened porch facing the river.

Innkeeper(s): M. Thomas & Brenda Ward.

Rates:$110-140. MC VISA. ContPlus Bkfst. 7 rooms. Beds:QT. AC in room. Tennis. Bicycling. Fishing.

Contact: M. Thomas Ward. Certificate may be used: Monday, Tuesday, Wednesday, Thursday, except holidays. January through April, October - December.

Massachusetts

Barnstable

Crocker Tavern B&B
3095 Main St
Barnstable 02630
(508)362-5115

1754. This historic Cape Cod inn once served as a headquarters for the Whigs during the Revolutionary era. The inn is part of the Olde Kings Highway Historic District, and also is listed with the National Register. Visitors choose from three guest rooms in the two-story Georgian-style inn, all with fireplaces, sitting areas and private baths. The antique-filled rooms feature Colonial decor, and the James Otis Room offers a four-poster queen bed and clawfoot tub. Cape Cod Bay is just a mile from the inn, and it's an easy walk to shops and activities of the village.

Innkeeper(s): Sue & Jeff Carlson

Rates:$75-95. ContPlus Bkfst. 3 rooms. Fireplaces. Beds:Q. AC in room. Swimming. Fishing.

Contact: Susan Faria. Certificate may be used: November - April excluding holidays and holiday weekends.

Barnstable Village

Beechwood Inn
2839 Main St
Barnstable Village 02630
(508)362-6618

1853. Beechwood is a carefully restored Queen Anne house offering period furnishings, fireplaces and ocean views. Its warmth and elegance make it

159

a favorite hideaway for couples looking for a peaceful return to the Victorian era. The inn is named for rare old beech trees that shade the veranda.

Innkeeper(s): Anne & Bob Livermore.

Rates:$105-140. MC VISA AX. Gourmet Brkfst. Teas. 6 rooms. Fireplaces. Beds:KQD. AC, Refrig. in room. Golf. Tennis. Skiing. Swimming. Horseback riding. Fishing.

Seen in: *National Trust Calendar.*

Contact: Anne Livermore. Certificate may be used: Nov. 1 - May 15, excluding holidays. Subject to availability.

"Your inn is pristine in every detail. We concluded that the innkeepers, who are most hospitable, are the best part of Beechwood."

Barre

The Jenkins House B&B Inn
Rt. 122/32 at Barre Common
Barre 01005
(508)355-6444

1834. Five guest rooms await visitors at this handsome Gothic Revival inn. Three of the rooms feature private baths, and other amenities include air conditioning, ceiling fans, desks and turndown service. One guest room boasts a romantic fireplace. The full breakfast may include chocolate waffles and homemade muffins or scones. The Woods Memorial Library is just a few steps from the inn, and Rutland State Park is within easy driving distance.

Innkeeper(s): David Ward.

Rates:$70-120. MC VISA. Full Bkfst. AP available. Gourmet Brkfst. Teas. Evening snacks. 5 rooms. 2 with shared baths. Fireplaces. Beds:KQT. AC in room. Golf. Bicycling. Skiing. Swimming. Horseback riding. Fishing.

Contact: David Ward. Certificate may be used: Year round Sunday through Thursday, no holidays.

Beverly

Bunny's B&B
PO Box 373
Beverly 01915
(508)922-2392

1940. This Dutch Colonial inn is located on a scenic route leading along the state's Northeastern coast. One room features a decorative fireplace and Oriental rug. Breakfasts in the formal dining room always feature homemade muffins and the innkeepers will make every effort to meet special dietary needs if notified in advance.

Innkeeper(s): Bunny & Joe Stacey.

Rates:$55-80. ContPlus Bkfst. 3 rooms. 2 with shared baths.

Fireplaces. Beds:QT. Swimming. Fishing.

Contact: Carol Stacey. Certificate may be used: All year except Oct. 25-31, 1994. All year except Oct. 25-31, 1995.

Boston

Beacon Hill B&B
27 Brimmer St
Boston 02108
(617)523-7376

1869. This six-story Victorian rowhouse overlooks the Charles River in a quiet residential area of downtown Boston. Rooms are spacious and each has a fireplace. Two guest rooms and the dining room have views of the river. There's an elevator for toting luggage. The Boston Common and Freedom Trail, Quincy Market, conference hotels and the Back Bay are all within walking distance.

Innkeeper(s): Susan Butterworth.

Rates:$115-140. Full Bkfst. 3 rooms. Fireplaces. Beds:QD. AC in room.

Contact: Susan Butterworth. Certificate may be used: Nov. 15 - April 1 (excluding holiday periods). Monday through Thursday (if open for business).

"Enjoyed your lovely home, your cooking, your friendliness and the vibrant, alive decor."

Brewster

Old Manse Inn
1861 Main St, PO Box 839
Brewster 02631
(508)896-3149

1800. This old sea captain's house is tucked behind tall trees and has a gracious mansard roof. It was built by Captain William Lewis Knowles, and served as a link in the Underground Railroad during the Civil War. The rooms are decorated with old-fashioned print wallpapers, original paintings and antiques.

Innkeeper(s): Sugar & Doug Manchester.

Rates:$70-100. MC VISA AX DS. Full Bkfst. Gourmet Dinner. Teas. 9 rooms. Fireplaces. Beds:QDT. TV, AC in room. Golf. Bicycling. Swimming. Fishing.

Seen in: *Travel & Leisure, Boston Herald, Boston Globe.*

Contact: Sugar Manchester. Certificate may be used: Sunday-Thursday.

"Our stays at the Old Manse Inn have always been delightful. The innkeepers are gracious, the decor charming and the dining room has a character all its own."

Old Sea Pines Inn

2553 Main St, PO Box 1026
Brewster 02631
(508)896-6114 Fax:(508)896-8322

1900. This turn-of-the-century mansion on three-and-one-half acres of lawns and trees was formerly the Sea Pines School of Charm and Personality for

Young Women, established in 1907. Recently renovated, the inn displays elegant wallpapers and a grand sweeping stairway. It is located near beaches and bike paths, as well as village shops and restaurants.

Innkeeper(s): Stephen & Michele Rowan.

Rates:$43-135. MC VISA AX DC CB. Full Bkfst. Gourmet Brkfst, Dinner. Picnic lunches. Evening snacks. 21 rooms. 5 with shared baths. Fireplaces. Beds:QT. Conference Rm. TV, AC in room. Golf. Tennis. Handicap access. Swimming. Horseback riding. Fishing.

Seen in: *New York Times, Cape Cod Oracle, For Women First.*

Contact: Stephen Rowan. Certificate may be used: Nov. 1 - April 30, weekdays only.

"The loving care applied by Steve, Michele and staff is deeply appreciated."

The Poore House

2311 Main St
Brewster 02631
(508)896-2094 (800)233-6662

1837. Once home to Brewster's poor, this historic Greek Revival inn now offers comfortable quarters

to inn visitors. Rooms are furnished with antiques and other eclectic stylings. Guests will find shops and outstanding eateries within easy walking distance. Roland C. Nickerson State Park is in the immediate vicinity.

Innkeeper(s): Paul Anderson & Randy Guy.

Rates:$45-85. VISA AX. ContPlus Bkfst. 5 rooms. Beds:QDT. Swimming. Fishing.

Contact: Randon Guy. Certificate may be used: November through

June.

Brookline

The Bertram Inn

92 Sewall Ave
Brookline 02146
(617)566-2234 (800)295-3822
Fax:(617)277-1887

1908. Antiques and authenticity are the rule at this turn-of-the-century Gothic Revival inn, found on a peaceful, tree-lined street. Innkeeper Bryan R.

Austin is well versed in the restoration of historical properties and furniture and that knowledge is evident at the Bertram Inn, with its old-English stylings and Victorian decor. Boston College, Boston University, Fenway Park and the F.L. Olmstead National Historic Site all are nearby. Shops and restaurants are within walking distance.

Innkeeper(s): Bryan Austin.

Rates:$49-124. MC VISA. ContPlus Bkfst. 12 rooms. 3 with shared baths. Fireplaces. Beds:KQT. TV, Phone, AC in room.

Contact: Bryan Austin. Certificate may be used: Only in the December through April season/not including holidays.

Cambridge

The Mary Prentiss Inn

6 Prentiss St
Cambridge 02140
(617)661-2929 Fax:(617)661-5989

1843. Just a half-mile from the center of Harvard Square is this historic Greek Revival inn, complete with Ionic columns and trim. Listed with the National Register, the inn offers 18 guest rooms, almost all with kitchenette. Each room sports unique furnishings and amenities. Guests often enjoy relaxing at umbrella-covered tables on the roomy outdoor deck. A fireplace in the parlor room is another popular spot where visitors may opt to eat their breakfasts. Two rooms are available with fireplaces for a special romantic occasion.

Innkeeper(s): Charlotte & Briar Forsythe.

Rates:$79-159. MC VISA. Cont. Bkfst. 18 rooms. Fireplaces. Beds:QT. TV, Phone, AC in room. Handicap access. Swimming.

Contact: Charlotte Forsythe. Certificate may be used: December-July.

Cape Cod

Dunscroft By the Sea Inn & Cottage
24 Pilgrim Rd, Harwich Port
Cape Cod 02646
(508)432-0810 (800)432-4345

1920. This gambrel-roofed house sits behind a split-rail fence at the end of a winding brick driveway. Inside the handsome columned entrance is an extensive library and a living room with a piano. Best of all is the candlelit bed chamber with turned-down bed and the music of ocean waves rolling onto the private beach on Nantucket Sound, 300 feet from the inn.

Innkeeper(s): Wally & Alyce Cunningham.

Rates:$85-165. MC VISA AX. Full Bkfst. EP. 9 rooms. Fireplaces. Beds:KQT. Conference Rm. TV, AC, Refrig. in room. Golf. Tennis. Skiing. Handicap access. Swimming. Horseback riding. Fishing.

Contact: Alyce Cunningham. Certificate may be used: Oct. 15 - May 15 except holidays.

"A quaint and delightful slice of New England. Your generous hospitality is greatly appreciated. Your place is beautiful."

Centerville

Copper Beech Inn on Cape Cod
97 Main St
Centerville 02632
(508)771-5488

1830. Shaded by a massive European beech tree is this white clapboard house, listed in the National Register. It was built by Captain Hillman Crosby, a

name long associated with boat builders and fast sailing ships. Preserved and restored, the inn is a walk away to Craigville Beach, considered one of the 10 best beaches in the United States. Summer theater and fine restaurants are also nearby.

Innkeeper(s): Joyce Diehl.

Rates:$80-90. MC VISA AX DS. Full Bkfst. Gourmet Brkfst. 3 rooms. Beds:KQ. AC in room. Golf. Tennis. Bicycling. Swimming. Horseback riding. Fishing.

Seen in: *Innsider, Cape Cod Life, Cape Cod Times, Country Magazine.*

Contact: Joyce Diehl. Certificate may be used: Monday through Thursday-May 15 through June 15 and Sept. 15 through Oct. 15. Anytime Oct. 16 through May 14.

"Everything we were looking for, clean and private, but best of all were our wonderful hosts."

Chatham

Carriage House Inn
407 Old Harbor Rd
Chatham 02633
(508)945-4688 Fax:(508)945-4688

1860. The charming Cape Cod resort town of Chatham is home to this Colonial Revival inn which features English and Traditional decor. Guests will enjoy the special touches, such as turn-down service and fresh chocolates on the pillows each night. The inn's garden helps furnish fresh flowers for its tasteful interior. Borrow a bike for a tour of the area, or relax in front of the fireplace. Beach towels are furnished for trips to the shore, just a quarter-mile mile away. The Monomoy National Wildlife Reserve also is nearby.

Innkeeper(s): Pam & Tom Patton.

Rates:$75-135. MC VISA AX. Full Bkfst. Teas. 3 rooms. Beds:Q. AC in room. Bicycling. Swimming.

Contact: Pam Patton. Certificate may be used: Oct. 16, 1994 - May 15, 1995, excluding holiday weekends (Columbus Day, Veteran's Day, Thanksgiving, Christmas, New Year's, Washington's Birthday).

Cyrus Kent House
63 Cross St
Chatham 02633
(508)945-9104 (800)338-5368
Fax:(508)945-9104

1877. A former sea captain's home, the Cyrus Kent House was built in the Greek Revival style. The award-winning restoration retained many original features such as wide pine floorboards, ceiling rosettes, and marble fireplaces. Although furnished with antiques and reproductions, all modern amenities are available. Most bedrooms have four-poster beds. Suites feature sitting rooms with fireplaces. Chatham's historic district is a short stroll away.

Innkeeper(s): Sharon Swan.

Rates:$75-155. MC VISA AX. ContPlus Bkfst. 9 rooms. Fireplaces. Beds:Q. TV, Phone in room. Swimming. Fishing.

Contact: Sharon Swan. Certificate may be used: October through April.

Old Harbor Inn
22 Old Harbor Rd
Chatham 02633
(508)945-4434 (800)942-4434
Fax:(508)945-2492

1936. This pristine New England bed & breakfast was once the home of "Doc" Keene, a popular physician in the area. A meticulous renovation has created an elegant, beautifully appointed inn offering antique furnishings, designer linens and lavish amenities. A continental breakfast, often featuring Sharon's homemade scones, is served in the sunroom or on the deck. The beaches, boutiques and galleries are a walk away and there is an old grist mill, the Chatham Lighthouse, and a railroad museum. Band concerts are offered Friday nights in the summer at Kate Gould Park.

Innkeeper(s): Tom & Sharon Ferguson.

Rates:$95-170. MC VISA DC DS CB. ContPlus Bkfst. Teas. 6 rooms. Beds:KQT. AC in room. Golf. Tennis. Swimming. Horseback riding. Fishing.

Seen in: *Herald News, Traveler.*

Contact: Sharon Ferguson. Certificate may be used: Sunday through Thursday, Oct. 15 through June 15.

Chilmark

Breakfast at Tiasquam
RR 1, Box 296, Martha's Vineyard
Chilmark 02535
(508)645-3685

1987. This unique farmhouse sits amid woodlands and rolling pastures. The multi-level decks look out to fields of wildflowers, oaks and evergreens. Relax in a hammock or in your comfortable guest room. The sinks in the bathrooms were hand-thrown by

potter Robert Parrott. The breakfast, as one might expect from the name, is delightful and varies season to season. Fresh corn-blueberry pancakes might

be topped with Vermont maple syrup, or freshly-caught fish may be found as part of the breakfast fare. Vacationers who just want to relax will appreciate the private, rural setting of this inn.

Innkeeper(s): Ron Crowe.

Rates:$70-195. Full Bkfst. 8 rooms. 6 with shared baths. Beds:QT. Golf. Tennis. Bicycling. Handicap access. Swimming. Fishing.

Contact: Ron Crowe. Certificate may be used: Sunday-Thursday nights, October-May.

"Best breakfast on the island, the perfect B&B."

Concord

Colonel Roger Brown House
1694 Main St
Concord 01742
(508)369-9119 (800)292-1369
Fax:(508)369-1305

1775. This house was the home of Minuteman Roger Brown who fought the British at the Old North Bridge. The frame for this center-chimney Colonial was raised April 19, the day the battle took place. Some parts of the house were built as early as 1708. The adjacent Damon Mill houses a fitness club available to guests. Both buildings are in the National Register.

Innkeeper(s): Sheila Carlton.

Rates:$65-80. MC VISA AX DC CB. ContPlus Bkfst. Evening snacks. 5 rooms. Conference Rm. Tennis. Skiing. Spa. Sauna. Swimming.

Seen in: *Middlesex News.*

Contact: Sheila Carlton. Certificate may be used: November-April or midweek.

"The Colonel Roger Brown House makes coming to Concord even more of a treat!"

Hawthorne Inn
462 Lexington Rd
Concord 01742
(508)369-5610

1870. The Hawthorne Inn is situated on land that once belonged to Ralph Waldo Emerson, the

Alcotts and Nathaniel Hawthorne. It was here that Bronson Alcott planted his fruit trees, made pathways to the Mill Brook, and erected his Bath

House. Hawthorne purchased the land and repaired a path leading to his home with trees planted on either side. Two of these trees still stand. Across the road is Hawthorne's House, The Wayside. Next to it is the Alcott's Orchard House, and Grapevine Cottage where the Concord grape was developed. Nearby is Sleepy Hollow Cemetery where Emerson, the Alcotts, the Thoreaus, and Hawthorne were laid to rest.

Innkeeper(s): Gregory Burch & Marilyn Mudry.

Rates:$85-160. MC VISA AX DS. ContPlus Bkfst. Teas. 7 rooms. Beds:T. AC in room. Skiing. Swimming. Fishing.

Seen in: *New York Times, Boston Globe, Yankee Magazine.*

Contact: Gregory Burch. Certificate may be used: November - March, excluding holidays and no Friday-Saturday in November.

"Surely there couldn't be a better or more valuable location for a comfortable, old-fashioned country inn."

Cummaquid

The Acworth Inn

4352 Old Kings Hwy, PO Box 256
Cummaquid 02637
(508)362-3330 (800)362-6363

1860. This inn, located on the Olde Kings Highway on the north side of Cape Cod, offers a strategic midway point for those exploring the area. The historic Cape-style farmhouse features four guest rooms, each with private bath and lovingly furnished. Innkeeper Reg Walter's hand-painted, restored furniture adds special charm to the inn's interior. Some of the pieces are available for purchase. Guests select from the Cummaquid, Chatham, Yarmouth Port and Barnstable rooms, all named for Cape Cod villages. Visitors will find the shore just a half-mile from the inn.

Innkeeper(s): Frank Gaynor.

Rates:$55-95. MC VISA AX. ContPlus Bkfst. EP. 4 rooms. Fireplaces.

Beds:QDT. Bicycling. Swimming. Fishing.

Contact: Frank Gaynor. Certificate may be used: September through June.

Danvers

Samuel Legro House

78 Centre St
Danvers 01923
(508)774-1860

1854. This Greek Revival inn features antique and country-style decor. There's a spinning wheel in the living room. Guests enjoy using the inn's swimming pool in the warmer months and listening to the player piano when they relax indoors. Extra touches, include fresh flowers, fresh-brewed coffee and homemade muffins. Boston is 25 miles away, and mystical Salem is a 10-minute drive. Bradley W. Palmer State Park also is found nearby.

Innkeeper(s): Peggie Blais.

Rates:$50-65. ContPlus Bkfst. 3 rooms. 3 with shared baths. Beds:QT. TV, Phone, AC in room. Skiing. Swimming. Fishing.

Contact: Peggie Blais. Certificate may be used: Sunday through Thursday, May through September.

Deerfield-South

Deerfield B&B - The Yellow Gabled House

111 N Main St
Deerfield-South 01373
(413)665-4922

1820. Huge maple trees shade the yard of this historic house, four miles from historic Deerfield and one mile from Route 91. Decorated with antiques and old lace, two of the guest rooms have their own cozy sofa. The battle of Bloody Brook Massacre in 1675 occurred at this site, now landscaped with perennial English gardens.

Innkeeper(s): Edna Julia Stahelek.

Rates:$65-95. Full Bkfst. Gourmet Brkfst. 3 rooms. 2 with shared baths. Beds:QT. TV, AC in room. Golf. Tennis. Skiing. Horseback riding. Fishing.

Seen in: *Recorder, Boston Globe.*

Contact: Edna Stahelek. Certificate may be used: Weekdays except September and October; weekends January-February only.

"We are still speaking of that wonderful weekend and our good fortune in finding you."

Dennis

Isaiah Hall B&B Inn

152 Whig St
Dennis 02638
(508)385-9928 (800)736-0160
Fax:(508)385-5879

1857. Adjacent to the Cape's oldest cranberry bog is this Greek Revival farmhouse built by Isaiah Hall, a cooper. His brother was the first cultivator of cranberries in America and Isaiah designed and

patented the original barrel for shipping cranberries. In 1948, Dorothy Gripp, an artist, established the inn. Many examples of her artwork remain.
Innkeeper(s): Marie Brophy.

Rates:$55-102. MC VISA AX. ContPlus Bkfst. EP. Evening snacks. 11 rooms. 1 with shared bath. Fireplaces. Beds:QT. Golf. Tennis. Bicycling. Swimming. Horseback riding. Fishing.

Seen in: *Cape Cod Life, New York Times.*

Contact: Marie Brophy. Certificate may be used: Any April, May, June 23, Sunday - Thursday except holidays.

Dennisport

Rose Petal B&B

152 Sea St, PO Box 974
Dennisport 02639
(508)398-8470

1872. This Cape Cod-style home was built for Almond Wixon, whose family was among the origi-

nal settlers of Dennisport. In 1918, Almond was lost at sea with all on board. The Wixon homestead was completely restored in 1986. Surrounded by a white picket fence and attractively landscaped yard, the Rose Petal is situated in the heart of Cape Cod, a short walk from the beach. Homebaked pastries highlight a full breakfast in the dining room.
Innkeeper(s): Gayle & Dan Kelly.

Rates:$45-84. MC VISA AX. Gourmet Brkfst. 3 rooms. 1 with shared bath. Beds:QT. AC in room. Golf. Tennis. Bicycling. Swimming. Fishing.

Contact: Gayle Kelly. Certificate may be used: Anytime except July, August, September and special events.

"Perfect. Every detail was appreciated."

East Falmouth

Bayberry Inn

226 Trotting Park
East Falmouth 02536
(508)540-2962

1985. This classic Cape Cod-style inn offers two upstairs guest rooms, both with a view of the neighboring woods. The Rose Room features a queen bed, while the Garden Room has a double bed and tub. The rooms also may be used together as a suite, offering sleeping quarters for up to seven guests. The area abounds with activities, including antiquing, ferry rides, golf, museums, an outlet mall, water sports and whale-watching. South Cape Beach and Washburn Island state parks are nearby.
Innkeeper(s): Joel & Anna Marie Peterson

Rates:$40-70. Full Bkfst. Gourmet Brkfst. Teas. Evening snacks. 2 rooms. Beds:Q. Swimming. Fishing.

Contact: Anna Marie Peterson Certificate may be used: Anytime except July, August

East Orleans

The Parsonage Inn

202 Main St, PO Box 1501
East Orleans 02643
(508)255-8217

1770. This 18th-century parsonage is a full Cape-style house, complete with ancient wavy glass in the windows and antique furnishings throughout. In addition to the five old Cape Cod rooms, an efficiency and a private cottage are available. "Breakfast in a basket" is served in the courtyard or in guest rooms. Main Street, the road to Nauset Beach, is lined with the old homes of sea captains and other early settlers.
Innkeeper(s): Ian & Elizabeth Browne.

Rates:$65-100. MC VISA. ContPlus Bkfst. 8 rooms. Beds:QT. AC in room. Golf. Tennis. Swimming. Fishing.

Seen in: *Miami Herald.*

Contact: Elizabeth Browne. Certificate may be used: Nov. 1 through April 30 except all holidays i.e. Thanksgiving, Christmas, New Year, Valentine's, President's.

"Your hospitality was as wonderful as your home. Your home was as beautiful as Cape Cod. Thank you!!"

Ship's Knees Inn
186 Beach Rd, PO Box 756
East Orleans 02643
(508)255-1312 Fax:(508)240-1351

1820. This 170-year-old restored sea captain's home is a three-minute walk from the ocean. Rooms are decorated in a nautical style with antiques. Several rooms feature authentic ship's knees, hand-painted

trunks, old clipper ship models and four-poster beds. Some rooms boast ocean views and the Master Suite has a working fireplace. The inn offers swimming and tennis facilities on the grounds. About three miles away, the innkeepers also offer a one-bedroom efficiency apartment and two ocean-side cottages. Head into town or spend the day basking in the beauty of Nauset Beach with its picturesque sand dunes.

Innkeeper(s): Donna Anderson & Peter Butcher.

Rates:$45-100. MC VISA. Cont. Bkfst. 25 rooms. 14 with shared baths. Fireplaces. Beds:KQT. TV, AC, Refrig. in room. Tennis. Swimming. Fishing.

Seen in: *Boston Globe.*

Contact: Donna Anderson. Certificate may be used: Exceptions: July, August and holidays.

"Warm, homey and very friendly atmosphere. Very impressed with the beamed ceilings."

East Sandwich

The Azariah Snow House
529 Route 6A
East Sandwich 02537
(508)888-6677

1917. Innkeeper Dia Bacon takes pride in her hospitality and gourmet breakfasts that might include lobster quiche and hazelnut French toast. Afternoon teas are given, especially on rainy days.

Bacon will cook dinner on occasion at the request of guests. The bedrooms are uniquely decorated with fresh cut flowers and handmade quilts. There are plenty of scenic areas for walking and bicycling and Hyannis with its shopping and fine restaurants is nearby.

Innkeeper(s): Dia Bacon.

Rates:$50-65. Full Bkfst. Gourmet Brkfst. Picnic lunches. Teas. 3 rooms. 3 with shared baths. Beds:Q. Bicycling. Swimming. Fishing.

Contact: Dia Bacon. Certificate may be used: Midweek.

Wingscorton Farm Inn
Rt 6A, Olde Kings Hwy
East Sandwich 02537
(508)888-0534

1757. Wingscorton is a working farm on seven acres of lawns, gardens and orchards. It adjoins a short walk to a private ocean beach. This Cape Cod manse, built by a Quaker family, is a historical landmark on what once was known as the King's Highway, the oldest historical district in the United States. All the rooms are furnished with working fireplaces (one with a secret compartment where runaway slaves hid), as well as fully restored antiques. Breakfast features fresh produce with eggs, meats and vegetables from the farm's livestock and gardens.

Innkeeper(s): Richard Loring.

Rates:$115-150. MC VISA AX. Full Bkfst. 3 rooms. Fireplaces. Beds:QT. Refrig. in room. Farm. Spa. Swimming. Fishing.

Seen in: *Boston Globe, New York Times.*

Contact: Richard Loring. Certificate may be used: Off season, November - April.

"Absolutely wonderful. We will always remember the wonderful time."

Eastham

Penny House Inn
4885 County Rd, PO Box 238
Eastham 02651
(508)255-6632 (800)554-1751

1751. Captain Isaiah Horton built this house with a shipbuilder's bow roof. Traditional wide-planked floors and 200-year-old beams buttress the ceiling of the public room. The Captain's Quarters, the largest guest room with its own fireplace, bears the motto: *Coil up your ropes and anchor here, Til better weather doth appear.*

Innkeeper(s): Bill & Margaret Keith.

Rates:$80-125. MC VISA AX DS. Full Bkfst. Teas. 12 rooms. Fireplaces. Beds:KQT. Conference Rm. AC, Refrig. in room. Skiing. Swimming. Fishing.

Contact: Margaret Keith. Certificate may be used: October - May excluding holiday weekends and special events. Space available, Sunday - Thursday.

"Enjoyed my stay tremendously. My mouth waters thinking of your delicious breakfast."

Edgartown

The Arbor
222 Upper Main St, PO Box 1228
Edgartown 02539
(508)627-8137

1880. Originally built on the adjoining island of Chappaquidick, this house was moved over to Edgartown on a barge at the turn of the century.

Located on the bicycle path, it is within walking distance from downtown and the harbor. Guests may relax in the hammock, have tea on the porch, or walk the unspoiled island beaches of Martha's Vineyard.

Innkeeper(s): Peggy Hall.

Rates:$65-135. MC VISA. Cont. Bkfst. Teas. 10 rooms. 2 with shared baths. Beds:QT. Golf. Tennis. Bicycling. Swimming. Horseback riding. Fishing.

Seen in: *Herald News, Yankee Traveler.*

Contact: Margaret Hall. Certificate may be used: May 1-June 14 and Sept. 16-Oct. 31, Monday-Thursday.

"Thank you so much for your wonderful hospitality! You are a superb hostess. If I ever decide to do my own B&B, your example would be my guide."

Ashley Inn
129 Main St, PO Box 650
Edgartown 02539
(508)627-9655 (800)477-9655

1860. A retired whaling captain built this gracious Georgian inn on Martha's Vineyard. Guest rooms are furnished in period antiques, brass and wicker. The inn is just four blocks from the beach, and its Main Street location offers easy access to Edgartown's many fine restaurants and shops. Breakfasts are served in the English tea room, and guests find the inn's grounds perfect for an after-

meal stroll. Others like to relax in the hammock or in the comfortable sitting room. A special honeymoon package is available.

Innkeeper(s): Fred & Janet Hurley.

Rates:$55-175. MC VISA AX. Cont. Bkfst. 11 rooms. 2 with shared baths. Beds:QT. TV, AC, Refrig. in room. Fishing.

Contact: Fred Hurley. Certificate may be used: Oct. 15, 1994 to May 15, 1995 & Oct. 15 to Dec. 31, 1995.

Captain Dexter House of Edgartown
35 Pease's Point Way, Box 2798
Edgartown 02539
(508)627-7289

1840. Located just three blocks from Edgartown's harbor and historic district, this black-shuttered sea merchant's house has a graceful lawn and terraced flower gardens. A gentle Colonial atmosphere is enhanced by original wooden beams, exposed floorboards, working fireplaces, old-fashioned dormers and a collection of period antiques. Luxurious canopy beds are featured.

Innkeeper(s): R. & S. Pieczenik.

Rates:$65-190. MC VISA AX DC. ContPlus Bkfst. Teas. 11 rooms. Fireplaces. Beds:QD. Conference Rm. AC in room. Bicycling. Swimming. Fishing.

Seen in: *Island Getaways, Vineyard Gazette.*

Contact: Roberta Pieczenik. Certificate may be used: May through June 15 and October.

"It was a perfect stay!"

The Governor Bradford Inn of Edgartown
128 Main St, PO Box 239
Edgartown 02539
(508)627-9510

1865. Located in the Island of Martha's Vineyard, this gracefully restored inn has rooms with ceiling fans and king-size brass or four-poster beds. A library room is complete with a fireplace and books, and there is a wicker room and parlor where you can sip complimentary sherry. Breakfast is served in the sunlit tea room where fresh flowers abound in the room's blue and white decor. The Victorian Age awaits guests to Edgartown where one can roam the streets for art galleries, antique shops and museums.

Innkeeper(s): Ray & Brenda Raffurty.

Rates:$60-210. MC VISA AX. Gourmet Brkfst. Teas. 16 rooms. Beds:KT. Conference Rm. TV, Refrig. in room. Golf. Tennis. Bicycling. Swimming. Horseback riding. Fishing.

Seen in: *The Herald News, The Sunday Enterprise.*

Contact: Raymond Raffurty. Certificate may be used: Oct. 15 through Nov. 15 Sunday through Thursday only. Nov. 16 through April 14 anytime except holiday and special-event weekends. April 15 through May 26 Sunday through Thursday only.

Essex

George Fuller House
148 Main St (Rt 133)
Essex 01929
(508)768-7766

1830. This three-story, Federal-style home is situated on a lawn that reaches to the salt marsh adjoining the Essex River. Original Indian shutters and Queen Anne baseboards remain. All the guest accommodations boast Boston rockers, and some feature canopy beds and fireplaces. For a view of the water, ask for the Andrews Suite. Belgian waffles and cranberry muffins are a house specialty. Your host offers sailing lessons on the Essex River aboard his 30-foot sailboat, the "Glass Jewel." Many of the town's 50 antique shops are within walking distance of the inn.

Innkeeper(s): Cindy & Bob Cameron.

Rates:$70-115. MC VISA AX DC DS CB. Full Bkfst. Teas. 7 rooms. Fireplaces. Beds:KQT. TV, Phone, AC, Refrig. in room. Skiing. Swimming. Fishing.

Seen in: *Gloucester Times, Yankee Traveller, Discerning Traveller.*

Contact: Cynthia Cameron. Certificate may be used: Nov. 1, 1994-May 15, 1995.

"Thank you for the wonderful time we had at your place. We give you a 5-star rating!"

Falmouth

Elms
PO 895, 495 W Falmouth Hwy
Falmouth 02574
(508)540-7232 Fax:(508)540-7232

1739. The breezes of Buzzards Bay, quality accommodations and a four-course gourmet breakfast greet guests at this Queen Anne Victorian inn. Chapoquoit Beach is a short walk and sports herb gardens and a romantic gazebo. Guests enjoy their 4 p.m. daily meeting time in the living room, where they may sample a complimentary glass of sherry. The Saconesset Homestead Museum is nearby, and South Cape Beach and Washburn Island state parks are within easy driving distance.

Innkeeper(s): Joe & Betty Mazzucchelli.

Rates:$65-85. AX. Full Bkfst. 9 rooms. 2 with shared baths. Beds:QT. Golf. Tennis. Handicap access. Swimming. Fishing.

Contact: Joe Mazzucchelli. Certificate may be used: Nov. 1 through May 30.

Gladstone Inn
219 Grand Ave S
Falmouth 02540
(508)548-9851 Fax:(508)548-9851

1895. A soft, ever-present ocean breeze ensures a sound night's sleep at this inn offering Cape Cod charm and homeyness. Wake up to a more than ample buffet breakfast on the enclosed porch overlooking the ocean. Guests can use the inn's bicycles for a ride on the Shining Sea Bike Path. After a day at the beach or a game of golf or tennis, enjoy the backyard area with its barbecue and picnic table. An enclosed shower and rest room adjoining the inn lets guests leave their room upon check-out but still take in one last swim.

Innkeeper(s): James & Gayle Carroll.

Rates:$57. MC VISA. Full Bkfst. 15 rooms. 15 with shared baths. Beds:KT. Bicycling. Swimming. Fishing.

Contact: James Carroll. Certificate may be used: May 20-June 23; Sept. 16-Oct. 9; excluding holidays and any other discounts.

The Inn at One Main Street
One Main St
Falmouth 02540
(508)540-7469

1892. In the historic district where the road to Woods Hole begins is this shingled Victorian with two-story turret, an open front porch and gardens framed by a white picket fence. It first became a tourist house back in the '50s. Cape Cod cranberry pecan waffles and gingerbread pancakes with whipped cream are favorite specialties. Within walking distance, you'll find the Shining Sea Bike Path, beaches, summer theater, tennis, ferry shuttle and bus station. The innkeepers are Falmouth natives and are available to offer their expertise on the area.

Innkeeper(s): Karen Hart & Mari Zylinski.

Rates:$65-95. MC VISA AX. Gourmet Brkfst. 6 rooms. Beds:QT. Conference Rm. Swimming. Fishing.

Contact: Karen Hart. Certificate may be used: January, February, March.

"The art of hospitality in a delightful atmosphere, well worth traveling 3,000 miles for."

Woods Hole Passage
186 Woods Hole Rd
Falmouth 02540
(508)548-9575 Fax:(508)540-9123

1890. This rustic home and barn are surrounded by blueberries, raspberries and trees. The barn was moved from an estate to its present location. Breakfasts are served in front of a multi-paneled window, on the patio or in the garden. Home-baked breads, souffles, fruit and quiche are just a few of the delicious items. If you want to get an early start, the inn offers a "breakfast-to-go" bag

with fruit, a muffin and juice. Walk through the woods or take a stroll on the Cape Cod shore. Other attractions include the Aquarium at Woods Hole and the Falmouth Playhouse. After a full day, the libraried living room offers a fireplace and a relaxing atmosphere.
Innkeeper(s): Cristina Mozo.
Rates:$65-95. MC VISA AX DC CB. Full Bkfst. Gourmet Brkfst. 5 rooms. Beds:Q. AC in room. Golf. Tennis. Bicycling. Swimming. Fishing.
Contact: Cristina Mozo. Certificate may be used: Oct. 28 to March 30, except special holiday days.

Great Barrington

Windflower Inn
684 S Egremont Rd
Great Barrington 01230
(413)528-2720 (800)992-1993
Fax:(413)528-5147

1850. This country manor is situated on 10 acres shaded by giant oaks and maples. Early American and English antiques fill the spacious guest rooms.

There is a piano room with shelves of books, and a clock collection is featured throughout. The inn's dinners have received excellent reviews and feature herbs, vegetables and berries from the garden. Guests may cross the street for tennis and golf at the country club.
Innkeeper(s): Barbara & Gerald Liebert, Claudia & John Ryan.

Rates:$160-210. AX. Full Bkfst. MAP available. Teas. 13 rooms. Fireplaces. Beds:KQ. AC in room. Skiing. Swimming. Fishing.
Seen in: *The Los Angeles Times, Boulevard Magazine.*
Contact: Barbara Liebert. Certificate may be used: Room only, midweek Sunday-Thursday, non-holiday, November-May.

"Every creative comfort imaginable, great for heart, soul and stomach."

Greenfield

The Brandt House
29 Highland Ave
Greenfield 01301
(413)774-3329 (800)235-3329
Fax:(413)772-2908

1890. Three-and-a-half-acre lawns surround this impressive three-story Colonial Revival house, situated hilltop. The library and pool room are popular for lounging. A full breakfast often includes homemade scones. There is a clay tennis court, nature trails, badminton, horseshoes and in winter, lighted ice skating at a nearby pond. Historic Deerfield is within five minutes.
Innkeeper(s): Phoebe Compton.
Rates:$60-135. MC VISA DC. Full Bkfst. 7 rooms. 2 with shared baths. Fireplaces. Beds:KQT. TV, Phone, AC, Refrig. in room. Tennis. Skiing. Fishing.
Contact: Phoebe Compton. Certificate may be used: November through April.

Hamilton

The Miles River Country Inn
823 Bay Rd, Box 149
Hamilton 01936
(508)468-7206 Fax:(508)468-3999

1779. This rambling Colonial sits on more than 30 acres and adjoins meadows, woodlands and wetlands. Sweeping lawns are graced with seven gar-

dens and two ponds. The Miles River flows through the property, which is set among Boston's fabled North Shore estates and is a haven for travelers and wildlife alike. Guests can see or hear Great Blue Heron, countless varieties of duck, great horned and screech owls. Many of the house's 12 fireplaces are in the bedrooms. One room's walls are covered with 19th-century wooden bedsteads imported from Brittany.

Innkeeper(s): Gretel T. & Peter B. Clark.

Rates:$70-90. Full Bkfst. Gourmet Brkfst. Teas. 8 rooms. 5 with shared baths. Fireplaces. Beds:KQT. Farm. Bicycling. Skiing. Exercise room. Swimming. Fishing.

Contact: Gretel T. Clark. Certificate may be used: Three-day weekends and Halloween weekend excluded.

Harwich Port

Captain's Quarters
85 Bank St
Harwich Port 02646
(508)432-1991 (800)992-6550

1850. This Victorian house features a classic wrap-around porch, gingerbread trim, an authentic turret room and a graceful, curving front stairway. It is situated on an acre of sunny lawns, broad shade trees and colorful gardens. The inn is a five-minute walk to sandy Bank Street Beach and is close to town.

Innkeeper(s): Ed & Susan Kennedy.

Rates:$69-89. MC VISA AX. ContPlus Bkfst. 5 rooms. Beds:KQT. TV in room. Swimming. Fishing.

Contact: Edward Kenney. Certificate may be used: March - June 15 and September - October excluding holiday and Harwich Cranberry Festival weekends.

"Accommodations are very comfortable and attractive. This is our favorite inn!"

Country Inn Acres
86 Sisson Rd
Harwich Port 02646
(508)432-2769 (800)231-1722

1780. Roses cascading over a picket fence frame this rambling Cape Cod house located on six-and-a-half acres. Comfortable furnishings and an unhurried pace set a relaxing tone. Hearty New England cookery is featured in the public dining room. An in-ground pool and three hard-surfaced tennis courts on the grounds are for guests' use.

Innkeeper(s): Kathleen & David Van Gelder.

Rates:$65-140. MC VISA AX. ContPlus Bkfst. 7 rooms. Fireplaces. Beds:KQT. Conference Rm. TV, AC in room. Tennis. Swimming. Fishing.

Contact: Kathleen Van Gelder. Certificate may be used: Nov. 1 through April 30, no holidays or holiday weekends.

Harbor Breeze
326 Lower County Rd
Harwich Port 02646
(508)432-0337 (800)272-4343

1940. Ideally located across the street from picturesque Allens Harbor and only a short walk from the Brooks Road beach, this inn is a classic Cape Cod home. A rambling connection of cedar shake additions, nestled in an attractive pine setting, surround a garden courtyard to form a guest wing. Flowered walkways lead to nine guest rooms, which are furnished in wicker, woods and country floral. There are restful sitting areas amid the pines and a swimming pool where you can enjoy the ocean breezes. A short walk down a shady tree-lined street brings you to a sandy beach on Nantucket Sound.

Innkeeper(s): Kathleen & David Van Gelder.

Rates:$65-125. MC VISA AX. ContPlus Bkfst. 9 rooms. Beds:KQT. TV, AC, Refrig. in room. Swimming. Fishing.

Contact: Kathleen Van Gelder. Certificate may be used: May 1 - June 20 and Sept. 8 - Oct. 31. Not valid on holidays or holiday weekends.

Harbor Walk
6 Freeman St
Harwich Port 02646
(508)432-1675

1880. There's always a breeze on the front porch of this Victorian inn built originally as a summer guest house. Handmade quilts and antiques enhance the Cape Cod spirit of the inn. A few steps from the house will bring you into view of the Wychmere Harbor area. The greater community of Harwich offers a large conservation area for walking and birdwatching which connects with a scenic bike path that stretches for 22 miles. There are two golf courses, three harbors for boating and fishing and sandy beaches with warm-water swimming.

Innkeeper(s): Marilyn & Preston Barry.

Rates:$60. ContPlus Bkfst. 6 rooms. 2 with shared baths. Beds:QT. Swimming. Fishing.

Contact: Marilyn Barry. Certificate may be used: Monday through Thursday, June through September, October all month.

Hyannis

The Inn on Sea Street
358 Sea St
Hyannis 02601
(508)775-8030

1849. This elegant two-story Victorian inn is listed on the town's register of historic houses. Its charms include Colonial portraits, fine Persian rugs and a grand curved staircase. Furnishings in the guest rooms include four-poster beds with lace canopies. A former sun room has been transformed into a guest room with its own entrance. Guests may enjoy home-baked breads and muffins with their breakfasts on the antique tables covered with lace cloths and set with sterling silver, crystal and flowers from the garden.

Innkeeper(s): Lois M. Nelson/J.B. Whitehead.

Rates:$70-98. MC VISA AX DS. Full Bkfst. Gourmet Brkfst. 9 rooms. 2 with shared baths. Fireplaces. Beds:QT. TV, Phone, AC, Refrig. in room. Swimming.

Seen in: *The Journal.*

Contact: Lois Nelson. Certificate may be used: May 1 - June 15; Oct. 1 - Nov. 1.

"A lot of people really don't know how much they are missing, until they visit you."

Lanesboro

Bascom Lodge

PO Box 1800
Lanesboro 01237
(413)443-0011 Fax:(413)442-9010

1937. Operated by the Appalachian Mountain club, this stone and wood retreat sits on the summit of Mount Greylock, which is the highest mountain in Massachusetts. The lodge is at the center of the 11,000-acre Mount Greylock State Reservation and 50 feet from the Appalachian Trail. Although the rooms are nothing fancy, hikers find the lodge a comfortable place to rest and enjoy the 100-mile views of the Berkshires. A lobby area features historical and educational displays, a trading post stocked with maps, trail guides and hiker paraphernalia, and a room with chairs and sofas.

Innkeeper(s): Jean Cowhig

Rates:$70-80. MC VISA. Full Bkfst. MAP available. Picnic lunches. 8 rooms. 8 with shared baths. Beds:DT. Handicap access. Fishing.

Contact: Jean Cowhig. Certificate may be used: Sunday through Friday nights only.

Whipple Tree B&B

10 Bailey Rd
Lanesboro 01237
(413)442-7468

1753. This restored Federal Colonial farmhouse is located at the base of Mount Greylock and offers a splendid view of the Berkshire Hills. Most of the guest rooms have random-width plank floors and hand-crafted items, and each is decorated in the spirit of a New England farmhouse. You may choose to eat breakfast in the sunny dining room, outside among the trees and flowers or by the side

of the pool. The inn is 20 minutes away from Williamstown where you will find the Clark Art Institute and the Williamstown Summer Theater and Museum. The immediate area offers outlet stores and antique shops.

Innkeeper(s): Charles & Kris Lynch.

Rates:$60-85. ContPlus Bkfst. 5 rooms. 3 with shared baths. Beds:QT. TV, AC, Refrig. in room. Farm. Skiing. Swimming. Fishing.

Contact: Charles Lynch. Certificate may be used: Anytime except July, August & October and holiday weekends, Christmas week and February President's holiday week.

Lee

Morgan House Inn

33 Main St
Lee 01238
(413)243-0181

1817. This classic Colonial inn reflects the stagecoach era with its stenciled wall coverings, comfortable antique-filled rooms and country prints. The innkeepers, Lenora and Stuart, are former owners of a Berkshire inn, a Cambridge fine dining restaurant, a wine and specialty food store and have years of experience in corporate dining. Lenora prepares contemporary and traditional New England cuisine. Her favorites include warm popovers, barbecued pork tenderloin with Boston baked beans and fresh corn relish, duckling with lemon bourbon sauce and wild rice pancakes.

Innkeeper(s): Lenora & Stuart Bowen.

Rates:$40-135. MC VISA AX DC DS. Full Bkfst. EP. 13 rooms. 10 with shared baths. Beds:KQT. TV, AC in room. Skiing. Fishing.

Contact: Stuart Bowen. Certificate may be used: November through June, September.

Lenox

Amadeus House

15 Cliffwood St
Lenox 01240
(413)637-4770 (800)205-4770
Fax:(413)637-4484

1820. Named to capture the feeling of Lenox as the nation's summer music capital, this original Colonial house, which was later updated during the Victorian era, is close to several performing arts companies. The area is the summer home of the Boston Symphony Orchestra, Shakespeare & Co., who perform stage classics and modern repertoire, and the Berkshire Performing Arts Center. Besides the love for music reflected at the inn, with its rooms named after great composers and a library of recordings and books, you can spend a relaxing summer afternoon on the porch, reading a good book and sipping lemonade.

Innkeeper(s): John Felton & Martha Gottron.

Rates:$55-175. Full Bkfst. Picnic lunches. Teas. 8 rooms. 2 with shared baths. Fireplaces. Beds:QDT. Skiing. Swimming. Fishing.

Contact: John Felton. Certificate may be used: Nov. 1, 1994 to April 30, 1995, excluding holidays.

Birchwood Inn
7 Hubbard St, Box 2020
Lenox 01240
(413)637-2600 (800)524-1646

1767. This Colonial Revival inn, once the Hubbard Tavern, is in the National Register. Overlooking the village from its hilltop location next to Kennedy Park, its lawns and delightful gardens are framed by old New England stone fences. Lavish Colonial interiors handsomely set off the library, parlor and guest rooms. A multi-course, homemade breakfast is abundant, yet caters to those maintaining health-conscious diets.

Innkeeper(s): Joan, Dick & Dan Toner.

Rates:$50-195. MC VISA AX DC DS CB. Full Bkfst. Gourmet Brkfst. Evening snacks. 12 rooms. 2 with shared baths. Fireplaces. Beds:KQT. Conference Rm. TV, Phone, Refrig. in room. Golf. Tennis. Skiing. Swimming. Horseback riding. Fishing.

Contact: Joan Toner. Certificate may be used: Sunday night through Thursday night Nov. 1-June 15 excluding holidays.

"Inn-credible! Inn-viting! Inn-spiring! Inn-comparable! Our ultimate getaway. Wonderful ambiance, great food and the finest hosts we ever met."

Brook Farm Inn
15 Hawthorne St
Lenox 01240
(413)637-3013 (800)285-7638

1879. Brook Farm Inn is named after the original Brook Farm, a literary commune that sought to combine thinker and worker through a society of intelligent, cultivated members. In keeping with that theme, this gracious Victorian inn offers poetry and writing seminars and has a 650-volume poetry library. Canopy beds, Mozart and a swimming pool tend to the spirit.

Innkeeper(s): Joe & Anne Miller.

Rates:$65-170. MC VISA DS. Full Bkfst. EP. Picnic lunches. Teas. 12 rooms. Fireplaces. Beds:KQT. AC in room. Golf. Tennis. Skiing. Swimming. Horseback riding. Fishing.

Seen in: *Berkshire Eagle, Country Inns, Travel & Leisure, Boston Magazine.*

Contact: Anne Miller. Certificate may be used: Nov. 1 - June 15, Sunday to Thursday only.

"We've been traveling all our lives and never have we felt more at home."

The Gables Inn
81 Walker St, Rt 183
Lenox 01240
(413)637-3416

1885. At one time, this was the home of Pulitzer Prize-winning novelist, Edith Wharton. The Queen Anne-style Berkshire cottage features a handsome

eight-sided library and Mrs. Wharton's own four-poster bed. An unusual indoor swimming pool with spa is available in warm weather.

Innkeeper(s): Mary & Frank Newton.

Rates:$75-195. MC VISA DS. ContPlus Bkfst. Gourmet Brkfst. 18 rooms. Fireplaces. Beds:Q. TV, AC, Refrig. in room. Golf. Tennis. Skiing. Spa. Swimming. Fishing.

Seen in: *P.M. Magazine, New York Times.*

Contact: Frank Newton. Certificate may be used: Nov. 1 to May 20, not valid Saturday.

"You made us feel like old friends and that good feeling enhanced our pleasure. In essence it was the best part of our trip."

Rookwood Inn
11 Old Stockbridge Rd, PO Box 1717
Lenox 01240
(800)223-9750

1886. This turn-of-the-century Queen Anne Victorian inn offers 21 elegant guest rooms, including two suites. Among the amenities in the air-conditioned guest rooms are ceiling fans and fireplaces. The inn's size makes it perfect for small meetings, reunions and weddings. The beautiful Berkshires are famous for cultural and recreational opportunities, including the Chesterwood Museum, cross-country and downhill skiing, fishing, Jacob's Pillow Dance Festival, the Mount, the Norman Rockwell Museum and numerous other performing arts attractions.

Innkeeper(s): Tom & Betsy Sherman.

Rates:$70-225. AX. ContPlus Bkfst. Teas. 21 rooms. Fireplaces. Beds:KQT. Conference Rm. AC in room. Golf. Tennis. Skiing. Swimming. Fishing.

Seen in: *New York Times, Boston Globe, London Times.*

Contact: Tom Sherman. Certificate may be used: Nov. 1 - May 31. Holidays excluded.

Underledge Inn
76 Cliffwood St
Lenox 01240
(413)637-0236

1870. Drive along Cliffwood Street under an archway of greenery, then up Underledge's winding drive to a peaceful setting overlooking the

Berkshire Hills. The inn sits resplendently atop four acres, providing rooms with sunset views. In the foyer you'll find an exquisite oak staircase and floor-to-ceiling oak fireplace. A solarium is the setting for breakfast. Just down the street are quaint shops and fine restaurants.

Innkeeper(s): Marcie Lanoue.

Rates:$60-175. MC VISA AX. ContPlus Bkfst. 8 rooms. Fireplaces. Beds:KQT. AC in room. Skiing. Fishing.

Contact: Marcie Lanoue. Certificate may be used: November through June, holidays excluded, 1994. November through June, holidays excluded, 1995.

"We were received like a guest in a luxurious private house. We now think of Underledge as our summer home."

Village Inn
16 Church St, PO Box 1810
Lenox 01240
(413)637-0020 (800)253-0917
Fax:(413)637-9756

1771. Four years after the Whitlocks built this Federal-style house, they converted it and two adjoining barns for lodging. Since 1775, it has operated as an inn. Recently renovated, there are stenciled wallpapers, maple floors and four-poster canopied beds. Rates do not include breakfast. An afternoon tea including scones and clotted cream, is available from $5.50.

Innkeeper(s): Clifford Rudisill & Ray Wilson.

Rates:$50-165. MC VISA AX DC DS CB. Full Bkfst. EP. Teas. 33 rooms. Fireplaces. Beds:KQT. Conference Rm. Phone, AC in room. Skiing. Handicap access. Spa. Swimming. Fishing.

Seen in: *The London Independent.*

Contact: Clifford Rudisill. Certificate may be used: November through May, excluding holidays. (June through October excluded.)

"Kathy and I stayed at your beautiful inn in early October. It was the highlight of our trip to New England."

Walker House
64 Walker St
Lenox 01240
(413)637-1271 (800)235-3098
Fax:(413)637-2387

1804. This beautiful Federal-style house sits in the center of the village on three acres of graceful woods and restored gardens. Guest rooms have fireplaces and private baths. Each is named for a favorite composer such as Beethoven, Mozart, or Handel. The innkeepers' musical backgrounds include associations with the San Francisco Opera, the New York City Opera, and the Los Angeles Philharmonic. Walker House concerts are scheduled from time to time.

Innkeeper(s): Richard & Peggy Houdek.

Rates:$60-170. ContPlus Bkfst. Teas. 8 rooms. Fireplaces. Beds:QT. Conference Rm. AC in room. Golf. Tennis. Bicycling. Skiing. Handicap access. Swimming. Horseback riding. Fishing.

Seen in: *Boston Globe, PBS, Los Angeles Times.*

Contact: Peggy Houdek. Certificate may be used: Monday-Thursday, November-April, holidays excluded.

"We had a grand time staying with fellow music and opera lovers! Breakfasts were lovely."

Lexington

Pacem
62 Sherburne Rd
Lexington 02173
(617)862-3337

1968. This contemporary inn, designed by Royal Barry Wills, offers modern amenities in an area renowned for its historic significance. Guests enjoy relaxing in the family room and music room, both of which boast fireplaces, in addition to the library and patio. Visitors may borrow three-speed bicycles if they wish. The Hancock Clarke House, Minute Man National Historic Park, Munroe Tavern and the Museum of our National Heritage are nearby.

Innkeeper(s): Carroll Ann Bottino.

Rates:$55-65. Cont. Bkfst. 6 rooms. 3 with shared baths. Beds:T. Phone, AC in room. Bicycling. Skiing. Swimming. Fishing.

Contact: Carroll Ann Bottino. Certificate may be used: Any Monday-Thursday.

Lynn

Diamond District B&B
142 Ocean St
Lynn 01902-2007
(617)599-4470 (800)666-3076
Fax:(617)599-4470

1911. This 22-room Georgian house was built for
shoe manufacturer P.J. Harney-Lynn. The Charles
Pinkham family (son of Lydia Pinkham - health

tonic producer) later purchased it. Many of the
original fixtures and wall coverings remain, and the
inn is suitably furnished with Oriental rugs and
antiques. There are several views of the ocean from
the house, but the porch is the most popular spot
for sea gazing. Breakfast is served in the dining
room or porch.

Innkeeper(s): Sandra & Gerard Caron.
Rates:$85-125. MC VISA AX DC DS CB. Full Bkfst. 6 rooms. Beds:QT.
Conference Rm. TV, Phone, AC, Refrig. in room. Bicycling. Swimming.
Seen in: *Lynn historic home tour.*
Contact: Gerard Caron. Certificate may be used: Monday through
Thursday excluding Oct. 1-31.

*"The room was spectacular and breakfast was served
beautifully."*

Marblehead

Harborside House B&B
23 Gregory St
Marblehead 01945
(617)631-1032

1850. Enjoy the Colonial charm of this home,
which overlooks Marblehead Harbor and Boston's
historic North Shore. Rooms are decorated with
antiques and period wallpaper. A third-story sundeck offers a lovely view. A generous continental
breakfast of home-baked breads, muffins and fresh
fruit is served each morning in the well-decorated
dining room or on the open porch. The village of
Marblehead provides many shops and restaurants.
Boston is 30 minutes away.

Innkeeper(s): Susan Livingston.

Rates:$65-75. ContPlus Bkfst. Teas. 2 rooms. 2 with shared baths.
Beds:DT. Tennis. Bicycling. Swimming.
Seen in: *Marblehead Reporter.*
Contact: Susan Livingston. Certificate may be used: November through
April, excluding holidays.

The Nesting Place B&B
16 Village St
Marblehead 01945
(617)631-6655

1890. Conveniently located one half-hour away
from Boston and Cape Ann, this Victorian inn
offers as much privacy as you require as well as the
opportunity for stimulating conversation. Discover
the world of the early clipper ships as you walk the
narrow winding streets and the beaches of
Marblehead's renowned harbor, only minutes away.
There's a relaxing hot tub to top off a day of browsing through art galleries, antique shops and quaint
boutiques.

Innkeeper(s): Louise Hirshberg.
Rates:$55-70. MC VISA. Cont. Bkfst. 2 rooms. 2 with shared baths.
Beds:KQT. Tennis. Skiing. Spa. Sauna. Swimming. Fishing.
Contact: Louise Hirshberg. Certificate may be used: Nov. 1 - May 1.

Spray Cliff on the Ocean
25 Spray Ave
Marblehead 01945
(508)744-8924 (800)626-1530
Fax:(508)744-8924

1910. Panoramic views stretch out in grand proportions from this English Tudor mansion set high
above the Atlantic. The inn provides a spacious
and elegant atmosphere inside. The grounds of the
inn include a brick terrace surrounded by lush
flower gardens where eider ducks, black cormorants
and seagulls gather.

Innkeeper(s): Richard & Diane Pabich.
Rates:$139-179. MC VISA AX DC DS CB. ContPlus Bkfst. 7 rooms.
Fireplaces. Beds:KQ. Skiing. Swimming. Fishing.
Seen in: *New York Times, Glamour.*
Contact: Diane Pabich. Certificate may be used: Nov. 15 - April 15.

"I prefer this atmosphere to a modern motel. It's more relaxed and love is everywhere!"

Menemsha

Beach Plum Inn

Box 98
Menemsha 02552
(508)645-9454 (800)528-6616

1952. A shady lawn, a patio and pavilion of this Cape Cod Shingle home overlook the harbor and Elizabeth Islands. Located on eight acres, the inn's rooms are either in the main house or private cottages and some have sea views. A four-star dining room features spectacular views from every table. The Cordon Bleu chefs, while famous for continental cuisine, are equally skilled in the preparation of fresh native seafood and New England dishes. Guests can swim off the shore of the inn's private beaches and miles of public beaches offering surf, sound and pond swimming minutes away.

Innkeeper(s): Janie & Paul Darrow.

Rates:$100-250. MC VISA AX DS. Full Bkfst. EP. MAP available. Gourmet Brkfst, Lunch, Dinner. Picnic lunches. Teas. Evening snacks. 11 rooms. Beds:KQT. Phone, AC in room. Tennis. Bicycling. Handicap access. Swimming. Fishing.

Contact: Janie Darrow. Certificate may be used: May-mid-June, excluding Memorial Day and weekends. Mid-September-October-excluding weekends.

Nantucket Island

The Carlisle House Inn

26 N Water St
Nantucket Island 02554
(508)228-0720 Fax:(508)228-6074

1765. For more than 100 years, the Carlisle House has served as a notable Nantucket lodging establishment. Three floors of picture-perfect rooms provide accommodations from the simple to the deluxe. Hand stenciling, polished wide-board floors, handsome color schemes and carpets fill each room. Special candlelight dinners are occasionally served at a harvest table in the kitchen. The ferry is a five-minute walk.

Innkeeper(s): Peter & Suzanne Conway.

Rates:$60-155. MC VISA AX. ContPlus Bkfst. Teas. 14 rooms. 4 with shared baths. Fireplaces. Beds:KQT. Swimming. Fishing.

Seen in: *Cape Cod Life, Boston Globe, Los Angeles Times.*

Contact: Peter Conway. Certificate may be used: April to mid-June except special holiday or event weekends and Oct. 1 - mid-December.

Eighteen Gardner Street Inn

18 Gardner St
Nantucket Island 02554
(508)228-1155 (800)435-1450

1835. Built by Captain Robert Joy, this charming home has been lovingly restored as a classic Nantucket country inn. Each of the rooms is decorated with antiques and period reproductions, including canopied or four-poster beds. The inn is a short stroll from many of Nantucket's finest restaurants, museums, galleries, boutiques and historic sites. Guests may use one of the inn's bicycles for an easy ride to many of the island's superb beaches. Breakfasts may include Nantucket Sweet Cakes topped with blueberry, strawberry or apple.

Innkeeper(s): Mary Schmidt.

Rates:$75-300. MC VISA AX DS. ContPlus Bkfst. Gourmet Brkfst. Picnic lunches. Teas. Evening snacks. 17 rooms. 2 with shared baths. Fireplaces. Beds:Q. TV, AC in room. Bicycling. Skiing. Swimming. Fishing.

Contact: Roger Schmidt. Certificate may be used: Oct. 20, 1994 to April 15, 1995.

The Folger Hotel & Cottages

71 Easton St, PO Box 628
Nantucket Island 02554
(508)228-0313 (800)365-4371
Fax:(508)228-4186

1891. This large Victorian hotel was built for turn-of-the-century vacationers who usually stayed a month at a time and brought the whole family. Its weathered, brown-shingled exterior is brightened with white trim, balustraded porches, white lawn furniture and a rose-covered picket fence. Several cottages are available and a restaurant adjoins the hotel.

Innkeeper(s): Bob & Barb Bowman.

Rates:$66-120. MC VISA AX DC DS. Full Bkfst. EP. 63 rooms. 25 with shared baths. Beds:KQT. Conference Rm. Phone in room. Tennis. Bicycling. Handicap access. Swimming. Fishing.

Seen in: *Boston Globe, Cape Cod Times.*

Contact: Bob Bowman. Certificate may be used: Sept. 18 - Oct. 31, 1994; April 1 - June 16, 1995; Sept. 18 - Oct. 31, 1995.

"A busy and fun hotel."

House of the Seven Gables
32 Cliff Rd
Nantucket Island 02554
(508)228-4706

1865. Originally the annex of the Sea Cliff Inn, one of the island's oldest hotels, this three-story Queen Anne Victorian inn offers 10 guest rooms. Beaches, bike rentals, museums, restaurants, shops and tennis courts are all found nearby. The guest rooms are furnished with king or queen beds and period antiques. Breakfast is served each morning in the guest rooms, and often include homemade coffee cake, muffins or Portuguese rolls.
Innkeeper(s): Suzanne Walton.
Rates:$40-150. MC VISA AX DS. Cont. Bkfst. 10 rooms. 2 with shared baths. Beds:KQ. Swimming. Fishing.
Contact: Suzanne Walton. Certificate may be used: Oct. 12 - May 15.

Martin House Inn
61 Centre St, PO Box 743
Nantucket Island 02554
(508)228-0678

1803. Known as Wonoma Inn in the '20s, this shingled mariner's house in the historic district is tucked behind a picket fence. In summer, roses climb to the six-over-six windows and the hammock gently sways on the side veranda. Authentic period pieces include Chippendale chests, Windsor rockers and Victorian settlers, and there are four-poster and canopy beds in the guest rooms. The cobblestone streets of Nantucket's Main Street are a stroll away.
Innkeeper(s): Channing & Cecilia Moore.
Rates:$65-140. MC VISA AX. ContPlus Bkfst. EP. 13 rooms. 4 with shared baths. Fireplaces. Beds:QT. Swimming. Fishing.
Seen in: *Cape Cod Life.*
Contact: T. Channing Moore. Certificate may be used: Nov. 1 to April 1, excluding holidays, Nantucket Christmas Stroll (first weekend in December) and Dec. 23 - Jan. 2.

The Sherburne Inn
10 Gay St
Nantucket Island 02554
(508)228-4425

1835. This inn once was home to the Atlantic Silk Company. On a quiet side street, it became an elegant guest house in 1872 and still retains its 19th-century charm. Two parlors, both with fireplaces, are available for guests wishing to read, relax or watch TV. Breakfasts may be enjoyed in front of the fireplace or in the flower garden. The inn offers easy access to Nantucket's fine restaurants and shops and the beach is just 500 feet away. The Steamship Authority dock is also nearby.

Innkeeper(s): Dale Hamilton & Susan Gasparich.
Rates:$75-145. MC VISA AX DS. Cont. Bkfst. 8 rooms. Fireplaces. Beds:KQT. TV, Phone, Refrig. in room. Swimming. Fishing.
Contact: Dale Hamilton. Certificate may be used: Nov. 1 - May 15 excluding Thanksgiving weekend, Dec. 2-4, Christmas weekend and April 21-23.

Stumble Inne
109 Orange St
Nantucket Island 02554
(508)228-4482 Fax:(508)228-4752

1704. This Nantucket Island inn is appointed with fine antiques. Six of the inn's rooms are across the street from the Stumble Inne at the Starbuck House, an early 19th-century Nantucket "half-house." Rooms feature wide pine floors, antique beds, ceiling fans and Laura Ashley decor.

Innkeeper(s): Mary Kay & Mal Condon.
Rates:$65-145. MC VISA. ContPlus Bkfst. 12 rooms. 1 with shared bath. Beds:QT. TV, AC, Refrig. in room. Tennis. Bicycling. Swimming. Fishing.
Seen in: *Innsider.*
Contact: Mary Kay Condon. Certificate may be used: Sunday through Thursday, October through May, excluding holidays and special events.

"We realize much of our happiness was due to the warm hospitality that was a part of every day."

The White House
48 Centre St
Nantucket Island 02554
(508)228-4677

1830. For more than 40 years a favorite hostelry of visitors to Nantucket, The White House is situated ideally in the heart of the historic district and an easy walk to the ferry terminal. The first floor houses an antique shop. Guests stay in rooms on the second floor or a housekeeping apartment. Afternoon wine and cheese is served in the garden.
Innkeeper(s): Nina Hellman.
Rates:$60-110. MC VISA AX. Cont. Bkfst. 4 rooms. Beds:KQT. Phone in room. Golf. Tennis. Bicycling. Swimming. Fishing.
Contact: Nina Hellman. Certificate may be used: Weekdays mid-April to mid-June and mid-September to mid-October. Anytime mid-October to December. Excluding holidays and special island events.

The Woodbox Inn
29 Fair St
Nantucket Island 02554
(508)228-0587

1709. Nantucket's oldest inn was built by Captain Bunker. In 1711, the Captain constructed an adjoining house. Eventually, the two houses were

made into one by cutting into the sides of both. Guest rooms are furnished with period antiques. The inn's gourmet dining room features an Early American atmosphere with low-beamed ceilings and pine-paneled walls.

Innkeeper(s): Dexter Tutein.

Rates:$120-195. Gourmet Brkfst, Dinner. 6 rooms. Fireplaces. Beds:KQT. Conference Rm. Refrig. in room. Golf. Tennis. Bicycling. Swimming. Horseback riding. Fishing.

Seen in: *Wharton Alumni Magazine, Cape Cod Life, Boston Magazine.*

Contact: Dexter Tutein, Jr. Certificate may be used: Midweek (mid October to end of December).

"Best breakfast on the island," Yesterday's Island.

Newburyport

Clark Currier Inn
45 Green St
Newburyport 01950
(508)465-8363

1803. Once the home of shipbuilder Thomas March Clark, this three-story Federal-style inn provides gracious accommodations to visitors in the Northeast Massachusetts area. Visitors will enjoy the inn's details, including window seats, Indian shutters and pumpkin pine flooring. Breakfast is served in the garden room, with an afternoon tea offered in the parlor. The inn's grounds also boast a picturesque garden and gazebo. Parker River National Wildlife Refuge and Salisbury Beach State Reserve are nearby.

Innkeeper(s): Mary, Bob & Melissa Nolan.

Rates:$65-125. MC VISA AX DS. ContPlus Bkfst. Teas. 8 rooms.

Beds:QDT. Phone, AC in room. Skiing. Swimming. Fishing.

Contact: Mary Nolan. Certificate may be used: Space available anytime, preferred dates January-March.

Windsor House
38 Federal St
Newburyport 01950
(508)462-3778 Fax:(508)465-3443

1786. This brick Federal-style mansion was designed as a combination home and chandelry (a ship's outfitter and brokerage company for cargo). The third floor served as a warehouse and the Merchant Suite was once the main office. This suite features a 14-foot ceiling with handhewn, beveled beams. It is appointed with a wing-back chair from the Old Boston Opera, a sleigh bed and an antique hope chest. The English innkeeper serves a hearty English country breakfast and a full English tea in the afternoon. Children are welcome.

Innkeeper(s): Judith & John Harris.

Rates:$75-115. MC VISA AX DS. Full Bkfst. Teas. 6 rooms. 3 with shared baths. Beds:KQT. Phone in room. Skiing. Fishing.

Seen in: *New York Times, Boston Magazine, Boston Herald Sunday Magazine.*

Contact: Judith Harris. Certificate may be used: Nov. 1-April 31 - Sunday-Thursday excluding holidays.

"You will find what you look for and be met by the unexpected too. A good time!"

North Adams

Twin Sisters Inn
1111 S State St, PO Box 311
North Adams 01247
(413)663-6933

1930. This inn, a converted carriage barn, now offers comfortable lodging to those visiting the state's Northwest corner and its many recreational

activities. The inn's 10-acre grounds provide a love-ly, quiet escape from the distractions of busy city life. Four guest rooms share two baths, and queen and twin accommodations are available. Nearby attractions include the Clark Art Institute, Clarksburg and Taconic Trail state parks, Tanglewood and the Williamstown Theatre Festival. Skiing may be enjoyed at Brodie Mountain, Jiminy Peak and Mt. Snow.
Innkeeper(s): John & Gabriella Bond.

Rates:$50-60. Cont. Bkfst. 4 rooms. 4 with shared baths. Beds:QT. Skiing. Fishing.

Contact: Gabriella Bond. Certificate may be used: Monday through Thursday.

North New Salem

Bullard Farm B&B
89 Elm St
North New Salem 01364
(508)544-6959 Fax:(508)544-6959

1796. This inn's four air-conditioned guest rooms are found in a farmhouse containing six working fireplaces. The farm has been in the family of the innkeeper's mother since 1864, and guests are wel-come to hike the inn's grounds, observing its histo-ry as a lumber mill and tannery. The inn features many original pieces used in its country-style decor. Full breakfasts may include banana sour cream cof-fee cake. Winter visitors may enjoy a sleigh ride or cross-country skiing on the inn's 300 acres. Shutesbury State Forest is a short drive from the inn.
Innkeeper(s): Janet F. Kraft.

Rates:$60-85. MC VISA. Full Bkfst. 4 rooms. 4 with shared baths. Fireplaces. Beds:QT. Conference Rm. Phone, AC in room. Farm. Golf. Bicycling. Skiing. Swimming. Horseback riding. Fishing.

Seen in: *Boston Globe, Worcester Telegram.*

Contact: Janet Kraft. Certificate may be used: Weekdays or weekends, January through March.

Oak Bluffs

The Beach Rose
PO Box 2352, Columbian Ave
Oak Bluffs 02557
(508)693-6135

1986. This Martha's Vineyard inn offers three guest rooms, all lovingly decorated in antique country style. The skylit guest rooms of the Cape Cod-style inn share two baths. Breakfasts may be enjoyed in the inn's country kitchen, an outdoor deck or in front of the fireplace. Help yourself to iced tea and

lemonade throughout the day. Within walking dis-tance of the inn is a lagoon pond where guests may enjoy fishing, sailing, sunbathing and windsurfing. The State Lobster Hatchery is a short distance from the inn.
Innkeeper(s): Gloria & Russ Everett.

Rates:$60-95. Full Bkfst. 3 rooms. 3 with shared baths. Beds:QT. Swimming. Fishing.

Contact: Gloria Everett. Certificate may be used: May 15 - June 30; Sept. 10 - Oct. 9 subject to availability and special events; Sunday - Thursday during July and August.

The Tucker Inn
46 Massasoit Ave, PO Box 2680
Oak Bluffs 02557
(508)693-1045

1872. Located on a quiet residential park within walking distance of retail establishments and the town beach, this two-story Victorian Stick/Shingle

inn offers visitors to Martha's Vineyard a choice of suites and guest rooms with shared and private baths. The former doctor's residence boasts an attractive veranda that is ideal for reading or relax-ing after a busy day exploring the island's many attractions, or a trip to nearby Chappaquiddick. Public transportation and boat lines are a five-minute walk from the inn.
Innkeeper(s): William Reagan.

Rates:$50-95. MC VISA. 9 rooms. 2 with shared baths. Beds:QT. Swimming. Fishing.

Contact: W.K. Reagan. Certificate may be used: Weekdays, May, June, September, October, 1994 & 1995.

Orleans

The Farmhouse at Nauset Beach
163 Beach Rd
Orleans 02653
(508)255-6654

1870. Feel the intimacy of Orleans and capture the flavor of Cape Cod at this quiet country inn resting in a seashore setting. Rooms in this Greek Revival-style inn are comfortably furnished to depict their

19th-century past. Guests enjoy the "at home" feeling with morning coffee and freshly baked muffins or coffee cake. Nauset Beach is a short walk away. Spend a day charter fishing in Cape Cod Bay or the Atlantic. To make your stay complete your itinerary can include antiquing, shopping, exploring quiet country lanes or a day at the beach.

Innkeeper(s): Dot Standish.

Rates:$42-95. MC VISA. ContPlus Bkfst. 8 rooms. 3 with shared baths. Beds:KDT. TV, Refrig. in room. Golf. Tennis. Swimming. Fishing.

Contact: Dorothy Standish. Certificate may be used: October to May except holiday weekends.

Petersham

Winterwood at Petersham

19 N Main St
Petersham 01366
(508)724-8885

1842. The town of Petersham is often referred to as a museum of Greek Revival architecture. One of the grand houses facing the common is Winterwood. It boasts fireplaces in almost every room and the two-room suite has twin fireplaces. Private dining is available for small groups.

Innkeeper(s): Jean & Robert Day.

Rates:$80. MC VISA AX. ContPlus Bkfst. 6 rooms. Fireplaces. Beds:QT. Conference Rm. Skiing. Fishing.

Seen in: *Boston Globe.*

Contact: Robert Day. Certificate may be used: Year-round with the exceptions of September and October.

"Between your physical facilities and Jean's cooking, our return to normal has been made even more difficult. Your hospitality was just a fantastic extra to our total experience."

Provincetown

Asheton House

3 Cook St
Provincetown 02657
(508)487-9966

1840. This elegant Greek Revival inn originally served as the home of a whaling captain. The inn's luscious furnishings include American, English, French and Oriental antiques. Accommodations include the Suite, with a lovely view of Cape Cod Bay, a dressing room and private bath; the Captain's Room, tastefully furnished in American antiques, including a queen-size four-poster bed and Queen Anne arm chairs, and boasting a view of the Pilgrim Memorial Monument and the English box-

wood garden; and the Safari Room, with two double beds, bamboo headboards and Oriental rug.

Innkeeper(s): Jim Bayard.

Rates:$55-95. 3 rooms. 2 with shared baths. Fireplaces. Beds:QT. Swimming. Fishing.

Contact: James Bayard. Certificate may be used: Sept. 15 to May 15 except holidays.

Elephant Walk Inn

156 Bradford St
Provincetown 02657
(508)487-2543 (800)889-9255

1917. This Craftsman-style inn on Cape Cod's northernmost tip has offered a home to guests for many years, including Naval officers during WWII when the inn was requisitioned by the Navy. Four guest rooms are found on each of the inn's two floors, all with cable TV, ceiling fans, mini-refrigerators and private baths. The rooms boast antiques, brass and ceramic lamps and a wide variety of artwork. A number of the rooms feature refinished oak floors with Oriental carpets. Guests often enjoy morning coffee in the Sun Room and also may find relaxation on an open-air deck with a view of the garden.

Innkeeper(s): Len Paoletti.

Rates:$40-85. MC VISA AX DC. Cont. Bkfst. 8 rooms. Beds:KQT. TV, AC, Refrig. in room. Swimming. Fishing.

Contact: Len Paoletti. Certificate may be used: Monday through Thursday, April 25 - May 25, June 1-22.

Rehoboth

Gilbert's B&B

30 Spring St
Rehoboth 02769
(508)252-6416

1836. This country farmhouse sits on 100 acres of woodland that includes an award-winning tree farm. Cross-country skiing, hiking, and pony-cart rides are found right outside the door. If they choose to, guests can even help with the farm chores, collecting eggs and gardening. A swimming pool is open during summer. Three antique-filled bedrooms share a second-floor sitting room. The nearby town of Rehoboth is almost 350 years old.

Innkeeper(s): Jeanne & Martin Gilbert.

Rates:$45-50. Full Bkfst. Teas. 3 rooms. 3 with shared baths. Beds:KT. Farm. Golf. Tennis. Skiing. Swimming. Horseback riding. Stables.

Seen in: *Attleboro Sun Chronicle, Country Magazine, Somerset Spectator.*

Contact: Jeanne Gilbert. Certificate may be used: Nov. 1 through April 30, 1995 and from Nov. 1, 1995-Dec. 31, 1995.

"This place has become my second home."

Richmond

A B&B in the Berkshires
1666 Dublin Rd
Richmond 01254
(413)698-2817 (800)795-7122
Fax:(413)698-3164

1962. This modern ranch home, with its striking mountain views, offers easy access to the area's many attractions. Guests choose from three air-con-

ditioned guest rooms, all with cable TV, king or queen beds, phones, private bath, turndown service and VCRs. Visitors also may borrow a bicycle for a refreshing ride around the inn's 3.5 acres. Bousque Ski Area, Pleasant Valley Wildlife Sanctuary and Tanglewood all are within easy driving distance of the inn.

Innkeeper(s): Doane Perry.

Rates:$75-125. MC VISA AX. ContPlus Bkfst. Teas. 3 rooms. Beds:KQ. TV, Phone, AC in room. Bicycling. Skiing. Swimming. Fishing.

Contact: T. Doane Perry. Certificate may be used: All except July, August, weekends.

Rockport

The Inn on Cove Hill
37 Mt Pleasant St
Rockport 01966
(508)546-2701

1791. Pirate gold found at Gully Point paid for this Federal-style house. An exquisitely crafted spiral staircase, random-width, pumpkin-pine floors, and hand-forged hinges display the artisan's handiwork. A picket fence and granite walkway welcome guests.

Innkeeper(s): John & Marjorie Pratt.

Rates:$45-99. Cont. Bkfst. 11 rooms. 2 with shared baths. Beds:Q. Bicycling. Swimming.

Seen in: *Boston Globe, Yankee Magazine.*

Contact: John Pratt. Certificate may be used: May, Sunday through Thursday nights.

"Everything was superb. Love your restorations, your muffins and your china."

Tuck Inn
17 High St
Rockport 01966
(508)546-7260

1790. Two recent renovations have served to make this charming Colonial inn all the more enticing. Period antiques and paintings by local artists are featured throughout the spacious inn. A favorite gathering spot is the living room with its fireplace, pine floors and tasteful furnishings. Guests may take a dip in the swimming pool or at local beaches. Within easy walking distance are the many art galleries, restaurants and shops of Bearskin Neck. A nearby train station offers convenient access to Boston.

Innkeeper(s): Liz & Scott Wood.

Rates:$47-107. MC VISA. ContPlus Bkfst. 12 rooms. Beds:KQT. TV, AC in room. Swimming. Fishing.

Contact: Scott & Elizabeth Wood. Certificate may be used: Nov. 1, 1994 through April 30, 1995 Sunday through Thursday and Nov. 1 - Dec. 31, 1995. No holidays.

Yankee Clipper Inn
Box 2399, 96 Granite St
Rockport 01966
(508)546-3407 (800)545-3699
Fax:(508)546-9730

1840. This white clapboard oceanfront mansion features sweeping views of the sea and the rocky shoreline. Gleaming mahogany woodwork and fireplaces combined with fine antiques create an old-fashioned, elegant ambiance in the main building. Some accommodations offer canopy beds and balconies. The Bulfinch House, a Greek Revival building housing extra guest rooms, is situated away from the water uphill from the main inn. A heated salt-water pool is in view of the ocean.

Innkeeper(s): Bob & Barbara Ellis.

Rates:$99-208. MC VISA AX DS. Full Bkfst. MAP available. Gourmet Dinner. Picnic lunches. 26 rooms. Beds:KQT. Conference Rm. Phone, AC in room. Swimming. Fishing.

Seen in: *Gloucester Daily Times, Los Angeles Times, North Shore Life.*

Contact: Barbara Ellis. Certificate may be used: Midweek only, Oct. 21 - May 21.

"The rooms were comfortable, the views breathtaking from most rooms, and the breakfasts delicious, with prompt and courteous service."

Salem

The Salem Inn
7 Summer St
Salem 01970
(508)741-0680 (800)446-2995
Fax:(508)744-8924

1834. Captain Nathaniel West, first owner of this historic building, believed that at all times his home should be maintained in readiness for his return from sea. Today that same philosophy is practiced for guests of the Salem Inn. The guest rooms are uniquely decorated with homey touches and there are two-room suites with kitchens for families.

Innkeeper(s): Richard & Diane Pabich.

Rates:$80-150. MC VISA AX DC DS CB. ContPlus Bkfst. EP. 21 rooms. Fireplaces. Beds:KQ. Conference Rm. TV, Phone, AC in room. Swimming. Fishing.

Seen in: *New York Times, Boston Sunday Globe.*

Contact: Diane Pabich. Certificate may be used: Nov. 15 - April 15, holidays excluded.

"Delightful, charming. Our cup of tea."

Sandwich

Captain Ezra Nye House
152 Main St
Sandwich 02563
(508)886-6142 (800)388-2278
Fax:(508)833-2897

1829. Captain Ezra Nye built this house after a record-shattering Halifax to Boston run, and the

stately Federal-style house reflects the opulence and romance of the clipper ship era. Hand-stenciled walls and museum-quality antiques decorate the interior. Within walking distance are the Doll Museum, the Glass Museum, restaurants, shops, the famous Heritage Plantation, the beach and marina.

Innkeeper(s): Elaine & Harry Dickson.

Rates:$55-90. MC VISA AX DS. Full Bkfst. 7 rooms. 2 with shared baths. Fireplaces. Beds:QT. Golf. Tennis. Bicycling. Swimming. Fishing.

Seen in: *Glamour, Innsider, Cape Cod Life, Toronto Life, Yankee Magazine.*

Contact: Elaine Dickson. Certificate may be used: Sunday-Thursday, Nov. 1-April 30.

"The prettiest room and most beautiful home we have been to. We had a wonderful time."

The Summer House
158 Main St
Sandwich 02563
(508)888-4991

1835. The Summer House is a handsome Greek Revival in a setting of historic homes and public buildings. (Hiram Dillaway, one of the owners, was a famous mold maker for the Boston & Sandwich Glass Company.) The house is fully restored  and decorated with antiques and hand-stitched quilts. Four of the guest rooms have black marble fireplaces. The porch overlooks an old-fashioned perennial garden, antique rose bushes, and a 70-year-old rhododendron hedge.

Innkeeper(s): David & Kay Merrell.

Rates:$55-75. MC VISA AX DS. Full Bkfst. Gourmet Brkfst. Teas. 5 rooms. 4 with shared baths. Fireplaces. Beds:KQT. Phone in room. Golf. Tennis. Skiing. Swimming. Fishing.

Seen in: *Country Living.*

Contact: Kay Merrell. Certificate may be used: Sunday - Thursday, November - March.

"This is just full of charm. As beautiful as a fairy world."

Sheffield

Ivanhoe Country House

254 S Undermountain Rd
Sheffield 01257
(413)229-2143

1780. Vast reaches of manicured lawns provide the setting for this country house on 25 acres, adjacent to the Appalachian Trail. The Chestnut Room is a popular gathering area with its fireplace, library and games. Antiques and comfortable country furnishings are found throughout the inn. Breakfast is brought to each guest bedroom. Genteely raised pets are welcome, though requirements are stringent.

Innkeeper(s): Carole & Dick Maghery.

Rates:$55-75. Cont. Bkfst. 9 rooms. Fireplaces. Beds:DT. AC, Refrig. in room. Skiing. Swimming.

Contact: Carole Maghery. Certificate may be used: September through June, Sunday through Thursday (no holidays).

"Everything was terrific, especially the blueberry muffins."

South Egremont

The Egremont Inn

Old Sheffield Rd
South Egremont 01258
(413)528-2111 (800)859-1780

1780. This three-story inn was once a stagecoach stop. Guest rooms are furnished with country antiques. Dinner is available Wednesday through

Sunday in the formal dinning room. There is a historic Tavern room. Five fireplaces are in the common rooms. The inn also has a wraparound porch. Tennis courts and a swimming pool are on the premises.

Innkeeper(s): Steve and Karen Waller.

Rates:$90-350. MC VISA AX. Cont. Bkfst. EP. MAP available. Gourmet Dinner. 22 rooms. Beds:QT. Conference Rm. Phone, AC in room. Tennis. Skiing. Swimming. Fishing.

Contact: Steve Waller. Certificate may be used: Sunday through Thursday only. November through May.

"All the beauty of the Berkshires without the hassle, the quintessential country inn."

South Lee

Merrell Tavern Inn

1565 Pleasant St
South Lee 01260
(413)243-1794 (800)243-1794
Fax:(413)243-1794

1794. This elegant stagecoach inn was carefully preserved under supervision of the Society for the Preservation of New England Antiquities. Architectural drawings of Merrell Tavern have been preserved by the Library of Congress. Eight fireplaces in the inn include two with original beehive and warming ovens. An antique circular birdcage bar serves as a check-in desk. Comfortable rooms feature canopy and four-poster beds with Hepplewhite and Sheraton-style antiques.

Innkeeper(s): Charles & Faith Reynolds.

Rates:$85-145. MC VISA. Full Bkfst. Teas. 9 rooms. Fireplaces. Beds:QD. Conference Rm. Phone, AC, Refrig. in room. Golf. Skiing. Fishing.

Seen in: *Americana, Country Living, New York Times, Boston Globe.*

Contact: Charles Reynolds. Certificate may be used: Weekdays November to June inclusive.

"Delightful place, we so loved the fireplace. You provided us with a much-needed relaxing weekend."

South Yarmouth

Captain Farris House B&B

308 Old Main St
South Yarmouth 02664
(508)760-2818 (800)350-9477
Fax:(508)398-1262

1845. Listed with the National Register, this inn offers accommodations at both the Captain Allen Farris House and the adjacent Elisha Jenkins House. Eight rooms are found at the Captain's house, with two suites next door. The architectural stylings are Greek Revival and French Second Empire. Breakfasts are served either in the dining room, on the terrace or in the inn's courtyard. Be sure to inquire about picnic lunches, ideal for an afternoon of exploring the Cape's many attractions. Two blocks away is the Bass River.

Innkeeper(s): Scott Toney.

Rates:$75-225. MC VISA AX. Gourmet Brkfst, Lunch. Picnic lunches.

Teas. 10 rooms. Beds:KQT. TV, Phone in room. Bicycling. Handicap access. Swimming. Fishing.

Contact: Scott Toney. Certificate may be used: Nov. 15, 1994-April 15, 1995 excluding holiday weekends, limited number of rooms available.

Sterling

Sterling Orchards B&B

60 Kendall Hill Rd
Sterling 01564-0455
(508)422-6595

1740. The orchards planted in 1920 by Robert Smiley's father provide a suitable setting to frame the 250-year-old farmhouse that has been thoroughly renovated. Original Indian shutters are still in place. A hiding place in the 12-square-foot center chimney, originally built by settlers, can still be found. The largest guest room (20x30) served as the town ballroom at the 1881 centennial. Afternoon tea is available in the Appleseed Tea Room, the inn's dining room.

Innkeeper(s): Robert & Shirley P. Smiley.

Rates:$65-80. Full Bkfst. Teas. Evening snacks. 2 rooms. Beds:QD. Conference Rm. Phone in room. Farm. Skiing. Swimming.

Seen in: *Boston Globe, Worcester Telegram.*

Contact: Shirley Smiley. Certificate may be used: July 7 - Oct. 7.

"It's like stepping back in time with every modern convenience."

Stockbridge

Arbor Rose Bed & Breakfast

8 Yale Hill, Box 114
Stockbridge 01262
(413)298-4744

1810. This New England-style clapboard home is surrounded by gardens and a mill pond. Antiques and floral wallpaper give the bed and breakfast a homey feel. A home-baked breakfast of muffins or pastries, cereals and fruit is served each day. On Sunday a full breakfast is served along with the weekly items. The Norman Rockwell Museum is nearby. Winter guests can take advantage of several cross-country and downhill ski areas.

Innkeeper(s): Christina Alsop.

Rates:$55-135. MC VISA AX. Full Bkfst. Teas. 5 rooms. 3 with shared baths. Beds:KQT. Farm. Tennis. Bicycling. Skiing.

Seen in: *Yankee Traveler.*

Contact: Christina Alsop. Certificate may be used: November - May 25.

Sturbridge

Commonwealth Cottage

11 Summit Ave, PO Box 368
Sturbridge 01566
(508)347-7708

1890. This 16-room Queen Anne Victorian house, on an acre near the Quinebaug River, is just a few minutes from Old Sturbridge Village. Both the din-

ing room and parlor have fireplaces. The Baroque theme of the Sal Raciti room makes it one of the guest favorites and it features a queen mahogany bed. Breakfast may be offered on the gazebo porch or in the formal dining room. It includes a variety of homemade specialties, such as freshly baked breads and cakes.

Innkeeper(s): Robert & Wiebke Gilbert.

Rates:$72-112. Full Bkfst. Evening snacks. 7 rooms. 2 with shared baths. Beds:QT. Skiing. Spa. Swimming. Fishing.

Contact: Wiebke Gilbert. Certificate may be used: November - December, 1994, Sunday - Thursday, holiday weekends excluded, January - April, 1995, Sunday - Thursday, holiday weekends excluded.

Vineyard Haven

Captain Dexter House of Vineyard Haven

100 Main St, PO Box 2457
Vineyard Haven 02568
(508)693-6564

1840. Captain Dexter House was the home of sea captain Rodolphus Dexter. Authentic 18th-century antiques, early American oil paintings and Oriental rugs are among the inn's appointments. There are Count Rumford fireplaces and hand-stenciled walls in several rooms. Located on a street of fine historic homes, the inn is a short stroll to the beach.

Innkeeper(s): Rick Fenstemaker.

Rates:$65-170. MC VISA AX DC. ContPlus Bkfst. Teas. 7 rooms. Fireplaces. Beds:KQD. Conference Rm. Bicycling. Swimming. Fishing.

Seen in: *Martha's Vineyard Times, Cape Cod Life.*

Contact: Roberta Pieczenik. Certificate may be used: January through June 15 and Oct. 15 through Dec. 31. Exclusive of holidays/special events. Space-available basis.

"The house is sensational. Your hospitality was all one could expect. You've made us permanent bed & breakfast fans."

Lothrop Merry House

Owen Park, PO Box 1939
Vineyard Haven 02568
(508)693-1646

1790. Eight yoke of oxen moved this house to its present beach-front location. A wedding gift from father to daughter, the house has a classic center chimney and six fireplaces. Breakfast is served in season on the flower-bedecked patio overlooking stunning harbor views. A private beach beckons at the end of a sloping lawn.

Innkeeper(s): John & Mary Clarke.

Rates:$68-169. MC VISA. Cont. Bkfst. 7 rooms. 3 with shared baths. Fireplaces. Beds:QT. AC in room. Skiing. Swimming. Fishing.

Seen in: *Cape Cod Life.*

Contact: Mary Clarke. Certificate may be used: Nov. 15-March 15, except Dec. 24-Jan. 2.

"It is the nicest place we've ever stayed."

Nancy's Auberge

102 Main St, PO Box 4433
Vineyard Haven 02568
(508)693-4434

1840. The former whaling village of Vineyard Haven is home to this Greek Revival inn, a block-and-a-half from the island's ferry service. From here it's easy to explore the area, either by bicycle, bus, car, trolley or on foot. Many fine restaurants are found nearby and the beach is one block away. The

inn is furnished with antiques and sports three fireplaces. Guests choose from the Gemini and Harbor Lights rooms, or Martha's Boudoir.

Innkeeper(s): Nancy Hurd.

Rates:$68-98. MC VISA. ContPlus Bkfst. 3 rooms. 2 with shared baths. Beds:QT. Swimming. Fishing.

Contact: Nancy Hurd. Certificate may be used: Monday through Thursday, except July and August.

Twin Oaks Inn

8 Edgartown Rd, PO Box 1767
Vineyard Haven 02568
(508)693-8633 (800)696-8633

1906. Pastels and floral prints provide a relaxing atmosphere at this Dutch Colonial inn on Martha's Vineyard, which offers four guest rooms and an apartment with its own kitchen. The breakfast specialty is applecrisp, and guests also enjoy afternoon tea on the enclosed wraparound front porch. The inn is within walking distance of the bicycle path, downtown businesses and the ferry, but its location off the main road affords a more relaxed and sedate feeling for visitors. The family-oriented inn accommodates family reunions, meetings and weddings, and its fireplace room is popular with honeymooners.

Innkeeper(s): Doris Stewart.

Rates:$65-180. MC VISA. ContPlus Bkfst. Teas. 5 rooms. 2 with shared baths. Fireplaces. Beds:QDT. Conference Rm. TV in room. Swimming. Fishing.

Contact: Doris Stewart. Certificate may be used: Sept. 15 - May 15, 1994/1995.

Ware

The Wildwood Inn

121 Church St
Ware 01082
(413)967-7798

1880. This yellow Victorian has a wraparound porch and a beveled-glass front door. American primitive antiques include a collection of New England cradles, a cobbler's bench, and a spinning wheel. The inn's two acres are dotted with maple, chestnut and apple trees. Through the woods you'll find a river.

Innkeeper(s): Fraidell Fenster, Richard Watson.

Rates:$38-80. MC VISA AX. Full Bkfst. 9 rooms. 2 with shared baths. Beds:KQT. AC in room. Skiing. Swimming. Fishing.

Seen in: *Boston Globe.*

Contact: Fraidell Fenster. Certificate may be used: Sunday - Thursday, Nov. 1 -April 30. Weekends and holidays excluded.

"Excellent accommodations, not only in rooms, but in the kind and thoughtful way you treat your guests. We'll be back!"

Wareham

Mulberry B&B
257 High St
Wareham 02571
(508)295-0684

1847. This former blacksmith's house is in the historic district of town and has been featured on the local garden club house tour. Frances, a former school teacher, has decorated the guest rooms in a country style with antiques. A deck, shaded by a tall mulberry tree, looks out to the back garden.

Innkeeper(s): Frances A. Murphy.

Rates:$45-55. AX DS. Full Bkfst. Teas. 4 rooms. 4 with shared baths. Beds:DT. AC in room. Bicycling. Skiing. Swimming. Fishing.

Seen in: *Brockton Enterprise.*

Contact: Frances A. Murphy. Certificate may be used: Sunday through Thursday, May through October; Anytime November through April.

"Thank you for your hospitality. The muffins were delicious."

Wellfleet

The Inn at Duck Creeke
PO Box 364
Wellfleet 02667
(508)349-9333

1815. The five-acre site of this sea captain's house features both a salt water marsh and a duck pond. The Saltworks house and the main house are appointed in an old-fashioned style with antiques, although the rooms are not luxurious. The inn is favored for its two restaurants; Sweet Seasons and the Tavern Room.

Innkeeper(s): Bob Morrill & Judy Pihl.

Rates:$40-90. MC VISA AX. Cont. Bkfst. Gourmet Dinner. 25 rooms. 8 with shared baths. Beds:QDT. AC in room. Swimming. Fishing.

Seen in: *The New York Times, Provincetown Magazine, The Providence Journal.*

Contact: Judith Pihl. Certificate may be used: May 5-June 30, 1995. September and October, 1994 and 1995 not including Labor Day and Columbus Day weekends.

"Duck Creeke will always be our favorite stay!"

West Stockbridge

Card Lake Inn
Main St PO Box 38
West Stockbridge 01266
(413)232-0272

1824. Located in the center of town, this Colonial Revival inn features a popular local restaurant on the premises. Norman Rockwell is said to have frequented its tavern. Stroll around historic West Stockbridge then enjoy the inn's deck cafe with its flower boxes and view of the sculpture garden of an art gallery across the street. Original lighting, hardwood floors and antiques are features of the inn. Chesterwood and Tanglewood are within easy driving distance.

Innkeeper(s): Ed & Lisa Robbins.

Rates:$40-130. MC VISA AX DS. ContPlus Bkfst. 7 rooms. 2 with shared baths. Beds:KQT. AC in room. Skiing. Swimming. Fishing.

Contact: Edward Robbins. Certificate may be used: Anytime except the months of June, July, August, October.

Williamsville Inn
Rt 41
West Stockbridge 01266
(413)274-6118 Fax:(413)274-3539

1797. At the foot of Tom Ball Mountain is this Federal-syle inn, formerly the Tom Ball farm. Some guest rooms feature fireplaces or woodstoves. The inn's grounds sport gardens, a swimming pool and tennis court. Guests often enjoy relaxing in a swing that hangs from an ancient elm. Chesterwood, Mission House, Old Corner House and Tanglewood are within easy driving distance.

Innkeeper(s): Peter J. Taggart, Gail Ryan & Kathleen Ryan.

Rates:$95-165. MC VISA AX. Full Bkfst. EP. Picnic lunches. 15 rooms. Fireplaces. Beds:KQT. AC in room. Farm. Tennis. Skiing. Swimming. Fishing.

Contact: Peter Taggart. Certificate may be used: Subject to projected availability.

Williamstown

The Williamstown B&B
30 Cold Spring Rd
Williamstown 01267
(413)458-9202

1881. Historic Williamstown is home to this inn, a two-story Victorian with three guest rooms. With its convenient location near the village circle, the inn is within walking distance of the Clark Art Institute, restaurants, shops and Williams College, with its excellent art museum. The full breakfasts always include a hot entree, and all breads, cakes, muffins and scones are homemade. Guests may relax in the living room as well as on the roomy front porch.

Innkeeper(s): Kim Rozell/Lucinda Edmonds.

Rates:$65-80. Full Bkfst. 3 rooms. Beds:QT. Skiing. Swimming. Fishing.

Contact: Lucinda Edmonds. Certificate may be used: Midweek, November - April.

Woods Hole

The Marlborough
320 Woods Hole
Woods Hole 02543
(508)548-6218 Fax:(508)457-7519

1942. This is a faithful reproduction of a Cape-style cottage complete with picket fence and rambling roses. Although the inn is beautifully decorated,

well-traveled children are welcome. An English paddle-tennis court, a swimming pool and a gazebo are popular spots in summer. In winter, breakfast is served beside a roaring fire. The inn is the closest bed and breakfast to the ferries to Martha's Vineyard and Nantucket.

Innkeeper(s): Diana M. Smith.

Rates:$65-105. MC VISA AX. Gourmet Brkfst. Teas. 5 rooms. Beds:QT. AC in room. Golf. Tennis. Bicycling. Swimming. Fishing.

Seen in: *Cape Cod Life.*

Contact: Diana Smith. Certificate may be used: Oct. 12, 1994 through April 30, 1995.

"Our stay at the Marlborough was a little bit of heaven."

Yarmouth Port

Liberty Hill Inn
77 Main St, Rt 6A
Yarmouth Port 02675
(508)362-3976 (800)821-3977
MA880304.TIF

1825. Just back from historic Old King's Highway, this country inn is a restored Greek Revival mansion. It is located on the site of the original Liberty Pole dating from Revolutionary times. A romantic decor includes fine antiques and thick carpets, 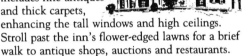 enhancing the tall windows and high ceilings. Stroll past the inn's flower-edged lawns for a brief walk to antique shops, auctions and restaurants.

Innkeeper(s): Beth & Jack Flanagan.

Rates:$70-125. MC VISA AX. Full Bkfst. Gourmet Brkfst. 5 rooms. Beds:KQT. Conference Rm. AC in room. Golf. Tennis. Skiing. Swimming. Horseback riding. Fishing.

Seen in: *Cape Cod Life, Colonial Homes.*

Contact: Elizabeth Flanagan. Certificate may be used: Nov. 1, 1994 to June 20, 1995 except President's weekend, Christmas to New Year and Memorial weekend. Nov. 1 to Dec. 20, 1995.

"Your homey hospitality makes us want to return."

Olde Captain's Inn on the Cape
101 Main St (Rt 6A)
Yarmouth Port 02675
(508)362-4496

1835. Located in the historic district and on Captain's Mile, this house is in the National Register. It is decorated in a traditional style, with coordinated wallpapers and carpets, and there are two suites that include kitchens and living rooms. Apple trees, blackberries and raspberries grow on the acre of grounds and often contribute to the breakfast menus. There is a summer veranda overlooking the property. Good restaurants are within walking distance.

Innkeeper(s): Betsy O'Connor.

Rates:$40-100. ContPlus Bkfst. 5 rooms. 2 with shared baths. Beds:QDT. TV in room. Golf. Tennis. Swimming. Horseback riding. Fishing.

Contact: Sven Tilly. Certificate may be used: Sunday through Thursday except holidays and July and August.

Michigan

Adrian

Briaroaks Inn
2980 N Adrian Hwy
Adrian 49221
(517)263-1659 (800)308-7279

1940. Lined with 100-year-old oak trees and over-looking meandering Beaver Creek, the Briaroaks

Inn offers American Colonial architecture with a Cape Cod influence. Visitors choose from three large guest rooms, all with TVs, fireplaces and whirlpool baths. Guests may enjoy their full gourmet breakfasts in the formal dining room or on the inn's patio, overlooking the creek. The inn also features a gazebo on the grounds. Fishing, cross-country skiing and antiquing all may be enjoyed in the area surrounding Adrian, a college town. Lake Hudson State Recreational Area and Hidden Lake Gardens are both nearby.

Innkeeper(s): Connie & Dallas Marvin.

Rates:$65-125. MC VISA. Gourmet Brkfst. 3 rooms. Fireplaces. Beds:KQ. Phone, AC in room. Skiing. Handicap access. Swimming. Fishing.

Contact: Connie Marvin. Certificate may be used: Year-round Sunday through Thursday, except holidays and race weekends.

Algonac

Linda's Lighthouse Inn
5965 Pte Tremble, Box 828
Algonac 48000
(810)794-2992

1920. Overlooking Dickerson Island, on the north branch of the St. Clair River, is this two-story Colonial inn, once used to aid bootleggers bringing in liquor from Canada during prohibition. Guests who arrive by boat and use the inn's 100 feet of dockage will have transportation to restaurants provided for them. Guests choose from the Jacuzzi, Lighthouse, Rose and Duck rooms, all featuring feather pillows. St. John's Marsh is less than a half-mile away.

Innkeeper(s): Ron & Linda (Russell) Yetsko.

Rates:$65-90. MC VISA AX. Gourmet Brkfst. 4 rooms. Beds:KQT. AC in room. Bicycling. Skiing. Swimming. Fishing.

Contact: Linda Russell. Certificate may be used: Sunday through Thursday, May 1 through Nov. 1.

Allegan

DeLano Inn
302 Cutler St
Allegan 49010
(616)673-2609

1863. This Italian Provincial mansion, surrounded by a wrought-iron fence, is listed in the National Register of Historic Places. The inn offers cozy sitting rooms and a summer porch. There are stenciled floors, lace curtains, marble fireplaces, crystal chandeliers, a spiral staircase, antique furnishings and European feather beds.

Innkeeper(s): Bob & Jean Ashley.

Rates:$65-85. MC VISA. Full Bkfst. 5 rooms. 5 with shared baths. Beds:QT. Conference Rm. AC in room. Skiing. Swimming. Fishing.

Seen in: *Allegan County News & Gazette.*

Contact: Robert Ashley. Certificate may be used: Jan. 2 through April 30.

"The world would be a much more peaceful place if we all celebrated hospitality the way you folks do."

Winchester Inn
524 Marshall St (M-89)
Allegan 49010
(616)673-3621 (800)582-5694

1864. This neo-Italian Renaissance mansion was built of double-layer brick and has been restored to its original beauty. Surrounded by a unique, hand-

poured iron fence, the inn is decorated with period antiques and romantically furnished bedchambers.

Innkeeper(s): Dave & Denise Ferber.

Rates:$65-85. MC VISA AX. Full Bkfst. 4 rooms. Beds:KQ. Conference Rm. Golf. Tennis. Skiing. Swimming. Horseback riding. Fishing.

Seen in: *Architectural Digest, Home and Away, Midwest Living, Detroit Free Press, Cleveland Plain Dealer, Grand Rapids Press.*

Contact: Denise Ferber. Certificate may be used: Sunday through Thursday, May-October, no weekends. November-April, weekends possible, plus weekdays. No holidays, tulip time.

"This is one of Michigan's loveliest country inns."

Bay City

Clements Inn
1712 Center Ave (M-25)
Bay City 48708
(517)894-4600 Fax:(517)895-8535

1886. The amber-paned windows and oak ceilings of this three-story Queen Anne Victorian inn are just a few of its impressive features. Built by William Clements, the home joined a number of other impressive estates on Center Avenue, most owned by lumber barons. The inn's well-appointed guest rooms are named for famous authors or fictional characters, continuing a strong tradition started by Clements, a collector of rare books. A winding staircase, original gas lighting fixtures and hand-carved woodwork have impressed many visitors, who also may enjoy spending time on the screened porch in the warmer months.

Innkeeper(s): Brian & Karen Hepp.

Rates:$75-125. MC VISA AX DS. ContPlus Bkfst. Teas. 6 rooms. Fireplaces. Beds:KQ. TV, Phone, AC in room. Skiing. Handicap access. Exercise room. Swimming. Fishing.

Contact: Karen Hepp. Certificate may be used: Anytime July, 1994-Dec. 30, 1995.

Stonehedge Inn
924 Center Ave (M-25)
Bay City 48708
(517)894-4342

1889. An exquisite oak staircase greets guests as they enter this 19th-century Tudor-style home. Marble fireplaces and original brass light fixtures add an elegant flair to the common rooms. The home was built by a lumber baron and many of the original features are still in operation including speaking tubes and a dumb-waiter. Spend an afternoon cruising the riverwalk or take a look at the historical district and museum.

Innkeeper(s): Ruth Koerber.

Rates:$75-85. MC VISA AX DS. ContPlus Bkfst. 7 rooms. 7 with shared baths. Beds:QT. Conference Rm. AC in room. Golf. Tennis. Skiing. Swimming. Fishing.

Seen in: *Bay City Times, Midwest Living, Great Lakes Getaway.*

Contact: Ruth Koerber. Certificate may be used: November, January-April.

"Your facilities provided a unique and warm atmosphere, and your friendly hospitality added a very personal touch."

Bellaire

Grand Victorian B&B Inn
402 North Bridge St
Bellaire 49615
(616)533-6111 (800)336-3860
Fax:(616)533-8197

1895. It's hard to believe that anything but joy has ever been associated with this beautiful Queen Anne Victorian inn, but its original owner, who built it in anticipation of his upcoming nuptials, left town broken-hearted when his wedding plans fell through. The eye-pleasing inn, with its gables, square corner towers, bays and overhangs, is listed with the National Register of Historic Places. There is much to do in this popular area of Northern Michigan, with its famous nearby skiing and fishing spots, but the inn's impressive interior may entice guests to stay on the premises. Guest rooms are well-appointed with period antiques and lavish touches. Visitors may borrow a bicycle built for two for a relaxing tour of town.
Innkeeper(s): Jill & George Watson.

Rates:$75-95. MC VISA AX. Full Bkfst. Gourmet Brkfst. Picnic lunches. Teas. 4 rooms. Fireplaces. Beds:QDT. AC in room. Tennis. Bicycling. Skiing. Exercise room. Swimming. Fishing.

Contact: Jill Watson. Certificate may be used: Anytime, 1994 & 1995, two-night minimum.

Big Bay

The Big Bay Point Lighthouse B&B
3 Lighthouse Rd
Big Bay 49808
(906)345-9957

1896. With 4,500 feet of frontage on Lake Superior, this landmark lighthouse commands 534 acres of forests and a five-acre lawn. The interior of the lighthouse features a brick fireplace. Several guest rooms look out to the water. The tower room on the top floor offers truly unforgettable views. Breakfast is light, so pack some extra food.
Innkeeper(s): Linda & Jeff Gamble.

Rates:$80-165. Full Bkfst. 7 rooms. 2 with shared baths. Beds:QDT. Bicycling. Skiing. Sauna. Swimming. Fishing.

Seen in: *Los Angeles Times, USA Today.*

Contact: Linda Gamble. Certificate may be used: Nov. 1, 1994-May 1, 1995.

Blissfield

Hiram D. Ellis Inn
415 W Adrian St (US 223)
Blissfield 49228
(517)486-3155

1883. This red brick Italianate house is in a village setting directly across from the 1851 Hathaway House, an elegant historic restaurant. Rooms at the Hiram D. Ellis Inn feature handsome antique bedsteads, armoires and floral wallpapers. Breakfast is served in the inn's common room, and the innkeeper receives rave reviews on her peach and apple dishes. (There are apple, peach, and pear trees on the property.) Bicycles are available for riding around town, or you can walk to the train station and board the murder mystery dinner train that runs on weekends.
Innkeeper(s): Christine Webster & Frank Seely.

Rates:$60-80. MC VISA. ContPlus Bkfst. 4 rooms. Beds:Q. Conference Rm. TV, Phone, AC, Refrig. in room. Bicycling. Swimming. Fishing.

Seen in: *Ann Arbor News, Michigan Living.*

Contact: Christine Webster. Certificate may be used: Sunday through Thursday nights only.

"I have now experienced what it is truly like to have been treated like a queen."

Brooklyn

Dewey Lake Manor
11811 Laird Rd
Brooklyn 49230
(517)467-7122

1860. This Italianate house overlooks Dewey Lake and is situated on 18 acres in the Irish Hills. The house is furnished in a country Victorian style with antiques. An enclosed porch is a favorite spot to relax and take in the views of the lake while having breakfast. Favorite pastimes include lakeside bonfires in the summertime and ice skating or cross-country skiing in the winter.
Innkeeper(s): Joe, Barbara, Barry & Tandy Phillips.

Rates:$55-65. MC VISA. ContPlus Bkfst. Picnic lunches. Evening snacks. 5 rooms. 1 with shared bath. Beds:DT. Conference Rm. TV, AC in room. Golf. Skiing. Swimming. Fishing.

Seen in: *Ann Arbor News.*

Contact: Barbara Phillips. Certificate may be used: Anytime November through April. Sunday through Thursday, October and May.

"I came back and brought my friends. It was wonderful."

Cadillac

American Inn B&B

312 E Cass St
Cadillac 49601
(616)779-9000

1896. This Colonial Revival inn, only a four-block walk from Lake Cadillac, provides visitors a year-round home. Beautiful fall colors, winter skiing and snowmobiling and the usual spring and summer attractions are all found in this area of Western Michigan. The inn's decor features original wood carving, hardwood floors and stained-glass windows. All guest rooms offer cable TV, private baths and phones, and there is a luxurious suite available that can accommodate up to six people. The suite boasts a three-person private spa and a spiral staircase that leads to an outdoor deck overlooking Lake Cadillac.

Innkeeper(s): Cathy & Mike Feister.

Rates:$75-150. MC VISA. ContPlus Bkfst. 5 rooms. Beds:KQ. TV, Phone, AC, Refrig. in room. Skiing. Sauna. Swimming. Fishing.

Contact: Cathy Feister. Certificate may be used: March - June, Sunday - Thursday, except holidays.

Essenmacher's Bed & Breakfast

204 Locust Lane
Cadillac 49601
(616)775-3828

1884. Guest rooms in this waterfront home overlook Lake Mitchell, just steps from the house. A country decor includes crafts and quilts. Swimming,

boating, water skiing and fishing are popular lake activites. Golf and restaurants are within walking distance.

Innkeeper(s): Doug & Vickie Essenmacher.

Rates:$55-65. MC VISA. Full Bkfst. Evening snacks. 2 rooms. Beds:Q. TV, Phone in room. Golf. Bicycling. Skiing. Swimming. Fishing.

Contact: Vickie Essenmacher. Certificate may be used: March, April, May, November, December - anytime (Sunday through Saturday) with advance notice.

"Host was very gracious and friendly! Room was very clean and scenic! The most delicious muffins!"

Charlevoix

Belvedere Inn

306 Belvedere Ave
Charlevoix 49720
(616)547-2251 (800)280-4667

1887. Guests at this attractive two-story inn enjoy a fine view of Round Lake and are just a short walk from a public beach. Visitors have their choice of seven rooms, including two suites. The Broqua Suite features a kitchen and private entrance, per-

fect for honeymooners or for those enjoying a longer-than-usual stay. All of the rooms offer private baths and most have queen beds. Cable TV and VCR can be found in a common room. Guests may opt to relax and enjoy the beautiful surroundings or take advantage of the many recreational activities available in the Charlevoix area, including Fisherman's Island State Park.

Innkeeper(s): Tim & Karen Watters.

Rates:$60-115. Full Bkfst. Evening snacks. 7 rooms. Beds:QT. Bicycling. Skiing. Swimming. Fishing.

Contact: Timothy Watters. Certificate may be used: September - May, excluding holidays.

Bridge Street Inn

113 Michigan Ave
Charlevoix 49720
(616)547-6606

1895. This three-story Colonial Revival structure recalls the bygone era when Charlevoix was home to many grand hotels. Originally a guest "cottage" of one of those large hotels, this inn boasts nine gracious guest rooms, many of which are available with private bath. The rooms sport antique furnishings, floral rugs and wooden floors and offer stunning views of the surrounding lakes. Guests are within walking distance of Lake Michigan's beaches, Round Lake's harbor and Lake Charlevoix's boating and fishing. Be sure to inquire in advance

about the inn's many discounts and special rate for small groups.

Innkeeper(s): Vera & John McKown.

Rates:$56-105. MC VISA. ContPlus Bkfst. 9 rooms. 6 with shared baths. Beds:Q. Skiing. Swimming. Fishing.

Contact: John McKown. Certificate may be used: November, December, January, February, March, April (Sunday through Thursday only).

Eaton Rapids

Dusty's English Inn
728 S Michigan Rd
Eaton Rapids 48827
(517)663-2500 (800)858-0598
Fax:(517)663-2643

1927. Guests at this Tudor-style inn are treated to an experience similar to what they would find in the English countryside. Originally built by Irving J. Reuter, the president of Oldsmobile, the inn is now on the state's register of historic homes. Golf, fishing, canoeing, birdwatching and hiking are available on the grounds or adjacent to the inn. The inn's accommodations include two cottages in addition to lovely rooms in the main house. Guests may socialize in three impressive common rooms, including a library and pub. The state capital, Lansing, is 18 miles north.

Innkeeper(s): Dusty Rhodes.

Rates:$75-155. MC VISA DS. Full Bkfst. Gourmet Dinner. Picnic lunches. 12 rooms. 1 with shared bath. Fireplaces. Conference Rm. TV, Phone, AC in room. Golf. Skiing. Handicap access. Swimming. Fishing.

Seen in: *Lansing State Journal.*

Contact: Dusty Rhodes. Certificate may be used: Sunday through Thursday.

Fennville

Crane House
6051 124th Ave (M-89)
Fennville 49408
(616)561-6931

1870. A restored 1870 farmhouse in a quiet rural setting, this inn is located on the grounds of a working fruit farm. Beautiful antique furnishings,

most from the owner's collection, are featured in each guest room and throughout the house. Handmade quilts and feather beds add to the country feeling, and the backyard even sports an old-fashioned outhouse. Holland, famous for its annual Tulip Festival and Saugatuck, the Cape Cod of the Midwest, is a short drive away.

Innkeeper(s): Nancy Crane McFarland.

Rates:$65-95. MC VISA DS. Full Bkfst. 5 rooms. 2 with shared baths. Beds:DT. Farm. Skiing. Handicap access. Swimming. Fishing.

Seen in: *Kalamazoo Gazette, Holland Sentinel, Country Living, Detroit Free Press.*

Contact: Nancy Crane McFarland. Certificate may be used: Anyday Nov. 1 through April 30.

"I'd been fretting for such a heavenly weekend all winter. Many thanks again."

Fruitport

Village Park B&B
60 W Park St
Fruitport 49415
(616)865-6289

1873. Located in the midst of Western Michigan's Tri-Cities area, this inn's small-town village location offers comfort and relaxation to those busy partaking of the many nearby activities. This farmhouse-style inn overlooks Spring Lake and a park where guests may picnic or play tennis. The inn offers six guest rooms, all with private bath. A library is just across the street. P.J. Hoffmaster State Park, the Gillette Nature Center and Pleasure Island water park are nearby. Fishing charters and sightseeing cruises on Lake Michigan can be arranged. Be sure to inquire about the inn's Wellness Weekends.

Innkeeper(s): John & Virginia Hewett.

Rates:$60-85. MC VISA. Full Bkfst. 6 rooms. Fireplaces. Beds:KDT. AC in room. Golf. Tennis. Skiing. Spa. Sauna. Exercise room. Swimming. Fishing.

Seen in: *Muskegon Chronicle, Detroit Free Press.*

Contact: John Hewett. Certificate may be used: Sunday through Thursday except Coast Guard festival week and holidays. Corporate rates and packages excluded. Subject to availability.

Garden

The Summer House
PO Box 107 State St
Garden 49835
(906)644-2457

1874. This two-story Victorian inn, in a picturesque village of Michigan's upper peninsula, can be found by following a scenic route leading down the Garden Peninsula. Once a busy railroad stop in the 1800s, Garden is now a serene historic village, with many original buildings. The inn, with its stately columns supporting its front porch, offers five guest rooms, all with ceiling fans. The Summer House's decor features English and Traditional furniture. Visitors will find ideal hunting conditions on the peninsula, and Fayette State Park is nearby. The city's park features a picnic area, playground, hiking and a sand beach.

Innkeeper(s): Jan M. McCotter.

Rates:$40-70. MC VISA AX DS. Full Bkfst. Evening snacks. 6 rooms. 3 with shared baths. Beds:KD. Skiing. Fishing.

Contact: Jan M. McCotter. Certificate may be used: May and October only.

Glen Arbor

White Gull Inn
PO Box 351
Glen Arbor 49636
(616)334-4486 Fax:(616)334-3998

1894. One of Michigan's most scenic areas is home to the White Gull Inn. With the Sleeping Bear Dunes and alluring Lake Michigan just minutes away, visitors will find no shortage of sightseeing or recreational activities during a stay here. The inn's farmhouse setting, country decor and five comfort-

able guest rooms offer guests a relaxing haven no matter what the season. Glen Lake is a block away, and guests also will enjoy the area's fine dining and shopping opportunities.

Innkeeper(s): Bill & Dotti Thompson.

Rates:$61. MC VISA AX DS. ContPlus Bkfst. 5 rooms. 5 with shared baths. Fireplaces. Beds:QT. Skiing. Swimming. Fishing.

Contact: Dorothy Thompson. Certificate may be used: Oct. 25 - Dec. 15; Jan. 1 - May 15.

Harrisville

Red Geranium Inn
508 E Main St, Box 613
Harrisville 48740
(517)724-6153

1910. On the shore of Lake Huron, in historic Harrisville, visitors will find the Red Geranium Inn, a Queen Anne Victorian home with a pleasing variety of furnishings. Wicker, Shaker and many unique items are featured throughout this waterfront inn, which offers five guest rooms sharing two baths. Visitors may borrow the inn's bicycles for a tour of town, or curl up with a book in the library or in front of the fireplace. Nearby is Harrisville State Park, also on the lakefront, and west of town is the Huron National Forest.

Innkeeper(s): Mary & Jim Hamather.

Rates:$45-50. ContPlus Bkfst. 5 rooms. 5 with shared baths. Beds:QT. Bicycling. Skiing. Swimming. Fishing.

Contact: Mary Hamather. Certificate may be used: Midweek, May, June, September, October. (Tuesday, Wednesday, Thursday).

Iron River

Pine Willow B&B
600 Selden Rd
Iron River 49935
(906)265-4287

1926. In the spring, the inn's apple and plum trees burst into bloom. Iron County's Historical Museum hosts many festivals during the summer season, each a unique view into the area's diverse culture. Wildlife is abundant and you may catch a glimpse of a Bald Eagle as it soars over the forest. The fall foliage season starts in September and lasts through October. Located in the western portion of the Upper Peninsula of Michigan, the Colonial Revival home was built by the Selden family who figured prominently in the area's mining industry.

Innkeeper(s): Jon & Kelly Nelson.

Rates:$49-59. MC VISA. Full Bkfst. Gourmet Brkfst. Picnic lunches. Teas. Evening snacks. 7 rooms. Fireplaces. Beds:Q. Bicycling. Skiing.

Swimming. Fishing.

Contact: Kelly Nelson. Certificate may be used: Anytime except weekends and holidays.

Ithaca

Chaffin Farms B&B
1245 W Washington RD
Ithaca 48847
(517)875-3410

1892. Located in central Michigan between Mount Pleasant and Lansing, this inn was once a large dairy farm with 12 barns housing various farm animals. Guests will be impressed with the inn's colorful stone wall, built with rocks hauled in from the surrounding area. The inn is furnished with antiques, and visitors will marvel at the inn's impressive kitchen, which was featured in Country Woman magazine. Antiquing is popular in the area and Alma College is nearby. Sue, a doll collector, is well known for her delicious blueberry muffins.

Innkeeper(s): Bob & Sue Chaffin.

Rates:$50. Full Bkfst. Teas. 3 rooms. 2 with shared baths. Beds:QT. Phone, AC in room. Farm.

Contact: Sue Chaffin. Certificate may be used: April 15 to July 1; Aug. 1 to Nov. 1 (not July or last weekend of May).

Jonesville

Munro House B&B
202 Maumee St
Jonesville 49250
(517)849-9292

1834. Ten fireplaces are found at the historic Munro House, named for George C. Munro, a Civil War brigadier general. The Greek Revival structure, Hillsdale County's first brick house, also served as a safe haven for slaves on the Underground Railroad. Visitors can still see a secret room, used for hiding slaves, above the bath area of the downstairs bedroom. The inn's five guest rooms all have private baths, cable TV and phones. Many guests enjoy reading one of the library's special-interest books. Breakfast is eaten overlooking the inn's gardens. Hillsdale College is just five miles away.

Innkeeper(s): Joyce Yarde.

Rates:$50-68. MC VISA. Full Bkfst. Evening snacks. 5 rooms. Fireplaces. Beds:QT. TV, Phone, AC in room. Skiing. Fishing.

Contact: Joyce Yarde. Certificate may be used: Sunday through Thursday.

Leland

Manitou Manor B&B
PO Box 864
Leland 49654
(616)256-7712

1900. This sprawling farmhouse offers a Florida porch that looks out over the inn's cherry orchards. Traditional furnishings are found throughout, and there is a fieldstone fireplace in the living room. Manitou Manor's breakfasts are served in the formal dining room and feature foods produced locally. Walk to a nearby winery for a self-guided tour, or drive to herb, hydroponic and maple syrup farms. Take a ferry from Leland to the Manitou islands, or visit the nearby Grand Traverse Lighthouse Museum.

Innkeeper(s): Penny & Walt Mace.

Rates:$85-115. MC VISA. Full Bkfst. 4 rooms. Beds:KQT. Golf. Tennis. Skiing. Swimming. Horseback riding. Fishing.

Seen in: *Booth Newspaper, Outsider Magazine.*

Contact: Penny Mace. Certificate may be used: Nov. 1 through Dec. 31, 1994; Jan. 1 through May 11, 1995; Oct. 29 through Dec. 31, 1995; Excluding all holidays.

Lowell

McGee Homestead B&B
2534 Alden Nash NE
Lowell 49331
(616)897-8142

1880. Just 18 miles from Grand Rapids, travelers will find the McGee Homestead B&B, an Italianate farmhouse with four charming, antique-filled guest rooms. Surrounded by orchards, it is one of the largest farmhouses in the area. Breakfasts feature the inn's own fresh eggs. Guests may golf at an adjacent course, or enjoy nearby fishing and boating. Lowell is home to Michigan's largest antique mall, and many historic covered bridges are found in the surrounding countryside. Travelers who remain on the farm may relax in a hammock or visit a barnful of petting animals.

Innkeeper(s): Bill & Ardis Barber.

Rates:$38-55. MC VISA. Full Bkfst. Evening snacks. 4 rooms. Beds:K. Farm. Golf. Skiing. Swimming. Fishing.

Contact: Ardis Barber. Certificate may be used: Anytime available.

Ludington

The Doll House Inn
709 E Ludington Ave
Ludington 49431
(616)843-2286

1900. Antique dolls are among the special family heirlooms found throughout this Victorian inn. Seven rooms, decorated in lace curtains and brass or antique beds, include a bridal suite with a canopy bed and whirlpool tub for two. Guests can enjoy a full "heart-smart" breakfast on the wicker-filled porch. The beach is a short stroll from the inn.

Innkeeper(s): Barbara & Joe Gerovac.

Rates:$60-95. MC VISA. Gourmet Brkfst. Picnic lunches. 7 rooms. Beds:KQT. TV, Phone, AC in room. Golf. Bicycling. Skiing. Swimming. Fishing.

Contact: Barbara Gerovac. Certificate may be used: May through November, weekdays only, Sunday - Thursday.

The Lamplighter B&B
602 E Ludington Ave
Ludington 49431
(616)843-9792 Fax:(616)845-6070

1894. A magnificent golden oak staircase greets guests at the Lamplighter B&B, which for years was home to an area physician. Many business travelers use this Queen Anne Victorian inn as their home base when in the area. The Lamplighter has managed to retain much of its original charm, including a brass mouthpiece on the front door that allowed the doctor to communicate with arriving patients. Freddy, the resident cocker spaniel, enjoys taking guests for walks. The innkeepers are fluent in German.

Innkeeper(s): Judy & Heinz Bertram.

Rates:$75-85. MC VISA DS. Full Bkfst. Gourmet Brkfst. 4 rooms. Beds:Q. TV, Phone, AC in room. Skiing. Swimming. Fishing.

Contact: Heinz Bertram. Certificate may be used: October through May.

The Inn at Ludington
701 E Ludington Ave
Ludington 49431
(616)845-7055

1889. This Victorian mansion features English country furniture and collectibles. Guest rooms offer four-poster and brass beds, handmade quilts, fresh flowers and carry a theme, such as the Teddy Bear Room. The Tower Room is decorated in hearts and roses. A full breakfast features locally grown products and "made in Michigan" food stuffs.

Innkeeper(s): Diane Shields/Dave Nemitz.

Rates:$55-85. MC VISA AX. Full Bkfst. Picnic lunches. 7 rooms. 1 with shared bath. Fireplaces. Beds:QDT. AC in room. Golf. Tennis. Skiing. Swimming. Horseback riding. Fishing.

Seen in: *Ludington Daily News, Detroit Free Press, Chicago Tribune, Country Accents Magazine.*

Contact: Diane Shields. Certificate may be used: November - May anytime (except holidays and special-event weekends).

"Loved the room and everything else about the house."

Mackinac Island

Haan's 1830 Inn
PO Box 123, Huron St
Mackinac Island 49757
(906)847-6244

1781. The clip-clopping of horses is still heard from the front porches of this inn as carriages and wagons transport visitors around the island. In the National Register of Historic Places, Haan's 1830 Inn is the oldest Greek Revival-style home in the Northwest Territory. It is behind a picket fence and just across the street from Haldiman Bay. Victorian and Early American antiques include a writing desk used by Colonel Preston, an officer at Fort Mackinac at the turn of the century, and a 12-foot breakfast table formerly used by local farmers when they harvested each other's crops.

Innkeeper(s): Nicholas & Nancy Haan.

Rates:$60-115. ContPlus Bkfst. 7 rooms. 2 with shared baths. Beds:QT. Horseback riding. Fishing.

Seen in: *Detroit Free Press, Chicago Tribune, Innsider Magazine, Sears Discovery Magazine, Chicago Sun-Times.*

Contact: Vernon Haan. Certificate may be used: May 19 through June 9, Sunday through Thursday; Sept. 19 through Oct. 16, Sunday through Thursday.

"The ambiance, service and everything else was just what we needed."

Metivier Inn
Box 285, Market St
Mackinac Island 49757
(906)847-6234

1877. The Metivier Inn is perched on a bluff over-looking the downtown historic district where horse-drawn carriages and bicyclists preside in the

absence of motorized vehicles. French and English decor is found throughout the turreted Victorian home. Guests can relax in the living room before the fire or out on the wicker-filled porch.
Innkeeper(s): Dr. & Mrs. Bacon/Mr. & Mrs. Neyer.
Rates:$98-145. MC VISA DS. ContPlus Bkfst. 21 rooms. Beds:Q.
Conference Rm. Golf. Tennis. Swimming. Horseback riding. Fishing.
Seen in: *Travel and Leisure, Michigan Living and Detroit News.*
Contact: Jane Bacon. Certificate may be used: May and October,
Sunday through Thursday only, no holidays.

"The accommodations were more than expected and our hosts made it even better."

Mendon

The Mendon Country Inn
440 W Main St
Mendon 49072
(616)496-8132 Fax:(616)496-8403

1843. This two-story inn was constructed with St. Joseph River clay bricks fired on the property. There are eight-foot windows, high ceilings and a walnut staircase. Country antiques are accentuated with rag rugs, collectibles and bright quilts. The Indian Room has a fireplace. A creek runs by the property, and a romantic courting canoe is avail-able to guests. Depending on the season, guests may also borrow a tandem bike or arrange for an Amish sleigh ride.
Innkeeper(s): Dick & Dolly Buerkle.
Rates:$65-150. MC VISA AX DS. ContPlus Bkfst. Picnic lunches. Teas.
Evening snacks. 18 rooms. Fireplaces. Beds:QD. Conference Rm. AC,
Refrig. in room. Golf. Tennis. Bicycling. Skiing. Handicap access. Spa.

Sauna. Swimming. Fishing.
Seen in: *Innsider, Country Home.*
Contact: Richard Buerkle. Certificate may be used: Sunday to Thursday,
Nov. 1 to April 15, does not include holidays.

"A great experience. Good food and great hosts. Thank you."

Muskegon

Blue Country B&B
1415 Holton Rd
Muskegon 49445
(616)744-2555

1910. Once known as the Brookside Tea House during prohibition, this Craftsman home now is known for its family-oriented atmosphere and

woodsy setting. Four guest rooms include the Blue Tea Rose Room, with a hand-carved sycamore bed and vanity, and the Whispering Woods Room, fea-turing wood furnishings and an attractive antique wall print. Guests will enjoy the teapot collection, and they are welcome to try the electronic organ and hammered dulcimer. The inn is just 10 min-utes from Lake Michigan. There are numerous area attractions, including Muskegon and Duck Lake state parks.
Innkeeper(s): John & Barbara Stevens.
Rates:$61. Full Bkfst. Teas. Evening snacks. 4 rooms. 4 with shared
baths. Beds:QT. AC in room. Skiing. Swimming. Fishing.
Contact: Barbara Stevens. Certificate may be used: July 5, 1994 to
Dec. 31, 1995. Sunday night through Thursday night.

Oscoda

Huron House
3124 N US-23
Oscoda 48750
(517)739-9255

1940. This is a great place to take long walks on the sandy beaches of Lake Huron and follow-up with a relaxing soak in the hot tub, or if you book the Jacuzzi Suite, enjoy your own private whirlpool.

Another favorite room overlooks the lake. Homemade Belgium waffles, crepes, muffins and quiche are some of the delicious breakfasts that await you, served in the privacy of your room, in the spacious second floor breakfast room overlooking Lake Huron or on the outdoor decks. The inn is near the River Road National Forest Scenic Byway. The 22-mile route along the AuSable River provides some of the most breathtaking scenery in Michigan.

Innkeeper(s): Dennis & Martie Lorenz.

Rates:$60-115. MC VISA. Full Bkfst. 7 rooms. Beds:KQ. TV, AC, Refrig. in room. Skiing. Spa. Swimming. Fishing.

Contact: Dennis Lorenz. Certificate may be used: Jan. 1 to May 15. Sunday through Thursday excluding holidays.

Owosso

Mulberry House
1251 N Shiawassee St (M-52)
Owosso 48867
(517)723-4890

1890. Each of the rooms at this late 19th-century inn reflects an individual atmosphere. The Sweet Annie Room is decorated with a nostalgic style and

features a ceiling fan. Other rooms provide a relaxing feel with their comfortable furniture and decor. Relax on the front porch swing or stroll through the gardens. The sites of historic Owasso include the Curwood Castle and the Shiawassee Arts Center. For a look at the lovely architecture take the Walking Tour through the streets of Owasso. Antiquing and herb farms are some other interesting attractions.

Innkeeper(s): Carol Holmes.

Rates:$60-70. MC VISA DS. ContPlus Bkfst. Gourmet Brkfst. 3 rooms. 1 with shared bath. Beds:DT. AC in room. Golf. Tennis. Bicycling.

Seen in: *Argus-Press.*

Contact: Carol Holmes. Certificate may be used: Sunday - Thursday all year.

"A serendipity in the middle of a fast-paced society."

Petoskey

Perry Hotel
Bay & Lewis Sts
Petoskey 49770
(616)347-4000 (800)456-1917
Fax:(616)347-0636

1899. This handsome Federal-style Queen Anne Victorian inn was the city's first brick hotel. Many of the hotel's rooms offer lovely views of Petoskey's picturesque Gaslight District or the waters of Little Traverse Bay. Guests choose from five room categories, all named after the city's other 19th-century resort hotels, now only a memory. Within walking distance are an arts center, library, museum, shopping establishments and the waterfront. Outdoor lovers will find the area a paradise, with nearby golfing and skiing establishments among the state's finest. Guests also may enjoy a hot tub or exercise bikes.

Innkeeper(s): Stafford Smith.

Rates:$60-165. MC VISA AX. Full Bkfst. EP. Gourmet Brkfst, Lunch, Dinner. Picnic lunches. Teas. Evening snacks. 81 rooms. Beds:KQT. Conference Rm. TV, Phone, AC in room. Tennis. Skiing. Handicap access. Spa. Exercise room. Fishing.

Contact: Judy Honor. Certificate may be used: November through May, not valid Christmas week or ski weekends.

Port Huron

Victorian Inn
1229 Seventh St
Port Huron 48060
(810)984-1437

1896. This finely renovated Queen Anne Victorian house has both an inn and restaurant. Gleaming carved-oak woodwork, leaded-glass windows and

fireplaces in almost every room reflect the home's gracious air. Authentic wallpapers and draperies provide a background for carefully selected antiques. Victorian-inspired menus include such entrees as partridge with pears and filet of beef Africane, all served on antique china.

Innkeeper(s): Kelly Lozano.

Rates:$55-65. MC VISA AX DC DS CB. ContPlus Bkfst. Gourmet Lunch, Dinner. 4 rooms. 2 with shared baths. Fireplaces. Beds:QT. AC in room. Golf. Tennis. Swimming. Fishing.

Seen in: *Detroit Free Press.*

Contact: Lynne Secory. Certificate may be used: Sunday through Thursday.

"In all of my trips, business or pleasure, I have never experienced such a warm and courteous staff."

Saginaw

Brockway House
1631 Brockway
Saginaw 48602
(517)792-0746 (800)383-5043

1864. Ancient walnut trees, 17 types of locust trees and several euwanumus trees accentuate Brockway House's acre of lawns. Corinthian columns adorn the front porch. If you want to be spoiled, check into the Zuehike Suite. In the morning, enjoy the full gourmet breakfast - sometimes available served in bed. Crabmeat quiche and baked puffed pancakes with sauteed fruit are favorites. The innkeeper is a history buff and an expert on the area, and enjoys making sure you get to explore the best of Saginaw's treasures.

Innkeeper(s): Ina (Zoe) Carpenter.

Rates:$85-175. MC VISA. Gourmet Brkfst. 4 rooms. Beds:KQ. Conference Rm. Phone in room. Golf. Tennis. Swimming. Fishing.

Seen in: *The Saginaw News.*

Contact: Ina Zoe Carpenter. Certificate may be used: One night must be weeknight (Sunday - Thursday). Coupons not valid with other discounts.

"I could not have chosen a more perfect place."

Heart House Inn
419 N Michigan Ave
Saginaw 48602
(517)753-3145

1860. Originally built during the Civil War by a lumberman who also had shipping business on the Saginaw River, this 8,000-square-foot house was renovated in the '80s by a heart surgeon, thus the name. Its features include black walnut beamed ceilings and stained glass. Furnishings are from the '30s and '40s.

Innkeeper(s): Kelly Zurvalec/Kim Bolin/Kurt Zurvalec

Rates:$55-75. MC VISA AX. ContPlus Bkfst. AP available. Gourmet

Dinner. Picnic lunches. Evening snacks. 8 rooms. Beds:T. Conference Rm. Phone, AC in room. Skiing. Handicap access. Swimming. Fishing.

Contact: Kelly Zurvalec. Certificate may be used: Anytime based on availability.

Saint Joseph

South Cliff Inn B&B
1900 Lakeshore Dr
Saint Joseph 49055
(616)983-4881 Fax:(616)983-7391

1917. Overlooking Lake Michigan is this charming English cottage, which features six luxurious guest rooms. One of the most popular is the teal-toned Sunset Suite, with its panoramic lake view and custom marble tub. Many guests enjoy relaxing in front of the inn's living room fireplace, or on one of two decks that provide vistas of the lake. St. Joseph, a popular getaway for Chicago and Detroit residents, offers many opportunities for visitors. Guests may walk downtown for shopping and dining, or borrow a bike for a relaxing ride. Several state parks are within easy driving distance.

Innkeeper(s): Bill Swisher.

Rates:$50-110. MC VISA AX DS. ContPlus Bkfst. 7 rooms. Fireplaces. Beds:KQT. TV, Phone, AC, Refrig. in room. Bicycling. Skiing. Swimming. Fishing.

Contact: Wm. Eugene Swisher. Certificate may be used: Nov. 1, 1994 through March 31, 1995.

Saugatuck

Bayside Inn
618 Water St Box 1001
Saugatuck 49453
(616)857-4321 (800)548-0077
Fax:(616)857-1870

1927. Located on the edge of the Kalamazoo River and across from the nature observation tower, this downtown inn was once a boathouse. The common

room now has a fireplace and view of the water. Each guest room has its own deck. The inn is near several restaurants, shops and beaches. Fishing for salmon, perch and trout is popular.

Innkeeper(s): Kathy & Frank Wilson.

Rates:$55-185. MC VISA AX DS. ContPlus Bkfst. 10 rooms. Fireplaces. Beds:KQ. Conference Rm. TV, Phone, AC, Refrig. in room. Golf. Skiing. Spa. Swimming. Fishing.

Contact: Kathleen Wilson. Certificate may be used: November through April midweek, excluding holidays.

The Park House
888 Holland St
Saugatuck 49453
(616)857-4535 (800)321-4535
Fax:(616)857-1065

1857. This Greek Revival-style home is the oldest residence in Saugatuck and was constructed for the first mayor. Susan B. Anthony was a guest here for

two weeks in the 1870s, and the local Women's Christian Temperance League was established in the parlor. A country theme pervades the inn, with antiques, old woodwork and pine floors. A cottage with a hot tub and a river-front guest house are also available.

Innkeeper(s): Lynda & Joe Petty.

Rates:$60-160. MC VISA AX DS. ContPlus Bkfst. 9 rooms. Fireplaces. Beds:KQT. Conference Rm. TV, Phone, AC in room. Skiing. Handicap access. Swimming. Fishing.

Seen in: *Detroit News, Innsider, Gazette, South Bend Tribune.*

Contact: Lynda Petty. Certificate may be used: Weekdays excluding July, August and holidays.

"Thanks again for your kindness and hospitality during our weekend."

The Red Dog B&B
132 Mason St
Saugatuck 49453
(616)857-8851

1879. In the heart of downtown Saugatuck, a charming resort town, visitors will find this two-story farmhouse, originally owned by the town barber. Guests will enjoy a trip to the ice cream shop next door that once served as the barbershop. The inn's six guest rooms include a two-room suite with kitchenette. A second-floor porch that runs the length of the inn is the perfect place for conversing or relaxing after a day of exploring the area's rolling sand dunes and lakefront boardwalk.

Innkeeper(s): Gary Kott.

Rates:$40-85. MC VISA DC DS. Full Bkfst. 6 rooms. 2 with shared baths. Beds:Q. TV, AC in room. Skiing. Swimming. Fishing.

Contact: Gary Kott. Certificate may be used: November, December, April.

Sherwood Forest B&B
938 Center St, PO Box 315
Saugatuck 49453
(616)857-1246 Fax:(616)857-1996

1900. While Robin and Marian may not be around, a stay at this Victorian home in the woods near Lake Michigan may make you a Merry Man (or woman). The heated swimming pool is decorated with a hand-painted mural of dolphins and the wide sandy beaches are only a half block away. The Black and White room (named for its color scheme) features a huge, six-jet Jacuzzi.

Innkeeper(s): Keith and Susan Charak.

Rates:$60-130. MC VISA. ContPlus Bkfst. Gourmet Dinner. 5 rooms. Fireplaces. Beds:Q. AC in room. Golf. Tennis. Bicycling. Skiing. Swimming. Horseback riding. Fishing.

Seen in: *Commercial Record.*

Contact: Keith Charak. Certificate may be used: November-April, holidays excluded, select rooms only.

Twin Oaks Inn
227 Griffith St, PO Box 867
Saugatuck 49453
(616)857-1600

1860. This large Queen Anne Victorian inn was a boarding house for lumbermen at the turn of the century. Now an old-English-sytle inn, it offers a variety of lodging choices, including three suites. Guests also may stay in the inn's cozy cottage, which boasts an outdoor hot tub. There are many diversions at the Twin Oaks, including a collection of videotaped movies numbering more than 600. An English garden with a pond and fountain provides a relaxing setting, and guests also may borrow bicycles or play horseshoes on the inn's grounds. Towels and free passes to Oval Beach are furnished.

Innkeeper(s): Jerry & Nancy Horney.

Rates:$64-94. MC VISA DS. Full Bkfst. Teas. 10 rooms. Beds:KQ. Conference Rm. TV, AC in room. Golf. Bicycling. Skiing. Spa. Swimming. Fishing.

Seen in: *Home & Away, Cleveland Plain Dealer.*

Contact: Nancy Horney. Certificate may be used: Nov. 1-April 1.

South Haven

Victoria Resort B&B
241 Oak St
South Haven 49090
(616)637-6414

1920. Less than two blocks from a sandy beach, this Classical Revival inn offers many recreational opportunities for its guests, who may choose from

bicycling, beach and pool swimming, basketball and tennis, among others. The inn's rooms and suites provide visitors several options, including cable TV, fireplaces, whirlpool tubs and ceiling fans. Cottages with maid service, for families or groups traveling together, also are available. A 10-minute stroll down tree-lined streets leads visitors to South Haven's quaint downtown, with its riverfront restaurants and shops.
Innkeeper(s): Bob & Jan Leksich.
Rates:$60-125. MC VISA DS. ContPlus Bkfst. 11 rooms. Fireplaces. Beds:QT. TV, AC, Refrig. in room. Tennis. Bicycling. Skiing. Swimming. Fishing.
Contact: Robert Leksich. Certificate may be used: Nov. 1, 1994 through April, 1995. Sunday through Thursday only, except holidays.

Swartz Creek

Pink Palace Farms
6095 Baldwin Rd
Swartz Creek 48473
(810)655-4076

1888. Ten miles southwest of Flint lies this historic Gothic Revival farmhouse. Home to a 150-head Holstein cattle operation, this farm-style inn offers a perfect getaway for those weary of the bustling city. The house has been preserved as closely as possible to its original condition, and the property is listed with the National Register. Breakfast is served in the guests' rooms or in the inn's country

dining room. The area surrounding Pink Palace Farms includes fields, streams and woods. Picnicking and fishing are enjoyed at a small spring-fed lake. Guests are encouraged to explore the farm's barns and grounds.
Innkeeper(s): Blaine & Jeannette Pinkston.
Rates:$45. Full Bkfst. 3 rooms. 2 with shared baths. Beds:KT. Conference Rm. Phone in room. Farm. Bicycling. Skiing. Swimming. Fishing.
Contact: Jeannette Pinkston. Certificate may be used: Weekdays. Weekends based upon availability.

Traverse City

The Grainery B&B
2951 Hartman Road
Traverse City 49684
(616)946-8325

1892. In a rural setting just outside the beautiful lakefront resort town of Traverse City is this two-story farmhouse that includes two golf greens on its 10-acre grounds. Country Victorian decor abounds at the Grainery, which offers visitors a choice of guest rooms or a romantic, secluded cottage with refrigerator, cable TV and easy access to the inn's outdoor hot tub. Ruth's Room features an antique canopy bed. Breakfast is enjoyed in the Pondview Room, where guests are treated to a variety of winged visitors, including cranes and herons. The world-famous Interlochen Arts Academy is 15 minutes away.
Innkeeper(s): Ron & Julie Kucera.
Rates:$65-85. MC VISA. AP available. Gourmet Brkfst. 4 rooms. 2 with shared baths. Beds:K. TV, Phone, AC, Refrig. in room. Farm. Skiing. Spa. Swimming. Fishing.
Contact: Julie Kucera. Certificate may be used: Weekdays.

Linden Lea on Long Lake
279 S Long Lake Rd
Traverse City 49684
(616)943-9182

1901. Guests are free to explore an island-filled lake at this inn, originally a summer cottage. A variety of fish are found at the lake, including bass, muskie, northern pike and perch. Guests have use of the private beach and rowboat. The guest rooms sport lake views, and visitors will enjoy the inn's multilevel sundecks. Beveled glass, a fireplace with hand-carved, solid cherry mantel and country furnishings add to the inn's considerable charm. Guests often are treated to the sights and sounds of the area's birdlife, including the haunting cry of the loon. Interlochen Center for the Arts is nearby.

Innkeeper(s): Jim & Vicky McDonnell.

Rates:$70-75. 2 rooms. 2 with shared baths. Beds:D. Skiing. Swimming. Fishing.

Contact: Victoria McDonnell. Certificate may be used: November, January-April, Sunday-Thursday only.

The Victoriana 1898
622 Washington St
Traverse City 49684
(616)929-1009

1898. Egbert Ferris, a partner in the European Horse Hotel, built this Italianate Victorian manor and a two-story carriage house. Later, the bell tower from the old Central School was moved onto the property and now serves as a handsome Greek Revival gazebo. The house has three parlors, all framed in fretwork. Etched and stained glass is found throughout. Guest rooms are furnished with family heirlooms. The house speciality is Belgian waffles topped with homemade cherry sauce.

Innkeeper(s): Flo & Bob Schermerhorn.

Rates:$55-75. MC VISA. Full Bkfst. 3 rooms. Fireplaces. Beds:KQD. AC in room. Bicycling. Skiing. Swimming. Fishing.

Seen in: *Midwest Living.*

Contact: Flo Schermerhorn. Certificate may be used: November through April, Sunday through Thursday, 1994-1995.

"We will long remember your beautiful home, those delectable breakfast creations and our pleasant chats."

Union Pier

Pine Garth Inn
15790 Lakeshore Rd
Union Pier 49129
(616)469-1642 Fax:(616)469-1642

1905. The rooms and five guest cottages at this charming bed & breakfast inn are individually decorated in a country style and each boasts something special. One room has a private deck and a wall of windows that look out to Lake Michigan. Other rooms feature Ralph Lauren linens, fireplaces and Laura Ashley decor. Albert Hall, the deluxe cottage, offers two queen-size beds, a wood-burning stove and an outdoor hot tub on a private deck.

Innkeeper(s): Russ & Paula Bulin.

Rates:$85-145. MC VISA AX DS. Full Bkfst. 5 rooms. Fireplaces. Beds:Q. Conference Rm. AC in room. Golf. Tennis. Bicycling. Skiing. Swimming. Horseback riding. Fishing.

Seen in: *Chicago Tribune, Travel and Leisure, Heritage Country, Detroit Free Press.*

Contact: Russell Bulin. Certificate may be used: Midweek November through April, no holidays.

The Inn at Union Pier
9708 Berrien, PO Box 222
Union Pier 49129
(616)469-4700 Fax:(616)469-4720

1920. Set on a shady acre across a country road from Lake Michigan, this inn features unique Swedish ceramic fireplaces, a hot tub and sauna, a

veranda ringing the house and a large common room with comfortable overstuffed furniture and a grand piano. Rooms offer such amenities as private balconies and porches, whirlpools, views of the English garden and furniture dating from the early 1900s. Breakfast includes fresh fruit and homemade jams made of fruit from surrounding farms.

Innkeeper(s): Joyce & Mark Pitts.

Rates:$100-160. MC VISA DS. MAP available. Gourmet Brkfst. Evening snacks. 16 rooms. Fireplaces. Beds:KQ. Conference Rm. Phone, AC, Refrig. in room. Bicycling. Skiing. Handicap access. Spa. Sauna. Swimming.

Seen in: *Chicago Tribune, USA Today, The Detroit News.*

Contact: Joyce Erickson Pitts. Certificate may be used: Sunday - Thursday only - Oct. 1, 1994 - May 25, 1995 and Oct. 1 - Dec. 31, 1995. Excluding holidays and special events. May not be used in conjunction with any other coupons, promotions or discounts.

"The food, the atmosphere, the accommodations, and of course, the entire staff made this the most relaxing weekend ever."

West Branch

The Rose Brick Inn
124 East Houghton Ave
West Branch 48661
(517)345-3702

1906. This Queen Anne Victorian is recognized as a state historical site. The inn features four guest rooms, all with phones, private bath, queen beds and Victorian decor. Nearby, guests will find antiquing, canoeing and cross-country skiing opportunities. The inn also is within easy driving distance of Houghton Lake, well known for its fishing and boating, and Higgins Lake, famous for its clear water and fine beaches. The lake also boasts two of Michigan's finest state parks.

Innkeeper(s): Leon Swartz.

Rates:$48-58. MC VISA. Cont. Bkfst. 4 rooms. Beds:Q. Conference Rm. Phone, AC in room. Golf. Tennis. Skiing. Spa. Swimming. Fishing.

Contact: Susan Grimske-Kai. Certificate may be used: Sunday through Thursday nights, holidays excluded.

Minnesota

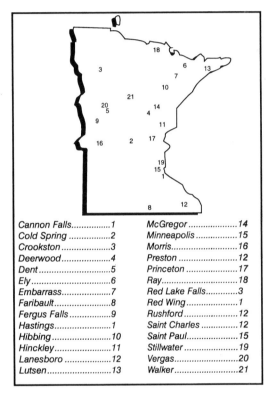

Cannon Falls

Candlewick Country Inn
300 W Mill St
Cannon Falls 55009
(507)263-0879

1880. An easy getaway from the Twin Cities, the Candlewick is perfect for a romantic weekend for guests who need a break from the rigors of the metropolitan area. Furnished in country decor, this quiet inn offers two rooms, both with private bath. The inn's player piano offers a nostalgic feel for bygone days, and guests may explore nearby museums, shopping and antiquing.

Innkeeper(s): Thomas & Dona Morgan.

202

Rates:$65-75. MC VISA. Full Bkfst. 2 rooms. Beds:QD. Phone in room. Skiing.

Contact: Dona Morgan. Certificate may be used: Sunday through Thursday.

Cold Spring

Pillow, Pillar & Pine Guest House
419 Main St
Cold Spring 56320
(612)685-3828

1908. This three-story Greek Revival mansion was built by businessman Marcus Maurin as a wedding gift for his daughter. The home has warmth and charm highlighted by stained glass, oak and maple floors, fireplaces, antique light fixtures and a wrap-around porch. Cold Spring is named for the natural spring that started the city's first industry - Cold Spring Brewing Company. In 1874, an immigrant German brewer discovered the spring and built a small brew-house. The popularity of his "Cold Spring" beer grew and expanded.

Innkeeper(s): Mike & Linda Carlson.

Rates:$52-94. MC VISA. Full Bkfst. Evening snacks. 4 rooms. 2 with shared baths. Beds:Q. AC in room. Skiing. Swimming. Fishing.

Contact: Linda Carlson. Certificate may be used: Monday - Thursday, Nov. 1-30, 1994; Monday - Thursday, January through March 31, 1995.

Crookston

The Elm Street Inn
422 Elm St
Crookston 56716
(218)281-2343 (800)568-4476
Fax:(218)281-1756

1910. Recently restored, the Elm Street Inn is within walking distance of the Crookston business area with 35 National Register buildings. Gleaming hardwood floors and stained-glass windows add to the enjoyment of this Arts and Crafts house. The innkeeper grew up in a family bakery and prepares

home-baked breakfast specialties. Crookston is in the heart of the Red River Valley, 25 miles east of Grand Forks, North Dakota.

Innkeeper(s): John & Sheryl Winters.

Rates:$55-65. MC VISA AX. Full Bkfst. Gourmet Brkfst, Lunch, Dinner. Picnic lunches. Teas. Evening snacks. 4 rooms. 2 with shared baths. Beds:D. Conference Rm. AC in room. Golf. Tennis. Bicycling. Skiing. Swimming. Fishing.

Seen in: *Grand Forks Herald.*

Contact: Sheryl Winters. Certificate may be used: Off-season (September-May).

Deerwood

Walden Woods B&B
16070 Hwy 18 SE
Deerwood 56444
(612)692-4379 (800)892-5336

1982. Located nearly in the center of the state, this log house could serve as a secluded getaway or as headquarters to exploring the abundant lakes and attractions nearby. Although there are a number of activities within driving distance, including the Paul Bunyan Amusement Center, Walden Woods offers plenty within its 40 acres to keep guests happy, including hiking trails, fishing, cross-country skiing and just relaxing. Be sure to inquire about the picnic lunches, perfect for an afternoon outing.

Innkeeper(s): Richard & Anne Manly.

Rates:$55-70. MC VISA AX. Full Bkfst. Gourmet Brkfst. Picnic lunches. Evening snacks. 4 rooms. 4 with shared baths. Beds:QT. Skiing. Handicap access. Swimming. Fishing.

Seen in: *Brainerd Dispatch, St. Paul Pioneer Press, Millelacs Messenger.*

Contact: Anne Manly. Certificate may be used: Sunday through Thursday, November through April.

"A cozy and charming place with the comforts of home. I'd recommend it to anyone!"

Dent

Heart O'Lakes Farm B&B
Rt 1 Box 30
Dent 56528
(218)758-2121 (800)770-6348

1975. This inn sits in the middle of Ottertail County's lake country, and there are woods and lakes on the large property. But Heart O' Lakes Farm also is known for its wonderful breakfasts, downhome feel and absolute relaxation. Innkeepers Carolann and Don Garber offer guests that extra-special family feeling inherent in the farm setting. With Carolann's regionally known cooking abilities, it is doubtful many guests will skip breakfast. The inn is also a working cattle and hog farm, and Don never tires of showing visitors around. Activities abound all year-long in the area, and Maplewood State Park sits just a short drive due west.

Innkeeper(s): Don & Carolann Garber.

Rates:$55-65. Full Bkfst. 4 rooms. 3 with shared baths. Beds:Q. Farm. Bicycling. Skiing. Spa. Swimming. Fishing.

Contact: Carolann Garber. Certificate may be used: No weekends in July and August.

Ely

Burntside Lodge
2755 Burntside Lodge Rd
Ely 55731
(218)365-3894

1913. "Staying here is like taking a vacation 60 years ago," states innkeeper Lou LaMontagne. Families have come here for 70 years to enjoy the

waterfront, woodside setting. The lodge and its cabins are in the National Register and much of the original hand-carved furnishings remain from the Jazz age. Fishing, listening to the cry of the loon and boating around the lake's 125 islands are popular activities. Breakfast and dinner are available in the waterside dining room. Some say Burntside Lake is the most beautiful lake in the world.

Innkeeper(s): Lou & Lonnie LaMontagne.

Rates:$80-110. MC VISA AX DS. EP. MAP available. 23 rooms. Beds:KT. Refrig. in room. Tennis. Handicap access. Sauna. Swimming. Fishing.

Contact: Lonnie LaMontagne. Certificate may be used: May 15 to June 23, August 19 to Sept. 23.

"Unforgettable."

Trezona House
315 E Washington St
Ely 55731
(218)365-4809

1906. Northeast Minnesota offers a vacationer's paradise no matter what the season, and Trezona House provides an ideal setting for those exploring the area. This turn-of-the-century Folk Victorian home, in town, is easily accessible to nearby Burntside Lake and the Hidden Valley Ski Area. The newly renovated home, which holds a membership in a local historical society, features unique decor throughout. Ask about the picnic lunches, just the ticket for an outing to nearby Bear Head Lake State Park.

Innkeeper(s): Lynn Olson & Jim Macdonald.

Rates:$40-55. MC VISA. ContPlus Bkfst. Picnic lunches. 4 rooms. 4 with shared baths. Beds:QT. Skiing. Swimming. Fishing.

Contact: Lynn Olson. Certificate may be used: January - April, 1995.

Embarrass

Finnish Heritage Homestead
4776 Waisanen Rd
Embarrass 55732
(218)984-3318

1901. This turn-of-the-century Finnish-American log house offers outdoor recreation and family-style full breakfasts to visitors, who receive many personal touches, such as bath robes, slipper socks and turndown service in their guest rooms. Guests also may utilize the inn's relaxing sauna and enjoy badminton, bocce ball, croquet and horseshoes on its spacious grounds. Terrific fishing and skiing are found nearby, and be sure to inquire about the availability of picnic lunches to take along. A gazebo and gift shop also are on the premises.

Innkeeper(s): Elaine Braginton.

Rates:$53. Full Bkfst. Picnic lunches. 4 rooms. 4 with shared baths. Beds:QT. Farm. Skiing. Sauna. Swimming. Fishing.

Contact: Elaine Braginton. Certificate may be used: Monday to Thursday nights only.

Faribault

Cherub Hill B&B Inn
105 NW 1st Ave
Faribault 55021
(507)332-2024 (800)332-7254

1896. Midway between the Twin Cities and Albert Lea, this Queen Anne Victorian inn offers romantic, Victorian accommodations to its guests, many of whom are honeymooners. Guests are treated to early coffee or tea before their full breakfasts are served. The three air-conditioned guest rooms, which all feature private baths and turndown service, also include one suite. Other available guest room amenities include a fireplace and whirlpool bath. The charming town features many historic buildings, fine restaurants and shops. Nerstrand-Big Woods and Sakatah Lake state parks are nearby.

Innkeeper(s): Kristi LeMieux.

Rates:$70-88. MC VISA AX. Full Bkfst. Teas. 3 rooms. Fireplaces. Beds:QD. AC in room. Golf. Tennis. Skiing. Swimming. Fishing.

Contact: Kristi LeMieux. Certificate may be used: Any Sunday through Thursday night, year-round.

Fergus Falls

Nims Bakketopp Hus
RR 2 Box 187A
Fergus Falls 56537
(218)739-2915

1978. This home is on a wooded hillside overlooking Long Lake. There are decks on the lakeside. Family heirlooms and Norwegian items are featured. There is a draped canopy bed in the French Room and a king-size waterbed under a skylight in the master bedroom.

Innkeeper(s): Dennis & Judy Nims.

Rates:$60-95. MC VISA DS. Full Bkfst. Gourmet Brkfst. Teas. Evening snacks. 3 rooms. Beds:Q. TV, Phone, AC in room. Skiing. Spa. Swimming. Fishing.

Seen in: *Minneapolis Tribune.*

Contact: Dennis Nims. Certificate may be used: Nov. 1 to March 31.

Hastings

Thorwood & Rosewood Historic Inns
315 Pine St
Hastings 55033
(612)437-3297 (800)992-4667

Fax:(612)437-4129

1880. This romantic Queen Anne Victorian has several verandas and porches. Grained cherry woodwork and nine fireplaces add elegance to the inn. Most rooms in The River Rose have fireplaces. In the Mississippi Under the Stars Room, a skylight shines down on the whirlpool tub. This 1,200-square-foot suite features a baby grand piano, tapestries, paisleys and a copper soaking tub as well as a round shower.

Innkeeper(s): Dick & Pam Thorsen.

Rates:$75-195. MC VISA AX DC DS. Full Bkfst. Gourmet Brkfst, Lunch, Dinner. Picnic lunches. Evening snacks. 15 rooms. Fireplaces. Beds:QT. Conference Rm. AC in room. Skiing. Handicap access. Swimming. Fishing.

Seen in: *Travel Holiday.*

Contact: Pamela Thorsen. Certificate may be used: Monday-Thursday only except October and December and holidays on $145 and $195 rooms only.

Hibbing

The Adams House
201 E 23rd St
Hibbing 55746
(218)263-9742

1927. This Tudor-style home gives guests a touch of England, complete with pleasing decor. The house's unique look, with slanted roof and windows of leaded glass, has been recognized by the city's historical society, and guests will enjoy its large bedrooms and antique-filled interior. Downtown shopping and several of the area's churches are within walking distance, and Hibbing is well known for its recreational offerings, including boating, fishing and skiing.

Innkeeper(s): Marlene & Merrill Widmark.

Rates:$43-48. ContPlus Bkfst. 5 rooms. 4 with shared baths. Beds:DT. Phone in room. Bicycling. Skiing. Swimming. Fishing.

Contact: Marlene Widmark. Certificate may be used: January through June, 1995 any day of the week.

Hinckley

Dakota Lodge
Rt 3, Box 178
Hinckley 55037
(612)384-6052

1976. The five-room log-siding house provides the perfect getaway for guests seeking relaxation and escape. The lodge's rustic exterior and country setting mesh perfectly with its gracious interior. Four of the rooms feature both fireplace and whirlpool.

Less than 90 miles from Minneapolis, the area surrounding the lodge offers canoeing, snowmobiling, fishing and swimming for outdoor enthusiasts. Others may want to explore Hinckley, with its Fire Museum, Grand Casino, zoo and 32-mile bicycle trail. St. Croix State Park is also in the vicinity.

Innkeeper(s): Mike Schmitz, Tad Hilborn.

Rates:$58-110. MC VISA DS. Full Bkfst. 5 rooms. Fireplaces. Beds:Q. AC in room. Farm. Skiing. Handicap access. Swimming. Fishing.

Contact: Michael Schmitz. Certificate may be used: Year-round, Sunday-Thursday.

Lanesboro

Birch Knoll Ranch R&R
Rt 2 Box 11
Lanesboro 55949
(612)475-2054

1910. Those seeking privacy in a country setting need look no further than Birch Knoll Ranch, where guests have the roomy, two-story farmhouse to themselves. Breakfast is brought to the house in the morning and may include blueberry French toast and apple dishes. Explore the 240-acre cattle, corn and soybean farm and its woods. Nearby is the 34-mile paved Root River Bike Trail, called one of the country's most scenic. The river itself, which is known for its large trout, runs right through the property. Other activities in Southeastern Minnesota's Bluff Country include antiquing, cross-country skiing, and exploring Amish country.

Rates:$40-75. MC VISA. Full Bkfst. 3 rooms. 2 with shared baths. Beds:QT. AC in room. Farm. Skiing. Fishing.

Contact: George Hust. Certificate may be used: Nov. 1 through May 31 or midweek if openings.

Lutsen

Cascade Lodge
HC 3 Box 445
Lutsen 55612
(218)387-1112 (800)322-9543
Fax:(218)387-1113

1938. A main lodge and 10 cabins (including log cabins) comprise Cascade Lodge, tucked away in the midst of Cascade River State Park which overlooks Lake Superior. Cascade Creek meanders between the cabins toward the lake. The lodge has a natural-stone fireplace and the lounge areas are decorated with hunting trophies of moose, coyote, wolves and bear. Canoeing, hiking to Lookout Mountain, walking along Wild Flower Trail and watching the sunset from the lawn swing are favorite summer activities. Skiing, snowshoeing, photography and fireside conversations are popular in winter.

Innkeeper(s): Gene & Laurene Glader.

Rates:$33-149. MC VISA AX DS. EP. MAP available. 30 rooms. Fireplaces. Beds:QT. Conference Rm. Phone, Refrig. in room. Golf. Tennis. Bicycling. Skiing. Handicap access. Swimming. Horseback riding. Fishing.

Seen in: *Country Inns.*

Contact: Gene Glader. Certificate may be used: Good only Sunday - Thursday, Oct. 23, 1994 to June 15, 1995. Two-night minimum. Lodge rooms only. (Breakfast not included, holidays excluded).

"We needed to get away and recharge ourselves. This was the perfect place."

Lindgren's B&B

County Rd 35, PO Box 56
Lutsen 55612-0056
(218)663-7450

1926. This '20s log home is in the Superior National Forest on the north shore of Lake Superior. The inn features massive stone fireplaces,

a baby grand piano and a Finnish-style sauna. The living room has tongue-and-groove, Western knotty cedar wood paneling and seven-foot windows offering a view of the lake.

Innkeeper(s): Bob & Shirley Lindgren.

Rates:$80-110. MC VISA. Full Bkfst. Evening snacks. 4 rooms. Beds:KT. Conference Rm. Phone in room. Golf. Tennis. Skiing. Sauna. Swimming. Horseback riding. Fishing.

Seen in: *Brainerd Daily Dispatch, Duluth News-Tribune, Tempo, Midwest Living.*

Contact: Shirley Lindgren. Certificate may be used: Anytime April, May, November. Midweek Monday-Thursday, Jan. 1 to April 1 and Dec. 1 to Dec. 15.

"Thanks so much for providing a home base for us as we explored the North Country."

McGregor

Savanna Portage Inn B&B

HCR 4, Box 96
McGregor 55760
(218)426-3500 (800)428-6108

1977. A lakeside getaway greets visitors at the Savanna Portage Inn, a perfect summer vacation or winter wonderland retreat. The two-story Colonial Revival home is nestled in a grove of trees, providing a cozy, relaxed feeling for visitors, who have their choice of four rooms, including the Daniel Greysolon, with two oversized beds. Nearby activities include golf, country dancing, antiquing, cross-country skiing and a state park.

Innkeeper(s): Clyde N. Johnson.

Rates:$60-75. MC VISA AX DS. Full Bkfst. 4 rooms. 2 with shared baths. Beds:KQT. TV, Phone in room. Golf. Tennis. Skiing. Handicap access. Swimming. Fishing.

Contact: Clyde Johnson. Certificate may be used: Anytime of year Sunday through Thursday. Advance registration on space available basis.

Minneapolis

The LeBlanc House

302 University Ave NE
Minneapolis 55413
(612)379-2570

1896. Visitors to the University of Minnesota area should look no further than the LeBlanc House. The restored Queen Anne Victorian offers guests a

historical perspective of life in the 1800s. The inn's convenient location also provides easy access to the Metrodome and downtown Minneapolis, while giving its guests a chance to relax in style after exploring the area. Amelia's Room has a view of the city lights and visitors may be treated to gourmet specialties such as pistachio quiche or rum raisin French toast.

Innkeeper(s): Barbara & Bob Zahaski.

Rates:$75-95. MC VISA AX. Full Bkfst. Gourmet Brkfst. 3 rooms. 2 with shared baths. Beds:Q. Conference Rm. Phone, AC in room. Skiing. Swimming. Fishing.

Contact: Barbara Zahaski. Certificate may be used: Year-round (no limited time).

Morris

The American House
410 E Third St
Morris 56267
(612)589-4054

1900. One block from the Morris campus of the University of Minnesota, this is a two-story house with a wide veranda. It is decorated in a country style with original stencil designs, stained glass and family heirlooms. The Elizabeth Room holds a Jenny Lind bed with a hand-crocheted bedcover.

Innkeeper(s): Karen Berget.

Rates:$35-50. MC VISA. Full Bkfst. 3 rooms. 3 with shared baths. Beds:D. AC in room. Skiing.

Seen in: *Forum, Hancock Record.*

Contact: Karen Berget. Certificate may be used: Anytime with advance reservations.

"It was most delightful!"

Preston

The Jail House Historic Inn
109 Houston 3 NW
Preston 55965
(507)765-2181 Fax:(507)765-2558

1869. The Old Fillmore County Jail is better known these days as the Jail House Inn. The current "jailers" are anything but gruff to their guests, who are treated to one of the Midwest's most unique inn settings. The striking Italianate structure, featured in the National Register of Historic Places, offers authentic Victorian decor in its 12 fascinating rooms, including the Cell Block, where guests actually sleep behind bars, the Detention Room and Master Bedroom, with a china tub weighing nearly half a ton. After guests are sprung for the day, they are free to explore the state's historic bluff country. Tours of nearby caves and a fish hatchery are just a few of the activities available.

Innkeeper(s): Marc & Jeanne Barre Sather

Rates:$40-140. MC VISA DS. Full Bkfst. MAP available. 12 rooms. Fireplaces. Beds:KQ. TV, AC in room. Skiing. Fishing.

Contact: Marc Sather. Certificate may be used: Sunday - Thursday, Nov. 1 through April 30.

Princeton

Oakhurst Inn B&B
212 8th Ave S
Princeton 55371
(612)389-3553 (800)443-2258

1906. The Spain family occupies the third floor of their handsomely restored late Victorian bed and breakfast. Located in a small, quiet community of

central Minnesota, Oakhurst was built originally for a local banker. Guests have access to a parlor where afternoon refreshments are served, a library room, and three cheery guest rooms furnished in four-poster, iron, and brass beds. Complimentary bicycles and horseshoes are also available.

Innkeeper(s): Suzie & Dave Spain.

Rates:$60-75. MC VISA. Full Bkfst. MAP available. Gourmet Brkfst. Teas. Evening snacks. 3 rooms. Beds:Q. AC in room. Golf. Tennis. Bicycling. Swimming. Fishing.

Contact: Suzie Spain. Certificate may be used: Year-round, anytime.

"It was like a dream to wake up in your lovely home."

Ray

Bunt's B&B Inns
Lake Kabetogama, 9906 Gappa Rd
Ray 56669
(218)875-2691

1913. Outdoor lovers don't need to settle for dreary lodgings when visiting the Voyageurs National Park area. Bunt's provides a wide range of options for guests with regard to privacy and comfort. A brand-new facility, the Kab-Inn, joins three existing B&B options at Bunt's. Bunt's variety of accommodations allows for family reunions and business groups. Lake Kabetogama is well known for its walleye fishing while other nearby lakes provide additional opportunities for boating and canoeing enthusiasts.

Innkeeper(s): Bob Buntrock.

Rates:$60-120. MC VISA AX DS. Cont. Bkfst. 8 rooms. Beds:KQT. Phone, AC in room. Skiing. Handicap access. Spa. Sauna. Swimming. Fishing.

Contact: Robert Buntrock. Certificate may be used: Anytime.

Red Lake Falls

Sleepy Hollow
155 Bottineau Ave NE
Red Lake Falls 56750
(218)253-2921 (800)210-2022

1917. Northern Minnesota's abundance of waterways is legendary, and visitors exploring the state's Northwestern region will want to know about Sleepy Hollow, which features a veranda overlooking the Clearwater River. A short drive from Thief River Falls, the four-room, two-story Colonial Revival home's property extends to the river bank. The inn's country decor features one room designated the "Lindbergh Room," since the home was built by Charles Lindbergh's half-sister.

Innkeeper(s): Tom & Myrtle Tydlacka

Rates:$45. Cont. Bkfst. 4 rooms. 4 with shared baths. Beds:KDT. Fishing.

Contact: Myrtle Tydlacka. Certificate may be used: May 1-Nov. 1

Red Wing

Pratt-Taber Inn
706 W Fourth St
Red Wing 55066-2414
(612)388-5945

1876. This 18th-century Italianate inn, recognized by the National Register of Historic Places, overlooks the Hiawatha Valley, near the Mississippi River. The decor and surroundings of the inn make visitors feel they have stepped into a bygone era. Early Renaissance Revival and country Victorian antiques add to the inn's authentic feel. Guests also will enjoy the white wicker porch and gingerbread woodwork, not to mention the many fireplaces and the innkeepers' tempting goodies. The well-appointed library and parlor are other favorite spots. No more than 20 minutes away are five scenic golf courses.

Innkeeper(s): Jane & Dick Molander.

Rates:$69-89. MC VISA. Gourmet Brkfst. Evening snacks. 6 rooms. 4 with shared baths. Fireplaces. Beds:KQT. Conference Rm. TV, Phone, AC in room. Bicycling. Skiing. Handicap access. Spa. Swimming. Fishing.

Seen in: *Better Homes & Gardens, Midwest Living.*

Contact: Jane Molander. Certificate may be used: November - August only. Midweek only (Sunday - Thursday nights). No holidays.

"When I need a peaceful moment I dream of the Pratt-Taber and the big screened-in porch with church bells chiming a favorite tune."

St. James Hotel
406 Main St
Red Wing 55066
(612)388-2846 (800)252-1875
Fax:(612)388-5226

1875. The historic St. James provides a glimpse back to the exciting Mississippi riverboat era. The elegant Italianate structure, listed with the

National Register, is filled with classy Victorian touches. Just a block from the riverfront, the St. James has at its back door a city park, providing a restful setting for guests. The inn's rooms, some of which boast river views, sport names such as Samuel Clemens, LaCrosse Queen and Huck Finn, and a third of them carry non-smoking designations. Guests will appreciate the distinctive and period-authentic room furnishings and the detail-oriented staff.

Innkeeper(s): Gene Foster.

Rates:$100-155. MC VISA AX DC DS CB. Full Bkfst. EP. 60 rooms. Beds:Q. Conference Rm. TV, Phone, AC in room. Skiing. Handicap access. Spa. Fishing.

Seen in: *Midwest Living.*

Contact: Marge Truve. Certificate may be used: Sunday through Thursday for free night.

Rushford

Meadows Inn
Box 703, 900 Pine Meadow Ln
Rushford 55971
(507)864-2378 Fax:(507)864-7501

1993. This European-style, two-story stucco home offers panoramic views of the lovely hill country in the Southeastern part of the state. The inn's Chateauesque exterior is complemented by its custom French and European-country interior, high-lighted by the romantic Bridal Chamber. A queen-size hand-crafted four-poster bed, luxurious patterned carpeting, French reproduction furnishings, whirlpool bath and pedestal sink make this room a perfect weekend getaway. The other guest rooms are graced with extra-special touches, such as a collection of music boxes, that add to the inn's elegant ambiance.

Innkeeper(s): Nancy Johnson.

Rates:$50-100. MC VISA DS. Full Bkfst. 6 rooms. 2 with shared baths. Beds:QT. Conference Rm. Phone, AC in room. Tennis. Skiing. Spa.

Contact: Nancy Johnson. Certificate may be used: November through May.

Saint Charles

Victorian Lace Inn
1512 Whitewater Ave
Saint Charles 55972-1234
(507)932-4496

1867. This newly restored brick Victorian features a pleasant front porch where guests often linger to watch an occasional Amish buggy pass by. Lace curtains and antique furnishings are features of the guest rooms.

Innkeeper(s): Sharon & Curt Vreeman.

Rates:$55-70. Full Bkfst. Gourmet Brkfst. Teas. 4 rooms. 4 with shared baths. Beds:QT. Golf. Bicycling. Skiing. Fishing.

Contact: Sharon Vreeman. Certificate may be used: Anytime, November-April. Sunday-Thursday, May-October.

"They have thought of everything."

Saint Paul

The Garden Gate B&B
925 Goodrich Ave
Saint Paul 55105
(612)227-8430 (800)967-2703

1907. One of the most striking of the city's Victoria Crossing neighborhood homes is this recently redecorated Prairie-style Victorian. The large, air-conditioned duplex features guest rooms named Gladiola, Rose and Delphinium, and the rooms are as lovely as they sound. Visitors to the Garden Gate will be enthralled with the treats within walking distance, including other beautiful neighborhood homes, and the well-known shops and restaurants on Grand and Summit avenues. After a busy day of exploring, guests may want to request a therapeutic massage or soak in a clawfoot tub.

Innkeeper(s): Miles & Mary Conway.

Rates:$60-85. ContPlus Bkfst. 5 rooms. 4 with shared baths. AC in room. Bicycling. Swimming.

Contact: Mary Conway. Certificate may be used: Sunday - Thursday only.

Prior's on DeSoto
1522 DeSoto St
Saint Paul 55101
(612)774-2695

1991. Walking distance from Phalen Lake and park, this modern, air-conditioned home, featuring a 20-foot vaulted ceiling, was custom-built by the innkeeper's husband, a building contractor. The attractive residence has been lovingly furnished by Mary, who along with husband Richard, is a seasoned traveler, with 50 states and 23 countries to her credit. This experience makes the innkeepers ideal travel guides for those in need of advice or assistance. Among Mary's breakfast specialties are caramel rolls and scones, and she gladly will meet any of her guests' special dietary needs.

Innkeeper(s): Mary E. Prior.

Rates:$59-79. Full Bkfst. Gourmet Brkfst. Picnic lunches. Teas. Evening snacks. 2 rooms. Beds:KQT. Conference Rm. Phone, AC, Refrig. in room. Golf. Tennis. Skiing. Swimming. Horseback riding. Fishing.

Contact: Mary Prior. Certificate may be used: Sunday through Thursday year-round.

Stillwater

James A. Mulvey Residence Inn
622 W Churchill
Stillwater 55082
(612)430-3453

1878. A charming river town is home to this Italianate-style inn, just a short distance from the Twin Cities, but far from the metro area in atmosphere. Visitors select from five air-conditioned guest rooms, including one suite. The rooms feature queen beds and Victorian furnishings. The inn, just nine blocks from the St. Croix River, is a popular stop with couples celebrating anniversaries. They enjoy the inn's convenient early coffee or tea service that precedes the full breakfasts. Great antiquing, fishing and skiing are enjoyed nearby, and there are many lovely picnic spots in the area.

Innkeeper(s): Trueh & Jill Lawson.

Rates:$95-139. MC VISA. Full Bkfst. 5 rooms. Fireplaces. Beds:Q. AC in room. Skiing. Fishing.

Contact: Jill Lawson. Certificate may be used: Sunday through Thursday.

Vergas

The Log House & Homestead on Spirit Lake
Box 130
Vergas 56587
(218)342-2318 (800)342-2318

1889. Either a log house or farmhouse setting greets guests at this inn, situated on 115 acres of woods and fields adjacent to loon-filled Spirit Lake in the heart of Minnesota's lake country. The three-story log home has recently been joined by a farmhouse, both lovingly restored and decorated, providing the opportunity for additional visitors to discover this romantic, restful setting. Those who desire a more active visit may use the inn's small boat. Hiking and swimming are other options. A favorite activity is just to relax in a porch rocker at sunset, enjoying a view of the lake.

Innkeeper(s): Lyle & Yvonne Tweten.

Rates:$75-105. MC VISA DS. ContPlus Bkfst. Gourmet Brkfst. 4 rooms. Fireplaces. Beds:KQ. AC in room. Farm. Skiing. Handicap access. Swimming. Fishing.

Contact: Yvonne Tweten. Certificate may be used: Sunday through Thursday excepting holidays.

Walker

Tianna Farms B&B
PO Box 968
Walker 56484
(218)547-1306 (800)842-6620
Fax:(218)547-2255

1922. Overlooking beautiful Leech Lake, this former dairy farm also was the site of a golf course, now named Tianna Country Club, where guests receive 50 percent off green fees. The inn's lakefront resort area lures many visitors, who may choose from five rooms, ranging from the Garden and Hunting rooms, with two twin beds, to the Suite, with a king and two twin beds. The family-oriented Tianna Farms also can be reserved at whole-house rates for weekends or full weeks. There are tennis facilities and a trampoline on the premises.

Innkeeper(s): Liza Vogt/Linda Wenzel.

Rates:$45-120. MC VISA DS. Full Bkfst. Evening snacks. 5 rooms. Beds:KQT. Tennis. Skiing. Swimming. Fishing.

Contact: Liza Vogt. Certificate may be used: Oct. 15-May 14.

Mississippi

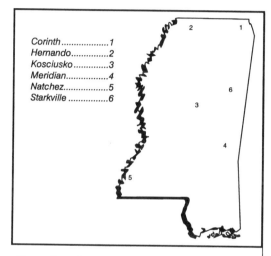

Corinth

Generals' Quarters B&B
924 Fillmore St, PO Box 1505
Corinth 38834
(601)286-3325 Fax:(601)287-4445

1870. History buffs will enjoy this inn, located 22 miles from Shiloh National Military Park, and in the historic district of Corinth, a Civil War village. Visitors to this Queen Anne Victorian, with its quiet, tree-lined lot, enjoy a full Southern breakfast. Three guest rooms and one suite are available. Innkeeper J.L. Aldridge often leads tours of the historic district. Fort Robinette and Corinth National Cemetery are nearby.
Innkeeper(s): J.L. & Rosemary Aldridge.
Rates:$75. MC VISA AX. Full Bkfst. 4 rooms. Fireplaces. Beds:QDT. TV, Phone, AC in room. Swimming. Fishing.
Contact: Rosemary Aldridge. Certificate may be used: Year-round.

Hernando

Sassafras Inn
785 Hwy 51 S
Hernando 38632
(601)429-5864 (800)882-1897
Fax:(601)429-5864

1985. This modern inn offers guests to the state's Northwest corner a delightful respite from their travels or from the hustle and bustle of Memphis, 10 miles north. An impressive indoor swimming pool and spa are guest favorites, and visitors also enjoy the cabana room for reading or lounging, or the recreation room with billiards, darts and ping pong. A romantic honeymoon cottage also is available. Arkabutla Lake is an easy drive from the inn.
Innkeeper(s): Frances & Dennis McClanahan.
Rates:$75-175. MC VISA AX DS. Full Bkfst. Gourmet Dinner. 5 rooms. Beds:Q. Conference Rm. TV, Phone, AC, Refrig. in room. Golf. Tennis. Skiing. Spa. Sauna. Exercise room. Swimming. Horseback riding. Fishing.
Contact: Frances McClanahan. Certificate may be used: Sunday through Thursday.

Kosciusko

The Redbudd Inn
121 N Wells St
Kosciusko 39090
(601)289-5086

1884. Kosciusko, the birthplace of Oprah Winfrey, is also home to this striking Queen Anne Victorian inn, which boasts a long and distinguished history as a traveler's haven. Beautiful woodwork and an impressive square staircase highlight the inn's interior, and its architectural details have made it a well-known local landmark. Five guest rooms are available, all filled with lovely antiques. An antique shop/tea room is on the premises.
Innkeeper(s): Maggie Garrett & Rose Mary Burge.
Rates:$70-100. MC VISA. Full Bkfst. Gourmet Brkfst, Lunch, Dinner. 5

rooms. 1 with shared bath. Fireplaces. Beds:QT. Conference Rm. TV,
Phone, AC in room. Golf. Tennis. Handicap access. Swimming.
Horseback riding. Fishing.

Seen in: *Colonial Homes Magazine.*

Contact: Maggie Garrett. Certificate may be used: Anytime available.

Meridian

Lincoln, Ltd. B&B
PO Box 3479, 2303 23rd Ave
Meridian 39303
(601)482-5483 (800)633-6477
Fax:(601)693-7447

1907. This private suite is in the rear of a Tudor-
style home in Meridian's historic district. It boasts
a carport, fireplace, kitchen, private bath, queen
bed, living room and private entrance. The kitchen
is equipped with the amenities needed for a continental breakfast. Antique furnishings and an abundance of windows, add a bright, cheery feel. The
suite's privacy makes it ideal for business travelers,
those relocating to the area or those desiring more
complete accommodations.

Innkeeper(s): Barbara Hall & Linda Carrier.

Rates:$70-75. MC VISA AX. ContPlus Bkfst. 3 rooms. 2 with shared
baths. Beds:Q. TV, Phone, AC, Refrig. in room. Spa. Swimming.
Fishing.

Seen in: *The Meridian Star, Country Inns, Woman's Day.*

Contact: Barbara Hall. Certificate may be used: Anytime except March,
April or December. Based on availability.

*"I would have missed 99 percent of Mississippi's charm
had I not stayed in your B&Bs. Thank you."*

Natchez

Harper House
201 Arlington Ave
Natchez 39120
(601)445-5557

1892. Located in the Arlington Heights section of
Natchez, this Queen Anne Victorian inn is a fine
example of the city's popular Victorian-style
homes. The inn's conve-
nient location, mid-
way between Baton
Rouge and Vicksburg,
make it an ideal stop
for those exploring
this beautiful and his-
tory-rich region.
Breakfast is served
in a charming gaze-
bo. Natchez-Under-
the-Hill and the
famous antebellum homes in the historic district
are within easy walking distance. Natchez National
Cemetery and Natchez State Park are nearby.

Innkeeper(s): John & Kay Warren.

Rates:$90. MC VISA. Full Bkfst. 2 rooms. Beds:DT. TV, AC in room.
Fishing.

Contact: Kay Warren. Certificate may be used: November, December,
January, February, 1994 and 1995.

Starkville

The Cedars B&B
2173 Oktoc Rd
Starkville 39759
(601)324-7569

1836. This historic plantation offers a glimpse of
life in the 19th-century South. The late
Colonial/Greek Revival structure was built primari-
ly by slaves, with construction lasting two years.
The inn's 183 acres boast fishing ponds, pasture
and woods, and guests love to explore, hike and
ride horses. Four guest rooms are available, two
with private bath. Visitors enjoy the inn's collection of 19th- and early 20th-century horse and farm
equipment. Noxubee Wildlife Refuge and the
Tombigbee National Forest are within easy driving
distance.

Innkeeper(s): Erin Scanlon.

Rates:$45-75. Full Bkfst. Evening snacks. 4 rooms. 2 with shared
baths. Fireplaces. Beds:DT. Conference Rm. Phone, AC in room. Farm.
Swimming. Fishing.

Contact: Erin Scanlon. Certificate may be used: Anytime based on
availability.

Missouri

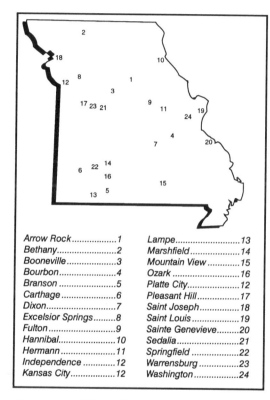

Arrow Rock

Borgman's B&B
706 Van Buren St
Arrow Rock 65320
(816)837-3350

1855. Borgman's B&B features a two-story porch and spacious guest rooms. Air conditioning and three new bathrooms have been added to this historic house. An old Victrola is available for guests' use in the parlor, and Grandma's trunk offers local hand-crafted gift items. Historic Arrow Rock and its Old Tavern are a short walk away.
Innkeeper(s): Kathy & Helen Borgman.

Rates:$45-50. ContPlus Bkfst. 4 rooms. 4 with shared baths. Beds:D. AC in room.

Contact: Kathy Borgman. Certificate may be used: Anytime except Friday and Saturday in June, July and August.

Miss Nelle's B&B
PO Box 122
Arrow Rock 65320
(816)837-3280 (800)795-2794

1853. Historic Arrow Rock, on the Santa Fe Trail, is home to this inn, listed in the National Register. Its Main Street location offers convenient access to

antique establishments, restaurants, shops and the famous Lyceum Theatre. The air-conditioned inn, with its comfy front porch swings, offers two large guest rooms. One of the rooms features a romantic fireplace. Antique furnishings highlight the interior, including the elegant dining room where breakfast is served. Missouri Valley College is nearby.
Innkeeper(s): Linda Hoffman.
Rates:$45. Cont. Bkfst. 2 rooms. 2 with shared baths. Fireplaces.

Beds:D. AC in room.

Contact: Linda Hoffman. Certificate may be used: Weeknights September, 1994-December, 1995.

Bethany

Unicorn Lodge B&B
119 S 15th St
Bethany 64424
(816)425-3676

1937. Midway between Kansas City and Des Moines, this art deco brick hotel offers a pleasant respite for Midwest travelers. Eleven air-conditioned guest rooms are available, and most feature king or queen accommodations. Guests may watch TV in the inn's sitting room or take a relaxing stroll of the town square, just a few steps away. The innkeepers chose the Unicorn name for their establishment because it symbolizes graciousness and tranquility, and visitors will find its likeness throughout. There is a restaurant on the premises.

Innkeeper(s): Bill & Wynn Pollock.

Rates:$40-70. Cont. Bkfst. Picnic lunches. 12 rooms. Beds:KQT. Conference Rm. AC in room.

Contact: Wynn Walter Pollock. Certificate may be used: May through December, 1994 & 1995.

Booneville

Morgan Street Repose B&B
611 E Morgan
Booneville 65233
(816)882-7195 (800)248-5061

1869. The historic Missouri River town of Boonville is home to this inn, composed of two Italianate structures on the site of what once was a hotel that served travelers on the Santa Fe Trail. The inn is listed with the National Register of Historic Places. More than 400 antebellum and Victorian homes and buildings are found in town. Visitors enjoy their gourmet breakfasts in one of three dining rooms or in the Secret Garden. Several state parks are within easy driving distance, and the University of Missouri-Columbia is 20 miles to the east.

Innkeeper(s): Robert & Doris Shenk.

Rates:$60-75. Gourmet Brkfst. Teas. Evening snacks. 3 rooms. Beds:QT. AC, Refrig. in room. Bicycling.

Contact: Doris Shenk. Certificate may be used: Anytime based on availability.

Bourbon

Meramec Farm Bed and Board
Star Route Box 50
Bourbon 65441
(314)732-4765

1883. This farmhouse inn and cedar guest cabin are found on a working cattle operation, little more than an hour's drive from St. Louis. Seven generations have lived and worked the farm, which boasts

460 acres. Visitors stay in the 1880s farmhouse or the cabin, built from cedar cut on the farm. The inn's proximity to the Meramec River and Vilander Bluffs provides lovely views and many outdoor activities. Spring visitors are treated to the sight of baby calves. Meramec Caverns and several state parks are nearby.

Innkeeper(s): Carol Springer & David Curtis.

Rates:$45-70. Full Bkfst. Gourmet Dinner. Picnic lunches. 6 rooms. 5 with shared baths. Fireplaces. Beds:QT. AC, Refrig. in room. Farm. Handicap access. Swimming. Horseback riding. Fishing.

Seen in: *Midwest Motorist, St. Louis Post Dispatch, St. Louis Magazine.*

Contact: Carol Springer. Certificate may be used: Sunday - Thursday, year-round.

Branson

Aunt Sadie's Garden Glade
163 Fountain
Branson 65616
(417)335-4063 (800)944-4250

1968. This secluded home is nestled in a wooded glade, just five minutes from Branson's many activities. The modern ranch home offers two lovely guest rooms and a cottage that sleeps up to five adults. The Paisley Room features a queen bed and fireplace, while the Rose Room boasts king and three-quarter beds and a spa. The inn's big country breakfast, served family style, includes homemade biscuits and gravy, several entrees, fruit and pastry.

A large outdoor deck is the perfect place for bird-watching, relaxing or socializing.

Innkeeper(s): Linda & Richard Hovell.

Rates:$65-85. MC VISA AX. Full Bkfst. 3 rooms. Fireplaces. Beds:KQT. AC, Refrig. in room. Swimming. Fishing.

Contact: Linda Hovell. Certificate may be used: Dec. 1, 1994-April 1, 1995 and Dec. 1-30, 1995.

Inn at Fall Creek

391 Concord Ave
Branson 65615
(417)336-3422 (800)280-3422
Fax:(417)336-5950

1982. Surrounded by 60 wooded acres, this modern inn offers five guest rooms, two of them suites. Less than two miles from Branson's "strip," the inn is ideally located for those taking advantage of the area's many attractions, including nearby Silver Dollar City and Talking Rocks. Guests are treated to early coffee or tea and an evening snack in addition to a full breakfast. The inn's guest rooms are furnished in country decor. Rooms with fireplace, kitchenette or spa are available.

Innkeeper(s): J. C. McCracken.

Rates:$65-105. MC VISA. Full Bkfst. Evening snacks. 5 rooms. Fireplaces. Beds:KQ. TV, AC, Refrig. in room. Spa. Swimming. Fishing.

Contact: J. C. McCracken. Certificate may be used: Dec. 1, 1994-March 30, 1995.

Carthage

Grand Avenue Inn

1615 Grand Ave
Carthage 64835
(417)358-7265

1893. Historic Carthage, site of the first major land battle of the Civil War after war was formally

declared by Congress, is home to many impressive Victorian structures, built after the war's end. This

Queen Anne Victorian inn is one of many examples of that architecture found in town. Five guest rooms are available, and Albert's and Belle's rooms may be combined to form a suite. Guests also are welcome to relax in the inn's outdoor pool. Be sure to visit the Jasper County Courthouse, a stunning Romanesque Revival structure found in Carthage Square. Truman's birthplace is within easy driving distance.

Innkeeper(s): Paula Hunt & Betty Nisich.

Rates:$55-85. MC VISA. Full Bkfst. Gourmet Brkfst. Teas. Evening snacks. 6 rooms. 1 with shared bath. Beds:QD. AC, Refrig. in room. Bicycling. Fishing.

Contact: Paula Hunt. Certificate may be used: Mondays through Thursdays preferred - weekday & weekend night OK, i.e. Thursday and Friday or Sunday and Monday evenings' stay. (January - March, 1995 preferred).

Dixon

Rock Eddy Bluff

HCR 62, Box 241
Dixon 65459
(314)759-6081

1975. This inn's rural, off-the-beaten-path location is ideal for those seeking a secluded, country retreat. Visitors choose from two guest rooms or the three-bedroom Turkey Ridge Cottage. The East and West rooms offer antique furnishings, queen beds and TVs, not to mention magnificent views. Amid a rolling river valley and wooded ridges, the inn's setting is a nature lover's delight, complete with canoeing, fishing and hiking. Canoes are provided, and the innkeepers will take guests on horse-drawn wagon excursions. More than 75 species of birds have been sighted here, including bald eagles and great blue herons.

Innkeeper(s): Tom & Kathy Corey.

Rates:$42-97. Full Bkfst. Picnic lunches. 5 rooms. 5 with shared baths. Fireplaces. Beds:Q. Phone, AC, Refrig. in room. Farm. Swimming. Fishing.

Contact: Tom Corey. Certificate may be used: Monday-Thursday nights.

Excelsior Springs

Crescent Lake Manor

1261 St. Louis Ave
Excelsior Springs 64024
(816)637-2958 (800)897-2958

Surrounded by a moat, this three-story Georgian-style house is just a half-hour drive from Kansas City. The three guest rooms are decorated with country and traditional touches, and a swimming pool and tennis court are found on the 21-acre grounds. Golfers will find a challenge at Excelsior Springs Golf Course, and many guests enjoy visiting the nearby Hall of Waters for a relaxing mineral bath and massage.

Innkeeper(s): Mary Elizabeth Leake.

Rates:$55-60. MC VISA. Full Bkfst. 3 rooms. 2 with shared baths. Fireplaces. Beds:QT. Conference Rm. TV, Phone, AC, Refrig. in room. Bicycling. Fishing.

Contact: Mary Elizabeth Leake. Certificate may be used: Monday through Thursday.

Fulton

Loganberry Inn
310 W 7th St
Fulton 65251
(314)642-9229

1899. The Loganberry Inn is decorated in berry shades and has antique furnishings in the English country-style. Upstairs are pegged doors from the 1850s that predate the house. Guests may relax in the parlor by the fireplace. The inn serves homemade bread and apple butter.

Innkeeper(s): Bob & Deb Logan.

Rates:$55-75. MC VISA. Full Bkfst. 4 rooms. 2 with shared baths. Beds:QT. AC in room. Fishing.

Seen in: *The Fulton Sun.*

Contact: Deborah Logan. Certificate may be used: Sunday through Thursday.

"Thank you for sharing your lovely home and gracious hospitality with us."

Hannibal

Fifth Street Mansion B&B
213 S Fifth St
Hannibal 63401
(314)221-0445 (800)874-5661

1958. This 20-room Italianate house displays extended eaves and heavy brackets, tall windows

and decorated lintels. A cupola affords a view of the town. Mark Twain was invited to dinner here by the Garth family and joined Laura Frazer (his Becky Thatcher) for the evening. An enormous stained-glass window lights the stairwell. The library features a stained-glass window with the family crest and is paneled with hand-grained walnut.

Innkeeper(s): Donalene & Mike Andreotti.

Rates:$40-95. MC VISA AX DS. Full Bkfst. 7 rooms. Beds:Q. Conference Rm. Phone, AC in room. Fishing.

Seen in: *Innsider.*

Contact: Michael Andreotti. Certificate may be used: Sunday-Thursday, November-March, except holiday weekends.

"We thoroughly enjoyed our visit. Terrific food and hospitality!"

Garth Woodside Mansion
RR 1 Box 304
Hannibal 63401
(314)221-2789

1871. This Italian Renaissance mansion is set on 39 acres of meadow and woodland. Original Victorian antiques fill the house. An unusual flying

staircase with no visible means of support vaults three stories. Best of all, is the Samuel Clemens Room where Mark Twain slept. Afternoon beverage is served, and there are nightshirts tucked away in your room.

Innkeeper(s): Irv & Diane Feinberg.

Rates:$65-105. MC VISA. Full Bkfst. Gourmet Brkfst. Teas. 8 rooms. Beds:QT. Conference Rm. AC in room. Golf. Tennis. Fishing.

Seen in: *Country Inns, Chicago Sun-Times, Glamour Magazine, Victorian Homes, Midwest Living, Innsider.*

Contact: Irv Feinberg. Certificate may be used: Sunday through Thursday, November through March.

"So beautiful and romantic and relaxing, we forgot we were here to work," Jeannie and Bob Ransom, Innsider.

Hermann

Reiff House B&B
306 Market St
Hermann 65041
(314)486-2994

1871. Hermann, once a busy Missouri River port city, now is home to a beautiful National Historic District, where the inn is found. A three-story former hotel, the first floor holds the Hermann visitor center. Guest rooms include the romantic Ivy Rose Suite. Breakfasts, which may feature freshly squeezed orange juice, German sausage, homemade muffins, quiche and sugar-free strawberry trifle, are enjoyed in the sitting room or courtyard, which turns into a German biergarten during Maifest and Oktoberfest weekends.

Innkeeper(s): Nancy Coleman.

Rates:$55. Full Bkfst. EP. Gourmet Brkfst. Evening snacks. 3 rooms. 2 with shared baths. Beds:Q. AC in room.

Contact: Nancy Coleman. Certificate may be used: All times excluding months of May and October.

Independence

Woodstock Inn
1212 W Lexington
Independence 64050
(816)833-2233

1900. This turn-of-the-century home is in the perfect location for sightseeing in historic Independence. Visit the home of Harry S. Truman or the Truman Library and Museum. The Old Jail Museum is another popular attraction. A large country breakfast is served each morning. Independence is less than 30 minutes from Kansas City where you may spend the day browsing through the shops at Country Club Plaza or Halls' Crown Center.

Innkeeper(s): Mona & Ben Crosby.

Rates:$45. MC VISA AX. Full Bkfst. 13 rooms. Beds:QDT. AC in room. Swimming. Fishing.

Seen in: *Country Magazine, San Francisco Chronicle.*

Contact: Mona Crosby. Certificate may be used: January, February, March, April-anytime. June, July, August, September-no weekend night (Friday-Saturday) Sunday-Thursday. October, November, December-anytime.

"Pleasant, accommodating people, a facility of good character."

Kansas City

Dome Ridge
14360 NW Walker Rd
Kansas City 64164
(816)532-4074

1982. The innkeeper custom-built this inn, a geodesic dome in a country setting just 10 minutes from the airport. One guest room boasts a king bed with a white iron and brass headboard, double spa and separate shower. In the inn's common areas, guest may enjoy a barbecue, CD player, fireplace, gazebo, library and pool table. The gourmet breakfasts, usually featuring Belgian waffles or California omelets, are served in the dining room, but guests are advised that the inn's kitchen is well worth checking out.

Innkeeper(s): William & Roberta Faust.

Rates:$50-95. Gourmet Brkfst. 4 rooms. 1 with shared bath. Beds:KQD. AC in room. Golf. Skiing. Spa. Swimming. Fishing.

Contact: Roberta Faust. Certificate may be used: Sunday through Thursday, all year.

Lampe

Grandpa's Farm B&B
Box 476, HCR1
Lampe 65681
(417)779-5106 (800)280-5106

1891. This limestone farmhouse in the heart of the Ozarks offers guests a chance to experience country life in a relaxed farm setting. Midway between Silver Dollar City and Eureka Springs, Ark., the inn boasts several lodging options, including a duplex with suites, guest room and honeymoon suite. All feature air conditioning, ceiling fans, private baths and private entrances. The innkeepers are known for their substantial country breakfast and say guests enjoy comparing how long the meal lasts before they eat again. Although the inn's 186 acres are not farmed extensively, domesticated farm animals are on the premises.

Innkeeper(s): Keith and Pat Lamb.

Rates:$65-85. MC VISA DS. Full Bkfst. 4 rooms. Fireplaces. Beds:KDT. Conference Rm. Phone, AC, Refrig. in room. Farm. Handicap access. Spa. Exercise room. Swimming. Fishing.

Contact: Pat Lamb. Certificate may be used: Nov. 1-April 30.

Marshfield

The Dickey House B&B Inn
331 S Clay St
Marshfield 65706
(417)468-3000 Fax:(417)468-3002

1913. This Colonial Revival mansion is framed by ancient oak trees and boasts eight massive two-story Ionic columns. Burled woodwork, beveled glass and

polished hardwood floors accentuate the gracious rooms. Interior columns soar in the parlor, creating a suitably elegant setting for the innkeeper's outstanding collection of antiques. A queen-size canopy bed, fireplace and balcony are featured in the Heritage Room.

Innkeeper(s): William & Dorothy Buesgen.

Rates:$45-95. MC VISA. Full Bkfst. Gourmet Brkfst. 6 rooms. Beds:KQD. TV, AC in room. Handicap access. Fishing.

Contact: Dorothy Buesgen. Certificate may be used: Anytime.

"Thanks so much for all that you did to make our wedding special."

Mountain View

Merrywood Guest House
PO Box 42
Mountain View 65548
(417)934-2210

1897. This turn-of-the-century farmhouse in South-Central Missouri offers visitors four guest rooms. Antique country furnishings, bay windows, beaded ceilings, ceiling fans and pine floors add to the inn's charming interior, and guests also will enjoy relaxing on the front porch, with its rockers and swing. Guests are treated to afternoon tea and an evening snack in addition to their full country breakfasts. The surrounding area offers antiquing,

birdwatching, fishing, golf, and canoeing trips on the nearby Jacks Fork River can be arranged.

Innkeeper(s): Henry & LaVonne Justis.

Rates:$60. Full Bkfst. Teas. Evening snacks. 4 rooms. 4 with shared baths. Beds:DT. Refrig. in room. Farm. Fishing.

Contact: LaVonne Justis. Certificate may be used: Sunday through Thursday except July and August.

Ozark

Country Lane Cabin
254 Carriage Ln
Ozark 65721
(417)581-7372 (800)866-5903

1993. Located between Springfield and Branson, this contemporary log cabin offers old-fashioned country charm. The inn is a popular honeymoon destination, with many comforts provided for a romantic getaway. A fireplace, queen bed, refrigerator and a whirlpool bath are some of the amenities provided. Guests also enjoy early coffee and tea plus a full country breakfast and evening snack. A cozy front porch, pine floors and a handmade quilt add to the atmosphere. Fine antiquing is found nearby.

Innkeeper(s): Aaron & Nancy Hughes.

Rates:$70. Full Bkfst. Evening snacks. 1 room. Fireplaces. Beds:Q. AC, Refrig. in room. Spa.

Contact: Nancy Hughes. Certificate may be used: January through May, 1995.

Dear's Rest Bed & Breakfast
1408 Capp Hill Ranch Rd
Ozark 65721
(417)485-3839 (800)588-2262

1988. Amish craftsmen fashioned this cedar log house in a beautiful, secluded wooded setting that is close to Southwest Missouri's many attractions. The B&B only accommodates one party at a time, providing guests extraordinary comfort and privacy. A fireplace and outdoor hot tub add to the allure. The surrounding area abounds with wildlife and many guests enjoy hiking along nearby Bull Creek in the Mark Twain National Forest.

Innkeeper(s): Linda & Allan Schilter.

Rates:$55. MC VISA. Full Bkfst. 1 room. Fireplaces. Beds:DT. Phone, AC, Refrig. in room. Skiing. Spa. Swimming. Fishing.

Seen in: *Voice and View, Ozark Headliner.*

Contact: Linda Schilter. Certificate may be used: Monday through Thursday only during September, January, February and March.

Merrywoods B&B

493 Bluff Dr
Ozark 65721
(417)581-5676 (800)381-2327

1980. Situated on a bluff overlooking the Finley River, this contemporary lodge home offers convenient access to nearby Branson, Silver Dollar City and Springfield. Merrywoods is home to hundreds of teddy bears, and many guests also have caught glimpses of living creatures, such as deer and turkey, on the inn's grounds. Furnished in country decor, each of the three air-conditioned guest rooms offers a private balcony, queen bed and sitting area with bench, chair and loveseat. Ozark is well known for its antique shops, and there is much to see in the vicinity, including Wilson's Creek National Battlefield.

Innkeeper(s): Gail & David Beard.

Rates:$55-85. MC VISA. ContPlus Bkfst. 3 rooms. Beds:Q. AC in room. Skiing. Handicap access. Swimming. Fishing.

Contact: Gail & David Beard. Certificate may be used: December - March, 1994 & 1995.

Platte City

Basswood Country Inn Resort

15880 Interurban Rd
Platte City 64079
(816)858-5556 (800)242-2775
Fax:(816)858-5556

1935. Once the country estate of A.J. Stephens, this unusual B&B combines an RV resort with a country inn. However, with more than 73 wooded acres, there's plenty of room for both. The setting is pristine with seven spring-fed fishing lakes stocked with bass, crappie and carp. We recommend the original red cottage situated at the water's edge. It features a large stone fireplace and a brass bed with bucolic views of water and woodland. The motel-like main building also has a lake view. The Celebrity House features such names as The Trumans, Bing Crosby and Rudy Vallee who stayed here in the '40s and '50s.

Innkeeper(s): Don & Betty Soper.

Rates:$63-125. MC VISA DS. Cont. Bkfst. 8 rooms. Fireplaces. Beds:KQT. Conference Rm. Phone, AC, Refrig. in room. Golf. Tennis. Skiing. Handicap access. Swimming. Fishing.

Seen in: *The Landmark, Platte Dispatch-Tribune, Electric Farmer.*

Contact: Betty Soper. Certificate may be used: Sept. 15-May 15.

"From the moment we walked into our cabin to the moment we left (although we didn't want to!), we experienced one of the most relaxing, enjoyable weekends we've had in years."

Pleasant Hill

Pleasant Stay Inn

140 First St
Pleasant Hill 64080
(816)987-5900

1886. Pleasant Hill's only three-story structure houses three unique guest rooms. Visitors choose from country, Southwest or Victorian decor in their rooms, which all sport dining areas. An easy getaway from the Kansas City metro area, Pleasant Hill offers a refreshing, small-town atmosphere and impressive antique shops. Honeymoon suite arrangements can be made. Central Missouri State University, Powell Gardens and the James A. Reed Memorial Wildlife Refuge are within easy driving distance.

Innkeeper(s): Randy & Marie Tarry.

Rates:$45-55. MC VISA. Full Bkfst. 3 rooms. Beds:DT. AC, Refrig. in room. Fishing.

Contact: Marie Tarry. Certificate may be used: July 1, 1994 through Oct. 31, 1994; July 1, 1995 through Oct. 31, 1995.

Saint Joseph

Harding House

219 N 20th St
Saint Joseph 64501
(816)232-7020

1905. This turn-of-the-century four-square home was built for George Johnson. At the time, Johnson was vice president and general manager of Wyeth Hardware, the world's largest hardware-supply company. Fourteen beveled leaded-glass windows, beautiful oak woodwork and gracious pocket doors are among its features. Furnishings are antique. Lemon bread and tea or other beverages are served in the late afternoon.

Innkeeper(s): Glen & Mary Harding.

Rates:$40-55. MC VISA AX DS. Full Bkfst. Gourmet Brkfst. Teas. Evening snacks. 5 rooms. 4 with shared baths. Fireplaces. Beds:Q. Conference Rm. AC in room.

Seen in: *Country Magazine, News Press Gazette, Saint Joseph Telegraph.*

Contact: Mary Harding. Certificate may be used: January - June, August - September, November - December. Excluding July & October.

"Our stay in your home has been an experience of pure delight."

Saint Louis

Doelling Haus
4817 Towne South
Saint Louis 63128
(314)894-6796

1965. This suburban, two-story Dutch Colonial serves as a home away from home for St. Louis-area visitors. Guests choose from the Blue Danube, Bavarian or Black Forest rooms. Central air ensures year-round comfort, and guests are welcome to park in the garage. A family room with cable TV, a patio and sitting room also are popular places to relax. The innkeepers sometimes can accommodate visitors' pets if prior agreement is reached. The inn offers convenient access to interstate highways, and the historic towns of Hermann, St. Charles and St. Genevieve are within easy driving distance.

Innkeeper(s): Carol & David Doelling.

Rates:$55-60. Full Bkfst. AP available. Gourmet Brkfst. Teas. 3 rooms. 2 with shared baths. Beds:Q. Phone, AC in room. Skiing. Swimming. Fishing.

Contact: Carol Haynes-Doelling. Certificate may be used: Year-round.

The Eastlake Inn Bed & Breakfast
703 N Kirkwood Rd
Saint Louis 63122
(314)965-0066

1920. Just minutes from St. Louis, in the town of Kirkwood, this inn features the turn-of-the-century style of decor made popular by furniture designer

Charles Eastlake. These period antiques add elegance and charm to the Colonial Revival inn. A collection of antique dolls and bears, and the dining room's 1,129-piece chandelier also receive attention. The full breakfasts sometimes are enjoyed on the inn's sun porch. The Ulysses S. Grant National Historic Site, Hidden Valley Ski Area and Six Flags over Mid-America are nearby.

Innkeeper(s): Lori & Dan Ashdown.

Rates:$55-70. MC VISA. Full Bkfst. Teas. 3 rooms. Beds:QD. Conference Rm. AC in room. Golf. Tennis. Skiing. Swimming.

Contact: Lori Ashdown. Certificate may be used: Oct. 1, 1994-Dec. 31, 1995, Sunday through Thursday, holidays excluded.

Soulard
1014 Lami
Saint Louis 63104
(314)773-3002

1850. One of the oldest buildings in St. Louis, this newly renovated Victorian inn now serves as a neighborhood showpiece. Its location in the historic district of Soulard accounts for the French influence found throughout the area, also known for its blues and jazz clubs. Guest rooms include the Queen Anne Suite, with cable TV, cherry wood furniture, clawfoot tub, lace curtains, queen bed and sitting room; and the Soulard Suite, which offers a lovely view of downtown and the arch from its window seats. Be sure to inquire about special-occasion packages, including anniversaries and sports or theater events.

Innkeeper(s): Raymond Ellerbeck.

Rates:$85. MC. Full Bkfst. AP available. 4 rooms. 3 with shared baths. Fireplaces. Beds:Q. TV, Phone, AC, Refrig. in room. Tennis. Bicycling. Swimming. Fishing.

Contact: Raymond Ellerbeck. Certificate may be used: Anytime.

The Winter House
3522 Arsenal St
Saint Louis 63118
(314)664-4399

1897. Original brass hardware, three fireplaces and a turret provide ambiance at this turn-of-the-century brick Victorian. Embossed French paneling adds

elegance. The suite features a balcony and the bedroom has a pressed-tin ceiling. The home is ideally located three miles from the downtown area. Exotic restaurants are within walking distance. Breakfast is served on antique Wedgewood china and includes freshly squeezed orange juice, gourmet coffees, teas and a selection of breads, muffins and fruit.

Innkeeper(s): Kendall & Sarah Winter.

Rates:$65-80. MC VISA AX DC DS CB. ContPlus Bkfst. 3 rooms. Fireplaces. Beds:QD. AC in room. Skiing. Swimming. Fishing.

Seen in: *Innsider.*

Contact: Sarah Winter. Certificate may be used: Monday-Thursday, November through February.

"A delightful house with spotless, beautifully appointed rooms, charming hosts. Highly recommended."

Sainte Genevieve

The Southern Hotel
146 S Third St
Sainte Genevieve 63670
(314)883-3493 (800)275-1412

1790. This Federal building is the largest and oldest brick home west of the Mississippi. It features a long front porch, large parlors and a spacious dining room. Highlights of the guest rooms include cedar bedposts carved in the shape of Old Man River, a hand-painted headboard and a delicately carved Victorian bed. The clawfoot tubs are hand-painted. Guests are invited to add their names to a quilt-in-progress, which is set out in the parlor.

Innkeeper(s): Mike & Barbara Hankins.

Rates:$80-110. MC VISA. Full Bkfst. Gourmet Brkfst. 8 rooms. Fireplaces. Beds:KQ. Conference Rm. AC in room. Swimming. Fishing.

Seen in: *Innsider, St. Louis Gourmet, River Heritage Gazette.*

Contact: Mike Hankins. Certificate may be used: Jan. 5 through Dec. 20, Sunday through Thursday except holidays.

"I can't imagine ever staying in a motel again! It was so nice to be greeted by someone who expected us. We felt right at home."

Sedalia

Sedalia House
Rt 4, Box 25
Sedalia 65301
(816)826-6615

1907. A working farm on 300 scenic acres is home to this spacious Colonial Revival inn, just two miles from town. Rolling hills, ponds and woods offer guests many outdoor recreational opportunities, including birdwatching and hiking. Guests enjoy a hearty country breakfast before heading out to explore the area's many attractions, including Bothwell Lodge, Katy Trail State Park and Whiteman Air Force Base, home of the stealth

bomber. Sedalia also hosts the Missouri State Fair and the Scott Joplin ragtime music festival.

Innkeeper(s): Daniel Ice.

Rates:$58-65. MC VISA. Full Bkfst. 6 rooms. 5 with shared baths. Beds:KQT. AC in room. Farm.

Contact: Daniel Ice. Certificate may be used: September through May.

Springfield

Walnut Street Inn
900 E Walnut St
Springfield 65806
(417)864-6346 (800)593-6346
Fax:(417)864-6184

1894. This three-story Queen Anne gabled house has cast-iron Corinthian columns and a veranda. Polished wood floors and antiques are featured throughout. Upstairs you'll find the gathering room with a fireplace. Ask for the McCann guest room with two bay windows. A full breakfast is served, including items such as peach-stuffed French toast.

Innkeeper(s): Nancy & Karol Brown.

Rates:$80-150. MC VISA AX DC DS CB. Full Bkfst. AP available. Gourmet Brkfst. 14 rooms. Fireplaces. Beds:Q. Conference Rm. TV, Phone, AC, Refrig. in room. Golf. Handicap access. Fishing.

Seen in: *Midwest Living, Victoria Magazine, Country Inns, Innsider Magazine.*

Contact: Karol Brown. Certificate may be used: Sunday - Thursday, excluding holidays.

Warrensburg

Cedarcroft Farm B&B
431 SE "Y" Hwy
Warrensburg 64093
(816)747-5728 (800)368-4944

1867. John Adams, a Union army veteran and Sandra's great grandfather, built this house. There are 80 acres of woodland, meadows and creeks where deer, fox, coyotes and wild turkeys still roam. Two original barns remain. The house offers

two upstairs rooms that share a downstairs bath. Bill participates in Civil War re-enactments and is happy to demonstrate clothing, weapons and customs of the era. Sandra cares for her quarter horses and provides the home-baked, full country breakfasts.

Innkeeper(s): Sandra & Bill Wayne.

Rates:$48-53. MC VISA DS. Full Bkfst. 2 rooms. 2 with shared baths. AC in room. Farm. Skiing. Horseback riding. Fishing.

Seen in: *Kansas City Star, Higginsville Advance, Midwest Motorist, and KCTV.*

Contact: Bill Wayne. Certificate may be used: Sunday-Thursday nights, except August.

"We enjoyed the nostalgia and peacefulness very much."

Washington

Schwegmann House
438 W Front St
Washington 63090
(314)239-5025 (800)949-2262

1861. John F. Schwegmann, a native of Germany, built a flour mill on the Missouri riverfront. His stately three-story home was constructed to provide extra lodging for overnight customers who traveled long hours to town. Today, guests enjoy the formal gardens and patios overlooking the river, as well as gracious rooms decorated with antiques and handmade quilts.

Innkeeper(s): Catherine & William Nagel.

Rates:$60-75. MC VISA. Full Bkfst. Gourmet Brkfst. Teas. Evening snacks. 10 rooms. 2 with shared baths. Beds:QD. AC in room. Handicap access. Swimming. Fishing.

Seen in: *St. Louis Post-Dispatch, West County Journal.*

Contact: Catherine Nagel. Certificate may be used: November-March, Monday through Friday only.

"Like Grandma's house many years ago."

Montana

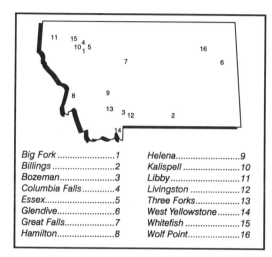

Big Fork

Burggraf's Countrylane B&B
Rainbow Dr
Big Fork 59911
(406)837-4608 (800)525-3344
Fax:(406)837-2468

1984. This contemporary log home on Swan Lake, minutes from Flathead Lake in the Rockies, offers fine accommodations in one of America's most beautiful settings. Upon arrival, visitors enjoy hors d'oeuvres, chilled wine, and fresh fruit. Ceiling fans, clock radios and turndown service are amenities. Picnic baskets are available and would be ideal for taking along on a paddle boat lake excursion. Excellent skiing and snowmobiling opportunities await winter visitors, and all will enjoy the inn's seven scenic acres.

Innkeeper(s): Natalie & RJ Burggraf.

Rates:$85. MC VISA. Full Bkfst. Gourmet Brkfst. Picnic lunches. Teas. Evening snacks. 6 rooms. Beds:KQT. Skiing. Handicap access. Swimming. Fishing.

Contact: Natalie Burggraf. Certificate may be used: Early spring, summer, early fall.

Billings

The Sanderson Inn
2038 S 56th St
Billings 59106
(406)656-3388

1905. This turn-of-the-century Folk Victorian inn is found in a farm setting just two miles out of town. Three guest rooms, all with ceiling fans, queen beds and private baths are available to visitors, who will enjoy the peaceful, family-oriented setting. Eastern Montana College is in busy Billings, where two interstates join together. Guests are treated to a full breakfast before heading out to explore local attractions and activities, which could include antiquing, fishing and visiting museums. Lake Elmo State Park and Pompey's Pillar are nearby.

Innkeeper(s): Margaret Sanderson.

Rates:$30-60. MC. Full Bkfst. 3 rooms. Beds:Q. Farm. Fishing.

Contact: Margaret Sanderson. Certificate may be used: Oct. 1-June 1.

Bozeman

The Torch & Toes B&B
309 S Third Ave
Bozeman 59715
(406)586-7285 (800)446-2138
Fax:(406)586-7285

1906. This Colonial Revival home, three blocks from the center of town, boasts an old-fashioned front porch and a carriage house. Antique furnishings in the parlor feature a Victrola. A pillared and carved oak fireplace and bay window seat adorn the

dining room. Ron is a professor of architecture at nearby Montana State University.

Innkeeper(s): Ron & Judy Hess.

Rates:$65-70. MC VISA. Full Bkfst. 4 rooms. Beds:KQT. Golf. Tennis. Skiing. Swimming. Horseback riding. Fishing.

Seen in: *Bozeman Chronicle, San Francisco Peninsula Parent, Northwest Magazine.*

Contact: Judith Hess. Certificate may be used: Off-season: Oct. 1, 1994 - April 30, 1995.

"Thanks for your warm hospitality."

Voss Inn

319 S Willson
Bozeman 59715
(406)587-0982

1883. The Voss Inn is a restored two-story house with a large front porch and a Victorian parlor. Old-fashioned furnishings include an upright piano and chandelier. A full breakfast is served, with fresh baked rolls kept in a unique warmer that's built into an ornate 1880s radiator.

Innkeeper(s): Bruce & Frankee Muller.

Rates:$70-85. MC VISA DC. Full Bkfst. Gourmet Brkfst. Picnic lunches. Teas. 6 rooms. Beds:KQT. Phone, AC in room. Golf. Bicycling. Skiing. Horseback riding. Fishing.

Seen in: *Sunset, Cosmopolitan, Gourmet, Countryside.*

Contact: Bruce Muller. Certificate may be used: Year-round.

"First class all the way."

Columbia Falls

Historic Plum Creek House

985 Vans Ave
Columbia Falls 59912
(406)892-1816 (800)682-1429
Fax:(406)892-1876

1957. Incredible views of the Flathead Valley's forests and mountains greet guests at this contemporary riverfront ranch inn. The inn offers something for everyone, even family pets who may stay in the sheltered outdoor kennel. Outdoor recreational opportunities are boundless, but guests who wish to put their feet up and relax also will find this air-conditioned inn to their liking. A heated pool and outdoor spa lure many guests. Glacier National Park can be seen from the inn and is just a short drive away.

Innkeeper(s): Caroline Stevens.

Rates:$60-95. MC VISA AX DC DS CB. Full Bkfst. Gourmet Brkfst, Dinner. Teas. Evening snacks. 5 rooms. Fireplaces. Beds:Q. TV, Phone, AC in room. Bicycling. Skiing. Spa. Swimming. Fishing.

Contact: Caroline Stevens. Certificate may be used: Jan. 5 to May 1, Sept. 15 - Dec. 15.

Essex

Izaak Walton Inn

123 Izaak Walton Rd, PO Box 653
Essex 59916
(406)888-5700 Fax:(406)888-5200

1939. The Izaak Walton Inn was built as an overnight lodging for Great Northern Railway workers. It is located now on the Burlington-Northern Mainline and is served twice daily by Amtrak. The inn is in a strategic location for enjoying Glacier National Park. You can take trails and rivers into the Rocky Mountain forests and meadows.

Innkeeper(s): Larry & Lynda Vielleux.

Rates:$72-92. MC VISA. Full Bkfst. AP available. Picnic lunches. 31 rooms. 20 with shared baths. Beds:QT. Conference Rm. Bicycling. Skiing. Sauna.

Seen in: *Outdoor America-Summer, Seattle Times.*

Contact: Cindy Dills. Certificate may be used: April 15 - June 15; Sept. 15 - Dec. 15; excluding all holidays.

"The coziest cross-country ski resort in the Rockies."

Glendive

The Hostetler House B&B

113 N Douglas
Glendive 59330
(406)365-4505 Fax:(406)365-8456

1912. Casual country decor mixed with handmade and heirloom furnishings are highlights at this two-story inn. The inn features many comforting touch-

es, such as a romantic hot tub and gazebo, enclosed sun porch and sitting room filled with books. The two guest rooms share a bath, and are furnished lovingly by Dea, an interior decorator. The full breakfasts may be enjoyed on Grandma's china on the dining room or on the deck or sun porch. The Yellowstone River is one block from the inn and downtown shopping is two blocks away. Makoshika

State Park, home of numerous fossil finds, is nearby.
Innkeeper(s): Craig & Dea Hostetler.
Rates:$45. Full Bkfst. Gourmet Brkfst. 2 rooms. 2 with shared baths. Beds:D. AC in room. Skiing. Spa. Swimming. Fishing.
Contact: Dea Hostetler. Certificate may be used: Anytime.

Great Falls

The Chalet B&B Inn
1204 4th Ave, N
Great Falls 59401
(406)452-9001 (800)786-9002

1909. This simple stick-style Victorian chalet features handsomely decorated rooms highlighted by polished woodwork, French doors, beamed ceilings and leaded-glass windows. Margie is a noted San Francisco interior designer, now back in her hometown. David continues to carry on a family tradition as a violin maker. The C.M. Russell Museum is across the street on Old West Trail.
Innkeeper(s): Margie Matthews-Anderson & David Anderson.
Rates:$40-50. AX DS. ContPlus Bkfst. Gourmet Dinner. Picnic lunches. Evening snacks. 5 rooms. 3 with shared baths. Beds:KQT. TV, Phone, AC, Refrig. in room. Bicycling. Skiing. Swimming. Fishing.
Seen in: *Great Falls Tribune.*
Contact: Marge Matthews-Anderson & Dave Anderson Certificate may be used: Open.

"Thanks for the royal treatment."

Three Feathers Inn
626 5th Ave N
Great Falls 59401
(406)453-5257

1904. This Victorian house, in the historic area, was built for A. T. Belzer. It was converted to a boarding house during the Depression and remained until the mid-1980s. The house was restored in 1987 and became the Three Pheasant Inn. Its common rooms include glassed-in sun porches, a parlor and library. Guest rooms are filled with Victorian-style antiques. The garden is graced with a 100-year-old fountain and a gazebo.
Innkeeper(s): Helen & Mike Pluhar.
Rates:$50-75. MC VISA. Full Bkfst. Picnic lunches. Teas. 5 rooms. 3 with shared baths. Beds:QT. Phone in room. Bicycling. Skiing. Swimming. Fishing.
Contact: Mike Pluhar. Certificate may be used: December, 1994; January, February, 1995.

"Have stayed at many B&Bs in England, Scotland and Ireland, but yours has been the nicest."

Hamilton

The Bavarian Farmhouse B&B
163 Bowman Rd
Hamilton 59840
(406)363-4063

1898. Bavarian hospitality and flavor is found at this farmhouse inn, nestled amid a grove of large trees. Five guest rooms, four with private baths, are available. Visitors are treated to a hearty German farm breakfast consisting of boiled eggs, breads, coffee, cereal, cheese, cold cuts, jam, juice, rolls and tea. The innkeepers, both experienced travelers, are happy to help arrange fishing, floating, horseback riding or hunting excursions if given advance notice. Efficiency cabins also are available. The Daly Mansion and Sleeping Child Hot Springs are within easy driving distance.
Innkeeper(s): Peter & Ahn Reuthlinger.
Rates:$45-55. Full Bkfst. Teas. 5 rooms. 1 with shared bath. Beds:QD. Skiing. Swimming. Fishing.
Contact: Ahn Reuthlinger. Certificate may be used: July and August, not over a Saturday night, otherwise anytime.

Helena

The Barrister B&B
416 N Ewing St
Helena 59601
(406)443-7330 Fax:(406)449-7759

1880. There is plenty of room to relax in this Victorian mansion with more than 2,000 square feet of common area, which includes a parlor, formal dining room, den and TV room, library, office and enclosed sun porch. The inn boasts six ornate fireplaces, original stained-glass windows, high ceilings and carved staircases. The beautiful St. Helena Cathedral is directly across the street. The spacious guest rooms are intimate and the decor in each room varies from nostalgic to elegant.
Innkeeper(s): Nick & Connie Jacques.
Rates:$75-90. MC VISA. Full Bkfst. Gourmet Brkfst, Lunch. Evening snacks. 5 rooms. Fireplaces. Beds:Q. Conference Rm. TV, Phone, AC in room. Bicycling. Skiing. Swimming. Fishing.
Contact: Nick Jacques. Certificate may be used: January, February, March.

Kalispell

Demersville School B&B
855 Demersville Rd
Kalispell 59901
(406)756-7587

1908. This turn-of-the-century schoolhouse, four miles south of Kalispell, offers guests the unique experience of sleeping in a classroom. The inn's

four guest rooms, filled with school memorabilia, are found in the school's addition, built in 1967. The inn's charming dining room is housed in one of the school's original classrooms, and breakfast there may include wild huckleberry muffins or Dutch Babies with chokecherry syrup. Guests will enjoy a visit to the antique-filled library. Lone Pine State Park is nearby.

Innkeeper(s): Sandi & Pat LaSalle.
Rates:$61-68. MC VISA. Full Bkfst. 4 rooms. Beds:QDT. Bicycling. Skiing. Spa. Fishing.
Contact: Sandra LaSalle. Certificate may be used: Sunday through Thursday, May 15 - Oct. 15. On availability Oct. 15 - May 15, regular rate.

Switzer House Inn
205 Fifth Ave E
Kalispell 59901
(406)257-5837 (800)257-5837

1910. Originally built for a lumberman from Minnesota, this Queen Anne Victorian is found on Kalispell's historic east side. Guests enjoy relaxing

on the wraparound porch or by taking a stroll to Woodland Park, two blocks away. Downtown gal-

leries, museums, restaurants, shops and theaters are just five blocks from the inn. Visitors select from the Queen Anne, Blanche's Corner, Lew's Retreat or Twin's rooms, all found on the inn's second floor. The gourmet breakfast is served buffet style and guests also may help themselves to hot chocolate or lemonade in the library.

Innkeeper(s): Heather Brigham.
Rates:$75-90. MC VISA. Full Bkfst. EP. Gourmet Brkfst. Teas. 4 rooms. 4 with shared baths. Beds:QT. Skiing. Swimming. Fishing.
Contact: Heather Brigham. Certificate may be used: Sept. 1 through May 31.

Libby

The Kootenai Country Inn
264 Mack Rd
Libby 59923
(406)293-7878

1980. Less than a mile from the Kootenai River, on a 40-acre ponderosa forest, this modern Craftsman home provides a relaxing getaway for visitors to the state's Northwest corner. The inn offers ideal accommodations for families or couples traveling together, and guests are encouraged to share the inn's full kitchen and laundry room. The inn's grounds are ideal for hiking and other outdoor activities, which also are plentiful in the area. Please notify the innkeepers in advance to see if your pet can be suitably accommodated.

Innkeeper(s): Amy & Mel Siefke.
Rates:$60-75. MC VISA AX. Full Bkfst. AP available. Gourmet Brkfst, Lunch, Dinner. Picnic lunches. Teas. Evening snacks. 7 rooms. 5 with shared baths. Fireplaces. Beds:QT. Conference Rm. Phone, AC, Refrig. in room. Skiing. Swimming. Stables. Fishing.
Contact: Amy Siefke. Certificate may be used: January - April 30.

Livingston

Talcott House
405 W Lewis St
Livingston 59047
(406)222-7699

1903. This 7,800-square-foot red brick mansion is in town, three blocks from the Yellowstone River. A portion of the inn's picket fence shows up in *A River Runs Through It*, as it was filmed next door. Tiffany light fixtures, leaded glass, hand-carved paneling, carved fireplaces and moldings, Doric columns, and parquet floors are a few of the many original features found in the house.

Innkeeper(s): Pam & Garry McCutcheon.
Rates:$50-70. MC VISA. Full Bkfst. 5 rooms. 2 with shared baths.

Beds:KQT. Conference Rm. Phone in room. Golf. Tennis. Bicycling. Skiing. Exercise room. Swimming. Horseback riding. Fishing.

Seen in: *House & Garden, USA Today, Town & Country, Minneapolis Star Tribune, Atlanta Journal.*

Contact: Pam McCutcheon. Certificate may be used: October-May, some dates available in June and September.

Three Forks

Sacajawea Inn
PO Box 648, 5 N Main St
Three Forks 59752
(406)285-6515 (800)821-7326
Fax:(406)285-4210

1910. Rocking chairs fill the wide front porch of this National Register hotel. Named after the famous guide who led Lewis and Clark through the Three Forks area, the hotel was founded by John Quincy Adams. The 30,000-square-foot building has been renovated recently and decorated in 1991. The inn's pleasant restaurant is popular for fine dining. Golf and hunting for deer, elk, and pheasants are all nearby. It's two hours to Yellowstone National Park.

Innkeeper(s): Smith & Jane Roedel.

Rates:$49-99. MC VISA AX DS. Full Bkfst. EP. 33 rooms. Beds:KQT. Conference Rm. TV, Phone, AC in room. Golf. Bicycling. Skiing. Swimming. Fishing.

Seen in: *Billings Gazette, Montana, Child.*

Contact: Mary Hardin. Certificate may be used: Oct. 2, 1994-May 1, 1995 (excluding Dec. 31, Feb. 10-15).

"You should be commended for the time, resources, and energy you put into this worthy landmark in our fine valley."

West Yellowstone

Sportsman's High B&B
750 Deer St
West Yellowstone 59758
(406)646-7865 (800)272-4227
Fax:(406)646-9434

1984. Nature lovers will have a delightful time at this inn, a large contemporary home that blends Colonial, farm and rustic stylings. Four guest rooms and a log cabin are the lodging choices, all with private baths. Three resident collies enjoy showing visitors the inn's aspen- and pine-filled grounds. Hiking trails, lakes and trout streams are found nearby and cross-country skiing and snowmobiling are enjoyed in winter. The innkeepers are avid birdwatchers, fly-fishers and fly-tiers, and a fly-tying

bench is available. Bring a camera to record some of the inn's plentiful wildlife, ranging in size from hummingbirds to moose.

Innkeeper(s): Diana & Gary Baxter.

Rates:$65-85. MC VISA AX. Full Bkfst. Gourmet Brkfst. Teas. 5 rooms. Beds:KQ. Golf. Skiing. Spa. Swimming. Horseback riding. Fishing.

Seen in: *Rocky Mountain Adventures, LA Times, West Yellowstone News.*

Contact: Diana Baxter. Certificate may be used: Good anytime during Oct. 1 to May 31, subject to availability, excluding Christmas week.

Whitefish

Castle B&B
900 S Baker Ave
Whitefish 59937
(406)862-1257

1931. In the National Register of Historic Places, the Castle features a two-story turret off the living room with views of the Rocky Mountains that surround Whitefish. The Queen's Room is decorated with blue and white wallpaper and features a queen-size bed topped with a hand-crocheted bedspread made by the host's mother. A library and piano are available to guests. The Amtrak station is one mile away.

Innkeeper(s): Jim & Pat Egan.

Rates:$63-95. MC VISA DS. Full Bkfst. Teas. 3 rooms. 2 with shared baths. Beds:QT. Golf. Tennis. Skiing. Sauna. Exercise room. Swimming. Horseback riding. Fishing.

Seen in: *St. Paul Star Tribune, Montana, Country Extra.*

Contact: Jim Egan. Certificate may be used: Sept. 15-Dec. 15,1994; Feb. 1-June 1,1995; Sept. 15-Dec. 15, 1995.

"The surroundings were gorgeous, but what made my stay most enjoyable were the hosts."

The Crenshaw House
5465 Hwy 93 S
Whitefish 59937-8410
(406)862-3496 (800)453-2863

1973. This contemporary farmhouse inn offers

three guest rooms, all with private bath. Many amenities are found at the inn, including satellite TV, turndown service and a wake-up tray, which precedes the tasty gourmet breakfast prepared by innkeeper Anni Crenshaw-Rieker. Guests also enjoy afternoon tea and an evening snack. The inn also boasts a fireplace and spa and child care can be arranged. Several state parks are found nearby.

Innkeeper(s): Anni Crenshaw-Rieker.

Rates:$65-115. MC VISA. Gourmet Brkfst. Teas. Evening snacks. 3 rooms. Beds:KQT. Phone, Refrig. in room. Farm. Skiing. Spa. Swimming. Fishing.

Contact: Anni Crenshaw-Rieker. Certificate may be used: Sept. 15-Dec. 15, 1994 upon availability. Jan. 5-May 31, 1995 upon availability.

Wolf Point

Forsness Farm Bed & Breakfast
Box 5035
Wolf Point 59201
(406)653-2492

1926. A working farm/ranch is home to this Prairie-style inn, which was built by Indian traders and moved to its present location in 1975. Cattle, chickens, horses, milk cows, sheep and even a burro reside at the ranch, and guests are welcome to help with egg gathering or milking. Fishing for coho salmon, pike and prehistoric paddlefish is found in the Missouri River, less than two miles from the inn. Two upstairs guest rooms, one with king bed and the other with twin beds, share a bath with whirlpool tub. Summertime guests often enjoy Indian celebrations and the area also hosts an authentic Wild West rodeo.

Innkeeper(s): Jo Ann & Dewey Forsness.

Rates:$40-60. Full Bkfst. Picnic lunches. Evening snacks. 2 rooms. 2 with shared baths. Beds:KT. AC in room. Farm. Bicycling. Swimming. Stables. Fishing.

Contact: JoAnn Forsness. Certificate may be used: Year-round.

Nebraska

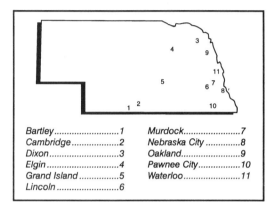

Bartley

Pheasant Hill Farm
HC 68 Box 12
Bartley 69020
(308)692-3278 Fax:(308)345-4281

1937. This stucco farmhouse offers the perfect setting for outdoor lovers. Hunters especially will be appreciative of the opportunities presented by the

60 state and wildlife recreation areas nearby, not to mention the fishing and boating at seven local lakes. The area is well known for its historical Indian and archeological sites. Pheasant Hill is a

wheat and corn farm of more than a thousand acres and it is home to a herd of Hereford cattle. The farmhouse also features a large lounge area ideal for relaxing with a game of darts or ping pong.

Innkeeper(s): Max & Dona Nelms.

Rates:$55. Full Bkfst. AP available. Gourmet Brkfst, Lunch, Dinner. Picnic lunches. Evening snacks. 5 rooms.

Contact: Dona Nelms. Certificate may be used: Year-round.

Cambridge

The Cambridge Inn
606 Parker, PO Box 239
Cambridge 69022
(308)697-3220

1907. The Prairie Lakes region of Southwest Nebraska is known for its abundant outdoor activities, and the Cambridge Inn offers an ideal setting for those exploring the area. A beautiful, historic Neoclassical home, the inn features both Ionic and Corinthian columns supporting its stories. Handsome woodwork is found throughout, and authentic decor such as a clawfoot tub, pedestal sink and stained glass add to the charm. Breakfasts are served in the formal dining room, and guests may relax in the parlor and library. The Ivy Court room offers a sitting area and a writing desk.

Innkeeper(s): Mike & Elaine Calabro.

Rates:$40-70. MC VISA DS. Full Bkfst. MAP available. Gourmet Brkfst. 5 rooms. 2 with shared baths.

Contact: Elaine Calabro. Certificate may be used: July 1 - Dec. 30, 1994; Feb. 14 - May 25 & May 31 - Dec. 30, 1995.

Dixon

The George Farm
Rt 1 Box 50
Dixon 68732
(402)584-2625

1926. Two miles south of Highway 20, west of Sioux City, lies this air-conditioned farmhouse furnished in country decor. Although in a rural setting, the farm offers a wide array of activities within easy driving distance. Wayne State College is nearby, as are an abundance of local crafts and antique establishments. Marie, an avid antiquer, can provide help for those searching the area for special items. Relax with a stroll through the farm's 640 acres, or just enjoy some peace and quiet in the library. The inn accepts children and pets, with prior arrangement.

Innkeeper(s): Marie George.

Rates:$35-40. Full Bkfst. 4 rooms. 4 with shared baths. Exercise room.

Contact: Marie George. Certificate may be used: When not previously booked. Not during pheasant-hunting-opening season (November).

Elgin

Plantation House
Rt 2 Box 17, 401 Plantation St
Elgin 68636
(402)843-2287

1916. This historic mansion sits adjacent to Elgin City Park, and guests will marvel at its beauty and size. Once a small Victorian farmhouse, the

Plantation House has evolved into a 20-room Greek Revival treasure. Visitors will be treated to a tour and a large family-style breakfast, and may venture to the park to play tennis or horseshoes. The antique-filled guest rooms include the Stained Glass Room, with a queen bed and available twin-bed anteroom, and the Old Master Bedroom, with clawfoot tub and pedestal sink.

Innkeeper(s): Merland & Barbara Clark.

Rates:$35-50. Full Bkfst. 5 rooms. 3 with shared baths. Conference Rm.

Seen in: *Omaha World Herald, Norfolk Daily News, Home & Away Magazine.*

Contact: Barbara Clark. Certificate may be used: Sunday-Thursday (all year), certain holidays excluded. Anytime (Oct. 1-April 1), certain holidays excluded.

"Gorgeous house! Relaxing atmosphere. Just like going to Mom's house."

Grand Island

Kirschke House B&B
1124 W 3rd St
Grand Island 68801
(308)381-6851

1902. A steeply sloping roofline and a two-story tower mark this distinctive, vine-covered brick Victorian house. Meticulously restored, there are

polished wood floors, fresh wallpapers and carefully chosen antiques. The Roses Roses Room is a spacious accommodation with a canopy bed, rocking chair and decorating accents of roses and vines. In the old brick wash house is a wooden hot tub. In winter and spring, the area is popular for viewing the migration of sandhill cranes and whooping cranes.

Innkeeper(s): Lois Hank/Marlynn Dexter.

Rates:$45-55. MC VISA AX DS. Full Bkfst. Gourmet Dinner. Evening snacks. 4 rooms. 4 with shared baths. Spa. Horseback riding. Fishing.

Seen in: *Grand Island Daily Independent.*

Contact: Lois Hank. Certificate may be used: Sunday through Thursday only.

"We have been to many B&Bs in England, Canada and America. The Kirschke House ranks with the finest we've stayed in."

Lincoln

Yellow House on the Corner
1603 N Cotner Blvd
Lincoln 68505
(402)466-8626

1912. Triple arches decorate the front of this Prairie Cottage-style home. It features stained-glass windows and a bay window. Nebraska crafts are featured in both the bed & breakfast and the Hearts 'n' Hands Gift Shop located behind the house. There is a whirlpool tub in one of the bathrooms.

Innkeeper(s): Joyce Converse.

Rates:$45. Full Bkfst. 3 rooms. 2 with shared baths. Exercise room.

Contact: Joyce Converse. Certificate may be used: Any available time.

"Staying at your house was a memory maker...and the food!"

Murdock

Farm House B&B
32617 Church Road
Murdock 68407
(402)867-2062

1896. Travelers weary of the monotony of the nearby interstate or the buzz of the big city can find relief at the Farm House B&B. Visitors experience what country life was like at the turn of the century. The innkeepers can accommodate pets on their back porch or large, fenced yard. No farm animals are kept here, so guests can expect a minimum of distractions during their relaxing stay. Several state parks are close by and the inn is within a half-hour's drive of Omaha and Lincoln.

Innkeeper(s): Mike & Pat Meierhenry.

Rates:$35. Full Bkfst. 2 rooms. 2 with shared baths.

Contact: Patricia Meierhenry. Certificate may be used: Monday through Thursday year-round.

Nebraska City

Whispering Pines
RR #2
Nebraska City 68410
(402)873-5850

1882. An easy getaway from Kansas City, Lincoln or Omaha, Nebraska City's Whispering Pines offers visitors a relaxing alternative from big-city life. Fresh flowers greet guests at this two-story brick Italianate, furnished with Victorian and country decor. Situated on more than six acres of trees, flowers and ponds, the inn is a birdwatcher's delight. Breakfast is served formally in the dining room, or guests may opt to eat on the deck with its view of garden and pines. The inn is within easy walking distance to Arbor Lodge, home of the founder of Arbor Day.

Innkeeper(s): Bud & Shirley Smulling.

Rates:$45-65. MC VISA DS. Full Bkfst. 5 rooms. 3 with shared baths.

Contact: W. B. Smulling. Certificate may be used: Sunday through Thursday.

Oakland

Benson B&B
402 N Oakland Ave
Oakland 68045-1135
(402)685-6051

1905. This inn is on the second floor of the Benson Building, a sturdy, turreted brick structure built of walls nearly 12 inches thick. Decorated throughout in mauve, blue and cream, the Benson B&B features four comfortable guest rooms, and a restful, small-town atmosphere. Guests may visit the Swedish Heritage Center and a lovely city park. An 18-hole golf course is a five-minute drive away, and outdoor activities are also nearby. Check out the craft and gift store on the building's lower level, the inn's collection of soft drink memorabilia and be sure to ask about the Troll Stroll.

Innkeeper(s): Stan & Norma Anderson.

Rates:$45-50. Full Bkfst. Evening snacks. 4 rooms. 4 with shared baths. Beds:QD. Spa. Fishing.

Contact: Norma Anderson. Certificate may be used: Monday, Tuesday, Wednesday or Thursday nights only.

Pawnee City

My Blue Heaven B&B
1041 Fifth St
Pawnee City 68420
(402)852-3131

1920. Not many travelers know that just a shade north of the Kansas state line, in Nebraska's Southeast corner, they may find heaven, as in My Blue Heaven B&B. Legend says that Pawnee City, the county seat, once was the area's largest Pawnee Indian village. The hosts pride themselves on hospitality and the small-town feel of their history-laden community, which also features a barbed wire museum of 800 varieties. The inn's two guest rooms, one of which is known as the Blue Berry Hill Room, are filled with antiques.

Innkeeper(s): Duane & Yvonne Dalluge.

Rates:$30-35. MC VISA. Full Bkfst. 2 rooms. 2 with shared baths.

Contact: Yvonne Dalluge. Certificate may be used: Nov. 15, 1994 to April 30, 1995 and Nov. 15 to Dec. 30, 1995.

Waterloo

Journey's End
102 Lincoln Ave, PO Box 190
Waterloo 68069-0190
(402)779-2704

1905. A short drive from Omaha, the Journey's End is an elegant, Neoclassical Greek Revival

home boasting two impressive Ionic columns. The inn, surrounded by large trees, is listed with the national and state historic registers. Antiques, including a stunning clock collection, are found throughout the attractive interior, and the Gone With the Wind Room offers a garden and orchard view. The home, built by seed company founder J.C. Robinson, also features a guest room in his name. Fishing and canoeing are a short walk away or guests may decide to soak up the village's relaxed atmosphere.

Innkeeper(s): John (Bill) Clark.

Rates:$45-75. Full Bkfst. Gourmet Lunch, Dinner. Teas. Evening snacks. 3 rooms. 2 with shared baths. Conference Rm.

Contact: John Clark. Certificate may be used: Year-round, but preferably Oct. 1 - April 1.

Nevada

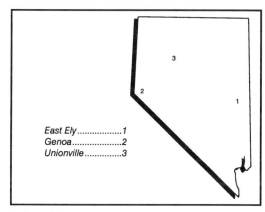

East Ely...................1
Genoa....................2
Unionville..............3

East Ely

Steptoe Valley Inn
PO Box 151110, 220 E 11th St
East Ely 89315
(702)289-8687

1907. Originally a grocery store at the turn of the century, this inn has been lovingly reconstructed to resemble a Victorian country cottage. Five uniquely decorated guest rooms are named for local pioneers, and all offer air conditioning, cable TV and ceiling fans. The rooms also have views of the inn's scenic surroundings, and three of them feature queen beds. A nearby railroad museum offers train rides and Great Basin National Park is nearby. Guests may rent a jeep at the inn for exploring the area's back country.

Innkeeper(s): Jane & Norman Lindley.

Rates:$69-84. MC VISA AX. Full Bkfst. Gourmet Brkfst. 5 rooms. Beds:QT. TV, Phone, AC in room. Fishing.

Contact: Jane Lindley. Certificate may be used: Anytime June through September except July 4th & Labor Day weekends & Pony Express Horse race weekends, which are normally last two weekends in August.

Genoa

Wild Rose Inn
2332 Main St, PO Box 256

Genoa 89411
(702)782-5697

1989. Located 15 miles from Lake Tahoe in Nevada's oldest settlement, this newly built Victorian is resplendent with gables, porches and a two-story turret. The Garden Gate Room is housed in the tower and features five windows overlooking the valley and the Sierras. Among the antiques is a collection of old toys. Freshly baked orange rolls are prepared often for breakfast.

Innkeeper(s): Sandi & Joe Antonucci.

Rates:$85-115. MC VISA AX. Full Bkfst. 5 rooms. Beds:QT. TV, AC in room. Skiing. Spa. Sauna. Exercise room. Fishing.

Seen in: *Sacramento Bee.*

Contact: Sandra Antonucci. Certificate may be used: Sunday through Thursday except August.

"We enjoyed our stay so much. The room was great!"

Unionville

Old Pioneer Garden Guest Ranch
79 Unionville Rd
Unionville 89418-9503
(702)538-7585

1862. Once a bustling silver mining town, Unionville now has only a handful of citizens, and Old Pioneer Garden Guest Ranch is just down the road from town. Accommodations are in a renovated blacksmith's house, a farmhouse and across the meadow in the Hadley House. A Swedish-style gazebo rests beside a bubbling stream, and there are orchards, grape arbors, vegetable gardens, sheep and goats. A country supper is available.

Innkeeper(s): Mitzi & Lew Jones.

Rates:$65-75. Full Bkfst. Gourmet Lunch, Dinner. Picnic lunches. Teas. 7 rooms. 4 with shared baths. Beds:T. Conference Rm. Bicycling. Handicap access. Stables.

Seen in: *Denver Post.*

Contact: Harold Jones. Certificate may be used: Midweek.

"An array of charm that warms the heart and delights the soul."

New Hampshire

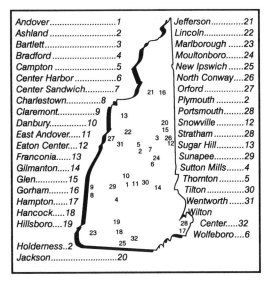

Andover

Andover Arms Guest House
Main St, PO Box 256
Andover 03216
(603)735-5953

1860. This family-oriented Victorian farmhouse inn boasts five guest rooms, including one suite. The furnishings include country and traditional decor.

Guests enjoy two sitting rooms, cable TV, VCR and walks on the inn's two acres. Popular with those celebrating anniversaries, Andover Arms is available for meetings, receptions and weddings. The innkeepers are able to accommodate most pets when prior arrangements are made. The Daniel

Webster Birthplace, King Ridge Ski Area and Winslow State Park are within easy driving distance.

Innkeeper(s): Rick & Michele Kittwig & Cynthia Zautner.

Rates:$50-75. ContPlus Bkfst. 5 rooms. 4 with shared baths.

Contact: Cynthia Zautner. Certificate may be used: Anytime except graduation weekends (end of May-beginning of June) and leaf-peeping weekends (usually middle of October).

Ashland

Glynn House Victorian Inn
43 Highland St, PO Box 719
Ashland 03217-0719
(603)968-3775 (800)637-9599

1895. A three-story turret, gables and verandas frosted with Queen Anne gingerbread come together in an appealing mass of Victoriana in the Glynn

House. Carved-oak woodwork and pocket doors accentuate the foyer. Period furnishings and ornate Oriental wall coverings decorate the parlor. The village of Ashland is a few minutes from "On Golden Pond" (Squam Lake) and the White Mountains.

Innkeeper(s): Karol & Betsy Paterman.

Rates:$60-125. MC VISA DC. Full Bkfst. Gourmet Brkfst. Teas. Evening snacks. 9 rooms. 2 with shared baths. Fireplaces. Beds:QT. Conference Rm. AC in room. Tennis. Bicycling. Skiing. Handicap access. Spa.

Swimming. Fishing.

Contact: Karol Paterman. Certificate may be used: November-June.

"Boston was fun, but the Glynn House is the place we'll send our friends."

Bartlett

The Country Inn at Bartlett
Rt 302 Box 327
Bartlett 03812
(603)374-2353 (800)292-2353
Fax:(603)374-2547

1885. This New England farmhouse, built as a summer home by a Portland sea captain, rests in a stand of tall pines adjacent to national forest land.

For the last 50 years it has provided a homey atmosphere for families and friends coming to the White Mountains. Accommodations are in the house or in cottage rooms. An outdoor hot tub takes advantage of the crisp, pine-scented air.

Innkeeper(s): Mark Dindorf & Heidi Lewis.

Rates:$56-96. MC VISA AX DC DS. Full Bkfst. 18 rooms. 6 with shared baths. Fireplaces. Beds:DT. TV, AC, Refrig. in room. Golf. Tennis. Skiing. Handicap access. Spa. Swimming. Horseback riding. Fishing.

Seen in: *Outside Magazine.*

Contact: Mark Dindorf. Certificate may be used: Sunday - Thursday (midweek), except holiday periods. Not valid Oct. 1-15, Dec. 20 - Jan. 2.

"Walking through your door felt like stepping back in time."

Bradford

The Bradford Inn
RFD 1 Box 40, Main St
Bradford 03221
(603)938-5309

1898. The Bradford Hotel was the most elaborate lodging in town when it first boasted of electricity, a coal furnace and a large dining room. Now

restored and polished to its original turn-of-the-century charm, guests can once again enjoy the grand staircase, the wide halls, parlors, high ceilings and sunny rooms.

Innkeeper(s): Connie & Tom Mazol.

Rates:$48-99. MC VISA AX DC DS CB. Full Bkfst. Picnic lunches. 12 rooms. Beds:T. Conference Rm. AC in room. Golf. Tennis. Skiing. Handicap access. Swimming. Horseback riding. Fishing.

Seen in: *New York Times, Granite State Vacationer, Family Times.*

Contact: Thomas Mazol. Certificate may be used: Anytime subject to availability.

"We enjoyed excellent breakfasts and dinners as well as a clean and spacious suite and a most pleasant host and hostess."

Candlelite Inn B&B
Rt 114, RR #1, Box 408
Bradford 03221
(603)938-5571

1897. Nestled on more than three acres of countryside in the valley of the Lake Sunapee region, this Victorian inn has a gazebo porch perfect for sipping lemonade on a summer day and a parlor with fireplace to keep warm on a winter day while relaxing with a good book. All of the guest rooms have mountain views and are decorated with fresh flowers and plants. Quilts on the beds and walls, cross stitch pillows and pictures, and tole painting that includes plaques to table top decorations are the innkeepers' creations.

Innkeeper(s): Marilyn & Les Gordon.

Rates:$65-75. MC VISA DS. Full Bkfst. Evening snacks. 6 rooms. Beds:Q. Skiing. Swimming. Fishing.

Contact: Marilyn Gordon. Certificate may be used: Subject to availability.

The Rosewood Country Inn
RR1, Box 225, Pleasant View Rd
Bradford 03221
(603)938-5253

1850. This three-story country Victorian inn in the White Mountains treats its guests to a candlelight and crystal breakfast and elegant accommodations that manage to avoid being stuffy. The inn prides itself on special touches; the innkeepers like to keep things interesting with ideas such as theme weekends and special breakfast fare, including cinnamon apple pancakes with cider sauce. Mount Sunapee Ski Area and Lake Sunapee are less than 20 minutes away.

Innkeeper(s): Dick & Lesley Marquis.

Rates:$69-99. MC VISA. Full Bkfst. Gourmet Brkfst. Picnic lunches. 8 rooms. Beds:KQT. Conference Rm. AC in room. Skiing. Swimming. Fishing.

Contact: Lesley Marquis. Certificate may be used: November through June and September.

Campton

The Campton Inn
RR 2, Box 12, Rt 175
Campton 03223
(603)726-4449

1836. Three steep gables mark the roof line of this historic country farmhouse. Simply but comfortably furnished rooms include a TV and game room, a large common room and a screened porch. A full breakfast is served, a good time to tap into the innkeepers' extensive knowledge of the area.

Innkeeper(s): Robbin & Peter Adams.

Rates:$50-65. Full Bkfst. 6 rooms. 5 with shared baths. Beds:DT. TV in room. Golf. Tennis. Bicycling. Skiing. Swimming.

Contact: Robbin Adams. Certificate may be used: April 1 through July 31 and Oct. 15 through Dec. 23.

"What a great week. Excellent service!"

Mountain-Fare Inn
Mad River Rd, PO Box 553
Campton 03223
(603)726-4283

1820. This white farmhouse is surrounded by flower gardens in the summer and unparalleled foliage in

the fall. Ski teams, family reunions and other groups often enjoy the outdoors here with Mountain Fare as a base. In the winter everyone seems to be a skier, and in the summer there are

boaters and hikers. The inn is decorated in a casual New Hampshire-style country decor. The hearty breakfast is a favorite of returning guests.

Innkeeper(s): Susan & Nicholas Preston.

Rates:$56-80. Full Bkfst. Teas. 10 rooms. 2 with shared baths. Beds:QT. AC in room. Tennis. Bicycling. Skiing. Sauna. Swimming. Fishing.

Seen in: *Ski, Skiing, Snow Country.*

Contact: Susan Preston. Certificate may be used: Any Sunday through Thursday except Dec. 15 - Jan. 2, February vacation week and Sept. 25 - Oct. 20.

"Thank you for your unusually caring attitude toward your guests."

Osgood Inn B&B
PO Box 419, Cross St
Campton 03223
(603)726-3543

1900. Guests may enjoy the village atmosphere of this New England-style farmhouse located in the White Mountains. A front parlor, country dining room and large common room with fireplace are areas of relaxation. The magic of the seasons can be viewed from the sunny back porch and garden-filled backyard. Cross-country skiers have miles of nearby trails available. Downhill skiing at Waterville Valley and Loon Mountain is 20 minutes away.

Innkeeper(s): Dexter & Patricia Osgood.

Rates:$50. Full Bkfst. Teas. 5 rooms. 4 with shared baths. Beds:KDT. Skiing. Fishing.

Contact: Dexter & Patricia Osgood. Certificate may be used: Sunday-Thursday - except holiday days, Christmas week, and first two weeks in October.

Center Harbor

Kona Mansion Inn
Box 458
Center Harbor 03226
(603)253-4900 Fax:(603)253-7350

1900. Located in the state's scenic lake region, this family-oriented Tudor inn sports a waterfront location on 125 acres. Six of the guest rooms boast kitchenettes, and some rooms are able to accommodate visitors' pets. The inn also hosts meetings, reunions and weddings, and it offers a variety of food services. Antiquing and fishing are other popular guest activities.

Innkeeper(s): The Crowleys.

Rates:$65-150. MC VISA. Full Bkfst. EP. MAP available. Gourmet Dinner. Picnic lunches. 10 rooms. Beds:KT. Conference Rm. AC in room. Tennis. Swimming. Fishing.

Contact: K.E. Crowley. Certificate may be used: May 15-Oct. 31.

Red Hill Inn

RD 1 Box 99M
Center Harbor 03226
(603)279-7001 (800)573-3445
Fax:(603)279-7003

1904. The mansion was once the centerpiece of a 1,000-acre estate. It was called "keewaydin" for the strong north wind that blows across Sunset Hill. When the Depression was over, the inn was sold. New owners included European royalty escaping from Nazi Germany. Now the mansion is a lovely restored country inn with spectacular views of the area's lakes and mountains. From your room you can see the site of the filming of "On Golden Pond."

Innkeeper(s): Don Leavitt & Rick Miller.

Rates:$85-145. MC VISA AX DC DS CB. Full Bkfst. 21 rooms. Fireplaces. Beds:KQT. Conference Rm. Phone in room. Tennis. Skiing. Handicap access. Spa. Swimming. Fishing.

Seen in: *New England Getaways*.

Contact: Rick Miller. Certificate may be used: Sunday through Thursday, Nov. 1 to June 30 excluding holiday weeks (Christmas, New Year's, President's Week).

"Our stay was very enjoyable."

Center Sandwich

Corner House Inn

Main St PO 204
Center Sandwich 03227
(603)284-6219 (800)832-7829
Fax:(603)284-6220

1849. Handstitched teddy bears greet visitors at this Victorian Stick inn, tucked between Squam Lake and the White Mountains. The picturesque village setting offers antique and craft shops, an art gallery, a museum and many fine eateries. The inn doubles as a popular lunch and dinner establishment, as well as a charming bed and breakfast inn. Five major downhill ski areas are within an hour's drive. All guest rooms feature complimentary maple syrup.

Innkeeper(s): Don & Jane Brown.

Rates:$80. MC VISA AX. Full Bkfst. Picnic lunches. 3 rooms. Beds:QT. Conference Rm. Golf. Tennis. Skiing. Swimming. Horseback riding. Fishing.

Seen in: *Country Living, New Hampshire Profiles*.

Contact: Donald Brown. Certificate may be used: Sunday-Thursday, November-June.

Charlestown

Maplehedge B&B

Rt 12, Box 638, S Main St
Charlestown 03603
(603)826-5237

1753. This elegantly restored summer home is set among acres of lawn and 200-year-old maple trees. The bed and breakfast boasts five distinctive bed-

rooms. The Beale Room is named for the innkeeper's grandparents and is full of sentimental treasures such as milk bottles from her grandfather's dairy and family photos. The Butterfly Suite is filled with white wicker, including an antique, glass-topped hamper and Victorian butterfly trays. The rooms are furnished in antiques, including some of the linens. A delectable three-course breakfast is served and may include fresh fruit salads and scones. Evening refreshments include California wine with Vermont cheese. Guests can go on antiquing tours or attend country auctions.

Innkeeper(s): Joan & Dick DeBrine.

Rates:$80-90. MC VISA. Gourmet Brkfst. 5 rooms. Fireplaces. Beds:QT. Phone, AC in room. Golf. Skiing. Swimming. Fishing.

Seen in: *Los Angeles Times, Buffalo News, Country Living, Yankee Traveler*.

Contact: Joan DeBrine. Certificate may be used: Upon availability Sunday-Friday excluding Sept. 25-Oct. 25.

"The highlight of my two weeks in New England."

Claremont

Goddard Mansion B&B

25 Hillstead Rd
Claremont 03743
(603)543-0603 (800)736-0603
Fax:(603)543-0001

1905. This mansion with its gazebo is set amid

acres of lawn. The living room has a large fireplace and there is a baby grand piano and a 1939

Wurlitzer jukebox with 78s. Many of the guest rooms have panoramic views of mountains in New Hampshire and Vermont. The airy French Country Room and the surreal Cloud Room are favorites. Homemade muffins are served with preserves made from fruit grown on the property.

Innkeeper(s): Frank & Debbie Albee.

Rates:$65-95. MC VISA AX DC DS CB. Full Bkfst. Teas. 8 rooms. 6 with shared baths. Beds:QDT. Conference Rm. AC in room. Skiing. Fishing.

Seen in: *Eagle Times.*

Contact: Debbie Albee. Certificate may be used: All year upon availability, excluding foliage season and major holidays (may sometimes include one weekend night).

"Our trip would not have been as enjoyable without having stayed at your inn."

Danbury

The Inn at Danbury
Rt 104
Danbury 03230
(603)768-3318 Fax:(603)768-3386

1850. This rambling farmhouse inn offers many charming touches and amenities. The inn is a favorite haven of cyclists and skiers, and also those who enjoy a relaxing getaway in a rural mountain atmosphere. The Danbury area offers many opportunities for both on- and off-road bicycle enthusiasts, and the inn's restored barn is home to a full-service bike shop. There's an indoor swimming pool and exercise equipment. The Ragged Mountain Ski Area is a short drive away. A full breakfast is served and other food service is available.

Innkeeper(s): April Williams & George Issa.

Rates:$59-79. MC VISA AX. Full Bkfst. AP available. MAP available. 14 rooms. Beds:KQT. Conference Rm. Bicycling. Skiing. Swimming. Fishing.

Contact: April Williams Issa. Certificate may be used: Midweek, non-vacation, December-March and October. Any other days in any other months.

East Andover

Highland Lake Inn B&B
PO Box 164, Maple St
East Andover 03231
(603)735-6426 Fax:(603)735-5355

1767. This waterfront Victorian inn overlooks three mountains, and all the rooms have views of either the lake or the mountains. The guest rooms feature handmade quilts and some have four-poster beds. Guests may relax in the inn's library, in front of its fireplace or walk the pretty 10-acre grounds, and enjoy old apple and maple trees, as well as the shoreline. Adjacent to a 21-acre nature conservancy, there are scenic trails and a stream to explore. Highland Lake is stocked with bass and also has trout. Fresh fruit salads, hot entrees, and homemade breads are featured at breakfast.

Innkeeper(s): The Petras Family.

Rates:$85-90. MC VISA AX. Full Bkfst. 10 rooms. Beds:KQT. Farm. Skiing. Swimming. Fishing.

Contact: Mary Petras. Certificate may be used: Jan. 1-May 31 (excluding Memorial Day).

Eaton Center

The Inn at Crystal Lake
Rt 153, Box 12
Eaton Center 03832
(603)447-2120 (800)343-7336
Fax:(603)447-3599

1884. A Greek Revival house with Victorian touches, this cozy inn is located a few steps from Crystal Lake. Victorian decor predominates with canopy, brass and iron beds and antique dressers. An inn since 1884, there are two balconies and a porch to capture the scenic views. Evening meals are served in the dining room with its fireplace and crystals. Walter is a former geology professor-metal sculptor-turned chef who trained at a French restaurant after purchasing the inn. His specialties include breast of duckling, shrimp steamed in Vermouth and chicken in brie sauce.

Innkeeper(s): Richard, Janice & Colleen Octeau.

Rates:$42-50. MC VISA AX DC DS. Full Bkfst. EP. MAP available. Gourmet Dinner. Evening snacks. 11 rooms. Beds:QT. Skiing. Swimming. Fishing.

Seen in: *The Boston Globe, Bon Appetit, Carroll County Independent.*

Contact: Janice Octeau. Certificate may be used: April, May, June, November.

"Thanks for a terrific time, good weather, fabulous food and equally fabulous company."

Franconia

The Inn at Forest Hills
Route 142, PO Box 783
Franconia 03580
(603)823-9550 Fax:(603)823-8701

1890. This Tudor-style inn in the White Mountains offers a solarium and a large common room with fireplace and cathedral ceilings.

Breakfast is served with a quiet background of classical music in the dining room where in the winter there's a blazing fireplace, and in summer the French doors open to the scenery. Guest rooms feature a casual country decor with quilts, flowered wall coverings and some four poster beds. Ski free on the inn's property and on the 240 acres adjoining it. Downhill facilities are found at Bretton Woods or Loon Mountain. Nearby Franconia Notch Park features trails designed for cycling, hiking, and snow mobiling.

Innkeeper(s): Joanne & Gordon Haym.

Rates:$60-95. MC VISA. Full Bkfst. Gourmet Brkfst. 8 rooms. 3 with shared baths. Beds:KQT. Tennis. Skiing. Swimming. Fishing.

Contact: Gordon Haym. Certificate may be used: July 1-July 31, 1994; Nov. 1-Dec. 22, 1994; March 15- July 31, 1995; Nov. 1-Dec. 21, 1995.

Franconia Inn
1300 Easton Rd
Franconia 03580
(603)823-5542 (800)473-5299
Fax:(603)823-8078

1934. Beautifully situated on 117 acres below the White Mountain's famous Franconia Notch, this white clapboard inn is three stories high. An oak-paneled library, parlor, rathskeller lounge and two

verandas offer relaxing retreats. The inn's rooms are simply decorated in a pleasing style and there is a special honeymoon suite with private Jacuzzi. Bach, classic wines and an elegant American cuisine are featured in the inn's unpretentious dining room.

Innkeeper(s): Alec & Richard Morris.

Rates:$58-123. MC VISA AX. Full Bkfst. EP. MAP available. Gourmet Brkfst, Dinner. Picnic lunches. 33 rooms. Beds:KQT. Conference Rm. Farm. Tennis. Bicycling. Skiing. Handicap access. Spa. Swimming. Horseback riding. Stables. Fishing.

Seen in: *Philadelphia Inquirer, Boston Globe, Travel Leisure.*

Contact: Alec Morris. Certificate may be used: Sunday through Thursday nights (non-holiday) during the months of November through March.

"The piece de resistance of the Franconia Notch is the Franconia Inn." Philadelphia Inquirer.

Gilmanton

The Historic Temperance Tavern
PO Box 369, Rt 107 & Rt 140
Gilmanton 03237
(603)267-7349 Fax:(603)267-7503

1793. This historic Colonial inn has been welcoming visitors for more than 200 years, and it acquired its name during a temperance movement in the early 19th century. The inn offers five guest rooms, including one suite, all of which feature private baths and turndown service. The rooms all boast furnishings that reflect an authentic Federal decor. Visitors enjoy the inn's many fireplaces, its common rooms and fine food. Guests often schedule outings to Gunstock Mountain Ski Resort, Loudon Raceway and Shaker Village.

Innkeeper(s): Steve & Kristie Owens.

Rates:$40-125. MC VISA. Full Bkfst. MAP available. Gourmet Brkfst, Lunch, Dinner. 5 rooms. Fireplaces. Beds:DT. Conference Rm. Skiing. Swimming. Fishing.

Seen in: *New Hampshire Magazine.*

Contact: Stephen Owens. Certificate may be used: Midweek, Monday through Thursday, no holidays or race days at local speedway. During April or November, 1994-1995 including weekends. No holidays or race days.

Glen

Bernerhof Inn
Box 240 Rt 302
Glen 03838
(603)383-4414 (800)548-8007
Fax:(603)383-0809

1894. This unusual house sports a variety of peaks

and gables and is fronted with a glassed-in greenhouse. There is a common room just inside the entrance called the Zumstein Room. A Finnish sauna is on the property and guests can stroll through the pines to the swimming pool. Celebrate friends' birthdays by asking for the customized cooking classes available to small groups.

Innkeeper(s): Ted & Sharon Wroblewski.

Rates:$69-139. MC VISA AX. Full Bkfst. MAP available. Gourmet Dinner. 9 rooms. Beds:KQ. TV, Phone, AC in room. Golf. Tennis. Skiing. Handicap access. Spa. Swimming. Horseback riding. Fishing.

Seen in: *Bon Appetit, New Hampshire Profiles, The Boston Globe.*

Contact: Hollie Smith. Certificate may be used: Midweek only, non-vacation/holidays not during foliage.

"When people want to treat themselves, this is where they come."

Gorham

The Gorham House Inn

PO Box 267, 55 Main St
Gorham 03581
(603)466-2271 (800)453-0023

1891. Located across from the town common, this Victorian is in the local historic register. There's a wraparound porch and the three guest rooms are decorated in a comfortable Victorian style. Blueberry pancakes with locally made syrup and cheddar eggs dishes are served frequently.

Innkeeper(s): Ron & Maggie Orso.

Rates:$55. MC VISA AX DC DS CB. Full Bkfst. Teas. Evening snacks. 3 rooms. 3 with shared baths. Beds:DT. Skiing. Swimming. Fishing.

Contact: Ronald Orso. Certificate may be used: November through June except holiday periods including Canadian holidays.

Hampton

The Inn at Elmwood Corners

252 Winnacunnet Rd
Hampton 03842-2627
(603)929-0443 (800)253-5691

1870. This old sea captain's house boasts a wide wraparound porch, filled with wicker in the summer. The inn is decorated with stencilled walls, braided rugs and collections such as antique teddy bears and dolls. Mary has stitched the quilts that top the beds. The library is jammed and guests may borrow a book and finish reading it at home. A favorite breakfast is John's poached brook trout or Eggs Benedict.

Innkeeper(s): John & Mary Hornberger.

Rates:$38-85. MC VISA. Full Bkfst. 7 rooms. 5 with shared baths. Beds:QT. Conference Rm. AC, Refrig. in room. Golf. Tennis. Skiing.

Swimming. Fishing.

Seen in: *Portsmouth Herald, Hampton Union, Boston Globe.*

Contact: Mary Hornberger. Certificate may be used: Not valid Friday/Saturday during June through October.

"Very hospitable, can't think of a thing you need to add."

The Victoria Inn

430 High St
Hampton 03842
(603)929-1437

1875. Elegance and style are featured at this Queen Anne Victorian inn just a half-mile from the ocean. A romantic gazebo, spacious guest rooms and Victorian furnishings throughout the inn add to its considerable charm. The Honeymoon Suite and Victoria Room are popular with those seeking privacy and luxury. Guests may borrow the inn's bicycles for a relaxing ride or read a book in its deluxe morning room. Other common areas include the living room, where visitors enjoy cable TV, and the sitting room, with its cozy fireplace.

Innkeeper(s): Ruth & Bill Muzzey.

Rates:$55-95. MC VISA. Gourmet Brkfst. 6 rooms. 3 with shared baths. Beds:KQT. TV, Phone, AC in room. Bicycling. Skiing. Swimming. Fishing.

Contact: William Muzzey. Certificate may be used: Nov. 1-May 1.

Hancock

The Hancock Inn

Main St
Hancock 03449
(603)525-3318 (800)525-1789
Fax:(603)525-9301

1789. Travelers have enjoyed this old inn, now in the National Register of Historic Places, since the days it served as a stagecoach stop more than 200 years ago. Canopied beds are found in some rooms and there are hooked rugs, wing-back chairs and rockers. The Mural Room boasts a pastoral mural painted in 1825. The Carriage Room lounge features tables of old bellows, seats from early buggies and a blazing hearth.

Innkeeper(s): Linda & Joe Johnston.

Rates:$88-120. MC VISA AX DC DS. Full Bkfst. EP. Teas. 11 rooms. Beds:QT. Conference Rm. Phone, AC in room. Skiing. Handicap access. Swimming. Fishing.

Seen in: *Country Inns, The Boston Globe, The Keene Sentinel, Yankee Homes.*

Contact: Linda Johnston. Certificate may be used: November - June, no holidays.

"The warmth you extended was the most meaningful part of our visit."

Hillsboro

The Inn at Maplewood Farm
447 Center Rd, PO Box 1478
Hillsboro 03244
(603)464-4242 Fax:(603)464-5859

1794. Antique-lovers will enjoy this historic inn, which not only features attractive American and European pieces, but a location in the heart of antique and auction country. An antique retail shop also is on the premises. Guests may borrow a canoe or mountain bike to explore the surrounding area. The inn borders scenic Fox State Forest and historic Hillsborough Center is just up the road. The Franklin Pierce Homestead and Pats Peak Ski Area are nearby.

Innkeeper(s): Laura & Jayme Simoes.

Rates:$50-65. MC VISA AX DS. Full Bkfst. EP. Picnic lunches. Teas. Evening snacks. 5 rooms. 2 with shared baths. Fireplaces. Beds:KQT. Conference Rm. Farm. Skiing. Swimming. Fishing.

Contact: Laura Simoes. Certificate may be used: Midweek stays, only Sunday-Thursday night off-season (Nov. 1-April 30).

Holderness

The Inn on Golden Pond
Rt 3, PO Box 680
Holderness 03245
(603)968-7269

1879. Framed by meandering stone walls and split-rail fences more than 100 years old, this inn is situated on 50 acres of woodlands. Most rooms overlook picturesque countryside and nearby is Squam Lake, setting for the film "On Golden Pond." An inviting, 60-foot screened porch provides a place to relax during the summer.

Innkeeper(s): Bill & Bonnie Webb.

Rates:$85-135. MC VISA AX. Full Bkfst. EP. 9 rooms. Beds:KQT. Golf. Tennis. Skiing. Swimming. Fishing.

Seen in: *Boston Globe, Baltimore Sun, Los Angeles Times.*

Contact: William Webb. Certificate may be used: Good except weekends in July, August, September and holiday weekends. Not available Sept. 15 - Oct. 31.

"Another sweet flower added to my bouquet of life."

Jackson

Dana Place Inn
Rt 16, Pinkham Notch Rd
Jackson 03846
(603)383-6822 (800)537-9276

Fax:(603)383-6822

1860. The original owners received this Colonial farmhouse as a wedding present. The warm, cozy atmosphere of the inn is surpassed only by the spec-

tacular mountain views. During autumn, the fall leaves explode with color, and guests can enjoy the surroundings while taking a hike or bike ride through the area. The beautiful Ellis River is the perfect place for an afternoon of fly-fishing or a picnic. After a scrumptious country breakfast, winter guests can step out the door and into skis for a day of cross-country skiing.

Innkeeper(s): The Levine Family.

Rates:$75-135. MC VISA AX DC DS CB. Full Bkfst. AP available. MAP available. Gourmet Dinner. Picnic lunches. Teas. 39 rooms. 4 with shared baths. Beds:KQT. Conference Rm. Phone, AC in room. Golf. Tennis. Skiing. Swimming. Horseback riding. Fishing.

Seen in: *Travel & Leisure, Inn Spots, Bon Appetit, Country Journal.*

Contact: Harris Levine. Certificate may be used: Oct. 23-Dec. 22, 1994, March 20-June 15, 1995, Oct. 22-Dec. 21, 1995, midweek only.

Ellis River House
Rt 16, Box 656
Jackson 03846
(603)383-9339 (800)233-8309
Fax:(603)383-4142

1893. Andrew Harriman built this farmhouse, as well as the village town hall and three-room schoolhouse where the innkeepers' child attends school. Classic antiques fill the guest rooms and riverfront "honeymoon" cottage and each window reveals views of magnificent mountains, the vineyard, or spectacular Ellis River. As a working farm, the Ellis River House includes a population of chickens, geese, ducks, pigs and a pony.

Innkeeper(s): Barry & Barbara Lubao.

Rates:$55-225. MC VISA AX DC DS. Full Bkfst. MAP available. Teas. 20 rooms. 3 with shared baths. Fireplaces. Beds:KQT. Conference Rm. TV, AC in room. Golf. Tennis. Bicycling. Skiing. Handicap access. Spa. Sauna. Swimming. Horseback riding. Fishing.

Seen in: *The Mountain Ear.*

Contact: Barbara Lubao. Certificate may be used: Not valid August-October. Not valid Dec. 20-March 30 on weekends. Not valid holidays or fall foliage. Valid Jan. 2-March 30, midweek. Valid April, May, June, July - midweek and weekends. Valid November-Dec. 19 midweek and weekends.

"We have stayed at many B&Bs all over the world and are in agreement that the beauty and hospitality of Ellis River House is that of a world-class bed & breakfast."

The Inn at Jackson

Thorn Hill Rd, Box 807
Jackson 03846
(603)383-4321

1902. Architect Stanford White built this inn over-looking the village and White Mountains. The atmosphere is comfortable and inviting, and breakfast is served in a glassed-in porch which provides a panoramic view. In winter, sleigh rides can be arranged and in summer, hay rides and horseback riding.

Innkeeper(s): Lori Tradewell.

Rates:$58-85. MC VISA AX DC DS CB. Full Bkfst. 9 rooms. Beds:QT. Golf. Tennis. Skiing. Spa. Swimming. Horseback riding. Fishing.

Seen in: *Country Inns.*

Contact: Lori Tradewell. Certificate may be used: April, May, June, November - anytime excluding holidays. July, August, January, March, December - Sunday through Thursday excluding holidays.

"We had a terrific time and found the inn warm and cozy and most of all relaxing."

The Inn at Thorn Hill

PO Box A, Thorn Hill Rd
Jackson 03846
(603)383-4242 (800)289-8990
Fax:(603)383-8062

1895. Follow a romantic drive through the Honeymoon Covered Bridge to Thorn Hill Road where this country Victorian stands, built by architect Stanford White. Its 10 acres are adjacent to the Jackson Ski Touring trails. Inside, the decor is Victorian and a collection of antique light fixtures accentuates the guest rooms, pub, drawing room, and parlor.

Innkeeper(s): Jim & Ibby Cooper.

Rates:$140-236. MC VISA AX DC. MAP available. Gourmet Brkfst, Dinner. Teas. 19 rooms. Fireplaces. Beds:KQT. Conference Rm. AC in room. Golf. Tennis. Skiing. Spa. Swimming. Horseback riding. Fishing.

Seen in: *Mature Outlook, The Reporter, New England GetAways, Bon Appetit.*

Contact: Jim Cooper. Certificate may be used: All year except: Sept. 23 - Oct. 16, 1994 - foliage, foliage, 1995. Dec. 23 - Jan. 1, 1995 - Christmas, Christmas, 1995. Winter weekends January - March, 1995.

"Magnificent, start to finish! The food was excellent but the mountain air must have shrunk my clothes!"

Whitneys' Inn

Rt 16B, Box W
Jackson 03846
(603)383-8916 (800)677-5737
Fax:(603)383-8916

1840. This country inn offers romance, family recreation and a lovely setting at the base of the Black Mountain Ski Area. The inn specializes in recreation, as guests enjoy cookouts, cross-country and downhill skiing, hiking, lawn games, skating, sledding, sleigh rides, swimming and tennis. Homemade corned beef hash is one of the breakfast specialties. Popular nearby activities include trying out Jackson's two golf courses and picnicking at Jackson Falls.

Innkeeper(s): Robert & Barbara Bowman.

Rates:$60-150. MC VISA AX DS. Full Bkfst. MAP available. Gourmet Dinner. Picnic lunches. Teas. 29 rooms. Fireplaces. Beds:KQT. Conference Rm. TV, Refrig. in room. Tennis. Skiing. Fishing.

Contact: Kevin Martin. Certificate may be used: Sept. 6-22, Oct. 16 - Nov. 23, Nov. 27 - Dec. 21, 1994. Jan. 2 - February, 1995 (Sunday - Thursday), Feb. 26 - March 16, March 19 - July 20, Sept. 5-21, Oct. 16 - Nov. 20, Nov. 27 - Dec. 21, 1995.

Jefferson

Applebrook B&B

Rt 115A, PO Box 178
Jefferson 03583
(603)586-7713 (800)545-6504

1800. Panoramic views surround this large Victorian farmhouse nestled in the middle of New Hampshire's White Mountains. Guests can awake

to the smell of freshly baked muffins made with locally picked berries. A comfortable, firelit sitting room boasts stained glass, a goldfish pool and a beautiful view of Mt. Washington. Test your golfing skills at the nearby 18-hole championship course, or spend the day antique hunting. A trout stream and spring-fed rock pool are nearby. Wintertime guests can ice skate or race through the powder at nearby ski resorts or by way of snowmobile, finish off the day with a moonlight toboggan ride.

Innkeeper(s): Sandra Conley & Martin Kelly.

Rates:$40-60. MC VISA. Full Bkfst. Teas. 11 rooms. 8 with shared baths. Beds:KQT. Golf. Tennis. Bicycling. Skiing. Spa. Swimming. Horseback riding. Fishing.

Contact: Sandra Conley. Certificate may be used: Anytime except weekends Aug. 1 - Oct. 15, Dec. 15 - March 15.

"We came for a night and stayed for a week."

Lincoln

Red Sleigh Inn B&B
Box 562
Lincoln 03251
(603)745-8517

1910. This house was built by J. E. Henry, owner of the Lincoln Paper Mill, a huge lumber business and dairy farm. The foundation was constructed of stones taken from the Pemigawasset River. Loretta's blueberry muffins are a guest favorite.
Innkeeper(s): Bill & Loretta Deppe.

Rates:$65-75. MC VISA. Full Bkfst. Teas. 6 rooms. 4 with shared baths. Beds:KQT. Skiing. Swimming. Fishing.

Seen in: *Newsday, Ski, Skiing.*

Contact: Loretta Deppe. Certificate may be used: Non-holiday weekends, midweek.

"Your ears must be ringing because we haven't stopped talking about the Red Sleigh Inn and its wonderful, caring owners."

Marlborough

Peep-Willow Farm
51 Bixby St
Marlborough 03455
(603)876-3807

1988. Just east of busy Keene lies this charming Colonial Gambrel Cape, a contemporary farmhouse featuring comfortable lodging in a rural setting. After enjoying the inn's full breakfast, visitors may explore the surrounding area, which boasts many recreational and sightseeing activities. The innkeeper keeps pets on the premises and allows visitors to bring theirs. Monadnock State Park is nearby.
Innkeeper(s): Noel Aderer.

Rates:$50. Full Bkfst. 3 rooms. 3 with shared baths. Beds:KQT. Farm. Skiing. Swimming. Fishing.

Contact: Noel Aderer. Certificate may be used: November-August.

Moultonboro

Olde Orchard Inn
RR 1, Box 256
Moultonboro 03254
(603)476-5004 (800)598-5845

1790. This farmhouse rests next to a mountain brook and pond in the midst of an apple orchard. Five guest rooms and one family suite are available,

all with private baths. After enjoying a large country breakfast, guests may borrow a bicycle for a ride to Lake Winnipesaukee, just a mile away. The inn is within an hour's drive of five downhill skiing areas, and guests also may cross-country ski on the inn's own trails. Visitors are encouraged to notify the innkeepers if bringing along a pet; arrangements usually can be made. The Castle in the Clouds and the Ossipee Ski Area are nearby.
Innkeeper(s): Jim & Mary Senner.

Rates:$70-80. AX. Full Bkfst. 8 rooms. Fireplaces. Beds:T. Farm. Bicycling. Skiing. Swimming. Fishing.

Contact: James Senner. Certificate may be used: November - April.

New Ipswich

The Inn at New Ipswich
11 Porter Hill Rd, Box 208
New Ipswich 03071
(603)878-3711

1790. A classic red barn gives this inn a country feel. The grounds are bordered with stone walls, gardens and fruit trees. Two of the bedrooms have

working fireplaces and all feature antiques. The front porch offers rockers for relaxing and the screened porch is an excellent place to take in the evening breezes. The Monadnock region offers mountain climbing and hiking as well as a summer theater, antiquing and incredible fall foliage. In cool months, homemade breakfasts are served in the keeping room in front of a crackling fire.
Rates:$65. MC VISA. Full Bkfst. Evening snacks. 5 rooms. Fireplaces. Beds:QT. Golf. Skiing. Fishing.

Contact: Virginia Bankuti. Certificate may be used: Anytime Nov. 1 thru June 30. Weekdays only from July 1 thru Oct. 31. Excludes holiday weekends.

"Breakfast alone is worth the trip."

North Conway

The 1785 Inn
PO Box 1785, 3582 White Mtn Hwy
North Conway 03860
(603)356-9025 (800)421-1785

Fax:(603)356-6081

1785. The main section of this center-chimney house was built by Captain Elijah Dinsmore of the New Hampshire Rangers. He was granted the land for service in the American Revolution. Original hand-hewn beams, corner posts, fireplaces, and a brick oven are still visible and operating.

Innkeeper(s): Charlie & Becky Mallar.

Rates:$59-199. MC VISA AX DC DS CB. Full Bkfst. MAP available. Gourmet Brkfst. Dinner. Teas. Evening snacks. 17 rooms. 5 with shared baths. Beds:KQT. Conference Rm. AC, Refrig. in room. Golf. Tennis. Bicycling. Skiing. Swimming. Horseback riding. Fishing.

Seen in: *New England Getaways, Valley Visitor, Bon Appetit, Ski Magazine, Connecticut Magazine.*

Contact: Charles Mallar. Certificate may be used: January, March, April, May June, November and December, excluding holidays.

"Occasionally in our lifetimes is a moment so unexpectedly perfect that we use it as our measure for our unforgettable moments. We just had such an experience at The 1785 Inn."

The Buttonwood Inn

Mt Surprise Rd, PO Box 1817
North Conway 03860
(603)356-2625 (800)258-2625
Fax:(603)356-3140

1820. This center-chimney, New England-style inn was once a working farm of more than 100 acres on the mountain. Of the original outbuildings, only the granite barn foundation remains. Through the years, the house has been extended to a total of 20 rooms.

Innkeeper(s): Claudia & Peter Needham.

Rates:$45-120. MC VISA AX DC. Full Bkfst. Picnic lunches. Teas. 9 rooms. 6 with shared baths. Beds:KQT. Golf. Skiing. Handicap access. Swimming. Fishing.

Seen in: *Northeast Bound, Skiing, Boston Globe, Yankee Travel.*

Contact: Claudia Needham. Certificate may be used: Midweek-Sunday through Thursday, non-peak times-exclusive of holiday weekends and weeks. Weekends-April through June exclusive of holiday weekends.

"The very moment we spotted your lovely inn nestled midway on the mountainside in the moonlight, we knew we had found a winner."

Cranmore Mt Lodge

Kearsarge Rd, PO Box 1194
North Conway 03860
(603)356-2044 (800)356-3596
Fax:(603)356-8963

1865. Babe Ruth was a frequent guest at this old New England farmhouse when his daughter was the owner. There are many rare Babe Ruth photos displayed in the inn and one guest room is still decorated with his furnishings. The barn on the property is held together with wooden pegs and contains dorm rooms.

Innkeeper(s): Dennis & Judy Helfand.

Rates:$69-94. MC VISA AX DC DS. Full Bkfst. MAP available. Picnic lunches. 20 rooms. 4 with shared baths. Beds:KQT. TV, AC in room. Tennis. Bicycling. Skiing. Spa. Swimming. Fishing.

Seen in: *New England Getaways, Ski Magazine, Snow Country, Montreal Gazette, Newsday.*

Contact: Judith Helfand. Certificate may be used: Sunday-Thursday except Sept. 15-Oct. 24, 1995.

"Your accommodations are lovely, your breakfasts delicious."

Eastman Inn

Main St, Box 882
North Conway 03860
(603)356-6707 (800)626-5855

1797. This classic three-story Victorian inn has been restored and decorated to retain the warmth and charm of the 18th century. The inn has panoramic views of the mountains in all directions. Fine restaurants and shopping outlets are a short walk away. The innkeepers can help you with packages that include everything from canoeing to llama treking.

Innkeeper(s): Craig Leitner.

Rates:$55-80. MC VISA. Full Bkfst. 14 rooms. 2 with shared baths. Beds:KQ. TV, AC in room. Bicycling. Skiing. Swimming. Fishing.

Contact: Craig Leitner. Certificate may be used: Anytime April 1-June 21 and Nov. 1-Dec. 21.

The Forest - A Country Inn

PO Box 1376, Rt 16A
North Conway 03860
(603)356-9772
(800)448-3534
Fax:(603)356-5652

1835. This spacious Second Empire Victorian offers easy access to the many attractions of the Mt. Washington Valley. The inn's 11 guest rooms are uniquely decorated with country antique furnishings. Honeymooners often enjoy the privacy of the inn's turn-of-the-century stone cottage. A stream runs through the inn's 25 wooded acres, and guests may cross-country ski right on the property. The inn also boasts a built-in swimming pool. Breakfast fare could include apple pancakes, rum raisin French toast or spiced Belgian waffles. Heritage New Hampshire and Story Land are nearby.

Innkeeper(s): Ken & Rae Wyman

Rates:$60-135. MC VISA DC DS. Full Bkfst. Teas. 13 rooms. 2 with shared baths. Fireplaces. Beds:KQT. AC in room. Golf. Tennis. Skiing. Swimming. Horseback riding. Fishing.

Contact: Rae Wyman. Certificate may be used: Anytime excluding holidays, fall foliage and winter weekends.

Stonehurst Manor

Rt 16
North Conway 03860-1937
(603)356-3113 (800)525-9100
Fax:(603)356-3217

1876. This English-style manor stands on lush, landscaped lawns and 30 acres of pine trees. It was built as the summer home for the Bigelow family, founder of the Bigelow Carpet Company. Inside the tremendous front door is an elegant display of leaded and stained-glass windows, rich oak woodwork, a winding staircase and a massive, hand-carved oak fireplace.

Innkeeper(s): Peter Rattay.

Rates:$75-155. MC VISA AX. Full Bkfst. EP. MAP available. Gourmet Brkfst, Dinner. Teas. 24 rooms. 2 with shared baths. Fireplaces. Beds:KQT. Conference Rm. TV, AC in room. Tennis. Bicycling. Skiing. Handicap access. Spa. Swimming. Fishing.

Seen in: *The Boston Globe, New York Daily News, Bon Appetit.*

Contact: Peter Rattay. Certificate may be used: Sunday - Thursday (except holiday weekends) for the months of January, February, March, April, May, June, November, December.

"An architecturally preserved replica of an English country house, a perfect retreat for the nostalgic-at-heart," Phil Berthiaume, Country Almanac.

Victorian Harvest Inn

28 Locust Ln, Box 1763
North Conway 03860
(603)356-3548 (800)642-0749

1850. Perched atop a hill in the Mt. Washington Valley, this Folk Victorian inn features comfortable

surroundings and attention to detail. The country Victorian furnishings are highlighted by homemade quilts and teddy bears that visitors may adopt during their stay. The Victoria Station Room boasts its own carousel horse, and the Nook & Cranny Room offers a view of the entire Moat Range. Guests also enjoy strolling the grounds, which include a footbridge, gardens and a Victorian decorated pool.

Innkeeper(s): Linda & Robert Dahlberg.

Rates:$65-90. MC VISA AX DS. Full Bkfst. EP. Teas. 6 rooms. 2 with shared baths. Beds:KQDT. Phone, AC, Refrig. in room. Skiing. Swimming. Fishing.

Contact: Linda Dahlberg. Certificate may be used: Sunday-Thursday, January-June, November-December, no Christmas week.

North Conway/Kearsarge

Isaac Merrill House Inn

PO Box 8, 720 Kearsarge Rd
North Conway/Kearsarge 03847
(603)356-9041 (800)328-9041
Fax:(603)356-9041

1773. The guest book at this inn dates from 1875. Since that time the inn has been renovated and placed on the federal map as a national landmark. Some of the rooms have skylights as well as brass beds or canopy beds and antique rockers. Breakfast is served fireside. Across the street flows a babbling brook.

Innkeeper(s): The Levine Family.

Rates:$45-138. MC VISA AX DS. Full Bkfst. MAP available. Picnic lunches. Teas. 22 rooms. 4 with shared baths. Beds:KQT. Conference Rm. AC in room. Golf. Tennis. Bicycling. Skiing. Spa. Sauna. Exercise room. Swimming. Horseback riding. Fishing.

Seen in: *The Standard-Times, The Irregular, Fosters Business Review, Granite State News, Boston Globe, Yankee Magazine.*

Contact: Richard Levine. Certificate may be used: July 1 - Sept. 16, 1994; Dec. 1, 1994 - Sept. 13, 1995.

"Although I expected this to be a nice, cozy place, I was not prepared for the royal treatment my family and I received. We cast our vote for Larry and Claire as innkeepers of the year."

Orford

White Goose Inn

Rt 10, PO Box 17
Orford 03777
(603)353-4812 (800)358-4267
Fax:(603)353-4543

1770. The White Goose Inn is bordered by a picket fence. An old elm tree was set in the Colonial

Revival circular porch and was a community conversation piece for many years. The inn is decorated in an authentic style accentuating the wide-pine floors, beamed ceilings and Colonial fireplaces. Area winter sports include ice skating, skiing and sleigh riding. Dartmouth College is nearby.

Innkeeper(s): Manfred & Karin Wolf.

Rates:$65-105. MC VISA. Full Bkfst. 15 rooms. 2 with shared baths. Beds:QT. AC in room. Golf. Tennis. Skiing. Swimming. Horseback riding. Fishing.

Seen in: *Country Living.*

Contact: Manfred Wolf. Certificate may be used: November-May.

Plymouth

Colonel Spencer Inn

Rt 3S, RFD 1, Box 206
Plymouth 03264
(603)536-3438

1763. This pre-Revolutionary Colonial boasts Indian shutters, gleaming plank floors and secret passageways. Benjamin Baker, one of the house's early owners, fought at Bunker Hill and with General Washington at Cambridge. Within view of the river and the mountains, the inn is now a cozy retreat with a cheery country Colonial decor. Afternoon tea and evening coffee and dessert are served. A suite with kitchen is also available. Occasional evening meals may be arranged by reservation.

Innkeeper(s): Carolyn & Alan Hill.

Rates:$35-65. Full Bkfst. 7 rooms. Beds:T. Golf. Tennis. Bicycling. Skiing. Swimming. Horseback riding. Fishing.

Contact: Alan Hill. Certificate may be used: All year except holiday weekends.

"You have something very special here and we very much enjoyed a little piece of it!"

Portsmouth

Governor's House B&B

32 Miller Ave
Portsmouth 03801
(603)431-6546
Fax:(603)427-0803

1917. This elegant Georgian Colonial inn served as the family home of former Gov. Charles M. Dale for 30 years. Innkeeper Nancy

Grossman, a professional artist and tile painter, added her creative touch to each of the private baths in the inn's four guest rooms. The Captain's Room sports a canopied, queen pencil-post bed, a mermaid on its shower wall and nautical antiques. The Governor's, Peacock and Prescott rooms are equally enchanting. The inn boasts a private tennis court and golfers will enjoy the beautiful course at nearby Wentworth by the Sea. The Coolidge Mansion and Fort Constitution are within easy driving distance.

Innkeeper(s): John & Nancy Grossman.

Rates:$75-140. MC VISA. Full Bkfst. Teas. 4 rooms. Beds:Q. AC in room. Golf. Tennis. Swimming. Horseback riding. Fishing.

Contact: John Grossman. Certificate may be used: Anytime except weekends mid-May through September, October, holidays and special events.

Snowville

Snowvillage Inn

Stuart Rd, Box 176
Snowville 03849
(603)447-2818 (800)447-4345

1916. Frank Simonds, noted World War I historian and government consultant, called his retreat here "Blighty." The beams in the main house are hand-hewn and were taken from the original 1850 farmhouse. The inn has a spectacular sweeping view of Mt. Washington, and resembles a European mountain home with an Austrian flavor. (The hostess was born in Austria.)

Innkeeper(s): Peter, Trudy & Frank Cutrone.

Rates:$76-136. MC VISA AX DC DS. Full Bkfst. MAP available. Gourmet Dinner. 18 rooms. Fireplaces. Beds:KQ. Conference Rm. Tennis. Skiing. Sauna. Swimming. Fishing.

Seen in: *New England GetAways, Los Angeles Times, The Boston Globe.*

Contact: Tom Spaulding. Certificate may be used: Applies to a standard room, midweek during July 1-Sept. 16, 1994, Oct. 17-Dec. 16, 1994, Jan. 1-Feb. 16, 1995, Feb. 27-Sept. 14, 1995; Oct. 16-Dec. 14, 1995.

"A jewel of a country inn with gourmet food."

Stratham

Maple Lodge B&B

68 Depot Rd
Stratham 03885
(603)778-9833

1900. Built by an old sea captain, the living room of Maple Lodge overlooks Great Bay. An enormous stone fireplace is a favorite place for guests in winter, while the screened veranda is popular in summer. Guest rooms are spacious with comfy beds and floral wallpapers. A gourmet breakfast is served in keeping with the country setting.

Innkeeper(s): John & Natalie Fortin.

Rates:$65. MC VISA DS. Full Bkfst. 3 rooms. 3 with shared baths. Beds:DT. Golf. Fishing.

Contact: Natalie Fortin. Certificate may be used: Oct. 30 through April 15.

"The personal, caring touch given to every small detail captured our satisfaction to the fullest."

Sugar Hill

The Hilltop Inn
Main St
Sugar Hill 03585
(603)823-5695

1895. This rambling Victorian guest house is located on the quiet main street of town. The rooms are decorated with antiques, and there are several cozy common rooms for relaxing after a day of canoeing, horseback riding or skiing. A spacious deck provides views of the sunsets. Pets are welcome.

Innkeeper(s): Meri & Mike Hern.

Rates:$60-110. MC VISA DS. Full Bkfst. Gourmet Dinner. Picnic lunches. Teas. 6 rooms. Beds:QD. Golf. Tennis. Skiing. Swimming. Horseback riding. Fishing.

Seen in: *Boston Globe, Littleton Courier, Baltimore Sun, Philadelphia Herald, Yankee, Outside, Victoria Magazine.*

Contact: Meri Hern. Certificate may be used: April 1 - May 15, Nov. 1 - Dec. 15.

"Relaxing and comforting, better than being home!"

Sunset Hill House
Sunset Hill Rd
Sugar Hill 03585
(603)823-5522 (800)786-4455
Fax:(603)823-5738

1882. This Second Empire Victorian has views of two mountain ranges. Three parlors, all with cozy fireplaces, are favorite gathering spots. The inn's lush grounds offer many opportunities for recreation or relaxing, and guests often enjoy special events, such as fly-fishing lessons and maple-sugar tours. The Cannon Mountain Ski Area and Franconia Notch State Park are nearby. Be sure to inquire about golf and ski packages.

Innkeeper(s): Michael, Frank, Retsy Coyle & Gloria Korta.

Rates:$70-110. MC VISA AX DS. Full Bkfst. MAP available. Gourmet Brkfst, Dinner. Evening snacks. 30 rooms. Beds:KQT. Skiing. Swimming. Fishing.

Contact: Gloria Korta. Certificate may be used: Not available first two weeks of October or holiday weekends.

Sunapee

Dexter's Inn
Stagecoach Rd, Box 703 NS
Sunapee 03782
(603)763-5571 (800)232-5571

1800. This beautiful country estate offers special amenities for sports lovers. A swimming pool and three all-weather tennis courts provide hours of fun. Improve your game with a lesson from the staff tennis pro, or take in 18 holes at one of three nearby golf courses. For the more shopping-inclined, the area offers many antique and gift boutiques. Guests who prefer relaxation can sit and take in the view, expansive lawns and flower gardens. The rooms are cozy and decorated with a Vermont country flair.

Innkeeper(s): Holly & Michael Durfor.

Rates:$130-188. MC VISA DS. Full Bkfst. MAP available. 18 rooms. Beds:KQT. Conference Rm. AC in room. Golf. Tennis. Swimming. Horseback riding.

Contact: Michael Durfor. Certificate may be used: Sunday through Thursday.

"Just like being at home."

Haus Edelweiss
Box 368
Sunapee 03782
(603)763-2100 (800)248-0713

1880. A quiet street near Sunapee Harbor is home to this Victorian inn, just 500 feet from a boat dock. The five guest rooms feature famous literary

names, and a favorite is the romantic Romeo and Juliet Room. The cozy Emily Dickinson Room is available for those travelling alone. Guests select their breakfast fare the night before, and choose from Bavarian, continental, traditional or Yankee offerings. A speciality is Apfelpfannkuchen, baked German apple pancakes with whipped cream. King Ridge and Mt. Sunapee ski areas are nearby.

Innkeeper(s): John & Jennifer Dixon.

Rates:$45-60. MC VISA DS. Full Bkfst. AP available. Gourmet Brkfst. Picnic lunches. Teas. Evening snacks. 5 rooms. 3 with shared baths.

Beds:QT. Refrig. in room. Skiing. Swimming. Fishing.

Contact: Jennifer Dixon. Certificate may be used: Good only on weekday non-peak weeks.

The Inn at Sunapee
Box 336, 125 Burke Haven Hill Rd
Sunapee 03782
(603)763-4444 (800)327-2466

1875. Formerly part of a dairy farm, this spacious farmhouse inn also is home to a restaurant. The innkeepers, who spent nearly 30 years in the Far

East and Southeast Asia, have blended that international flavor into the traditional antique furnishings and New England menu items. The inn offers three sitting rooms, an impressive fieldstone fireplace, a library, swimming and tennis. The family-oriented inn also hosts meetings, reunions and weddings. Mt. Sunapee State Park and ski area are nearby.

Innkeeper(s): Ted & Susan Harriman.

Rates:$70-80. MC VISA AX. Full Bkfst. EP. MAP available. Gourmet Dinner. 16 rooms. Beds:QDT. Conference Rm. Farm. Golf. Tennis. Skiing. Swimming. Fishing.

Seen in: *New London-Gadabouts, Yankee Magazine.*

Contact: Susan Harriman. Certificate may be used: Anytime, except holiday weekends, Christmas week, first two weeks of August and first two weeks of October. Limited space.

Sutton Mills

Village House At Sutton Mills
Box 151, Grist Mill Rd
Sutton Mills 03221
(603)927-4765

1857. This country Victorian inn overlooks the village and offers charming accommodations along with convenient access to the area's many attractions. The three guest rooms sport antique furnishings and country quilts. Visitors also enjoy turn-down service and a full country breakfast. Wadleigh State Beach is nearby, and neighboring New London offers antiquing, fine dining and summer theater.

Innkeeper(s): Peggy & Norm Forand.

Rates:$50. Full Bkfst. 3 rooms. 3 with shared baths. Beds:DT. Skiing. Swimming. Fishing.

Contact: Norman & Peggy Forand. Certificate may be used: November and December except Thanksgiving weekend and Christmas plus March 15 through May 15, subject to room availability.

Thornton

Amber Lights Inn B&B
Route 3
Thornton 03223
(603)726-4077

1815. A breakfast to remember will delight this inn's guests, who are served a six-course, homemade meal in the Hannah Adams dining room. The Colonial inn offers five antique-filled guest rooms, all with queen beds and handmade quilts. Guests enjoy the inn's copper collection, on display in its country kitchen. They also like to relax in the sunny garden room, where wintertime visitors can watch other guests as they cross-country ski on the inn's grounds. Be sure to inquire about the inn's Murder Mystery weekend packages. Fine downhill skiing is found within easy driving distance of the inn.

Innkeeper(s): Carola Warnsman & Paul Sears.

Rates:$60-75. MC VISA AX DS. Full Bkfst. Gourmet Brkfst. 5 rooms. 4 with shared baths. Beds:QT. Golf. Skiing. Swimming. Horseback riding. Fishing.

Seen in: *New Hampshire, An Explorer's Guide.*

Contact: Carola Warnsman. Certificate may be used: Midweek only Jan. 1 - March 30, anytime April 1 - July 31 and anytime Nov. 1 - Dec. 24. Reservations required.

Tilton

Tilton Manor
28 Chestnut St
Tilton 03276
(603)286-3457

1889. This turn-of-the-century Folk Victorian inn is just two blocks from downtown Tilton. The inn's comfortable guest rooms are furnished with antiques and sport handmade afghans. Guests are treated to a hearty country breakfast featuring freshly baked muffins, and dinner is available with advance reservations. Visitors enjoy relaxing in the sitting room, where they may play games, read or watch TV after a busy day exploring the historic area. Gunstock and Highland ski resorts are nearby and the Daniel Webster Birthplace and Shaker Village are within easy driving distance.

Innkeeper(s): Chip and Diane Sasses.

Rates:$60-65. AX DS. Full Bkfst. AP available. MAP available. 5 rooms. 2 with shared baths. Fireplaces. Beds:KDT. Skiing. Swimming. Fishing.

Contact: Diane Sassis. Certificate may be used: No holidays.

Wentworth

Hilltop Acres
Box 32
Wentworth 03282
(603)764-5896

1806. This cozy inn is located in the White Mountains on 20 acres of woodland and fields. There is a brook that winds through the woods.

Guests may choose from rooms in the farmhouse or housekeeping cottages with fireplaces. There is a knotty-pine paneled recreation room with games and a piano.

Innkeeper(s): Marie A. Kauk & Cecilia Egger.

Rates:$65-80. MC VISA AX. ContPlus Bkfst. 6 rooms. Conference Rm. Skiing. Swimming. Fishing.

Contact: Marie Kauk. Certificate may be used: Monday-Thursday.

Wentworth Inn & Art Gallery
Ellsworth Hill Rd, Off Rt 25
Wentworth 03282
(603)764-9923 (800)258-7372

1800. This Federal Colonial-style inn is located on Baker Pond Brook in the foothills of the White Mountains. The guest rooms are elegantly decorated. A full country breakfast and afternoon snacks are offered. Gourmet candlelight dining is available in the evening. The New Hampshire Vacations Tourist Information is located on the property and there is an art gallery and gift shop. A double-tiered veranda overlooks Mount Stinson.

Innkeeper(s): Jim & Barbara Moffat.

Rates:$60-80. MC VISA AX DC CB. Full Bkfst. EP. AP available. MAP available. Gourmet Dinner. 7 rooms. 3 with shared baths. Beds:Q. Conference Rm. Golf. Skiing. Swimming. Horseback riding. Fishing.

Seen in: *Eagle-Tribune, Union Leader.*

Contact: James Moffat. Certificate may be used: Anytime.

Wilton Center

Stepping Stones
Bennington Battle Tr
Wilton Center 03086
(603)654-9048

1895. Decks and terraces overlook the enormous gardens of this Greek Revival house, in the local historic register. Guest rooms feature white-washed pine, cherry or Shaker-style country pieces accented with botanical prints. Poached eggs on asparagus with hollandaise sauce, blueberry Belgian waffles and jumbo apple muffins with streusel topping are guests' favorite breakfast choices. The innkeeper is both a garden designer and weaver.

Innkeeper(s): Ann Carlsmith.

Rates:$45-50. Full Bkfst. Teas. Evening snacks. 3 rooms. 2 with shared baths. Beds:QT. AC in room. Skiing.

Contact: Ann Carlsmith. Certificate may be used: 1994 and 1995 excluding Sept. 20-Oct. 30, 1994 and 1995.

Wolfeboro

Tuc'Me Inn B&B
68 N Main St, Rt 109N, PO Box 657
Wolfeboro 03894
(603)569-5702

1850. This Federal Colonial-style house features a music room, parlor, and screen porches. Afternoon tea with home-baked scones is served in the

Victorian garden room. Chocolate chip or strawberry pancakes are often presented for breakfast in the dining room. The inn is a short walk to the quaint village of Wolfeboro and the shores of Lake Winnipesaukee.

Innkeeper(s): Ernie, Terry, Tina Foutz & Isabel Evans.

Rates:$59-75. MC VISA. Full Bkfst. Teas. 7 rooms. 4 with shared baths. Beds:QT. AC in room. Skiing. Swimming. Horseback riding. Fishing.

Seen in: *Granite State News, Wolfeboro Times ("The Times").*

Contact: Terrille Sue Foutz. Certificate may be used: Nov. 1 to April 15, anytime; April 15 to Oct. 31, weekdays (Sunday-Thursday) only.

"Super in every detail."

New Jersey

Avon-by-the-Sea

The Avon Manor B&B Inn
109 Sylvania Ave
Avon-by-the-Sea 07717-1338
(908)774-0110

1907. The Avon Manor was built as a private summer residence in the Colonial Revival style. The handsome facade is graced by a 100-foot wrap-

around porch. Light, airy bedrooms are decorated in Laura Ashley pastels. Guests breakfast in a sunny dining room.
Innkeeper(s): Kathleen & Jim Curley.
Rates:$60-110. Full Bkfst. Teas. 8 rooms. 2 with shared baths.

Beds:QT. AC in room. Swimming. Horseback riding. Fishing.
Contact: Kathleen Curley. Certificate may be used: Anytime except July and August, holiday and special weekends.

The Sands B&B Inn
42 Sylvania Ave
Avon-by-the-Sea 07717
(908)776-8386

1896. Just seven houses from a white sandy beach is this Queen-Anne-style house, featuring some rooms with ocean views. There are ceiling fans and refrigerators in the rooms. The owners have operated the inn since 1958.
Innkeeper(s): Joseph & Ann Suchecki.
Rates:$50-75. Full Bkfst. 9 rooms. 9 with shared baths. Beds:QDT. TV, AC, Refrig. in room. Swimming. Fishing.
Contact: Ann Suchecki. Certificate may be used: Early May or late September excluding holidays.

Bay Head

Bay Head Harbor Inn
676 Main Ave
Bay Head 08742
(908)899-0767

1890. This three-story Shingle-style inn, just a block from the beach and the bay, boasts several rooms with private porches. The inn is decorated with folk art and country antiques. Afternoon tea and evening snacks are served. Walk to fine restaurants, unique shops and Twilight Lake.
Innkeeper(s): Janice & Dan Eskesen.
Rates:$75-125. MC VISA. ContPlus Bkfst. Teas. Evening snacks. 6 rooms. 6 with shared baths. Beds:KQT. AC in room.
Contact: Janice Eskesen. Certificate may be used: Oct. 1, 1994-Dec. 31, 1994; Jan. 31, 1995-May 1, 1995; Oct. 1, 1995-Dec. 31, 1995.

Beach Haven

Green Gables
212 Centre St
Beach Haven 08008
(609)492-3553 Fax:(609)492-2507

1890. This Queen Anne Victorian located in the Beach Haven Historic District is in the National Register. Decorated in an elegant Victorian style, the inn's dining room provides romantic candle-light dinners rated "four-star" by many. (If you plan to dine here, be sure and make reservations at the same time you reserve your room.) Among some guest favorites are enjoying the inn's flower gardens from front porch rockers, strolling on the beach a block and a half away, and walking to shops, concerts in the park and nearby clubs. New Broadway plays may be seen at the summer stock theater, Surflight, just around the corner.

Innkeeper(s): Rita & Adolfo De Martino.

Rates:$70-115. MC VISA AX DC. Gourmet Dinner. Picnic lunches. Teas. 6 rooms. 5 with shared baths. Beds:DT. Tennis. Swimming. Fishing.

Contact: Rita Rapella. Certificate may be used: January, February, March, April, October, November, December.

Belmar

The Seaflower B&B
110 9th Ave
Belmar 07719
(908)681-6006

1907. This comfortable Dutch Colonial inn is a half-block from the beach and boardwalk. Guest rooms feature the sound of ocean waves and the scent of fresh flowers. Wallpapers set off an eclectic mixture of antiques, new four-poster and canopy beds, and an abundance of paintings. Guests enjoy the ocean views from the porch's teak Adirondack chairs. One of the major deep-sea fishing ports on the Northeast Coast is nearby at the mouth of the Shark River, and your hosts can help set up charters.

Innkeeper(s): Pat O'Keefe & Knute Iwaszko.

Rates:$60-90. AX. Full Bkfst. Gourmet Brkfst. 6 rooms. 2 with shared baths. Beds:KQT. Golf. Tennis. Bicycling. Swimming. Horseback riding. Fishing.

Seen in: *New Jersey Monthly Magazine.*

Contact: Knute Iwaszko. Certificate may be used: Anytime except weekends July, August, mid-September.

Cape May

The Inn at 22 Jackson
22 Jackson St
Cape May 08204
(609)884-2226 (800)452-8177
Fax:(609)884-2226

1898. The gingerbread on this Queen Anne Victorian is painted purple, white and navy. The inn boasts a three-story tower. Suites are outfitted with wet bars, refrigerators and microwaves, as well as cable TV and private baths. The inn is decorated in a light, bright eclectic style with furnishings ranging from 1860 Victorian antiques, pieces from the '30s and antique toy and game collections. The inn's four porches are popular for rocking and having breakfast.

Innkeeper(s): Barbara Carmichael & Chip Masemore.

Rates:$95-265. MC VISA AX. Full Bkfst. Teas. 5 rooms. Beds:KQT. TV, AC, Refrig. in room. Bicycling. Swimming. Fishing.

Contact: Chip Masemore. Certificate may be used: Sunday-Thursday, November, January-April 30. Weekends November, January and February.

The Abbey
34 Gurney St at Columbia Ave
Cape May 08204
(609)884-4506

1869. This inn consists of two buildings, one a seaside Gothic Revival villa with a 60-foot tower, Gothic arched windows and shaded verandas. Furnishings include floor-to-ceiling mirrors, ornate gas chandeliers, marble-topped dressers and beds of carved walnut, wrought iron and brass. The cottage adjacent to the villa is a Second Empire-style home with a mansard roof. A full breakfast is served in the dining room in spring and fall and on the veranda in the summer. Late afternoon refreshments and tea are served each day at 4:30 p.m.

Innkeeper(s): Jay & Marianne Schatz.

Rates:$90-190. MC VISA DS. Full Bkfst. Teas. 14 rooms. Beds:KQD. Conference Rm. AC, Refrig. in room. Golf. Tennis. Swimming. Horseback riding. Fishing.

Seen in: *Richmond Times-Dispatch, New York Times, Glamour, Philadelphia Inquirer, National Geographic.*

Contact: Jay Schatz. Certificate may be used: Monday through Thursday, April, May, October (except week of Oct. 7-17) and November.

"Staying with you folks really makes the difference between a 'nice' vacation and a great one!"

Abigail Adams B&B

12 Jackson St
Cape May 08204
(609)884-1371

1888. The front porch of this Victorian, one of the
Seven Sisters, is only 100 feet from the ocean.
There is a free-standing circular staircase, as well as

original fireplaces and woodwork throughout. The
decor is highlighted with flowered chintz and
antiques, and the dining room is hand-stenciled.
Innkeeper(s): Kate Emerson.
Rates:$75-140. MC VISA AX. Full Bkfst. Gourmet Brkfst. Teas. 5 rooms.
2 with shared baths. Beds:QD. AC in room. Swimming.
Contact: Kate Emerson. Certificate may be used: Oct. 15-May 15,
Sunday through Thursday.

"What a wonderful time. Comfortable & homey."

Albert G. Stevens Inn

127 Myrtle Ave
Cape May 08204
(609)884-4717 (800)890-2287

1898. If you feel right at home, even before you
reach the front door, it may be because you've seen
this Queen Anne Free Classic Victorian house on
local postcards. Next door to the Wilbrahan
Mansion, it features a wraparound veranda, a
tower, Victorian antiques and carved woodwork. A
full country breakfast is served and during fall and
winter dinners are included. The beach is three
blocks away. Beach tags are available.
Innkeeper(s): Curt & Diane Rangen.
Rates:$65-155. MC VISA AX DS. Full Bkfst. Teas. 9 rooms. Beds:QDT.
AC in room. Sauna. Exercise room. Swimming. Fishing.
Seen in: *The Jersey Shore.*
Contact: Curtis Rangen. Certificate may be used: February - June,
October - January; Sunday through Thursday.

Alexander's Inn

653 Washington St
Cape May 08204
(609)884-2555 Fax:(609)884-8883

1883. This mansard-roofed Victorian has been
recently renovated and fitted with sprinkler system,
private baths and central air conditioning, yet the
inn still maintains its elegant Victorian atmosphere. There are Oriental rugs, antiques and oil
paintings in abundance. The gourmet dining room
provides white-glove service with silver, crystal,
linen and lace. Located on Washington Street are
the trolley tours, horse-and-carriage rides, bicycle
rentals, museums and shops. Saturday night guests
at the inn are treated to a five-course Sunday
brunch.
Innkeeper(s): Larry & Diane Muentz.
Rates:$90-150. MC VISA AX DS. ContPlus Bkfst. Gourmet Dinner. Teas.
6 rooms. Beds:Q. AC in room. Swimming. Fishing.
Contact: Diane Muentz. Certificate may be used: Winter (January,
February, March).

Captain Mey's B&B Inn

202 Ocean St
Cape May 08204
(609)884-7793

1890. Named after a Dutch West India captain
who named the area, the inn displays its Dutch
heritage with table-top Persian rugs, Delft china
and imported Dutch lace curtains. The dining room
features chestnut and oak Eastlake paneling.
Breakfast is served by candlelight.
Innkeeper(s): George & Kathleen Blinn.
Rates:$89-169. MC VISA. Full Bkfst. 10 rooms. 3 with shared baths.
Fireplaces. Beds:QT. AC, Refrig. in room. Golf. Tennis. Swimming.
Horseback riding. Fishing.
Seen in: *Atlantic City Magazine, Americana Magazine, Country Living,
New Jersey Monthly.*
Contact: Kathleen Blinn. Certificate may be used: January, February,
March, April, May; midweek only.

*"The innkeepers pamper you so much you wish you
could stay forever."*

The Carroll Villa B&B

19 Jackson St
Cape May 08204
(609)884-9619 Fax:(609)884-0264

1882. This Victorian hotel is located one-half block
from the ocean on the oldest street in the historic
district of Cape May. Breakfast at the Villa is a
memorable event, featuring dishes acclaimed by the
New York Times and Frommers. Homemade fruit
breads, Italian omelets and Crab Eggs Benedict are
a few specialties. Meals are served in the Mad

Batter Restaurant on a European veranda, a secluded garden terrace or in the skylit Victorian dining room. The decor of this inn is decidedly Victorian with period antiques and wallpapers.

Innkeeper(s): Mark Kulkowitz & Pam Huber.

Rates:$61-121. MC VISA. Full Bkfst. Gourmet Brkfst, Lunch, Dinner. Picnic lunches. 21 rooms. Beds:QT. Conference Rm. Phone, AC in room. Golf. Tennis. Swimming. Fishing.

Seen in: *Atlantic City Press, Asbury Press, Frommer's, New York Times, Washington Post.*

Contact: Mark Kulkowitz. Certificate may be used: Sept. 26 - May 25, Sunday - Thursday only. Holiday periods and special events excluded.

"Mr. Kulkowitz is a superb host. He strives to accommodate the diverse needs of guests."

Fairthorne B&B
111 Ocean St
Cape May 08204
(609)884-8791 (800)438-8742

1892. Antiques abound in this three-story Colonial Revival. Lace curtains and a light color scheme complete the charming decor. The signature break-

fasts include special daily entrees along with an assortment of home-baked breads and muffins. A light afternoon tea also is served with refreshments. The proximity to the beach will be much appreciated by guests, and the innkeepers offer the use of beach towels, bicycles and sand chairs. The nearby historic district is full of fun shops and restaurants.

Innkeeper(s): Diane & Ed Hutchinson.

Rates:$110-190. MC VISA. Full Bkfst. Teas. 7 rooms. 2 with shared baths. Beds:K. TV, AC, Refrig. in room. Bicycling. Swimming. Fishing.

Seen in: *New Jersey Women's Magazine.*

Contact: Diane Hutchinson. Certificate may be used: October through June, Sunday through Thursday, excludes holidays, Christmas week through New Year's Eve.

"Give us more brochures. We'll send them to our friends."

Humphrey Hughes House
29 Ocean St
Cape May 08204
(609)884-4428 (800)582-3634

1903. Stained-glass windows mark each landing of

the staircase, and intricately carved American chestnut columns add to the atmosphere in this 30-room mansion. The land was purchased by the Captain Humphrey Hughes family in the early 1700s and remained in the family till 1980. Dr. Harold Hughes' majestic grandfather clock remains as one of many late-Victorian antiques.

Innkeeper(s): Lorraine & Terry Schmidt.

Rates:$80-205. MC VISA. Full Bkfst. Teas. 10 rooms. Beds:KQ. AC in room. Handicap access. Fishing.

Seen in: *New York Times.*

Contact: Lorraine Schmidt. Certificate may be used: End of October through end of April weekdays only (Sunday - Thursday) excluding the week between Dec. 24 - Jan. 3.

"Thoroughly enjoyed our stay."

Leith Hall Historic Seashore Inn
22 Ocean St
Cape May 08204
(609)884-1934

1885. Each guest room of this Second Empire Victorian features an ocean view. There is a handsome library and parlor and opulently decorated bed chambers with Victorian beds, mahogany tables and multi-patterned wallpapers. First-floor rooms have stained-glass French doors that open onto the verandas. Quiches, crepes and egg entrees are served on antique silver, crystal and Royal Worcester china. An English afternoon tea is offered.

Innkeeper(s): Elan & Susan Zingman-Leith.

Rates:$85-150. Full Bkfst. Teas. 7 rooms. Beds:Q. Conference Rm. AC, Refrig. in room. Swimming. Fishing.

Contact: Elan Zingman-Leith. Certificate may be used: Sunday through Thursday, October through June, except holiday weekends.

Mainstay Inn & Cottage
635 Columbia Ave
Cape May 08204
(609)884-8690

1872. This was once the elegant and exclusive Jackson's Clubhouse popular with gamblers. Many

of the guest rooms and the grand parlor look much as they did in the 1840s. Fourteen-foot-high ceilings, elaborate chandeliers, a sweeping veranda and a cupola add to the atmosphere. Tom and Sue Carroll received the annual American Historic Inns award in 1988 for their preservation efforts.

Innkeeper(s): Tom & Sue Carroll.

Rates:$95-210. Full Bkfst. Gourmet Brkfst. Teas. 16 rooms. Fireplaces. Beds:KQT. Conference Rm. TV, Phone, AC, Refrig. in room. Golf. Tennis. Bicycling. Handicap access. Swimming. Horseback riding. Fishing.

Seen in: *Washington Post, Good Housekeeping, New York Times.*

Contact: Thomas E. Carroll. Certificate may be used: Oct. 24, 1994 to April 27, 1995 with the exception of Christmas week; available Sunday through Thursday. Available again Oct. 22, 1995.

"By far the most lavishly and faithfully restored guesthouse...run by two arch-preservationists." Travel and Leisure.

The Mason Cottage
625 Columbia Ave
Cape May 08204
(609)884-3358 (800)716-2766

1871. Since 1946, this elegant seaside inn has been open to guests. The curved-mansard, wood-shingle roof was built by local shipyard carpenters. Much of

the original furniture remains in the house, and it has endured both hurricanes and the 1878 Cape May fire.

Innkeeper(s): Dave & Joan Mason.

Rates:$65-135. MC VISA. Full Bkfst. Teas. 5 rooms. Fireplaces. Beds:QD. Conference Rm. AC, Refrig. in room. Golf. Tennis. Swimming. Horseback riding. Fishing.

Contact: Joan Mason. Certificate may be used: April 1 to June 15; Sept. 15 to Jan. 1 Monday - Thursday.

"We look forward so much to coming back each summer and enjoying your hospitality and very special inn."

Mooring
801 Stockton Ave
Cape May 08204
(609)884-5425 Fax:(609)884-1357

1882. Rose gardens and lush flower beds greet guests visiting this Second Empire Victorian inn. The grand entrance hall boasts a spiral staircase

leading to rooms decorated with Renaissance-era antiques. Ask for "Old Ironsides" and you'll enjoy a 1700s-era four-poster bed, Tiffany paintings and a step-down bath. Breakfast is family style and features pink Depression Glass and gold flatware, with generous servings of peach pancakes, California egg puffs and other dishes. Afternoon tea is offered on the front veranda or fireside in the parlor.

Innkeeper(s): Leslie Valenza.

Rates:$75-175. MC VISA. Full Bkfst. Teas. 12 rooms. Beds:QT. AC in room. Fishing.

Contact: Leslie Valenza. Certificate may be used: Sunday through Thursday during October - June, excluding holidays.

The Inn on Ocean
25 Ocean Street
Cape May 08204
(609)884-7070 (800)304-4477

1880. Pansies and petunias blossom in front of this Second Empire Victorian and accentuate the green, white and yellow color scheme and strawberry pink roof. Inside, a light Victorian decor creates a bright and airy, yet elegant atmosphere. The inn boasts the only Victorian billiard room in town.

Innkeeper(s): Jack & Katha Davis.

Rates:$95-165. MC VISA AX. Full Bkfst. Teas. 5 rooms. Beds:KQT. TV, AC, Refrig. in room. Swimming. Fishing.

Contact: Katha Davis. Certificate may be used: Sunday through Thursday, November, February, March, April.

"The food was fabulous and served with a delicate flair. We enjoyed the family warmth and Victorian elegance." J.T., New York.

Poor Richard's Inn
17 Jackson St
Cape May 08204
(609)884-3536

1882. The unusual design of this Second-Empire house has been accentuated with five colors of paint. Arched gingerbread porches tie together the distinctive bays of the house's facade. The combination of exterior friezes, ballustrades and fretwork has earned the inn an individual listing in the National Register. Some rooms sport an eclectic country Victorian decor with patchwork quilts and pine furniture, while others tend toward a more traditional turn-of-the-century ambiance. All rooms are air-conditioned. A few apartment suites are available.

Innkeeper(s): Harriett & Richard Samuelson.

Rates:$39-128. MC VISA AX. Cont. Bkfst. 9 rooms. 5 with shared baths. Beds:QT. TV, AC in room. Golf. Swimming. Fishing.

Seen in: *Washington Post, New York Times, National Geographic.*

Contact: Richard Samuelson. Certificate may be used: Sept. 26, 1994 - May 15, 1995, Sunday through Thursday, except holidays.

"Hold our spot on the porch. We'll be back before you know it."

The Queen Victoria

102 Ocean St
Cape May 08204
(609)884-8702

1881. Christmas is a special festival at this beautifully restored Victorian manor. Tree-trimming workshops, Charles Dickens feasts and costumed

carolers crowd the calendar. The rest of the year, well-stocked libraries, and long porches lined with antique rocking chairs provide for more sedate entertainment. *Victorian Homes* featured 23 color photographs of the inn. Amenities include afternoon tea and mixers, a fleet of bicycles, and evening turndown service. Suites feature a whirlpool tub, fireplace or private porch.
Innkeeper(s): Dane & Joan Wells.

Rates:$100-260. MC VISA. Full Bkfst. Teas. 23 rooms. Fireplaces. Beds:QD. Conference Rm. TV, AC, Refrig. in room. Golf. Tennis. Bicycling. Handicap access. Swimming. Horseback riding. Fishing.

Seen in: *Discerning Traveler, New York Magazine, Cover Girl Magazine, Washington Post, Victorian Magazine.*

Contact: Dane Wells. Certificate may be used: November through March, Monday through Thursdays, excluding holidays.

"Especially impressed by the relaxed atmosphere and the excellent housekeeping."

Rhythm of the Sea

1123 Beach Ave
Cape May 08204
(609)884-7788

1910. A three-story Craftsman building, Rhythm of the Sea is filled with mission oak and furniture from the L. & J.G. Stickley Company. There are lanterns, wooden blinds, rocking chairs, window benches and other decorative items in the Mission style. For a full breakfast, choose a Wednesday, Saturday or Sunday stay. Continental breakfast is offered on other mornings. Four o'clock refresh-

ments are served on the porch.
Innkeeper(s): Richard & Carol Macaluso.

Rates:$135-210. MC VISA AX. Full Bkfst. Gourmet Brkfst. Picnic lunches. Teas. 6 rooms. Beds:Q. AC in room. Bicycling. Swimming. Fishing.

Contact: Carol Macaluso. Certificate may be used: Anytime excluding July 1 through Labor Day and other holidays.

Sea Holly B&B Inn

815 Stockton Ave
Cape May 08204
(609)884-6294

1875. The home-baked cuisine at this charming three-story Gothic cottage is an absolute delight. Innkeeper Christy Igoe began her love for baking in childhood and at 12, she created her own chocolate chip cookie recipe and now has her own cookbook. Her goodies are served at breakfast and in the afternoons with tea and sherry. The beautiful home is decorated with authentic Renaissance Revival and Eastlake antique pieces. Some rooms boast ocean views. The inn is a wonderful place for a special occasion as the Igoes offer honeymoon, birthday and anniversary specials.
Innkeeper(s): Christy & Chris Igoe.

Rates:$95-180. MC VISA AX. Full Bkfst. Teas. 8 rooms. Beds:QD. AC in room. Golf. Tennis. Bicycling. Swimming. Horseback riding. Fishing.

Seen in: *Mid-Atlantic Newsletter.*

Contact: Christy Igoe. Certificate may be used: Monday - Thursday, mid-February, March, April, May, June, September, October, November, December. Excludes holidays.

"You have shown us what a real B&B is supposed to be like."

Seventh Sister Guesthouse

10 Jackson St
Cape May 08204
(609)884-2280

1888. Most of the Seventh Sister's guest rooms have ocean views. The inn is in the National Register. Extensive wicker and original art collections are featured and three floors are joined by a spectacular central circular staircase. The center of town is one block away.
Innkeeper(s): Bob & JoAnne Myers.

Rates:$65-85. MC VISA AX. EP. 6 rooms. 6 with shared baths. Swimming. Fishing.

Seen in: *New York Times, 1001 Decorating Ideas.*

Contact: JoAnne Echevarria-Myers. Certificate may be used: November, December, January, February, March - excluding holidays.

Stetson B&B Inn

725 Kearney Ave
Cape May 08204
(609)884-1724

1915. This bed & breakfast features country English

and Victorian decor with stenciling and hardwood floors. There are two porches and a sitting room with fireplace available to guests. Breakfast is served in a sunny dining room. Located one block from the beach, the inn has a dressing room and beach shower for you to use on your last day when you wish to stay at the beach, past check-out time.
Innkeeper(s): Carol & Lou Elwell.

Rates:$75-115. MC VISA. Full Bkfst. 7 rooms. Beds:D. AC in room. Fishing.

Contact: Carol Elwell. Certificate may be used: Anytime February-March. Sunday-Thursday all other months (except July-August). Closed January. Call last-minute for weekends in April and November. Excludes special events.

Summer Cottage Inn
613 Columbia Ave
Cape May 08204
(609)884-4948

1867. A cupola tops this Italianate-style inn located on a quiet tree-lined street in the Historic District. It's close to the beach (one block) and the Victorian Mall. Period Victorian pieces are featured in the parlor and the veranda is filled with plants, ferns and wicker rockers. Your host is an avid restorer and carries that passion to antique auto restoration.
Innkeeper(s): Linda & Skip Loughlin.

Rates:$85-150. MC VISA. Full Bkfst. Teas. 8 rooms. 4 with shared baths. Beds:QT. AC in room. Bicycling. Fishing.

Contact: Linda Loughlin. Certificate may be used: January - March (Monday through Thursday).

White Dove Cottage
619 Hughes St
Cape May 08204
(609)884-0613 (800)321-3683

1866. The beautiful octagonal slate on the Mansard roof of this Second Empire house is just one of the inn's many handsome details. Bright sunny rooms are furnished in American and European antiques, period wallpapers, paintings, prints and handmade quilts. Breakfast is served to the soft music of an antique music box and boasts heirloom crystal, fine china and lace. Located on a quiet gas-lit street, the inn is two blocks from the beach, restaurants and shops. Ask about mystery weekends and the inn's Honeymoon and Romantic Escape packages.
Innkeeper(s): Frank & Sue Smith.

Rates:$75-175. Full Bkfst. Teas. 6 rooms. Fireplaces. Beds:QD. TV, AC in room. Golf. Tennis. Swimming. Horseback riding. Fishing.

Contact: Frank Smith. Certificate may be used: Sundays through Thursdays, Sept. 10, 1994 to June 12, 1995; Sept. 10 to Dec. 31, 1995.

The Wooden Rabbit
609 Hughes St
Cape May 08204
(609)884-7293

1838. Robert E. Lee brought his wife to stay at this sea captain's house to ease her arthritis. The house was also part of the Underground Railroad.

Throughout the inn are whimsical touches such as the "rabbit hutch" in the living room which holds a collection of Beatrix Potter figures. The decor is country, with folk art and collectibles. Children are welcome.
Innkeeper(s): Greg & Debby Burow.

Rates:$75-165. MC VISA. Full Bkfst. Teas. 3 rooms. Beds:KQ. TV, AC in room. Swimming. Fishing.

Seen in: *The Sandpiper.*

Contact: Deborah Burow. Certificate may be used: No holidays, special events, weekends (Friday, Saturday, Sunday). Good only Monday through Thursday, good mid-October-Dec. 20, 1994, good Jan. 5 through March 31, 1995.

"The room was perfect, our breakfast delicious. We will be back."

Chatham

Parrot Mill Inn
47 Main St
Chatham 07928
(201)635-7722

1780. More than 100 years ago, this Victorian Shingle-style mill house was moved from its Fishawak River location to Main Street. It features a Dutch Gambrel roof and is decorated in a Colonial style befitting its origins. Your hostess will assist you with any special arrangements you may require for business meetings, touring, small wedding or graduation plans. The inn is 20 miles (60 minutes) from New York City by car and 14 miles from Newark.

Innkeeper(s): Betsy Kennedy.

Rates:$95. MC VISA AX. Cont. Bkfst. 11 rooms. 1 with shared bath. Beds:QT. Conference Rm. Phone, AC in room.

Contact: Betsy Kennedy. Certificate may be used: We are open 12 months of the year. Reservations must be made in advance.

Flemington

The Cabbage Rose Inn
162 Main St
Flemington 08822
(908)788-0247

1891. This pink and white Victorian mansion boasts a three-story turret with an open gingerbread porch on the tower's third floor. Oriental rugs,

antiques and fabrics with large cabbage rose motifs are featured throughout. "Romance and Roses" is a package that offers the inn's best room with a four-poster bed, champagne, a box of Cabbage Rose Inn chocolates, long-stemmed red roses, and a four-course dinner.

Innkeeper(s): Pam Venosa & Al Scott.

Rates:$80-115. MC VISA AX. Full Bkfst. 5 rooms. Fireplaces. Beds:Q. Phone, AC in room. Golf. Bicycling. Skiing. Swimming. Horseback riding. Fishing.

Seen in: *Innsider Magazine, New Jersey Monthly.*

Contact: Pam Venosa. Certificate may be used: Sunday - Thursday, all year. Anytime, January - March.

"Incredible hospitality. Made our stay in New Jersey wonderful."

Glenwood

Apple Valley Inn B&B and Antiques
Corner Rts 517 & 565, PO Box 302
Glenwood 07418
(201)764-3735

1831. This three-story Colonial farmhouse is set on three acres with its own apple orchard (more than 40 trees) and in-ground pool. A brook running next to the house is a great trout-fishing spot. The innkeeper is an avid antique collector and guest rooms (named after varieties of apples) include American antiques. Try the Red Delicious room. Across the street is a popular pick-your-own-fruit farm. Check with the innkeeper to find when the strawberries, peaches, cherries and apples are ripe so you can gather your favorites. Action Park, ski slopes, and the Appalachian Trail are nearby.

Innkeeper(s): Mitzi & John Durham.

Rates:$65-75. Full Bkfst. Picnic lunches. Teas. 6 rooms. 5 with shared baths. Beds:DT. Conference Rm. Farm. Skiing. Swimming. Fishing.

Contact: Mildred Durham. Certificate may be used: Sunday through Thursday.

Island Heights

Studio of John F. Peto
102 Cedar Ave
Island Heights 08732
(908)270-6058

1889. This Victorian home is listed on the National Register of Historic Places and is of note because it was built by renowned artist John F. Peto. His granddaughter has opened the home for guests. Filled with artifacts, eclectic furnishings, memorabilia and reproductions of his art, the studio is decorated much as it was originally. There is a large screened porch with rocking chairs providing views down the hill to the river. A full breakfast is usually served.

Innkeeper(s): Joy Peto Smiley.

Rates:$75-85. AX DS. Full Bkfst. 4 rooms. 4 with shared baths. Fireplaces. Beds:DT. AC, Refrig. in room. Golf. Tennis. Swimming. Fishing.

Seen in: *House and Gardens Magazine, Observer Entertainer.*

Contact: Joy Peto Smiley. Certificate may be used: Anytime.

"Breakfast is so great—we won't need any lunch."

Mays Landing

Abbott House
6056 Main Street
Mays Landing 08330
(609)625-4400

1863. Guests at this Victorian-style mansion can relax on the bluff overlooking the Great Egg Harbor River, read on the second-floor veranda with its intricate fretwork or take afternoon tea in the belvedere (cupola) with spectacular views of historic Mays Landing. The inn is within walking distance to Lake Lenape and its various summer attractions. Each room is individually decorated with antiques, wicker, handmade quilts and other special touches. The Victorian Parlor is a place for games, reading and conversation. Refreshments can be enjoyed on one of the many porches and verandas.

Innkeeper(s): Donna & Cliff Melder.

Rates:$79-95. Cont. Bkfst. Gourmet Brkfst. Teas. 5 rooms. Beds:QT. AC in room. Bicycling. Swimming. Fishing.

Contact: Cliff Melder. Certificate may be used: Year-round, no restrictions.

Ocean City

BarnaGate B&B
637 Wesley Ave
Ocean City 08226
(609)391-9366

1895. Three-and-a-half blocks from the ocean, the BarnaGate B&B offers Victorian-style guest rooms with paddle fans and country quilts. The top floor of the four-story inn features a private sitting room. Guests enjoy fresh fruit and homemade breads at breakfast.

Innkeeper(s): Lois & Frank Barna.

Rates:$65-75. MC VISA. Full Bkfst. 5 rooms. 4 with shared baths. Beds:KT. Swimming. Fishing.

Seen in: *The Star-Ledger, The Intelligencer-Record, The Press of Atlantic City.*

Contact: Frank Barna. Certificate may be used: October, 1994 to April, 1995; Weekdays Monday - Thursday.

"You two must have invented the meaning of the word 'hospitality'."

Northwood Inn B&B
401 Wesley Ave
Ocean City 08226
(609)399-6071

1894. This gracious three-story Queen Anne Victorian with Colonial Victorian touches has been restored recently by the innkeeper, who is a wooden boatbuilder and custom-home builder. There are gleaming plank floors, a sweeping staircase and library. The Tower Room in the turret is a favorite as is the Lotus Blossom Suite with a separate sitting room. The inn is within walking distance of the beach and boardwalk.

Innkeeper(s): Marj & John Loeper.

Rates:$75-150. MC VISA. Full Bkfst. Gourmet Brkfst. 8 rooms. Beds:QT. AC in room. Swimming. Fishing.

Contact: Marj Loeper. Certificate may be used: Oct. 15, 1994 - May 1, 1995; Oct. 15 - Dec. 15, 1995. Sunday - Thursday.

Scarborough Inn
720 Ocean Ave
Ocean City 08226
(609)399-7968 (800)258-1558
Fax:(609)399-4472

1895. Painted in wedgewood, rose, and soft creams, the Hotel Scarborough is a familiar Victorian landmark in this seaside resort. Family-owned and operated, the inn is filled with the innkeepers' artwork and an upright piano for informal singalongs. Shuffleboard, ping pong, a library, and card room are available to guests. A continental breakfast is served in a cozy, plant-filled parlor or on the wraparound porch. The beach and boardwalk are a short stroll from the inn.

Innkeeper(s): Gus & Carol Bruno.

Rates:$50-100. MC VISA DS. Cont. Bkfst. 25 rooms. Beds:QDT. AC, Refrig. in room. Swimming. Fishing.

Contact: Gus Bruno. Certificate may be used: May through October (excluding holidays and weekends). Sunday - Thursday.

"Your hospitality is truly unsurpassed...anywhere. A million thanks."

Ocean Grove

Pine Tree Inn
10 Main Ave
Ocean Grove 07756
(908)775-3264

1870. This small Victorian hotel is operated by long-standing residents of the area. Guest rooms are decorated in antiques and all the rooms are equipped with sinks. Bicycles and beach towels are available.

Innkeeper(s): Karen Mason & Francis Goger.

Rates:$45-95. MC VISA. ContPlus Bkfst. Teas. 12 rooms. 8 with shared baths. Beds:QDT. TV, Phone, AC, Refrig. in room. Bicycling. Fishing.

Seen in: *Country Living.*

Contact: Karen Mason. Certificate may be used: Sunday through Thursday nights only (all year) 1994 and 1995.

Pemberton

Isaac Hilliard House B&B
31 Hanover St (Towne Centre)
Pemberton 08068
(609)894-0756 (800)371-0756

1750. A wrought-iron fence sets off this two-story green and white Victorian. The inn is filled with antique bric-a-brac and collections such as plates and books. There's an antique bridal gown in one of the guest rooms. Walk two minutes to the canoe rental, then paddle along the Rancocas River. The Grist Mill Village and good restaurants are close by.

Innkeeper(s): Marian & Dan Michaels.

Rates:$50-125. MC VISA. Full Bkfst. Picnic lunches. 4 rooms. Beds:Q. TV, AC, Refrig. in room. Bicycling. Swimming. Fishing.

Contact: Marian Michaels. Certificate may be used: Sunday through Thursday only, excluding holidays.

Salem

Brown's Historic Home B&B
41-43 Market St
Salem 08079
(609)935-8595

1738. Brown's Historic Home originally was built as a Colonial house. About 1845 the house was

modernized to the Victorian era. The inn is furnished with antiques and heirlooms, including a handmade chess set and quilt. The fireplaces are made of King of Prussia marble. The backyard garden
features a lily pond, wildflowers and a waterfall.

Innkeeper(s): Bill & Marge Brown.

Rates:$75-100. MC VISA DS. Full Bkfst. Evening snacks. 4 rooms. 2 with shared baths. Fireplaces. Beds:T. TV, Phone, AC, Refrig. in room. Golf. Fishing.

Seen in: *Newsday, Mid-Atlantic Country, Early American Life, Today's Sunbeam.*

Contact: William Brown. Certificate may be used: Anytime if space is available.

"Down-home-on-the-farm breakfasts with great hospitality."

Sea Girt

Holly Harbor Guest House
112 Baltimore Blvd
Sea Girt 08750
(908)974-8389 (800)348-6999

1905. Holly trees border the lawn of this three-story shingled cottage located eight houses from the beach. A wide front porch is framed by a border of peonies. In the summer, a full buffet breakfast is served.

Innkeeper(s): Bill & Kim Walsh.

Rates:$50-125. MC VISA AX. Full Bkfst. EP. 13 rooms. 12 with shared baths. Beds:KQT. TV, AC in room. Golf. Tennis. Swimming. Fishing.

Seen in: *Fodors, New Jersey Monthly.*

Contact: William Walsh. Certificate may be used: May - September, but will do all year.

"Your hospitality and warmth are unequaled."

Spring Lake

Ashling Cottage
106 Sussex Ave
Spring Lake 07762
(908)449-3553 (800)237-1877

1877. Surrounded by shady sycamores on a quiet residential street, this three-story Victorian residence features a mansard-and-gambrel roof with

hooded gambrel dormers. One of the two porches has a square, pyramid-roofed pavilion which has been glass-enclosed and screened. Guests can watch the sun rise over the ocean one block away or set over Spring Lake. A full buffet breakfast can be enjoyed in the plant- and wicker-filled pavilion.

Innkeeper(s): Goodi & Jack Stewart.

Rates:$75-145. Full Bkfst. 10 rooms. 2 with shared baths. Beds:Q. Golf. Tennis. Bicycling. Swimming. Horseback riding. Fishing.

Seen in: *New York Times, New Jersey Monthly, Town & Country Magazine, Country Living Magazine, New York Magazine.*

Contact: Jack Stewart. Certificate may be used: Sunday through Thursday, April, May, June, October, November, subject to availability.

Stanhope

Whistling Swan Inn
110 Main St
Stanhope 07874
(201)347-6369 Fax:(201)347-3391

1900. This Queen Anne Victorian has a limestone wraparound veranda and a tall steep-roofed turret. Family antiques fill the rooms and highlight the

polished ornate woodwork, pocket doors and winding staircase. It is a little over a mile from Waterloo Village and the International Trade Zone.

Innkeeper(s): Paula & Joe Mulay.

Rates:$75-110. MC VISA AX DS. Full Bkfst. Picnic lunches. 10 rooms. Beds:Q. Conference Rm. Phone, AC in room. Golf. Tennis. Bicycling. Skiing. Handicap access. Swimming. Horseback riding. Fishing.

Seen in: *Sunday Herald, New York Times, New Jersey Monthly Magazine, Mid-Atlantic Country Magazine, Star Ledger, Daily Record.*

Contact: Paula Williams. Certificate may be used: Sundays through Thursdays, November through April.

Woodbine

Henry Ludlam Inn
Cape May County 1336 Rt 47
Woodbine 08270
(609)861-5847

1740. This country inn borders picturesque Ludlam Lake. Canoeing, birding, biking and fishing are popular activities, and the innkeepers make sure

you enjoy these at your peak by providing you with a full country breakfast. Some of the bedrooms have fireplaces, and all feature antique double feather beds topped with handmade quilts.

Innkeeper(s): Ann & Marty Thurlow.

Rates:$85-99. MC VISA AX. Full Bkfst. Gourmet Brkfst. Picnic lunches. Teas. 5 rooms. Fireplaces. Beds:QDT. Conference Rm. AC in room. Golf. Tennis. Bicycling. Skiing. Swimming. Horseback riding. Fishing.

Seen in: *Atlantic City Press, New Jersey Bride, Mid-Atlantic Country Magazine, Atlantic City Magazine, New Jersey Outdoors.*

Contact: Ann Thurlow. Certificate may be used: Sunday through Thursday; Oct. 1, 1994-May 15, 1995; Oct. 1-Dec. 15, 1995. Cannot be used holiday weekends.

"An unforgettable breakfast."

New Mexico

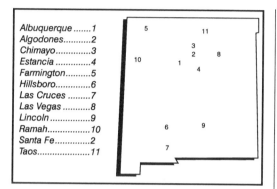

Albuquerque

Las Palomas Valley B&B

2303 Candelaria Rd NW
Albuquerque 87107
(505)345-7228 Fax:(505)345-7328

1939. This adobe inn in Albuquerque's historic North Valley Region features eight individually decorated guest rooms, three of them in casitas near an orchard. The Boxcar Suite is a renovated railroad car that boasts a king bed, kitchenette, sun porch and view of the Sandia Mountains. Other rooms sport New Orleans, Oriental or Spanish country themes. The full breakfasts include specialty omelets and fresh fruit. The inn's barbecue, hot tub and tennis court are favorite guest amenities. Old Town is nearby and Coronado State Park is within easy driving distance.

Innkeeper(s): Lori & Andrew Caldwell.

Rates:$59-125. MC VISA AX. Full Bkfst. Gourmet Brkfst. 8 rooms. Fireplaces. Beds:KQT. TV, AC, Refrig. in room. Tennis. Skiing. Handicap access. Spa.

Contact: Lori Caldwell. Certificate may be used: Nov. 1 - March 31.

The Ranchette

2329 Lakeview Rd SW
Albuquerque 87105
(505)877-5140

1982. This adobe-style homestay is situated on two acres with horse corrals and views of extinct volcanoes and the Sandia and Monzano mountains. The

hostess has facilities for those traveling with their horses. Gourmet vegetarian meals are specialties.

Innkeeper(s): Rev. Janis Hildebrand.

Rates:$50-110. Full Bkfst. Gourmet Brkfst, Dinner. Picnic lunches. Teas. Evening snacks. 3 rooms. 2 with shared baths. Beds:KD. Phone, AC in room. Bicycling. Skiing. Spa. Stables. Fishing.

Contact: Janis Hildebrand. Certificate may be used: Off-season, year-round midweek.

"The Ranchette offers great views and a warm hospitable atmosphere. It's a little bit of paradise in a land known for its enchantment."

W.E. Mauger Estate

701 Roma Ave NW
Albuquerque 87102
(505)242-8755

1897. This former boarding house is now an elegantly restored Victorian in the National Register. Rooms are done in Victorian style with views of downtown Albuquerque and the Sandia Mountains beyond. The second floor is decorated with antiques and lace. The inn is located in an area undergoing renovation, six blocks from the convention center.

Innkeeper(s): Chuck Silver & Brian Miller.

Rates:$69-109. MC VISA AX DC CB. Full Bkfst. Evening snacks. 8 rooms. Beds:KQT. Conference Rm. AC, Refrig. in room. Golf. Tennis.

Skiing. Horseback riding. Fishing.

Seen in: *Albuquerque Journal, Phoenix Home and Garden, Albuquerque Monthly.*

Contact: Charles Silver. Certificate may be used: Nov. 1-15, Dec. 1-15, January and February.

"Because of your hospitality, kindness and warmth, we will always compare the quality of our experience by the W.E. Mauger Estate."

The W.J. Marsh House

301 Edith SE
Albuquerque 87102
(505)247-1001

1895. This three-story brick Queen Anne mansion and its one-time servants' cottage are located in the Huning Highland Historic District. Original redwood doors and trim, porcelain fixtures and an ornate hand-carved fireplace are highlighted by country-Victorian decor. A friendly ghost is said to inhabit the main house, occasionally opening drawers and rearranging the furniture. The inn is listed in the national and state historic registers.

Innkeeper(s): Janice Lee Sperling, MD.

Rates:$59-109. Full Bkfst. Gourmet Brkfst. 10 rooms. 8 with shared baths. Fireplaces. Beds:QDT. Conference Rm. AC in room. Golf. Tennis. Skiing. Swimming. Horseback riding. Fishing.

Seen in: *Albuquerque Monthly.*

Contact: Janice Lee Sperling, MD. Certificate may be used: Any except during Balloon Fiesta and major holidays, Monday - Thursday nights only.

The Windmill Ranch

6400 Coors Blvd Northwest
Albuquerque 87120
(505)898-6864 Fax:(505)898-6864

1894. Visitors to this peaceful Pueblo Revival inn often are treated to the sight of colorful hot air balloons floating overhead. Its lovely setting, amid tall elms and just a stone's throw from the Rio Grande, offers guests a relaxing haven. Many visitors enjoy strolling tree-lined paths along the river, and a garden patio is another favorite spot. The inn's guest rooms are named after the famous Western figures Billy the Kid, Wyatt Earp, Doc Holliday and Pancho Villa.

Innkeeper(s): Stephen & Michelle Sutor.

Rates:$85-105. MC VISA DS. Gourmet Brkfst. Teas. Evening snacks. 4 rooms. Fireplaces. Beds:K. Conference Rm. TV, Phone, AC, Refrig. in room. Farm. Skiing. Spa. Sauna. Stables.

Contact: Michelle Sutor. Certificate may be used: Anytime upon availability.

Algodones

Hacienda Vargas

PO Box 307
Algodones 87001-0307
(505)867-9115

1700. Nestled among the cottonwoods and mesas of the middle Rio Grande Valley, Hacienda Vargas has seen two centuries of Old West history. It once served as a trading post for Native Americans as well as a 19th-century stagecoach stop between Santa Fe and Albuquerque. The grounds contain an adobe chapel, courtyard, and gardens. The main house features five *kiva* fireplaces, Southwest antiques, Spanish tile, a library and art gallery.

Innkeeper(s): Pablo & Jule DeVargas.

Rates:$69-129. MC VISA. Full Bkfst. 4 rooms. Fireplaces. Beds:Q. Conference Rm. Phone, AC, Refrig. in room. Golf. Skiing. Spa. Swimming. Horseback riding. Fishing.

Contact: Jule DeVargas. Certificate may be used: Nov. 1 - Feb. 28 anytime except holidays. March 1 - Nov. 1, Monday - Thursday except Balloon Fiesta Sept. 30 - Oct. 11 and holidays.

Chimayo

La Posada De Chimayo

Box 463
Chimayo 87522
(505)351-4605

1891. The rustic charm of this adobe inn is matched only by the enthusiasm of innkeeper Sue Farrington, who built the original two-room guest house herself. Sturdy pine vigas, brick floors and a kiva fireplace offer guests an authentic New Mexico experience. A newly restored adobe farmhouse provides two additional rooms. The natural, no-frills setting of the inn is a treat for those weary of city life, and many guests make frequent return visits to relax and partake of the generous and delicious meals. Historic weaving and woodworking shops are nearby.

Innkeeper(s): Sue Farrington.

Rates:$80-90. MC VISA. Full Bkfst. 4 rooms. Fireplaces. Beds:QD.

Seen in: *Chicago Tribune, Sage Magazine, St. Louis Post-Dispatch, Albuquerque Journal.*

Contact: Sue Farrington. Certificate may be used: Monday through Thursday, Nov. 1-22, 1994; anyday Nov. 28 - Dec. 19, 1994; anyday Jan. 4 - April 8.

"Thank you for this retreat and your thoughtfulness in all details."

Estancia

The Roundhouse
PO Box 347
Estancia 87016
(505)384-5370

1985. This unusual inn is an easy getaway from Albuquerque. Guests are intrigued by its geodesic dome shape, and will be charmed by its Southwestern decor. Located on the high plains of the central part of the state, the inn provides its guests a restful stay away from big-city life. Guests may relax in the inn's sitting room or do some antiquing, sightseeing or shopping in the surrounding area. Manzano Mountains State Park is within easy driving distance of the inn.
Innkeeper(s): Jay & Del Foley.

Rates:$55. MC VISA. ContPlus Bkfst. Evening snacks. 2 rooms. 2 with shared baths. Beds:QT. TV, Refrig. in room. Skiing.

Contact: Jay Foley. Certificate may be used: Fall, winter.

Farmington

Silver River Inn
3151 W Main, PO Box 3411
Farmington 87499
(505)325-8219 (800)382-9251

1989. Guests at this contemporary adobe house enjoy a view of the San Juan River from the patio of their private suite. Amenities in the suite include a dining/living room with twin daybeds, kitchen with microwave and refrigerator, Mexican tile bathroom, phone and queen bed. Guests also may relax in the library or take a refreshing walk in the nearby cottonwood forest, a perfect spot for birdwatching. The peaceful setting caters to those wishing to get away from it all, while those interested in sightseeing will find many opportunities in the area, such as the Aztec and Salmon ruins and Four Corners Monument.
Innkeeper(s): Diana Ohlson & David Beers.

Rates:$65-85. MC VISA. ContPlus Bkfst. 1 room. Beds:Q. Phone, Refrig. in room. Skiing. Handicap access. Swimming. Fishing.

Contact: Diana Ohlson. Certificate may be used: November through February.

Hillsboro

The Enchanted Villa
PO Box 456
Hillsboro 88042
(505)895-5686

1941. Originally built as a romantic retreat for an English nobleman, this adobe inn is a favorite spot for family reunions, receptions, seminars and wed-

dings. The large guest rooms feature Southwest decor, and a suite with sleeping alcove is perfect for families. The inn has added an in-house restaurant, serving dinner on most weekends and offering picnic lunches for special occasions. A kennel on the premises accommodates guests' pets. Visitors delight in exploring the many charms of Hillsboro, a designated historic district. Sightseeing opportunities also are available at nearby Gila National Forest.
Innkeeper(s): Maree Westland.

Rates:$50. Full Bkfst. Gourmet brkfst, Lunch, Dinner. Picnic lunches. Teas. Evening snacks. 5 rooms. 2 with shared baths. Beds:KQT. Bicycling. Handicap access. Swimming. Fishing.

Contact: Maree Westland. Certificate may be used: Anytime, other than holidays.

Las Cruces

Lundeen Inn of the Arts
618 S Alameda Blvd
Las Cruces 88005
(505)526-3327 Fax:(505)526-3355

1920. Art lovers will enjoy this historic adobe inn/art gallery, where almost every wall sports an impressive painting. The 17 guest rooms all bear the name of a famous New Mexican or Indian artist, including Maria Martinez and Georgia O'Keeffe. The Mexican Territorial inn is made up of separate two-story structures joined by an impressive living room, which features dark hardwood floors, an 1855 imported piano and pressed-tin ceiling. Guests often are treated to adobe brick-making demonstrations or Indian dancing. New Mexico State University is nearby and Leasburg Dam State Park is a short drive away.

Innkeeper(s): Linda & Gerald Lundeen.

Rates:$58-90. MC VISA AX DC DS. Full Bkfst. Teas. 17 rooms. Fireplaces. Beds:QT. Conference Rm. Phone, AC, Refrig. in room. Golf. Tennis. Swimming. Horseback riding. Fishing.

Seen in: *New Mexico Magazine.*

Contact: Linda Lundeen. Certificate may be used: Yearly May 1-Nov. 1.

Las Vegas

Plaza Hotel

230 Old Town Plaza
Las Vegas 87701
(505)425-3591 (800)328-1882
Fax:(505)425-9659

1882. This brick Italianate Victorian hotel, once frequented by the likes of Doc Holliday, Big Nose Katy and Billy the Kid, was renovated in 1982. A stencil pattern found in the dining room inspired the selection of Victorian wallpaper borders in the guest rooms, decorated with a combination of contemporary and period furnishings. Guests are still drawn to the warm, dry air and the hot springs north of town.

Innkeeper(s): Wid & Kak Slick.

Rates:$56-110. MC VISA AX DC DS. 37 rooms. Beds:KQ. Conference Rm. TV, Phone, AC in room. Skiing. Fishing.

Contact: Judy Finley. Certificate may be used: Nov. 1 - May 1. Not good on holidays or for special events.

Lincoln

Casa de Patron

PO Box 27
Lincoln 88338
(505)653-4676 Fax:(505)653-4671

1860. This historic adobe once was used to imprison Billy the Kid and played an integral part in the colorful frontier days of Lincoln County. A shaded courtyard and walled garden add to the

authentic Old West atmosphere, and the comfortable rooms are supplemented by two contemporary adobe casitas. Cleis plays the inn's pipe organ and arranges soapmaking and quilting workshops for guests. Salon evenings feature classical music and Old World cookery. Dinner is available by advance reservation.

Innkeeper(s): Jeremy & Cleis Jordan.

Rates:$79. MC VISA. Full Bkfst. 3 rooms. Beds:QT. Skiing. Horseback riding. Fishing.

Seen in: *Albuquerque Journal, Preservation News, Sunset, Travelin', Rocky Mountain News, Milwaukee Journal.*

Contact: Jeremy Jordan. Certificate may be used: All year, Sunday through Thursday, subject to holidays (local and national).

"The time with you at Casa de Patron is truly a treasure to me."

Ramah

The Vogt Ranch B&B

PO Box 716
Ramah 87321
(505)783-4362

1915. This secluded inn, located at the foot of the Zuni Mountains, was constructed of rock from a nearby Indian ruin. The inn's charming interior includes a bear pelt on the wall, Navajo rugs and woodplanked floors. One of the guest rooms boasts a Zuni corner fireplace, the other a wood stove. Guests have the place to themselves, as innkeeper Anita Davis drops by in the morning with breakfast, sometimes consisting of blue-corn pancakes, sausage, fresh fruit, eggs and juice. Guests enjoy exploring nearby cliffs and gazing at the beautiful panoramas. Be sure to visit nearby Zuni Pueblo, famous for its fetish necklaces.

Innkeeper(s): Anita Davis & Scott Clifford.

Rates:$65-75. Full Bkfst. 2 rooms. Beds:Q. Farm. Fishing.

Contact: Anita Davis. Certificate may be used: May, June and Nov. 15 through Dec. 20.

Santa Fe

The Inn on Alameda

303 E Alameda
Santa Fe 87501
(505)984-2121 (800)289-2122
Fax:(505)986-8325

1987. This contemporary country inn offers the style and charm of old Santa Fe. With its kiva fireplaces, Spanish tile accents and authentic Southwestern-style guest rooms, the inn provides just the right touches of comfort and elegance. Guest rooms feature handmade furnishings showcasing the talents of local craftsmen and artists. Visitors may relax in the inn's lobby, lounge and spa, or visit the nearby art galleries, boutiques, restaurants and shops. The gourmet breakfast buffet is enjoyed in the country kitchen or guests' rooms. The Agoyo Room lounge is home to the inn's world-famous turquoise margarita.

Innkeeper(s): Fritz Mercer.

Rates:$140-215. MC VISA AX DC DS. Cont. Bkfst. Gourmet Brkfst. Evening snacks. 64 rooms. Fireplaces. Beds:KQ. Conference Rm. TV, Phone, AC, Refrig. in room. Skiing. Handicap access. Spa. Sauna. Exercise room. Fishing.

Contact: Fritz Mercer. Certificate may be used: Not valid for the months of July, August, September and October.

The Don Gaspar Compound

617 Don Gaspar
Santa Fe 87501
(505)986-8664 Fax:(303)385-4088

1912. Each accommodation of this compound is a completely private casita. They surround a flower-filled courtyard with a fountain. Features include antiques, original art and porches. Heirloom flowers are brought from the inn's working ranch and nursery, Blue Lake Ranch and Bed & Breakfast in Durango.

Innkeeper(s): David & Shirley Alford.

Rates:$85-220. ContPlus Bkfst. 6 rooms. Fireplaces. Beds:KQ. TV, Phone, AC, Refrig. in room. Golf. Tennis. Skiing. Swimming. Horseback riding. Fishing.

Contact: Shirley Alford. Certificate may be used: Monday to Thursday, Nov. 1-May 1. All holiday weeks and weekends excluded.

Taos

The Mildred & Don Cheek Stewart House

46 Hwy 150 N, PO Box 2326
Taos 87571
(505)776-2913 Fax:(505)758-1399

1970. The surrounding landscape of this eclectic inn is an artist's dream. The Sangre de Cristo mountains to the east lend sharp contrast to the gentle sweeping views across the volcanic basin to the west. The magnificent colors produced by the sunrise and sunset add to this spectacular scene. Built by an eccentric artist, the inn features hand-hewn logs, vigas and doors from a convent, gates made of old harps and volcanic rock in the chimney. Year-round activity attracts a wide variety of people and breakfasts may include chatting with a well-known artist, writer or fellow adventurer.

Innkeeper(s): Mildred & Don Cheek.

Rates:$75-120. MC VISA. Full Bkfst. 5 rooms. Fireplaces. Beds:KQT. Phone, Refrig. in room. Skiing. Spa. Swimming. Fishing.

Contact: Mildred & Don Cheek. Certificate may be used: Jan. 2-15; April 20 - May 30, holidays excluded; Nov. 1 - Dec. 15, holidays excluded.

New York

Addison

Addison Rose B&B
37 Maple Ave
Addison 14801
(607)359-4650

1892. Located on a scenic highway south of the Finger Lakes, this Queen Anne Victorian "painted lady" inn is an easy getaway from Corning or Elmira. The inn was built by a doctor for his bride and was presented to her on Christmas Eve, their wedding day. The three guest rooms offer authentic Victorian furnishings. Many fine examples of Victorian architecture exist in Addison. Pinnacle State Park is just east of town.

Innkeeper(s): Bill & Mary Ann Peters.

Rates:$65-75. Full Bkfst. Gourmet Brkfst. Teas. 3 rooms. Beds:DT. Skiing. Swimming. Fishing.

Contact: William Peters. Certificate may be used: Anytime subject to availability.

Albany

Mansion Hill Inn
115 Philip St at Park Ave
Albany 12202
(518)465-2038 Fax:(518)434-2313

1861. This Victorian houses guest rooms and apartment suites on the top two floors and a restaurant on the street level. Originally the home of brush maker Daniel Brown, it later served as a bulk grocery store. It is located in the historic district just around the corner from the Governor's Executive Mansion in the Mansion Neighborhood. It is a few minutes' walk to the State Capitol and the downtown Albany business district.

Innkeeper(s): Maryellen, Elizabeth & Steve Stofelano, Jr.

Rates:$69-155. MC VISA AX DC DS CB. Full Bkfst. Gourmet Brkfst, Dinner. 8 rooms. Beds:Q. Conference Rm. TV, Phone, AC, Refrig. in room. Handicap access.

Seen in: *Albany Review, Hudson Valley Magazine, Albany Times Union.*

Contact: Stephen Stofelano, Jr. Certificate may be used: Weekends, year-round (subject to availability), 1994 and 1995.

"Rooms were beautiful and comfortable down to the shower curtain."

Angelica

Angelica Inn
64 W Main St
Angelica 14709
(716)466-3295
NY907627.TIF

1886. Located in the Allegany foothills, the Angelica Inn features stained glass, crystal chandeliers, parquet floors, an oak staircase, carved woodwork, antique furnishings and scented rooms. Guest rooms offer such amenities as fireplaces, a porch and a breakfast alcove area.

Innkeeper(s): John & Fleurette Pelletier.

Rates:$60-70. MC VISA AX DC DS CB. Full Bkfst. 5 rooms. Fireplaces. Beds:QT. Conference Rm. Skiing. Fishing.

Contact: Fleurette Pelletier. Certificate may be used: Monday to Thursday - two-night minimum.

"Victorian at its best!"

Auburn

The Irish Rose - A Victorian B&B
102 South St
Auburn 13021
(315)255-0196 Fax:(315)255-0899

1870. A Victorian setting and Irish hospitality are blended at this National Register Queen Anne Victorian. The inn features cherry hardwood floors, cherry fireplace mantels, and cherry doors. An uncluttered Victorian style includes some antiques. The innkeeper, once a head chef, provides a full gourmet buffet breakfast. On the grounds are a swimming pool and rose garden.

Innkeeper(s): Patricia Fitzpatrick & Kevin McElligatt.

Rates:$55-95. MC VISA DS. Full Bkfst. Gourmet Brkfst. Evening snacks. 5 rooms. 2 with shared baths. Fireplaces. Beds:KQT. Conference Rm. Phone in room. Golf. Tennis. Skiing. Swimming. Horseback riding. Fishing.

Seen in: *Auburn Citizen, Syracuse News Times, Fingerlakes Magazine.*

Contact: Kevin McElligatt. Certificate may be used: September until May 31.

"My first B&B experience, won't be my last. Romantic."

Averill Park

Ananas Hus B&B
Rt 3 Box 301
Averill Park 12018
(518)766-5035

1962. This ranch home in the mountains east of Albany offers stunning views of the Hudson River Valley. Visitors enjoy gourmet breakfasts and relaxing afternoon teas. There are 29 acres available to guests who wish to hike or play lawn games. The surrounding area offers antiquing, downhill skiing and shopping, and the inn's location provides convenient access to the recreation and sightseeing opportunities of three states. Cherry Plain State Park is nearby.

Innkeeper(s): Clyde & Thelma Tomlinson.

Rates:$55-65. AX. Gourmet Brkfst. Teas. 3 rooms. 3 with shared baths. Beds:DT. Golf. Skiing. Swimming. Fishing.

Seen in: *Discovery Press.*

Contact: Thelma Tomlinson. Certificate may be used: Sunday through Thursday, Oct. 11-Dec. 29, 1994; Feb. 5-Dec. 28, 1995 except holidays and holiday weekends.

Avon

Avon Inn
55 E Main St
Avon 14414
(716)226-8181 Fax:(716)226-8185

1820. This Greek Revival mansion, in both the state and national historic registers, has been providing lodging for more than a century. After 1866, the residence was turned into a health center that provided water cures from the local sulphur springs. The guest registry included the likes of Henry Ford, Thomas Edison, and Eleanor Roosevelt. Though the inn is no longer a health spa, guests can still relax in the garden with its gazebo and fountain or on the Grecian-pillared front porch. A full-service restaurant and conference facilities are on the premises.

Innkeeper(s): Linda Reusch.

Rates:$60-75. MC VISA AX DC DS CB. Full Bkfst. Picnic lunches. 15 rooms. Fireplaces. Beds:KQD. Conference Rm. Phone, AC, Refrig. in room. Golf. Skiing. Horseback riding.

Contact: Linda Reusch. Certificate may be used: Anytime except holidays or special events, not valid Saturdays May 1 - Labor Day.

Bainbridge

Berry Hill Farm B&B
Box 128, RD #1
Bainbridge 13733
(607)967-8745 Fax:(607)967-8745

1820. Surrounded by flower and herb gardens, this farmhouse presides over 180 acres. Guest rooms are furnished in antiques and decorated with bunches

of fresh and dried flowers. Organic gardens provide 100 varieties of annuals and perennials. There are tulips, poppies, lilacs, sweet peas and in May, the fruit trees are in bloom. A full country breakfast is served. By advance reservation you can arrange for a sleigh ride or horse-drawn wagon to take you through the woods and meadows of the Berry Hill Farm, or you may stroll through the gardens and woods on your own.

Innkeeper(s): Jean Fowler & Cecilio Rios.

Rates:$60-70. MC VISA AX. Full Bkfst. Gourmet Brkfst. 4 rooms. 4 with shared baths. Beds:QDT. Farm. Golf. Tennis. Skiing. Swimming. Horseback riding. Fishing.

Seen in: *Tri-Town News, Daily Star.*

Contact: Jean Fowler. Certificate may be used: Anytime Jan. 2 to May 15 except holidays and special events.

"The house is just wonderful and our rooms were exceptionally comfortable."

Baldwinsville

Pandora's Getaway
83 Oswego St
Baldwinsville 13027
(315)638-8668

1845. Nestled amid large trees on a hill in a tranquil village setting, this Greek Revival inn is listed in the National Register of Historic Places. Guests enjoy breakfasts of fresh fruit, homemade breads and quiche or a favorite family recipe in the formal dining room on Depression glassware. Guests who stay in the Master Suite enjoy color TV, a fireplace and private bath, while the Front Guest Room

boasts eight windows, offering village views. The inn is a block from the village center and its restaurants, shops and working river lock. Just minutes away are Fort Saint Marie, the state fairgrounds and Syracuse University.

Innkeeper(s): Sandy Wheeler.

Rates:$50-80. MC VISA AX. Full Bkfst. Gourmet Brkfst. 4 rooms. 2 with shared baths. Fireplaces. Beds:KQ. TV in room. Skiing. Swimming. Fishing.

Contact: Sandy Wheeler. Certificate may be used: Sunday-Friday. Not during August or September.

Bellport

The Great South Bay Inn
160 S Country Rd
Bellport 11713
(516)286-8588 Fax:(516)286-3628

1890. Long Island's south shore is home to this Cape Cod-style inn, filled with turn-of-the-century antiques. Six guest rooms are available, four with private baths and all featuring original wainscotting. Favorite relaxing spots include the garden room and parlor. The innkeepers are fluent in French, and pride themselves on serving guests' individual needs, including pet accommodations or train station pick-ups. Fire Island National Seashore and the Wertheim National Wildlife Refuge are nearby.

Innkeeper(s): Michael & Judith Harvey.

Rates:$70-95. MC VISA. ContPlus Bkfst. Picnic lunches. Teas. 6 rooms. 2 with shared baths. Fireplaces. Beds:QT. TV in room. Bicycling. Swimming. Fishing.

Contact: Judith Harvey. Certificate may be used: January - May upon availability.

Shell Cottage B&B
21 Brown's Ln
Bellport 11713
(516)286-9421

1880. This Folk Victorian inn is located in charming Bellport Village. Visitors choose from Elizabeth's Room, with its sitting area and dressing room; Kate's Room, a cozy getaway for two; or the spacious Lily's Room, with its romantic whirlpool tub. Guests will enjoy the adventure of taking a ferry across the bay to Fire Island to swim and sunbathe. Those who remain at the inn may relax or watch TV in the sitting room, or take a nap on the grand south porch. Others may borrow a bike to view the lovely homes on Bellport Lane. Fine dining and the Gateway Playhouse, a well-known summer theater, are nearby.

Innkeeper(s): Carol Buck.

Rates:$65-95. Full Bkfst. 3 rooms. Beds:DT. Bicycling.

Contact: Carol Buck. Certificate may be used: Except summer weekend May 1, 1994 through Sept. 30, 1994.

Berlin

The Sedgwick Inn
Route 22, Box 250
Berlin 12022
(518)658-2334 (800)845-4886
Fax:(518)658-3998

1791. The Sedgwick Inn sits on 12 acres in the Taconic Valley in the Berkshire Mountains. The main house features guest rooms, the low-ceilinged

Coach Room Tavern and a glass-enclosed dining porch facing an English garden. A Colonial-style motel behind the main house sits beside a rushing brook. A small antique shop, once a Civil War recruiting station, is designed in the Neoclassical style of the early 19th century. A converted carriage house with a hardwood dance floor and handhewn beams serves as a gift shop with prints, paintings, sculptures and a selection of unusual craft and gourmet items.

Innkeeper(s): Edith Evans.

Rates:$65-95. MC VISA AX DC DS CB. Full Bkfst. Gourmet Dinner. 11 rooms. Beds:KQ. Conference Rm. TV, Phone in room. Farm. Golf. Tennis. Skiing. Swimming. Fishing.

Seen in: *Berkshire Eagle, Hudson Valley Magazine, Albany Times Union, Good Housekeeping.*

Contact: Edith Evans. Certificate may be used: June, July, August,

October - Sunday through Thursday. Rest of year depending on availability except for holiday weekends.

"We were absolutely enchanted. We found this to be a charming place, a rare and wonderful treat."

Brockport

The Portico B&B
3741 Lake Rd
Brockport 14420
(716)637-0220

1850. Named for its three porches, called porticos, this Greek Revival inn is situated amid blue spruce, maple and sycamore trees in a historic district. Tall columns and a cupola add to its charm. Three antique-filled guest rooms are available to visitors, who enjoy a full Victorian breakfast and kettledrum, also known as afternoon tea. The surrounding area offers many attractions, including the Cobblestone Museum, Darien Lake Amusement Park, George Eastman House and Strasenburgh Planetarium. Several colleges, golf courses and parks are nearby.

Innkeeper(s): Anne & Ronn Klein.

Rates:$55. Full Bkfst. Teas. 3 rooms. 2 with shared baths. Fireplaces. Beds:QT. Skiing. Swimming. Fishing.

Contact: Anne Klein. Certificate may be used: July 1, 1994 - Dec. 31, 1995.

The Victorian B&B
320 Main St
Brockport 14420
(716)637-7519 (800)836-1929
Fax:(716)637-7519

1890. Within walking distance of the historic Erie Canal, this lovely Queen Anne Victorian inn is located on Brockport's Main Street. Visitors select from eight second-floor guest rooms, all with phones, private baths and TVs. Victorian furnishings are found throughout the inn. A favorite spot is the solarium, with its three walls of windows, perfect for curling up with a book or magazine. Two first-floor sitting areas also provide relaxing havens for guests. Lake Ontario is just 10 miles away, and visitors will find much to explore in nearby Rochester.

Innkeeper(s): Sharon Kehoe.

Rates:$59. Full Bkfst. 8 rooms. Beds:QT. Phone, AC in room. Skiing. Fishing.

Contact: Sharon Kehoe. Certificate may be used: Nov. 1 through March 31.

Brookfield

Bivona Hill Bed and Breakfast
Academy Rd, PO Box 201
Brookfield 13314
(315)899-8921

1974. Rekindle your romance at this country home which overlooks the Beaver Creek Valley. The romantic getaway package includes a five-course candlelight dinner in a beautifully decorated queen suite that boasts its own fireplace. Every guest room offers a view of the valley. The smell of freshly ground coffee draw even the sleepiest guest into the dining room for homemade baked goods, jam and a delicious country breakfast. Homemade chocolates are special extras for each guest. More than 130 miles of state-maintained horse trails are nearby, and guests are welcome to bring their horses and house them at the inn's stables. If antiques are your passion, the inn is ideally located 20 minutes from the largest antique community in the state.
Innkeeper(s): Michael Bivona.
Rates:$48-75. MC VISA AX. Full Bkfst. Gourmet Brkfst, Lunch, Dinner. Picnic lunches. Teas. 5 rooms. 3 with shared baths. Fireplaces. Beds:QT. TV, Phone, Refrig. in room. Farm. Golf. Skiing. Horseback riding. Stables. Fishing.
Seen in: *Country Inns, Travel Magazine.*
Contact: Michael Bivona. Certificate may be used: All year, based upon availability.

"The room was ideal, the food was exceptional and your dedication appreciated."

Gates Hill Homestead
PO Box 96, Dugway Rd
Brookfield 13314
(315)899-5837

1974. This early American salt-box inn is found on 64 acres of forested farmland, and is home to a working farm and prize-winning Percheron horses. Early American furnishings highlight the inn's four guest rooms. The innkeepers also lead horse-drawn stagecoach tours of the history-rich area, complemented by a delicious, family-style dinner. Sleigh rides are available in winter, with or without dinner. Colgate University and the Upstate Auto Museum are within easy driving distance.
Innkeeper(s): Charles & Donna Tanney.
Rates:$64. MC VISA. Full Bkfst. Gourmet Dinner. 4 rooms. 2 with shared baths. Beds:DT. AC in room. Farm. Skiing. Stables. Fishing.
Contact: Donna Tanney. Certificate may be used: April, Sunday through Thursday; Oct. 20 through Nov. 30, Sunday through Thursday.

Burdett

The Red House Country Inn
4586 Picnic Area Rd
Burdett 14818-9716
(607)546-8566

1844. Nestled within the 13,000-acre Finger Lakes National Forest, this old farmstead has an in-ground swimming pool, large veranda overlooking groomed lawns, flower gardens and picnic areas. Pet Samoyeds and goats share the seven acres. Next to the property are acres of wild blueberry patches and stocked fishing ponds. The Red House is near Seneca Lake, world-famous Glen Gorge, and Cornell University.
Innkeeper(s): Sandy Schmanke & Joan Martin.
Rates:$60-85. MC VISA AX DS. Full Bkfst. 5 rooms. 5 with shared baths. Fireplaces. Beds:QDT. Golf. Tennis. Bicycling. Skiing. Swimming. Fishing.
Seen in: *New York Alive, Discerning Traveler, New York Magazine.*
Contact: Joan Martin. Certificate may be used: November-April, Sunday-Thursday inclusive.

"Delightful. Beautifully located for hiking, cross-country skiing. Guest rooms are charming."

Canandaigua

The Acorn Inn
PO Box 334, 4508 Rt 64 S
Canandaigua 14424
(716)229-2834

1795. Visitors to this Federal Stagecoach inn may enjoy afternoon tea before a blazing fire in the large colonial fireplace equipped with antique crane and hanging iron pots. Guest rooms are furnished with antiques, canopy beds, luxury linens and bedding, and each has a sitting area. Books are provided in each guest room as well as in the libraries. After a day of skiing and dinner at a local restaurant, guests will find a carafe of ice water and chocolates in their room. Beds are turned down nightly and in colder weather, warmed to await your return.
Innkeeper(s): Louis & Joan Clark.
Rates:$95-140. MC VISA DS. Full Bkfst. 4 rooms. Beds:Q. TV, AC in room. Golf. Skiing. Swimming. Fishing.
Contact: Joan Clark. Certificate may be used: Tuesday-Thursday inclusive, November-April inclusive. Discount available on Bristol and Hotchkiss rooms only.

Nottingham Lodge B&B

5741 Bristol Valley Rd, Rt 64
Canandaigua 14424
(716)374-5355

1825. South of Canandaigua Lake in the heart of the Bristol Mountain Ski Center area, this Tudor-style inn offers stunning views of the nearby mountain from its valley setting. Visitors select from the Michelle Room, with its canopy bed; Valerie Room, four-poster; and Katheryn, iron and brass. The inn's full breakfast features fresh fruit and homemade baked goods, and it is served in the dining room with its breathtaking view of Bristol Mountain. Guests enjoy gathering around the cobblestone fireplace or hiking along the stream behind the inn.

Innkeeper(s): Bill & Bonnie Robinson.

Rates:$60-65. MC VISA DS. Gourmet Brkfst. 3 rooms. Beds:Q. Skiing. Swimming. Fishing.

Contact: Bonnie Robinson. Certificate may be used: No limit except Dec. 26, 1994-Jan. 2, 1995.

Oliver Phelps Country Inn

252 N Main St
Canandaigua 14424
(716)396-1650

1834. Century-old chestnut trees frame this stately Federal-style inn, which offers elegant accommodations to Finger Lakes visitors. The inn features poster beds, a charming clock collection, and period antiques. Arched entryways, handsome fireplaces, stenciled walls, wine keg paneling and wooden floors add to the authentic aura. The surrounding area has many attractions, including sailing lessons and winery tours. Don't miss the nearby Granger Homestead or Sonnenberg Gardens.

Innkeeper(s): John & Joanne Sciarratta.

Rates:$65-105. MC VISA DS. Full Bkfst. 4 rooms. Fireplaces. Beds:KQT. AC in room. Bicycling. Skiing. Swimming.

Contact: Joanne Sciarratta. Certificate may be used: November - May 15.

Candor

The Edge Of Thyme, A B&B Inn

6 Main St
Candor 13743
(607)659-5155 (800)722-7365

1860. Originally the summer home of John D. Rockefeller's secretary, this two-story Georgian-style inn offers gracious accommodations a short drive from Ithaca. The inn sports many interesting features, including an impressive stairway, marble

fireplaces, parquet floors, pergola (arbor) and windowed porch with leaded glass. Guests may relax in front of the inn's fireplace, catch up with reading in its library or watch television in the sitting room. An authentic turn-of-the-century full breakfast is served, and guests also may arrange for special high teas.

Innkeeper(s): Prof. Frank & Eva Mae Musgrave.

Rates:$55-75. MC VISA. Gourmet Brkfst. Teas. 5 rooms. 3 with shared baths. Beds:QDT. Skiing. Fishing.

Contact: Eva Mae Musgrave. Certificate may be used: Sunday through Thursday, not during major weekends i.e. graduations, parent's weekends.

Chemung

Halcyon Place B&B

197 Washington St, PO Box 244
Chemung 14825
(607)529-3544

1825. The innkeepers chose the name "halcyon" because it signifies tranquility and a healing richness. The historic Greek Revival inn and its lovely

grounds offer just that to guests, who will appreciate the fine period antiques, paneled doors, six-over-six windows of hand-blown glass and wide plank floors. An herb garden and screen porch also beckon visitors. Full breakfasts may include omelets with garden ingredients, raspberry muffins, rum sticky buns or waffles. The inn's three guest rooms feature double beds, and one boasts a romantic fireplace. Fine antiquing and golfing are found nearby.

Innkeeper(s): Douglas & Yvonne Sloan.

Rates:$50-60. Full Bkfst. Gourmet Brkfst. Teas. 3 rooms. 2 with shared baths. Fireplaces. Beds:D. Bicycling. Skiing. Swimming. Fishing.

Contact: Yvonne Sloan. Certificate may be used: Sept. 1, 1994 - May 1, 1995 and September - December, 1995.

Chestertown

Balsam House Inn
Atateka Dr, RR 1 Box 365
Chestertown 12817
(518)494-2828 (800)441-6856
Fax:(518)494-4431

1845. This Stick Victorian offers the refreshing air and scenic wonders of the Adirondack Mountains. Each of the four seasons provides its own lures, including bicycling, canoeing, cross-country and downhill skiing, horseback riding, hot air ballooning, ice fishing, sleigh rides and white-water rafting. Guest rooms all feature country furnishings and some have fireplaces. Nearby Gore Mountain boasts the only gondola in the state.

Innkeeper(s): Josef & Maggie Roettig.

Rates:$75-185. MC VISA AX DC. Full Bkfst. Gourmet Dinner. 22 rooms. Fireplaces. Beds:KQ. AC in room. Bicycling. Skiing. Fishing.

Contact: Josef Roettig. Certificate may be used: Sepember, 1994 - June, 1995. Excludes holidays.

The Friends Lake Inn
Friends Lake Rd
Chestertown 12817
(518)494-4751 Fax:(518)494-4616

1910. Formerly a boardinghouse for tanners who worked in the area, this Mission-style inn now offers its guests elegant accommodations and fine

dining. Overlooking Friends Lake, the inn provides easy access to many well-known skiing areas, including Gore Mountain. Guests are welcome to borrow a canoe for a lake outing and use the inn's private dock and beach. Guest rooms are well-appointed and include brass and iron beds. Many have breathtaking lake views. An outdoor hot tub is a favorite spot after a busy day of recreation.

Innkeeper(s): Sharon Taylor.

Rates:$80-225. MC VISA. Full Bkfst. MAP available. Gourmet Brkfst, Lunch, Dinner. Picnic lunches. Teas. Evening snacks. 14 rooms. Beds:Q. Conference Rm. AC in room. Bicycling. Skiing. Spa. Swimming. Fishing.

Contact: Sharon Taylor. Certificate may be used: Available only Sunday-Thursday.

Cold Spring

Pig Hill
73 Main St
Cold Spring 10520
(914)265-9247 Fax:(914)265-2155

1830. The antiques at this stately three-story inn can be purchased and range from Chippendale to chinoiserie style. Rooms feature formal English and

Adirondack decor, with special touches such as four-poster or brass beds, painted rockers and, of course, pigs. The lawn features a tri-level garden. The delicious breakfasts can be shared with guests in the dining room or garden, or you can take it in the privacy of your room. The inn is about an hour out of New York City, and the train station is only two blocks away.

Innkeeper(s): Wendy O'Brien.

Rates:$100-150. MC VISA AX. Full Bkfst. Teas. 8 rooms. 4 with shared baths. Fireplaces. Beds:Q. Conference Rm. AC in room. Swimming. Fishing.

Seen in: *National Geographic, Woman's Home Journal, Country Inns, Getaways for Gourmets.*

Contact: Wendy O'Brien. Certificate may be used: Weekdays/any time of year.

"Some of our fondest memories of New York were at Pig Hill."

Corinth

Agape Farm B&B
4894 Rt 9N
Corinth 12822
(518)654-7777

1990. Amid 33 acres of fields and woods, this Adirondack farmhouse inn is home to chickens and horses, as well as guests seeking a refreshing get-

away. Visitors have their choice of six guest rooms, all with ceiling fans, phones, private baths and views of the tranquil surroundings. The inn's wrap-around porch lures many visitors, who often enjoy a glass of icy lemonade. Homemade breads, jams, jellies and muffins are part of the full breakfast served here, and guests are welcome to pick berries or gather a ripe tomato from the garden. A trout-filled stream on the grounds flows to the Hudson River, a mile away.

Innkeeper(s): Fred & Sigrid Koch.

Rates:$50-99. MC VISA. Full Bkfst. 5 rooms. Beds:KQDT. Phone in room. Farm. Golf. Tennis. Skiing. Handicap access. Swimming. Horseback riding. Fishing.

Seen in: *Oneida Daily Dispatch.*

Contact: Fred Koch. Certificate may be used: Sept. 15 to June 15, 1994 and 1995.

"Clean and impeccable, we were treated royally."

The Inn at the Edge of the Forest
11 East Dayton Dr
Corinth 12822
(518)654-6656 (800)654-3343

1972. Situated among fragrant pines and tall trees, this contemporary chalet-style inn offers a respite from the rigors of city life even though it is just 12 miles from the many exciting attractions of Saratoga Springs. The enchanting woodland setting is ideal for romantic getaways and is a popular site for weddings and honeymoons. Guests often gather in front of the inn's fireplaces with a mug of hot chocolate and a platter of fresh-baked cookies. Moreau State Park and Grant's Cottage are within

easy driving distance.

Innkeeper(s): Mike & Pam DeJoseph.

Rates:$50-165. Full Bkfst. Gourmet Brkfst. 3 rooms. 1 with shared bath. Beds:KQT. Skiing. Swimming. Fishing.

Contact: Michael DeJoseph. Certificate may be used: Anytime except racing season and a few selected weekends (Jazz Festival and fall foliage).

Corning

1865 White Birch B&B
69 E First St
Corning 14830
(607)962-6355

1865. This Victorian is a short walk from historic Market Street, the Corning Glass Museum and many restaurants. Guests will appreciate the detailed woodwork, hardwood floors, an impressive

winding staircase and many antiques. The rooms are decorated in a cozy, country decor. Home-baked breakfasts provide the perfect start for a day of visiting wineries, antique shops or museums.

Innkeeper(s): Kathy & Joe Donahue.

Rates:$60-65. MC VISA AX. Gourmet Brkfst. 4 rooms. 2 with shared baths. Beds:QT. Golf. Tennis. Skiing. Swimming. Fishing.

Contact: Kathy Donahue. Certificate may be used: November-December, 1994, Monday through Thursday, no holidays-weekends when available. January-March, 1995, November-December, 1995-Monday-Thursday, no holidays-weekends, subject to availability.

"This is a beautiful home, decorated to make us feel warm and welcome."

Delevan House
188 Delevan Ave
Corning 14830
(607)962-2347

1933. Visitors to the Corning area will find a touch of home at this comfortable Colonial Revival house on a hill overlooking town. The inn's screened porch offers the perfect spot for reading, relaxing or sipping a cool drink. A full breakfast is served before guests head out for a day of business, sightseeing or travel. The Finger Lakes are 30 miles away, and just two miles from the inn visitors will find the city's historic district. The Mark Twain Home and Pinnacle State Park are nearby.

Innkeeper(s): Mary DePumpo.

Rates:$55-85. Full Bkfst. 3 rooms. 2 with shared baths. Beds:D. Swimming. Fishing.

Contact: Mary M. DePumpo. Certificate may be used: November thru March.

Crown Point

Crown Point B&B
Box 490, Main Street
Crown Point 12928
(518)597-3651

1886. This Queen Anne Victorian inn north of Fort Ticonderoga offers a fascinating vantage point from which to view the historical area. Crown Point served as a fortress guarding Lake Champlain during the Revolutionary War. The inn, originally owned by a local banker, boasts cherry, chestnut, mahogany, oak, pine and walnut woodwork. The spacious guest rooms, furnished with period antiques, all feature private baths. The Master Bedroom Suite features a highback walnut bed and marble-topped dresser and the Crown Room sports a queen-size brass bed. Three parlors are available for relaxing and socializing.

Innkeeper(s): Jan & Al Hallock.

Rates:$50-65. MC VISA. ContPlus Bkfst. Picnic lunches. 5 rooms. Beds:QDT. Bicycling. Skiing. Swimming.

Contact: Sandy Johnson. Certificate may be used: Oct. 16-May 14.

Deposit

Chestnut Inn at Oquaga Lake
RD #1, Box 135, Oquaga Lake Rd
Deposit 13754
(607)467-2500 (800)467-7676
Fax:(607)467-5911

1927. This spacious Craftsman-style inn east of Binghampton offers a variety of rooming and dining options. The family-oriented inn is well-equipped to handle meetings, receptions and weddings, and guests will find no shortage of activities or amenities. Bicycles, child care and swimming are offered. The inn features picnic lunches, perfect for a day by the lake. Oquaga Creek State Park is a short drive away.

Innkeeper(s): Richard Post.

Rates:$49-179. MC VISA AX DC DS. Full Bkfst. MAP available. Gourmet Brkfst, Lunch, Dinner. Picnic lunches. Teas. Evening snacks. 27 rooms. 20 with shared baths. Beds:KQT. Conference Rm. Bicycling. Skiing. Handicap access. Swimming. Fishing.

Contact: James Gross. Certificate may be used: Anytime.

The White Pillars Inn
82 Second St
Deposit 13754
(607)467-4191 Fax:(607)467-2264

1820. Guests are greeted with freshly baked cookies at this exquisite Greek Revival inn. This is only the beginning of a food adventure to remember. After a restful night's sleep on a hand-carved, high-

board bed, guests linger over a five-course breakfast, which might include an overstuffed omelette or a baked apple wrapped in pastry and topped with caramel sauce. Dinner is a gourmet's treat, and all meals are prepared by innkeeper Najla Aswad, whose recipes have been recommended by Gourmet magazine. The inn is decorated with beautiful antiques, rich Persian carpets and colorful floral arrangements.

Innkeeper(s): Najla R. Aswad.

Rates:$75-125. MC VISA AX DC DS CB. Full Bkfst. Gourmet Brkfst, Dinner. 3 rooms. Beds:KT. Conference Rm. TV, Phone, AC in room. Golf. Tennis. Skiing. Swimming. Horseback riding. Fishing.

Seen in: *Gourmet*.

Contact: Najla Aswad. Certificate may be used: Oct. 20 - May 1.

"The perfect place to do nothing but eat!"

Dolgeville

Adrianna B&B
44 Stewart St
Dolgeville 13329
(315)429-3249 (800)335-4233

1965. In the foothills of the Adirondacks, this two-story raised ranch home awaits visitors to the central New York area. Three guest rooms are available, one with private bath and all with ceiling fans. Barney, the resident cat, often curls up in front of the fireplace, and guests are welcome to

join him there for afternoon tea. The inn's swimming pool is another favorite relaxation area, especially after a day spent antiquing or touring the area's many points of interest, including Beaversprite Sanctuary and the Herkimer House. The National Baseball Hall of Fame at Cooperstown is within easy driving distance.

Innkeeper(s): Adrianna Naizby.

Rates:$50-65. MC VISA. Full Bkfst. 3 rooms. 2 with shared baths. Beds:QT. AC in room. Skiing. Fishing.

Contact: Adrianna Naizby. Certificate may be used: Anytime except July, August, Christmas.

Dover Plains

Old Drovers Inn
Old Rt 22
Dover Plains 12522
(914)832-9311 Fax:(914)832-6356

1750. Luxurious accommodations and fine food are featured at this historic Colonial Revival inn, located in the Harlem Valley at the foot of the

Berkshires. The inn once served as a resting spot for area drovers, or cowboys, who were leading cattle to market in New York City. Visitors select from the Cherry, Meeting, Rose or Sleigh rooms. The handsome furnishings and service found at the inn are matched by its cuisine, which is well known in the area. Tour the inn's 12 acres or borrow bicycles and enjoy the scenery. On weekends a full breakfast and dinner are available.

Innkeeper(s): Alice Pitcher & Kemper Peacock.

Rates:$120-365. MC VISA DC CB. ContPlus Bkfst. MAP available. Gourmet Brkfst, Lunch, Dinner. Picnic lunches. Teas. 4 rooms. Fireplaces. Beds:D. Conference Rm. AC in room. Farm. Bicycling. Skiing. Swimming. Fishing.

Contact: Alice Pitcher. Certificate may be used: Monday through Thursday.

Dundee

The 1819 Red Brick Inn
2081 State Route 230
Dundee 14837-9424
(607)243-8844

1819. This Federal-style inn's impressive exterior, with its 15-inch-thick brick walls, is complemented by its antique-filled interior. Many fine wineries are found in the area, and that influence is reflected in the guest rooms, named Bordeaux, Burgundy, Chablis and Champagne. The inn sits on 60 acres, near a mineral springs that in the late 1800s attracted many health-conscious visitors. Keuka Lake and Watkins Glen state parks are within easy driving distance.

Innkeeper(s): Sigurd & Helen Kristiansen.

Rates:$60. Full Bkfst. 4 rooms. 2 with shared baths. Beds:DT. Farm. Skiing. Swimming. Fishing.

Contact: Sigurd Kristiansen. Certificate may be used: Monday through Thursday.

East Hampton

Maidstone Arms
207 Main St
East Hampton 11937
(516)324-5006 Fax:(516)324-5037

1860. Overlooking the village green and pond, this historic Colonial Revival inn offers elegant accommodations to those visiting the Eastern portion of Long Island. The inn's guest rooms, all individually furnished, feature air conditioning, cable TV, phones, private baths and turndown service. Many rooms also boast fireplaces and refrigerators. An outstanding restaurant is on the premises. Recreational activities abound in the area, including fishing, golf, sailing and tennis. Amagansett National Wildlife Reserve and the Town Marine Museum are nearby.

Innkeeper(s): Christophe M. Bergen.

Rates:$132-375. MC VISA AX. Full Bkfst. EP. Gourmet Lunch, Dinner. Picnic lunches. Teas. Evening snacks. 19 rooms. Fireplaces. Beds:QT. Conference Rm. TV, Phone, AC, Refrig. in room. Swimming. Fishing.

Contact: Christophe Bergen. Certificate may be used: Oct. 15 to Dec. 15, 1994; Jan. 2 to June 1, 1995.

Elka Park

The Redcoat's Return
Dale Ln
Elka Park 12427
(518)589-9858

1910. Styled as an English country inn, the four-story Redcoat's Return is set in the northern Catskill Mountains at the center of the Catskill

Game Preserve. Originally, it was built as a summer boarding house for vacationers. Dinner is served fireside in the library dining room. The Wrights have served as innkeeper/owners for more than 20 years.
Innkeeper(s): Tom and Peggy Wright.
Rates:$80-95. MC VISA AX. Full Bkfst. 14 rooms. 7 with shared baths. Beds:D. Golf. Tennis. Skiing. Fishing.
Seen in: *New York Times, Ski Magazine, Golf Magazine.*
Contact: Thomas Wright. Certificate may be used: Sunday through Thursday except Christmas and New Year and October.

"Loved the place even more than last time."

Essex

The Stone House
Box 43
Essex 12936
(518)963-7713

1826. Just a two-minute walk from the ferry that traverses Lake Champlain, this stately Georgian stonehouse offers a tranquil English country setting. Breakfast may be eaten in the elegant dining room or on the garden terrace, and guests also enjoy an evening snack and glass of wine by candlelight on the inn's porch. The charming hamlet of Essex, listed in the National Register, is waiting to be explored and visitors may do so by borrowing one of the inn's bicycles. Antiquing, fine dining and shopping are found in town, and Lake Champlain and nearby Lake George provide many recreational activities.

Innkeeper(s): Sylvia Hobbs.
Rates:$60-95. ContPlus Bkfst. Evening snacks. 4 rooms. 2 with shared baths. Beds:QDT. AC in room. Bicycling. Skiing. Swimming. Fishing.
Contact: Sylvia Hobbs. Certificate may be used: May 15-Oct. 15 mid-week only. Sunday through Thursday.

Fair Haven

Black Creek Farm B&B
PO Box 390
Fair Haven 13064
(315)947-5282

1888. Pines and towering birch trees frame this Victorian farmhouse inn, filled with an incredible assortment of authentic antiques. Set on 20 acres

in the countryside west of Fair Haven, this inn offers a refreshing escape from big-city life. The inn's impressive furnishings come as no real surprise, since there is an antique shop on the premises. Guests enjoy relaxing in a hammock, on the porch, or by taking a stroll along the peaceful country roads. The inn is two miles from Lake Ontario's shoreline and within easy reach of Fair Haven Beach State Park and Thorpe Vineyard.
Innkeeper(s): Bob & Kathy Sarber.
Rates:$50-60. MC VISA. Full Bkfst. Evening snacks. 3 rooms. 3 with shared baths. Beds:D. AC in room. Farm. Bicycling. Skiing. Swimming. Fishing.
Contact: Kathy Sarber. Certificate may be used: Not to be used during July and August on Saturday night.

Frost Haven B&B Inn
14380 West Bay Rd, PO Box 241
Fair Haven 13064
(315)947-5331

1870. This Federal-style inn near Lake Ontario offers a relaxing getaway for residents of nearby Rochester and Syracuse. Four guest rooms are available, all furnished with Victorian stylings and featuring bath robes and ceiling fans. Guests enjoy a full breakfast before beginning a busy day of antiquing, fishing, sightseeing, swimming or sunbathing. Fair Haven Beach State Park is nearby, and Fort Ontario is within easy driving distance.

Innkeeper(s): Brad & Chris Frost.

Rates:$60-66. MC VISA AX. Full Bkfst. 4 rooms. 4 with shared baths. Beds:QDT. Swimming. Fishing.

Contact: Christine Frost. Certificate may be used: Excludes weekends July through Labor Day.

Fleischmanns

River Run
Main St, Box D4
Fleischmanns 12430
(914)254-4884

1887. The backyard of this large three-story Victorian slopes to the river where the Little Red Kill and the Bushkill trout streams join. Guests are invited to bring their well-behaved pets with them. (They are given a spot on the back porch where there are doggie towels for wiping dusty paws before entering the inn.) Kennel crates are provided when guests want to explore the area without their pets. Inside, stained-glass windows shine on the hardwood floors of the dining room, and there's a pleasant fireplace in the parlor. Adirondack chairs are situated comfortably on the front porch.

Innkeeper(s): Larry Miller & Jeanne Palmer.

Rates:$45-90. MC VISA. Full Bkfst. Teas. 8 rooms. 3 with shared baths. Beds:KQT. Golf. Tennis. Bicycling. Skiing. Handicap access. Swimming. Horseback riding. Fishing.

Seen in: *Catskill Mountain News, Kingston Freeman, New York Times.*

Contact: Lawrence Miller. Certificate may be used: Weekends: April-June, September, November-December. Midweek: all year. Note: all holiday periods excluded.

"We are really happy to know of a place that welcomes all of our family."

Forestburgh

The Inn at Lake Joseph
400 St Joseph Rd
Forestburgh 12777
(914)791-9506 Fax:(914)794-1948

1865. This Queen Anne Victorian, with a massive screened veranda, is set on 20 acres and was once the vacation home of Cardinal Hayes and Cardinal Spellman. The inn is surrounded by rolling lawns and woodlands and a small swimming beach is located within a short walk. It is in the National Register.

Innkeeper(s): Ivan Weinger & Dee Millar.

Rates:$138-238. MC VISA AX. Full Bkfst. AP available. Gourmet Brkfst,

Lunch, Dinner. Picnic lunches. Teas. 10 rooms. Fireplaces. Beds:KQT. Conference Rm. Phone in room. Tennis. Skiing. Handicap access. Spa. Swimming. Fishing.

Seen in: *New York Times, Kaatskill Life Magazine.*

Contact: Ivan Weinger. Certificate may be used: Midweek. Weekends, space-available basis.

"This is a secluded spot where every detail is attended to, making it one of the country's best inns."

Fredonia

The White Inn
52 E Main St
Fredonia 14063
(716)672-2103 Fax:(716)672-2107

1868. Built on the homesite of the county's first physician, this elegant mansion features a 100-foot-long veranda where refreshments are served. Period antiques and reproductions are found in every bedroom. Guests enjoy gourmet meals at this inn, a charter member of the Duncan Hines "Family of Fine Restaurants." Local wineries offer tours and wine tastings. Specialty and antique shops are nearby. Chautauqua Institute is a short drive from the inn, and guests can arrange Chautauqua-White Inn packages. Fredonia is also the summer home of the Buffalo Bills. Lake Erie provides relaxation and an opportunity to enjoy a sail aboard the inn's 37-foot sloop.

Innkeeper(s): Robert Contiguglia & Kathleen Dennison.

Rates:$59-159. MC VISA AX DC DS. Full Bkfst. AP available. Gourmet Dinner. 23 rooms. Fireplaces. Beds:KQ. Conference Rm. TV, Phone, AC, Refrig. in room. Skiing.

Seen in: *Country Living, Innsider.*

Contact: Kathleen Dennison. Certificate may be used: Sunday - Thursday nights, excluding holiday weekends.

"Thanks again for another wonderful stay."

Freeville

LoPinto Farm Lodge
355 Sheldon Rd
Freeville 13068
(607)347-6556 (800)551-5806
Fax:(607)347-4085

1953. A hunter's paradise is found at this country inn, a hunting lodge on 320 acres of recreation-rich land between Cortland and Ithaca. Deer and turkey hunting and bass fishing are just a few of the inn's specialties, which also include cross-country skiing and hay and sleigh rides. A handsome, well-lit sitting room, with fireplace, piano and TV, is a favorite gathering place where the inn's guests may compare notes on the day's activities. Cayuga Lake is within easy driving distance and the innkeepers are happy to arrange fishing charters there or elsewhere.

Innkeeper(s): Joe & Mary LoPinto & Tracy Grooms.

Rates:$90-100. MC VISA AX DC DS. Full Bkfst. Picnic lunches. Evening snacks. 5 rooms. 5 with shared baths. Beds:QT. Conference Rm. Farm. Skiing. Handicap access. Swimming. Stables. Fishing.

Contact: Joseph LoPinto. Certificate may be used: Anytime except May, October, November, December.

Friendship

A Merry Maid Inn B&B
53 W Main St
Friendship 14739
(716)973-7740

1883. Relaxation is the key word at this charming Victorian inn in a small Alleghany Mountain hamlet. The innkeepers specialize in stress-reduction therapies and are happy to share this expertise with their visitors. The inn's guest rooms are named after four goddesses: Demeter, Gaia, Isis and Persephone. The Gaia and Isis rooms feature romantic fireplaces, and three other fireplaces are found in the inn. Guests will be impressed with the breakfast offerings, which may include Amish friendship bread with cream cheese, fresh fruit salad or French toast. Antiquing, golf and tennis are found nearby.

Innkeeper(s): Moon & Mark Beiferman-Haines.

Rates:$45-65. MC VISA DC CB. Full Bkfst. Gourmet Dinner. 4 rooms. 3 with shared baths. Fireplaces. Beds:KQ. Skiing. Fishing.

Contact: Moon Beiferman-Haines. Certificate may be used: Sunday - Thursday except holidays (call for availability).

Garrison

The Bird & Bottle Inn
Rt 9, Old Albany Post Rd
Garrison 10524
(914)424-3000 Fax:(914)424-3283

1761. Built as Warren's Tavern, this three-story yellow farmhouse served as a lodging and dining spot on the old New York-to-Albany Post Road, now a National Historic Landmark. George Washington, Hamilton, Lafayette and many other

historic figures frequently passed by. The inn's four acres include secluded lawns, a bubbling stream and Hudson Valley woodlands. Timbered ceilings, old paneling and fireplace mantels in the inn's notable restaurant maintain a Revolutionary War era ambiance. Second-floor guest rooms have canopied or four-poster beds and each is warmed by its own fireplace.

Innkeeper(s): Ira Boyar.

Rates:$195-215. MC VISA AX DC. Full Bkfst. MAP available. Gourmet Dinner. Picnic lunches. 4 rooms. Fireplaces. Beds:Q. Conference Rm. AC in room. Golf. Bicycling. Skiing. Handicap access. Swimming. Horseback riding. Fishing.

Seen in: *Colonial Homes, Hudson Valley, Westchester Spotlight.*

Contact: Ira Boyar. Certificate may be used: Wednesday, Thursday, Friday-Feb. 1 to Sept. 30.

Greenfield Center

The Wayside Inn
104 Wilton Rd
Greenfield Center 12833
(518)893-7249 Fax:(518)893-2884

1786. This Federal-style inn and arts center provides a unique atmosphere to visitors of the Saratoga Springs area. Situated on 10 acres amid a brook, herb gardens, pond, wildflowers and willows, the inn originally served as a stagecoach tavern. Many interesting pieces, gathered during the innkeepers' 10 years living abroad highlight the inn's interior. Visitors select from the Colonial American, European, Far East and Middle East rooms. The inn shares space with an arts center, located in the big, blue barn that serves as a local landmark. Migrating birds are known to frequent the inn's picturesque pond.

Innkeeper(s): Dale & Karen Shook.

Rates:$55-135. MC VISA DC CB. Gourmet Brkfst. 5 rooms. Beds:KQ. Conference Rm. AC in room. Farm. Bicycling. Skiing. Swimming. Fishing.

Contact: Karen Shook. Certificate may be used: November-April.

Hadley

Saratoga Rose B&B

PO Box 238, 4174 Rockwell St
Hadley 12835
(518)696-2861 (800)942-5025
Fax:(518)696-5319

1885. This romantic Queen Anne Victorian offers a small, candlelit restaurant perfect for an evening for two. Breakfast specialties include Grand Marnier French Toast and Eggs Anthony. Rooms are decorated in period style. The Queen Anne Room, decorated in blue, boasts a wood and tile fireplace and a quilt-covered bed. The Garden Room offers a private sunporch and an outside deck with a Jacuzzi spa. Each of the rooms features something special. Guests can take in the mountain view or relax on the veranda while sipping a cocktail.

Innkeeper(s): Anthony & Nancy Merlino.

Rates:$70-140. MC VISA DS. Full Bkfst. MAP available. Gourmet Brkfst, Lunch, Dinner. Picnic lunches. Evening snacks. 4 rooms. Fireplaces. Beds:K. AC in room. Tennis. Bicycling. Skiing. Spa. Swimming. Horseback riding. Fishing.

Seen in: *Getaways for Gourmets.*

Contact: Nancy Merlino. Certificate may be used: September-June.

"A must for the inn traveller."

Hague

Trout House Village Resort

Lake Shore Dr (Rt 9 N), PO Box 510
Hague 12836-0510
(518)543-6088 (800)368-6088

1930. On the shores of beautiful Lake George is this resort inn, offering accommodations in the lodge, authentic log cabins or cottages. Many of the guest rooms in the lodge boast lake views while the log cabins offer jetted tubs and fireplaces. Outstanding cross-country skiing, downhill skiing and snowmobiling are found nearby. The inn furnishes bicycles, canoes, kayaks, paddle boats, rowboats, sleds, skis and toboggans. Summertime evenings offer evening games of capture-the-flag and soccer. Other activities include basketball, horseshoes, ping pong, a putting green and volleyball.

Innkeeper(s): Scott & Alice Patchett.

Rates:$39-257. MC VISA AX DS. Full Bkfst. MAP available. Gourmet Dinner. 26 rooms. Fireplaces. Beds:QT. Conference Rm. TV, Phone, Refrig. in room. Tennis. Bicycling. Skiing. Exercise room. Swimming. Fishing.

Contact: Robert Patchett. Certificate may be used: Sept. 15 to June 15.

Hamburg

Sharon's B&B Lake House

4862 Lakeshore Rd
Hamburg 14075
(716)627-7561

1935. This historic lakefront house is located 10 miles from Buffalo and 45 minutes from Niagara Falls. Overlooking Lake Erie, the West Lake Room and the Upper Lake Room provide spectacular views. The home's beautiful furnishings offer additional delights.

Innkeeper(s): Sharon DiMaria.

Rates:$100-110. Full Bkfst. Gourmet Brkfst, Lunch, Dinner. Evening snacks. 2 rooms. Beds:T. TV, Phone in room. Golf. Skiing. Spa. Swimming. Fishing.

Contact: Sharon DiMaria. Certificate may be used: Anytime only by reservation.

"Spectacular view, exquisitely furnished."

Hamlin

Sandy Creek Manor House

1960 Redman Rd
Hamlin 14464-9635
(716)964-7528

1910. Six acres of woods and perennial gardens provide the setting for this English Tudor house. Stained glass, polished woods and Amish quilts add warmth to the home. Breakfast is served on the open porch in summer. Fisherman's Landing, on the banks of Sandy Creek, is a stroll away. Bullhead, trout and salmon are popular catches.

Innkeeper(s): Shirley Hollink & James Krempasky.

Rates:$55-65. MC VISA DS. Full Bkfst. AP available. Teas. Evening snacks. 3 rooms. 2 with shared baths. Beds:KQDT. AC in room. Skiing. Swimming. Fishing.

Seen in: *Rochester Times Union.*

Contact: Shirley Hollink. Certificate may be used: Anytime.

"Delightful in every way."

Hammondsport

J.S. Hubbs B&B

17 Sheather St, PO Box 366
Hammondsport 14840
(607)569-2440

1840. At the Southern tip of Keuka Lake is the village of Hammondsport, home to this Greek Revival inn, with its charming cupola. The village square

and lake are just one-half block from the inn. Because of its interesting architecture, the inn has come to be known as the ink bottle house, one of the village's major landmarks. The inn offers five guest rooms, including one in the cupola. Guests enjoy relaxing in the living room and parlor. Many fine wineries are found in the area, and the Greyton H. Taylor Wine Musuem is nearby.

Innkeeper(s): Walter & Linda Carl.

Rates:$58-134. MC VISA. Full Bkfst. 6 rooms. 2 with shared baths. Beds:QD. AC in room. Fishing.

Contact: Walter Carl. Certificate may be used: Mid-October to mid-May (1994-1995), Monday-Thursday.

Hempstead

Country Life B&B
237 Cathedral Ave, Garden City Brdr
Hempstead 11550
(516)292-9219

1929. For vacationers who want to spend time in New York City but don't want to stay amidst all the hustle and bustle, this cozy home is only minutes from the city by train. Even if you don't venture into the city, the surrounding areas offer deluxe shopping at Bloomingdales and Saks Fifth Avenue, a five-minute drive. Breakfast may include Dutch pancakes or cheese strata. Wine and cheese are served in the late afternoon. Guest rooms boast antiques, and one features twin four-poster beds with hand-crocheted spreads. Baby furniture is available.

Innkeeper(s): Richard & Wendy Duvall.

Rates:$60-95. Full Bkfst. 5 rooms. 2 with shared baths. Beds:KQT. AC in room. Golf. Tennis. Bicycling. Skiing.

Seen in: *Garden City News, New York Times, Newsday.*

Contact: Wendy Duvall. Certificate may be used: July 1-Dec. 13, 1994, midweek; or weekends last-minute only. Jan.1-May 30, 1995, midweek or weekends one week in advance. June 1-Dec. 31, 1995 midweek, or weekends last-minute only.

Hobart

Breezy Acres Farm B&B
RD 1, Box 191
Hobart 13788
(607)538-9338

1830. Maple syrup, fields of corn and hay, heifers and a fruit and vegetable stand assure you that you are truly staying at a working farm. The rambling farmhouse is filled with family antiques. The innkeeper, a professional home economist, serves a full country breakfast. There is a pond and the Delaware River runs past the property. Guest often enjoy hiking the farm's 300 acres, working their way up to the log cabin hideaway.

Innkeeper(s): Joyce and David Barber.

Rates:$50-60. MC VISA. Full Bkfst. 3 rooms. Beds:KQD. Farm. Golf. Tennis. Skiing. Spa. Swimming. Horseback riding. Fishing.

Seen in: *Catskill Country.*

Contact: Joyce Barber. Certificate may be used: Sunday-Thursday year-round. May call at last-minute for weekend availability.

"Nicest people you'd want to meet."

Hudson

The Inn at Blue Stores
Box 99, Star Route
Hudson 12534
(518)537-4277

1908. A rural Hudson Valley setting may seem an unusual place for a Spanish-style inn, but this former gentlemen's farm now provides a lovely and unique setting for those seeking a relaxing getaway. Visitors

will enjoy the inn's clay tile roof and stucco exterior, along with its impressive interior, featuring black oak woodwork, leaded-glass entry and stained glass. Visitors are treated to full breakfasts and refreshing afternoon teas. The spacious porch and swimming pool are favorite spots for relaxing and socializing.

Innkeeper(s): Linda Saulpaugh.

Rates:$95-150. MC VISA AX. Full Bkfst. Teas. Evening snacks. 5 rooms. 2 with shared baths. Beds:KQT. AC in room. Farm. Skiing. Fishing.

Contact: Linda Saulpaugh. Certificate may be used: November - April excluding major holidays, Christmas, New Year's, Thanksgiving, President's Day, Easter.

Ithaca

La Tourelle Country Inn
1150 Danby Rd (96B)
Ithaca 14850
(607)273-2734 (800)765-1492
Fax:(607)273-4821

1986. This white stucco European-style country inn is located on 70 acres three miles from town, allowing for wildflower walks, cross-country skiing and all-season hiking. Adjacent Buttermilk Falls State Park provides stone paths, waterfalls and streams. The inn is decorated with a hint of European decor and includes fireplace suites and tower suites. A continental breakfast arrives at your door in a basket, French Provincial style, and guests often tote it to the patio or gazebo to enjoy views of the rolling countryside. There is an indoor tennis court.
Innkeeper(s): Leslie Leonard.

Rates:$60-125. MC VISA AX. Cont. Bkfst. Gourmet Dinner. Evening snacks. 34 rooms. Fireplaces. Beds:KQ. Conference Rm. TV, Phone, AC, Refrig. in room. Tennis. Skiing. Handicap access. Swimming. Fishing.

Contact: Leslie Leonard. Certificate may be used: Sunday through Thursday year-round except New Year's Eve and Valentine's Day.

Rose Inn
Rt 34 N, Box 6576
Ithaca 14851-6576
(607)533-7905 Fax:(607)533-7908

1851. This classic Italianate mansion has long been famous for its circular staircase of Honduran mahogany. It is owned by Sherry Rosemann, a noted interior designer specializing in mid-19th-century architecture and furniture, and her husband Charles, a hotelier from Germany. On 20 landscaped acres, it is 10 minutes from Cornell University. The inn has been the recipient of many awards for its lodging and dining.
Innkeeper(s): Sherry & Charles Rosemann.

Rates:$100-250. MC VISA. Full Bkfst. EP. Gourmet Brkfst, Dinner. 15 rooms. Fireplaces. Beds:KQT. Conference Rm. Phone, AC in room. Farm. Golf. Tennis. Skiing. Swimming. Horseback riding. Fishing.

Seen in: *Country Inn, New York Times, Ithaca Times, New Woman.*

Contact: Charles Rosemann. Certificate may be used: April 1-Nov. 30, Monday through Thursday. Dec. 1-March 31, Sunday through Friday.

"The blending of two outstanding talents, which when combined with your warmth, produce the ultimate experience in being away from home. Like staying with friends in their beautiful home."

Jeffersonville

The Griffin House
RD 1 Box 178, Maple Ave
Jeffersonville 12748
(914)482-3371

1895. Visitors are in for a visual treat when they enter this three-story Victorian inn. The inn, which required five years to complete at the turn of the century, remains a shining example of the master craftsmanship evident in those days. Filled with gorgeous examples of hand-carved American chestnut, including the main staircase, the inn also has brick fireplaces, stained-glass windows and wooden floors. Often, guests are treated to a sample of the talents of the innkeepers, both world-class musicians, and musical touches are found throughout, including in the guest rooms.
Innkeeper(s): Paul & Irene Griffin.

Rates:$75-95. Full Bkfst. Gourmet Brkfst. Teas. 4 rooms. 2 with shared baths. Beds:D. Conference Rm. Bicycling. Skiing. Fishing.

Contact: Irene Griffin. Certificate may be used: Year-round.

Keene

The Bark Eater Inn
Alstead Mill Rd
Keene 12942
(518)576-2221 Fax:(518)576-2071

1830. Originally a stagecoach stop on the old road to Lake Placid, The Bark Eater (English for the Indian word Adirondacks) has been in almost continuous operation since the 1800s. Then, it was a full day's journey over rugged, mountainous terrain with two teams of horses. The inn features wideboard floors, fireplaces and rooms filled with antiques. It has become a special haven for those seeking simple but gracious accommodations and memorable dining.
Innkeeper(s): Jodi Downs.

Rates:$81-110. MC VISA AX DS. Full Bkfst. AP available. MAP available. Gourmet Dinner. Picnic lunches. Teas. Evening snacks. 12 rooms. 6 with shared baths. Beds:KQT. Conference Rm. Farm. Skiing. Stables. Fishing.

Contact: Jodi Downs. Certificate may be used: Sunday-Thursday except holiday periods.

"Staying at a country inn is an old tradition in Europe, and is rapidly catching on in the United States... A stay here is a pleasant surprise for anyone who travels."
William Lederer, author, Ugly American.

Keene Valley

Trail's End
PO Box 562
Keene Valley 12943
(518)576-9860 (800)281-9860

1902. This charming mountain inn is in the heart
of the Adirondack's High Peaks. Surrounded by
woods and adjacent to a small pond, the inn offers
spacious guest rooms with antique furnishings and
country quilts. All-you-can-eat morning meals in
the glassed-in breakfast room not only provide a
lovely look at the countryside, but often a close-up
view of various bird species. Fresh air and gorgeous
views abound, and visitors enjoy invigorating hikes,
trout fishing and fine cross-country skiing.
Downhill skiiers will love the challenge of nearby
White Mountain, with the longest vertical drop in
the East.

Innkeeper(s): Cherie & Erik Van den Berg.
Rates:$52-90. MC VISA. Full Bkfst. MAP available. Picnic lunches. 11
rooms. 7 with shared baths. Fireplaces. Beds:KT. TV, Refrig. in room.
Skiing. Fishing.
Contact: Laura Nardelli. Certificate may be used: All year weekdays and
April 1-May 20 and Nov. 1-Dec. 20.

Lake Geo/Warrensburg

House on the Hill B&B
Box 248, Rt 28
Lake Geo/Warrensburg 12885
(518)623-9390 (800)221-9390

1750. This historic Federal-style inn on a hill in
the Adirondacks offers five guest rooms. After they
are treated to coffee and baked goods in their
rooms, guests enjoy the inn's full breakfasts in the
Sun Room, which offers wonderful views of the surrounding fields and woods from its many windows.
Cross-country skiing and hiking may be enjoyed on
the spacious grounds, covering 176 acres. Gore
Mountain Ski Area is close and Lake George is a
10-minute drive.

Innkeeper(s): Joseph & Lynn Rubino.
Rates:$75-99. MC VISA. Full Bkfst. Picnic lunches. Evening snacks. 5
rooms. 4 with shared baths. Beds:Q. TV, Phone, AC in room. Skiing.
Swimming. Fishing.
Contact: Joseph Rubino. Certificate may be used: Anytime subject to
availability.

Lake Luzerne

Lamplight Inn B&B
PO Box 70, 2129 Lake Ave
Lake Luzerne 12846
(518)696-5294 (800)262-4668
Fax:(518)696-5256

1891. Howard Conkling, a wealthy lumberman,
built this Victorian Gothic estate on land that had
been the site of the Warren County Fair. The

home was designed for entertaining since Conkling
was a very eligible bachelor. It has 12-foot beamed
ceilings, chestnut wainscoting and moldings, and a
chestnut keyhole staircase crafted in England.

Innkeeper(s): Gene & Linda Merlino.
Rates:$80-150. MC VISA AX. Gourmet Brkfst. 10 rooms. Fireplaces.
Beds:QT. Conference Rm. AC in room. Golf. Tennis. Skiing. Swimming.
Horseback riding. Fishing.
Seen in: *New York Magazine, Newark Star-Ledger, Newsday.*
Contact: Linda Merlino. Certificate may be used: September through
May, midweek only, Sunday - Thursday, excluding holidays.

*"Rooms are immaculately kept and clean. The owners
are the nicest, warmest, funniest and most hospitable
innkeepers I have ever met."*

Lake Placid

Highland House Inn
3 Highland Pl
Lake Placid 12946
(518)523-2377 Fax:(518)523-1863

1910. This three-story inn is situated on the hill
just above Main Street and the Olympic Center.
The rooms are decorated in a charming
Adirondack-country-style, and boast birch-tree furnishings and antiques. A large deck built around
clumps of birch trees features a hot tub. The cottage offers all the comforts of home, including a
fireplace. Breakfast is served in the glass-walled dining room.

Innkeeper(s): Ted & Cathy Blazer.

Rates:$55-75. MC VISA. Full Bkfst. 8 rooms. Fireplaces. Beds:QT. TV, AC in room. Bicycling. Skiing. Spa. Swimming. Fishing.

Seen in: *Ski Magazine, Weekender.*

Contact: Cathy Blazer. Certificate may be used: April, Monday-Thursday; May, Monday-Thursday; November, Monday-Thursday (excluding Thanksgiving Day).

"You have the perfect place to rest and relax."

Interlaken Inn
15 Interlaken Ave
Lake Placid 12946
(518)523-3180 (800)428-4369

1906. The five-course dinner at this beautiful Victorian inn is prepared by innkeeper Carol Johnson and her son, Kevin, a graduate of the

Culinary Institute of America. The high-quality cuisine is rivaled only by the rich decor of this cozy inn. Walnut paneling covers the dining room walls, which are topped with a tin ceiling. Bedrooms are carefully decorated with wallpapers, fresh flowers and luxurious bed coverings. Spend the afternoon gazing at the mountains and lakes that surround this Adirondack hideaway, or visit the Olympic venues.

Rates:$50-170. MC VISA AX. Full Bkfst. MAP available. Gourmet Dinner. Teas. 12 rooms. Beds:KQT. Golf. Tennis. Bicycling. Skiing. Swimming. Horseback riding. Fishing.

Seen in: *Outside Magazine.*

Contact: Carol Johnson. Certificate may be used: Midweek - Sunday through Thursday anytime for bed and breakfast rates $50-$110. Dinner is additional.

The Stagecoach Inn
370 Old Military Rd
Lake Placid 12946
(518)523-9474

1833. This old inn was once a stagecoach stop and post office on the Elizabethtown-Saranac Lake route. The long wraparound porch and interior birch trim add authenticity to the experience. Each room has its own design and decor with brass beds, white iron beds, quilts, wicker and antiques.

Innkeeper(s): Andrea Terwillegar.

Rates:$60-85. VISA. Full Bkfst. 9 rooms. Fireplaces. Beds:DT. Golf. Tennis. Skiing. Swimming. Horseback riding. Fishing.

Seen in: *New York Times, Country Inns, Newsday, Vogue.*

Contact: Peter Moreau. Certificate may be used: May and June, 1994, May, June, November, 1995.

"This inn is really special."

Lewiston

The Cameo Inn
4710 Lower River Rd
Lewiston 14092
(716)745-3034

1875. This classic Queen Anne Victorian inn offers a breathtaking view of the lower Niagara River. Located on the Seaway Trail, the inn offers convenient access to sightseeing in this popular region. The inn's interior features family heirlooms and period antiques, and visitors choose from four guest rooms, including a three-room suite overlooking the river. Breakfast is served buffet-style, and the entrees, which change daily, may include crepes Benedict, German oven pancakes or Grand Marnier French toast. Area attractions include Old Fort Niagara, outlet malls and several state parks.

Innkeeper(s): Greg & Carolyn Fisher.

Rates:$65-115. MC VISA DS. Full Bkfst. 4 rooms. 2 with shared baths. Beds:QT. TV in room. Golf. Tennis. Skiing. Swimming. Horseback riding. Fishing.

Seen in: *Country Folk Art Magazine, Esquire, Journey Magazine.*

Contact: Gregory Fisher. Certificate may be used: Anytime Nov. 15 - April 30; Sunday through Thursday May 1 - Nov. 14; holiday periods and special events excluded. All as available.

The Little Blue House B&B
115 Center St
Lewiston 14092
(716)754-9425

1906. Located in the heart of the village's main street, this Colonial inn offers charming accommodations and convenient access to area activities. Three unique guest rooms are available, including a Chinese-themed room with a king bed and a Victorian-style room with a queen bed. The inn's decor includes antiques, collectibles and contemporary art. Ten minutes away are the American and Canadian Falls.

Innkeeper(s): Michael & Margot Kornfeld.

Rates:$60-160. ContPlus Bkfst. 4 rooms. 2 with shared baths. Beds:KQ. TV, AC in room. Fishing.

Contact: Michael Kornfeld. Certificate may be used: Anytime Nov. 15-Feb. 5; Sunday-Tuesday March 16-Nov. 14 (or as available on short notice).

Malone

Kilburn Manor

59 Milwaukee St
Malone 12953
(518)483-4891 (800)454-5287
Fax:(518)481-5028

1820. Hospitality, lovely scenery and abundant recreational opportunities await visitors at this spacious Greek Revival inn in Northern New York.

Six guest rooms feature cable TV, decks and turndown service. Although many guests will enjoy venturing out to explore the outdoors, those who remain at the inn also will find plenty to do, including reading and relaxing in the inn's library.

Innkeeper(s): Suzanne Hogan.

Rates:$65-75. AX. Full Bkfst. 6 rooms. 2 with shared baths. Beds:KQT. TV in room. Bicycling. Skiing. Swimming.

Contact: Suzanne Hogan. Certificate may be used: No holiday weekends.

Milford

The 1860 Spencer House

RD 1, PO Box 65
Milford 13807
(607)286-9402 Fax:(607)286-9402

1860. A pine-lined estate in the countryside near Milford is home to this Italianate inn, originally

the residence of a professor at what is now Hartwick College in neighboring Oneonta. Featuring a lovely view of the Susquehanna River Valley, the inn offers a variety of accommodations to visitors, including an efficiency apartment and family suite. Guests enjoy their full breakfasts on the sunny deck or in the formal dining room. Popular Cooperstown, with its National Baseball Hall of Fame, is 10 minutes away, and Gilbert Lake State Park is nearby.

Innkeeper(s): Karl & Anne Marie Hosnedl.

Rates:$45-75. MC VISA AX. Full Bkfst. Teas. 8 rooms. 3 with shared baths. Beds:QT. TV, Phone in room. Golf. Tennis. Exercise room. Swimming. Horseback riding. Fishing.

Contact: Karl Hosnedl. Certificate may be used: Off-peak times, during the week in May, June, July, any time after Labor Day.

Mount Tremper

Mt. Tremper Inn

Rt 212 & Wittenberg Rd, PO Box 51
Mount Tremper 12457
(914)688-5329

1850. Nettie & Charles Lamson built this Victorian inn to accommodate guests who would stay all summer with husbands and fathers commuting by rail from New York City on the weekends. Now with Hunter Mountain skiing 16 miles away, the inn is popular all year. Romantic classical music wafts through the Victorian parlor which is decorated with velvet Empire sofas, burgundy velvet walls, Oriental carpets and museum-quality

antiques. A large blue stone fireplace warms guests who gather for nighttime chats. Each bedchamber has Victorian wallpapers, French lace curtains, luxury linens and antique bedsteads.

Innkeeper(s): Lou Caselli & Peter LaScala.

Rates:$65-95. MC VISA. Full Bkfst. 12 rooms. 10 with shared baths. Beds:DT. Conference Rm. Skiing. Exercise room. Swimming. Fishing.

Seen in: *New York Times, Mature Outlook, New York, Victorian Homes, Ski.*

Contact: Peter LaScala. Certificate may be used: June 1 to Nov. 1, Monday to Thursday (no Friday-Saturday-Sunday).

"Two fantastic hosts, thank you! Great place, great people!"

Mumford-Rochester

Genesee Country Inn
948 George St
Mumford-Rochester 14511-0340
(716)538-2500

1833. This stone house with two-and-a-half-foot-thick limestone walls served as a plaster mill and later as a hub and wheel factory. Now it is an inn set on six acres with views of streams, woodlands and ponds. There is a deck adjacent to a 16-foot waterfall. Ask for a garden room and enjoy a fireplace and your own balcony overlooking the mill ponds.

Innkeeper(s): Gregory & Glenda Barcklow.

Rates:$85-125. MC VISA DC. Gourmet Brkfst. Teas. 8 rooms. Fireplaces. Beds:QT. Conference Rm. Phone, AC, Refrig. in room. Skiing. Swimming.

Contact: Glenda Barcklow. Certificate may be used: November through April except holidays.

"You may never want to leave..."

Naples

Naples Valley B&B
7161 County Rd #12
Naples 14512
(716)374-6397

1962. This Craftsman-style inn provides easy access to the many attractions of the Southwestern Finger Lakes region. The inn's location, north of town on the high road, offers a lovely view of the Bristol Hills in a relaxed setting. Visitors select from three guest rooms: Kingsbury, with its king bed and country furnishings; Fourposter, an English garden setting with double bed; and Twin Iris, with French Provincial decor and twin beds. Guests love to mingle in the Gathering Room, with its cobblestone fireplace and library. Many winery tours are available in the area, in addition to skiing at Bristol Mountain.

Innkeeper(s): Nadina Stevens.

Rates:$60-65. Full Bkfst. AP available. Teas. 3 rooms. 3 with shared baths. Beds:KQT. Skiing. Fishing.

Contact: Nadina K. Stevens. Certificate may be used: March 1-June 1.

Niagara Falls

The Cameo Manor North
3881 Lower River Rd
Niagara Falls 14174
(716)745-3034

1860. This Colonial Revival inn offers a restful setting ideal for those seeking a peaceful getaway. The inn's three secluded acres add to its romantic setting, as does an interior that features several fireplaces. Visitors select from three suites, which feature private sun rooms, or two guest rooms that share a bath. Popular spots with guests include the library, outdoor deck and solarium. Fort Niagara and Wilson-Tuscarora state parks are nearby, and the American and Canadian Falls are within easy driving distance of the inn.

Innkeeper(s): Greg & Carolyn Fisher.

Rates:$75-125. MC VISA DS. Full Bkfst. 5 rooms. 2 with shared baths. Beds:QT. TV in room. Golf. Tennis. Skiing. Swimming. Horseback riding. Fishing.

Seen in: *Buffalo News, Country Folk Art Magazine, Esquire.*

Contact: Gregory Fisher. Certificate may be used: Anytime Nov. 15 - April 30; Sunday through Thursday May 1 - Nov. 14; holiday periods and special events excluded. All as available.

North Hudson

Pine Tree Inn B&B
Rt 9, PO Box 10
North Hudson 12855-0010
(518)532-9255 (800)645-5605

1865. The Pine Tree Inn is a classic Adirondack structure bordering the Schroon River. The main house, built in 1865, was known as the Schroon River Inn until a three-story wing was added in 1928. Original oak floors, a tin ceiling, and hanging globe fixtures highlight the dining room, where a hearty country breakfast is served. There is also a TV lounge for guests and a one-acre lawn with picnic tables and grills. It is ideally situated to nearby cross-country skiing.

Innkeeper(s): Peter & Patricia Schoch.

Rates:$50-55. MC VISA. Full Bkfst. 5 rooms. 5 with shared baths. Beds:DT. Refrig. in room. Skiing. Swimming. Fishing.

Seen in: *Poughkeepsie Journal.*

Contact: Patricia B. Schoch. Certificate may be used: Sunday - Thursday nights - all year.

North River

Highwinds Inn
Barton Mines Rd
North River 12856
(518)251-3760 (800)241-1923

1932. This mountain retreat offers panoramic views of the Siamese wilderness area and the Adirondacks. Every room has a view of the mountains. The inn offers a garnet stone fireplace and a view of the sunset on the dining porch.

Innkeeper(s): Kim Repscha.

Rates:$98-150. MC VISA. Full Bkfst. MAP available. Gourmet Dinner. Picnic lunches. 4 rooms. Beds:KD. Tennis. Bicycling. Skiing. Swimming. Fishing.

Seen in: *The Post Star.*

Contact: Kimberly Repscha. Certificate may be used: Labor Day to Columbus Day. March 1 - April 1.

Penn Yan

Finton's Landing
661 E Lake Rd
Penn Yan 14527
(315)536-3146

1867. This Victorian house is located on the east shore of Keuka Lake, with 165 feet of private beach. Wonderful views of green lawns, hills and the crystal-clear water may be enjoyed from the porch. The inn features a country decor. Nearby are Mennonite shops and craft stores to explore.

Innkeeper(s): Doug & Arianne Tepper.

Rates:$79. MC VISA. Full Bkfst. 4 rooms. Skiing. Swimming. Fishing.

Contact: Doug Tepper. Certificate may be used: Sunday-Thursday.

Pine City

Rufus Tanner House
1016 Sagetown Rd
Pine City 14871
(607)732-0213

1864. This charming Greek Revival farmhouse sits among century-old sugar maple and dwarf fruit trees. Its spacious rooms are filled with antiques and other period furnishings that add greatly to the inn's ambiance. The four guest rooms include the first-floor Master Bedroom, with its marble-topped high Victorian furniture, and a bath with two-person shower, whirlpool and black marble floor. Guests are welcome to use the treadmill and weight machine in the basement. The Elmira-Corning area near the inn offers many attractions, including Mark Twain's Burial Site and the National Soaring Museum.

Innkeeper(s): Bill Knapp & John Gibson.

Rates:$55-95. MC VISA. Full Bkfst. Gourmet Dinner. Evening snacks. 4 rooms. Beds:Q. Spa. Exercise room.

Contact: William Knapp. Certificate may be used: Not during race or graduation weekends.

Queensbury

The Crislip's B&B
693 Ridge Rd
Queensbury 12804
(518)793-6869

1805. This Federal-style house was built by Quakers and was once owned by the area's first doctor, who used it as a training center for young interns. There's an acre of lawns and annual gardens and a Victorian Italianate veranda overlooks the Green Mountains. The inn is furnished with 18th-century antiques and reproductions, including four-poster canopy beds, and highboys. There's a keeping room with a huge fireplace. Historic stone walls flank the property.

Innkeeper(s): Ned & Joyce Crislip.

Rates:$55-75. MC VISA. Full Bkfst. 3 rooms. Beds:K. TV, AC, Refrig. in room. Skiing. Swimming. Fishing.

Contact: Joyce Crislip. Certificate may be used: Winter months - January, February, March.

Sanford's Ridge B&B

749 Ridge Rd
Queensbury 12804
(518)793-4923

1797. Visitors to the Adirondacks will find a bit of history and more than a little hospitality at this Federal-style inn, built by David Sanford after the Revolutionary War. The inn has retained its original elegance and added a few modern touches such as a slate billiard table in the carriage house, an in-ground swimming pool and a sunny outdoor deck. Visitors select from the Haviland, Sanford and Webster rooms, all with private baths and each with its special charms. The full breakfasts include a special entree of the day and grape jam from fruit grown on the premises. Lake George is a short drive away.

Innkeeper(s): Carolyn & Bob Rudolph.

Rates:$65-95. MC VISA. Full Bkfst. 3 rooms. Fireplaces. Beds:QD. AC in room. Skiing. Swimming. Fishing.

Contact: Carolyn Rudolph. Certificate may be used: November - April, 1994-1995.

Rochester

Strawberry Castle B&B

1883 Penfield Rd, Rt 441
Rochester 14526
(716)385-3266

1870. A rosy brick Italianate villa, Strawberry Castle was once known for the grapes and strawberries grown on the property. Ornate plaster ceilings

and original inside shutters are special features. There are six roof levels, carved ornamental brackets, and columned porches topped by a white cupola.

Innkeeper(s): Anne Felker & Robert Houle.

Rates:$75-95. MC VISA AX. Full Bkfst. 3 rooms. Beds:D. Conference Rm. AC, Refrig. in room. Golf. Skiing. Swimming. Fishing.

Seen in: *Upstate Magazine*.

Contact: Anne Felker. Certificate may be used: November-February excluding major holiday weekends.

"You have a most unusual place. We applaud your restoration efforts and are thankful you've made it available to travelers."

Saratoga Springs

The Inn on Bacon Hill B&B

PO Box 1462
Saratoga Springs 12866
(518)695-3693

1862. State legislator Alexander Baucus built his mid-Victorian mansion in the country a few miles from Saratoga Springs. A guest parlor, marble fireplaces, a carved staircase and original moldings add to the gracious "country gentleman" lifestyle. Antique beds are piled with flowered quilts in the guest rooms.

Innkeeper(s): Andrea Collins-Breslin.

Rates:$60-85. MC VISA. Full Bkfst. 5 rooms. 2 with shared baths. Beds:QT. Farm. Bicycling. Skiing. Swimming. Fishing.

Seen in: *Boston Globe, The Saratogian, Early American Life, Americana*.

Contact: Andrea Collins-Breslin. Certificate may be used: Anytime except holiday weekends from November-March; Sunday-Thursday during April-June, September and October. Not available July and August.

"We'll long remember the warmth and pleasures of sharing a little piece of summer with you."

Six Sisters B&B

149 Union Ave
Saratoga Springs 12866
(518)583-1173 Fax:(518)587-2470

1880. The unique architecture of this charming Victorian home, features a large second-story bay window, a hardwood front door decked with

stained glass and a veranda accentuated with plants and rocking chairs. Inside, the antiques, ceiling fans and Oriental rugs create an elegant atmosphere. During racing season, guests can rise early and take a short walk to the local race track to watch the horses prepare. Upon their return, guests are greeted with the smells of a delicious breakfast. Visit Saratoga Springs' lovely downtown area with its shops and many restaurants.

Innkeeper(s): Kate Benton & Steve Ramirez.

Rates:$60-125. MC VISA AX. Full Bkfst. Gourmet Brkfst. 4 rooms. Beds:KQD. AC, Refrig. in room. Golf. Tennis. Skiing. Swimming. Horseback riding. Fishing.

Seen in: *Gourmet, Country Inns, Country Folk Art Magazine.*

Contact: Kate Benton. Certificate may be used: Sunday-Thursday except July and August.

"The true definition of a bed and breakfast."

The Westchester House Bed & Breakfast
102 Lincoln Ave, PO Box 944
Saratoga Springs 12866
(518)587-7613

1885. This gracious Queen Anne Victorian has been welcoming vacationers for more than 100 years. Antiques from four generations of the

Melvin's family grace the high-ceilinged rooms. Oriental rugs top gleaming wood floors, while antique clocks and lace curtains set a graceful tone. Guests gather on the wraparound porch, in the parlors or gardens for an afternoon refreshment of old-fashioned lemonade. Racing season rates are quoted separately.

Innkeeper(s): Bob & Stephanie Melvin.

Rates:$100-225. MC VISA AX. ContPlus Bkfst. Teas. 7 rooms. Beds:QT. Conference Rm. AC in room. Golf. Tennis. Skiing. Swimming. Horseback riding. Fishing.

Seen in: *Getaways for Gourmets, Albany Times Union, Saratogian, Capital, Country Inns, New York Daily News, WNYT, Newsday, Hudson Valley Magazine.*

Contact: Stephanie Melvin. Certificate may be used: Sunday through Thursday, not available June, July, August, October and holiday weekends.

"I adored your B&B and have raved about it to all.

One of the most beautiful and welcoming places we've ever visited."

Severance

The Red House
Sawmill Rd, PO Box 125
Severance 12872
(518)532-7734

1850. Twenty feet from the banks of Paradox Brook, on the West end of Paradox Lake, is this two-story farmhouse inn that boasts a multitude of recreational offerings for its guests. The inn features three guest rooms, one with private bath. The inn's full breakfasts include homemade breads and regional specialties. Be sure to plan a day trip to Fort Ticonderoga and ride the ferry across Lake Champlain to Vermont.

Innkeeper(s): Helen Wildman.

Rates:$55-65. Full Bkfst. 3 rooms. 2 with shared baths. Beds:QT. Phone in room. Farm. Tennis. Skiing. Swimming. Fishing.

Contact: Helen Wildman. Certificate may be used: From Oct. 1, 1994 to June 1, 1995.

Sodus Bay

Bonnie Castle Farm B&B
PO Box 188, 6603 Bonnie Castle Rd
Sodus Bay 14590
(315)587-2273 Fax:(315)587-4003

1889. Bonnie Castle Farm is surrounded by expansive lawns and trees overlooking the east side of Great Sodus Bay, a popular resort area at the turn of the century. Accommodations include a suite and large guest room with water views, plus anoth-

er wainscotted room with cathedral ceilings. The country setting offers a wide variety of recreational activities, including cross-country skiing, skating, fishing, and swimming.

Innkeeper(s): Eric & Georgia Pendleton.

Rates:$55-95. MC VISA AX. Gourmet Brkfst. 9 rooms. 2 with shared

baths. Beds:KQ. TV in room. Bicycling. Skiing. Spa. Swimming. Fishing.
Contact: Eric Pendleton. Certificate may be used: Anytime except Friday and Saturday in July and August.

Southold

Goose Creek Guesthouse
1475 Waterview Dr, Box 377
Southold 11971
(516)765-3356

1862. Grover Pease left for the Civil War from this house, and after his death his widow Harriet ran a summer boarding house here. The basement actual-

ly dates from the 1780s and is constructed of large rocks. The present house was moved here and put on the older foundation. Southold has many old historic homes and a guidebook is provided for visitors. The inn is close to the New London ferry and the ferry to South Shore via Shelter Island.
Innkeeper(s): Mary J. Mooney-Getoff.
Rates:$60-75. Gourmet Brkfst. Picnic lunches. Teas. 4 rooms. 4 with shared baths. Beds:KQT. Golf. Tennis. Swimming. Horseback riding. Fishing.
Seen in: *New York Times, Newsday.*
Contact: Mary Mooney-Getoff. Certificate may be used: Anyday September through June. Sunday through Thursday night during summer.

"We will be repeat guests. Count on it!!"

Spencer

A Slice of Home
178 N Main St
Spencer 14883
(607)589-6073

1843. This Italianate inn's location, approximately equidistant from Ithaca and Elmira, offers a fine vantage point for exploring the Finger Lakes region. Although the area is well known for its scenery, many recreational opportunities also are available. The innkeeper has a special fondness for those traveling by bicycle, and is happy to help with ride planning or other special arrangements. The inn offers four guest rooms, furnished in coun-

try decor and featuring king and queen beds. Guests may relax in the library or by taking a stroll on the inn's 12 acres. Cross-country skiing and winery tours are found in the area.
Innkeeper(s): Beatrice Brownell.
Rates:$35-80. Full Bkfst. Picnic lunches. 4 rooms. 3 with shared baths. Beds:KQ. TV in room. Bicycling. Skiing.
Contact: Beatrice Brownell. Certificate may be used: Oct. 1, 1994 to May 1, 1995.

Springville

The Franklin House
432 Franklin St
Springville 14141-1130
(716)592-7877 Fax:(716)592-5388

1843. Once the home of a well-known area chicken farm, this Queen Anne Victorian inn now serves visitors to attraction-rich Western New York. An easy getaway from Buffalo, the inn offers three guest rooms, including a suite. Visitors will enjoy cross-country skiing on the inn's five acres, hot tubbing in the Hawaiian Room, or using the IBM computer with modem. An award-winning, homemade country-style breakfast is served before guests set out for their day's activities, which could include hitting the slopes at the Kissing Bridge Ski Area or a visit to Letchworth State Park, the Grand Canyon of the East.
Innkeeper(s): Richard & Penny Timm.
Rates:$60-110. MC VISA AX. Full Bkfst. Teas. Evening snacks. 3 rooms. 2 with shared baths. Beds:QT. TV, AC in room. Skiing. Handicap access. Spa. Fishing.
Contact: Paulette Timm. Certificate may be used: April - September.

Stillwater

Lee's Deer Run B&B
411 County Rd, #71
Stillwater 12170
(518)584-7722

1830. In an idyllic countryside setting between Saratoga Lake and Saratoga National Historic Park, this inn, lovingly crafted from a 19th-century barn, now is home to four charming guest rooms, some with four-poster beds. The inn's full breakfasts are served in the dining room or on a deck with a view of the surrounding area. Bennington Battlefield and the Willard Mountain Ski Area are nearby.
Innkeeper(s): Rose & Don Lee.
Rates:$85-135. Full Bkfst. 4 rooms. Beds:K. Farm. Skiing. Fishing.
Contact: Donald Lee. Certificate may be used: Sept. 15 to June 15.

Syracuse

Bed & Breakfast Wellington
707 Danforth St
Syracuse 13208
(315)474-3641 (800)724-5006
Fax:(315)474-2557

1914. The breakfasts at this home feature healthy dishes, but that doesn't mean they're bland and boring. Pear Hawaiian French toast is the house specialty, and innkeeper Wendy Wilber serves up sides of turkey sausage and yogurt with fresh fruit she picks herself. Guests are pampered with pretty china table settings and lacy tablecloths. The rich wood interior accentuates the fireplaces, canvas floors and antiques. The area is booming with activities, including a zoo, the Carousel Center, nature centers and wildlife preserves. The innkeepers will help you plan meetings or get-togethers such as a rehearsal or birthday dinner, bridal or baby shower.

Innkeeper(s): Ray Borg & Wendy Wilber.

Rates:$65-85. MC VISA AX. Full Bkfst. Gourmet Brkfst. Lunch, Dinner. Picnic lunches. Teas. Evening snacks. 5 rooms. Beds:K. TV in room. Skiing. Fishing.

Seen in: *Syracuse Herald-Journal.*

Contact: Wendy Wilber & Ray Borg. Certificate may be used: Space available, Sunday through Thursday all year and weekends that are not peak weekends.

Warrensburg

Country Road Lodge
HCR #1, Box 227 Hickory Hill Rd
Warrensburg 12885
(518)623-2207

1929. This simple farmhouse lodge is situated on 35 acres along the Hudson River at the end of a country road. Rooms are clean and comfortable but not fancy. A full breakfast is provided with homemade breads and muffins. The sitting room reveals panoramic views of the river and Sugarloaf Mountain. Bird watching, hiking and skiing are popular activities. Groups often reserve all four guest rooms.

Innkeeper(s): Steve & Sandi Parisi.

Rates:$55-58. Full Bkfst. MAP available. 4 rooms. 2 with shared baths. Beds:DT. Skiing. Swimming. Fishing.

Contact: Stephen Parisi. Certificate may be used: All excluding January through March.

"Homey, casual atmosphere."

The Merrill Magee House
2 Hudson St
Warrensburg 12885
(518)623-2449

1839. This stately Greek Revival home offers beautiful antique fireplaces in every guest room. The Sage, Rosemary, Thyme and Coriander rooms fea-

ture sitting areas, and a family suite includes two bedrooms, a sitting room with a television, refrigerator and a bathroom with a clawfoot tub. The decor is romantic and distinctly Victorian. Romantic getaway packages include complimentary champagne and candlelight dinners. The local area hosts arts and crafts festivals, an antique car show, white-water rafting and Gore Mountain Oktoberfest. Tour the Adirondack's from the sky during September's balloon festival or browse through the world's largest garage sale in early October.

Innkeeper(s): Ken & Florence Carrington.

Rates:$95-115. MC VISA AX DC DS. Full Bkfst. EP. Gourmet Dinner. 11 rooms. Fireplaces. Beds:KQT. Conference Rm. AC in room. Golf. Tennis. Skiing. Handicap access. Swimming. Horseback riding. Fishing.

Seen in: *Cleveland Plain Dealer, NY Daily News, Saratogian, Adirondack Life.*

Contact: Florence Carrington. Certificate may be used: Sunday through Thursday (only) year-round.

"A really classy and friendly operation - a real joy."

Waterville

B&B of Waterville
211 White St
Waterville 13480
(315)841-8295

1871. This two-story Italianate Victorian is in the Waterville Historic Triangle District, one block from Rt. 12 and 20 minutes away from Hamilton College and Colgate University. The hostess is an avid quiltmaker and the house is filled with her handiwork. La Petite Maison, a fine French restaurant, is a few steps away.

Innkeeper(s): Carol & Stanley Sambora.

Rates:$45-55. MC VISA. Full Bkfst. Gourmet Brkfst. 3 rooms. 2 with shared baths. Beds:DT. Golf. Tennis. Skiing. Horseback riding. Fishing.

Seen in: *Observer Dispatch.*

Contact: Carol Sambora. Certificate may be used: Anytime, as available.

"Don't change a thing ever."

Webster

Country Schoolhouse B&B
336 Basket Rd
Webster 14580
(716)265-4720

1863. A few miles east of Rochester, this 19th-century former schoolhouse features three guest rooms in a quiet, country setting. The surrounding area abounds with activities, including antiquing, crafts, fishing, museums and shopping. Lake Ontario is tantalizingly close and visitors new to the area will enjoy a visit to the nearby Erie Canal. The Brantling Ski Slopes are within easy driving distance of the inn.

Innkeeper(s): Mary Ann "Betty" Hess.

Rates:$50-60. Full Bkfst. 3 rooms. 3 with shared baths. Beds:DT. Skiing. Swimming. Fishing.

Contact: Mary Ann Hess. Certificate may be used: September through November, Sunday through Thursday, 1994 and 1995.

Westfield

Westfield House
E Main Rd, PO Box 505, Rt 20
Westfield 14787
(716)326-6262

1840. Westfield was part of the Granger Homestead. Benjamin Hopson, a local ice merchant, built a magnificent Gothic Revival addition in 1860. His daughter, Lucy, used the living room, with its large crystal windows, as a tea room. The Gothic detailed interiors include a winding staircase to the six upstairs bed chambers.

Innkeeper(s): Betty & Jud Wilson.

Rates:$60-95. MC VISA. Gourmet Brkfst. 8 rooms. Fireplaces. Beds:KQT. Conference Rm. AC in room. Golf. Tennis. Bicycling. Skiing. Swimming. Fishing.

Seen in: *Canadian Leisure Ways, Buffalo News, Innsider.*

Contact: Betty Wilson. Certificate may be used: According to availability.

"Your accommodations and hospitality are wonderful! Simply outstanding. The living room changes its character by the hour."

The William Seward Inn
RD 2, S Portage Rd, Rt 394
Westfield 14787
(716)326-4151 (800)338-4151
Fax:(716)326-4163

1821. This two-story Greek Revival estate stands on a knoll overlooking the forest and Lake Erie. Seward was a Holland Land Company agent before becoming governor of New York. He later served as Lincoln's Secretary of State and is known for the Alaska Purchase. George Patterson bought Seward's home and also became governor of New York. Most of the mansion's furnishings are dated 1790 to 1870 from the Sheraton-Victorian period.

Innkeeper(s): Jim & Debbie Dahlberg.

Rates:$85-145. MC VISA DS. Full Bkfst. Gourmet Brkfst, Dinner. 14 rooms. Fireplaces. Beds:KQT. Conference Rm. AC in room. Golf. Tennis. Skiing. Handicap access. Swimming. Fishing.

Seen in: *Intelligencer, Evening Observer, New-York-Pennsylvania Collector, New York Times, Pittsburgh Post-Gazette, Toronto Globe & Mail.*

Contact: James Dahlberg. Certificate may be used: Anytime except Friday - Saturday, July through October or holiday weekends.

"The breakfasts are delicious. The solitude and your hospitality are what the doctor ordered."

Willsboro

Champlain Vistas
183 Lake Shore Road
Willsboro 12996
(518)963-8029

1860. Incredible views of the Adirondack High Peaks, Lake Champlain and Vermont's Green Mountains are enjoyed at this inn in the state's Northeast region. The original farm buildings are listed in the National Register of Historic Places. The living room boasts a stone fireplace, Oriental carpet and spinning wheel. Two miles south of the property guests may board a ferry that travels across Lake Champlain to Vermont.

Innkeeper(s): Barbara Moses.

Rates:$60-85. Full Bkfst. AP available. 4 rooms. 2 with shared baths. Beds:Q. Conference Rm. Farm. Skiing. Handicap access. Swimming. Fishing.

Contact: Barbara Moses. Certificate may be used: Off-season, November - April.

Windham

Country Suite B&B
Rt 23 W, PO Box 700
Windham 12496
(518)734-4079

1874. This spacious country farmhouse in the Catskill Mountains offers easy access to the many scenic attractions of the region. Seven guest rooms, three with private baths, are available to visitors. The inn's country-style furnishings include antiques and family heirlooms. After a busy day of exploring the area, guests often gather in the inn's comfortable living room to relax. The Ski Windham ski area is just two miles from the inn and several others are within a 30-minute drive.

Innkeeper(s): Sondra Clark & Lorraine Seidel.

Rates:$65-75. AX. Full Bkfst. 7 rooms. 4 with shared baths. Beds:QT. Farm. Skiing. Fishing.

Contact: Sondra Clark. Certificate may be used: Anytime excluding holiday weekends.

Danske Hus B&B
361 South St
Windham 12496
(518)734-6335

1865. Located just across the road from Ski Windham, this farmhouse-style inn offers countryside and mountain views to its guests. Eclectic furnishings are found throughout the inn and its four guest rooms. Breakfast may be enjoyed in the dining room or outside on a picturesque deck. Guests also enjoy a large living room, piano, sauna, TV room and woodburning fireplace. Windham Golf Course is within walking distance. The Catskills provide many other tourist attractions, including caverns, fairs and ethnic festivals.

Innkeeper(s): Barbara Jensen.

Rates:$50-85. AX. Full Bkfst. Teas. 4 rooms. 1 with shared bath. Beds:KQT. Skiing. Sauna. Swimming. Fishing.

Contact: Barbara Jensen. Certificate may be used: Weekdays, non-holidays, not during Christmas week, President's week.

Youngstown

The Mill Glen Inn
1102 Pletcher Rd
Youngstown 14174
(716)754-4085

1880. This two-story 19th-century farmhouse inn offers easy access to the many attractions found in the Niagara Falls area. Visitors select from three charming guest rooms that feature ceiling fans and turndown service. Breakfasts are served in the Wagner dining room or on the inn's covered porch. Fort Niagara State Park and the Artpark are nearby, and the American and Canadian Falls are just a short drive from the inn. Great fishing can be found on Lake Ontario and the lower Niagara River.

Innkeeper(s): Peter & Milly Brass.

Rates:$40-65. ContPlus Bkfst. 3 rooms. 2 with shared baths. Beds:DT. Farm. Skiing. Swimming. Fishing.

Contact: Mildred Brass. Certificate may be used: Oct. 1-April 31-anytime; May 1-Sept. 30-Sunday-Thursday only; Last-minute okay anytime.

North Carolina

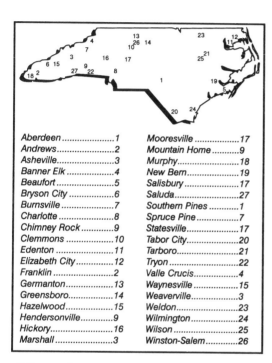

Aberdeen

The Inn at Bryant House
214 N Poplar St
Aberdeen 28315
(910)944-3300 (800)453-4019
Fax:(910)944-8898

1913. This Colonial Revival inn has been completely restored to its original Southern splendor. Pastel colors flow through the entire house and the sitting, dining and living rooms open to one another for easy access. Breakfast is served buffet-style in the dining or garden room. With advance notice, lunches and dinners can be served for small business meetings, wedding parties, family gatherings, club activities and weekend retreats. The Pinehurst area is known for its quiet rolling hills and more than 30 championship-quality golf courses.

Innkeeper(s): Bill & Abbie Gregory
Rates:$45-70. MC VISA AX DS. ContPlus Bkfst. 8 rooms. 2 with shared baths. Beds:QT. AC in room.
Contact: Phyllis A. Gregory. Certificate may be used: Subject to availability, year-round.

Andrews

The Walker Inn of Old Valleytown
39 Junaluska Rd, PO Box 1567
Andrews 28901
(704)321-5019

1840. This inn was originally a refuge for weary travelers on the stagecoach line between Franklin

and Murphy. The rooms of this spacious Colonial inn have their own histories. The Post Office Bedroom contains the original boxes of the Old Valleytown Post Office, before the town became Andrews. The Judge's Bedroom, with its large four-poster bed and cozy fireplace, was always reserved for the circuit court judge and other distinguished guests. The grounds surrounding the inn suggest a miniature plantation, displaying both English and Colonial design.

Innkeeper(s): Patricia & Peter Cook.
Rates:$45-55. MC VISA AX. Full Bkfst. 5 rooms. 2 with shared baths. Beds:QD. Conference Rm. AC in room. Swimming. Fishing.
Contact: Patricia B. Cook. Certificate may be used: Sunday through Thursday, May 1 through Nov. 1 excluding holidays.

Asheville

Acorn Cottage B&B
25 St. Dunstans Circle
Asheville 28803
(704)253-0609

1925. Built by Ronald Green, a prominent architect in the Asheville area who designed many of the historic buildings, this English country cottage is found in the heart of town. The inn, with its eclectic decor and beautiful gardens, is close to many nearby attractions. Guests can enjoy a cool drink during summer afternoons or warm themselves by the fire in the living room during cool evenings. Bedrooms feature fine linens and private baths with special soaps.

Innkeeper(s): Elizabeth & Emil Stahl.

Rates:$75-90. MC VISA. Full Bkfst. Teas. 4 rooms. Beds:Q. TV, Phone, AC in room. Skiing. Fishing.

Contact: Connie Stahl. Certificate may be used: Weekdays only, none in October or December or July.

Corner Oak Manor
53 Saint Dunstans Rd
Asheville 28803
(704)253-3525

1924. Surrounded by oak, maple and pine trees, this English Tudor inn is decorated with many fine oak antiques and handmade items. Innkeeper

Karen Spradley has handstitched something special for each room and the house features handmade items by local artisans. Breakfast delights include entrees such as Blueberry Ricotta Pancakes, Four Cheese and Herb Quiche and Orange French Toast. When you aren't enjoying local activities, you can sit on the shady deck, relax in the Jacuzzi, play a few songs on the piano or curl up with a good book.

Innkeeper(s): Karen & Andy Spradley.

Rates:$85-100. MC VISA DS. Full Bkfst. Gourmet Brkfst. Picnic lunches. 4 rooms. Beds:Q. AC in room. Spa. Fishing.

Contact: Karen Spradley. Certificate may be used: January, February, March anytime except holidays. April - September, November weekdays only (Sunday - Thursday) except holidays. October and December, none.

Dogwood Cottage
40 Canterbury Rd N
Asheville 28801-1535
(704)258-9725

1910. This Carolina mountain home is located a mile-and-a-half from downtown Asheville, on Sunset Mountain. The veranda, filled with white wicker and floral chintz prints, is the focal point of the inn during summer. It affords tree-top views to the Blue Ridge Mountains. Wing chairs and fresh country pieces accent the inn's gleaming hardwood floors. Breakfast is served in the formal dining room or on the covered porch.

Innkeeper(s): Joan & Don Tracy.

Rates:$90-95. MC VISA AX. Full Bkfst. Evening snacks. 4 rooms. Fireplaces. Beds:QT. Handicap access. Swimming. Fishing.

Contact: Joan Tracy. Certificate may be used: January through March, anytime. April through December, Sunday - Thursday only.

"Cozy, warm and gracious."

Banner Elk

Archers Mountain Inn
Rt 2 Box 56-A
Banner Elk 28604
(704)898-9004 Fax:(704)898-4285

1984. Perched on the side of Beech Mountain, the Archers Inn offers spectacular views of the Elk River Valley and the Sugar and Grandfather Mountains. Rooms offer such amenities as stone fireplaces with love seats, a sunken tub and private decks. The living room features a huge fieldstone fireplace and a piano. A country-style breakfast is served with homemade jams and homemade biscuits.

Innkeeper(s): Bill & Toni Coleman.

Rates:$50-125. MC VISA. Full Bkfst. Picnic lunches. 14 rooms. Fireplaces. Beds:Q. TV, Refrig. in room. Skiing. Swimming. Fishing.

Seen in: *Blue Ridge Country.*

Contact: William Coleman. Certificate may be used: April-May, Sept. 1-10.

"There have been few times in my life when I have encountered such warmth and friendliness."

Beaufort

Pecan Tree Inn B&B
116 Queen Street
Beaufort 28516
(919)728-6733

1866. Originally built as a Masonic lodge, this state historic landmark is in the heart of Beaufort's historic district. Gingerbread trim, Victorian porches, turrets,

and two-century-old pecan trees grace the exterior. Guests can relax in the parlor, on the porches, or pay a visit to the flower and herb gardens. The Bridal Suite boasts a king-size canopied bed and Jacuzzi.
Innkeeper(s): Susan & Joe Johnson.
Rates:$65-120. MC VISA. ContPlus Bkfst. 7 rooms. Beds:KQT. AC in room. Golf. Bicycling. Swimming. Horseback riding. Fishing.
Seen in: *Sunday Telegram, This Week Magazine*.
Contact: Susan Johnson. Certificate may be used: Sunday - Thursday.

"After visiting B&Bs far and wide I give Pecan Tree Inn a Five-Star rating in all respects."

Bryson City

Randolph House
PO Box 816, 223 Fryemont Rd
Bryson City 28713
(704)488-3472

1895. Randolph House is a mountain estate tucked among pine trees and dogwoods, near the entrance of Great Smoky Mountain National Park. The house provides an unforgettable experience, not the least of which is the gourmet dining provided on the terrace or in the dining room.
Innkeeper(s): Bill & Ruth Randolph Adams.
Rates:$110-150. MC VISA AX DS. Full Bkfst. MAP available. 5 rooms. 2 with shared baths. Beds:DT. Conference Rm. AC in room. Handicap access. Horseback riding. Fishing.
Seen in: *Tourist News*.
Contact: W. L. Adams. Certificate may be used: Mid-April, May and September.

"Very enjoyable, great food."

Burnsville

The NuWray Inn
PO Box 156, Town Square
Burnsville 28714
(704)682-2329 (800)368-9729

1833. This Colonial Revival home is the oldest country inn in the Western part of the state. There are featured events each month as well as theater packages in the summer season of the acclaimed Parkway Playhouse in Burnsville. Shindig-on-the-Square takes place every other weekend in front of the inn, where many of the townspeople enjoy live music and street dancing. The mountains in the area offer unique beauty with the change of the seasons.
Innkeeper(s): Chris & Pam Strickland.
Rates:$70-110. MC VISA AX. Full Bkfst. 26 rooms. Beds:KQT. TV in room. Skiing. Handicap access. Swimming. Fishing.
Contact: Chris Strickland. Certificate may be used: Sunday - Thursday anytime except October.

Charlotte

The Homeplace B&B
5901 Sardis Rd
Charlotte 28270
(704)365-1936

1902. Situated on two-and-one-half wooded acres in Southeast Charlotte, this peaceful setting is an oasis in one of the South's fastest-growing cities. Bedrooms have 10-foot ceilings, heart-of-pine floors and blends of Country/Victorian decor. Special touches include quilts, fine linens, handmade accessories, family antiques and original primitive paintings by innkeeper Peggy Dearien's father. Spend the afternoon or evening relaxing on the porches or walking the secluded gardens. While touring the grounds, you will see a 1930s log barn that was moved to the property in 1991.
Innkeeper(s): Frank & Peggy Dearien.
Rates:$78-88. MC VISA AX. Full Bkfst. Gourmet Brkfst. 4 rooms. 2 with shared baths. Beds:QT. AC in room.
Seen in: *Charlotte Observer, Charlotte Magazine, Birmingham News, Country Magazine*.
Contact: Margaret Dearien. Certificate may be used: Sunday through Thursday only.

"Everything was perfect. The room was superb, the food excellent!"

Chimney Rock

Esmeralda Inn
Hwy 74, PO Box 57
Chimney Rock 28720
(704)625-9105

1890. Nestled in the Blue Ridge Mountains, this rustic country lodge served as home base for production of several silent movies, and notables such

as Mary Pickford, Gloria Swanson, Douglas Fairbanks, Clark Gable and many others used the Esmeralda as a hideout. Lew Wallace, noted author, finished the script for "Ben Hur" in room No. 9. The lobby, constructed of natural trees and filled with local artifacts, is a favorite place for visitors to take refuge and relax.

Innkeeper(s): Ackie & JoAnne Okpych.

Rates:$40-63. MC VISA DS. Cont. Bkfst. Gourmet Dinner. 13 rooms. 6 with shared baths. Beds:KQ. Swimming. Fishing.

Contact: JoAnne Okpych. Certificate may be used: March, May, June, July, August, September, November and December.

Clemmons

Tanglewood Manor
PO Box 1040
Clemmons 27012
(910)766-0591 Fax:(910)766-8723

1859. Located on 1,152 acres, this is a full-service establishment offering facilities for groups of any size. Tanglewood Park is a showcase for plant varieties from around the world. The rose garden, in front of the Manor House, contains more than 800 rosebushes, including more than 400 American Rose Society winners. For nature lovers, Tanglewood's Little Walden Nature Trail contains

three self-guided walks. The park has two modern, fully equipped playgrounds, a miniature golf course and an Olympic-size swimming pool.

Innkeeper(s): Angela Schultz.

Rates:$77-107. MC VISA AX DC CB. ContPlus Bkfst. 10 rooms. Beds:KD. Conference Rm. TV, Phone, AC in room. Tennis. Bicycling. Skiing. Handicap access. Swimming. Stables. Fishing.

Contact: Angela Schultz. Certificate may be used: Dec. 1, 1994 to Feb. 28, 1995.

Edenton

The Lords Proprietors' Inn
300 N Broad St
Edenton 27932
(919)482-3641 (800)348-8933
Fax:(919)482-2432

1801. On Albemarle Sound, Edenton was one of the Colonial capitals of North Carolina. The inn consists of three houses, providing elegant accom-

modations in Edenton's Historic District. Breakfast and dinner are served in a separate dining room on a patio. A guided walking tour from the Visitor's Center provides an opportunity to see museum homes.

Innkeeper(s): Arch & Jane Edwards.

Rates:$140-180. Full Bkfst. MAP available. Gourmet Brkfst, Dinner. Teas. 20 rooms. Beds:KQT. Conference Rm. TV, Phone, AC in room. Handicap access. Swimming. Fishing.

Seen in: *Southern Living, Mid-Atlantic Country, House Beautiful, Washington Post.*

Contact: Jane F. Edwards. Certificate may be used: Second night may not be Saturday or national holiday.

"One of the friendliest and best-managed inns I have ever visited."

Elizabeth City

Culpepper Inn
609 West Main St
Elizabeth City 27909
(919)335-1993

1935. The inn is the town's most impressive brick Colonial Revival-style house built by William and Alice Culpepper. Guests can come here to pick a peach from the tree, sit by the pool or in a hammock, read a book by the goldfish pond or relax by the fireplace. A Roman-style swimming pool was added in the mid-1980s. The town is situated on the Pasquotank River in the heart of the historical Albermarle area and is home to the Museum of the Abermarle, numerous antique stores, historic homes and restaurants.

Innkeeper(s): Judy Smith & Henry Brinkman.

Rates:$85-105. MC VISA AX. Gourmet Brkfst. Teas. 11 rooms. Fireplaces. Beds:KQT. Conference Rm. AC in room. Handicap access. Swimming. Fishing.

Contact: Judy Smith. Certificate may be used: January and February any night. November and December, Sunday - Friday night.

Franklin

Buttonwood Inn
190 Georgia Road
Franklin 28734
(704)369-8985

1925. Tall pine trees surround this two-story batten board house located adjacent to the Franklin Golf Course. Local crafts and handmade family quilts accent the country decor. Wonderful breakfasts are served here - often Eggs Benedict, baked peaches and sausage and freshly baked scones with homemade lemon butter. On a sunny morning enjoy breakfast on the deck and savor the Smoky Mountain vistas. Afterward you'll be ready for white-water rafting, hiking and fishing.

Innkeeper(s): Liz Oehser.

Rates:$55-70. Full Bkfst. 4 rooms. 2 with shared baths. Beds:DT. Golf. Swimming.

Contact: Mary Oehser. Certificate may be used: Sunday-Thursday except October (only if available). No weekends or holidays unless three-day booking, buy (2) get (1).

Germanton

MeadowHaven B&B
NC Hwy 8, PO Box 222
Germanton 27019
(910)593-3996 Fax:(910)593-3996

1976. In this contemporary chalet, a "comfy" chair, writing desk, ceiling fan, phone, remote control TV, VCR, free movies, hair dryer and hooded

bathrobes are standard in each room in the main house. The Loft Room is a private hideaway where you'll find family antiques alongside new pieces from the Bob Timberlake collection. The private "birdhouse" bathroom offers tree-top views of Sauratown Mountain. Bathe in an antique "hearts afire" clawfooted tub/shower, then fall asleep on an antique iron bed.

Innkeeper(s): Sam & Darlene Fain.

Rates:$65-225. MC VISA AX. Full Bkfst. Evening snacks. 7 rooms. Fireplaces. Beds:QD. TV, Phone, AC, Refrig. in room. Spa. Sauna. Exercise room. Swimming. Fishing.

Contact: Darlene Fain. Certificate may be used: January, March, November; Monday through Wednesday, subject to availability. Main house only.

Greensboro

Greenwood B&B
205 N Park Dr
Greensboro 27401
(910)274-6350 (800)535-9363
Fax:(910)274-9943

1911. Greenwood is a fully renovated, stick-style chalet on the park in the historic district. President W. H. Taft was once a guest here. The inn is decorated with wood carvings and art from around the world. There are two living rooms, each with a fireplace and a swimming pool is in the backyard.

Innkeeper(s): Jo Anne Green & Robert Broussard.

Rates:$75-90. MC VISA AX DS. ContPlus Bkfst. Evening snacks. 4 rooms. Fireplaces. Beds:KQT. Phone, AC in room. Golf. Tennis. Swimming. Fishing.

Seen in: *Triad Style*.

Contact: Jo Anne Green. Certificate may be used: January through March, 1994 and 1995; May through September, 1994 and 1995; November and December, 1994 and 1995.

"Marvelous renovation. Courteous, helpful, knowledgeable hostess and perfectly appointed room and bath. Interesting fine-art interior decorating."

Hazelwood

Belle Meade Inn
804 Balsam Rd
Hazelwood 28738
(704)456-3234

1908. Located near Asheville in the mountains of the Western part of the state, this Craftsman home was named *Belle Meade*, a French phrase meaning

"beautiful meadow." Chestnut woodwork provides the background for antiques and traditional furnishings. A fieldstone fireplace is featured in the living room. The Great Smoky Mountain Railroad ride is nearby.

Innkeeper(s): Gloria & Al DiNofa.

Rates:$55-60. MC VISA DS. Full Bkfst. Teas. 4 rooms. Beds:QDT. TV, AC in room. Skiing. Fishing.

Seen in: *Blue Ridge Magazine, Asheville Citizen Times, St. Petersburg Times.*

Contact: Gloria DiNofa. Certificate may be used: Dec. 1 through April 30, excluding holidays.

"Immaculately clean. Distinctively furnished. Friendly atmosphere."

Hendersonville

Claddagh Inn at Hendersonville
755 N Main St
Hendersonville 28792
(704)697-7778

1898. Claddagh has been host for more than 90 years to visitors staying in Hendersonville. The wide, wraparound veranda is filled with rocking chairs, while the library is filled with inviting books. Many of North Carolina's finest craft and antique shops are just two blocks from the inn. Carl Sandburg's house and the Biltmore Estate are nearby, and within a short drive are spectacular sights in the Great Smoky Mountains.

Innkeeper(s): Dennis & Vickie Pacilio.

Rates:$69-99. MC VISA AX DC DS. Full Bkfst. 14 rooms. Beds:KQT. Conference Rm. Phone, AC in room. Golf. Tennis. Fishing.

Seen in: *Country Inn, Blue Ridge Country, Southern Living.*

Contact: Vickie Pacilio. Certificate may be used: January, February, March, April, May, November, December; Sunday-Thursday. No holiday periods.

"Excellent food, clean, home atmosphere."

Echo Mountain Inn
2849 Laurel Park Hwy
Hendersonville 28739
(704)693-9626 Fax:(704)697-2047

1896. This massive stone and wood structure sits on top of Echo Mountain and has spectacular views from the dining room and many guest rooms. Guest rooms are decorated with antiques and reproductions, including many rooms with a fireplace or mountain view. The inn is three miles from the heart of historic Hendersonville. Special services are available by advance reservation. Select from gourmet picnic baskets, roses, champagne, wine, sparkling juice, balloon bouquets, fruit baskets, cheese boards, special-occasion cakes and more.

Innkeeper(s): Frank & Karen Kovacik.

Rates:$37-175. MC VISA AX DS. ContPlus Bkfst. Gourmet Dinner. Picnic lunches. 33 rooms. Beds:KQT. Conference Rm. TV, Phone, AC, Refrig. in room. Skiing. Fishing.

Contact: Karen Kovacik. Certificate may be used: Anytime (except holidays) January, February, March, April, May, September, November, December. Sunday-Thursday, June, July, August. Excludes October, excludes holidays.

The Waverly Inn

783 N Main St
Hendersonville 28792
(704)693-9193 Fax:(704)692-1010

1898. In the National Register, this three-story Victorian and Colonial Revival house has a two-tiered, sawn work trimmed porch and widow's walk. A beautifully carved Eastlake staircase and an original registration desk grace the inn. There are four-poster canopy beds and clawfoot tubs. Breakfast is served in the handsome dining room. The Waverly is the oldest surviving inn in Hendersonville.

Innkeeper(s): John & Diane Sheiry & Darla Olmstead.

Rates:$79-165. MC VISA AX DS. Full Bkfst. Picnic lunches. Teas. 16 rooms.

Beds:KQT. Phone, AC in room. Golf. Tennis. Swimming. Horseback riding. Fishing.

Seen in: *The New York Times, Country Magazine, Blue Ridge Country Magazine.*

Contact: John Sheiry, Jr. Certificate may be used: January, February, March, anytime. Four rooms/night maximum. April, May, September, November, December, Sunday through Thursday. Does not apply on holidays or during special package weekends.

"Our main topic of conversation while driving back was what a great time we had at your place."

Hickory

The Hickory B&B

464 7th St SW
Hickory 28602
(704)324-0548 (800)654-0548
Fax:(704)345-1112

1908. Bedrooms in this Georgian-style inn are decorated with antiques, collectibles, fresh flowers and a country flavor. There's a parlor to sit in and chat and a library to enjoy a good book or to play a game. Homemade tea and lemonade, with something from the oven are served to guests in the late afternoon. The inn is located in a city that has evolved from a furniture and textile mill town of yesteryear into a cultural arts mecca of mountain communities. From mountains to malls, Hickory satisfies the shopper as well as the sportsperson.

Innkeeper(s): Suzanne & Bob Ellis.

Rates:$55-70. Full Bkfst. Picnic lunches. Teas. 4 rooms. Fireplaces. Beds:QT. TV, Phone in room. Golf. Skiing. Swimming. Horseback riding. Fishing.

Seen in: *Mid-Atlantic Country, Hickory Daily News and Charlotte Observer.*

Contact: Suzanne Ellis. Certificate may be used: Not available mid-September to mid-November. Available Sunday through Thursday only.

Marshall

Marshall House

5 Hill St, PO Box 865
Marshall 28753
(704)649-9205 (800)562-9258
Fax:(704)649-2999

1903. Richard Sharp Smith, a resident architect for the Biltmore Estates, designed this house with a large veranda to maximize the view of the French Broad River and Appalacian Mountains. Pebbledash, a type of masonry brought to the area by George Vanderbilt, was applied to the exterior. The 5,200-square-foot house has a bountiful supply of antiques to complement the original pocket doors, wavy glass and wood floors.

Innkeeper(s): Jim & Ruth Boylan.

Rates:$39-75. MC VISA AX DC DS CB. ContPlus Bkfst. 9 rooms. 7 with shared baths. Fireplaces. Conference Rm. Bicycling. Skiing. Handicap access. Swimming. Fishing.

Seen in: *Asheville Citizen Times, Blue Ridge Business.*

Contact: Ruth Boylan. Certificate may be used: October only during week. July only during week. Depending on availability, acceptable all other times.

"Thank you for your hospitality. We felt right at home."

Mooresville

24 Spring Run B&B

Located on Lake Norman
Mooresville 28115
(704)664-6686

1989. Situated on Lake Norman, 24 Spring Run is a modern three-story brick home in a new residential area. Inside are fine antiques and stained glass. Guests have use of a private sitting room and fireplace. A three-course gourmet breakfast is served in the formal dining room or on the deck overlooking the lake. Most of the breakfast recipes are from a 70-year-old collection belonging to the innkeeper's grandmother. The Mallard Head Country Club offers golfing next door. Complimentary golf cart, paddle boat, and exercise equipment are provided to guests.

Innkeeper(s): Mary Farley.

Rates:$89. MC VISA. MAP available. Gourmet Brkfst. 2 rooms. Beds:QD. TV, AC in room. Golf. Exercise room. Swimming. Fishing.

Seen in: *Charlotte Observer, Statesville Gazette.*

Contact: Mary Farley. Certificate may be used: Monday, Tuesday, Wednesday, Thursday - June and September, 1995. Except holidays.

Mountain Home

Mountain Home Inn

PO Box 234, 10 Courtland Blvd
Mountain Home 28758
(704)697-9090 (800)397-0066

1988. Located near Asheville and the Great Smoky Mountains, Mountain Home is the site of an old stagecoach stop. Within the three-story home are antiques, Oriental rugs, and a red velvet Victorian parlor with fireplace. Guests have the use of a kitchen and laundry room. Two of the seven bedrooms feature Jacuzzi tubs.

Innkeeper(s): Bill & Lynn Romero.

Rates:$65-90. MC VISA AX DS. Full Bkfst. 9 rooms. 2 with shared baths. Beds:KQ. Conference Rm. TV, Phone, AC in room. Skiing. Handicap access. Swimming. Fishing.

Contact: Lynnette Romero. Certificate may be used: January - May.

"Great hosts, food and cleanliness."

Murphy

Huntington Hall B&B

500 Valley River Ave
Murphy 28906
(704)837-9567 (800)824-6189
Fax:(704)837-2527

1881. This two-story country Victorian home was built by J.H. Dillard, the town mayor and twice a member of the house of representatives. Clapboard siding and tall columns accent the large front

porch. An English country theme is highlighted throughout. Afternoon refreshments and evening turndown service are included. Breakfast is served in the dining room or on the sun porch. Murder-

mystery, summer-theater, and white-water-rafting packages available.

Innkeeper(s): Bob & Kate DeLong.

Rates:$55-85. MC VISA AX DC DS CB. Full Bkfst. Gourmet Brkfst. Evening snacks. 5 rooms. Fireplaces. Beds:QDT. Conference Rm. TV, AC in room. Golf. Tennis. Swimming. Horseback riding. Fishing.

Seen in: *Atlanta Journal, Petersen's 4-Wheel Magazine.*

Contact: Robert Delong. Certificate may be used: Sunday through Thursday.

"Your skill and attitude make it a pleasant experience to stay and rest at HH."

New Bern

King's Arms Inn

212 Pollock St
New Bern 28560
(919)638-4409 (800)872-9306

1848. Four blocks from the Tryon Palace, in the heart of the New Bern Historic District, this Colonial-style inn features a mansard roof and touches of Victorian architecture. Guest rooms are decorated with antiques, canopy and four-poster beds and fireplaces. An old tavern in town was the inspiration for the name of the inn.

Innkeeper(s): Richard & Pat Gulley.

Rates:$55-76. MC VISA AX. ContPlus Bkfst. 10 rooms. 2 with shared baths. Beds:KQ. TV, Phone, AC in room.

Seen in: *Washington Post, Southern Living.*

Contact: Patricia Gulley. Certificate may be used: January - February only.

"Delightful."

New Berne House

709 Broad St
New Bern 28560
(919)636-2250 (800)842-7688

1923. Using bricks salvaged from Tryon Palace, this stately red brick Colonial Revival replica was built by the Taylor family, known for its historic preservation work in North Carolina. Located in the historic district, it is one block to the governor's mansion, Tryon Palace, now a Williamsburg-style living museum. The splendidly refurbished formal parlor is the setting for afternoon tea, and a graceful sweeping staircase leads to guest rooms with canopy beds and antique furnishings.

Innkeeper(s): Marcia Drum & Howard Bronson.

Rates:$80. MC VISA AX. Gourmet Brkfst. Teas. Evening snacks. 7 rooms. Beds:KQT. Conference Rm. Phone, AC in room. Bicycling.

Seen in: *Charlotte Observer, Raleigh News & Observer, Pinehurst Outlook.*

Contact: Marcia Drum. Certificate may be used: Anytime except weekends, holidays and special events.

"In six months of traveling around the country New Berne House was our favorite stop!"

Salisbury

Rowan Oak House
208 S Fulton St
Salisbury 28144
(704)633-2086 (800)786-0437

1901. This Queen Anne house, in the middle of the Salisbury Historic District, features a carved-oak front door, leaded and stained glass, meticulously carved mantels and the original ornate electric and gaslights. Guests may enjoy afternoon tea in the Victorian parlor or on the columned, wrap-around porch overlooking a garden. Guest rooms have antiques, historic wallpaper, down comforters, fresh flowers and fruit. One room has a double Jacuzzi.

Innkeeper(s): Bill & Ruth Ann Coffey.

Rates:$65-95. MC VISA DS. Full Bkfst. Teas. 4 rooms. 2 with shared baths. Fireplaces. Beds:KQDT. Phone, AC in room. Tennis. Spa. Swimming. Fishing.

Seen in: *Salisbury Post, Daily Independent, Country Victorian Accents.*

Contact: Ruth Ann Coffey. Certificate may be used: Sunday-Thursday except April and October.

"A stay at the Rowan Oak House is the quintessential B&B experience. Their home is as interesting as it is beautiful, and they are the most gracious host and hostess you can imagine."

Saluda

The Oaks
PO Box 1088, Greenville St
Saluda 28773
(704)749-9613

1894. Once you look past the huge oak tree out front, you'll see a beautiful Victorian turreted, three-story home. A front porch with blue ceiling and contrasting gingerbread trim curves around the turret to a hidden nook where a porch swing hangs. The floors inside are a patchwork of old heart pine flooring, oak parquet, rugs and carpets. Saluda is home to many artists, and interesting bargains abound in the nearby antique

shops. Visit the Thompson & Pace Country Stores, which have served Saluda for generations and have stories to prove it.

Innkeeper(s): Ceri & Peggy Dando.

Rates:$55-64. MC VISA. Full Bkfst. Teas. 4 rooms. Beds:Q. Golf. Tennis. Skiing. Swimming. Horseback riding. Fishing.

Contact: Ceri Dando. Certificate may be used: All season, all year.

Orchard Inn
Hwy 176, PO Box 725
Saluda 28773
(704)749-5471 (800)581-3800
Fax:(704)749-9805

1910. This inn combines the casual feel of a country farmhouse with the elegance of a Southern plantation. It has Oriental rugs, original artwork, quilts and Flow Blue china. The dining room is in a long, glassed-in porch overlooking the Warrior Mountain Range. Dinner is available by reservation and the chef's creations include chilled peach soup, catfish scampi and broiled fresh mountain trout. For dessert there's lemon gateau, Victoria creams and pecan pie from a special New Orleans recipe. Guests can explore the area on superb country roads.

Innkeeper(s): Veronica & Newell Doty.

Rates:$105-175. MC VISA. Full Bkfst. Gourmet Dinner. Picnic lunches. 12 rooms. Fireplaces. Beds:KQT. Conference Rm. Phone, AC in room. Handicap access. Fishing.

Contact: Newell Doty. Certificate may be used: Sunday - Thursday nights, except holidays and October.

Southern Pines

Knollwood House
1495 W Connecticut Ave
Southern Pines 28387
(910)692-9390 Fax:(910)692-0609

1925. Fairway dreams await golfers at this English-manor-style inn where upstairs sitting rooms overlook the 14th and 15th holes of the beautiful Mid-Pines golf course. The inn's lawns roll down 100 feet or so to the course, which is a masterpiece by Scottish golf course architect Donald Ross. More than 30 golf courses are within 20 miles. There have been many celebrations under the crystal chandelier and 10-foot ceilings, and the Glenn Miller Orchestra once played on the back lawn.

Innkeeper(s): Dick & Mimi Beatty.

Rates:$75-120. VISA. Full Bkfst. Gourmet Brkfst. 4 rooms. Fireplaces. Beds:KQT. AC in room. Tennis.

Contact: Richard Beatty. Certificate may be used: July 5 to Sept. 20; Nov. 20 to March 1.

Spruce Pine

The Richmond Inn
101 Pine Ave
Spruce Pine 28777
(704)765-6993

1939. The flagstone terrace of the Richmond Inn overlooks the valley of the North Toe River and the Blue Ridge Mountains beyond. Family treasures and antiques warm the interiors and many rooms feature four-poster beds. Three blocks away is the village and within a half-hour drive are Roan Mountain, the world's largest rhododendron gardens, and Linvill Caverns, Linville Falls and Linville Gorge Widerness Area.
Innkeeper(s): Bill Ansley/Lenore Boucher.
Rates:$45-70. MC VISA. Full Bkfst. Evening snacks. 7 rooms. Beds:QT. Skiing. Swimming. Fishing.
Contact: Bill Ansley. Certificate may be used: All year long, Sunday - Thursday. Limited certificates accepted on Friday and Saturday. Excludes holidays, special events and the month of October.

Statesville

Aunt Mae's
532 E Broad St
Statesville 28677
(704)873-9525

1891. The past is well preserved at this Victorian inn where Aunt Mae spent her 90 years collecting and storing treasures. Enjoy a library filled to the brim with nostalgia, and browse through books, magazines and news articles from the early 1900s. Read love notes written long ago. Turn-of-the-century Valentine and Christmas cards are displayed at the appropriate times. Guests can sit in the formal downstairs parlor and listen to the antique radio and play the popular records of a day gone by on one of the antique record players.
Innkeeper(s): Sue & Richard Rowland.
Rates:$60. MC VISA. Gourmet Brkfst. Picnic lunches. Evening snacks. 2 rooms. AC in room. Bicycling. Swimming. Fishing.
Contact: Sue Rowland. Certificate may be used: All year.

Tabor City

Four Rooster Inn
205 Pireway Rd.
Tabor City 28463
(910)653-3878

1949. This brick house is located on more than an acre of lawns and camellias. Elegantly appointed with antiques and new furnishings, the rooms are accentuated with coordinating fabrics and fine linens. Arrive early for afternoon tea served in one of the inn's Florida rooms. Breakfast trays with coffee are brought up first thing in the morning, then a full breakfast is served in the dining room. The innkeepers sailed the Intracoastal Waterways for several years before settling down in Tabor City.
Innkeeper(s): Gloria & Bob Rogers.
Rates:$55-75. MC VISA. Full Bkfst. Gourmet Brkfst. Teas. Evening snacks. 3 rooms. 2 with shared baths. Beds:QD. Phone, AC in room. Farm. Bicycling. Swimming. Fishing.
Contact: Bob Rogers. Certificate may be used: March 1 - Dec. 31.

Tarboro

Little Warren
304 E Park Ave
Tarboro 27886
(919)823-1314

1913. The wide, wraparound front porch of this gracious family home overlooks the Town Common, said to be one of two originally chartered commons remaining in the United States. The house is in the historic district and is designated with a National Register plaque.
Innkeeper(s): Patsy & Tom Miller.
Rates:$65. MC VISA AX DS. Full Bkfst. 3 rooms. Beds:DT. Phone, AC in room. Fishing.
Contact: Thomas Miller. Certificate may be used: Not during Christmas holiday.

"It is indeed a unique ambiance."

Tryon

Mimosa Inn
One Mimosa Inn Lane
Tryon 28782
(704)859-7688

1903. The Mimosa is situated on the southern slope of the Blue Ridge Mountains. With its long rolling lawns and large columned veranda, the inn has been a landmark and social gathering place for almost a century. There is a stone patio and outdoor fireplace. During fox hunting season there are two hunts a week in the area as well as two annual steeplechases.
Innkeeper(s): Jay & Sandi Franks.
Rates:$55-85. Full Bkfst. 9 rooms. Beds:QT. Conference Rm. AC in room. Golf. Fishing.
Contact: Sandra Franks. Certificate may be used: Anytime except holidays and special events in January - March. Sunday - Thursday only April - December.

Pine Crest Inn
200 Pine Crest Ln
Tryon 28782
(704)859-9135 (800)633-3001
Fax:(704)859-9135

1906. Carter Brown purchased this former sanitarium on a wooded knoll close to the center of town and in 1917 opened a small resort. Each of the cabins he added to the complex were given a secluded porch, a terrace, a fireplace and a private bath. The inn's dining room has rough-hewn decor reminiscent of a Colonial tavern. Mr. Brown initiated the fox hunts, steeplechase racing and horse shows that have made Tryon a popular equine center.

Innkeeper(s): Jennifer & Jeremy Wainwright.

Rates:$125-165. MC VISA AX DS. Full Bkfst. Gourmet Dinner. Picnic lunches. 30 rooms. Fireplaces. Beds:KQT. Conference Rm. TV, Phone, AC in room. Bicycling. Fishing.

Seen in: *Southern Living.*

Contact: Jeremy Wainwright. Certificate may be used: No weekends or holidays.

"We felt pampered and at home in your lovely refurbished Pine Crest Inn."

Tryon Old South B&B
107 Markham Pl
Tryon 28782
(704)859-6965

1910. This Colonial Revival inn is located just two blocks from downtown and Trade Street's antique and gift shops. Located in the Thermal Belt, Tryon

is known for its pleasant, mild weather although an occasional thunderstorm makes things interesting. Guests don't go away hungry from innkeeper Terry Cacioppo's large Southern-style breakfasts. Unique woodwork abounds in this inn and equally as impressive is a curving staircase. Behind the property is a large wooded area and several waterfalls are just a couple of miles away.

Innkeeper(s): Terry Cacioppo

Rates:$45-75. MC VISA. Full Bkfst. 3 rooms. Beds:Q. AC in room.

Fishing.

Contact: Terry Cacioppo. Certificate may be used: November - May.

Valle Crucis

Mast Farm Inn
PO Box 704
Valle Crucis 28691
(704)963-5857 Fax:(704)963-6404

1885. Listed in the National Register of Historic Places, this 18-acre farmstead includes a main house and seven outbuildings. The inn features a wraparound porch with rocking chairs, swings and a view of the mountain valley. Homemade breads and vegetables fresh from the garden are specialties. Rooms are furnished with antiques, quilts and mountain crafts.

Innkeeper(s): Sibyl & Francis Pressly.

Rates:$85-165. MC VISA. ContPlus Bkfst. MAP available. 12 rooms. 2 with shared baths. Fireplaces. Beds:KQT. Farm. Golf. Tennis. Skiing. Handicap access. Horseback riding. Fishing.

Seen in: *Southern Bride, News and Observer, Blue Ridge Country, Country, Southern Living, Mid-Atlantic Country.*

Contact: Francis Pressly. Certificate may be used: January through June and September and Sunday through Thursday except holidays.

"Your warm hospitality is a rare find and one that we will remember for a long time."

The Inn at the Taylor House
PO Box 713
Valle Crucis 28691
(704)963-5581 Fax:(704)963-5818

1910. A wraparound porch encircling this farmhouse-style inn communicates the feeling of real hospitality and sets the tone for the entire house.

There's old and new wicker on the porch with bright fabrics, lots of plants and flower boxes. An old-fashioned porch swing adds to the feeling, and from the breakfast area, you can look out on a field of grazing Charlais cattle. The town was founded by Scottish Highlanders when they first came to this country. Every summer, the area hosts the largest gathering of Scottish clans in the United States.

Innkeeper(s): Chip Schwab.

Rates:$110-145. MC VISA. Gourmet Brkfst. 7 rooms. Beds:KQT. Farm. Handicap access. Fishing.

Contact: Chip Schwab. Certificate may be used: Sunday - Thursday.

Waynesville

Grandview Lodge
809 Valley View Cir Rd
Waynesville 28786
(704)456-5212 (800)255-7826
Fax:(704)452-5432

1890. Grandview Lodge is located on two-and-a-half acres in the Smoky Mountains. The land surrounding the lodge has an apple orchard, rhubarb patch, grape arbor and vegetable garden for the inn's kitchen. Rooms are available in the main lodge and in a newer addition. The inn's dining room is known throughout the region and Linda, a home economist, has written "Recipes from Grandview Lodge."

Innkeeper(s): Stan & Linda Arnold.

Rates:$90-105. Full Bkfst. MAP available. Gourmet Dinner. 11 rooms. Fireplaces. Beds:KQT. TV in room. Golf. Tennis. Skiing. Swimming. Fishing.

Seen in: *Asheville Citizen, Winston-Salem Journal, Raleigh News and Observer.*

Contact: Stanley Arnold. Certificate may be used: Not participating in August and October or on holidays. Anytime November through May. Sunday through Thursday, June, July, September.

"It's easy to see why family and friends have been enjoying trips to Grandview."

Weaverville

Dry Ridge Inn
26 Brown St
Weaverville 28787
(704)658-3899 (800)839-3899

1849. This house was built as the parsonage for the Salem Campground, an old religious revival camping area. Because of the high altitude and pleasant weather, it was used as a camp hospital for Confederate soldiers suffering from pneumonia during the Civil War. The area was called Dry Ridge by the Cherokee Indians before the campground was established.

Innkeeper(s): Paul & Mary Lou Gibson.

Rates:$65-80. MC VISA. Full Bkfst. Gourmet Brkfst. 7 rooms. Fireplaces. Beds:QT. Conference Rm. AC in room. Golf. Skiing. Spa. Swimming. Horseback riding. Fishing.

Seen in: *Asheville Citizen Times, Marshall News Record.*

Contact: Paul Gibson. Certificate may be used: Anytime except April, July, August and October.

"Best family vacation ever spent."

Weldon

Weldon Place Inn
500 Washington Ave
Weldon 27890
(919)536-4582 (800)831-4470

1913. Homemade strawberry bread is a pleasant way to start your morning at this Colonial Revival home. Located in the historic area, it is two miles from I-95. Wedding showers and other celebrations are popular here. There are beveled-glass windows, canopy beds and Italian fireplaces. Most of the inn's antiques are original to the house, including a horse-hair stuffed couch with its original upholstery. Select the Romantic Retreat package and you'll enjoy flowers, sparkling cider, a whirlpool tub and breakfast in bed.

Innkeeper(s): Angel & Andy Whitby.

Rates:$45-85. MC VISA. Full Bkfst. Evening snacks. 4 rooms. 1 with shared bath. Fireplaces. AC in room. Fishing.

Contact: Andy Whitby. Certificate may be used: Sunday-Thursday, April-September, Sunday-Saturday, October-March.

Wilmington

Historic Stemmerman's 1855 Inn
130 S Front St
Wilmington 28401
(910)763-7776

1886. Overlooking the waters of the Cape Fear River, this Federal-style inn has deluxe executive suites with elegant period furnishings and fully equipped kitchenettes. A Southern gourmet restaurant and a mini-mart are on the premises as well as a cocktail lounge with billiards and music. Area attractions include the Azalea Festival in spring, the Piney Woods Festival and Cape Fear Marlin Tournament in summer, the Riverfest in fall and the Christmas Candlelight Tour in winter.

Innkeeper(s): Joseph & Rita Khoury.

Rates:$59-179. MC VISA AX DC. Cont. Bkfst. 7 rooms. Beds:KQT. Conference Rm. TV. Phone, AC, Refrig. in room. Swimming. Fishing.

Contact: Joseph Khoury. Certificate may be used: Sept. 15, 1994 - Feb. 28, 1995 (except holidays).

Wilson

Miss Betty's B&B Inn
600 Nash St, NE
Wilson 27893-3045
(919)243-4447 (800)258-2058

1858. This inn is on Nash Street, which was once described as one of the 10 most beautiful streets in the world. Comprised of two historic houses—the

Davis-Whitehead-Harriss house and the adjacent Riley house—the exteriors are highlighted by bold Italianate details. The inn provides a touch of Victorian elegance and comfort with Victorian wallpapers, antiques and furnishings featured throughout.

Innkeeper(s): Betty & Fred Spitz.

Rates:$60-75. MC VISA AX DC DS CB. Full Bkfst. 10 rooms. Fireplaces. Beds:KDT. Conference Rm. TV, Phone, AC in room. Golf. Tennis. Handicap access. Swimming. Fishing.

Seen in: *Wilson Daily Times, Enterprise.*

Contact: Frederick Spitz. Certificate may be used: All times subject to last-minute availability only.

"Yours is second to none."

Winston-Salem

Augustus T. Zevely Inn
803 S Main St
Winston-Salem 27101
(910)748-9299 (800)929-9299
Fax:(910)721-2211

1844. Each room of this Georgian-style inn is individually decorated in authentic Moravian style. A spacious covered porch, shaded by a spreading magnolia, offers a relaxing space to enjoy breakfast or escape the heat of the day or cool of the evening when wine and cheese is served. A line of Old Salem furniture has been designed by Lexington Furniture Industries, with a few pieces especially created for the Zevely House. A replanted orchard screens the parking spaces for guests at the rear of the lot where stables and outbuildings once stood.

Innkeeper(s): Thomas Lantry.

Rates:$85-175. MC VISA AX. Full Bkfst. Gourmet Brkfst. Picnic lunches. Teas. Evening snacks. 13 rooms. Fireplaces. Beds:KQT. TV, Phone, AC, Refrig. in room. Tennis. Bicycling. Handicap access. Swimming. Fishing.

Contact: Thomas Lantry. Certificate may be used: November-March, July-August; non-holidays and special events (furniture mart, Easter sunrise service, etc.) for 1994 and 1995 as available and appropriate.

Wachovia B&B
513 Wachovia St
Winston-Salem 27101
(910)777-0332

1913. This rose and white Victorian cottage with a wraparound porch is located on a quiet, tree-lined street. The inn is located only a few blocks from the Winston-Salem city center and the Old Salem Historic District. Guests may choose to eat their breakfast in the large dining room, in their rooms, or on the porch. The innkeepers like to provide flexible check-in and check-out times and there is no rigid breakfast schedule. Within walking distance is the Stevens Center for performing arts, gourmet restaurants, antique and specialty shops and several exercise facilities and parks.

Innkeeper(s): Susan Bunting.

Rates:$60-65. MC VISA. Full Bkfst. Teas. 5 rooms. 3 with shared baths. Beds:QDT. AC in room. Golf. Tennis. Bicycling. Horseback riding. Fishing.

Seen in: *Parentips Magazine, Winston-Salem Magazine.*

Contact: Susan Bunting. Certificate may be used: December - February.

North Dakota

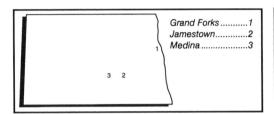

Grand Forks

The Big Red House
729 Belmont Rd
Grand Forks 58201
(701)775-3332

1909. Visitors to Grand Forks may stay at this spacious inn on an elm-lined street near a historic district. The turn-of-the-century home features many antiques and Oriental collectibles. The inn has easy access to downtown, either on foot or by city bus. Both IBM and Apple computers are on the premises.

Small pets are allowed in the basement kennel. The Red River is just a block away, and the city offers many fine parks. Ask about anniversary, birthday and wedding specials.

Innkeeper(s): Rick & Becky Schoeneck.

Rates:$50. MC VISA. Full Bkfst. Gourmet Brkfst. Evening snacks. 2 rooms. 2 with shared baths. Skiing. Fishing.

Contact: Rebecca Schoeneck. Certificate may be used: July 1, 1994 through Dec. 31, 1995.

Jamestown

Country Charm B&B
RR 3 Box 71
Jamestown 58401
(701)251-1372 (800)331-1372

1897. Jamestown not only offers convenience, centrally located at the intersection of the state's east-west interstate and main north-south highway, it features the Country Charm, a prairie farmhouse six miles from town and a short hop from I-94. The inn's tranquil setting is accented by the surrounding pines and cottonwood trees. The blue-dominated Patches and Lace Room features a multi-shaded patchwork quilt. Activities and places of interest abound in the Jamestown area, including Frontier Village and North Dakota's oldest courthouse.

Innkeeper(s): Ethel & Tom Oxtoby.

Rates:$50-52. Full Bkfst. 3 rooms. 3 with shared baths. Beds:D. AC in room. Golf. Tennis. Bicycling. Skiing. Swimming. Fishing.

Contact: Ethel Oxtoby. Certificate may be used: Monday - Thursday.

Medina

Chase Lake Country Inn
2967 56th Ave SE
Medina 58467
(701)486-3502

1916. Named for the national wildlife refuge just 10 miles away, this three-story farmhouse was once home to a state senator. This inn is a favorite of hunters, and the innkeepers can provide information about the area's wildlife. On the main floor, guests may stay in the handicap accessible Antique Allie. Four rooms are found on the inn's second floor, and the third level features the secluded Lover's Loft. The inn, which shares space on the property with the innkeeper's working farm, offers an exercise room and cable TV. Pets and hunting dogs may be kept on the premises.

Innkeeper(s): Craig & Debra Hoffmann.

Rates:$40-50. MC VISA. Full Bkfst. AP available. Picnic lunches. Teas. 7 rooms. 4 with shared baths. Beds:Q. TV, Phone, AC in room. Farm. Skiing. Handicap access. Exercise room. Swimming. Fishing.

Contact: Debra Hoffmann. Certificate may be used: Anytime.

Ohio

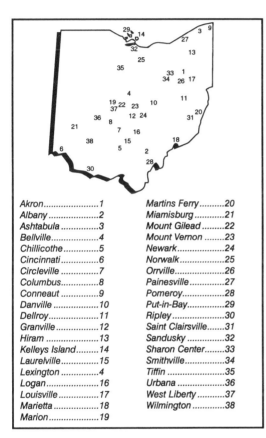

Akron

O'Neil House
1290 W Exchange
Akron 44313
(216)867-2650 Fax:(216)867-2650

1923. This 20,000-square-foot English Tudor mansion was built for the William O'Neil family, founder of General Tire. There are four acres, separated into seven English gardens divided by natural stone walls. An oak-paneled foyer and a secret bar hidden behind a bookshelf in the library represent an opulent '20s lifestyle. Breakfast is served in the room overlooking the reflecting pond or on the terrace. "The Gatsby," an Eggs Benedict-style dish with filet mignon is the inn's specialty.

Innkeeper(s): Gayle & Jay Johnson.

Rates:$95-140. MC VISA DS. ContPlus Bkfst. Gourmet Brkfst. 4 rooms. Fireplaces. Beds:KQ. Phone, AC in room.

Contact: Gayle Johnson. Certificate may be used: Sunday through Thursday any week, except Nov. 15-Jan. 1.

Albany

Albany House
9 Clinton St
Albany 45710
(614)698-6311

1860. Located seven miles from Ohio University in a quaint village setting, this inn is filled with antiques, quilts, Oriental rugs, and collectibles.

Because of four two-story columns, it is often referred to as "Tara North." A new addition includes an indoor pool, showers and changing room.

Innkeeper(s): Sarah & Ted Hutchins.

Rates:$60-85. ContPlus Bkfst. Evening snacks. 4 rooms. 3 with shared baths. Beds:T. AC in room. Swimming. Fishing.

Contact: Sarah Hutchins. Certificate may be used: Weekdays but weekends okay if we have rooms.

Ashtabula

Michael Cahill B&B
1106 Walnut Blvd
Ashtabula 44004
(216)964-8449

1887. This two-story early Victorian "Stick Style" home is situated on a bluff overlooking Lake Erie. It was built by Irish immigrants who profited in the 1880s and 1890s as saloon keepers. Walnut Boulevard was then known as "Captain's Row" because of the many ship captains who lived there. The inn features cherry woodwork, original electric chandeliers and antique and period furnishings. A large wraparound porch allows guests to enjoy Lake Erie breezes. Within easy walking distance is the Marine Museum, antique shopping in restored Bridge Street shops and charter boat fishing. Wineries and many covered bridges are nearby.
Innkeeper(s): Paul & Pat Goode.

Rates:$45-55. Full Bkfst. 4 rooms. 2 with shared baths. Beds:T. AC in room. Fishing.

Contact: Paul Goode. Certificate may be used: November-May, anytime. June-October, weekdays only.

Bellville

Frederick Fitting House
72 Fitting Ave
Bellville 44813
(419)886-2863

1863. This pretty blue and white Italianate Victorian commands a corner of the town of Bellville, 10 minutes from Ohio University. Rooms include the Colonial Room with a queen canopy bed and the Shaker Room with twin beds that can be converted to a king. Breakfast is served in the Victorian dining room or garden gazebo, but you may wish to carry it to the front porch or to the library where you can settle down during the winter to a roaring fire in its fireplace. Malabar Farms is nearby as is the Mohican River.
Innkeeper(s): Suzanne & Ramon Wilson.

Rates:$58-72. Full Bkfst. Gourmet Brkfst, Dinner. Picnic lunches. Evening snacks. 3 rooms. Beds:KQT. Skiing. Swimming. Fishing.

Contact: Suzanne Wilson. Certificate may be used: Sunday-Thursday, May-October; any nights, November-April.

Chillicothe

The Greenhouse B&B
47 E 5th St
Chillicothe 45601
(614)775-5313

1894. This beautifully restored Queen Anne Victorian is framed by green lawns, flowerbeds and an original iron fence. Stained-glass windows and leaded-glass doors cast prisms of light onto the polished-oak entrance hall complete with its own Italian fireplace. A cherry wood dining room, a library and a Greek-style parlor are all open to guests. The innkeepers will be happy to arrange carriage rides for you, or you may wish to walk to the antique shops and restaurants in the neighborhood.
Innkeeper(s): Tom & Dee Shoemaker.

Rates:$60. MC VISA AX. Full Bkfst. 4 rooms. Beds:DT. TV, AC in room. Fishing.

Contact: Dee Shoemaker. Certificate may be used: November through April.

Old McDill-Anderson Place
3656 Polk Hollow Rd
Chillicothe 45601
(614)774-1770

1820. This brick Italianate house is blessed with a veranda and screened breakfast porch that overlooks lawns on the inn's two acres. This is home to

Del, a wood-turner and university dean, and Ruth, a caring cook known for her gourmet breakfasts and snacks featuring historic recipes using local produce and garden herbs. There is a one-family suite in addition to the bed & breakfast rooms. Feather beds and woodstoves add to the coziness, and guests often enjoy the billiard table and old piano.
Innkeeper(s): Ruth & Del Meyer.

Rates:$55-65. Full Bkfst. Evening snacks. 4 rooms. 1 with shared bath. Fireplaces. Beds:DT. Conference Rm. Phone, AC in room. Fishing.

Seen in: *Cleveland Plain Dealer.*

Contact: Ruth Meyer. Certificate may be used: Monday through Thursday, holiday weeks excluded.

"I felt I was staying in the place described by many novelists."

Cincinnati

Prospect Hill B&B
408 Boal St
Cincinnati 45210
(513)421-4408

1867. Nestled in a wooded hillside in the Prospect Hill Historic District, this Italianate townhouse offers spectacular views of downtown Cincinnati. The inn has original woodwork, doors and light fixtures. Each guest room is decorated in a particular historical period. Guests may relax under a shade tree or on the side porch and enjoy the view. There is ample off-street parking and downtown activities are just a short walk away.

Innkeeper(s): Gary Hackney & Tony Jenkins.

Rates:$69-99. MC VISA. ContPlus Bkfst. 3 rooms. 2 with shared baths. Fireplaces. Beds:Q. TV, AC in room. Skiing. Spa. Fishing.

Seen in: *Cincinnati Downtowner, Cincinnati Enquirer, Travel Holiday.*

Contact: Tony Jenkins. Certificate may be used: Non-weekend nights only, Room #1-$79 rate, 1994 and 1995.

"A truly beautiful setting and warm hospitality makes it a truly memorable experience."

Circleville

Castle Inn
610 S Court St
Circleville 43113
(614)477-3986 (800)477-1541

1899. Arches, battlements, towers and stained glass bedeck this medieval castle-like house constructed over a two-year period. Affording romantic anniver-

saries and honeymoons, the Round Tower Room boasts an ornate Victorian bedstead and a pink marble bathroom. Breakfast is served on English china in a handsome dining room overlooking the Shakespeare Garden, which displays only flowers and herbs featured in Shakespeare's plays. Weekends often include imaginative packages such as an "Elizabethan House Party," a "Dickens Theatre Party" or murder mysteries.

Innkeeper(s): Jim & Sue Maxwell.

Rates:$65-85. MC VISA AX. Full Bkfst. Gourmet Brkfst. 4 rooms. Fireplaces. Beds:DT. TV, AC in room. Fishing.

Seen in: *Circleville Herald, Packet, Southeast Ohio, Akron Beacon-Journal, Ohio Heartlander, Senior Times.*

Contact: Susan Maxwell. Certificate may be used: November - March, Sunday - Thursday.

"The atmosphere is romantic, the food excellent, the hospitality super!"

Columbus

Penguin Crossing B&B
295 E N Broadway
Columbus 43214
(614)261-7854 (800)736-4846
Fax:(614)261-0778

1923. Roses and a large covered porch greet guests of this three-story brick house. The Classics Room boasts a brass and porcelain bed, an oak dresser and

D. OSTER

period wallpaper, while the Jenny Lind Room has an heirloom Jenny Lind bed. Breakfasts include a selection of natural foods, and the innkeeper is happy to cater to special dietary needs. The inn is within walking distance to antique shops, bookstores and delicatessens, and Ohio State University is two miles away.

Innkeeper(s): Ross & Tracy Irvin.

Rates:$75-135. MC VISA. Full Bkfst. Gourmet Brkfst. Evening snacks. 4 rooms. 3 with shared baths. Beds:QD. Phone, AC in room. Exercise room.

Contact: Tracey Irvin. Certificate may be used: Sunday through Thursday.

Conneaut

Campbell Braemar

390 State St
Conneaut 44030
(216)599-7362

1910. This little Colonial Revival house is decorated in a Scottish style, and a Scottish breakfast is provided. Guests are invited to use the kitchen for

light cooking as the hosts live next door. Wineries, golf, fishing, sandy beaches and hunting are nearby.

Innkeeper(s): Mary & Andrew Campbell.

Rates:$55-65. Full Bkfst. Teas. 4 rooms. Beds:KQT. AC in room. Swimming. Fishing.

Contact: Mary Campbell. Certificate may be used: July 25 - Dec. 31, 1995; Monday-Thursday.

Danville

Red Fox Country Inn

26367 Danville-Amity Rd
Danville 43014
(614)599-7369

1830. More than 50 dogwood, crab apple and magnolia trees blume in spring on the 15 acres surrounding this farm home, originally built as an inn for coach travelers along the Danville-Amity Wagon Road. Amish woven rugs and hand-crafted, large oak beds furnish the rooms. Dining room cupboards boast collections of redware, early pewter and toys. The innkeepers' antique shop in the renovated horse stable features country and primitve

furnishings, as well as more collectibles. Invite friends to join you for breakfast (notifying the innkeeper the night before) and afterwards play crochet on the lawn or settle in on the porch swing while Amish carts pass by.

Rates:$60-75. MC VISA. Full Bkfst. Gourmet Dinner. Evening snacks. 4 rooms. Beds:QD. AC in room. Skiing. Fishing.

Contact: Ida L. Wolff Certificate may be used: Sunday through Thursday year round. Weekends November through March. Exclude all holidays and special events at area colleges.

The White Oak Inn

29683 Walhonding Rd (SR 715)
Danville 43014
(614)599-6107

1915. Large oaks and ivy surround the wide front porch of this three-story farmhouse situated on 13 green acres. It is located on the former Indian trail and pioneer road that runs along the Kokosing River, and an Indian mound has been discovered on the property. The inn's woodwork is all original white oak, and guest rooms are furnished in antiques. Visitors often shop for maple syrup, cheese and handicrafts at nearby Amish farms. Three cozy fireplace rooms provide the perfect setting for romantic dinners for two.

Innkeeper(s): Yvonne & Ian Martin.

Rates:$75-150. MC VISA DS. Full Bkfst. Gourmet Dinner. 10 rooms. Fireplaces. Beds:QDT. Conference Rm. Phone, AC in room. Golf. Bicycling. Skiing. Horseback riding. Fishing.

Seen in: *Ladies Home Journal, Columbus Monthly, News Journal-Mansfield, Cleveland Plain Dealer.*

Contact: Yvonne Martin. Certificate may be used: Sunday-Thursday night year-round, holidays excluded.

"The dinner was just fabulous and we enjoyed playing the antique grand piano."

Dellroy

Whispering Pines B&B

SR 542, PO Box 340
Dellroy 44620
(216)735-2824

1880. This Victorian is located on picturesque Atwood Lake and boasts a wonderful view. Each bedroom has a view of the lake and is decorated with 19th-century antiques. A fireplace adds a romantic touch to one guest room. The large brick courtyard boasts Victorian lighting and gardens. An elegant breakfast is served outside on the enclosed porch or in the formal dining room. The innkeepers offer special Valentine's Day packages.

Innkeeper(s): Bill & Linda Horn.

Rates:$85-90. MC VISA. Full Bkfst. Gourmet Brkfst. 4 rooms.

Fireplaces. Beds:KQ. Conference Rm. AC in room. Golf. Tennis. Bicycling. Skiing. Spa. Swimming. Horseback riding. Fishing.

Seen in: *Canton Repository, Akron Beacon Journal, Times Reporter, Standard Free Press.*

Contact: Linda Horn. Certificate may be used: Nov. 1-May 1, Sunday-Thursday.

"Gracious hospitality, tranquil."

Granville

Granville Manor
4058 Columbus Rd
Granville 43023
(614)587-4677

1850. Twelve acres surround this Italian-style home. Depending on the time of year you visit, you may want to enjoy one of the late-Sunday afternoon Concerts-on-the-Green, picking apples at a nearby orchard, spending time at the antiques fair, or taking the walking tour of historic homes. Narrowly escaping the bulldozer, the Granville Manor is now being restored room by room. The parlor boasts a polished-oak floor and an oak and marble fireplace. Butter rum cake, poppy seed muffins and fresh, warm cherry cobbler are popular breakfast items.

Innkeeper(s): Marc & Sharon Gubkin.

Rates:$50-60. MC VISA. ContPlus Bkfst. 3 rooms. Beds:QDT. AC in room. Spa.

Contact: Marc Gubkin. Certificate may be used: Anytime, subject to availability except the months of May, June, August, September and October.

Hiram

The Lily Ponds B&B
6720 Wakefield Rd, PO Box 322
Hiram 44234
(216)569-3222 (800)325-5087
Fax:(216)569-3223

1950. This homestay is located on 22 acres of woodland dotted with clumps of rhododendron and mountain laurel. There are two large ponds and an old stone bridge. Your hostess works with a tour company and has traveled around the world. The inn's decor includes her collections of Eskimo art and artifacts and a variety of antiques. Pecan waffles served with locally harvested maple syrup are a favorite breakfast. Guests enjoy borrowing the canoe or hiking the inn's trails.

Innkeeper(s): Marilane Spencer.

Rates:$55-65. Full Bkfst. 3 rooms. Beds:KQT. Phone, AC in room. Bicycling. Skiing. Fishing.

Seen in: *Record-Courier, Record-News.*

Contact: Marilane Spencer. Certificate may be used: Weekdays year-round (no Friday or Saturday).

"We felt like we were staying with friends from the very start."

Kelleys Island

Eagles Nest
PO Box 762, Cameron Rd
Kelleys Island 43438
(419)746-2708

1895. Built one hundred years ago, this rustic country house is surrounded by woodland. A lacy country decor is spiced with quilts, skylights, a wood-

beamed bedroom and sun decks off the back. There is one room in the main house and the guest house has a suite and two efficiency rooms, all with accommodations for light cooking. A full breakfast is served on the screened porch in the main house. Often, fresh herb omelets are created with herbs gleaned from the innkeeper's garden.

Innkeeper(s): Mark & Robin Volz.

Rates:$70-85. MC VISA DS. Full Bkfst. 4 rooms. Beds:Q. AC, Refrig. in room. Bicycling. Swimming. Fishing.

Contact: Robin Volz. Certificate may be used: Sunday-Thursday, May, June, September, October, November. Buy one night-get one night free.

The Inn on Kelleys Island
Box 11
Kelleys Island 43438
(419)746-2258

1876. With a private deck on the shore of Lake Erie, this waterfront Victorian offers an acre of grounds. Built by the innkeeer's ancestor, Captain Frank Hamilton, the house features a black marble fireplace and a porch with a spectacular Lake Erie view. The Pilot House is a room with large windows looking out to the lake. The inn is close to the ferry and downtown with restaurants, taverns and shops.

Innkeeper(s): Patrick & Lori Hayes.

Rates:$65-85. Cont. Bkfst. 4 rooms. 4 with shared baths. Bicycling. Swimming. Fishing.

Contact: Lori Hayes. Certificate may be used: Sunday through Thursday during the months of May, June, September, October and November, excluding holidays.

Laurelville

Hocking House B&B
18596 Laurel St, Box 118
Laurelville 43135
(614)332-1655 (800)477-1541

1880. A wide wraparound front porch filled with flowers, swings and rockers greet guests at this farmhouse. Furnished with antique dressers, guest rooms

are accented with old and new quilts, some created by Amish neighbors. The nearby Amish settlement provides shops for baskets, aprons and seasonal produce. Rock climbing, wildflower walks, canoeing and picnicking are popular in the area as well as scenic drives through the countryside.

Innkeeper(s): Jim & Sue Maxwell.

Rates:$45-65. MC VISA. Full Bkfst. 4 rooms. Beds:DT. AC in room. Handicap access. Swimming.

Contact: Susan Maxwell. Certificate may be used: November - May, Sunday - Thursday.

Lexington

The White Fence Inn
8842 Denman Rd
Lexington 44904
(419)884-2356

1895. This picturesque Ohio farm is set on 73 acres of pasture and farmland. The inn is decorated in a

country style, and each guest room has a theme such as the Victorian Room, the Amish Room and the Primitive Room. Giant willow trees hang from a small vineyard and over a creek that meanders through the property. The innkeepers harvest Concord grapes to make grape juice for their guests. Tom Sawyer-style bamboo fishing poles are available for those who want to angle bass or bluegill from the fish pond. Sleigh and hay rides are available.

Innkeeper(s): Bill & Ellen Hiser.

Rates:$64-95. Full Bkfst. 6 rooms. 2 with shared baths. Fireplaces. Beds:KQT. Refrig. in room. Farm. Skiing. Handicap access. Fishing.

Seen in: *Adventure Road, Mainstream, Mansfield News Journal.*

Contact: William Hiser. Certificate may be used: All year, Sunday - Thursday. No major holidays.

"I feel very lucky to have found a little corner of heaven in Lexington."

Logan

The Inn at Cedar Falls
21190 State Rt 374
Logan 43138
(614)385-7489

1820. This barn-style inn was constructed in 1987 on 80 acres adjacent to Hocking State Park and a half mile from the waterfalls. The kitchen and din-

ing room is in a 19th-century log house with a wood-burning stove, plank floor and 18-inch-wide logs. Accommodations in the new barn building are simple and comfortable, each furnished with antiques. Verandas provide sweeping views of woodland and meadow. The grounds include gardens for the inn's gourmet dinners, and animals that have been spotted include mink, weasel, red fox, wild turkey and whitetail deer.

Innkeeper(s): Ellen Grinsfelder.

Rates:$75-150. MC VISA. Full Bkfst. Gourmet Brkfst, Lunch, Dinner. Picnic lunches. 12 rooms. Fireplaces. Beds:QT. Conference Rm. AC, Refrig. in room. Handicap access. Fishing.

Seen in: *The Post.*

Contact: Ellen Grinsfelder. Certificate may be used: Sunday through Thursday, December through April only.

"Very peaceful, relaxing and friendly. Couldn't be nicer."

Louisville

The Mainstay B&B
1320 E Main St
Louisville 44641
(216)875-1021

1886. Built by a Civil War veteran, this Victorian still has the original fish scale on its gables, and inside, it features carved-oak woodwork and oak doors. Guests are treated to a complimentary basket of fruit and cheese in their air-conditioned rooms. Outside are flower gardens with birdbaths and a water fountain. This is a great stop in the middle of a long trip because laundry facilities are available to guests. Nearby colleges are Malone, Walsh, Mount Union and Kent State University.

Innkeeper(s): Joseph & Mary Shurilla.

Rates:$50-60. MC VISA. Full Bkfst. Teas. 4 rooms. Beds:QT. TV, Phone, AC, Refrig. in room. Spa.

Contact: Mary Shurilla. Certificate may be used: Sunday through Thursday nights excluding Hall of Fame week (last in July) and major holidays.

Marietta

The Buckley House
332 Front St
Marietta 45750
(614)373-3080

1879. A double veranda accents this gablefront Greek Revival house and provides views of Muskingum Park and river as well as Lookout Point and the "Valley Gem," a traditional Mississippi river boat. Guests are served tea, evening aperitifs and breakfast from the inn's parlor, porches and dining room. Within a five-block area are museums, a mound cemetery, the W.P. Snyder Jr. Sternwheeler, boat rides, trolley tours and shops and restaurants.

Innkeeper(s): Alf & Dell Nicholas.

Rates:$60-70. MC VISA DS. ContPlus Bkfst. 3 rooms. Beds:QD. Phone,

AC in room. Bicycling. Swimming. Fishing.

Contact: Dell Nicholas. Certificate may be used: Nov. 1 through March 31. Based on availability.

Marion

Olde Towne Manor
245 St James St
Marion 43302
(614)382-2402

1920. This beautiful stone house, located in the heart of Marion's historic district, won Marion's most attractive building award in 1990. The home offers bookworms the chance to browse through a 1,000-volume library. A gazebo or sauna are ideal settings for relaxation. The nearby home of President Warren G. Harding and the Harding Memorial will attract history buffs. In August, the town hosts the U.S. Open Drum and Bugle Corps National Championships, and the Marion Popcorn Festival is a unique attraction the weekend after Labor Day.

Innkeeper(s): Mary-Louisa Rimbach.

Rates:$55-65. MC VISA. Full Bkfst. 4 rooms. Beds:QDT. AC in room. Golf. Tennis. Sauna. Swimming. Horseback riding. Fishing.

Contact: Mary-Louisa Rimbach. Certificate may be used: Anytime except Dec. 24 and 25, 1994 and 1995.

Martins Ferry

Mulberry Inn B&B
53 N 4th St
Martins Ferry 43935
(614)633-6058

1868. The Roosevelt Room in this Victorian inn once housed Eleanor Roosevelt during a "Bond Drive." Mrs. Blackford, goddaughter of Jefferson Davis, was the hostess during that time and was well known for her hospitality during the Depression. The inn is decorated with country antiques and quilts. All the rooms are air-conditioned.

Innkeeper(s): Charles & Shirley Probst.

Rates:$45. MC VISA DS. Full Bkfst. Evening snacks. 4 rooms. 4 with shared baths. Beds:QDT. AC in room. Golf. Tennis. Skiing. Swimming. Fishing.

Contact: Shirley Probst. Certificate may be used: Anytime January through March. April through December Sunday through Thursday.

Miamisburg

English Manor B&B
505 E Linden Ave
Miamisburg 45342
(513)866-2288 (800)676-9456

1924. This is a beautiful English Tudor mansion situated on a tree-lined street of Victorian homes. Well-chosen antiques combined with the innkeepers' personal heirlooms added to the inn's polished floors, sparkling leaded- and stained-glass windows and shining silver, make this an elegant retreat. Breakfast is served in the formal dining room or by the fireplace in your room, and in the afternoon, tea is served. Fine restaurants, a waterpark, baseball and theater are close by, as is The River Corridor bikeway on the banks of the Great Miami River.
Innkeeper(s): Marilyn & Jack DiDrichson.

Rates:$65-75. MC VISA AX DC DS. Full Bkfst. AP available. 8 rooms. 5 with shared baths. Beds:KQT. Conference Rm. Phone, AC in room. Bicycling. Swimming. Fishing.

Contact: Jack DiDrichson. Certificate may be used: Sunday through Thursday.

Mount Gilead

Holiday House
88 E High St
Mount Gilead 43338
(419)947-8804

1895. Located in the village of Mount Gilead, Holiday House is just a few blocks from the downtown area with its assortment of antique and specialty shops. The inn is adorned with cut glass windows and doors, intricate oak woodwork, two impressive fireplace mantles and pocket doors. First-level parquet floors with fancy borders add to the elegance of the mansion. The innkeepers are happy to share their experience and knowledge in restoring their Victorian mansion.
Innkeeper(s): Ralph & Mary Kay Robins

Rates:$60. ContPlus Bkfst. Evening snacks. 4 rooms. 1 with shared bath. Beds:KQT. Phone, AC in room. Skiing. Fishing.

Contact: Mary Kay Robins. Certificate may be used: Jan. 1 through April 15.

Mount Vernon

The Russell-Cooper House
115 E Gambier St
Mount Vernon 43050
(614)397-8638

1829. Dr. John Russell and his son-in-law Colonel Cooper modeled a simple brick Federal house into a unique Victorian. Its sister structure is the

Wedding Cake House of Kennebunk, Maine. There is a hand-painted plaster ceiling in the ballroom and a collection of Civil War items and antique medical devices. Woodwork is of cherry, maple and walnut, and there are etched and stained-glass windows. Hal Holbrook called the town America's Hometown.
Innkeeper(s): Tim & Maureen Tyler.

Rates:$45-75. MC VISA AX. Full Bkfst. Gourmet Brkfst. Teas. 6 rooms. Fireplaces. Beds:QDT. Conference Rm. AC in room. Golf. Skiing. Swimming. Fishing.

Seen in: *Ohio Business, Victorian Homes, Columbus Monthly, Innsider, Country, Americana, Columbus Dispatch.*

Contact: Maureen Tyler. Certificate may be used: Sunday - Thursday.

"A salute to the preservation of American history and culture. Most hospitable owners!"

Newark

Pitzer-Cooper House B&B
6019 White Chapel Rd SE
Newark 43056
(614)323-2680 (800)833-9536

1858. In the National Register, this historic farmhouse boasts an elegant entry and a two-story veranda overlooking lawns and perennial and herb gardens. A common room has views of the shaded pond, and there is a music room with a baby grand piano. Borrow the inn's bikes and visit the famed Dawes Arboretum a mile away. Also close by are the Olde Mill Velvet Ice Cream factory and parlor, bike trails and Blackhand Gorge Nature Preserve. There are nine museums and several fairs and festivals in the county.

Innkeeper(s): Joe & Teresa Cooper.

Rates:$55. Full Bkfst. 2 rooms. 2 with shared baths. Beds:D. Phone, AC, Refrig. in room. Bicycling. Skiing. Swimming. Fishing.

Contact: Teresa Cooper. Certificate may be used: Anytime, year-round, through Dec. 31, 1995.

Norwalk

Boos Family Inn B&B

5054 St Rt 601
Norwalk 44857
(419)668-6257 Fax:(419)668-7722

1860. To see the modern additions to this former farm home, you would not at first realize that parts of this home date back to the mid-1800s. There are two acres of flowers, lawns and trees. Five minutes away is Thomas Edison's home, Ohio's largest outlet mall and Cedar Point.

Innkeeper(s): Don & Mary Boos.

Rates:$45-60. MC VISA DS. ContPlus Bkfst. 4 rooms. Beds:QD. TV, Phone, AC, Refrig. in room. Farm. Swimming. Fishing.

Contact: Mary Boos. Certificate may be used: September through May or Monday through Thursday, June, July, August.

Orrville

Grandma's House B&B

5598 Chippewa Rd
Orrville 44667
(216)682-5112

1860. Wheat and corn fields surround this friendly brick farmhouse. It has been in the same family for the last 60 years. The inn is furnished with antique bedsteads, homemade quilts and a collection of old rolling pins. An old-fashioned porch entices guests to relax, and behind the house is a 16-acre wooded hillside with walking paths. Marilyn specializes in hot cinnamon rolls and home-baked breads.

Innkeeper(s): Marilyn & Dave Farver.

Rates:$55-90. ContPlus Bkfst. 5 rooms. 2 with shared baths. Beds:QT. Farm. Skiing. Handicap access.

Seen in: *Wooster Daily Record, Northeast Ohio Avenues.*

Contact: Marilyn Farver. Certificate may be used: Sunday through Thursday - all year. Anytime from November through April.

"What a delight. We will definitely be back. Perfect."

Painesville

Rider's 1812 Inn

792 Mentor Ave
Painesville 44077
(216)354-8200 (800)354-8200

1812. In the days when this inn and tavern served the frontier Western Reserve, it could provide lodging and meals for more than 100 overnight guests. Restored in 1988, the pub features an original fireplace and wavy window panes. Most of the inn's floors are rare, long-needle pine. A passageway in the cellar is said to have been part of the Underground Railroad. An English-style restaurant is also on the premises. Guest rooms are furnished with antiques. Breakfast in bed is the option of choice.

Innkeeper(s): Elaine Crane & Judge Gary Herman.

Rates:$70-90. MC VISA AX DS. ContPlus Bkfst. Gourmet Dinner. Picnic lunches. Teas. 8 rooms. Beds:KQT. Conference Rm. TV, Phone, AC, Refrig. in room. Skiing. Swimming. Fishing.

Seen in: *Business Review, News-Herald.*

Contact: Elaine Crane. Certificate may be used: Anytime Sunday through Friday night; no Saturdays or holidays.

"The hospitality of yourself and your employees is unbeatable, so personal yet professional."

Pomeroy

Holly Hill Inn

114 Butternut Ave
Pomeroy 45769-1202
(614)992-5657

1836. This gracious clapboard inn with its many shuttered windows is shaded by giant holly trees. Original window panes of blown glass remain, as well as wide-board floors, mantels and fireplaces. The family's antique collection includes a crocheted canopy bed in the Honeymoon Room overlooking a working fireplace. Dozens of antique quilts are displayed and for sale. Guests are invited to borrow an antique bike to ride through the countryside.

Innkeeper(s): John, Marc & Marilyn Fultz.

Rates:$59-79. MC VISA DS. Full Bkfst. 4 rooms. 4 with shared baths. Fireplaces. Beds:QT. Conference Rm. TV, Phone in room. Bicycling. Swimming. Fishing.

Seen in: *Sunday Times-Sentinel.*

Contact: J. Marcus Fultz. Certificate may be used: Anytime except special weekends.

"Your inn is so beautiful, and it has so much historic charm."

Put-in-Bay

Fether B&B
1539 Langram Rd
Put-in-Bay 43456
(419)285-5511

1870. English country gardens of the Victorian period are featured on the three acres that surround this Queen Anne Victorian. When the hammock is already occupied, the wraparound porch filled with rocking chairs and a swing affords wonderful views of Lake Erie. More active times may find you at the volleyball/badminton net or you may wish to follow the nature trail through the inn's wooded area.
Innkeeper(s): Fred & Eleanor Fether.
Rates:$60-85. MC VISA DS. Full Bkfst. 5 rooms. 4 with shared baths. Beds:KQT. Farm. Golf. Tennis. Bicycling. Swimming. Fishing.
Contact: Eleanor Fether. Certificate may be used: Sunday through Thursday, April through October.

Ripley

Baird House B&B
201 N Second St
Ripley 45167
(513)392-4918

1825. A lacy wrought-iron porch and balcony decorate the front facade of this historic house, while the second-floor porch at the rear offers views of the Ohio River, 500 feet away. There are nine marble fireplaces and an enormous chandelier in the parlor. A full breakfast is served.
Innkeeper(s): Glenn & Patricia Kittle.
Rates:$60-85. Full Bkfst. Gourmet Brkfst. Teas. Evening snacks. 3 rooms. 2 with shared baths. Fireplaces. Beds:KDT. Phone, AC in room. Golf. Tennis. Swimming.
Seen in: *Ohio Magazine, Country Inn Cookbook.*
Contact: Patricia Kittle. Certificate may be used: Monday through Thursday - year-round - 1994 and 1995.

"Anxious to return."

Saint Clairsville

My Father's House B&B
173 S Marietta St
Saint Clairsville 43950
(614)695-5440

1810. Ohio's first senator, Benjamin Ruggles, built this Federal home. Decorated with both antiques and contemporary pieces, the house's living room features an open fireplace. Guest rooms are air-conditioned. Several museums are nearby along with a covered bridge, the Great Western School House and Dysart Woods.
Innkeeper(s): Mark & Polly Loy.
Rates:$50-55. MC VISA AX DS. ContPlus Bkfst. 4 rooms. Beds:QT. TV, Phone, AC in room. Skiing. Fishing.
Contact: Polly Loy. Certificate may be used: January - April.

Sandusky

The 1890 Queen Anne B&B
714 Wayne St
Sandusky 44870
(419)626-0391

1890. Built by John T. Mack, publisher of the city's first newspaper, the Queen Anne Bed & Breakfast is an exquisitely maintained, historical home which

opened its doors to travelers in the summer of 1991. Only seven blocks away is Sandusky Bay, where travelers can book passages on local ferries to Kelleys Island, the Bass Islands, or as far away as Canada's Pelee Island. Sandusky is most popular for its summertime activities, including the largest tour destination in Ohio, Cedar Point Amusement Park. It alone attracts nearly five million visitors to the north coast each summer.
Innkeeper(s): Robert & Joan Kromer.
Rates:$50-75. MC VISA DS. ContPlus Bkfst. 3 rooms. 1 with shared bath. Beds:K. AC in room. Swimming. Fishing.
Contact: Joan Kromer. Certificate may be used: January, February, March and April.

Wagner's 1844 Inn
230 E Washington St
Sandusky 44870
(419)626-1726

1844. This inn was originally constructed as a log cabin. Additions and renovations were made, and the house evolved into an Italianate-style accented with brackets under the eaves and black shutters on the second-story windows. A wrought-iron fence frames the house, and there are ornate wrought-iron porch rails. A billiard room and screened-in porch are available to guests. The ferry to Cedar Point and Kelleys Island is within walking distance.

Innkeeper(s): Walt & Barbara Wagner.

Rates:$50-80. MC VISA DS. ContPlus Bkfst. 3 rooms. Fireplaces. Beds:QD. AC in room. Swimming. Fishing.

Seen in: *Lorain Journal.*

Contact: Barbara Wagner. Certificate may be used: Nov. 1-May 1.

"This B&B rates in our Top 10."

Sharon Center

Hart & Mather B&B

1343 Sharon-Copley Rd, PO 93
Sharon Center 44274
(216)239-2801 (800)352-2584

1840. Listed in the National Register, this Greek Revival house is furnished with handsome antiques and reproductions. Ask for the Sharon Center Suite with its own fireplace, sitting room and mahogany double bed. Or try Mr. Hart's Room, with a balcony overlooking the village green. The Hart & Mather Gift Shop and Cake Shop are on the premises. A continental breakfast is served or a full breakfast is available by special arrangement. (The pecan Belgian waffles are favorites.) The innkeepers own Belgian Draft horses, and you can treat yourself to a fabulous ride in a beautiful Cinderella-like white carriage.

Innkeeper(s): T. T. Thompson.

Rates:$69-119. MC VISA AX DS. Full Bkfst. 4 rooms. Fireplaces. Beds:QD. TV, AC, Refrig. in room. Fishing.

Contact: Deborah Troy. Certificate may be used: Sunday-Thursday only. Anytime in 1994 or 1995.

Smithville

The Smithville B&B

171 W Main St, PO Box 142
Smithville 44677
(216)669-3333 (800)869-6425

1850. Situated in the heart of the village, this historic brick house is owned by the founders of "Cat's Meow" collectibles of historic villages. Each guest room features a different series of the villages. Ask for the balcony suite and you'll enjoy a romantic room that overlooks the town. The inn's favorite spot is the dining room with beamed ceilings, cherry wood walls and floor, and a handsome chande-

lier. The owners grow blueberries on their farm a few miles away, and in summer, blueberry muffins and waffles are often served.

Innkeeper(s): Lori Kubik.

Rates:$52-62. MC VISA DS. Full Bkfst. 5 rooms. Beds:QT. TV, AC, Refrig. in room.

Contact: Robert Welker. Certificate may be used: October through May, not available June through September.

Tiffin

Zelkova Inn

2348 S CR#19
Tiffin 44883
(419)447-4043

1952. Zelkova trees (Japanese elms) greet you as you drive up to the entrance of this 7,500-square-foot mansion set on 37 acres. Designed by local architect Ned Porter and built as a residence for Dr. William Funderburg, the brick mansion has outdoor fountains, a large deck, a swimming pool and is nestled comfortably among trees, gardens and extensive landscaping. The back of the inn overlooks the woods with nature trails leading down to Honey Creek. Guests can enjoy canoeing on this tributary to the Sandusky River. The bedrooms are named after families who also had their homes designed by Ned Porter. Handmade quilts cover the beds. Decor throughout is in the French country-style.

Innkeeper(s): Michael Pinkston.

Rates:$65-95. MC VISA DS. Full Bkfst. MAP available. Gourmet Brkfst, Lunch, Dinner. Picnic lunches. Teas. Evening snacks. 4 rooms. Beds:KQT. Conference Rm. Phone, AC in room. Bicycling. Swimming.

Seen in: *Courier, Advertiser Tribune.*

Contact: Michael Pinkston. Certificate may be used: October 1, 1994 through June 30, 1995.

"The food was wonderful and plentiful, and the beds are great!!"

Urbana

Northern Plantation B&B

3421 E Route 296
Urbana 43078
(513)652-1782 (800)652-1782

1913. This Victorian farmhouse, located on 100 acres, is occupied by fourth-generation family members. (Marsha's father was born in the downstairs bedroom in 1914.) The Homestead Library is decorated traditionally and has a handsome fireplace, while the dining room features a dining set and a china cabinet made by the innkeeper's great-grandfather. Most of the guest rooms have canopy beds. A large country breakfast is served. On the property is a fishing pond, corn fields, soybeans and woods with a creek. Nearby are Ohio Caverns and Indian Lake.

Innkeeper(s): Mary Carol Scott.

Rates:$65-90. MC VISA DS. Full Bkfst. 4 rooms. 3 with shared baths. Beds:KD. Farm. Skiing. Handicap access. Fishing.

Contact: Marsha Martin. Certificate may be used: Anytime.

West Liberty

Liberty House B&B

208 N Detroit St, US Rt 68
West Liberty 43357-0673
(513)465-1101 (800)437-8109
Fax:(513)465-9880

1906. Flower gardens and a welcoming wraparound veranda with an old-fashioned swing beckon guests to this folk Victorian inn. There are patterned oak floors and woodwork, and rooms are furnished with Oriental rugs and antiques. The guest room beds are adorned with fine linens and both antique and new quilts. A gracious breakfast is served and candlelight dinners are available if you reserve ahead. Within walking distance is Mad River trout fishing, craft and antique shops, a general store and restaurants.

Innkeeper(s): Russ & Sue Peterson.

Rates:$50-65. MC VISA DS. Full Bkfst. 3 rooms. Beds:QDT. AC in room.

Contact: Sue Peterson. Certificate may be used: Oct. 1 through March 1.

Wilmington

Cedar Hill B&B in the Woods

4003 St, Rt 73W
Wilmington 45177
(513)383-2525

1992. The guest rooms in the second floor of this rustic log carriage house overlook the trees of its 10 wooded acres. The innkeeper is the owner of Cedar Hill Design, a country and Shaker needlework company. Many of her works are featured throughout the inn and guests are welcome to tour her studio on the premises. A spacious common room features a limestone fireplace with a large open hearth. Trails meander through the woods where you may spot deer, raccoon and other wildlife. Hearty breakfast menus might include Parmesan Baked Eggs, steamed asparagus and smoked Amish bacon. The inn is 10 minutes from Waynesville, the antique capital of Ohio. David Smith's Shaker-design studio is nearby.

Innkeeper(s): Linda & Jim Higgins.

Rates:$65. MC VISA. Full Bkfst. Gourmet Brkfst. Evening snacks. 2 rooms. Beds:Q. AC in room. Golf. Swimming. Fishing.

Contact: Linda Higgins. Certificate may be used: Sunday through Thursday. Friday/Saturday if rooms are available.

Oklahoma

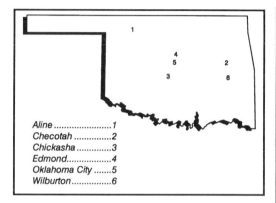

Aline

Heritage Manor
RR 3, Box 33
Aline 73716
(405)463-2563

1903. A wonderful way to experience Oklahoma history is to stay at the Heritage Manor, two turn-of-the-century restored homes. One is an American Four-Square house and the other, a glorified Arts-and-Crafts-style home. Antiques were gathered from area pioneer homes and include an Edison Victrola Morning Glory Horn and a cathedral pump organ. Antique sofas and English leather chairs fill the sitting room. Mannequins dressed in pioneer clothing add to the decor. There are several fireplaces, and a widow's walk tops the main house.

Innkeeper(s): A.J. & Carolyn Rexroat.

Rates:$50. Full Bkfst. Gourmet Dinner. Teas. 4 rooms. 4 with shared baths. Beds:D. Conference Rm. Phone, AC in room. Farm. Handicap access. Spa. Swimming. Fishing.

Seen in: *Country, Enid Morning News, Daily Oklahoman.*

Contact: Carolyn Rexroat. Certificate may be used: Anytime available.

Checotah

Sharpe House
301 NW 2nd
Checotah 74426
(918)473-2832

1911. Built on land originally bought from a Creek Indian, this Southern plantation-style inn was a teacherage—the rooming house for single female teachers. It is furnished with heirlooms from the innkeepers' families and hand-crafted accessories. The look of the house is antebellum, but the specialty of the kitchen is Mexican cuisine. Family-style evening meals are available upon request. Checotah is located at the junction of I-40 and U.S. 69. This makes it the ideal base for your day trips of exploration or recreation in Green Country.

Innkeeper(s): Kay Kindt & Armando Corral.

Rates:$50. Full Bkfst. EP. Gourmet Brkfst. Evening snacks. 3 rooms. TV, AC in room. Swimming. Fishing.

Contact: Kay Kindt. Certificate may be used: Anytime.

Chickasha

Campbell-Richison House B&B
1428 Kansas
Chickasha 73018
(405)222-1754

1909. Upon entering this prairie-style home, guests will notice a spacious entryway with a gracious stairway ascending to the second-floor guest rooms. The front parlor is a wonderful spot for relaxing, reading or just soaking up the history of the home. The dining room has a stained-glass window that gives off a kaleidoscope of beautiful colors when the morning sun shines through. A spacious yard encompasses one-quarter of a city block and has large shade trees that can be enjoyed on a swing or from the wicker-lined porch.

Innkeeper(s): David & Kami Ratcliff.

Rates:$30-55. ContPlus Bkfst. Teas. 3 rooms. 2 with shared baths.

Beds:T. Phone, AC, Refrig. in room.

Contact: David Ratcliff. Certificate may be used: Anytime as space available.

Edmond

The Arcadian Inn B&B
328 E First St
Edmond 73034
(405)348-6347 (800)299-6347

1908. Unwind in the garden spa of this Victorian inn or on the wraparound porch to enjoy the Oklahoma breeze. Breakfast may be served privately in your suite or in the dining room flooded with morning sunlight, beneath the ceiling paintings of angels and Christ done by a local artisan. Located next to the University of Central Oklahoma, the inn is four blocks from downtown antique shopping. Guests will enjoy the private baths with Jacuzzis and clawfoot tubs.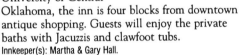

Innkeeper(s): Martha & Gary Hall.

Rates:$65-120. MC VISA AX DS. Full Bkfst. Gourmet Dinner. 5 rooms. Fireplaces. Beds:KQT. Phone, AC in room. Golf. Tennis. Spa. Swimming. Fishing.

Seen in: *Daily Oklahoman, Antique Traveler Newspaper.*

Contact: Martha Hall. Certificate may be used: Sunday - Thursday, excluding holidays.

Oklahoma City

The Grandison
1841 NW 15th
Oklahoma City 73106
(405)521-0011 (800)240-4667

1912. This brick and shingled three-story house is shaded by pecan, apple and fig trees. You'll find a pond and gazebo among the lawns and gardens. The building's original Belgian stained glass remains, and the decor is an airy country Victorian. The bridal suite includes a working fireplace, white lace curtains and a clawfoot tub.

Innkeeper(s): Bob & Claudia Wright.

Rates:$55-125. MC VISA AX DS. Full Bkfst. Evening snacks. 5 rooms. Fireplaces. Beds:QD. Phone, AC, Refrig. in room.

Seen in: *The Daily Oklahoman, Oklahoma Pride.*

Contact: Claudia Wright. Certificate may be used: Sunday through Thursday.

"Like going home to Grandma's!"

Willow Way B&B
27 Oakwood Dr
Oklahoma City 73121
(405)427-2133 Fax:(405)427-8907

1950. Each unique suite of this Tudor-style inn boasts rich colors and luxurious linens. Guests will find an eclectic blending of florals, horses and folk art among the pieces displayed. Birds, squirrels, an occasional rooster's crow and regular flights of geese and ducks lend to the pastoral feeling at Willow Way. The innkeepers are long-time residents of Oklahoma City and will be happy to give you information on attractions, theater, art, restaurants and shops.

Innkeeper(s): Lionel & Johnita Turner.

Rates:$60-80. MC VISA. Full Bkfst. 5 rooms. 2 with shared baths. Beds:Q. Phone, AC in room.

Contact: Johnita Turner. Certificate may be used: Sunday through Thursday.

Wilburton

The Dome House
315 E Main
Wilburton 74578
(918)465-0092

1908. An area landmark since it was built, the Victorian inn's unique feature is its distinctive dome-topped, two-story turret. A sitting area in the turret and wide porches invite guests to relax and remember a simpler time. A parlor where guests can meet and enjoy conversation includes a fireplace. Situated in the heart of the beautiful Kiamichi Mountains, the inn is centrally located to a wide variety of outdoor activites. The Court House, Federal Building, post office and restaurants are all within walking distance.

Innkeeper(s): Raymon & LaVerne McFerran.

Rates:$45-75. ContPlus Bkfst. Teas. 3 rooms. Beds:QDT. TV, Phone, AC, Refrig. in room. Bicycling. Swimming. Fishing.

Contact: LaVerne McFerran. Certificate may be used: Anytime rooms are available, July 1, 1994 - Dec. 31, 1995.

Oregon

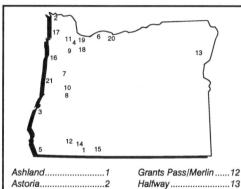

Ashland

Ashland's Victory House
271 Beach St
Ashland 97250
(503)488-4428

1940. The era of the '40s provides the theme for this inn, run by a former college professor. Furnishings include eclectic collections from the era including Depression glass. Rooms are named after World War II leaders such as Winston, Eleanor, and Harry. FDR's studio features a kitchenette and has a queen bed and backyard view. Your host is an expert on the area's activities and inn bicycles and picnic baskets await your excursions.
Innkeeper(s): Dale Swire.
Rates:$59-85. Full Bkfst. 5 rooms. Beds:KQT. TV, AC in room. Golf. Tennis. Bicycling. Skiing. Handicap access. Spa. Swimming. Horseback riding. Fishing.
Contact: Dale Swire. Certificate may be used: Exclude June through September and holidays.

Buckhorn Springs
2200 Buckhorn Springs Rd
Ashland 97520
(503)488-2200

1891. Located on 120 secluded acres in a mountain valley 12 miles east of Ashland, Buckhorn Springs is a newly renovated resort. In the National Register, it was once a sacred healing site for Modoc, Takilma, Rogue and Klamath Indians. At the turn of the century it became a health spa popular for its mineral spring waters. Four restored cabins are located beside a bubbling stream, Emigrant Creek. Each guest room in the lodge is decorated in a different era important to the history of Buckhorn and each has a clawfoot tub outfitted with a third spigot which pipes in hot mineral bath waters.
Innkeeper(s): Bruce & Leslie Sargent.
Rates:$45-100. MC VISA DS. Full Bkfst. Gourmet Dinner. Picnic lunches. Teas. 16 rooms. 9 with shared baths. Beds:KQT. Conference Rm. Refrig. in room. Skiing. Spa. Swimming. Fishing.
Seen in: *Ashland Daily Tidings, Medford Mail Tribune, Sunset.*
Contact: Bruce Sargent. Certificate may be used: Anytime except weekends June through September, excluding holidays.

"A tremendous addition to the usable historic sites in this area."

Chanticleer B&B Inn
120 Gresham St
Ashland 97520
(503)482-1919 Fax:(503)482-1919

1920. This gray clapboard, Craftsman-style house has been totally renovated and several rooms added. The inn is light and airy and decorated with antiques. Special features include the open hearth fireplace and bricked patio garden.
Innkeeper(s): Jean Penney.
Rates:$90-155. MC VISA. Full Bkfst. Gourmet Brkfst. 6 rooms. Beds:QT. Phone, AC in room. Skiing. Swimming. Fishing.
Seen in: *Country Home, Pacific Northwest.*
Contact: Pebby Kuan. Certificate may be used: Nov. 1 - March 31.

"Chanticleer has set the standard by which all others will be judged."

Iris Inn

59 Manzanita St
Ashland 97520
(503)488-2286

1905. The Iris inn is a restored Victorian set on a large flower-filled yard. It features simple American country antiques. The upstairs guest rooms have views of the valley and mountains. Evening sips of wine often are taken out on the large deck overlooking a rose garden. Breakfast boasts an elegant presentation with dishes such as buttermilk scones and peaches and cream French toast.

Innkeeper(s): Vicki Lamb.

Rates:$60-92. MC VISA. Gourmet Brkfst. 5 rooms. Beds:QDT. AC in room. Golf. Tennis. Skiing. Swimming. Horseback riding. Fishing.

Contact: Vicki Lamb. Certificate may be used: Sunday - Thursday, March, April, May; Any night, November, December, January, February.

"It's like returning to home to be at the Iris Inn."

Mt. Ashland Inn

550 Mt Ashland Rd
Ashland 97520
(503)482-8707

1987. Elaine and Jerry Shanafelt built their log lodge with 300 cedar trees harvested from their 160-acre fir and cedar forest. Situated a mile high on a mountain ridge, this handsome lodge provides a unique romantic getaway when visiting the Shakespeare Festival. The inn's parlor is warmed with a fabulously crafted stone fireplace. Ask for the honeymoon suite to enjoy a Jacuzzi for two and a view of Mount McLoughlin. Lowfat delectables are a speciality for breakfast. Guests may hike along the Pacific Crest Trail that runs through the property. Downhill skiing is just up the road.

Innkeeper(s): Elaine & Jerry Shanafelt.

Rates:$77-130. MC VISA. Full Bkfst. 5 rooms. Beds:KQT. Conference Rm. Refrig. in room. Skiing. Spa. Swimming. Fishing.

Seen in: *Pacific Northwest, Edward Carter's Travels, Snow Country, Oregon, Glamour, Travel and Leisure.*

Contact: Elaine Shanafelt. Certificate may be used: Sunday through Thursday, Oct. 16, 1994 through June 8, 1995 and Oct. 15-Dec. 21, 1995, excluding all holiday periods.

"The romantic atmosphere and special personal touches you've provided made our stay doubly enjoyable."

Oak Hill Country B&B

2190 Siskiyou Blvd
Ashland 97520
(503)482-1554

1910. Decorated with hints of French country, this Craftsman farmhouse has a fine front porch that creates a relaxing spot for enjoying the less crowded

South end of town. A hearty country gourmet breakfast is served family style in the dining room. There are bicycles for exploring the area.

Innkeeper(s): Ron & Tracy Bass.

Rates:$60-90. MC VISA. Full Bkfst. 5 rooms. Beds:Q. TV, AC in room. Bicycling. Skiing. Swimming. Fishing.

Contact: Ron Bass. Certificate may be used: November - April, no holidays.

Pinehurst Inn at Jenny Creek

17250 Hwy 66
Ashland 97520
(503)488-1002

1920. Twenty-four acres surround this former roadhouse, now decorated with cozy country pieces. The dining room features handmade willow highback chairs, lace curtains and tablecloths. Organically raised beef and local produce are served in the dining room. The inn's owners also operate the 1,000-acre Box-R Ranch and you can stay there in one of the four guest houses. You can enjoy riding and trout fishing or plan ahead for a wagon or sleigh ride with the ranch's Belgian draft horses.

Innkeeper(s): Mike & Mary Jo, Dan & Melissa Moloney.

Rates:$64-105. MC VISA. Full Bkfst. Gourmet Dinner. 6 rooms. Beds:KQ. Bicycling. Skiing. Fishing.

Contact: William Moloney. Certificate may be used: Monday through Thursday except holidays.

The Woods House B&B

333 N Main St
Ashland 97520
(503)488-1598 (800)435-8260
Fax:(503)482-7912

1908. Built and occupied for almost 40 years by a prominent Ashland physican, each room of this Craftsman-style inn boasts special detail. Many guest rooms offer canopied beds and skylights. Full breakfasts are served either in the sunny dining room or in the garden under a spreading walnut tree. After breakfast, take a stroll through the half-

acre of terraced, English gardens. Located in the historic district, the inn is four blocks from Ashland's Shakespearean theaters.

Innkeeper(s): Francoise & Lester Roddy.

Rates:$65-110. MC VISA. Full Bkfst. Gourmet Brkfst. 6 rooms. Beds:KQT. AC in room. Bicycling. Skiing. Swimming. Fishing.

Seen in: *The Times.*

Contact: Francoise Roddy. Certificate may be used: November-March, any night, excluding holidays.

"Within this house lies much hospitality, friendship and laughter. What more could a home ask to be?"

Astoria

Grandview B&B
1574 Grand Ave
Astoria 97103
(503)325-5555 (800)488-3250

1896. To fully enjoy its views of the Columbia River, this Victorian house sports both a tower and

a turret. Antiques and white wicker furnishings contribute to the inn's casual, homey feeling. The Meadow Room is particularly appealing to bird lovers with its bird cage, bird books and bird wallpaper. Breakfast, served in the main-floor turret, frequently includes smoked salmon with bagels and cream cheese.

Innkeeper(s): Charleen Maxwell.

Rates:$46-102. MC VISA DS. ContPlus Bkfst. 9 rooms. 3 with shared baths. Beds:QT. Golf. Tennis. Fishing.

Seen in: *Pacific Northwest, Northwest Discoveries, Los Angeles Times.*

Contact: Charleen Maxwell. Certificate may be used: Jan. 1 - May 17 and Nov. 1 - Dec. 31.

"We're still talking about our visit and the wonderful

breakfast you served."

Bandon

Lighthouse B&B
650 Jetty Rd, PO Box 24
Bandon 97411
(503)347-9316

1980. This contemporary redwood house stands alone on an oceanfront jetty across the mouth of the Coquille River. Its splendid setting affords views of surfing seals and the Bandon Lighthouse. Simply furnished rooms include the Sunset View Room overlooking the lighthouse and the Greenhouse Room with a whirlpool for two. Salmon fishing boats, a sternwheeler and sailboarders ply the waters.

Innkeeper(s): Bruce & Linda Sisson.

Rates:$80-100. MC VISA. ContPlus Bkfst. 4 rooms. Fireplaces. Beds:KQ. TV, Phone, Refrig. in room. Golf. Tennis. Spa. Swimming. Horseback riding. Fishing.

Seen in: *Sunset, National Geographic Travel Guide.*

Contact: Bruce Sisson. Certificate may be used: Oct. 20 through June 20. Restricted some weekends and all holidays.

"Thank you for your warm welcome and charming hospitality."

Beaverton

The Yankee Tinker B&B
5480 SW 183rd Ave
Beaverton 97007
(503)649-0932 (800)846-5377

1970. This suburban ranch house is decorated with New England family heirlooms, antiques and country accents. Handmade quilts, flower gardens, and a large deck provide for a comfortable stay 10 miles from Portland, in Washington County's wine country. Peaches and cream French toast and herbed omelets are among the breakfast offerings.

Innkeeper(s): Jan & Ralph Wadleigh.

Rates:$60-70. MC VISA AX DC. Full Bkfst. 3 rooms. 2 with shared baths. Beds:QT. Phone, AC in room.

Contact: Ralph Wadleigh. Certificate may be used: Excluding holidays and special events.

Brookings

Chetco River Inn
21202 High Prairie Rd
Brookings 97415
(503)469-8128 (800)327-2688

1987. Situated on 35 wooded acres and the Chetco River, this modern B&B offers a cedar fishing lodge exterior and a marble- and antique-filled interior. A

collection of crafts, Oriental rugs and leather sofas add to your enjoyment. Because it's 18 miles from Brookings, you may wish to arrange ahead for a dinner. Then you can enjoy the sounds of the rushing river without interruption.

Innkeeper(s): Sandra Brugger.

Rates:$85. MC VISA. Full Bkfst. Gourmet Brkfst. Evening snacks. 3 rooms. Beds:KQT. Swimming. Fishing.

Contact: Sandra Brugger. Certificate may be used: All year except holidays.

South Coast Inn
516 Redwood St
Brookings 97415
(503)469-5557 (800)525-9273
Fax:(503)469-6615

1917. Enjoy panoramic views of the Pacific from two guest rooms at this Craftsman-style inn built by San Francisco architect Bernard Maybeck. All rooms are furnished with antiques, ceiling fans and TVs. A floor-to-ceiling stone fireplace and beamed ceilings make the parlor a great place to gather with friends. There are sun decks, a strolling garden and an indoor hot tub and sauna. Brookings is in the warm "Banana Belt" of the South Coast.

Innkeeper(s): Ken Raith & Keith Pepper.

Rates:$69-89. MC VISA AX DS. Full Bkfst. 4 rooms. Beds:Q. TV in room. Handicap access. Spa. Sauna. Exercise room. Swimming. Fishing.

Contact: Keith Pepper. Certificate may be used: October - May.

Cascade Locks

Shahala at the Locks
1280 NE Forest Ln, PO Box 39
Cascade Locks 97014
(503)374-8222 Fax:(503)374-8328

1960. This brick ranch-style house is situated on a bluff overlooking the Columbia Gorge. Forest and mountain views add to the natural wonders of the setting. Cutting through the inn's 16 acres, Herman Creek rushes to meet the river below. A three-course breakfast is served, featuring jams made from berries grown on the property.

Innkeeper(s): The Carters.

Rates:$50-100. MC VISA. Full Bkfst. 8 rooms. 6 with shared baths. Beds:Q. AC in room. Skiing. Handicap access. Swimming. Fishing.

Contact: Jean Carter. Certificate may be used: Anytime except weekends, July and August.

Coos Bay

The Upper Room Chalet
306 N 8th St
Coos Bay 97420
(503)269-5385

1906. Evergreens and rhododendrons frame this Victorian chalet-style house. It is furnished with country Victorian pieces mingled with family antiques and dolls. The master suite has a clawfoot tub and huge brass bed. Biscuits and gravy, ham, eggs and hashbrowns are served.

Innkeeper(s): Carl & Barbara Solomon.

Rates:$60-70. MC VISA. Full Bkfst. Evening snacks. 5 rooms. 3 with shared baths. Beds:KDT. Swimming. Fishing.

Contact: Barbara Solomon. Certificate may be used: November, 1994-April, 1995.

Corvallis

Harrison House
2310 NW Harrison Blvd
Corvallis 97330
(503)752-6248

1939. In a Dutch Colonial style, this house is adjacent to Oregon State University. The favorite guest room faces west, overlooking a side yard with beds of flowers and a crab apple tree, which in summer, shades an oversized hammock. Family antiques fill the inn and there are four-poster and other antique bedsteads, most topped with down comforters. Dutch Babies (puffed German pancakes filled with fruit) are served with whipped cream at breakfast. Rates:$50-65. MC VISA AX. Full Bkfst. Evening snacks. 4 rooms. 2 with shared baths. Beds:KQD. Conference Rm. TV, Phone in room. Golf. Tennis. Bicycling. Skiing. Swimming. Horseback riding. Fishing.

Contact: Jim Berry. Certificate may be used: Sunday through Thursday.

Cottage Grove

Lea House Inn
433 Pacific Hwy
Cottage Grove 97424
(503)942-5686

1891. Situated on a large lot, this pretty Victorian house has leaded windows, a veranda and a second-story sun porch. The house was built by a photogra-

pher who was also an architect and carpenter, so he fashioned the gables, shingled exterior and handsome stair railings. Antique bedroom sets furnish the guest rooms. English tea is served in the afternoon, and you may want to schedule your covered bridge or vintage train outings around it. If you reserve dinner, you'll be treated to five courses, which may include Veal Scaloppini Edwardo or Cherry Apricot Gingered Chicken.
Innkeeper(s): Michelle Lawhorn.
Rates:$50-65. MC VISA. Full Bkfst. Picnic lunches. Teas. Evening snacks. 3 rooms. 2 with shared baths. Beds:KQT. Bicycling. Swimming. Fishing.
Contact: Michelle Aileen Lawhorn. Certificate may be used: Year-round, July 1, 1994 - Dec. 31, 1995.

Dayton

Wine Country Farm
6855 Breyman Orchards Rd
Dayton 97114
(503)864-3446

1910. Surrounded by vineyards and orchards, Wine Country Farm is an eclectic French house sitting

on a hill overlooking the Cascade Mountain Range. Arabian horses are raised here and five varieties of grapes are grown. Request the master bedroom and you'll enjoy a fireplace. The innkeepers can arrange for a horse-drawn buggy ride and picnic, and you may borrow the inn's bikes for excursions to the area's vineyards. Downtown Portland and the Oregon coast are each an hour away.
Innkeeper(s): Joan Davenport.
Rates:$55-75. 4 rooms. 2 with shared baths. Golf. Tennis. Skiing. Swimming. Horseback riding. Fishing.
Seen in: *Wine Spectator.*
Contact: Joan Davenport. Certificate may be used: Monday through Thursday.

Eugene

Atherton Place, a B&B Inn
690 W Broadway
Eugene 97402
(503)683-2674

1988. Within a few minutes' walk of the City Center Mall, Hult Center and the University of Oregon, Atherton Place is a Dutch Colonial-style home. A library, sun room and sitting room offer cozy places to read. Crown moldings, polished oak floors and built-in cabinets attest to a craftsmanship of former days. Guest rooms have new queen beds and a casual country decor.
Innkeeper(s): Marne Krozek.
Rates:$50-70. Gourmet Brkfst. Teas. Beds:QT. Phone in room. Bicycling. Skiing. Swimming. Fishing.
Contact: Marne Krozek. Certificate may be used: November - May.

Campbell House Inn
252 Pearl St
Eugene 97401
(503)343-1119 Fax:(503)343-2258

1892. An acre of grounds surrounds this Victorian inn, built by a local timber owner and gold miner. The rooms range from a basement room featuring fly-fishing paraphernalia and knotty-pine panel-  ing to an elegant two-room honeymoon suite on the second floor, complete with fireplace, bathtub for two and a view of the mountains. The Campbell House, located in Eugene's historic Skinner Butte District, is within walking distance of restaurants, the Hult Center for the Performing Arts, the 5th Street Public Market and antique shops. Outdoor activities include jogging or biking along riverside paths.

Innkeeper(s): Myra Plant & Sonja Cruthers.

Rates:$85-225. MC VISA AX. Full Bkfst. Teas. 14 rooms. Fireplaces. Beds:KQT. Conference Rm. TV, Phone, Refrig. in room. Handicap access. Swimming. Fishing.

Contact: Myra Plant. Certificate may be used: November - December, 1994; January - February, 1995.

Campus Cottage
1136 E 19th Ave
Eugene 97403
(503)342-5346

1922. A block south of the University of Oregon is Eugene's first bed & breakfast. This charming country French cottage features special touches such as fresh flowers and cozy comforters, which accentuate the antiques in each guest bedroom. The innkeepers provide bicycles as a fun way to travel around the campus. Refrigerators are available and other amenities include home-baked cookies. The morning paper accompanies a full breakfast of fruits, pastries and egg dishes.

Innkeeper(s): Ursula Bates.

Rates:$87-127. Full Bkfst. 4 rooms. Beds:QT. Conference Rm. Phone, Refrig. in room. Skiing. Swimming. Fishing.

Seen in: *New York Times, PM Magazine, Los Angeles Times.*

Contact: Ursula Bates. Certificate may be used: Dec. 1 through May 1 excluding holidays and conventions.

Kjaer's House in the Woods
814 Lorane Hwy
Eugene 97405
(503)343-3234

1910. This handsome Craftsman house on two landscaped acres was built by a Minnesota lawyer. It was originally accessible by streetcar. Antiques include a square grand piano of rosewood and a collection of antique wedding photos. The house is attractively furnished and surrounded by flower gardens.

Innkeeper(s): Eunice & George Kjaer.

Rates:$50-65. Full Bkfst. Teas. Evening snacks. 2 rooms. 1 with shared bath. Beds:Q. Conference Rm. Tennis. Bicycling. Swimming. Fishing.

Seen in: *Register-Guard, Oregonian.*

Contact: Eunice Kjaer. Certificate may be used: Sunday-Thursday, January, February, March.

"Lovely ambiance and greatest sleep ever. Delicious and beautiful food presentation."

The Oval Door
988 Lawrence at 10th
Eugene 97401
(503)683-3160 Fax:(503)485-5339

1990. This is a New England farm-style house, complete with wraparound porch. It is located in a residential neighborhood 15 blocks from the University of Oregon. Guest rooms feature ceiling fans and antiques. There is a whirlpool room, library and parlor. Breakfast can be catered to your dietary needs.

Innkeeper(s): Judith McLane.

Rates:$65-83. MC VISA. Full Bkfst. 4 rooms. Beds:QT. Phone in room. Bicycling.

Contact: Judith McLane. Certificate may be used: Anytime.

Pookie's B&B on College Hill
2013 Charnelton St
Eugene 97405
(503)343-0383 (800)558-0383
Fax:(503)343-0383

1918. Pookie's is a charming Craftsman house with an English influence. Surrounded by maple and fir trees, the B&B is located in the College Hill neigh-

borhood. Mahogany and oak antiques decorate the rooms. The innkeeper worked for many years in the area as a concierge and can offer you expert help with excursion planning or business needs.

Innkeeper(s): Pookie & Doug Walling.

Rates:$65-80. Full Bkfst. AP available. Teas. Evening snacks. 3 rooms. 2 with shared baths. Beds:KQT. Conference Rm. Phone in room. Skiing. Swimming. Fishing.

Contact: Pookie Walling. Certificate may be used: All year based upon availability.

Forest Grove

Main Street B&B
1803 Main St
Forest Grove 97116
(503)357-9812

1913. Located in a college town 20 miles from Portland, this Craftsman bungalow is in the local historical register. There is a formal dining room where a bountiful gourmet breakfast is served, often featuring local nuts, dairy items and fruit. From the patio you may listen to the fountain. Evening refreshments are presented fireside or on the front porch.

Innkeeper(s): Marie Mather.

Rates:$50-55. MC VISA. Full Bkfst. Evening snacks. 2 rooms. 2 with shared baths. Beds:KQ. Phone, AC in room. Swimming. Fishing.

Contact: Marie Mather. Certificate may be used: Oct. 15, 1994-Jan. 30, 1995; Oct. 15-Dec. 30, 1995.

Grants Pass

The Ahlf House B&B
762 NW 6th St
Grants Pass 97526
(503)474-1374 (800)863-1374

1902. This four-story Queen Anne Victorian stands on a hill, framed by tulip, pine and cedar trees. With 5,500 square feet, it is the largest historic house in Grants Pass. Delicately painted in three shades of blue, the house boasts a double-tiered veranda and bay with fish-scale siding. A gracious Victorian home feeling is carried out in antique decor. Stop by the gift shop for that special remembrance.

Innkeeper(s): Ken & Cathy Neuschafer.

Rates:$50-85. MC VISA. Full Bkfst. Teas. Evening snacks. 4 rooms. Beds:QT. Conference Rm. TV, AC in room. Swimming. Fishing.

Seen in: *Daily Courier, Horizon Air Magazine.*

Contact: Cathy Neuschafer. Certificate may be used: Weeknights, weekends, no holidays.

"We felt very pampered and relaxed. The atmosphere is much more than money can buy."

The Clemens House B&B Inn
612 NW Third St
Grants Pass 97526
(503)476-5564

1905. Antiques and family treasures can be found throughout this historic turn-of-the-century home.

Bedrooms feature lace curtains and handmade quilts. One suite has its own kitchenette and another room boasts a fireplace. Breakfasts always include daily specials and homemade breads and jam. In spring, the gardens are blooming with azaleas, camellias and rhododendrons. The surrounding area offers antique car shows, boat races, concerts and river rafting.

Innkeeper(s): Gerry & Maureen Clark.

Rates:$50-80. MC VISA. Full Bkfst. Gourmet Brkfst. Teas. 3 rooms. Beds:QT. AC, Refrig. in room. Swimming. Fishing.

Contact: Maureen Clark. Certificate may be used: Sunday-Thursday, June-September. Anytime October-May except holidays.

"We will never stay at a motel again...business travel has never been so good."

Martha's House
764 NW 4th St
Grants Pass 97526
(503)476-4330 (800)261-0167

1912. If you pass by this inn in the morning, you may hear the happy chatter of guests on the veranda enjoying a breakfast of freshly baked breads,

farm fresh eggs and local produce. And Felix the cat may be nearby. This Victorian farmhouse is close to the center of town. Antique toys are a feature in Rachel's Room, which also harbors a Jacuzzi tub, queen brass bed and antiques. There are terry robes, air conditioning and TVs. Enjoy the area's river rafting and nearby Shakespearean Festival.

Innkeeper(s): Glenn & Martha Evelyn Hawkins.

Rates:$50-65. MC VISA. Full Bkfst. Teas. Evening snacks. 4 rooms. 1 with shared bath. Beds:KQT. Conference Rm. TV, Phone, AC in room. Bicycling. Handicap access. Fishing.

Contact: Martha Evelyn Hawkins. Certificate may be used: Sunday - Thursday.

The Washington Inn
1002 Washington Blvd
Grants Pass 97526
(503)476-1131

1864. This beautifully preserved Victorian is in the National Register. Patties Parlor, a favorite guest room, offers a fireplace, queen bed and clawfoot tub. The back lawn and flower gardens may be enjoyed from the deck off the breakfast room, and plum, pear and apple trees grow on the side yard. Glide quietly on the front porch swing, or pedal away on the inn's bicycles to explore the area.

Innkeeper(s): Bill Thompson.

Rates:$40-65. ContPlus Bkfst. 3 rooms. 1 with shared bath. Fireplaces. Beds:Q. Golf. Tennis. Bicycling. Skiing. Exercise room. Swimming. Fishing.

Contact: William Thompson. Certificate may be used: Monday through Thursday.

Grants Pass/Merlin

Pine Meadow Inn
1000 Crow Road
Grants Pass/Merlin 97532
(503)471-6277 Fax:(503)471-6277

1992. Built on a wooded knoll, this handsome yellow farmhouse looks out on a four-acre meadow, which the innkeepers call their front yard. Views of

Mt. Walker, Mt. Sexton and Buckhorn Mountain are seen. Five acres of private forest feature walking paths, gardens and private sitting areas. A large deck and hot tub are available under towering pines. Below the gardens is a koi pond and waterfall where one can relax and contemplate. The inn is easily accessible from I-5, yet feels worlds away.

Innkeeper(s): Maloy & Nancy Murdock.

Rates:$95-110. Full Bkfst. Gourmet Brkfst. 3 rooms. Beds:Q. Phone, AC in room. Skiing. Spa. Swimming. Fishing.

Contact: Nancy Murdock. Certificate may be used: October - March.

Halfway

The Birch Leaf Farm B&B
Route 1, Box 91
Halfway 97834
(503)742-2990

1902. Nestled in the middle of a 42-acre farm near the Oregon Trail and halfway between the Eagle

Cap Wilderness and Hells Canyon, this National Register farmhouse boasts original woodwork and hardwood floors. Each guest room has a view of the Wallowa Mountains. A country-style breakfast is served complete with locally made jams and honey. Nearby activities include white-water rafting, jet-boat trips, pack trips and skiing through local mountains.

Innkeeper(s): David & Maryellen Olson.

Rates:$55-65. MC VISA DC. Full Bkfst. Gourmet Brkfst, Dinner. 6 rooms. 5 with shared baths. Beds:KQT. Conference Rm. Farm. Skiing. Swimming. Horseback riding. Fishing.

Seen in: *Hells Canyon Journal.*

Contact: Maryellen Olson. Certificate may be used: Major holidays excluded.

"I will always remember the warmth and quiet comfort of your place."

Jacksonville

Reames House
540 E California St, PO Box 128
Jacksonville 97530
(503)899-1868

1868. This white frame house, in the National Register of Historic Places, was built for Thomas Reames, Wells Fargo banker and town sheriff. Perennial gardens bloom throughout the yard and climbing roses frame the front veranda. The plant-filled, white-wicker sitting room is brightened by hand-stenciled pink roses. The Colonial Room features a canopy bed, while The Victoria boasts a carved walnut bed and clawfoot tub. In spring and summer, guests enjoy boarding the horse-drawn wagon that passes nearby and meanders through Jacksonville. Bicycles, tennis rackets and gold-panning equipment may be borrowed.

Innkeeper(s): George & Charlotte Winsley.

Rates:$75-90. Full Bkfst. 5 rooms. 2 with shared baths. Beds:QT. AC in room. Golf. Tennis. Bicycling. Skiing. Swimming. Horseback riding. Fishing.

Seen in: *Oregonian, Mail Tribune.*

Contact: Charlotte Winsley. Certificate may be used: July 1-Oct. 1, 1994 Monday-Wednesday; Oct. 1, 1994-May 31, 1995 anytime; June 1-Oct. 1, 1995 Monday-Wednesday; Oct. 1-Dec. 31, 1995 anytime.

"Such a beautiful house and location."

Klamath Falls

Klamath Manor B&B
219 Pine St
Klamath Falls 97601
(503)883-5459 (800)956-5459

1921. This house has been renovated to include

French doors, polished oak floors and moldings, and there is an expansive oak staircase. Ice cream sundaes and homemade desserts are served each evening (if you haven't stuffed yourself by frequenting the innkeeper's bottomless cookie jar too many times.) There is a library, Jacuzzi and deck. Bed chambers are furnished with antiques.

Innkeeper(s): Teresa & Harry Pastorius.

Rates:$55-70. MC VISA. Full Bkfst. MAP available. Evening snacks. 3 rooms. 2 with shared baths. Fireplaces. Beds:KQ. Golf. Skiing. Spa. Swimming. Fishing.

Contact: Teresa Pastorius. Certificate may be used: Oct. 1, 1994 through March 31, 1995.

Thompsons' B&B
1420 Wild Plum Ct
Klamath Falls 97601
(503)882-7938

1987. The huge picture windows in this comfortable retreat look out to a spectacular view of Klamath Lake and nearby mountains. Popular Moore Park is practically next door, providing a day of hiking, picnicking or relaxing at the marina. The inn is a perfect site to just relax and enjoy the view. Bird watching is a must, as the inn is home to pelicans, snow geese and many varieties of wild ducks.

Innkeeper(s): Mary & Bill Pohll.

Rates:$55-75. Full Bkfst. 4 rooms. Beds:K. TV, Phone, AC in room. Golf. Tennis. Skiing. Swimming. Fishing.

Contact: Mary Pohll. Certificate may be used: September through June.

"Hospitality as glorious as your surroundings."

Lincoln City

The Enchanted Cottage
4507 SW Coast
Lincoln City 97367
(503)996-4101 Fax:(503)996-2682

1945. This 4,000-square-foot house is 300 feet from the beach and a short walk from Siletz Bay with its herd of sea lions. Victoria's Secret is a favorite romantic guest room that features a queen canopy bed, antique furnishings and, best of all, the sounds of the Pacific surf. Ask for Natalie's Garden Room if you must see and hear the ocean. But everyone takes in the view in the morning when homemade biscuits and breakfast casseroles are specialties served in the dining room.

Innkeeper(s): Cynthia & David Fitton.

Rates:$95. MC VISA. Full Bkfst. Evening snacks. 4 rooms. 2 with shared baths. Beds:KQD. TV, Phone in room. Golf. Tennis. Handicap access. Swimming. Horseback riding. Fishing.

Seen in: *Oregonian.*

Contact: Cynthia Fitton. Certificate may be used: Anytime between Oct. 15, 1994 and May 15, 1995.

Manzanita

The Arbors at Manzanita
78 Idaho Ave, PO Box 68
Manzanita 97130
(503)368-7566

1920. This old-English-style cottage is a half block from the wide sandy beaches that the area is known for. The Neakahnie Mountains are in view as well as the panoramic stretches of the Pacific coastline. Ask for the Waves View room to enjoy the largest view. Enjoy the library, garden and the innkeeper's evening snacks.

Innkeeper(s): Judd & Lee Burrow.

Rates:$75-95. Full Bkfst. 2 rooms. Beds:Q. Golf. Swimming. Horseback riding. Fishing.

Contact: Lee Burrow. Certificate may be used: Midweek May 1 through Oct. 31, 1994; Anytime Nov. 1, 1994 through April 30, 1995. Holidays excluded.

Newberg

Smith House
415 N College St
Newberg 97132-2650
(503)538-1995

1904. This quaint Victorian is furnished in antiques. Located two blocks from George Fox College, the B&B offers a hot tub, fresh fruit and flowers when you arrive. In the morning, you'll be treated to a breakfast of jumbo muffins and homemade raspberry jam and syrups. The innkeepers share Tequila, a double yellow nape Amazon parrot, and the family's Old English sheepdog among other pets. The Rose Room is outfitted with an oak bedroom suite, rocking chair, desk and filled bookcase.

Innkeeper(s): Glen & Mary Post.

Rates:$55. Full Bkfst. 2 rooms. 2 with shared baths. Beds:Q. Phone in room. Spa. Swimming. Fishing.

Contact: Mary Post. Certificate may be used: Sept. 1 through May 15.

Springbrook Farm
30295 N Hwy 99W
Newberg 97132
(503)538-4606 (800)793-8528

1912. An ancient silver maple tree shades the main house, one of four Craftsman-style buildings on this farm. There are 10 acres of gardens, a pool, tennis court and a 60-acre hazelnut orchard. A blue heron monitors the inn's pond and you may paddle around in the canoe. Walking through the orchard to the adjoining winery is a must, as is a bicycle ride to other wineries in the area. Ask for the Carriage House and you'll enjoy a pond and garden

view. It has a kitchen and if you "eat in" you may choose from the garden's offerings for your dinner.

Innkeeper(s): Charles & Ellen McClure.

Rates:$90-125. Gourmet Brkfst. 5 rooms. 4 with shared baths. Beds:Q. AC in room. Farm. Tennis. Bicycling.

Contact: Ellen McClure. Certificate may be used: Oct. 30-April 1, carriage house only (no weekends or major holidays). No summer-season discounts in carriage house.

"An incredible, wonderful refuge! We are beautifully surprised!"

Oregon City

The Inn of the Oregon Trail

416 S McLoughlin
Oregon City 97045
(503)656-2089

1867. This National Register home was built by Captain Fellows, shipbuilder and sternwheeler captain on the Willamette. Located in the historic dis-

trict of Canemah (all 67 acres of which are in the National Register), the house is Gothic Revival with three cathedral windows. Elvira's Suite has vaulted ceilings, a king bed, balcony, pot-bellied stove and gothic arch. Enjoy the inn's lunchtime restaurant or order sandwiches to take on a walk to

Willamette Falls.

Innkeeper(s): Mary & Tom DeHaven.

Rates:$48-85. MC VISA. Full Bkfst. Gourmet Brkfst, Dinner. 4 rooms. Fireplaces. Beds:KQDT. Conference Rm. AC in room. Skiing. Handicap access. Swimming. Fishing.

Contact: Mary DeHaven. Certificate may be used: Jan. 15 - May 15; Sept. 15 - Nov. 30; space available; excluding holidays.

Jagger House B&B

512 Sixth St
Oregon City 97045
(503)657-7820

1880. The Jagger House is in the historic McLoughlin neighborhood with four museums nearby. Decorated in country style, the guest rooms feature pine and oak furnishings, stenciling and folk art. A full breakfast is served at a pine harvest table in the morning. The innkeeper often leads historic walking tours of the neighborhood.

Innkeeper(s): Claire & Tom Met.

Rates:$65-75. MC VISA. Full Bkfst. AP available. Teas. 3 rooms. 2 with shared baths. Beds:QT. AC in room. Skiing. Handicap access. Swimming. Fishing.

Contact: Claire Met. Certificate may be used: October, 1994 through March, 1995 (holidays excluded). October through December, 1995.

"Truly a treasure."

Portland

A Victorian Rose

3729 SW Kelly Ave
Portland 97201
(503)223-7673 Fax:(503)241-7220

1904. Hand-painted roses and a grand crystal chandelier greet guests when they enter this three-story Victorian. Arrive in the afternoon and you'll most

likely be served tea and scones, (by the fireside in cool weather). Try to stay in a different room each time you come, for they are decorated by different Portland interior designers. There is a French country room with a canopy bed, the Victorian Garden Room with a summer theme in soft teal and coral, and the English Rose with a royal four-poster bed, cabbage roses and bay window that overlooks the Willamette River and Mt. Hood.

Innkeeper(s): Linda Alexander, Gene Nudelman, Rebecca Radish.

Rates:$90-110. MC VISA. Full Bkfst. EP. Gourmet Brkfst. 3 rooms. Beds:KQT. Skiing. Swimming. Fishing.

Contact: Linda Alexander. Certificate may be used: October through April, any night/holidays subject to availability. May through September - Sunday night through Thursday night subject to availability.

Seaside

The Boarding House
208 N Holladay Dr
Seaside 97138
(503)738-9055 (800)995-4013

1898. Situated by the Necanicum River, two blocks from the convention center, is this Victorian with beamed ceilings, paneling and tongue-and-groove walls. Rooms offer down quilts, wicker pieces and family heirlooms. The Cottage is a small Victorian on the river bank with a kitchen, two sleeping areas and deck with river views that include ducks, seals and cranes. Breakfast is served in the dining room or on the wraparound porch. The innkeepers will help you find the best places to dig for clams, explore tide pools, dine, discover shipwrecks and picnic.

Innkeeper(s): Barbara Harlan Edwards.

Rates:$65-80. MC VISA. Full Bkfst. 7 rooms. Beds:QT. TV in room. Swimming. Fishing.

Contact: Barbara Harlan Edwards. Certificate may be used: Sunday through Thursday, Nov. 1, 1994 to June 1, 1995 and Nov. 1, 1995 through Dec. 31, 1995 (holidays excluded).

Custer House B&B
811 First Ave
Seaside 97138
(503)738-7825

1903. Wicker furnishings and a clawfoot tub are features of one of the rooms in this farmhouse-style B&B. It is located four blocks from the ocean and two blocks from the Seaside Convention Center. Your host is retired from the Air Force. Enjoy exploring the area's historic forts and beaches.

Innkeeper(s): George A. (Skip) Custer III.

Rates:$60-70. MC VISA. Full Bkfst. 3 rooms. 2 with shared baths. Beds:QT. Golf. Tennis. Swimming. Horseback riding. Fishing.

Seen in: *Oregon Adventures Magazine.*

Contact: George Custer. Certificate may be used: Oct. 15 through May 15, no special events.

The Dalles

Williams House Inn
608 W 6th St
The Dalles 97058
(503)296-2889

1899. This handsome, green-and-white gingerbread Victorian possesses a veranda, gazebo and belvedere. Lush green lawns, trees and shrubs slope down to Mill Creek. The popular Harriet's Room overlooks Klickitat Hills and the Columbia River, and has a canopied four-poster bed, chaise lounge and period writing desk. Each summer the hosts harvest their 25-acre cherry orchard. They are active in the historic preservation of the area.

Innkeeper(s): Don & Barbara Williams.

Rates:$55-75. MC VISA AX DS. Full Bkfst. 3 rooms. 2 with shared baths. Fireplaces. Beds:D. Conference Rm. TV, Phone, AC in room. Golf. Tennis. Skiing. Swimming. Fishing.

Seen in: *Oregonian, New York Times, Glamour.*

Contact: E. D. Williams. Certificate may be used: Oct. 15, 1994 to May 15, 1995.

"A fantasy come true, including the most gracious, delightful company in conversation, Barb and Don Williams!"

Yachats

Sea Quest
95354 Hwy 101
Yachats 97498
(503)547-3782 Fax:(503)547-3782

1980. This 6,000-square-foot cedar and glass house is only 100 feet from the ocean, located on two-and-one-half acres. Each guest room has a Jacuzzi tub and outside entrance. A wood-burning stove warms the living room. The second-floor breakfast room is distinguished by wide views of the ocean, forest and Ten Mile Creek.

Innkeeper(s): Elaine & George Rozsa.

Rates:$105-245. MC VISA. Full Bkfst. 5 rooms. Beds:Q. Conference Rm. Golf. Spa. Swimming. Horseback riding. Fishing.

Contact: George Rozsa. Certificate may be used: Jan. 5 to May 15.

Pennsylvania

Airville

Spring House
Muddy Creek Forks
Airville 17302
(717)927-6906

1798. Spring House, the prominent home in this pre-Revolutionary War village, was constructed of massive stones over a spring that supplies water to most of the village. The walls are either white-washed or retain their original stenciling. Furnished with country antiques, quilts, Oriental rugs, and paintings, the guest rooms are cozy with featherbeds in winter. The inn boasts a library and grand piano.
Innkeeper(s): Ray Constance Hearne.

Rates:$60-95. Gourmet Brkfst. Evening snacks. 5 rooms. 2 with shared baths. Beds:QT. Skiing. Swimming. Fishing.

Seen in: *Woman's Day, Country Decorating, Innsider Magazine.*

Contact: Ray Hearne. Certificate may be used: Winter weeks: December through March, Sunday - Thursday not on weekends. Also: November weekdays except Thanksgiving; April weekdays, all holidays excluded.

"What a slice of history! Thank you for your hospitality. We couldn't have imagined a more picturesque setting."

332

Annville

Swatara Creek Inn
Box 692, Rd 2
Annville 17003
(717)865-3259

1860. A former boys' home, this bed & breakfast now boasts canopy beds and lacy curtains. The first floor of this Victorian mansion provides a sitting

room, dining room and gift shop. A full breakfast is served in the dining room, but honeymooners can request their meal in the comfort of their rooms. For chocolate lovers, nearby Hershey is a treat. Several shopping outlets are about an hour away or visit the Mount Hope Estate and Winery. For an unusual day trip, tour the Seltzer and Weaver Bologna plant in Lebanon. Each August, the town hosts a popular bologna festival. Nearby Lancaster County is the home of Amish communities.

Innkeeper(s): Dick & Jeannette Hess.

Rates:$43-75. MC VISA AX DC DS. Full Bkfst. 10 rooms. Beds:QT. AC in room. Farm. Golf. Handicap access. Fishing.

Seen in: *Daily News, Patriot-News.*

Contact: Jeannette Hess. Certificate may be used: Sundays through Thursdays - year-round but no holiday weekends.

"Peaceful."

Avella

Weatherbury Farm
579 Chestnut Rd
Avella 15312
(412)587-3763 Fax:(412)587-7363

1863. Meadows, fields, gardens and valleys fill the 104 acres of this working farm where sheep, chickens, rabbits and cattle are raised. Stenciled walls,

ceiling fans, wide-plank floors and fireplaces add to the country comforts. Peach French toast or garden vegetable eggs often are served and you may choose the garden, dining room or gazebo for your morning meal location. Enjoy porches, picnic spots, a swimming pool and the hammock.

Innkeeper(s): Marcy Tudor.

Rates:$60. MC VISA. Full Bkfst. Evening snacks. 2 rooms. Fireplaces. Beds:D. Farm. Bicycling. Skiing. Fishing.

Contact: Marcy Tudor. Certificate may be used: Monday - Thursday nights.

Avondale

B&B at Walnut Hill
541 Chandler's Mill Rd
Avondale 19311
(610)444-3703

1840. The family that built this pre-Civil War home ran a grist mill on the premises. Innkeepers Sandy and Tom Mills moved into the home as newlyweds. Today Sandy, a former caterer, serves up gourmet breakfasts, such as cottage cheese pancakes with blueberry sauce, in the formal dining room with homemade teas, lemon butter and currant jam. Her cooking expertise was recognized in Good Housekeeping's Christmas issue. The guest rooms are cozy and welcoming and filled with antiques. One room features a Laura Ashley canopy bed. Another boasts Victorian wicker. The house overlooks horses grazing in a meadow, and a nearby creek is visited by Canadian geese, deer and an occasional fox.

Innkeeper(s): Tom & Sandy Mills.

Rates:$80. Gourmet Brkfst. 2 rooms. 2 with shared baths. Beds:DT. TV, AC in room. Golf. Tennis. Bicycling. Skiing. Spa. Horseback riding. Fishing.

Seen in: *Times Record, Suburban Advertiser.*

Contact: Sandra Mills. Certificate may be used: Sunday - Thursday, no holidays. January through March.

"The only thing left to do is move in."

Beach Lake

East Shore House B&B
PO Box 250
Beach Lake 18405
(717)729-8523 Fax:(717)729-8080

1900. This Victorian-style home boasts a wrap-around porch perfect for rest and relaxation. The gazebo, which sits on top of a bubbling brook, offers another enchanting rest spot. Rooms feature decor typical of turn-of-the-century boardinghouse rooms. Each season brings a host of new activities. In warm months, enjoy canoeing and hiking at nearby Delaware River. The "Fall Foliage Express" takes tourists on a train excursion through the local countryside. In winter, guests can snuggle up by the woodstove after a day of skiing or ice skating.

Innkeeper(s): Amy & Mike Wood.

Rates:$45-65. MC VISA. Full Bkfst. 6 rooms. 2 with shared baths. Beds:DT. Golf. Skiing. Fishing.

Contact: Amy Wood. Certificate may be used: Sunday through Thursday nights year-round with the exception of holidays.

Bethlehem

Wydnor Hall
3612 Old Philadelphia Pike
Bethlehem 18015
(610)867-6851 Fax:(610)866-2062

1810. On the Old Philadelphia Pike, this Georgian fieldstone mansion is close to Lehigh University and the historic district. Tall trees shade the acre of

grounds. Meticulously restored, the house is appointed with an English decor. Amenities include pressed linens, down comforters and terry cloth robes. The breakfast table is set with fine china and silver. Homemade pastries, breads and cakes are served at tea time.

Innkeeper(s): Kristina Taylor.

Rates:$110-125. MC VISA AX DC CB. Full Bkfst. Teas. 5 rooms. Beds:QT. Conference Rm. TV, Phone, AC in room.

Contact: Kristina Taylor. Certificate may be used: Sunday through Thursday, subject to availability.

Bloomsburg

Irondale Inn B&B
100 Irondale Ave
Bloomsburg 17815
(717)784-1977

1913. A few blocks from Bloomsburg University, this fieldstone Georgian house is down a quiet road with lawns and gardens that reach to Fishing

Creek. There are seven working fireplaces, some in guest rooms, which are appointed with antiques, reproductions and queen-size beds. There is a game room with a pool table.

Innkeeper(s): Linda Wink.

Rates:$75-85. Full Bkfst. 4 rooms. 4 with shared baths. Fireplaces. Beds:Q. Skiing. Spa. Fishing.

Contact: Linda Wink. Certificate may be used: Anytime January through March. Sunday through Thursday all year, weekends also if available. Excludes special events and holidays.

Magee's Main Street Inn
20 W Main St
Bloomsburg 17815
(717)784-3200 (800)331-9815
Fax:(717)784-5517

1870. For a hotel-sized stay with the quaint comfort of a bed and breakfast, Magee's 45-room inn offers regular rooms and deluxe double rooms with separate living rooms. An expansive breakfast is served and coffee is available throughout the day. Rooms are stocked with sparkling waters and fruit juices. The inn boasts a ballroom for wedding receptions and parties. Harry's Grille, an adjoining restaurant, serves lunch and dinner in a cozy atmosphere.

Innkeeper(s): Norman Mael.

Rates:$60-90. MC VISA AX DC DS CB. Full Bkfst. AP available. Picnic lunches. 46 rooms. Beds:KQT. Conference Rm. TV, Phone, AC in room. Skiing. Fishing.

Contact: Norman Mael. Certificate may be used: Not available last week in September or weekends in October.

Bradford

Fisher Homestead B&B
253 E Main St
Bradford 16701
(814)368-3428 Fax:(814)368-7053

1847. Located in Northwestern Pennsylvania, the Fisher Homestead is constructed of fieldstone and wood. It offers a long front porch, decks and patios for relaxation. Period antiques furnish the guest rooms. A full breakfast is served on weekends, while a continental breakfast is provided during the week.

Innkeeper(s): Fred & Brenda Ruth.

Rates:$61-70. MC VISA AX DC. Full Bkfst. 7 rooms. Beds:QD. TV, Phone, AC in room. Skiing. Swimming.

Contact: Brenda Ruth. Certificate may be used: Nov. 1 to April 30 (except holidays).

Buckingham

Mill Creek Farm B&B
PO Box 816
Buckingham 18912
(215)794-0776 (800)562-1776

1750. One hundred Bucks Country acres surround this Federal farmhouse, a state historical site. Guest rooms are furnished with pleasing country antiques.

Visit the inn's pastures and paddocks to enjoy the thoroughbred mares and yearlings. You also may wish to walk through the orchard or fish in the pond. The countryside provides lush scenery for cycling and jogging.

Innkeeper(s): Paul Hoskinson.

Rates:$85-125. MC VISA AX. Full Bkfst. Teas. 5 rooms. 2 with shared baths. Beds:Q. Conference Rm. TV, AC in room. Farm. Tennis. Bicycling. Skiing. Exercise room. Swimming. Stables. Fishing.

Contact: James Brame. Certificate may be used: Midweek year-round.

Canadensis

Brookview Manor B&B Inn
RR #1 Box 365, Rt 447
Canadensis 18325
(717)595-2451

1911. By the side of the road, hanging from a tall evergreen, is the welcoming sign to this forest retreat. There are brightly decorated common rooms and four fireplaces. The carriage house has three bedrooms and is suitable for small groups. The innkeepers like to share a "secret waterfall" within a 20-minute walk from the inn.

Innkeeper(s): Nancie & Lee Cabana.

Rates:$90-145. MC VISA AX DC DS CB. Full Bkfst. 6 rooms. Fireplaces. Beds:KQT. Conference Rm. Skiing. Swimming. Fishing.

Seen in: *Mid-Atlantic Country.*

Contact: Nancie Cabana. Certificate may be used: Anytime, except weekends in July - October or any holidays.

"Thanks for a great wedding weekend. Everything was perfect."

Carlisle

Line Limousin Farmhouse B&B
2070 Ritner Highway
Carlisle 17013
(717)243-1281

1870. The grandchildren of Bob and Joan are the ninth generation of Lines to enjoy this 200-year-old homestead. A stone and brick exterior accents the farmhouse's graceful style, while inside, family heirlooms attest to the home's longevity. This is a breeding stock farm of 110 acres and the cattle raised here, Limousin, originate from the Limoges area of France. Giant maples shade the lawn and there are woods and stone fences.

Innkeeper(s): Bob & Joan Line.

Rates:$53-69. Full Bkfst. 4 rooms. 2 with shared baths. Beds:KDT. TV, Phone, AC, Refrig. in room. Farm. Skiing. Stables. Fishing.

Contact: Joan Line. Certificate may be used: Monday through Thursday all year, except special events.

Pheasant Field B&B
150 Hickorytown Rd
Carlisle 17013
(717)258-0717 Fax:(717)258-0717

1790. Located on eight acres of central Pennsylvania farmland, this brick, two-story Federal-style farmhouse features wooden shutters and a covered front porch. An early 17th-century stone barn is on the property, and horse boarding often is available. The Appalachian Trail is a mile away. Fly-fishing is popular at Yellow Breeches and Letort Spring. Dickinson College and Carlisle

Fairgrounds are other points of interest.
Innkeeper(s): Denise Fegan, Chuck DeMarco.

Rates:$65-95. MC VISA AX DS. Full Bkfst. 4 rooms. 2 with shared baths. Beds:KQ. AC in room. Farm. Tennis. Skiing. Stables. Fishing.

Contact: Denise Fegan. Certificate may be used: November through March.

Columbia

The Columbian
360 Chestnut St
Columbia 17512
(717)684-5869 (800)422-5869

1897. This stately three-story mansion is a fine example of Colonial Revival architecture. Antique beds, a stained-glass window and home-baked breads are among its charms. Guests may relax on the wraparound sun porches.
Innkeeper(s): Chris & Becky Will.

Rates:$70-80. MC VISA DS. Full Bkfst. 6 rooms. Fireplaces. Beds:QT. TV, AC in room. Swimming. Fishing.

Seen in: *Philadelphia Inquirer, Lancaster Intelligencer Journal, Columbia News, Washington Post.*

Contact: Chris Will. Certificate may be used: Sunday night-Thursday night.

"In a word, extraordinary!"

Cooksburg

Clarion River Lodge
River Rd-Cook Forest, PO Box 150
Cooksburg 16217
(814)744-8171 (800)648-6743
Fax:(814)744-8553

1962. The Clarion River Lodge is a rustic retreat above the Clarion River surrounded by Cook Forest. Its pegged-oak flooring, oak beams, pine ceiling, wild cherry and butternut paneling and fieldstone fireplace add to the lodge's natural character. A distinctive glassed-in breezeway leads from the main building to the guest wing. Rooms are decorated with modern Scandinavian decor.
Innkeeper(s): Ellen O'Day.

Rates:$89-129. MC VISA AX. Full Bkfst. MAP available. Picnic lunches.

20 rooms. Beds:KQ. Conference Rm. Phone, AC, Refrig. in room. Golf. Skiing. Swimming. Horseback riding. Fishing.

Seen in: *Pittsburgh Press, Pittsburgh Women's Journal.*

Contact: John Brandon. Certificate may be used: Sunday to Thursday nights, except August & October.

"If your idea of Paradise is a secluded rustic retreat surrounded by the most beautiful country this side of the Rockies, search no more."

Dallas

Ponda-Rowland B&B Inn
RR 1, Box 349
Dallas 18612
(717)639-3245 (800)854-3286
Fax:(717)639-5531

1850. Situated on a 130-acre farm, this historic house overlooks a 30-acre wildlife sanctuary with six ponds, feeding stations and trails visited by

whitetail deer, fox, turkeys, mallard ducks, Canadian geese and occasionally, blue herons. The home is filled with beautiful American country antiques and collections. There are beamed ceilings and a stone fireplace in the living room. The scenic setting, hospitable hosts, farm animals and hearty country breakfast make this a perfect place to have a great time you will remember for years to come. Hayrides may be arranged by advance reservations.
Innkeeper(s): Jeanette & Cliff Rowland.

Rates:$38-85. MC VISA AX DS. Full Bkfst. Picnic lunches. Teas. Evening snacks. 5 rooms. Fireplaces. Beds:KT. Conference Rm. Phone in room. Farm. Skiing. Swimming. Horseback riding. Stables. Fishing.

Seen in: *Philadelphia Inquirer, Newage Examiner, Times-Leader.*

Contact: Clifford Rowland. Certificate may be used: Nov. 14, 1994-May 17, 1995, Nov. 15, 1995-Dec. 28, 1995, Sunday to Thursday except holiday weeks.

"Warm and friendly people who made us feel right at home."

Dillsburg

The Peter Wolford House
440 Franklin Church Rd
Dillsburg 17019
(717)432-0757

1804. A Federal farmhouse in the National Register, the Peter Wolford House was constructed of Flemish Bond brick by a prominent gristmill operator. His brick-patterned bank barn, a unique

Pennsylvania and Maryland barn style, still stands. There are pine floors and many fireplaces, including a 10-foot-wide, walk-in fireplace used for cooking. Antiques and handmade quilts fill the guest rooms. Outside on the 10 acres are meadows, an herb garden and perennial borders accented by a handmade picket fence. State gamelands are adjacent to the inn.

Innkeeper(s): Ted & Loretta Pesano.

Rates:$60-65. Full Bkfst. Teas. Evening snacks. 3 rooms. 3 with shared baths. Fireplaces. Beds:Q. AC in room. Skiing. Fishing.

Contact: Loretta Pesano. Certificate may be used: Excluding months of May & October, Christmas, New Year's & Easter.

Donegal

Mountain View B&B & Antiques
Mountain View Rd
Donegal 15628
(412)593-6349

1853. Six wooded acres surround this Georgian-style farmhouse, a county historic landmark. The innkeepers own Donegal antiques and have selected many

fine 18th- and 19th-century pieces to furnish the inn. There is a large barn on the property. Guests enjoy the rural setting for its outstanding views of the Laurel Mountains. Fallingwater, a famous Frank Lloyd Wright house, is 20 minutes away.

Innkeeper(s): Lesley & Gerard O'Leary.

Rates:$85-140. MC VISA AX DC DS CB. Full Bkfst. Gourmet Brkfst. Teas. Evening snacks. 6 rooms. 3 with shared baths. Beds:QD. Phone, AC in room. Golf. Tennis. Skiing. Handicap access. Swimming. Horseback riding. Fishing.

Contact: Lesley O'Leary. Certificate may be used: All times except holiday weekends and October weekends.

Doylestown

The Inn at Fordhook Farm
105 New Britain Rd
Doylestown 18901
(215)345-1766 Fax:(215)345-1791

1750. Three generations of Burpees (Burpee Seed Company) have dispensed hospitality on this 60-acre farm. Guest rooms are in the family's 18th-century fieldstone house and Victorian carriage house. The inn is filled with family heirlooms and guests can sit at the famous horticulturist's desk in the secluded study where Mr. Burpee wrote his first seed catalogs.

Innkeeper(s): Elizabeth Romanella & Blanche Burpee Dohan.

Rates:$93-175. MC VISA AX. Full Bkfst. Teas. 7 rooms. 3 with shared baths. Fireplaces. Beds:KQ. Conference Rm. AC in room. Swimming. Fishing.

Seen in: *Bon Appetit, Mid-Atlantic Country, Gourmet.*

Contact: Elizabeth Romanella. Certificate may be used: Sunday - Thursday, year-round. Not October or holidays.

"The inn is absolutely exquisite. If I had only one night to spend in Bucks County, I'd do it all over again at Fordhook Farms!"

Eagles Mere

Shady Lane B&B Inn
Allegheny Ave, PO Box 314
Eagles Mere 17731
(717)525-3394

1947. This ranch-style house rests on two mountaintop acres. Eagles Mere is a Victorian town with gaslights and old-fashioned village shops. Crystal clear Eagles Mere Lake is surrounded by Laurel Path, a popular scenic walk. The Endless Mountains provide cross-country skiing, fishing and hiking. Tobogganing is popular on the Eagles Mere Toboggan Slide.

Innkeeper(s): Pat & Dennis Dougherty.

Rates:$75. Full Bkfst. Teas. 8 rooms. Beds:KQT. Skiing. Fishing.

Contact: Dennis Dougherty. Certificate may be used: Sunday through Thursday from Sept. 1 to June 30 (not in July or August).

East Berlin

The Bechtel Mansion Inn
400 W King St
East Berlin 17316
(717)259-7760 (800)331-1108

1897. The town of East Berlin, near Lancaster and Gettysburg, was settled by Pennsylvania Germans prior to the American Revolution. William Leas, a

wealthy banker, built this many-gabled romantic Queen Anne mansion, now listed in the National Register. The inn is furnished with an abundance of museum-quality antiques and collections. Mennonite quilts top many of the handsome bedsteads.

Innkeeper(s): Ruth Spangler.

Rates:$70-135. MC VISA AX DC DS. Full Bkfst. Gourmet Brkfst. 10 rooms. 3 with shared baths. Beds:QDT. Conference Rm. AC, Refrig. in room. Skiing. Swimming.

Seen in: *Washington Post*.

Contact: Charles Bechtel. Certificate may be used: Anytime space is available except weekends in October and holiday weekends. Anytime at the last minute, if cancellations make space available.

"Ruth was a most gracious hostess and took time to describe the history of your handsome museum-quality antiques and the special architectural details."

Elizabethtown

Apple Abound Inn B&B
518 S Market St
Elizabethtown 17022
(717)367-3018 Fax:(717)367-9793

1907. In the local historic register, this three-story Victorian has a tower and a wide, wraparound veranda. Cranberry-colored glass comprise the transoms and there are bay windows and a stained-glass window. Chestnut doors and built-in china cabinets are other features. The inn's apple theme continues

to the guest rooms and add to the country decor. Lancaster is nearby.

Innkeeper(s): Jennifer Sheppard

Rates:$65-75. MC VISA. Full Bkfst. Teas. Evening snacks. 3 rooms. 2 with shared baths. Beds:QD. AC in room. Skiing. Fishing.

Contact: Jennifer and Jon Sheppard. Certificate may be used: November through April.

Emlenton

Whippletree Inn & Farm
RD 3, Box 285
Emlenton 16373
(412)867-9543

1905. The 100 hilltop acres of Whippletree Farm overlook the Allegheny River, and a trail on the property leads down to the river. The restored farmhouse contains many functional antiques. If you have your own horse, you are invited to use the farm's race track. The oldest continuously operated public country club in the United States is five miles away in Foxburg and the American Golf Hall of Fame is there. The innkeepers host team penning events for 4H.

Innkeeper(s): Warren & Joey Simmons.

Rates:$45-50. Full Bkfst. Gourmet Brkfst. Teas. Evening snacks. 5 rooms. 3 with shared baths. Beds:KQT. Farm. Skiing. Handicap access. Swimming. Fishing.

Contact: JoAnne Simmons. Certificate may be used: November through August.

Emmaus

Leibert Gap Manor B&B
4502 S Mountain Dr, PO Box 623
Emmaus 18049
(800)964-1242

1987. This three-story Williamsburg-style house is on 17 acres. Random-width pine floors, open-beam ceilings and a Colonial fireplace are on the main floor. Primitive and cottage pieces, along with canopy beds and antiques, are found in the guest

rooms. A solarium overlooks the Leibert Gap flyway and you may watch hawks and other birds pass by. In the afternoon, enjoy tea and scones on the long brick porch. Nearby are 10 colleges as well as many antique shops and factory outlets.

Innkeeper(s): Wayne & Pauline Sheffer.

Rates:$90-125. MC VISA AX DC CB. Full Bkfst. 4 rooms. Conference Rm. AC in room. Bicycling. Skiing. Exercise room. Fishing.

Contact: Pauline Sheffer. Certificate may be used: Anytime space available.

Ephrata

The Guesthouse at Doneckers
318-324 N State St
Ephrata 17522
(717)738-9502 Fax:(717)738-9554

1910. Jacob Gorgas, devout member of the Ephrata Cloister and a clock maker (noted for crafting 150 eight-day Gorgas grandfather clocks), built this stately home. It was restored and filled with European antiques collected by Bill Donecker, owner of the Community of Doneckers, a village with shops, a restaurant and the 19-room Guesthouse of Doneckers. Rooms feature amenities such as spas, fireplaces, inlaid floors or stained-glass windows.

Innkeeper(s): Jan Grobengeiser.

Rates:$59-175. MC VISA AX DC DS CB. ContPlus Bkfst. 40 rooms. 2 with shared baths. Fireplaces. Beds:QT. Conference Rm. Phone, AC, Refrig. in room. Bicycling. Handicap access. Spa.

Seen in: *Daily News, Country Inns.*

Contact: Jill Brown. Certificate may be used: Sunday through Thursday, excluding holidays, year-round.

"A peaceful refuge."

Smithton Inn
900 W Main St
Ephrata 17522
(717)733-6094 Fax:(717)733-3333

1763. Henry Miller opened this inn and tavern on a hill overlooking the Ephrata Cloister, a religious society he belonged to, known as Seventh Day

Baptists. Several of their medieval-style German buildings are now a museum. This is a warm and welcoming inn with canopy beds or four-posters, candlelight, fireplaces and nightshirts provided for each guest. If you're not allergic, ask for a lavish feather bed to be put in your room.

Innkeeper(s): Dorothy Graybill.

Rates:$65-115. MC VISA AX. Full Bkfst. Teas. 16 rooms. 8 with shared baths. Fireplaces. Beds:KQT. Phone, AC, Refrig. in room. Handicap access. Spa.

Seen in: *New York Magazine, Country Living, Early American Life.*

Contact: Allan Smith. Certificate may be used: Jan. 15 through Feb. 28, Monday through Thursday.

"After visiting over 50 inns in four countries, Smithton has to be one of the most romantic, picturesque inns in America. I have never seen its equal!"

Erie

Spencer House B&B
519 West 6th St
Erie 16507
(814)454-5984 (800)890-7263
Fax:(814)456-5091

1876. Still under renovation, this three-story Victorian Stick house features gabled windows and a wraparound porch. Original woodwork, much of it carved with scrolls and scripture, is one of the inn's most outstanding features. Twelve-foot ceilings, interior folding shutters and a well-stocked library with black walnut bookshelves are other highlights. The Tree Top Room offers a ceiling-to-floor canopy and a reading nook.

Innkeeper(s): Pat & Keith Hagenbuch.

Rates:$65-110. MC VISA AX DS. Full Bkfst. Teas. 5 rooms. Fireplaces. Beds:Q. TV, Phone, AC in room. Skiing. Swimming. Fishing.

Contact: Patricia Hagenbuch. Certificate may be used: Nov. 1, 1994-March 31, 1995; Nov. 1-Dec. 31, 1995. Midweek stay.

Erwinna

Evermay-on-the-Delaware
River Rd
Erwinna 18920
(610)294-9100 Fax:(610)294-8249

1700. Twenty-five acres of Bucks County at its best — rolling green meadows, lawns, stately maples and the silvery Delaware River, surround this three-story manor. Serving as an inn since 1871, it has hosted such guests as the Barrymore family. Rich walnut wainscotting, a grandfather clock and twin fireplaces warm the parlor, scented by vases of roses or gladiolus. Antique-filled guest rooms overlook the river or gardens.

Innkeeper(s): Ron Strouse & Fred Cresson.

Rates:$85-160. MC VISA. ContPlus Bkfst. Gourmet Dinner. Teas. 16 rooms. Beds:Q. Conference Rm. Phone, AC in room. Golf. Tennis. Skiing. Handicap access. Swimming. Horseback riding. Fishing.

Seen in: *New York Times, Philadelphia, Travel and Leisure, Food and Wine.*

Contact: Ronald Strouse. Certificate may be used: Sunday through Thursday, excluding holidays.

"It was pure perfection. Everything from the flowers to the wonderful food."

Gettysburg

Baladerry Inn at Gettysburg
40 Hospital Rd
Gettysburg 17325
(717)337-1342 (800)220-0025

1812. Set on the edge of Gettysburg Battlefield, this brick country manor was used as a hospital during the Civil War. Additions were built in 1830 and 1977. Fully restored today, the Baladerry offers spacious grounds, gardens, a tennis court, dining terrace, great room and full country breakfasts.

Innkeeper(s): Tom & Caryl O'Gara.

Rates:$78-98. MC VISA AX DC CB. Full Bkfst. Teas. Evening snacks. 8 rooms. Fireplaces. Beds:KQT. Conference Rm. AC in room. Tennis. Skiing. Fishing.

Contact: Caryl O'Gara. Certificate may be used: Monday through Thursday; December, January, February, March.

The Brafferton Inn
44 York St
Gettysburg 17325
(717)337-3423

1786. The earliest deeded house in Gettysburg, the inn was designed by James Gettys and is listed in the National Register of Historic Places. The walls

of this huge brownstone range from 18 inches to two-and-one-half-feet thick. There are skylights in all the guest rooms and a primitive mural of famous scenes in the area painted on the four dining room walls.

Innkeeper(s): Jane & Sam Back.

Rates:$75-120. MC VISA. ContPlus Bkfst. 10 rooms. Fireplaces. Beds:QT. TV, AC in room. Skiing. Swimming. Fishing.

Seen in: *Early American Life, Country Living.*

Contact: Samuel Back. Certificate may be used: Sunday through Thursday except long holiday weekends.

"Your house is so beautiful - every corner of it - and your friendliness is icing on the cake. It was fabulous!"

The Doubleday Inn
104 Doubleday Ave
Gettysburg 17325
(717)334-9119

1929. Located directly on the Gettysburg Battlefield and bordered by original stone breastworks, this restored Colonial home is furnished

with Victorian sofas and period antiques. Available to guests is one of the largest known Civil War libraries with volumes devoted exclusively to the Battle of Gettysburg. On selected evenings, guests can participate in discussions with a Civil War historian, who brings the battle alive with accurate accounts and authentic memorabilia and weaponry. Candlelight country breakfasts are served.

Innkeeper(s): Joan & Sal Chandon.

Rates:$79-100. MC VISA. Full Bkfst. Picnic lunches. Teas. 9 rooms. 4 with shared baths. Beds:DT. AC in room. Golf. Skiing. Fishing.

Seen in: *Innsider, New York, State College, Washingtonian.*

Contact: Sal Chandon. Certificate may be used: Sunday-Thursday all year excluding holidays for the full term of promotion.

"What you're doing for students of Gettysburg & the Civil War in general is tremendous! Our stay was wonderful!!"

Keystone Inn B&B

231 Hanover St
Gettysburg 17325
(717)337-3888

1913. Furniture-maker Clayton Reaser constructed this three-story brick Victorian with a wide-columned porch hugging the north and west sides. Cut stone graces every door and windowsill, each with a keystone. A chestnut staircase ascends the full three stories, and the interior is decorated with comfortable furnishings, ruffles and lace.

Innkeeper(s): Wilmer & Doris Martin.

Rates:$59-100. MC VISA. Full Bkfst. EP. Teas. 5 rooms. 2 with shared baths. Beds:KQT. Phone, AC in room. Bicycling. Skiing. Fishing.

Seen in: *Gettysburg Times, Hanover Sun.*

Contact: Doris Martin. Certificate may be used: Sunday through Thursday, November to April.

"We slept like lambs. This home has a warmth that is soothing."

The Old Appleford Inn

218 Carlisle St
Gettysburg 17325
(717)337-1711 Fax:(717)334-6228

1867. Located in the historic district, this Italianate-style brick mansion offers a taste of 19th-century charm and comfort. Among its inviting features are a plant-filled sunroom and a parlor with a baby grand piano and pump organ from a nearby settlement.

Innkeeper(s): Maribeth & Frank Skradski.

Rates:$93-103. MC VISA AX DS. Full Bkfst. Teas. Evening snacks. 10 rooms. Beds:QD. AC in room. Farm. Golf. Tennis. Skiing. Horseback riding. Fishing.

Seen in: *Innsider, Gettysburg Times, Baltimore Sun.*

Contact: Maribeth Skradski. Certificate may be used: Sunday through Thursday only, excluding all holidays. May not be used with any other promotion or gift certificate. Not available in May and October months.

"Everything in your place invites us back."

Greensburg

Huntland Farm B&B

Rd 9, Box 21
Greensburg 15601
(412)834-8483 Fax:(412)834-8483

1848. Porches and flower gardens surround the three-story, columned, brick Georgian manor that presides over the inn's 100 acres. Corner bedrooms are furnished with English antiques. Fallingwater, the Frank Lloyd Wright house, is nearby. Other attractions include Hidden Valley, Ohiopyle water rafting, Bushy Run and Fort Ligonier.

Innkeeper(s): Robert & Elizabeth Weidlein.

Rates:$70. AX. Full Bkfst. Teas. 4 rooms. 4 with shared baths. Fireplaces. Beds:KQT. Farm. Skiing.

Contact: Robert Weidlein. Certificate may be used: Anytime - subject to availability.

Hanover

Beechmont Inn

315 Broadway
Hanover 17331
(717)632-3013 (800)553-7009

1834. This gracious Georgian inn was a witness to the Civil War's first major battle on free soil, the Battle of Hanover. Decorated in Federal-period antiques, several guest rooms are named for the battle's commanders. The romantic Diller Suite contains a marble fireplace and queen canopy bed. The inn is noted for

elegant breakfasts, often served by candlelight.

Innkeeper(s): William & Susan Day.

Rates:$80-135. MC VISA AX. Gourmet Brkfst. Picnic lunches. Teas. Evening snacks. 7 rooms. Fireplaces. Beds:QD. TV, Phone, AC, Refrig. in room. Golf. Tennis. Bicycling. Skiing. Handicap access. Swimming. Horseback riding. Fishing.

Seen in: *Evening Sun, York Daily Record.*

Contact: William Day. Certificate may be used: Sunday night through Thursday night.

"I had a marvelous time at your charming, lovely inn."

Harford

9 Partners Inn

1 N Harmony Rd, PO Box 300
Harford 18823
(717)434-2233 Fax:(717)434-2801

1794. A bright red door welcomes guests to this white three-story, salt-box New England house. There are several fireplaces, original to the building, and the rooms are furnished with a mix of antiques and maple pieces. A large deck to the side of the house overlooks 24 acres of rolling meadows and the mountains beyond. Breakfast is offered in the dining room.

Innkeeper(s): Rudy Sumpter & Jim DeCoe.

Rates:$55-85. MC VISA. Full Bkfst. Gourmet Brkfst. 3 rooms. Beds:Q. Bicycling. Skiing. Fishing.

Contact: Rudy Sumpter. Certificate may be used: July 7 - Dec. 16, 1994; April 1 - Dec. 15, 1995.

Harrisburg

Abide With Me B&B

2601 Walnut St
Harrisburg 17103-1952
(717)236-5873

1879. A city historical site, this B&B is a brick Second Empire Victorian. There are three stories with shuttered windows, a large bay and a rounded front veranda. Oak, parquet and wide-plank floors and fireplaces add to the interest inside. Modestly furnished, the B&B offers some antiques and country pieces. The Harrisburg State Capital is a mile-and-a-half away.

Innkeeper(s): Don & Joyce Adams.

Rates:$48-55. Gourmet Brkfst. 3 rooms. 3 with shared baths. Beds:KQT. AC in room. Golf. Swimming. Fishing.

Contact: Joyce K. Adams. Certificate may be used: Except Sept. 25-Oct. 9.

(Harrisburg) New Kingstown

Kanaga House B&B

US Rt 11/Carlisle Pike
New Kingstown 17072-0092
(717)697-2714

1775. This gracious three-story German stonehouse is built of limestone. Steeped in the Colonial era, the innkeepers have gathered historic information that links the builder of the home, Joseph Junkin, with the Revolutionary War, the Puritans and the first Covenanter's Communion. A Joseph Junkin letter to his son, commander of the Battle of Brandywine, is in the parlor. The Elizabeth Junkin Room features a hope chest dated 1796, while the Eleanor Junkin Room offers a canopy bed with rose and blue bed hangings. Outside, an enormous gazebo creates a focal point for garden weddings.

Innkeeper(s): Don & Mary Jane Kretzing.

Rates:$60-75. MC VISA. Full Bkfst. Picnic lunches. 6 rooms. 1 with shared bath. Fireplaces. Beds:Q. Conference Rm. AC, Refrig. in room. Golf. Skiing. Fishing.

Contact: Mary Jane Kretzing. Certificate may be used: Sunday through Thursday, no special event weekends.

Hawley

Settlers Inn at Bingham Park

4 Main Ave
Hawley 18428
(717)226-2993 (800)833-8527
Fax:(717)226-1874

1927. When the Wallenpaupack Creek was dammed up to form the lake, the community hired architect Louis Welch and built this Grand Tudor Revival-style hotel featuring chestnut beams, leaded-glass windows and an enormous stone fireplace. The dining room, the main focus of the inn, is decorated with handmade quilts, hanging plants and chairs that once graced a Philadelphia cathedral. If you're looking for trout you can try your luck fishing the Lackawaxen River which runs behind the inn.

Innkeeper(s): Jeanne & Grant Genzlinger.

Rates:$75-115. MC VISA AX. Full Bkfst. Gourmet Lunch. 15 rooms. Beds:QT. Conference Rm. TV, Phone, AC, Refrig. in room. Tennis. Bicycling. Skiing. Swimming. Fishing.

Seen in: *Travel Holiday, New Jersey Monthly, Philadelphia, Philadelpia Inquirer.*

Contact: Jeanne Genzlinger. Certificate may be used: Anytime but weekends July-October.

"Country cozy with food and service fit for royalty."

Hershey-Palmyra

The Hen-Apple B&B
409 S Lingle Ave
Hershey-Palmyra 17078
(717)838-8282

1825. Located at the edge of town, this Georgian farmhouse is surrounded by an acre of lawns and old fruit trees. There are antiques and country pieces, along with a collection of wicker in the Wicker Room. Breakfast is provided in the dining room or the screened porch. Hershey is two miles away.

Innkeeper(s): Flo & Harold Eckert.

Rates:$65. MC VISA. Full Bkfst. Teas. 6 rooms. Beds:KDT. AC in room. Swimming. Fishing.

Contact: Flo Eckert. Certificate may be used: Jan. 5-April 30-Friday, Saturday, Sunday. Year-round Sunday through Thursday excluding holidays and first week in October.

Holicong

Barley Sheaf Farm
Rt 202 Box 10
Holicong 18928
(215)794-5104 Fax:(215)794-5565

1740. Situated on part of the original William Penn land grant, this beautiful stone house with white shuttered windows and mansard roof is set on 30 acres of farmland. Once owned by noted playwright George Kaufman, it was the gathering place for the Marx Brothers, Lillian Hellman and S. J. Perlman. The bank barn, pond, and majestic old trees round out a beautiful setting.

Innkeeper(s): Ann & Don Mills, Heather Knight.

Rates:$95-175. MC VISA AX DC CB. Full Bkfst. 10 rooms. Fireplaces. Beds:KQT. Conference Rm. AC in room. Farm. Handicap access. Swimming. Fishing.

Seen in: *Country Living.*

Contact: Don Mills. Certificate may be used: Sunday through Thursday - all year.

Intercourse

Carriage Corner B&B
3705 E Newport Rd, PO Box 371
Intercourse 17534-0371
(717)768-3059 (800)209-3059

1980. Located on two acres, this is a two-story, white Colonial house. The inn is decorated with folk art and country furnishings. Homemade breads

and hot cereals are served in the dining room. Walk five minutes to the village and explore shops displaying local crafts, pottery and handmade furniture.

Innkeeper(s): Gordon & Gwen Schuit.

Rates:$48-68. MC VISA. Full Bkfst. 4 rooms. 2 with shared baths. Beds:QD. TV, AC in room. Farm.

Contact: Gordon Schuit. Certificate may be used: June through October. Weekends not available. All other times okay.

Jim Thorpe

The Inn at Jim Thorpe
24 Broadway
Jim Thorpe 18229
(717)325-2599 (800)329-2599
Fax:(717)325-9145

1848. This massive New Orleans-style structure, now lovingly restored, hosted some colorful 19th-century guests, including Thomas Edison, John D. Rockefeller and Buffalo Bill. All rooms are appointed with Victorian furnishings and have private baths with pedestal sinks and marble floors. Also on the premises are a Victorian dining room, bar, shops, conference center and cabaret theater. The inn is situated in the heart of Jim Thorpe, a quaint Victorian town that was known at the turn of the century as the "Switzerland of America."

Innkeeper(s): John, David & Dale Drury.

Rates:$65-100. MC VISA AX DC DS. ContPlus Bkfst. MAP available. Gourmet Dinner. 22 rooms. Beds:Q. Conference Rm. TV, Phone, AC in room. Bicycling. Skiing. Handicap access. Swimming. Fishing.

Seen in: *Philadelphia Inquirer, Pennsylvania, Allentown Morning Call.*

Contact: David Drury. Certificate may be used: Sunday-Thursday year round. Anytime at last minute if available.

"Thank you for having provided us a relaxing getaway."

Kane

Kane Manor Country Inn
230 Clay St
Kane 16735
(814)837-6522 (800)837-8885
Fax:(814)837-6664

1896. This Georgian Revival inn, on 250 acres of woods and trails, was built for Dr. Elizabeth Kane, the first female doctor to practice in the area.

Many of the family's possessions dating back to the American Revolution and the Civil War remain. (Ask to see the attic.) Decor is a mixture of old family items in an unpretentious country style. There is a pub, popular with locals, on the premises. The building is in the National Register.

Innkeeper(s): Bruce David.

Rates:$95. MC VISA AX DS. Full Bkfst. Gourmet Dinner. Picnic lunches. Teas. 10 rooms. 4 with shared baths. Fireplaces. Beds:T. Conference Rm. TV in room. Golf. Tennis. Bicycling. Skiing. Swimming. Fishing.

Seen in: *Pittsburgh Press, News Herald, Cleveland Plain Dealer, Youngstown Indicator.*

Contact: Bruce David. Certificate may be used: Year-round subject to availability.

"It's a place I want to return to often, for rest and relaxation."

Kennett Square

Scarlett House
503 W State St
Kennett Square 19348
(610)444-9592

1910. This stone foursquare home features an extensive wraparound porch and front door surrounded by leaded-glass windows. Beyond the foyer are two downstairs parlors, while a second-floor parlor provides a sunny setting for afternoon tea. Rooms are furnished in romantic Victorian decor. Beds are turned down with a flower and chocolate at night. When served in the dining room, breakfast is by candlelight with fine china and lace

linens. Mushroom-shaped chocolate chip scones are a novel breakfast specialty at the inn—a reminder that this is the acclaimed mushroom capital of the world.

Innkeeper(s): Susan Lalli-Ascosi & Andy Ascosi.

Rates:$65-105. ContPlus Bkfst. Teas. Evening snacks. 4 rooms. 2 with shared baths. Beds:Q. AC in room.

Contact: Susan Lalli-Ascosi. Certificate may be used: Monday through Thursday only; January, February, March, July, August only, excludes holidays, cannot be used in combination with other promotions.

"Truly an enchanting place."

Lackawaxen

Roebling Inn on the Delaware
PO Box 31, Scenic Dr
Lackawaxen 18435
(717)685-7900

1870. This Greek Revival house is in the National Register of Historic Places and once was the home of Judge Ridgway, tallyman for the Delaware and Hudson Canal Company. Country furnishings are supplemented with some antiques, and there is a long front porch for relaxing. Full country breakfasts are provided. Afterward, ask the innkeepers for directions to nearby hidden waterfalls, or walk to the Zane Grey Museum, Roebling's Delaware Aqueduct or Minisink Battleground Park.

Innkeeper(s): Don & JoAnn Jahn.

Rates:$65-100. MC VISA AX. Full Bkfst. 6 rooms. Beds:QT. TV, AC in room. Skiing. Swimming. Fishing.

Contact: JoAnn Jahn. Certificate may be used: Monday, Tuesday, Wednesday, Thursday and non-holiday and November through April.

Lampeter

Bed & Breakfast - The Manor
PO Box 416, 830 Village Rd
Lampeter 17537
(717)464-9564

1934. In a Dutch Colonial building, The Manor is located on almost five acres. Adirondack chairs provide viewing spots from the large front porch. Among the creative elements of the country decor, is an Amish dress and cap that hangs in one of the guest rooms. A former restaurant owner, Mary Lou offers gourmet and low-fat breakfasts. By prior arrangement, the innkeepers will reserve a dinner for you with an Old Order Amish farm family.

Innkeeper(s): Mary Paolini.

Rates:$79-99. MC VISA. Full Bkfst. Gourmet Brkfst. Teas. Evening snacks. 6 rooms. 2 with shared baths. Beds:QT. AC in room. Fishing.

Contact: Jackie Curtis. Certificate may be used: Nov. 1 to May 15.

Walkabout Inn B&B

837 Village Rd, PO Box 294
Lampeter 17537
(717)464-0707 Fax:(717)464-2678

1925. The Walkabout Inn offers hospitality
Australian-style thanks to Australian Richard
Mason, one of the innkeepers. Tea is imported

from down under and breakfasts are prepared from
Australian recipes. From the wraparound porch,
guests can watch Amish buggies pass by. Bed chambers have antique furniture, Pennsylvania Dutch
quilts and hand-painted wall stencilings. Each room
is named from the image stenciled on its walls.

Innkeeper(s): Richard & Margaret Mason.

Rates:$99-159. MC VISA AX. Full Bkfst. Gourmet Dinner. Teas. 6
rooms. Fireplaces. Beds:QT. Conference Rm. TV, AC in room. Bicycling.
Spa.

Seen in: *New York Post, Intelligencer Journal.*

Contact: Richard Mason. Certificate may be used: Sunday through
Thursday no holidays or weekends.

*"You anticipated our every need and that is not done in
too many places."*

Lancaster

Hollinger House

2336 Hollinger Rd
Lancaster 17602
(717)464-3050

1870. A peach bottom slate roof tops this large
Adams-style brick house, and there is a wraparound

veranda and a double balcony. Several fireplaces
and original hardwood floors have been restored.
Adding to the setting's pastoral beauty, sheep
meander over the meadow and woodland stream.
The innkeepers serve hors d'oeuvres upon arrival,
tea in the afternoon, and additional goodies at bedtime. In the morning, a bountiful breakfast is provided.

Innkeeper(s): Gina & Jeff Trost.

Rates:$75-90. MC VISA DS. Full Bkfst. Gourmet Brkfst. Picnic lunches.
Evening snacks. 5 rooms. Beds:KQT. AC in room. Bicycling. Skiing.
Fishing.

Contact: Gina Trost. Certificate may be used: Between November and
March.

The King's Cottage, A B&B Inn

1049 E King St
Lancaster 17602
(717)397-1017 Fax:(717)397-3447

1913. This Mission Revival house features a red-tile
roof and stucco walls, common in many stately
turn-of-the-century houses in California and New

Mexico. Its elegant interiors include a sweeping
staircase, a library with marble fireplace, stained-
glass windows, and a solarium. The inn is appointed with Oriental rugs and antiques and fine 18th-
century English reproductions. The formal dining
room provides the location for gourmet morning
meals.

Innkeeper(s): Karen & Jim Owens.

Rates:$80-125. MC VISA DS. Full Bkfst. Teas. 8 rooms. Beds:KQ.
Conference Rm. AC in room. Golf. Tennis. Skiing. Swimming. Fishing.

Seen in: *Country, USA Weekend, Bon Appetit, Intelligencer Journal,
Times.*

Contact: James Owens. Certificate may be used: December through
July, Monday through Thursday, excluding holidays/special events. Not
valid with other offers.

*"I appreciate your attention to all our needs and look
forward to recommending your inn to friends."*

New Life Homestead B&B

1400 E King St (Rt 462)
Lancaster 17602
(717)396-8928

1912. This two-story brick home is situated within six miles of the Amish farms. Hosts Carol and Bill Giersch often host evening discussions about the culture and history of the surrounding Pennsylvania Dutch Country, and they will, with advance notice, arrange tours and meals in Amish homes. Their full country breakfasts are made from produce purchased at local Amish markets.

Innkeeper(s): Carol & Bill Giersch.

Rates:$50-70. Full Bkfst. Evening snacks. 4 rooms. 2 with shared baths. Beds:QT. AC in room. Golf. Tennis. Swimming. Fishing.

Seen in: *Keystone Gazette, Pennsylvania Dutch Traveler.*

Contact: Carol Giersch. Certificate may be used: December through March, Sunday through Thursday.

"Reminded me of my childhood at home."

Patchwork Inn

2319 Old Philadelphia Pike
Lancaster 17602
(717)293-9078

1850. Quilts provide the decor for this farmhouse located next to a working Amish farm. Guest room furniture is antique oak, and three of the beds have six-foot carved headboards. Breakfast, served in the dining room, often includes baked egg dishes, Dutch Baby pancakes and quilt talk. Afterwards, walk to Millstream Park and enjoy its trails and arboreteum. The innkeepers will be happy to guide you to out-of-the-way quilt and fabric stores and advise you on selections, if desired.

Innkeeper(s): Anne & Lee Martin.

Rates:$60-80. MC VISA DS. Full Bkfst. 4 rooms. 2 with shared baths. Beds:Q. AC in room.

Contact: Warren Martin. Certificate may be used: Sunday - Thursday all months except August and October.

Witmer's Tavern - Historic 1725 Inn

2014 Old Philadelphia Pike
Lancaster 17602
(717)299-5305

1725. This pre-Revolutionary War inn is the sole survivor of 62 inns that once lined the old Lancaster-to-Philadelphia turnpike. Immigrant Conestoga wagon trains were made here for the Western and Southern journeys to wilderness homesteads. Designated as a National Landmark, the property is restored to its original and simple, rustic pioneer style. There are sagging wide-board floors and antiques with original finish. History buffs will enjoy seeing the Indian escape tunnel

entrance and knowing President John Adams once stayed here. Guest rooms feature antiques, old quilts and fresh flowers.

Innkeeper(s): Brant, Pamela, Keith, Melissa & Jeanne Hartung.

Rates:$60-90. ContPlus Bkfst. 7 rooms. 5 with shared baths. Fireplaces. Beds:D. Conference Rm. AC in room. Bicycling. Skiing. Swimming. Fishing.

Seen in: *Stuart News.*

Contact: Brant Hartung. Certificate may be used: Sunday through Thursday, November through July, excluding holidays.

"Your personal attention and enthusiastic knowledge of the area and Witmer's history made it come alive and gave us the good feelings we came looking for."

Landenberg

Cornerstone B&B Inn

RD 1 Box 155
Landenberg 19350
(610)274-2143 Fax:(610)274-0734

1704. The Cornerstone is a farmhouse with a pleasant wicker-filled veranda. Eighteenth-century furnishings and two fireplaces make the parlor inviting. Wing chairs, fresh flowers, and working fireplaces add enjoyment to the guest rooms. A greenhouse, Jacuzzi and bicycles are additional amenities. Stay in one of two apartments in the renovated stone barn if you'd like more space and a kitchen and laundry.

Innkeeper(s): Linda Chamberlin & Mary Mulligan.

Rates:$75-150. MC VISA AX DS. Full Bkfst. 7 rooms. 1 with shared bath. Fireplaces. Beds:KQ. TV, AC in room. Farm. Bicycling.

Contact: Linda Chamberlin. Certificate may be used: Sunday-Thursday, no holidays/holiday weeks.

Lebanon

Zinns Mill Homestead
243 N Zinns Mill Rd
Lebanon 17042
(717)272-1513

1800. Zinn's Mill Homestead is a 200-year-old stone house overlooking a stream that once powered a local grain mill. There are 13 wooded acres and a gazebo now marks the spot where the mill once stood. Pennsylvania German antiques furnish the inn and there is a walk-in Colonial fireplace in the family room. Mount Hope Winery and Renaissance Faire are five miles away.
Innkeeper(s): Judy & Bob Heisey.
Rates:$75-95. MC VISA. Full Bkfst. 4 rooms. 3 with shared baths. Beds:QT. TV, AC in room. Farm. Bicycling. Sauna. Fishing.
Contact: Judith Heisey. Certificate may be used: April - October.

Lewisburg

Brookpark Farm B&B
100 Reitz Blvd
Lewisburg 17837
(717)523-0220

1914. Twenty-five acres surround this three-story brick house. The innkeepers operate the Pennsylvania House Gallery in their enormous barn on the property. The inn, therefore, includes traditional, transitional and country designs from these furniture collections including cherry, pine and mahogany woods.
Innkeeper(s): Crystale & Todd Moyer.
Rates:$55-65. MC VISA. Full Bkfst. Teas. 5 rooms. 2 with shared baths. Beds:Q. Conference Rm. AC in room. Farm. Skiing. Fishing.
Contact: Todd Moyer. Certificate may be used: Year-round - anytime.

Lima

Hamanassett B&B
P O Box 129
Lima 19037
(610)459-3000 Fax:(610)459-3000

1856. Ancestors of the innkeeper purchased this estate in 1870 and the property later hosted The Lima Hunt. The inn's 48 acres offer fields of wildflowers and gardens of rhododendrons, azaleas and daffodils. Inside the three-story Federal manor, 2,000 books fill the library shelves. A corner fireplace warms the dining room, overlooking the lawns and gardens. There is a formal drawing room where tea is presented. Canopied beds are featured in the guest rooms.
Innkeeper(s): Mrs. Evelene H. Dohan.
Rates:$85-120. Full Bkfst. Gourmet Brkfst. Teas. 9 rooms. 2 with shared baths. Beds:KQT. Conference Rm. Phone, AC, Refrig. in room.
Contact: Evelene Dohan. Certificate may be used: Not available May and June, October, November or any holiday weekend.

Lock Haven

Victorian Inn B&B
402 E Water St
Lock Haven 17745
(717)748-8688

1859. Located on the West Branch of the Susquehanna River, this Victorian inn offers an old-fashioned porch overlooking the water. Wine and cheese is served in the garden atrium, and the cheerful Victorian dining room is the spot for breakfast. Bicycles may be borrowed for pedaling along the Island Route.
Innkeeper(s): J & B Rogers.
Rates:$49. MC VISA AX DC DS. Full Bkfst. 9 rooms. Beds:KQT. TV, Phone, AC in room. Bicycling. Skiing. Swimming. Fishing.
Contact: Barbara Rogers. Certificate may be used: Mid-December to mid-April.

Malvern

The Great Valley House of Valley Forge
110 Swedesford Rd, RD 3
Malvern 19355
(610)644-6759 Fax:(610)644-7019

1690. This Colonial stone farmhouse sits on four acres just two miles from Valley Forge Park. Boxwoods line the walkway and ancient trees surround the house. Each of the three guest rooms are hand-stenciled and feature canopied or brass beds topped with handmade quilts. Guests enjoy a full breakfast before a 14-foot fireplace in the "summer kitchen," the oldest part of the house. On the grounds are a swimming pool, walking and hiking trails.
Innkeeper(s): Pattye Benson.
Rates:$75-85. Full Bkfst. 4 rooms. 2 with shared baths. Beds:QT. TV, Phone, AC, Refrig. in room. Golf. Tennis. Skiing. Swimming. Horseback riding. Fishing.
Seen in: *Main Line Philadelphia, Philadelphia Inquirer, Washington Post.*
Contact: Patricia Benson. Certificate may be used: Year-round, Sunday-Thursday.

"Our favorite, an excellent breakfast in an enchanting old stone kitchen."

Manheim

Herr Farmhouse Inn
2256 Huber Dr
Manheim 17545
(717)653-9852 (800)584-0743

1750. This pre-Revolutionary War stone farmhouse is one of the oldest buildings in Lancaster County. The woodwork, including the moldings, cabinets and doors is original. Early American antiques and reproductions set the scene for a truly Colonial vacation. Two rooms include fireplaces. The kitchen, where a hearty continental breakfast is served, boasts a walk-in fireplace. Antique shopping, historic attractions and Amish dining are nearby.

Innkeeper(s): Barry Herr.

Rates:$63-95. MC VISA. ContPlus Bkfst. 4 rooms. 2 with shared baths. Fireplaces. Beds:DT. AC in room. Farm. Golf. Tennis. Bicycling. Skiing. Handicap access. Swimming. Fishing.

Seen in: *Country Inns.*

Contact: Barry Herr. Certificate may be used: Sunday through Thursday, holidays excluded.

"Your home is lovely. You've done a beautiful job of restoring and remodeling."

Penn's Valley Farm & Inn
6182 Metzler Rd
Manheim 17545
(717)898-7386

1826. This picture-perfect farm was purchased by the Metzler's ancestors in 1770, but it was originally owned by the three Penn brothers. The guest house, built in 1826, features stenciled farm animals painted along the winding stairway that leads to the bedrooms. An open hearth is in the living room. Breakfast is served in the dining room of the main farmhouse.

Innkeeper(s): Melvin & Gladys Metzler.

Rates:$55-65. MC VISA AX. Full Bkfst. 2 rooms. 1 with shared bath. Beds:QT. AC, Refrig. in room. Farm. Swimming.

Contact: Gladys Metzler. Certificate may be used: December, 1994 through February, 1995.

Marietta

Vogt Farm B&B
1225 Colebrook Rd
Marietta 17547
(717)653-4810

1868. Twenty-eight acres surround this farmhouse. There are three porches from which to enjoy the pastoral scene of cattle and sheep. Keith offers a walking tour of the farm, including the grain elevator. The innkeepers have hosted guests for 20 years and have created a comfortable setting for overnight stays. Desks, private phones and a copier are available to business travelers.

Innkeeper(s): Kathy Vogt.

Rates:$55. MC VISA AX DC DS. Full Bkfst. 3 rooms. 3 with shared baths. Beds:KQT. Phone, AC in room. Farm.

Contact: Kathy Vogt. Certificate may be used: Sunday - Thursday, except October.

Meadville

Fountainside B&B
628 Highland Ave
Meadville 16335
(814)337-7447

1855. A long front porch extends across the front of this farmhouse-style B&B. A full breakfast is served on the weekends, a continental breakfast during the week. Both Victorian and modern pieces are combined to furnish the rooms. Allegheny College is next door.

Innkeeper(s): Maureen Boyle.

Rates:$55-60. MC VISA AX DS. Full Bkfst. Gourmet Brkfst. Teas. Evening snacks. 5 rooms. 4 with shared baths. Beds:QT. Conference Rm. Bicycling. Skiing. Swimming. Fishing.

Contact: Maureen Boyle. Certificate may be used: Weekdays April - November. Weekdays or weekends December - April.

Mercersburg

The Mercersburg Inn
405 S Main St
Mercersburg 17236
(717)328-5231 Fax:(717)328-3403

1909. Situated on a hill overlooking the Blue Ridge Mountains, the valley and village, this 20,000-square-foot Georgian Revival mansion was built for industrialist Harry Byron. Six massive columns mark the entrance, which opens to a majestic hall featuring chestnut wainscoting and an elegant double stairway and rare scagliola (marbleized) columns. All the rooms are furnished with antiques and reproductions. A local craftsman built the inn's four-poster, canopied king-size beds. Many of the rooms have their own balconies and a few have fireplaces. The inn's chef is noted for his elegant six-course dinners, but the menu also includes a la carte choices. This menu changes seasonally.

Innkeeper(s): Frances Wolfe & John Mohr.

Rates:$110-180. MC VISA DS. Full Bkfst. Gourmet Dinner. Picnic lunches. 15 rooms. Fireplaces. Beds:KQT. Conference Rm. Phone, AC in room. Skiing. Swimming. Fishing.

Seen in: *Mid-Atlantic Country, Washington Post, The Herald-Mail, Richmond News Leader, Washingtonian, Philadelphia Inquirer.*

Contact: Frances Wolfe. Certificate may be used: Sunday through Thursday, subject to availability (excluding holidays).

"Elegance personified! Outstanding ambiance and warm hospitality."

Mertztown

Longswamp B&B
RD 2, PO Box 26
Mertztown 19539
(610)682-6197 Fax:(610)682-4854

1789. Country gentleman Colonel Trexler added a mansard roof to this stately Federal mansion in 1860. Inside is a magnificent walnut staircase and pegged wood floors. As the story goes, the colonel discovered his unmarried daughter having an affair and shot her lover. He escaped hanging, but it was said that after his death his ghost could be seen in the upstairs bedroom watching the road. In 1905, an exorcism was reported to have sent his spirit to a nearby mountaintop.

Innkeeper(s): Elsa & Dean Dimick.

Rates:$70-75. MC VISA. Full Bkfst. Teas. 10 rooms. 4 with shared baths. Fireplaces. Beds:QT. AC in room. Farm. Tennis. Bicycling. Skiing. Swimming. Horseback riding. Fishing.

Seen in: *Washingtonian, Weekend Travel, The Sun.*

Contact: Elsa Dimick. Certificate may be used: November through April.

"The warm country atmosphere turns strangers into friends."

Millersburg

Victorian Manor Inn
312 Market St
Millersburg 17061
(717)692-3511

1871. In the Second Empire style, this three-story inn was fully renovated over a period of four years. Nineteenth-century furnishings are found in most rooms, which include walnut beds and marble-topped dressers. A side veranda and a gazebo offer wicker furnishings. The nearby Millersburg Ferry has offered passage across the Susquehanna River for more than 100 years.

Innkeeper(s): Skip & Sue Wingard.

Rates:$55-65. MC VISA AX. Full Bkfst. Gourmet Brkfst. Teas. 3 rooms. 2 with shared baths. Beds:DT. AC in room. Swimming. Fishing.

Contact: Suzanne Wingard. Certificate may be used: Sept. 1, 1994 - June 30, 1995.

Milton

Pau-lyn's Country B&B
RR 3, Box 676
Milton 17847
(717)742-4110

1850. Recently renovated, this three-story Victorian brick home offers a formal dining room with a fireplace and antique musical instruments. A porch and patio overlook the large lawn. Nearby are working farms and dairies, covered bridges, mountains, hills and valleys.

Innkeeper(s): Paul & Evelyn Landis.

Rates:$45-50. Full Bkfst. 7 rooms. 5 with shared baths. Beds:QT. AC in room. Bicycling. Skiing. Handicap access. Swimming. Fishing.

Contact: Evelyn Landis. Certificate may be used: Sunday through Thursday year-round, weekends as available.

Tomlinson Manor B&B
250 Broadway
Milton 17847
(717)742-3657

1927. In the Georgian style, this appealing three-story stone manor was designed by Dr. Charles Tomlinson, a local physician and amateur architect. Shutters border the small-paned windows, and there are gardens all around. All the rooms, including the library, are furnished with antiques. Next door to the B&B is a dinner theater.

Innkeeper(s): Michael & Nancy Slease.

Rates:$55. MC VISA. ContPlus Bkfst. 3 rooms. Beds:Q. AC in room. Fishing.

Contact: Nancy Slease. Certificate may be used: Weekdays (Sunday-Thursday) through the entire promotion period.

Montoursville

The Carriage House at Stonegate
RD 1, Box 11A
Montoursville 17754
(717)433-4340 Fax:(717)433-4536

1830. President Herbert Hoover was a descendant of the original settlers of this old homestead in the Loyalsock Creek Valley. Indians burned the original house, but the present farmhouse and numerous outbuildings date from the early 1800s. The Carriage House is set next to a lovely brook.

Innkeeper(s): Harold & Dena Mesaris.

Rates:$70. ContPlus Bkfst. 2 rooms. 1 with shared bath. Beds:QT. TV, Phone, Refrig. in room. Farm. Golf. Tennis. Skiing. Swimming. Horseback riding. Fishing.

Contact: Harold Mesaris. Certificate may be used: March, April, May, November.

Mount Joy

Cedar Hill Farm

305 Longenecker Rd
Mount Joy 17552
(717)653-4655

1817. Situated on 51 acres overlooking Chiques Creek, this stone farmhouse boasts a two-tiered front veranda affording pastoral views of the surrounding fields. The host was born in the house and is the third generation to have lived here since the Swarr family first purchased it in 1878. Family heirlooms and antiques include an elaborately carved walnut bedstead, a marble-topped washstand and a "tumbling block" quilt. In the kitchen, a copper kettle, bread paddle and baskets of dried herbs accentuate the walk-in fireplace, where guests often linger over breakfast. Cedar Hill is a working poultry and grain farm.

Innkeeper(s): Russel & Gladys Swarr.
Rates:$60-70. MC VISA AX DS. ContPlus Bkfst. 5 rooms. Beds:KQT. AC in room. Farm. Golf. Tennis. Skiing. Fishing.
Seen in: *Women's World, Lancaster Farming, Philadelphia, New York Times, Ladies Home Journal.*
Contact: Gladys Swarr. Certificate may be used: Nov. 1 to April 1 (no holiday weekends).

"Dorothy can have Kansas, Scarlett can take Tara, Rick can keep Paris — I've stayed at Cedar Hill Farm."

Hillside Farm B&B

607 Eby Chiques Rd
Mount Joy 17552
(717)653-6697 Fax:(717)653-6697

1863. This comfortable farm has a relaxing homey feel to it. Rooms are simply decorated and special extras such as handmade quilts and antiques add an

elegant country touch. The home is a true monument to the cow. Dairy antiques, cow knickknacks and antique milk bottles abound. Some of the bot-

tles were found during the renovation of the home and its grounds. Spend the day hunting for bargains in nearby antique shops, malls and factory outlets, or tour local Amish and Pennsylvania Dutch attractions. The farm is a good vacation spot for families with children above the age of 10.

Innkeeper(s): Gary & Deb Lintner; Wilma & Bob Lintner.
Rates:$50-63. Full Bkfst. AP available. 5 rooms. 2 with shared baths. Beds:KQDT. AC in room. Farm. Golf. Swimming. Fishing.
Seen in: *Antiques & Auction News, Intelligencer Journal.*
Contact: Deb Lintner. Certificate may be used: Anytime except weekends in September and October.

"Warm, friendly, comfortable...feels like home."

The Olde Square Inn

127 E Main St
Mount Joy 17552
(717)653-4525 (800)742-3533
Fax:(717)653-0976

1917. Located on the town square, this Neoclassical house features handsome columned fireplaces and leaded-glass windows. The innkeepers operate a food concessions stand at Columbia Market and provide fresh homemade croissants, muffins and rolls for breakfast. Mills, Amish farms and marketplaces are nearby.

Innkeeper(s): Fran & Dave Hand.
Rates:$65-75. MC VISA. ContPlus Bkfst. 4 rooms. Beds:KQT. TV, AC in room. Swimming. Fishing.
Contact: Frances Hand. Certificate may be used: Anytime, except holiday weekends.

Mount Pocono

Farmhouse B&B

HCR 1, Box 6B Grange Rd
Mount Pocono 18344
(717)839-0796

1850. Located on six acres, this red and white farmhouse offers a country decor with accents of heirloom antiques. All the rooms are suites, and there is a two-story private cottage (once an ice house) with original stone walls. The suites have fireplaces and sunken tubs. Homemade cookies await in your room upon check-in, and there is tea service. Breakfast choices are invented by Jack, a professional chef, and may include Bacon Double Cheeseburger Omelets or Blueberry Stuffed French Toasted Croissants.

Innkeeper(s): Jack & Donna Asure.
Rates:$85-105. MC VISA DS. Full Bkfst. 3 rooms. Fireplaces. Beds:Q. TV, Phone, AC, Refrig. in room. Skiing. Swimming. Fishing.
Contact: Donna Asure. Certificate may be used: Sunday-Thursday, Jan. 1-May 31 and Nov. 1-Dec. 15. No holidays. First-time guests only, non-smokers only.

Muncy

The Bodine House B&B
307 S Main St
Muncy 17756
(717)546-8949

1805. This Federal-style townhouse, framed by a white picket fence, is in the National Register. Antique and reproduction furnishings beautifully

highlight the inn's four fireplaces, the parlor, study and library. A favorite guest room features a pine canopy bed, hand-stenciled and bordered walls, and a framed sampler by the innkeeper's great-great-great-grandmother. Candlelight breakfasts are served beside the fireplace in a gracious Colonial dining room.

Innkeeper(s): David & Marie Louise Smith.

Rates:$55-70. MC VISA AX. Full Bkfst. 5 rooms. Fireplaces. Beds:T. TV, AC in room. Golf. Tennis. Bicycling. Skiing. Swimming. Horseback riding. Fishing.

Seen in: *Colonial Homes.*

Contact: David Smith. Certificate may be used: Weekdays (Sunday through Thursday nights).

Nazareth

The Classic Victorian B&B
35 N New St
Nazareth 18064
(215)759-8276

1907. This brick and stone Colonial Revival house is located in the Nazareth Historic District, once a closed Moravian community. Chintz-covered wicker furniture and overflowing flower baskets fill the wraparound veranda in summer. The inn features chestnut pocket doors, bay windows, Oriental carpets and Chippendale and other antique furniture. The Polo Room is decorated in paisley with a pheasant border near the ceiling and a four-poster mahogany bed. Breakfast is served under a wisteria-

covered arbor overlooking the back garden, in the formal candlelit dining room with china and sterling, or in a basket brought to your room. Afternoon tea and evening turndown service are provided.

Innkeeper(s): Irene & Dan Sokolowski.

Rates:$70-90. MC VISA AX. Full Bkfst. Gourmet Brkfst. Picnic lunches. Teas. 3 rooms. 2 with shared baths. Beds:DT. Conference Rm. TV, Phone, AC in room. Skiing.

Seen in: *Express Times, Home News.*

Contact: Irene Sokolowski. Certificate may be used: No weekends or holidays, Monday through Thursday all year.

"We felt so at home it was like staying with family."

New Bloomfield

The Tressler House B&B
41 W Main St, P O Box 38
New Bloomfield 17068
(717)582-2914

1830. A white picket fence frames the acre of lawn surrounding this Federal-period home. A spider web window transom marks the front entrance. Oriental rugs, coordinated fabrics and wallcoverings fill the 22 rooms. Old mill stones, collected by the former owner, are woven into the brick patio and sidewalk. There is a covered porch filled with antique wicker, and a walled duck pond. Smoked turkey sausages and blueberry pancakes often are featured at breakfast.

Innkeeper(s): David & Carol Ulsh.

Rates:$50-60. Full Bkfst. Gourmet Brkfst. 4 rooms. 2 with shared baths. Fireplaces. Beds:DT. TV, AC in room. Golf. Tennis. Skiing. Swimming. Horseback riding. Fishing.

Seen in: *Perry County Times, Perry County Shopper, Antiques & Auction News.*

Contact: Carol Ulsh. Certificate may be used: Sunday through Thursday upon availability all year.

New Hope

Aaron Burr House
80 W Bridge St
New Hope 18938
(215)862-2520

1870. This inn is one of the Wedgewood Collection inns. A Victorian Shingle style, it is in the National Register. Its three stories, including the spacious parlor, are appointed with antiques and reproductions. Guest rooms offer amenities such as private baths, telephones, TVs and many have fireplaces. Within walking distance are fine restaurants, shops and art galleries. The grounds offer two gazebos, stately old trees and a flagstone patio.

Innkeeper(s): Carl & Nadine Glassman.

Rates:$100-190. MC VISA AX. ContPlus Bkfst. AP available. Teas. 10 rooms. Fireplaces. Beds:KQT. Conference Rm. Phone, AC, Refrig. in room. Tennis. Bicycling. Skiing. Exercise room. Swimming. Fishing.

Contact: Carl Glassman. Certificate may be used: Monday-Thursday, non-holidays, January-April.

Hollyhedge B&B
6987 Upper York Rd
New Hope 18938
(215)862-3136 Fax:(215)862-0960

1730. This handsome stone manor rests on 20 acres with green lawns, a natural pond and a small stream. French, American and English antiques are found throughout the inn. Some rooms have private entrances and some feature fireplaces. The innkeepers are former restaurateurs and provide a notable breakfast. Catered weddings and corporate retreats are popular here.

Innkeeper(s): Joe & Amy Luccaro.

Rates:$65-150. MC VISA AX. Full Bkfst. Gourmet Brkfst. 15 rooms. Fireplaces. Beds:KQT. Conference Rm. AC in room. Tennis. Bicycling. Swimming. Fishing.

Contact: Joe Luccaro. Certificate may be used: Not on holiday weekends.

Hotel Du Village
2535 N River Rd
New Hope 18938
(215)862-9911

1907. Once part of a William Penn land grant, the Hotel du Village features 10 acres of trees, lawns and a creek. The Tudor-style hotel once served as a boarding school for girls, while the restaurant is part of the old White Oaks estate. Chestnut paneling, Persian carpets and three working fireplaces provide a backdrop to chef Omar Arbani's French cuisine.

Innkeeper(s): Barbara & Omar Arbani.

Rates:$85-100. AX DC CB. ContPlus Bkfst. Gourmet Dinner. 20 rooms. Beds:KQT. Conference Rm. AC in room. Tennis. Swimming.

Seen in: *Trenton Times, The Burlington County Times.*

Contact: Barbara Arbani. Certificate may be used: Non-holiday Sundays through Thursdays.

"The food is wonderful - fireplaces burning makes everything so romantic!"

The Whitehall Inn
1370 Pineville Rd
New Hope 18938
(215)598-7945

1794. This white-plastered stone farmhouse is located on 13 country acres studded with stately maple

and chestnut trees. Inside, a winding walnut staircase leads to antique-furnished guest rooms that offer widepine floors, wavy-glass windows, high ceilings and some fireplaces. An antique clock collection, Oriental rugs and late Victorian furnishings are found throughout. Afternoon tea, evening chocolates and a candlelight breakfasts served with heirloom china and sterling reflect the inn's many amenities. There are stables on the property and horseback riding may be arranged.

Innkeeper(s): Mike & Suella Wass.

Rates:$130-180. MC VISA AX DC DS CB. Gourmet Brkfst. Teas. 6 rooms. 2 with shared baths. Fireplaces. Beds:QD. AC in room. Tennis. Skiing. Swimming. Stables. Fishing.

Contact: Mike Wass. Certificate may be used: Monday through Thursday year-round.

New Oxford

Flaherty House
104 Lincoln Way
New Oxford 17350
(717)624-9494 (800)217-0618

1888. This three-story brick Victorian has a large bay, a long front porch, and stained-glass and shuttered windows. Located in the middle of what is considered Pennsylvania's antique capital, there are more than 200 antique dealers within walking distance of the inn. Heirlooms and antiques are featured throughout the house. A full country breakfast is served.

Innkeeper(s): Joe & Bonnie Masslofsky.

Rates:$60-90. Full Bkfst. 3 rooms. 2 with shared baths.

Contact: Bonnie Masslofsky. Certificate may be used: Sunday through Thursday except June 30 to July 7.

Newtown

Hollileif B&B
677 Durham Road (Rt 413)
Newtown 18940
(215)598-3100

1700. This handsome former farmhouse sits on more than five rolling acres of scenic Bucks County countryside. The name "hollileif," which means "beloved tree," refers to the 40-foot holly trees that grace the entrance. Bedrooms are appointed with lace and fresh flowers. Afternoon refreshments in the parlor or patio are provided, as well as evening turndown service. Guests can enjoy croquet, badminton, volleyball, horseshoes and hammocks during the summer and sledding in winter.

Innkeeper(s): Ellen & Richard Butkus.

Rates:$80-125. MC VISA AX DS. Full Bkfst. Gourmet Brkfst. Teas. 5 rooms. Fireplaces. Beds:QD. AC in room. Golf. Tennis. Skiing. Swimming. Horseback riding. Fishing.

Seen in: *Trentonian.*

Contact: Ellen Butkus. Certificate may be used: Sunday through Thursday excluding all holidays and Dec. 26-29, 1994 and Dec. 26-28, 1995.

"The accommodations were lovely and the breakfasts delicious and unusual, but it is really the graciousness of our hosts that made the weekend memorable."

North Wales

Joseph Ambler Inn
1005 Horsham Rd
North Wales 19454
(215)362-7500 Fax:(215)362-7500

1734. This beautiful fieldstone-and-wood house was built over a period of three centuries. Originally, it was part of a grant that Joseph Ambler, a Quaker wheelwright, obtained from William Penn in 1688. A large stone bank barn and tenant cottage on 12 acres constitute the remainder of the property. Guests enjoy the cherry wainscoting and walk-in fireplace in the schoolroom.

Innkeeper(s): Steve & Terry Kratz.

Rates:$95-140. MC VISA AX DC DS CB. Full Bkfst. Gourmet Dinner. 28 rooms. Beds:QD. Conference Rm. TV, Phone, AC in room. Skiing. Handicap access. Swimming. Fishing.

Seen in: *Colonial Homes, Country Living.*

Contact: Wendy Hammel. Certificate may be used: Anytime.

"What a wonderful night my husband and I spent. We are already planning to come back to your wonderful getaway."

Northumberland

Campbell's B&B
707 Duke St
Northumberland 17857
(717)473-3276

1859. This old farmhouse has three stories and there are porches overlooking the well-planted grounds and rose gardens. A few antiques and reproductions add to the country decor. Lake Augusta is a mile away for fishing and boating.

Innkeeper(s): Bob & Millie Campbell.

Rates:$50-60. Full Bkfst. Evening snacks. 4 rooms. 2 with shared baths. Beds:QT. AC in room. Golf. Tennis. Skiing. Swimming. Horseback riding. Fishing.

Contact: Robert Campbell. Certificate may be used: Anytime except college weekends and holidays.

Philadelphia

The Independence Park Inn
235 Chestnut St
Philadelphia 19106
(215)922-4443 Fax:(215)922-4487

1856. This five-story urban inn is listed in the National Register of Historic Places. The high-ceilinged guest rooms feature rich draperies and Chippendale writing tables. In the parlor lobby, guests may enjoy tea and cucumber sandwiches by the fireplace. Breakfast is served on the skylighted court. Conference rooms are available for business travelers.

Innkeeper(s): Terry Bompard.

Rates:$135-165. MC VISA AX DC DS CB. Cont. Bkfst. Teas. 36 rooms. Beds:KQT. Conference Rm. TV, Phone, AC in room. Swimming.

Seen in: *The Philadelphia Inquirer, The Atlanta Journal and Constitution.*

Contact: Terry Bompard. Certificate may be used: Weekends with two-night minimum.

"Everything possible seems to have been planned for our comfort and needs."

Shippen Way Inn
416-18 Bainbridge St
Philadelphia 19147
(215)627-7266 (800)245-4873

1750. In the National Register of Historic Places, Shippen Way is located close to Independence Hall. Working fireplaces, timbered walls and ceiling beams create an authentic Colonial decor. This era is reinforced with a cobbler's bench, pencil-post beds, a stenciled kitchen floor and a flax wheel.

Old-fashioned roses and herbs are set in a walled garden where breakfast is often served.

Innkeeper(s): Ann Foringer & Raymond Rhule.

Rates:$70-105. MC VISA AX. ContPlus Bkfst. 9 rooms. Fireplaces. Beds:QDT. TV, Phone, AC in room. Handicap access.

Seen in: *Life Today, Mid-Atlantic Country.*

Contact: Ann Foringer. Certificate may be used: Sunday through Thursday, year-round.

Thomas Bond House

129 S 2nd St
Philadelphia 19106
(215)923-8523 (800)845-2663
Fax:(215)923-8504

1769. One way to enjoy the history of Philadelphia is to treat yourself to a stay at this Colonial row house in Independence National Historic Park. White shutters and cornices accentuate the brick exterior, often draped in red, white and blue bunting. A finely executed interior renovation provides a handsome background for the inn's collection of Chippendale reproductions, four-poster beds, and dropfront desks. Working fireplaces, phones, television and whirlpool tubs provide additional comforts.

Innkeeper(s): Thomas F. Lantry.

Rates:$85-150. MC VISA AX DC. Full Bkfst. Gourmet Brkfst. Teas. Evening snacks. 12 rooms. Fireplaces. Beds:QT. Conference Rm. Phone, AC in room. Golf. Tennis. Bicycling. Sauna.

Seen in: *Mid-Atlantic Country, Washingtonian, Washington Post, Philadelphia Inquirer.*

Contact: Thomas Lantry. Certificate may be used: November - March; July - August; non-holidays for 1994 and 1995, as applicable and space available.

Pine Bank

Cole's Log Cabin B&B

Rural Delivery 1, Box 98
Pine Bank 15341
(412)451-8521

1820. For a simple getaway in the country, book a B&B room in the main log cabin or the private log cabin. Country furniture, not antiques, fill the rooms. The Spiral Staircase Room has exposed logs, and both a double and three-quarter-size bed. The property has 160 acres and you may arrange to use the inn's deer stands if you'd like to hunt on 15,000 acres of nearby Pennsylvania game land. Grouse, turkey, squirrel and deer may be found.

Innkeeper(s): Terry & Jane Cole.

Rates:$55-60. ContPlus Bkfst. 4 rooms. 2 with shared baths. Beds:Q. AC in room. Farm.

Contact: Jane Cole. Certificate may be used: Year-round on availability.

Pine Grove Mills

Split-Pine Farmhouse B&B

P O Box 326
Pine Grove Mills 16868
(814)238-2028

1830. Filled with generations of antiques layered into an English Country look, this Federal farmhouse is located a few minutes away from State College. Belleek china is used during tea time and the candlelight breakfast, which is served in the elegantly appointed dining room. The breakfast menu features dishes such as Mushroom Charlottes with Currant Sauce, Santa Fe Strata and Champagne Granita.

Innkeeper(s): Mae McQuade.

Rates:$63-180. MC VISA DS. Full Bkfst. Gourmet Brkfst, Dinner. Picnic lunches. Teas. 3 rooms. 1 with shared bath. Beds:KQT. TV, AC in room. Skiing. Swimming. Fishing.

Contact: Mae McQuade. Certificate may be used: Jan. 15-April 1, 1995; May 20-July 1, 1995; after Thanksgiving-Dec. 15, 1994 and 1995.

Point Pleasant

Tattersall Inn

PO Box 569
Point Pleasant 18950
(215)297-8233

1740. This plastered fieldstone house with its broad porches and wainscoted entry hall was the home of local mill owners for 150 years. The walls are 18 inches thick. Breakfast is usually served in the dining room where a vintage phonograph collection is on

display. The Colonial-style common room features a beamed ceiling and walk-in fireplace. Guests gather here for apple cider and cheese in the late afternoon.

Innkeeper(s): Gerry & Herb Moss.

Rates:$70-109. MC VISA AX DS. ContPlus Bkfst. Teas. Evening snacks. 6 rooms. Beds:QT. AC in room. Tennis. Skiing. Swimming. Horseback riding. Fishing.

Seen in: *Courier Times.*

Contact: Herbert Moss. Certificate may be used: Monday-Thursday, holidays excluded.

Ronks

Candlelight Inn B&B
2574 Lincoln Hwy E
Ronks 17572
(717)299-6005 (800)772-2635

1920. Located in the Pennsylvania Dutch area, this Federal-style house offers a side porch for enjoying the home's acre of tall trees and surrounding Amish farmland. The guest rooms are on the second floor at the end of a winding staircase. Lancaster is five miles to the east.

Innkeeper(s): Heidi & Tim Soberick.

Rates:$65-95. MC VISA DS. Full Bkfst. Teas. 6 rooms. 2 with shared baths. Beds:KQT. AC in room.

Contact: Heidi Soberick. Certificate may be used: Sunday through Thursday from Nov. 15 through July 15.

Shippensburg

Field & Pine B&B
2155 Ritner Hwy
Shippensburg 17257-9756
(717)776-7179

1790. Local limestone was used to build this stone house located on the main wagon road to Baltimore and Washington. Originally, it was a tavern and weigh station, and the scales are still attached to the stagecoach barn on the property. The house is surrounded by stately pines, and sheep graze on the inn's 80 acres. The bedrooms are hand-stenciled and furnished with quilts and antiques.

Innkeeper(s): Mary Ellen & Allan Williams.

Rates:$65-75. MC VISA. Gourmet Brkfst. 3 rooms. 2 with shared baths. Fireplaces. Beds:QDT. AC in room. Farm. Bicycling. Horseback riding. Fishing.

Seen in: *Valley Times-Star.*

Contact: Mary Ellen Williams. Certificate may be used: Sunday through Thursday.

"Our visit in this lovely country home has been most delightful. The ambiance of antiques and tasteful decorating exemplifies real country living."

McLean House B&B
80 W King St
Shippensburg 17257
(717)530-1390

1798. This inn is filled with an eclectic collection of furnishings, gathered from the innkeepers' 30 years of moves while in the army. Located in the historic district, the house is a combination of Victorian Stick style and Victorian Shingle style. Trout-filled Branch Creek borders the property and attracts mallard ducks, often seen from the dining area during breakfast. The innkeepers will advise you on visiting the dozens of antique and flea markets in the area. If you'd like, they also will arrange to escort you to your first auction.

Innkeeper(s): Bob & Jan Rose.

Rates:$40-45. Full Bkfst. Gourmet Brkfst. Evening snacks. 3 rooms. 2 with shared baths. Beds:DT. AC in room. Fishing.

Contact: Janet Rose. Certificate may be used: Anytime, no restrictions except Dec. 20 - Jan. 6.

Spruce Creek

Cedar Hill Farm
HC-01 Box 26, Rt 45
Spruce Creek 16683
(814)632-8319

1820. The original stone section of this house is joined by a later addition. The area overlooks Spruce Creek, famous for fly-fishing. Ask for the

room with the brass bed and fireplace. If you have children you'll want to bring them in the spring when the newborn calves, pigs, chickens and beagle dogs arrive. Vegetables, pumpkins, corn and hay are grown on the farm's 100 acres. Nearby, a working dairy farm allows visitors during milking hours. A hearty Pennsylvania Dutch breakfast is served.

Innkeeper(s): Sharon & Jim Dell.

Rates:$40-55. MC VISA. Full Bkfst. 4 rooms. 4 with shared baths. Beds:T. Farm. Skiing. Fishing.

Contact: Sharon Dell. Certificate may be used: January through April, December.

"Lovely surroundings, delightful hosts."

Starlight

The Inn at Starlight Lake
PO Box 27
Starlight 18461
(717)798-2519 (800)248-2519
Fax:(717)798-2672

1909. Acres of woodland and meadow surround the last surviving railroad inn on the New York, Ontario and Western lines. Originally a boarding house, the inn had its own store, church, school, blacksmith shop and creamery. Platforms, first erected to accommodate tents for the summer season, were later replaced by individual cottages. The inn is situated on the 45-acre, spring-fed Starlight Lake, providing summertime canoeing, swimming, fishing and sailing. (No motorboats are allowed on the lake.)

Innkeeper(s): Jack & Judy McMahon.

Rates:$110-154. MC VISA. Full Bkfst. EP. MAP available. Gourmet Dinner. Picnic lunches. Evening snacks. 6 rooms. 5 with shared baths. Conference Rm. Golf. Tennis. Bicycling. Skiing. Swimming. Fishing.

Seen in: *New York Times, Philadelphia Inquirer, Newsday.*

Contact: Judy McMahon. Certificate may be used: Midweek except July and August.

"So great to be back to our home away from home."

State College

The Vincent Douglas House
490 Meckley Rd
State College 16808
(814)237-4490

1834. This is a restored brick farmhouse. The inn's antique decor includes an oak bedroom set with a high bed and French country wallcoverings. Breakfast is served in the dining room and offers specialties such as apple omelets with amaretto and cream cheese. A stream on the property is often visited by wild ducks, deer and other wildlife. State College and Penn State are four miles away.

Innkeeper(s): Beverly Wiker.

Rates:$80-100. Full Bkfst. 4 rooms. Beds:QT. AC in room. Skiing. Fishing.

Contact: Beverly Wiker. Certificate may be used: January to May.

Stroudsburg

Stroudsmoor Country Inn
PO Box 153
Stroudsburg 18360
(717)421-6431 Fax:(717)421-8042

1840. Built of clapboard and stone, this country inn is located on 150 acres. There are 17 buildings, including the main house, cottages and a cluster of country shops which make up The Marketplace. A fieldstone fireplace is the focal point of the lobby. Rooms offer televisions and country antiques and the cottages have porches. There is both an indoor and outdoor pool. The dining room decor features bentwood chairs, copper kettles and linen napkins. A four-course breakfast is provided and on Sundays there is a champagne brunch.

Innkeeper(s): Andrew Forte & Linda Pirone-Forte.

Rates:$50-145. MC VISA AX. Full Bkfst. AP available. MAP available. Gourmet Dinner. Picnic lunches. 30 rooms. Fireplaces. Beds:KQT. Conference Rm. TV, AC, Refrig. in room. Skiing. Handicap access. Spa. Swimming. Fishing.

Contact: Linda Forte. Certificate may be used: January through March, 1995.

Troy

Silver Oak Leaf B&B
196 Canton St
Troy 16947
(717)297-4315 (800)326-9834

1880. Silver oak trees shade this large three-story house with gabled windows and a two-story bay. A wide veranda wraps around two sides of the house. The interiors feature Victorian and country pieces, set off with floral bedspreads and priscilla curtains. Oven pancakes, homemade breads and omelets are frequently served. There are vegetable and flower gardens on the property.

Innkeeper(s): Steve & June Bahr.

Rates:$50. Full Bkfst. Gourmet Brkfst. 4 rooms. 3 with shared baths. Beds:Q. Skiing. Fishing.

Contact: June and Steve Bahr. Certificate may be used: Tuesday or Wednesday night.

Warfordsburg

Buck Valley Ranch
Route 2, Box 1170
Warfordsburg 17267-9667
(717)294-3759 (800)294-3759

1930. Trailriding is a popular activity on the ranch's 64 acres in the Appalachian Mountains of Northern Pennsylvania. State game lands and forests border the ranch. The guest house, decorated in a ranch/cowboy style, is a private farmhouse that can accommodate eight people. Meals are prepared using homegrown vegetables and locally raised meats. Some rates include horseback riding.
Innkeeper(s): Nadine & Leon Fox.
Rates:$90-170. MC VISA. Full Bkfst. Gourmet Brkfst, Lunch, Dinner. Picnic lunches. Evening snacks. 4 rooms. 4 with shared baths. Beds:QT. Farm. Skiing. Sauna. Stables. Fishing.
Contact: Nadine Fox. Certificate may be used: Weekdays only Sunday night - Thursday night.

Washington Crossing

Inn to the Woods
150 Glenwood Drive
Washington Crossing 18977
(215)493-1974 (800)982-7619
Fax:(215)493-3774

1980. Located on 10 forested acres, this chalet offers seclusion and trails for hiking. Victorian furnishings and framed art add to the pleasingly appointed guest rooms. There is an indoor garden and fishpond. The chalet has beamed ceilings and parquet floors. On weekdays a continental breakfast is served, while on Saturday a full breakfast is provided. The fare for Sunday is a champagne brunch.
Innkeeper(s): Barry & Rosemary Rein.
Rates:$75-145. MC VISA AX. ContPlus Bkfst. Gourmet Brkfst. Teas. 6 rooms. Beds:KQT. Conference Rm. TV, AC in room. Bicycling. Skiing. Swimming. Fishing.
Contact: Barry Rein. Certificate may be used: Sunday - Thursday, January - May, November, December. No holidays.

Wellsboro

Auntie M's B&B
3 Sherwood St
Wellsboro 16901
(717)724-5771

1933. Gaslights lend a soft evening glow to the streets of this old-fashioned town. Auntie M's is a

Colonial Revival house in a quiet neighborhood close to tennis courts, stores, a museum and theater. The innkeepers operate a gift shop that features hand-carved duck decoys, kaleidoscopes, and stained glass.
Innkeeper(s): Carmella & Allan Rupert.
Rates:$55. Full Bkfst. Gourmet Brkfst. 3 rooms. 3 with shared baths. Beds:QT. Phone in room. Bicycling. Skiing. Fishing.
Contact: Carmella Rupert. Certificate may be used: January through April.

Four Winds B&B
58 West Ave
Wellsboro 16901
(800)368-7963

1872. This is a Victorian carpenter-style house on one acre, located nine miles from the Pennsylvania Grand Canyon. The rooms are decorated with country Victorian pieces. In the evening, walk along sidewalks illuminated by old-fashioned gas lamps and enjoy the fountain and village green. Seven lakes are nearby and there are miles of trails for hiking and cycling.
Innkeeper(s): Deborah & Charles Keister.
Rates:$42. MC VISA AX. Full Bkfst. 4 rooms. 4 with shared baths. Beds:DT. Skiing. Swimming. Fishing.
Contact: Deborah Keister. Certificate may be used: Spring, summer, winter - anytime. Fall - weekdays.

Kaltenbach's B&B
RR #6 Box 106A, Stony Fork Rd
Wellsboro 16901
(717)724-4954 (800)722-4954

1975. Seventy-two acres of farmland, pasture, forest and meadows surround this ranch house in North-central Pennsylvania. Children of all ages enjoy hanging around the sheep, pigs, rabbits and cattle. A mounted elk head above the fireplace is the focal point of the living room. There are two honeymoon suites, both with a two-person tub. Country breakfasts feature eggs, breakfast meats, blueberry muffins and homemade jams. White-water rafting is popular in the nearby Grand Canyon of Pennsylvania.
Innkeeper(s): Lee Kaltenbach.
Rates:$60-125. MC VISA. Full Bkfst. Picnic lunches. Teas. Evening snacks. 10 rooms. 2 with shared baths. Fireplaces. Beds:KQ. Conference Rm. TV, Phone, AC, Refrig. in room. Farm. Tennis. Skiing. Handicap access. Swimming. Fishing.
Contact: Lee Kaltenbach. Certificate may be used: Sunday through Thursday, year-round except holidays.

West Chester

Bankhouse B&B

875 Hillsdale Rd
West Chester 19382
(610)344-7388

1765. Built into the bank of a quiet country road, this 18th-century house overlooks a 10-acre horse  farm and pond. The interior is decorated with country antiques, stenciling, and folk art. Guests have their own private entrance and porch. Two bedrooms share a common sitting room library. Hearty country breakfasts include German apple souffle pancakes, custard French toast and nearly a hundred other recipes. West Chester and the Brandywine Valley attractions are conveniently close.

Innkeeper(s): Diana & Michael Bove.

Rates:$65-85. Full Bkfst. Evening snacks. 3 rooms. 2 with shared baths. Beds:DT. Phone, AC in room. Golf. Skiing. Swimming.

Seen in: *Philadelphia Inquirer, Mercury, Bucks County Town & Country Living, Sunday Mercury, Chester County Living.*

Contact: Diana Bove. Certificate may be used: Monday through Thursday nights only.

"Everything was so warm and inviting."

Monument House

1311 Birmingham Rd
West Chester 19382
(610)793-2986

1820. In the Pennsylvania Historic Register, this house was constructed of German clapboard siding. The monument, which stands adjacent to the inn, is in memory of General Lafayette who was wounded here during the Battle of the Brandywine. From the inn's front porch, you can enjoy the rolling countryside and its farms. The innkeeper is a ceramic designer who works on the premises.

Innkeeper(s): Maureen & Richard Brockman.

Rates:$70-80. Full Bkfst. 2 rooms. 2 with shared baths. Beds:KT. AC in room. Swimming.

Contact: Maureen Brockman. Certificate may be used: Monday through Thursday (departing Friday) year-round. Deposit required on all reservations.

White Horse

Fassitt Mansion B&B

6051 Old Philadelphia Pike (Rt 340)
White Horse 17527

(717)442-3139 (800)653-4139

1845. Located on two acres, this Federal home is six miles from the town of Intercourse in Lancaster County. There are 12-foot-high ceilings and six

fireplaces. A continental breakfast offers local butters and fruit jams, served in the dining room.

Innkeeper(s): Tara L. Golish.

Rates:$65-80. MC VISA. Full Bkfst. Gourmet Brkfst. Teas. Evening snacks. 4 rooms. Fireplaces. Beds:KQT. AC in room. Golf. Tennis. Fishing.

Contact: Tara Golish. Certificate may be used: Anytime subject to availability - no holidays.

York

The Smyser-Bair House B&B

30 S Beaver St
York 17401
(717)854-3411

1880. This four-story red brick house stands on a corner in downtown York. Its green shutters and Italianate styling add a welcoming touch. The house is decorated in cheerful colors highlighting finely carved moldings, a walnut staircase, high ceilings and parquet floors. It is appointed with crystal chandeliers, floor-to-ceiling gold leaf pier mirrors and Victorian antiques.

Innkeeper(s): Bob & Hilda King.

Rates:$60-80. MC VISA. Full Bkfst. Teas. 5 rooms. 3 with shared baths. Beds:QDT. AC in room. Golf. Skiing. Fishing.

Seen in: *York Daily Record.*

Contact: Thomas King. Certificate may be used: Anytime except April, June and October, subject to availability.

"We really enjoyed the warmth and hospitality of the innkeepers. They really care about their guests."

Rhode Island

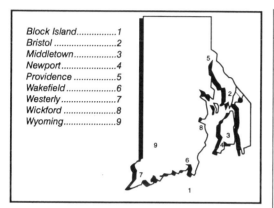

Block Island

1661 Inn & Hotel Manisses

1 Spring St, PO Box 1
Block Island 02807
(401)466-2421 (800)626-4773
Fax:(401)466-2858

1875. Five buildings comprise this island inn and overlook grassy lawns and the ocean. Common rooms and guest rooms are furnished with antiques and art. The newest luxury rooms in the Nicholas Ball Cottage (a replica of an Episcopal church) offer both Jacuzzis and fireplaces. Dinner is available each night in the summer and on weekends other times of the year. Visit the inn's animal farm to watch the antics of the Indian runner ducks, black swans, pygmy goats, llamas and Sicilian donkeys. Flower, vegetable and herb gardens are adjacent to the farm.

Innkeeper(s): Joan & Justin Abrams.

Rates:$59-325. MC VISA AX. Full Bkfst. EP. Gourmet Brkfst, Lunch, Dinner. Picnic lunches. Teas. Evening snacks. 38 rooms. 4 with shared baths. Fireplaces. Beds:KQT. Conference Rm. Phone, Refrig. in room. Handicap access. Swimming. Fishing.

Contact: Joan Abrams. Certificate may be used: Anytime except weekends. November-June and September & October.

The Bellevue House

PO Box 1198 High St
Block Island 02807
(401)466-2912

1882. Offering a hilltop perch, meadow-like setting and ocean views, this Colonial Revival farmhouse inn in the Block Island Historic District has served

guests for more than a century. A variety of accommodations includes five guest rooms with shared bath, five suites and two cottages. The Old Harbor Ferry, restaurants and shops are just a five-minute walk from the inn. Guests may use ferries from New London, Conn., Montauk Point, N.Y., and Newport, Point Judith and Providence, R.I., to reach the island. Block Island National Wildlife Reserve and Rodmans Hollow Natural Area are nearby.

Innkeeper(s): Neva Flaherty & Read Kingsbury.

Rates:$60-90. MC VISA. ContPlus Bkfst. 10 rooms. 5 with shared baths. Beds:QT. Swimming. Fishing.

Contact: Neva Flaherty. Certificate may be used: Sunday - Thursday, May, June, September, October excluding holiday weekends.

Blue Dory Inn

Box 488, Dodge St
Block Island 02807
(401)466-2254 (800)992-7290
Fax:(401)466-2909

1897. This Shingle Victorian inn on Crescent Beach offers many guest rooms with ocean views.

The Cottage, The Doll House and The Tea House are separate structures for those desiring more room or privacy. Antiques and Victorian touches are featured throughout. Year-round car ferry service taking approximately one hour is found from Point Judith, R.I. The island also may be reached by air on New England Airlines or by charter. Mohegan Bluffs Scenic Natural Area is nearby.

Innkeeper(s): Ann Loedy.

Rates:$65-175. MC VISA AX. ContPlus Bkfst. 18 rooms. Beds:KQT. Conference Rm. TV, AC, Refrig. in room. Tennis. Swimming. Horseback riding. Fishing.

Contact: Ann Loedy. Certificate may be used: After Sept. 15, 1994 and 1995; before June 25, 1994 and 1995.

The White House
Box 447
Block Island 02807
(401)466-2653

1792. This Colonial-style bed & breakfast is furnished with French Provincial antiques and has sweeping views of the ocean, rolling lawns and gardens. The Captain's Quarters has a bedroom-sitting room that encompasses the entire ocean side of the house. The room also has a canopied double bed and outdoor balcony. Guests have a private north portico entrance and main floor drawing room with TV. Arrangements can be made to be met at the airport or ferry.

Innkeeper(s): Joseph Connolly.

Rates:$55-120. MC VISA AX. Gourmet Brkfst. Teas. 5 rooms. 4 with shared baths. Beds:QT. TV in room. Fishing.

Contact: Joseph Connolly. Certificate may be used: Monday, Tuesday, Wednesday and Thursday only in season. All days of week in winter.

Bristol

Rockwell House Inn B&B
610 Hope St
Bristol 02809-1945
(401)253-0040

1809. In the National Register, this inn is one block away from Narragansset Bay. It's a Federal and Greek Revival home with eight-foot pocket doors, Italianate mantels and working fireplaces. Double parlors open to the dining room and its inlaid parquet floors. There is a sun porch with a stone turret and leaded-glass windows. Private parties of up to 100 people often enjoy the house and garden. Afternoon tea is served.

Innkeeper(s): Debra & Steve Krohn.

Rates:$55-95. MC VISA AX. Full Bkfst. Gourmet Brkfst. Picnic lunches. Teas. 4 rooms. Fireplaces. Beds:KQ. Conference Rm. Handicap access. Swimming. Fishing.

Seen in: *Ocean State Traveler.*

Contact: Debra Krohn. Certificate may be used: November through May 15 - or by availability.

"Next time I'll bring company. It's much too romantic to be here alone! This is such a lovely home."

William's Grant Inn
154 High St
Bristol 02809
(401)253-4222 (800)596-4222

1808. This handsome Federal Colonial home was built by Governor William Bradford for his son. There are two beehive ovens and seven fireplaces as well as original wide-board pine floors and paired interior chimneys. Antique furnishings and folk art make the guest rooms inviting. A hearty continental breakfast is served in the country kitchen.

Innkeeper(s): Mary & Michael Rose.

Rates:$55-95. MC VISA AX DC. Full Bkfst. 5 rooms. 2 with shared baths. Beds:Q. Conference Rm. Swimming. Fishing.

Contact: Mary Weaver Rose. Certificate may be used: November-March, 1994-1995.

Middletown

The Briar Patch
42 Briarwood Ave
Middletown 02840
(401)841-5824

1920. This European-style inn offers a convenient location and several dining options to its visitors, who also will enjoy the country accents in each comfortable guest room. The inn's full breakfasts are served in its charming dining room, attractively accented in blue and brown. Visitors are encouraged by the attentive innkeeper to inquire about breakfast or other meal options. Feel free to borrow a bicycle for a relaxing ride. Easton's Beach is just a five-minute walk from the inn, providing the perfect opportunity to sample one of the inn's picnic lunches.

Innkeeper(s): Maureen McCracken.

Rates:$50-85. Full Bkfst. Picnic lunches. Teas. 3 rooms. Beds:QT. Bicycling. Swimming. Fishing.

Contact: Maureen McCracken. Certificate may be used: October and November, 1994 and 1995. April and May, 1995.

Finnegan's Inn
120 Miantonomi Ave
Middletown 02842
(401)849-1298 (800)828-0000

1840. This elegant, two-story Stick Victorian inn offers a glimpse of fine living in an earlier age. The innkeepers' attention to detail is evident throughout, with French crystal chandeliers, stained-glass windows and Tiffany lighting in the library as a few of the highlights. Parlors are found on each of the inn's floors. Newport's many attractions, including the Art Museum, the Artillery Museum and Belcourt Castle, are just a short drive from the inn, which also offers a daily shuttle to the city.
Innkeeper(s): Randy & Selma Fabricant.

Rates:$60-115. MC VISA. ContPlus Bkfst. Teas. 8 rooms. Fireplaces. Beds:KQT. Phone, AC, Refrig. in room. Bicycling. Swimming. Fishing.

Contact: Randy Fabricant. Certificate may be used: Nov. 1 through March 31, excluding holiday weekends (Thanksgiving, Christmas, New Year's, Valentine's Day).

Lindsey's Guest House
6 James St
Middletown 02842
(401)846-9386

1955. This contemporary split-level home in a residential area features three guest rooms, including one on the ground level that boasts a private entrance and is handicapped-accessible. Breakfast is served in the dining room and usually includes cereal, coffee cake, fruit, juice, muffins and jam, and coffee or beverage of choice. The innkeeper has worked in the hospitality industry for more than 30 years and is happy to offer sightseeing tips. The Norman Bird Sanctuary and Sachuest Point National Wildlife Reserve are nearby.
Innkeeper(s): Anne T. Lindsey.

Rates:$55-75. MC VISA. ContPlus Bkfst. 3 rooms. 2 with shared baths. Beds:KQDT. Golf. Tennis. Handicap access. Swimming. Horseback riding. Fishing.

Contact: Anne Lindsey. Certificate may be used: November through April.

Newport

The Brinley Victorian Inn
23 Brinley St
Newport 02840
(401)849-7645 (800)999-8523

1875. This is a three-story Victorian with a mansard roof and long porch. A cottage on the property dates from 1850. There are two parlors and a library providing a quiet haven from the bustle of the Newport wharfs. Each room is decorated with period wallpapers and furnishings. There are fresh flowers and mints on the pillows. The brick courtyard is planted with bleeding hearts, peonies and miniature roses, perennials of the Victorian era.
Innkeeper(s): John & Jennifer Sweetman.

Rates:$49-145. MC VISA. Cont. Bkfst. 17 rooms. 4 with shared baths. Beds:KQT. AC, Refrig. in room. Swimming. Fishing.

Seen in: *New Hampshire Times, Boston Woman, Country Victorian, Yankee.*

Contact: John Sweetman. Certificate may be used: Nov. 1 through to April 30.

"Ed and I had a wonderful anniversary. The Brinley is as lovely and cozy as ever! The weekend brought back lots of happy memories."

Cliffside Inn
2 Seaview Ave
Newport 02840
(401)847-1811 (800)845-1811
Fax:(401)848-5850

1880. The governor of Maryland, Thomas Swann, built this Newport summer house in the style of a Second Empire Victorian. It features a mansard

roof and many bay windows. The rooms are decorated in a Victorian motif set off by ceiling moldings painted in pastel colors. The Cliff Walk is located one block from the inn.
Innkeeper(s): Stephan Nicolas.

Rates:$115-325. MC VISA AX DC DS. Gourmet Brkfst. Teas. Evening snacks. 12 rooms. Fireplaces. Beds:KQT. Conference Rm. TV, Phone, AC, Refrig. in room. Swimming. Fishing.

Seen in: *Country Inns, Philadelphia Inquirer, Discerning Traveler, New York, Newsday.*

Contact: Stephan Nicoles. Certificate may be used: Nov. 1-March 31 (weekdays only).

"...it captures the grandeur of the Victorian age."

Halidon Hill Guest House

Halidon Ave
Newport 02840
(401)847-8318 (800)227-2130

1968. This contemporary, two-story Georgian style inn offers a convenient location and comfortable accommodations for those exploring the Newport area. The two spacious suites both boast kitchenettes. The inn is just a 10-minute walk to Hammersmith Farm and provides easy access to the area's mansions, restaurants and shopping. Guests will enjoy lounging on the roomy deck near the in-ground pool, or in front of the fireplace in cooler weather. Newport Harbor and the Tennis Hall of Fame are nearby.

Innkeeper(s): Helen & Paul Burke.

Rates:$55-200. AX DC DS. ContPlus Bkfst. 2 rooms. Handicap access. Fishing.

Contact: Helen Burke. Certificate may be used: Spring, fall and winter anytime. Summer during the week.

The Historical John Banister Mansion

56 Pelham St at Spring
Newport 02840
(401)846-0059

1751. This Georgian Colonial home, listed in the National Register, was built by a man who ran merchant ships from the colonies to Europe. He was thought to have been a smuggler. During the Revolutionary War, the house was used by General Prescott as British headquarters. The home has been restored in great detail down to matching original interior paint colors. Antique coverlets top the beds. A gourmet breakfast is served on a table dating back to the 1750s. Some rooms have views of the harbor, only one block away.

Innkeeper(s): Dr. Rui & Claire Rodriques.

Rates:$135-200. 14 rooms. 2 with shared baths. Fireplaces. Beds:QT. Conference Rm. Refrig. in room. Golf. Tennis. Swimming. Horseback riding. Fishing.

Seen in: *Rhode Island, Boston Sunday Globe, Country Inns.*

Contact: R. Rodriguez. Certificate may be used: Mid-week summer season only, from Tuesday to Thursday only.

The Melville House

39 Clarke St
Newport 02840
(401)847-0640 Fax:(401)847-0956

1750. This attractive, National Register two-story Colonial inn once housed aides to General Rochambeau during the American Revolution. Early American furnishings decorate the interior. There is also an unusual collection of old appli-

ances, including a cherry-pitter, mincer and dough maker. A full breakfast includes Portuguese Quiche, Jonnycakes, homemade bread and Portuguese egg

sandwiches. The inn is a pleasant walk from the waterfront and historic sites.

Innkeeper(s): Vince DeRico & David Horan.

Rates:$50-110. MC VISA AX. ContPlus Bkfst. Picnic lunches. Teas. 7 rooms. 2 with shared baths. Beds:KDT. Golf. Tennis. Bicycling. Swimming. Horseback riding. Fishing.

Seen in: *Country Inns, "Lodging Pick" for Newport.*

Contact: Vince DeRico. Certificate may be used: Sunday - Thursday nights, November - March.

"Comfortable with a quiet elegance."

The Pilgrim House

123 Spring St
Newport 02846
(401)846-0040 (800)525-8373
Fax:(401)846-0357

1876. Next door to historic Trinity Church, this mansard-roofed Victorian features a third-floor deck to savor expansive views of Newport Harbor, two

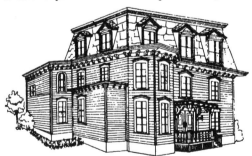

streets away. The inn is decorated with Victorian period furnishings. A working fireplace in the living room invites a guest to browse through restaurant menus. Eucalyptus wreaths pleasantly scent the air when it's not filled with the fragrance of freshly baked breads and muffins.

Innkeeper(s): Pam & Bruce Bayuk.

Rates:$55-140. MC VISA. Cont. Bkfst. Teas. 11 rooms. 2 with shared baths. Beds:DT. Conference Rm. AC in room. Golf. Tennis. Swimming. Fishing.

Seen in: *The Times.*

Contact: Pam Bayuk. Certificate may be used: Nov. 1-April 30, mid-week (Sunday-Thursday).

"What can I say, it's a perfect hideaway. Great time was had by all."

The Victorian Ladies
63 Memorial Blvd
Newport 02840
(401)849-9960 Fax:(701)849-9960

1850. Guests of this restored three-story Victorian building can stroll to Newport's beaches, the Cliff Walk, the Colonial town and the harbor front. At the Victorian Ladies, a charming latticed courtyard connects the main house to the smaller house in back. Reproduction period furniture, crystal and lush floral prints add to the Victorian ambiance in the rooms that innkeeper Helene O'Neill decorated.

Rates:$85-185. MC VISA. Gourmet Brkfst. 11 rooms. Beds:QT. Phone, AC in room. Swimming.

Seen in: *Country Inns, Glamour, Bride Magazine.*

Contact: Helene O'Neill. Certificate may be used: Weekends and holidays excluded. July and August months excluded from promotion.

"We want to move in!"

Providence

State House Inn
43 Jewett St
Providence 02908
(401)351-6111 Fax:(401)351-4261

1889. Shaker and Colonial furniture fill this turn-of-the-century home, located in the midst of a quaint and peaceful Providence neighborhood. The rooms provide amenities that will please any busi-

ness traveler and have the country comfort and elegance of days gone by. The common room contains a small library for guest use. A famed historic district featuring restored homes and buildings is three blocks away, and the capitol is a five-minute walk.

Innkeeper(s): Frank & Monica Hopton.

Rates:$69-99. MC VISA AX. Full Bkfst. EP. 10 rooms. Fireplaces. Beds:KQT. TV, Phone, AC, Refrig. in room.

Seen in: *Phoenix Newspaper.*

Contact: Frank Hopton. Certificate may be used: Anytime except weekends in May, June, July, September and October.

"Thank you again for the warm, comfortable and very attractive accommodations."

Wakefield

Larchwood Inn
521 Main St
Wakefield 02879
(401)783-5454 (800)275-5450
Fax:(401)783-1800

1831. The Larchwood Inn and its adjacent sister inn, the Holly House, were both constructed in the same era. The two inns are antique-filled and fami-

ly-run, with 20th-century amenities. Scottish touches are sprinkled throughout the interior. The birthday of poet Robert Burns is celebrated complete with "piper and haggis." Three dining rooms offer breakfast, lunch and dinner. (Breakfast is an extra charge.) A cocktail lounge and weekend dancing also are on the premises.

Innkeeper(s): Francis & Diann Browning.

Rates:$40-100. MC VISA AX DC DS CB. Full Bkfst. EP. Gourmet Brkfst. 19 rooms. 7 with shared baths. Fireplaces. Beds:QT. Conference Rm. Phone in room. Bicycling. Skiing. Swimming. Horseback riding. Fishing.

Contact: Francis Browning. Certificate may be used: Oct. 15, 1994-May 1, 1995; Oct. 15-Dec. 30, 1995.

"I certainly would not hesitate to recommend your inn and look forward to staying there whenever in the area."

Westerly

Grandview B&B
212 Shore Rd
Westerly 02891
(401)596-6384 (800)447-6384
Fax:(401)596-6384

1910. An impressive wraparound stone porch high-lights this majestic Shingle Victorian inn, which also boasts a lovely ocean view from its hilltop site. The inn features 12 guest rooms, a family room with cable TV and player piano, a spacious living room with a handsome stone fireplace, and a sun porch, where visitors enjoy a hearty breakfast buffet. A black labrador retriever named Nike welcomes all visitors, but respectfully requests they leave their pets at home. Antiquing, fishing, golf, swimming and tennis are found nearby and Misquamicut State Beach is withing easy driving distance.

Innkeeper(s): Pat Grande.

Rates:$50-90. MC VISA AX. ContPlus Bkfst. 12 rooms. 10 with shared baths. Beds:DT. Golf. Tennis. Swimming. Fishing.

Contact: Patricia Grande. Certificate may be used: Sunday night through Thursday night only year-round/not valid on holidays.

Shelter Harbor Inn
10 Wagner Rd, Rt 1
Westerly 02891
(401)322-8883 (800)468-8883
Fax:(401)322-7907

1810. This farmhouse at the entrance to the community of Shelter Harbor has been renovated and transformed to create a handsome country inn. Rooms, many with fireplaces, are in the main house, the barn and a carriage house. A third-floor deck provides panoramic views of Block Island Sound. The dining room features local seafood and other traditional New England dishes. Nearby are secluded, barrier beaches, stone fences and salt ponds.

Innkeeper(s): Jim Dey.

Rates:$76-112. MC VISA AX DC DS CB. Full Bkfst. MAP available. Gourmet Brkfst, Lunch, Dinner. Picnic lunches. 23 rooms. Fireplaces. Beds:QT. Conference Rm. Phone, AC in room. Farm. Spa. Exercise room. Swimming. Fishing.

Seen in: *Rhode Island Monthly, The Day.*

Contact: Jim Dey. Certificate may be used: Weeknights only Sunday - Thursday, Oct. 1, 1994 - June 1, 1995.

"This inn was, on the whole, wonderful."

Wickford

Meadowland
765 Old Baptist Rd
Wickford 02852
(401)294-4168

1836. Situated on a half-acre of land surrounded by fruit trees, Meadowland was once the site of a Victorian-era celery farm. Bedrooms are furnished in wicker, and each of the three floors has a sitting room. A formal breakfast is served by candlelight. The innkeeper can arrange a half-day sail or sunset dinner cruise on the 46-foot Morning Star.

Innkeeper(s): Linda Iavarone.

Rates:$65. Gourmet Brkfst. 7 rooms. 6 with shared baths. Beds:D. AC in room. Golf. Tennis. Swimming. Horseback riding. Fishing.

Seen in: *Ocean State Traveler.*

Contact: Linda Iavarone. Certificate may be used: Anytime, subject to availability.

"Serenity at its best."

Wyoming

The Cookie Jar B&B
64 Kingstown Rd (Rt 138)
Wyoming 02898
(401)539-2680 (800)767-4262

1732. The living room of this historic farmhouse inn once served as a blacksmith shop. The inn's original stone walls and wood ceiling remain, along with a granite fireplace built by an Indian stonemason after the forge was removed. Years later, as rooms were added, the building became the Cookie Jar restaurant, a name the innkeepers judged worth keeping. Visitors select their full breakfast fare from a menu listing the night before. The inn's grounds boast more than 50 fruit trees, a flower garden, a barn and a swimming pool. Those who love the beach or fishing will find both fresh and salt water within a 20-minute drive.

Innkeeper(s): Dick & Madelein Sohl.

Rates:$48-65. Full Bkfst. 3 rooms. 2 with shared baths. Beds:KQDT. Skiing. Handicap access. Swimming. Fishing.

Contact: Charles Sohl. Certificate may be used: Anytime except Friday and Saturday during months May through October. Not valid on holidays or special events.

South Carolina

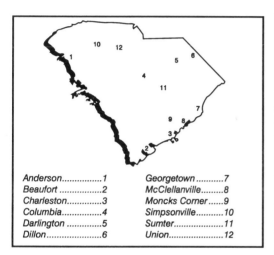

Anderson...............1
Beaufort................2
Charleston.............3
Columbia...............4
Darlington..............5
Dillon....................6
Georgetown...........7
McClellanville.........8
Moncks Corner......9
Simpsonville..........10
Sumter..................11
Union....................12

Anderson

River Inn
612 E River St
Anderson 29624
(803)226-1431 Fax:(803)296-2203
1914. This three-story, dormered Georgian
Plantation house borders the historic district of
Anderson. Leaded glass, 10-foot beamed ceilings
and working coal fireplaces mark this country
manor. An eclectic collection of antiques include a
mahogany dining set and leaded china cabinets.
Each room has its own fireplace and bath. Mounds
of azaleas, 70-year-old fragrant camillia sasanqua
trees, roses and crepe myrtles add grace to the inn's
five acres.
Innkeeper(s): Pat Clark & Wayne Hollingsworth.
Rates:$60-65. MC VISA AX. Full Bkfst. Gourmet Brkfst. Dinner. Picnic
lunches. 3 rooms. Fireplaces. Beds:QT. Conference Rm. TV, AC in
room. Golf. Tennis. Spa. Swimming. Fishing.
Contact: Patricia Clark. Certificate may be used: Sunday-Thursday.

Beaufort

Old Point Inn
212 New St
Beaufort 29902
(803)524-3177 Fax:(803)525-6544
1898. Built by William Waterhouse as a wedding
present for his wife, Isabelle Richmond, this Queen
Anne Victorian has wraparound verandas in the

"Beaufort Style." Guests often rock, swing or
recline in the hammock while watching boats ply
the Intracoastal Waterway. Four pillared fireplaces,
pocket doors and eyelash windows are features of
the house. The inn is located in the historic dis-
trict, with a waterfront park, a marina, restaurants
and downtown shopping nearby.
Innkeeper(s): Joe & Joan Carpentiere.
Rates:$70-100. MC VISA AX. ContPlus Bkfst. 4 rooms. Beds:KQT.
Conference Rm. AC in room. Golf. Tennis. Bicycling. Swimming.
Horseback riding. Fishing.
Seen in: *Islander.*
Contact: Joan Carpentiere. Certificate may be used: November-
February, Sunday through Wednesday.

*"We are still cruising on our memories of a wonderful
honeymoon. It certainly had a great start staying at the
Old Point Inn. We couldn't have done better."*

The Rhett House Inn

1009 Craven St
Beaufort 29902
(803)524-9030 Fax:(803)524-1890

1820. Most people cannot pass this stunning two-story clapboard house without wanting to step up to the long veranda and try the hammock. Guest rooms are furnished in antiques, with quilts and fresh flowers. Many guest rooms have fireplaces. Handsome gardens feature a fountain and are often the site for romantic weddings. Bicycles are available.

Innkeeper(s): Steve & Marianne Harrison.

Rates:$125-175. MC VISA. Full Bkfst. Gourmet Brkfst, Dinner. Picnic lunches. Teas. Evening snacks. 10 rooms. Fireplaces. Beds:KQ. Conference Rm. TV, Phone, AC in room. Bicycling. Handicap access. Swimming. Fishing.

Seen in: *Innsider, Family Business Magazine, The Lowcountry Ledger.*

Contact: Stacey Colebaugh. Certificate may be used: Sunday - Thursday, not valid October, November, March, April and May.

"A dream come true!"

Charleston

1837 B&B

126 Wentworth St
Charleston 29401
(803)723-7166

1837. Originally owned by a cotton planter, this three-story home and brick carriage house is located centrally in the Charleston Historic District within walking distance to shops, restaurants, and the convention center. Red cypress wainscoting, cornice molding and heart-of-pine floors adorn the formal parlor where a full gourmet breakfast is served. Guest rooms offer iron or rice beds. Afternoon tea is served on the inn's piazzas.

Innkeeper(s): Sherri Weaver & Richard Dunn.

Rates:$49-99. MC VISA AX. Full Bkfst. Gourmet Brkfst. Teas. 8 rooms. Fireplaces. Beds:Q. AC, Refrig. in room. Golf. Tennis. Swimming. Fishing.

Seen in: *New York Newsday, Kansas City Star, New York Times.*

Contact: Sherri Weaver. Certificate may be used: Nov. 1 to March 9 excludes Christmas period.

"This cozy room added that special touch to a much-needed weekend getaway."

The Battery Carriage House Inn

20 S Battery
Charleston 29401
(800)775-5575 Fax:(803)727-3130

1843. Just outside the door of this antebellum house you can enjoy the serenity of a Charleston garden. And outside the wrought iron gates lies

beautiful White Point Gardens, the Battery and Charleston Harbor. Renovations in many rooms have preserved the charm of the past, while increasing amenities, including steam baths or Jacuzzis, cable television, computer hookups for the business traveler and fax and copy machines. The inn was used in the filming of "North and South" and the interior rooms have been filmed for "Queen."

Innkeeper(s): Katharine Hastie.

Rates:$149-199. MC VISA AX DS. Cont. Bkfst. 11 rooms. Beds:KQT. TV, Phone, AC in room. Swimming. Fishing.

Contact: J. D. Hastie, Jr. Certificate may be used: Monday - Thursday only; Feb. 15-March 9; June 6-Sept. 30; Nov. 1-Dec. 21.

King George Inn & Guests

32 George St
Charleston 29401
(803)723-9339

1790. This inn is a Federal-style home with a Greek Revival parapet-style roofline. There are four stories with three levels of Charleston porches. All the rooms have fireplaces, 10-foot ceilings and six-foot windows. Several fireplaces and moldings are the original Adamesque architectural detail. The house was lived in for many years by Peter Freneau, who was a prominent Charleston journalist, merchant, ship owner and Jeffersonian politician. The inn is within one minute's walk to shopping and restaurants.

Innkeeper(s): Debbie, BJ, Mike.

Rates:$70-110. MC VISA. Cont. Bkfst. 7 rooms. Fireplaces. Beds:QT. AC, Refrig. in room. Swimming. Fishing.

Contact: Lynn Robertson. Certificate may be used: Weekdays in November and December (except Christmas week). Also good all days in January and weekends in February.

Lodge Alley Inn

195 E Bay St
Charleston 29401
(803)722-1611 (800)845-1004
Fax:(803)722-1611

1800. Each room of this inn is appointed with Oriental carpets, fireplaces, lustrous pine floors and period reproductions that reflect Charleston's

European heritage. A lavish two-room penthouse has a private roof-top patio and views of Charleston's historic district and waterfront. The Charleston Tea Party Lounge, gardens and 18th-century parlor are perfect places to relax. Not to be missed is The French Quarter restaurant that overlooks the courtyard gardens and fountain. The noted chef prepares roast duckling, Chateaubriand and other house specialties on a grand rotisserie.

Innkeeper(s): Norma Armstrong.

Rates:$105-299. MC VISA AX. AP available. 94 rooms. Fireplaces. Beds:KQT. Conference Rm. TV, Phone, AC, Refrig. in room. Golf. Swimming. Fishing.

Seen in: *Travel Host, Southern Living.*

Contact: Tammy Faust. Certificate may be used: Anytime based on availability.

Maison Du Pre

317 E Bay St
Charleston 29401
(803)723-8691 (800)844-4667
Fax:(803)723-3722

1804. In the downtown Ansonborough Historic District is this inn with its frame and brick buildings. Courtyards, with three fountains, are surrounded by tall garden walls and wrought-iron gates. The inn has a drawing room with a baby grand piano. Guest rooms are furnished with antiques and Oriental carpets. The inn offers "Lowcountry tea" every afternoon.

Innkeeper(s): Lucille, Robert & Mark Mulholland.

Rates:$98-145. MC VISA. ContPlus Bkfst. Teas. 15 rooms. Fireplaces. Beds:QT. Conference Rm. TV, Phone, AC in room. Swimming. Fishing.

Seen in: *Country Inns, Americana.*

Contact: R.J. Mulholland. Certificate may be used: Sundays through Thursdays only.

Columbia

Chesnut Cottage B&B

1718 Hampton St
Columbia 29201
(803)256-1718 (800)898-8555

1850. This inn was originally the home of Confederate General James Chesnut and his wife, writer Mary Boykin Miller Chesnut. She authored "A Diary From Dixie," written during the Civil War but published posthumously in 1905. The white frame one-and-a-half-story house has a central dormer with an arched window above the main entrance. The small porch has four octagonal columns and an ironwork balustrade. Hearty breakfasts are served in the privacy of your room, on the porch or in the main dining room. The innkeepers

can provide you with sightseeing information, make advance dinner reservations, as well as cater to any other special interests you might have.

Innkeeper(s): Diane & Gale Garrett.

Rates:$65-125. MC VISA AX DC DS. Full Bkfst. Gourmet Brkfst. Picnic lunches. Teas. 4 rooms. Fireplaces. Beds:KQ. TV, Phone, AC, Refrig. in room. Tennis. Bicycling. Swimming. Fishing.

Seen in: *TV show "Breakfast with Christie."*

Contact: Diane Garrett. Certificate may be used: December - January - August and November (exempt September, October).

Darlington

Croft Magnolia Inn

306 Cashua St
Darlington 29532
(803)393-1908

1800. The Southern-style country inn is a popular place during stock car racing season and is only one mile away from the Darlington Raceway. One of the inn's halls is dedicated to NASCAR racing with stock car memorabilia. A foyer is decorated with English furniture and original paintings, created by family members, of jousting knights and other English themes. Complimentary wine is delivered to the rooms during the evening, and the innkeeper takes pride in making guests feel at home. Outside the inn, tree-lined streets and large homes make for enjoyable walks.

Innkeeper(s): Joan Pearmain-Jackson.

Rates:$75-85. Full Bkfst. Evening snacks. 4 rooms. Beds:QDT. AC in room.

Contact: Joan Pearmain-Jackson. Certificate may be used: Unable to participate holidays and race weekends.

Dillon

Magnolia Inn B&B

601 E Main St - Hwy 9
Dillon 29536
(803)774-0679

1903. This Southern Colonial-style home was built by a prominent local family who used long-leaf heart pine wood among other fine materials in the construction. Stately columns flank the entry. On the ground floor is a library, parlor, and dining room where such breakfast treats as pecan-apple pancakes and breakfast casseroles are served. The upstairs guest rooms feature handsome four-postered, white iron, and oak beds.

Innkeeper(s): Jim & Pam Lannoo.

Rates:$55-65. MC VISA AX. Full Bkfst. Picnic lunches. 4 rooms. Fireplaces. Beds:Q. AC in room. Golf. Bicycling. Swimming. Fishing.

Seen in: *Sandlapper.*

Contact: James Lannoo. Certificate may be used: Anytime except some special events.

"Your home is beautiful and our first Bed and Breakfast experience has won us over to do it again...and again."

Georgetown

1790 House
630 Highmarket St
Georgetown 29440
(803)546-4821

1790. Located in the heart of a historic district, this beautifully restored West Indies Colonial just celebrated its 200th birthday. The spacious rooms feature 11-foot ceilings and seven fireplaces, three

in the guest bedrooms. The inn decor reflects the plantations of a bygone era. Guests can stay in former slave quarters, renovated to include a queen bedroom and sitting area. Each of the romantic rooms feature special touches, such as the red and deep blue decor of the Indigo Room, and the antique white iron and brass bed in the Prince George Suite. The Dependency Cottage is a perfect honeymoon hideaway with a private entrance enhanced with gardens and a patio, and the room also includes a Jacuzzi tub.

Innkeeper(s): Patricia & John Wiley.

Rates:$63-115. MC VISA AX DS. Full Bkfst. Gourmet Brkfst. 7 rooms. Beds:QT. AC in room. Golf. Tennis. Bicycling. Fishing.

Contact: John Wiley. Certificate may be used: Year-round.

"The 1790 House always amazes me with its beauty."

Ashfield Manor
3030 S Island Rd
Georgetown 29440
(803)546-0464

1960. Breakfast with many homemade items is served in guests' rooms, the parlor or on the inn's long, screened porch. Georgetown is conveniently located 30 miles from Myrtle Beach and 60 miles from Charleston. A beautiful public beach is 15 minutes away at Pawleys Island. Located on

Winyah Bay, the town's seaport offers area restaurants with abundant fresh seafood. Many homes and churches date back to the 1700s and can be seen on a walking tour or by carriage or tour train. Also available are harbor tours that allow you to see Georgetown and its plantations from the water.

Innkeeper(s): Carol & Dave Ashenfelder.

Rates:$45-65. MC VISA AX DC DS CB. ContPlus Bkfst. 4 rooms. 4 with shared baths. Beds:Q. TV, AC in room. Golf. Tennis. Swimming. Fishing.

Contact: Carol Ashenfelder. Certificate may be used: All year.

The Shaw House B&B
613 Cypress Ct
Georgetown 29440
(803)546-9663

1976. Near Georgetown's historical district is the Shaw House. It features a beautiful view of the Willowbank marsh which stretches out for more than 100 acres. Sometimes giant turtles come up and lay eggs on the lawn. Guests enjoy rocking on the inn's front and back porches and identifying the large variety of birds that live here. A Southern home-cooked breakfast often includes grits, quiche and Mary's heart-shaped biscuits.

Innkeeper(s): Mary & Joe Shaw.

Rates:$50-60. Full Bkfst. 3 rooms. Fireplaces. Beds:KQT. TV, Phone, AC, Refrig. in room. Golf. Tennis. Bicycling. Swimming. Horseback riding. Fishing.

Seen in: *Charlotte Observer, Country.*

Contact: Mary Shaw. Certificate may be used: When available.

"Your home speaks of abundance and comfort and joy."

McClellanville

Laurel Hill Plantation
8913 N Hwy 17, PO Box 190
McClellanville 29458
(803)887-3708

1850. From the large wraparound porch of this plantation house is a view of salt marshes, islands and the Atlantic Ocean. A nearby creek is the perfect location for crabbing, and there is a fresh-water pond for fishing. The home was destroyed by Hurricane Hugo, but has been totally reconstructed in its original Low Country style. It is furnished with antiques, local crafts and folk art. The inn has a gift shop that features books, antiques, baby clothes and decorative items.

Innkeeper(s): Jackie & Lee Morrison.

Rates:$65-85. MC VISA. Full Bkfst. 4 rooms. Beds:QDT. AC in room. Farm. Fishing.

Seen in: *Country Living, Seabreeze.*

Contact: Jackie Morrison. Certificate may be used: Sunday - Thursday except April, May, September, October. No promos in above months.

"The total privacy yet friendliness was very much appreciated."

Moncks Corner

Rice Hope Plantation Inn
206 Rice Hope Dr
Moncks Corner 29461
(803)761-4832 (800)569-4038
Fax:(803)884-0223

1927. Resting on 11 acres of natural beauty, the inn is set among live oaks on a bluff overlooking the Cooper River. Also, on the property are formal gardens that boast 200-year-old camellias and many old varieties of azaleas and other trees and plants. Nearby attractions include the Trappist Monastery at Mepkin Plantation, Francis Marion National Forest, Cypress Gardens and historic Charleston. Outdoor occasions are great because of the inn's formal gardens and the Cooper River backdrop.

Innkeeper(s): Doris Kasprak.

Rates:$60-75. MC VISA. ContPlus Bkfst. Gourmet Lunch, Dinner. Teas. 4 rooms. 2 with shared baths. Beds:Q. Conference Rm. AC in room. Tennis. Bicycling. Fishing.

Seen in: *The Post & Courier.*

Contact: Doris Kasprak. Certificate may be used: All year.

Simpsonville

Hunter House B&B
201 E College St
Simpsonville 29681
(803)967-2827

1906. Stained-glass windows, hand-carved woodwork, pine staircase and 10-foot ceilings are a few of the features that make this Victorian inn a pleasant place to stay. The innkeepers will be happy to assist you with special-occasion arrangements such as catering, floral decorations, photography, live music or even a horse-drawn carriage. The wood-paneled hallway leads to the Victorian parlor, with its French doors, piano and pump organ. Guests need not go far for antiquing because there's an antique shop on the premises.

Innkeeper(s): Dianne & Earl Neely.

Rates:$65-85. Full Bkfst. Evening snacks. 3 rooms. 2 with shared baths. Fireplaces. Beds:QD. Conference Rm. TV, Phone, AC, Refrig. in room. Fishing.

Contact: Dianne Neely. Certificate may be used: January - March and July - September, excluding Fridays & Saturdays.

Sumter

Magnolia House
230 Church St
Sumter 29150
(803)775-6694

1907. Each room of this Greek Revival home with its five fireplaces is decorated in antiques from a different era. Also gracing the inn are inlaid oak floors and stained-glass windows. Sumter's Historic District includes neighborhood heroes such as George Franklin Haynesworth, who fired the first shot of The War Between the States. Guests may enjoy an afternoon refreshment in the formal backyard garden. Breakfast is served in the large dining room with massive French antiques.

Innkeeper(s): Carol & Buck Rogers.

Rates:$65. MC VISA AX. Full Bkfst. 4 rooms. Fireplaces. Beds:D. AC in room. Bicycling. Swimming. Fishing.

Contact: Carol Ann Rogers. Certificate may be used: Anytime except Dec. 15-30, 1994.

Union

The Inn at Merridun
100 Merridun Pl
Union 29379
(803)427-7052 Fax:(803)427-7052

1855. Nestled on nine acres of wooded ground, this Greek Revival inn is in a small Southern college town. During spring, see the South in its colorful splendor—blooming azaleas, magnolias and wisteria. Sip an iced drink on the inn's marble verandas and relive memories of a bygone era. Soft strains of Mozart and Beethoven, as well as the smell of freshly baked cookies and country suppers, fill the air of this antebellum country inn.

Innkeeper(s): Jim & Peggy Waller.

Rates:$75-85. MC VISA DS. Full Bkfst. Gourmet Brkfst, Lunch, Dinner. Picnic lunches. Teas. Evening snacks. 5 rooms. Fireplaces. Beds:KQT. TV, Phone, AC, Refrig. in room. Bicycling. Handicap access. Swimming. Fishing.

Contact: Jim Waller. Certificate may be used: Anytime 94/95.

South Dakota

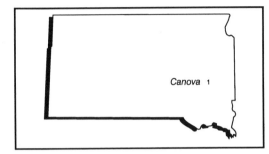

Canova 1

Canova

B&B at Skoglund Farm
Rt 1, Box 45
Canova 57321
(605)247-3445

1917. This is a working farm on the South Dakota prairie. Peacocks stroll around the farm along with cattle, chickens and other fowl. Guests can enjoy an evening meal with the family. Children under 5 years old stay for free.

Innkeeper(s): Alden & Delores Skoglund.

Rates:$60. Full Bkfst. Gourmet Dinner. 4 rooms. 4 with shared baths. Beds:QDT. Farm. Golf. Tennis. Bicycling. Swimming. Horseback riding. Fishing.

Contact: Delores Skoglund. Certificate may be used: Anytime rooms are available.

"Thanks for the down-home hospitality and good food."

Tennessee

Altamont

Woodlee House B&B
P O Box 310
Altamont 37301
(615)692-2368

1895. This Colonial Revival house, in the National Register of Historic Places, is located on Cumberland Mountain near the Stone Door, a 150-

foot crevice. Lone Rock Cake Ovens, 7,000-foot-long Wonder Cave, Foster Falls and the many outstanding waterfalls of Savage Gulf State Natural Area are all in the vicinity. The inn is built around an original pre-Civil War log cabin, now the par-

lor. Rooms are decorated with antiques, collections of books, quilts, miniature houses and flow blue china.

Innkeeper(s): Earlene Speer.

Rates:$50. Full Bkfst. 2 rooms. 2 with shared baths. AC in room.

Contact: Earlene Speer. Certificate may be used: Anytime except October.

Bolivar

Magnolia Manor
418 N Main St
Bolivar 38008
(901)658-6700

1849. Two acres of landscaped grounds surround this Colonial Georgian inn with stately columns and exquisitely decorated rooms. (The innkeeper is an interior designer.) The walls are 13-inch thick, sun-dried red brick. During the Civil War, Magnolia Manor served as headquarters for a time for General Grant and there are many stories centering around its visitors, Generals Sherman, Logan and McPherson. Request the suite with the massive carved bed.

Innkeeper(s): Elaine & Jim Cox.

Rates:$75-85. Full Bkfst. Picnic lunches. 6 rooms. 3 with shared baths. Fireplaces. Beds:Q. AC in room. Fishing.

Contact: Elaine Cox. Certificate may be used: Anytime except Thanksgiving and Christmas holidays.

Brentwood

English Manor B&B Inn & Catering Service
6304 Murray Ln
Brentwood 37027
(615)373-4627 (800)332-4640

1970. An elegant Colonial Revival mansion, the English Manor offers 7,000 square feet on five landscaped acres. A barn and horse are situated behind the house. All guest rooms feature phones, TVs and private baths. Rocking chairs on the porch and a swing in the backyard provide spots to rest after a stroll along the creek or a visit to the barnyard. A hearty breakfast is served and the innkeeper is known for her homemade fudge, offered in the evening. Southern meals are available by arrangement. The inn is popular for weddings and corporate meetings because of its private wooded setting.

Innkeeper(s): William Shackelford.

Rates:$70. MC VISA AX. Full Bkfst. Gourmet Brkfst, Lunch, Dinner. Picnic lunches. Teas. Evening snacks. 6 rooms. Conference Rm. Skiing. Swimming. Fishing.

Contact: Willia Dean English. Certificate may be used: Upon availability.

Chattanooga

The Milton House B&B
508 Fort Wood Pl
Chattanooga 37403
(615)265-2800

1915. Ionic columns, pilasters and a slate gabled roof accent this elegant Greek Revival mansion in the National Register. Features include three pillared fireplace mantels and an American Gothic window highlighting the grand winding staircase. Maple and heart pine floors provide a sparkling background for the Victorian, Eastlake and Renaissance antiques that fill the inn. It's a few blocks to the University of Tennessee at Chattanooga, the Tennessee River and the Tennessee Aquarium, the world's largest freshwater aquarium. Rooms offer amenities such as a private porch, fireplace or Jacuzzi for two.

Innkeeper(s): Susan Mehlen.

Rates:$65-135. Full Bkfst. 5 rooms. 2 with shared baths. Fireplaces. Beds:D. AC in room. Bicycling. Swimming. Fishing.

Contact: Susan Mehlen. Certificate may be used: November through February.

Cookeville

Scarecrow Country Inn
1720 E Spring St
Cookeville 38501
(615)526-3431 Fax:(615)528-5707

1967. This unobtrusively located inn, on seven acres, surprises most who discover it. Known locally for its fine dinners served Wednesday through Sundays, the inn was assembled from 14 log houses and cabins, some 150 to 200 years old. Guest rooms maintain the log-cabin atmosphere, and there's an old copper-lined bathtub.

Innkeeper(s): Wanda Fitzpatrick.

Rates:$70. MC VISA. Full Bkfst. Gourmet Brkfst. 4 rooms. 1 with shared bath. Fireplaces. Beds:QT. TV, Phone, AC in room. Handicap access.

Seen in: *Detroit Free Press.*

Contact: Wanda Fitzpatrick. Certificate may be used: Monday through Thursday nights, no holidays.

"Many thanks to you and your staff."

Cordova

The Bridgewater House
7015 Raleigh La Grange Rd
Cordova 38018
(901)372-3413

1890. This century-old schoolhouse sits on more than two acres shaded by stately oak trees. Upon entering, you will find the original hardwood floors, leaded-glass windows and hand-marbleized moldings. Awake to a gourmet breakfast prepared by the innkeeper, a caterer and former manager of corporate test kitchens. Specialities include Strawberries Romanoff, Broccoli with Hollandaise or a Cheese Blintz souffle. The Bridgewater Inn promises to be an experience not soon forgotten.

Innkeeper(s): Katherine Mistilis.

Rates:$75-100. Gourmet Brkfst. 2 rooms. Beds:KD. AC in room. Fishing.

Contact: Katherine Mistilis. Certificate may be used: Sunday-Thursday.

Ducktown

The White House B&B
104 Main St, PO Box 668
Ducktown 37326
(615)496-4166 (800)775-4166

1906. In the National Register, this Queen Anne Victorian offers a wraparound porch with a swing. Rooms are air-conditioned and decorated in a traditional style with family antiques. The Ocoee River, selected for Olympic white-water events, is 10 minutes away.

Innkeeper(s): Dan & Mardee Kauffman.

Rates:$50-60. MC VISA. Full Bkfst. Gourmet Brkfst. Evening snacks. 3 rooms. 2 with shared baths. Beds:QT. Golf. Swimming. Horseback riding. Fishing.

Contact: Mardee Kauffman. Certificate may be used: Excluding weekends in October and local white-water events on the Ocoee River.

Franklin

Magnolia House B&B
1317 Columbia Ave
Franklin 37064
(615)794-8178

1905. In summer, a blooming Magnolia tree shades the wicker-filled front porch of this gabled Craftsman cottage. The land is where the Battle of

Franklin was fought. Furnishings range from 19th-century Victorian and Empire pieces to an Eastlake bedroom suite. The most popular breakfast here is Tennessee country ham, biscuits, cheese grits casserole and fresh fruit. An English flower garden and herb garden are in the back. Walk five blocks through a maple shaded neighborhood of historic houses to downtown Franklin, 15 blocks of which are in the National Register of Historic Places.

Innkeeper(s): Bill & Betty Blankenship.
Rates:$70-85. MC VISA. Full Bkfst. 3 rooms. Beds:Q. Phone, AC in room.
Contact: Betty Blankenship. Certificate may be used: Tuesday, Wednesday, Thursday, year-round.

Gatlinburg

7th Heaven Log Inn on the Golf Resort
3944 Castle Rd
Gatlinburg 37738
(615)430-5000 (800)248-2923
Fax:(615)436-7748

1991. Wake up to Eggs Benedict Mountain Style served on the deck among the tree tops and you'll start to understand the inn's name. There are views of the golf course, dogwood trees, wild ducks and hummingbirds. Decks stretch for two stories all around the inn. Across the road is the Smoky Mountain National Park. Ride America's largest aerial tram, try the 1,800-foot Alpine Slide or hike and picnic in the Smoky Mountain National Park.

Innkeeper(s): Ginger & Paul Wolcott.

Rates:$77-117. MC VISA. Gourmet Brkfst. Evening snacks. 4 rooms. Beds:Q. AC in room. Golf. Tennis. Skiing. Spa. Swimming. Horseback riding. Fishing.
Contact: Paul Wolcott. Certificate may be used: Weekdays; January, February, March & April.

"Five days was not enough. We'll be back." D.L., London.

Goodlettsville

Woodshire B&B
600 Woodshire Dr
Goodlettsville 37072
(615)859-7369

1850. A gentle gray and white salt-box house, the Woodshire also includes a reconstructed mid-19th-century log cabin. John's woodcrafts and Beverly's weavings and paintings add to the home's antiques to provide a warm and personal decor. Homemade breads and biscuits are offered at breakfast. Opryland is eight miles away.

Innkeeper(s): John & Beverly Grayson.
Rates:$50-60. ContPlus Bkfst. 3 rooms. Beds:D. TV, Phone, AC in room. Swimming. Fishing.
Contact: John Grayson. Certificate may be used: Spring and fall.

Greeneville

Hilltop House B&B
6 Sanford Circle
Greeneville 37743
(615)639-8202

1920. This manor house is located on a bluff overlooking the Nolichuckey River Valley, and guests can enjoy the mountain view from their bedrooms. The Elizabeth Noel room, named for the former owner, boasts a canopy bed, a sitting area and a veranda perfect for sunset watching. A relaxing afternoon can be spent discovering wildflowers and bird watching. Innkeeper Denise Ashworth, a horticulturist and landscape architect, hosts a variety of gardening workshops at the inn.

Innkeeper(s): Denise M. Ashworth.
Rates:$60-70. MC VISA AX. Full Bkfst. Gourmet Brkfst, Lunch, Dinner. Picnic lunches. Teas. 3 rooms. Fireplaces. Beds:KQD. TV, Phone, AC, Refrig. in room. Golf. Bicycling. Swimming. Fishing.
Seen in: *Country Inns.*
Contact: Denise Ashworth. Certificate may be used: January - March.

"Peaceful and comfortable, great change of pace."

Hampshire

Ridgetop Bed & Breakfast
P O Box 193
Hampshire 38461
(615)285-2777 (800)377-2770

1979. This contemporary Western cedar house rests on 20 cleared acres along the top of the ridge. A quarter-mile below is a waterfall. Blueberries grow in abundance on the property and guests may pick them in summer. (These provide the filling for luscious breakfast muffins, waffles and pancakes year-round.) There are 170 acres in all, mostly wooded. Picture windows and a deck provide views of the trees and wildlife: flying squirrels, birds, raccoons and deer. The inn is handicap-accessible.

Innkeeper(s): Kay & Bill Jones.

Rates:$60-80. MC VISA. Full Bkfst. 2 rooms. Beds:DT. AC, Refrig. in room. Handicap access. Swimming. Horseback riding. Fishing.

Seen in: *Columbia Daily Herald*.

Contact: Kay Jones. Certificate may be used: Nov. 15 - March 15. Months of July and August.

Jackson

Highland Place B&B
519 N Highland Ave
Jackson 38301
(901)427-1472

1911. This two-story house in the North Highland Historical District is five blocks from downtown. The inn is popular for bridal showers and dinners. There is a library, game room with pool table and a dining room where breakfast is served. Chinese rugs and a wood-burning fireplace are features of the Hamilton Room.

Innkeeper(s): Danette & Greg Davis

Rates:$65-75. MC VISA. ContPlus Bkfst. Teas. 3 rooms. 2 with shared baths. Fireplaces. Beds:KQ. Conference Rm. Swimming. Fishing.

Contact: Danette Davis. Certificate may be used: Anytime - excluding holidays.

Jefferson City

Branner-Hicks House
1169 N Chucky Pk
Jefferson City 37760
(615)475-2302

1850. Built by Confederate Colonel Branner, this handsome farmhouse is now in the National Register of Historic Places. There are 11 acres

along Mossy Creek. Fine woodwork, chandeliers, antique mirrors and furnishings fill the inn. Ask for

the Cherokee Suite with its walnut fireplace and beamed ceiling. It's five minutes to Cherokee Lake, 40 minutes to Knoxville.

Innkeeper(s): Polly Hicks.

Rates:$65. Full Bkfst. 3 rooms. Beds:DT. Phone, AC in room.

Contact: Polly Hicks. Certificate may be used: Anytime except October.

Jonesborough

Aiken-Brow House
104 3rd Ave S
Jonesborough 37659
(615)753-9440

1850. There's a beautiful gazebo on the grounds of this historic Greek Revival home, a half-block from Main Street. All the rooms have air conditioning and there are porches for rocking. Victorian furnishings prevail. The inn is located in the Jonesborough Historic District.

Innkeeper(s): Calvin & Ann Brow.

Rates:$45-65. Full Bkfst. 3 rooms. 2 with shared baths. Fireplaces. Beds:DT. AC in room. Golf. Tennis. Skiing. Swimming. Horseback riding. Fishing.

Seen in: *Blue Ridge, East Tennessee*.

Contact: Calvin Brow. Certificate may be used: Monday, Tuesday, Wednesday, Thursday only, not Friday, Saturday, Sunday - except April 8-12, August 25-30, October first full weekend.

Bowling Green Inn B&B
901 W College St
Jonesborough 37659
(615)753-6356

1805. Eleven acres surround this recently restored farmhouse that once was a stagecoach stop on the Old Stage Road between Bristol and Leesburg. Antique furnishings and country items decorate the inn. Jonesborough is Tennessee's oldest town and has retained its beautiful historic houses. Special events include Civil War re-enactment weekend with its Confederate Memorial Ball, quilting festivals, historic days and the National Storytelling Festival.

Innkeeper(s): Esther & Frank Congo.

Rates:$55. MC VISA. Cont. Bkfst. 3 rooms. Beds:DT. AC, Refrig. in room. Handicap access. Swimming. Fishing.

Contact: Esther Congo. Certificate may be used: Anytime except Oct. 7-8, 1994; April 8-9, 1995; Aug. 25-26, 1995 and Oct. 6-7, 1995.

Limestone

Snapp Inn B&B
1990 Davy Crockett Rd
Limestone 37681
(615)257-2482

1815. From the second-story porch of this red brick Federal, guests enjoy views of local farmland as well as the sounds of Big Limestone Creek. The Smoky

Mountains are seen from the back porch. Decorated with locally gathered antiques, the home is within walking distance of Davy Crockett Birthplace State Park. A full country breakfast often includes Ruth's homemade biscuits.

Innkeeper(s): Ruth & Dan Dorgan.

Rates:$50. Full Bkfst. Evening snacks. 3 rooms. Fireplaces. Beds:Q. AC in room. Farm. Golf. Tennis. Swimming. Fishing.

Seen in: *Greenville Sun*.

Contact: Ruth Dorgan. Certificate may be used: Availability by reservation.

Loudon

The Mason Place B&B
600 Commerce St
Loudon 37774
(615)458-3921

1865. In the National Register, Mason Place received an award for its outstanding restoration. In the Greek Revival style, the inn has a red slate roof, graceful columns and a handsome double-tiered balcony overlooking three acres of lawns,

trees and gardens. There are 10 working fireplaces, a Grecian swimming pool, gazebo, and wisteria-covered arbor. A grand entrance hall, fine antiques and tasteful furnishings make for an elegant decor, suitable for the mansion's 7,000 square feet.

Innkeeper(s): Bob & Donna Stewert.

Rates:$96. MC VISA. Gourmet Brkfst. Picnic lunches. Teas. Evening snacks. 5 rooms. Fireplaces. Beds:Q. Conference Rm. AC in room. Golf. Tennis. Bicycling. Skiing. Swimming. Horseback riding. Fishing.

Contact: Donna Jean Stewert. Certificate may be used: February and March.

Monteagle

Adams Edgeworth Inn
Monteagle Assembly
Monteagle 37356
(615)924-2669 Fax:(615)924-3236

1896. This National Register Victorian inn recently has been refurbished in an English manor style. Original paintings and sculptures and fine English

antiques are found throughout. Wide verandas are filled with white wicker furnishings and breezy hammocks, and there's a prize-winning rose garden. You can stroll through the 96-acre Victorian village that surrounds the inn and enjoy rolling hills, creeks and Victorian cottages. Waterfalls, natural caves and scenic overlooks are along the 150 miles of hiking trails of nearby South Cumberland State Park.

Innkeeper(s): Wendy & David Adams.

Rates:$60-150. MC VISA AX. Full Bkfst. EP. Gourmet Lunch, Dinner. Picnic lunches. 12 rooms. Fireplaces. Beds:KQT. Conference Rm. TV, AC, Refrig. in room. Golf. Tennis. Bicycling. Handicap access. Spa. Sauna. Swimming. Horseback riding. Fishing.

Seen in: *Country Inns, Chattanooga News Free Press, Tempo*.

Contact: Wendy Adams. Certificate may be used: November, December, January, February, March, April, May - Monday-Thursday only. Holidays and special local events are also excluded.

"Leaving totally rejuvenated."

Nashville/Ashland

Birdsong Country Inn B&B
1306 Hwy 49E
Nashville/Ashland 37015
(615)792-4005

1910. This rambling lodge-style house, in the
National Register of Historic Places, was built with
cedar logs by the Cheek family of Maxwell House

coffee fame. Handsome furnishings and an art collection set off the chinked walls and beamed ceilings. The inn boasts a screened-in front porch,
English gardens and green lawns. Hammocks swing
underneath walnut and cedar trees, and there are
peach and pear trees on the 10 acres. Hike or picnic along Sycamore Creek, visit the barn or soak in
the heated spa.

Innkeeper(s): Anne & Brooks Parker.
Rates:$85-100. MC VISA AX DS. ContPlus Bkfst. Teas. Evening snacks.
5 rooms. 2 with shared baths. Beds:Q. AC in room. Spa. Stables.
Fishing.
Contact: Alton Brooks Parker. Certificate may be used: Weekdays or
weekends (space available) year-round.

Nashville/Goodlettsville

The Drake Farm on Lumsley Creek
5508 Brick Church Pike, PO Box 875
Nashville/Goodlettsville 37070
(615)859-2425 (800)586-7539
Fax:(615)859-3671

1850. A 15-mile drive from downtown Nashville
will bring you to this 116-acre farm. The Greek
Revival house still stands along Lumsley Creek as it
did during the Civil War. It has been home to five
generations of Drakes. There are pastures, woodlands, hammocks, swings and fields for croquet and
volleyball. Bees work in the apiary to produce
honey for your breakfasts. All the guest rooms have
fireplaces. Plan ahead and you may reserve a candlelight dinner, picnic, rehearsal dinner or even a
wedding.

Innkeeper(s): Rose Mary Drake.

Rates:$55. MC VISA AX. Full Bkfst. Gourmet Dinner. Picnic lunches.
Teas. 2 rooms. 2 with shared baths. Fireplaces. Beds:QT. AC in room.
Farm. Handicap access. Swimming. Fishing.
Contact: Rose Mary Drake. Certificate may be used: January, August.

Pikeville

Fall Creek Falls B&B
Rt 3, Box 298B
Pikeville 37367
(615)881-5494 Fax:(615)881-5040

1981. An abundance of gables marks the architecture of this 6,000-square-foot country manor, surrounded by 40 acres of woodland and meadow.

Victorian and country furnishings are found in
rooms such as the Sweet Heart Room, which offers
a heart-shaped, red whirlpool tub. Breakfast is
served in the dining room or the Florida room overlooking the fields and deer trails. Strawberry bread
with strawberry cream cheese is a specialty. Fall
Creek Falls State Park is a mile away where you
can hike trails that meander past scenic waterfalls.

Innkeeper(s): Doug & Rita Pruett.
Rates:$54-79. MC VISA. Full Bkfst. 8 rooms. 2 with shared baths.
Beds:QT. Conference Rm. AC in room. Golf. Tennis. Swimming.
Horseback riding. Fishing.
Contact: Rita Pruett. Certificate may be used: From Feb. 1 to May 1.

Rockford

Wayside Manor
4009 Old Knoxville Hwy
Rockford 37853
(615)970-4823 (800)675-4823
Fax:(615)981-1890

1932. Three separate buildings comprise this inn; a
Classical Revival main house, Cape Cod house and
a cottage. There are seven acres of grounds with
flower gardens, tall maples strung with hammocks,
a bubbling creek, gazebo and spa. Guest rooms feature French doors, soft carpeting, high ceilings,
original art, private porches, antique quilts and
fresh flowers. Two suites have Jacuzzis and fireplaces. Business meetings, retreats, reunions and
weddings often are held here.

Innkeeper(s): Abby & Becky Koella.

Rates:$85-195. MC VISA DS. Full Bkfst. MAP available. Gourmet Lunch, Dinner. Picnic lunches. Teas. Evening snacks. 11 rooms. 3 with shared baths. Fireplaces. Beds:KQT. Conference Rm. TV, Phone, AC in room. Tennis. Bicycling. Skiing. Handicap access. Spa. Swimming. Fishing.

Contact: Becky Koella. Certificate may be used: June, July, August, January, February or March.

Townsend

Richmont Inn
220 Winterberry Ln
Townsend 37882
(615)448-6751

1991. This unusual inn is a new Appalachian-style cantilever barn, built on 11 acres. The common room and dining room are decorated with French paintings and English antiques. The Francis Asbury room has a private balcony and mountain view while Nancy Ward offers spacious quarters with a conference table, skylights, wet bar, king bed and valley, forest and mountain views. It has its own fireplace and private balcony. A candlelight dessert is served in the evening.
Innkeeper(s): Jim & Susan Hind.

Rates:$85-135. Full Bkfst. Gourmet Brkfst. Picnic lunches. Evening snacks. 10 rooms. Fireplaces. Beds:KQ. AC, Refrig. in room. Skiing. Handicap access. Fishing.

Contact: James Hind. Certificate may be used: Sunday - Thursday, November - March and September (exclude holidays).

Watertown

Watertown B&B
116 Depot St
Watertown 37184
(615)237-9999

1898. Upper and lower verandas encircle this graceful house. There are two-story columns and double porches. It once served as the hotel for the old railroad that passed through. The bed & breakfast offers a fully stocked library. The Van Wert Room

has a queen bed and full private bath. There are tandem bikes to borrow for cycling in the area. Nashville is a 40-minute drive.
Innkeeper(s): Bob & Sharon McComb.

Rates:$48-53. MC VISA. Full Bkfst. Evening snacks. 3 rooms. 1 with shared bath. Beds:QD. AC in room. Bicycling. Swimming. Fishing.

Contact: Sharon McComb. Certificate may be used: No restrictions.

Texas

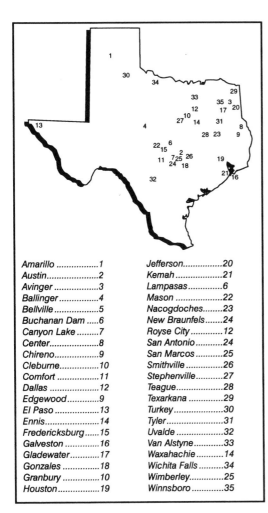

Amarillo

Parkview House B&B
1311 S Jefferson
Amarillo 79101
(806)373-9464

1908. Ionic columns support the wraparound wick-er-filled front porch of this gabled grandma's Victorian. Herb and rose gardens surround the property and the back garden has a Victorian gazing ball. Antique mahogany, walnut and oak pieces are found throughout. The French, Colonial and Victorian Rose rooms all feature draped bedsteads. Sticky buns and homemade granola are served in the mornings after which even new guests sometimes depart with a hug and "Bye Mom, I'll see you next time."

Innkeeper(s): Carol & Nabil Dia.

Rates:$60-80. MC VISA. ContPlus Bkfst. Evening snacks. 6 rooms. 2 with shared baths. Beds:QD. Phone, AC in room. Tennis. Bicycling. Spa. Swimming. Horseback riding. Fishing.

Seen in: *Lubbock Avalanche, Amarillo Globe News, Accent West, Sunday Telegraph Review.*

Contact: Carol Dia. Certificate may be used: Anytime based on availability except Friday and Saturday and major holidays, Christmas, Thanksgiving, Valentine and Mother's Day, Easter/Spring Break.

"We have been spoiled and will never want to stay at a dull motel again."

Austin

Southard House
908 Blanco
Austin 78703
(512)474-4731

1890. This house, an Austin historic landmark, originally had a single story, but was raised to accommodate an additional level at the turn of the century. Eleven-foot ceilings provide a background for antiques and paintings.

Innkeeper(s): Jerry & Rejina Southards.

Rates:$59-159. MC VISA AX DC DS CB. Full Bkfst. 10 rooms. Fireplaces. Beds:QT. Phone, AC, Refrig. in room. Bicycling.

Seen in: *Southern Living, New York Times, US Air, Austin Home & Garden.*

Contact: Kara Southards. Certificate may be used: Sunday through Thursday, no holidays, weekends, or special events.

"A memory to be long cherished. We especially enjoyed the home atmosphere and the lovely breakfasts in the garden."

Avinger

McKenzie Manor
Rt 1 Box 404A
Avinger 75630
(903)755-2240

1960. Nature trails with private ponds are right outside the door of this rustic, rock lodge set on the shore of Lake O' The Pines. Guests can sit on wide

decks and watch eagles soar, beavers build dams and deer graze. Relax in the gazebo or by the large rock fireplace with a good book from the private library of the innkeeper, historian and author Fred McKenzie. This four-generation family home is designed with a large meeting room, vaulted ceilings and stained-glass windows. All rooms are adjacent to sitting areas and each room is decorated in its own unique style with lovely antiques and family possessions.

Innkeeper(s): Fred & Anne McKenzie.

Rates:$65-95. MC VISA. Full Bkfst. Gourmet Dinner. Picnic lunches. 7 rooms. 2 with shared baths. Fireplaces. Beds:KQ. Conference Rm. TV, AC in room. Handicap access. Spa. Swimming. Fishing.

Contact: Carol Harrell. Certificate may be used: January, any week night, Monday-Thursday.

Ballinger

Miz Virginia's B&B
107 S 6th St
Ballinger 76821
(915)365-2453

1886. Serving the community as a hotel and boarding house since before the turn of the century, this inn stands as one of the oldest buildings in town. An antique store and restaurant are now on the premises of the B&B. Guests can browse through 20 rooms of antiques and collectibles. After getting a taste of shopping, there's more to be found in town with quaint shops of antiques, pottery, woodmaking, arts and crafts. Courthouse Square hosts many festivities, including an annual Ethnic Festival and Christmas in Olde Ballinger.

Innkeeper(s): S. C. & Juanita Chrisco.

Rates:$38-85. MC VISA DS. Full Bkfst. MAP available. Gourmet Dinner.

Teas. 7 rooms. 5 with shared baths. Beds:D. AC in room. Fishing.

Contact: Juanita Chrisco. Certificate may be used: Year-round.

Bellville

High Cotton Inn
214 S Live Oak
Bellville 77418
(409)865-9796 (800)321-9796
Fax:(409)865-5588

1906. Use of the downstairs parlor, fenced swimming pool and bottomless cookie jar is encouraged at this Victorian B&B. Porch swings are strategically located on the balcony and front porch. There's a cozy upstairs sitting room for reading, television or conversation. Around 9 a.m. each morning, guests gather in the old family dining room for a full Southern-style breakfast. Innkeepers can provide information on excursions to Blue Bell Creamery, Winedale, Round Top and Festival Hill.

Innkeeper(s): George & Anna Horton.

Rates:$50. MC VISA DS. Full Bkfst. EP. 5 rooms. 5 with shared baths. Beds:QT. AC in room. Swimming. Fishing.

Contact: Anna Horton. Certificate may be used: Sunday through Thursday only. Not available April or October.

Buchanan Dam

Mystic Cove B&B
RR 1 Box 309B
Buchanan Dam 78609
(512)793-6642

1987. This two-story, rock and cedar inn located on the West shore of Lake Buchanan offers small group retreats with plans made to order. Workshops include stress management, meditation, yoga and dream interpretation. There are lots of covered porches for relaxing, a sandy beach for swimming and docks for boating and fishing. A private, fully equiped cottage (breakfast extra) is located at water's edge with an attached fishing dock. The Queen Anne Room, which is decorated Victorian style, has a great lake view.

Innkeeper(s): Ralph & Loretta Dueweke.

Rates:$55-85. Full Bkfst. EP. 3 rooms. Beds:KQ. AC, Refrig. in room. Exercise room. Swimming. Fishing.

Contact: Loretta Dueweke. Certificate may be used: Sept. 15 - May 15.

Canyon Lake

Aunt Nora's B&B
120 Naked Indian Trail
Canyon Lake 78132
(210)905-3989

1983. Nestled on four acres, amid oak, cedar and Indian trees, this Texas country inn has many nearby scenic areas that include a walk to the top of the hill to view Canyon Lake. The sitting room is a perfect place to relax among handmade furnishings, antiques, paintings, lacy crafts, wood stove and natural wood floors. Enjoy the private collection of Pigtails & Lace hand-crafted dolls. The guest rooms are decorated with country curtains, natural woodwork, handmade maple and cherry wood furnishings, ceiling fans and quilts.

Innkeeper(s): Alton & Iralee Haley.

Rates:$55-125. Full Bkfst. 4 rooms. 2 with shared baths. Beds:Q. Phone, AC, Refrig. in room. Spa. Swimming. Fishing.

Contact: Iralee Haley. Certificate may be used: January through April and October through December (excludes May through September) and preferable Sunday through Thursday (excludes all holidays).

Center

Pine Colony Inn
500 Shelbyville St
Center 75935
(409)598-7700

1945. The inn is a restored hotel with more than 8,000 square feet of antique-filled rooms. Artwork from local artist Woodrow Foster adorns the walls.

These limited-edition prints are framed and sold by the innkeepers. The town is located between Toledo Bend, which is one of the largest man-made lakes in the United States, and Lake Pinkston, where the state record bass (just under 17 pounds) was caught in 1986. Ask the innkeepers about all the little-out-of-the-way places to see either by foot, bicycle or car.

Innkeeper(s): Marcille Hughes

Rates:$45-55. MC VISA. Full Bkfst. 12 rooms. 4 with shared baths. Beds:KT. Conference Rm. TV, Phone, AC, Refrig. in room. Swimming. Fishing.

Contact: Marcille Hughes. Certificate may be used: Anytime.

Chireno

Gingerbread House
Gingerbread St, Box 94
Chireno 75937
(409)362-2365

1895. This Victorian home was first built as a wedding present. The home took two years to complete, by which time the would-be bride changed her mind. The home was never occupied and the man never married. Later, the home was purchased for $1,500 and was used as a boarding house for teachers. The next owners used the Gingerbread House as a summer home and added a charming gazebo, built in a grove of magnolias. As a B&B, the house has guest rooms filled with vintage furnishings and whimsical decorative touches.

Innkeeper(s): Bob & Dorothy Bates

Rates:$55-80. MAP available. Gourmet Brkfst. 3 rooms. 2 with shared baths. Beds:KQ. TV, AC in room. Fishing.

Contact: Dorothy Bates. Certificate may be used: Only Tuesday, Wednesday and Thursday, excluding holidays.

Cleburne

Anglin Queen Anne B&B
723 N Anglin St
Cleburne 76031
(817)645-5555

1892. This home, which was once owned by a cattle baron, is dominated by a three-story cupola set between two second-story porches. The first story includes a large round veranda with porch posts and gingerbread fretwork. The mansion's interior is embellished with wood paneling, molding and fancy carvings. Two main staircases have elaborate grillwork, paneling and stained glass. The dining rooms include a Northwind dining set, Oriental warlord's chair and a carved chair set from a European guest house.

Innkeeper(s): Dan & Billie Anne Leach.

Rates:$50-125. MC VISA. ContPlus Bkfst. Gourmet Brkfst, Lunch, Dinner. Picnic lunches. Teas. Evening snacks. 5 rooms. Fireplaces. Beds:Q. Conference Rm. Phone, AC in room. Handicap access. Swimming. Fishing.

Contact: Billie Anne Leach. Certificate may be used: Anytime, flexible.

Comfort

Idlewilde

115 Hwy 473
Comfort 78013
(210)995-3844

1902. This Western-style farmhouse and cottages has come to be known as "Haven in the Hills." The home and surrounding grounds were a girls' summer camp for more than 60 years. The inn has no set check-in or check-out times. The innkeepers offer breakfast either in the main house dining area or at your specified spot (which could be breakfast in bed). The large, unique hallways and center rooms are open and airy with lots of windows. Antiques and country French furniture decorate the entire lodge.

Innkeeper(s): Hank Engel & Connie Cazel.

Rates:$93. MC VISA. Full Bkfst. AP available. Gourmet Dinner. Picnic lunches. Teas. 5 rooms. 2 with shared baths. Beds:QT. Conference Rm. AC in room. Golf. Tennis. Bicycling. Handicap access. Swimming. Horseback riding. Stables. Fishing.

Contact: Hank Engel. Certificate may be used: Weekdays, Sunday through Thursday night, all year 1994 through Dec. 31, 1995. No holidays.

Dallas

Inn on Fairmount

3701 Fairmount
Dallas 75219
(214)522-2800 Fax:(214)522-2898

1930. Located in the heart of the Oak Lawn/Turtle Creek area, this Federal-style inn is just minutes from dozens of restaurants and clubs. It's less than two minutes from the Dallas Market Center and just 10 minutes from the Arts District of Dallas. Each morning, just outside your door, freshly brewed coffee and the morning newspaper await you. The bedrooms and suites have fine furnishings, direct-dial phones and remote-control color televisions.

Innkeeper(s): Michael C. McVay.

Rates:$80-120. MC VISA. Cont. Bkfst. Evening snacks. 7 rooms. Beds:KQT. TV, Phone, AC in room. Spa.

Contact: Michael McVay. Certificate may be used: Anytime.

Edgewood

Crooked Creek Farm B&B

Rt 1, Box 180
Edgewood 75117
(903)896-1284 (800)766-0790

1977. This traditional brick farmhouse, which is found in a rural community of 1,300, is nestled on the edge of the East Texas timberline. The farm covers more than 100 acres. Cattle are raised here and there are trees, creek, a nature trail, ponds and four fishing tanks on the property. A hearty breakfast may feature country ham and bacon, eggs, biscuits and gravy and a fruit dish. In town, an ongoing bicentennial project includes a museum and 14 authentically restored and furnished structures representing rural life in 1900.

Innkeeper(s): Dorothy Thornton.

Rates:$65-75. Full Bkfst. 6 rooms. 4 with shared baths. Beds:KQDT. AC in room. Farm. Fishing.

Contact: Dorthy Thornton. Certificate may be used: Anytime except first weekend each month.

El Paso

Sunset Heights B&B Inn

717 W Yandell Ave
El Paso 79902
(915)544-1743 (800)767-8513
Fax:(915)544-5119

1905. This luxurious inn is accentuated by palm trees and Spanish-style arches. Inside, bedrooms are filled with antiques and boast brass and four-poster

beds. Breakfast is a five- to eight-course feast prepared by innkeeper Richard Barnett. On any morning a guest might awake to sample a breakfast with Southwestern flair, including Eggs Chillquillas and pit-smoked Machakas, a combination of smoked beef, avocado and onion. Juice, fresh coffee, tea, dessert and fresh fruits top off the meal, which might begin with caviar and quiche. Enjoy the morning meal in the dining room or spend breakfast in bed.

Innkeeper(s): Richard Barnett.

Rates:$80-165. MC VISA AX. Full Bkfst. Gourmet Brkfst, Dinner. Picnic lunches. 5 rooms. Fireplaces. Beds:KQT. Conference Rm. TV, Phone, AC, Refrig. in room. Golf. Tennis. Skiing. Spa. Exercise room. Swimming.

Seen in: *Southwest Profile.*

Contact: Richard Barnett. Certificate may be used: January - April, but accept all year. Not valid on: Thanksgiving, Christmas, Sun Bowl Weekend, Valentine's.

Ennis

Raphael House
500 W Ennis Ave
Ennis 75119
(214)875-1555 Fax:(214)875-0308

1906. Built and owned by the Raphael family for many decades, this Greek Revival house is highlighted with a three-story porch. Century-old pecan trees border a gracious English garden. Inside, the open foyer flows to a parlor, separated only by massive, polished, clear pine Doric columns. There are gleaming heart pine floors throughout and many original furnishings. Spacious bedchambers include handsome antique bedsteads and canopied beds, all with down comforters. A carriage pulled by Belgian horses stops to pick up riders across the street from the inn.

Innkeeper(s): Brian & Danna Cody Wolf.

Rates:$58-98. MC VISA AX DC DS CB. Full Bkfst. Evening snacks. 6 rooms. Beds:KQ. Conference Rm. TV, Phone, AC in room. Swimming. Fishing.

Seen in: *Dallas Morning News, Dallas Times-Herald, Ft. Worth Star-Telegram.*

Contact: Danna Cody Wolf. Certificate may be used: Sunday through Thursday (excluding holidays and special events). Friday - Saturday with 24-hour notice.

"This house has been refurbished to a truly magnificent standard by a perfectionist."

Fredericksburg

Country Cottage Inn
249 E Main St
Fredericksburg 78624
(210)997-8549

1850. This beautifully preserved house was built by blacksmith and cutler Frederick Kiehne. With two-foot-thick walls, it was the first two-story limestone house in town. The Country Cottage holds a collection of Texas primitives and German country antiques, accentuated by Laura Ashley linens. Some of the baths include whirlpool tubs. The innkeepers have restored a second historic house, a block away, which is also available. Full regional-style breakfasts are brought to each room.

Innkeeper(s): Jeffery Webb.

Rates:$75-110. MC VISA. Full Bkfst. 5 rooms. Fireplaces. Beds:KQ. TV, Phone, AC, Refrig. in room. Spa. Swimming. Fishing.

Seen in: *Weekend Getaway, Dallas Morning News.*

Contact: Jean Sudderth. Certificate may be used: Monday, Tuesday, Wednesday, January and February only (excluding holidays).

"A step back in time in 1850 style."

East of the Sun-West of the Moon
512 W Austin
Fredericksburg 78624
(210)997-4981

1903. Having been recently remodeled to restore its charm and pioneer spirit, this yellow house has furnishings and decor that include an eclectic mix of Western, country antiques and a few contemporary pieces. Upon arrival, guests join the innkeepers for wine and cheese during a "get-acquainted time." Located one block north of Main Street, the inn is within walking distance of shopping, restaurants and entertainment. The living room has a wood-burning fireplace for cool, hill country evenings.

Innkeeper(s): Mark & Teresa Ray.

Rates:$60-70. MC VISA. Full Bkfst. AP available. Evening snacks. 2 rooms. 2 with shared baths. Fireplaces. Beds:QT. TV, AC in room. Swimming. Fishing.

Contact: Teresa Ray. Certificate may be used: Jan. 2-31, 1995 and Feb. 1-9 and 16-28, 1995.

Galveston

Michael's B&B Inn
1715 35th St
Galveston 77550
(409)763-3760 (800)776-8302

1916. Built by Hans Guldman, Galveston's one-time vice-consul for Denmark, the massive red brick home sits on an acre of gardens that include Mrs. Guldman's greenhouse and fish pond. Guests can have breakfast in the formal dining room or in the sunroom overlooking the garden. The house holds a cache of family antiques with con-temporary pieces and original art. Common rooms include a large dining room, parlor, sunroom and study.

Innkeeper(s): Mikey & Allen Isbell.

Rates:$85. MC VISA. Full Bkfst. 4 rooms. 4 with shared baths. Beds:KD. AC, Refrig. in room. Bicycling. Swimming.

Contact: Mikey Isbell. Certificate may be used: Anytime space available except special event weekends.

The Inn on the Strand
2021 Strand
Galveston 77550
(409)762-4444

1856. This Greek Revival-style inn is an award-winning restoration in the heart of a National Historic District and a stop for the town trolley and horse carriages. The spacious accommodations are in an antebellum warehouse with high ceilings, cypress doors and brick walls. Guests can relax in large, elegant sitting rooms. The building served many functions during its time, including being a cotton warehouse, pre-Civil War armory, ship store and sail-making shop. The area, with its large collection of buildings from the 1800s, was once known as the Wall Street of the South.

Innkeeper(s): Dan & Carol Craig.

Rates:$115-150. MC VISA AX DC CB. Full Bkfst. 6 rooms. Beds:K. AC in room. Swimming. Fishing.

Contact: Carol Craig. Certificate may be used: Sunday-Thursday.

Gladewater

The Carousel House Complex-Fireside Inn
201 W Commerce
Gladewater 75647
(903)845-6830

1930. The overall theme of this bed & breakfast, which was transformed from the upstairs firemen's quarters and courtroom areas, is in keeping with the town's notoriety as "The Antique Capital of East Texas." The building is a two-story, solid concrete and brick structure that originally housed the Gladewater City Hall, including the Fire House, Water Department, Tax Office, City Jail, City Courtroom and Council Chambers. Where the polished red fire trucks once stood, The Ole City Hall Restaurant now serves dinner. The mug shot and fingerprinting room is now a small private club known as The Station. A complimentary membership comes with a stay at the inn.

Innkeeper(s): Annette Wilson.

Rates:$45. Full Bkfst. 10 rooms. Beds:KDT. Conference Rm. AC in room. Fishing.

Contact: Annette Wilson. Certificate may be used: July 1, 1994 up to April, 1995.

Gonzales

St. James Inn
723 St James
Gonzales 78629
(210)672-7066

1914. Ann and J.R. Covert spent three years restoring this massive cattle baron's mansion in the Texas Hill Country. On the main floor is a tiled

solarium and living room. The second-floor guest rooms all have working fireplaces. On the third and top level is a unique wind tunnel—a long crawl space with windows on either end—which provides natural air conditioning. Gourmet candlelight dinners are available in addition to the full breakfasts.

Innkeeper(s): Ann & J.R. Covert.

Rates:$65-95. MC VISA AX. Full Bkfst. MAP available. Gourmet Brkfst, Lunch, Dinner. Picnic lunches. Teas. 6 rooms. 2 with shared baths. Fireplaces. Beds:KQ. Conference Rm. TV, AC in room. Golf. Fishing.

Seen in: *Gonzales Inquirer, Houston Chronicle, Victoria Advocate.*

Contact: Ann Covert. Certificate may be used: July-Sept. 15; Dec. 15-March 15.

"We had a wonderful weekend. It's a marvelous home and your hospitality is superb. We'll be back."

Granbury

Dabney House B&B
106 S Jones
Granbury 76048
(817)579-1260

1907. Built during the Mission Period, this Craftsman-style country manor boasts original hardwood floors, stained-glass windows and some of the original light fixtures. The parlor and dining rooms have large, exposed, wooden beams and the ceilings throughout are 10-feet high. The Dabney Suite has a private entrance into an enclosed sun porch with rattan table and chairs that allow for a private breakfast. The bedroom of this suite is furnished with a four-post tester bed with drapes and an 1800 dresser.

Innkeeper(s): John & Gwen Hurley.

Rates:$60-105. MC VISA AX. Full Bkfst. 4 rooms. Beds:QD. AC in room. Swimming. Fishing.

Contact: Gwen Hurley. Certificate may be used: Good only on Sunday through Thursday night reservations.

Pearl Street Inn B&B
319 W Pearl St
Granbury 76048
(817)279-PINK

1912. Known historically as the B. M. Estes House, the inn is decorated with a mix of English, French and American antiques. The English Garden Suite

is fashioned in a green, peach and ivy motif and features a king-size iron and brass bed, English antique furniture, airy sitting room and full bath accented by a cast iron tub and 1912 wall sink. Other guest rooms include clawfoot tubs, crystal lamps and lace.

Innkeeper(s): Danette Hebda.

Rates:$79-98. Full Bkfst. Gourmet Brkfst. 4 rooms. Beds:KD. AC in room. Swimming. Fishing.

Contact: Danette Hebda. Certificate may be used: Sunday - Thursday excluding certain holidays and special events.

Houston

Durham House B&B Inn
921 Heights Blvd
Houston 77008
(713)868-4654 Fax:(713)868-7965

1902. Located 10 minutes from downtown Houston, this Victorian house, listed in the National Register of Historic Places, was built by the area's first fire chief. Antique furniture, a gazebo, player piano, tandem bicycle and tapes of old radio programs create an atmosphere reminiscent of the early 1900s. Breakfast in bed and romantic dining locations are available for guests, and innkeeper

Marguerite Swanson offers escorted tours of the city.

Innkeeper(s): Marguerite Swanson.

Rates:$60-85. MC VISA AX DS. Full Bkfst. Picnic lunches. Teas. Evening snacks. 6 rooms. 2 with shared baths. Beds:QT. Conference Rm. AC in room. Golf. Tennis. Bicycling. Swimming. Horseback riding. Fishing.

Seen in: *Victorian Homes, Houston Chronicle.*

Contact: Marguerite Swanson. Certificate may be used: Sunday through Thursday.

"Another comfortable, wonderful stay."

The Highlander
607 Highland Ave
Houston 77009
(713)861-6110 (800)807-6110
Fax:(713)861-6110

1922. Nestled among stately pecan trees, this four-square-style home is conveniently close to downtown Houston, yet removed from the city hustle and bustle. Lace and family heirlooms fill the four guest rooms.

Innkeeper(s): Arlen & Georgie McIrvin.

Rates:$75. MC VISA AX DS CB. Full Bkfst. 4 rooms. 2 with shared baths. Beds:KQ. Phone, AC in room.

Contact: Georgie McIrvin. Certificate may be used: Sunday through Thursday.

"Best night's sleep in years."

La Colombe D'or
3410 Montrose Blvd
Houston 77006
(713)524-7999 Fax:(713)524-8923

1923. Renowned as the "World's Smallest Luxury Hotel," the inn houses six suites having a mixture of original art and antiques. Each has its own dining room, allowing for a luxurious alternative to the public dining areas. Guests also may enjoy the romantic main dining rooms, the intimate walnut-paneled bar and cozy firelit library. Breakfast is an extra charge but can be served in your room upon request. The home originally belonged to W. W. Fondren, the founder of Humble Oil.

Innkeeper(s): Gina Bradshaw.

Rates:$195-575. MC VISA AX DC DS. Cont. Bkfst. AP available. Gourmet Lunch, Dinner. 6 rooms. Beds:K. Conference Rm. TV, Phone, AC, Refrig. in room. Handicap access.

Contact: Gina Bradshaw. Certificate may be used: July, August, September.

Robin's Nest
4104 Greeley St
Houston 77006
(713)528-5821 (800)622-8343

Fax:(713)942-8297

1895. Legend denotes this former dairy farm as one of the oldest homes in Houston. The inn features elegant, tall windows and ceiling fans. Beautiful flowers decorate the front lawn of this home. Guests will appreciate the inn's proximity to downtown Houston, theaters and gourmet restaurants. Located in the Montrose area of the city, the inn is less than an hour from popular attractions such as NASA and Galveston.

Innkeeper(s): Robin Smith.

Rates:$70-85. MC VISA AX DC DS CB. Full Bkfst. 4 rooms. Beds:QDT. Conference Rm. TV, Phone, AC in room. Golf. Tennis. Swimming. Horseback riding. Fishing.

Seen in: *Houston Home and Garden, Houston Business Journal, Woman's Day, Houston Metropolitan, Houston Post.*

Contact: Robin Smith. Certificate may be used: Sunday-Thursday, all year.

"Fanciful and beautiful, comfortable and happy."

Webber House B&B
1011 Heights Blvd
Houston 77008
(713)864-9472

1907. Built by a local bricksman, the inn features intricate masonry inside and outside, leaded, curved and stained glass, 11-foot-high ceilings, molasses-

colored cypress woodwork and a three-level staircase anchored by large, carved posts. These many attributes were responsible for its selection as the residence of actor Glenn Ford in the movie, "Final Verdict." Tree-lined Heights Boulevard, patterned after Commonwealth Avenue in Boston, is the area's central thoroughfare with many turn-of-the-century homes and numerous antique shops.

Innkeeper(s): JoAnn Jackson.

Rates:$65-110. MC VISA AX DS. ContPlus Bkfst. 3 rooms. Fireplaces. Beds:Q. TV, Phone, AC, Refrig. in room.

Contact: JoAnn Jackson. Certificate may be used: Sunday through Thursday all year except holidays; Thanksgiving, Christmas, Easter, New Year's.

Jefferson

McKay House
306 E Delta St
Jefferson 75657
(903)665-7322

1851. Both Lady Bird Johnson and Alex Haley have enjoyed the gracious Southern hospitality offered at the McKay House. Accented by a Williamsburg-style picket fence, the Greek Revival cottage features a pillared front porch. Heart-of-pine floors, 14-foot ceilings and documented wallpapers complement antique furnishings. Orange and pecan French toast or home-baked muffins and shirred eggs are served on vintage china. Victorian nightshirts and gowns await guests in each of the bedchambers. A "gentleman's" style breakfast is served.

Innkeeper(s): Alma Anne & Joseph Parker.

Rates:$75-125. MC VISA AX. Full Bkfst. Teas. 7 rooms. Fireplaces. Beds:Q. AC in room. Golf. Fishing.

Seen in: *Southern Accents, Dallas Morning News, Country Home, Southern Bride.*

Contact: Peggy Taylor. Certificate may be used: July 1, 1994-Dec. 31, 1995, Sunday through Thursday nights except holiday and festival times. Regular posted rates apply to one night.

"The facilities of the McKay House are exceeded only by the service and dedication of the owners."

Pecan Place
PO Box 38, 402 W. Lafayette
Jefferson 75657
(903)665-8481

1920. Located on a large picturesque lot covered with pecan and oak trees, this inn is just one block away from restaurants, shops, museums and activities. Each spacious room includes shower or footed tub, antique furnishings, ceiling fans and working vintage radio. After strolling the town's brick streets, guests can relax on the swing or in front of the fireplace in the parlor. Be sure to sample the homemade pecan pie. Pick up your key at Jefferson General Store before 5 p.m. as the innkeeper does not reside on premises, but is only a phone call away.

Innkeeper(s): Cliff & Anna Bode.

Rates:$55-85. MC VISA AX. Cont. Bkfst. 6 rooms. 2 with shared baths. Beds:KQ. AC in room. Fishing.

Contact: Clifford Bode. Certificate may be used: Sunday through Thursday only excluding holidays.

Pride House

409 Broadway
Jefferson 75657
(903)665-2675 (800)894-3526

1888. Mr. Brown, a sawmill owner, built this Victorian house using fine hardwoods, sometimes three layers deep. The windows are nine-feet tall on both the lower level and upstairs. The rooms

include amenities such as fireplaces, balconies, canopy beds and private entrances. Each one boasts an original stained-glass window. The West Room is decorated in crimson reds and features a gigantic clawfoot tub that has received an award from *Houston Style Magazine* for "best tub in Texas." A wide veranda stretches around two sides of the house.

Innkeeper(s): Christel & Carol.

Rates:$65-100. MC VISA. Full Bkfst. 10 rooms. Fireplaces. Beds:KQDT. Conference Rm. Golf. Skiing. Fishing.

Seen in: *Woman's Day, Country Home, Texas Highways, Texas Homes.*

Contact: Sandra Spaldy. Certificate may be used: Sunday-Wednesday (Thursday can be second night) except 1 week in March, Thanksgiving and Christmas weeks and first two weeks in December, Wed/Thurs and Mardi Gras week.

"Like Goldilock's porridge - just right."

Kemah

Captains Quarters

701 Bay Ave
Kemah 77565
(713)334-4141

1931. This cozy cottage is a Galveston Bay landmark, standing watch over an endless stream of pleasure and fishing boats. Two of the three bedrooms feature balconies facing the water. The inn

can accommodate large parties, including two or three couples traveling together or family reunions. A wraparound porch overlooks the bay. Historical

sights, gift shops and waterfront seafood restaurants are within walking distance. The Disney-designed Space Center Houston and NASA are 15 minutes away.

Innkeeper(s): Mary & Royston Patterson.

Rates:$40-60. MC VISA AX. ContPlus Bkfst. EP. 3 rooms. Fireplaces. Beds:QD. TV, Phone, AC, Refrig. in room. Swimming. Fishing.

Contact: Mary Patterson. Certificate may be used: Thursday-Friday or Saturday-Sunday or any two week nights - Monday, Tuesday, Wednesday, Thursday, Friday.

Lampasas

Historic Moses Hughes B&B

Rt 2, Box 31
Lampasas 76550
(512)556-5923 Fax:(512)556-6922

1856. Nestled among ancient oaks in the heart of the Texas Hill Country, this native stone ranch house rests on 45 acres that include springs, a creek, wildlife and other natural beauty. The ranch was built by Moses Hughes, the first white settler and founder of Lampasas. He and his wife decided to stay in the area after her health dramatically improved after visiting the springs. Guests can join the innkeepers on the stone patio or upstairs wooden porch for a taste of Texas Hill Country life.

Innkeeper(s): Al & Bevery Solomon.

Rates:$75-85. Full Bkfst. AP available. Teas. 2 rooms. Beds:D. AC in room. Fishing.

Contact: A.A. Solomon Certificate may be used: Year round, no weekends or holidays.

Mason

Hasse House

1221 Ischar St, PO Box 58
Mason 76856
(915)347-6463

1883. Guests may explore the 320-acre Hasse ranch, which is a working ranch where deer, wild turkey, feral hogs and quail are common sights. After purchasing the land, Henry Hasse and his

wife lived in a log cabin on the property before building the rock home 23 years later. Three generations of Hasses have lived here, and today it is owned by a great-granddaughter who restored the home in 1980. The inn is located in the small German village of Art, Texas, which is located six miles east of Mason.
Innkeeper(s): Laverne Lee.
Rates:$80. MC VISA. Cont. Bkfst. 2 rooms. Beds:D. AC, Refrig. in room. Swimming. Fishing.
Contact: Laverne Lee. Certificate may be used: July 1 through Oct. 31, 1994; Jan. 1 through Oct. 31, 1995.

Mason Square B&B

134 Ft. McKavett, PO Box 298
Mason 76856
(915)347-6398 (800)369-0405

1895. A fine collection of framed, historically significant maps of Texas and the Southwest that span centuries of discovery and settlement are throughout the guest rooms and hallway of this inn. Located on the second floor of a historic commercial building, the B&B has original pressed-tin ceilings, Victorian woodwork and doors, stained-glass transoms and oak floors. Guests can step outside for a stroll down memory lane as the inn is part of the courthouse square with buildings dating from 1879. Several antique shops, galleries and some local businesses have occupied the same buildings for generations.
Rates:$45-60. Cont. Bkfst. 3 rooms. Beds:KQ. AC in room. Fishing.
Contact: Brent Hinckley. Certificate may be used: All times, subject to availability.

Nacogdoches

Llano Grande Plantation

Rt 4 Box 9400
Nacogdoches 75961
(409)569-1249

1840. A collection of three lodgings sits on this 600-acre property of rivers and pine forest. The land was home to Native Americans for many centuries, and in 1867 La Salle's expedition passed through. One of the first Spanish missions in this huge region, north of the Rio Grande, was established here 30 years later. Carefully chosen period antiques resemble those of the original owners. A farmhouse is from the Texas Republic period and another building is Southern Country Georgian.
Innkeeper(s): Charles & Ann Phillips.
Rates:$70. Full Bkfst. 3 rooms. Fireplaces. Beds:DT. Phone, AC, Refrig. in room. Farm. Fishing.
Contact: Ann Phillips. Certificate may be used: Monday through Thursday, all year except holiday weeks and local events.

New Braunfels

The Rose Garden B&B

195 S Academy
New Braunfels 78130
(210)629-3296

1930. In a town full of rich German heritage, this Colonial Revival inn features designer bedrooms, fluffy towels, scented soaps and potpourri-filled rooms. Take a stroll along the cool, Comal Springs or browse antique shops which are all within walking distance. Relax in the parlor by the fireplace or in the rose garden. Breakfast is served in the formal dining room, garden, or brought to your room on a specially prepared tray. The inn is only one block from downtown.
Innkeeper(s): Dawn Mann.
Rates:$75. Full Bkfst. Gourmet Brkfst. 2 rooms. Beds:Q. Phone in room. Swimming. Fishing.
Contact: Dawn Mann. Certificate may be used: Sunday-Thursday excluding holidays and special events.

Royse City

Country Lake B&B

Rt 2, Box 94B
Royse City 75189
(214)636-2600 Fax:(214)635-2300

1992. During their combined years working for Warner Bros. and Paramount in Hollywood, the innkeepers have collected movie and Western memorabilia, which can be seen throughout the two-story B&B. From the Fireside Room with original oil paintings to the halls lined with autographed photos of the stars, guests can enjoy the eclectic decor that includes the Mae West and Europa rooms. Rock on the veranda or screened porch, catch fish in the private pond or stroll acres of lawns and gardens. Enjoy "hootenanny" nights with plenty of washboards and kazoos for everyone.

Innkeeper(s): James & Annie Cornelius.

Rates:$45-85. MC VISA. Full Bkfst. MAP available. Gourmet Brkfst, Dinner. Picnic lunches. Evening snacks. 5 rooms. 2 with shared baths. Beds:QD. Phone, AC, Refrig. in room. Farm. Handicap access. Swimming. Fishing.

Contact: James Cornelius. Certificate may be used: Monday through Friday.

San Antonio

Adams House B&B

231 Adams St
San Antonio 78210
(210)224-4791 Fax:(210)223-5125

1902. Built in what is now known as the King William Historic District, this Georgian-style inn is a reflection of Southern tradition. Guests can partake of a hearty Southern/Texana breakfast served in the dining room or on one of the airy verandas. For your musical pleasure, a parlor has a piano and stereo equipment. A library boasts a large collection of books and records, including a law library. A short trolley ride takes you to the Alamo, Spanish Governor's Palace, Tower of the Americas and other attractions.

Innkeeper(s): Betty Lancaster.

Rates:$75-95. MC VISA AX DS. Gourmet Brkfst. 5 rooms. Beds:Q. TV, Phone, AC in room.

Contact: Betty Lancaster. Certificate may be used: Weekday.

Beckmann Inn & Carriage House B&B

222 E Guenther St
San Antonio 78204
(210)229-1449 (800)945-1449

1886. A beautiful wraparound porch with white wicker furniture warmly welcomes guests to the main house of this Victorian inn. Through the entrance and into the living room, guests stand on an intricately designed wood mosaic floor imported from Paris. Arch-shaped pocket doors with framed opaque glass open to the formal dining room, where breakfast is served. All the guest rooms feature 12- to 14-foot ceilings with fans, tall, ornately

carved queen-size antique Victorian beds and colorful floral accessories.

Innkeeper(s): Betty Jo & Don Schwartz.

Rates:$90-130. MC VISA AX DC. Gourmet Brkfst. 5 rooms. Fireplaces. Beds:Q. TV, AC in room. Swimming.

Contact: Don & Betty Jo Schwartz. Certificate may be used: Midweek, based on availability; Monday through Thursday no holidays or fiesta or spring break.

Bonner Garden

145 E Agarita
San Antonio 78212
(210)733-4222 (800)396-4222
Fax:(210)733-6129

1910. Mary Bonner was internationally renowned for her etchings and printmaking skills. Selected Bonner prints and works by other artists, including the Bonner House's owner, are displayed through-

out the house. This Italian Renaissance inn has a rooftop patio/spa and exercise room. The house made history when it was constructed by Atlee Ayres, who was one of the few architects in the Southwest who first used concrete. The home was built of concrete, reinforced with steel and cast iron, and clad in stucco. Exercise facilities include a 50-foot pool, Nordic Track exerciser and stationary bicycle.

Innkeeper(s): Randall & Cynthia Stenoien.

Rates:$75-95. MC VISA AX DS. Full Bkfst. 5 rooms. Fireplaces. Beds:KQ. TV, Phone, AC in room. Swimming. Fishing.

Contact: Noel Stenoien. Certificate may be used: Sunday through Thursday nights-all year. Friday/Saturday nights-selective.

Classic Charms
302 King William
San Antonio 78204
(210)271-7171 (800)209-7171

1902. Located in the King William Historic District, this Victorian inn is one block from the Riverwalk, six blocks from downtown and eight blocks from the Alamo and the Mexican Market. King William Street has been called the "prettiest street in Texas" by *Texas Monthly* and the innkeeper contributes her share by keeping gardens of jasmine, hibiscus and crepe myrtle. Sun-dried sheets, high-ceilings, three octogon-shaped guest rooms and Texas-sized cinnamon rolls add to experience. After a day of sightseeing, guests can relax on the large wraparound porches.

Innkeeper(s): Edith Stockhardt.

Rates:$75-115. Full Bkfst. 5 rooms. 1 with shared bath. Fireplaces. Beds:KQT. TV, Phone, AC in room. Fishing.

Contact: Edith Stockhardt. Certificate may be used: Not during regular school holidays, last two weeks of April (Fiesta), Christmas season.

San Marcos

Crystal River Inn
326 W Hopkins
San Marcos 78666
(512)396-3739

1883. This Greek Revival inn with its tall white columns has a fireside dining room with piano and wet bar. Innkeepers encourage a varied itinerary, including sleeping until noon and having breakfast in bed to participating in a hilarious murder mystery. Guests can rock the afternoon away on the veranda or curl up by the fireplace in their bedroom. Guest rooms include clawfoot tubs, four-poster and canopied beds. A designer outlet mall, not too far away, features more than 75 bargain stores.

Innkeeper(s): Mike & Cathy Dillon.

Rates:$55-100. MC VISA AX DC DS CB. Full Bkfst. 11 rooms. Fireplaces. Beds:KQT. TV, Phone, AC, Refrig. in room. Bicycling. Swimming. Fishing.

Contact: Cathy Dillon. Certificate may be used: Weekdays only.

Smithville

The Katy House
201 Ramona St
Smithville 78957
(512)237-4262 (800)843-5289

1905. The Italianate exterior is graced by an arched portico over the bay-windowed living room. The Georgian columns reflect the inn's turn-of-the-century origin. Cypress floors, pocket doors and a graceful stairway accent the completely refurbished interior. The inn is decorated almost exclusively in American antique oak. A leisurely 10-minute bicycle ride (innkeepers provide bikes) will take you to the banks of the Colorado River. Also available are maps that outline walking or biking tours with lists of some of the historical and interesting information of the area.

Innkeeper(s): Bruce & Sallie Blalock.

Rates:$75-95. MC VISA. Full Bkfst. Picnic lunches. Evening snacks. 4 rooms. 1 with shared bath. Beds:QT. TV, Phone, AC, Refrig. in room. Bicycling. Swimming.

Contact: Sallie Blalock. Certificate may be used: Anytime.

Stephenville

The Oxford House
563 N Graham
Stephenville 76401
(817)965-6885 Fax:(817)965-7555

1898. A $3,000 lawyer's fee provided funds for construction of The Oxford House, and the silver was brought to town in a buckboard by W. J. Oxford, Esq. The house was built of cypress with porches

three-quarters of the way around. Hand-turned, gingerbread trim and a carved wooden ridgerow are special features.

Innkeeper(s): Paula & Bill Oxford.

Rates:$65-72. MC VISA. Full Bkfst. Gourmet Brkfst. Teas. 4 rooms. Beds:KQ. TV, AC in room. Farm. Tennis. Handicap access. Fishing.

Seen in: *Glamour.*

Contact: Paula Oxford. Certificate may be used: Weekdays or weekends in January, March, August, September, December. Holidays subject to availability.

"A perfect evening of serenity sitting on the front porch with such kind hosts."

Teague

Hubbard House Inn B&B

621 Cedar St
Teague 75860-1617
(817)739-2629

1903. Having served as the Hubbard House Hotel for railroad employees during part of its history, this red brick and white frame Georgian home is furnished mostly with early American antiques. There's a second-floor balcony porch with swings, which offer guests a place to relax. A country breakfast is served in the large formal dining room on a glass-topped antique pool table. A garden on the west side of the house provides vegetables that the innkeeper offers to guests.

Innkeeper(s): John Duke.

Rates:$60. MC VISA AX DC. Full Bkfst. Evening snacks. 6 rooms. 6 with shared baths. Beds:K. TV, AC in room. Farm. Handicap access. Fishing.

Contact: John W. Duke. Certificate may be used: October through May.

Texarkana

Mansion on Main B&B

802 Main St
Texarkana 75501
(903)792-1835

1895. Spectacular two-story columns salvaged from the St. Louis World's Fair accent the exterior of this Neoclassical-style inn. Victorian nightgowns and sleepshirts are provided and whether you are on a business trip or your honeymoon, expect to be pampered. Six bedchambers vary from the Butler's Garret to the Governor's Suite and are all furnished with antiques and period appointments. The inn is located in the downtown historic area. Enjoy a fireside cup of coffee or a lemonade on the veranda.

Innkeeper(s): Kay & Jack Roberts.

Rates:$55-120. MC VISA AX. Full Bkfst. Teas. 6 rooms. Fireplaces. Beds:Q. TV, Phone, AC, Refrig. in room. Handicap access. Fishing.

Contact: Peggy Taylor. Certificate may be used: July 1, 1994-Dec. 31, 1995. Anytime on space available basis, one week in advance, regular rates apply to one night.

Turkey

Hotel Turkey Living Museum

3rd & Alexander, PO Box 37
Turkey 79261
(806)423-1151 (800)657-7110

1927. Guests can enjoy ranch cookouts and entertainment provided by a cowboy balladeer and cowboy poet. Performers entertaining at the inn have become a tradition since Bob Willis, "The King of Western Swing," played in small evening concerts and dances in the dining room of the hotel when he was not cutting hair at Ham's Barber Shop on main street during 1929. At this inn with its Victorian/Western decor, a petting barnyard includes the likes of Miss Molly and Tinker Bell, the alpine goats, and Thunder and Lightning, the potbellied pigs.

Innkeeper(s): Scott & Jane Johnson.

Rates:$49-59. MC VISA AX DS. Full Bkfst. Evening snacks. 17 rooms. 5 with shared baths. Beds:T. Conference Rm. AC in room. Tennis. Handicap access. Swimming. Stables. Fishing.

Contact: Scott Johnson. Certificate may be used: Anytime open.

Tyler

Chilton Grand

433 S Chilton Ave
Tyler 75702
(903)595-3270 Fax:(903)595-3270

1910. This Greek Revival mansion is surrounded by oak, maple, magnolia and pecan trees. The inn is located in the brick-streeted Azalea District, on what was formerly known as Silk Stocking Row. Many celebrations and festivals take place in town, and within walking distance are other historic mansions, Brickstreet Playhouse, Midtown Arts Center, downtown Tyler and many antique shops. Guests are within minutes of eight championship golf courses, theaters, restaurants and shopping malls.

Innkeeper(s): Jerry & Carole Glazebrook.

Rates:$75-150. MC VISA AX. Full Bkfst. 3 rooms. Beds:DT. Phone, AC, Refrig. in room. Swimming. Fishing.

Contact: Carole Glazebrook. Certificate may be used: November to February.

Uvalde

Casa de Leona

1149 Pearsall Rd, PO Box 1829
Uvalde 78802
(210)278-8550 Fax:(210)278-8550

1972. This Spanish-style hacienda surrounds a courtyard and each bedroom looks out to the fountain and flower gardens. There is also a guest cottage with its own kitchenette. The local area offers many activities. Tour museums or browse through an antique mall. The Mexican border is nearby and a tour-guide service is available.

Innkeeper(s): Carolyn & Ben Durr.

Rates:$55-80. MC VISA AX. Full Bkfst. Gourmet Brkfst. 6 rooms. 2 with shared baths. Beds:QT. Conference Rm. TV, Phone, AC in room. Golf. Swimming. Fishing.

Seen in: *Innsider, Wake Up & Smell the Coffee Cookbook.*

Contact: Carolyn Durr. Certificate may be used: January-March.

Van Alstyne

The Durning House B&B and Tea Room

205 W Stephens, PO Box 1173
Van Alstyne 75495
(903)482-5188

1901. Decorated with American oak and antiques, the inn has been host to many events, including weddings, office parties, Christmas parties, club meetings and Murder Mystery Dinners. Three life-size pigs grace the east garden. The innkeepers have published a cookbook titled "Hog Heaven" that includes more than 400 recipes featured at the inn. Your hosts also appear regularly on a TV show preparing recipes from "Hog Heaven."

Innkeeper(s): Brenda Hix & Sherry Heath.

Rates:$95. MC VISA. Cont. Bkfst. 2 rooms. Beds:Q. AC, Refrig. in room. Swimming. Fishing.

Contact: Sherry Heath. Certificate may be used: Anytime.

Waxahachie

Bonnynook Inn

414 W Main St
Waxahachie 75165
(214)938-7207 Fax:(214)937-7700

1887. This gingerbread Victorian was the birthplace of Paul Richards, former baseball manager of the Baltimore Orioles and Chicago White Sox.

The inn has two porches overlooking a yard filled with 30 varieties of flowers. Four antique-filled guest rooms (two with whirlpool tubs) feature English, French, Belgian, and Art Deco furnishings. By advance reservation, guests may enjoy a multi-course dinner served in an Austrian-style dining room. Waxahachie has the largest concentration of Victorian gingerbread homes in the state. The historic town square is two blocks away.

Innkeeper(s): Vaughn & Bonnie Franks.

Rates:$70-95. MC VISA AX DS. Cont. Bkfst. Gourmet Brkfst. Dinner. Picnic lunches. Evening snacks. 5 rooms. Conference Rm. Phone, AC in room. Golf. Swimming. Fishing.

Seen in: *Great Escapes, Texas Highways, Dallas Morning News, Fort Worth Star Telegram, Plano Profiles.*

Contact: Vaughn Franks. Certificate may be used: Sunday - Thursday.

"This was a wonderful retreat from the everyday hustle and bustle and we didn't hear a phone ring once!"

Wichita Falls

Harrison House B&B

2014 Eleventh St
Wichita Falls 76301
(817)322-2299 (800)327-2299

1919. This prairie-style inn features 10-foot ceilings, narrow-board oak floors, a hand-carved mantelpiece, gumwood paneling and detailed molding. The home was built by oilman, developer and philanthropist N.H. Martin. After the discovery of oil on the family ranch in nearby Jolly, Martin and his partner went on to build the Country Club Estates. They donated the land on which Hardin Junior College (now Midwestern State University) was built. The inn also caters to special occasions and as many as 200 guests can be accommodated for a stand-up buffet.

Innkeeper(s): Suzanne Staha & Judith McGinnis.

Rates:$65. MC VISA AX. Full Bkfst. 6 rooms. 4 with shared baths. Beds:QDT. AC in room.

Contact: Suzanne Staha. Certificate may be used: Advance registration.

Wimberley

Southwind B&B

Rt 2, Box 15
Wimberley 78676
(512)847-5277 (800)508-5277

1985. Located three miles east of the quaint village of Wimberly, this early Texas-style inn sits on 25 wooded acres. Roam the unspoiled acres and discover deer crossing your path and armadillos, raccoons and foxes skittering just beyond your footsteps. During the wet season, enjoy clear natural springs and waterfalls. There's a porch outside guest rooms where one can sit in a rocking chair, feel gentle breezes and listen to birds sing. The parlor is a cool retreat in the summer and provides a warm fireplace in winter weather.

Innkeeper(s): Carrie Watson.

Rates:$70-80. MC VISA DS. Full Bkfst. 3 rooms. Fireplaces. Beds:KQ. AC in room. Spa. Swimming. Fishing.

Contact: Carrie Watson. Certificate may be used: Monday - Thursday nights, September - April.

Winnsboro

Thee Hubbell House

307 W Elm
Winnsboro 75494
(903)342-5629 (800)227-0639
Fax:(903)342-6627

1888. Gen. Robert E. Lee's cousin, B.W. Lee, at one time owned the land that this inn sits on and later sold it for $550 in gold. After someone built a house on the property, Col. J.A. Stinson, Wood County plantation owner and Confederate Army Veteran, purchased the home in 1906 and reconstructed it into its present Colonial style. Common areas include a formal living room with fireplace and piano, dining rooms for breakfast, spacious verandas, an upstairs gallery, garden room, patio and gazebo.

Innkeeper(s): Dan & Laurel Hubbell.

Rates:$75-175. MC VISA AX DC DS CB. Full Bkfst. Gourmet Brkfst, Dinner. 12 rooms. Fireplaces. Beds:KQT. Conference Rm. AC, Refrig. in room. Handicap access. Spa. Swimming. Fishing.

Contact: Dan Hubbell. Certificate may be used: Sunday through Thursday.

Utah

Cedar City

Bard's Inn
150 S 100 West
Cedar City 84720
(801)586-6612

1910. This handsome bungalow features stained-glass windows, a wide front porch and a second-story porch. The Katharina Room has an antique,

high-back queen bed and a twin size walnut sleigh bed. Homemade pastries and fruit are served on the porch or in the formal dining room.

Innkeeper(s): Jack & Audrey Whipple.

Rates:$70-80. MC VISA. ContPlus Bkfst. 7 rooms. Beds:QT. AC in room. Golf. Skiing. Fishing.

Contact: Jack & Audrey Whipple. Certificate may be used: Sept. 15, 1994 to June 15, 1995.

Paxman's Summer House
170 N 400 W
Cedar City 84720
(801)586-3755

1905. This steeply-gabled, turn-of-the-century Victorian offers a small veranda overlooking a residential street, two blocks from the Shakespearean Festival. Early Mormon pioneer pieces furnish the Pine Room, while walnut and marble Victorian furnishings fill the Master bedroom on the downstairs level. Breakfast includes fruit, cheese and homemade bread. Brian Head Ski Resort

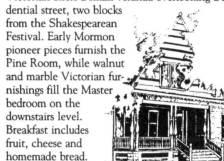

and Zion National Park are a short drive away.

Innkeeper(s): Karlene Paxman.

Rates:$55-78. MC VISA. ContPlus Bkfst. 4 rooms. Beds:Q. AC in room. Skiing. Fishing.

Contact: Karlene Paxman. Certificate may be used: Oct. 1 - May 1 except holidays and their weekends.

Eden

The Snowberry Inn
1315 N Hwy 158
Eden 84310
(801)745-2634

1992. This rustic log house features a gambrel roof and is situated on four acres with views of Wasatch Mountains and Pineview Reservoir. The Indian Room has a log bed, Indian artifacts and Navajo rugs. A country breakfast is served with hash browns and egg dishes or whole-wheat waffles. There is a hot tub on the property.

Innkeeper(s): Roger & Kim Arave.

Rates:$75. MC VISA. Full Bkfst. Gourmet Brkfst. 5 rooms. Beds:Q. Conference Rm. Skiing. Handicap access. Spa. Swimming. Fishing.

Contact: Kimberly Arave. Certificate may be used: Oct. 1-Dec. 24, 1994; April 1-May 15, 1995; Oct. 1-Dec. 20, 1995.

Ephraim

Ephraim Homestead

135 W 100 North (43-2)
Ephraim 84627
(801)283-6367

1860. Three buildings comprise this Mormon pioneer homestead. The Granary, circa 1860, is furnished in Mormon pioneer items and resembles a museum reproduction with its fireplace, cast-iron cookstove, rustic kitchen, antique beds and cradle. The barn offers two rustic rooms on the top floor, while the Victorian Gothic house, fashioned of adobe, is furnished in Eastlake antiques. It features Scandinavian/Victorian stencilings in its two tiny guest rooms located up steep stairs off the kitchen. Apple muffins and French toast are prepared on the wood stove for guests.

Innkeeper(s): McKay & Sherron Andreasen.

Rates:$35-75. Full Bkfst. Evening snacks. 4 rooms. 2 with shared baths. Fireplaces. Beds:DT. Phone, AC, Refrig. in room. Skiing. Swimming. Fishing.

Contact: Sherron Adreasen. Certificate may be used: Anytime except July 6-15, 1995; December, 1994 & 1995; Memorial Day weekend.

Huntsville

Jackson Fork Inn

7345 E, 900 S
Huntsville 84317
(801)745-0051 (800)255-0672

1940. This former dairy barn was named after the hay fork that was used to transport hay into the barn. The romantic inn now includes eight guest rooms and a restaurant. Five rooms include two-person Jacuzzi tubs, and all are cozy and comfortable. A self-serve continental breakfast is prepared each day with muffins and fresh coffee. The inn is ideal for skiers and located near Powder Mountain, Nordic Valley and Snowbasin ski resorts.

Innkeeper(s): Vicki Petersen.

Rates:$40-110. MC VISA AX DS. Cont. Bkfst. 8 rooms. Beds:Q. Conference Rm. Golf. Skiing. Swimming. Fishing.

Contact: Vicki Petersen. Certificate may be used: Monday through Thursday night stays.

Moab

Canyon Country B&B

590 N 500 W
Moab 84532
(801)259-5262 (800)435-0286

1960. Nestled between the snow-capped La Sal Mountains and the red-rock canyons of the Colorado River, this ranch-style inn offers a casual atmosphere. The inn is within walking and bicycling distance to local shops, museums, art galleries and restaurants. Special touches include a warm Southwestern decor, freshly cut flowers in each room, a mint on your pillow and an adventure travel library. Nutritious country breakfasts include freshly baked quiche, a variety of breads, muffins, bagels and whole grain cereal.

Innkeeper(s): Paul Miller.

Rates:$60-90. MC VISA AX DS. Full Bkfst. 6 rooms. 1 with shared bath. Beds:Q. AC, Refrig. in room. Golf. Tennis. Bicycling. Skiing. Spa. Sauna. Swimming. Horseback riding. Fishing.

Seen in: *Outside Magazine.*

Contact: Jeanne Lambla. Certificate may be used: Anytime.

Monroe

Peterson's B&B

95 N 300 W, PO Box 142
Monroe 84754-0142
(801)527-4830

1890. Although it appears to be a modern ranch house, this home has sections more than 100 years old. For 20 years Mary Ann has hosted bed and

breakfast guests here. A former cooking teacher, she offers breakfasts of Hawaiian French Toast, Pannokoken with Applesauce and eggs benedict. The fenced yard is shaded by an ancient apple tree. Visit Fremont Indian State Park and discover petroglyphs and pictographs carved into the cliffs, as well as pit dwellings of the Fremonts. The waters of Monroe Hot Springs, seven blocks away, have the color of lemonade and are non-sulfurous.

Innkeeper(s): Mary Ann Peterson.

Rates:$45-90. Full Bkfst. AP available. 4 rooms. 2 with shared baths.

Beds:KDT. TV, AC, Refrig. in room. Tennis. Skiing. Swimming. Fishing.
Contact: Mary Ann Peterson. Certificate may be used: April to September.

Nephi

The Whitmore Mansion B&B
110 S Main St, PO Box 73
Nephi 84648
(801)623-2047

1898. This exquisitely crafted, fanciful Queen Ann Victorian, listed in the National Register, features hand-carved stairways, fireplace mantels and mas-

sive oak pocket doors. Old books, plants, hand-made coverlets and antiques furnish the home. Request the three-room tower suite at the top of the turret for a unique experience. Homemade ice cream is served on the front porch in summer, and a hearty breakfast specialty, such as German strata, is offered each morning. Weddings are popular here. (The hosts are wedding consultants.)
Innkeeper(s): Robert & Dorothy Gliske.
Rates:$60-85. MC VISA AX. Full Bkfst. Evening snacks. 5 rooms. Beds:QT. Golf. Tennis. Skiing. Swimming. Fishing.
Contact: Dorothy Gliske. Certificate may be used: Anytime, subject to availability.

Park City

The Old Miners' Lodge A B&B Inn
615 Woodside Ave, PO Box 2639
Park City 84060-2639
(801)645-8068 (800)648-8068
Fax:(801)645-7420

1889. This originally was established as a miners'

boarding house by E. P. Ferry, owner of the Woodside-Norfolk silver mines. A two-story Victorian with Western flavor, the lodge is a significant structure in the Park City National Historic District. Just on the edge of the woods beyond the house is a deck and a steaming hot tub.
Innkeeper(s): Hugh Daniels, Susan Wenne, Liza Simpson.
Rates:$50-190. MC VISA AX DS. Full Bkfst. 10 rooms. Beds:KQT. Conference Rm. Refrig. in room. Golf. Tennis. Bicycling. Skiing. Handicap access. Spa. Swimming. Horseback riding. Fishing.
Seen in: *Boston Herald, Los Angeles Times, Detroit Free Press, Washington Post, Ski.*
Contact: Hugh Daniels. Certificate may be used: April 15-June 15 and Sept. 15-Nov. 15.

"This is the creme de la creme. The most wonderful place I have stayed at bar none including ski country in the U.S. and Europe."

Saint George

Greene Gate Village Historic B&B Inn
76 W Tabernacle
Saint George 84770
(801)628-6999 (800)350-6999
Fax:(801)628-5068

1872. This is a cluster of four restored pioneer homes all located within one block. The Bentley House has a comfortable Victorian decor while the Supply Depot is decorated in a style reflective of its origin as a shop for wagoners on their way to California. The Orson Pratt House and the Carriage House are other choices, all carefully restored.
Innkeeper(s): John & Barbara Greene.
Rates:$45-110. MC VISA AX. Full Bkfst. AP available. 16 rooms. Fireplaces. Beds:KQT. Conference Rm. TV, Phone, AC, Refrig. in room. Tennis. Skiing. Handicap access. Spa. Sauna. Swimming. Fishing.
Seen in: *Deseret News, Spectrum.*
Contact: John Greene. Certificate may be used: Anytime.

"You not only provided me with rest, comfort and wonderful food, but you fed my soul."

Salina

The Victorian Inn
190 W Main St
Salina 84654
(801)529-7342 (800)972-7183

1896. A courtyard filled with a rose garden,
stained-glass windows and fine
wood floors and moldings set
the tone for this
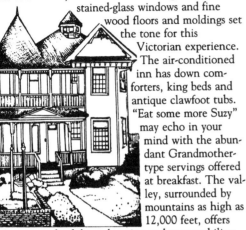
Victorian experience.
The air-conditioned
inn has down com-
forters, king beds and
antique clawfoot tubs.
"Eat some more Suzy"
may echo in your
mind with the abun-
dant Grandmother-
type servings offered
at breakfast. The val-
ley, surrounded by
mountains as high as
12,000 feet, offers
close spots for fishing, hunting and snowmobiling.
Innkeeper(s): Debbie & Ron Van Horn.

Rates:$75-90. MC VISA. Full Bkfst. 3 rooms. Beds:K. AC in room.
Skiing. Fishing.

Contact: Debbie Van Horn. Certificate may be used: June 20-Aug. 20,
1995; Sunday - Thursday.

Salt Lake City

The Anton Boxrud B&B
57 S 600 E
Salt Lake City 84102
(801)363-8035 (800)524-5511

1901. This home was created in the Victorian
"Eclectic" style, and it features two levels of porches, beveled and stained
glass, hardwood floors,
pocket doors and
burled woodwork
interiors. The
innkeepers have cre-
ated an "Old World"
tone with the
antique decor. A
honeymoon suite is
offered with the option
of a champagne breakfast in bed. The Governor's
Mansion is a half-block away. Temple Square,
Hansen Planetarium, the Family History Library

and the Delta Sports and Convention Center are
nearby.
Innkeeper(s): Mark Brown & Keith Lewis.

Rates:$55-109. MC VISA AX. Full Bkfst. Evening snacks. 7 rooms. 3
with shared baths. Beds:KQT. Skiing. Spa. Swimming. Fishing.

Contact: Mark A. Brown. Certificate may be used: Oct. 15-Dec. 15,
1994; Jan. 4-Jan. 30, 1995; April 15-May 30, 1995; Oct. 15-Dec. 15,
1995.

Springdale

O'Toole's Under The Eaves
980 Zion Park Blvd, PO Box 29
Springdale 84767
(801)772-3457

1929. Once a post office, kindergarten and library,
this Scandinavian-influenced house was built of
sandstone blocks cut from the canyon walls by
architect Gilbert Stanley Underwood. Resembling
an English country cottage, the house is noted for
its steep gables. The decor is an eclectic mix of traditional furnishings and antiques. The terraced gardens offer a Jacuzzi, and a private whirlpool is also
available in one of the guest rooms. The hosts
moved to the area because of their interest in hiking, golf and cycling, and they are happy to help
you make the most of your visit.
Innkeeper(s): Rick & Michelle O'Toole.

Rates:$45-100. MC VISA. Full Bkfst. 6 rooms. 2 with shared baths.
Beds:QT. AC in room. Skiing. Sauna. Fishing.

Contact: Michelle O'Toole. Certificate may be used: November-March
only.

Torrey

Sky Ridge B&B
PO Box 750220
Torrey 84775-0220
(801)425-3222 Fax:(801)425-3222

1993. Located on 75 acres, this gabled, three-story
territorial-style farmhouse offers views of Capitol
Reef, Boulder Mountain and Torrey Valley.

Antiques, art and furnishings made by the nationally known artist/innkeeper fill the rooms and some guest chambers offer a hot tub, Jacuzzi or private deck. Breakfast is served in the dining room overlooking forested Boulder Mountain. Guests are welcome to pick fruit from the ancient orchards during summer and fall. Wilderness tours on horseback or four-wheel drive may be arranged. The natural arches, sheer canyon walls and multi-colored cliffs and domes of Capitol Reef National Park are five minutes away.

Innkeeper(s): Sally Elliot & Karen Kesler.

Rates:$59-95. MC VISA. Full Bkfst. Gourmet Brkfst. 5 rooms. Beds:QT. Phone in room. Skiing. Fishing.

Contact: Sally Elliot. Certificate may be used: Jan. 1 through April 30, 1995 (Sunday through Thursday).

Vermont

Alburg

Thomas Mott Homestead B&B
Blue Rock Rd, Rt 2 Box 149-B
Alburg 05440-9620
(802)796-3736 (800)348-0843

1838. Each room in this restored farmhouse provides a special view of Lake Champlain, yet guests often may be found enjoying the view from the sit-

ting room as they warm by the fireplace. There are also full views of Mt. Mansfield and nearby Jay Peak. Montreal Island is one hour away. Full gourmet dinners may be arranged by advance reservations. Patrick is a noted wine consultant.

Innkeeper(s): Patrick J. Schallert, Sr.

Rates:$55-80. MC VISA DS. Gourmet Brkfst, Dinner. Evening snacks. 5 rooms. Fireplaces. Beds:KQT. Conference Rm. Golf. Tennis. Bicycling. Skiing. Swimming. Fishing.

Seen in: *Los Angeles Times, St. Alban's Messenger, Yankee Traveler, Boston Globe.*

Contact: Patrick Schallert. Certificate may be used: 1994-March, April, May, November-December. 1995-January through May 31; November-December.

"Hospitality reigns."

Andover

The Inn at High View
RR #1, Box 201A
Andover 05143
(802)875-2724 Fax:(802)875-4021

1789. Relaxation is stressed at this spacious farmhouse inn in the Green Mountains. A fireplace, rock garden swimming pool and sauna add to

guests' enjoyment. Cross-country ski trails are found on the grounds, hooking up with a series of others to provide up to 15 kilometers of uninterrupted skiing. The inn offers advance-reservation dinner service for its guests on weekends, specializing in Italian fare.

Innkeeper(s): Gregory Bohan & Salvatore Massaro.

Rates:$80-125. MC VISA. Full Bkfst. EP. MAP available. Gourmet Dinner. 8 rooms. Fireplaces. Beds:KQT. Conference Rm. Skiing. Sauna. Fishing.

Contact: Gregory Bohan. Certificate may be used: Midweek anytime except first two weeks of October, Christmas week, President's week. Midweek or weekend from April through July only. Discount off full-rate only.

Arlington

The Arlington Inn
Historic Rt 7A, PO Box 369
Arlington 05250
(802)375-6532

1848. The Arlington Inn is one of Vermont's finest examples of Greek Revival architecture. Set on lushly landscaped grounds, the inn boasts elegantly appointed guest rooms filled with period antiques. Norman Rockwell once used the carriage house as a studio.

Innkeeper(s): Mark & Deborah Gagnon.

Rates:$75-165. MC VISA. ContPlus Bkfst. EP. MAP available. Picnic lunches. 13 rooms. Fireplaces. Beds:KQT. Conference Rm. AC in room. Golf. Tennis. Bicycling. Skiing. Swimming. Horseback riding. Fishing.

Seen in: *San Diego Times, Bon Appetit, Country Inns, Vermont Life.*

Contact: Mark Gagnon. Certificate may be used: Weekdays excluding Sept. 22 - Oct. 22.

"What a romantic place and such outrageous food!"

Arlington Manor House B&B
Buck Hill Rd
Arlington 05250
(802)375-6784

1908. A view of Mt. Equinox is enjoyed from the spacious terrace of this Dutch Colonial inn in the Battenkill River Valley. The inn also sports its own lighted tennis courts and is within easy walking distance of the Battenkill River, where canoeing, fishing and river tubing are popular activities. A variety of accommodations is offered, and two of the inn's guest rooms have romantic fireplaces. A bikers' workshop and bench stand are on the premises.

Innkeeper(s): Al & Kathleen McAllister.

Rates:$50-130. MC VISA. Full Bkfst. AP available. Gourmet Brkfst. Teas. Evening snacks. 5 rooms. 3 with shared baths. Fireplaces. Beds:QDT. Conference Rm. Phone, AC in room. Farm. Tennis. Skiing. Swimming. Fishing.

Contact: Al McAllister. Certificate may be used: Nov. 1 through Sept. 1 except all three-day federal holiday weekends. Sept. 2 through Oct. 31 not available - some discounts midweek.

Hill Farm Inn
RR 2, Box 2015
Arlington 05250
(802)375-2269

1790. One of Vermont's original land grant farmsteads, Hill Farm Inn has welcomed guests since 1905 when the widow Mettie Hill opened her

home to summer vacationers. One section of the house was hauled by 40 yoke of oxen to its present location. The farm has recently benefited from a community conservancy group's efforts to save it from becoming a subdivision.

Innkeeper(s): Regan & John Chichester.

Rates:$70-120. MC VISA AX DS. Full Bkfst. MAP available. Gourmet Dinner. Teas. Evening snacks. 13 rooms. 5 with shared baths. Beds:KQT. Phone in room. Farm. Bicycling. Skiing. Handicap access. Swimming. Fishing.

Seen in: *Providence Journal, Boston Globe, Innsider.*

Contact: Regan Chichester. Certificate may be used: November through June, Sunday through Thursdays only, holiday times excluded also.

"A superb location with lots to do indoors and out. Beautifully kept rooms and excellent home cooking."

Ira Allen House
Rural Delivery 2, Box 2485
Arlington 05250
(802)362-2284

1759. Built by Ethan Allen's brother, this historic Colonial Revival inn is a state historic site. Hand-

blown glass panes, hand-hewn beams, handmade bricks and wide-board floors provide evidence of the inn's longevity. Surrounded by farms and forest, the inn's setting is perfect for those searching for some peace and quiet. Plenty of recreational activities also are found nearby, including fine trout fishing in the Battenkill River, just across the street. Saturday night dinners are available in winter, and guests are welcome to raid the living room fridge, where they will find complimentary soda and non-alcoholic beer.

Innkeeper(s): Rowland & Sally Bryant.

Rates:$55-70. MC VISA AX. Full Bkfst. 11 rooms. 5 with shared baths. Beds:T. Skiing. Swimming. Fishing.

Contact: Rowland Bryant. Certificate may be used: Anytime except for holidays and Sept. 23-Oct. 23.

Bellows Falls

Blue Haven Christian B&B

227 Westminster Rd
Bellows Falls 05101
(802)463-9008 (800)228-9008
Fax:(802)463-1454

1830. This Folk Victorian inn served as a school for nearly a century, until 1929. Guests still will find the wide oak flooring used in the school, and a crude stone fireplace added by the next owner. The visitors of today relax on canopied beds under goose-down quilts in air-conditioned guest rooms. Bathrobes and turndown service also are enjoyed by visitors. Tea and scones are popular afternoon snacks and homemade granola and freshly baked shortbreads often are served at breakfast. The Connecticut River is nearby.

Innkeeper(s): Helene Champagne.

Rates:$58-75. MC VISA AX. Full Bkfst. Teas. 6 rooms. 2 with shared baths. Beds:KT. AC, Refrig. in room. Skiing. Fishing.

Contact: Helene Champagne. Certificate may be used: Month of June, month of September, August, midweek preferred.

River Mist B&B

7 Burt St
Bellows Falls 05101
(802)463-9023

1903. The scenic village of Bellows Falls is home to this turn-of-the-century Queen Anne Victorian inn, with its inviting wraparound porch and charming country Victorian interior. Guests may relax in any of three sitting rooms or in front of its fireplace. Enjoy for a day of antiquing, skiing or just wandering around the picturesque environs. Be sure to take a ride on the Green Mountain Flyer before leaving town.

Innkeeper(s): John & Linda Maresca.

Rates:$50-75. MC VISA AX. Full Bkfst. 5 rooms. 3 with shared baths. Beds:QT. Skiing. Swimming. Fishing.

Contact: Linda Maresca. Certificate may be used: Anytime except peak foliage and holiday weekends.

Bennington

Molly Stark Inn

1067 E Main St
Bennington 05201
(802)442-9631 (800)356-3076

1890. This attractive Queen Anne Victorian inn has been serving travelers for more than 50 years. Careful restoration has enabled it to retain its

Victorian charm while offering the comforts today's guests have come to expect. Features include antique furnishings, clawfoot tubs, hardwood floors, handmade quilts and a woodstove. The inn's convenient Main Street location puts it within walking distance of many restaurants and shops, and just minutes from Historic Old Bennington. The Bennington Museum boasts paintings by Grandma Moses.

Innkeeper(s): Reed & Cammi Fendler.

Rates:$65-85. MC VISA AX DS. Full Bkfst. Gourmet Brkfst. 6 rooms. 4 with shared baths. Beds:KQT. Phone, AC, Refrig. in room. Skiing. Fishing.

Contact: Reed Fendler. Certificate may be used: Sunday through Thursday, November - April.

Bethel

Greenhurst Inn

River St, RD 2, Box 60
Bethel 05032-9404
(802)234-9474

1890. In the National Register of Historic Places, Greenhurst is a gracious Victorian mansion built for the Harringtons of Philadelphia. Overlooking the White River, the inn's opulent interiors include etched windows once featured on the cover of *Vermont Life*. There are eight masterpiece fireplaces and a north and south parlor.

Innkeeper(s): Lyle & Claire Wolf.

Rates:$55-100. MC VISA DS. ContPlus Bkfst. 13 rooms. 6 with shared baths. Fireplaces. Beds:QT. Conference Rm. AC in room. Golf. Tennis.

Bicycling. Skiing. Swimming. Horseback riding. Fishing.

Seen in: *Los Angeles Times, Time, New York Times, Vermont Life.*

Contact: Lyle Wolf. Certificate may be used: All year except holiday weekends and Sept. 15-Oct. 15.

"The inn is magnificent! The hospitality unforgettable."

Brandon

Old Mill Inn
Rd #2
Brandon 05733
(802)247-8002

1786. Tucked away on 10 acres of woods, meadows and farmland, this inn overlooks the Green Mountains. It was originally a grist mill, then a dairy farm. The guest rooms feature handmade quilts, antique furniture, American folk art, fresh flowers, mints and juices. Wine and cheese are served in the woodsy sitting room. Breakfast includes fresh eggs from the inn's chickens, home-made breads and jams made from berries grown on the property.

Innkeeper(s): Annemarie & Karl Schreiber.

Rates:$55-85. MC VISA. Full Bkfst. Teas. Evening snacks. 6 rooms. Beds:DT. AC in room. Farm. Golf. Tennis. Bicycling. Skiing. Swimming. Horseback riding. Fishing.

Seen in: *Times Herald Record.*

Contact: Annemarie Schreiber. Certificate may be used: May through Sept. 15, November through Dec. 20.

"Absolutely fantastic and delightful!"

Rosebelle's Victorian Inn
31 Franklin St, Route 7
Brandon 05733
(802)247-0098

1839. This elegant Second Empire Victorian inn with mansard roof is listed in the National Register of Historic Places. Impressive both inside and out, the inn and its six guest rooms have been lovingly furnished with authentic Victorian pieces by the

innkeepers. Favorite gathering spots include the comfortable common rooms and the wicker-filled porch. Guests also enjoy strolling the grounds where they often experience close encounters with butterflies and hummingbirds.

Innkeeper(s): Ginette and Norm Milot.

Rates:$65-85. MC VISA. Full Bkfst. Gourmet Brkfst. Picnic lunches. Teas. 6 rooms. 4 with shared baths. Beds:QDT. Skiing. Fishing.

Contact: Ginette Milot. Certificate may be used: Sunday through Thursday - April, May, June, November, December, January, February (with exception of President's week) and March. Excluded is July, August, September, and October.

Brattleboro

"40 Putney Road" B&B
40 Putney Rd
Brattleboro 05301
(802)254-6268

1928. A riverfront setting and unique architecture attract guests to this inn in Southeastern Vermont. The French Baronial estate with chateauesque sty-ings is well known as an area landmark. Enjoy relaxing in the inn's library or on its sun porch, with a view of the garden. Breakfast may be eaten on the patio, overlooking beautifully mani-cured grounds. The area along the West and Connecticut rivers provides spectacular fall foliage.

Innkeeper(s): James Fairbanks & Alain Beret.

Rates:$75-90. MC VISA DS. Full Bkfst. 4 rooms. Fireplaces. Beds:Q. Conference Rm. TV, Phone, AC in room. Skiing. Swimming. Horseback riding. Fishing.

Seen in: *Vermont, An Explorers Guide.*

Contact: Alain Beret. Certificate may be used: Nov. 1, 1994 through March 31, 1995 - Sunday through Thursday only, excluding holidays.

Brookfield

Green Trails Country Inn
PO Box 494
Brookfield 05036
(802)276-3412 (800)243-3412

1790. Two historic houses join to provide the space for the inn's guest rooms, furnished with quilts and antiques. The Stencil Room features original sten-cils painted over a century ago on its plaster walls. The inn's spacious lawns and pleasant gardens are popular and just across the road is Sunset Lake with a floating bridge and more scenic views. A

Vermont-style dinner is usually available. The inn has 25 miles of cross-country ski trails.

Innkeeper(s): Pat & Peter Simpson.

Rates:$68-85. Full Bkfst. MAP available. 15 rooms. 6 with shared baths. Beds:DT. Conference Rm. Skiing. Fishing.

Seen in: *Sunday Republican.*

Contact: Peter Simpson. Certificate may be used: Anytime except mid-September to mid-October.

"The inn is really lovely, the welcome very warm and food is scrumptuous."

Brownsville

Mill Brook B&B
PO Box 410, Rt 44
Brownsville 05037
(802)484-7283

1880. Once known as the House of Seven Gables, Mill Brook has been in constant use as a family home and for a while, a boarding house for mill loggers. Old German Fraktur paintings decorate the woodwork and there are three sitting rooms for guests. Antique furnishings are found throughout. Popular activities in the area include hang gliding, bike tours and canoeing.

Innkeeper(s): Kay Carriere.

Rates:$45-139. MC VISA. Full Bkfst. Gourmet Brkfst. Teas. Evening snacks. 11 rooms. 3 with shared baths. Beds:KQT. Farm. Skiing. Spa. Fishing.

Contact: K. Carriere. Certificate may be used: Nov. 1 to Dec. 15 excluding Thanksgiving holidays. April 1 to May 30 excluding Memorial Day weekend.

"Splendid hospitality. Your B&B was beyond our expectation."

Chelsea

Shire Inn
8 Main St, PO Box 37
Chelsea 05038
(802)685-3031

1832. This handsome Federal-style home is highlighted by massive granite lintels over each window and the front door. Accentuated with a picket fence, the inn is on 17 acres of woods and fields, and a stream from the White River flows on the property. Wide-plank flooring is a fine backdrop for a collection of antiques.

Innkeeper(s): Jay & Karen Keller.

Rates:$76-194. MC VISA AX DS. Full Bkfst. AP available. MAP available. Gourmet Dinner. Picnic lunches. 6 rooms. Fireplaces. Beds:KQT. Golf. Tennis. Bicycling. Skiing. Swimming. Horseback riding. Fishing.

Seen in: *Country Inn Review, Vermont Life.*

Contact: Jay Keller. Certificate may be used: Nov. 1 - June 30.

"Max and I really enjoyed our stay in your wonderful inn and the meals were great."

Chester

Inn Victoria and Tea Pot Shoppe
On the Green, PO Box 788
Chester 05143
(802)875-4288 (800)732-4288
Fax:(802)875-4323

1820. High tea is the one of the highlights for guests who can keep the memory alive by purchasing from the innkeeper's Tea Pot Shop. This Second Empire Victorian is among several historic houses and seven churches found in Chester's On the Green area. Many weekends include Victorian fairs and festivals. Overture to Christmas is a festive time for townspeople and visitors dressing Victorian and caroling door-to-door. Two summer theater groups are nearby.

Innkeeper(s): Tom, KC Lawagan.

Rates:$75-125. MC VISA DC CB. Gourmet Brkfst, Dinner. Teas. 3 rooms. Beds:Q. Conference Rm. TV, Phone in room. Skiing. Swimming. Fishing.

Contact: Kathleen Lawagan. Certificate may be used: Special weekends excluded.

The Madrigal Inn & Fine Arts Center, Ltd.
61 Williams River Rd
Chester 05143
(802)463-1339 (800)854-2208

1992. This contemporary post-and-beam inn in the Green Mountains provides a peaceful and romantic getaway. Its guest rooms feature views of the farmland, meadows, rivers and woods of the surrounding area. Breakfasts are enjoyed in the barnboard-paneled dining room and often feature Vermont

French toast with local maple syrup. For those choosing to relax at the inn, the loft library and patio are popular locations. A Steinway grand piano is available for the musically inclined and an art studio is on the premises.

Innkeeper(s): Raymond & Nancy Dressler.

Rates:$85. MC VISA. Full Bkfst. MAP available. Teas. Evening snacks. 12 rooms. Beds:KQT. Conference Rm. Farm. Bicycling. Skiing. Handicap access. Exercise room. Fishing.

Contact: Raymond Dressler. Certificate may be used: Anytime except foliage season, Sept. 15-Oct. 30, Martin Luther King weekend (mid-January), President's Day weekend (mid-February) or between Dec. 24 and Jan. 3.

Old Town Farm Inn

RR 4, Box 383B, State Rt 10
Chester 05143
(802)875-2346

1861. This comfortable New England inn with its elegant spiral staircase was called the Town Farm of Chester because anyone who needed food and lodging were provided for, in return for a day's work on the farm. Fred R. Smith, famous as "Uncle Sam" in the '20s and '30s resided here. Artists have been inspired by the scenic views, which include a pond and meadow and woodlands inhabited by deer and wild turkey. Maple syrup from surrounding trees is served, as is the family's popular "Country Inn Spring Water."

Innkeeper(s): Fred & Jan Baldwin.

Rates:$54-68. MC VISA. Full Bkfst. 11 rooms. 8 with shared baths. Beds:T. Farm. Bicycling. Skiing. Fishing.

Seen in: *Yankee Magazine.*

Contact: Fred Baldwin. Certificate may be used: Mid-March through mid-September.

"A warm haven! Very friendly and comfortable."

Chittenden

Mountain Top Inn & Resort

Mountain Top Rd
Chittenden 05737
(802)483-2311 (800)445-2100

Fax:(802)483-6373

1870. This secluded inn is situated in the Green Mountains of Central Vermont and affords a spectacular view of the lake and surrounding mountains. Room selections include cottages and chalets with fireplaces or rooms with a view.

Innkeeper(s): Bill Wolfe/Bud McLaughlin

Rates:$98-238. MC VISA AX. Full Bkfst. EP. AP available. MAP available. Gourmet Dinner. Picnic lunches. 50 rooms. Beds:KQT. Conference Rm. Phone, AC in room. Tennis. Bicycling. Skiing. Spa. Sauna. Swimming. Horseback riding. Stables. Fishing.

Contact: Bud McLaughlin. Certificate may be used: Year-round. Some weekends and holidays may not be available.

"Twenty years ago we spent a very enjoyable week here with our daughter. The inn, the service and atmosphere were superior at that time and we are glad to report that it hasn't changed."

Craftsbury

Craftsbury Inn

Main St, Box 36
Craftsbury 05826-0036
(802)586-2848 (800)336-2848

1850. Bird's-eye maple woodwork and embossed tin ceilings testify to the history of this Greek Revival inn, which also features random-width floors with square nails and a foundation and porch steps of bullseye granite, quarried in town. The living room fireplace once graced the first post office in Montpelier. Guest rooms sport country antiques and handmade quilts. The dining room is open to the public by advance reservation and features two dinner seating times.

Innkeeper(s): Blake & Rebecca Gleason.

Rates:$64-160. MC VISA. Full Bkfst. MAP available. Gourmet Dinner. 10 rooms. 4 with shared baths. Beds:DT. Conference Rm. Skiing. Swimming. Fishing.

Contact: Rebecca Gleason. Certificate may be used: Weekends mid-May to October except holidays & foliage. Sunday - Thursday December to mid-April except holidays.

Finchingfield Farm B&B

RR 1, Box 1195
Craftsbury 05826
(802)586-7763

1902. A distinctly English flavor is found at this Greek Revival farmhouse. The innkeepers have operated bed & breakfasts in England and Vermont

and enjoy sharing their enthusiasm for the experience with guests. Surrounded by gardens, fruit trees, meadows and pastures that are used mainly to graze dairy cows and horses, the inn offers a relaxing setting for exploring the Northeast Kingdom. The four spacious guest rooms feature British bedding, English antiques and feather pillows. Nearby Barr Hill Nature Conservancy offers hiking and Caspian Lake is a five-minute drive.

Innkeeper(s): Janet & Bob Meyer.

Rates:$60-80. MC VISA. Full Bkfst. 4 rooms. 2 with shared baths. Beds:KQT. Farm. Skiing. Fishing.

Contact: Robert Meyer. Certificate may be used: When open except: Sept. 1 to Oct. 15 and holiday (3-day) weekends.

Danby

Quail's Nest B&B

PO Box 221, Main St
Danby 05739
(802)293-5099

1835. Located in the village, this Greek Revival inn features six guest rooms, and on each bed is found a handmade quilt. Full breakfasts are made to order by your innkeepers, who also provide early morning coffee or tea, afternoon tea and an evening snack. The Green Mountain National Forest is just to the east of the inn, providing many outstanding recreational opportunities. Outlet shopping is found just a few miles south in Manchester, and Alpine skiing is enjoyed at Bromley, Killington, Okemo, Pico and Stratton ski areas, all within easy driving distance.

Innkeeper(s): Nancy & Gregory Diaz.

Rates:$60-75. MC VISA. Full Bkfst. Teas. Evening snacks. 6 rooms. 2 with shared baths. Beds:QDT. Conference Rm. Skiing. Swimming. Fishing.

Contact: Nancy Diaz. Certificate may be used: Oct. 24 to Thanksgiving (not including Thanksgiving); Dec. 1-15, Sunday through Thursday Jan. 2 to June15.

Silas Griffith Inn

RR 1, Box 66F
Danby 05739
(802)293-5567

1891. Originally on 55,000 acres, this stately Queen Anne Victorian mansion features solid cherry, oak, and bird's-eye maple woodwork.

Considered an architectural marvel, an eight-foot, round, solid-cherry pocket door separates the original music room from the front parlor.

Rates:$69-96. MC VISA AX. Full Bkfst. Gourmet Brkfst. Dinner. Picnic lunches. Teas. 17 rooms. 3 with shared baths. Beds:KQT. Conference Rm. Bicycling. Skiing. Swimming. Fishing.

Seen in: *Vermont Weathervane, Rutland Business Journal, Vermont.*

Contact: Lois Dansereau. Certificate may be used: Jan. to Sept. 20. Not usable Sept. 20 through Oct. 20, New Year's or President's weekend.

"Never have I stayed at a B&B where the innkeepers were so friendly, sociable and helpful. They truly enjoyed their job."

Dorset

Dovetail Inn

Rt 30 Box 976
Dorset 05251
(802)867-5747 Fax:(802)867-0246

1820. The historic village of Dorset is home to this 19th-century Federal-style inn, located on the Dorset Green. Guest rooms feature country furnishings. Visitors enjoy the fireplace, library and pool, and may opt to eat breakfast in the guest rooms or the keeping room. Fine dining and shopping are within easy walking distance. Winter guests enjoy nearby Bromley and Stratton ski areas and those who come in summer often attend the Dorset Theatre Festival or visit the Southern Vermont Art Center in Manchester Village.

Innkeeper(s): Jim & Jean Kingston.

Rates:$60-125. MC VISA. ContPlus Bkfst. 11 rooms. Beds:KQT. AC in room. Skiing. Fishing.

Contact: Jean Kingston. Certificate may be used: Midweek Sunday-Thursday throughout the year except Dec. 22, 1994-Jan. 1, 1995.

Marble West Inn

PO Box 847, Dorset West Rd
Dorset 05251
(802)867-4155 (800)453-7629

1840. This historic Greek Revival inn boasts many elegant touches, including stenciling in its entrance hallways done by one of the nation's top craftsmen. Guests also will enjoy Oriental rugs, handsome marble fireplaces and polished dark oak floors. Visitors delight at the many stunning views enjoyed at the inn, including Green Peak and Owl's Head mountains, flower-filled gardens and meadows and two trout-stocked ponds. Emerald Lake State Park is nearby.

Innkeeper(s): Wayne & June Erla.

Rates:$55-125. MC VISA AX. Full Bkfst. MAP available. 8 rooms. Beds:KQT. Skiing. Swimming. Fishing.

Contact: June Erla. Certificate may be used: Anytime except holidays and fall foliage. Subject to availability.

East Burke

Mountain View Creamery

Darling Hill Rd, PO Box 355
East Burke 05832
(802)626-9924 Fax:(802)626-9924

1890. Formerly the creamery of a large gentleman's farm, this red brick Georgian inn, with its butter churn cupola, once was home to 100 Jersey cows. Now the upper level features 10 antique-filled guest rooms, all with private baths and handmade quilts. A cozy parlor, perfect for curling up with a book, is downstairs. There are 440 acres and guests may cross-country ski and hike on the inn's trails, and Burke Mountain and Lake Willoughby are just minutes away.

Innkeeper(s): John & Marilyn Pastore.

Rates:$70-120. MC VISA. Full Bkfst. Gourmet Brkfst. Teas. 10 rooms. Beds:QT. Conference Rm. Farm. Skiing. Swimming. Stables. Fishing.

Contact: John Pastore. Certificate may be used: May 1 through June 15; Oct. 15 through Dec. 15.

Fair Haven

Maplewood Inn

Rt 22A South
Fair Haven 05743
(802)265-8039 (800)253-7729

1795. This beautifully restored Greek Revival house was once the family home of the founder of Maplewood Dairy, Isaac Wood. Period antiques and reproductions grace the inn's spacious rooms and

suites. A collection of antique spinning wheels and yarn winders is displayed. A porch wing is thought to have been a tavern formerly located down the road. Overlooking three acres of lawn, the inn offers an idyllic setting.

Innkeeper(s): Cindy & Doug Baird.

Rates:$70-105. MC VISA AX DC DS CB. ContPlus Bkfst. Teas. 5 rooms. Fireplaces. Beds:QDT. TV, Phone, AC, Refrig. in room. Golf. Tennis. Bicycling. Skiing. Swimming. Horseback riding. Fishing.

Seen in: *Country, Innsider, Americana, New England Getaways.*

Contact: Cindy Baird. Certificate may be used: Sunday through Thursday, January-Sept. 15; Nov. 1 through Dec. 23. Call to check for possible weekend stays.

"Your inn is perfection. Leaving under protest."

Vermont Marble Inn

12 W Park Pl
Fair Haven 05743
(802)265-8383 (800)535-2814
Fax:(802)265-4226

1867. Built by descendants of Ethan Allen, the inn sits on five elegantly landscaped acres and is made entirely of locally quarried clouded marble. The decor includes Victorian sculpted marble fireplaces, crystal chandeliers and exquisite mohagany furniture. Guest rooms are named for famous English authors whose books can be found by each bedside. Canopied beds, antique trunks, intimate love seats and one-of-a-kind quilts and bedspreads decorate the rooms. Guests who want to be coddled and treated like family, will find this the right place, because the innkeepers are known for their genuine hospitality.

Innkeeper(s): Bea & Richard Taube & Shirley Stein.

Rates:$145-225. MC VISA AX. Full Bkfst. MAP available. Gourmet Dinner. Teas. 12 rooms. Fireplaces. Beds:QT. Conference Rm. Phone in room. Bicycling. Skiing. Swimming. Fishing.

Contact: Bea Taube & Shirley Stein. Certificate may be used: Jan. 2 - April 30.

Fairlee

Silver Maple Lodge & Cottages
S Main St, RR 1, Box 8
Fairlee 05045
(802)333-4326 (800)666-1946

1790. This old Cape farmhouse was expanded in the 1850s and became an inn in the '20s when Elmer & Della Batchelder opened their home to

guests. It became so successful that several cottages, built from lumber on the property, were added and for 60 years the Batchelder family continued the operation. They misnamed the lodge, however, mistaking silver poplar trees on the property for what they thought were silver maples. Guest rooms are decorated with many of the inn's original furnishings and the new innkeepers have carefully restored the rooms and added several bathrooms. A screened-in porch surrounds two sides of the house.
Innkeeper(s): Scott & Sharon Wright.

Rates:$48-68. MC VISA AX DS. Cont. Bkfst. 16 rooms. 2 with shared baths. Fireplaces. Beds:KT. AC, Refrig. in room. Golf. Tennis. Bicycling. Skiing. Handicap access. Swimming. Fishing.

Seen in: *Boston Globe, Vermont Country Sampler, Travel Holiday.*

Contact: Scott Wright. Certificate may be used: Sunday-Thursday year-round except Sept. 15-Oct. 15.

"Your gracious hospitality and attractive home all add up to a pleasant experience."

Hancock

Kincraft Inn
Rt 100 Box 96
Hancock 05748
(802)767-3734

1820. This farmhouse features hand-crafted cabinetry and Shaker-style furniture along with a convenient location near skiing and fishing. Innkeeper Ken Neitzel's woodworking talents are showcased throughout, and a furniture showroom also is on the premises. Talented Ken is handy in the

kitchen, and along with wife Irene, pleases guests with their hearty homemade country breakfasts. The inn offers easy access to Killington, Mad River, Middlebury, Pico and Sugarbush ski areas, and the White River is within walking distance.
Innkeeper(s): Irene & Ken Neitzel.

Rates:$48. MC VISA. Full Bkfst. MAP available. 6 rooms. 6 with shared baths. Beds:DT. Skiing. Fishing.

Contact: Irene Neitzel. Certificate may be used: Excluding holidays and Sept. 15 - Oct. 15.

Hardwick

Somerset House B&B
24 Highland Ave
Hardwick 05843
(802)472-5484

1894. After having been away for two years in England, the innkeepers returned home to Vermont and settled in this gracious Victorian house to provide lodging for those visiting this beautiful part of the country. The home is located in the heart of the village and set amid lawns and flower gardens. Many nearby attractions can be reached by bicycle. Breakfast is served in the dining room.
Innkeeper(s): Ruth & David Gaillard.

Rates:$65. MC VISA. Gourmet Brkfst. Teas. 4 rooms. 4 with shared baths. Beds:QT. Skiing. Swimming. Fishing.

Contact: Ruth Gaillard. Certificate may be used: Anytime except August, September and October.

Hartford

House of Seven Gables
221 Main St, Box 526
Hartford 05047
(802)295-5884

1891. This historic inn is said to have been one of the first homes in Hartford to have electricity. It also served as the Bible Institute of New England and later as a restaurant bearing the name the inn retains today. Its unique architecture, a blend of Georgian, Gothic Revival and Stick Victorian, only adds to its charm. Victorian touches are found throughout the guest rooms, each featuring its own unique decor, and including brass, highback and poster beds. Luscious homemade breakfasts sometimes feature apple-filled pancakes or maple-cured sausage. Dartmouth College is four miles to the east.
Innkeeper(s): Lani & Kathy Janisse.

Rates:$50-95. MC VISA AX. Full Bkfst. Gourmet Brkfst. Teas. 8 rooms.

7 with shared baths. Beds:QT. Conference Rm. Skiing. Exercise room. Swimming. Fishing.

Contact: Kathy Janisse. Certificate may be used: January-June 30, 1995.

Killington

The Cascades Lodge & Restaurant
RR 1, Box 2848
Killington 05751
(802)422-3731 (800)345-0113
Fax:(802)422-3351

1980. Breathtaking views and modern amenities are found at this contemporary three-story country lodge in the heart of the Green Mountains. Guests enjoy an exercise area, indoor pool with sundeck, sauna and whirlpool. A bar and restaurant are on the premises, and the inn's amenities make it an ideal spot for meetings, reunions or weddings. Within walking distance is an 18-hole golf course and the Killington Summer Theater.
Innkeeper(s): Bob, Vickie & Andrew MacKenzie.

Rates:$50-198. MC VISA AX DS. Full Bkfst. EP. MAP available. 46 rooms. Beds:QD. Conference Rm. TV, Phone in room. Skiing. Handicap access. Spa. Sauna. Exercise room. Swimming. Fishing.

Contact: Robert MacKenzie. Certificate may be used: May 2, 1995 to Sept. 16, 1995.

The Peak Chalet
PO Box 511, South View Path
Killington 05751
(802)422-4278

1979. This contemporary chalet-style inn is located in the heart of the Killington Ski Resort. That convenience is matched by the inn's elegant accommodations and attention to detail. Guest rooms feature either a four-poster, iron, panel or sleigh bed, all queen-size. The living room, with its impressive stone fireplace and view of the surrounding area, is a favorite gathering spot for those not on the slopes.
Innkeeper(s): Gregory & Diane Becker.

Rates:$50-110. MC VISA AX DC CB. ContPlus Bkfst. 4 rooms. Beds:QT. Skiing. Swimming. Fishing.

Contact: Diane & Gregory Becker. Certificate may be used: All year round, midweek only (Sunday - Thursday) except during foliage season and Christmas holidays.

The Vermont Inn
Rt 4
Killington 05751
(802)775-0708 (800)541-7795

1840. Surrounded by mountain views, this rambling

red-and-white farmhouse has provided lodging and superb cuisine for many years. Exposed beams add to the atmosphere in the living and game rooms.

The award-winning dining room provides candle-light tables beside a huge fieldstone fireplace.
Innkeeper(s): Susan & Judd Levy.

Rates:$45-70. MC VISA AX DC. Full Bkfst. EP. MAP available. Gourmet Dinner. Teas. 19 rooms. 4 with shared baths. Beds:QT. Tennis. Skiing. Handicap access. Spa. Sauna. Exercise room. Swimming. Fishing.

Seen in: *New York Daily News, New Jersey Star Leader, Rutland Business Journal, Bridgeport Post Telegram.*

Contact: Judd Levy. Certificate may be used: Good anytime Sunday-Thursday except during foliage season.

"We had a wonderful time. The inn is breathtaking. Hope to be back."

Lake Willoughby

Fox Hall B&B
Willoughby Lake Rd
Lake Willoughby 05822
(802)525-6930 (800)566-6930

1890. This whimsical Cottage Revival building was a former girl's camp, Camp Songadeewin of Keewaydin. The gambrel-roofed mid-section is flanked by round towers. From the veranda are spectacular views of Willoughby Lake, steep granite cliffs and gentle mountains. Designated a National Landmark, much of the lake area is protected parkland. The inn is decorated in a country-style with ruffled curtains and bed covers.
Innkeeper(s): Ken & Sherry Pyden.

Rates:$33-90. MC VISA AX DS. Full Bkfst. Teas. Evening snacks. 9 rooms. 5 with shared baths. Beds:QDT. Bicycling. Skiing. Swimming. Fishing.

Seen in: *Toronto Globe & Mail, The Boston Sunday Globe.*

Contact: Sherry Pyden. Certificate may be used: Anytime, reservation required.

"A wonderful experience. What a beautiful room!"

Londonderry

The Village Inn At Landgrove

RD Box 215, Landgrove Rd
Londonderry 05148
(802)824-6673 (800)669-8466

1820. This rambling inn is located along a country lane in the valley of Landgrove in the Green Mountain National Forest. The Rafter Room is a game room with a fireside sofa for 12. Breakfast and dinner are served in the timbered dining room. Evening sleigh or hay rides are sometimes arranged. Rooms vary from dorm style to newly decorated rooms with country decor, so inquire when making your reservation.

Innkeeper(s): Kathy and Jay Snyder.

Rates:$55-105. MC VISA AX DS. Full Bkfst. MAP available. Picnic lunches. 16 rooms. Beds:QT. Conference Rm. Golf. Tennis. Skiing. Spa. Swimming. Horseback riding. Fishing.

Contact: D. Jay Snyder. Certificate may be used: Midweek, non-holiday periods.

"A superb example of a country inn."

Ludlow

Black River Inn

100 Main St
Ludlow 05149
(802)228-5585

1835. This inn is located on the banks of the Black River, across from the gazebo at the village green. One guest room features an original copper-lined bathtub, and Abraham Lincoln is said to have slept in the 1794 walnut four-poster featured in another room. There is a two-bedroom suite available for families. A full country breakfast is served. Dinner and cocktails are available by reservation in the inn's dining room.

Innkeeper(s): Rick & Cheryl Del Mastro.

Rates:$85-125. MC VISA AX. Full Bkfst. MAP available. Gourmet Dinner. 10 rooms. 2 with shared baths. Beds:QD. Golf. Tennis. Bicycling. Skiing. Swimming. Horseback riding. Fishing.

Contact: Rick Del Mastro. Certificate may be used: April-Sept. 15 and Nov. 1-Dec. 15, anytime. Sept. 16-Oct. 31, Dec. 16-March 31, Sunday through Thursday only. Christmas week and holiday weekends excluded.

Echo Lake Inn

PO Box 154
Ludlow 05149
(802)228-8602 (800)356-6844

Fax:(802)228-3075

1840. Just minutes from Killington and Okemo ski areas, this New England country-style inn offers full dining service, a library and parlor. Guests also may

borrow canoes and are allowed to pick wildflowers and berries in season. Within easy driving distance, guests will find golf, horseback riding, waterfalls and wineries.

Innkeeper(s): John & Yvonne Pardieu & Chip Connelly.

Rates:$76-170. MC VISA AX. Full Bkfst. EP. MAP available. Gourmet Dinner. Picnic lunches. 26 rooms. 15 with shared baths. Beds:QDT. AC in room. Tennis. Skiing. Spa. Exercise room. Swimming. Fishing.

Contact: Charles Connelly. Certificate may be used: July 5-Sept. 22, 1994; Nov. 24-Dec. 22, 1994; March 5-April 3, 1995; May 8-Sept. 21, 1995; Nov. 22-Dec. 21, 1995.

Fletcher Manor B&B

1 Elm St
Ludlow 05149
(802)228-3548

1837. Situated on two acres in the heart of Ludlow Village, this three-story brick Federal and Greek Revival house is bordered by the Black River.

Guest rooms feature views of Okemo Mountain, the river and the inn's manicured lawns. Furnishings are Victorian and country antiques. Handmade quilts top the beds. There is a baby grand piano in the music room and a fireplace in the parlor.

Innkeeper(s): Bob & Jill Tofferi.

Rates:$45-95. MC VISA. ContPlus Bkfst. 4 rooms. 4 with shared baths. Beds:QDT. Refrig. in room. Bicycling. Skiing. Swimming. Fishing.

Seen in: *Okemo Mt. Magazine.*

Contact: Jill Tofferi. Certificate may be used: Sunday - Thursday all year. Anytime May 1 - Sept. 1. Excluding holiday periods and foliage.

"Beautiful home and very gracious hosts."

Lyndonville

Wheelock Inn B&B

RR 2, Box 160, South Wheelock Rd
Lyndonville 05851
(802)626-8503 Fax:(802)626-3403

1809. This 19th-century farmhouse features hand-hewn beams and wide pine flooring. Renovations have added to the charm and attractiveness. Spacious grounds and a quiet setting make it ideal for both outdoor enthusiasts and those seeking an escape. A guest lounge provides a place for games or reading. Bean Pond and Branch Brook offer boating, fishing and swimming opportunities. The inn's gardens furnish flowers, fruit and vegetables. Burke Mountain is nearby.

Innkeeper(s): John & Betty Ayers.

Rates:$45-75. MC VISA. Full Bkfst. Picnic lunches. Evening snacks. 3 rooms. 2 with shared baths. Fireplaces. Beds:KT. Phone in room. Farm. Skiing. Fishing.

Contact: John Ayers. Certificate may be used: Any except Sept. 15-Oct. 15, President's week (February).

Manchester

The Battenkill Inn

Box 948
Manchester 05254
(802)362-4213 (800)441-1628

1840. There is something for everyone at this Victorian farmhouse inn. Guest rooms are filled with antiques, and four of them boast wood-burning

fireplaces. Fine fishing is found in the Battenkill River on the inn's grounds and guests also are welcome to stroll down to the pond to feed the ducks or play croquet on the lush lawns. Two sitting rooms with fireplaces are popular gathering areas. Dining and shopping experiences await visitors in Manchester Village and Emerald Lake State Park is a short drive from the inn.

Innkeeper(s): Mary Jo & Ramsay Gourd.

Rates:$70-185. MC VISA AX. Full Bkfst. Picnic lunches. Evening snacks. 10 rooms. Fireplaces. Beds:KQT. Farm. Skiing. Handicap access. Swimming. Fishing.

Contact: Mary Jo Gourd. Certificate may be used: Winter, Spring, November-June.

Manchester Center

Manchester Highlands Inn

Highland Ave, Box 1754A
Manchester Center 05255
(802)362-4565 (800)743-4565
Fax:(802)362-4028

1898. This Queen Anne Victorian mansion sits proudly on the crest of a hill overlooking the village. From the three-story turret, guests can look out over Mt. Equinox, the Green Mountains and

the valley below. Feather beds and down comforters adorn the beds in the guest rooms. A game room with billiards and a stone fireplace are popular in winter, while summertime guests enjoy the outdoor pool, croquet lawn and veranda. Gourmet country breakfasts and home-baked afternoon snacks are served.

Innkeeper(s): Robert & Patricia Eichorn.

Rates:$95-125. MC VISA AX. Full Bkfst. Gourmet Brkfst. Teas. 15 rooms. Beds:QT. Golf. Tennis. Bicycling. Skiing. Swimming. Horseback riding. Fishing.

Seen in: *Toronto Sun, Vermont, Asbury Park Press, Vermont Weathervane.*

Contact: Patricia Eichorn. Certificate may be used: Sunday through Thursday, all year except Sept. 15-Oct. 25 and any holiday periods.

"We couldn't believe such a place existed. Now we can't wait to come again."

Manchester Village

Birch Hill Inn
West Rd, PO Box 346
Manchester Village 05254
(802)362-2761 (800)372-2761

1790. It's rare to meet a Vermont innkeeper actually from Vermont, but at Birch Hill the hostess is the fourth generation to live in this old farmhouse. The bedrooms are elegantly furnished, and some have mountain views and fireplaces. There are eight miles of groomed, picturesque cross-country trails that lead past a small pond and flowing brook.

Innkeeper(s): Jim & Pat Lee.

Rates:$105-130. MC VISA AX. Full Bkfst. AP available. Teas. Evening snacks. 6 rooms. Fireplaces. Beds:KQT. Farm. Golf. Bicycling. Skiing. Swimming. Fishing.

Seen in: *Rye Chronicle.*

Contact: Patricia Lee. Certificate may be used: Jan. 2 through March 20 & June 1 through Sept. 15, Sunday through Thursday, non-holiday.

"Without a doubt the loveliest country inn it has ever been my pleasure to stay in," I. Pastarnack, The Rye Chronicle.

Village Country Inn
PO Box 408, Rt 7A
Manchester Village 05254
(802)362-1792 (800)370-0300
Fax:(802)362-7238

1889. Townsfolk refer to the Village Country Inn as the old summer house of the Kellogg cereal family. A Grecian columned porch spans 100 feet

across the front of the house and is filled with chintz-covered rockers and pots of flowers. Decorated in a French Country style, rooms feature French lace and antiques. Dinner is served in a garden dining room, which overlooks marble terraces and fountains.

Innkeeper(s): Anne & Jay Degen.

Rates:$150-190. MC VISA AX DS. Full Bkfst. MAP available. Gourmet Brkfst, Dinner. Teas. 31 rooms. Beds:KQT. TV, Phone, AC in room. Golf. Tennis. Bicycling. Skiing. Swimming. Fishing.

Seen in: *Country Inns, Albany Times Union.*

Contact: Jay Degen. Certificate may be used: Midweek (Sunday through Thursday) non-holiday and non-foliage season.

"An inn for choosy guests," Albany Times Union.

Middlebury

Middlebury Inn
14 Courthouse Sq, PO Box 798
Middlebury 05753
(802)388-4961 (800)842-4666

1827. For more than 160 years this red brick, white-shuttered inn has been host to travelers. Many guests return repeatedly for Chef Tommie

Phelps' afternoon teas and dinner fare. Sunday brunch is served in what some consider Vermont's most beautiful dining room. A National Historic Landmark, the inn is comprised of several properties that overlook the village green of this picturesque New England college town with its waterfall and historic buildings.

Innkeeper(s): Frank & Jane Emanuel.

Rates:$70-170. MC VISA AX DC DS. Full Bkfst. Gourmet Dinner. Picnic lunches. Teas. 75 rooms. Beds:QDT. Conference Rm. TV, Phone, AC, Refrig. in room. Golf. Skiing. Handicap access. Fishing.

Seen in: *Chicago Tribune, Glamour, Burlington Free Press, New York Times.*

Contact: Frank Emanuel. Certificate may be used: To Dec. 31, 1995; Sunday through Thursday only, except not valid July through October. All subject to availability.

"Books everywhere, reader's delight."

Montgomery Village

Black Lantern Inn
Route 118
Montgomery Village 05470
(802)326-4507 (800)255-8661

1803. This brick inn and restaurant originally served as a stagecoach stop. There is a taproom with beamed ceilings, and two downstairs lounges. A large three-bedroom suite has its own spa. Vermont antiques fill all the guest rooms. A few minutes from the inn, skiers (novice and expert) can ride the tramway to the top of Jay Peak.

Innkeeper(s): Rita & Allan Kalsmith.

Rates:$65-120. MC VISA AX. Full Bkfst. EP. MAP available. Gourmet Dinner. 16 rooms. Fireplaces. Beds:KQT. Skiing. Fishing.

Seen in: *Burlington Free Press, Los Angeles Times, Bon Appetit, Ottawa Citizen.*

Contact: Rita Kalsmith. Certificate may be used: Not during holiday weeks.

"...one of the four or five great meals of your life," Jay Stone, Ottawa Citizen.

Montpelier

Betsy's B&B
74 E State St
Montpelier 05602
(802)229-0466 Fax:(802)229-0466

1895. Within walking distance of downtown and located in the state's largest historic preservation district, this Queen Anne Victorian with romantic

turret and carriage house features lavish Victorian antiques throughout its interior. Bay windows, carved woodwork, high ceilings, lace curtains and wood floors add to the authenticity. An exercise room, hot tub and porch tempt many visitors. The full breakfast varies in content but not quality, and guest favorites include chocolate chip waffles and sourdough banana pancakes.

Innkeeper(s): Jon & Betsy Anderson.

Rates:$45-75. MC VISA. Full Bkfst. 5 rooms. 2 with shared baths. Beds:QT. TV, Phone in room. Skiing. Spa. Exercise room.

Contact: Betsy Anderson. Certificate may be used: Nov. 1 through May 15.

Moretown

Honeysuckle Inn
RD1 Box 740
Moretown 05660
(802)496-6200 (800)227-8135

1799. Four major ski areas are found within a half-hour's drive of this 18th-century Federal-style inn, whose grounds are framed by honeysuckle and lilacs. Guests will enjoy taking a look at the basement, which once served as a kitchen. Its old cooking fireplace with beehive oven is still intact. Another popular feature is a roomy wraparound porch, featuring wicker furnishings and an abundance of lush plants. The Belding Room boasts a highback brass and iron double bed and private bath with shower. Breakfast fare sometimes includes French toast made from home-made cinnamon raisin bread.

Innkeeper(s): Maryanne & Ed Wood.

Rates:$50-76. MC VISA. AP available. Gourmet Brkfst. Evening snacks. 6 rooms. 4 with shared baths. Beds:QT. Golf. Tennis. Skiing. Swimming. Horseback riding. Fishing.

Seen in: *Travel & Leisure, Ski.*

Contact: Maryanne Wood. Certificate may be used: Anytime except fall foliage and Christmas week.

North Troy

Rose Apple Acres Farm
RR 2, Box 300, East Hill Rd
North Troy 05859
(802)988-4300

1900. Surrounded by panoramic views, this 52-acre working farm is the perfect place for relaxing vacations. Rest on the porch and take in the view or tour the grounds, lush with gardens, woods and ponds. The innkeepers house sheep, goats, cows and Belgian horses on the farm. Homemade goodies abound on the breakfast table and guests can purchase farm-made maple syrup, jams, jellies and honey. Homespun yarn also is available. The surrounding area boasts a number of factories, including the Cabot Cheese Factory and Ben and Jerry's Ice Cream Factory. Tour the Bread and Puppet Museum or the Haskell Free Library and Opera House. In winter, skiing the slopes at Jay Peak is a must.

Innkeeper(s): Jay & Camilla Mead.

Rates:$50-60. ContPlus Bkfst. 3 rooms. 2 with shared baths. Beds:DT. Farm. Golf. Tennis. Bicycling. Skiing. Swimming. Horseback riding. Fishing.

Seen in: *Washington Times, Vermont Life, Montreal Gazette.*

Contact: Camilla Mead. Certificate may be used: Anytime except holiday weekends.

"So relaxing, non-stress here."

Orleans

Valley House Inn
4 Memorial Sq
Orleans 05860
(802)754-6665 (800)545-9711

1873. There has been a Valley House in existence since 1833, though the present structure was built in 1873. A small dining room serves a hearty

Vermont breakfast, and visitors also will find a tavern, a hair salon and florist shop.
Innkeeper(s): David & Louise Bolduc.
Rates:$35-70. MC VISA AX DS. Full Bkfst. Picnic lunches. Teas. 20 rooms. Beds:KQT. Conference Rm. TV, AC, Refrig. in room. Golf. Bicycling. Skiing. Swimming. Fishing.
Contact: David Bolduc. Certificate may be used: September through March, excluding April and May.

"The grand lobby and half-moon front desk made us feel like we were stepping back to the turn of the century."

Orwell

Historic Brookside Farms
Rt 22A, PO Box 36
Orwell 05760
(802)948-2727 Fax:(802)948-2015

1789. Nineteen stately Ionic columns grace the front of this Neoclassical Greek Revival farmhouse,

which was designed by James Lamb. This is a working farm with Hereford cattle, Hampshire sheep, maple syrup production and poultry. There are 300 acres of lush country landscape with several miles of cross-country skiing and a 26-acre pond for boating and fishing. Innkeeper Murray Korda is a concert violinist and speaks seven languages.
Innkeeper(s): Joan & Murray Korda & family.
Rates:$85-150. Full Bkfst. Gourmet Dinner. Picnic lunches. Teas. Evening snacks. 6 rooms. 3 with shared baths. Beds:DT. Conference Rm. Farm. Golf. Tennis. Bicycling. Skiing. Handicap access. Horseback riding. Fishing.
Seen in: *New York Times, Burlington Free Press, Los Angeles Times, Preservation Magazine.*
Contact: Joan Korda. Certificate may be used: June 1-June 30, Nov. 1-April 15.

"A wonderful piece of living history."

Poultney

Tower Hall B&B
2 Bentley Ave
Poultney 05764
(802)287-4004

1895. A three-story peaked turret lends its name to this Queen Anne inn located next to Green Mountain College. Stained glass, polished woodwork and original fireplace mantels add to the Victorian atmosphere and the guest rooms are furnished with antiques of the period. A sitting room adjacent to the guest rooms has its own fireplace. Kathy's cranberry nut and date nut breads are especially popular breakfast items.
Innkeeper(s): Kathy & Ed Kann.
Rates:$55-65. MC VISA. Full Bkfst. 3 rooms. 2 with shared baths. Fireplaces. Beds:D. TV, Refrig. in room. Golf. Tennis. Bicycling. Skiing. Swimming. Fishing.
Seen in: *Rutland Herald, Rutland Business Journal.*
Contact: Kathleen Kann. Certificate may be used: November, 1994 - April, 1995.

"Your beautiful home was delightful and just the best place to stay!"

Randolph

Foggy Bottom Farm B&B
RR 2, Box 121A
Randolph 05060
(802)728-9201

1840. Guests traveling with horses will find this country farmhouse to their liking, as will any visitor who enjoys fine art, good food and a pastoral setting. The 125 acres are well cared for and feature biking, hiking and skiing trails. Horses may be corralled for $15 per night and innkeeper Sarah Shields, a horse breeder and trainer, will take riders out on the inn's riding trails. A hearty full breakfast is served, and visitors also enjoy afternoon tea. Trout fishing is found nearby.

Innkeeper(s): Sarah Shields & Bill Dunkelberger.

Rates:$50-85. Full Bkfst. Teas. 5 rooms. 2 with shared baths. Beds:DT. Farm. Golf. Tennis. Bicycling. Skiing. Swimming. Horseback riding. Stables. Fishing.

Contact: Sarah Shields. Certificate may be used: Jan. 1-June 30; Oct. 15-Dec. 31; Sunday-Saturday (all week).

Reading

The Peeping Cow B&B
Rt 106 Box 178
Reading 05062
(802)484-5036 Fax:(802)484-9558

1818. This 19th-century farmhouse prides itself on pampering its guests and providing them with a relaxing and peaceful getaway. No televisions are found here, but guests enjoy other diversions, such as fireplace chats, hikes on the inn's 30 acres, naps underneath goose down comforters, and explorations of the area's many attractions. Picnic lunches are available with advance notice for a day trip to nearby Woodstock, with its historic Federal homes and Paul Revere bells. Ascutney, Killington and Okemo ski areas are within easy driving distance.

Innkeeper(s): Nancy & Frank Lynch.

Rates:$60-80. ContPlus Bkfst. EP. Picnic lunches. 4 rooms. 1 with shared bath. Beds:QDT. AC in room. Farm. Skiing. Swimming. Fishing.

Contact: Anne Lynch. Certificate may be used: September from after Labor Day to Sept. 15 and Oct. 25 until Dec. 22.

Rochester

Liberty Hill Farm
RR 1 Box 158, Liberty Hill Rd
Rochester 05767
(802)767-3926

1825. A working dairy farm with a herd of registered Holsteins, this farmhouse offers a country setting and easy access to recreational activities. The inn's location, between the White River and the Green Mountains, is ideal for outdoor enthusiasts and animal lovers. Barn cats, chickens, a dog, ducks, horses and turkeys are found on the grounds, not to mention the Holstein herd. Fishing, hiking, skiing and swimming are popular pastimes of guests, who are treated to a family-style dinner and full

breakfast, both featuring many delicious homemade specialties.

Innkeeper(s): Bob & Beth Kennett.

Rates:$100. Full Bkfst. MAP available. Teas. 7 rooms. 7 with shared baths. Beds:QT. Farm. Skiing. Swimming. Fishing.

Contact: Elizabeth Kennett. Certificate may be used: Nov. 1-Dec. 24, 1994 and 1995 excluding Thanksgiving weekend; Jan. 6-May 25, 1995 excluding holidays.

Roxbury

The Inn at Johnnycake Flats
RR1, Carrie Howe Road
Roxbury 05669
(802)485-8961

1806. The guest rooms in this registered historical site include family antiques, Shaker baskets and handmade quilts. The innkeepers can help you identify local wildflowers and birds. In winter, enjoy cross-country skiing and come home to sip hot cider beside the fire. Ask Debra and Jim about their hobby, cold climate gardening. A popular toboggan ride is down the lane in front of the inn. An old swimming hole known to locals for many years is popular.

Innkeeper(s): Debra & Jim Rogler.

Rates:$55-65. DS. Full Bkfst. Picnic lunches. Teas. Evening snacks. 4 rooms. 3 with shared baths. Beds:DT. Farm. Golf. Tennis. Bicycling. Skiing. Swimming. Horseback riding. Fishing.

Contact: Debra Rogler. Certificate may be used: Anytime except end of May, mid-July, September and October.

"You've nurtured a bit of paradise here, thanks for the lovely stay."

Rutland

Betty Phelps B&B
19 North St
Rutland 05701
(802)775-4480

1914. This California ranch inn is considered the state's first Frank Lloyd Wright house. Guests will be intrigued by the custom wall murals, hand-crafted dolls and parquet floors. Children of all ages will enjoy the basement, which features foosball, ping pong and pool. The inn's location, next door to a city playground, also will please the recreation-minded. Guests play tennis on the inn's own clay court, adjacent to a barn boasting a 30-foot mural painted by the innkeeper.

Innkeeper(s): Betty Phelps.

Rates:$50-65. Full Bkfst. 6 rooms. 4 with shared baths. Beds:QDT. Tennis. Skiing. Fishing.

Contact: Betty Phelps. Certificate may be used: April 1 to Oct. 1.

The Inn at Rutland

70 N Main St
Rutland 05701
(802)773-0575 Fax:(802)773-0575

1890. This distinctive Victorian mansion is filled with many period details, from high, plaster-worked ceilings to leather wainscotting in the dining room.

Leaded windows and interesting woodwork are found throughout. Guest rooms have been decorated to maintain Victorian charm without a loss of modern comforts. A wicker-filled porch and common rooms are available to guests. Located in central Vermont, The Inn at Rutland is only 15 minutes from the Killington and Pico ski areas.

Innkeeper(s): Bob & Tanya Liberman.

Rates:$65-140. MC VISA. ContPlus Bkfst. 11 rooms. Beds:KQT. Conference Rm. TV, Phone in room. Golf. Tennis. Bicycling. Skiing. Swimming. Horseback riding. Fishing.

Contact: Robert Liberman Certificate may be used: Nov. 1-Dec. 15, 1994; April 1, 1995-Aug. 31, 1995; Nov. 1-Dec. 15, 1995; off-season only.

"A lovely page in the 'memory album' of our minds."

Saint Johnsbury

Looking Glass Inn

Rt 18 Box 199
Saint Johnsbury 05819
(802)748-3052

1806. This historic Second Empire Victorian once served travelers in the early 19th century. Visitors today enjoy the same lovely Northeast Vermont setting and old-time hospitality, including special romantic candlelight dinners that can be arranged by reservation. Visitors start their day with a large

country breakfast served in the mauve-accented dining room. Later in the day, guests are welcome to relax with a cup of tea or glass of sherry. Idyllic country roads are found throughout the surrounding area, perfect for exploring year-round.

Innkeeper(s): Barbara Haas.

Rates:$60-80. MC VISA. Full Bkfst. Gourmet Brkfst, Dinner. 6 rooms. 4 with shared baths. Farm. Skiing. Handicap access. Swimming. Fishing.

Contact: Barbara Haas. Certificate may be used: Anytime.

Shoreham Village

Shoreham Inn & Country Store

On The Green, Main St
Shoreham Village 05770
(802)897-5761 (800)255-5081

1790. Located just five miles east of Fort Ticonderoga, this Federal-style inn is a favorite of nature-lovers. Fascinating antique shops and many lovely covered bridges are found in the area. The inn's dining

Circa 1790

room, with its large open fire, is a popular gathering spot, and guests also are drawn to the restored 19th-century sitting rooms. Guest rooms are furnished with country antiques. A country store is on the premises.

Innkeeper(s): Cleo & Fred Alter.

Rates:$75. Full Bkfst. Picnic lunches. 10 rooms. 9 with shared baths. Beds:QT. Skiing. Exercise room. Swimming. Fishing.

Contact: Fred Alter. Certificate may be used: On space-available basis.

South Londonderry

Londonderry Inn

PO Box 301-93, Rt 100
South Londonderry 05155
(802)824-5226 Fax:(802)824-3146

1826. For almost 100 years, the Melendy Homestead, overlooking the West River and the village, was a dairy farm. In 1940, it became an inn. A tourist brochure promoting the area in 1881 said, "Are you overworked in the office, counting room or workshop and need invigorating influences? Come ramble over these hills and mountains and try the revivifying effects of Green Mountain oxygen."

Innkeeper(s): Jim & Jean Cavanagh.

Rates:$33-87. ContPlus Bkfst. EP. 25 rooms. 5 with shared baths. Beds:KQT. Conference Rm. Golf. Tennis. Skiing. Handicap access. Swimming. Horseback riding. Fishing.

Seen in: *New England Monthly, Ski, McCall's.*

Contact: Esther Fishman. Certificate may be used: Good anytime except holiday periods and winter weekends. All other times subject to availability.

"A weekend in a good country inn, such as the Londonderry, is on a par with a weekend on the ocean in Southern Maine, which is to say that it's as good as a full week nearly anyplace else," The Hornet.

Springfield

Hartness House Inn

30 Orchard St
Springfield 05156
(802)885-2115 (800)732-4789
Fax:(802)885-2115

1903. Once the home of inventor and former Gov. James Hartness, this Newport-style inn offers elegant lodging in the main house and two contemporary wings. Charles Lindbergh once stayed here as a guest of the governor, and a spacious room with carved double bed and window seat bears his name. The impressive staircase in the main house will intrigue guests, as will the historic observatory with its 600- power Turret Equatorial Telescope. Several ski areas are within easy driving distance, and guests may enjoy hiking, swimming and tennis on the inn's grounds.

Innkeeper(s): Eileen Coughlin.

Rates:$69-139. MC VISA AX DC. Full Bkfst. AP available. MAP available. Picnic lunches. 40 rooms. Beds:QT. Conference Rm. TV, Phone, AC in room. Tennis. Skiing. Handicap access. Fishing.

Contact: Eileen Coughlin. Certificate may be used: November-July.

Stockbridge

Stockbridge Inn B&B

PO Box 45, Rt 100 N
Stockbridge 05772
(802)746-8165 (800)588-8165

1860. This Italianate inn has a history involving Justin Morgan, who was instrumental in developing the Morgan horse breed. The inn's location in the

countryside outside Stockbridge provides easy access to the nearby White River, famed for its canoeing, trout fishing and white-water rafting. Killington Mountain skiing is within easy driving distance, and autumn colors in the surrounding area are hard to beat.

Innkeeper(s): Jan Hughes & Tim Bird.

Rates:$50-90. MC VISA. Full Bkfst. AP available. Teas. 6 rooms. 4 with shared baths. Beds:DT. Farm. Skiing. Swimming. Fishing.

Contact: Janice Hughes. Certificate may be used: Anytime except holidays/holiday weeks/foliage. Not applicable Oct. 1-15, Feb. 10-24, Dec. 24 - Jan. 4.

The Wild Berry Inn

Rt 100 HC65 #23
Stockbridge 05772
(802)746-8141

1780. This historic farmhouse inn in the foothills of the Green Mountains retains much of its 18th-century charm. Its picturesque Tweed River Valley location offers outstanding opportunities for bicy-

The ·Wild· Berry· Inn

cling, canoeing, cross-country skiing and fishing. Golf is enjoyed at the Killington and White River courses and Killington also provides cultural activities in art, music and theater. Autumn visitors enjoy a chairlift or gondola ride at Killington Ski Area to better view the season's colors.

Innkeeper(s): Janet Heider & Barbara Havelka.

Rates:$60-110. MC VISA AX DS. Full Bkfst. Teas. 5 rooms. 2 with shared baths. Beds:KQD. Farm. Skiing. Fishing.

Contact: Janet Heider. Certificate may be used: All times except holiday weekends, holiday week and fall foliage.

Stowe

The Siebeness Inn
3681 Mountain Rd
Stowe 05672
(802)253-8942 (800)426-9001
Fax:(802)253-9232

1952. A multi-course full breakfast enjoyed with a view of majestic Mt. Mansfield is a highlight of this New England Colonial inn. The charming village

of Stowe is just a few miles away, and a free trolley shuttle takes visitors there to partake of the town's many attractions. The inn offers bicycles, an exercise room, hot tub and pool for relaxing and recreation. Cable TV, a fireplace, a library and VCR are available in the inn's common areas. Favorite guest activities include tours of Ben & Jerry's Ice Cream Factory, Green Mountain Chocolate Factory and the Shelburne Museum.

Innkeeper(s): Sue & Nils Andersen.

Rates:$60-130. MC VISA AX DC DS CB. Full Bkfst. MAP available. Picnic lunches. Teas. 10 rooms. Beds:KQT. AC in room. Golf. Tennis. Bicycling. Skiing. Exercise room. Swimming. Horseback riding. Fishing.

Contact: Susan Andersen. Certificate may be used: April 1-June 30; Nov. 1-Dec. 16.

The Inn at the Brass Lantern
717 Maple St
Stowe 05672
(802)253-2229 (800)729-2980
Fax:(802)253-7425

1800. This rambling farmhouse and carriage barn

rests at the foot of Mt. Mansfield. A recent award-winning renovation has brought a new shine to the inn from the gleaming plank floors to the polished woodwork and crackling fireplaces. Quilts and antiques fill the guest rooms and some, like the Honeymoon Room, have their own fireplace and mountain view. A complimentary afternoon and evening tea is provided along with a full Vermont-style breakfast. This is a non-smoking, three diamond inn.

Innkeeper(s): Andy Aldrich.

Rates:$70-150. MC VISA AX. Full Bkfst. Teas. Evening snacks. 9 rooms. Fireplaces. Beds:QT. Conference Rm. AC in room. Golf. Tennis. Bicycling. Skiing. Spa. Sauna. Exercise room. Swimming. Horseback riding. Fishing.

Seen in: *Vermont, Vermont Life, Innsider, Discerning Traveler.*

Contact: Andy Aldrich. Certificate may be used: April to mid-June and mid-October to mid-December exclusive of U.S. and Canadian holidays.

"The little things made us glad we stopped."

Ye Olde England Inne
433 Mountain Rd
Stowe 05672
(802)253-7558 (800)477-3771
Fax:(802)253-8944

1850. Originally a farmhouse, Ye Olde England Inne has acquired a Tudor facade, interior beams and stone work. Brass and copper pieces, Laura

Ashley decor and English antiques add to the atmosphere. The inn sponsors polo events and features a polo package. Gliding, golf and ski packages are also available. A popular honeymoon package includes champagne sleigh rides. Nightly entertainment is provided at Mr. Pickwick's Polo Pub and romantic dining is available at Copperfields.

Innkeeper(s): Christopher & Linda Francis.

Rates:$90-275. MC VISA AX DS. EP. AP available. MAP available. Gourmet Brkfst, Lunch. 25 rooms. Fireplaces. Beds:KQ. Conference Rm. TV. Phone, AC, Refrig. in room. Golf. Skiing. Spa. Swimming. Fishing.

Seen in: *National Geographic Traveler, Channel 5 TV in Boston.*

Contact: Christopher Francis. Certificate may be used: April, May, first two weeks in June, November, first two weeks in December. Holidays not included.

"Even more perfect than we anticipated."

Townshend

Boardman House
Box 112
Townshend 05353
(802)365-4086

1840. This stately Greek Revival is located on the village green of Townshend in Southeast Vermont. Guests enjoy a full breakfast before beginning their day, which could include antiquing, canoeing or

kayaking in the West River or skiing at Bromley, Magic Mountain or Stratton ski areas, all within easy driving distance. The inn boasts a large, lush lawn and pretty gardens, a parlor with a library and a refreshing sauna. Early coffee or tea is served and picnic lunches are available.

Innkeeper(s): Paul Weber & Sarah Messenger.

Rates:$65-75. Full Bkfst. AP available. Gourmet Brkfst. Picnic lunches. 7 rooms. 2 with shared baths. Beds:QT. Golf. Tennis. Skiing. Sauna. Swimming. Horseback riding. Fishing.

Contact: Sarah Messenger. Certificate may be used: November, December, March, April, May, June, July, August.

Townshend Country Inn
RR 1, Box 3100
Townshend 05353
(802)365-4141

1776. Perennial gardens grace the front and back of this Colonial farmhouse, situated on four riverfront acres. The inn is decorated with quilts, stenciling, antiques and reproductions. The innkeeper serves homemade muffins and fruit breads at breakfast.

Innkeeper(s): Joseph & Donna Peters.

Rates:$65-85. MC VISA DS. Cont. Bkfst. Gourmet Dinner. 3 rooms. 3 with shared baths. Beds:QT. Farm. Skiing. Swimming. Fishing.

Contact: Joseph Peters. Certificate may be used: May 1-July 30; Oct. 25-Dec. 20; March 1-March 31.

Vergennes

Strong House Inn
82 W Main St
Vergennes 05491
(802)877-3337

1834. In the National Register of Historic Places, this graceful Federal-style house is suitably appointed. Ask for Samuel's Suite and you will enjoy an

English country library, a sun room and your own fireplace. With its gently rolling hills and country lanes, the area is popular for cycling. Shelburne Museum, Otter Creek and Lake Champlain are nearby.

Innkeeper(s): Mary and Hugh Bargiel.

Rates:$65-155. MC VISA AX. Full Bkfst. Picnic lunches. Teas. 7 rooms. 2 with shared baths. Fireplaces. Beds:KQT. TV, Phone, AC in room. Farm. Skiing. Swimming. Fishing.

Contact: Mary Bargiel. Certificate may be used: November through May, excluding weekends and holidays.

"Blissful stay...Glorious breakfast!"

Waitsfield

Lareau Farm Country Inn
Rt 100, Box 563
Waitsfield 05673
(802)496-4949 (800)833-0766

1790. This Greek Revival house was built by Simeon Stoddard, the town's first physician. Old-fashioned roses, lilacs, delphiniums, iris and peonies fill the gardens. The inn sits in a wide meadow next to the crystal-clear Mad River. A canoe trip or a refreshing swim are possibilities here.

Innkeeper(s): Dan & Susan Easley.

Rates:$63-125. MC VISA. Full Bkfst. Gourmet Brkfst. 14 rooms. 2 with shared baths. Beds:KQT. Conference Rm. Farm. Golf. Tennis. Skiing. Swimming. Horseback riding. Fishing.

Seen in: *Pittsburgh Press, Philadelphia Inquirer, Los Angeles Times.*

Contact: Susan Easley. Certificate may be used: Midweek (Sunday-Thursday) excluding holidays and foliage season.

"Hospitality is a gift. Thank you for sharing your gift so freely with us."

The Inn at Mad River Barn
Rt 17 PO Box 88
Waitsfield 05673
(802)496-3310

1948. The inn consists of two farmhouses and a converted barn. One farmhouse was recently remodeled to include a two-story lounge, game room, bar and restaurant. Guests may stay in the barn or the more luxurious farmhouse. Just beyond the barn is a path to the mountain. Old stone walls and lumber trails run through the property.

Innkeeper(s): Betsy Pratt.

Rates:$50-75. MC VISA AX. Full Bkfst. MAP available. Gourmet Dinner. 15 rooms. Beds:QT. Conference Rm. TV, Refrig. in room. Tennis. Skiing. Swimming. Fishing.

Seen in: *Boston Globe.*

Contact: Betsy Pratt. Certificate may be used: Spring-summer only.

"If I plan a ski trip to Vermont, the Mad River Barn will be where I park myself."

Mad River Inn
Tremblay Rd, PO Box 75
Waitsfield 05673
(802)496-7900 (800)832-8278
Fax:(800)496-5124

1860. Surrounded by the Green Mountains, this Queen Anne Victorian sits on seven scenic acres along the Mad River. The charming inn boasts attractive woodwork throughout, highlighted by ash, bird's-eye maple and cherry. Guest rooms feature European featherbeds and include the Hayden Breeze Room, with a king brass bed, large windows and sea relics; and the Abner Doubleday Room, with a queen ash bed and mementos of baseball's glory days. The inn sports a billiard table, gazebo and organic gardens. Autumn visitors are free to take home a pumpkin from the inn's prolific patch.

Innkeeper(s): Rita & Luc Maranda.

Rates:$69-125. MC VISA AX. Full Bkfst. Teas. 9 rooms. Beds:KQT. Conference Rm. Skiing. Spa. Swimming. Fishing.

Contact: Rita Maranda. Certificate may be used: Jan. 1 - Sept. 15; Oct. 15 - Dec. 15.

Millbrook
RFD Box 62
Waitsfield 05673
(802)496-2405

1850. Guests enter Millbrook through the warming room, where an antique Glenwood parlor stove is usually roaring. This classic Cape-style farmhouse is known for its individually stenciled guest rooms, Green Mountain views, and one of the valley's best dining rooms.

Innkeeper(s): Joan & Thom Gorman.

Rates:$50-60. Full Bkfst. 7 rooms. 3 with shared baths. Beds:QDT. Golf. Tennis. Bicycling. Skiing. Swimming. Horseback riding. Fishing.

Seen in: *Daily News, Los Angeles Times, Boston Globe, Travel Today, Gourmet.*

Contact: Joan Gorman. Certificate may be used: Weekdays only: not available Christmas week, February or Sept. 15-Oct. 15.

"A weekend at your place is just what the doctor had in mind."

Newtons' 1824 House Inn
Rt 100, Box 159
Waitsfield 05673
(802)496-7555 (800)426-3986
Fax:(802)496-7558

1824. Surrounded by the Green Mountains, Newtons' 1824 House Inn is a white clapboard farmhouse on 52 acres. The Mad River passes

through the property and there's a private swimming hole. The inn is decorated with Oriental rugs, original art, Victorian wallpaper, crystal and Venetian glass chandeliers and thick European down quilts. Guests may enjoy homemade breads, freshly squeezed orange juice and maple syrup tapped from the inn's own maples.

Innkeeper(s): Nick & Joyce Newton.

Rates:$75-125. MC VISA DS. Gourmet Brkfst. Teas. 6 rooms. Beds:KQT. Conference Rm. AC in room. Farm. Golf. Tennis. Skiing. Spa. Swimming. Fishing.

Seen in: *Los Angeles Times, Miami Herald, Chicago Tribune, New York Post.*

Contact: N.D. Newton. Certificate may be used: Weekdays Sunday - Thursday, no foliage, no holidays.

"Established hospitality - unusual breakfast specialties."

The Inn at Round Barn Farm
RR 1, Box 247
Waitsfield 05673
(802)496-2276 Fax:(802)496-8832

1810. The Bates family built this farmhouse and in 1910, added a round barn that was a working dairy barn for almost 60 years. One of the few remaining in Vermont, it has 12 sides and is capped with a windowed cupola. Eighty-five acres of ponds, meadows, fields and woods surround the inn. Romantic rooms include Jacuzzi tubs, fireplaces, canopied beds and steamshowers.

Innkeeper(s): Anne Marie DeFreest and Jack & Doreen Simko.

Rates:$85-175. MC VISA AX. Gourmet Brkfst. Teas. 11 rooms. Fireplaces. Beds:KQT. Conference Rm. Phone, AC, Refrig. in room.

Farm. Golf. Tennis. Skiing. Sauna. Swimming. Horseback riding. Fishing.

Seen in: *Vermont Life, Country Inns, Colonial Homes, Bon Appetit.*

Contact: Anne Marie DeFreest. Certificate may be used: Nov. 1-Dec. 15 and April 1-May 15.

"Felt like home. Appreciate the champagne, flowers, love poems and mostly the warm, welcomed feeling. Perfect honeymoon spot."

Waitsfield Inn

Rt 100, Box 969
Waitsfield 05673
(802)496-3979 (800)758-3801

1825. This former parsonage rambles over a large yard, behind a picket fence. The old barn is now the common room and features original wood-planked flooring and a fireplace. Guest rooms are filled with period antiques. Roast duckling is a favorite choice for romantic dining in the glow of old-fashioned oil lamps in the inn's restaurant.
Innkeeper(s): Ruth & Steve Lacey.

Rates:$69-119. MC VISA AX DS. Full Bkfst. Evening snacks. 14 rooms. Beds:D. Golf. Tennis. Bicycling. Skiing. Swimming. Horseback riding. Fishing.

Contact: Ruth Lacey. Certificate may be used: June through September, December and January excluding holidays.

Warren

Beaver Pond Farm Inn

RD Box 306, Golf Course Rd
Warren 05674
(802)583-2861

1840. Formerly a working dairy and sheep farm, this Vermont farmhouse is situated in a meadow overlooking several beaver ponds. It has been taste-

fully and graciously restored by its present owners, with antiques and Laura Ashley wallpapers adding to the decor. Mrs. Hansen holds cooking classes here. The inn is adjacent to the Sugarbush Golf Course and close to the downhill ski trails of Sugarbush and Mad River Glen.
Innkeeper(s): Betty & Bob Hansen.

Rates:$72-96. MC VISA AX. Full Bkfst. Gourmet Dinner. Picnic lunches. Evening snacks. 6 rooms. 2 with shared baths. Beds:KQT. Conference Rm. Golf. Skiing. Swimming. Fishing.

Seen in: *Los Angeles Times, New Woman, Innsider, Diners Club.*

Contact: Elizabeth Hansen. Certificate may be used: On a space-available basis. Not available in February, October, Christmas-New Year's holiday week or major holidays.

"The inn is simply magnificent. I have not been in a nicer one on three continents. Breakfast was outrageous."

West Hill House

RR #1, Box 292
Warren 05674
(802)496-7162

1862. This attractive inn boasts a great location, just a mile from the Sugarbush Ski Area and next to the Sugarbush Golf Course/cross-country ski cen-

ter. The grounds include a beaver pond, meadows, pretty perennial gardens and spectacular views of the Green Mountains. Guests enjoy early coffee or tea before the delicious full breakfasts, and later are served afternoon tea and bedtime snacks. Candlelight gourmet dinners are served in the English antique dining room by special arrangement.
Innkeeper(s): Dotty Kyle & Eric Brattstrom.

Rates:$85-95. MC VISA. Full Bkfst. Gourmet Brkfst, Dinner. Picnic lunches. Teas. Evening snacks. 4 rooms. Beds:QDT. TV in room. Golf. Tennis. Skiing. Swimming. Horseback riding. Fishing.

Seen in: *Yankee Magazine, Innsider Magazine.*

Contact: Dorothy Kyle. Certificate may be used: Any Sunday-Thursday year-round except holiday weekends which include Sunday or Monday and February weeks before and after President's weekend.

Waterbury

The Inn at Blush Hill
Blush Hill Rd, Box 1266
Waterbury 05676
(802)244-7529 (800)736-7522
Fax:(802)244-7314

1790. This shingled Cape-style house was once a stagecoach stop en route to Stowe. A 12-foot-long

pine farmhand's table is set near the double fire-place and the kitchen bay window, revealing views of the Worcester Mountains. A favorite summer-time breakfast is pancakes with fresh blueberries, topped with ice cream and maple syrup.
Innkeeper(s): Pamela & Gary Gosselin.

Rates:$85-90. MC VISA AX DS. Full Bkfst. Gourmet Brkfst. Teas. Evening snacks. 6 rooms. 4 with shared baths. Fireplaces. Beds:QD. AC in room. Golf. Tennis. Bicycling. Skiing. Swimming. Fishing.

Seen in: *Vermont, Charlotte Observer, Yankee, New York Times, Ski.*

Contact: Pamela Gosselin. Certificate may be used: Sunday through Thursday only, January, February, March, April, May, June, November, December, excluding holidays.

"Our room was wonderful - especially the fireplace. Everything was so cozy and warm."

Grunberg Haus Bed & Breakfast
RR 2, Box 1595, Rt 100 S
Waterbury 05676
(802)244-7726 (800)800-7760

1972. This hillside Tyrolean chalet was hand-built by George and Irene Ballschneider. The Grunberg

Haus captures the rustic charm of country guest homes in Austria with its wall of windows over-looking the Green Mountains, a massive fieldstone fireplace and a self-service Austrian pub. Rooms are furnished with antique furniture and cozy quilts. All rooms open onto the second-floor balcony that surrounds the chalet. Attractions in Stowe, the Mad River Valley, Montpelier and the Lake Champlain region are close at hand. Innkeepers regularly entertain their guests at the Steinway Grand piano.
Innkeeper(s): Christopher Sellers & Mark Frohman.

Rates:$55-140. MC VISA AX DS. Full Bkfst. Gourmet Brkfst. Teas. Evening snacks. 16 rooms. 10 with shared baths. Beds:QDT. Conference Rm. Golf. Tennis. Bicycling. Skiing. Spa. Sauna. Swimming. Horseback riding. Fishing.

Seen in: *Hudson Dispatch, Innsider, Ski, Toronto Globe, Vermont, Washington Times, Yankee.*

Contact: Christopher Sellers. Certificate may be used: Oct. 20-Dec. 20, 1994 and 1995; March 20-June 20, 1995.

"You made an ordinary overnight stay extraordinary."

Thatcher Brook Inn
PO Box 490
Waterbury 05676
(802)244-5911 (800)292-5911
Fax:(802)244-1294

1899. Listed in the Vermont Register of Historic Buildings, this restored Victorian mansion features a porch with twin gazebos. A covered walkway leads to the historic Wheeler House. Guest rooms are decorated in Laura Ashley-style with canopy beds. The inn specializes in Country French cuisine and Bailey's Fireside Tavern is on the premises.
Innkeeper(s): Peter & Kelly Varty.

Rates:$75-175. MC VISA AX DC DS. Full Bkfst. AP available. MAP available. Gourmet Brkfst, Dinner. Teas. 24 rooms. Fireplaces. Beds:KQT. Conference Rm. Phone in room. Skiing. Handicap access. Spa. Fishing.

Contact: Kelly Varty. Certificate may be used: Sunday through Thursday (non-peak periods).

"I'd have to put on a black tie in Long Island to find food as good as this and best of all it's in a relaxed country atmosphere. Meals are underpriced."

Weathersfield

The Inn at Weathersfield
Rt 106 Box 165
Weathersfield 05151
(802)263-9217 (800)477-4828
Fax:(802)263-9219

1795. Built by Thomas Prentis, a Revolutionary

War veteran, this was originally a four-room farmhouse set on 237 acres of wilderness. Two rooms were added in 1796, and a carriage house in 1830. During the Civil War, the inn served as a station on the Underground Railroad. Six pillars give the inn a Southern Colonial look, and there are 12 fireplaces, a beehive oven, wide-plank floors and period antiques throughout.

Innkeeper(s): Mary Louise & Ron Thorburn.

Rates:$149-220. MC VISA AX DC DS CB. Full Bkfst. MAP available. Gourmet Brkfst, Dinner. Picnic lunches. Teas. 12 rooms. Fireplaces. Beds:KQT. Conference Rm. Phone in room. Bicycling. Skiing. Handicap access. Sauna. Exercise room. Stables. Fishing.

Seen in: *The Boston Herald, Los Angeles Times, Country Inns, Colonial Homes, Better Homes & Gardens, National Geographic Traveler.*

Contact: Mary Louise Thorburn. Certificate may be used: Sunday through Thursday except month of October, Christmas through New Year and holidays. Call at the last minute for availability during restricted times.

"There isn't one thing we didn't enjoy about our weekend with you and we are constantly reliving it with much happiness."

Weston

Darling Family Inn
Rt 100
Weston 05161
(802)824-3223

1830. This charming two-story inn also features two cottages. Located in the Green Mountains, just minutes from Bromley, Okemo and Stratton ski areas, the inn provides a taste of life from the early Colonial days. Guest rooms feature handmade quilts crafted locally. The cottages include kitchenettes, and pets are welcome in the cottages if prior arrangements are made.

Innkeeper(s): Chapin & Joan Darling.

Rates:$65-95. Full Bkfst. Teas. 7 rooms. Beds:KQT. Farm. Skiing. Fishing.

Contact: Chapin Darling. Certificate may be used: Sundays through Thursday (excluding Sundays of holiday weekends) January through June; Sept. 1 through Sept. 15; Oct. 15 through Dec. 23.

Wilder Homestead Inn
25 Lawrence Hill Rd
Weston 05161
(802)824-8172

1827. Within walking distance of the Green Mountain National Forest, this inn with both Federal and Greek Revival stylings features seven guest rooms, all with private baths and views. Five of the rooms sport log-burning fireplaces. Large country breakfasts may include eggs, homemade biscuits with jam, hotcakes with genuine Vermont

maple syrup, Lumberjack mush or sausage. Spring visitors enjoy an abundance of wildflowers. A craft shop is on the premises.

Innkeeper(s): Roy & Peggy Varner.

Rates:$60-105. MC VISA. Full Bkfst. Teas. 7 rooms. 2 with shared baths. Beds:QT. Skiing. Exercise room. Fishing.

Contact: Margaret Varner. Certificate may be used: Midweek only, Sunday through Thursday (except Sunday of holidays) Jan. 1 through July 31; Sept. 1-15; Oct. 21 through Dec. 21.

Williamstown

Autumn Crest Inn
Clark Rd, Box 1540
Williamstown 05679
(802)433-6627 (800)339-6627

1810. This carefully restored farmhouse sits atop a ridge overlooking Williamstown Valley and is surrounded by the thick Vermont woods and rolling pastures. In the summer, the White River beckons to canoers, and in the winter, sleigh rides and cross-country ski trails lead guests through the countryside. The inn also features two lit clay tennis courts and a well-stocked bar in its Great Hall.

Innkeeper(s): Kenneth Eden & Richard Casson.

Rates:$98-148. MC VISA AX DC CB. Full Bkfst. MAP available. Gourmet Brkfst. 18 rooms. Fireplaces. Beds:QT. Conference Rm. Tennis. Skiing. Handicap access. Swimming. Stables. Fishing.

Seen in: *Gourmet, Vermont.*

Contact: Kenneth Eden. Certificate may be used: Year-round.

"Casual elegance."

Wilmington

The Inn at Quail Run
HCR 63, Box 28 Smith Rd
Wilmington 05363
(802)464-3362 (800)343-7227

1968. Enjoy the serenity of the Vermont countryside at this inn surrounded by 12 private acres and mountain views. Brass and antique beds are covered with comforters perfect for snuggling. A hearty country breakfast is served each morning. Murder mystery and Christmas Inn Vermont packages add an extra flair to vacations. Relax in the sauna after working out in the exercise room or solar-heated pool. Skiing and sleigh rides make good use of the Vermont winter. Country Theatre, flea markets and the Marlboro Music Festival are nearby attractions.

Innkeeper(s): Thomas & Marie Martin.

Rates:$85-125. MC VISA AX DS. Full Bkfst. Gourmet Brkfst. Teas. Evening snacks. 15 rooms. Fireplaces. Beds:KQT. Tennis. Skiing. Sauna. Exercise room. Swimming. Fishing.

Contact: Thomas Martin. Certificate may be used: Anytime space available.

Woodstock

The Canterbury House
43 Pleasant St
Woodstock 05091
(802)457-3077

1880. National Geographic tabbed Woodstock as one of America's most beautiful villages, and this Victorian inn offers a convenient stopping place for

those exploring the area. Visitors find themselves within easy walking distance of antique stores, art galleries, museums, restaurants and shopping. The inn has bicycles available for guest use, perfect for an outing on the area's scenic country roads.

Innkeeper(s): Fred & Celeste Holden.

Rates:$95-135. MC VISA AX. Gourmet Brkfst. Teas. 8 rooms. Beds:QT. AC in room. Tennis. Bicycling. Skiing. Handicap access. Fishing.

Contact: Fred Holden. Certificate may be used: Jan. 1-July 30, 1995.

Woodstocker B&B
61 River St, Rt 4
Woodstock 05091
(802)457-3896 (800)457-3896

1830. Enjoy the sights of historic Woodstock at this inn. Each room is unique and cozy and the suites feature kitchens and living rooms. After a day of sightseeing or skiing, relax in the hot tub.

Woodstock boasts many quaint shops and art galleries. The Calvin Coolidge Homestead, Plymouth Cheese Factory and the Billings Farm and Museum are nearby. Watch glass being made at a local glass factory, or try out the Alpine slide at Pico.

Innkeeper(s): Jerry & JaNoel Lowe.

Rates:$90-125. MC VISA. Full Bkfst. Gourmet Brkfst. Teas. 9 rooms. Beds:Q. TV, AC in room. Golf. Tennis. Bicycling. Skiing. Handicap access. Spa. Swimming. Horseback riding. Fishing.

Contact: Jerry Lowe. Certificate may be used: Jan. 2-Feb. 11; March 1-Sept. 14 (except holidays); Oct. 18-Dec. 19.

Woodstock (Reading)

Bailey's Mills B&B
Box 117, RR 1
Woodstock (Reading) 05062
(802)484-7809 (800)639-3437

1820. This historic Federal-style inn features the architectural stylings of a Southern manor and boasts a ballroom and 11 fireplaces, with two original beehive ovens. The suite sports a king bed and private sun porch. Two rooms have working fireplaces. The inn's sun porch overlooks the ruins of the old mill dam of the original house. The quiet country setting is perfect for bike rides and relaxing strolls, and terrific photo opportunities are found at Jenne Farm, just a few minutes away.

Innkeeper(s): Barbara Thaeder & Don Whitaker.

Rates:$65-105. MC VISA. ContPlus Bkfst. 3 rooms. Fireplaces. Beds:KQ. Farm. Skiing. Fishing.

Contact: Barbara Thaeder. Certificate may be used: Nov. 1-Dec. 15, March 10-April 30 except Thanksgiving week or call last-minute anytime.

Virginia

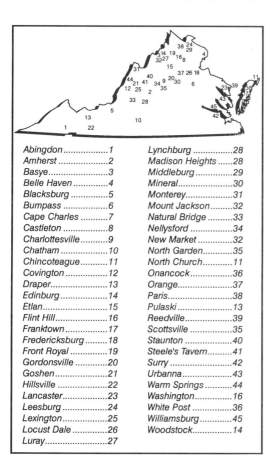

Abingdon

Victoria & Albert Inn
224 Oak Hill St
Abingdon 24210
(703)676-2797 Fax:(703)676-0898

1892. Situated behind a white picket fence and rose arbor gate, this handsome green and white three-story Victorian features a shaded porch, bay windows and a Victorian decor. Your host is a col-

lege instructor at nearby Emory and Henry.
Innkeeper(s): Jeanette & Donald Darby.

Rates:$60-90. MC VISA. Gourmet Brkfst. Evening snacks. 3 rooms. 2 with shared baths. Fireplaces. Beds:KQT. TV, Phone, AC in room. Bicycling.

Contact: Jeanette Darby. Certificate may be used: November through March (1994-1995).

Amherst

Dulwich Manor B&B Inn
Rt 5, Box 173A, Rt 60E
Amherst 24521
(804)946-7207

1912. This red Flemish brick and white columned English Manor sits on five secluded acres at the end of a country lane and in the midst of 85 acres of woodland and meadow. The Blue Ridge Mountains may be enjoyed from the veranda. The entry features a large center hall and a wide oak staircase. Walls are 14 inches thick. The 18 rooms include a 50-foot-long ballroom on the third floor. The inn is decorated with a creative mix of antiques, reproductions and modern art. Your host is a professional singer and actor and your hostess is a costumer.
Innkeeper(s): Bob & Judy Reilly.

Rates:$69-89. Full Bkfst. 6 rooms. 2 with shared baths. Fireplaces. Beds:QT. AC in room. Skiing. Spa. Swimming. Fishing.

Contact: Judith Reilly. Certificate may be used: Sunday-Thursday except May and October. Anytime December-February excluding holidays and holiday eves.

Basye

Sky Chalet Country Inn and Restaurant
PO Box 300, Route 263 W
Basye 22810
(703)856-2147 Fax:(703)856-2436

1937. This Bavarian-style inn tucked atop Supin Lick Ridge in Shenandoah Valley has offered hospitality for many decades, and it is believed to be the longest-operating inn in the Shenandoah Valley. There are verandas, a gazebo and a patio, with mountain and valley views. An open stone fireplace in the dining room sets the tone for home-style cuisine. Guest rooms are rustic and comfortable and some feature fireplaces.

Innkeeper(s): Mona & Ken Seay.

Rates:$59-95. MC VISA DC DS. ContPlus Bkfst. EP. Gourmet Dinner. Evening snacks. 8 rooms. Fireplaces. Beds:DT. Skiing. Swimming. Fishing.

Contact: Mona Seay. Certificate may be used: Sunday through Thursday, year-round excluding major holidays. All week - December through April, excluding major holidays.

Belle Haven

Bay View Waterfront B&B
35350 Copes Dr
Belle Haven 23306
(804)442-6963 (800)442-6966

1797. This rambling inn stretches more than 100 feet across and has five roof levels. There are heart-pine floors, high ceilings and several fireplaces. The hillside location affords bay breezes and wide views of the Chesapeake, Occohannock Creek and the inn's surrounding 140 acres. The innkeepers are descendants of several generations who have owned and operated Bay View. If you come by water to the inn's deep water dock, look behind Channel Marker 16.

Innkeeper(s): Wayne & Mary Will Browning.

Rates:$80-95. Full Bkfst. 4 rooms. 2 with shared baths. Fireplaces. Beds:D. AC in room. Farm. Bicycling. Fishing.

Contact: Mary Will Browning. Certificate may be used: Monday - Thursday, April - October excluding holidays. Anytime November - March, excluding holidays.

Blacksburg

Sycamore Tree B&B
PO Box 10937
Blacksburg 24062
(703)381-1597

1990. Although not historic, this inn has a lovely setting on 126 acres at the foot of Hightop Mountain. Decorated in a traditional style, all the guest rooms have private baths. The innkeepers enjoy offering advice on local activities such as nearby hiking on the Appalachian Trail and the walk to a 60-foot waterfall at the Cascades.

Innkeeper(s): Charles & Gilda Caines.

Rates:$95-110. MC VISA. Full Bkfst. Evening snacks. 6 rooms. Beds:KQT. AC in room. Skiing. Handicap access. Swimming. Fishing.

Contact: Gilda Caines. Certificate may be used: Sunday through Thursday - January, February, March, April, June, July, November, December. Not available May, August, September, October.

Cape Charles

Sunset Inn B&B
108 Bay Avenue
Cape Charles 23310
(804)331-2424

1915. Located waterfront on the Chesapeake Bay, this inn offers delightful breezes from its Victorian porch. Guest rooms are spacious, boasting both air

conditioning and ceiling fans. The Victoria Room offers a window seat, queen sleigh bed, daybed and cable TV. Favorite activities are exploring the uncrowded beach and historic district, or bird-watching, fishing and cycling in the area.

Innkeeper(s): Albert Longo & Joyce Tribble.

Rates:$45-85. MC VISA. Full Bkfst. Teas. 4 rooms. 1 with shared bath. Beds:Q. TV, AC in room. Bicycling. Spa. Swimming. Fishing.

Contact: Albert Longo. Certificate may be used: Sunday - Thursday.

Castleton

Blue Knoll Farm

Rt 1, Box 141
Castleton 22716
(703)937-5234

1900. The original house of the Blue Knoll Farm is pre-Civil War, and many Civil War battles were fought in the area. The farmhouse is in the scenic valley of Castleton Mountain. Guest rooms feature antiques, family mementos and cozy comforters. Some rooms have fireplaces. Guests may relax on the wicker chairs on the Victorian porch.

Innkeeper(s): Mary & Gil Carlson.

Rates:$95-125. MC VISA. Full Bkfst. 4 rooms. Fireplaces. Beds:KQ. AC in room. Farm. Spa. Fishing.

Contact: Mary Carlson. Certificate may be used: January through March, 1995; November & December of 1994.

"The weekend was better than we had hoped. You both are more than partly responsible."

Charlottesville

Silver Thatch Inn

3001 Hollymead Dr
Charlottesville 22901-7422
(804)978-4686 Fax:(804)973-6156

1780. This white clapboard inn, shaded by tall elms, was built for British officers by Hessian soldiers who were prisoners during the Revolutionary

War. Before its current life as a country inn, Silver Thatch was a boys' school, a melon farm and a tobacco plantation. Many additions have been made to the original house, now called the Hessian Room. The inn is filled with antiques. There are three intimate dining rooms featuring fresh American cuisine.

Innkeeper(s): Rita & Vince Scoffone.

Rates:$110-125. MC VISA AX DC. ContPlus Bkfst. EP. Gourmet Dinner. 7 rooms. Fireplaces. Beds:Q. Conference Rm. AC in room. Tennis. Fishing.

Seen in: *Travel & Leisure, Washington Post, Los Angeles Times, New York Magazine.*

Contact: A. Vincent Scoffone. Certificate may be used: Sunday through Thursday, all year except April, May and October.

"Everything was absolutely perfect! The room, the food and above all, the people!"

Chatham

House of Laird

335 S Main St, PO Box 1131
Chatham 24531
(804)432-2523

1880. This Greek Revival house is in the National Register. Lavishly appointed with handsome antiques, imported draperies, Oriental rugs and grand canopy beds, the inn offers a truly luxurious experience. Heated towels, personal bathrobes, evening turndown service and cable TV are among the amenities. Best of all is the full breakfast served in the exquisitely decorated dining room on china and silver with linen tablecloths.

Innkeeper(s): Mr. & Mrs. Ed Laird.

Rates:$40-99. MC VISA AX. Full Bkfst. Gourmet Brkfst. Teas. Evening snacks. 4 rooms. Fireplaces. Beds:Q. TV, Phone, AC in room. Handicap access. Swimming. Fishing.

Contact: Ed Laird. Certificate may be used: January through March.

Sims-Mitchell House B&B

Box 429, 242 Whittle St SW
Chatham 24531-0429
(804)432-0595 (800)967-2867

1870. This Italianate house boasts 11 fireplaces, original horsehair-based plaster, furnishings from several generations of Mitchells and original art by Southern artists. (Art created by your host also is displayed.) There is a two-bedroom suite and a separate two-bedroom cottage at the side yard offering pastoral views. Hargrave Military Academy and Chatham Hall are within a five-block walk. Henry operates the local planetarium and Patricia is the author of several cookbooks and specializes in health-conscious Southern cuisine.

Innkeeper(s): Henry & Patricia Mitchell.

Rates:$60-70. MC VISA. ContPlus Bkfst. 2 rooms. Phone, AC, Refrig. in room.

Contact: Patricia B. Mitchell. Certificate may be used: Any.

Chincoteague

The Watson House
4240 Main St
Chincoteague 23336
(804)336-1564

1898. Situated in town, this white Queen Anne Victorian has a large front porch overlooking Main Street. The porch is a favorite spot of guests and

often the location for afternoon tea and refreshments. The rooms have air conditioning and ceiling fans. Beach towels, chairs and bicycles are complimentary, and there is an outdoor shower for cleaning up after sunning.
Innkeeper(s): Tom & Jacque Derrickson, David & Jo Anne Snead.
Rates:$65-105. MC VISA. Full Bkfst. Teas. 6 rooms. Beds:Q. AC in room. Bicycling. Swimming. Fishing.
Contact: Thomas Derrickson. Certificate may be used: March, April, May, October - Monday through Thursday.

Chincoteague/NChurch

The Garden and the Sea Inn
4188 Nelson Rd, Rt 710, PO Box 275
Chincoteague/NChurch 23415
(804)824-0672 (800)824-0672
Fax:(804)824-5605

1802. This European-style inn is situated near the Assateague Wildlife Refuge and beach. The interior abounds with Victorian detail with bay windows and stained glass. Guests are treated to a deluxe continental breakfast and afternoon tea with cookies or brownies each day. The French, four-star restaurant offers gourmet dinners. Fresh sauteed softshell crabs are a specialty, created by chef and innkeeper Victoria Olian. The inn hosts many special events such as dinner concerts and movie weekends. (If you're celebrating a special occasion, request an elegant room in the newly renovated garden house and you'll be able to enjoy a private whirlpool tub.)

Innkeeper(s): Victoria Olian & Jack Betz.
Rates:$70-140. MC VISA AX DC DS CB. ContPlus Bkfst. EP. Gourmet Dinner. Teas. 5 rooms. Beds:Q. Phone, AC, Refrig. in room. Farm. Golf. Tennis. Bicycling. Swimming. Fishing.
Seen in: *Eastern Shore News, Salisbury Daily Times, Washington Post, Washingtonian, Virginian Pilot-Ledger Star, Los Angeles Times.*
Contact: Victoria Olian. Certificate may be used: During season, Monday through Thursday nights excluding holiday weekends and last week of July. When dinner is being served, guest must dine at Inn one night of stay.

"The meals were masterpieces."

Covington

Milton Hall B&B Inn
207 Thorny Ln
Covington 24426
(703)965-0196

1874. This historic 44-acre estate adjoins the George Washington National Forest, and the inn appears as an exquisite English country manor with its buttressed porch towers, gables and Gothic trimmings. The home was built for the Viscountess of Milton, Maria Theresa Fitzwilliam, whose brother found the site while living in America and serving in the Union Army. Each spacious, romantic room boasts its own fireplace and is decorated in a different  color scheme. The rooms reflect the styles of the late 1800s. A full English breakfast is served each morning and a proper afternoon tea also is included. With the abundance of excellent hunting and fishing, the innkeepers offer a special sporting package.
Innkeeper(s): John & Vera Eckert.
Rates:$75-95. MC VISA. Full Bkfst. Picnic lunches. Teas. 6 rooms. Fireplaces. Beds:QT. Conference Rm. TV, Phone, AC in room. Golf. Tennis. Skiing. Swimming. Horseback riding. Fishing.
Seen in: *Alleghany Highlander, Washington Post, Country Inns.*
Contact: John Eckert. Certificate may be used: Anytime.

Draper

Claytor Lake Homestead Inn
Rt 651, PO Box 7
Draper 24324
(703)980-6777 (800)676-5253
Fax:(703)980-8320

1800. This inn was once a two-story log cabin built by slaves for the Ross family. It has been enlarged several times over the past century. The dining room's bay window overlooks Claytor Lake and a private beach. There is also a spectacular view of the lake from the brick-and-stone wraparound porch, which has rocking chairs and a swing. Furnishings include early American and country antiques, many collected from the historic Hotel Roanoke. Home-ground and seasoned breakfast sausage is a house specialty.

Innkeeper(s): Don & Judy Taylor.

Rates:$55-70. MC VISA AX. Full Bkfst. 5 rooms. 4 with shared baths. Beds:KQ. Conference Rm. Phone, AC in room. Golf. Swimming. Fishing.

Seen in: *Roanoke Times, Smyth County News, Southwest Times, Blue Ridge Country Magazine, Blue Ridge Digest.*

Contact: Judy Taylor. Certificate may be used: Anytime except May 6-7 and May 13-14 and parent's weekends.

"The total environment, including innkeepers, is first-class."

Edinburg

Edinburg Inn B&B Ltd.
218 S Main St, Route 2, Box 4
Edinburg 22824
(703)984-8286

1850. Next to a beautifully restored old mill and stream, this Queen Anne Victorian offers wide verandas and perennial and rose gardens. Ducks and geese meander to the door of Judy's kitchen, where she is often found baking nut rolls, cinnamon strudel coffee cake and other delectables for breakfast or evening refreshments. Fresh flowers bedeck the country decor in the spacious, airy guest rooms and sitting rooms. At dinner time, cross over to the mill, which now houses a new restaurant.

Innkeeper(s): Judy & Clyde Beachy.

Rates:$70-85. MC VISA. Full Bkfst. Evening snacks. 4 rooms. 2 with shared baths. Beds:D. AC in room. Skiing. Handicap access. Fishing.

Contact: Clyde Beachy. Certificate may be used: Sunday through Thursday.

Etlan

Dulaney Hollow at Old Rag Mountain B&B
Star Rt 6, Box 215
Etlan 22719
(703)923-4470

1900. Period furnishings decorate this Victorian manor house on 15 acres in the foothills of the Blue Ridge Mountains. There are shaded lawns and old farm buildings. A country breakfast is served, and picnic baskets may be packed for you to take on a bicycle-built-for-two jaunt or for hiking the hills around the Shenandoah River and National Park. A walk up the inn's pasture provides a great view of the Blue Ridge. Monticello and Montpelier are within an hour's drive.

Innkeeper(s): Susan Allen & Louis Cable.

Rates:$55-95. Full Bkfst. Picnic lunches. 4 rooms. 3 with shared baths. Beds:QT. Skiing. Fishing.

Contact: Louis Cable. Certificate may be used: Exclude months of September, October, November and designated holiday weekends.

Flint Hill

Caledonia Farm B&B
Rt 1, Box 2080
Flint Hill 22627
(703)675-3693 (800)262-1812

1812. This gracious Federal-style stone house in the National Register is beautifully situated on 52 acres adjacent to Shenandoah National Park. It was built

by a Revolutionary War officer, and his musket is displayed over a mantel. The house, a Virginia Historic Landmark, has been restored with the original Colonial color scheme retained. All rooms provide views of Skyline Drive and the Blue Ridge Mountains. The innkeeper is a retired broadcaster.

Innkeeper(s): Phil Irwin.

Rates:$80-140. MC VISA DS. Full Bkfst. Gourmet Brkfst. Teas. Evening snacks. 4 rooms. 2 with shared baths. Fireplaces. Beds:D. Conference Rm. Phone, AC, Refrig. in room. Farm. Golf. Tennis. Bicycling. Skiing.

Handicap access. Swimming. Horseback riding. Fishing.

Seen in: *Country, Country Almanac, Country Living, Blue Ridge Country, Discovery, Washington Post, Baltimore Sun.*

Contact: Phil Irwin. Certificate may be used: Non-holiday, Sunday through Wednesday check-in, Jan. 2 through Sept. 15, 1994 and 1995.

"We've stayed at many, many B&B's. This is by far the best!"

Franktown

Stillmeadow Inn B&B
7423 Bayside Rd, P O Box 144
Franktown 23354
(804)442-2431 Fax:(804)442-5567

1895. Located on Virginia's Eastern Shore, on an acre of dogwood, magnolia, white pines and drifts of azaleas and rhododendron, this Victorian home warmly welcomes guests with its elegant foyer, handsome library and carefully decorated guest rooms. Breakfast and afternoon tea are served in the dining room.

Innkeeper(s): Irene B. Walker.

Rates:$55-95. MC VISA. Full Bkfst. Teas. 3 rooms. Beds:KQT. Conference Rm. TV, Phone, AC in room. Golf. Bicycling. Swimming. Fishing.

Contact: Irene Walker. Certificate may be used: Monday through Thursday year-round.

Fredericksburg

La Vista Plantation
4420 Guinea Station Rd
Fredericksburg 22408
(703)898-8444 Fax:(703)898-1041

1838. La Vista has a long and unusual past, rich in Civil War history. Both Confederate and Union armies camped here, and this is where the Ninth Cavalry was sworn in. A Classical Revival structure with high ceilings and pine floors, the house sits on 10 acres of pasture and woods. There is a pond stocked with bass. Note: Area code will change in July, 1995. The new area code will be 540.

Innkeeper(s): Michele & Edward Schiesser.

Rates:$85. MC VISA. Full Bkfst. 1 room. Fireplaces. Beds:KDT. Conference Rm. Phone, AC, Refrig. in room. Farm. Tennis. Bicycling. Horseback riding. Fishing.

Seen in: *Free Lance Star.*

Contact: Michele Schiesser. Certificate may be used: Dec. 1-30, 1994, Monday-Thursday; Jan. 1-March 30, 1995, Monday-Thursday; Dec. 1-30, 1995, Monday-Thursday. No holidays.

"Thanks for the best weekend we've ever had."

Front Royal

Chester House Inn
43 Chester St
Front Royal 22630
(703)635-3937 (800)621-0441

1905. This stately Georgian-style estate rests on two acres of terraced gardens, which include vast plantings of boxwood, wisteria arbors, a fountain and brick walkways and walls. Elaborately carved marble mantels from London remain, and an original speaker tube extends from the second-floor bedroom to the kitchen. Just down the street is the renovated village commons, the Confederate Museum and the Belle Boyd Cottage.

Innkeeper(s): Bill & Ann Wilson.

Rates:$85-110. MC VISA AX. ContPlus Bkfst. Teas. 5 rooms. Fireplaces. Beds:KQT. Conference Rm. AC in room. Golf. Tennis. Skiing. Swimming. Horseback riding. Fishing.

Seen in: *Winchester Star, Northern Virginia Daily, Blue Ridge Country.*

Contact: William Wilson. Certificate may be used: Sunday-Thursday, January through April and July and August.

"A home of greater charm would be hard to find."

Killahevlin B&B Inn
1401 N Royal Ave
Front Royal 22630
(703)636-7335 (800)847-6132
Fax:(703)636-8694

1905. This Edwardian Mansion is in the National Register due in part to its builder, William Carson, creator of Skyline Drive, Williamsburg, Jamestown and Yorktown. Each guest room in the main house enjoys handsome decor and a working fireplace with antique mantels. Three rooms offer whirlpool tubs. Both the innkeepers share a common Irish heritage with Will Carson. Nineteenth-century Irish cottage wallpapers and Waterford crystal add to the atmosphere. In addition to views of the Blue Ridge Mountains, the inn's three acres include two restored gazebos, a circular driveway and formal boxwood gardens.

Innkeeper(s): Susan & John Lang.

Rates:$85-105. MC VISA. Full Bkfst. Teas. Evening snacks. 6 rooms. Fireplaces. Beds:Q. Conference Rm. AC in room. Skiing. Swimming. Fishing.

Contact: John Lang. Certificate may be used: All year except May and October.

Gordonsville

Sleepy Hollow Farm B&B
16280 Blue Ridge Turnpike
Gordonsville 22942
(703)832-5555 (800)215-4804
Fax:(703)832-2515

1788. Many generations have added on to this brick farmhouse with its 18th-century dining room and bedrooms. The pink and white room was fre-

quently visited by a friendly ghost from Civil War days, according to local stories. She hasn't been seen for several years since the innkeeper, a former missionary, had the house blessed. The grounds include an herb garden, a pond with gazebo, a chestnut slave cabin, terraces and abundant wildlife.

Innkeeper(s): Beverly Allison.

Rates:$60-95. MC VISA. Full Bkfst. Picnic lunches. Teas. 6 rooms. Fireplaces. Beds:QT. Conference Rm. TV, Phone, AC, Refrig. in room. Farm. Skiing. Handicap access. Fishing.

Seen in: *Orange County Review.*

Contact: Beverly Allison. Certificate may be used: Sunday through Thursday only.

"This house is truly blessed."

Goshen

The Hummingbird Inn
Wood Lane, PO Box 147
Goshen 24439
(703)997-9065 (800)397-3214
Fax:(703)997-9065

1780. This early Victorian mansion is located in the Shenandoah Valley against the backdrop of the Blue Ridge Mountains. Both the first and second floors offer wraparound verandas. Furnished with antiques, the inn features a library and sitting room with fireplaces. Family-style suppers are available by advance reservations. An old barn and babbling creek are on the grounds. Lexington, the Virginia

Horse Center, Natural Bridge, the Blue Ridge Parkway and antiquing are all nearby.

Innkeeper(s): Diana & Jeremy Robinson.

Rates:$50-75. MC VISA. Full Bkfst. Gourmet Dinner. Picnic lunches. Teas. 4 rooms. Fireplaces. Beds:Q. Skiing. Swimming. Fishing.

Contact: Jeremy Robinson. Certificate may be used: Nov. 1-March 31, 1994 and 1995.

"We enjoyed our stay so much that we returned two weeks later on our way back. . .for a delicious home-cooked dinner, comfortable attractive atmosphere, and familiar faces to welcome us after a long journey. We knew we'd find all that at the Hummingbird Inn."

Hillsville

Bray's Manor B&B Inn
PO Box 385
Hillsville 24343
(703)728-7901 (800)753-2729

1991. This farmhouse was newly built to accommodate guests and now boasts air conditioning, private baths and a two-room apartment with its own Jacuzzi. The front porch overlooks the valley where Hereford cattle are usually found grazing. You can play croquet or badminton on the five acres or simply enjoy the view from the porch. Country breakfasts are served.

Innkeeper(s): Dick & Helen Bray.

Rates:$65. MC VISA DS. Full Bkfst. 3 rooms. Beds:Q. AC in room. Farm.

Contact: Helen Bray. Certificate may be used: April, May, June, July, November, December.

Lancaster

The Inn at Levelfields
State Rt 3, Box 216
Lancaster 22503
(804)435-6887 (800)238-5578

1857. This hip-roofed Georgian Colonial house stands a quarter of a mile from the road bordered by hedges of 250-year-old English boxwood. Once

the center of a large plantation, the mansion has been completely refurbished and filled with family antiques and Oriental rugs, offering the finest in Virginia tradition.

Innkeeper(s): Warren & Doris Sadler.

Rates:$85. MC VISA. Full Bkfst. Gourmet Brkfst. 4 rooms. Fireplaces. Beds:KQT. AC in room. Swimming. Fishing.

Seen in: *Richmond Times-Dispatch, Newport News Daily Press, Woman's Day, Colonial Homes.*

Contact: Doris Sadler. Certificate may be used: Sunday through Thursday.

"Your hospitality far exceeds any we've experienced and truly made our stay one we'll treasure."

Leesburg

The Norris House Inn

108 Loudoun St SW
Leesburg 22075
(703)777-1806 (800)644-1806
Fax:(703)771-8051

1806. The Norris brothers, Northern Virginia's foremost architects and builders, purchased this building in 1850 and began extensive renovations

several years later. They used the finest wood and brick available, remodeling the exterior to an Eastlake style. Beautifully restored, the inn features built-in bookcases in the library and a cherry fireplace mantel.

Innkeeper(s): Pam & Don McMurray.

Rates:$90-140. MC VISA DC. Full Bkfst. Teas. 6 rooms. 6 with shared baths. Fireplaces. Beds:Q. Conference Rm. AC in room. Golf. Swimming. Horseback riding. Fishing.

Seen in: *New York Times, Better Homes and Gardens, Washingtonian, Country Home.*

Contact: Pamela McMurray. Certificate may be used: Sunday through Friday stays only. Good for 1994 and 1995.

"Thank you for your gracious hospitality. We enjoyed everything about your lovely home, especially the extra little touches that really make the difference."

Lexington

Historic Country Inns of Lexington

11 N Main St
Lexington 24450
(703)463-2044 Fax:(703)463-7262

1789. Three inns comprise this group of country inns. Maple Hall, a beautiful three-story, columned plantation in the country, boasts a stocked fishing pond, dining facilities, tennis court and swimming pool. Or you can choose from two in-town locations: the Georgian-style Alexander-Winthrow House or the McCampbell Inn. All three are handsomely furnished with antiques, paintings and Oriental rugs. The 18 rooms at Maple Hall have fireplaces.

Innkeeper(s): Don Fredenburg.

Rates:$95-135. MC VISA. ContPlus Bkfst. MAP available. Gourmet Dinner. Teas. 23 rooms. Beds:QT. Conference Rm. TV, Phone, AC, Refrig. in room. Skiing. Fishing.

Contact: Mrs. Peter Meredith. Certificate may be used: July - August, November - December, 1994; January - March, July - August, November - December, 1995.

Llewellyn Lodge at Lexington

603 S Main St
Lexington 24450
(703)463-3235 (800)882-1145

1939. This brick Colonial shaded by tall trees, features three gables on the third story. It is decorated in antique and traditional furnishings. Nearby historic attractions include the home of Stonewall Jackson, the Natural Bridge and the Robert E. Lee house.

Innkeeper(s): Ellen & John Roberts.

Rates:$70-85. MC VISA AX. Full Bkfst. Gourmet Brkfst. Teas. 6 rooms. Beds:KQT. Conference Rm. AC in room. Skiing. Fishing.

Seen in: *News-Gazette, New York Times.*

Contact: Ellen Roberts. Certificate may be used: January, 1995 - anytime. February - March 15, 1995 - weekdays only.

"Like being at home! The breakfast was the best ever."

Seven Hills Inn

408 S Main St
Lexington 24450
(703)463-4715 Fax:(703)463-6526

1928. This Colonial Revival house stands in the heart of the Shenandoah Valley. Carefully renovated, the inn's white columns and brick exterior are reminiscent of a Southern plantation. The guest rooms, named after area homesteads, are furnished with antiques and reproductions, and the Fruit Hill room offers a Jacuzzi tub. Within a 10-minute walk is Washington and Lee University, the Virginia Military Institute and the Lexington Visitors Center.

Innkeeper(s): Ben & Carol Grigsby.

Rates:$75-95. MC VISA. Cont. Bkfst. 7 rooms. 2 with shared baths. Conference Rm.

Contact: Jeanne Tomlinson. Certificate may be used: November, 1994 - April, 1995.

Locust Dale

The Inn at Meander Plantation
HCR 5, Box 460A
Locust Dale 22948
(703)672-4912

1766. This elegant country estate was built by Henry Fry, close friend of Thomas Jefferson, who often stopped here on his way to Monticello. Ancient formal boxwood gardens, woodland and meadows are enjoyed by guests as well as views of the Blue Ridge Mountains from the rockers on the back porches. The mansion is decorated serenely with elegant antiques and period reproductions, including queen-size, four-poster beds. The innkeeper is a food writer and will prepare special breakfasts for individual diets. Full dinner service and picnic baskets are available with advance reservations.

Innkeeper(s): Bob & Suzie Blanchard, Suzanne Thomas.

Rates:$95-175. MC VISA. Full Bkfst. Gourmet Lunch, Dinner. Picnic lunches. Teas. Evening snacks. 5 rooms. Beds:Q. Conference Rm. AC, Refrig. in room. Farm. Stables. Fishing.

Contact: Suzanne Thomas. Certificate may be used: Jan. 1-Aug. 31, 1995 - anyday. Monday - Thursday only (no weekends), Sept. 1-Dec. 31, 1994 and 1995.

Luray

Spring Farm B&B
13 Wallace Ave
Luray 22835
(703)743-4701 Fax:(703)743-5871

1795. Spring Farm is on 10 acres two miles from Luray Caverns. Hite's Springs runs through the land. The Greek Revival home has double front and back verandas. Rooms feature a mix of antique and new furnishings, and there is a fireplace in the living room. Ask the innkeepers for advice on shopping, dining and activities in the Shenandoah and they'll be happy to help you plan a getaway you'll long remember.

Innkeeper(s): Thelma Mayes.

Rates:$75-145. MC VISA. Full Bkfst. Picnic lunches. Teas. Evening snacks. 5 rooms. 2 with shared baths. Beds:Q. Skiing. Fishing.

Contact: Thelma Mayes. Certificate may be used: January - June except weekend holidays.

Lynchburg

Lynchburg Mansion Inn B&B
405 Madison St
Lynchburg 24504
(804)528-5400 (800)352-1199

1914. This stately Spanish Georgian mansion is located in the Garland Hill Historic District. Drive in on Madison Street, still paved in turn-of-the-

century brick, and pull up under the columned porte-cochere. A massive portico surrounded by six Greek Revival columns welcomes guests to this elegant and romantic B&B. The grand hall showcases an oak and cherry staircase, which leads three stories up to a solarium and the guest rooms. Breakfast is served in the formal dining room on antique china. As a bonus, explore the secret passageway near the back hall.

Innkeeper(s): Bob & Mauranna Sherman.

Rates:$89-119. MC VISA AX DC. Full Bkfst. Gourmet Brkfst. 5 rooms. Fireplaces. Beds:KQ. Conference Rm. TV, Phone, AC, Refrig. in room. Skiing. Spa.

Seen in: *News & Advance, Roanoker.*

Contact: Mauranna Sherman. Certificate may be used: All year, Sunday through Thursday. No holidays or holiday eves.

Madison Heights

Winridge B&B
Rt 1, Box 362 Winridge Dr
Madison Heights 24572
(804)384-7220

1910. This is a Colonial Revival home on 14 acres, five miles from Lynchburg. The Habecker Room is a favorite with its large four-poster bed, rocking

chair and desk. All the rooms have ceiling fans and two have air conditioning. The host was a professional caterer and serves full breakfasts.
Innkeeper(s): Lois Ann & Ed Pfister.

Rates:$59-69. Full Bkfst. Evening snacks. 3 rooms. 2 with shared baths. Beds:QT. AC in room. Farm. Golf. Tennis. Skiing. Swimming. Horseback riding. Fishing.

Seen in: *News & Advance.*

Contact: Lois Ann Pfister. Certificate may be used: November, December, 1994; January, February, March, 1995.

Middleburg

Tuscany Inn
101 S Madison St
Middleburg 22117
(703)687-6456 Fax:(703)837-1913

1787. Once owned by the town's first doctor and later the mayor, this historic inn is the second oldest building in Middleburg. Located in the middle of "Hunt Country," the inn is close to equestrian event sites and wineries. A restaurant on premises offering lunch and dinner features regional Italian cuisine served in four elegant dining rooms, including the main, bar, drawing and sun rooms.
Innkeeper(s): Michel Golden & Gino Ballarin.

Rates:$95-125. Cont. Bkfst. Gourmet Lunch, Dinner. Picnic lunches. 3 rooms. 2 with shared baths. Fireplaces. Beds:KDT. AC in room. Farm. Handicap access. Fishing.

Contact: Michel Golden. Certificate may be used: Excluding holidays and weekends (except Sunday).

Mineral

Littlepage Inn
15701 Monrovia Rd
Mineral 23117
(703)854-9861 (800)248-1803

1811. Two old fieldstone posts mark the country lane to this large plantation home, in the National Register. Heart pine floors and original glass window panes were preserved in a recent prize-winning restoration. The spacious rooms are filled with period furnishings with many original to the house. There is a separate cottage with fireplace, grate room and kitchen. The inn's 125 acres offer gardens, fields, a wooded spring, a 19th-century smokehouse, ice house, barn and stable.
Innkeeper(s): Bob Overton.

Rates:$75-125. MC VISA AX DC. Full Bkfst. Gourmet Dinner. Picnic lunches. Teas. Evening snacks. 4 rooms. Beds:Q. Phone, AC in room. Farm. Spa. Swimming. Fishing.

Contact: Robert Overton. Certificate may be used: Monday through Thursday year-round.

Monterey

Highland Inn
Main Street, PO Box 40
Monterey 24465
(703)468-2143

1904. Listed in the National Register, this clapboard Victorian hotel has outstanding Eastlake wraparound verandas. Small-town life may be viewed from rocking chairs and swings. Guest rooms are furnished in country fashion, with iron beds and antiques. Sheep outnumber people in a pastoral setting surrounded by three million acres of National Forest.
Innkeeper(s): Michael Strand & Cynthia Peel-Strand.

Rates:$49-69. MC VISA. Cont. Bkfst. 21 rooms. Conference Rm. Golf. Fishing.

Seen in: *Washington Post, Rural Living, Richmond Times Dispatch, Roanoker.*

Contact: Michael Strand. Certificate may be used: Anytime except holiday weekends November-April. Midweek only May-October.

"The most beautiful place I've been."

Mount Jackson

The Widow Kip's Country Inn
Rt 1 Box 117
Mount Jackson 22842
(703)477-2400

1830. This lovingly restored farmhouse with its sweeping view of the Massanutten Mountains is situated on seven acres. It's a stone's throw from a fork of the Shenandoah River. Locally crafted quilts enhance the four-poster, sleigh and hand-carved Victorian beds. Two restored cottages (the Silk Purse and Sow's Ear) as well as a gift shop, create a Williamsburg-style courtyard. Cows graze unexpectedly a few feet away from the swimming pool.

Innkeeper(s): Betty Luse.

Rates:$65-85. MC VISA. Gourmet Brkfst. Picnic lunches. 8 rooms. Fireplaces. Beds:Q. TV, AC, Refrig. in room. Golf. Tennis. Bicycling. Skiing. Swimming. Horseback riding. Fishing.

Seen in: *Country Inns, Mid-Atlantic Country, Americana, Sojourner.*

Contact: Betty Luse. Certificate may be used: Monday - Thursday. Not month of October.

"Everything sparkled. The rooms were decorated with flair and imagination."

Natural Bridge

Burger's Country Inn B&B
Rt 2 Box 564
Natural Bridge 24578
(703)291-2464

1921. This inn was first opened to guests in the '20s when it was operated by the Burger family (Francis Burger runs it now) and it was called

Petunia Inn. Located 12 miles south of Lexington, it is one mile from Natural Bridge. Thomas Jefferson owned the land here, having been granted 157 acres in 1774. The graceful yellow and white Colonial farmhouse has columns, bay windows and double porches. It rests on 10 acres.

Innkeeper(s): Frances Burger.

Rates:$45-50. ContPlus Bkfst. 4 rooms. 2 with shared baths. Fishing.

Contact: Frances B. Burger. Certificate may be used: Weekdays - Sunday through Thursday - May - September. Anytime November - April.

Nellysford

Trillium House
PO Box 280, Wintergreen
Nellysford 22958
(804)325-9126 (800)325-9126
Fax:(804)325-1099

1983. This handsomely designed inn is located in the mountain resort of Wintergreen on the 17th hole of the golf course. The inn has a large library, common room, television room and garden room. Breakfast is served in the dining room that looks out to trees and fairways. Trillium House guests may participate in resort features such as English riding, health spa, tennis, hiking trails, golf and skiing (at varying rates).

Rates:$90-105. MC VISA. Full Bkfst. Gourmet Brkfst, Dinner. 12 rooms. Beds:QT. Conference Rm. TV, Phone in room. Skiing. Handicap access. Fishing.

Contact: Ed Dinwiddie. Certificate may be used: Midweek, non-holiday, not October, no weekends, Nov. 1, 1994-Sept. 29, 1995.

New Market

A Touch of Country B&B
9329 Congress St
New Market 22844
(703)740-8030

1873. This white clapboard Shenandoah Valley I-frame house has a second-story pediment centered above the veranda entrance. It was built by Captain William Rice, commander of the New Market Cavalry, and the house sits on what was once a battleground of the Civil War. Rice's unit was highly praised by General Lee. Guest chambers are in the main house and in the handsome carriage house.

Innkeeper(s): Jean Schoellig & Dawn M. Kasow.

Rates:$60-70. MC VISA. Full Bkfst. 6 rooms. Beds:QT. AC in room. Golf. Tennis. Skiing. Swimming. Horseback riding. Fishing.

Seen in: *USA Today Weekend.*

Contact: Jean Schoellig. Certificate may be used: Anytime, December-March; Sunday-Thursday, April-November excluding October; no holidays.

"Every morning should start with sunshine, bird song and Dawn's strawberry pancakes."

Red Shutter Farmhouse B&B

Rt 1 Box 376
New Market 22844-9306
(703)740-4281

1790. For generations, the veranda at the Red Shutter has been the location of choice during summer to view the valley and mountains. Located on 20 acres, the inn offers large rooms and suites and a library/conference room. Breakfast is in the dining room. Enjoy drives to the many area caverns, New Market Battlefield and Skyline Drive.
Innkeeper(s): George & Juanita Miller.

Rates:$55-70. MC VISA. Full Bkfst. 6 rooms. 2 with shared baths. Fireplaces. Beds:KQT. Conference Rm. Farm. Skiing. Fishing.

Contact: George Miller. Certificate may be used: Dec. 1 through Feb. 29, anytime; March 1 through Nov. 30, Monday through Thursday, subject to availability.

North Garden

The Inn at Crossroads

RR 692 Rt 2, Box 6
North Garden 22959
(804)979-6452

1820. This four-story brick inn was built as a tavern on the road from Shenandoah Valley to the James River. The long front porch and straightforward, Federal-style architecture was common to ordinaries of that era. Each guest room has a theme carried out in its books and decor, such as the Country Garden Room, the Storybook Room and the Country Squire Room. The grounds offer a boxwood cave, an old well and a swing hung under a grand oak tree. A full breakfast is served in the Keeping Room. Charlottesville is nine miles away.
Innkeeper(s): Lynn Neville & Christine Garrison.

Rates:$59-69. MC VISA. Full Bkfst. Gourmet Brkfst. Picnic lunches. 5 rooms. 5 with shared baths. Fireplaces. Beds:KD. AC in room. Skiing. Swimming. Fishing.

Contact: Lynn L. Neville. Certificate may be used: January-March; April and May week nights Sunday-Thursday; June-August; September and October week nights Sunday-Thursday; November-December.

Onancock

Colonial Manor Inn

PO Box 94, 84 Market St
Onancock 23417
(804)787-3521

1892. Converted to a guest house in 1936, this Victorian inn has remained in the same family for more than 55 years. There are 20 comfortably fur-

nished rooms, including the parlor which offers collections of books on the Eastern Shore and its history. A glassed-in sun porch overlooks the front yard, planted with English boxwood, tulips, dogwoods and crepe myrtles. A Victorian gazebo with a brick floor is in the back garden. Onancock Wharf, a deep-water wharf on the Chesapeake Bay, is five blocks away.
Innkeeper(s): June & Jerry Evans.

Rates:$50-65. Cont. Bkfst. 14 rooms. 10 with shared baths. Beds:QT. TV, AC in room. Fishing.

Contact: June Evans. Certificate may be used: No holidays or holiday weekends.

The Spinning Wheel B&B

31 North St
Onancock 23417
(804)787-7311

1890. This folk Victorian with its veranda and green shutters is a welcoming spot from which to enjoy the Eastern Shore. Spinning wheels and antiques are found throughout the house. You can walk to shops and the harbor or explore even further with the tandem bicycles available from the innkeepers. Enjoy the beaches, bay and ocean, then return to the inn in time for wine and  hors d'oeuvres in the late afternoon. Chef David produces a hearty breakfast and by special arrangement, you may have it delivered to your room.
Innkeeper(s): Karen & David Tweedie.

Rates:$75-85. MC VISA. Full Bkfst. 5 rooms. Beds:Q. AC in room. Bicycling. Swimming. Fishing.

Contact: David Tweedie. Certificate may be used: Monday - Thursday.

Orange

Hidden Inn
249 Caroline St
Orange 22960
(703)672-3625 Fax:(703)672-5029

1880. Acres of huge old trees can be seen from the wraparound veranda of this Victorian inn nestled in the Virginia countryside. Meticulous attention has been given to every detail of the inn's restoration, right down to the white lace and fresh cut flowers. Monticello, Blue Ridge, Montpelier and several wineries are located nearby.

Innkeeper(s): Barbara & Ray Lonick.

Rates:$79-159. MC VISA. Full Bkfst. Gourmet Dinner. Teas. 10 rooms. Fireplaces. Beds:KQT. Conference Rm. AC, Refrig. in room. Golf. Tennis. Spa. Swimming. Horseback riding. Fishing.

Seen in: *Forbes Magazine, Washington Post.*

Contact: R.C. Lonick. Certificate may be used: Monday through Thursday, except May and October. No holidays.

"It just doesn't get any better than this!"

The Holladay House
155 W Main St
Orange 22960
(703)672-4893 (800)358-4422
Fax:(703)672-3028

1890. Each room in this Federal-style inn is furnished with family pieces and comes with its own sitting area. Rooms are decorated with fresh cut flowers. Breakfast is served to guests in their rooms. Specialties include peach muffins and apple puffs. Nearby attractions include wineries, antique shops, arts and crafts stores and President James Madison's home, which is 90-minutes away.

Innkeeper(s): Pete & Phebe Holladay.

Rates:$75-145. MC VISA. Full Bkfst. 6 rooms.

Contact: Pete Holladay. Certificate may be used: Sunday through Thursday.

Paris

The Ashby Inn
Rt 1 Box 2A
Paris 22130
(703)592-3900 Fax:(703)592-3781

1829. The graceful proportions of this Federal-style inn predict the elegance of its traditional decor featuring American antiques, canopy beds, fireplaces and polished-wood floors. Some rooms boast private verandas, affording views of the four acres of land-scaped gardens. The taproom's original walnut beams and stone fireplace have seen many a trainer, breeder and rider. The stellar reputation of the

dining room is one of the reasons Ashby Inn was selected as one of the "Top Inns Worldwide" by Conde Nast Traveler and "North America's 20 Most Romantic Hideaways" by the Washington Post.

Innkeeper(s): John & Roma Sherman.

Rates:$80-200. MC VISA. Full Bkfst. Gourmet Dinner. Picnic lunches. 10 rooms. 2 with shared baths. Fireplaces. Beds:Q. Conference Rm. Phone, AC in room. Skiing. Fishing.

Contact: Roma Sherman. Certificate may be used: Wednesday or Thursday.

Pulaski

The Count Pulaski B&B and Garden
821 N Jefferson Ave
Pulaski 24301
(703)980-1163 (800)980-1163

1910. The innkeeper's many travels to Europe and Asia form the core of the inn's furnishings, which are combined with family antiques. The 80-year-old Colonial Revival house is located in the historic district on a half-acre of lawn and gardens. Nearby are lakes, mountains, national and state parks, museums, art galleries and antique shops. Ask about the dinner cruise on the Pioneer Maid.

Innkeeper(s): Florence Stevenson.

Rates:$75. MC VISA. Gourmet Brkfst. Evening snacks. 3 rooms. Fireplaces. Beds:KQT. Phone, AC, Refrig. in room. Bicycling. Swimming. Fishing.

Contact: Florence Stevenson. Certificate may be used: Anytime space is available.

Reedville

Cedar Grove B&B Inn
Rt 1 Box 2535
Reedville 22539
(804)453-3915 Fax:(804)453-3915

1913. Overlooking the Chesapeake Bay and the

lighthouse standing over the entrance to the Great Wicomico River, this Colonial Revival home is situated on 10 acres. If you opt for the Lighthouse

Suite, you'll enjoy not only the period antiques, but water views in all directions. A window seat overlooking the pond, a large cherry four-poster bed and a screened balcony are included. Enjoy a bountiful breakfast in the formal dining room with chamber music, crystal chandelier, china and silver. The innkeepers hope you'll make use of their tennis court, bicycles and a bicycle built for two.

Innkeeper(s): Susan & Bob Tipton.

Rates:$60-90. Full Bkfst. Gourmet Brkfst. 3 rooms. Beds:QD. AC in room. Tennis. Bicycling. Swimming. Fishing.

Contact: Susan Tipton. Certificate may be used: Midweek (Monday-Thursday) anytime. Weekends also November through April.

Scottsville

High Meadows Vineyard
Rt 4, Box 6, Rt 20 S
Scottsville 24590
(804)286-2218 (800)232-1832

1832. Minutes from Charlottesville on the Constitution Highway (Route 20), High Meadows stands on 50 acres of gardens, forests, ponds, a

creek and a vineyard. Listed in the National Register, it is actually two historic homes joined by a breezeway as well as a turn-of-the-century Queen Anne manor house. The inn is furnished in Federal and Victorian styles. Guests are treated to gracious Virginia hospitality in an elegant and peaceful setting with wine tasting and a romantic candlelight dinner every evening.

Innkeeper(s): Peter Sushka & Mary Jae Abbitt.

Rates:$84-155. MC VISA. Full Bkfst. EP. Gourmet Brkfst, Dinner. 12 rooms. Fireplaces. Beds:KQT. Conference Rm. AC, Refrig. in room. Skiing. Handicap access. Swimming. Horseback riding. Fishing.

Seen in: *Washington Times, Cavalier Daily, Daily Progress, Washington Post, Richmond Times Dispatch, Mid-Atlantic.*

Contact: Peter Sushka. Certificate may be used: Sunday-Thursday all year, no holidays, for 1994 and 1995. Sunday-Saturday, Dec. 1-March 1, no holiday weekends.

"We have rarely encountered such a smooth blend of hospitality and expertise in a totally relaxed environment."

Staunton

Belle Grae Inn
515 W Frederick St
Staunton 24401
(703)886-5151 Fax:(703)886-6641

1870. Located in the Newton Historic District, this Victorian-Italianate inn offers 15 distinctive lodging rooms decorated with antiques and keepsakes. Guests can listen to the innkeeper relate the colorful history of the house as they sit and sip refreshments on the veranda and take in the view of nearby Betsy Bell and Mary Gray Mountains, for which the inn is named. Live piano music every Friday and Saturday night can be found in The Bistro. The restaurant is an indoor/outdoor cafe serving dishes with a Southern flavor. Within walking distance of the inn are President Woodrow Wilson's birthplace, the Statler Brother's Museum and antique shops.

Innkeeper(s): Michael Organ.

Rates:$99-139. MC VISA AX DC. Full Bkfst. AP available. Gourmet Brkfst, Dinner. 20 rooms. Fireplaces. Beds:QT. Conference Rm. TV, Phone, AC in room. Skiing. Handicap access. Fishing.

Contact: Michael Organ. Certificate may be used: Non-holiday, Sunday through Thursday nights.

Frederick House
28 N New St
Staunton 24401
(703)885-4220 (800)334-5575

1810. Across from Mary Baldwin College, this inn consists of five renovated town houses, the oldest of which is believed to be a copy of a home designed by Thomas Jefferson. A full breakfast is served in Chumley's Tea Room. Guest rooms are furnished with antiques and feature ceiling fans. Original staircases and woodwork are highlighted throughout. Suites are available.

Innkeeper(s): Joe & Evy Harman.

Rates:$55-150. MC VISA AX DC DS. Full Bkfst. EP. Gourmet Brkfst. Teas. 14 rooms. Conference Rm. Golf. Tennis. Skiing. Spa. Sauna.

Exercise room. Swimming. Horseback riding. Fishing.

Seen in: *Richmond Times-Dispatch, News Journal.*

Contact: Joe Harman. Certificate may be used: December, January, February.

"Thanks for making the room so squeaky-clean and comfortable! I enjoyed the Virginia hospitality. The furnishings and decor are beautiful."

Thornrose House At Gypsy Hill

531 Thornrose Ave
Staunton 24401
(703)885-7026 (800)861-4338

1912. A columned veranda wraps around two sides of this gracious red brick Georgian-style house. Two sets of Greek pergolas grace the lawns and gardens

of azalea, rhododendron and hydrangea. The inn is furnished with a mix of antique oak and walnut period pieces and overstuffed English country chairs. Bircher muesli, and hot-off-the-griddle whole grain banana pecan pancakes are popular breakfast items, served in the dining room (fireside on cool days). Across the street is a 300-acre park with lighted tennis courts, an 18-hole golf course and swimming pool.

Innkeeper(s): Suzanne & Otis Huston.

Rates:$55-75. Full Bkfst. EP. Teas. 5 rooms. Beds:KQT. AC in room. Fishing.

Contact: Otis Huston. Certificate may be used: Dec. 1 through March 31, Sunday through Thursday only. Holidays excluded.

Steele's Tavern

The Osceola Mill Country Inn

Steele's Tavern 24476
(703)377-6455 (800)242-7352
Fax:(703)377-6455

1849. Eleven acres and three buildings comprise Osceola Mill Country Inn, once part of the McCormick Farm where Cyrus McCormick farmed.

A 27-foot wheel, once driven by the waters of Marl Creek, serves as a constant reminder of the rich history of the area. The inn's open beams retain the rustic feel of the original mill. A 5,000-pound millstone serves as a coffee table. The honeymoon cottage, formerly the mill store, boasts a great stone fireplace and whirlpool spa. The property provides a babbling brook, river, inviting paths and views of the Blue Ridge Mountains.

Innkeeper(s): Shane Tattersall.

Rates:$89-169. MC VISA. Full Bkfst. Gourmet Dinner. 13 rooms. Fireplaces. Beds:KQT. Conference Rm. AC, Refrig. in room. Golf. Tennis. Skiing. Spa. Swimming. Horseback riding. Fishing.

Seen in: *Richmond News Leader.*

Contact: Shane Tattersall. Certificate may be used: Sunday - Thursday only. Cannot be used during October.

Surry

The Seward House Inn

PO Box 352
Surry 23883
(804)294-3810

1902. A long white porch, festooned with gingerbread and flowers, invites you to an old-fashioned visit at "Grandma's house." Family pieces and collections from three generations include toys, needlework and china. Ask for the Seward House omelet, a house specialty. Afterwards, enjoy the Chippokes Plantation State Park or cross the James River by ferry and visit Colonial Williamsburg.

Innkeeper(s): Jackie Bayer & Cindy Erskine.

Rates:$55-75. AX. Full Bkfst. Picnic lunches. 4 rooms. 2 with shared baths. Beds:QDT. AC, Refrig. in room.

Contact: Jackie Bayer & Cindy Erskine. Certificate may be used: Anytime subject to availability.

Urbanna

Hewick Plantation
VSH 602/615, Box 82
Urbanna 23175
(804)758-4214 (800)484-7514

1678. A driveway lined with large oak trees leads to this two-story brick Colonial located on 66 acres. There is an ancient family cemetery on the

grounds, and at the rear of the house is an archeological dig conducted by the College of William and Mary. A cross-stitch kit of Hewick Plantation, made by the Heirloom Needlecraft company, is available at the inn and is being used to help fund the current restoration of the manor. The innkeeper is a ninth-generation descendant of Christopher Robinson, builder of Hewick Plantation and an original trustee of the College of William and Mary.

Innkeeper(s): Helen & Ed Battleson.

Rates:$70-100. MC VISA. ContPlus Bkfst. 2 rooms. Beds:DT. Conference Rm. Swimming. Fishing.

Seen in: *Richmond Times Dispatch, Daily Press, Pleasant Living, WRIC-TV.*

Contact: Helen Battleson. Certificate may be used: Monday through Thursday.

Warm Springs

The Inn at Gristmill Square
Box 359
Warm Springs 24484
(703)839-2231

1800. The inn consists of five restored buildings.

The old blacksmith shop and silo, the hardware store, the Steel House and the Miller House all contain guest rooms. (The old mill is now the

Waterwheel Restaurant.) A few antiques and old prints appear in some rooms, while others are furnished in a contemporary style. There are tennis courts and a swimming pool at the inn. A short walk over Warm Springs Mill Stream and down the road brings travelers to historic Warm Springs Pools.

Innkeeper(s): The McWilliams family.

Rates:$80-95. MC VISA DS. Cont. Bkfst. MAP available. Gourmet Dinner. Picnic lunches. 16 rooms. Fireplaces. Beds:KQ. Conference Rm. TV, Phone, AC, Refrig. in room. Golf. Tennis. Skiing. Sauna. Exercise room. Swimming. Horseback riding. Fishing.

Seen in: *New York Times, Bon Appetit, Colonial Homes.*

Contact: Janice McWilliams. Certificate may be used: Sunday, Monday, Tuesday, Wednesday, Thursday.

"You have such a wonderful inn - such attention to detail and such a considerate staff."

Washington

The Foster-Harris House
PO Box 333
Washington 22747
(703)675-3757 (800)666-0153

1900. This Victorian farmhouse stands on a lot laid out by George Washington and is situated at the edge of the village. The streets of the town are exactly as surveyed 225 years ago, and the town is the first of the 28 Washingtons in the United States. The village has galleries and craft shops as well as the Inn at Little Washington, a five-star restaurant.

Innkeeper(s): Phyllis Marriott.

Rates:$95-135. MC VISA AX DS. Full Bkfst. Gourmet Brkfst. Picnic lunches. Teas. 4 rooms. Fireplaces. Beds:Q. AC in room. Skiing. Horseback riding. Fishing.

Seen in: *Culpeper News, Richmond Times-Dispatch.*

Contact: Phyllis Marriott. Certificate may be used: November-March.

"The View Room is charming, as are the hosts."

Gay Street Inn
PO Box 237
Washington 22747
(703)675-3288

1855. After a day of Skyline Drive, Shenandoah National Park and the caverns of Luray and Front Royal, come home to this stucco, gabled farm-

house. If you've booked the fireplace room, a canopy bed will await you. Furnishings include period Shaker pieces. The innkeepers will be happy to steer you to the most interesting vineyards, "pick-your-own" fruit and vegetable farms and Made-In-Virginia food and craft shops.
Innkeeper(s): Donna & Robin Kevis.
Rates:$95-110. Full Bkfst. Picnic lunches. Teas. 3 rooms.
Contact: Donna Kevis. Certificate may be used: Weekdays anytime 1994 and 1995. No Friday/Saturday or Saturday/Sunday combinations.

White Post

L'Auberge Provencale
PO Box 119
White Post 22663
(703)837-1375 (800)638-1702
Fax:(703)837-2004

1753. This farmhouse was built with fieldstones gathered from the area. Hessian soldiers crafted the woodwork of the main house, Mt. Airy. It contains three of the inn's dining rooms. Guest rooms are decorated in Victorian antiques.
Innkeeper(s): Alain & Celeste Borel.
Rates:$145-185. MC VISA AX DC. Gourmet Brkfst. Dinner. Picnic lunches. 10 rooms. Beds:QT. Conference Rm. AC in room. Farm. Golf. Tennis. Bicycling. Skiing. Swimming. Horseback riding. Fishing.
Seen in: *Bon Appetit, Glamour, Washington Dossier, Washington Post, Baltimore Magazine, Richmond Times.*
Contact: Celeste Borel. Certificate may be used: January - April, July - September, November - December. October not available. No Saturdays or holidays.

"Peaceful view and atmosphere, extraordinary food and wines. Honeymoon and heaven all in one!"

Williamsburg

The Cedars
616 Jamestown Rd
Williamsburg 23185
(804)229-3591 (800)296-3591

1930. This three-story brick house is one-half mile from Colonial Williamsburg and directly across from William and Mary College. Traditional antiques and Colonial reproductions are enhanced by handmade quilts. Tucked behind the inn is a cottage for six.
Innkeeper(s): Carol, Jim & Brona Malecha.
Rates:$85-150. MC VISA. Full Bkfst. Gourmet Brkfst. 9 rooms. Beds:KQT. AC in room.
Contact: Carol Malecha. Certificate may be used: Jan. 2 through March 15.

Fox Grape B&B
701 Monumental Ave
Williamsburg 23185
(804)229-6914

1947. This brick Cape Cod house has an herb garden in the front yard. The inn features stenciled walls, needlepoint wallhangings, stained glass, antiques and decoys. Guests may relax in the parlor. Breakfast is served in the decoy dining room.
Innkeeper(s): Pat & Bob Orendorff.
Rates:$78-84. MC VISA DS. ContPlus Bkfst. 4 rooms. Beds:QT. AC in room. Fishing.
Contact: Robert Orendorff. Certificate may be used: January, February, March. Cannot be used with any other promotion.

"Your home is just beautiful, and your warm, helpful and humorous manner made our trip memorable."

Homestay B&B
517 Richmond Rd
Williamsburg 23185
(804)229-7468 (800)836-7468

1933. This Colonial Revival house is decorated with Victorian pieces inherited from the innkeeper's family. A screened back porch and fireplace in the living room are gathering spots. Collections of hand-crafted Noah's arks may be found throughout the house. The College of William and Mary is adjacent, and Williamsburg's Colonial area is four blocks away.
Innkeeper(s): Barbara & Jim Thomassen.
Rates:$70-85. MC VISA. Full Bkfst. 3 rooms. Beds:KT. AC in room. Bicycling.
Contact: James J. Thomassen Certificate may be used: Anytime Jan. 3, 1995 - March 31, 1995, certain weekends excepted.

Piney Grove at Southall's Plantation

PO Box 1359
Williamsburg 23187-1359
(804)829-2480

1800. The Gordineers welcome you to their two historic homes. Piney Grove is a rare Tidewater log building, in the National Register of Historic Places, located on the Old Main Road among farms, plantations, country stores and quaint churches. Ladysmith House is a modest antebellum plantation house (c. 1857). Both homes are furnished with a unique collection of artifacts and antiques that illustrates the history of the property and area. Guests also enjoy meandering among the gardens, grounds and nature trail.

Innkeeper(s): Brian & Cindy Rae Gordineer.

Rates:$125-150. Full Bkfst. MAP available. 4 rooms. Fireplaces. Beds:DT. Conference Rm. AC, Refrig. in room. Farm. Swimming. Fishing.

Seen in: *New York Times, Richmond Times-Dispatch, Washington Post.*

Contact: Brian Gordineer. Certificate may be used: January-December, 1995 (not on holiday weekends). One room is set aside for participants.

"Thank you for your warm gracious hospitality. We really enjoyed ourselves and look forward to returning."

Williamsburg Manor B&B

600 Richmond Rd
Williamsburg 23185
(804)220-8011 Fax:(804)220-0245

1927. Built during the reconstruction of Colonial Williamsburg, this Georgian brick Colonial is just three blocks from the historic village. A grand

staircase, culinary library, Waverly fabrics, Oriental rugs and antiques are offered. The hosts are culinary professionals, and Michael was the former Executive Chef of Berkeley Plantation. Gourmet regional Virginia dinners are available.

Innkeeper(s): Laura & Michael MacKnight.

Rates:$125. Full Bkfst. Gourmet Dinner. 5 rooms. Beds:Q. TV, AC in

room. Golf. Tennis. Bicycling. Handicap access. Swimming. Fishing.

Seen in: *Williamsburg Magazine.*

Contact: Michael Macknight. Certificate may be used: January, February, March, June, July, August, September, November, Monday-Thursday only.

Woodstock

Azalea House B&B

551 S Main St
Woodstock 22664
(703)459-3500

1892. A white picket fence and garden archway invite guests to this Victorian house. Filled with family antiques and decorated with stenciled ceil-

ings, the inn provides balcony views of the mountains. Margaret is an azalea expert and her gardens proclaim the fact. Nearby are caverns, vineyards, Civil War sites and good antiquing.

Innkeeper(s): Margaret & Price McDonald.

Rates:$50-70. MC VISA AX. Gourmet Brkfst. Teas. 3 rooms. Beds:QD. AC in room. Skiing. Fishing.

Contact: Price McDonald. Certificate may be used: Weekdays Monday through Thursday, excluding the month of October and the day Monday when part of a holiday weekend.

Washington

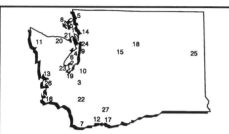

Anacortes

Albatross Bed & Breakfast
5708 Kingsway
Anacortes 98221
(206)293-0677

1927. This Cape Cod-style house is located on an acre, a block away from Skyline Marina. Most of the guest rooms and the inn's deck have views of Burrows Bay, islands or the harbor. Each guest room is individually furnished in a traditional-style decor. The innkeepers will pick up guests from the ferry landing (three minutes away) or from the airport.

Innkeeper(s): Barbie & Ken Arasim.

Rates:$65-85. MC VISA. Full Bkfst. Teas. Evening snacks. 4 rooms. Beds:KQ. Golf. Tennis. Bicycling. Skiing. Handicap access. Swimming. Horseback riding. Fishing.

Seen in: *Apropos Magazine, Business Pulse.*

Contact: Ken Arasim. Certificate may be used: Oct. 15 - June 1 excluding holidays.

"Our stay with you was a comfortable, enjoyable experience. Such cordiality!"

Campbell House
3617 Commercial
Anacortes 98221
(206)293-4910 (800)484-9596

1916. This Victorian farmhouse-style inn is minutes from downtown shopping, beautiful parks, waterfront and the San Juan Ferry. Two of the guest

rooms feature a view of Mt. Baker and Fidalgo Bay. The innkeepers prepare special picnic breakfasts for those catching the early ferry.

Innkeeper(s): Sarah & Doug Jones.

Rates:$60-69. MC VISA. Full Bkfst. Gourmet Brkfst. 2 rooms. Beds:QT. Swimming. Fishing.

Contact: Sarah Jones. Certificate may be used: September-May.

Channel House
2902 Oakes Ave
Anacortes 98221
(206)293-9382 (800)238-4353

1902. Built by an Italian count, the Channel House is designated the Krebs House by the

Historical Home Tour. Guest rooms view Puget Sound and the San Juan Islands, and the ferry is minutes away. The inn has a Victorian flavor, with a library, three fireplaces, and a dining room with French doors leading out to the garden.

Innkeeper(s): Dennis & Patricia McIntyre.

Rates:$69-95. MC VISA AX DS. Full Bkfst. Evening snacks. 6 rooms. Fireplaces. Beds:KQ. Bicycling. Spa. Swimming. Fishing.

Seen in: *Skagit Valley Herald.*

Contact: Dennis McIntyre. Certificate may be used: November-April, Sunday-Thursday only.

"The house is spectacular and your friendly thoughtfulness is the icing on the cake."

Hasty Pudding House

1312 8th Street
Anacortes 98221
(206)293-5773 (800)368-5588

1913. This Edwardian Craftsman house is located in a quiet neighborhood near historic downtown, the waterfront and Causland Park. The front porch solarium contains wicker furnishings, while the house is decorated with antiques, lace curtains and coordinated wallpapers.

Innkeeper(s): Melinda & Mikel Hasty.

Rates:$60-85. MC VISA AX DS. Full Bkfst. 4 rooms. Beds:KQT. Golf. Tennis. Swimming. Fishing.

Contact: Melinda Hasty. Certificate may be used: November - March, Sunday - Thursday only.

"You and your beautiful bed and breakfast really made our trip."

Outlook B&B

608 "H" Ave
Anacortes 98221
(206)293-3505

1910. This Craftsman home has been in the Robinson family for more than 75 years. The yard is filled with azaleas, rhododendrons, camellias and some of the original landscaping. A recently added deck and living room enhance the water and mountain views from Mount Baker to Guemes

Channel and the San Juans. Enjoy the antiques and six-foot Jacuzzi tub in Edythe's Room, then watch sailboat races, sea lions, bald eagles and, occasionally, the Northern Lights. Walk downtown for shops, restaurants and galleries.

Innkeeper(s): Ralph & Trish Robinson.

Rates:$69-85. MC VISA. Full Bkfst. Gourmet Brkfst. 2 rooms. Beds:Q. TV in room. Skiing. Swimming. Fishing.

Contact: Patricia Robinson. Certificate may be used: Oct. 15 to April 15.

Sunset Beach B&B

100 Sunset Beach
Anacortes 98221
(206)293-5428 (800)359-3448

1972. Located next to Washington Park and on two waterfront acres, this ranch house offers views of seven of the San Juan Islands. There are two decks, a hot tub and flower gardens that bloom next to each guest room. The Honeymoon Suite has Oriental decor. Full breakfasts feature biscuits and gravy, strawberry waffles or blueberry pancakes. The ferry to the San Juans is three minutes away.

Innkeeper(s): Joann & Hall Harker.

Rates:$63-79. MC VISA. Full Bkfst. 3 rooms. 2 with shared baths. Beds:Q. Phone in room. Handicap access. Spa. Swimming. Fishing.

Contact: Harold Harker. Certificate may be used: Jan. 10, 1995 to May 10, 1995.

Anderson Island

The Inn at Burg's Landing

8808 Villa Beach Rd
Anderson Island 98303
(206)884-9185

1987. A short ferry trip from Steilacoom and Tacoma, this log homestead boasts beautiful views of Mt. Rainier, Puget Sound and the Cascade Mountains. The master bedroom features a skylight and a private whirlpool bath. After a full breakfast, guests can spend the day at the inn's private beach. Golf, hiking and freshwater lakes are nearby, and the area has many seasonal activities, including Fourth of July fireworks, the Anderson Island fair and parade in September and a February Sweetheart Dance and Dinner.

Innkeeper(s): Ken & Annie Burg.

Rates:$65-90. MC VISA AX. Full Bkfst. Picnic lunches. 3 rooms. Beds:Q. Golf. Tennis. Bicycling. Skiing. Spa. Swimming. Horseback riding. Fishing.

Seen in: *Sunset, Tacoma News Tribune, Portland Oregonian.*

Contact: Annie Burg. Certificate may be used: June-September, Sunday through Thursday; October-May anytime.

Ashford

Growly Bear B&B
37311 SR 706, PO Box 103
Ashford 98304
(206)569-2339 (800)700-2339

1890. Guests at Growly Bear will appreciate the cozy, rustic setting of this 100-year-old mountain home located only a mile from the entrance of Mt. Rainier National Park. Guest rooms are large and feature comfortable furnishings, quilts and a sitting room. A full gourmet mountain country breakfast is served each morning with fresh pastries made at a bakery located on the premises. The breakfast is a great start to a day of hiking or cross-country skiing. The inn is an ideal location for park visitors and is four miles from the village of Ashford.
Innkeeper(s): Susan Jenny.

Rates:$70-90. MC VISA AX. Full Bkfst. 2 rooms. Beds:Q. Skiing. Fishing.

Contact: Susan Jenny. Certificate may be used: Anytime except June, July, August.

Mountain Meadows Inn B&B
28912 SR 706E
Ashford 98304
(206)569-2788

1910. Originally built for the superintendent of the Pacific National Lumber Company, the house boasts hanging baskets of fuchsias which accentuate the veranda. Comfortable guest rooms feature a view of the woodland setting, occasionally visited by deer and elk. An unusual collection of railroad artifacts, including museum-quality model trains, is found throughout the inn. Breakfasts are prepared on an 1889 wood cooking stove. The innkeeper also operates the Hobo Inn, six miles away, which features guest rooms in renovated railroad cabooses, one with its own Jacuzzi.
Innkeeper(s): Chad Darrah.

Rates:$65-95. MC VISA. Full Bkfst. 5 rooms. Beds:KQT. Conference Rm. Skiing. Swimming. Horseback riding. Fishing.

Seen in: Seattle Times, Pacific Northwest, Eastside Weekly, Prime Times.

Contact: Chad Darrah. Certificate may be used: October through May.

"Our stay here will be one of the nicest memories of our vacation."

Bainbridge Island

Bombay House
8490 Beck Rd NE
Bainbridge Island 98110
(206)842-3926 (800)598-3920

1907. This Victorian captain's house is set atop Blakely Hill, amidst colorful, unstructured gardens. It boasts a quaint widow's walk and an old-fash-

ioned gazebo overlooking picturesque sailboats and ferries cruising through Rich Passage. Take the scenic Seattle ferry ride six miles to Bainbridge.
Innkeeper(s): Bunny Cameron & Roger Kanchuk.

Rates:$55-125. MC VISA AX. ContPlus Bkfst. AP available. Gourmet Brkfst. Teas. 4 rooms. 2 with shared baths. Beds:KQT. Conference Rm. AC in room. Farm. Golf. Tennis. Bicycling. Swimming. Fishing.

Seen in: Bainbridge Review.

Contact: Roger Kanchuk. Certificate may be used: Sunday-Wednesday all year.

"We had a great time thanks to you and your husband for your hospitality."

Bellingham

Anderson Creek Lodge B&B
5602 Mission Rd
Bellingham 98226
(206)966-2126 (800)441-5585
Fax:(206)966-3465

1979. Take a plunge in the indoor heated pool or workout in the exercise room at this woodland and meadow inn. The Lodge presents an atmosphere of Pacific Northwest individuality and distinctive character in each room. Secluded in the woods behind the Lodge is the Retreat Center. Modern dormitories and six conference rooms can be utilized for a variety of group functions accommodating up to 70 people. Guests can hike the wilderness trail by Anderson Creek or take advantage of 25 acres of sports fields. The Lodge is centrally located between Seattle and Vancouver.

Innkeeper(s): Carol Mobley.

Rates:$90-125. MC VISA AX DS. Full Bkfst. Gourmet Brkfst. Picnic lunches. Evening snacks. 5 rooms. 3 with shared baths. Fireplaces. Beds:KT. Conference Rm. Skiing. Swimming. Fishing.

Contact: Robert Bell. Certificate may be used: Sunday-Thursday excluding holidays. Sept. 30, 1994-June 15, 1995 and Sept. 30-Dec. 31, 1995.

Bremerton

Willcox House
2390 Tekiu Rd
Bremerton 98312
(206)830-4492 Fax:(206)830-0506

1936. Colonel Julian Willcox and his family, once members of San Francisco high society, selected Lionel Pries to build this home on a wooded bluff overlooking Hood Canal. Holding court thereafter, the family entertained fashionable Northwest personalities, including Clark Gable. The 7,800-square-foot manse was constructed with a slate tile exterior, copper roofing and vast expanses of small-paned windows, affording views of the shimmering waters, the Olympic mountains and forested hillsides. There are five marble and copper fireplaces, silk wallpaper, oak floors, fine antiques and period pieces throughout. The Julian Room sports a double whirlpool tub.

Innkeeper(s): Cecilia & Phillip Hughes.

Rates:$115-175. MC VISA. Full Bkfst. Gourmet Dinner. Picnic lunches. Evening snacks. 5 rooms. Fireplaces. Beds:KQT. Swimming. Fishing.

Seen in: *Country Inns, Seattle Times, The Olympian, Journal American.*

Contact: Cecilia Hughes. Certificate may be used: October - June, Monday - Thursday excluding holidays.

"Diane & I and Clark love the place and delight in the knowledge that all Californians aren't bad - in fact some are downright wonderful."

Camas

Washingtonia Inn
602 NE 18th Loop
Camas 98607
(206)834-7629

1902. This Dutch Colonial farmhouse is on more than an acre at the entrance to the Columbia River Gorge. The innkeepers are a designer and artist, and rooms feature original artwork, period furniture, cable TVs, and best of all, stunning views of both the gorge and Mt. Hood. The master suite has a Jacuzzi tub and fireplace. There are more than two acres of lawns, with hammocks, a waterfall, rose garden and swings that hang from two walnut

trees. By prior arrangement you may have special gourmet dinners as well as sailing excursions on the river.

Innkeeper(s): Denys Larsen, Jay Chapman.

Rates:$55-175. MC VISA. Full Bkfst. Gourmet Brkfst, Lunch, Dinner. Picnic lunches. Teas. Evening snacks. 5 rooms. 4 with shared baths. Fireplaces. Beds:KQ. TV in room. Skiing. Spa. Exercise room. Swimming. Fishing.

Contact: Denys Larsen. Certificate may be used: All dates except national holidays.

Coupeville

Captain Whidbey
2072 W Captain Whidbey Inn Rd
Coupeville 98239
(206)678-4097 (800)366-4097
Fax:(206)678-4110

1907. Overlooking Whidbey Island's Penn Cove, this log house inn has comfortable rooms featuring down comforters, feather beds and views of lagoons and gardens. The dining room also has a magnificent view and guests can enjoy their meals by the fireplace. The chef utilizes local catches like steelhead fish, salmon, Dungeness crab, spot prawns and Penn Cove mussels. The innkeeper is also a sailing captain and guests often book an afternoon on his 52-foot ketch Cutty Sark. The innkeeper's family has run the inn for more than 30 years.

Innkeeper(s): Captain John Colby Stone.

Rates:$85-195. MC VISA AX DC DS CB. Full Bkfst. EP. Gourmet Brkfst, Dinner. Picnic lunches. Evening snacks. 29 rooms. 12 with shared baths. Fireplaces. Beds:KQT. Conference Rm. Phone, Refrig. in room. Bicycling. Swimming. Fishing.

Seen in: *Gourmet Magazine, USA-Weekend.*

Contact: John Colby Stone. Certificate may be used: October - May, Sunday - Thursday.

"I visit and stay here once a year and love it."

Colonel Crockett Farm
1012 S Ft. Casey Rd
Coupeville 98239
(206)678-3711

1855. In the National Register, this Victorian farmhouse presides over 40 island acres of lawns, meadows and country gardens. Sweeping views of Crockett Lake and Admiralty Inlet may be enjoyed from the inn and its grounds. The Crockett Room, a favorite of newlyweds, has a blue chintz canopied bed and fainting couch. Danny DeVito and Michael Douglas stayed at the inn during the Coupeville filming of *War of the Roses.*

Innkeeper(s): Robert & Beulah Whitlow.

Rates:$65-95. MC VISA. Full Bkfst. 5 rooms. Beds:KQT. Farm. Fishing.

Seen in: *Peninsula, Portland Oregonian, Country Inns, Glamour.*

Contact: Beulah Whitlow. Certificate may be used: October through April, Sunday (except on three-day holiday weekends) through Thursday (except Thanksgiving and Christmas).

"Everyone felt quite at home...such a beautiful spot."

The Inn at Penn Cove

702 N Main, PO Box 85
Coupeville 98239
(206)678-8000 (800)688-2683

1887. Two restored historic houses, one a fanciful peach and white Italianate confection in the National Register, comprise the inn. Each house contains only three guest rooms affording a multitude of small parlors for guests to enjoy. The most romantic accommodation is Desiree's Room with a fireplace, a whirlpool tub for two and mesmerizing views of Puget Sound and Mt. Baker.

Innkeeper(s): Gladys & Mitchell Howard.

Rates:$60-125. MC VISA AX DS. Full Bkfst. 6 rooms. 2 with shared baths. Fireplaces. Beds:KQ. Conference Rm. Spa. Exercise room.

Seen in: *Whidbey News-Times, Country Inns, Glamour.*

Contact: Mitchell Howard. Certificate may be used: Monday-Thursday (Memorial Day through Labor Day); Sunday-Friday (April 1-Memorial Day and Labor Day-Oct. 31); any night Nov. 1-March 31.

"Our hosts were warm and friendly, but also gave us plenty of space and privacy - a good combination."

The Victorian B&B

PO Box 761, 602 N Main
Coupeville 98239
(206)678-5305

1889. This graceful Italianate Victorian sits in the heart of one of the nation's few historic reserves. It was built for German immigrant Jacob Jenne, who became the proprietor of the Central Hotel on Front Street. Noted for having the first running water on the island, the house's old wooden water tower stands in the back garden. An old-fashioned storefront, once the local dentist's office, sits demurely behind a picket fence, now a private hideaway for guests.

Innkeeper(s): Al & Marion Sasso.

Rates:$65-100. MC VISA DS. Full Bkfst. 3 rooms. Beds:Q. Golf. Horseback riding. Fishing.

Seen in: *Seattle Times, Country Inns.*

Contact: Alfred Sasso. Certificate may be used: Sunday through Thursday - September through May.

"If kindness and generosity are the precursors to success (and I certainly hope they are!), your success is assured."

Deer Harbor

Deep Meadow Farm B&B

PO Box 321
Deer Harbor 98243
(206)376-5866

1939. Located on 40 acres, this homestead is one of the few family farms still remaining on Orcas Island. It served for many years as the local dairy farm. Now, with an added wing and new front

porch it serves as a handsome B&B. Midwestern farm furniture and Civil War memorabilia furnish the inn, including a certificate from President Lincoln signed to the innkeeper's great-great-great Grandfather. There are two horses, a border collie and two cats. Kayaking and whale watching are popular pastimes.

Innkeeper(s): Gary & Anna Boyle.

Rates:$85-95. Full Bkfst. Teas. 2 rooms. Farm. Spa. Swimming. Fishing.

Contact: Anna Boyle. Certificate may be used: Oct. 1, 1994-April 30, 1995; Oct. 1, 1995-Dec. 31, 1995.

Edmonds

Harrison House

210 Sunset Ave
Edmonds 98020
(206)776-4748

1982. This new, Beaux Arts-style inn is a waterfront home with a sweeping view of Puget Sound and the Olympic Mountains. Large guest rooms include a private deck on which you may entertain and view the boating activities. The inn is located one block north of the Edmonds-Kingston Ferry Dock. The ferry crosses Puget Sound to the Olympic Peninsula on which sits the beautiful Olympic National Park with its abundance of wildlife and enchanting rain forest. Guests can walk to the boat harbor, fishing pier, beaches and shopping.

Innkeeper(s): Jody & Harve Harrison.

Rates:$55-65. Full Bkfst. 2 rooms. Beds:KQ. TV, Phone, Refrig. in room. Skiing. Swimming. Fishing.

Contact: Harve Harrison. Certificate may be used: Nov. 1, 1994 through March 30, 1995.

Enumclaw

White Rose Inn
1610 Griffin Ave
Enumclaw 98022
(206)825-7194

1922. Axel Hanson, owned the White River Lumber Company and built this 22-room, 8,500 square-foot Colonial mansion with Honduran

mahogany and quarter-sawn oak. A large canopied four-poster cherry bed, crystal chandelier, and original fresco ceilings appropriately adorn the Paradise Room. There is a rose garden, sunroom, and formal dining room. Guests enjoy walking to town for dinner and shopping.

Innkeeper(s): Linda Klein.

Rates:$85-95. MC VISA. Gourmet Brkfst. Teas. 4 rooms. Beds:QD. Conference Rm. Skiing. Fishing.

Contact: Linda Klein. Certificate may be used: Not during major holidays or last weekend in July. Not on Saturday nights.

Ferndale

Slater Heritage House B&B
1371 W Axton
Ferndale 98248
(206)384-4273 Fax:(206)384-4273

1904. Two acres surround this three-story Princess Ann Victorian. An unusual double tiered wraparound porch offers inviting views and respite. It was originally built beside Nook Sack River and in 1989 moved to its present location. Elegance in Ebony is a popular room with black accents, and no maid who previously inhabited The Maid's Room had it so good, for there is now a jetted tub.

Innkeeper(s): Dave & Laura Armitage.

Rates:$57-79. VISA. Full Bkfst. Gourmet Brkfst. Teas. 4 rooms. Beds:Q. TV in room. Farm. Skiing. Handicap access. Fishing.

Contact: Laura Armitage. Certificate may be used: October through May.

Forks

Miller Tree Inn
PO Box 953, 654 E Division St
Forks 98331
(206)374-6806

1917. The Miller Tree Inn is a modernized farmhouse set on three acres adjacent to a favorite grazing spot for local elk. The inn caters to steelhead, salmon and trout fishermen, and will serve breakfast at 4:30 a.m. with advance notice. Comfortable rooms and economical rates make it a popular stopover in this logging town.

Innkeeper(s): Ted & Prue Miller.

Rates:$50-55. MC VISA. Full Bkfst. Teas. Evening snacks. 6 rooms. 4 with shared baths. Beds:DT. Farm. Skiing. Spa. Fishing.

Seen in: *Peninsula Business Journal, Walking Magazine.*

Contact: Prue Miller. Certificate may be used: October - May.

"The homey and warm atmosphere was wonderful. You've spoiled us."

Freeland-Whidbey Island

Seaside Cottage
213 E Sandpiper Rd
Freeland-Whidbey Island 98249
(206)331-8455 Fax:(206)331-8636

1920. Located on a sandy beach, Seaside Cottage provides views of the San Juan Islands and the Olympic Mountains from the living room and kitchen. You also may wish to enjoy the view without getting out of bed in the morning. A breakfast tray and easy set up is organized for you upon your arrival so you can have breakfast at your leisure. Afterwards, walk through the old-growth forest, fish from the beach or boat from the dock. Don't miss the Berry Farm Winery while on the island.

Innkeeper(s): Cliff & Virginia Lindsey.

Rates:$60-95. Full Bkfst. 2 rooms. Fireplaces. Beds:KQ. TV, Phone, Refrig. in room. Handicap access. Swimming. Fishing.

Contact: Cliff Lindsey. Certificate may be used: Oct. 15, 1994 to April 30, 1995 and Oct. 15, 1995 to Dec. 31, 1995.

Friday Harbor

Friday's
35 First St
Friday Harbor 98250-2023
(206)378-5848 (800)352-2632

1891. This hotel once served as the hostelry for Chinese laborers who worked at the old cannery.

Now, newly renovated, it boasts flower-filled window boxes, stained-glass windows and ceiling fans. Oak antiques, limited-edition wildlife prints and Victorian carpeting provide pleasant touches. Adding to the happy ambiance

are double showers and whirlpool tubs. Friday's is a short walk from the ferry terminal. Rent a bicycle while on the island and visit Lime Kiln Park, a whale-watching park.

Innkeeper(s): Debbie & Steve Demarest.

Rates:$55-155. MC VISA AX. ContPlus Bkfst. 11 rooms. 7 with shared baths. Beds:KQT. Golf. Swimming. Fishing.

Seen in: *Island Sounder, Journal of the San Juan Island.*

Contact: Steve Demarest. Certificate may be used: Nov. 1-April 30 excluding holidays.

"Clean and restful."

Mariella Inn & Cottages
630 Turn Pt Rd
Friday Harbor 98250
(206)378-6868 Fax:(206)378-6822

1902. This Queen Anne Victorian rests on nine acres, surrounded on three sides by water. There are 11 rooms and seven waterfront cottages. An

English flower garden, long stretches of lawn, a trout-filled pond, apple orchard and clumps of blackberries offer pleasant strolls. Panoramic water views are enjoyed from the dining room where breakfast is served. (Dinner is available by advance reservations.) For a special occasion choose Arequipa, with an antique walnut bed and spectacular view of the water, or the Ivy Cottage with its waterfront deck.

Innkeeper(s): Arthur & Alison Lohrey.

Rates:$70-225. MC VISA. Full Bkfst. Gourmet Brkfst. Dinner. Evening snacks. 11 rooms. 7 with shared baths. Beds:KQ. Bicycling. Spa. Fishing.

Contact: Arthur Lohrey. Certificate may be used: Oct. 1 - May 20.

San Juan Inn B&B
PO Box 776, 50 Spring St
Friday Harbor 98250
(206)378-2070 (800)742-8210
Fax:(206)378-6437

1873. In the National Register, this old European-style hotel is filled with stained glass, old photographs and flowers picked from the inn's garden. A Victorian settee is situated under a cherry tree within sniffing distance of the lilacs and roses. It's a half block to the ferry landing. The innkeeper speaks Danish, German, Norwegian, French, Swedish and English.

Innkeeper(s): Annette & Eugene "Skip" Metzger.

Rates:$65-93. MC VISA AX DS. ContPlus Bkfst. EP. 10 rooms. 6 with shared baths. Beds:QDT. Swimming. Fishing.

Contact: Eugene Metzger. Certificate may be used: October-December, 1994. January-May, October-December, 1995. Not available on holidays or during holiday periods of 1994 and 1995.

Tucker House B&B with Cottages
260 B St
Friday Harbor 98250
(206)378-2783 (800)742-8210
Fax:(206)378-6437

1898. Only two blocks from the ferry landing, the white picket fence bordering Tucker House is a welcome sight for guests. The spindled entrance leads to the parlor and the simply furnished five guest rooms in the house. A separate cottage next to the hot tub is popular with honeymooners.

Innkeeper(s): Eugene & Annette Metzger.

Rates:$75-125. MC VISA AX DS. EP. Gourmet Brkfst. 5 rooms. 2 with shared baths. Fireplaces. Beds:Q. TV, Refrig. in room. Spa. Swimming. Fishing.

Seen in: *Sunset Magazine, Pacific Northwest Magazine, Western Boatman.*

Contact: Eugene Metzger. Certificate may be used: October- December, 1994; January - June, 1995, October - December, 1995. Not valid on holidays or during holiday seasons.

"A lovely place, the perfect getaway. We'll be back."

Gig Harbor

Krestine, A Tall Ship
3311 Harborview Dr, PO Box 31
Gig Harbor 98335
(206)858-9395

1903. This is your chance to stay overnight on a tall ship. The handsome ketch is a historic 100-foot sailing vessel. The focal point of the living quarters is the 20-square-foot Great Saloon with its wood

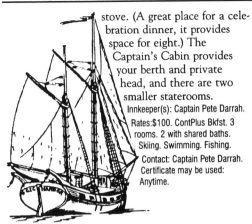

stove. (A great place for a celebration dinner, it provides space for eight.) The Captain's Cabin provides your berth and private head, and there are two smaller staterooms.

Innkeeper(s): Captain Pete Darrah.

Rates:$100. ContPlus Bkfst. 3 rooms. 2 with shared baths. Skiing. Swimming. Fishing.

Contact: Captain Pete Darrah. Certificate may be used: Anytime.

Greenbank

Guest House Cottages, A B&B Inn
3366 S Hwy 525, Whidbey Island
Greenbank 98253
(206)678-3115

1920. These storybook cottages and log home are nestled within a peaceful forest on 25 acres. The Hansel and Gretel cottage features stained-glass and

criss-cross pared windows that give it the feel of a gingerbread house. Ask for the Lodge and you'll enjoy a private setting with a pond just beyond your deck. Inside is a Jacuzzi tub, stone fireplace, king bed, antiques and an intimate hunting lodge atmosphere.

Innkeeper(s): Mary Jane & Donald Creger.

Rates:$135-285. MC VISA AX DS. ContPlus Bkfst. 7 rooms. Fireplaces. Beds:KQT. TV, AC, Refrig. in room. Golf. Spa. Exercise room. Swimming. Horseback riding. Fishing.

Seen in: *Los Angeles Times, Woman's Day, Sunset, Country Inns, Bride's.*

Contact: Mary Jane Creger. Certificate may be used: Only from Oct. 15 through March 15, Monday through Thursday, holiday periods exempt and holiday weeks, 1994 and 1995, discount is offered on regular rates.

"The wonderful thing is to be by yourselves and rediscover what's important."

Home Valley

Sojourner Inn
MP 0.39 L Berge Rd
Home Valley 98648
(509)427-7070 Fax:(509)427-4229

1979. A contemporary tri-level cedar house, the Sojourner is set on a ridge with unparalleled views of the confluence of the Columbia and Wind Rivers. National forests surround the inn's four acres, and a pair of bald eagles reside on the property. In addition to the stunning river views, the inn offers an excellent library, back deck and patio. The innkeeper is a Cordon Bleu chef and can provide dinners and receptions for special occasions.

Innkeeper(s): Judith Yeckel & Robert Davis.

Rates:$50-100. MC VISA. Full Bkfst. Gourmet Brkfst, Lunch, Dinner. Picnic lunches. Evening snacks. 5 rooms. 2 with shared baths. Beds:QD. Phone, AC in room. Skiing. Handicap access. Swimming. Fishing.

Contact: Judith Yeckel. Certificate may be used: All year except for national-holiday weekends and special events.

Hoquiam

Lytle House
509 Chenault
Hoquiam 98550
(206)533-2320 (800)677-2320
Fax:(206)533-4025

1889. Set high on a hill overlooking the harbor, this massive three-story Queen Anne Victorian was built by a lumberman. There are graceful sun porches, arches and gingerbread trim. The Treehouse Room is shaded by a 100-foot copper beech tree, while the Rose Room offers a view of

the harbor. Afternoon tea is available. The innkeepers will host a murder mystery dinner party or elegant high tea by prior arrangement.
Innkeeper(s): Robert & Dayna Bencala.

Rates:$65-105. MC VISA AX. Full Bkfst. AP available. Teas. Evening snacks. 9 rooms. 6 with shared baths. Beds:QT. Fishing.

Contact: Dayna Bencala. Certificate may be used: Sept. 30 - May 31.

Kirkland

Shumway Mansion
11410 99th Place NE
Kirkland 98033
(206)823-2303 Fax:(206)822-0421

1909. This resplendent 22-room, 10,000 square-foot mansion is situated on more than two acres over-looking Juanita Bay. With a large ballroom and veranda with water views, few could guess that a short time ago, the building was hoisted on hydraulic lifts. It was then pulled three miles across town to its present site, near the beach.
Innkeeper(s): Richard & Salli Harris & family.

Rates:$65-95. MC VISA AX. Full Bkfst. Evening snacks. 8 rooms. Beds:Q. Conference Rm. Phone in room. Handicap access. Spa. Sauna. Exercise room. Swimming. Fishing.

Seen in: *Northgate Journal, Journal American, Northwest Living.*

Contact: R. W. Harris. Certificate may be used: Sunday through Thursday.

"Guests enjoy the mansion so much they don't want to leave." Northwest Living.

La Conner

Heather House
505 Maple St, PO Box 237
La Conner 98257-0237
(206)466-4675

1979. Built as a careful replica of a shingled Cape Cod house in Massachusetts, Heather House features wainscoting, mantels and floors of oak. Next door is a salt-box cottage, home to the innkeepers. The Fireplace Room offers a queen bed, sofa and wood-burning fireplace. Freshly baked scones are

the specialty of the house. You are invited to raid the refrigerator for snacks throughout the day, and there are bicycles to borrow.
Innkeeper(s): Wayne & Bev Everton.

Rates:$50-70. MC VISA. ContPlus Bkfst. 3 rooms. 3 with shared baths. Beds:QT. Farm. Bicycling. Fishing.

Contact: Wayne Everton. Certificate may be used: Anytime except month of August.

Ridgeway B&B
1292 McLean Rd, PO Box 475
La Conner 98257
(206)428-8068 (800)428-8068

1928. A Dutch Colonial farmhouse, Ridgeway is on two acres. From here you can watch migrating swans and snow geese in the fall. Homemade

desserts are served each evening and in the morning, a full farm breakfast. Your host is a pilot and can arrange a private flight over the Skagit Valley and the San Juan Islands.
Innkeeper(s): Louise & John Kelly.

Rates:$75-125. MC VISA AX DS. Full Bkfst. Evening snacks. 6 rooms. 3 with shared baths. Beds:KQT. Farm. Skiing. Swimming. Fishing.

Contact: John Kelly. Certificate may be used: Sept. 15 through March 15, Sunday through Thursday except US and Canadian holidays.

"We've stayed in a lot of B&Bs and this is one of our top five. It was great!" D.L., Calif.

Langley

Twickenham House B&B Inn
5023 Langley Rd
Langley 98260
(206)221-2334 (800)874-5009

1991. If the beauty of Puget Sound isn't enough, this island inn will be sure to satisfy. Innkeepers Maureen and Ray Cooke take the idea of bed and breakfast seriously. They offer comfortable rooms with French Canadian and European pine furniture, and a gourmet, three-course breakfast each morning. The home offers three living rooms with fireplaces and a British pub area. The inn shares the expansive 10-acre grounds with Northwest evergreens, ducks, sheep, hens and roosters. The island has many restaurants, boutiques and shops. Langley holds several seasonal events, including a country fair and a mystery weekend.

Innkeeper(s): Maureen & Ray Cooke.

Rates:$85-120. MC VISA. Gourmet Brkfst. 6 rooms. Beds:QT. Golf. Tennis. Bicycling. Handicap access. Swimming. Horseback riding. Fishing.

Seen in: *Sunset, Country Living, Oregonian, Odyssey.*

Contact: Maureen Cooke. Certificate may be used: Sunday-Thursday, November, December, January, February, March, April, May, and June. Not available July, August, September and October.

"Gracious and friendly hosts."

Leavenworth

Bavarian Meadows B&B

11099 Eagle Creek Rd
Leavenworth 98826
(509)548-4449

1982. Following a European country theme, Bavarian Meadows offers Belgian waffles, Dutch honey, bratwurst and fresh eggs or muesli for breakfast. There is a hot tub that is open all year, and hay and sleigh rides are available at a farm nearby. Kitchen and laundry privileges are extended to guests.

Innkeeper(s): Bob & Judy Riley.

Rates:$55-80. Full Bkfst. Gourmet Brkfst. Picnic lunches. Evening snacks. 3 rooms. Beds:Q. TV, AC, Refrig. in room. Bicycling. Skiing. Spa. Fishing.

Contact: Judith Riley. Certificate may be used: January through April, June through Sept. 15.

Bosch Garten B&B

9846 Dye Rd
Leavenworth 98826
(509)548-6900 Fax:(509)548-6076

1992. This is a new house on one acre, offering mountain and orchard views. Guest rooms are on the second floor. Wedge Mountain and the

Cascades may be seen. The garden has a hot tub, waterfall and stream and there is a covered deck. There are also herb, flower, rose, rock, alpine and Japanese gardens.

Innkeeper(s): Myke & Cal Bosch.

Rates:$85. MC VISA. Full Bkfst. Gourmet Brkfst. 3 rooms. Beds:K. TV, Phone, AC in room. Bicycling. Skiing. Swimming. Fishing.

Contact: Ruth Bosch. Certificate may be used: Not applicable during festivals (Autumn Leaf, Christmas Lighting, Maifest), good any other time.

Haus Rohrbach Pension

12882 Ranger Rd
Leavenworth 98826
(509)548-7024 (800)548-4477

1975. This inn is located two minutes away from the village. Private fireplaces and whirlpools for two are features of each of three suites. Sourdough pancakes and cinnamon rolls are specialties of the house. Guests often take breakfast out to the deck to enjoy pastoral views that include grazing sheep and a pleasant pond. In the evening, return from white-water rafting, tobagganning, skiing or sleigh rides to soak in the hot tub or indulge in the inn's complimentary desserts served in front of the wood stove.

Innkeeper(s): Robert & Kathryn Harrild.

Rates:$65-160. MC VISA AX DS. Full Bkfst. EP. Picnic lunches. Evening snacks. 12 rooms. 4 with shared baths. Fireplaces. Beds:KQ. Conference Rm. AC, Refrig. in room. Bicycling. Skiing. Handicap access. Spa. Swimming. Horseback riding. Fishing.

Contact: Kathryn Harrild. Certificate may be used: September through June 1994 and 1995-otherwise subject to availability.

Old Blewett Pass B&B

3470 Hwy 97
Leavenworth 98826
(509)548-4475

1908. Turn-of-the-century travelers stopped at this inn before crossing the mountain passes in search of their destiny. Today, weary travelers still will find this rustic inn a refreshing place for rest and relaxation. A traditional breakfast with bacon, eggs, sausages, waffles or perhaps omelettes, cereals and muffins are sure to satisfy. Innkeepers Dave and Laura Wagner are happy to show guests the secrets of gold panning, and you can try your luck in Peshastin Creek, which runs through the property. Leavenworth is 15 minutes away.

Innkeeper(s): Dave & Laura Wagner.

Rates:$75-90. MC VISA. Full Bkfst. Teas. 4 rooms. Beds:QT. Bicycling. Skiing. Swimming. Fishing.

Contact: Laura Wagner. Certificate may be used: Anytime except during local festivals and holidays.

"So glad we were sent this way."

Pine River Ranch
19668 Highway 207
Leavenworth 98826
(509)763-3959

1940. Thirty-five acres surround this old farmhouse, which originally served as Skiland Dairy. A block barn and silo still stand. To announce the full ranch breakfast, the breakfast triangle is rung. Guests enjoy walking along the creek, gathering eggs or checking out the barn, wildlife trails, beaver dams and meadows. The guest house is a separate cabin for eight with its own hot tub and view of the pond, valley and mountains. The Ponderosa Suite offers a private Jacuzzi, fireplace, pine canopy bed and forest-green slate floors.

Innkeeper(s): Michael & Mary Ann Zenk.
Rates:$75-145. MC VISA. Full Bkfst. AP available. Gourmet Brkfst. Picnic lunches. Teas. Evening snacks. 5 rooms. 2 with shared baths. Fireplaces. Beds:Q. TV, AC, Refrig. in room. Farm. Bicycling. Skiing. Handicap access. Spa. Swimming. Fishing.
Contact: Mary Ann Jackson-Zenk. Certificate may be used: March through May, anytime excluding holidays; June through February, excluding weekends, holidays and month of December.

Long Beach

Boreas B&B
607 N Boulevard, PO Box 1344
Long Beach 98631
(206)642-8069

1920. This inn started as a beach house and was remodeled eclectically with decks and a massive stone fireplace. There are two living rooms that offer views of the beach. Guest rooms all have ocean or mountain views (depending on the weather). Guests can enjoy the hot tub on the sun deck, take the path that winds through the dunes to the surf, or walk to the boardwalk, restaurants and shopping.

Innkeeper(s): Sally Davis & Coleman White.
Rates:$65-95. MC VISA. Full Bkfst. Teas. 4 rooms. 2 with shared baths. Beds:QT. Bicycling. Spa. Fishing.
Contact: Sally Davis. Certificate may be used: Between Sept. 15 - May 15 excluding holiday and festival weekends.

Scandinavian Gardens Inn
Rt 1, Box 36, 1610 S California St
Long Beach 98631-9801
(206)642-8877 (800)988-9277

Fax:(206)642-8763

1977. You are asked to honor a Scandinavian custom of removing your shoes upon entering this B&B. White wool carpeting and blond-wood pieces decorate the living room. A recreation room offers a hot tub and Finnish sauna. The Icelandic Room has an antique armoire and hand-painted cabinets, while the Swedish Suite features a two-person soaking tub tucked into a private nook. Breakfast items such as creamed rice, shrimp au gratin and Danish pastries are served smorgasbord style with the hosts in costume.

Innkeeper(s): Rod & Marilyn Dakan.
Rates:$65-110. MC VISA. Full Bkfst. EP. Gourmet Brkfst. 5 rooms. Beds:QT. Refrig. in room. Spa. Sauna. Exercise room. Swimming. Fishing.
Contact: Marilyn Dakan. Certificate may be used: Year-round except holiday and festival weekends. If Saturday night included, must be three-night minimum.

Lyle

Lyle Hotel Restaurant and Bar
PO Box 838
Lyle 98635
(509)365-5953 Fax:(509)365-2128

1905. Located one block from the mouth of the Klickitat and Columbia Rivers, this concrete and stucco structure was originally built as a railroad hotel. All the rooms have river views, including the hotel dining room. Dinner here offers specialties such as grilled halibut with cilantro citrus salsa complemented by a wide selection of Northwest brews. Nearby is a hunting preserve for game birds and prized spots for river rafting and kayaking.

Innkeeper(s): Cal Wood & Valya Coole.
Rates:$45-48. MC VISA. Gourmet Dinner. 9 rooms. 9 with shared baths. Beds:KQT. Bicycling. Skiing. Swimming. Fishing.
Contact: Calvin Wood. Certificate may be used: Sept. 15-Jan. 1; April 1-May 15.

Manson

Proctor House
495 Lloyd Rd, Rt 1, Box 104
Manson 98831
(509)687-6361 (800)441-1233
Fax:(509)687-6106

1986. Eleven acres surround this newly built European farmhouse, a mile from the lake. The Lake Chelan suite provides a panoramic water and orchard view. A private deck, sitting area and fireplace are included. Lake Chelan is 55 miles long

and with the surrounding mountains rising to 6,000 feet, it affords scenic vistas. Be sure to book the boat tour.

Innkeeper(s): Gail D. Proctor.

Rates:$77-125. MC VISA AX. Full Bkfst. AP available. 4 rooms. Fireplaces. Beds:KQ. AC in room. Skiing. Spa. Sauna. Exercise room. Swimming. Fishing.

Contact: Gail Proctor. Certificate may be used: Nov. 1 - April 15.

Nahcotta

Our House in Nahcotta B&B
PO Box 33
Nahcotta 98637
(206)665-6667

1930. Located across the street from Willapa Bay, this three-story Victorian Stick house has been decorated by the innkeeper, an interior designer and master gardener. Guests enjoy a private parlor, homemade breads and the inn's special fruit plate. The highly rated Ark Restaurant is a few steps away. The Long Beach Peninsula offers a boardwalk, salmon fishing, cranberry bogs, bird watching and a hard-sand public driving beach.

Innkeeper(s): Norma Riley.

Rates:$85. MC VISA. Full Bkfst. Gourmet Brkfst, Dinner. Picnic lunches. 3 rooms. 1 with shared bath. Fireplaces. Beds:Q. Bicycling. Swimming. Fishing.

Contact: Norma Riley. Certificate may be used: Monday through Thursday, all year.

Olga

Spring Bay Inn
PO Box 97
Olga 98279-0097
(206)376-5531 Fax:(206)376-2193

1993. Adjacent to Obstruction Pass State Park, Spring Bay Inn is a new lodge with its own waterfront and 57 wooded acres. All guest rooms have

fireplaces, views of the bay, antique clawfoot tubs, showers and high ceilings. Explore the private bay, beach, forest, hiking trails or wetland. There is a bayside spa, picnic spot and beach-front campfire area. The innkeepers are former park rangers and enjoy giving complimentary after-breakfast kayak tours (weather permitting) to guests.

Innkeeper(s): Sandy Playa.

Rates:$145-165. MC VISA. Full Bkfst. Gourmet Brkfst. Teas. Evening snacks. 4 rooms. Fireplaces. Beds:KQT. Conference Rm. Phone in room. Spa. Swimming. Fishing.

Contact: Sandy Playa. Certificate may be used: Monday through Thursday nights, October, November and December, 1994, January, February, March, April, November and December, 1995.

Olympia

Harbinger Inn
1136 E Bay Dr
Olympia 98506
(206)754-0389

1910. The inn is built of finely detailed, grey, ashler block construction with white pillars and wide balconies—all completely restored. Original distinctive features include a street-to-basement tunnel and a hillside waterfall fed by an artesian well. Turn-of-the-century furniture has been used in keeping with the original wall stencils and oak pocket doors of the first floor. Guests can borrow books from the library for night reading, enjoy late afternoon tea and cookies or just make themselves comfortable in the sitting room while gazing over the water and marina to the nearby capitol.

Innkeeper(s): Terrell & Marisa Williams.

Rates:$60-90. MC VISA AX. ContPlus Bkfst. 4 rooms. 3 with shared baths. Beds:KQ. Bicycling. Swimming. Fishing.

Contact: Marisa Williams. Certificate may be used: October - March.

Port Angeles

Bavarian Inn B&B
1126 E 7th
Port Angeles 98362
(206)457-4098

1982. Built in the style of a Bavarian Chalet, this inn provides views of the shipping traffic to the San Juan Islands and the local ferry as it rounds the end of the Hook. Down comforters top the beds, and there are fresh flowers in the guest rooms. The innkeepers are happy to point you to special attractions in the area including mushrooming, the Olympic National Park, salmon migrations and local scenic drives.

Innkeeper(s): Gene & Joy Robinson.

Rates:$80-95. MC VISA. Full Bkfst. 3 rooms. Beds:KQT. Skiing. Fishing.

Contact: Joy Robinson. Certificate may be used: Nov. 1 to April 30, Sunday through Thursday nights, excluding holidays.

Tudor Inn
1108 S Oak
Port Angeles 98362
(206)452-3138

1910. This English Tudor inn has been tastefully restored to display its original woodwork and fir stairway. Guests enjoy stone fireplaces in the living room and study. A terraced garden with 100-foot oak trees graces the property.

Innkeeper(s): Jane & Jerry Glass.

Rates:$55-90. MC VISA. Full Bkfst. Teas. 5 rooms. 3 with shared baths. Beds:KQT. Skiing. Swimming. Fishing.

Seen in: *Seattle Times, Oregonian, Los Angeles Times, Olympic Magazine.*

Contact: Jerry Glass. Certificate may be used: November through May.

"Delicious company and delicious food. Best in hospitality and warmth. Beautiful gardens!"

Port Orchard

Northwest Interlude
3377 Sarann Ave E
Port Orchard 98366
(206)871-4676

1971. Antiques such as Grandma's four-poster bed fill this contemporary Northwest home, overlooking Puget Sound and the Olympic Mountain range. Snacks are offered when you check in, and visitor's enjoy evening turndown service and gourmet breakfasts. Pike Street Market in Seattle is a short ferry ride away.

Innkeeper(s): Barbara Cozad & Frances Scott.

Rates:$55-75. MC VISA. Full Bkfst. Gourmet Brkfst. 4 rooms. 2 with shared baths. Fireplaces. Beds:KD. TV, Phone, Refrig. in room. Skiing. Swimming. Fishing.

Contact: Barbara Cozad. Certificate may be used: October through March (except Thanksgiving and Christmas holiday season).

"It was appropriate that we had a king-sized bed, since the moment we met Frances & Barbara we were treated royally."

Port Townsend

A Rose Cottage B&B
1310 Clay St
Port Townsend 98368
(206)385-6944 (800)232-6944

1868. This Gothic Revival inn offers water and mountain views and a back garden filled with beds of roses and pink, red and white poppies. The inn's French Room provides mahogany inlaid furnishings and a French armoire, while other rooms include English and Eastlake Victorian pieces. Scones and fruit cobblers are popular breakfast items.

Innkeeper(s): Mike & Jo Reynolds.

Rates:$70-102. MC VISA. Gourmet Brkfst. 4 rooms. Beds:KQD. Swimming. Fishing.

Contact: Jo Reynolds. Certificate may be used: Sunday through Thursday, October to May.

Ann Starrett Mansion Victorian B&B Inn
744 Clay St
Port Townsend 98368
(206)385-3205 (800)321-0644
Fax:(206)385-2976

1889. George Starrett came from Maine to Port Townsend and became the major residential builder. By 1889, he had constructed one house a week, totaling more than 350 houses. The Smithsonian believes the Ann Starrett's elaborate free-hung spiral staircase is the only one of its type in the United States. A frescoed dome atop the octagonal tower depicts four seasons and four virtues. On the first day of each season, the sun causes a ruby red light to point toward the appropriate painting.

Innkeeper(s): Bob & Edel Sokol.

Rates:$65-195. MC VISA AX DS. Full Bkfst. Gourmet Brkfst. Picnic lunches. Teas. 11 rooms. 2 with shared baths. Fireplaces. Beds:KQT. Conference Rm. TV in room. Golf. Tennis. Skiing. Swimming. Fishing.

Seen in: *Peninsula, New York Times, Vancouver Sun, San Francisco Examiner, London Times, Colonial Homes.*

Contact: Edel Sokol. Certificate may be used: Sunday - Friday, November - April, no festival or long weekends.

"A wonderful experience for aspiring time travelers."

Arcadia Country Inn
1891 S Jacob Miller Rd
Port Townsend 98368
(206)385-5245 Fax:(206)379-0191

1904. This red and white Craftsman-style house is situated on 80 acres of woodland and pasture. It is owned by the Flying Karamazov Brothers who sometimes practice in the barn where dances and theater are held. Guest rooms are decorated with antiques. One room features a view of the Olympic Mountains.

Innkeeper(s): Andrea Grahn & Brad Roy.

Rates:$60-120. MC VISA. Full Bkfst. 5 rooms. Beds:KQT. Conference Rm. Spa. Swimming. Fishing.

Contact: Andrea Grahn. Certificate may be used: October through April.

The English Inn

718 "F" St
Port Townsend 98368
(206)385-5302 Fax:(206)385-5302

1885. A garden, gazebo and hot tub are amenities offered at this Italianate Victorian B&B, in the National Register of Historic Places. Guest rooms are named for famous English poets such as Longfellow, Keats and Wordsworth, and books of poetry are found in each room. Borrow bicycles and explore the historic district and uptown shops or walk to a nearby restaurant.

Innkeeper(s): Juliette & John Swenson.

Rates:$65-95. MC VISA. Full Bkfst. Gourmet Brkfst. Teas. 5 rooms. Beds:KQ. Bicycling. Spa. Swimming.

Contact: Juliette Swenson. Certificate may be used: Monday-Thursday, October through June.

Manresa Castle

PO Box 564, 7th & Sheridan
Port Townsend 98368
(206)385-5750 (800)732-1281
Fax:(206)385-5883

1892. This 30-room mansion was built by Charles Eisenbeis, a merchant and the first mayor of Port Townsend. Later it was a school for priests and finally in 1973 was restored by the Smith family for overnight lodging. From the romantic guest rooms there are panoramic views of the Olympic Range, the Cascades, and the city. There is a full-service restaurant on the premises.

Innkeeper(s): Vernon & Lena Humber.

Rates:$65-180. MC VISA. Cont. Bkfst. EP. 40 rooms. Beds:KQT. Conference Rm. TV, Phone in room. Spa. Fishing.

Contact: Roger O'Connor. Certificate may be used: November, 1994 - April, 1995, excluding Dec. 31.

Ravenscroft Inn

533 Quincy St
Port Townsend 98368
(206)385-2784 Fax:(206)385-6724

1987. Some of the most elegant rooms in Port Townsend may be found at Ravenscroft. A Charleston Shingle-style house, the inn is decorated appropriately in a serene Colonial style with four-poster beds, wing chairs and highboy dressers. For the past two years special rooms have been entered in the Waverly Contest featured in "Country Inns Magazine." Porches on two levels wrap around the inn, affording mountain and bay views. Cooking classes are popular here and the inn has its own cookbook. John is a musician and has produced a tape called "The Ravenscroft," with classical pieces and some original compositions performed on the piano.

Innkeeper(s): Leah Hammer & John Ranney.

Rates:$65-160. MC VISA AX DS. Gourmet Brkfst. Teas. 9 rooms. Fireplaces. Beds:KQT. Skiing. Sauna. Swimming. Fishing.

Contact: Leah Hammer. Certificate may be used: Sunday through Thursday, Oct. 15, 1994 - May 15, 1995. Holidays and special events excluded.

Salkum

The Shepherd's Inn B&B

168 Autumn Heights Dr
Salkum 98582
(206)985-2434

1984. This contemporary B&B affords guests a 50-mile view of the Cowlitz Valley and rolling hills. There is a wraparound deck and inside, floor-to-ceiling windows to take advantage of the wooded setting. Wild huckleberry crepes and homemade cinnamon rolls are house specialities. The DeGoede Bulb Farm is nearby. Water skiing is one mile away.

Innkeeper(s): Richard & Ellen Berdan.

Rates:$55-70. AX DS. Full Bkfst. Gourmet Brkfst. 5 rooms. 2 with shared baths. Beds:KQT. Skiing. Handicap access. Spa. Swimming. Fishing.

Seen in: *Lewis County News.*

Contact: Ellen Berdan. Certificate may be used: Nov. 1-May 30, Sunday-Thursday, except holidays.

"The room is beautiful and the view breathtaking. Food was delicious!"

Seabeck

The Walton House

12340 Seabeck Hwy Northwest
Seabeck 98380
(206)830-4498

1903. Situated on two waterfront acres, this New England salt-box-style house affords each guest room splendid views of Hood Canal and the

Olympic Mountains. Ray and Shirley are the third generation of Waltons to live here, and the old ash tree was planted by Ray's grandfather. The Mountain Ash Room is decorated in green and cream and is filled with family antiques. Seabeck Store and Marina and the Seabeck Conference Grounds are just a little more than a mile away.

Innkeeper(s): H. Ray & Shirley Walton.

Rates:$63-72. Full Bkfst. 3 rooms. 1 with shared bath. Beds:D. Fishing.

Contact: Shirley Walton. Certificate may be used: Thursday through Sunday nights.

Seattle

Capitol Hill Inn

1713 Belmont Ave
Seattle 98122
(206)323-1955

1903. This elegant Queen Anne-style home may once have served as a brothel. Recently renovated, the inn features Victorian-era antiques, chandeliers and custom-designed wall coverings. Bedrooms are decorated in the themes of different nations and boast brass beds topped with down comforters. A full breakfast is complemented with an espresso bar. Guests enjoy proximity to popular shops and restaurants.

Innkeeper(s): Katherine & Joanne Godmintz.

Rates:$75-105. MC VISA. Gourmet Brkfst. 5 rooms. 3 with shared baths. Beds:KQDT. Conference Rm.

Seen in: *Capitol Hill Times.*

Contact: Katherine Godmintz. Certificate may be used: December, January, February, March, December.

"Elegant, original, comfortable & memorable. Cooking is fabulous."

Green Gables Guesthouse

1503 2nd Ave W
Seattle 98119
(206)282-6863 (800)400-1503
Fax:(206)286-1025

1904. In the late Victorian Foursquare-style, this

house on Queen Anne Hill is filled with antiques and costumes. The inn's costume shop, "The Emperor's New Clothes," features attire from the Victorian, Great Gatsby and medieval periods. The Chestnut Bower Room offers a wraparound corner window and bench overlooking the chestnut tree, while Queen Anne's Lace provides a view of downtown Seattle and the Space Needle.

Microbreweries, coffee houses, performing art and sport centers are easily accessed. The inn has a private garden and separate house for longer visits.

Innkeeper(s): Lila & David Chapman.

Rates:$65-110. Full Bkfst. Picnic lunches. Teas. Evening snacks. 4 rooms. 2 with shared baths. Beds:KQT. Conference Rm. Phone, Refrig. in room. Bicycling. Handicap access. Swimming. Fishing.

Contact: Lila Chapman. Certificate may be used: January-March, no holidays.

Mildred's B&B

1202 15th Ave E
Seattle 98112
(206)325-6072

1890. Coffee and juice comes to your room half-an-hour before breakfast at this large, white Victorian inn. Across the street is historic, 44-acre Volunteer Park with a flower conservatory and tennis courts. An electric trolley stops right out the front door and the surrounding area is one of stately old homes and tree-lined streets. Making the trip-to-Grandmother's fantasy come alive are a grand piano, lace curtains, red carpets and a wrap-around veranda. A sitting area adjacent to the guest rooms has a pull-down ironing board.

Innkeeper(s): Mildred & Melodee Sarver.

Rates:$85-95. MC VISA AX DC CB. Full Bkfst. 3 rooms. Beds:Q. TV, Refrig. in room. Skiing. Swimming. Fishing.

Contact: Mildred Sarver. Certificate may be used: November through February.

Prince of Wales

133 Thirteenth Ave E
Seattle 98102
(206)325-9692 (800)327-9692
Fax:(206)322-6402

1903. This three-story Queen Anne Victorian features a tower and covered porch. Its Capitol Hill location allows for walks to shops, parks and local restaurants. The Prince's Retreat guest room offers a private rooftop deck, complete with telescope for viewing the Seattle skyline. There is a clawfoot tub. Early breakfasts may be accommodated by advance arrangement. Downtown is a mile and a half away.

Innkeeper(s): Carol Norton

Rates:$60-95. MC VISA AX. Full Bkfst. 4 rooms. 2 with shared baths.

Beds:KQ. Skiing. Fishing.

Contact: Carol Norton. Certificate may be used: Sunday through Thursday, no holidays. Dec. 1, 1994 - March 15, 1995.

Seaview

Gumm's B&B Inn
PO Box 447
Seaview 98644
(206)642-8887

1911. This gracefully restored Northwest Craftsman home and its yard take up one city block a mile from the ocean. It offers a massive stone fireplace in the living room, a sun porch and outdoor hot tub. Ask for Barbara's Room to enjoy a four-poster rice bed, TV and armoire. Special accommodations for families make the inn popular for small weddings, family reunions and anniversaries. Walk a half block to the cranberry bogs or come to the cranberry festival in the fall. Other local celebrations include sandcastle building, whale watching, antique auto parades and a water music festival.

Innkeeper(s): Esther M. Slack.

Rates:$65-80. MC VISA. Full Bkfst. Teas. 4 rooms. 2 with shared baths. Beds:QD. TV in room.

Contact: Esther M. Slack. Certificate may be used: Good from October to May.

Sequim

Greywolf Inn
395 Keeler Rd
Sequim 98382
(206)683-5889

1976. Built in a farmhouse style, this house is located on five acres. If you prefer a canopy bed, request the Pamela Room and enjoy Bavarian decor. Salmon and egg dishes are presented at breakfast. Decks surround the house, affording views of an occasional eagle, ducks in the pond and Mount Baker. A nature trail provides a pleasant walk through the fields, tall fir trees and over a small stream. Visit the buffalo that come up to the road at the Olympic Game Farm. Birdwatching and

beachcombing are popular on the Dungeness Spit.

Innkeeper(s): Peggy & Bill Melang.

Rates:$75-140. MC VISA AX. Full Bkfst. 6 rooms. Beds:KQT. Phone in room. Skiing. Spa. Swimming. Fishing.

Contact: Peggy Melang. Certificate may be used: Sunday through Thursday, Oct. 15 through May 15.

Shelton

Twin River Ranch B&B
E 5730 Hwy 3
Shelton 98584
(206)426-1023

1918. This farmhouse commands 140 acres on a saltwater bay on the Southern Olympic Peninsula. Once a duck hunting lodge, the farmhouse still has its huge stone fireplace and beamed ceilings. A stream where salmon spawn in the fall flows past the guest rooms. Otter often fish here. The innkeeper is a cattleman and has created a wildlife sanctuary on the property.

Innkeeper(s): Ted & Phlorence Rohde.

Rates:$50-55. MC VISA. Full Bkfst. AP available. Teas. 2 rooms. 2 with shared baths. Beds:DT. Farm.

Contact: Phlorence Rohde. Certificate may be used: Oct. 1 through May 31, 1994 and 1995.

Silverdale

Seabreeze Beach Cottage
16609 Olympic View Rd, NW
Silverdale 98383
(206)692-4648

1975. Moor your boat directly in front of this cottage, or drive up on Olympic View Road, just South of Bangor Submarine Base. Located on two acres, Seabreeze is 20 minutes from Seattle. High tide rises to within two feet of the deck. The cottage is rented to one couple or family at a time so you can enjoy the fireplace, a private spa overlooking the water and the views over Hood Canal all to yourself. The little house was once part of the Maple Beach Resort, but it now stands alone.

Innkeeper(s): Dennis Fulton.

Rates:$119-149. ContPlus Bkfst. AP available. 2 rooms. Fireplaces. Beds:QT. TV, Phone, Refrig. in room. Spa. Swimming. Fishing.

Contact: Dennis Fulton. Certificate may be used: Sunday evening through Friday mornings, October-April.

Snohomish

Eddy's B&B
425 9th St
Snohomish 98290
(206)568-7081

1884. Only six blocks from downtown, this blue and white Country Victorian is located on an acre of landscaped grounds. Ask for the room with the

queen-size pine canopy bed, handmade quilts and country antiques. Breakfast is served on the pool terrace or in the dining room.

Innkeeper(s): Ted & Marlene Bosworth.

Rates:$70-80. MC VISA. Full Bkfst. 2 rooms. Beds:KQT. Skiing. Fishing.

Contact: Marlene Bosworth. Certificate may be used: Nov. 1 through Dec. 15, Sunday through Thursday; Jan. 2 through May 31, Sunday through Thursday; no holidays.

Spokane

Fotheringham House
2128 W 2nd Ave
Spokane 99204
(509)838-1891 Fax:(509)838-1807

1891. A vintage Victorian in the National Register, this inn was built by the first mayor of Spokane, David Fotheringham. There are tin ceilings, a carved staircase, gabled porches and polished woodwork. Victorian furnishings and stained-glass pieces are featured. Across the street is Coeur d'Alene Park and the Patsy Clark Mansion, a

favorite Spokane restaurant. Walk two blocks to the Elk Drug Store to enjoy sitting at the old-fashioned soda fountain.

Innkeeper(s): Graham & Jackie Johnson.

Rates:$70-85. MC VISA. Full Bkfst. Teas. 3 rooms. 2 with shared baths. Beds:Q.

Contact: Jacquelin M. Johnson. Certificate may be used: Sunday through Thursday; November through April.

Marianna Stoltz House
E 427 Indiana
Spokane 99207
(509)483-4316

1908. Located on a tree-lined street, two miles from downtown Spokane, is this American Foursquare

Victorian. It is in the local historic register and features a wraparound porch, high ceilings, and leaded-glass windows. Furnishings include Oriental rugs and period pieces. Peach Melba Parfait and Stoltz House Strada are breakfast specialties.

Innkeeper(s): Marie McCarter, Phyllis & Jim Maguire.

Rates:$65-75. MC VISA AX DC DS. Full Bkfst. 4 rooms. 2 with shared baths. Beds:KQT. AC in room. Skiing. Swimming. Fishing.

Contact: Phyllis Maguire. Certificate may be used: Nov. 1-Dec. 15, 1994; Jan. 1-Feb. 28, 1995.

Tokeland

Tokeland Hotel
100 Hotel Rd
Tokeland 98590
(206)267-7006

1870. This hotel, a National Historical Site, is on three acres of meadow overlooking Willapa Bay. The old farmhouse first became a hotel in 1889 when steamer ships made trips from South Bend to Tokeland. The innkeeper met the boats with a horse-drawn cart. Original furnishings are featured

in the lobby and authentic turn-of-the-century guest rooms are on the second floor with bathrooms down the hall. Cranberry pot roast and crab and cheddar on sourdough are featured in the hotel restaurant, open for all three meals. Westport is 15 minutes away for those planning to fish for salmon.

Innkeeper(s): Scott & Katherine White.

Rates:$49-65. MC VISA DC DS. Full Bkfst. Gourmet Brkfst, Lunch, Dinner. Picnic lunches. Evening snacks. 18 rooms. 17 with shared baths. Beds:QT. Conference Rm. Bicycling. Swimming. Fishing.

Contact: Scott White. Certificate may be used: Nov. 15, 1994 - March 15, 1995.

Trout Lake

The Farm
490 Sunnyside Rd
Trout Lake 98650
(509)395-2488 Fax:(509)395-2121

1904. Four acres surround this three-story yellow farmhouse, 25 miles north of the Columbia Gorge and Hood River. The old rail fence, meadow and forested foothills of Mount Adams create a pastoral scene appropriate for the inn's herd of Cashmere goats. A big farm breakfast is served. Inside, entertainment centers around the player piano, wood stove and satellite dish. Outdoors, take a flight from Trout Lake into Mount St. Helens, or gear up for huckleberry picking, trout fishing and hiking at nearby Gifford Pinchot National Forest. Ask the innkeepers about the fairs, rodeos and Saturday markets.

Innkeeper(s): Eric & Dewey Skemp.

Rates:$60-75. Full Bkfst. 2 rooms. 2 with shared baths. Beds:QDT. Farm. Bicycling. Skiing. Swimming. Fishing.

Contact: Dewey Skemp. Certificate may be used: All of November and free night one time Monday through Thursday all year 1994 and 1995 during promo.

Vashon Island

Sweetbriar B&B
16815 129th Lane SW
Vashon Island 98070
(206)463-9186 Fax:(206)463-1957

1989. Located on two wooded acres overlooking Colvos Passage and the Olympic Mountains, this B&B includes a separate cabin. Decorated in a cottage style with period furnishings, it features pine floors, leaded-glass windows, a wood-burning stove, four-poster bed, covered porch and kitchen. The main house rooms include antiques and local art. Laundry and kitchen privileges are available.

Innkeeper(s): Glenn & Sally Priest.

Rates:$65-90. MC VISA. Full Bkfst. Gourmet Brkfst. 3 rooms. Fireplaces. Beds:KQ. TV, Refrig. in room. Bicycling. Spa. Swimming. Fishing.

Contact: Glenn Priest. Certificate may be used: On a two-day booking only.

Washington, D.C.

Washington

The Embassy Inn
1627 16 St NW
Washington 20009
(202)234-7800 (800)423-9111
Fax:(202)234-3309

1922. This restored inn is furnished in a Federalist style. The comfortable lobby offers books and evening sherry. Conveniently located, the Adams Morgan area of ethnic restaurants is seven blocks away. The Embassy's philosophy of innkeeping includes providing personal attention and cheerful hospitality. Concierge services are available.
Innkeeper(s): Jennifer Schroeder & Susan Stiles.

Rates:$55-110. MC VISA AX DC CB. ContPlus Bkfst. 38 rooms. Beds:DT. Phone, AC in room.

Seen in: *Los Angeles Times, Inn Times, Business Review.*

Contact: Jennifer Schroeder. Certificate may be used: Winter and summer.

"When I return to D.C., I'll be back at the Embassy."

Morrison-Clark Inn
1015 L St NW
Washington 20001
(202)898-1200 (800)332-7898
Fax:(202)289-8576

1864. This elegant inn is comprised of two Italianate-Victorian mansions, which once housed the Soldiers, Sailors and Marines Club from 1923 to 1983. The older part of the inn contains guest rooms with 12-foot-high ceilings and authentic period furnishings. All modern amenities are provided with many luxurious touches. Lunch and dinner are served in a beautiful, intimate dining room, which is renowned for its fine cuisine.
Innkeeper(s): Michael Rawson.

Rates:$99-185. MC VISA AX DC DS CB. ContPlus Bkfst. Gourmet Lunch, Dinner. Picnic lunches. Evening snacks. 54 rooms. Beds:QT. Conference Rm. TV, Phone, AC, Refrig. in room. Handicap access. Exercise room.

Seen in: *Country Inns Magazine, Washington Post.*

Contact: Paige Dunn. Certificate may be used: July, August, November, December, January, February.

Reeds B&B
PO Box 12011
Washington 20005
(202)328-3510 Fax:(202)332-3885

1887. This three-story Victorian townhouse was built by John Shipman, who owned one of the first construction companies in the city. The turn-of-the-century revitalization of Washington began in Logan Circle, considered to be the city's first truly residential area. During the house's restoration, flower gardens, terraces and fountains were added. Victorian antiques, original wood paneling, stained glass, chandeliers, as well as practical amenities, such as air conditioning and laundry facilities, make this a comfortable stay.
Innkeeper(s): Charles & Jackie Reed.

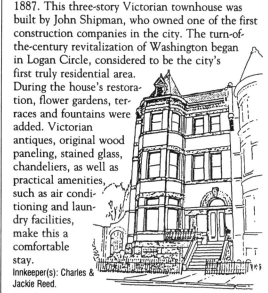

Rates:$50-85. MC VISA AX DC. ContPlus Bkfst. 7 rooms. 6 with shared baths. Fireplaces. Beds:Q. TV, Phone, AC in room.

Seen in: *Philadelphia Inquirer, Washington Gardner, Washington Post.*

Contact: Jacqueline Reed. Certificate may be used: Dec. 1-15 and Jan. 2-March 15.

"This home was the highlight of our stay in Washington!"

The Windsor Inn
1842 16th St NW
Washington 20009
(202)667-0300 (800)423-9111
Fax:(202)667-4503

1922. Recently renovated and situated in a neighborhood of renovated townhouses, the Windsor Inn is the sister property to the Embassy Inn. It is larger and offers suites as well as a small meeting room. The lobby is in an art deco style. Carved, marbletop antiques are in abundance, and a private club atmosphere prevails. The White House is 14 blocks away. It is five blocks to the Metro station at Dupont Circle. There are no elevators.

Innkeeper(s): Jennifer Schroeder & Susan Stiles.

Rates:$55-150. MC VISA AX DC CB. ContPlus Bkfst. 46 rooms. Beds:QDT. Conference Rm. Phone, AC, Refrig. in room.

Seen in: *Los Angeles Times, Inn Times.*

Contact: Jennifer Schroeder. Certificate may be used: Summer/winter.

"Being here was like being home."

West Virginia

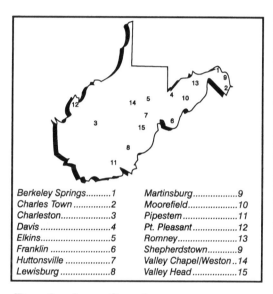

Berkeley Springs

The Manor Inn
415 Fairfax St
Berkeley Springs 25411
(304)258-1552

1878. In the National Register, this Second Empire Victorian features 12-foot ceilings, a mansard roof, large porch and French doors. The innkeeper collects antique quilts and is herself a quilter. George Washington is said to have bathed in the warm mineral springs in town where he owned a property a block from the Manor Inn. Roman and Turkish baths are featured in The Baths, a West Virginia State Park.

Innkeeper(s): Donald & Dorothy Trask.

Rates:$75-95. MC VISA. Full Bkfst. Gourmet Brkfst. 4 rooms. 1 with shared bath. Beds:Q. AC in room. Skiing. Swimming. Fishing.

Contact: Dorothy Trask. Certificate may be used: Sunday through Thursdays excluding holidays.

Charles Town

Gilbert House B&B of Middleway
PO Box 1104
Charles Town 25414
(304)725-0637

1760. A magnificent graystone of early Georgian design, the Gilbert House boasts the state's oldest flagstone sidewalk. During restoration, graffiti found

on the upstairs bedroom walls included a drawing of President James Polk and a child's growth chart from the 1800s. Elegant appointments include fine Oriental rugs, tasteful art and antique furnishings. The inn is located in the 18th-century village of Middleway, which contains one of the country's most well-preserved collections of log houses.

Innkeeper(s): Jean & Bernie Heiler.

Rates:$80-140. MC VISA AX. Full Bkfst. 4 rooms. Fireplaces. Beds:QDT. Conference Rm. AC in room. Fishing.

Contact: Bernard Heiler. Certificate may be used: March 1-June 15.

"We have stayed at inns for 15 years, and yours is at the top of the list as best ever!"

The Washington House Inn
216 S George St
Charles Town 25414
(304)725-7923 (800)297-6957

1891. This three-story brick Victorian is said to have been built by the descendants of President Washington's brothers, John Augustine and Samuel. Carved oak mantels, fireplaces, spacious air-conditioned guest rooms, antique furnishings and refreshments served on the wraparound porch make the inn memorable. Harpers Ferry National Historic Park, Antietam, and the Shenandoah and Potomac rivers are

all within a 15-minute drive, as is Martinsburg outlet shopping.

Innkeeper(s): Mel & Nina Vogel.

Rates:$70-95. Full Bkfst. EP. Teas. 6 rooms. Fireplaces. Beds:QT. Conference Rm. AC in room. Bicycling. Skiing. Swimming. Fishing.

Contact: Nina Vogel. Certificate may be used: January - June, 1995.

Charleston

Historic Charleston B&B
114 Elizabeth St
Charleston 25311
(304)345-8156 (800)225-5982

1905. A U.S. Marshal built this American Foursquare house, a city historical site one block west of the capitol. It features a front porch, upper sunroom and many fireplaces. The innkeepers have decorated it with antiques, collectibles and country crafts.

Innkeeper(s): Robert & Jean Lambert.

Rates:$65. MC VISA AX. Full Bkfst. 3 rooms.

Contact: Jean A. Lambert. Certificate may be used: October through April.

Davis

Meyers House B&B
PO Box 360
Davis 26260
(304)259-5451

1885. Decorated informally in a country style, this three-story shingled Victorian features a sun room

and lending library. It is situated in a small town, atop a mountain, nine miles from Canaan Valley State Park and Ski Resort, and one mile from Blackwater Falls State Park. Your host is a scuba diver and has tank fills available to you on the premises. Rental bikes are available nearby.

Innkeeper(s): Elmer & Deborah Plum.

Rates:$60-75. MC VISA. Full Bkfst. 5 rooms. 4 with shared baths. Beds:QT. TV, AC in room. Skiing. Handicap access. Swimming. Fishing.

Contact: Deborah Plum. Certificate may be used: November & March.

Elkins

The Retreat at Buffalo Run
214 Harpertown Rd
Elkins 26241
(304)636-2960

1903. This turn-of-the-century home is located near Davis and Elkins College, in the heart of West Virginia's beautiful Potomac Highland, gateway to the 840,000-acre Monongahela National Forest. Lounge in the sun or on shady porches and enjoy the warm days and cool nights of a mountain summer. Spectacular fall foliage on the hills surrounding the house, and spring-through-fall flowers are enjoyed by guests. Choose one of many activities in the area and let the innkeepers point you in the right direction with maps and a gourmet picnic.

Innkeeper(s): Bertha & Earl Rhoad.

Rates:$49. ContPlus Bkfst. 6 rooms. 6 with shared baths. Beds:QDT. Conference Rm. Skiing. Fishing.

Contact: Bertha Rhoad. Certificate may be used: November - Dec. 15, 1994 and 1995; January - May 15, 1995.

Tunnel Mountain B&B
Rt 1, Box 59-1
Elkins 26241
(304)636-1684

1939. Nestled on five acres of wooded land, this charming three-story Fieldstone home offers privacy in a peaceful setting. Rooms are tastefully decorated with antiques, collectibles and crafts. Each bedroom boasts a view of the surrounding mountains.

The chestnut and knotty pine woodwork accentuate the decor. The fireplace in the large common room is a great place for warming up after a day of touring or skiing. The area is home to a number of interesting events, including a Dulcimer festival.
Innkeeper(s): Anne & Paul Beardslee.

Rates:$55-65. Full Bkfst. 3 rooms. Beds:Q. TV, AC in room. Golf. Bicycling. Skiing. Swimming. Fishing.

Contact: Paul Beardslee. Certificate may be used: November through May, Sunday through Thursday nights.

Franklin

Candlelight Inn
PO Box 147
Franklin 26807
(304)358-3025

1908. Francis Evick, ancestor to the innkeepers, settled the town of Franklin, situated between two mountain ranges. The inn's parlor has a fireplace and the sitting room opens to a deck with a hot tub, available any time. Breakfast is served in the formal dining room or in the gazebo or poolhouse. A new indoor pool is open to guests. The south branch of the Potomac River is two blocks away.
Innkeeper(s): Carey & Claudia Evick.

Rates:$45-55. MC VISA. Full Bkfst. Evening snacks. 3 rooms. 2 with shared baths. Beds:Q. TV, Phone, AC in room. Skiing. Spa. Swimming. Fishing.

Contact: Claudia Evick. Certificate may be used: Nov. 1, 1994 through April 30, 1995.

Huttonsville

Hutton House
Route 250/219, PO Box 88
Huttonsville 26273
(304)335-6701

1898. This rambling Queen Anne Victorian in the National Register sits above the village, providing views of Tygart River Valley and the Laurel Mountains. Ornate windows, a three-story turret, pocket doors, wraparound porch and gingerbread trim are features. The inn is comfortably decorated with antiques and suitable Victorian touches. A full breakfast is served with antique Depression glass collected by the innkeeper.
Innkeeper(s): Loretta Murray, Dean Ahren.

Rates:$60-70. MC VISA. Full Bkfst. Evening snacks. 6 rooms. Beds:QDT. Golf. Tennis. Skiing. Swimming. Horseback riding. Fishing.

Contact: Loretta Murray. Certificate may be used: September - May, Monday - Thursday excluding Dec. 25-Jan. 1.

Lewisburg

The General Lewis
301 E Washington St
Lewisburg 24901
(304)645-2600 (800)628-4454
Fax:(304)645-2600

1834. This gracious Federal-style inn boasts a columned veranda, flower gardens and long lawns. Patrick Henry and Thomas Jefferson registered at the inn's walnut desk which was retrieved from an old hot springs resort in the area. A stagecoach that once delivered travelers to springs on the James River and Kanawha Turnpike, rests under an arbor. American antiques are featured throughout the inn and Memory Hall displays household items and tools once used by local pioneers. Nearby are state parks, national forests, streams and rivers, as well as sites of the Revolutionary and Civil wars.
Innkeeper(s): Mary Noel & James Morgan.

Rates:$75-95. MC VISA AX. Full Bkfst. Picnic lunches. 25 rooms. Fireplaces. Beds:QD. TV, Phone, AC in room. Skiing. Handicap access. Swimming. Fishing.

Seen in: *Southern Living.*

Contact: Nancy Morgan. Certificate may be used: Dec. 1, 1994 - March 31, 1995.

"The staff is wonderful at making us feel at home, and we can be as much a part of the inn as we want."

Martinsburg

Aspen Hall Inn
405 Boyd Ave
Martinsburg 25401
(304)263-4385

1745. This limestone Georgian manor, listed in the National Register, overlooks four acres of lawns, gardens and a stream. The rooms are decorated in a Southern plantation style, and there are double parlors, a library, and a dining room. Second-floor guest rooms feature canopy beds and are furnished with antiques. Afternoon tea is served in the library or the garden gazebo. The property is mentioned in journals kept by George Washington, and he attended a wedding here. During the French and Indian War, Washington sent troops to protect the Quaker-owned building.
Innkeeper(s): Gordon & Lou Anne Claucherty.

Rates:$95-110. MC VISA. Full Bkfst. Teas. 5 rooms. Fireplaces. Beds:QT. Conference Rm. TV, AC in room. Skiing. Swimming. Fishing.

Contact: Lou Anne Claucherty. Certificate may be used: March, April, November, Dec. 1-18.

Pulpit & Palette Inn

516 W John St
Martinsburg 25401
(304)263-7012

1875. Listed in the National Register, this Victorian inn is set off by a handsome iron fence. The interiors are filled with a mix of American antiques, Tibetan rugs and art, setting off moldings and other architectural details in the library, drawing room and upstairs veranda. Your British-born innkeeper prepares afternoon tea for guests. The Blue Ridge Outlet Center is two blocks away.

Innkeeper(s): Bill & Janet Starr.

Rates:$75. MC VISA. Gourmet Brkfst. Teas. 2 rooms. 2 with shared baths. Beds:Q. AC in room.

Contact: William Starr. Certificate may be used: June 1 to Oct. 31 (except Friday or Saturday).

Moorefield

McMechen House Inn

109 N Main St
Moorefield 26836
(304)538-7173 (800)298-2466

1853. This handsomely restored three-story brick Greek Revival townhouse is in the National Register. There are polished pine floors, a spectacular cherry staircase winding up to the third floor, walnut doors and woodwork, cranberry glass light fixtures and indoor folding shutters. Two parlors and a library add to the gracious dining room that houses the inn's restaurant. There is an antique and gift shop on the premises. Small weddings are often held at the inn.

Innkeeper(s): Linda, Bob & Larry Curtis.

Rates:$65-85. MC VISA AX DC. Full Bkfst. EP. Teas. 7 rooms. 3 with shared baths. Beds:D. AC in room. Swimming. Fishing.

Contact: Linda Curtis. Certificate may be used: December - March

Pipestem

Walnut Grove Inn

HC 78, Box 260
Pipestem 25979
(304)466-6119 (800)225-5982

1860. Located on 38 acres, this red shingled country farmhouse also has a century-old log barn and ancient cemetery with graves of Confederate soldiers and others prior to the Civil War. The farmhouse is decorated eclectically and the front porch is furnished with rocking chairs and a swing. Swimming, basketball, badminton and horseshoes are available. A country breakfast of biscuits and gravy, fresh eggs and homemade preserves is served in the dining room or screen room.

Innkeeper(s): Bonnie & Larry Graham.

Rates:$55-65. MC VISA. Full Bkfst. 4 rooms. Beds:KQDT. AC in room. Bicycling. Skiing. Fishing.

Contact: Larry Graham. Certificate may be used: Between Nov. 15 to March 31.

Pt. Pleasant

Stone Manor

12 Main St
Pt. Pleasant 25550
(304)675-3442

1885. This stone Victorian sits on the banks of the Kanawha River with a front porch that faces the river. Point Pleasant Battle Monument Park, adjacent to the inn, was built to commemorate the location of the first battle of the Revolutionary War. In the National Register, the inn was once the home of a family that ran a ferry boat crossing for the Ohio and Kanawha Rivers. Now restored, the house is decorated with Victorian antiques and offers a pleasant garden with a Victorian fish pond and fountain.

Innkeeper(s): Janice & Tom Vance.

Rates:$50. Full Bkfst. 3 rooms. 3 with shared baths. Fireplaces. Beds:QD. AC in room. Fishing.

Contact: Janice Vance. Certificate may be used: Anytime, 1994. Anytime, 1995.

Romney

Hampshire House 1884

165 N Grafton St
Romney 26757
(304)822-7171

1884. Located near the South branch of the Potomac River, the garden here has old boxwoods and walnut trees. The inn features ornate brickwork, tall, narrow windows, and fireplaces with handsome period mantels. A sitting room with a well-stocked library, a cozy patio and a music room with an antique pump organ are favorite places.

Innkeeper(s): Jane & Scott Simmons.

Rates:$65-80. MC VISA AX DC DS. Full Bkfst. 4 rooms. Fireplaces. Beds:QT. Conference Rm. TV, AC in room. Tennis. Bicycling. Swimming. Horseback riding. Fishing.

Seen in: *Hampshire Review, Mid-Atlantic Country, Weekend Journal.*

Contact: Jane Simmons. Certificate may be used: Anytime except Saturday night, June, July, August, September or anytime in October.

"Your personal attention made us feel at home immediately."

Shepherdstown

Stonebrake Cottage
Shepherd Grade Rd, PO Box 1612
Shepherdstown 25443
(304)876-6607

1880. Situated at the edge of a 140-acre farm, Stonebrake Cottage has been refurbished and decorated with antique country chests and four-poster beds. This completely private Victorian cottage contains three bedrooms, a living room and a kitchen stocked with the makings for a full country breakfast. A 10-acre woodland is nearby for private picnics.
Innkeeper(s): Anne & Dennis Small.

Rates:$80-90. MC VISA. ContPlus Bkfst. 3 rooms. 1 with shared bath. Beds:QDT. Phone, AC, Refrig. in room. Farm. Skiing. Swimming. Fishing.

Seen in: *The Washington Post, Martinsburg Journal.*

Contact: Anne Small. Certificate may be used: Sunday, Monday, Tuesday, Wednesday, Thursday. No Fridays or Saturdays.

"Absolutely charming...food was wonderful."

Thomas Shepherd Inn
Box 1162, 300 W German St
Shepherdstown 25443
(304)876-3715

1868. Spreading oaks and towering pines shade this two-story brick Federal house, in the National Register. Formerly a Lutheran parsonage, it was

built on land once owned by Thomas Shepherd, founder of Shepherdstown, West Virginia's oldest town. Furnishings are American antiques.
Innkeeper(s): Margaret Perry.

Rates:$85-125. MC VISA AX DS. Gourmet Brkfst, Lunch, Dinner. 7 rooms. Fireplaces. Beds:KQT. Conference Rm. AC in room. Bicycling. Skiing. Swimming. Fishing.

Seen in: *Baltimore Sun, Herald Mail, Travel & Leisure, New York Times.*

Contact: Margaret Perry. Certificate may be used: Sunday - Thursday except holidays and October.

"The elegance and tastefulness of the inn, the breakfast and the trip back into time that it affords can only be exceeded by Margaret's hospitality."

Valley Chapel/Weston

Ingeberg Acres
PO Box 199
Valley Chapel/Weston 26446
(304)269-2834

1979. Enjoy the privilege of hunting turkey, grouse and deer on private, posted land on the 450 acres of this horse and cattle farm. Wildflowers, blackberries and raspberries may be gathered as well. A pond on the property is stocked with game fish for anglers. Guest rooms are air-conditioned. Breakfast is served family style and you are invited to participate in or observe everyday farm chores.
Innkeeper(s): Inge & John Mann.

Rates:$59. Full Bkfst. Evening snacks. 3 rooms. 3 with shared baths. Beds:KD. AC in room. Farm. Swimming. Stables. Fishing.

Contact: Ingeberg Mann. Certificate may be used: Monday-Thursday all year, weekends off-season, no other discounts applicable.

Valley Head

Nakiska Chalet B&B
HC 73, Box 24
Valley Head 25064
(304)339-6309 (800)225-5982

1982. On the way to this B&B, you'll be traveling the mountainous roads of West Virginia and the hosts remind you to slow down and enjoy the scenery. Their A-frame house on 11 acres is surrounded by forests of sugar maples that display the best of foliage in autumn. Breakfast, served buffet style, often includes local maple syrup atop blueberry pancakes. Wild turkey, deer, fox and grouse have been spotted from the deck.
Innkeeper(s): Joyce & Doug Cooper.

Rates:$60-70. Full Bkfst. Picnic lunches. Evening snacks. 3 rooms. 2 with shared baths. Beds:QT. Skiing. Fishing.

Contact: Joyce Cooper. Certificate may be used: Sunday through Thursday, non-holiday.

Wisconsin

Albany

Albany Guest House
405 S Mill St
Albany 53502
(608)862-3636

1908. This quaint three-story home is a comforting stop for weary travelers. The red-tiled foyer, lacy curtains and abundance of plants and flowers make

guests feel at home, and an upright piano and fireplace in the living room further emphasize this atmosphere. The guest rooms have special touches, including picture windows and hand-carved antiques. The expansive six acres boasts a number of maple trees, which the innkeepers tap for homemade syrup. Breakfast is a treat with homemade muffins, special egg dishes and traditional Wisconsin cheeses and meats. Tour a cheese factory or visit New Glarus, a village dubbed "America's little Switzerland," a short drive away.

Innkeeper(s): Bob & Sally Braem.

Rates:$50-68. Full Bkfst. 4 rooms. Fireplaces. Beds:KQ. AC in room. Golf. Bicycling. Skiing. Fishing.

Seen in: *Silent Sports, Madison.*

Contact: Sally Braem. Certificate may be used: Monday through Thursday, May through October. Anytime November through April.

"Was even more than I expected."

Oak Hill Manor B&B
401 E Main St
Albany 53502
(608)862-1400

1908. The state's scenic Hidden Valley region is home to this American Foursquare inn, just 30 minutes south of Madison. Sylvia's Room boasts a five-foot iron and brass headboard on its queen bed, a view of the garden and a fireplace. The romantic Judith's Room features a heart-shaped queen canopy bed. Guests enjoy a three-course gourmet breakfast, including a sample of some of the area's outstanding cheeses. Nearby recreational activities include canoeing the Sugar River, hiking the Ice Age Trail or riding the inn's bikes on the Sugar River Trail.

Innkeeper(s): Lee & Mary DeWolf.

Rates:$55-60. MC VISA. Gourmet Brkfst. Teas. Evening snacks. 4 rooms. Fireplaces. Beds:Q. AC in room. Bicycling. Skiing. Swimming. Fishing.

Contact: Mary DeWolf. Certificate may be used: Monday-Thursday, May 1 through Oct. 31; anytime Nov. 1 through April 30.

Algoma

Amberwood Beach Inn
N7136 Hwy 42, Lakeshore Dr
Algoma 54201
(414)487-3471

1925. Double French doors in the guest rooms open to private decks overlooking Lake Michigan. In the evening, from your room, you can hear the waves

lapping ashore. Breakfast in bed is available when you book the bridal suite for a honeymoon or anniversary. A favorite activity is to picnic under the trees at the edge of the water.

Innkeeper(s): Jan Warren & George Davies.

Rates:$55-85. MC VISA. Full Bkfst. 5 rooms. Beds:KQT. Conference Rm. TV, Refrig. in room. Golf. Bicycling. Skiing. Sauna. Swimming. Fishing.

Seen in: *Wisconsin Country Life, Milwaukee, Wisconsin Trails.*

Contact: Jan Warren. Certificate may be used: Sunday through Thursday.

Bayfield

Apple Tree Inn
Rt 1, Box 251
Bayfield 54814
(715)779-5572

1911. The Apple Tree Inn is a fully restored farmhouse overlooking Lake Superior. It was once owned by a dairy farmer/landscape artist. A rustic old barn on the grounds now serves as an antique store. Breakfast is served on the porch before the lake. Guest rooms are furnished in early Americana style and two have lake views.

Innkeeper(s): Joanna Barningham.

Rates:$65-70. MC VISA. Full Bkfst. Gourmet Brkfst. Picnic lunches. Teas. Evening snacks. 5 rooms. Beds:KQ. TV in room. Farm. Golf. Tennis. Bicycling. Skiing. Handicap access. Swimming. Horseback riding. Fishing.

Seen in: *Lake Superior Magazine.*

Contact: Joanna Barningham. Certificate may be used: Jan. 1-June 30, August 20-Dec. 31.

Cooper Hill House
33 S Sixth St, PO Box 1288
Bayfield 54814
(715)779-5060

1888. This inn, built from native hemlock and white pine, offers a view of Lake Superior. Guest rooms are sunny and feature antiques, family heir-

looms and quilts. A cozy sitting room offers a place for relaxing, reading and playing games. The inn serves homemade breads, fresh fruit and specially blended coffee.

Innkeeper(s): Larry & Julie MacDonald.

Rates:$70-80. MC VISA. ContPlus Bkfst. 4 rooms. Beds:Q. AC in room. Golf. Bicycling. Skiing. Swimming. Fishing.

Seen in: *Wintertime, Lake Superior, Outside.*

Contact: Julie MacDonald. Certificate may be used: Nov. 1-Dec. 23, 1994; Jan. 2-Feb. 16, 1995; Feb. 21-May 25, 1995; Nov. 1-Dec. 23, 1995.

"Thanks for the great time, great food and great company."

Thimbleberry Inn B&B

15021 Pagent Rd, PO Box 1007
Bayfield 54814
(715)779-5757

1993. The waters of Lake Superior sparkle beside the 400 feet of shoreline adjacent to this natural wood home. The peaceful forest setting adds to the romance of the rooms which include fireplaces. Innkeeper Sharon Locey writes a food column and currently is writing her first cookbook. Her culinary expertise makes breakfast a gourmet treat. While enjoying your morning meal, watch for wildlife and bald eagles as they soar over the Loceys' 40 acres. The deck features a cedar hot tub perfect for relaxing after skiing, hiking or just spending the day by the lake's side.

Innkeeper(s): Sharon & Craig Locey.

Rates:$65-105. MC VISA. Gourmet Brkfst. 4 rooms. Fireplaces. Beds:KQ. Golf. Skiing. Swimming. Fishing.

Contact: Sharon Locey. Certificate may be used: Jan. 3 - May 1, Sunday - Thursday; Nov. 1 - Dec. 20, Sunday - Thursday.

Cedarburg

The Washington House Inn

W 62 N 573 Washington Ave
Cedarburg 53012
(414)375-3550 (800)554-4717
Fax:(414)375-9422

1886. Completely renovated, this brick building is decorated in a light-hearted country Victorian style, featuring antiques, whirlpool baths and fireplaces. The original guest registry, more than 100 years old, is displayed proudly in the lobby.

Innkeeper(s): Wendy Porterfield.

Rates:$59-159. MC VISA AX DC DS. ContPlus Bkfst. EP. Gourmet Dinner. Picnic lunches. Teas. 34 rooms. Fireplaces. Beds:KQ. Conference Rm. TV, Phone, AC, Refrig. in room. Golf. Tennis. Bicycling. Handicap access. Spa. Sauna. Horseback riding.

Seen in: *Country Home, Chicago Sun-Times.*

Contact: Michelle Sladky. Certificate may be used: Valid Sunday - Thursday only.

"A piece of time lost to all but a fortunate few who will experience it. Please save it for my children."

Chetek

Canoe Bay Inn & Cottages

W16065 Hogback Rd
Chetek 54728
(800)568-1995 Fax:(715)924-2078

1930. This country inn offers lodge-style surroundings with the finest of amenities. On the shore of a 50-acre, private, spring-fed lake and surrounded by nearly 300 acres of forest, the inn provides a year-round escape from city life. Two of the more luxurious rooms are the Adirondack and Sheridan suites, boasting just about every extra imaginable. The inn, less than a two-hour drive from the Twin Cities, is a favorite anniversary and honeymoon destination.

Innkeeper(s): Dan & Lisa Dobrowolski.

Rates:$89-189. MC VISA DS. MAP available. Gourmet Brkfst, Dinner. Teas. Evening snacks. 8 rooms. Fireplaces. Beds:KQ. Conference Rm. TV, AC, Refrig. in room. Skiing. Swimming. Fishing.

Contact: Lisa Dobrowolski. Certificate may be used: October-April.

Cochrane

The Rosewood B&B

203 S Main St
Cochrane 54622-7228
(608)248-2940

1913. This spacious inn, located on the village's Main Street, features an attractive stone exterior

and Victorian decor. Visitors select from three guest rooms, all featuring fireplaces and queen beds. Many recreational activities are available in the vicinity, just a short distance from the Mississippi River. Merrick and Perrot state parks are nearby, and the inn is within easy driving distance of Eau Claire and La Crosse.

Innkeeper(s): Debra & Steven Knutson.

Rates:$58-78. Cont. Bkfst. 3 rooms. 2 with shared baths. Fireplaces.

Beds:Q. TV in room. Skiing. Swimming. Fishing.

Contact: Debra Knutson. Certificate may be used: October & November, 1994; Jan. 2 - April 15, 1995.

Colfax

Son-ne-vale Farm B&B
Rt 1, Box 132
Colfax 54730
(715)962-4342

1900. This farmhouse inn, nestled amid large trees on its 125-acre grounds, offers two guest rooms to those exploring this area of the state. A gourmet

breakfast is served to the inn's guests. Area activities include antiquing and fishing. Eau Claire is 30 miles from the inn, and the Hoffman Hills State Recreational Area is nearby.

Innkeeper(s): Lillian Sonnenberg.

Rates:$45. Gourmet Brkfst. 2 rooms. 2 with shared baths. Beds:KQT. Farm. Fishing.

Contact: Lillian Sonnenberg. Certificate may be used: Anytime not filled with other reservations. Call to check.

Crandon

Courthouse Square B&B
210 E Polk St
Crandon 54520
(715)478-2549

1905. Situated on the shores of Surprise Lake, this Victorian Shingle also manages to provide the conveniences of town with its location. The inn features antique and country furnishings, and each of its guest rooms offers a lake or park view. The area provides excellent antiquing and shopping opportunities, in addition to cross-country and downhill skiing. Visitors also enjoy borrowing a bike to explore the town, relaxing on the inn's porch or venturing across the street to a city park.

Innkeeper(s): Les & Bess Aho.

Rates:$45-60. Gourmet Brkfst. Teas. Evening snacks. 4 rooms. 4 with shared baths. Beds:QT. Bicycling. Skiing. Swimming. Fishing.

Contact: Bess Aho. Certificate may be used: Sunday through Thursday, holidays excluded.

Cumberland

The Rectory
1575 Second Ave, Box 1042
Cumberland 54829
(715)822-3151

1905. This city's unique island setting makes it an ideal stopping point for those exploring the state's lake-rich Northwest. The German Gothic inn, once home to the parish priest, features charming guest rooms, all filled with antiques, heirlooms and items of interest. The Mae Jenet Room, with its striking corner turret, features a doll collection and other unique toys. Breakfasts, served in the roomy parlor, often feature the inn's famous Breakfast Pie. A gaming casino is nearby, and 50 lakes are found within a 10-mile radius of Cumberland.

Innkeeper(s): Gerald & Ethel Anderson.

Rates:$60-65. MC VISA. Full Bkfst. 4 rooms. 2 with shared baths. Beds:QT. Conference Rm. Skiing. Swimming. Fishing.

Contact: Ethel Anderson. Certificate may be used: Excludes Memorial Day and Labor Day weekend; weekend before Labor Day weekend; February 14, July 3, 4, 5; December 24, 25, 31.

Eagle

Eagle Centre House B&B
W370 S9590 Hwy 67
Eagle 53119
(414)363-4700

1846. Modeled after the mid-19th-century stage-coach inns, this two-story Greek Revival house, less than an hour's drive from Milwaukee, offers a wide variety of vintage antiques in its attractive interior. The two second-story rooms offer relaxing whirlpool tubs. Full breakfasts may include Danish kringles from nearby Racine. The inn's location, near the Kettle Moraine State Forest, provides easy access for cross-country skiing and hiking. Old World Wisconsin is within walking distance.

Innkeeper(s): Riene Wells.

Rates:$85-125. MC VISA AX. Full Bkfst. 5 rooms. Beds:DT. Phone, AC in room. Golf. Skiing. Swimming. Horseback riding. Fishing.

Seen in: *Country Living Magazine, Milwaukee Journal, Waukesha Freement, Chicago Tribune, Chicago Sun-Times.*

Contact: Riene Wells. Certificate may be used: Sunday through Thursday nights, holidays excluded, whirlpools excluded.

Eagle River

Brennan Manor
1079 Everett Rd
Eagle River 54521
(715)479-7353

1928. This Tudor-style manor evokes images of a baronial hunting lodge with its 35-foot ceilings, timber rafters, and suit of armor at the entry. Hand-

carved woodwork, arched windows, and a 30-foot stone fireplace in the Great Room completes the Old World ambiance. On the grounds are two stone patios, expansive lawns leading to the lake, a private swimming beach, wet boat house, and two piers. A lake-view guest house is available, as well as four lavishly decorated bedrooms that lead to an open balcony overlooking the Great Room.
Innkeeper(s): Robert & Connie Lawton.
Rates:$69-89. MC VISA. Full Bkfst. 4 rooms. Beds:Q. Golf. Tennis. Bicycling. Skiing. Swimming. Horseback riding. Fishing.
Seen in: *Wisconsin Trails, Country Extra, Silent Sports, Northern Action and Best of the Northwoods.*
Contact: Robert Lawton. Certificate may be used: Sunday through Thursday, except July, August, Christmas, New Year.

Eau Claire

Fanny Hill Inn
3919 Crescent Ave
Eau Claire 54703
(715)836-8184 (800)292-8026
Fax:(715)836-8180

1989. This modern inn, built in the Queen Anne Victorian style, provides an elegant lodging experience with its well-appointed guest rooms and dinner theater. Many of the romantic rooms boast fireplaces and whirlpool baths. Each offers Victorian furnishings, but still retains its own unique ambiance, including several with city, garden, river or woods views. Special dinner/theater packages are available.
Innkeeper(s): Dennis & Carol Heyde.
Rates:$74-149. MC VISA AX DC DS CB. Full Bkfst. 11 rooms. Fireplaces. Beds:KQ. Conference Rm. TV, Phone, AC in room. Skiing. Handicap access. Swimming. Fishing.
Contact: Mark Luedtke. Certificate may be used: Sunday - Thursday.

Otter Creek Inn
2536 Hwy 12
Eau Claire 54701
(715)832-2945

1950. On a hillside overlooking a creek is this Tudor-style inn, surrounded by oaks and pines. Visitors immediately feel welcome as they make their way up the inn's curved pebblestone walk to the front door. The Palm Room sports an antique sleigh bed, romantic loveseat and sunken whirlpool tub. The Rose Room, often the choice of honeymooners, features a cloverleaf-shaped whirlpool tub that overlooks the gardens and gazebo. The spacious inn provides many spots for relaxation, including a gazebo, the great room with its inviting fireplace and a roomy patio.
Innkeeper(s): Randy & Shelley Hansen.
Rates:$59-129. MC VISA AX DS. ContPlus Bkfst. 5 rooms. Beds:Q. Conference Rm. TV, Phone, AC in room. Golf. Skiing. Handicap access. Spa. Swimming. Fishing.
Seen in: *Country Magazine.*
Contact: Shelley Hansen. Certificate may be used: Sunday through Thursday evenings, excluding holidays.

Endeavor

Neenah Creek Inn & Pottery
W7956 Neenah Rd
Endeavor 53930-9756
(608)587-2229

1900. Wildlife lovers will enjoy the creekfront setting of this turn-of-the-century Portage brick farmhouse. The Circus Room honors nearby Baraboo, and features a brass queen bed. Country furnishings are found throughout the inn. Guests enjoy relaxing in the common room, on the outdoor porch, in the solarium and in the spacious dining-living room. The inn's 11 acres are filled with walking paths. Don't be shy about asking for a demonstration of the potter's wheel. Wisconsin Dells is an easy drive away.
Innkeeper(s): Pat & Doug Cook.
Rates:$65-105. MC VISA. Full Bkfst. Gourmet Brkfst. Evening snacks. 4 rooms. Beds:QT. AC in room. Farm. Skiing. Swimming. Fishing.
Contact: Patricia Cook. Certificate may be used: Nov. 1-Dec. 15, April 1-30.

Fish Creek

White Gull Inn
4225 Main St, PO Box 160
Fish Creek 54212
(414)868-3517 Fax:(414)868-2367

1896. This Folk Victorian inn offers a variety of lodging options, and all feature charming and comfortable accommodations. Breakfasts may include Eggs Benedict, hash browns or buttermilk pancakes with Door County maple syrup. Recreational opportunities abound in the area, including bicycling, charter fishing, cross-country skiing, golf, hiking and wind surfing. The inn's traditional Door County fish boil is available at least two evenings per week. Peninsula State Park is nearby and several fascinating museums are within easy driving distance.

Innkeeper(s): Andy & Jan Coulson.

Rates:$67-126. MC VISA AX DC DS CB. Full Bkfst. EP. 13 rooms. 5 with shared baths. Fireplaces. Beds:QDT. TV, Phone, AC in room. Skiing. Swimming. Fishing.

Contact: Andrew Coulson. Certificate may be used: Sunday through Thursday nights; Oct. 23 through Dec. 23, 1994; Jan. 2 through May 11, 1995; Oct. 22 through Dec. 21, 1995.

Fontana-on-Geneva Lake

Emerald View House
PO Box 322
Fontana-on-Geneva Lake 53125
(414)275-2266

1932. This Colonial Revival inn near picturesque Lake Geneva offers an easy getaway for those in Chicago, Milwaukee or Madison. The family-oriented inn offers a fireplace, library and sitting rooms. Guests enjoy a full gourmet breakfast before heading out for a day of antiquing, fishing, skiing, shopping or just exploring their lovely surroundings. Alpine Valley and Big Foot Beach State Park are nearby.

Innkeeper(s): Suzanne Brooks.

Rates:$65-95. Full Bkfst. Gourmet Brkfst. 4 rooms. 2 with shared baths. Beds:KDT. Skiing. Handicap access. Swimming. Fishing.

Contact: Suzanne Brooks. Certificate may be used: Anytime there is availability.

Hayward

Edgewater Inn
Rt 1, Box 1293, Turners Rd
Hayward 54843
(715)462-9412

1905. Those seeking a tranquil getaway or a host of recreational activities will find both at this lakefront farmhouse inn. Nature lovers will delight in

the animal and birdlife found here, as well as fishing, hiking and golfing at a nine-hole course adjacent to the inn. The Lakeview Suite boasts a fireplace, king bed and sitting room. The Island View Room features a canopy bed, a deck with a lake view and Shirley Temple memorabilia in a curio cabinet. The area is home to several museums and the fall colors are exceptional.

Innkeeper(s): Ron & Wendy Rudd.

Rates:$65-90. Full Bkfst. Gourmet Brkfst. 5 rooms. Fireplaces. Beds:KQD. AC, Refrig. in room. Skiing. Swimming. Fishing.

Contact: Wendy Rudd. Certificate may be used: October, 1994 through May, 1995 excluding holidays and special events. October, 1995 through December, 1995 excluding holidays and special events.

Ross' Teal Lake Lodge
Rt 7, Ross Rd
Hayward 54843
(715)462-3631

1908. Located on 250 acres bordering Teal Lake and Teal River, this is a great vacation spot for families and fishermen. Most of the Northwoods fishing cabins here are of vertical log construction, and some feature fireplaces and kitchens. There are two beds in each room. Fishing guides and a fishing school for children and adults offer both fishing expertise and local folklore. (You'll learn how to catch the prized muskie, a fierce freshwater game fish.) Bicycles, tricycles and water bicycles are available to use. A telescope in the lounge is trained on a family of eagles that nest on the island, and you can watch them feed and learn to fly. Early springtime guests enjoy the otters that scramble around the inn's docks.

Innkeeper(s): Tim & Prudence Ross.

Rates:$100-250. MC VISA. Full Bkfst. EP. AP available. MAP available. Picnic lunches. 25 rooms. Fireplaces. Beds:KT. Conference Rm. Refrig. in room. Tennis. Bicycling. Skiing. Handicap access. Spa. Sauna. Swimming. Fishing.

Contact: Prudence Ross. Certificate may be used: June, September, October.

Houlton

Shady Ridge Farm B&B
410 Highland View
Houlton 54082
(715)549-6258

1890. Every inch of this 22-acre farm boasts something unique. The home features a parlor with musical instruments, including an antique pump

organ. The bedrooms are decorated with stenciling patterns, ceiling fans and handmade quilts. Oliver's Room includes a four-poster bed and antique stained glass. The innkeepers raise friendly llamas and encourage guests to take the animals on walks or pack picnic lunches on their backs. They also offer children's llama parties. The llamas can be purchased as can some antiques and local artwork. Breakfasts include unusual fare such as Norwegian baked pancakes with rosehip syrup from the farm. The homegrown fruits that complement the meal are raised organically.

Innkeeper(s): Sheila & Britt Fugina.

Rates:$65-85. Full Bkfst. Evening snacks. 3 rooms. 2 with shared baths. Beds:QT. Farm. Golf. Bicycling. Skiing. Sauna. Swimming. Horseback riding. Fishing.

Seen in: *Minneapolis Tribune*.

Contact: Sheila Fugina. Certificate may be used: Sunday through Thursday anytime. Friday and Saturday, November through March.

"Garrison Keillor says a certain calmness comes from being in the right place and knowing it. We have felt that calmness here."

Hudson

Grapevine Inn B&B
702 Vine St
Hudson 54016
(715)386-1989

1901. Guests at this Queen Anne Victorian/Greek Revival inn enjoy a wake-up tray of coffee and baked breads before sitting down to a three-course gourmet breakfast. Three elegant, antique-filled guest rooms will delight visitors. The St. Croix River and the scenic riverway are within walking distance, and tubing excursions down the Apple River are popular. Willow River State

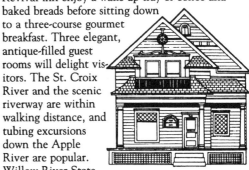

Park is nearby, and the impressive Mall of America is just a 30-minute drive from the inn.

Innkeeper(s): Avery & Barbara Dahl.

Rates:$75-119. Gourmet Brkfst. Teas. Evening snacks. 3 rooms. Beds:Q. Conference Rm. AC in room. Bicycling. Skiing. Fishing.

Contact: Barbara Dahl. Certificate may be used: Non-holiday weekends. Combination weekday/weekend night okay. Not Friday-Saturday. Sunday - Monday or Thursday - Friday options okay.

Kansasville

The Linen & Lace B&B
26060 Washington Ave
Kansasville 53139
(414)534-4966

1900. This romantic, three-story farmhouse inn provides a pleasant getaway from the rigors of everyday life yet allows convenient access to the area's many attractions. Kenosha, Lake Geneva,

Milwaukee and Racine are within easy driving distance. Visitors select from the French Lilac, Raspberry and Wild Primrose rooms, all featuring antiques, ceiling fans, down comforters, family heirlooms and, not surprisingly, lots of linen and lace. Guests enjoy walks on the inn's 4.5-acre grounds, and a favorite destination is a garden created from the stone foundation of the farm's original barn.

Innkeeper(s): Nancy & David Reckhouse.

Rates:$60-70. MC VISA. Full Bkfst. Evening snacks. 4 rooms. 3 with shared baths. Beds:QD. Farm. Skiing. Swimming. Fishing.

Contact: Nancy Reckhouse. Certificate may be used: January - April.

Kewaunee

The "Gables"
821 Dodge St
Kewaunee 54216
(414)388-0220

1883. Milwaukee architect Henry Koch designed this 22-room mauve and green Queen Anne Victorian. The Windsor Room features a king-size canopy bed. Earl's garden bursts forth each spring with hundreds of daffodils, tulips and lilacs. Zelda, a Russian Blue cat, and Baron, a handsome dachshund, are the inn's mascots. Wisconsin cheeses, cherries, and sausages are featured in the full breakfast served in the formal dining room. A secret recipe, "Cheese Cake Coffee Cake," is often served but never revealed. Penny is a dietician and teaches B&B classes. Nine miles of scenic beach start three blocks from the inn. A salmon collection station and Door County are close by.

Innkeeper(s): Earl & Penny Dunbar.

Rates:$50-65. AX. Gourmet Brkfst. Evening snacks. 5 rooms. 4 with shared baths. Beds:KQT. Golf. Skiing. Spa. Swimming. Fishing.

Seen in: *The Kewaunee Star, Green Bay Press-Gazette, Chicago Tribune.*

Contact: Penny Dunbar. Certificate may be used: Anytime on availability.

"You both have a knack for making people feel welcome and at ease. Your home is just beautiful, and the breakfast was delicious."

La Pointe

Woods Manor
Nebraska Row, PO Box 7
La Pointe 54850
(715)747-3102

1927. Lake Superior's Madeline Island is home to this inn, which provides a unique setting for a romantic escape or family vacation. The six guest rooms vary in size and amenities, but all are comfortably appointed with antiques and family heirlooms. One of the rooms boasts a screened-in porch in addition to its king bed. Guests are welcome to borrow a bicycle or canoe, or take advantage of the inn's private beach for sunbathing or swimming. Hikers will enjoy the trails at nearby Big Bay Island Park or Big Bay State Park. The innkeepers are able to accommodate pets.

Innkeeper(s): Gail Petersen.

Rates:$94-109. MC VISA. ContPlus Bkfst. Teas. 6 rooms. Beds:KQ. Tennis. Bicycling. Sauna. Swimming. Fishing.

Contact: Gail Petersen. Certificate may be used: Weekends in May and June or weekdays in September and October.

Lake Delton

The Swallow's Nest B&B
141 Sarrington, PO Box 418
Lake Delton 53940
(608)254-6900

1988. This inn has a picturesque view of the Wisconsin Dells and Lake Delton. The Swallow's Nest features a two-story atrium with skylights, and cathedral windows and ceiling. Guests may relax on the screened deck, in the library by the fireplace or in the gazebo by the waterfall. The inn is furnished with English period furniture, rocking chairs, lace curtains, handmade quilts and goose-down comforters.

Innkeeper(s): Mary Ann Stemo.

Rates:$60-70. MC VISA. Full Bkfst. Teas. 4 rooms. Beds:QT. Phone, AC in room. Skiing. Swimming. Fishing.

Seen in: *Milwaukee Journal, Wisconsin Trails Magazine.*

Contact: Mary Ann Stemo. Certificate may be used: Sunday night through Thursday night, no holidays.

"Your home is beautiful, and the breakfasts were wonderful!"

Lake Geneva

T.C. Smith Inn B&B
865 Main St
Lake Geneva 53147
(414)248-1097 (800)423-0233

1845. Listed in the National Register of Historic Places, this High Victorian-style inn blends elements of Greek-Revival and Italianate architecture. The inn has massive carved wooden doors, hand-painted moldings and woodwork, a high-ceilinged foyer, an original parquet floor, Oriental carpets, museum-quality period antiques and European oil paintings. Guests may enjoy tea in the Grand

Parlor by a marble fireplace or enjoy breakfast on an open veranda overlooking Lake Geneva.

Innkeeper(s): Maureen Marks.

Rates:$75-250. MC VISA AX DC DS. Full Bkfst. 8 rooms. Fireplaces. Beds:KQ. Phone, AC, Refrig. in room. Golf. Tennis. Bicycling. Skiing. Swimming. Horseback riding. Fishing.

Seen in: *Keystone Country Peddler, Pioneer Press Publication.*

Contact: Maureen Marks. Certificate may be used: Midweek Monday-Thursday, no holidays.

"As much as we wanted to be on the beach, we found it impossible to leave the house. It's so beautiful and relaxing."

Maiden Rock

Harrisburg Inn
W3334 Hwy 35, PO Box 15
Maiden Rock 54750
(715)448-4500

1892. A breathtakingly beautiful view of Lake Pepin greets guests of this historic country house, which overlooks the Great Mississippi River Valley from its location high on the bluff. All rooms offer handmade quilts, and the Evening Primrose Suite and Morning Glory Room boast private decks to further enjoy the lake view. Country-style breakfasts may be served on the porch, in the kitchen or in the rooms for guests who desire their morning meal in bed. The inn is a pleasant drive from the Twin Cities. Nearby shops will delight those with an eye for the unique.

Innkeeper(s): Carol Crisp & Bern Paddock.

Rates:$58-88. MC VISA DS. Full Bkfst. Evening snacks. 4 rooms. Beds:Q. AC in room. Golf. Skiing. Swimming. Fishing.

Seen in: *Chicago Tribune, Milwaukee Journal, Hastings Star Gazette.*

Contact: Carol Crisp. Certificate may be used: Sunday - Thursday, April - September; anytime during November - March except Saturdays and holidays.

"Thanks for your hospitality and good food!"

Manawa

Ferg Haus Inn
N8599 Ferg Rd
Manawa 54949
(414)596-2946 Fax:(414)596-2946

1912. A German immigrant family built this Bavarian-German country inn on farmland that now is home to a charming Bavarian Village. The inn's four guest rooms all have views of the flower-filled village, lush lawn or picturesque ponds. For guests' convenience, the dining area, guest rooms

and sitting room all are located on the second floor. Boating, fishing, golf and hiking are found nearby. Those who visit during the winter holiday season will be impressed with the village's Christmas decorations and display.

Innkeeper(s): Lloyd & Shirley Ferg.

Rates:$55-65. Full Bkfst. Evening snacks. 4 rooms. 3 with shared baths. Beds:KQT. Conference Rm. Farm. Skiing. Fishing.

Contact: Shirley Ferg. Certificate may be used: January, February, March, April, May.

Manitowoc

Arbor Manor B&B
1304 Michigan Ave
Manitowoc 54220
(414)684-6095

1858. Nestled in the woods on the city's historic Northside, this spacious Neoclassical Greek Revival inn offers elegant accommodations in a romantic setting. Guests select from Albert's Master Suite, Anna's Chamber or Dorothy's Chamber, each providing its own special ambiance. A favorite gathering spot is the marble-floored Garden Room, where visitors will find a television, fireplace, jukebox, magazines and newspapers. The car ferry across the lake to Ludington, Mich., docks just a short distance away.

Innkeeper(s): Lou Ann & Jay Spaanem.

Rates:$90-95. MC VISA. Gourmet Brkfst. 3 rooms. Fireplaces. Beds:KQ. AC in room. Swimming. Fishing.

Contact: Lou Ann Spaanem. Certificate may be used: Monday - Thursday all year 1994 and 1995.

Mayville

The Audubon Inn
45 N Main
Mayville 53050
(414)893-0552

1896. This Neoclassical inn, listed in the National Register of Historic Places, is a favorite with honeymooners and those celebrating anniversaries. Located south of Fond du Lac and just minutes from the well-known Horicon Marsh Wildlife Area, the inn is an easy getaway for Madison and Milwaukee residents seeking a respite from big-town rigors. Guest rooms offer double whirlpools. Dining facilities are on the premises. Excellent cross-country skiing and fishing are found nearby.

Innkeeper(s): Rip O'Dwanny.

Rates:$70-120. MC VISA AX DC DS CB. Full Bkfst. Gourmet Brkfst, Lunch, Dinner. 17 rooms. Beds:Q. Conference Rm. TV, Phone, AC in room. Skiing. Handicap access. Fishing.

Contact: Rip O'Dwanny. Certificate may be used: Sunday through Thursday, November through May.

Mequon

Sonnenhof Inn
13907 N Port Washington
Mequon 53097
(414)375-4294

1845. Easy access to alluring Lake Michigan is a highlight of this Dutch Colonial inn, just north of Milwaukee. The family-oriented inn's countryside setting on 21 acres makes it an attractive alternative to big-city lodging. The inn's amenities include a fireplace, library and tennis courts. Visitors enjoy a full breakfast before they begin their day's activities. Lake Michigan is only a mile from the inn, and Pike Lake State Park is nearby.

Innkeeper(s): Georgia & Tom Houle.

Rates:$65-115. MC VISA. Full Bkfst. 5 rooms. 2 with shared baths. Beds:Q. Conference Rm. Phone, AC, Refrig. in room. Farm. Tennis. Skiing. Swimming. Fishing.

Contact: Georgia Houle. Certificate may be used: Sunday through Thursday only.

Milton

Chase on the Hill
11624 State Rd 26
Milton 53563
(608)868-6646

1848. Found in the rolling hills of the state's South-central region, this farmhouse inn offers charming accommodations and convenient access to the area's many attractions. Guest rooms are decorated with antique country furnishings. Full breakfasts and afternoon teas are offered, which are ideal after a busy day exploring nearby Kettle Moraine State Forest, Milton House Museum and Old World Wisconsin. Farm animals are found at the inn, along with pet cats. The area is rich with bird-watching, fishing, golfing and hiking opportunities.

Innkeeper(s): Michael Chase & Jesse Garza.

Rates:$35-55. Full Bkfst. Teas. 4 rooms. 3 with shared baths. Beds:QT. Farm. Skiing. Swimming. Fishing.

Contact: Michael Chase. Certificate may be used: Anytime.

Mineral Point

Knudson's Guest House
415 Ridge St
Mineral Point 53565
(608)987-2733

1922. This red brick Colonial Revival inn is found in one of the state's most historic and scenic regions. Decor includes antiques and country fur-

nishings, and one of the inn's two sitting rooms, which boasts a fireplace, is a favorite relaxing area. Guests will appreciate the full breakfast served in the formal dining room before they head out for a day of sightseeing. The area's many nearby attractions include Governor Dodge State Park, House on the Rock and antique-rich Spring Green.

Innkeeper(s): Agnes & Jim Knudson

Rates:$63. Full Bkfst. 3 rooms. Beds:Q. TV, Phone, AC in room. Skiing. Fishing.

Contact: Agnes Knudson. Certificate may be used: Anytime.

Oconomowoc

The Inn at Pine Terrace
351 Lisbon Rd
Oconomowoc 53066
(414)567-7463 (800)421-4667
Fax:(414)893-1800

1881. This inn's convenient location, midway between Madison and Milwaukee and just north of the interstate that connects them, makes it equally appealing to business travelers and those seeking a romantic retreat. Some rooms boast whirlpool tubs and visitors are welcome to use the inn's inground swimming pool. A conference room is available for meetings and seminars.

Innkeeper(s): Mary.

Rates:$60-120. MC VISA AX DC DS CB. Full Bkfst. 13 rooms. Beds:QT. Conference Rm. TV, Phone, AC in room. Skiing. Swimming. Fishing.

Contact: Rip O'Dwanny. Certificate may be used: Sunday through Thursday.

Osceola

Pleasant Lake Inn

2238 60th Ave
Osceola 54020
(715)294-2545 (800)294-2545

1989. This country-style home commands a view of Pleasant Lake from its picturesque forest setting. All the rooms have their own sun room or private deck and two have double whirlpools. The original farm, a quarter of a mile from the inn, has been in the Berg family for more than 130 years.

Maintained trails wind along the lake and through the woods, and an apple orchard is a favorite spot for picture-taking in the spring and apple-gathering in the fall. A full breakfast often includes Dutch pancakes made from freshly ground flour and served with honey from the innkeepers' beehives.

Innkeeper(s): Richard & Charlene Berg.
Rates:$55-100. MC VISA. Full Bkfst. 4 rooms. Beds:Q. AC in room. Bicycling. Skiing. Swimming. Fishing.
Contact: Charlene Berg. Certificate may be used: Sunday-Thursday year round except September, October and New Year's Eve.

"We enjoyed sharing our mornings with the hummingbirds and the evenings by the bonfire."

Plainfield

Johnson Inn

231 W North St, Box 487
Plainfield 54966
(715)335-4383

1850. Located in a scenic region of Central Wisconsin well known for its antiques, flea markets, lakes and hunting, this inn offers a fine stopping point for those exploring the area's attractions. Antiques, birch flooring, carved oak paneling and tall ceilings highlight the interior. The lacy Rathermel Room features a pink, blue and white color scheme, with wicker furnishings, queen bed and private bath, while the Sherman Safari Room boasts a unique jungle print decor and a queen bed. The innkeep-

ers' well-tended garden helps furnish some of the inn's foodstuffs.

Innkeeper(s): Burrell & Nancy Johnson.
Rates:$65-75. Gourmet Brkfst. Teas. Evening snacks. 4 rooms. 2 with shared baths. Beds:Q. Bicycling. Skiing. Swimming. Fishing.
Contact: Lois Johnson. Certificate may be used: Sept. 1, 1994 to May 1, 1995.

Platteville

The Cunningham House

110 Market St
Platteville 53818
(608)348-5532

1906. Settled by lead and zinc miners, Platteville is one of the oldest communities in Wisconsin. The Cunningham House is a three-story Classical Revival building with a front porch overlooking a tree-filled park in the historic district. Purchased from the local historical society, the innkeepers renovated the house into a comfortable bed & breakfast. Fresh baked muffins, as well as pancake-and-sausage breakfasts may be enjoyed on the back deck filled with flowers and porch swings. The nearby Shakespeare Festival runs July through August.

Innkeeper(s): Jud & Arletta Giese.
Rates:$50. Full Bkfst. 3 rooms. 3 with shared baths. Beds:QT. AC in room. Skiing. Swimming. Fishing.
Contact: Arletta Giese. Certificate may be used: Nov. 1 through March 31.

Plymouth

Yankee Hill Inn B&B

405 Collins St
Plymouth 53073
(414)892-2222

1870. Two outstanding examples of 19th-century architecture comprise this inn, one a striking Italianate Gothic listed in the National Register, and the other a lovely Queen Anne Victorian with many custom touches. Between the two impressive structures, visitors will choose from 11 spacious guest rooms, all featuring antique furnishings and handmade quilts. Visitors may walk to downtown, where they will find an antique mall, shopping and fine dining.

Innkeeper(s): Jim & Peg Stahlman.
Rates:$68-94. MC VISA. Full Bkfst. 11 rooms. Beds:QD. Skiing. Fishing.
Contact: Jim Stahlman. Certificate may be used: Nov. 1 through April 30, anytime except for holiday weekends or holidays. May 1 through Oct. 31, Monday through Thursday.

Port Washington

The Inn at Old Twelve Hundred
806 W Grand Ave
Port Washington 53074
(414)268-1200

1890. Beautiful antiques cover every inch of this huge Queen Anne home. Oak woodwork accents the careful decorating and attention to detail. The

William Guy Room has a working fireplace and a sitting area, the windows boast lace curtains and stained-glass insets. Gather around the sitting room fireplace or spend time on one of three enclosed porches. The expansive yard features a gazebo that adds to the Victorian feel of the home. Croquet, horseshoes and a tandem bicycle are available.

Innkeeper(s): Stephanie & Ellie Bresette.

Rates:$65-145. MC VISA AX. ContPlus Bkfst. 5 rooms. Fireplaces. Beds:KQD. TV, Phone, AC, Refrig. in room. Bicycling. Skiing. Swimming. Fishing.

Seen in: *Lake Shore Life, News Graphic, Ozaukee Press.*

Contact: Stephanie Bresette. Certificate may be used: Sunday through Thursday.

"I can't think of a more romantic or relaxing place to be."

Port Washington Inn
308 W Washington St
Port Washington 53074
(414)284-5583

1903. This blue and white, three-story Second Empire Victorian boasts original woodwork that remains in excellent condition. Stained-glass windows, a built-in fainting bench, gas lamps, polished oak floors and many original wall coverings are featured. The inn's suite offers a large four-poster bed, a sitting room, private balcony, and a view of the lake. Strawberry-stuffed French toast or Lemon Raspberry Streusel are favorite breakfast items. Harrington Beach State Park

is an easy drive from the inn.

Innkeeper(s): Connie Evans & Craig Siwy.

Rates:$60-95. MC VISA. Full Bkfst. 4 rooms. 2 with shared baths. Beds:Q. TV, AC in room. Bicycling. Skiing. Swimming. Fishing.

Contact: Connie Evans. Certificate may be used: Nov. 1 through April 30 (excluding December and Valentine's weekend).

Portage

The Inn at Grady's Farm
W10928 Hwy 33
Portage 53901
(608)742-3627

1903. The Baraboo River runs through this 300-acre farm. Guests will find a host of things to do without leaving the inn. The library contains a good collection of special-interest books and video

selections. Relax in the tub or Jacuzzi, or tour the beauty of the grounds. Test your canoeing skills on the river or simply take in the flower gardens. During warm weather, breakfast is served on the screened-in veranda. During winter months, ski aficionados will appreciate the proximity to the Cascade Mountain Ski Area.

Innkeeper(s): Carol Moeller & Donna Obright.

Rates:$55-105. MC VISA. Full Bkfst. 4 rooms. Beds:KQ. AC in room. Farm. Golf. Tennis. Skiing. Spa. Swimming. Horseback riding. Fishing.

Contact: Carol Moeller. Certificate may be used: Anytime, excluding holidays, September through June. Sunday through Thursday, July and August.

"We will never stay in a motel again."

Prescott

The Oak Street Inn B&B
506 Oak St
Prescott 54021
(715)262-4110

1854. The innkeepers at this inviting historic home believe every vacation at their inn should be a romantic experience. To encourage this, rooms are specially decorated with antiques, family heirlooms and soft, inviting colors. The Elizabeth Room includes a four-poster bed, separate dressing room and a clawfoot tub. The Avery Room is decked in dark blue and rose and has a private dining area. The Jenna Room features unique woodwork and windows. Each room is stocked with fresh flowers, and the homemade cookies are a special treat. Start off your morning with fresh muffins and a steaming mug of coffee before settling down to a hearty breakfast.

Innkeeper(s): Stan & Ann-Marie Johnson.

Rates:$60-85. MC VISA. Full Bkfst. 2 rooms. Beds:Q. AC in room. Golf. Tennis. Bicycling. Skiing. Swimming. Fishing.

Seen in: *Chicago Tribune, The Shopper, St. Croix Views.*

Contact: Ann-Marie Johnson. Certificate may be used: Anytime November through April. Sunday through Friday, May through October.

"We're now relaxed, refreshed and ready (though reluctant) to re-enter the rat race."

Racine

Lochnaiar Inn
1121 Lake Ave
Racine 53043
(414)633-3300

1915. This elegant three-story English Tudor mansion is situated on a bluff overlooking Lake Michigan. It is conveniently located within walking distance of downtown and the marina, which is well known for its year-round festivals and recreational activities. The finely furnished guest rooms offer visitors European-style comforts, including canopied four-poster beds, empress tubs and fresh-cut flowers. Business travelers will appreciate the many amenities offered for their convenience, while the more casual guests will marvel at the inn's historic grandeur.

Innkeeper(s): Jenny & Dawn Weisbrod.

Rates:$75-175. MC VISA AX DS. Full Bkfst. Gourmet Brkfst. 8 rooms. Fireplaces. Beds:KQ. Conference Rm. TV, Phone, AC in room. Skiing. Handicap access. Swimming. Fishing.

Seen in: *Racine Journal Times.*

Contact: Dawn Weisbrod. Certificate may be used: Nov. 1, 1994 - April 30, 1995.

"The inn is an absolute gem and you are both a delight."

Reedsburg

Parkview B&B
211 N Park St
Reedsburg 53959
(608)524-4333

1895. Tantalizingly close to Baraboo and Wisconsin Dells, this central Wisconsin inn overlooks a city park in the historic district. The gracious innkeepers delight in tending to their guest's desires and offer wake-up coffee and a morning paper. The home's first owners were in the hardware business, so there are many original, unique fixtures, in addition to hardwood floors, intricate woodwork, leaded and etched windows and a suitors' window. The downtown business district is just a block away.

Innkeeper(s): Tom & Donna Hofmann.

Rates:$55-70. MC VISA AX. Full Bkfst. 4 rooms. 2 with shared baths. Beds:KQT. AC in room. Skiing. Swimming. Fishing.

Seen in: *Reedsburg Times Press.*

Contact: Donna Hofmann. Certificate may be used: Sunday through Thursdays, June - October. Anytime remainder of the year except holidays.

"Your hospitality was great! You all made us feel right at home."

Richland Center

Lambs Inn B&B
Rt 2, Box 144
Richland Center 53581
(608)585-4301

1800. An old-fashioned family farm in a scenic hidden valley is the setting for this inn, with four guest rooms and an adjacent cottage. Ann's Room, with its cream walls, lace curtains and rose carpet,

is highlighted by a quilt handpieced by Donna's grandmother. Marie's Room, with its yellow and blue tones, offers a stunning view of the valley. The country kitchen is a favorite gathering place. Breakfast fare sometimes features bread pudding or kringle.

Innkeeper(s): Donna & Dick Messerschmidt.

Rates:$70-105. MC VISA. Full Bkfst. Evening snacks. 4 rooms. Beds:KQT. Farm. Skiing. Swimming. Fishing.

Contact: Donna Messerschmidt. Certificate may be used: Anytime.

The Mansion
323 S Central
Richland Center 53581
(608)647-2808

1916. As the birthplace of Frank Lloyd Wright, Richland Center attracts its share of visitors. Guests at this Mission Inn, with its Prairie-style overtones, are within walking distance of the Warehouse, designed by Wright during his Mayan period. The Warehouse also is home to the Frank Lloyd Wright Museum. The inn's visitors select from the Mandarin, Meadowlands, Oakwood and Scandia guest rooms. Other fine examples of Wright's work are found less than a half-hour's drive in Spring Green, site of his home and school, Taliesin. Summer visitors enjoy the Farmer's Market, a short walk from the inn.

Innkeeper(s): Beth Caulkins & Harvey Glanzer.

Rates:$45-55. ContPlus Bkfst. 5 rooms. 4 with shared baths. Fireplaces. Beds:KQT. Conference Rm. AC, Refrig. in room. Skiing.

Contact: Beth Caulkins. Certificate may be used: Sunday through Thursday, subject to availability.

Sister Bay

The Wooden Heart Inn
11086 Highway 42
Sister Bay 54234
(414)854-9097

1992. This contemporary log home in the woods of beautiful Door County offers antique furnishings, ceiling fans and queen beds. An adjoining loft is

available to read, relax or watch TV. Guests also are welcome to join the innkeepers on the main floor to enjoy the fireplace and refreshments, which are served each evening. The full country breakfasts are served in the great room. A gift shop, specializing in Christmas, country and Scandinavian items, is on the premises.

Innkeeper(s): Mike & Marilyn Hagerman.

Rates:$80-90. MC VISA. Full Bkfst. 3 rooms. Beds:Q. AC in room. Skiing. Swimming. Fishing.

Contact: Michael Hagerman. Certificate may be used: Sunday - Thursday, Nov. 1 - April 30.

Soldiers Grove

Old Oak Inn & Acorn Pub
Rt 1 Box 1500, Hwy 131 S
Soldiers Grove 54655
(608)624-5217

1902. Guests will find lodging and dining at this spacious Queen Anne Victorian turreted inn, a mile from town. Beautiful etched and stained glass

and woodcarving dominate the interior, while the guest rooms boast antique-style furnishings and imported woodwork. The area is well known for its antiquing, cross-country skiing and fishing, and many visitors just enjoy soaking up the abundant local scenery. The inn's facilities make it a natural location for meetings and receptions, and it also is popular with those celebrating anniversaries.

Innkeeper(s): Karen Raschella-Norbert.

Rates:$40-62. MC VISA. Full Bkfst. Gourmet Brkfst, Lunch, Dinner. Picnic lunches. Teas. Evening snacks. 7 rooms. 7 with shared baths. Beds:KT. TV, AC in room. Farm. Skiing. Fishing.

Contact: Karen Raschella-Norbert. Certificate may be used: Anytime Nov. 1 - April 1; Sunday through Thursday balance of the year.

Sparta

The Franklin Victorian
220 E Franklin St
Sparta 54656
(608)269-3894 (800)845-8767

1890. Built for a banker when Sparta was the hub of social life, this house still boasts of such splendid woods as black ash, curly birch, quarter-cut white oak, and red birch. Features include leaded windows in the library and dining room, many of the original filigreed brass light fixtures, and a magnificent sunset stained-glass window. Sparta is nestled

among the hills of Wisconsin's Coulee Region. Area attractions include rivers, trout streams, craft and antique shops.

Innkeeper(s): Lloyd & Jane Larson

Rates:$60-80. MC VISA. Full Bkfst. Gourmet Brkfst. Teas. 4 rooms. 2 with shared baths. Beds:KQ. Conference Rm. Bicycling. Skiing. Swimming. Fishing.

Contact: Lloyd Larson. Certificate may be used: No restrictions.

Just-N-Trails B&B
Rt 1 Box 274
Sparta 54656
(608)269-4522 (800)488-4521

1920. Nestled in a scenic valley sits the 200-acre dairy farm. Guests are welcome to share in the dairy operations and encouraged to explore the hiking and cross-country ski trails. In addition to delightfully decorated rooms in the farmhouse, there are a Scandinavian log house and plush restored granary for those desiring more privacy. The well-cared-for grounds and buildings reflect the innkeepers' pride in their home, which was built by Don's grandfather.

Innkeeper(s): Donna & Don Justin.

Rates:$65-245. MC VISA AX DS. Gourmet Brkfst. 9 rooms. 2 with shared baths. Fireplaces. Beds:KQ. Conference Rm. AC in room. Farm. Skiing. Spa. Swimming. Fishing.

Seen in: *Milwaukee Journal, Country, Wisconsin Woman, Wisconsin Trails.*

Contact: Donna Justin. Certificate may be used: Monday through Thursday year-round except holidays.

"Everything was perfect, but our favorite part was calling in the cows."

Spring Green

Hill Street B&B
353 Hill St
Spring Green 53588
(608)588-7751

1900. A lovely Queen Anne Victorian located in a historic city near the Wisconsin River, the Hill Street Bed & Breakfast is a real traveler's treat. Many buildings in the area bear the mark of

renowned architect Frank Lloyd Wright, and one of the inn's rooms is named in his honor. The inn also features a spacious wraparound porch, a turret alcove and beautifully carved antique woodwork. Madison and Wisconsin Dells are within easy driving distance.

Innkeeper(s): Kelly Phelps.

Rates:$50-80. Full Bkfst. 7 rooms. 2 with shared baths. Conference Rm. Sauna.

Seen in: *Wisconsin Trails, Milwaukee Magazine.*

Contact: Kelly Phelps. Certificate may be used: Oct. 1 through June 1, Sunday through Thursday except holidays.

"The best part of our stay was your wonderful breakfast and your company while we ate."

Spring Green (Plain)

Bettinger House B&B
855 Wachter Ave, Hwy 23
Spring Green (Plain) 53577
(608)546-2951 Fax:(608)546-2951

1904. This two-story brick inn once was home to the town's midwife, (and the innkeeper's grandmother) who delivered more than 300 babies here. The current innkeepers are just as eager to bring new guests into their home. The Elizabeth Room, named for the midwife, boasts a round king-size bed and private bath. Lavish country breakfasts often include potatoes dug from the innkeeper's off-site farm, sour cream cucumbers, breakfast pie with eggs and sausage, rhubarb coffeecake, and sorbet. Area attractions are plentiful, including the House on the Rock, St. Anne's Shrine and the Wisconsin River. Be sure to visit the nearby Cedar Grove Cheese Factory.

Innkeeper(s): Marie & Jim Neider.

Rates:$45-55. MC VISA. Full Bkfst. 3 rooms. 3 with shared baths. Beds:KQT. AC in room. Skiing. Fishing.

Contact: Marie Neider. Certificate may be used: Anytime except Friday, Saturday and holidays.

Springbrook

The Stout Trout B&B
Rt 1 Box 1630
Springbrook 54875
(715)466-2790

1900. Located on 40 acres of rolling, wooded countryside, The Stout Trout overlooks a lily-ringed bay on Gull Lake. The lake can be viewed from the living room, dining areas and second-floor guest rooms. The inn features wood-plank floors, folk art, classic prints and country-style furniture.

Homemade jams and maple syrup are served.

Innkeeper(s): Kathleen Fredricks.

Rates:$65. Full Bkfst. 4 rooms. Beds:Q. Bicycling. Skiing. Swimming. Fishing.

Seen in: *Chicago Tribune, Wisconsin West Magazine*.

Contact: Kathleen Fredricks. Certificate may be used: All year, Monday - Thursday, except July, August, September.

"Thank you again for the comfortable setting, great food and gracious hospitality!"

Stevens Point

Dreams of Yesteryear
1100 Brawley St
Stevens Point 54481
(715)341-4525 Fax:(715)344-3047

1901. This elegant Queen Anne Victorian inn, listed in the National Register of Historic Places, is within walking distance of downtown, the Wisconsin River and the University of Wisconsin-Stevens Point. Visitors to the Isabella Suite will be charmed by its footed

tub, queen-size Victorian bed, reading nook and high tank water closet. The inn features golden oak woodwork, hardwood floors and leaded glass. The full breakfasts are served in the formal dining room. An excellent hiking trail is found just one block from the inn.

Innkeeper(s): Bonnie & Bill Maher.

Rates:$55-110. MC VISA DS. Full Bkfst. Gourmet Brkfst. Teas. Evening snacks. 5 rooms. Beds:KQT. TV, AC in room. Bicycling. Skiing. Swimming. Fishing.

Contact: Bonnie Maher. Certificate may be used: September - April, Sunday through Thursday.

Marcyanna's B&B
440 N Old Wausau Rd
Stevens Point 54481
(715)341-9922

1990. Sixty-five wooded acres on the Wisconsin River make up the grounds of this contemporary farmhouse inn, which offers convenient access to many recreational activities. Visitors select either the Old-Fashioned or Oriental guest rooms, both filled with many antiques and family heirlooms. The grounds provide wonderful opportunities for hiking, picnicking and relaxing. Fine cross-country skiing, golfing and snowmobiling are found nearby, and Bukolt Park, with its public boat landing, is just a short distance from the inn.

Innkeeper(s): Dennis & Marcy Ferriter.

Rates:$55-60. Full Bkfst. Gourmet Brkfst. 2 rooms. Beds:DT. Skiing. Fishing.

Contact: Marcyanna Ferriter. Certificate may be used: January - April; June - August.

Stone Lake

New Mountain B&B
Rt 1, Box 73C
Stone Lake 54876
(715)865-2486 (800)639-6822

1991. Visitors enjoy a hilltop view of Big Sissabagama Lake at this Scandinavian-style inn. Its four charming guest rooms include the Loon's Nest and Winterwood Room, which occupy the inn's second floor. The family-style breakfasts are served on the screen porch in warm weather. The innkeepers cannot accommodate visitors' pets, but encourage guests to lavish attention on the resident animals. Fishing aficionados will appreciate the lake's offerings, including bass, muskies and walleyes. Guests may borrow boats, canoes and a paddleboat. Dock space is available and be sure to try the sauna.

Innkeeper(s): Jim & Elaine Nyberg.

Rates:$50-60. Full Bkfst. 4 rooms. 3 with shared baths. Beds:QD. Skiing. Handicap access. Sauna. Swimming. Fishing.

Contact: James Nyberg. Certificate may be used: Oct. 1 through May 1, 1995.

Sturgeon Bay

The Inn at Cedar Crossing
336 Louisiana St
Sturgeon Bay 54235
(414)743-4200

1884. This historic hotel, in the National Register, is a downtown three-story brick building, that once

housed street-level shops with second-floor apartments for the tailors, shopkeepers and pharmacists who worked below. The upstairs, now guest rooms, is decorated with floral wallpapers, stenciling and antiques. The Anniversary Room, for instance, has a mahogany bed and a whirlpool tub. There are two dining rooms, both with fireplaces, on the lower level. The waterfront is three blocks away.
Innkeeper(s): Terry Wulf.

Rates:$79-135. MC VISA. Full Bkfst. Gourmet Dinner. Picnic lunches. Evening snacks. 9 rooms. Fireplaces. Beds:KQ. Phone, AC in room. Skiing. Handicap access. Spa. Swimming. Fishing.

Seen in: *New Month Magazine, Milwaukee Sentinel, Chicago Sun-Times, Green Bay Press Gazette.*

Contact: Terry Wulf. Certificate may be used: Sunday through Thursday nights; November through April, excluding holidays.

"Your warmth and friendliness is the reason for our returning time and again."

The Scofield House B&B
908 Michigan St, PO Box 761
Sturgeon Bay 54235
(414)743-7727

1900. Mayor Herbert Scofield, prominent locally in the lumber and hardware business, built this late Victorian house with a sturdy square tower and inlaid floors that feature intricate borders patterned

in cherry, birch, maple, walnut, and red and white oak. Oak moldings throughout the house boast raised designs of bows, ribbons, swags and flowers. Equally lavish decor is featured in the guest rooms with fluffy flowered comforters and cabbage rose wallpapers highlighting romantic antique bedsteads. Door County cherry muffins are a house specialty.
Rates:$69-180. Gourmet Brkfst. Teas. 6 rooms. Fireplaces. Beds:Q. TV, AC, Refrig. in room. Golf. Tennis. Skiing. Spa. Swimming. Fishing.

Seen in: *Innsider, Glamour, Country, Wisconsin Trails, Green Bay Press Gazette, Chicago Tribune.*

Contact: Frances Cecil. Certificate may be used: Nov. 15 - April 30, Monday - Thursday (no holidays)(two-night minimum reservation).

"Lovely accommodations and warm hospitality."

Viola

The Inn at Elk Run
S 4125 County Hwy SS
Viola 54664
(608)625-2062 (800)729-7313
Fax:(608)625-4310

1910. This Dutch Colonial farmhouse in the scenic Mississippi River Valley region offers a relaxing getaway from city life. Visitors select from the Sarah, Simplicity or Sunrise rooms, all featuring ceiling fans, clock radios, desks, phone and turndown service. Guests are treated to full country breakfasts and afternoon teas. The area is well known for its antiquing, apple orchards, bike trails and cross-country skiing. In addition, many guests enjoy exploring the local Amish settlement and shops or taking a canoe trip on the nearby Kickapoo River.
Innkeeper(s): Janet & Roger Hugg.

Rates:$40-55. Full Bkfst. Teas. 3 rooms. 3 with shared baths. Beds:QT. Phone in room. Farm. Skiing. Swimming. Fishing.

Contact: Janet Hugg. Certificate may be used: November - April.

Viroqua

Viroqua Heritage Inn
220 E Jefferson St
Viroqua 54665
(608)637-3306

1890. The three-story turret of this gabled Queen Anne mansion houses the sitting rooms of two guest chambers and the formal first-floor parlor. Columns, spindles and assorted gingerbread spice the exterior while beveled glass, ornate fireplaces and crystal chandeliers grace the interior. An antique baby grand piano, a violin and Victrola reside in the music room. Breakfast is served on the original carved-oak buffet and dining table.
Innkeeper(s): Nancy Rhoades.

Rates:$45-75. MC VISA AX DS. Full Bkfst. 4 rooms. 2 with shared baths. Beds:QD. Conference Rm. Bicycling. Skiing. Swimming. Fishing.

Seen in: *Milwaukee Magazine, Lax.*

Contact: Nancy Rhoades-Seevers. Certificate may be used: Oct. 15, 1994 to June 1, 1995.

"Wonderful house, great hosts."

Walworth

Arscott House B&B
PO Box 946, 241 S Main
Walworth 53184
(414)275-3233

1903. Built by a master carpenter at the turn of the century, this turreted Queen Anne Victorian has been lovingly restored to its original stylings. A

new addition is the inn's Arizona Suite, with Southwestern decor, a spacious sitting room and a private, outside entrance. A roomy front porch and two outside decks are favorite relaxing spots, and guests may breakfast in their rooms if they wish. The inn is just minutes from Lake Geneva's many attractions.

Innkeeper(s): Valerie C. Dudek.
Rates:$45-65. MC VISA DS. Full Bkfst. EP. Teas. 5 rooms. 3 with shared baths. Beds:QD. TV, AC in room. Bicycling. Skiing. Swimming. Fishing.
Contact: Valerie Dudek. Certificate may be used: October - December, Sunday through Thursday (example: Full charge for Saturday stay, Sunday night free).

Waupaca

Crystal River B&B
E1369 Rural Rd
Waupaca 54981
(715)258-5333

1853. The stately beauty of this historic Greek Revival farmhouse is rivaled only by its riverside setting. Each room features a view of the water, garden, woods or all three. A Victorian gazebo, down comforters and delicious breakfasts, with pecan sticky buns, a special favorite, add to guests' enjoyment. Exploring the village of Rural, which is in the National Register, will delight those interested in bygone days. Recreational activities abound, with the Chain O'Lakes and a state park nearby.

Innkeeper(s): Gene & Lois Sorenson.
Rates:$55-95. MC VISA. Full Bkfst. 7 rooms. 2 with shared baths. Fireplaces. Beds:KQ. AC in room. Bicycling. Skiing. Swimming. Fishing.
Seen in: *Resorter, Stevens Point Journal, Wisconsin Trail Magazine.*
Contact: Lois Sorenson. Certificate may be used: Monday through Thursday.

"It was like being king for a day."

Thomas Pipe Inn
11032 Pipe Rd
Waupaca 54981
(715)824-3161

1855. A former stagecoach stop in the pre-railroad days, this historic Greek Revival inn offers four elegant guest rooms to visitors, many who have come to explore the Chain O'Lakes and its many attractions. Elizabeth's Room boasts a clawfoot tub and canopy bed, while the Florence Pipe Room features a brass bed loaded with pillows. The Thomas Pipe Room sports a beautiful view of the woods and Marjorie's Suite has an antique bed and sitting room with sleeper sofa and fireplace. Hartman's Creek State Park is a 10-minute drive from the inn.

Innkeeper(s): Dick & Marcie Windisch.
Rates:$65-95. MC VISA. Full Bkfst. 4 rooms. Fireplaces. Beds:Q. AC in room. Farm. Skiing. Swimming. Fishing.
Contact: Marcella Windisch. Certificate may be used: January to April, Sunday to Thursday.

Waupun

The Rose Ivy Inn
228 S Watertown St
Waupun 53963
(414)324-2127

1900. This elegant Queen Anne Victorian with distinctive turret features four guest rooms. The rooms boast antiques, lace and romantic Victorian touches. Visitors will enjoy the city's five original bronze statues, including James Earl Fraser's well-known "End of the Trail," a national historical landmark. The area boasts many outstanding antique, craft and specialty shops, and the Horicon Marsh Wildlife Refuge and Wild Goose State Trail are less than two miles from the inn.

Innkeeper(s): Melody & Kenneth Kris.
Rates:$59-79. MC VISA AX DS. Full Bkfst. Teas. Evening snacks. 4 rooms. 2 with shared baths. Beds:QD. AC in room. Bicycling. Skiing.
Contact: Melody Kris. Certificate may be used: November through April excluding Friday and Saturday nights Nov. 15 through Dec. 31, excluding Christmas Eve, Christmas, New Year's Eve, New Year's Day and Valentine's Day.

Whitewater

Victoria-On-Main B&B
622 W Main St
Whitewater 53190
(414)473-8400

1895. This Queen Anne Victorian is located in the heart of Whitewater National Historic District, adjacent to the University of Wisconsin. It was built for Edward Engebretson, mayor of Whitewater. Each guest room is named for a Wisconsin hardwood. The Red Oak Room, Cherry Room and Bird's Eye Maple Room all feature antiques, Laura Ashley prints and down comforters. A hearty breakfast is served and there are kitchen facilities available for light meal preparation. Whitewater Lake and Kettle Moraine State Forest are five minutes away.

Innkeeper(s): Nancy S. Wendt.

Rates:$65-75. MC VISA. Full Bkfst. 3 rooms. 2 with shared baths. Fireplaces. Beds:QDT. TV in room. Skiing. Swimming. Fishing.

Contact: Nancy Wendt. Certificate may be used: November through March.

"We loved it. Wonderful hospitality."

Winter

Chippewa River Inn B&B
N4836 County Rd G
Winter 54896
(715)266-2662 (800)867-2447
Fax:(715)266-2662

1905. Guests may choose relaxation or recreation at this northwoods inn, surrounded by pines and with easy access to the river. Each of the inn's pine-paneled guest rooms has its own theme. Guests enjoy a full breakfast and evening snack and often like to stroll the grounds looking for birds and other wildlife, such as deer and otters. Those in search of muskies and walleye like to use the Chippewa Flowage, 15 minutes from the inn.

Innkeeper(s): Sue & Dean Hesselberg, Karen & Charles Nielsen.

Rates:$55. Full Bkfst. Evening snacks. 8 rooms. 5 with shared baths. Beds:QT. Skiing. Swimming. Fishing.

Contact: Karen Nielsen. Certificate may be used: Anytime Sept. 6 through May 26.

Wisconsin Dells

The Dells Carver Inn
1270 E Hiawatha Dr
Wisconsin Dells 53965
(608)254-4766

1991. This contemporary lakefront inn, built in the chateau style, offers family-oriented lodging to those visiting one of the state's most popular sites. The full breakfasts may be enjoyed in the dining area or on the deck or sun porch. After breakfast, guests may move to the inn's conversation areas in the large living room, soak up the sun on the private beach or try their hands at parasailing or jet skiing. Also a popular destination of honeymooners and those celebrating anniversaries, the inn boasts a hot tub and several romantic guest rooms, including Eileen's Victorian Reminiscence and Samantha's Sugar and Spice.

Innkeeper(s): Tom & Eileen Gruman.

Rates:$55-65. Full Bkfst. 5 rooms. 2 with shared baths. Beds:KQ. TV, Phone, AC in room. Skiing. Spa. Swimming. Fishing.

Contact: Eileen Gruman. Certificate may be used: October, 1994 through April, 1995.

Wisconsin Rapids

The Nash House
1020 Oak Street
Wisconsin Rapids 54494
(715)424-2001 Fax:(715)424-2001

1903. A former lieutenant governor was born in this Stick Victorian inn still bearing his name. A full breakfast is served in the dining room, on the outdoor patio or screened porch. Guests will enjoy the works of local artists featured throughout the rooms. The inn is well-equipped to handle business travelers, who often manage to squeeze in a round at one of the area's five golf courses. Other visitors take advantage of tours offered at a local cheese factory, cranberry marsh, dairy farm or paper mill.

Innkeeper(s): Jim & Phyllis Custer.

Rates:$50. MC VISA AX DS. Full Bkfst. 3 rooms. Beds:Q. AC in room. Bicycling.

Contact: Phyllis Custer. Certificate may be used: Oct. 1, 1994 - May 31, 1995, as rooms are available.

Wyoming

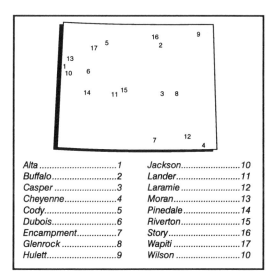

Alta

High Country Comforts
Route 1, Box 3720
Alta 83422
(307)353-8560 (800)254-2331
Fax:(307)353-8486

1977. Flannel sheets, down comforters and luxurious towels await guests at this log house inn where the innkeeper describes the decor as American country with rustic elegance. Located above the majestic Teton Valley and just minutes from Grand Targhee Ski & Summer Resort and Driggs, Idaho, the inn offers a base for a myriad of outdoor activities. Guests can enjoy an upstairs pool table, bar and lounge area that overlooks the center of the home and its cozy, warm atmosphere.

Innkeeper(s): Terry Whelan.

Rates:$60-90. MC VISA DS. Full Bkfst. 4 rooms. 4 with shared baths. Beds:QT. Conference Rm. Farm. Golf. Bicycling. Skiing. Spa. Swimming. Horseback riding. Stables. Fishing.

Seen in: *Jackson Hole News, Jackson Hole Guide, Teton Valley News.*

Contact: Terry Whelan. Certificate may be used: Anytime.

Buffalo

Cloud Peak Inn
590 N Burritt Ave
Buffalo 82834
(307)684-5794

1906. Built at the turn of the century by a wealthy rancher, this inn features a graceful staircase, elegant parlor and spacious bedrooms. At the end of the day, guests can relax in front of the "fossilized" fireplace, soak in the Jacuzzi or unwind on the porch or balcony. Arrangements can be made for dinner although there are some excellent restaurants in the area. A fine golf course is only two blocks from the inn. The innkeepers will tell you about some "secret" fishing spots in the mountains that are sure bets. Geologic tours of the area can be arranged with prior notice.

Innkeeper(s): Rick & Kathy Brus.

Rates:$45-75. MC VISA AX. Full Bkfst. Gourmet Brkfst. Evening snacks. 5 rooms. 2 with shared baths. Beds:KQT. Skiing. Spa. Swimming. Fishing.

Contact: Kathleen Brus. Certificate may be used: May 1, 1994 to April 30, 1995.

Casper

Durbin Street Inn B&B
843 S Durbin
Casper 82601
(307)577-5774 Fax:(307)266-5441

1917. This American Foursquare house is located along a street lined with tall trees, within a national historic district and close to downtown and Caspar College. Rooms include a huge living room with a fireplace and library, and a separate conference room. Family-style breakfasts including blueberry pancakes, eggs, sausage, biscuits and gravy are served in the dining room. Casper has a walking tour of its buildings dating from the late 1800s and early 1900s. Many of the buildings are striking because of the corbelling of the brickwork.

Innkeeper(s): Don & Sherry Frigon.

Rates:$55-70. MC VISA AX DC DS CB. Full Bkfst. Gourmet Dinner. Teas. Evening snacks. 5 rooms. 4 with shared baths. Fireplaces. Beds:QD. Conference Rm. Refrig. in room. Skiing. Swimming. Fishing.

Contact: Sherry Frigon. Certificate may be used: Anytime upon availability.

Cheyenne

A. Drummonds Ranch B&B
399 Happy Jack Rd, Hwy 210
Cheyenne 82007
(307)634-6042 Fax:(307)635-6744

1990. With 120 acres of Wyoming wilderness and a nearby National Forest and State Park, this Old English farmhouse offers a quiet retreat. An outside hot tub, adjacent to the house, provides a view of the surrounding area and for evening soakers, an unmatched night sky. Boarding is available for those traveling with horses and pets. A. Drummonds Ranch is located half way between Cheyenne and Laramie.

Rates:$65-80. Full Bkfst. Picnic lunches. Teas. Evening snacks. 3 rooms. 2 with shared baths. Beds:QT. Bicycling. Skiing. Spa. Swimming. Stables. Fishing.

Contact: Taydie Drummond. Certificate may be used: January - March, October - December.

Adventurers' Country B&B Raven Cry Ranch
3803 I-80 S. Service Rd
Cheyenne 82009
(307)632-4087

1989. Situated behind an adobe fence, this Southwestern-style inn rests on a knoll overlooking 102 acres of prairie. Guests enjoy the tree-lined

adobe courtyard, flower gardens and a front veranda filled with rocking chairs and swings. The inn offers murder mystery weekends and a Western Adventure package. Weekly rodeos, a scenic rail excursion, and crystal and granite lakes are nearby.

Innkeeper(s): Fern & Chuck White.

Rates:$65-75. Full Bkfst. Gourmet Brkfst. Dinner. Picnic lunches. Evening snacks. 4 rooms. Beds:KQ. Phone in room. Farm. Skiing. Horseback riding. Stables. Fishing.

Contact: Fern White. Certificate may be used: Not July 22-31, or holidays.

"The service was superbly personalized with great attention to detail and a great down-home cowboy atmosphere."

The Howdy Pardner B&B
1920 Tranquility Rd
Cheyenne 82009
(307)634-6493

1981. This secluded ranch home is perched high on a hill where nearby wildlife includes elk, deer, antelope and geese. Cathedral ceilings and a buckstove fireplace are features of the living room. Guest rooms offer a western decor. The innkeeper is known for her huge breakfasts which may include biscuits and gravy, Texas potatoes, baked cheese grits and country breakfast pie with eggs and sausage. The area is known for its great stream and lake fishing. Cheyenne attractions that shouldn't be missed are the Old West Museum at Frontier Park, Historic Governor's Mansion, and Terry Bison Ranch.

Innkeeper(s): Jan Peterson.

Rates:$50-65. MC VISA. Gourmet Brkfst. Evening snacks. 3 rooms. 2 with shared baths. Beds:QT. TV in room. Skiing. Handicap access. Fishing.

Contact: Jan Peterson. Certificate may be used: Anytime except last two weeks of July each year. All other times okay.

Porch Swing B&B
712 E 20th St
Cheyenne 82001
(307)778-7182

1907. At this Victorian inn, breakfast is served on the back porch in summer and by the dining room fire in cold weather. Guests can enjoy items like

yeast waffles with maple syrup and fresh strawberries, orange pecan French toast and German pancakes with Swiss honey butter. All these recipes and more are found in the innkeepers' cookbook available for sale. The property's summer gardens are colorful and fragrant with a variety of perennials, aromatic and culinary herbs, wildflowers and annuals. The innkeepers would be happy to send you home with a cutting or seeds of something that's taken your fancy.

Innkeeper(s): Thomas & Carole Eppler.

Rates:$43-54. MC VISA. Full Bkfst. Gourmet Brkfst. Teas. Evening snacks. 3 rooms. 2 with shared baths. Beds:QD. Bicycling. Skiing.

Contact: Carole Eppler. Certificate may be used: Anytime except last 10 days in July.

Cody

The Lockhart Inn
109 W Yellowstone Ave
Cody 82414
(307)587-6074 (800)377-7255
Fax:(307)587-8644

1890. Once the home of author and journalist Caroline Lockhart, the veranda of this Victorian inn has beautiful mountain views. Rooms are deco-

rated with antiques, old-fashioned beds and a claw-foot tub. Breakfast is served on fine china at your private table in the dining room. Airport pick-up service is offered, as well as making reservations for dining, river rafting, golfing, rodeo events and more.

Innkeeper(s): Cindy Baldwin & Steven Farnes.

Rates:$55-90. MC VISA AX DC DS CB. Full Bkfst. Gourmet Dinner. Picnic lunches. Teas. 7 rooms. Beds:QT. TV, Phone, AC in room. Skiing. Handicap access. Swimming. Fishing.

Contact: Cindy Baldwin. Certificate may be used: October through April.

Parson's Pillow
1202 14th St
Cody 82414
(307)587-2382 (800)377-2348

1902. This historic building originally served as the Methodist-Episcopal Church. Surrounded by a picket fence and a flower-filled garden, it features a bell tower complete with the original bell donated by a cousin of Buffalo Bill. A baby grand piano sits in the parlor, once the meeting room. Guest rooms feature antiques and quilts. Early breakfasts and box

lunches are available for hunters and fishermen. The Buffalo Bill Historical Center and the Cody Historic Walking Tour are nearby.

Innkeeper(s): Lee & Elly Larabee.

Rates:$55-75. MC VISA DS. Full Bkfst. Teas. 4 rooms. 2 with shared baths. Beds:Q. Golf. Tennis. Skiing. Swimming. Horseback riding. Fishing.

Contact: Lee Larabee. Certificate may be used: September through May.

Dubois

Jakey's Fork Homestead
Box 635
Dubois 82513
(307)455-2769

1896. Nestled on a hillside, this farmhouse-style inn overlooks the original turn-of-the-century log buildings and Jakey's Fork Creek, an unspoiled trout stream. This rustic home is heated by a wood

stove and large brick fireplace. The rooms are decorated with mountain artwork and photography. Through the gardens and down the boardwalk are the original sod-covered homestead buildings. One of the buildings has been converted to a workshop where the innkeeper crafts unique handmade knives.

Innkeeper(s): Irene & Justin Bridges.

Rates:$60. VISA. Full Bkfst. Picnic lunches. 2 rooms. 2 with shared baths. Beds:Q. Skiing. Sauna. Fishing.

Contact: Irene Bridges. Certificate may be used: Labor Day 1994 to June 30, 1995 except Dec. 15-31. Labor Day, 1995 to Dec. 15, 1995.

Encampment

Grand & Sierra Lodge
1016 Lomax, Box 312
Encampment 82325
(307)327-5200

1978. Nestled in the Medicine Bow National Forest, this hand-crafted Lodgepole Pine inn has a deck that overlooks the Encampment River Canyon. The innkeepers have 38 years of experience in guiding and outfitting, and they offer a variety of packages that include fishing float trips on the North Platte River and family sightseeing trips to view waterfowl, mountain sheep, eagles, deer, elk, beaver, mink and moose. After a day trip, which can be custom-made, guests may relax in the outdoor spa or by the rock fireplace and the large den.

Innkeeper(s): Glen, Skyler & Marcy Knotwell.

Rates:$39-65. MC VISA. Full Bkfst. 5 rooms. 3 with shared baths. Beds:KDT. Conference Rm. Skiing. Spa. Swimming. Fishing.

Contact: Marcy Knotwell. Certificate may be used: July 1 - Oct. 31, 1994; May 28 - Oct. 31, 1995.

Glenrock

Hotel Higgins
PO Box 741, 416 W Birch
Glenrock 82637
(307)436-9212 (800)458-0144
Fax:(307)436-9213

1916. Elm trees and juniper frame this restored hotel, in the National Register. Located on the Oregon Trail, it is near the home station of the

Pony Express. There are many period furnishings original to the hotel, including brass and iron beds. Polished tile floors and beveled-glass doors add to the inn's ambiance. Each morning a full gourmet breakfast is served with champagne. The Paisley Shawl is a restaurant on the premises.

Innkeeper(s): Jack & Margaret Doll.

Rates:$58-68. MC VISA DC CB. Full Bkfst. Gourmet Lunch, Dinner. 12 rooms. 6 with shared baths. Beds:KT. Conference Rm. TV, Phone, AC in

room. Skiing. Handicap access. Swimming. Fishing.

Seen in: *Travel & Leisure, Rapid City Journal.*

Contact: Carol Thomas. Certificate may be used: December, 1994 through April, 1995.

Hulett

Diamond L Guest Ranch
PO Box 70
Hulett 82720
(307)467-5236 (800)851-5909

1979. The main lodge is built of cedar logs and is more than 4,000 square feet. There's a 10-foot-high rock fireplace and open-beam ceiling in the main parlor. The innkeepers like to limit the number of guests per week to 12 so they can personally cater to each of them. Besides horseback riding, guests can fill their days by moving cattle, splitting wood, feeding the livestock or collecting the eggs and feeding the chickens. Spend an hour, a day or a week being a "real" ranch hand. Guests also may do nothing but relax by soaking in the hot tub or sitting on the deck and enjoying the scenery.

Innkeeper(s): Gary & Carolyn Luther.

Rates:$60-110. MC VISA AX. Full Bkfst. MAP available. 5 rooms. 3 with shared baths. Beds:DT. Skiing. Spa. Swimming. Stables. Fishing.

Contact: Carolyn Luther. Certificate may be used: March 15 to June 1; Oct. 1-28; Dec. 1-31.

Jackson

H. C. Richards B&B
Box 2606, 160 W Deloney
Jackson 83001
(307)733-6704 Fax:(307)733-0930

1969. Many afternoons at this ranch-style stone home are filled with the smells of baking scones, eccles cakes, crumpets or other special items from the large kitchen. Located just one-and-a-half blocks west of the town square, the inn is within walking distance to many museums, art galleries, restaurants, theaters and shops. A tennis court, basketball court and park are just out the back door and skiing is a short six blocks away. The area is a paradise for outdoor enthusiasts, as the Grand Teton and Yellowstone national parks are nearby.

Innkeeper(s): Jackie Williams.

Rates:$65-90. MC VISA. Full Bkfst. Gourmet Brkfst. Teas. 3 rooms. Beds:QD. TV, Phone in room. Skiing. Swimming. Fishing.

Contact: Jackie Williams. Certificate may be used: October, November, December, January, February, March, April, May.

The Sassy Moose Inn
HC 362, Teton Village Rd
Jackson 83001
(307)733-1277 (800)356-1277
Fax:(307)739-0793

1992. All of the rooms at this log-house-style inn have spectacular Teton views. The Mountain Room has a rock fireplace, queen bed and mountain cabin decor. The River Room's decor is dominated by the colors of the Snake River and accented with antiques. The inn is five minutes from Teton Village and the Jackson Hole Ski Resort. Teton Pines Golf Course and Nordic Trails are just across the road. After a day of activities, enjoy sharing your experiences over tea or relaxing in the large hot tub.

Innkeeper(s): Polly Englant.

Rates:$99-154. MC VISA. Full Bkfst. Teas. 5 rooms. Fireplaces. Beds:KQT. Skiing. Spa. Swimming. Fishing.

Contact: Craig Kelley. Certificate may be used: All times except: months of July and August and Dec. 15 - Jan. 5.

Twin Trees B&B
575 S Willow at Snow King, Box 7533
Jackson 83001
(307)739-9737 (800)728-7337

1991. This country-ranch-style inn is located at the base of Snow King, Jackson's ski mountain. Skiers are within walking distance to the ski area and transportation is readily available to other nearby ski areas. The three rooms have their own personality and benefit from sunshine and close mountain views. Luxury appointments include down  comforters, plush linens and bathrobes. Breakfasts are served in the sunny dining room or (weather permitting) on the decks.

Innkeeper(s): Patricia Martin.

Rates:$79-105. MC VISA AX. Full Bkfst. Gourmet Brkfst. Teas. 3 rooms. Beds:KQT. Bicycling. Skiing. Spa. Swimming. Fishing.

Contact: Patricia Martin. Certificate may be used: Nov. 1 - Dec. 15, 1994; April 1 - May 15, 1995; Nov. 1 - Dec. 15, 1995.

Lander

Piece of Cake B&B
2343 Baldwin Creek Rd, PO Box 866
Lander 82520
(307)332-7608

1992. View roaming wildlife and the breathtaking

Wind River mountains from more than 1,000 square feet of deck attached to this lodge-style log home. Guest rooms include a Jacuzzi tub in a private bath. If you want to touch bases with the outside world, a satellite dish brings more than 200 stations for your viewing pleasure. The inn is open year-round and winter guests can enjoy the Continental Divide Snowmobile Trail. In the summer, mountain bikes are available.

Innkeeper(s): Ed & Betty Lewis.

Rates:$65-80. Full Bkfst. Gourmet Dinner. Picnic lunches. Evening snacks. 2 rooms. 1 with shared bath. Fireplaces. Beds:QT. Conference Rm. Phone, Refrig. in room. Bicycling. Skiing. Swimming. Fishing.

Contact: Betty Lewis. Certificate may be used: Anytime.

Laramie

Annie Moore's Guest House
819 University
Laramie 82070
(307)721-4177 (800)552-8992

1910. Aspens and a terraced flower garden mark the entrance to this Queen Anne Victorian across the street from the University of Wyoming. The decor is in an eclectic style with some mission pieces featured. The Purple Room offers a king bed, a bay window and deep purple carpet. Over muffins and coffee, guests enjoy breakfast conversations with many international travelers. Walk seven blocks to downtown and the Laramie Plains Museum or go across the street to the University of Wyoming's American Heritage Center, art museum or library.

Innkeeper(s): Ann Acuff & Joe Bundy.

Rates:$50-60. MC VISA AX DS. ContPlus Bkfst. 6 rooms. 6 with shared baths. Beds:KQT. Phone in room. Skiing. Fishing.

Contact: Ann Acuff. Certificate may be used: October through March.

Moran

The Inn at Buffalo Fork
18200 E Hwy 287, PO Box 311
Moran 83013
(307)543-2010

1994. This farmhouse with covered porch, shutters and gables has the incredible Teton Range as its backdrop. Herds of elk pass by and sandhill cranes visit this five-acre property, located in the heart of the Buffalo Valley ranchlands. Breakfast is served beside a rustic, river-rock hearth. The host has more than 25 years of experience guiding Snake River scenic tours and fishing expeditions. He is also the grandson of one of the original Jackson

Hole homesteaders and a lifelong resident who is well-versed in the history and geography of the area.

Innkeeper(s): Eugene & Jeannie Ferrin.

Rates:$85-140. MC VISA AX. Full Bkfst. AP available. Picnic lunches. Teas. Evening snacks. 5 rooms. Beds:KQT. Skiing. Handicap access. Spa. Swimming. Fishing.

Contact: Jeannie Ferrin. Certificate may be used: From Oct. 1 through May 15 (with Christmas- Dec. 20-Jan. 1- and Spring vacations excluded).

Diamond D Ranch-Outfitters
Buffalo Valley Rd, Box 211
Moran 83013
(307)543-2479

1972. Located on the scenic Buffalo Valley Road, this log house inn serves many purposes including being an old hunting lodge, guest ranch, pack trip outfitter, cross-country skiing lodge and snowmobile and base lodge for touring Yellowstone and Grand Teton national parks. There's a relaxed atmosphere with a flexible schedule. The main lodge has two units each with private baths and the cabins have two units also with private baths. The staff teaches Western horsemanship and has horses for each guest's ability.

Innkeeper(s): Rod & Rae Doty.

Rates:$99. MC VISA. Full Bkfst. 11 rooms. 4 with shared baths. Fireplaces. Beds:QT. TV, Refrig. in room. Bicycling. Skiing. Spa. Stables. Fishing.

Contact: Rod Doty. Certificate may be used: Dec. 15 to May 15.

Pinedale

Window on the Winds
10151 Hwy 191, PO Box 135
Pinedale 82941
(307)367-2600 Fax:(307)367-2395

1968. At the base of the Wind River Mountains, this log house inn has lodgepole pine queen beds, down comforters and rustic furnishings. A grand

room with a breathtaking view of the mountains offers a hearth for warmth and comfort. There is a sun room with a hot tub. Pinedale was the location for the Green River Rendezvous. In the early 1800s, trappers, traders, Indians and others in the

area would gather to trade goods. The Mountain Men and Indians of Pinedale re-enact The Rendezvous every year.

Innkeeper(s): Leanne McClain & Doug McKay.

Rates:$52-60. MC VISA DS. Full Bkfst. Picnic lunches. Evening snacks. 4 rooms. 4 with shared baths. Beds:QT. Conference Rm. Golf. Skiing. Spa. Horseback riding. Stables. Fishing.

Contact: Leanne McClain. Certificate may be used: September through May.

Riverton

Cottonwood Ranch B&B
951 Missouri Valley Rd
Riverton 82501
(307)856-3064

1976. This is a working farm ranch of 250 acres in the heart of cowboy country and 15 minutes away from Riverton. Farm tours are available as time permits to view the cow, calf and lamb operation, as well as the raising of corn, oats, malting barley and alfalfa. Farm dogs and cats also roam the property. Good hunting and fishing in three lakes, three rivers and multiple streams are within a half-hour's drive. Guests are served a full farm breakfast featuring homemade breads, home-canned preserves and the farm's own honey.

Innkeeper(s): Judie & Earl Anglen.

Rates:$40-45. Full Bkfst. Evening snacks. 3 rooms. 3 with shared baths. Beds:QDT. Farm. Swimming. Fishing.

Contact: Judith Anglen. Certificate may be used: October - May.

Story

Piney Creek Inn B&B
11 Skylark Ln, PO Box 456
Story 82842
(307)683-2338

1957. There's an abundance of wildlife on the property of this secluded log-house-style inn nestled in the Big Horn Mountains. For the Old West buff, historic sites that are only minutes away include Fort Phil Kearny, Bozeman Trail, numerous Indian battle sites and museums and galleries. At the end of the day, relax on the deck or in the common area, where visitors will find a TV, books, magazines and games. Guests also can relax by the campfire for conversation and viewing the stars.

Innkeeper(s): Vicky & Mel Hoff.

Rates:$45-65. Full Bkfst. MAP available. Picnic lunches. Evening snacks. 3 rooms. 2 with shared baths. Beds:Q. Skiing. Handicap access. Swimming. Fishing.

Contact: Vicky Hoff. Certificate may be used: Oct. 15, 1994 - April 30, 1995.

Wapiti

The Lodge at June Creek
Box 110
Wapiti 82450
(307)587-2143 (800)295-6343
Fax:(307)587-2143

1910. Tucked beneath the trees covering the Absaroka Range of the Rocky Mountains, each cabin of this lodge has a different theme and features knotty pine or log interiors, fluffy comforters, ruffled bed skirts, and rustic furnishings. The inn has a full-time children's counselor, who helps with activities such as nature crafts, hiking, riding, games and treasure hunts.

Innkeeper(s): Tom & Carrie Kruczek.

Rates:$62-95. MC VISA. Full Bkfst. EP. MAP available. Picnic lunches. Evening snacks. 11 rooms. Fireplaces. Beds:QT. Handicap access. Swimming. Stables. Fishing.

Contact: Tom Kruczek. Certificate may be used: Aug. 16 to Sept. 30, 1994; May 15 to June 15, 1995; Aug. 15 to Sept. 30, 1995.

Wilson

Teton View B&B
Box 652
Wilson 83014
(307)733-7954

1987. All of the bedrooms have a magnificent mountain view, large beds and country decor. In the winter, after a day of skiing or other outdoor activities, guests can relax with large fluffy bath towels, snuggle between flannel sheets and comforters and warm up with a welcome hot cordial drink. A lounge area includes a small refrigerator, coffee maker and games such as chess and backgammon. There are also books and brochures on the area and high-power binoculars to view the peaks.

Innkeeper(s): John & Joanna Engelhart.

Rates:$50-90. MC VISA. Full Bkfst. Gourmet Brkfst. 3 rooms. 1 with shared bath. Beds:KQT. Phone in room. Bicycling. Skiing. Swimming. Fishing.

Contact: Joanna Engelhart. Certificate may be used: May, June, October, February and March.

U. S. Territories

Puerto Rico

Ceiba

Ceiba Country Inn
PO Box 1067
Ceiba 00735
(809)885-0471 Fax:(809)885-0471

1969. A large Spanish patio is available at this tropical country inn perched on rolling, green hills. Situated 500 feet above the valley floor, the inn affords a view of the ocean with the isle of Culebra on the horizon. A continental buffet is served in the warm and sunny breakfast room. The inn is four miles from Puerto Del Rey, the largest marina in the Caribbean, and 10 miles from Luquillo Beach, which is a mile of white sand, dotted with coconut palms.

Innkeeper(s): Nicki Treat & Don Bingham.

Rates:$60. MC VISA AX DC DS CB. ContPlus Bkfst. 9 rooms. Beds:QT. Phone, AC in room. Handicap access. Swimming.

Contact: Nicki Treat. Certificate may be used: July - December, 1994; July - December, 1995.

Virgin Islands

Frederiksted, Saint Croix

The Prince Street Inn
402 Prince St
Frederiksted, Saint Croix 00840
(809)772-9550

1800. Located in the historic district of Frederiksted, this inn once served as a Danish Lutheran parsonage. Each room is unique in design and named after an old St. Croix estate. Guests are only a short stroll away from beaches, duty-free shopping and a wide variety of restaurants. Guest rooms include a rustic, wood cottage that sits in the shade of an African Baobab tree. Another room's entryway consists of a shady atrium with decorative ironwork. All rooms have fully equipped kitchens and ceiling fans.

Innkeeper(s): Paul & Charlotte Pyles.

Rates:$44-85. EP. 6 rooms. Beds:KT. TV, Refrig. in room. Swimming. Fishing.

Contact: Charlotte Pyles. Certificate may be used: July 1 - Dec. 14, 1994; April 16 - Dec. 14, 1995.

Saint Thomas

The Villas at Fort Recovery Estate
Box 11156
Saint Thomas 00801
(809)495-4354 (800)367-8455
Fax:(809)495-4036

1969. These villas are built around the 17th-century Dutch Fort Recovery. Bright masses of bougainvillea and hibiscus decorate the patios of the villas. Each villa is steps away from the inn's sandy beach. Villas one and two have an especially stunning water view. Beachcombing, snorkeling, fishing for marlin and tuna, or picnicking on one of the uninhabited islands are popular activities. There is no complimentary breakfast, but each villa has its own kitchenette.

Innkeeper(s): Pamelah Jills Jacobson.

Rates:$108-170. MC VISA AX. Cont. Bkfst. EP. Gourmet Dinner. 9 rooms. 1 with shared bath. Beds:KQT. Conference Rm. TV, AC, Refrig. in room. Golf. Tennis. Bicycling. Exercise room. Swimming. Horseback riding. Fishing.

Seen in: *New York Times, Caribbean Travel and Life and Islands Magazine.*

Contact: Pam Jacobson. Certificate may be used: September and October.

"On the Caribbean Sea, Fort Recovery Estates is the epitome of back to nature aesthetics with all the necessary amenities."

Canada

British Columbia

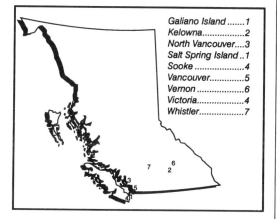

Galiano Island

Woodstone Country Inn
RR#1, Galiano Island
Galiano Island V0N 1P0
(604)539-2022 Fax:(604)539-2097

1989. Each of the inn's spacious rooms are comfortably furnished and decorated to reflect the unique nature of the Gulf Islands. The inn has nine acres

to explore and wander on pathways through towering cedar and fir trees and moss-covered glades.

Help yourself to boots, binoculars and a guidebook and visit the marsh to view birds. The innkeepers can make your trip complete with adventure packages and referrals to activities like exploring the island coves and bays by canoe or kayak.

Innkeeper(s): Andrew & Gail Nielsen-Pich.

Rates:$C80-130. MC VISA AX. Full Bkfst. Gourmet Dinner. Teas. 12 rooms. Fireplaces. Beds:KQT. Handicap access. Fishing.

Contact: Andrew Nielsen-Pich. Certificate may be used: Oct. 12 - Dec. 20; Jan. 3 - May 15.

Kelowna

The Gables Country Inn
Box 1153, 2405 Bering Rd
Kelowna V1Y 7P8
(604)768-4468 Fax:(604)768-4468

1890. This Victorian inn is Okanagan's only Heritage Award-winning bed & breakfast home. The inn is just a 10-minute drive to downtown Kelowna. Each upstairs guest room is furnished with antiques and other treasures from days gone by. The famous Gables breakfast features a wide variety of fresh fruits, as 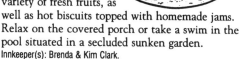 well as hot biscuits topped with homemade jams. Relax on the covered porch or take a swim in the pool situated in a secluded sunken garden.

Innkeeper(s): Brenda & Kim Clark.

Rates:$C55-65. Cont. Bkfst. EP. 4 rooms. 4 with shared baths. Beds:QT. Bicycling. Skiing. Swimming. Fishing.

Contact: Kim Clark. Certificate may be used: Oct. 1 - April 30, excluding Christmas to New Year's and Easter weekend.

North Vancouver

Laburnum Cottage B&B
1388 Terrace Ave
North Vancouver V7R 1B4
(604)988-4877 Fax:(604)988-4877

1945. Set in a half-acre of beautifully kept English gardens, this country-style inn is surrounded by virgin forest, yet is only 15 minutes from downtown Vancouver. Afternoon tea is offered on the covered porch overlooking the award-winning gardens and meandering creek. Besides the guest rooms, there are two self-contained cottages. Both cottages include a fireplace, kitchen facilities and a private bath. Check-in time is flexible and two major bus routes are only two blocks away.

Innkeeper(s): Margot & Wyn Seg.
Rates:$C115-150. MC VISA. Full Bkfst. Teas. 6 rooms. Fireplaces. Beds:KQT. Tennis. Skiing. Fishing.
Contact: Delphine Masterton. Certificate may be used: October-March.

Salt Spring Island

Weston Lake Inn
813 Beaver Point Rd
Salt Spring Island V8K 1X9
(604)653-4311

1976. Set on a 10-acre hobby farm overlooking the lake, this cozy inn features a hot tub built into the mountainside, providing an unobstructed view of

Salt Spring nature. Each room is individually appointed with Petipoint (done by the innkeeper), Eskimo art and sailboats. There are many original pieces of Canadian and Chilean art throughout the house. Breakfasts are served in the antique-filled dining room and are accompanied with soft, classical music. Breakfast may include buckwheat and banana pancakes, served with maple syrup and homemade blueberry and Triple Sec sauce.

Innkeeper(s): Susan Evans & Ted Harrison.
Rates:$C85-105. MC VISA AX. Full Bkfst. Gourmet Brkfst. Teas. 3 rooms. Beds:QT. Farm. Swimming. Fishing.
Contact: Susan Evans. Certificate may be used: Sunday through Thursday, Oct. 15 to March 25, Thanksgiving holiday and Christmas excluded.

Sooke

Ocean Wilderness Country Inn
109 W Coast Rd, RR 2
Sooke V0S 1N0
(604)646-2116 Fax:(604)646-2116

1940. The hot tub of this log house inn is in a Japanese gazebo overlooking the ocean. Reserve your time for a private soak and terry bathrobes are supplied. The innkeepers are pleased to prepare picnic lunches and arrange fishing charters, nature walks and beachcombing. Guests can enjoy wonderful seafood cookouts on Ocean Wilderness beach. Coffee is delivered to your room a half-hour before breakfast is served. Two of the rooms have hot tubs for two with spectacular ocean and Olympic Mountain views.

Innkeeper(s): Marion Rolston
Rates:$C85-175. MC VISA. Full Bkfst. 9 rooms. Beds:KQT. Refrig. in room. Handicap access. Fishing.
Contact: Marion Rolston. Certificate may be used: October to May.

Vancouver

The Albion Guest House
592 W 19th Ave
Vancouver V5Z 1W6
(604)873-2287 (800)879-5682

1906. Close to Vancouver's popular West End, Wreck Beach, Stanley Park and other attractions, this Victorian inn is a quiet retreat only minutes away from the action. The innkeeper takes special care in making his guests feel comfortable by starting off with an evening greeting of cognac, sherry and cookies laid out on a table. Earlier arrivals are offered tea, wine and appetizers. The rooms have down comforters and feather mattresses.

Innkeeper(s): David Ehrlich.
Rates:$C50-118. MC VISA. ContPlus Bkfst. Teas. 5 rooms. 3 with shared baths. Beds:KQ. Phone in room. Bicycling. Skiing. Spa. Swimming.
Contact: David Ehrlich. Certificate may be used: January-March.

Vernon

Pleasant Valley B&B
4008 Pleasant Valley Rd
Vernon V1T 4M2
(604)545-9504

1893. Because of its central location, outdoor enthusiasts can make this Victorian inn their home base for daily activities. The ski area of Silverstar Mountain is a 30-minute drive and two major lakes (Okanagan and Kalamalka) are 10 minutes from the inn. A fireplace in the living room brings warmth in the winter months and an outdoor deck and hot tub is enjoyed year-round. The innkeeper can direct you to adventure travel packages and local wineries. Breakfasts can include a variety of quiches or stuffed French toast with peach sauce.

Innkeeper(s): Christine & Doug Somerville.

Rates:$C45-55. VISA. Full Bkfst. 3 rooms. 3 with shared baths. Beds:QDT. Skiing. Spa. Swimming. Fishing.

Contact: Christine Somerville. Certificate may be used: January-June, September and November.

Victoria

Crow's Nest
71 Linden Ave
Victoria V8V 4C9
(604)383-4492 Fax:(604)383-3140

1911. This American chalet-style bed & breakfast is 10 minutes away from Victoria by bus. The inn has unrestricted views of the Olympic Mountains across the strait of Juan de Fuca. The town is one of Victoria's original neighborhoods with a variety of architecture to admire and tree-lined streets to stroll along. On nearby Cook Street, you'll discover a neighborhood pub, tea room, cafe and interesting shops. Guests can spend cozy evenings by the fireplace.

Innkeeper(s): Kit & Dene Mainguy.

Rates:$C65-85. MC VISA. Gourmet Brkfst. 3 rooms. 2 with shared baths. Beds:KQT.

Contact: Christopher Mainguy. Certificate may be used: September to May.

Dashwood Seaside Manor
Number One Cook St
Victoria V8V 3W6
(604)385-5517 Fax:(604)383-1760

1912. Dashwood Manor is an Edwardian Tudor Revival mansion with a rare oceanfront location. It can be seen from the ferry on the bluffs just to the right of Beacon Hill Park. Choose between a first-floor suite with a fireplace, chandelier and beamed ceilings, a second-story family unit or a top-floor suite for spectacular balcony views of the ocean and the Olympic Mountains. To reach downtown Victoria, take a short walk through the park.

Innkeeper(s): Derek Dashwood.

Rates:$C65-285. MC VISA AX DC. Full Bkfst. 15 rooms. Beds:Q. TV, Refrig. in room. Tennis. Bicycling.

Seen in: *San Francisco Chronicle*.

Contact: Derek Dashwood. Certificate may be used: Not weekends, not June to Sept. 30 and not at Christmas.

"Enchanting, very soothing."

Holland House Inn
595 Michigan St
Victoria V8V 1S7
(604)384-6644 Fax:(604)384-6117

1934. Fine art is displayed everywhere in this eclectic French inn. The luxurious guest rooms have been designed individually and feature original works by the premier artists of Victoria. The Gallery Lounge, where you may relax by the fire or browse in the art library, boasts still more original paintings. Some of the rooms have fireplaces and all have goose-down duvets, antique furnishings and small balconies. The inn is located two blocks from Victoria's Inner Harbor and the Seattle and Port Angeles ferry terminals.

Innkeeper(s): Lance Olsen/Robin Birsner.

Rates:$C80-210. MC VISA AX DC. Full Bkfst. 10 rooms. Fireplaces. Beds:KQT. TV, Phone in room. Handicap access. Fishing.

Contact: Lance Olsen. Certificate may be used: October, 1994 through April, 1995 (closed November).

Rose Cottage B&B
3059 Washington Ave
Victoria V9A 1P7
(604)381-5985 Fax:(604)592-5221

1912. The well-traveled hosts of this Folk-Victorian inn know the value their visitors place on a warm

welcome. The innkeepers have plenty of inside information about Victoria to make your visit as adventurous or as relaxing as you want. The inn sits on a peaceful street close to downtown and a short distance from the Gorge Park Waterway. The decor includes large, high ceilings, period furniture, a guest parlor that boasts a nautical theme and a large dining room with library.

Innkeeper(s): Robert & Shelley Bishop.

Rates:$C65-80. MC VISA. Full Bkfst. 3 rooms. 3 with shared baths. Beds:Q. Phone in room.

Contact: Robert Bishop. Certificate may be used: May 1-June 20 and Sept. 15-Dec. 31.

Wellington B&B

66 Wellington Ave
Victoria V8V 4H5
(604)383-5976 Fax:(604)385-0477

1912. Only one block from the ocean, this Folk Victorian inn is quiet, yet close to all the downtown activities. A nearby promenade boasts an incredible panoramic view of Victoria. The inn is just minutes away from Beacon Hill Park and is within easy walking distance of shopping, restaurants and outdoor activities.

Innkeeper(s): Inge & Sue Ranzinger.

Rates:$C55-95. MC. Full Bkfst. 4 rooms. Fireplaces. Beds:KQT. AC in room. Bicycling. Swimming. Fishing.

Contact: Inge Ranzinger. Certificate may be used: Oct. 15 to April 15.

Whistler

Golden Dreams B&B

6412 Easy St
Whistler V0N 1B6
(604)932-2667 (800)668-7055
Fax:(604)932-7055

1986. This private homestay boasts hearty vegetarian breakfasts that include homemade jam. The Victorian, Oriental and Aztec guest rooms feature duvets, sherry and slippers. Enjoy views of the mountains and the herb and flower gardens. One of the innkeepers is a coach for the National Ski Team and you may arrange for your own private coaching.

Innkeeper(s): Ann & Terry Spence.

Rates:$C65-95. MC VISA. Full Bkfst. MAP available. 4 rooms. 3 with shared baths. Beds:Q. Golf. Skiing. Spa. Swimming. Fishing.

Contact: Ann Spence. Certificate may be used: April 15-June 15 and Sept. 15-Nov. 15.

"Great house, great food, terrific people."

Ontario

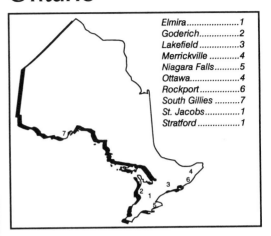

Elmira

Teddy Bear B&B Inn

Wyndham Hall, RR1
Elmira N3B 2Z1
(519)669-2379

1907. Canadian antiques, collectibles and Mennonite quilts fill the guest rooms of this home, once the area's schoolhouse. Favorite choices include the Daffodil Room and the Blue Room. The house has been featured on heritage tours and on the local television station.

Innkeeper(s): Gerrie & Vivian Smith.

Rates:$C65-75. MC VISA. Full Bkfst. 3 rooms. Beds:DT. TV, AC in room. Skiing. Swimming. Fishing.

Contact: Gerald Smith. Certificate may be used: Monday to Thursday inclusive.

"Prelude to paradise."

Goderich

La Brassine

Kitchigami Camp Rd, RR2
Goderich N7A 3X8
(519)524-6300

1908. The perfect escape for city folk, this farmhouse sits on 103 acres of wheat, corn and soybean fields. The shores of Lake Huron are at one end of the farm, which is a 10-minute walk away. The outside and inside of the inn are plain and simple with the downstairs decorated in antiques. People come here for the peace and quiet. Evenings may include catching a play at the Stratford, Grand Bend or Bligh theaters, where outstanding productions have been put on. Local annual events include sailing competitions and the Celtic Festival.

Innkeeper(s): Tom & Nicky Blanchard-Hublet.

Rates:$C40-60. MC VISA. Full Bkfst. Gourmet Dinner. 5 rooms. 5 with shared baths. Beds:QDT. Farm. Swimming. Fishing.

Contact: Tom Blanchard-Hublet. Certificate may be used: No weekends (Friday through Sunday).

Lakefield

Windmere
Selwyn, RR3
Lakefield K0L 2H0
(705)652-6290 (800)465-6327
Fax:(705)652-6949

1840. Windmere is a 100-acre working farm set in the heart of the Kawartha Lakes. Joan and Wally Wilkins' lovingly restored home, one of Peterborough County's original homesteads, overlooks shaded grounds and a deep-water swimming pond. Their livestock consists of Rob, the resident horse.

Innkeeper(s): Joan & Wally Wilkins.

Rates:$C45-65. Full Bkfst. Evening snacks. 4 rooms. 2 with shared baths. Beds:DT. AC in room. Farm. Golf. Bicycling. Skiing. Sauna. Swimming. Fishing.

Contact: Wallace & Jan Wilkins. Certificate may be used: Oct. 15, 1994 to April 27, 1995 and Oct. 15, 1995 to Dec. 31, 1995.

"Beautiful house and lovely people."

Merrickville

Sam Jakes Inn
118 Main St E, Box 580
Merrickville K0G 1N0
(613)269-3711 (800)567-4667
Fax:(613)269-3713

1861. During the 1860s, Sam Jakes operated the largest department store between Chicago and Montreal. His stone mansion has been renovated into a country inn that houses 24 guest rooms and six fireplace suites. Period decor includes folk art throughout. The inn has a main dining room with old hearth fireplace, a small private dining room, guest common room, library, whirlpool, sauna, and exercise room. A tavern features collections of nautical photographs. Outside are verandas and a garden patio.

Innkeeper(s): Gary Clarke.

Rates:$C112-145. MC VISA AX DC CB. Full Bkfst. AP available. MAP available. Gourmet Brkfst, Lunch, Dinner. Picnic lunches. Teas. 30 rooms. Fireplaces. Beds:KQ. Conference Rm. TV, Phone, AC in room. Golf. Bicycling. Skiing. Handicap access. Spa. Sauna. Exercise room. Swimming. Horseback riding. Fishing.

Contact: Gary Clarke. Certificate may be used: March/November.

Niagara Falls

Butterfly Manor
4917 River Rd
Niagara Falls L2E 3G5
(905)358-8988 Fax:(905)358-8988

1985. Within walking distance of Niagara Falls, this Tudor-style inn overlooks the Niagara River.

The inn is also a short drive from Niagara-on-the-Lake and a five-minute walk from the train and bus stations. Many points of interest on both sides of the U.S.-Canadian border are minutes away. The warm kitchen with fireplace delights guests with home-baked smells and pleasant atmosphere. The hostess will help you find a good place to dine and make suggestions on what you should include on your itinerary.

Innkeeper(s): L. Siciliano.

Rates:$C55-100. MC VISA AX. Full Bkfst. Gourmet Brkfst. 8 rooms. Fireplaces. Beds:Q. TV, AC in room. Fishing.

Contact: Luciana Siciliano. Certificate may be used: Oct. 1 to June 15.

Ottawa

Auberge McGee's Inn
185 Daly Ave
Ottawa K1N 6E8
(613)237-6089 Fax:(613)237-6201

1886. The portico of this restored Victorian mansion is reminiscent of the McGee's Irish roots featuring pillars that were common in Dublin architecture. The home was built for John McGee, Canada's first Clerk of the Privy Council. Rooms are comfortable and decorated in soft, pleasing colors. Amenities such as stocked mini-bars and

mounted hair dryers add a touch of modern convenience. For extended stays, the inn provides the use of laundry facilities and a guest kitchenette. May is a wonderful time to visit as the lawns are blooming with tulips. There is no end to what guests can see and do in Ottawa. Visit the Byward Market, the many museums, or 230-store Rideau center.

Innkeeper(s): Anne Schutte & Mary Unger.

Rates:$C48-150. MC VISA. Full Bkfst. 14 rooms. 4 with shared baths. Fireplaces. Beds:KQT. TV, Phone, AC, Refrig. in room. Golf. Skiing.

Seen in: *Country Inns, Ottawa Citizen, LaPresse, Ottawa Magazine.*

Contact: Anne Schutte. Certificate may be used: Except holiday periods.

"All we could ask for."

Rideau View Inn

177 Frank St
Ottawa K2P 0X4
(613)236-9309 (800)268-2082
Fax:(613)237-6842

1907. This large Edwardian home is located on a quiet residential street near the Rideau Canal. A hearty breakfast is served in the dining room. Guests are encouraged to relax in front of the fireplace in the living room. Owner George Hartsgrove also heads the physiology department's technical staff at the University of Ottawa.

Innkeeper(s): George Hartsgrove.

Rates:$C62-75. MC VISA AX DC. Full Bkfst. 7 rooms. 5 with shared baths. Fireplaces. Beds:QT. Phone, AC in room. Skiing.

Seen in: *Toronto Star.*

Contact: George Hartsgrove. Certificate may be used: Oct. 1 - March 31, not including holiday or festival weekends.

Rockport

Houseboat Amaryllis Inn

Rockport K0E 1V0
(613)659-3513

1920. Originally built as a private hunting and fishing lodge to float around the St. Lawrence and

Rideau Rivers, this docked houseboat is double-decked, 100 feet long and located on its own island of 7.5 acres. Situated in the middle of 1,000 Islands, the houseboat has a large veranda deck, living room with fireplace and a dining room overlooking the water and forested shores. The atmosphere and decor are a blend of traditional and contemporary design, unique to the St. Lawrence and island area.

Innkeeper(s): Pieter & Karin Bergen.

Rates:$C90-120. Full Bkfst. Gourmet Brkfst. Picnic lunches. 5 rooms. Beds:QT. Conference Rm. Swimming. Fishing.

Contact: Pieter Bergen. Certificate may be used: Sept. 1-30, 1994; June and September, 1995.

South Gillies

Unicorn Inn & Restaurant

RR 1
South Gillies P0T 2V0
(807)475-4200 Fax:(807)475-4200

1902. While the restaurant part of this B&B has gained worldwide notoriety as one of Canada's best places to eat, this turn-of-the-century farmhouse is nestled in a secluded valley amid 440 acres of spectacular rural scenery. Streams meander through the property, which includes the hills and cliffs of the Canadian Shield. Guests can enjoy abundant wildlife while hiking through the land's fields and mountains. Breakfasts to the sounds of Vivaldi and Mozart can include such items as souffled German pancakes with a Grand Marnier and strawberry sauce and oven-fresh scones or buttermilk biscuits.

Innkeeper(s): David & Arlan Nobel.

Rates:$C59-89. MC VISA DC CB. Full Bkfst. MAP available. Gourmet Brkfst, Dinner. 4 rooms. 3 with shared baths. Beds:KD. Conference Rm. Farm. Skiing. Swimming. Fishing.

Contact: David Nobel. Certificate may be used: Feb. 15 - May 31, Oct. 1 - Dec. 30.

St. Jacobs

Jakobstettel Guest House, Inc.

16 Isabella St
St. Jacobs N0B 2N0
(519)664-2208 Fax:(519)664-1326

1898. Coffee is always on at this Victorian inn, and guests also will find cookies in the cookie jar, juice in the fridge and a selection of teas. Common rooms include a library, game room and breakfast nook. Some of the guest rooms have a sitting room tucked into an alcove, a porch or stained-glass windows. The inn, with its five acres of trees and rose garden, is nestled in a quiet street. Around the corner, attractions include a wooded walking trail, specialty shopping in the village, restaurants, farmer's market and cultural attractions.

Innkeeper(s): Ella Brubacher.

Rates:$C90-150. MC VISA AX. ContPlus Bkfst. Picnic lunches. Teas. Evening snacks. 12 rooms. Beds:QT. Conference Rm. Phone, AC in room. Tennis. Bicycling. Skiing. Fishing.

Contact: Ella Brubacher. Certificate may be used: Sunday to Thursday only.

Stratford

Stone Maiden Inn
123 Church St
Stratford N5A 2R3
(519)271-7129

1872. The inn is named for the stone maidenheads in the front hallway of this Victorian house. Canopy beds, fireplaces and handmade quilts are featured. Ask for the room with the massive 17th-century French canopy bed and you will enjoy a 13-foot ceiling, whirlpool tub, bar refrigerator and TV. Afternoon refreshments are served. The Stratford Shakespearean Festival is held from May to October.

Innkeeper(s): Len & Barb Woodward.

Rates:$C90-160. MC VISA. Full Bkfst. 14 rooms. Fireplaces. Beds:KQT. TV, AC, Refrig. in room.

Contact: Len Woodward. Certificate may be used: Anytime except mid-June to Sept. 30.

Prince Edward Island

Charlottetown

Anne's Ocean View Haven B&B Inn
Box 2044, Kinloch Rd
Charlottetown C1A 7N7
(902)569-4456 (800)665-4644

1986. Situated in a countryside setting with a panoramic view of Northumberland strait, this B&B offers quiet surroundings while being close to downtown. With both traditional and modern decor, the inn's guest rooms have sitting rooms, refrigerators and four-piece baths. The island boasts beautiful, white sandy beaches and fertile red fields of potatoes. The beauty of the island attracts photographers from around the world and the many summer festivals provide much culture.

Innkeeper(s): R. Anne Olson.

Rates:$C65-125. Full Bkfst. Picnic lunches. 4 rooms. Beds:KQT. TV, Refrig. in room. Skiing. Swimming. Fishing.

Contact: Anne Olson. Certificate may be used: October-May only.

Inns of Interest

Lighthouses

The Keeper's House . . . . . . .Isle Au Haut, Maine
Big Bay Point Lighthouse B&B . . .Big Bay, Mich.

Schoolhouses

Ridgeview B&B . . . . .Elizabeth, Ill.
Old Sea Pines Inn . . . . Brewster, Mass.
The Bagley House . . . . Durham, Maine
Bridgewater Inn . . . . Cordova, Tenn.

Stagecoach Stops

Fensalden Inn . . . . Albion, Calif.
The Stagecoach Inn . . . . Lake Placid, N.Y.
The Walker Inn of Old Valleytown
. . . . Andrews, N.C.
Bowling Green Inn B&B . . . Jonesborough, Tenn.
Inn at Blush Hill . . . . Waterbury, Vt.

Jail Houses

The Jail House Historic Inn . . . . . Preston, Minn.
Casa de Patron . . . . Lincoln, N.M.

Activities

Dogmushing

Alaska's 7 Gables . . . . Fairbanks, Alaska

Bagpipes

Over Look Inn . . . . Eastham, Mass.

Horse & Carriage Rides

Old Louisville Inn . . . . Louisville, Ky.
Diamond D Ranch-Outfitters . . . . . Moran, Wyo.

Wildlife/Animals

"The Farm" B&B . . . . Seward, Ala.

Triangle L Ranch B&B Retreat . . Oracle, Arizona
Annie's B&B . . . . Springville, Calif.
Scrubby Oaks B&B . . . . Durango, Colo.
Wakulla Springs Lodge & Conference Center
. . . . Wakulla Springs, Fla.
Mississippi Memories . . . . Nauvoo, Ill.
The Woodlands . . . . Princeton, Iowa
Thistle Hill B&B . . . . WaKeeney, Kansas
The Miles River Country Inn . . . Hamilton, Mass.
Spray Cliff on the Ocean . . . . . Marblehead, Mass.
The Keeper's House . . . . Isle Au Haut, Maine
Sunset House . . . . West Gouldsboro, Maine
The Chesapeake Club . . . . . Chestertown, Maine
Black Walnut Point Inn
. . . . Tilghman Island, Maine
Thompsons' B&B . . . . Klamath Falls, Ore.
Ponda-Rowland B&B Inn . . . . Dallas, Pa.
Cole's Log Cabin B&B . . . . Pine Bank, Pa.
The Shaw House B&B . . . . Georgetown, R.I.
Hasse House . . . . Mason, Texas
Pine River Ranch . . . . Leavenworth, Wash.
Thimbleberry Inn B&B . . . . Bayfield, Wis.
Ross' Teal Lake Lodge . . . . Hayward, Wis.
Chippewa River Inn B&B . . . . Winter, Wis.
The Howdy Pardner B&B . . . . . Cheyenne, Wyo.
Grand & Sierra Lodge . . . . . . Encampment, Wyo.
The Inn at Buffalo Fork . . . . Moran, Wyo.
Woodstone Country Inn
. . . . . . Galiano Island, British Columbia, Canada
Unicorn Inn & Restaurant
. . . . South Gillies, Ontario, Canada

Plantations

Poipu B&B Inn . . . . Koloa, Kauai, Hawaii
Green Springs Plantation . . Saint Francisville, La.

Rice Hope Plantation Inn . . . Moncks Corner, R.I.
Littlepage Inn . . . . Mineral, Va.

Ranches

Fool's Cove Ranch B&B . . . . . Kingston, Arizona
Juniper Well Ranch . . . . Prescott, Arizona
Paz Entera Ranch . . . . Tucson, Arizona
Random Oaks Ranch . . . . Julian, Calif.
Rainbow Tarns
    . . . . . . Mammoth/Crowley Lake, Calif.
Tradewinds Bed & Breakfast
    . . . . Point Reyes Station, Calif.
Howard Creek Ranch . . . . Westport, Calif.
Shamrock Ranch . . . . Coalmont, Colo.
Kaia Ranch & Co . . . . Hana, Maui, Hawaii
The Ranchette . . . . Albuquerque, N.M.
Pinehurst Inn at Jenny Creek . . . . . Ashland, Ore.
Wine Country Farm . . . . Dayton, Ore.
Whippletree Inn & Farm . . . . Emlenton, Pa.
Diamond L Guest Ranch . . . . Hulett, Wyo.

Inns with Cookbook Authors

Dairy Hollow House . . . . Eureka Springs, Arizona
"Dairy Hollow House Cookbook"
"Dairy Hollow House Soup & Bread"

Campbell Ranch Inn . . . . Geyserville, Calif.
"The Campbell Ranch Inn Cookbook"

Grandview Lodge . . . . Waynesville, N.C.
"Recipes from Grandview Lodge"

Sea Holly Inn . . . . Cape May, N.J.
"Sea Holly Bed and Breakfast, A Sharing of Secrets"

The Durning House B&B and Tea Room
    . . . . Van Alstyme, Texas
"Hog Heaven"

Sims-Mitchell House B&B . . . . Chatham, Va.
"Waking Up Down South"
"Well Bless Your Heart", Vol. I & II
"Butter 'em While They're Hot"

Hill Farm Inn . . . . Arlington, Vt.
"Recipes from the kitchen of..."

Bombay House . . . . Bainbridge Island, Wash.
"Breakfast with Bunny"

Ravenscroft Inn . . . . Port Townsend, Wash.
"Something's CookINN"

English Gardens/Herb & Flower Gardens

Gingerbread Mansion . . . . Ferndale, Calif.
Bee and Thistle Inn . . . . Old Lyme, Conn.
Clark Cottage at Wintergreen
    . . . . Pomfret Center, Conn.
Green Tree Inn . . . . Elsah, Ill.
Berry Hill Farm B&B . . . . Bainbridge, N.Y.
Tanglewood Manor . . . . Clemmons, N.C.
The Peter Wolford House . . . . Dillsburg, Pa.
Lareau Farm Country Inn . . . . . . Waitsfield, Vt.
Laburnum Cottage B&B
    . . . . North Vancouver, British Columbia, Canada

Hunting Lodges

LoPinto Farm Lodge . . . . Freeville, N.Y.
Ingeberg Acres . . . . Valley Chapel/Weston, W.V.
Houseboat Amaryllis Inn
    . . . . Rockport, Ontario, Canada

Barns

Woods Hole Passage . . . . Falmouth, Mass.
Brannon-Bunker Inn . . . . . . Damariscotta, Maine
Cornerstone B&B Inn . . . . Landenberg, Pa.
Richmont Inn . . . . Townsend, Tenn.
Jackson Fork Inn . . . . Huntsville, Texas
The Inn at Mad River Barn . . . . . . Waitsfield, Vt.
The Inn at Round Barn Farm . . . . Waitsfield, Vt.
Waitsfield Inn . . . . Waitsfield, Vt.

Old Mills

Silvermine Tavern . . . . Norwalk, Conn.
The Osceola Mill Country Inn
    . . . . Steele's Tavern, Va.
The Inn at Gristmill Square . . Warm Springs, Va.
Old Mill Inn . . . . Brandon, Vt.

Old Taverns

Silvermine Tavern . . . . Norwalk, Conn.
Birchwood Inn . . . . Lenox, Mass.

Merrell Tavern Inn . . . . South Lee, Mass.
Bird & Bottle Inn . . . . Garrison, N.Y.
Rider's 1812 Inn . . . . Painesville, Ohio
Witmer's Tavern-Historic 1725 Inn
. . . . Lancaster, Pa.

Tunnels, Secret Passageways, Caves

Wingscorton Farm . . . . East Sandwich, Mass.
Sterling Orchards B&B . . . . Sterling, Mass.
Merry Sherwood Plantation . . . . . . Berlin, Maine
Pine Willow B&B . . . . Iron River, Mich.
Munro House B&B . . . . Jonesville, Mich.
Colonel Spencer Inn . . . . Plymouth, N.H.
Witmer's Tavern-Historic 1725 Inn
. . . . Lancaster, Pa.
Lynchburg Mansion Inn . . . . Lynchburg, Va.

Train Stations & Renovated Railroad Cars

Melitta Station Inn . . . . Santa Rosa, Calif.
Trout City Inn . . . . Buena Vista, Colo.
Varners' Caboose . . . . Montpelier, Iowa
Las Palomas Valley B&B . . . . Albuquerque, N.M.
Mountain Meadows Inn B&B . . . Ashford, Wash.

Unusual Sleeping Spaces

In a Winery

Cavender Castle Winery . . . . Dahlonega, Ga.

Blacksmith Shop

The Cookie Jar B&B . . . . Wyoming, R.I.

In a Church

Old Church House Inn B&B . . . . . Mossville, Ill.

50 yards from a reversing white water rapids

The Weskeag Inn . . . . . South Thomaston, Maine

On a houseboat

Houseboat Amaryllis Inn
. . . . Rockport, Ontario, Canada

Next to a Native American Archeological Dig

The White Oak Inn . . . . Danville, Ohio

Unusual Architecture

The Oscar Swan Country Inn . . . . . . Geneva, Ill.
Haan's 1830 Inn . . . . . . Mackinac Island, Mich.
Castle Inn . . . . Circleville, Ohio

Llama Ranches

Canaan Land Farm B&B . . . . . . Harrodsburg, Ky.
1661 Inn & Hotel Manisses . . . . Block Island, R.I.
Shady Ridge Farm B&B . . . . Houlton, Wis.

Revolutionary War

Crocker Tavern B&B . . . . Barnstable, Mass.
Colonial Roger Brown House . . . . Concord, Mass.
Lincoln House Country Inn . . Dennysville, Maine
Kanaga House B&B
. . . . . . Harrisburg, North Kingston, Pa.
The Historical John Banister Mansion
. . . . Newport, R.I.
The Melville House . . . . Newport, R.I.
Caledonia Farm B&B . . . . Flint Hill, Va.

Civil War

The Sedgwick Inn . . . . Berlin, N.Y.
Dry Ridge Inn . . . . Weaverville, N.C.
The Russell-Cooper House . . Mount Vernon, Ohio
The Doubleday Inn . . . . Gettysburg, Pa.
Beechmont Inn . . . . Hanover, Pa.
Kane Manor Country Inn . . . . Kane, Pa.
Chestnut Cottage B&B . . . . Columbia, R.I.
Magnolia Manor . . . . Bolivar, Tenn.
Branner-Hicks House . . . . . . Jefferson City, Tenn.
La Vista Plantation . . . . Fredericksburg, Va.
A Touch of Country B&B . . . . . New Market, Va.

Associated with Literary Figures

Edith Wharton
The Gables Inn . . . . Lenox, Mass.
Longfellow's The Courtship of Miles Standish
The Isaac Randall House . . . . Freeport, Maine
Ralph Waldo Emerson, Louisa Mae Alcott, Nathaniel Hawthorne
Hawthorne Inn . . . . Concord, Maine
Mark Twain
Fifth Street Mansion B&B . . . . . . Hannibal, Mo.
Garth Woodside Mansion . . . . Hannibal, Mo.
Becky Thatcher
Fifth Street Mansion B&B . . . . . . Hannibal, Mo.

Black History

Old Manse Inn . . . . Brewster, Mass.
Wingscorton Farm Inn . . . . East Sandwich, Mass.
The Isaac Randall . . . . Freeport, Maine
Munro House B&B . . . . Jonesville, Mich.
The Wooden Rabbit . . . . Cape May, N.J.
Rider's 1812 Inn . . . . Painesville, Ohio
The Inn at Weathersfield . . . . . Weathersfield, Vt.

Farms & Orchards

Apple Blossom Inn B&B . . . . . Ahwahnee, Calif.
Apple Lane Inn . . . . Aptos, Calif.
Scarlett's Country Inn . . . . Calistoga, Calif.
Rockin' A B&B . . . . Julian, Calif.
The Inn at Shallow Creek Farm . . . Orland, Calif.
Mama Bear's Orchard B&B . . . . Orosi, Calif.
Living Spring Farm & Guest Ranch
. . . . Platina, Calif.
Howard Creek Ranch . . . . Westport, Calif.
Black Forest B&B . . . . . . Colorado Springs, Colo.
Applewood Farms Inn . . . . Ledyard, Conn.
The Shaw House . . . . Anamosa, Iowa
Loy's B&B . . . . Marengo, Iowa
Centennial Farm B&B . . . . . . Webster City, Iowa
Country Charm B&B . . . . Sycamore, Ill.
Lear Acres B&B . . . . Bern, Kansas
Peaceful Acres B&B . . . . Great Bend, Kansas
Canaan Land Farm B&B . . . . . . Harrodsburg, Ky.

Gilbert's B&B . . . . Rehoboth, Mass.
Crane House . . . . Fennville, Mich.
Pink Palace Farms . . . . Swartz Creek, Mich.
Chase Lake Country Inn . . . . Medina, N.C.
Ellis River House . . . . Jackson, N.H.
Apple Valley Inn B&B and Antiques
. . . . Glenwood, N.J.
Berry Hill Farm B&B . . . . Bainbridge, N.Y.
Hart & Mather B&B . . . . . . Sharon Center, Ohio
Weatherbury Farm . . . . Avella, Pa.
Mill Creek Farm B&B . . . . Buckingham, Pa.
The Inn at Fordhook Farm . . . . . Doylestown, Pa.
Cedar Hill Farm . . . . Mount Joy, Pa.
Field & Pine B&B . . . . Shippensburg, Pa.
Dells B&B at Cedar Hill Farm . Spruce Creek, Pa.
B&B at Skoglund Farm . . . . Canova, S.D.
Llano Grande Plantation . . . . Nacogdoches, Texas
Hotel Turkey Living Museum . . . . . Turkey, Texas
Historic Brookside Farms . . . . Orwell, Vt.
Liberty Hill Farm . . . . Rochester, Vt.
Cottonwood Ranch B&B . . . . Riverton, Wyo.

Gold Mines/Gold Panning

Pearson's Pond Luxury Inn . . . . . . Juneau, Alaska
Julian Gold Rush Hotel . . . . Julian, Calif.
Dunbar House 1880 . . . . Murphys, Calif.
Old Blewett Pass B&B . . . . . Leavenworth, Wash.

Log Houses

Old Carson Inn . . . . Lake City, Colo.
The Log House . . . . Russellville, Ky.
Lindgren's B&B . . . . Lutsen, Minn.
The Inn at Burg's Landing
. . . . Anderson Island, Wash.

Hot Springs

Lithia Springs B&B . . . . Gassville, Arizona
Rainbow Tarns . . Mammoth/Crowley Lake, Calif.
Vichy Hot Springs Resort & Inn . . . Ukiah, Calif.

Waterfalls

St. Mary's Glacier B&B . . . . Idaho Springs, Colo.
Fall Creek Falls B&B . . . . Pikeville, Tenn.

Sycamore Tree B&B . . . . Blacksburg, Va.

Three-seat Outhouse

Maple Hill Farm B&B . . . . Coventry, Conn.

Oldest Continuously Operated Inns

Florida House Inn . . . . Amelia Island, Fla.
The York House . . . . Mountain City, Ga.
Village Inn, Lenox . . . . Mass.
The Bark Eater . . . . Keene, N.Y.
The Bellevue House . . . . Block Island, R.I.
The Inn at Gristmill Square . . Warm Springs, Va.

Inns Prior to 1799

1678 Hewick Plantation . . . . Urbanna, Va.
1690 The Great Valley House of Valley Forge
. . . . Malvern, Pa.
1700 Hacienda Vargas . . . . Algodones, N.M.
1700 Evermay-on-the-Delaware . . . . . Erwinna, Pa.
1700 Hollileif B&B . . . . Newtown, Pa.
1704 Stumble Inne . . . . . Nantucket Island, Mass.
1704 Cornerstone B&B Inn . . . . Landenberg, Pa.
1709 The Woodbox Inn . Nantucket Island, Mass.
1710 The Mill House B&B . . . . North East, Md.
1725 Witmer's Tavern - Historic 1725 Inn
. . . . Lancaster, Pa.
1730 Hollyhedge B&B . . . . New Hope, Pa.
1731 Maple Hill Farm B&B . . . . Coventry, Conn.
1732 Under Mountain Inn . . . . . Salisbury, Conn.
1732 The Cookie Jar B&B . . . . . . Wyoming, R.I.
1734 Joseph Ambler Inn . . . . . . North Wales, Pa.
1738 Brown's Historic Home B&B . . . Salem, N.J.
1739 Elms . . . . Falmouth, Mass.
1740 Sterling Orchards B&B . . . . Sterling, Mass.
1740 Henry Ludlam Inn . . . . Woodbine, N.J.
1740 Barley Sheaf Farm . . . . Holicong, Pa.
1740 Tattersall Inn . . . . Point Pleasant, Pa.
1743 The Inn at Mitchell House
. . . . Chestertown, Md.
1745 Aspen Hall Inn . . . . Martinsburg, W.V.
1750 Isaac Hilliard House B&B . . Pemberton, N.J.
1750 Old Drovers Inn . . . . Dover Plains, N.Y.

1750 House on the Hill B&B
. . . . Lake Geo/Warrensburg, N.Y.
1750 Mill Creek Farm B&B . . . . Buckingham, Pa.
1750 The Inn at Fordhook Farm . Doylestown, Pa.
1750 Herr Farmhouse Inn . . . . Manheim, Pa.
1750 Shippen Way Inn . . . . Philadelphia, Pa.
1750 The Melville House . . . . Newport, R.I.
1751 Penny House Inn . . . . Eastham, Mass.
1751 The Historical John Banister Mansion
. . . . Newport, R.I.
1753 Whipple Tree B&B . . . . . . Lanesboro, Mass.
1753 Maplehedge B&B . . . . . . Charlestown, N.H.
1753 L'Auberge Provencale . . . . . White Post, Va.
1754 Crocker Tavern B&B . . . . Barnstable, Mass.
1756 Bee and Thistle Inn . . . . . Old Lyme, Conn.
1757 Wingscorton Farm Inn
. . . . East Sandwich, Mass.
1759 Ira Allen House . . . . Arlington, Vt.
1760 Gilbert House B&B of Middleway
. . . . Charles Town, W.V.
1761 The Bird & Bottle Inn . . . . Garrison, N.Y.
1763 Colonel Spencer Inn . . . . . Plymouth, N.H.
1763 Smithton Inn . . . . Ephrata, Pa.
1765 The Carlisle House Inn
. . . . Nantucket Island, Mass.
1765 Bankhouse B&B . . . . West Chester, Pa.
1766 The Inn at Meander Plantation
. . . . Locust Dale, Va.
1767 Birchwood Inn . . . . Lenox, Mass.
1767 Highland Lake Inn B&B
. . . . East Andover, N.H.
1769 Thomas Bond House . . . . . Philadelphia, Pa.
1770 Silvermine Tavern . . . . Norwalk, Conn.
1770 The Parsonage Inn . . . . . East Orleans, Mass.
1770 White Goose Inn . . . . Orford, N.H.
1771 Village Inn . . . . Lenox, Mass.
1772 The Bagley House . . . . Durham, Maine
1773 Isaac Merrill House Inn
. . . . North Conway(Kearsg), N.H.
1775 Colonel Roger Brown House
. . . . Concord, Mass.
1775 Kanaga House B&B
. . . . Harrisburg/N Kingstn, Pa.
1776 The Inn at Chester . . . . Chester, Conn.

1776 Townshend Country Inn . . . Townshend, Vt.

1779 Miles River Country Inn . . Hamilton, Mass.

1780 Lake House . . . . Waterford, Maine

1780 Catoctin Inn and Antiques

. . . . Buckeystown, Md.

1780 Country Inn Acres . . . . Harwich Port, Mass.

1780 Ivanhoe Country House . . . . Sheffield, Mass.

1780 The 1780 Egremont Inn

. . . . South Egremont, Mass.

1780 Parrot Mill Inn . . . . Chatham, N.J.

1780 The Wild Berry Inn . . . . . . Stockbridge, Vt.

1780 Silver Thatch Inn . . . . . Charlottesville, Va.

1780 The Hummingbird Inn . . . . . . Goshen, Va.

1781 Haan's 1830 Inn . . . Mackinac Island, Mich.

1785 The 1785 Inn . . . . North Conway, N.H.

1786 Kenniston Hill Inn . . . . . . Boothbay, Maine

1786 Windsor House . . . . Newburyport, Mass.

1786 The Wayside Inn . . Greenfield Center, N.Y.

1786 The Brafferton Inn . . . . Gettysburg, Pa.

1786 Old Mill Inn . . . . Brandon, Vt.

1787 Lincoln House . . . . Dennysville, Maine

1787 Tuscany Inn . . . . Middleburg, Va.

1788 Sleepy Hollow Farm B&B . Gordonsville, Va.

1789 Merryvale B&B . . . . Woodbury, Conn.

1789 Captain Josiah Mitchell House

. . . . Freeport,Maine

1789 The Hancock Inn . . . . Hancock, N.H.

1789 Longswamp B&B . . . . Mertztown, Pa.

1789 The Inn at High View . . . . . . Andover, Vt.

1789 Historic Brookside Farms . . . . . . Orwell, Vt.

1789 Historic Country Inns of Lexington

. . . . Lexington, Va.

1790 Tuck Inn . . . . Rockport, Mass.

1790 Lothrop Merry House

. . . . Vineyard Haven, Mass.

1790 The Southern Hotel . Sainte Genevieve, Mo.

1790 Olde Orchard Inn . . . . . Moultonboro, N.H.

1790 The Inn at New Ipswich . New Ipswich, N.H.

1790 Pheasant Field B&B . . . . Carlisle, Pa.

1790 Field & Pine B&B . . . . . . Shippensburg, Pa.

1790 King George Inn & Guests . Charleston, S.C.

1790 1790 House . . . . Georgetown, S.C.

1790 Hill Farm Inn . . . . Arlington, Vt.

1790 Green Trails Country Inn . . . Brookfield, Vt.

1790 Silver Maple Lodge & Cottages . Fairlee, Vt.

1790 Birch Hill Inn . . . . . Manchester Village, Vt.

1790 Shoreham Inn & Country Store

. . . . Shoreham Village, Vt.

1790 Lareau Farm Country Inn . . . Waitsfield, Vt.

1790 The Inn at Blush Hill . . . . . Waterbury, Vt.

1790 Red Shutter Farmhouse B&B

. . . . New Market, Va.

1791 St. Francis Inn . . . . . . Saint Augustine, Fla.

1791 The Inn on Cove Hill . . . . Rockport, Mass.

1791 The Sedgwick Inn . . . . Berlin, N.Y.

1792 The White House . . . . . Block Island, R.I.

1793 Cove House . . . . Kennebunkport, Maine

1793 The Historic Temperance Tavern

. . . . Gilmanton, N.H.

1794 Merrell Tavern Inn . . . . . . South Lee, Mass.

1794 The Inn at Maplewood Farm

. . . . Hillsboro, N.H.

1794 9 Partners Inn . . . . Harford, Pa.

1794 The Whitehall Inn . . . . New Hope, Pa.

1795 The Inn on Lake Waramaug

. . . . New Preston, Conn.

1795 Canaan Land Farm B&B . . Harrodsburg, Ky.

1795 The Acorn Inn . . . . . . Canandaigua, N.Y.

1795 Maplewood Inn . . . . Fair Haven, Vt.

1795 The Inn at Weathersfield . Weathersfield, Vt.

1795 Spring Farm B&B . . . . Luray, Va.

1796 Babbling Brook B&B Inn . Santa Cruz, Calif.

1796 National Pike Inn . . . . . New Market, Md.

1796 Bullard Farm B&B . North New Salem, Mass.

1797 Williamsville Inn . . West Stockbridge, Mass.

1797 Eastman Inn . . . . North Conway, N.H.

1797 Sanford's Ridge B&B . . . . Queensbury, N.Y.

1797 Bay View Waterfront B&B Belle Haven, Va.

1798 Spring House . . . . Airville, Pa.

1798 McLean House B&B . . . . Shippensburg, Pa.

1799 Honeysuckle Inn . . . . Moretown, Vt.

Still in the Family

Crystle's B&B . . . . Concordia, Kansas

The Sherwood Inn . . . . New Haven, Ky.

Green Springs Plantation . . Saint Francisville, La.

Bullard Farm B&B . . . . . North New Salem, Mass.

Sterling Orchards B&B . . . . Sterling, Mass.

Northern Plantation B&B . . . . Urbana, Ohio

Line Limousin Farmhouse B&B . . . . . Carlisle, Pa.

The Inn at Fordhook Farm . . . . . Doylestown, Pa.

Hamanassett B&B . . . . Lima, Pa.

The Drake Farm on Lumsley Creek
. . . . . . Nashville, Goodletsville, Tenn.

Hasse House . . . . Mason, Texas

Bay View Waterfront B&B . . . . Belle Haven, Va.

Burger's Country Inn B&B . . . Natural Bridge, Va.

Hewick Plantation . . . . Urbanna, Va.

Birch Hill Inn . . . . Manchester Village, Vt.

Who Slept Here

Jack London, Mark Twain, Teddy Roosevelt

Vichy Hot Springs Resort & Inn . . . Ukiah, Calif.

Bat Masterson, Bob Ford, Calamity Jane

Creede Hotel . . . . Creede, Colo.

Margaret Mitchell (Gone With the Wind)

The Veranda . . . . Senoia, Ga.

Martin Van Buren

Old Hoosier House . . . . Knightstown, Ind.

Mary Pickford, Gloria Swanson, Douglas Fairbanks, Clark Gable

Esmeralda Inn . . . . Chimney Rock, N.C.

Doc Holliday, Big Nose Katy, Billy the Kid

Plaza Hotel . . . . Las Vegas, N.M.

Billy the Kid

Casa de Patron . . . . Lincoln, N.M.

John James Audubon

Lincoln House Country Inn . . Dennysville, Maine

Weston House . . . . Eastport, Maine

Samuel Clemens

Garth Woodside Mansion . . . . Hannibal, Mo.

Architect Stanford White

The Inn at Jackson . . . . Jackson, N.H.

Babe Ruth

Cranmore Mt. Lodge . . . . . . North Conway, N.H.

Robert E. Lee

The Wooden Rabbit . . . . Cape May, N.J.

William Seward

The William Seward Inn . . . . Westfield, N.Y.

William O'Neil Family, founder of General Tire

O'Neil House . . . . Akron, Ohio

Eleanor Roosevelt

Mulberry Inn B&B . . . . Martins Ferry, Ohio

Burpee family

The Inn at Fordhook Farm . . . . . Doylestown, Pa.

The Barrymore family

Evermay-on-the-Delaware . . . . Erwinna, Pa.

President John Adams

Witmer's Tavern-Historic 1725 Inn . Lancaster, Pa.

President Herbert Hoover

The Carriage House at Stonegate
. . . . Montoursville, Pa.

Thomas Jefferson

The Inn at Meander Plantation . Locust Dale, Va.

Abraham Lincoln

Black River Inn . . . . Ludlow, Vt.

Kellogg family

Village Country Inn . . . . Manchester Village, Vt.

George Washington

Aspen Hall Inn . . . . Martinsburg, W.V.

Additional Publications
From American Historic Inns

Bed & Breakfast and Country Inns, Sixth Edition

By Tim & Deborah Sakach

Imagine the thrill of receiving this unique book with its FREE night certificate as a gift. Now you can let someone else experience the magic of America's country inns with this unmatched offer. *Bed & Breakfasts and Country Inns* is the most talked about guide among inngoers.

This fabulous guide features more than 1,800 inns from across the United States and Canada. Best of all, no other "bookstore" guide offers a FREE night certificate.* This certificate can be used at any one of the inns featured in the guide.

Tim and Deborah Sakach have been writing about bed and breakfasts since 1981. Their books and the FREE night offer have been recommended by many travel writers and editors, and featured in: *The New York Times, Washington Post, Boston Globe, Chicago Sun Times, USA Today, Good Housekeeping, Cosmopolitan, Consumer Reports* and more.

*With purchase of one night at the regular rate required. Subject to limitations.

528 pages, paperback, 500 illustrations.   **Price $19.95**

The Official Guide to American Historic Inns,
Completely Revised and Updated

By Tim & Deborah Sakach

Open the door to America's past with this fascinating guide to historic inns that reflect our colorful heritage. From Dutch Colonials to Queen Anne Victorians, these bed & breakfasts and country inns offer experiences of a lifetime.

This special edition guide includes certified American Historic Inns that provide the utmost in hospitality, beauty, authentic restoration and preservation. Inns have been carefully selected so as to provide readers with the opportunity to visit genuine masterpieces.

With inns dating back to as early as 1637, this guide is filled with treasures waiting to be discovered. Full descriptions, illustrations, guest comments and recommendations are all included to let you know what's in store for you before choosing to stay at America's historic inns.

Send away for your copy today! Books available in Spring 1995.   **Price $14.95**

the Road Best Traveled – Monthly Newsletter

Here's the only way to make sure you don't get left out of the latest bed & breakfast and country inn promotions. This travel newsletter is packed with information about more FREE night offers, huge discounts on lodgings and family vacation opportunities.

And that's not all! *The Road Best Traveled* is your one-stop travel shopping source to help you plan your next vacation. This outstanding publication includes the latest hotel bargains, ways to get the cheapest air fare, unbelievable cruise deals and affordable excursion packages to exotic and far off places.

Wait, there's more! As a special offer to readers of this book, you'll

508

receive *Bed & Breakfasts and Country Inns* FREE with your subscription. Remember, this book includes a FREE night certificate! A great gift for a friend or another FREE night for you!

One-year subscription (12 issues)	**$39.95**
Save more! Special two-year subscription rate	**$69.95**

Bed & Breakfasts and Country Inns Travel Club
Charter Membership From American Historic Inns, Inc.

SAVE! SAVE! SAVE! Now, for the first time ever, we offer an exclusive discount club that lets you enjoy the excitement of bed & breakfast and country inn travel again and again. As a charter member of this once-in-a-lifetime offer you'll receive benefits that include savings of 25% to 50% off every night's stay!

Your membership card will entitle you to tremendous savings at some of the finest inns in America. Members receive an information-packed guide with more than 1,800 bed & breakfasts and country inns to choose from. Plan affordable getaways to inns nearby or visit an area of the country you've always wanted to experience.

The best part of being an American Historic Inns Travel Club Member is that the card can be used as many times as you like.*

In addition to your card, you will get a FREE night's stay certificate.** Truly a club membership that's hard to pass up!

That's not all! Sign up for a charter membership now and receive a one-year subscription to *The Road Best Traveled*, the only monthly newsletter that keeps you up to date on all of the latest bed & breakfast and country inn promotions. Not only will you find out about saving on inn stays, but you will also find travel bargains on air fare, car rentals, cruises, vacation packages and more.

As an added bonus, first-year members will receive a copy of *The Official Guide to American Historic Inns*. This completely revised and updated edition includes inns of unique interest and historical value. Your library collection will be complete with this book.

All travel club members receive:

- Travel club card entitling holder to 25% to 50% off lodging.
- FREE night's stay certificate.
- Guide to more than 1,800 inns across America.
- *The Road Best Traveled,* a monthly newsletter with discount updates.
- *The Official Guide to American Historic Inns,* completely revised and updated.

* Membership is good through Dec. 31, 1995. Subject to limitations.

** With purchase of one night at the regular rate required. Subject to limitations.

Introductory price with full benefits	**$59.95**

How To Start & Run Your Own Bed & Breakfast Inn

By Ripley Hotch & Carl Glassman

In this book you'll discover the secrets of the best inns. Learn how to decide whether owning or leasing an inn is right for you. Find out what business strategies characterize a successful inn and learn how to incorporate them in your own business.

If you've always dreamed of owning a bed & breakfast then this book is for you!

182 pages, paperback.	**Price $14.95**

AMERICAN HISTORIC INNS
INCORPORATED

PO Box 669
Dana Point
California
92629-0669
(714) 499-8070
Fax (714) 499-4022

Order Form

Name: _____

Street: _____

City/State/Zip: _____

Phone: (__ __ __) __ __ __ - __ __ __ __

Date: __ __ / __ __ / __ __

QTY.	Prod. No.	Description	Amount	Total
_____	AHI6	Bed & Breakfasts and Country Inns (Includes FREE night certificate)	$19.95	_____
_____	AHIH	The Official Guide to American Historic Inns	$14.95	_____
_____	AHIN	The Road Best Traveled Newsletter (Includes B&B and Country Inns AHI6)	$39.95	_____
_____	AHIN2	The Road Best Traveled Newsletter Special two-year rate	$69.95	_____
_____	AHIC	Bed & Breakfasts and Country Inns Travel Club – Charter Membership (Includes one-year of The Road Best Traveled and Official Guide to American Historic Inns)	$59.95	_____
_____	CB03	How to Start Your Own B&B	$14.95	_____

	Subtotal	_____
California buyers add 7.75% sales tax		_____
(Book and Travel Club Orders) Add $1.75 per copy for Shipping & Handling		_____
	TOTAL	_____

❑ Check/Money Order ❑ Mastercard ❑ Visa ❑ American Express

Account Number __ __ __ __ __ __ __ __ __ __ __ __ __ __ __ __   Exp. Date __ __ / __ __

Name on card _____

Signature _____

AMERICAN HISTORIC INNS
INCORPORATED

PO Box 669
Dana Point
California
92629-0669
(714) 499-8070
Fax (714) 499-4022

Order Form

Name: _____

Street: _____

City/State/Zip: _____

Phone: (__ __ __) __ __ __ - __ __ __ __

Date: __ __ / __ __ / __ __

QTY.	Prod. No.	Description	Amount	Total
_____	AHI6	Bed & Breakfasts and Country Inns (Includes FREE night certificate)	$19.95	_____
_____	AHIH	The Official Guide to American Historic Inns	$14.95	_____
_____	AHIN	The Road Best Traveled Newsletter (Includes B&B and Country Inns AHI6)	$39.95	_____
_____	AHIN2	The Road Best Traveled Newsletter Special two-year rate	$69.95	_____
_____	AHIC	Bed & Breakfasts and Country Inns Travel Club – Charter Membership (Includes one-year of The Road Best Traveled and Official Guide to American Historic Inns)	$59.95	_____
_____	CB03	How to Start Your Own B&B	$14.95	_____

		Subtotal	_____
	California buyers add 7.75% sales tax		_____
(Book and Travel Club Orders) Add $1.75 per copy for Shipping & Handling			_____
		TOTAL	_____

❑ Check/Money Order   ❑ Mastercard   ❑ Visa   ❑ American Express

Account Number __ __ __ __ __ __ __ __ __ __ __ __ __ __ __ __   Exp. Date __ __ / __ __

Name on card _____

Signature _____

INN EVALUATION FORM

Please copy and complete this form for each stay and mail to the address shown. Since 1981 we have maintained files that include thousands of evaluations from inngoers who have sent this form to us. This information helps us follow the changes in the inns listed in this guide.

Name of Inn: _____

City and State: _____

Date of Stay: _____

Your Name: _____

Address: _____

City/State/Zip: _____

Phone: (_ _ _) _ _ _ _ - _ _ _ _

Please use the following rating scale for the next items.
1: Outstanding. 2: Good. 3: Average. 4: Fair. 5: Poor.

Location	1	2	3	4	5
Cleanliness	1	2	3	4	5
Food Service	1	2	3	4	5
Privacy	1	2	3	4	5
Beds	1	2	3	4	5
Bathrooms	1	2	3	4	5
Parking	1	2	3	4	5
Handling of reservations	1	2	3	4	5
Attitude of staff	1	2	3	4	5
Overall rating	1	2	3	4	5

Please attach any comments on above.

MAIL THE COMPLETED FORM TO:
American Historic Inns, Inc.
PO Box 669
Dana Point, California 92629-0669
(714) 499-8070

Notes

Notes